WRITERS FOR CHILDREN

WRITERS FOR CHILDREN

Critical Studies of Major Authors
Since the Seventeenth Century

JANE M. BINGHAM, Editor

Charles Scribner's Sons · *New York*

Library of Congress Cataloging-in-Publication Data

Writers for children / Jane M. Bingham, editor.

p.   cm.
Bibliography: p.
Includes index.
ISBN 0-684-18165-7
1. Children's literature—History and criticism.
PN1009.A1W73 1987
809'.89282—dc19   87-16011CIP

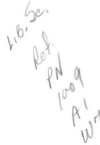

Acknowledgment is gratefully made to those publishers and individuals who have permitted the use of the following materials in copyright.

James Daugherty

Lines from "The Corps of Discovery" from *Of Courage Undaunted: Across the Continent with Lewis and Clark* by James Daugherty. Copyright 1951 by James Daugherty, renewed © 1979 by Charles Daugherty. "Women of the Wagons" from *Marcus and Narcissa Whitman* by James Daugherty. Copyright 1953 by James Daugherty, renewed © 1981 by Charles Daugherty. "Independent" from *West of Boston* by James Daugherty. Copyright 1956 by James Daugherty, renewed © 1984 by Charles Daugherty. All selections reprinted by permission of Viking Penguin.

Walter de la Mare

"Silver" from *Peacock Pie: A Book of Rhymes* and lines from "Now Silent Falls" from *Crossings: A Fairy Play;* both in *The Complete Poems of Walter de la Mare.* Copyright © 1969 by the Literary Trustees of Walter de la Mare. Reprinted by permission of the Literary Trustees of Walter de la Mare and the Society of Authors as their representative.

Eleanor Farjeon

"Poetry" by Eleanor Farjeon. Copyright 1938, 1966 by Eleanor Farjeon. Reprinted by permission of Harper and Row, Publishers, Inc., and by Harold Ober Associates Incorporated. "The Night Will Never Stay" by Eleanor Farjeon. Copyright 1951 by Eleanor Farjeon. Reprinted by permission of Harper and Row, Publishers, Inc., and by Harold Ober Associates Incorporated. Lines from "A Morning Song" from *The Children's Bells* by Eleanor Farjeon. Reprinted by permission of Harold Ober Associates Incorporated.

Langston Hughes

Excerpts from *The Dream Keeper and Other Poems* by Langston Hughes. Copyright 1932 by Alfred A. Knopf, Inc., renewed 1960 by Langston Hughes. Reprinted by permission of Alfred A. Knopf, Inc. Lines from "Mother to Son" and from "Suicide's Note" by Langston Hughes. Copyright 1920 by Alfred A. Knopf, Inc., renewed 1954 by Langston Hughes. Reprinted by permission of Alfred A. Knopf, Inc. Lines from "Merry-Go-

Round" by Langston Hughes. Copyright 1942 by Langston Hughes, renewed 1970 by Arna Bontemps and George Houston Bass. Reprinted by permission of Alfred A. Knopf, Inc. Excerpts from *The Big Sea* by Langston Hughes. Copyright 1940 by Langston Hughes. Copyright renewed © 1968 by Arna Bontemps and George Houston Bass. Reprinted by permission of Hill and Wang, a division of Farrar Straus and Giroux, Inc., and Harold Ober Associates Incorporated. Lines from "Good Morning" by Langston Hughes. Copyright 1951 by Langston Hughes. Copyright renewed 1979 by George Houston Bass. Reprinted by permission of Harold Ober Associates Incorporated from *Montage of a Dream Deferred.*

A. A. Milne

Lines from "Rice Pudding" and "Vespers" from *When We Were Very Young* by A. A. Milne. Copyright 1924 by E. P. Dutton, renewed 1952 by A. A. Milne. Lines from "Buttercup Days" and "A Thought" from *Now We Are Six* by A. A. Milne. Copyright 1927 by E. P. Dutton, renewed 1955 by A. A. Milne. Lines from "Coddleston Pie" from *Winnie-the-Pooh* by A. A. Milne. Copyright 1926 by E. P. Dutton, renewed 1954 by A. A. Milne. All selections reprinted by permission of the publisher, E. P. Dutton, a division of NAL Penguin Inc.; the Canadian publishers, McClelland and Stewart Ltd., Toronto; and the British publisher, Methuen and Company Ltd., London.

Elizabeth Madox Roberts

Lines from "Christmas Morning" and "On the Hill" from *Under the Tree* by Elizabeth Madox Roberts. Copyright 1922 by B. W. Huebsch, Inc., renewed 1950 by Ivor S. Roberts. Copyright 1930 by the Viking Press, Inc., renewed © 1958 by Ivor S. Roberts and the Viking Press, Inc. Reprinted by permission of Viking Penguin.

Carl Sandburg

"Splinter" from *Good Morning, America,* copyright 1928, 1956 by Carl Sandburg. Reprinted by permission of Harcourt Brace Jovanovich, Inc. "Buffalo Dusk" from *Smoke and Steel* by Carl Sandburg, copyright 1920 by Harcourt Brace Jovanovich, Inc.; renewed 1948 by Carl Sandburg. Reprinted by permission of the publisher.

EDITORIAL STAFF

CONTENTS

CONTENTS

INTRODUCTION

Writers for Children, a critical guide to selected classics in children's literature, is a major reference work on important writers from the seventeenth century to the first part of the twentieth century. It includes eighty-four original critical essays, alphabetically arranged with selected bibliographies, on writers ranging from Charles Perrault (1628–1703) to Carol Ryrie Brink (1895–1981). These critical essays are designed to assist a wide readership: high school and college students will find this volume valuable when writing research papers; parents, teachers, and librarians will find it useful in determining which authors they want to introduce to children; scholars, critics, and reviewers will be able to sharpen their own critical stance by knowing their colleagues' points of view. The index of titles and authors should prove helpful to all readers.

The authors selected as subjects for this volume have either written expressly for children (defined here as young people up to age sixteen), or their works have been appropriated by or relegated to young readers. Through the years these authors have continued to hold either popular or scholarly status, or sometimes both, such as Jonathan Swift, Lewis Carroll, and Mark Twain; or they are valued as important collectors of folk literature, such as Asbjørnsen and Moe, the Brothers Grimm, and Joseph Jacobs; or, although they have faded from popularity, they were highly respected in their own day, such as Elizabeth Madox Roberts, Cornelia Meigs, and Hendrik Willem van Loon; or they are known principally through translations of their works, such as Johanna Spyri, Heinrich Hoffmann, and C. Collodi. Not all of each author's books are still available, but at least one book by each author is in print. Many have been published as children's classics and are available in both hardback and paperback editions, as are those books that have been awarded the John Newbery Medal or the Randolph Caldecott Medal for the year's most distinguished novel or picture book for children. (The Newbery Medal for writing has been given by the American Library Association since 1922, and the Caldecott Medal for illustration has been given since 1938.)

Additional criteria for selection of author-subjects were the following: (1) they are deceased; (2) their work was in print for at least two generations after the original publication date and was still in print in the 1950s (the only exception here being C. S. Lewis, whose works came out in the early 1950s but who was nevertheless included because of the widespread serious critical reception of his *Narnia* books as well as the popularity of the series); and (3) their work has been widely acclaimed as worthwhile for children. The decision to include only deceased authors was prompted in part by the desire to include works not currently influenced by a particular author's personality or promotion but that rather have withstood the test of time and seem to have enduring value, most having been read for well over two generations.

Another factor influencing inclusion of authors was my own concern for the use adults make of children's books. Many of these authors' books have been longtime favorites of parents, teachers, and librarians and have been recommended on numerous reading lists. These works are sometimes found in basal readers (frequently in excerpted form) or are often read aloud or used for storytelling or dramatization. Many are used in high-school- or college-level children's literature courses, and some are used for bibliotherapy by psychologists and social workers.

The sixty-four contributing essayists represented here are qualified critics who have either published books or articles or have done extensive research on their subjects. Some are editors of major periodicals in the field, and others are well-established teachers of literature.

The essayists represent a variety of backgrounds, although the majority come from English departments in American colleges and universities. Representative exceptions include Roderick McGillis and Jon C. Stott from Canadian universities, Peter Hunt from the University of Wales, Jill P. May from the College of Education at Purdue, Margaret Coughlan from the Library of Congress, and Barbara T. Rollock from the New York Public Library.

Some contributors have published major resource books on their subjects, such as Michael Patrick Hearn, James T. Teahan, Walter James Miller, Lois Kuznets, Glenn Edward Sadler, and Ruth K. MacDonald.

A few of the essayists are also authors of literature for children: Gillian Avery and Ann Thwaite of England; Peter Hunt of Wales, Erik Haugaard, a Dane living in Ireland; Alison Lurie of Cornell University (a winner of the Pulitzer Prize); Francelia Butler of the University of Connecticut (the founder of the journal *Children's Literature*); Margaret Hodges, Professor Emeritus of the University of Pittsburgh; Avi (a recipient of the O'Dell and Christopher awards); Robin McKinley (the winner of the 1984 Newbery Medal); Myra Cohn Livingston (a recipient of the National Council of Teachers of English Poetry Award).

While *Twentieth Century Children's Writers* (1978) was the first reference book in the field of children's literature to include critical essays, its entries are brief (over seven hundred living and dead authors are presented), and the primary focus of the volume is biographical and bibliographical. The essays in *Writers for Children* range from twenty-five hundred to six thousand words and include eighty-four deceased authors who have been selected because they are generally accepted as having enduring value. Most of the books discussed in the essays in this volume have been in print for a minimum of fifty years, but usually longer, and at least one book by each author is still in print today and is being read by children.

The multivolume, periodically updated reference book *Something About the Author* (1971–   ) covers over three thousand authors of children's books; its brief reviews are biographical and descriptive rather than critical. A two-volume companion set, *Yesterday's Authors of Books for Children* (1977–1978), presents authors "from early times to 1960," but each entry presents only "facts and pictures" about the author or illustrator.

Writers for Children represents a major step forward in the critical evaluation of children's literature in that it presents concise in-depth studies by thoughtful scholars that go beyond biographical and bibliographical information (although each essayist does provide a list of selected primary and secondary works) and presents criticism of writers who are still popular as well as writers who are neglected but still important, such as Hendrik Willem van Loon, the winner of the first Newbery Medal. While the works of some popular authors, such as Laura Ingalls Wilder, are often reviewed, until now they have received little or no in-depth critical consideration.

Criticism in the field of children's literature has a relatively short history. Few scholars have devoted themselves to serious criticism, especially of new children's books; however, the picture is slowly changing. In the early 1970s Francelia Butler founded *Children's Literature,* a journal devoted to the publication of critical essays on children's literature. Today several journals publish critical essays about children's books, including *Children's Literature in Education,* the *Children's Literature Association Quarterly, Signal,* and the *Lion and the Unicorn.*

Over the past two decades, the critical reviewing of children's books—as opposed to in-depth criticism—has also increased in quantity and quality in such periodicals as the *Horn Book Magazine* (a notable pioneer in the field), the *School Library Journal,* and *Booklist,* as well as in sections of such diverse professional journals as *Language Arts,* the *Reading Teacher,* and *Social Education,* and in newspapers such as the *New York Times* and the *Christian Science Monitor,* which often carry children's book supplements.

Writers for Children substantially adds to the growing body of criticism in the field of children's literature. Because the essayists were free to determine their own critical stances from which to assess their subjects, the essays are not prescriptive, but deal with the same tenets of criticism that are dealt with in adult literature—audience, purpose, content, style, form, and context.

One issue, for instance, that any critic faces is determination of audience: who is the reader and for whom is the work intended? In children's literature, audience is often blurred. Is *Pilgrim's Progress,* for example, a book for children or adults? It was written in 1678 as an allegory for adults, but it was soon read by children as well as adults. Today profusely illustrated children's editions are available. John Bunyan has often been the subject of critical study as a writer for an adult audience, but he has had comparatively little criticism as a writer for children. Robert Bator's essay on Bunyan in this volume corrects this. He analyzes the work's child-appealing elements, from the subtitle's promise of a "dangerous journey" to Christian's confrontation with an assortment of lively characters in fantastic struggles and scenes, all of which have engrossed generations of children.

Alice's Adventures in Wonderland, on the other hand, which was written for children (in fact, for a specific child), has most often been critiqued as a book for adults. While it has been universally recommended for children's reading, it has had little in-depth evaluation as a book for children, readers who are typically caught between the world of instruction and reason and the world of imagination and fancy.

Anita Moss's essay on Lewis Carroll explores this point—the "tension between the didactic forces in children's literature on the one hand and the defenders of fantasy and imagination on the other." She astutely points out that "Carroll realizes an entirely new view of childhood at a time when children use their imaginations and intelligence not in the service of redeeming a fallen creation but as a way of protecting themselves from stifling adult authority and of acquiring more secure identities for themselves."

It was intended that the essays in *Writers for Children* reflect a diversity of approaches and styles. Some essayists focus on literary explication, as does Roderick McGillis in "Christina Rossetti" and "William Blake," Myra Cohn Livingston in "Edward Lear," and Jon C. Stott in "Nathaniel Hawthorne" and "L. M. Montgomery." Alison Lurie examines themes in E. Nesbit's works, one of which is "the aesthetic unpleasantness and threat to health of modern cities." Fred Erisman examines the essence of "westering" in the works of Laura Ingalls Wilder.

Robin McKinley's reaction to her reading of J. R. R. Tolkien reveals her uniquely personal style, while Erik Haugaard tells of Hans Christian Andersen's fairy-tale life in a narrative that is itself reminiscent of Andersen's tales.

Other essayists explore social, political, aesthetic, or moral issues. The concerns expressed in Grayce Scholt's "Hilaire Belloc," Donnarae MacCann's "Hugh Lofting," and Opal J. Moore's "Joel Chandler Harris," for example, may cause some readers to reconsider if and how they will present these authors' works to today's children.

One last word: it seems fitting that this volume, which represents a main building block in the field of children's literature, should be issued by Charles Scribner's Sons, the publisher of so many outstanding books for the young, including the respected *Children's Classics* series. The publication of this volume reflects Scribners' continuing commitment to children's literature.

I am pleased to see *Writers for Children* take its place in Scribners' important series of reference works, alongside such titles as *Ancient Writers, American Writers, British Writers,* and *European Writers.*

Finally, I wish to thank Clare Costello, Editorial Director, Charles Scribner's Sons, Books for Young People, and Charles Scribner, Jr., who invited me to take on this project; the Scribner Reference Books Division, whose assistance was invaluable; and Grayce Scholt, my first teacher of children's literature, my best critic, and my good friend.

JANE M. BINGHAM

WRITERS FOR CHILDREN

LOUISA MAY ALCOTT

1832-1888

W IIEN SHE CONSIDERED her achievements in writing for children, as opposed to her voluminous if little-known works for adults, Louisa May Alcott thought of her role in creating them as that of a craftsperson and an independent working woman, but certainly never as an artist. Her fiction for children kept her parents and siblings fed, clothed, sheltered, and out of debt, a financial feat that she accomplished much more successfully than either of her parents; but such writing never really satisfied her craving for artistic achievement. However, it is her children's novels that are remembered; had her writing been confined to and valued only for her adult fiction, she would now be considered a minor footnote in the history of American literature. But because of her successes in depicting faulty but sympathetic characters, her portrayal of the warmth of domestic life, her simple but accurate style, and her ability to evoke local color, she ranks among the foremost creators of realistic fiction for children, especially for her March family novels.

Louisa May Alcott, the second of the four daughters of Abigail and Bronson Alcott, was born in Germantown, Pennsylvania, on 29 November 1832, her father's thirty-third birthday. One would think that sharing a birthday with a child would make a parent feel particularly attracted to that child, but such was not the case in this family. Louisa favored her mother's side of the family, and her father did not really appreciate until late in his life the admirable characteristics this likeness conferred upon his daughter. Both parents were edu-

cational and social reformers from New England; at the time of Louisa's birth they were temporarily living in Germantown, where they started an elementary school based on Bronson Alcott's newfangled ideas about education of the "whole" child (and not just the child's intellect), coeducation of the sexes, and interracial opportunities for education. He also incorporated in his theories a number of vague and sketchy notions of the innate goodness of the child, loosely derived from transcendentalism.

The school was not a success, and its failure soon after Louisa's birth began a long line of unsuccessful ventures that left the Alcott family nearly indigent. But the parents never abandoned their commitment to social justice and educational reform, and through their connections with reform movements the Alcotts introduced their daughters to some of the most influential thinkers of the day (William Lloyd Garrison, Henry David Thoreau, Ralph Waldo Emerson, Julia Ward Howe, and Samuel Gridley Howe, among others), especially when the family returned to Boston in 1835 to start a school there. When the Alcotts moved again, this time to Concord after the demise of the Boston school, they found themselves living among the major transcendentalists of the mid-nineteenth century: Emerson was a neighbor and financial patron; Thoreau was the Alcott sisters' botany tutor. If the Alcott sisters did not have enough to eat, at least there was plenty to feed their minds. Bronson Alcott did odd jobs in Concord, but the family lived largely

1

off the charity of relatives and of Emerson until they moved back to Massachusetts in 1843.

When Louisa was twelve, her father's business ventures—this time an attempt to establish a communal farm in Harvard, Massachusetts—failed once again. A family council was called, and though Bronson showed some signs of wanting to leave his family to start a venture in communal living, the family decided to stay together. Abigail Alcott took over the reins of family management and decided to move them first to a rented farm and then to Boston so that she could support them as a social worker. In the city her daughters could help by taking on teaching and sewing jobs. The threat of family dissolution so alarmed the impressionable Louisa that from that point on she determined to do her duty by helping to support the family and to make something of herself, although exactly what was not yet clear to her.

In her twenties Alcott tried a number of occupations: teaching, social work, needlework, even domestic service. She also attempted some writing, mostly gothic short stories, which paid well and satisfied her flair for the exciting and dangerous, if only vicariously. She started two adult novels, *Moods* (1864) and *Work* (1873), though the books did not reach a stage that prompted her to contemplate publishing them at the time. She also wrote and published a collection of short stories for children, entitled *Flower Fables* (1855), which she had written for Emerson's daughter Ellen while serving as her tutor. The stories are fantasies, moral lessons taught by personified flowers; they received little notice from the public, and justly so, since Alcott was never successful at combining fantasy with heavy-handed moralities.

At thirty Alcott looked for a way to contribute to the Civil War effort, found a place for herself by enlisting in Dorothea Dix's nursing corps, and went to work in a hotel turned Army hospital in Washington, D.C. Her tour of duty was brief—only six weeks—because she contracted typhoid fever, the effects of which damaged her health for the rest of her life. But while she was at home recuperating, she turned her hand to revising the letters she had sent home into a series of short stories, which were collected and published as *Hospital Sketches* in 1863. The public was eager for any information, fictional or otherwise, about their "boys" in service, and the book was widely acclaimed. The public was accurate in its evaluation of the work, for in it Alcott found opportunity to use her most accomplished skills: a plain, colloquial style, as befit the rank-and-file soldier; characterization of ordinary people and realization of their heroism in everyday life; a sense of local color in the specifics of hospital life; and wry, understated humor. The commercial and popular success of the book led Alcott to revise and publish a novel that she had started writing in 1860. Though *Moods* was always her favorite book, she never felt that anyone appreciated her artistry or message. But then, the high-flown diction of the book—"Only a month betrothed, and yet so cold and gloomy, Adam!"—and the transcendental notions that informed her point of view about love, marriage, and divorce were not popular, or even widely understood. And the novel really did not call forth Alcott's finest literary abilities, as had *Hospital Sketches*.

With the profits from the two adult books, Alcott left on a European tour in 1865 as the paid companion of an invalid girl, but when she returned over a year later her road to success and family solvency was no clearer. The editor of *Hospital Sketches*, Thomas Niles of Roberts Brothers, approached her about writing a novel for girls, primarily because his firm wished to enter the juvenile market in competition with the "Oliver Optic" adventure books for boys published by a rival Boston firm, Lee and Shepard. Though Alcott claimed not to know anything about girls or writing for them, she turned to the four young women whom she did know to inspire her story: herself and her three sisters as they were growing up in Concord nearly twenty years earlier. The result was *Little Women* (1868), Alcott's greatest literary achievement and most enduring work.

She wrote the book in six weeks, barely editing it. She was suspicious of this kind of writing experience, for the work in which she found the most emotional satisfaction was characterized by feverish composition, intense concentration, and utter exhaustion when she finally finished. Perhaps because she was writing about her own family and therefore did not need to labor intensely to create solely from her own invention, and because the project did not involve her emotionally to the degree her gothic fiction or adult novels did, the result is much more natural and less contrived than her earlier works.

Jo March, the heroine of *Little Women*, remains to this day one of children's literature's best-loved characters. In Jo, Alcott found and revealed herself: faulty, impetuous, temperamental, energetic, highly motivated, and iconoclastic. Child readers found much to identify with in both her struggles to be ladylike and self-controlled and her competing desires to try the limits of socially acceptable behavior. Though modern children may complain that the girls are really too well-behaved to be true, by the standards of her own time Alcott had created in the sisters flaws that no writer had previously dared to attribute to fictional characters for children (like selfishness, greed, temper, vanity, and shyness).

The book also has much enduring appeal because of its portrayal of the Alcotts as the all-American family, intimate and fulfilled in their closeness. Critics and biographers have argued that the Alcott home could hardly have been like the March home, but Alcott was, after all, writing fiction for public consumption; airing the family's dirty linen would hardly have been appropriate. But Americans of the nineteenth century were unusually ready to believe in domestic life as warm and nurturing, and so most readers were willing to accept Alcott's somewhat sentimentalized picture of the Marches.

The accurate details of education, housekeeping, and social events—the balls that Jo and Meg attend, the sisters' misguided efforts to keep the household going and to entertain an unexpected guest in their mother's absence, the Christmas-night dramatic presentation for the girls of the neighborhood, the lessons in womanliness at their mother's knee—all maintain the modern reader's interest for much the same reason that historical fiction does. Though Alcott did not try to write historical fiction, she did give a realistic account of nineteenth-century family life for her readers. The satisfaction that the details give readers today arises from her accuracy. It is also possible that the reader's indulgence in the physical pleasures that the March sisters enjoy—details of clothing lovingly dwelt upon, the minutiae of the sisters' social lives, the decorations in their home—renders vicarious pleasure. Elsewhere, Alcott tries to persuade readers that the book is concerned with spiritual and moral matters. She suggests, for example, that Christmas is about something more than receiving presents and that following the way of the Pilgrim (in John Bunyan's *Pilgrim's Progress*) is more appropriate for the sisters than pursuing the worldly pleasures of some of their acquaintances.

Almost as soon as *Little Women* was published, readers began clamoring for a sequel, in order to see how the teenage girls grew up. Alcott turned not to her own life but to her creative powers this time to present her readers with *Good Wives* (1869), now published with *Little Women* as one volume. In *Good Wives*, Meg, Jo, and Amy marry, and Beth dies prematurely. The sisters go on to re-create in their own families the warm family circle that they themselves had grown up in. Jo, however, does not marry at once. Alcott boldly embodies in her character the idea of prolonged spinsterhood and the satisfactions one might find therein. But eventually even Jo, who had earlier vowed never to marry, succumbs to a more or less traditional happy ending in marriage and family, although her husband is hardly the handsome young man the reader might have expected to be her life's partner. Together they become directors of a boarding school, thus allowing Jo to have the career she so fervently desires. The writing of *Good Wives*, which apparently was also not as emotionally involving as writing gothic romances for adults, proceeded with little hesitation or revision. The public was satisfied for a while, especially since even boyish Jo had found an appropriate fictional partner, but the demand for more stories about the March girls continued throughout Alcott's life.

Even though she professed not to have enjoyed writing *Little Women* and *Good Wives*, Alcott found in these books the financial success she had been hoping for since the age of twelve. But if she did not find the kind of artistic recognition she had been seeking, at least public popularity conferred literary preeminence on the books. These two first books for children also provided Alcott with a number of formulas—sensible, practical education for girls; hard work and rewarding professions when they grew up (if not so rewarding as marriage); young men redeemed by the examples of good women—that she continued to use in her later books. Since these two books gained her critical acclaim as a children's writer, perhaps Alcott felt that repeating the formulas in later works would guarantee a steady stream of royalty checks, if not continued literary growth.

Among these successful formulas is the death of the virtuous child. Alcott usually uses death to make a saint out of the child victim, who is already spiritually rarified, just waiting for translation into sainthood. In *Little Women* the potential angel is Beth March, the homebody with no real faults, the sister most likely to remind her siblings by her good example of their own inadequacies. Though Alcott did not indulge in the lachrymose excesses found in other sentimental novels of her time, the detailed description of Beth's death affords the reader a moment of tearful pathos, which was clearly a popular feeling for her readers, as Alcott must have realized when she resorted to such incidents again in later novels.

The sequels to *Little Women* and *Good Wives*, *Little Men* (1871) and *Jo's Boys* (1886), follow the March sisters through their marriages and through Jo's establishment first of a boarding school and then of a college. In both later books, Alcott presents Bronson Alcott's educational ideas in practical form, showing both his educational methods and their long-term results: students who are educated in body and mind and who are both commonsensical and socially aware. Alcott also continues to deal with the issue of women combining career and marriage. Jo March succeeds in both, becoming a famous author, a teacher, and a wife and mother, with the support of her professor-husband. So it seems that as traditional as Jo's happy ending appeared in *Good Wives*, in *Little Men* she becomes more than just a "little woman" confined to her immediate family.

Spinsterhood is not necessary to pursue a career, although Alcott does include in *Jo's Boys* a female physician for whom the single life is both satisfying and appropriate. In the same book, the girls in Jo March's college are treated to a course in women's rights as part of their training, so that they, too, can choose to be wives, career women, or both. Being such an outspoken advocate of social reform could have been risky for Alcott early in her career, which might explain why she did not have Jo remain unmarried. But in both *Good Wives* and *Little Men* she suggests the possibility of women combining a profession and marriage. By the time she wrote *Jo's Boys*, her established popularity meant that she could give a fictional form to her social schemes, such as equal rights and opportunities for women, without risking her commercial success.

Alcott eventually became tired of the public's demand for more March family stories. *Jo's Boys*, composed over a period of six years while her health slowly declined, was her last novel about the March family. The writing of the book reminded her of family members who had died since she began writing the series (her mother and youngest sister among them), and compounded the difficulty of writing. The attitude of farewell to her readers is clear even in the book's opening pages, where Jo

and one of her sisters sit together, reminiscing. Though the book is more adventurous than its predecessors with regard to the themes of women's suffrage and occupational opportunities, it is also tired. In order to avoid any more demands from her public, Alcott duly married off or consigned the characters to professions or death, almost defying her readers to think of any story line that she could continue in a sequel.

In three mid-career novels, *An Old-Fashioned Girl* (1870), *Eight Cousins* (1875), and *Rose in Bloom* (1876), Alcott pursues her examination of education, but focuses more specifically on education for girls. In *An Old-Fashioned Girl*, Alcott criticizes the notion that rich girls need to learn no more than how to dress up like ladies before they are old enough to do so. Alcott contends that by following the current fashion fads and by courting young men, marriage to whom will assure them of the continuation of their vacuous lifestyles, young women guaranteed for themselves lives of meaningless motion and utter boredom.

The heroine of *An Old-Fashioned Girl*, Polly Milton, is no such rich girl; she becomes a model for her wealthy friend, Fanny Shaw, when the Shaw family loses its fortune. Polly knows how to make family members feel loved and appreciated; she knows how to manage her own money and career, how to run a household comfortably yet economically, and how to choose the appropriate partner for her life. Furthermore she knows what means she can use, besides the unthinkable flirtation practiced by Fanny's friends, to attract that partner. She is virtuous, honest, hard-working, and an accomplished homemaker. Polly values the ability to support herself independently and acquire self-confidence; she gains mental discipline and remains active in order to keep away lethargy and depression; in short, she gives meaning to her life. Idle Fanny and her friends have little to do, and so resort to activities that neither improve their own lives nor contribute to the well-being of others. They do not know how to take care of themselves and do not even care to know. As a result, their own inner resources are woefully underdeveloped. Though Polly is hardly the women's suffrage reformer and iconoclast that Jo March is, she understands a woman's need to be an active, honorable, contributing member in a society that might otherwise see her as a silly social decoration. The book does not really posit a new system for educational reform as much as it criticizes the contemporary curriculum for girls and reaffirms the value of women's work, both within and outside of the home.

Rose Campbell in *Rose in Bloom* is the guinea pig who undergoes the rigors of the new-fashioned education that Alcott outlines for the ideal woman. She is an orphaned heiress, the ward of her bachelor physician-uncle. Yet even though Rose has enough money to avoid housework and to indulge herself in any way she pleases, under her uncle's plan she still must learn to sew and cook; to choose clothing that is comfortable and practical but still attractive; to learn traditional school subjects, such as arithmetic and geography; and even to master some newer disciplines for women, such as anatomy, physical education, and philanthropic investment. Alcott makes Rose strong-minded and outspoken about women's rights, perhaps because she herself was active in the women's suffrage movement at the time the book was written. But even if Rose Campbell is a prototype for the "new woman" as Alcott imagined her, she does not totally abandon feminine pursuits or a desire for a happy ending in marriage and family.

In *Rose in Bloom*, Rose sets out to improve and educate her perfect partner, to make sure he is truly perfect before she will marry him; she goes one step beyond Polly Milton in not only luring him but also molding him into the "new man" and mate to her "new woman." But even after she marries him, she still follows a career as a lady bountiful, hardly an unusual profession for a rich woman of her time. Alcott does not suggest that women go into the more male-dominated careers, such as medicine, until *Jo's Boys*, which appeared much later in her career.

Of all her books for children, *Under the Lilacs* (1878) is Alcott's least satisfactory. Perhaps because while writing it she was also nursing her mother through her last illness, and was suffering both from grief over her mother's imminent death and from worry over the mounting medical bills, the work seems particularly bland and unimaginative. It is likely that Alcott decided to write the story only to make money rather than to express a new social concern as well as to make money, a motive she clearly reveals in her other novels. This might be the reason for the novel's otherwise uninspired plot. The book is a circus story about a ten-year-old orphan performer who runs away from the circus and finds himself in a foster home. (Ben's father has mysteriously disappeared from the circus, and his mother is dead.) Though Ben still remembers the glory of his acrobatic performances, he relinquishes them in order to follow a life of "respectability," that Victorian cliché for middle-class, unprovocative virtues. Ben needs only to pass by a school to realize his need and desire for schooling; a bed with clean sheets converts the former wanderer into a homebody. The only remnants of the circus that Alcott permits the boy to retain are his performing dog—the most attractive character in the book—and a farewell performance for friends, as a birthday indulgence. When Ben decides to sneak off to see a circus in a nearby town, he is punished by the theft of his dog; here is Alcott at her most punitive, for the transgression is such an understandable one that the writer seems unnecessarily harsh in depriving the boy of his only companion in the world. Ben's dog and missing father both return to him in the end, but there is no return to life under the big top for the reunited family; instead, the father marries Ben's foster mother and all settle down to a safe and obscure life full of the respectability Ben purports to long for.

Alcott betrays her true sympathies, however, when she makes the pet dog and the furtive visit to the circus so attractive. One suspects that while most of the events in the story are invented to carry on the plot line, the parts about circus life are drawn from Alcott's recollections of her own excitement as a child at seeing the visiting shows. The life of a circus performer may not be glamorous, as Ben's tale of abuse at the hands of the circus master and his unfortunate separation from his father are supposed to convince the reader. But the vigor of the writing in the circus scenes and the care invested in making the circus pet so attractive are at odds with Alcott's thematic intention to promote bland respectability.

By the time Alcott wrote her next novel, her health had seriously declined, but she had recovered at least some of her ability to write a lively novel about believable children. *Jack and Jill* (1880) is set in Harmony Village, the fictional equivalent of Concord, where Alcott was then living. Again, one finds many of Bronson Alcott's educational ideas, especially about the perils of developing the mind at the expense of the body; thus the children in the story are treated to a year's vacation from formal instruction in order to investigate their own interests, to rest their minds, and to indulge in healthful recreation and exercise. Many of the most interesting scenes in the book are drawn from actual school celebrations in Concord: the May Day rituals, the sledding party, the Washington's Birthday recitations, the science exhibition that marks the close of the school year. And it seems likely that many of the characters were drawn from Alcott's school-aged acquaintances in Concord. It is certain that the character of Ed Devlin is modeled after Ellsworth Devens, a well-mannered Concord teenager who had recently died. Ed does not sicken and die until halfway into the book, and he does not loom as a morose invalid in the opening chapters. But his death provides an inspirational moment and personal model for all the children of Harmony Village; in other words, he becomes a Beth March. But rather than the tried-and-true themes of educational reform and the inspiring death of a child, the book's greatest successes are the felicitous descriptions of the Concord children's parties and other details of local color, which, while they are really not central to the story, happily punctuate the otherwise predictable course of the narrative.

Throughout her career as a writer for children, Alcott also wrote short stories and serialized some of her novels for publication in children's magazines. *An Old-Fashioned Girl* appeared in *Merry's Museum*. Mary Mapes Dodge of *St. Nicholas* magazine also published Alcott's short stories and serialized *Under the Lilacs* and *Jack and Jill* for her readers. Alcott was ever mindful of the potential for her stories to make money; she always made sure that they saw print twice, once in a magazine, for which she could command top dollar, and once again in collections, of which she published fourteen for children. Though many of the stories betray their origins in Alcott's attempts to make money, some of them, particularly those in the volume entitled *A Garland for Girls* (1888), show to advantage her ability to tell an interesting, realistic tale about believable teenage girls and their problems. This last volume was published posthumously. On 6 March 1888, only two days after her father's death, Louisa May Alcott died of complications from her declining health, leaving a legacy of books for girls that still remain popular in spite of the passage of time and the sometimes dated ideals that the author expressed in them.

Selected Bibliography

WORKS OF LOUISA MAY ALCOTT

Flower Fables. Boston: G. W. Briggs, 1855.

Hospital Sketches. Boston: James Redpath, 1863.

Moods. Boston: Loring, 1864.

Little Women; or, Meg, Jo, Beth and Amy. Boston: Roberts Brothers, 1868.

Good Wives: Part Second of "Little Women." Boston: Roberts Brothers, 1869.

An Old-Fashioned Girl Boston: Roberts Brothers, 1870.

Little Men: Life at Plumfield with Jo's Boys. Boston: Roberts Brothers, 1871.

Work: A Story of Experience. Boston: Roberts Brothers, 1873.

Eight Cousins; or, The Aunt-Hill. Boston: Roberts Brothers, 1875.

Rose in Bloom: A Sequel to "Eight Cousins." Boston: Roberts Brothers, 1876.

Under the Lilacs. Boston: Roberts Brothers, 1878.

Jack and Jill: A Village Story. Boston: Roberts Brothers, 1880.

Jo's Boys and How They Turned Out: A Sequel to "Little Men." Boston: Roberts Brothers, 1886.

A Garland for Girls. Boston: Roberts Brothers, 1888.

CRITICAL AND BIOGRAPHICAL STUDIES

Bedell, Madelon. *The Alcotts*. New York: Clarkson Potter, 1981.

Cheney, Ednah Dow. *Louisa May Alcott, Her Life, Letters, and Journals*. Boston: Roberts Brothers, 1889.

Elbert, Sarah. *A Hunger for Home: Louisa May Alcott and Little Women*. Philadelphia: Temple University Press, 1984.

MacDonald, Ruth K. *Louisa May Alcott*. Twayne United States Authors Series, No. 457. Boston: Twayne Publishers, 1983.

Marsella, Joy. *The Promise of Destiny: Children and Women in the Short Stories of Louisa May Alcott*. Contributions to the Study of Childhood and Youth, No. 2. Westport, Conn.: Greenwood Press, 1983.

Payne, Alma J. *Louisa May Alcott: A Reference Guide*. Boston: G. K. Hall, 1980.

Saxton, Martha. *Louisa May: A Modern Biography of Louisa May Alcott*. Boston: Houghton Mifflin, 1977.

Stern, Madeleine B. *Critical Essays on Louisa May Alcott*. Boston: G. K. Hall, 1984.

———. *Louisa May Alcott*. Norman: University of Oklahoma Press, 1950; 2nd rev. ed., 1971.

—RUTH K. MacDONALD

HANS CHRISTIAN ANDERSEN

1805–1875

IN A LETTER to a friend, Hans Christian Andersen described himself as "a plant from the swamp." In our own day we are so used to such plants bearing flowers that it is difficult to imagine the conditions for those born far below a socially acceptable class at the beginning of the nineteenth century. Yet, in order fully to understand Andersen's success and the themes of his fairy tales, it is necessary to consider his background.

When Andersen was born, the town of Odense had only seven thousand inhabitants, though it did have a castle where a prince resided and a bishop's palace as well. Odense was a miniature copy of the society of its time: it contained all classes, and its very minuteness ensured that its citizens could not be unaware of one another. The governor was a crown prince who had been "banished" to the island of Fyn as a punishment by his father the king. At that time Denmark was still ruled by an absolute monarch who firmly believed in his divine right.

Because the governor was a crown prince, the court at the castle in Odense had an unusual splendor. Some of the nobles of the island had town houses, and there were officers in splendid uniforms to gape at—a world not too different from the one Andersen later described in "The Tinderbox" (1835).

Below the court and aristocrats were merchants and skilled tradesmen. Far below these, but numbering half of the inhabitants of Odense, were the unskilled and journeymen: artisans who were not members of the guilds and who were forbidden to keep apprentices. Andersen's father was such a journeyman shoemaker, who patched the shoes and boots of those almost as poor as he was.

Andersen was born two months after his parents' wedding. His father had rented one room in a house near the Odense River, which served not only as home for the family but also as a workshop. From a ladder in the tiny kitchen it was possible to climb out onto the roof, where his mother had a box of earth for growing parsley and chives. "It was my mother's whole garden, and in my fairy tale 'The Snow Queen' it still blooms."

In *The Fairy Tale of My Life* (1855), Andersen has described his childhood charmingly, if not always accurately. His parents were an oddly matched pair, his father some seven years younger than his mother. She was an illiterate and very superstitious woman; for her the world of dark powers, ghosts, and goblins was a reality. His father could both read and write and would have liked to have been more broadly educated. In the evenings and on Sundays he would read aloud to his son from the plays of the Danish playwright Ludvig Holberg. He claimed to be a freethinker, and his hero was Napoleon.

Little Hans Christian's paternal grandfather was mad, though his insanity was in no way dangerous and he was not confined to an asylum. He was a well-known "character" in the town, where he would roam the streets fantastically dressed, with flowers in his hat. He carved strange animals in wood, which he sold for pence to whoever would buy them. He did not come into his son's home, and only once did he speak to his grandchild. His influence on the highly strung boy was indeed negative. Andersen feared that he would become mad, like his grandfather.

However, he saw his paternal grandmother nearly every day. She earned a few coppers by working in a home for old people that had been established in the old Greybrothers' cloister. In his memoirs Andersen describes her as a quiet woman with mild blue eyes who was much loved. This is probably not a true picture. In a conversation with a friend, he admitted that she had been both jealous and vain. She often took her grandson with her to the cloister, and there he heard the old women tell fairy tales while they spun.

Andersen's descriptions of his childhood are more idyllic than truthful. Though he probably never starved, his parents' financial position was always precarious. The first time he attended the local theater with his parents, his comment was: "If we had as many buckets of butter as here are people, my, I would eat!"

In 1812 his father, who was a restless person, enlisted in the army. He had dreams of fighting for his hero, Napoleon, and returning a lieutenant. In those times in Denmark a soldier was despised even by the poorest of the poor. It was a hard blow for his wife. In September of that year his regiment was sent to Holstein. Six months later a truce was declared, and Andersen's father returned to Odense, not as a lieutenant but as a physical wreck. From then on his wife had to support the family by washing clothes in the Odense River.

Shortly after Andersen's eleventh birthday his father died. "The Icemaiden has taken him," was his mother's comment. Only a few months earlier, during the winter, his father had shown the boy that the frost had drawn a picture of a woman with outstretched hands on the glass of the window. As a joke he said, "That is the Icemaiden. She wants to take me." On 26 April 1816, she did.

There is no doubt that the inspiration for most of Andersen's fairy tales (like "The Icemaiden") can be found in his childhood. His style was probably developed at that time, too. The genre of the fairy tale is oral, not written. The words used are simple and not abstract; the message is seldom moralistic; and the wisdom is drawn from the experience of everyday life. The old women in the poorhouse who told fairy tales while they spun were probably all illiterate. Hans Christian heard the stories as they had been told for hundreds of years in the hovels of the poor.

That he was an extraordinary child there can be no doubt, for in a society in which the classes were sharply divided he soon managed to count some of the more wealthy and influential citizens among his friends. Andersen had a good voice and could sing as well as declaim whole scenes from Holberg. It amused the wealthy to invite the poor boy into their drawing rooms to entertain them. Even Prince Christian heard about him and gave him an audience. One of his friends, Colonel Høegh-Guldberg, advised the boy to ask the prince to help him get an education. Hans Christian sang songs he had composed himself and recited excerpts from plays. The prince then asked him if he wished to go on the stage. The little boy immediately said yes and then added, rather foolishly, that friends had advised him to ask for help to study but that he would rather become an actor. This frank reply did not please the prince, who suggested that an artisan skill, such as potting, would be more appropriate and that if he wished, His Royal Highness would help him secure an apprenticeship.

Hans Christian Andersen had no desire to learn a craft. He wanted to be famous. Even as a small child his ambitions were enormous. If he had not had this desire for fame, which as an adult often left him open to ridicule, he might have ended up a potter.

Exactly when the meeting between the prince and the pauper boy took place is not certain. Andersen seldom gave dates in his memoirs, and when he did they were often incorrect. There is a fairy-tale quality to this first meeting between the future king—who was later to help and support Andersen —and the young boy. The kings in the fairy tales are kind and familiar. Although Prince Christian did not wear slippers like the emperor in "The Swineherd," he was not above taking an interest in the meanest of his subjects.

How much schooling Andersen received is uncertain—again, the author is vague about such facts. He did attend a school that an old lady—a woman almost as ignorant as her pupils—held in the room of her cottage. Later he attended a school for Jewish children, which was closed after a year because of a decline in numbers. Read he could, and he borrowed books from everyone, though even in later life he spelled badly.

In 1818 his mother remarried. Again she chose a journeyman shoemaker. Her second husband was a poor choice, for although he was good-natured, he was also lazy and more willing to be supported than to support anyone. He took no particular interest in his stepson. As the family's finances went from bad to worse, it became increasingly important to find some sort of job for the boy. His mother wanted him to become a tailor and envisaged his having a shop with apprentices on the main street. Andersen did not find this plan acceptable. After he had been confirmed in the church a decision had to be made about his future. In Denmark, especially among the poor, the dividing line between childhood and adulthood was confirmation in the Lutheran faith.

It is difficult to understand how a child of fourteen could manage to convince his mother and all her friends that he should be allowed to go into the world to seek his fortune. Several factors probably helped. Andersen's father had told his wife that their son should always be allowed to do whatever he wished. Second, an old woman had predicted that one day the boy would become famous and that the city of Odense would be illuminated in his honor. (Both predictions came true. Odense was illuminated on 6 December 1867.) Possibly there was also a third reason: Hans Christian did not get along with his stepfather, and the atmosphere in the little household was difficult for the mother to handle. Whatever the reason, on 4 September 1819 Hans Christian Andersen set out for Copenhagen to become an actor. His clothes, which he carried in a bundle, were mere rags; in his purse he had ten rix-dollars. He started out like the hero in his fairy tale "The Traveling Companion" (1836).

The time in Copenhagen probably did less to form the fairy-tale author than his childhood had. There he was to experience a poverty worse than he had in Odense, and hunger was often his guest. But he survived because he had taken the fairy tales he had heard as a child for truth. He believed that you could win the princess and half a kingdom. He never married or received a kingdom, but through his fairy tales he did conquer the world. The hero —protagonist is not quite the right word—of a fairy tale is naive and clever. This combination accounts for his success. He is never worldly-wise; his intelligence is not blemished by sophistication. The "kings"—the people in power—who do know the world feel an urge to protect and help him. For naiveté once lost cannot be regained. And Andersen was helped!

His first successful literary venture was a slim volume written after the horrendous years spent acquiring an education, paid for by some of the most important people in Denmark, including the king. This was *A Journey on Foot from Copenhagen to the Eastern Point of Amager.* It tells of a young student who, on New Year's Eve, takes a walk on the little island of Amager, south of the capital. He meets an amazing array of characters on his wanderings, among them Saint Peter, the shoemaker of Jerusalem, and a cat that can talk. This book gave promise of what was to come. Here is to be found the same fantasy and literary style that he would later use in his fairy tales.

A Journey was published in 1829, and it took six years before he returned to a world where cats could talk. It was important for him to write a "serious" novel first, one that friends and critics would consider a major work. He achieved this with *The Improvisator* (1835), written after a long journey to Italy.

His first little pamphlet of fairy tales appeared the same year. It included "The Tinderbox," "Little Claus and Big Claus," "The Princess and the Pea," and "Little Ida's Flowers." Only the latter is totally original. The others are retellings of stories he had heard in his childhood. However, he borrowed only the basic plots. He seems never to have been interested in collecting and preserving fairy tales. They belonged to him; the fairy tale is the dream of the poor, and he had been poor.

The second little booklet was published the following year, in 1836. It contained "Inchelina" (or "Thumbelina," as it is called in most translations), "The Naughty Boy," and "The Traveling Companion."

The third booklet (1837) included two of his most famous tales: "The Little Mermaid" and "The Emperor's New Clothes." The three pamphlets were bound in one volume and published in book form in 1837, with an introduction by the author. From then on, almost every year until shortly before his death, new fairy tales appeared.

In a letter to the Danish author Bernhard Ingemann, after he had written his first tales, Andersen explains: "I have written them in a manner that I would tell them to a child." Most of the romantic authors, including Ingemann, had tried their hand at writing fairy tales, but their results were "literary" works not intended to be read aloud. Andersen "told" his fairy tales. You have the impression, even when you read them alone, of sitting next to the author. He establishes an intimacy between the reader and the poet that must have existed when the storyteller told his tales in the marketplace. In order to achieve this intimacy very few abstract words or long sentences are used. Even when the later tales were written "for adults as well, but in such a manner that a child can listen to them," he did not change his style.

The universe of the fairy tale is not that of ordinary life. In it what we consider fantastic is often the norm. One of the differences between the world portrayed in the fairy tales of the Brothers Grimm and those of Andersen is individuality. Andersen's trolls or witches are characters in their own right, they are not stereotypes. They have families, children, and lots of relatives. The old troll king of Norway in "The Hill of the Elves" (1846) is a lovable person with two sons who have been brought up a little too freely. We can identify with the inhabitants of this realm of fantasy. We are also given, in short sentences, details about the home life of the king of the elves. We are told the menu at the banquet and that his old housekeeper was distantly related to him. Anderson gives a personality to even a less important guest, such as the Hell horse. When the elfin girls dance, "the poor Hell horse got so dizzy watching it that he began to feel sick and had to leave the table."

Although the fantastic world in Andersen's fairy tales is strange, it is, at the same time, familiar. Its inhabitants may be able to perform and use magic, but they are also subject to the same vices as human beings. The pixie in "The Pixie and the Gardener's Wife" (1861) is vain, and in "The Pixie and the Grocer" (1853) he is materialistic. These are traits we easily recognize in others, though possibly not in ourselves.

The animals in the fairy tales are also individuals, easily distinguishable from each other. In the fables of Jean de La Fontaine they are used to illustrate a moral; they are stereotypes. In Andersen's tales animals live a life of their own. Like the figures of fantasy, they manifest the same virtues and vices as human beings, but the world with which they are familiar is the animal's. The rats in "The Pine Tree" (1846) do not consider the story of Humpty Dumpty worth listening to, and they comment: "It is a particularly uninteresting story. Don't you know any about bacon or candle stumps? No stories that take place in a larder?"

Andersen is very careful to differentiate each animal's knowledge of the world. The mole and the swallow cannot have had similar experiences, nor could they ever agree upon what is pleasant or worthwhile. The dung beetle is fond of dampness and dung, which is only natural if you have been born in a stable. The world is seen from the animal's point of view and human beings seldom play a part. In "The Happy Family" (1848) two elderly snails are busy trying to find a wife for their only son. They are the only survivors of the original family of large snails that once lived in the forest of burdock plants near a manor house. Having no children of their own, they have adopted a common garden snail. It is for him that a wife has to be found. When the wife wonders what lies beyond the forest of burdocks, her husband answers definitively: "Nothing. . . . There can be no better place than this, and what is beyond does not interest me." In "The Ugly Duckling" (1845) the mother duck explains the hugeness of the world to her little ones by saying: "The world is much larger than this. It stretches as far as the minister's wheat fields, though I have not been there." The world is no larger than that which is familiar.

Plants and flowers, too, have their own individuality besides the characteristic of their kind. In "The Snow Queen" (1846) each one tells a story: the daisy's is sentimental, the tiger lily's is ferocious, and the hyacinth's is unbearably sad. The rose appears in many of his stories and was obviously a favorite flower of Andersen's. It has the particular characteristic of being satisfied with its limited life. To bloom in the warm sunlight seems to have been enough to make it happy. It is amusing that it should have been the poet's favorite—he who was so ambitious and so seldom satisfied with his lot in life.

But if creatures of fantasy, animals, and flowers appeared in other fairy tales, Andersen was among the first to give life to inanimate objects. Teapots, weathercocks, fire tongs, a piggy bank, and even a spittoon, besides all the toys a child might possess, come to life in his fairy tales. As with animals and flowers, inanimate objects have only the knowledge of the world that they could have obtained through experience. Universal vices they all have, pride and vanity among them. In "The Flying Trunk" (1839) the merchant's son tells a story that takes place in the kitchen. Every one of the pots and pans and other objects to be found in such an establishment thinks himself the most important "person" there. They each speak from their own experience. For instance, only the market basket can speak with any assurance of the outside world, which makes it believe that it indeed should rule the kitchen.

All the flowers, animals, and objects act according to their natures and abilities. Andersen is very careful not to allow them to do things we know they cannot do. When it is put afloat by the street urchins, the darning needle does not become seasick, because a needle cannot. An exception to this rule is the reindeer in "The Snow Queen" (1846), which is allowed to shed two tears. It is this sort of realism that helps to make such stories so extraordinarily believable.

In the fairy tales where animals, plants, or objects are the heroes, human beings are merely incidental. They exist only insofar as they are meaningful to the real heroes of the stories. The cook in "The Darning Needle" (1847) is barely mentioned, except for her fingers—the only part the needle knows. The human world is hardly comprehensible to the animals; it often seems absurd or ridiculous. The objects are usually of the impression that the human race was created because of them, not vice versa. People had feet so that boots and bootjacks could exist, and necks to accommodate collars.

In most literary fairy tales, for example those of Oscar Wilde, a basic moral principle forms the core of the tale. Everything that happens is intended to illustrate and elucidate the central theme. In Andersen's fairy tales this is not so. What exactly is the moral of "The Story of a Mother" (1848)? It is difficult to find, yet it is a strangely moving story. "The Red Shoes" (1847) is one of the exceptions. Here, a basic moral point is followed almost to absurdity.

The world in Andersen's fairy tales is not just. The little mermaid becomes foam on the ocean. She does not marry the prince she has saved from drowning. Andersen's fairy tales are essentially realistic; we recognize his world because we know it. Virtue is not necessarily rewarded, nor evil punished. This is a fundamental difference between his fairy tales and those of other writers. It is a difference that must have been shocking in the nineteenth century. Because of the poverty of his youth, Andersen knew only too well that few were strong enough to swim against the tide; most succumbed. The hero of "Under the Willow Tree" (1853) does not have the strength to prevail and dies a lonely and miserable failure. It is interesting that in his notes Andersen declares that the tale "contains some pages from the story of my own life."

"The Snow Queen," one of his most famous stories, is an attempt to establish an accord between science and religion. Andersen was intensely interested in the technological world, which was then in its infancy. He called the machine "Master Bloodless," and, in coining this name, indicated his own fears of what was to come. At the same time, the discoveries and inventions made during his lifetime fascinated him, and he hailed their positive aspects in many stories. That Andersen was religious—believed in God—there can be no doubt. But no sect of Christianity could count him a member. His God was the one he had known as a child: ever good, kind, and uncomplicated. Andersen took no interest in religious controversy. In the short tale called simply "A Story" (1851), his dislike of the more severe and puritanical sects of Christianity is clearly shown.

Gerda in "The Snow Queen" represents his own Christian beliefs, a faith that was never questioning, and Kai represents science, ever searching in abstractions to prove an eternal truth. As philosophy the tale is not convincing, but the question it poses is far from irrelevant.

If "The Snow Queen" fails as philosophy, it is certainly successful as a story. Again, as in most of his fairy tales, we lose sight of the moral as we meet a group of enchanting characters: the robber girl and her mother, the Lapp woman who writes a letter on a dried codfish, and the Finnish woman who makes supper of it after she reads it. Typical of Andersen is the scene with the crows who are offered the choice between freedom and "permanent positions as royal court crows, with permission to eat all leftovers." Naturally, the crows choose the latter, saying: "To be secure is better than to fly." From the world of fantasy, Andersen draws us back to reality, to the familiar. We have all known "crows" who preferred security to freedom.

This realism in the fairy tales explains why they are still read and why they were so popular while Andersen lived. He had no "philosophy of life." He was an observer, and his perception was keen. Moral codes and philosophy can change with fashion, but human folly remains ever constant.

To one single theme he returned again and again: the poet and his relationship to those less gifted. "The Nightingale," written in 1845, and "The Gardener and His Master," written in 1871, four years before his death, are two of many stories about the artist and his relationship to society. It is interesting to compare the tales. In "The Nightingale" the artist is idealized—a bird with a beautiful voice serving an emperor. In "The Gardener and His Master," the artist is merely a gardener, the master a wealthy landowner. The emperor and the nightingale come to a mutual respect, the landowner and the gardener do not. It appears that in his old age, Andersen realized that the poet—the artist—will never be accepted as an equal by his "master." He must be content with being "outside," even in a society that may accept his art. This topic is explored further in "In the Duckyard," written in 1861, and "The Snail and the Rosebush," published the same year. Both stories are savage attacks on the poet's audience. In his notes, Andersen declares that the latter tale "belongs to that group of stories that I experienced myself."

For an author every experience—even the most sacred, the most personal—is material for his books. Andersen fell in love several times in his life: in 1830 with the sister of one of his friends. Her name was Riborg Voigt. Unlike the top in "The Sweethearts," Andersen never proposed. He met her again years later when time and motherhood had transformed the young girl into a matron. From this meeting stems the story of the top and the ball, with its rather cynical ending.

The last time Andersen fell in love the object of his affection was Jenny Lind. He met her when she was still unknown, before her world fame made every young man fall in love with her. They had much in common. Their backgrounds were similar —they were both artists, she a singer and he an author. She inspired his best-known fairy tale, "The Nightingale." Improbable as it may sound, he started the fairy tale the evening after having attended a performance at the Royal Theater in which Jenny appeared. Andersen proposed to Jenny Lind and she turned him down. He was more than infatuated; he was in love, and the refusal must have been painful. Again, experience was put to good use; the episode inspired "The Butterfly" (1861). One wonders if Jenny Lind used the same words as the mint plant did to the amorous butterfly: "Friendship, but no more!" They remained friends, for Jenny Lind was truly fond of him.

Not all of his fairy tales were written with such inspiration that a perfect story could be born overnight. Ideas often occurred that were tucked away for later use. The plot of "The Shadow" came to him while he lived in Rome, but the actual story was written much later, in Denmark. This tale of how a shadow became the master of a man, hiring the man to act as its shadow and finally having him killed, could have been written by Franz Kafka. It is one of the few that probably cannot be understood and enjoyed by children. This leads to the question, is Andersen a children's author? The answer is, not exclusively. If he had been, his fairy tales and stories would probably not have survived. Great books for children are for adults as well.

Looking back on all of them, what are the main differences between Andersen's fairy tales and those collected by the Brothers Grimm? First of all, there is very little cruelty in Andersen's fairy tales. Witches are often kind and use their magic to help rather than to destroy the hero. Magic is sparingly employed and seldom essential, as it is in so many folktales. The evil stepmother, who is introduced as a matter of course in the fairy tales of the Grimms, appears only in "The Wild Swans" (1838), which is a retelling of a Danish folktale. The bewitched princess, a stock character in folktales, is seldom found in Andersen's stories. She appears only in "The Traveling Companion." Unlike the Grimms, Andersen does not clearly define good and evil. Most of his characters—humans, animals, plants, or objects—are neither good nor bad. They are as human beings usually are—a mixture of the two. But to compare the fairy tales of the Brothers Grimm with those of Andersen is to do justice to neither. The only similarity between them is that the Grimms collected their fairy tales at approximately the same time as Andersen wrote his. Andersen used fairy tales for his own purposes and thus reformed the genre, whereas the Grimms were interested only in preserving them.

Andersen's fame was almost immediate. The first translation appeared in German, a language with which Andersen was sufficiently familiar to be able to correct the worst errors. Many of the English and American translations were made from the German edition; others were done by persons who had an incomplete knowledge of Danish. It would be more correct to classify these early attempts as retellings rather than translations. The sharpness of Andersen's writing was blunted to fit the sentimental Victorian concept of the fairy tale. Andersen was aware of the editing that had been done to his tales in America, but he was unable to do anything about it. Authors' copyrights simply did not exist, and most publishers pirated at will. Although his fairy tales sold widely, Andersen never received any money from America. One reputable English publisher finally refused to print any more of Andersen's fairy tales because he knew that within weeks, or even days, the edition would be pirated and would appear on sale at half the price.

Andersen can still fare badly, especially in books for younger children. In many picture books his stories have been retold in such a manner that they bear little resemblance to the original. In some, even the titles have been changed. "The Nightingale" becomes "The Emperor's Nightingale" in most translations in spite of the fact that the whole point of the fairy tale is that the nightingale—the poet—can never belong to the emperor. But even with bowdlerizing and often poor translations, the genius of Andersen cannot be destroyed. He belongs among those few authors whose fame will last.

Selected Bibliography

WORKS OF HANS CHRISTIAN ANDERSEN IN ENGLISH

"It's Perfectly True!" and Other Stories. Translated by Paul Leyssac. With illustrations by Vilhelm Pedersen. London: Macmillan, 1937.

Andersen's Fairy Tales. Translated by Jean Hersholt. With illustrations by Fritz Kredel. New York: Heritage Press, 1942.

Fairy Tales. Translated by R. P. Keigwin. With illustrations by Vilhelm Pedersen. Odense: Flensted, 1950–1958.

Fairy Tales and Stories. Translated by Reginald Spink. With illustrations reproduced from paper cuts made by Hans Christian Andersen. London: J. M. Dent, 1960; New York: E. P. Dutton, 1960.

Fairy Tales. Translated by L. W. Kingsland. With illustrations by Ernest H. Shepard. London: Oxford University Press, 1961; New York: H. Z. Walck, 1961.

Hans Christian Andersen: The Complete Fairy Tales and Stories. Translated by Erik C. Haugaard. With cover illustration by Maurice Sendak. Garden City, N.Y.: Doubleday, 1974.

EDITIONS OF ANDERSEN'S AUTOBIOGRAPHY

The True Story of My Life. Translated from the German by Mary Howitt. London: Longman, Brown, 1847.

The True Story of My Life. Translated by D. Spillan. London, 1852.

The Story of My Life. Translated by Horace E. Scudder. New York, 1871.

The Fairy Tale of My Life. Translated by W. Glyn Jones. New York: British Book Centre, 1954.

CRITICAL AND BIOGRAPHICAL STUDIES

Bredsdorff, Elias. *Hans Christian Andersen: The Story of His Life and Work.* New York: Scribners, 1975.

Grønbech, Bo. *Hans Christian Andersen.* Boston: Twayne Publishers, 1980.

Toksvig, Signe. *The Life of Hans Christian Andersen.* London: Macmillan, 1933; New York: Harcourt, Brace, 1934.

—ERIK HAUGAARD

EDWARD ARDIZZONE

1900–1979

WHEN EDWARD ARDIZZONE died in 1979, he left behind an abundant legacy of books and paintings for children and adults in his clearly recognizable literary and artistic styles. Ardizzone felt very strongly about the importance of writing, that it should have a flow, a cadence, to make reading aloud pleasurable, and that it should never condescend to a child. The illustrations should extend the text, revealing more about characters and events. Text and illustrations are interdependent in his work, and since he illustrated his own texts as well as those written by others, both text and illustrations must be considered here. Many of his stories for children capture characters and scenes from his childhood, softened by time and the quirks of memory.

Ardizzone came from a long line of artists. His great-grandfather was an amateur watercolorist who claimed to be a direct descendant of Joshua Kirby, a famous eighteenth-century painter and friend of Gainsborough. Ardizzone's mother, half Scottish and half English, had studied painting in Paris before her marriage; her father, Captain Kirby, was an artist as well as a sailing master. Ardizzone's father, Auguste, a fine linguist but unappreciative of the arts, worked for the Eastern Extension Telegraph Company in Haiphong, in the province of Tonkin (part of French Indochina), where Ardizzone was born on 16 October 1900.

The oldest of five children, Ardizzone had an unusual childhood. Although his father remained in the Far East, visiting England occasionally, in 1905 Ardizzone's mother brought him and his two younger sisters (two brothers were born later) to England to stay. She later departed abruptly to rejoin her husband for a few years, leaving two of her children in England with their grandmother. Despite his grandmother's frequent outbursts, Ardizzone's time with her was essentially happy, for he was given plenty of freedom. When an older cousin, Arthur, came to visit for a month, the two boys became fast friends.

After his mother's return to England with a new baby, she encouraged her children in the arts and gave them dramatic readings. They seemed to take after her rather than their father in their interests. When Ardizzone and his two sisters were still children, they submitted drawings and poems to magazine contests, and Ardizzone won a prize. He also read widely. In addition to children's books such as *Little Black Sambo* and the works of Beatrix Potter, he was fascinated by Captain Kirby's illustrated log books of his frigate, *Owen Glendower*, Gustave Doré's pictures for Dante's *Inferno*, and John Bunyan's *Pilgrim's Progress*, which he was sure he would illustrate himself one day. The influence of the sea surfaced early, too: Frederick Marryat's sea stories were favorites.

Soon after Ardizzone's mother returned to England, she and her children moved to Ipswich so that Edward could attend Ipswich Grammar School. Big, overweight, and shy, he was bullied and physically abused by the other boys. In classes his timidity made him tongue-tied, unable to function properly because of his emotional turmoil.

Those were difficult days. During his last year there his cousin Arthur joined him, making life much easier. Together the boys explored the docks, barges, and steamers that were to appear later in the Little Tim books.

Not having money for art school, Ardizzone took a six-month commerce course at Cannings College, where he was a superior student. Then he went to work, eventually spending six years in the statistical department of the Eastern Extension Telegraph Company. Bored, he began to draw again, doodling and caricaturing. He started attending the Westminster School of Art three nights a week, where he met Gabriel White, who was to become his brother-in-law and biographer. Those evenings were happy times, full of beer drinking and art discussions with their teacher at a local pub after class.

When Ardizzone's father gave him and his sisters £500 each for a nest egg, Ardizzone and his sister Betty promptly quit their jobs and toured the Continent. Ardizzone had decided to become a professional artist. His first commission of £75 was for 125 drawings to illustrate a 1929 edition of Sheridan Le Fanu's *In a Glass Darkly*. Five years elapsed before he was given another book to illustrate. During that time he met and married Catherine Anderson.

During the early thirties Ardizzone wrote the first Little Tim book, which was rejected by several publishers before Oxford University Press accepted it in 1935; *Little Tim and the Brave Sea Captain* was published the following year. Sales were slow at first, but steady, and Ardizzone's career blossomed. Other children's books quickly followed: *Lucy Brown and Mr. Grimes* (1937) and *Tim and Lucy Go to Sea* (1938). Then World War II intervened; Ardizzone was appointed an official war artist after brief service in a territorial anti-aircraft regiment.

After the war Ardizzone produced illustrations for *Pilgrim's Progress*, fulfilling the earlier promise he had made to himself. The Little Tim books began anew, too. In 1952 UNESCO sent him to India to attend a seminar and teach classes in silk-screen printing, and the following year he became an art tutor at the Royal College of Art, a position he held until 1961.

Ardizzone continued to draw and paint, illustrating several books by James Reeves, Eleanor Farjeon, Anthony Trollope, Eleanor Estes, and many others; his illustrations graced later editions of *Tom Sawyer* (1961), *Huckleberry Finn* (1961), and *Robinson Crusoe* (1968). His output was prodigious, but a fall in 1975 left him crippled. The following year he suffered another fall, and in 1979 he died, leaving a rich artistic and literary legacy.

In his essay "Creation of a Picture Book," Ardizzone tells of the origins of the Little Tim stories and how vital it is for the writer to think visually:

> At the turn of each page . . . the text must end with a natural break, a note of interrogation or suspense. With rare exceptions, the professional writer who is no artist finds this extremely difficult, if not impossible, to do. Not being visually minded, he cannot leave out enough. . . . And this, I think, is why the best picture books have been created by artists who have written their own text.

He explained why words should be carefully chosen, not only for sense but for sound, for cadence. Authors should not condescend to the child, yet the language should be clear and understandable. Furthermore, whether in poetry or prose, a reading aloud should delight the ear. Ardizzone attempted to carry out his beliefs in all of his own work, and a close look at some of his children's books reveals his success.

Little Tim and the Brave Sea Captain began as an entertainment for Ardizzone's two children. As the stories were retold and embellished, Edward realized that other children might enjoy them, too. He felt that good illustrations were crucial to elaborate on the narrative, set mood, and develop character. Speech balloons were an additional aid, but he used them sparingly; otherwise his work would look like comic books. The seaside setting was a mixture of the actual and the remembered: Tim's home was based on the one where Ardizzone visited his brother David; the various sea and ship scenes were remembered from Ipswich and the author's many experiences. His tale is full of long rolling sentences:

> When it was fine he spent the day on the beach playing in and out of the boats, or talking to his friend the old boatman who taught him all about the sea and ships.

Ardizzone also speaks directly to the reader in the manner of a storyteller: "You can imagine how pleased Tim was to see his daddy and his mummy and his old friends again." In addition to the cadenced prose there are challenging, rich words, like "barquentine," "anchored," "clambered," "grog," and others, especially sea and ship terms ("galley," "stowaway," "quay"). The illustrations extend the text, even those showing the backs of characters (Ardizzone felt that people's backs were very expressive).

The illustrations for *Little Tim and the Brave Sea Captain* extend the characterizations and reveal mood. When Tim announces his desire to go to sea, his parents laugh, telling him he is much too young. The next illustration displays Tim's disappointment as he stands on the beach facing the sea, body bent forward, hands clasped behind his back. There is no question about his dejection. As with most children, though, his moods swing abruptly; in the next illustration Tim is dancing for joy at being invited to accompany the boatman to the steamer. Ardizzone adds humor for adults, too. As the boatman and Tim chug along, in the foreground are a broken spar and a crate labeled, respectively, "flotsam" and "jetsam." In the text the taste of grog "made Tim want to be a sailor more than ever."

Tim is a delightful, well-developed protagonist, thoughtless as children are: what of his parents' worry when he disappears? He also gets seasick, cries about the work he has to do, and is frightened and tearful when the ship is about to sink. But he has courage, perseverance, and a kind of indomitable spirit that keeps him going through the bad times. His adventurous spirit is admirable; he is willing to take risks and suffer the consequences.

The next two books introduce a new protagonist. *Lucy Brown and Mr. Grimes* (1937) was written for Ardizzone's daughter, Christianna. Lucy meets and talks to a strange man in the park, a plot line that created a furor in the United States after its publication there; many years later (1970) a new version with new illustrations appeared revealing Mr. Grimes as an old family friend. In the sequel, *Tim and Lucy Go to Sea,* their voyage is threatened by mutineers. Again rich seafaring vocabulary is used: "lee shore," "after hatch," "figurehead," plus other difficult words ("desperate," "guardian"), and once more Ardizzone speaks directly to his audience: "You can imagine how excited Lucy was!" He also uses foreshadowing: "Then an adventure happened which made a great difference to all of them." The first editions of these first Little Tim books were hand-colored and completely in color instead of alternating color with black-and-

white drawings, as in subsequent editions and later Tim books. Although the switch to the alternating use of color was most likely prompted by economic considerations, Ardizzone also enjoyed drawing.

After the long war hiatus, the Little Tim books began again, three in fairly rapid succession: *Little Tim to the Rescue* (1949), *Tim and Charlotte* (1951), and *Tim in Danger* (1953). In the first book the reader is introduced to Ginger, a boy who is a foil for the industrious Tim; Ginger gets into mischief with almost tragic results. When Ginger disobeys the captain's orders to go below during a fierce storm, Tim also disobeys, saving Ginger and the ship's cat and receiving a gold medal for bravery. Tim is studious, too, earning firsts in all his exams when he returns from the sea. The admirable qualities of courage and bravery, especially when friends are involved, are stressed repeatedly in the Little Tim books.

When *Tim All Alone* was published in 1956, it was awarded the Kate Greenaway Medal for the best illustrated book of the year in Great Britain. The book has a startling beginning: Tim returns home from a long holiday to find his parents gone and a "to let" sign on his house. Tim cries, says his prayers, then determinedly sets out to find them wherever they may be. He hires on as a cabin boy to broaden his search. The vocabulary continues to be challenging ("inquire," "fret," "quayside," "hove-to," "dismay"), and once again the narrator speaks directly to the reader: "Now don't forget this cat because, later on, he is going to play a very important part in this tale." There are other direct asides to the audience as the story unfolds. The reader learns that life at sea is difficult as Tim is put to work "painting, scrubbing, running errands and helping the steward serve the officers' meals," and is often soaked with rain or salt sea spray. Foreshadowing plays its part again ("But Tim's troubles were not over yet") in a tale that involves quite a bit of coincidence to create the satisfying ending so enjoyed by children.

Tim's expressive back and postures are most notable when he returns to his ship after fruitless dockside inquiries about his parents. The speech balloons reveal the sympathy of captain and crew, later providing contrast to the heartless comments of another captain and crew. Watercolor illustrations capture the charm of some interiors and the several moods of the sea, in addition to highlighting and revealing characters. The black-and-white drawings add to characterization and drama. The story bears a strong resemblance to its precursors (Tim's tears; stowing away; getting sick; shipboard chores; disaster at sea; the happy reunion). Similar patterns are found in the later books as well.

Tim's Friend Towser (1962), *Tim and Ginger* (1965), and *Ship's Cook Ginger* (1977) reunite Tim and Ginger. The latter two books begin at home as most of the books do, include a variety of adventures at sea, and end at home or en route there. *Tim and Ginger* stresses bravery and friendship as Tim, worried when Ginger fails to return from shrimping, sets out to find him, "borrowing" a boat. Each boy eventually rescues the other. Again the narrator speaks directly to the reader, sometimes with long, rolling sentences: "You can imagine how anxiously Tim's father and mother waited all that night for news, and how tired and sad they were when the dawn came and still the boys had not been found." The vocabulary remains challenging ("grimly," "miserable") as Ardizzone writes about the qualities little boys admire: honesty, bravery, and loyalty.

In *Ship's Cook Ginger,* the last of the Little Tim books, when Tim and Ginger go to sea, Tim's parents accompany them as passengers. They soon disembark because of a crucial business matter, Tim and Ginger seeing them off at the train station and fortuitously missing their meal aboard ship. Captain, cook, first mate, and half the crew become ill, leaving the stubborn second mate in charge, a near disaster. Ginger, made cook after boasting about his culinary ability, produces a mouse in his first stew; the other meals grow progressively worse. Tim, with help, again saves the day and is rewarded for bravery. Ginger is taken under the recovered cook's wing and learns to make good meals and "scrumptious pies."

The writing pattern set in the earlier books is repeated here, the cadenced prose often with compound or complex sentences, the rich vocabulary ("bosun," "poltroon," "mooched about"), the direct talk to the reader: "You can just imagine how excited were Tim and Ginger as they packed." Ardizzone injects his own brand of humor when he writes that "it [a tonic] was especially good for boys because it was so nasty that they hurried up and became better." He creates page-turning suspense either by the use of oversized capital letters at the end of a page ("THEN THE BLOW FELL . . .") or by intriguing circumstances: "Sadly Tim crept into his bunk. He was frightened because he knew he was right." Foreshadowing plays a pivotal role as well in keeping the reader in suspense: "In fact,

when they [Tim and Ginger] arrived on board they were too full to eat even a tiny bit of the cook's scrumptious meat pie, which, as you will find out later, was lucky for them."

The illustrative pattern was to remain the same throughout the Little Tim books, watercolors alternating with expressive black-and-white drawings, speech balloons used sparingly, but adding important information ("It's poisonous!"). The American edition of *Ship's Cook Ginger* published by Macmillan, unlike some of the earlier editions, uses a stark white rather than cream-colored paper, which creates a harsher effect in the drawings. *Tim All Alone* also uses stark white, but the lines in it seem lighter, less muddy.

Ardizzone wrote children's books with other protagonists but with essentially the same format. In *Johnny the Clockmaker* (1960) a young boy loves to make things with wood. When Johnny announces that he plans to make a grandfather clock, everyone except Susannah, a classmate, laughs at him (one teasing child looks like Ginger). Since Johnny, like Tim, is determined and resourceful, he succeeds and gains the respect of all. There are more traditional storytelling elements here than in the Little Tim stories. *Johnny* begins, "Once upon a time"; contains a refrain ("JOHNNY IS UP TO HIS NONSENSE AGAIN"); and has a hero whose cleverness is repeatedly stressed, who listens to and heeds advice when going in search of something tangible, and who is successful on his third attempt to make the clock, with the help of Susannah. Ardizzone continues to use foreshadowing and direct comments to the reader.

Ardizzone's portrayal of women should be noted. As a rule they emerge as types—worried or concerned, but reassured by their husbands; motherly; or well-meaning do-gooders. Except for Mrs. Smawley in *Tim and Lucy Go to Sea*, the women do lots of hugging, caring, and providing of nourishment, but little else. The few girl protagonists are not strong, nontraditional role models: for example, Lucy spends most of her time darning socks (*Tim and Lucy Go to Sea*). The men, on the other hand, have the active dramatic roles, which may explain why the books are especially popular with boys.

Ardizzone's collaborations with other children's writers are also noteworthy, especially considering his strong feelings about the bond between text and illustrations. Except for picture books, he usually worked with pen and ink, creating expressive, detailed illustrations. Eleanor Farjeon's collection of stories *The Little Bookroom* (1955), one of Ardizzone's most successful collaborations and winner of the Carnegie Medal, shows the artist's drawing ability at its best. One of the half-page illustrations for "The King's Daughter Cries for the Moon" contains a variety of people: soldiers with a prisoner; a detective looking for clues on his knees; another on a rooftop looking through a spyglass; yet another flat against a building wall trying to stay hidden, while around the corner from him a man enters the building; and a boy being chased in the background while two people in windows converse. All of this activity plus architectural embellishments form a simple, uncluttered drawing. It is an amazing feat, and it captures the text perfectly, too.

Other illustrations in the book are equally successful. The introductory one for "The Little Dressmaker" is intentionally cluttered, creating a strong sense of place (fabric scattered about, dressmaker patterns on the walls). The drawing for "The Lady's Room" is simpler, a mood piece with little to distract our attention from the pensive, bored lady seated at the window. Other drawings capture the mood and essence of each story for a perfect blending of prose and art. Eleanor Farjeon wrote Ardizzone: "All of childhood is here, all I feel about childhood in the dim recesses where that part of me still lives. Thank you with all my heart."

Ardizzone illustrated ten books by James Reeves, more than for any other writer. *Titus in Trouble* (1959), a picture book, resembles the Little Tim books in format except that the ink drawings are covered with a green watercolor wash and, at times, a drawing and a watercolor painting appear opposite one another. The paintings are especially well done, rich and full of detail. In a much longer Reeves book, *Sailor Rumbelow and Other Stories* (1962), the numerous drawings, all less than half a page in size, range from simple sketches to more complicated compositions, all ideally suited to their subjects. Some sketches have heavy cross-hatchings forming blotches, yet despite their opacity many details are visible, giving the illustrations a strong personality.

An artist must be especially careful when illustrating poetry so that he does not distract the reader from the poem, so that he highlights it instead of competing with the poem for attention. Ardizzone succeeds admirably from his first drawing in Robert Graves's *Ann at Highwood Hall: Poems for Children*

(1964), showing Ann shrinking in fear from the plate her drunken father has hurled at her, through a series of fortuitous events, to the final illustration in the title poem showing Ann's back as she works at her loom by starlight. The book is representative of his other illustrations of poetry; the pictures are ideally suited to the content.

What values does Ardizzone offer children in his books? Through Tim and other characters he stresses an indomitable spirit and a willingness to work hard and to persevere despite setbacks and hardships. As in the traditional folktale pattern, Ardizzone rewards good and punishes folly, but gently. "Good" in Ardizzone's estimation includes the qualities mentioned earlier: courage and bravery; friendship and all that it implies; honesty; the willingness to listen to good advice; and studiousness, the desire to learn. These traits are within a child's grasp; the characters are human, to be admired and emulated. Excitement and drama may propel the reader from book to book even when events are contrived or improbable, but the personalities of Tim and others bind the books together and give them a lasting value.

What will endure of Ardizzone's work for children? His contribution to Farjeon's *A Little Bookroom* will last. In particular, the Little Tim books should remain favorites for the qualities of the spirit expressed in them and captured in the illustrations. His earliest book, *Little Tim and the Brave Sea Captain*, has been popular for almost fifty years, a testament to its staying power. It received the Lewis Carroll Shelf Award, which is given to those books deserving a prominent place on the shelf with *Alice in Wonderland*. The other books in the series are always in demand. Children obviously love the distinctive and memorable adventures Ardizzone has created for them.

Selected Bibliography

The following bibliography, except for the Little Tim books, is sharply truncated, since Ardizzone's work was extensive.

WORKS WRITTEN AND ILLUSTRATED BY EDWARD ARDIZZONE

Little Tim and the Brave Sea Captain. London and New York: Oxford University Press, 1936. Rev. ed. London: Oxford University Press, 1955; New York: H. Z. Walck, 1955.

Lucy Brown and Mr. Grimes. London and New York:

Oxford University Press, 1937. Rev. ed. London: Bodley Head, 1970; New York: H. Z. Walck, 1971.

Tim and Lucy Go to Sea. London and New York: Oxford University Press, 1938. Rev. ed. London: Oxford University Press, 1958; New York: H. Z. Walck, 1958.

Tim to the Rescue. London and New York: Oxford University Press, 1949.

Tim and Charlotte. London and New York: Oxford University Press, 1951.

Tim in Danger. London and New York: Oxford University Press, 1953.

Tim All Alone. London: Oxford University Press, 1956; New York: H. Z. Walck, 1961.

Johnny the Clockmaker. London: Oxford University Press, 1960; New York: H. Z. Walck, 1960.

Tim's Friend Towser. London: Oxford University Press, 1962; New York: H. Z. Walck, 1962.

Tim and Ginger. London: Oxford University Press, 1965; New York: H. Z. Walck, 1965.

Tim to the Lighthouse. London: Oxford University Press, 1968; New York: H. Z. Walck, 1968.

Tim's Last Voyage. London: Bodley Head, 1972; New York: H. Z. Walck, 1973.

Ship's Cook Ginger. London: Bodley Head, 1977; New York: Macmillan, 1978.

WORKS ILLUSTRATED BY ARDIZZONE

The Pilgrim's Progress (John Bunyan). London: Faber, 1947.

Titus in Trouble (James Reeves). London: Bodley Head, 1959; New York: H. Z. Walck, 1960.

The Little Bookroom (Eleanor Farjeon). London: Oxford University Press, 1955; New York: H. Z. Walck, 1956.

The Witch Family (Eleanor Estes). New York: Harcourt, Brace and World, 1960.

Sailor Rumbelow and Other Stories (James Reeves). London: Heinemann, 1962; New York: E. P. Dutton, 1962.

The Alley (Eleanor Estes). New York: Harcourt, Brace and World, 1964.

Ann at Highwood Hall: Poems for Children (Robert Graves). Garden City, N.Y.: Doubleday, 1964.

CRITICAL AND BIOGRAPHICAL STUDIES

Ardizzone, Edward. "Creation of a Picture Book." In *Only Connect: Readings on Children's Literature*, edited by Sheila Egoff et al. 2nd ed. New York: Oxford University Press, 1980. (Reprinted from *Top of the News*, December 1959.)

Ardizzone, Edward. *The Young Ardizzone*. London: Studio Vista, 1970.

Doyle, Brian, ed. *The Who's Who of Children's Literature*. New York: Schocken Books, 1968.

Reeves, James. "Edward Ardizzone." In *Twentieth-Century Children's Writers*, edited by Daniel Kirkpatrick. 2nd ed. New York: St. Martin's Press, 1983; London: Macmillan, 1983.

White, Gabriel. *Edward Ardizzone: Artist and Illustrator*. London: Bodley Head, 1979; New York: Schocken Books, 1980.

—MARILYN F. APSELOFF

ASBJØRNSEN AND MOE

1812–1885 and 1813–1882

IN THE MID-NINETEENTH century northern Europe enjoyed a cultural renaissance nourished in large part by the deep roots of national folk life. By 1815 Jacob and Wilhelm Grimm had already collected and published *Kinder- und Hausmärchen*, later published in English as *German Household Stories* and more popularly known as *Grimm's Fairy Tales*, which encouraged the romantic revival of folklore elsewhere. In Norway, newly independent after centuries of domination by Denmark and Sweden, Peter Christen Asbjørnsen and Jørgen Moe collaborated on four volumes of *Norske folkeeventyr* (Norwegian Folk Tales, 1841–1844). Asbjørnsen and Moe were inspired by the Brothers Grimm and by the research of Ivar Aasen into Norwegian rural dialects. Previously, literate Norwegians had written in Danish, but now patriotic linguists campaigned for a written language to reflect current Norwegian popular speech. As a result, the importance of Asbjørnsen and Moe lay not only in their collection of folktales but also in their pioneer work to develop a Norwegian written language with its own character, independent of Danish. Newly awakened pride in their native land brought the tales a wide audience at home, and this was followed by international success in Europe and America.

The Norwegian tales were added to the literature of English-speaking children when the eminent Oxford scholar George Webbe Dasent published his English translation of the Asbjørnsen and Moe collection, *Popular Tales from the Norse*, in 1859. This translation was soon being read and loved by American as well as English children. Dasent had sensed the homely, vigorous, humorous flavor of Norwegian storytelling and put the texts into what he called "mother English, which anyone that runs may read." The two Norwegian writers considered Dasent's translation "the best and happiest rendering . . . that has appeared. . . . The translator has understood and grasped the relation in which these tales stand to Norse nature and the life of the people, and how they have sprung out of both." Later translations of the tales into English usually follow the tone of Dasent's renderings.

When Asbjørnsen and Moe spoke of Norse nature and the life of the people, they did so from intimate knowledge of Norwegian folk language and folk music, the scenic beauty of Norway, and Norwegian peasant life. Jørgen Moe spent his boyhood in an inland region of eastern Norway, Ringerike, where the country people still kept to their old ways and knew a phenomenal number of traditional tales. Jørgen heard these as a child. Like a true folklore hero, he was a younger son who had to leave home to seek his fortune in some other career than the management of family property. Showing academic promise, he was sent to school at Norderhof, north of Christiania (now Oslo), and there in 1826 met Peter Christen Asbjørnsen, who at the age of fifteen had shown no academic inclinations whatever and had been sent to Norderhof in the hope of improvement. In spite of their different habits and temperaments, the two boys hit it off at once and formed a friendship that was to last a lifetime.

Asbjørnsen was soon sent home to Christiania, but in 1833 the two young men met again at the university there. This was the year when Andreas Faye's *Norske Sagn* (Norwegian Legends) appeared, modeled after the Grimms' tales. Faye's collection was small, but it was the first serious effort to publish traditional Norwegian stories. Faye was a pastor who hoped that the tales would help to root out superstition among his parishioners as well as to entertain children; he said that superstition exposed to the light would burst as trolls do in the sunshine. Both Asbjørnsen and Moe were attracted to the project and offered to add to Faye's collection.

The following year Moe was forced to leave Christiania because of poor health, returning from time to time until 1842 to pursue his studies. Although he had now decided on a career in the church, he had already written to Asbjørnsen, "If I can ever get well again I am going to start telling folk tales . . . that shall be Norwegian!" At Christmastime 1837 public interest in Norwegian folklore was given an impetus by a little picture book of traditional stories called *Nor: En Billedbog for den norske Ungdom* (Nor: A Picture Book for Norwegian Youth). The first part had been collected by Bernt Moe, Jørgen's cousin, who wanted to give children models of Norwegian virtues—courage, simplicity, fairness. The second part of the book, arranged by Asbjørnsen, was full of tales with rollicking action. These were even more well received than the moralizing tales. Jørgen Moe contributed an anonymous poem as introduction. At the same time, he and Asbjørnsen were planning a joint publication of some of the stories they had collected.

By 1840 Moe was writing a prospectus for the new book, proclaiming that the soul of a people shone forth in their national tales. Furthermore, he said, "No cultivated person now doubts the scientific importance of the folk tales; . . . they help to determine a people's unique character and outlook." This was a potent idea, forcefully stated: the old tales not only reflected national character but also were a strong influence in forming that character.

Within a year after the collection's publication in 1841, Moe claimed that the book was "a great success, almost a furor." The announced title, *Norske folke- og børne-eventyr* (Norse Folk and Children's Stories), suggested a child audience, but the book was reviewed as a serious piece of significant literature. A controversy developed. Were these primitive tales, told in a peasant dialect, really worthy to represent the soul of Norway? Romanticists enthusiastically championed the stories as symbols of true Norwegian identity. But in the view of academic conservatives such childish, naive tales could not be accepted as typical of Norway's best heritage. Some considered the language and style offensive, objectionably full of colloquialisms—the idiom of illiteracy. It was not until Jacob Grimm and other acknowledged German authorities praised the collection to the skies that critics at home were silenced. By 1844 three supplements had completed the first edition of *Norske folke-eventyr*.

Following its publication the university gave grants-in-aid to both collaborators to enable them to travel farther afield through the remoter parts of Norway to look for more stories. Few were found, but Asbjørnsen and Moe could now fairly claim that their collection was as complete as possible, and they could prepare a definitive edition. For this Moe wrote a long and scholarly introduction that proved to be a substantial contribution to the literature of international folklore. The university gave the stamp of its approval by asking Moe to lecture on folklore. His concept was that similar themes and motifs appeared in the folktales of many nations, and were probably disseminated very early by the invasions of nomadic Aryans of Indo-European origin. However, once these stories had crossed the borders of Norway, they had taken on a Norwegian identity to a remarkable degree, embodying national traits—humor in the face of difficulties and sturdy common sense in the round of daily life. In their folktales the Norwegian people were saying clearly and unforgettably, "This is who we are." The new edition appeared in 1851–1852 with critical notes and variant texts, relating the stories to those of other countries. A glowing review by P. A. Munch in the Christiania *Morgenbladet* (1852) called attention to the importance of this work for future studies in history, ethnic research, and comparative mythology. Most of all the style was praised—that very style which had been the thorniest point of controversy. Munch called it a " superb, national . . . style, a mode of expression that spoke directly to the childlike mind and heart." Not childish, it should be noted, but childlike; the tales were ageless and for all ages.

During the first years of his work on the folktales, Jørgen Moe showed an unlimited admiration for the traditions of the Norwegian peasant, but he was not sympathetic when in 1848 these same peasants began to stir with the rising tide of democracy throughout northern Europe and to make political demands. Moe was, in fact, a conservative by nature. Speaking to a student audience he exalted not the folktales but the sagas of Norway's glorious past as a spur to youth in "the noblest of all struggles, the battle to secure the full, free, and true development of our folk character." By 1853 he had turned entirely to the duties of his work in the church; he spent the last five years of his career in the honored position of bishop in the diocese of Kristiansand on the south coast. His son, Moltke Moe, collaborated with Asbjørnsen as a folklorist in his own right. One of his special interests was the mythical concepts of Norse folklore.

Jørgen Moe's temperament was serious and high-minded. During the folklore years he suffered from an inner tension and wrote to Asbjørnsen, "I need what you in your unobstructed perception of life's phenomena do not need—a system [of thought, a philosophical attitude]." Moe's work on the folktales evidently helped him to achieve an emotional equilibrium. His portrait as an older man appears with one of Asbjørnsen in *The Fairy World*, translated by H. L. Braekstad in the 1890's. Here Moe is seen in his role as pastor, calm and restrained, wearing a formal cravat and tightly fitting coat; he is smooth shaven, with a long upper lip and firm mouth. He could be a brother of Ralph Waldo Emerson.

In the eyes of Jørgen Moe, his friend Peter Christen Asbjørnsen had an enviable natural equilibrium. Asbjørnsen's portrait shows a bush of curly hair and a short beard framing his round face; he looks out through spectacles with a relaxed, benign expression. The son of a glazier in Christiania, in his early years he spent his free time in his father's workshop listening to the talk of the apprentices and their friends, who were usually from the country. Some were great storytellers, and Peter Christen became a gifted storyteller himself. He wasted his time at school in Norderhof and later at the university, showing some interest now in journalism, now in geology, and tentatively choosing medicine as a career, but never focusing his energies enough to succeed at anything. Studies in natural science and forestry occasionally brought him a position with the government forest service or other similar work, and meanwhile he was collecting folktales. In a letter to Andreas Faye written in 1835 he called himself Faye's "legend ambassador

extraordinary." But Asbjørnsen soon became dissatisfied with the moralistic tone of Faye's treatment of the tales and began collaborating with Moe on a separate publication. When Moe later retired from that role to devote his energies to the church, Asbjørnsen went on to edit *Norske huldreeventyr og folkesagn* (Norwegian Fairy Tales and Folk Legends, 1845–1848), framing each story with a sketch of peasant life in the region where the tale was told. These sketches had great appeal, even for the intelligentsia who had been dubious about the original work of the two folklorists. The *Huldreeventyr* went through many editions comprising various combinations of stories and notes and giving credit to all who had helped compile them. Asbjørnsen had accomplished a remarkable feat, the creation of a written language that employed the Dano-Norwegian words already in use by men of letters as well as words from Norwegian popular speech, giving acceptable spellings. By keeping to a middle path and demonstrating his sensitivity to what was appropriate, he had managed to please both literary conservatives and patriotic romanticists. Even those who thought that Asbjørnsen had made too many concessions to the Danish usage of literary circles conceded that Norwegian youth would be well served by the tales.

Sigrid Undset's introduction to *True and Untrue and Other Norse Tales* (1945) tells how children looked on Asbjørnsen's house in a suburb of Christiania almost as a shrine. The house was old and rambling. He had lived there in an apartment, a bachelor all his days, surrounded by the gifts of many friends, whom he loved to entertain. He was also a fine cook and writer of cookbooks in a day when a man who "minded the house" was a rarity.

Children have little or no interest in the sources, parallels, and variants of folktales; they simply want to hear the stories. The tales give pleasure like wild flowers. But like wild flowers, folktales have roots that give them life, and storytellers like to be aware of the roots. In this regard we owe a debt to Dasent, later knighted for his contributions to literature; he wrote a long introduction for his translation of *Popular Tales from the Norse*, basing his work on Moe's introduction to the definitive Norwegian edition of *Norske folkeeventyr*. Dasent pays tribute to Jacob Grimm for raising all folktales "to a study fit for the energies of grown men, and to all the dignity of a science." He makes two striking analogies to explain the resemblances of stories told in different countries, though coming from a common Aryan tribal source. "They are like as sisters of one house are like. . . . They are like the sleeping thoughts of many men upon one and the same thing."

Dasent then shows how the eddas and sagas, the ancient tales preserved "incorrupt" in isolated Iceland, evolved into the folktales of Norway, which were nourished by the same primal needs, hopes, and fears. The battles of the old Norse gods against the Frost Giants become the combats of mortal men against the giants and trolls. The mantle of the gods falls on the shoulders of the Norse hero Cinderlad; the magic sword of the Volsungs is in his hand. The kings of the sagas had descended from the gods; now the king stands on the porch of his farmstead palace at the end of the day, surveying his crops and herds. The word "wish," which once meant the perfect ideal, realized in the godhood of Odin, "the actual fruition of all joy and desire," comes to mean a longing for blessings unobtainable except by magic, by way of a "wishing stone," or an adopted "luck child," or a mill that grinds out anything one's heart desires. The fearsome Norns, who dispensed fate in the ancient eddas, become the hags of folktales, giving bane or blessing according to the deserts of adventuring boys or girls. In Dasent's translation of "Shortshanks," three hags each have one eye, which Shortshanks steals; here the genealogy can be traced back even farther than the Norns to the three Graeae of Greek mythology, the "Gray Sisters," whose eye Perseus stole.

The eddas and sagas had no Devil in the Christian sense; instead, Loki's daughter, Hel, presided over a cold world of the unheroic dead. In the Norse tales of the Christian era, Hel becomes a place where fires are lit at Christmastime to dispel the cold, and the Devil is as slow-witted and easy to deceive as the old Frost Giants. In the far north live great numbers of witches, the Devil's consorts, who have the malevolent intelligence ascribed to witches worldwide. They are killed with savage ruthlessness: torn to pieces, burned alive, or thrown into a snake pit. A wicked stepmother is often a witch in disguise.

Less frightening than the transmogrified gods and monsters are humans transformed into beasts and birds by witches or wizards or by their own eerie powers. The great white bear of "East of the Sun and West of the Moon" is a prince bewitched by a troll stepmother and her ugly troll daughter. (The heroine of this famous tale, a Norse Psyche, is "so lovely that there was no end to her loveli-

ness" and performs the difficult tasks necessary for the release of the prince.) The horse in "The Widow's Son" is a prince under a spell. In "Lord Peter," a parallel for "Puss in Boots," the cat is a bewitched princess. The princes transformed into "The Twelve Wild Ducks" are saved by their brave and beautiful sister, who is very nearly burned as a witch.

Animals abound in Norse fables and beast tales; the horse, the bull, the fox, the dog, the cock, and the hen play parts. Perhaps the best loved of all Norse folk animals are "The Three Billy Goats Gruff," the heroes of a brief, tightly constructed, exciting, and rib-tickling little drama that is an all-time favorite of children. In her 1957 picture book *The Three Billy Goats Gruff* Marcia Brown brilliantly portrays the troll as the darkness of the forest and the roar of water over rocks in a mountain brook; he loses his power when the biggest billy goat boldly confronts him on the bridge. The moral is typical of Norse folktales: use your wits; face up to your fear and it will vanish. With the exception of two exclusively British terms—"curling stones" and "burn" (" brook")—Dasent's text has become the most popular version of the story for American as well as for English children. And change from his translation of "Gruff" (for *bruse*) will not do. Other titles, such as "The Three Billikins Whiskers" or "The Three Bushy Billy Goats," have been used and may be closer to the Norwegian original, but they put us off as much as we would be if someone changed the name of Yankee-Doodle.

Most often the protagonist of Norse folktales is human. If young and feminine, she is seen as the men of Norway pictured their ideal golden girls; Moe wrote in his introduction to *Norske folkeeventyr* that the stories are told "with a manly mouth." As in "The Mastermaid," the heroine may be as wise as she is beautiful, outwitting all comers with the courage of a British Mollie Whuppie or Kate Crackernuts. Occasionally she may be a proud shrew who must be tamed by a "Hakon Grizzlebeard" or, as the wife of "Gudbrand on the Hillside," she may be laughably complacent. Typically she shows the quality of mercy toward all things in nature, and all things respond to her tenderness; little birds guide her in her hour of need.

But the most familiar protagonist met in the tales of Asbjørnsen and Moe is Askelad (Norwegian *Askefis*), Cinderlad, or Boots, as Dasent calls him. He is the male counterpart of Cinderella, the Norse parallel of Jack of England, Hans of Germany, or

Ivan of Russia, always considered a fool by his arrogant older brothers. He sits by the hearth, poking among the ashes, stupidly idling away his days—or so his brothers think. But in the fullness of time he will catch up with them as they go along the road to fame and fortune. They will be put to shame, and he will win the princess and half the kingdom through his quick wits and resourcefulness in making use of everything that comes his way. For him the ax or shovel heard at work in the forest are tools of magic. For him a walnut shell pours out an unfailing stream of pure water. He never turns a hair, no matter what betides, and only says, "Well, if it isn't worse than this, I can stand it well enough." Whenever he returns home, he has such fine clothes on his back that his old parents do not know him as the lazy boy who once sat in rags among the ashes. In his introduction to *Popular Tales from the Norse* (1912), Dasent says of this Norse hero:

> He is the man whom heaven helps, because he can help himself; and so, after his brothers try and fail, he alone can watch in the barn, and tame the steed, and ride up the glass hill, and gain the princess and half the kingdom. . . . In this way the consciousness of a nation, and the mirror of its thought, reflect the image and personification of a great moral truth, that modesty, endurance, and ability will sooner or later reap their reward, however much they may be degraded, scoffed at, and despised by the proud, the worthless, and the overbearing.

But as Moe well knew and stated, it is not only by noting the plots and characters that we see what is essentially Norwegian in Norse tales; it is the manner of telling, forthright and wryly humorous, that goes to the heart of the matter. It is true that the Norwegian texts contained occasional obscenities or other coarse details that most translators have deleted. But the general tone, in any translation, is unmistakably that of a decent, kindly people who learned to survive through all hardships and to laugh at themselves while they waited for the dawn of a day of independence after a long night of national humiliation.

The work of Asbjørnsen and Moe had a quick impact both at home and abroad. Henrik Ibsen, their contemporary, found in their texts a language in which he could speak for Norway; his *Peer Gynt* (1867) was written in response to the rediscovery of folk legends.

Ole Bull, a Norwegian world famous as a violin virtuoso, was associated with Jørgen Moe in evoking the rising flood of enthusiasm for Norwegian folk arts, and came to the United States with a wealth of lore. He was admired and entertained by Henry Wadsworth Longfellow and other eminent literary Americans. Ole Bull is the musician who tells Norse legends in Longfellow's *Tales of a Wayside Inn* (1863). Howard Pyle read the Norse tales as a child and in his early twenties wrote to his mother, "Some of the stories of trolls and kaboutermannekins are funny in the extreme and could be woven with some shaping into amusing and quaint stories." The Norwegian influence can be detected in the plots and style of Pyle's *Pepper and Salt* (1885) and *The Wonder Clock* (1888). "How Boots Befooled the King" shows this most clearly. Peter and Paul are the two older brothers, as in Norse tales; Boots is the youngest:

> Nobody thought anything of him except that he was silly, for he did nothing but sit poking in the warm ashes all of the day. . . . Boots asked if he might have the old tattered hat that hung back of the chimney. Oh yes, he might have that if he wanted it, for nobody with good wits was likely to wear such a thing.

This is pure Asbjørnsen and Moe, out of Dasent.

In 1889 Andrew Lang's famous *Blue Fairy Book* appeared, the first of his series of "Color Fairy Books," comprising the stories that Lang considered the best from all over the world; *The Blue Fairy Book* included four from Asbjørnsen and Moe—"East of the Sun and West of the Moon," "The Master Maid," "Why the Sea Is Salt," and "The Princess on the Glass Hill." The collection came out at a time when critics and educationists were inveighing against fairy tales in favor of real-life stories, proclaiming that children neither enjoyed nor should be allowed to escape into fantasy. The success of Lang's Color Fairy Books reinstated the realm of imagination in the world of children's literature on both sides of the Atlantic, incidentally establishing the tales of Asbjørnsen and Moe as perennial favorites.

The popularity of Norwegian folklore was again given impetus at about the time of World War I, when storytelling by children's librarians came into its own. Frances Clarke Sayers, a writer and storyteller par excellence, had a lifelong memory of "East of the Sun and West of the Moon" as told by a teacher to introduce the course in storytelling at

Carnegie Library School in Pittsburgh. The great event of the library school year was the arrival of Gudrun Thorne-Thomsen, who was at the University of Chicago with her husband in the School of Education under John Dewey. Gudrun Thorne-Thomsen lectured and taught seminars throughout the country in the uses of folklore and storytelling. She was a small, intense woman, with luminous dark eyes, ash-blond hair, and a richly musical and moving voice. From her childhood days she remembered Ole Bull and became, like him, the voice of Norway. Her American students were enchanted. When they left library school to head children's services across the United States, they enthusiastically carried to young readers and story-hour audiences the Norwegian tales to which Gudrun Thorne-Thomsen had introduced them. Her arrangements of *East o' the Sun and West o' the Moon, with Other Norwegian Folk Tales* (1912) were already in use in schools. The American Library Association made recordings of her storytelling. Pleasure in the Norwegian tales continued through library recommendations; the Carnegie Library of Pittsburgh's eighth edition of *Stories to Tell to Children* (1974) still listed twenty-one of the Norwegian stories as "tested with children for interest, popularity, and quality."

Among the many editions of the Norwegian tales collected by Asbjørnsen and Moe, a few deserve mention for their illustrations. In 1879 the first illustrated edition of *Norske folkeeventyr* employed the talents of a number of well-known Norwegian artists and of one who was as yet unknown. This was Erik Werenskiold, who had grown up in southeastern Norway and was steeped in the Norse myths, sagas, and folktales told to him by his father. At twenty-two he had drawn an illustration that Asbjørnsen saw and liked. When asked to submit more of his work for the proposed new edition, Werenskiold traveled to the Gudbrandsdal valley to draw pictures of farms and country people. In Pat Shaw Iversen's introduction to *Norwegian Folk Tales* (1960), he is quoted as saying:

> Behind this primitive life, behind these vigorous, strongly pronounced human types, and this unique architecture, one could sense the Middle Ages; and behind the large forest lay the Troll world of the Jotunheim mountains. I have never since found anything that seemed more Norwegian to me.

For the second illustrated edition, Werenskiold recommended that Theodor Kittelsen, another unknown artist, be asked to join him. He wrote to Asbjørnsen, "[Kittelsen] should be the man to do that side of your *eventyr* which none of the rest of us has yet been able to accomplish, namely the purely fantastic creations!" Between the two of them, Werenskiold found exactly the right style for each story in the collection to show how the storytellers and listeners of mid-nineteenth-century Norway pictured the tales, putting themselves in the leading roles, encompassing both workaday farm life and all the bright or dark fancies of the folk mind. A charming folktale picture by Kittelsen hung, and perhaps still hangs, in most Norwegian schools. It is reproduced in full color as the frontispiece for Gudrun Thorne-Thomsen's *East o' the Sun and West o' the Moon*.

The cultural and educational offices of both Norway and the United States made possible the Viking Press edition of *Norwegian Folk Tales* (1960), initiated by Carl Norman and translated by him in collaboration with Pat Shaw Iversen from Asbjørnsen and Moe in an effort to come closer than Dasent to the original Norwegian text. For this important work the heirs of Kittelsen and Werenskiold made available the plates of the original drawings, which are reproduced with admirable clarity. Shaw Iversen's introduction for this edition opens with a resounding statement:

> If Norway were to show the world a single work of art which would most truly express the Norwegian character, perhaps the best choice would be the folk tales, published for the first time more than a hundred years ago and later illustrated by Erik Werenskiold and Theodor Kittelsen.

Totally different are the illustrations by Kay Nielsen for his *East of the Sun and West of the Moon* (1917). Nielsen's work is aptly described as *bizarrerie*; the sophisticated figures are attenuated, often dressed in exotic costumes of no recognizable nationality. Far from childlike, they are posed in attitudes of extreme tension, in moods ranging from ecstasy to anguish. The insights are psychoanalytical, international, and ageless. The simple folk who told the tales would not recognize themselves. Yet so skillful is Nielsen's artistry and so rich are his colors that his illustrations for the chosen stories are well received and never to be forgotten by children who come upon them.

Ingri and Edgar Parin d'Aulaire have made a splendid contribution to the list of Asbjørnsen and Moe editions. Ingri Parin d'Aulaire was born and spent her childhood in Norway; her husband, who was half American, had painted murals there. Between them they knew Norwegian and the idiom of modern English very well, and in childhood both had loved the folktales of Asbjørnsen and Moe. They had a reverence for Dasent's translation and adapted their own translations from his. To prepare for their *East of the Sun and West of the Moon* (1938) they went to live on a little hillside farm surrounded by forests and at the foot of the mountains. It is possible to quibble with a few of the changes that the d'Aulaires made in Dasent's text, such as "The Maid on the Glass Mountain" for the familiar "Princess of the Glass Hill," and changes throughout the text in their "Three Bushy Billy Goats"; but the genius of the d'Aulaires lies in the illustrations, which reveal the motifs of Norse folk art and the architectural detail of the Norwegian domestic settings in a way no other edition has attempted. The tales are interpreted in a manner addressed to the tastes and understanding of children, yet are worthy to be judged by the most discriminating critic. The choice of stories too is admirable; only those most typically Norwegian are included. As a result, this handsome collection seems to be as quintessentially Norse as anything that is likely to be published for children in our time.

Asbjørnsen and Moe were born at the right time and in the right place to render an inestimable service to Norway and the world. The old storytellers who had sat telling tales by the hearth in the long dark northern nights were about to disappear. Another few years and their words would have been irretrievably lost. Ole Bull and Gudrun Thorne-Thomsen also came at the right time to carry the live spark from their homeland hearth to America and to make it shine again with the warmth of their personalities.

In recent times the audience of children listening to folktales has dwindled in the big cities, where the gadgets of technology hold sway. But in small-town libraries children still look forward each week to the story hour. Meanwhile, a new generation of storytellers has risen, finding big audiences of adults as well as children in the city park or the community hall. Here is where the Norwegian tales still flourish along with those of all the world. The northern United States, Canada, and Alaska saw Norwegian emigrants coming to till new farmlands, and those vast spaces should be fertile fields for the continuing spread of tales gathered by Asbjørnsen and Moe, whose names may now be unknown to the descendants of those emigrants. For those who do know, the names are linked together for all time.

Selected Bibliography

WORKS OF ASBJØRNSEN AND MOE IN NORWEGIAN AND IN ENGLISH TRANSLATION

Nor; en Billedbog for den norske Ungdom. With illustrations. Christiania: n.p., 1837. 2nd ed. Christiania: Guldberg and Dzwonkowski, 1843.

Norske folkeeventyr. Christiania: n.p., 1841–1844. Rev. ed., Christiania: n.p., 1851–1852.

Norske huldreeventyr og folkesagn. Christiania: W. C. Fabritius, 1845–1848.

Popular Tales from the Norse. Translated by Sir George Webbe Dasent. With an introductory essay by Dasent on the origin and diffusion of popular tales. Edinburgh: Edmonston and Douglas, 1859; New York: D. Appleton, 1859. New edition, with a memoir by Arthur Irwin Dasent. Edinburgh: David Douglas, 1903.

Tales from the Fjeld: A Second Series of Popular Tales from the Norse of Peter Christen Asbjørnsen. Translated by Sir George Webbe Dasent. With illustrations by Moyr Smith. London: Gibbings, 1896; New York: G. P. Putnam, 1896.

The Fairy World. Translated by H. L. Braekstad. With an introduction by Edmund W. Gosse. Boston: De Wolfe, Fiske, n.d.

East o' the Sun and West o' the Moon, with Other Norwegian Folk Tales. Retold by Gudrun Thorne-Thomsen, with some new translations and adaptations from Sir George Webbe Dasent. Chicago: Row, Peterson, 1912.

East of the Sun and West of the Moon: Old Tales from the North. Translated by Sir George Webbe Dasent. With illustrations by Kay Nielsen. London: Hodder and Stoughton, 1914; New York: George H. Doran, 1917.

East of the Sun and West of the Moon: Twenty-one Norwegian Folk Tales. Edited and adapted from the Sir George Webbe Dasent translation by Ingri and Edgar Parin d'Aulaire. With illustrations by Ingri and Edgar Parin d'Aulaire. New York: Viking Press, 1938.

True and Untrue and Other Norse Tales. Edited and compiled by Sigrid Undset. With illustrations by Frederick C. Chapman. New York: Knopf, 1945.

The Three Billy Goats Gruff. From the translation of Sir George Webbe Dasent. With illustrations by Marcia Brown. New York: Harcourt, 1957.

Norwegian Folk Tales, from the Collection of Peter Christen Asbjørnsen and Jørgen Moe. Translated by Pat Shaw

Iversen and Carl Norman. With illustrations by Erik Werenskiold and Theodor Kittelson. New York: Viking Press, 1960.

East of the Sun and West of the Moon and Other Tales. Translated by Sir George Webbe Dasent. Afterword by Clifton Fadiman. With illustrations by TomVroman. New York: Macmillan, 1963.

A Time for Trolls: Fairy Tales from Norway. Translated by Joan Roll-Hansen. With illustrations by Kai Øvre. Oslo: Johan Grundt Tanum Forlag, 1962; Vero Beach, Fla.: Arthur Vanous, 1982.

CRITICAL AND BIOGRAPHICAL STUDIES

Brittan, Jasmine. "Gudrun Thorne-Thomsen: Storyteller from Norway" *Horn Book* 34:17–28. (February 1958).

Falnes, Oscar J. *National Romanticism in Norway*. New York: Columbia University Press, 1933. (Contains the best and fullest account of the lives of Asbjørnsen and Moe.)

—MARGARET HODGES

J. M. BARRIE

1860–1937

JAMES MATTHEW BARRIE dedicated *Peter Pan*, his play for children, "To the Five," that is, to five boys: George, Jack, Peter, Michael, and Nicholas Llewelyn Davies, the sons of Arthur and Silvia Llewelyn Davies. They were boys whom Barrie entertained as children in Kensington Gardens, playing games and telling them stories about a boy "who would not grow up," but wanted always to be a little boy and to have fun. Together Barrie and the Davies children made believe that the Gardens were the haunt of fairies. The Round Pond became a sea where stick boats turned into real boats, fighting pirate ships and adventuring in search of treasure and coral islands. The little island in the Serpentine was a "Never-Never Land" that could be reached by flying, or by floating there in a bird's nest.

The dedication of *Peter Pan* is a long essay in which Barrie reveals much about himself, his past, and how the play came to be. With typical Barrie whimsy he sets out to "prove" that he wrote the play, although he claims that he cannot remember doing so:

> I think one remains the same person throughout [life], merely passing, as it were, in these lapses of time from one room to another, but all in the same house. If we unlock the rooms of the far past we can peer in and see ourselves, busily occupied in beginning to become you and me. Thus, if I am the author in question, the way he should go should already be showing in the occupant of my first compartment, at whom I now take the liberty to peek.

The occupant of his "first compartment" is Barrie as a little Scottish boy, putting on a play with a friend in the "washing-house" behind his home in Kirriemuir. This washhouse, by Barrie's own account, was the origin of the little house that the Lost Boys were to build for Wendy in the Never-Never Land.

In the nineteenth century Kirriemuir, sixteen miles north of Dundee, was a town of weavers. Its only claim to fame is the fact that Barrie was born there in 1860. His father, David Barrie, was a weaver, and later a clerk. He was respected as a hard-working man, self-educated, but unwilling for his sons to be "put to the weaving" early in life, as he had been.

His wife, Margaret Ogilvy, kept her maiden name among her friends, as was the Scottish custom of the time. Left motherless in childhood, she had taken care of her little brother and kept house for her father—washing, mending, cooking, then rushing out to play with other children. A womanly, motherly child with an eager, loving spirit appears repeatedly in Barrie's writing: she is Wendy mothering the Lost Boys in *Peter Pan*; she is the valiant little heroine of *A Kiss for Cinderella* (1920), mothering war orphans; she is Irene in *The Little White Bird* (1902), still a child, but proud to wear a nursemaid's starched cap as she wheels a pram through Kensington Gardens. Margaret Ogilvy was the heart and soul of the Barrie family life, and Jamie, the ninth of her ten children, returned her love with intense devotion. He sensed her pride when the oldest son, Alexander, became a teacher; only the ministry was a higher calling, and the second son, David, was destined for it by his parents. He was handsome and sweet-tempered, a fine student, and his mother's idol. When he was killed in a skating accident just before his fourteenth birthday, his mother never recovered from the blow. An older daughter, Jane Ann, took on the household duties, giving her life to her mother's care. Jamie's life too was deeply and permanently affected, because he despaired of taking David's place in his mother's love. (Barrie was to use the name David repeatedly in his novels and plays.) In *Margaret Ogilvy* (1896), his biographical account of her life, he tells how Jane Ann one day asked him to go to his grieving mother

> and say to her that she had still another boy. In the darkness of the room I heard her asking listlessly, "Is that you?" . . . I thought it was the dead boy she was speaking to, and I said in a little lonely voice, "No, it's no' him, it's just me." Then I heard a cry, and my mother turned in bed, and though it was dark I knew that she was holding out her arms.

Barrie's love for his mother has been called obsessive and was to remain a dominant force in his life and in his writing.

As a child Margaret Ogilvy had attended only a dame's school, where children were informally taught in the teacher's own home, but she had the Scottish passion for learning. In Barrie's words, she was "a great reader, and with ten minutes to spare before the starch was ready would begin the *Decline and Fall* [*of the Roman Empire*]—and finish it, too, that winter." Jamie was no scholar, but he was an avid reader. Like most boys of his time he read *Robinson Crusoe*, *The Swiss Family Robinson*, and the romances of Frederick Marryat, Robert Ballantyne, Jules Verne, and James Fenimore Cooper, all of them adventure stories with pirates, Indians—and islands. Islands never lost their lure for Barrie. In his preface to the 1913 edition of Ballantyne's *Coral Island*, he wrote: "To be born is to be wrecked on an island." Jamie also had a boy's natural appetite for "penny dreadfuls," the nineteenth century's equivalent of comic books, and his mother encouraged him to write some of his own. On looking back years later, he thought that this was the stage when he first decided "there could be no hum-dreadful-drum profession for me; literature was my game." He also recalled that after school he and his friends "became pirates in a sort

of Odyssey that was long afterwards to become the play of *Peter Pan*. . . . The next best thing to being boys is to write about them." To make believe was a link with childhood that Barrie never gave up.

At the age of eight he was sent to Glasgow Academy, where his older brother Alexander was classics master, and in the following years he attended other Scottish academies, always under the care of his own family or relatives. The last and happiest of his school days were spent at Dumfries Academy, south of Glasgow. At the time, Alexander was married and living in Dumfries; he and his wife made Jamie welcome. The academy offered new friendships and sports. Jamie wrote for the school magazine, made the football team, and became a good cricketer. Dumfries had a theater, the first Barrie had ever entered; this experience led to the founding of a school dramatics club for which he wrote his first play, *Bandelero the Bandit* (1877). Two of the characters were desperate villains, foreshadowing *Peter Pan*'s Captain Hook, but a local clergyman saw nothing funny about the skulduggery and wrote a newspaper article venting his wrath on the head of the young playwright. Even London newspapers took note of the uproar in faraway Dumfries, and Barrie was pleased.

One sorrow secretly gnawed at young Barrie's sense of self-esteem, as he was to openly confess through his later writing—for some reason he stopped growing. Dumfries Academy was coeducational, and Barrie was interested in the girls, but they were not interested in him. Going back to the academy as an honored guest in 1893, he told how the girls had voted for him as the boy with the sweetest smile in school. "The tragic thing," said Barrie, "was that my smile disappeared that day and has never been seen since." It is true that Barrie as an adult had an unsmiling face, but he who did not smile made others laugh about it. "Laugh at me," he seemed to say, with his self-deprecating humor, "but remember that I laughed first."

His small size continued to plague him. We see this in his early novel *The Little Minister* (1891), as the hero, Gavin Dishart, confides to his mother: " 'It's a pity I'm so little.' " Even his mother "was not aware [that] Gavin's shortness had grieved him all his life." For Barrie, it was a grief that partly accounted for his career as a writer. In a 1931 letter to a woman friend of his last years, he wrote:

> Six feet three inches. . . . If I had really grown to this it would have made a great difference in my

life. I would not have bothered turning out reels of printed matter. My one aim would have been to become a favourite of the ladies which between you and me has always been my sorrowful ambition. The things I could have said to them if my legs had been longer.

(Birkin, p. 21)

He was only half joking. Nothing he writes can be taken at face value; that is part of the Barrie charm.

When Jamie failed to win a scholarship, Alexander decided to pay his university tuition. A university education was worth any suffering. Families poorer than the Barries sacrificed for it; many students willingly starved in garret lodgings. Jamie was not enthusiastic, but his mother cast the deciding vote by saying gently that David would have gone. In 1878, at the age of eighteen, Jamie was duly enrolled as a student at Edinburgh University. He had no family or friends there, and he wanted only to be a writer. A fellow student remembered him as being "exceedingly shy and diffident," always alone, "a sallow-faced, round-shouldered, slight, somewhat delicate-looking figure," not much noticed by others "but himself observing all and measuring up men and treasuring up impressions." There was no social life. Twenty years later, when the university conferred an honorary degree on Barrie, he commented on the changes that time had wrought: "Perhaps greatest change of all, Woman—yes. 'Female forms whose gestures beam with mind.'" In Barrie's opinion the physical hardships and lack of feminine companionship in university days had maimed some students for life. A notebook entry read:

——He is very young looking—trial of his life that he is always thought a boy.——Far finer and nobler things in the world than loving a girl & getting her. ——Greatest horror—dream I am married—wake up shrieking.——Grown up & have to give up marbles—awful thought.

(Birkin, p. 12)

Barrie did enjoy the university debating society, where he distinguished himself as a wit. He also earned a little money as a free-lance drama critic for the *Edinburgh Courant*, but most of his hours were given over to what he called "grind, grind, grind"; he began to have migraine headaches. He was thankful to receive his degree in 1882 and to put the university behind him. His family knew then that he would never be a teacher or a minister and

made no objection when he took an attic room in Edinburgh and settled down—unsuccessfully at first—to write for his living. It was his quiet sister Jane Ann who encouraged him to answer an advertisement from the English paper the *Nottingham Journal* for an editorial writer. Barrie got the job and for eighteen months, at twelve pounds a month, filled columns with anything he cared to write about. His work was also appearing in London papers. When the *Nottingham Journal* failed, he returned to Kirriemuir and was inspired to write the first of his "Auld Licht Idylls," sketches of his mother's pious, God-fearing church congregation. The London *St. James's Gazette* accepted these articles (published in book form in 1888) and asked for more. Barrie was developing the style that was to be his hallmark, playing out his own experiences and intuitions in a blend of humor, whimsy, and pathos, rather like Charlie Chaplin's style in films.

In 1885 Barrie took the step longed for, though often feared, by so many ambitious Scots: he moved to London. He worked prodigiously, and success was not long in coming. Now he could send money home and give his mother every comfort. But there was a price to pay: the migraine headaches were a continuing torment. He had begun to smoke and soon had a chronic cough as well. Still, life had its rewards. He made a circle of friends, talented men and women. They noted his long silences, demanded by intense concentration on writing, but he could exert an irresistible charm. He and Robert Louis Stevenson carried on a cordial correspondence, though they never met. Barrie admired Stevenson's writing, particularly *Treasure Island*, and Stevenson urged him to come to Samoa for his health. "You take the boat to San Francisco," he wrote, "and then my place is second to the left." (In *Peter Pan*, Peter tells Wendy where he lives—"Second to the right, and then straight on till morning.")

Barrie was using friends, family, and everyone he met as grist for his mill, fitting them into roles for future novels and plays. His early novel *Sentimental Tommy* (1896) is about himself, a born actor, moving between dreams and reality "as through tissue-paper" with the faculty of "stepping into other people's shoes and remaining there until he became someone else."

An avid theatergoer, Barrie fell in love with one pretty actress after another, although always at a safe distance. Then, at a time when he himself was beginning to write successful plays, he met an extremely pretty young actress, Mary Ansell, and chose her for the second lead in his comedy *Walker, London* (1893). Barrie was very much in love with Mary and proposed marriage, though his notebooks suggest that he was afraid of marriage. His notes for *Sentimental Tommy* read in part:

> Such a man, if an author, wd be studying his love affair for a book. Even while proposing, the thought of how it wd *read* wd go thro' him.—Had he even a genuine deep feeling that wasn't merely sentiment? Was he capable of it? Perhaps not.

What Mary Ansell expected is not known. She once wrote: "I have never been really happy with people." But she accepted Barrie's proposal. At least she would have affluence: Barrie was now established as a playwright on both sides of the Atlantic. The wedding took place in 1894 at his parents' house at Kirriemuir, and the bridal pair went to Switzerland for their honeymoon. It was evidently a disaster for both of them; one of Barrie's notebook entries during his honeymoon read: "*Scene in Play. Wife*—Have you given me up? Have nothing to do with me? *Husband* calmly kind, no passion &c. (à la self)." In 1909 Mary left him, and they were divorced.

The one happy memento of Switzerland had been Barrie's wedding present to Mary, a Saint Bernard puppy named Porthos after the dog in George du Maurier's novel *Peter Ibbetson*. Mary adored her dog and found him an acceptable substitute for the children the Barries were never to have. When Porthos died, his place was taken by a Newfoundland dog, Luath, who became the model for the dog-nurse, Nana, in *Peter Pan*. Barrie gave his love to other people's children with whom he and Porthos made friends, especially on their walks in Kensington Gardens. It was there that the Davies boys entered Barrie's life. His mother and Jane Ann had died in 1885; now Barrie concentrated the full force of his affection and his imagination on "his boys," first George, Jack, and Peter, with their little nursemaid, and later Michael and Nicholas. The boys' parents soon met the Barries at a dinner party where they learned that Barrie was the man about whom George and Jack had talked, the man with the big dog in Kensington Gardens. Arthur Llewelyn Davies was a struggling young barrister of impeccable family background but limited income. His wife, Silvia, was the daughter of George du Maurier, and their son Peter was named for the

hero of *Peter Ibbetson*. *The Little White Bird*, the first of Barrie's Peter Pan creations, was the result of Barrie's encounters with the boys in the Gardens, of his own childhood memories, and of his extraordinary empathy with children. He simply stepped back into that "first compartment" of his life.

Barrie did not write *The Little White Bird* for children. It is a fanciful tribute to his love for Silvia and her boys. Writing in the first person, the author is thinly disguised as a retired army officer, a bachelor, who is sentimentally attached to a little nursery governess, Mary A——, whom he knows only by sight. She is engaged to a struggling young artist, and Captain W—— helps them with anonymous gifts and other kindly attentions. When the young couple are married and on the eve of their first child's birth, he anxiously walks the street with Mary's husband, pretending that he too has a wife who is giving birth. David A—— is born safely, but Captain W—— tells the proud father that his own son, "Timothy," has died, thus giving an excuse to present David with baby clothes and toys. Soon Captain W—— is telling David stories about fairies and playing with him in Kensington Gardens under the watchful eye of a young nursemaid, Irene. David learns from the captain that babies start as birds, flying from the Gardens to the homes that are waiting for them. One of these babies is Peter Pan, who takes over the story in the middle of the book, and disappears only at the end, as David reaches school age. It is left for Mary A—— to point out that the entire book is really about Timothy, "the little white bird," one of those who never find a mother. Timothy is Captain W——'s (Barrie's) dream child. Many "in" jokes in the Peter Pan chapters refer to the Gardens as seen by a child, or by an adult remembering a London childhood. Barrie's friend, the artist H. F. Ford, drew a detailed "Peter Pan's Map of Kensington Gardens" that was reproduced in some editions of *The Little White Bird*. In 1906 the middle section of the book was published separately for children as *Peter Pan in Kensington Gardens*, with Ford's map and with exquisite illustrations by Arthur Rackham.

Even before *The Little White Bird* appeared, Barrie had had a new Peter Pan idea. At Christmastime 1901, he had taken the Davies boys to a play, *Bluebell in Fairyland*, which was more than a run-of-the-mill Christmas pantomime. It had a plot and was not based on a book. (Lewis Carroll's Alice books, Thackeray's *The Rose and the Ring*, and Charles Kingsley's *Water Babies* had been dramatized.) Barrie conceived the idea of a "fairy play" about Peter Pan, with suitably young actors in leading roles. The idea was connected with summers the Barries had spent in an attractive house called Black Lake Cottage near Farnham in Surrey. The Davies family were nearby. The boys were then old enough to come every day to play at pirates and Indians with Barrie in the woods and on the little lake, which in their adventures became a South Seas lagoon. Barrie took many photographs during the wonderful days of 1901 and put them into a book, *The Boy Castaways of Black Lake Island* "by Peter Llewelyn Davies." Two copies were professionally bound and printed, but with no text except an introduction and chapter headings in the style of Ballantyne's *Coral Island*. For example: "VII. We finish the Hut—George and Jack set off on a Voyage of Exploration round the Island—Startling Discovery that the Island is the Haunt of Captain Swarthy and his Pirate Crew." *The Boy Castaways* went into the making of the play *Peter Pan*.

"Peter," of course, could no longer be a baby. In his dedication "To the Five" Barrie wrote, "I made Peter by rubbing the five of you violently together as savages with two sticks produce a flame. That is all he is, the spark I got from you." There would be pirates, Indians, wild animals, a villain with the traits of a fearsome schoolmaster—and an island. In *The Little White Bird* the fairies had built a house to fit a four-year-old girl, Maimie, who was lost in the Gardens after lock-up time. The little house appeared again in the play, but a new heroine was needed, a motherly child like Margaret Ogilvy. The poet William Ernest Henley had a small daughter who tried to call Barrie her "friend," but it came out as "Wendy." Barrie took the name for the heroine of *Peter Pan*, with John and Michael Darling as her younger brothers. The schoolmaster-villain evolved into Captain James Hook, whose suave manners and evil heart owed much to Stevenson's Long John Silver. The island was the "Never-Never Land" of children's dreams, and the Darling children were lured there by Peter Pan's promise to teach them to fly. An added attraction for Wendy was that she could be a mother to the Lost Boys who lived on the island. When the play was staged, Barrie arranged for a specially devised apparatus that would allow Peter and the three Darling children to fly about their London nursery and out the window. The staging was elaborate and costly; nothing quite like it had ever been attempted, certainly not in a play for children. But Barrie was

fortunate in finding the right producer, Charles Frohman, an American who was genial, generous, and willing to take a chance. Five sets and costumes for fifty characters were designed by the eminent artist William Nicholson; special music was written by the composer John Crock. Barrie attended rehearsals, polishing dialogue and stage business. No expense or trouble was spared.

The rest is history. On opening night at the Duke of York's Theatre, 27 December 1904, when the young actress who played Peter Pan asked the mostly adult audience to clap their hands if they believed in fairies, the response was so tumultuous that she burst into tears. From that time on for many years it was impossible to imagine an English Christmas for children without a production of *Peter Pan*. Roger Lancelyn Green's definitive *Fifty Years of "Peter Pan"* (1954) covers every stage of its history, including the roll call of illustrious actors and actresses who played leading roles, the performances in foreign languages, the silent film version, and the Disney cartoon. There was even a Peter Pan Club whose members knew all the words by heart. Soldiers on leave during World War I booked rows of seats for the play months in advance. Girls were named Wendy. Peter Pan collars came into fashion, in the style of the one worn by the inimitable Maude Adams in her role as the first American Peter Pan. And the end is not in sight—Peter Pan has become part of folklore.

Printed versions of Barrie's texts, and variations, proliferated. *J. M. Barrie's Peter Pan in Kensington Gardens* (1929) was "retold for Little People with the Permission of the author" (by May Byron), using the Rackham illustrations but taking great liberties with Barrie's wording; *The Nursery Peter Pan* (1961) stayed much closer to the original text. In 1911 Barrie made the play into a novel, *Peter and Wendy*, which has been republished under other titles, including *Peter Pan and Wendy* and *Peter Pan*, with various illustrators. The play itself was published as a book in 1928. It made delightful reading because of the interpretive directions and revelations that Barrie always added to his published plays, turning dramatic scripts into pieces of literature. In 1962 Eleanor Graham, English critic and editor, rewrote the story of the play as "presented by Eleanor Graham and Edward Ardizzone." The illustrations are charming, but Miss Graham's text is neither simpler nor shorter than Barrie's and is completely lacking in the Barrie touch.

It is generally agreed that Arthur Llewelyn Davies grew tired and resentful of Barrie's full-scale intrusion into the Davies family life. (Arthur lost his copy of *The Boy Castaways*, perhaps deliberately.) As the boys grew older, they were often plagued by their connection with "Peter Pan." Headlines appeared: "Peter Pan Enlists"; "Peter Pan Fined for Speeding"; "Peter Pan Becomes Publisher." Yet on the whole, the boys appreciated and returned Barrie's affection. Both Arthur and Silvia died while their children were still young. Barrie adopted them and took on their full support. Peter Davies wrote feelingly of Barrie's kindness, devotion, and generosity to the parents in their last illnesses, and added: "It would be interesting to have a list of all the impoverished authors and their families whom J.M.B. helped out of his own pocket at one time or another." In 1929 Barrie made a gift of all rights and royalties from *Peter Pan* to London's Great Ormond Street Hospital for Sick Children.

Barrie also supported two other hospitals, one of which appears in his 1916 play *A Kiss for Cinderella*. This is a wartime play about a Cockney waif who mothers some little orphans (one of them a German) while dreaming that she is Cinderella; the complete faith of a storyteller and the listeners is a recurring theme with Barrie. In the second act of this play we see the ball at the royal palace as a Cockney child might imagine it. The conception is as original as *Peter Pan*, and the play belongs in any list of Barrie's work as a writer for children. Here it should be said that children in the first quarter of the twentieth century were taken by their parents as a matter of course to Barrie matinees, not only to *Peter Pan* and *A Kiss for Cinderella*, but also to *Quality Street*, *Dear Brutus*, *Mary Rose*, and *The Little Minister*. Before it was dramatized, *The Little Minister* had been published serially in *Good Words*, which was edited by ministers of the Church of Scotland for young readers.

Barrie's work moved easily and naturally between the child world and the adult world, between fancy and fact. Like P. L. Travers of Mary Poppins fame, he might have said: "I don't think I write for children, any more than the great Miss Potter. For what? Whom? Well, myself, perhaps; I never think of an audience, that would kill everything" (as quoted in *Tellers of Tales*). But in the public perception Barrie was clearly identified with children. When he wrote the introduction for *The Young Visiters* [*sic*] (1919), he was suspected of writing the entire book, though the author was later proved to be, as claimed, Daisy Ashford, aged nine.

Lady Cynthia Asquith, Barrie's secretary, nurse, and close friend in his last years, called him "an extraordinary plural personality. . . . The art of weaving fantasy with fact—the art which made his fortune—had come to be his master as well as his servant. . . . Of what he really thought, of what he really was, he gave scarcely a clue" (as quoted in Dunbar). But Barrie himself gave a clue to at least one important role of his "plural personality," that of intent and intense worker. When in 1930 he was installed as chancellor of Edinburgh University, he delivered an address describing "The Entrancing Life" he had led: "What is the entrancing life? . . . Carlyle held that genius was an infinite capacity for taking pains . . . the entrancing life, I think, must be an infinite love of taking pains." And again in a 1932 speech at an Authors' Club dinner: "The most precious possession I ever had [was] my joy in hard work. . . . I fell in love with hard work one fine May morning. . . . Hard work, more than any woman in the world, is the one who stands up best for her man." Hard work was the one mistress he had wooed successfully; it made up for much that he had never had, or had lost. (He was crushed by the deaths of two of the Davies boys; George was killed in the war, and Michael was drowned during his college years while bathing in the Thames near Oxford.) But Nicholas, the youngest of "his boys," saw Barrie in another light, calling him

> the most wonderful of all companions, and the wittiest man I shall ever know, and all of the talk about his being obsessed with thoughts of his mother and with general gloom is largely distortion. . . . A creature of moods . . . hours of silence, but many more hours of humour.
>
> (Birkin, p. 201)

Sir James Matthew Barrie died in June 1937. Honors had been heaped upon him; many words of praise spoken. But perhaps the best summing-up of his "entrancing life" and of his gifts is not in honors nor in words. On 1 May 1912 a statue was unveiled in Kensington Gardens, commissioned and paid for by Barrie, and secretly erected the night before, so that it seemed to appear by magic. The design of the base shows children and fairies and small animals; at the top Peter Pan plays his pipes and dances, alone.

Selected Bibliography

WORKS OF J. M. BARRIE

Editions of Peter Pan

Peter Pan in Kensington Gardens. With illustrations by Arthur Rackham. London: Hodder and Stoughton, 1906; New York: Charles Scribner's Sons, 1906. (The middle section of *The Little White Bird*.)

Peter and Wendy. With illustrations by F. D. Bedford. London: Hodder and Stoughton, 1911; New York: Charles Scribner's Sons, 1911.

Peter Pan and Wendy. With illustrations by Mabel Lucie Attwell. London: Hodder and Stoughton, 1921; New York: Charles Scribner's Sons, 1921.

Peter Pan; or, The Boy Who Would Not Grow Up. London: Hodder and Stoughton, 1928; New York: Charles Scribner's Sons, 1928. (The original play version.)

J. M. Barrie's Peter Pan in Kensington Gardens. Retold by May Byron for Little People with the Permission of the author. With illustrations by Arthur Rackham. London: Hodder and Stoughton, 1929; New York: Charles Scribner's Sons, 1930.

Peter Pan. With illustrations by Edmund Blampied. New York: Charles Scribner's Sons, 1953. (The original text of *Peter Pan*.)

The Nursery Peter Pan. Edited by Olive Jones. With illustrations by Mabel Lucie Attwell and J. S. Goodall. Leicester, England: Brockhampton, 1961.

Peter Pan: The Story of the Play. Presented by Eleanor Graham and Edward Ardizzone. New York: Charles Scribner's Sons, 1962.

Peter Pan. With illustrations by Trina Schart Hyman. New York: Charles Scribner's Sons, 1980.

Other Works

Bandelero the Bandit. Dumfries, 1877.

The Little Minister. London: Cassell, 1891; New York: Street and Smith, 1891.

Margaret Ogilvy, by Her Son. London: Hodder and Stoughton, 1896; New York: Charles Scribner's Sons, 1896.

Sentimental Tommy. London: Cassell, 1896; New York: Charles Scribner's Sons, 1896.

The Boy Castaways of Black Lake Island. London: published by the author, 1901. (Only two copies printed.)

The Little White Bird; or, Adventures in Kensington Gardens. London: Hodder and Stoughton, 1902; New York: Charles Scribner's Sons, 1902.

A Kiss for Cinderella. London: Hodder and Stoughton, 1920; New York: Charles Scribner's Sons, 1921. (A play.)

CRITICAL AND BIOGRAPHICAL STUDIES

Ashford, Daisy. *The Young Visiters; or, Mr. Salteena's Plan*. With a preface by J. M. Barrie. London: Chatto and Windus, 1919; Garden City, N.Y.: Doubleday, 1919. Rev. ed., with illustrations by William Pène du Bois. Garden City, N.Y.: Doubleday, 1951.

Asquith, Lady Cynthia, ed. *The Flying Carpet*. New York: Charles Scribner's Sons, 1925. (See Barrie's "Neil and Tintinnabulum.")

————. *Portrait of Barrie*. London: J. Barrie, 1954; New York: Dutton, 1955.

————. *The Treasure Ship*. New York: Charles Scribner's Sons, 1926. (See Barrie's "The Blot on Peter Pan.")

Barrie, J. M. *The Entrancing Life*. London: Hodder and Stoughton, 1930; New York: Charles Scribner's Sons, 1930. (Text of speech given at Edinburgh University.)

————. *M'Connachie and J. M. B.: Speeches by J. M. Barrie*. London: Peter Davies, 1938; New York: Charles Scribner's Sons, 1939.

Birkin, Andrew. *J. M. Barrie and the Lost Boys: The Love Story That Gave Birth to Peter Pan*. New York: Clarkson Potter, 1979.

Darton, F. J. Harvey. *J. M. Barrie*. London: Nisbet, 1929.

Dunbar, Janet. *J. M. Barrie, the Man Behind the Image*. Boston: Houghton Mifflin, 1970.

Green, Roger Lancelyn. *Fifty Years of "Peter Pan."* London: Peter Davies, 1954. (See Barrie's "Scenario for a Proposed Film of *Peter Pan*.")

————. *J. M. Barrie*. London: Bodley Head, 1961; New York: H. Z. Walck, 1961. (A Bodley Head and Walck monograph.)

————. "J. M. Barrie and the Fairies." In *Tellers of Tales*. Rev. ed. London: Ward, 1965; New York: Franklin Watts, 1965.

Mackail, Denis G. *The Story of J. M. B.: A Biography*. London: Peter Davies, 1941; New York: Charles Scribner's Sons, 1941.

Meynell, Viola, ed. *Letters of J. M. Barrie*. London: Peter Davies, 1942; New York: Charles Scribner's Sons, 1947.

Roy, James A. *James Matthew Barrie: An Appreciation*. London: Jarrold's, 1937; New York: Charles Scribner's Sons, 1938.

—MARGARET HODGES

L. FRANK BAUM
1856–1919

"I remember. Yes, now I do. A long time ago. When I was a child. A book I read. A story. Oz, I think it was. Yes, Oz. *The Emerald City of Oz*...."

"Oz? Never heard of it."

"Yes, Oz, that's what it was. I saw it just now, like in the story. I saw it fall."

"Smith!"

"Yes, sir?"

"Report for psychoanalysis tomorrow."

(Ray Bradbury, "The Exiles," 1950)

IT IS NO use. No matter how hard and how long the librarians, teachers, critics, and other experts on what children ought to read have tried to pull it down, the Emerald City just will not fall. Boys and girls still take that perilous journey along the Road of Yellow Bricks just as their parents and grandparents and great-grandparents have done over the last eighty-five years. Few other works of American juvenile literature have inspired such passions as have L. Frank Baum's *Oz* books. While some of their elders have aggressively hated them, the children have loved the adventures of Dorothy and her many friends on the other side of the rainbow.

Perhaps Baum was guilty of outliving his vogue. With the publication of *The Wonderful Wizard of Oz* in 1900, he was universally acknowledged as a new master of American children's literature. But by the time of his death in 1919, a new attitude prevailed. A pedestrian realism usurped the fanciful and the fantastic from Yankee children's books. Fairyland itself became suspect, and there was no place for an American fairy tale in the new literature. Those who were now demanding tales of steam shovels and skyscrapers had no sympathy for Baum's talking scarecrows and humbug wizards. The *Oz* books must have begun to appear terribly retrogressive. But their author was progressive in his own way. He gave perhaps the best defense of his efforts in the preface to *The Lost Princess of Oz* (1917):

Some of my youthful readers are developing wonderful imaginations. This pleases me. Imagination has brought mankind through the Dark Ages to the present state of civilization. Imagination led Columbus to discover America. Imagination led Franklin to discover electricity. Imagination has given us the steam engine, the telephone, the talking-machine and the automobile, for these things had to be dreamed of before they became realities. So I believe that dreams—day dreams, you know, with your eyes wide open and your brain-machinery whizzing—are likely to lead to the betterment of the world. The imaginative child will become the imaginative man or woman most apt to create, to invent, and therefore to foster civilization.

Some of those youthful readers whom Baum was addressing included John Steinbeck, James Thurber, Ray Bradbury, Wanda Gág, Shirley Jackson, David McCord, Lloyd Alexander, Russell Baker, Walter Kerr, Nora Ephron, Erica Jong, and Frederick Buechner.

No one could ever accuse Baum of lacking a vivid imagination. That was both his principal strength and principal weakness. He was incapable of keeping his mind on one subject for any great length of time. He drifted from one unlikely job to another before he began writing children's stories in earnest at age forty. The variety of professions he attempted is amusing: job printer, stamp dealer, store clerk, chicken farmer, theater owner, actor. And in all of them he seemed to be just on the verge of succeeding when his house of cards fell. Baum was dazzled by the promise of the Gilded Age. The longest time he spent in one position was after his marriage to Maud Gage and the birth of his first child, when he entered the family oil business in Syracuse, New York, manufacturing and selling an axle grease called Baum's Castorine. But the day-to-day drudgery of the office and the road finally got to him, and he ran off to the prairies of the recently opened Dakota Territory to make his fortune during the local land boom. Here he failed not once but twice, first as proprietor of an extravagant variety store and then as editor of a rural newspaper. Prospects of prosperity surely to come with the World's Fair lured him to Chicago. Again he tried everything from journalism to selling crockery and fireworks to support his growing family.

During all of this time Baum was writing on the side. From the age of fourteen he wrote sporadically on topics as varied as his jobs. He had some brief success at the time of his marriage as a playwright of Irish melodramas, but on the whole his early efforts were of no consequence. Finally, in 1896, his mother-in-law, Matilda Joslyn Gage, a prominent women's rights activist, convinced him to write down the bedtime stories he made up for his four sons. These were the tales of the Beautiful Valley of Phunniland, where the rivers flow with milk, the rain is lemonade, and purple dragons raid the caramel bushes. But no publisher was interested in this unknown author's whimsical wonder stories.

Baum, however, did succeed in placing another manuscript. While his boys were growing up, he often recited popular nursery rhymes to them, and invariably they demanded to know more about Old King Cole, Little Bo-Peep, and all of the other Mother Goose characters. Inspired by events from the famous verses, their father dutifully invented elaborate fairy tales for them. Again his mother-in-law insisted that he seek a publisher for the stories, and he was fortunate to find one in Chicago who was considering a new edition of the Mother Goose

rhymes in order to highlight the work of a young, gifted Philadelphia artist. The publisher immediately saw the novelty of Baum's manuscript, so in the fall of 1897 the firm issued a sumptuous edition of *Mother Goose in Prose,* the first children's book by L. Frank Baum and the first one illustrated by Maxfield Parrish.

Although *Mother Goose in Prose* did not sell well (its high price was prohibitive), this first publication nevertheless encouraged Baum to write more aggressively for children. For a few years Baum had had limited success in selling topical verse to the newspapers and had recently published some of his doggerel, *By the Candelabra's Glare* (1898), in a limited edition. Capitalizing on his reputation as author of *Mother Goose in Prose,* he pulled together a collection of his own nursery rhymes, which he appropriately titled *Father Goose, His Book.* But when he and his collaborator, the newspaper cartoonist William Wallace Denslow, tried to secure a publisher for their Americanized Mother Goose rhymes, no one would touch the volume. Baum and Denslow insisted that it be illustrated in color, and only when they agreed to pay the printing costs was *Father Goose, His Book* finally published in the fall of 1899. To everyone's pleasant surprise, *Father Goose, His Book* became a runaway best-seller, and it immediately established Baum and Denslow as the most exciting children's book team of the day.

But no one was prepared for the book they produced in 1900. Even today *The Wonderful Wizard of Oz* is an impressive achievement. The most immediate appeal of their new collaboration was certainly its striking pictures—twenty-four color plates plus countless spreads in alternating gray, blue, red, green, yellow, and brown. Again author and artist had to pay the printing costs for their book, and so they were in complete control of its design and its publication. Like *Father Goose, His Book, The Wonderful Wizard of Oz* set high standards not only for the quality of production but also for the skill evidenced in the pictures themselves. In Denslow, Baum had surely found his John Tenniel. The drawings contained a humor and a charm distinctively their own, being refreshingly free of the excessive style so characteristic of children's books of the period.

The pictures, however, would mean little without the text. Admitting that his own contribution to *Father Goose, His Book* had been negligible, Baum was determined to try something entirely new in his first novel for boys and girls. Here finally was an American juvenile book whose story and art were intended, Baum said, "solely to pleasure children of today . . . , a modernized fairy tale, in which the wonderment and joy are retained and the heartaches and nightmares are left out." There are no grave lessons strewn along the Road of Yellow Bricks. There are no heavy, pedagogical asides meant to instruct the young how to better their lives. While Yankee Puritanism was being challenged in almost every other area of American life, its didacticism still dominated juvenile literature. *The Wonderful Wizard of Oz* did much to weaken its grip on the American publishing industry. Here finally was a full-blooded romance for the boys and girls of the United States.

Baum welcomed the new century with a new attitude toward childhood. *The Wonderful Wizard of Oz* was the right book at the right time. It offered its young readers an escape from a society in rapid transition. The American frontier had been proclaimed officially closed in 1890, and so by the decade's end, many were looking far beyond its borders, to other lands and other cultures as yet unspoiled by the Industrial Revolution. Just as their parents were exploring the possibilities of Hawaii, Cuba, Puerto Rico, Guam, and the Philippines, American boys and girls now discovered their own fairyland. They were immediately seduced by the novelty of a wonderland woven out of commonplace material. A Kansas cyclone could transport one as easily as could an Arabian magic carpet from *A Thousand and One Nights.* A scarecrow in a cornfield could be as desirable a companion as any fairy godmother in a French fairy tale. If anything, Baum taught the boys and girls of America to look and marvel at the world around them. "All the magic isn't in fairyland," the Shaggy Man explains in *Tik-Tok of Oz* (1914). "There's lots of magic in all Nature, and you may see it as well in the United States, where you and I once lived, as you can here."

Of course Baum *was* writing a fairy tale, not a story about contemporary American life. *The Wonderful Wizard of Oz* was designed to engage what the author called the child's "wholesome and instinctive love for stories fantastic, marvelous and manifestly unreal." Something is always happening in Baum's fairyland, something wonderful and unexpected. The transition from Baum's real world to his imaginary world is skillfully achieved through vivid contrast. Dorothy is introduced living in

nothing but the great broad sweep of flat country that reached the edge of the sky in all directions. The sun had baked the plowed land into a gray mass, with little cracks running through it. Even the grass was not green, for the sun had burned the tops of the long blades until they were the same gray color to be seen everywhere. Once the house was painted, but the sun blistered the paint and the rains washed it away, and now the house was as dull as everything else.

Even Dorothy's foster parents have been beaten gray by their environment. They rarely speak; they never laugh. But what a different place is the new country where the cyclone drops her house. Dorothy opens the door to discover

a country of marvelous beauty. There were lovely patches of green sward all about, with stately trees bearing rich and luscious fruits. Banks of gorgeous flowers were on every hand, and birds with rare and brilliant plumage sang and fluttered in the trees and bushes. A little way off was a small brook, rushing and sparkling along between green banks, and murmuring in a voice very grateful to a little girl who had lived so long on the dry, gray prairies.

Baum was a master at creating locale and atmosphere. With the greatest economy, he beautifully defines both Kansas and the Land of the Munchkins. The latter is an inviting country for the poor little girl from the great American prairie. Gray has become green. The stillness, the silence of the farm is nowhere to be found in fairyland; while Aunt Em has nothing to say to her niece, Nature herself now beckons the child to explore her wonders. Here the natives paint everything bright blue, their favorite color; back in Kansas, no one can even detect what color Dorothy's house was once painted. The abundance of a foreign land has replaced the barrenness of home.

But practical Dorothy is not dazzled by the beauties of this brave new world. She is from Kansas after all. She is perhaps the key to the story's continued popularity. Here at last is a living, breathing American child in fairyland, not some European princess called Beauty for want of another name. Unlike her celebrated predecessors in Grimm and Andersen tales, this heroine couldn't care less for riches and Prince Charming. She wants to get home. Any child can sympathize with her simple desire. What child has not felt the pangs of being lost? The Scarecrow cannot understand why anyone would wish to leave this beautiful country to go back to dull Kansas. "That is because you have no brains," Dorothy bluntly informs him. "No matter how dreary and gray our homes are, we people of flesh and blood would rather live there than in any other country, be it ever so beautiful. There is no place like home." And every child knows exactly what Dorothy means—even if the Scarecrow does not.

If Dorothy is this fairyland's Columbus, she also becomes its Lincoln. Through no fault of her own, her house kills the Wicked Witch of the East and liberates the Munchkins. Likewise she accidentally destroys the Wicked Witch of the West with a bucket of water and thus releases the Winkies from bondage. Nothing can daunt this American girl. When the Good Witch of the North twirled three times on her left heel and vanished into thin air, matter-of-fact Dorothy, "knowing her to be a witch, had expected her to disappear in just that way, and was not surprised in the least." Dorothy has the true pioneering spirit. When lost, she does not wait for Aunt Em and Uncle Henry to find her; she goes out and finds them. When told she must destroy the Wicked Witch of the West, she goes and does it. Baum's Dorothy is one of the first positive female characters in American juvenile fiction. She may be protected by the Good Witch's kiss, but it is her own will that helps her to overcome her problems. Certainly one major reason for the book's universal appeal to boys and girls is that here finally is a child who is like them, yet who is always able to take control of her situation. In Oz she discovers a great power within herself.

No fairy godmother hovers over Dorothy every step of her way along the Road of Yellow Bricks. Instead she is accompanied by the oddest trio in American fiction. Even in the wonderful Emerald City of Oz, people look upon Dorothy and her entourage with wondering eyes. The Scarecrow, the Tin Woodman, and the Cowardly Lion are of an entirely new breed of fairy companions. The members of this motley crew appeal immediately to the child's innate love of toys, mechanical gadgetry, and animals. Of course there are many other grotesques in children's literature, but few so beloved as these three. Dorothy's friends are related to the six comrades who aid the soldier in the German story, the five brothers of the Chinese version, the seven Simeons of Russian tradition, and so many others. But Baum's characters differ significantly from these other fairy helpers. Each in the older

tradition possesses some superhuman trait—the ability to blow a great gust of wind in one puff of breath, or to swallow a great sea in one gulp, or to run to the ends of the earth in a single bound. By contrast, the Scarecrow, the Tin Woodman, and the Cowardly Lion are known for what they do *not* have—a brain, a heart, and courage. At first appearance, they seem as lost as Dorothy. As they travel with the little girl, they must prove themselves worthy of receiving these great gifts from the Wonderful Wizard of Oz. Of course, all along the way, it is the Scarecrow who uses his head to get them out of difficulty, the Tin Woodman who demonstrates great kindness, and the Cowardly Lion who shows his bravery in coping with every obstacle in their path.

Baum's grotesques differ from their folklore predecessors in that they develop distinctive personalities. The others are merely plot devices with no characters beyond their particular extraordinary abilities. Baum, however, takes time for Dorothy and the reader to get to know the three companions. He succeeds beautifully in making them both believable and sympathetic. Another author might have made them merely bizarre. Baum supplies each with his own fascinating history. They do not simply act, but interact with one another. For example, the Scarecrow and the Tin Woodman dispute which is more desirable, a brain or a heart. "I shall ask for brains instead of a heart," the Scarecrow explains to his new friend, "for a fool would not know what to do with a heart if he had one." The Tin Woodman replies, "I shall take a heart, for brains do not make one happy, and happiness is the best thing in the world." Practical Dorothy is puzzled as to which one is correct and says nothing; she is more concerned with where she will find her next meal. The heroes of Oz are so vividly portrayed that each seems to have a life of his own outside the story's pages. It is no surprise, therefore, that almost from the date of the book's publication, its author was bombarded with letters from children demanding to know more about the Scarecrow and the Tin Woodman.

It is a rare child indeed who does not want to know what happened next to Dorothy and her friends. The story is briskly told in a clear, almost biblical prose. In this book at least, Baum's abundant invention never fails him. The Winged Monkeys, the Forest of Fighting Trees, the Deadly Poppy Field, not to mention the Emerald City itself, are just a few of the marvels to be found here.

Few other children's books are so brimming with such extraordinary characters and adventures as is *The Wonderful Wizard of Oz.* True, Baum's tale was in part anticipated by *Alice's Adventures in Wonderland* (1865) and *Through the Looking-Glass* (1872), but most children (just like Alice herself) are not as comfortable in Wonderland or beyond Lewis Carroll's Looking-Glass as they are in Oz. And no one really cares what happened to the March Hare and Mad Hatter next. True, there are some unpleasant elements in Baum's story. He did not succeed in eliminating all horrible and bloodcurdling incidents, heartaches, and nightmares from his book as stated in its introduction. (The kindhearted Tin Woodman is a bit too free with the ax in decapitating wildcats and wolves.) Nevertheless all the story's dangers and delights leave children wanting more stories about Oz.

One quality of *The Wonderful Wizard of Oz* that cannot be overemphasized is Baum's wit. His weakness for puns is evident everywhere in his fairy tale. The Scarecrow speaks in a "husky" voice; the Tin Woodman cracks jokes about "heart disease"; and the Wizard fills the Scarecrow's brains with bran to show him that they are indeed "bran-new." (And Baum implies that the word "brains" is no more than a portmanteau word for "bran" and "pins.") Such wordplay may make some adults groan, but in its simplicity and lack of verbal sophistication, it is exactly the kind of comedy quick-thinking young children enjoy. The story is enlivened throughout with Baum's sly, understated, gentle humor. When the Wizard first introduces himself to Dorothy as "Oz, the Great and Terrible," she replies aptly and directly, "I am Dorothy, the Small and the Meek." One fine passage, so characteristic of Baum's good spirits, describes Dorothy's first use of the Wicked Witch's Golden Cap:

> "Ep-pe, pep-pe, kak-ke!" she said, standing on her left foot.
>
> "What did you say?" asked the Scarecrow, who did not know what she was doing.
>
> "Hil-lo, hol-lo, hel-lo!" Dorothy went on, standing this time on her right foot.
>
> "Hello!" said the Tin Woodman, calmly.

At first, Baum apparently was not fully aware of what he had achieved. He had created a new American myth that he himself could not control. Both *Mother Goose in Prose* and *Father Goose, His Book* were comparatively tame experiments, deriving much from popular nursery lore. The enormous popularity of the latter gave him the confidence to attempt many different kinds of literature, with varying degrees of skill, within a remarkably short period of time. Baum could now devote his full attention to writing for children. In 1900 alone he published—in addition to *The Wonderful Wizard of Oz,* his "modernized fairy tale"—two collections of verse (*The Army Alphabet* and *The Navy Alphabet*), a song album (*The Songs of Father Goose*), and his Phunniland book (*A New Wonderland*). Uncertain of his public, Baum was cautiously testing the marketplace with novel experiments in juvenile publications.

In the twenty years during which Baum produced his children's books, this highly prolific writer went through several distinct periods of literary development. When *The Wonderful Wizard of Oz* proved to be nearly as popular as *Father Goose, His Book,* his early experimental phase gave way to a stream of fantasies with American themes and contemporary settings. The most overt of these, of course, was his *American Fairy Tales* (1901), a dozen loosely connected short stories (expanded to fifteen stories and published as *Baum's American Fairy Tales* in 1908). Baum's purpose in this anthology was to provide new wonder tales that "bear the stamp of our own times and depict the progressive fairies of today." Some of the stories do, some do not; but the best of them, such as "The Magic Bon-Bons" and "The Capture of Father Time," have a distinctive charm and humor that place them among Baum's most entertaining short fantasies.

Although subtitled "an electrical fairy tale," *The Master Key* (1901) is another of Baum's distinctly American fairy tales. It is also one of the earliest examples of juvenile science fiction in American literature. Set in contemporary Chicago, it relates how a red-blooded American boy accidentally summons the Demon of Electricity and thus receives several marvelous talismans. Being his first book written specifically for boys, *The Master Key* is a fast-paced adventure story in the tradition of Jules Verne and H. G. Wells. It is also a moral tale about the wise and foolish uses of scientific advancement. Another book published in 1901, *Dot and Tot of Merryland,* was intended for younger readers than those of *The Master Key.* As a companion to *The Wonderful Wizard of Oz* (and the last of Baum's books illustrated by Denslow), this fantasy also sends a little American girl to fairyland. But instead of beginning on the great gray prairies of Kansas,

Dot and Tot of Merryland is located in fertile central New York, on the farm of Baum's childhood, Rose Lawn. While out boating one afternoon, Dot and her friend Tot are taken underground to a wonderful land full of clowns, dolls, candy, and all the things boys and girls dream about. It is a pleasant travelogue, but lacks the vitality and invention of its more influential predecessor.

Baum's next major work, *The Life and Adventures of Santa Claus* (1902), was a transitional work in his canon. At first glance, it might appear to be another fairy tale in Baum's American tradition. After all, Santa Claus is largely a Yankee legend, immortalized by New Yorker Clement Clarke Moore's "A Visit from St. Nicholas" (1843). Baum's mock biography does include its American references; for example, the first Christmas tree is planted to entertain some Indian children. Nevertheless, *The Life and Adventures of Santa Claus* is really the first of what Baum called his "old-fashioned fairy tales." As he did in *Mother Goose in Prose,* Baum elaborates on old traditions in this revisionist history of the children's great benefactor. After describing in detail the pagan origin of Santa Claus, he speculates on the circumstances surrounding the first Christmas tree, the first Christmas stocking, the first flight of the reindeer, and the name of the jolly old elf. Baum's book, however, is unlike any of the current myths. It is surprisingly free of all mention of saints and Romans. His is the story of Santa Claus, not Saint Nicholas. Nowhere does Baum touch on the birth of Christ. Still, *The Life and Adventures of Santa Claus* is a moral tale, as witnessed in the climactic battle between Good and Evil. It may not preach about shepherds and wise men, but it still retains the Christmas spirit of giving within its otherwise pagan mythology.

Baum followed his Santa Claus book with an even more inventive fantasy, *The Enchanted Island of Yew,* his principal book of 1903. (That year also saw a reissue of *A New Wonderland* as *The Magical Monarch of Mo and His People,* with all references to Phunniland changed to Mo.) Again his story begins "once upon a time" in an enchanted forest. A fairy longs for adventure and becomes a mortal for a year. As Prince Marvel, she explores the wonders of an unusual new fairyland. Yew, like Oz, is cut into quarters, with a fifth country in the exact center. Each land has its own peculiarities, but none is more amusing than the Kingdom of Twi, a place of doubles, where everyone and everything has an identical twin. The highlight of the story, however, is Prince Marvel's reformation of a deformed tyrant who hates everyone because of his great ugliness. While each incident may be entertaining in itself, the work as a whole does not add up to much. There is no specific motivation for Prince Marvel's travels; he is not even on a quest for something. In the end, after a year of enough adventures to last a lifetime, he complacently returns to his original form, admitting unconvincingly, "There are, I find, some advantages to being a fairy."

A similar lesson is taught in the last of Baum's full-length old-fashioned fairy tales: Oh, what fools these mortals be! First serialized in *St. Nicholas* magazine in 1904 and 1905, *Queen Zixi of Ix* (1905) is perhaps the best book within this genre. Baum himself admitted that it was one of the best of all of his stories. Here he unblushingly and freely takes from classic European fairy lore. Foolish and wise wishes, wicked foster mothers, abused orphans, strange laws, eccentric and enchanted counselors are just some of the marvelous stuff out of which Baum weaves his romance, one worthy of Madame D'Aulnoy and the other ladies of the seventeenth-century French court. One evening, to pass away the time, the fairies weave a magic cloak to aid poor mortals. Unfortunately the mortals do not know how to use so extraordinary a gift properly, and by the story's end, the fairies return to retrieve it. It is also the story of Zixi of Ix, a beautiful witch-queen, and her mad passion to possess the cloak. Although it is certainly the most highly polished of any of Baum's stories, *Queen Zixi of Ix* is perhaps also the subtlest in its perceptions of human folly.

Of a completely different sort, but surely within the same fairy-tale tradition, are Baum's "Animal Fairy Tales," which began appearing in the *Delineator* in 1905 just as *Queen Zixi of Ix* was finishing its run in *St. Nicholas.* In the new series Baum was playing with the traditions of Aesop's fables and Rudyard Kipling's *Jungle Books* (1894, 1895). Baum argued that just as mortal men have their fairy guardians, so too must the beasts of the forest and of the plain. But here was a harsher reality than that of his other fairylands. These nine stories derive their moral power from the instincts and laws of the jungle. Of course, as in all fables, what is revealed as animal nature really reflects human behavior. All are infused with a good dose of social Darwinism: the most mentally fit always survive. Other examples of this genre are the six little books *The Twinkle Tales* (1906) and their full-length sequel, *Policeman Bluejay* (1907). Written under the pseudonym "Laura Bancroft," for a younger audience than the *Delineator* series, these stories may be sunnier than Baum's "Animal Fairy Tales," but they are no less earnest in their plea for human kindness to all creatures. Yet by comparison with "Animal Fairy Tales," some of which are among Baum's best short fiction, *The Twinkle Tales* are slight.

Within a decade Baum had produced an extraordinary body of work, not only in number but also in variety. The author himself now bragged that he was the greatest writer of fairy tales of his day. Certainly none of his contemporaries was as ambitious as he. While appearing to be working within the European tradition of fairy lore, Baum was actually developing a new attitude toward fantasy literature. He believed that children did not like stories of love and marriage, so his fairy tales were stripped of any romantic interest. "Love, as depicted in literature," Baum declared, "is a threadbare and unsatisfactory topic, and children can comprehend neither its esoteric nor its exoteric meaning. Therefore it has no place in their storybooks." What Baum offered instead of the old fairy tales were simple, clear plots full of stirring adventure to grab the young reader's full attention. He also believed that he could now secure his full effect without introducing any acts of violence. Thus these later wonder tales are refreshingly free of all killing and any undue painful punishments for one's sins.

Each of these early stories (even with their flaws) is fine in its own right. Children can and do still pick them up from time to time and enjoy them. Yet none has achieved the extraordinary popularity of *The Wonderful Wizard of Oz.* Even in his own day, the first *Oz* book outsold all of Baum's other fairy tales. Perhaps one just could not believe in his other fairylands as one could in Oz. Burzee, Yew, and Ix exist in the distant past. Oz seems always here and now. The tales of *Mother Goose in Prose* and *A New Wonderland* (or *The Magical Monarch of Mo*) are clever literary conceits, but they have no existence beyond the printed page. Even the Chicago of *American Fairy Tales* and *The Master Key* lacks the immediacy of Baum's most famous fairyland. And Merryland, unlike Oz, has nothing more for us to see after its seven valleys have been charted. None of Baum's other fairy tales in other lands has so vivid a central character as Dorothy in *The Wonderful Wizard of Oz.* No one seems to have

cared much what happened to Dot and Tot, Prince Marvel, and Princess Fluff.

It was inevitable that Baum would return to Oz. The children demanded it. When the book became the basis for a highly successful musical comedy in 1902, a sequel was imminent. Readers across the country were now introduced to the singing and dancing Scarecrow and Tin Woodman of the play. Baum was spoiled by the show's profits. Although the libretto had been heavily reworked by a team of script doctors until it barely resembled the children's story, Baum was eager to capitalize on his new fame as a playwright by composing countless libretti, which were never produced. Finally he realized that the best way to capitalize on his success was with a true sequel to the popular book.

The Marvelous Land of Oz (1904) was the result. Although Dorothy, the Cowardly Lion, and the Wizard do not reappear in this new fairy tale, the second *Oz* book, beautifully illustrated by John R. Neill, was an excellent continuation of the adventures of the Scarecrow and the Tin Woodman. It is really the story of Tip, a boy who escapes from Mombi the Witch, his cruel foster mother. While surprisingly thin in magic, *The Marvelous Land of Oz* contains as fine a cast of odd characters as its predecessor: Jack Pumpkinhead, the Animated Sawhorse, the Flying Gump, and the Woggle Bug. Baum also introduces his mild satire of the current women's suffrage movement in the overthrow of the Scarecrow's regime by General Jinjur's Army of Revolt, a band of angry housewives from all four corners of Oz. Such an incident does seem odd for a fairy tale, but *The Marvelous Land of Oz* was designed to be adapted to the musical stage. As one reviewer noted, the reader can almost see the colored tights on the chorus line of Jinjur's lady soldiers. The book is particularly heavily ladened with puns and dialogue somewhat out of place in a children's book but perfect for the popular stage. Within a year of the book's publication, it did finally reach the stage as the musical comedy *The Woggle Bug.* But the play was a financial failure.

Undaunted, Baum followed *The Marvelous Land of Oz* with another children's book, *John Dough and the Cherub* (1906), designed to become a musical comedy. John Dough, the Gingerbread Man, might have stepped off a Broadway stage himself. Baum describes him as "a delicatessen: a friend in knead . . . a Pan-American." His constant companion is Chick the Cherub, a child whose actual sex is never revealed and who is thus a perfect candidate for the part of the Principal Boy from English pantomime, what was called a "trouser role" for any young soubrette. There is a steady stream of eccentric characters, both specialties and possible choruses, clearly more appropriate for the theater than for the nursery; the most obvious is Sir Austed Alfrin, the Poet Laureate of the Isle of Phreex, a reference to Sir Alfred Austin, then poet laureate of England. Some incidents too seem more tailored for adult sensibilities than for children's; the Palace of Romance, for example, might easily inspire several interpolated numbers about falling in and out of love. Unfortunately, another playwright came up with a musical comedy called *The Gingerbread Man,* and the principal character in that play was also named John Dough!

With *The Wizard of Oz* play still successfully touring the country, Baum's publishers convinced him to continue the *Oz* series for a few more years. Baum was at first reluctant. He said he had other tales to tell. He compromised. Although technically within the series, the events of the next few books rarely take place in the Land of Oz. *Ozma of Oz* (1907), for example, occurs almost exclusively on the other side of the Deadly Desert, in the Land of Ev and the underground dominions of the Nome King. It is one of Baum's finest works. The opening alone demonstrates the author's full mastery of his art. Slowly and skillfully Baum builds the mystery of his fairy tale. While sailing to Australia with her ailing uncle, Dorothy is cast adrift in a chicken coop. The next morning she finds a yellow hen named Billina who suddenly has the ability to talk. They land on a lovely beach with an ominous message written in the sand, "Beware the Wheelers!" In the meantime, the hen is pecking for her breakfast and uncovers a little golden key that Dorothy wisely puts in her pocket. They are certain they are in fairyland when the Wheelers *do* appear —hideous creatures with wheels instead of hands and feet. They chase Dorothy and Billina into the rocky hills, where the girl coincidentally finds a keyhole in the mountainside in which the little golden key fits. Inside the cavern Dorothy discovers one of the greatest of Baum's whimsical characters, Tik-Tok, the Clockwork Man, who can walk, who can talk, who can think, who can do everything but live. It is he who saves Dorothy and Billina from the frightful Wheelers.

The Land of Ev is ruled by a most unusual villainess. The Princess Langwidere ("languid air") always wears the same simple white gown but keeps a great glass cabinet full of beautiful girls' heads that she dons as easily as other women change their dresses. And she wants Dorothy's head for her collection, so she locks the girl up in a tower. Fortunately the child is quickly rescued by the new ruler of Oz, Princess Ozma. Accompanied by the Scarecrow, the Tin Woodman, and the Cowardly Lion, Ozma is on a mission of mercy to release the Queen of Ev and her children from the Nome King's bondage. This task proves to be far more difficult than anticipated, for their adversary is a clever and treacherous sorcerer. But the Nome King is finally outwitted by the yellow hen in one of the most tightly constructed and exciting of Baum's many stories.

The principal interest of Baum's next *Oz* book is the reappearance of the little Wizard himself. Having previously journeyed to fairyland by air and by sea, Dorothy returns in *Dorothy and the Wizard in Oz* (1908) as a result of a California earthquake. The same upheaval swallows up the Wizard in his circus balloon. Their adventures underground (like those in the Nome King's dominions) are more frightening than any experienced above ground. They first encounter a race of vegetable people, living in great ornate hothouses, who decide to "plant" the intruders. They must battle the Wooden Gargoyles and escape the hungry Dragonettes. There is also an extraordinary adventure in the Valley of Voe. At first glance, although it appears to be deserted, all seems in harmony in this lovely land. They hear a bird sing, but none can be seen. They enter an inviting house where the dishes, utensils, and furniture seem to move on their own. They hear voices, but see no one. This is a land of invisible people who prove gracious and kind to the travelers, but the dream soon turns into a nightmare. There also dwell here fierce invisible bears who can see them but cannot be seen. The dangers beneath the earth build almost uncontrollably until Ozma steps in and sends the travelers to Oz. The last third of the book is a dull holiday in the Emerald City that pales after the power and terror of the previous adventures.

The Road to Oz (1909) is largely a reworking of *Dorothy and the Wizard in Oz,* but with the nightmares left out. Consequently it is also the least exciting of the *Oz* stories. But what *The Road to Oz* lacks in dramatic tension, it more than makes up for by introducing several of the most durable characters in Baum's fiction: the Shaggy Man, Polychrome the Rainbow's Daughter, and that lost little boy, Button-Bright. The parallels between the two books are obvious. The Wizard of Oz becomes the Shaggy Man. Toto the dog replaces Eureka the kitten. Dorothy's cousin Zeb, who acted as an older brother in *Dorothy and the Wizard in Oz,* is now Button-Bright, a younger brother. Now there are Scoodlers to fight instead of Wooden Gargoyles. Unfortunately the latter part of the book is dominated by preparations for Ozma's birthday party. In the climactic scene, Baum draws all of his fairy tales together as the Queen of Merryland, Queen Zixi of Ix, John Dough and the Cherub, and even Santa Claus pay tribute to the little princess of Oz. *The Road to Oz* is no more than a pleasant interlude in the history of Oz.

Baum returned to his high standards in *The Emerald City of Oz* (1910). Here he tries to define his ideal of fairyland. Under Ozma's rule Oz has evolved considerably from its state during the Wizard's regime. Benevolence has transformed the kingdom into a child's utopia. There are no poor in Oz, for there is no such thing as money there. A land of abundance, the country provides everyone with exactly what he needs to make him content. Everyone works half the time and plays half the time. Disease and aging are unknown in Oz, and it is extremely difficult to kill anyone. By contrast, Aunt Em and Uncle Henry are about to lose their farm in Kansas. They are growing old and cannot work any longer. Therefore Ozma invites them to join Dorothy to live in her fairyland, where they can be free of death and taxes.

Little is Ozma aware at first that beyond her land's borders the Nome King is planning his dreadful revenge. Hate is his principal motivation. Gathering increasingly terrifying goblin hordes behind him, the Nome King vows to conquer the Land of Oz and make all of its people his slaves. But when Ozma learns of his terrible plan, she refuses to fight him. "Because the Nome King intends to do evil is no excuse for my doing the same," she maintains. "No one has the right to destroy any living creatures, however evil they may be, or to hurt them or make them unhappy." But this is a fairy tale after all, so Ozma employs magic just in time to protect her subjects.

The Emerald City of Oz was intended to be Baum's last *Oz* book. He had already written five stories in the successful series and wanted to explore other wonderlands. Therefore Glinda the Good, at the tale's end, erects a Barrier of Invisibility, which not only protects Oz but also cuts it off from the Great Outside World. The book concludes with a sad note from Dorothy, saying, "You will never hear anything more from Oz. . . . But Toto and I will always love you and all the other children who love us."

For many years Baum had been wanting to write about a fairyland under the ocean. Even before *The Emerald City of Oz* was back from the printers, Baum embarked on a new series of wonder tales concerning a little girl from California named Trot and her constant companion, an old peg-legged sailor named Cap'n Bill. Their first adventure is with the mermaids, in *The Sea Fairies* (1911). Trot and Cap'n Bill are transformed into mermaids so they can view the wonders under the sea and confront a deformed magician named Zog, perhaps the first personification of pure unredeemed evil in Baum's work since the Wicked Witch of the West. Unfortunately, although the *Oz* books were best-selling juvenile works, *The Sea Fairies* did poorly. To ensure higher sales for the second book in the new series, Baum hastily introduced two of his Oz characters, Button-Bright and Polychrome from *The Road to Oz,* to Trot and Cap'n Bill in *Sky Island* (1912). Fresh from their adventures underwater, the little girl and the old sailor now visit a country in the clouds. They become embroiled in the bitter racial war between the feuding Blues and Pinks, two of the most bizarre of Baum's fairy tribes, whom they eventually unite under one just ruler. *Sky Island* is a fast-paced narrative, full of magic and wild escapes. Baum himself admitted that the book was his best next to *The Wonderful Wizard of Oz.*

But the children would have none of it. All they wanted was more about Oz. The disappointing sales of both *The Sea Fairies* and *Sky Island* convinced his publishers that his young readers were not as interested in the latest Baum title as they were in the latest *Oz* book. He now resolved to write an *Oz* story a year as long as the boys and girls demanded it. Perhaps to make up for lost time, Baum published two *Oz* projects in 1913. The first, *The Little Wizard Series,* consisted of six little books (later a single volume entitled *The Little Wizard Stories of Oz,* 1914) that were no more than delightful anecdotes about the most famous of the Oz characters intended for a younger audience. Also published in 1913, *The Patchwork Girl of Oz* is one of the longest and liveliest of the series. It is the first since *The Marvelous Land of Oz* to take place entirely within the Land of Oz and to feature a boy hero. Although Dorothy does appear about mid-adventure, the story really belongs to Ojo the Unlucky, a little Munchkin boy who must seek the many peculiar ingredients for an antidote to release his Unc Nunkie from an accidental enchantment. The child is accompanied by perhaps the craziest cast of Oz characters since that of *The Wonderful Wizard of Oz.* Principal among them is the Patchwork Girl, an energetic maid made out of an old crazy quilt. Unfortunately Ojo mixed a bit too many brains for her before she was brought to life, so she is spoiled for servitude. There is also Bungle the Glass Cat, conceited about her pink brains and ruby heart, and the square Woozy, a Cubist's nightmare. *The Patchwork Girl of Oz* is one of the lightest and funniest of all of Baum's *Oz* stories, obviously written with the thought of turning it into another of the author's musical comedies. There are numerous topical references, most obviously the walking, talking phonograph, Victor Columbia Edison, who acts as a running commentator of Baum's attitudes toward popular music. However, unlike that in *John Dough and the Cherub,* the stage machinery never gets in the way of the story of *The Patchwork Girl of Oz.*

The new story reflects Baum's growing enthusiasm for the stage; at the time, he was adapting *Ozma of Oz* and *The Road to Oz*, along with scenes and characters from *The Marvelous Land of Oz* and *Dorothy and the Wizard in Oz,* as a new musical extravaganza entitled *The Tik-Tok Man of Oz* (1913). Conveniently Baum's libretto differed enough from the earlier stories to use it as the basis for his next book, *Tik-Tok of Oz.* Still, an atmosphere of *déjà vu* hovers about the tale, and not until the appearance of Quox the Blue Dragon does the adventure finally take flight.

The Patchwork Girl of Oz was made into an elaborate early silent motion picture. It was the first production of the Oz Film Manufacturing Company, which Baum founded a few years after he moved to Hollywood, California. With his usual economy, Baum also reused material from one of his movies, *His Majesty, the Scarecrow of Oz,* in the next *Oz* book, *The Scarecrow of Oz* (1915). The resulting story is an odd mulligan stew of incidents relating to various sources. Although it finally brings Trot, Cap'n Bill, and Button-Bright to live in Oz, the story is primarily concerned with the troubled courtship of a gardener's boy and a princess, an unusual theme for Baum's fairy tales that was lifted from the plot of his motion picture. But romantic love had already

been fleetingly but successfully tested in his children's books, in the affair of Princess Ozma and Private Files in *Tik-Tok of Oz.*

Tik-Tok of Oz also gave the first indication of the last phase of Baum's work. With the growing agitations in Europe and the ultimate outbreak of World War I, Baum became increasingly concerned with the stupidities of war and monarchy. It was now time to publish *Rinkitink in Oz* (1916). Although written as early as 1905 as just another of his fairy tales, Baum pulled it out of his safety deposit box and added a new ending involving Dorothy and the Little Wizard. What came before was one of the most exciting of any of Baum's children's stories. With the aid of three enchanted pearls, Prince Inga of faraway Pingaree must rescue his parents, who have been imprisoned by fierce warriors who have invaded their island home. There is no indication in the book as published as to how exactly the original manuscript concluded, but by transforming it into an *Oz* story, Baum diminished its chances of being considered among his best efforts.

Baum was deeply troubled by events in Europe, and the last four of his fourteen *Oz* books express his disgust with the war. Ozma is constantly in danger of losing her throne. In *The Lost Princess of Oz* a discontented shoemaker kidnaps the princess and steals most of the greatest magic in all Oz in an attempt to make himself ruler of the fairyland. In *The Magic of Oz* (1919), the Nome King returns to conquer Oz, and this time conspires with a sullen Munchkin boy who knows a powerful magic word. In the posthumously published *Glinda of Oz* (1920), Ozma and Dorothy intervene in a stupid war between the Skeezers and Flatheads and are themselves imprisoned until Glinda and the Wizard can release them from a mysterious underwater palace. At first glance, *The Tin Woodman of Oz* (1918) seems to break the pattern, in describing how Nick Chopper searches for the Munchkin girl he once loved before he became tin. But even here Baum explores the primary theme of his last *Oz* books, the abuse of power. The most extraordinary episode in the book concerns a giant sorceress named Mrs. Yoop, who amuses herself by transforming innocent travelers into strange creatures against their wills. Baum suggests that when magic, like any technology, falls into the wrong hands, its results are always disastrous.

L. Frank Baum died in 1919, but Oz refused to

die with him. His widow contracted with his publishers to have the series continued, and twenty-six additional titles were published by numerous writers of varying abilities. And despite the growing protests from children's book experts against these American fairy tales, the *Oz* stories continued to sell and delight young readers. They remain an extraordinary contribution to American juvenile literature. "We cannot measure a child by a standard of size or age," Baum once explained. "The big folk who are children will be our comrades; the others we need not consider at all, for they are self-exiled from our domain." And what marvels they have denied themselves!

Selected Bibliography

WORKS OF L. FRANK BAUM

Mother Goose in Prose. With illustrations by Maxfield Parrish. Chicago: Way & Williams, 1897.

Father Goose, His Book. With illustrations by William Wallace Denslow. Chicago: George M. Hill, 1899; London: Werner, 1899.

A New Wonderland. With illustrations by F. Verbeck. New York: R. H. Russell, 1900. Republished as *The Surprising Adventures of the Magical Monarch of Mo and His People.* Indianapolis: Bobbs-Merrill, 1903.

The Army Alphabet. With illustrations by Harry Kennedy. Chicago: George M. Hill, 1900.

The Navy Alphabet. With illustrations by Harry Kennedy. Chicago: George M. Hill, 1900.

The Songs of Father Goose. Music by Alberta N. Hall. With illustrations by William Wallace Denslow. Chicago: George M. Hill, 1900.

The Wonderful Wizard of Oz. With illustrations by William Wallace Denslow. Chicago: George M. Hill, 1900. Republished as *The New Wizard of Oz.* Indianapolis: Bobbs-Merrill, 1903; London: Hodder and Stoughton, 1906.

Dot and Tot of Merryland. With illustrations by William Wallace Denslow. Chicago: George M. Hill, 1901.

American Fairy Tales. With illustrations by Ike Morgan, Harry Kennedy, and N. P. Hall. Chicago: George M. Hill, 1901; London: Hutchinson, 1926. Enlarged as *Baum's American Fairy Tales.* With illustrations by George F. Kerr. Indianapolis: Bobbs-Merrill, 1908.

The Master Key. With illustrations by F. Y. Cory. Indianapolis: Bowen-Merrill, 1902; London: Stevens and Brown, 1901.

The Life and Adventures of Santa Claus. With illustrations by Mary Cowles Clark. Indianapolis: Bowen-Merrill, 1902; London: Stevens and Brown, 1902.

The Enchanted Island of Yew. With illustrations by F. Y. Cory. Indianapolis: Bobbs-Merrill, 1903.

The Marvelous Land of Oz. With illustrations by John R. Neill. Chicago: Reilly and Britton, 1904; London: Revell, 1904.

Queen Zixi of Ix. With illustrations by Frederick Richardson. New York: Century, 1905; London: Hodder and Stoughton, 1905.

The Woggle-Bug Book. With illustrations by Ike Morgan. Chicago: Reilly and Britton, 1905.

John Dough and the Cherub. With illustrations by John R. Neill. Chicago: Reilly and Britton, 1906.

Twinkle Tales, under the pseudonym "Laura Bancroft." 6 vols. With illustrations by Maginel Wright Enright. Chicago: Reilly and Britton, 1906. (Includes *Bandit Jim Crow, Mr. Woodchuck, Prairie Dog Town, Prince Mud-Turtle, Sugar-Loaf Mountain,* and *Twinkle's Enchantment.*) Republished as *Twinkle and Chubbins.* Chicago: Reilly and Britton, 1911.

Ozma of Oz. With illustrations by John R. Neill. Chicago: Reilly and Britton, 1907.

Policeman Bluejay, under the pseudonym "Laura Bancroft." With illustrations by Maginel Wright Enright. Chicago: Reilly and Britton, 1907. Republished as *Babes in Birdland.* Chicago: Reilly and Britton, 1911.

Dorothy and the Wizard in Oz. With illustrations by John R. Neill. Chicago: Reilly and Britton, 1908.

The Road to Oz. With illustrations by John R. Neill. Chicago: Reilly and Britton, 1909.

The Emerald City of Oz. With illustrations by John R. Neill. Chicago: Reilly and Britton, 1910.

The Sea Fairies. With illustrations by John R. Neill. Chicago: Reilly and Britton, 1911.

Sky Island. With illustrations by John R. Neill. Chicago: Reilly and Britton, 1912.

The Patchwork Girl of Oz. With illustrations by John R. Neill. Chicago: Reilly and Britton, 1913.

The Little Wizard Series. 6 vols. With illustrations by John R. Neill. Chicago: Reilly and Britton, 1913. (Includes *Jack Pumpkinhead and the Sawhorse, Little Dorothy and Toto, Ozma and the Little Wizard, The Cowardly Lion and the Hungry Tiger, The Scarecrow and the Tin Woodman,* and *Tik-Tok and the Nome King.*) Republished as *Little Wizard Stories of Oz.* Chicago: Reilly and Britton, 1914.

Tik-Tok of Oz. With illustrations by John R. Neill. Chicago: Reilly and Britton, 1914.

The Scarecrow of Oz. With illustrations by John R. Neill. Chicago: Reilly and Britton, 1915.

Rinkitink in Oz. With illustrations by John R. Neill. Chicago: Reilly and Britton, 1916.

The Snuggle Tales. 6 vols. With illustrations by John R. Neill. Chicago: Reilly and Britton, 1916–1917. (Includes *Little Bun Rabbit, Once Upon a Time, The Yellow Hen, The Magic Cloak, The Gingerbread Man,* and *Jack Pumpkinhead.*) Republished as *Oz-Man Tales.* 6 vols. Chicago: Reilly and Britton, 1920.

The Lost Princess of Oz. With illustrations by John R. Neill. Chicago: Reilly and Britton, 1917.

The Tin Woodman of Oz. With illustrations by John R. Neill. Chicago: Reilly and Britton, 1918.

The Magic of Oz. With illustrations by John R. Neill. Chicago: Reilly and Lee, 1919.

Glinda of Oz. With illustrations by John R. Neill. Chicago: Reilly and Lee, 1920.

A Kidnapped Santa Claus. Indianapolis: Bobbs-Merrill, 1961.

Animal Fairy Tales. Chicago: International Wizard of Oz Club, 1969. (Includes the fables originally published in *The Delineator* in 1905.)

CRITICAL AND BIOGRAPHICAL STUDIES

Baum, Frank Joslyn, and Russell P. MacFall. *To Please a Child.* Chicago: Reilly and Lee, 1961.

Gardner, Martin, and Russell B. Nye. *The Wizard of Oz and Who He Was.* East Lansing: Michigan State University Press, 1957.

Greene, David L., and Dick Martin. *The Oz Scrapbook.* New York: Random House, 1977.

Hearn, Michael Patrick, ed. *The Annotated Wizard of Oz.* New York: Clarkson N. Potter, 1973.

————. *The Wizard of Oz.* New York: Schocken Books, 1983. (Critical Heritage Series: contains a selection of critical articles on Baum and his work, together with a bibliography.)

Moore, Raylyn. *Wonderful Wizard, Marvelous Land.* Bowling Green, Ohio: Bowling Green University Press, 1974.

—MICHAEL PATRICK HEARN

HILAIRE BELLOC
1870–1953

ON 27 JULY 1870, during the worst thunderstorm that the village of La Celle-St.-Cloud had seen in fifty years, Joseph Hilaire Pierre René Belloc was born. The storm signaled a thunderous life.

Louis, his father, standing at the baptismal font, said, "I should like him to be called Pierre." But out of the four given names, the one that stuck was Hilaire. Belloc was proud of his name because he felt that it showed he belonged to a great republic, a "perfect nation," France. For most of his life, however, his family and friends would address him as Hilary, the English equivalent.

The name confusion suggests the ambivalence in national loyalties that plagued the young Belloc. The child came from strong families on both sides. He was born to an English mother, Bessie Parkes, who had come from a long tradition of English radicalism. The granddaughter of the scientist and clergyman Joseph Priestley, she was on close terms with George Eliot, Elizabeth Barrett Browning, and George Sand, as well as Trollope and Thackeray. All her life she supported women's suffrage. Belloc's father, Louis, a semi-invalid, was the son of a well-known academic painter, Hilaire Belloc, who had studied under Théodore Gericault. The grandfather's reputation as a fine teacher of art was well established, as was his flamboyant temperament. He once said, "We have always been a family of guts."

Almost at the moment of Belloc's birth the Franco-Prussian War was breaking out. By September the Bellocs had fled to England. It was on a return visit to their war-damaged home two years later that Louis Belloc sickened and died. Bessie never fully recovered. Belloc's biographer Robert Speaight says, "Had Louis Belloc survived, his son would have been a Frenchman with an English mother instead of being an Englishman with a French father." Grief over her husband's death strengthened Bessie's ties with Roman Catholicism, causing the young Belloc's religious education to begin early. Throughout his life he would be a militant Roman Catholic.

Although much of the family's time was spent in England after Louis's death, summers were spent in the French village, and according to Speaight, most of Belloc's strongest youthful impressions come from those days. His major preparatory education was completed at the Oratory School, Edgbaston, England, where he was grounded in the classics, and where he came under the influence of John Cardinal Newman, famed Catholic theologian and founder of the school. By age seventeen the family had moved to Sussex, and Belloc began his lifelong love affair with that countryside. In 1892 he matriculated at Balliol College, Oxford, where he won first-class honors in history in 1895.

As a student at Balliol, he quickly became known for his vigor, high spirits, and strong opinions. He frequently went on long walks, celebrating the Diamond Jubilee, for example, by walking from York to Edinburgh. He also drank a lot of wine (which he would do the rest of his life) and regaled his many friends with his witticisms and songs. By this time he had served for nine months in the French army and was full of the spirited army songs he had so loved on the march, but he also dazzled his listeners with his own often extemporaneous verses, which he recited or sang in his strong tenor, in a "roaring" style.

In the summer of 1890 he met Elodie Hogan, a Californian traveling in Europe. Elodie had been contemplating a vocation with the Sisters of Charity, but the love-smitten Hilaire vowed to change her mind. They were married in 1896. Shortly after, he left the university for public life.

Because his career at Oxford had been so remarkably successful, he was bitterly disappointed when he was refused an All Souls Fellowship. He never recovered from the humiliation. While reasons for the refusal are unknown, Speaight and others think that the dons were aware of his strong anti-Semitism. His hostility toward Jews began when he was young, probably during the few months he spent at Collège Stanilas in Paris when he was seventeen. The Collège was a center for Catholic reactionaries and anti-Semites. Whatever the reason, the loss of the fellowship changed his life. Instead of obtaining a comfortable teaching post with a salary allowing him to support his family, he felt he had no choice but to begin "the grinding out of books."

By the end of his life he had published 147 books —biographies, collections of essays, novels, travel books based on his walking tours and sea journeys (especially on his beloved boat, *Nona*), poetry, and children's books. He had also edited several magazines and gone on numerous speaking tours of Europe and America—all to make money. Wilfred Sheed says he "howled and hacked" for money all his life. Speaight also refers to Belloc's ongoing need for money: he sometimes gave four lectures in one day. In a letter to J. S. Phillimore in 1909, Belloc said, "I will lecture on anything in any manner for money: and don't you forget it. . . . I can lecture on my hand, on my head or between my legs or with the dumb alphabet" (quoted in Speaight).

Early in his career his name was linked with Bernard Shaw, G. K. Chesterton, and H. G. Wells as the most significant writers of the period because they all reacted fiercely against the "Dr. Pangloss with a stiff upper lip" atmosphere that was so pervasive at the end of Victoria's reign. Each writer's response was different, but Renée Haynes says:

> All four writers . . . set out to shock, Shaw by rationalist and Chesterton by Christian paradox, Wells by angry, comic, compassionate fiction, and Belloc by satire of much that was assumed to be good, by an exuberant boastfulness that deliberately outraged all the current canons of gentlemanly modesty.
>
> (p. 5)

Belloc's first published work was *Verses and Sonnets* (1896), a group of mostly serious, often "delicately sacred" poems, although one section is labeled "grotesques." In the same year, his first children's book, *The Bad Child's Book of Beasts,* was published. Consciously or not, this book began Belloc's protest against the didacticism rampant in the early part of the century, especially evident in Elizabeth Turner's *The Daisy; or, Cautionary Tales in Verse* (1807). Although the ground had already been broken by Lewis Carroll with his parodies and by Edward Lear with his nonsense verse, Belloc went further than either. He made uproarious jokes of the moral admonitions that had once been given to youth as serious lessons.

While Belloc had his imitators, such as Harry Graham in *Ruthless Rhymes for Heartless Homes* (1899) and Mrs. Ernest Ames in *Wonderful England!* (1902), Belloc's satires were exceedingly skillful in that he not only made fun of the moralistic themes, but he also used meters so expertly that he created his own brand of macabre humor.

His first collection of comic verses, *The Bad Child's Book of Beasts,* which sold four thousand copies in three months, begins: "I call you bad, my little child, / Upon the title page, Because a manner rude and wild / Is common at your age." With these words the rudeness and wildness takes over; he jabs at "evil children" who imitate the bounding of the kangaroo, who "eat like little Hogs" and "whine like Puppy Dogs" and "take their manners from the Ape." Perhaps Belloc's best (and most anthologized) verses appear in this first volume, such as "The Yak," whom the child can lead about on a string; "The Lion," whose "shoulders are stark, and his jaws they are grim, / And a good little child will not play with him"; and "The Elephant," who has "such a / LITTLE tail behind, / So LARGE a trunk before."

But not all of Belloc's verses hold up as well as these. Many of the rhymes are so sophisticated and require so much background that Carpenter and Prichard observe that they will probably not be understood by today's children and will, presumably, not endure. It seems likely, however, that his best cautionary tales, the most outlandish spoofs on

Victorian tracts, will live forever, at least for collectors. In *Cautionary Tales for Children* (1907), twelve verses about blighted youth, the reader meets (and probably never forgets) Matilda, "Who told Lies, and was Burned to Death," as well as such other misfits as Rebecca, "Who slammed Doors for Fun and Perished Miserably," and Jim, "Who ran away from his Nurse, and was eaten by a Lion." In *New Cautionary Tales* (1930) the reader meets Sarah Byng, "Who could not read and was tossed into a thorny hedge by a Bull," along with the equally hilarious Maria, "Who made Faces and a Deplorable Marriage."

Although it must have pleased a wide British audience at the time of publication, one of the least satisfactory elements in some of Belloc's verses is the notion of Britain's presumed superiority over other cultures. In *The Bad Child's Book of Beasts,* for example, "The Dromedary is a cheerful bird; / I cannot say the same about the Kurd." These lines are accompanied by a doleful, stereotypic sketch of the Kurd, illustrated by "B. T. B." Six of Belloc's eight children's books were illustrated by B. T. B., Lord Basil Blackwood, a friend from Oxford days and a fine comic artist. One of these volumes, *The Modern Traveller* (1898), was about the satiric adventures of Commander Sin and Captain Blood; it was generally read by adults and almost unanimously praised by the critics, including Sir Arthur Quiller-Couch. After Blackwood's death, Nicolas Bentley illustrated *New Cautionary Tales* (1930) and *Ladies and Gentlemen* (1932). Belloc was fortunate in both of his illustrators. Carpenter and Prichard say of Blackwood's pictures that they "were not infrequently funnier than the verse."

Whether the verses or the illustrations were intended primarily for children is impossible to say. At least one publisher advertised the books as "nursery furniture," but adults may always have found them more fun than children. Part of that fun, unfortunately, was based on the notion that people who were different, that is, not British, were worthy objects for humor. The lords in the verses from *More Peers* (1911) are not *genuine* Englishmen: Lord Uncle Tom is "as black as Tar," and Lord Ali Baba is a "Turk / Who hated every kind of work."

While the six verses in *Ladies and Gentlemen,* whose subtitle is *For Adults Only and Mature at That,* take swipes at British judges, lords, statesmen, and even "the author," the reader also finds the xenophobic "The Three Races," in which the Nordic has a "slow" mind, the Alpine is "foolish" and has dirty yellow skin, and the Mediterranean is "the

most degraded of all" with his "crisp hair" that "even curls." Readers at the time might not have found these xenophobic remarks offensive, but they did find his anti-Semitism upsetting. His strong anti-Semitic feelings were well known at Oxford, and as Speaight suggests, they might have resulted in his being refused the teaching post he so clearly wanted. A. N. Wilson, however, says the dons didn't like him on personal grounds as well, since "he had hectored them" and was so often rude and drunk. Speaight states that his Oxford companions, who revered him personally, were embarrassed about his obstinate stand on the Dreyfus affair.

Alfred Dreyfus, a Jewish French army officer, had been sentenced to life imprisonment on Devil's Island for treason. After a much publicized scandal, he was retried, acquitted, and eventually promoted to the Legion of Honor. Belloc never believed Dreyfus was innocent. He was outspoken against those who supported him and argued that ninety-nine out of one hundred Frenchmen shared his belief. He said that the retrial had been directed by a small minority who held the money power, that is, the Jews. He railed against Émile Zola, whose *J'accuse* had done much to save Dreyfus; in short he abhorred the Dreyfusards. While it is true that the Dreyfusards were not necessarily seeking justice, but rather an undermining of army and church, Belloc brought much harm to himself by continuing his attacks. Speaight says the case revealed the contradictions in Belloc's political philosophies and caused many to question this liberal's search for truth, which "was so manifestly impaired by prejudice."

Charges of anti-Semitism were revived in 1922 when he published *The Jews,* in which he outlined a policy of separation. He insisted that he did not hate Jews, but that he wanted to protect them by creating a "Jewish nation . . . [with] registration and charters, Jewish courts. . . ." He said his stand was righteous because he made his points openly and was not like those who defended assimilation while saying "the vilest things about the Jews behind their backs."

Speaight defends Belloc to a point. While acknowledging his "chronic preoccupation" with Judaism, Speaight says, "*The Jews* was anything but an anti-Semitic tract, and it is a tragedy that for a hundred people who know the rhyme about Lord Swaythling or the 'little curly-headed men' there is not one who has read Belloc's sober examination of the problem." But Speaight concludes that even though Belloc "saluted the virtues of Israel" and genuinely wanted the Jews to have peace, his "solution" of separation was unacceptable.

Belloc honestly may have felt that protected segregation for Jews was preferable to "villainous assimilation," but he himself made vile comments. As with Protestants, he sometimes "teased" Jews: "The poor darlings, I'm awfully fond of them, but it's their own silly fault—they ought to have left God alone." Such ill-conceived banter, even though the comment was written in a private letter to Robert Speaight, reveals considerable condescension and scorn.

Like his friend and kindred spirit G. K. Chesterton, Belloc was an outspoken Roman Catholic. Belloc, in particular, was often "strident" in his fight against English Protestantism. His books on religion, especially *Europe and the Faith* (1920) and *The Great Heresies* (1938), clearly reveal his point of view, but he was most militant in (and most criticized for) his four-volume *History of England* (1925–1931), in which he "corrected" what he considered was the overly Protestant view of English history.

In spite of his Catholic militancy, he was elected as a Liberal to Parliament in 1906 and again in 1910. (He had become a British citizen in 1902.) With revolutionary zeal but on conservative principle, he opposed the Education Act of 1902 on the ground that a parent should be able to choose his child's religious influence (that is, if a school was in a region of mixed denominations, it should remain neutral); he opposed the importation of Chinese labor; and he opposed women's suffrage because it would upset the relationship between the sexes. With equal energy he went to great pains to serve his constituents: he advised a walking club on which were the best routes; he conducted classes in military history, conversational French, and medieval history. *Punch* said he was the most hardworking of the young M.P.s in that "the weekend brings him no respite from his labours as he invariably spends it in the grimy heart of Salford among his constituents."

Shortly into his second term, thoroughly disillusioned, he resigned his seat, saying that he was "relieved to be quit of the dirtiest company it has ever been my misfortune to keep." He had entered Parliament sympathizing with Herbert Asquith's Liberal party as it moved toward a welfare state, but by the time he resigned in 1910 he had only contempt for the compromises that being a Liberal

required. By then he had also published thirty-nine books, including four for children, and he had gone on countless lecture tours. As always, his energy was boundless, his wit sharp. Although he suffered from severe insomnia, he labored doggedly on whatever he undertook, sometimes working on several volumes at the same time—even while on tour.

He apparently created his prose works and his rambunctious satires with relative ease. His serious poetry, however, was written with considerable pain. George Sampson says that Belloc's best work is probably his sonnets, which are "slight in quantity, exquisite in quality." Belloc's friend J. B. Morton describes Belloc's making of sonnets as "chiselling and polishing with the utmost care." On his seventy-first birthday Belloc said he would be happy if he could feel he had contributed anything substantial to English poetry. He was forever in awe of the poetic process. The mystery of it, he said, could not be explained or understood "this side of the grave."

In retrospect, Belloc is difficult to assess. That he was a revolutionist steeped in the republican spirit of his French ancestors is clear. He abhorred government by privilege, by "cads," as he called them. It is also clear that he could argue conservative issues just as fiercely as liberal ones and see no contradiction. His belief in "distributism" (the redistribution of land to the people, an idea that had grown out of the Victorian medievalism of John Ruskin and William Morris) was part of a "leftist" movement affecting intellectuals on both sides of the Atlantic, from T. S. Eliot and Wyndham Lewis to Allen Tate and Robert Penn Warren. But Belloc's interpretation of distributism was "rightist" in that he believed it could work only under the dictates of a strong leader (Mussolini perhaps) and a revival of the Catholic Church in Europe.

His popularity during his lifetime was immense. An international celebrity, he had audiences with Pope Pius XI, whom he called a "greasy monsignore"; he visited Franklin D. Roosevelt, whom he liked; and he made a pilgrimage to Rome to visit Mussolini in 1924 after Mussolini had reconciled with the church in 1923. (A. N. Wilson says Belloc thought the "Italian *Duce* was the new Caesar.") And he received many honors, including an honorary doctorate from Glasgow University in 1920 and a knighthood in the Order of St. Gregory in 1934.

Morton's memoir is almost worshipful. But it is obvious that Belloc's brilliance was at times nearly overpowering. Stories abound of his wit in conversation; of his breaking into song in both English and French on all sorts of subjects and occasions; of his drinking wine and malt liquor (from which came his well-known "West Sussex Drinking Song"); of his endless entertaining even when he was exhausted from writing, traveling, and lecturing. A frequent, often unannounced visitor in many households as he wandered over Europe and America, he was a welcome and considerate guest. He came wearing his greatcoat, his pockets stuffed with bread.

As the father of three sons and two daughters to raise after his beloved wife, Elodie, died in 1914, he was devoted. It was not until his son Peter died in 1941 in World War II that his energy seriously deteriorated, probably the result of several small strokes beginning as early as 1933. (His son Louis had been listed as missing in action in the First World War.) Although Belloc strove valiantly to meet every occasion with his usual spirit, he never recovered from the shock of Peter's death. He never wrote again.

Belloc died in Sussex in the family home, King's Land, at Guildford, Surrey, on 12 July 1953, at age 82, as the result of an accident.

If Belloc had lived up to his own romantic ideal of the egalitarian spirit of the French Revolution and of distributism, late-twentieth-century assessments of his work for both adults and children might be different. That he was an individualist and a great personality loved by many is without question. That he was a brilliant craftsman and superb wit cannot be debated. That he was humane and sensitive to many facets of life, as revealed for the most part in his sonnets, is without doubt. But his sonnets are rarely read today. Only some of his children's verse is. In spite of the accolades still heaped on his children's verses (McCabe calls them "his most brilliant compositions"), many of his cleverest "pastiches of Victorian children's didactic verses" are unreadable. When Wilfred Sheed says that "most of his admirers today are children" because of his "delicate touch, exquisite phrasing, metrical wizardry and high spirits," one can only wonder if Sheed has read much of that verse. Craftsmanship notwithstanding, Belloc's prejudices obscure his contribution to children's literature as well as to adult literature. Out of a lifetime of extraordinary vitality and prodigious

work, Hilaire Belloc will probably be remembered for a dozen or so children's rhymes, but only those few that poke good-natured fun at the humanity of all peoples.

Selected Bibliography

WORKS OF HILAIRE BELLOC

The Bad Child's Book of Beasts. With illustrations by Basil Blackwood. Oxford: Alden, 1896; New York: Dutton, 1896.

Verses and Sonnets. London: Ward and Downey, 1896.

The Modern Traveller. With illustrations by Basil Blackwood. London: Arnold, 1898; London: Campion Press, 1959.

Cautionary Tales for Children: Designed for the Admonition of Children Between the Ages of Eight and Fourteen Years: Verses. With illustrations by Basil Blackwood. London: Eveleigh Nash, 1907; New York: Knopf, 1922.

More Peers. With illustrations by Basil Blackwood. London: Stephen Swift, 1911.

Europe and the Faith. London: Constable, 1920.

The Jews. London: Constable, 1922.

A History of England. 4 vols. London: Methuen, 1925–1931.

New Cautionary Tales. With illustrations by Nicolas Bentley. London: Duckworth, 1930; New York: Harper and Brothers, 1931.

Ladies and Gentlemen: For Adults Only and Mature at That. With illustrations by Nicolas Bentley. London: Duckworth, 1932.

The Great Heresies. New York: Sheed and Ward, 1938.

Matilda, Who Told Lies and Was Burned to Death. With illustrations by Steven Kellogg. New York: Dial Press, 1970.

The Yak, the Python, and the Frog. With illustrations by Steven Kellogg. New York: Parents' Magazine Press, 1975. (Verses from *The Bad Child's Book of Beasts* and others.)

CRITICAL AND BIOGRAPHICAL STUDIES

Belloc-Lowndes, Marie. *The Young Hilaire Belloc.* New York: Kenedy and Sons, 1956.

Carpenter, Humphrey, and Mari Prichard. *The Oxford Companion to Children's Literature.* Oxford: Oxford University Press, 1984.

Commire, Anne, ed. *Yesterday's Authors of Books for Children.* Vol. 1. Detroit: Gale Research, 1977.

Hamilton, Robert. *Hilaire Belloc.* London: Douglas Organ, 1945.

Haynes, Renée. *Hilaire Belloc.* London: Longmans, Green, 1953.

Jebb, Eleanor and Reginald. *Testimony to Hilaire Belloc.* London: Methuen, 1956.

Kirkpatrick, D. L., ed. *Twentieth-Century Children's Writers.* New York: St. Martin's Press, 1978.

Mandell, C. Creighton and Edward Shanks. *Hilaire Belloc.* London: Methuen, 1916.

McCabe, Bernard. "A Cautionary Career." *New York Review of Books* (7 Nov. 1985).

Morton, J. B. *Hilaire Belloc: A Memoir.* London: Sheed and Ward, 1955.

Sampson, George. *The Concise Cambridge History of English Literature.* New York: Macmillan, 1946.

Sheed, Wilfred. "Tantrums of a Literary Man." *New York Times Book Review.* (2 Sept. 1984).

Speaight, Robert. *The Life of Hilaire Belloc.* London: Hollis and Carter, 1957.

Wilhelmsen, Frederick. *Hilaire Belloc: No Alienated Man.* London: Sheed and Ward, 1954.

Wilson, A. N. *Hilaire Belloc.* New York: Atheneum, 1985.

—GRAYCE SCHOLT

LUDWIG BEMELMANS

1898–1962

IT IS SYMPTOMATIC of Ludwig Bemelmans' enduring reputation and also of the commercialism rampant in the present-day world of children's books that in 1985—twenty-three years after the author's death—a new book about his much-loved Madeline should be issued with noisy fanfare and hailed by its publishers as "a rediscovered classic." This new addition to the series, *Madeline's Christmas*, a rejuvenated edition of a tale that appeared in *McCall's* magazine's Christmas issue in 1956, is strikingly inferior in text and illustration to other Madeline stories. Yet it still reminds us of the amiable man who created an irresistible small girl, endowed her with heroic qualities, and pictured her adventures with exuberance, originality, and beauty.

Born on 27 April 1898 in Meran, a small city in the Austrian Tyrol—now a part of Italy known as Merano—Ludwig Bemelmans was the son of Lambert Bemelmans, a somewhat ne'er-do-well painter, and of Frances Fisher Bemelmans, the daughter of a prosperous Bavarian brewer. It was probably prophetic that Ludwig was born in a hotel, for all his life he retained a predilection for a cosmopolitan milieu, for travel, for the art of fine dining, for elegant hostelries, and for international friends of culture or wealth.

Soon after his birth, Bemelmans' family moved to Gmunden in Austria, to a hotel owned by his father; here he spent the first six years of his life in an idyllic setting with his adored French governess—speaking only French, singing the children's songs of France, and listening to its stories. Although he loved the Tyrol throughout his life, he scarcely spoke a word of German as a child (later on, he became proficient in six languages). Although hotel life was gracious and fascinating, it was also a rather unconventional and lonely existence for a child. "The only people you met were odd ones, below stairs and upstairs," Bemelmans tells his small daughter years later in *Father, Dear Father* (1953), a delightful, witty book that is chiefly a conversational, loosely constructed narrative of a trip he took to Europe with her. "In my youth the upstairs was a collection of Russian grand dukes and French countesses, English lords and American millionaires. Backstairs there were French cooks, Roumanian hairdressers, Chinese manicurists, Italian bootblacks, Swiss managers, English valets. All those people I got to know very well." He goes on to say that in America he ran into the same kind of people: "I can write about them, and one ought to write about what one knows. . . . I can't write about what you call 'ordinary people' because I don't know them well enough."

Eventually, Ludwig's father abandoned the family, and the boy was sent to be raised by his maternal grandfather in Regensburg, a Bavarian city on the Danube. Here he found offensive the transition from the amenities of hotel life to the earthiness of the brewery. As he grew into adolescence, he began to rebel against family and school—and even against Regensburg itself, which he considered dull and provincial. In *Hotel Bemelmans* (1946) Bemelmans says, "All my professors came to eat in the restaurant of Grandfather's brewery, so that he was always informed that I would not pass the examinations, that I was unruly, impertinent, never serious, always late, and kept bad company." Removed from the school, the boy was then sent to a private academy in Rothenburg—an educational venture that proved no more successful—and was later apprenticed to an uncle who owned a string of resort hotels in the Bavarian Alps. When Ludwig fell into trouble once again, this time in an incident in which a hotel manager was wounded, he was given the choice of reform school or emigration to America. Possibly the aggrieved uncle also felt that in New York the youth would learn modern, efficient techniques of hotel management. One also suspects that at this time the young man may have felt the first stirrings of a taste for a peripatetic life; surely this first real journey was the most far-reaching in its implications that he ever undertook.

Bemelmans arrived in New York armed with letters of reference to the managers of several prestigious hotels, and he found work easily enough; but just as easily he lost a series of jobs through careless accidents and various arrogant transgressions, until he finally found a place for himself in the dining room of what he calls the "Hotel Splendide"—actually the old Ritz-Carlton, a long-vanished monument of grandeur and beauty. During this time he was drawing everything that surrounded him, and he took some drawing lessons in the studio of a German artist. In the studio he was happy—it was a refuge from the hotel: "Here was freedom and integrity and good work. All my troubles would leave me on the ride down to the studio. But also this work was making my other life, the life of the Splendide, tolerable, for I was learning to see."

In 1918, having become a naturalized American citizen, Bemelmans enlisted in the United States Army and was dispatched first to Georgia and later to Buffalo, New York, where he volunteered to be an attendant in a hospital for the mentally ill. His first book for adults, *My War with the United States* (1937), was based upon translations from the German diary he kept at that time; it presents the young soldier's hilarious yet poignant account of army life —his views on military discipline and his descriptions of the peculiar problems created by his heavy German accent.

After the war Bemelmans returned to the Ritz-Carlton, this time to the banqueting department. But he continued to draw, and in the face of countless disappointments he was determined to become

a cartoonist. In 1925 he became part owner of a New York East Side restaurant, Hapsburg House, where he decorated the walls with lively trompe l'oeil murals and played the genial host to its devoted clientele of writers, editors, and publishers. Gradually these people became enchanted with the personality behind the paintings and began to use his drawings in their publications. With terrible timing he finally decided to leave the security and the sumptuous food and drink of the hotel and to strike out on his own; two weeks later came the stock market crash of September 1929.

The early 1930's were difficult years for Bemelmans; he was now living in a bleak studio on Eighth Street and feeling like a failure. To combat his homesickness—and to hide the dingy view from the windows—he pulled down the shades and painted Tyrolean scenes on them, and embellished the walls as well. In the same building lived a lithographer, who saw the colorful decorations and brought a visitor to see them—May Massee, editor of children's books for the Viking Press. She easily persuaded Bemelmans to do a children's book, thus adding the young man to the distinguished list of artists and writers she had discovered. At dinner, using a folded napkin, she showed him how a book is made, deploying colored pictures here, black-and-white ones there. Within a few months he handed her the manuscript for *Hansi* (1934), his first book, based on nostalgic memories of his beloved Tyrol. Although the large-sized book is somewhat clumsy in its dimensions, haphazard in page design, and wordy in text, its ingenuousness is captivating; brimming with spontaneity and warmth, it tells of a little boy who leaves his mother in Innsbruck to spend Christmas with his uncle's family in their mountain home. The grainy crayon drawings Bemelmans created to illustrate it are entirely appropriate to the naive charm of the story. His friend Kurt Wiese did the unglamorous work of preparing the color separations for the lithographic printing process.

There soon came marriage to Madeleine Freund and, later, the birth of their only child, Barbara, to whom Bemelmans remained a devoted, affectionate father for the rest of his life. "When Barbara was born, we were romantically poor—the garret kind of existence," he once said; but their saving grace was his father-in-law, who was a bank president.

The Golden Basket (1936), Bemelmans' second book, is not a picture book but it is a resplendently illustrated production about two little English girls —and, incidentally, their father—who live for a time in a small hotel in the beautiful old Belgian city of Bruges. Here, in this beguiling book that has long and undeservedly been out of print, one easily detects many facets of the author-illustrator: Bemelmans the innkeeper; the kindly, indulgent father; and the hearty devotee of good food. And here, too, is history in the making, for one day in a cathedral the two small sightseers meet a string of twelve little girls walking in two straight rows with their lovely, tall teacher. "The name of the smallest girl is Madeleine [*sic*]. Her hair is copper-red, she has blue eyes," and in the succeeding pages she presents a delectable foretaste of the enchanting heroine to come.

Returning to the locale of Austria, to a small town on the Danube, Bemelmans now wrote and illustrated *The Castle Number Nine* (1937). Baptiste, the protagonist, is a retired servant who has worked in the castles of dukes, kings, and princes. Bored and unhappy, he answers a newspaper advertisement and then, packing all his seven splendid liveries—a different color for every day in the week— he goes off to serve an eccentric count. The beautifully fluent narrative comes across as a stylish, sophisticated version of the English folktale "Master of All Masters." With its lovely deep-toned watercolors and its characteristic two-color drawings, it is almost a picture book—and quintessentially Bemelmans in text and illustrations. In the same year he also created the spirited drawings in sepia for Munro Leaf's *Noodle* (1937), the only children's book he ever illustrated for which he did not write the text. The faintly didactic story deals with a dachshund eager to change his shape and size until, predictably, he decides that he is best as he is.

An impulsive trip to Ecuador—he had just read a *National Geographic* article on the country—generated *Quito Express* (1938); its tiny hero, Pedro, an unwitting stowaway on a train, is modeled after a baby actually encountered in the same situation by Ludwig and Madeleine during their visit. The monochrome illustrations, done entirely in terra cotta, are freely drawn in a style reminiscent of modern primitivism; they exhibit the artist's usual pleasing blend of droll humor and sympathetic understanding.

The year 1939 was a high point in Bemelmans' career, for *Madeline* appeared and has ever since universally captivated young and old. Its creator once observed that initially nobody wanted to pub-

lish the book; its artwork was considered too sophisticated for young children. The artist traced the creation of the character Madeline to stories his mother told him of her life as a little girl in a Bavarian convent school. He had once even visited the place with her and seen the little beds in rows and the line of washbasins where the children brushed their teeth. But the essence of the plot— the appendectomy and Madeline's hospital sojourn —evolved from a bicycle accident he suffered one summer in France, which sent him to the hospital, where he met a little girl whose appendix had just been removed. The whole traumatic episode is detailed with typical Bemelmans élan in his 1954 Caldecott Medal acceptance speech for *Madeline's Rescue* (1953).

In the first, superb book about Madeline, art and text are so mutually supportive that it would be difficult to imagine a more beautifully integrated picture book. Bemelmans took himself seriously as a painter, and now, at last, he had a proper showcase for a lavish display of his talent. In his Caldecott speech he spoke of his dissatisfaction with the "self-advertisement" of art exhibitions and the trendy commercialism of the art galleries:

> I looked for another way of painting, for privacy; for a fresh audience, vast and critical and remote, to whom I could address myself with complete freedom I wanted to paint purely that which gave me pleasure, scenes that interested me; and one day I found that the audience for that kind of painting was a vast reservoir of impressionists who did very good work themselves, who were very clear-eyed and capable of enthusiasm. I addressed myself to children.

Whether the illustrations are line drawings of domestic activity shown against a yellow background or full-color outdoor scenes highly suggestive of Raoul Dufy, with scurrying line over colored wash, *Madeline* shows a strong sense of composition and design; note, for example, how the twelve little girls form themselves into constantly changing patterns. And the illustrations are full of humor, energy, and movement, too; while for dramatic emphasis the artist exaggerates—as in the elongation of the figure accompanying the lines "And afraid of a disaster / Miss Clavel ran fast / and faster."

Unlike most naturalized Americans, Bemelmans, a suave cosmopolitan, never entirely settled in

America; he had friends everywhere and felt at home wherever he happened to find himself. Throughout much of his mature life he maintained a pied-à-terre in Paris; he loved the city and spoke French more spontaneously than any other language. In a way Paris is the chief character in the book, and is portrayed just as vividly as the enchanting Madeline. Parisian images remain fixed in the mind—Notre Dame, the Eiffel Tower, the Place Vendôme, the Opéra, the Luxembourg Gardens—and all are supported by an orderly, secure, tightly plotted story.

Fourteen years and another world war passed before Bemelmans published the long-awaited sequel to *Madeline*. In *Madeline's Rescue* the protagonist shares the spotlight with a dog "of uncertain race" named Genevieve. The scribbly Dufy-like charm of the illustrations in *Madeline* is now much less noticeable; the paintings, deeper in tone and more purposeful in design, are less integral to the story and serve chiefly as a stage on which the children's drama unfolds. One misses the patterning, the terseness, and the elegant economy of the visual and verbal storytelling of the first *Madeline*. The artist continues his painterly celebration of Paris: the market Les Halles, the Church of St. Germain des Près, the Tuileries, the Pont Neuf, and a splendid view—with apologies to Utrillo—from a street in Montmartre of Sacre Coeur.

In frightening Miss Clavel, Madeline pushes her luck too far; she falls into the Seine, and dragging "her safe from a watery grave," the noble dog Genevieve almost displaces the little girl as the real heroine of the book. The villains of the story, so useful to the plot, resemble the villains of Bemelmans' adult books—petty officials who misuse their power to trample on the rights of good people—and good dogs. Of course, the naive but stalwart child retains her status as the emblematic picture-book hero—the kind of strong, individualistic personality young readers found abundant in the past, such as Little Tim, Harold (of the purple crayon), and the anthropomorphic Peter Rabbit, Curious George, and Ferdinand.

Invigorated by receiving the Caldecott Medal, Bemelmans soon produced *Madeline and the Bad Hat* (1957). As in succeeding *Madeline* books, both story and pictures lack Bemelmans' early buoyancy, creative imagination, and subtlety. Installed in the house next door to the famous "old house in Paris that was covered with vines" is the Spanish ambas-

sador. And "what bliss, what joy! His Excellency has a boy." But the ambassador's son, Pepito, proves to be a sneaky mischief-maker, playing tricks on everyone and especially on defenseless animals. Echoes of earlier textual cadences and pictorial designs appear throughout the book as the children range farther afield in pursuit of the "Bad Hat" and his diabolical high jinks. But when he invites his twelve lively neighbors to a gypsy carnival in *Madeline and the Gypsies* (1959), Pepito shares Madeline's inevitable tendency to become involved in misadventure. The two children go off to live for a time with the gypsies; they have a taste of the roving life and become performers in the carnival.

Finally, after the Spanish ambassador is transferred to London and Pepito begins to pine for his brood of young friends in *Madeline in London* (1961), Madeline and the rest join the jet set and fly over to London, where the mischievous pair again have a private adventure—this one a ludicrous escapade with a retired horse from the Queen's Life Guards. These last two books, in particular, exhibit an extravagance of color and incident and a frenetic diffusion of the order, integration, and aesthetic stability so beautifully evident in the first *Madeline*. Realism verges on whimsy, and the artist employs tonal brilliance and rapid movement in a slapdash manner. Humor becomes absurdity; the stories seem forced. One need only read these later books aloud to realize how unmemorable they are.

Madeline's Christmas is a weak attempt to turn an unknown tale into a holiday treasure. The publishers claim that "the art has been photographically enlarged and recolored by Jody Wheeler to prepare it for reproduction." But since the artist's style altered considerably during the 1950's, it is impossible to decide where Bemelmans leaves off and Jody Wheeler steps in. The story and, more important, the character of the heroine in both text and pictures are sadly impoverished. Gone are the beautiful cityscapes and the escapades all over Paris; instead, Madeline is mired in dull domesticity, for all eleven girls, along with a rather grotesque Miss Clavel, are in bed with colds, and only Madeline is well enough to play nurse. Suddenly, a rug merchant appears at the door, and since he is —conveniently—a magician as well, his carpets transport the twelve little maids, now miraculously recovered, to their parents in the nick of time for Christmas. Aesthetically, the book is a failure: a hodgepodge of artwork with careless drawing and garish color.

Curiously enough, Bemelmans' other works for children after the publication of the first *Madeline* volume were for the most part disappointing. *Fifi* (1940) resembles *Madeline* only in dimensions and in the fact that the text is rhymed. But it is a far-fetched tale told in limping verse. A wife of a foreign service officer in Africa—a big-bosomed dowager type—lives in Uganda "in a house with a veranda." The silly woman takes Fifi, her pampered poodle, by airplane to the dentist in Zanzibar; but when they have to land for refueling, Fifi narrowly escapes being cooked by the natives: "'Perhaps with cabbage,' says Mrs. Savage." Text and illustrations are entirely inconsequential, hastily executed, and blatantly racist. The scrappy drawings include ugly caricatures of black Africans.

Rosebud (1942) tells a kind of fable to prove that "one must never make fun of the little people." A perfectly contented rabbit reads in a book that the lion is the king of animals, that the whale is celebrated for his enormous size and the elephant for his strength, patience, and memory; sadly, the rabbit is described as "scared, shy and hysterical." Rosebud grows "madder and madder and madder" and finally begins to write his own book—"about the strength and smartness and the great courage of rabbits." The cartoonlike drawings are not improved by the addition of bright, irrelevant color, nor does there seem to be any artistic point in a purple whale, a pink camel, or a blue elephant.

Fifi and *Rosebud* at least share the merit of simplicity and directness. In *Sunshine: A Story About the City of New York* (1950), Bemelmans embarked on a project much more ambitious, though no more significant. Once again, rhymed couplets are set forth in a large book featuring a combination of full-color paintings and line drawings against a pastel background—the whole package obviously designed to claim kinship with the beloved *Madeline*. The story is built upon the problem of the postwar housing shortage in New York City—not a particularly childlike theme, especially as Bemelmans develops it. An avaricious landlord, satirically called Mr. Sunshine, advertises an apartment to let; unwittingly, he rents it to a woman who runs a music school, and—needless to say—the enthusiastic cacophony nearly drives him mad. In order to effect the rhymes, the text is strained, wordy, and digressive—unrewarding to read aloud. Lacking both verbal and visual unity, the book ends with the words and music of "O Holy Night" and with a merry Christmas for all, thus giving the impression that Mr. Sunshine has become some kind of reformed Scrooge.

The Happy Place (1952) is a meager tale of an Easter bunny sold as a pet but ultimately set free in New York's Central Park. The small volume is decorated with line drawings and a few paintings, none of which succeeds in enlivening the unexciting fantasy. Recalling the ambience of *Hansi* is *The High World* (1954). Set in the Austrian Tyrol, the story tells of simple, peaceful mountain people whose quiet lives are disrupted by the construction of a hydroelectric plant—and by a rude, overbearing government official who becomes a reformed character when an avalanche threatens the lives of children. Filled with the warmth and gemütlichkeit of the Alpine people, the book is generously illustrated with scraggly line drawings; in addition, there are four paintings, poorly integrated with the text, two of which are curiously muddy in tone and seem to be deliberately awkward and naive, while the other two are more pleasing in color and composition.

During the mid-1950's Bemelmans became almost obsessed with the desire to be a serious studio painter. In *My Life in Art* (1958) he indicates a change in his point of view toward his work:

> Art is mostly emotion and emotion fades away when purposeful thinking takes the upper hand. This happened to me. There came many, many years in which I had the desire to paint, but I created only pictures with a purpose. I came to America, illustrated the books and stories I wrote. I painted theatrical scenery. I did pictures and covers for magazines.

In 1953 he began to paint in earnest, and although he used oils, the work strongly resembles his painterly book illustrations—done in gouache—of the same period: the later *Madeline* books, *The High World*, and especially *Parsley* (1955) and *Welcome Home!* (1960). In *Father, Dear Father* Bemelmans offers his daughter a rather conventional reason why he *could* have been a great painter but was not: "Because I love living too much. If I were unhappy . . . or otherwise burdened, so that I would turn completely inward, then I would be a good painter. As is, I'm not sufficiently devoted." He felt then that, unfortunately, his greatest inspiration was a low bank balance. And a few years later he wrote in *My Life in Art*: "I am not a practical person, not logical and not a thinker. I can't learn anything except by my senses and I am impeded by a self-indulgent strain for pleasure and comfort."

First published in *Woman's Day*, the story "The Old Stag and the Tree" became the text for *Parsley*, a large, splendid picture book about a stag in the forest and his friend, a twisted old pine tree that stands on the edge of an abyss. In this tale of mutual dependence and survival, both the text and the glowing, dramatic illustrations are filled with humor as well as the peace and pain of life—and also with rejoicing over the bounty of the natural world. Uniform in size with *Parsley* is *Welcome Home!* A brief poem about a sly fox outwitting the hunters serves as the text for some of the most striking paintings Bemelmans ever created for a picture book. Broad sweeps of action and humor, all executed in radiant color, depict horses, hunters, and hounds, while contrasting scenes of snug domesticity feature the fox and his triumphant family.

The artist's final picture book, *Marina* (1962), follows the same generous format, but, sadly, the great straining for humor and effect results in much ado about very little. Anthropomorphism is raised to preposterous heights in the story of Marina, the child of a trained seal, who is swallowed by a shark and eventually rescued with the aid of six porpoises. The inept verses embellished with unchildlike puns arrive at a didactic conclusion, and the hasty color-washed drawings add nothing.

From the publication of *My War with the United States* until the end of his life, Bemelmans produced many works for adults, all illustrated with his inimitable drawings. Henry Pitz, the artist and critic, observed in *American Artist* of May 1951:

> The Bemelmans drawings will never be hoarded as great works of draftsmanship. . . . But they contain some precious ingredients that are missing from the great mass of skillful work. They contain delight and spontaneity and charm, a power to reveal seemingly artlessly, a hundred and one tiny facets of humanity's maneuvers.

Indeed, Ludwig Bemelmans' sparkling novels, short stories, and anecdotal sketches are laced with autobiographical reminiscences; fact and fiction are interspersed in literary pieces memorable for their wit, mischief, irreverence, compassion, and great understanding. For this sophisticated bon vivant,

brimming with joie de vivre and goodwill, lived and worked in a unique, private, completely furnished world of his own creation. "I find it hard to hate anybody, and impossible to hate anybody for long," he remarked to his daughter in *Father, Dear Father*. In addition to his books he also wrote hundreds of stories and articles for many important magazines such as the *New Yorker*, *Town and Country*, *Holiday*, and *Vogue*; a libretto for a ballet; and scripts for motion pictures and musical stage productions. One must acknowledge that his best writing is found in this prodigious output for adults —writing that matches the drawing in the way it glorifies the ironic humor, the ludicrousness and absurdities, of the human situation.

Not surprisingly, Bemelmans' work for adults created an enormous, almost cultlike, following of ardent, devoted readers. But much of this work has been unavailable in recent years; so, for a new generation of readers, Madeleine Bemelmans has gathered together a fresh volume of selected writings— *Tell Them It Was Wonderful* (1985). In an appreciative foreword Norman Cousins writes:

> Bemelmans was the least inarticulate and most delightful personality I ever encountered. . . . He was elegant, ebullient, expansive. He could discourse on writing, painting, food, wine, hotels, and great cities with a combination of overview and minute detail. . . . He was less tortured by self-doubt (at least visibly) than any writer I know. He was not only the supreme man-about-town but the man at the center of the town, the compleat continental and cosmopolitan.

Apart from the *Madeline* books, *Parsley* is the only one of Bemelmans' children's books remaining in print. But even if the fame of the genial, gentle citizen of the world were to rest solely upon these few books, his double reputation as writer and illustrator would be assured. Bemelmans' *La Bonne Table* (1964) contains this bit of self-evaluation:

> A curious, complicated being who is driven by an excess of energy. . . . He works with fury, and lives as if it were his last day on earth. He is overly kind, overly generous—and hides it under a cloak of arrogance. He paints or writes the night through, is never where he says he will be . . . drinks, smokes, eats to excess, but fortunately has the constitution of an ox.
>
> (p. 17)

Unfortunately, he was wrong. After more than a year of illness and misery, he died—far too young —on 1 October 1962.

Selected Bibliography

WORKS OF LUDWIG BEMELMANS

Hansi. With illustrations by the author. New York: Viking Press, 1934.

The Golden Basket. With illustrations by the author. New York: Viking Press, 1936. (Honor Book, Newbery Medal, 1937.)

The Castle Number Nine. With illustrations by the author. New York: Viking Press, 1937.

My War with the United States. New York: Viking Press, 1937.

Noodle, with Munro Leaf. Philadelphia: Frederick A. Stokes, 1937. (Illustrations by Bemelmans, text by Leaf.)

Quito Express. With illustrations by the author. New York: Viking Press, 1938.

Madeline. With illustrations by the author. New York: Simon and Schuster, 1939. (Honor Book, Caldecott Medal, 1940.)

Fifi. With illustrations by the author. New York: Simon and Schuster, 1940.

Rosebud. With illustrations by the author. New York: Random House, 1942.

Hotel Bemelmans. New York: Viking Press, 1946.

Sunshine: A Story About the City of New York. With illustrations by the author. New York: Simon and Schuster, 1950. (*New York Herald Tribune* Children's Spring Book Festival Award, 1950.)

The Happy Place. With illustrations by the author. Boston: Little, Brown, 1952.

Father, Dear Father. With illustrations by the author. New York: Viking Press, 1953.

Madeline's Rescue. With illustrations by the author. New York: Viking Press, 1953. (Caldecott Medal, 1954.)

The High World. With illustrations by the author. New York: Harper, 1954.

Parsley. With illustrations by the author. New York: Harper, 1955.

Madeline and the Bad Hat. With illustrations by the author. New York: Viking Press, 1957. (*New York Herald Tribune* Children's Spring Book Festival Award, 1957.)

My Life in Art. New York: Harper, 1958.

Madeline and the Gypsies. With illustrations by the author. New York: Viking Press, 1959.

Welcome Home! With illustrations by the author. New York: Harper, 1960.

Madeline in London. With illustrations by the author. New York: Viking Press, 1961.

Marina. With illustrations by the author. New York: Harper & Row, 1962.

La Bonne Table. Selected and edited by Donald and Eleanor Friede. New York: Simon and Schuster, 1964.

Tell Them It Was Wonderful: Selected Writings. Edited by Madeleine Bemelmans. New York: Viking Press, 1985.

Madeline's Christmas. With illustrations by the author. New York: Viking Press, 1985.

CRITICAL AND BIOGRAPHICAL STUDIES

Bemelmans, Ludwig. "Caldecott Award Acceptance" *Horn Book* 30: 270–275 (August 1954).

Commire, Anne, ed. *Something About the Author*. Vol. 15. Detroit: Gale Research, 1979.

Fuller, Muriel, ed. *More Junior Authors*. New York: H. W. Wilson, 1963.

Kingman, Lee, et al., eds. *Illustrators of Children's Books: 1957–1966*. Boston: Horn Book, 1968.

Kunitz, Stanley J., ed. *Twentieth-Century Authors*. New York: H. W. Wilson, 1955. (First supplement.)

Miller, Bertha Mahony, et al., eds. *Illustrators of Children's Books: 1946–1956*. Boston: Horn Book, 1958.

Pitz, Henry C. "The Illustrator's Page: Ludwig Bemelmans" *American Artist* 15: 48–49 (May 1951).

—ETHEL HEINS

MARGERY WILLIAMS BIANCO
1881–1944

MARGERY WILLIAMS BIANCO once commented that she "would still rather dig in the garden or talk to the cat or make patchwork quilts than write." This seems an improbable remark coming from one who published over thirty books in her lifetime, but perhaps not so improbable judging by her life itself. Margery Williams was born on 22 July 1881 in London, and her childhood was lived close to nature and to books. Her father, a distinguished classical scholar, did not believe in formal education for children. Consequently, Margery was taught to read early and then left to explore the world of books with very few restrictions. Her favorite book was Wood's *Natural History,* and her passionate love of nature shaped all her childhood games and adventures.

By 1906, when she was twenty-five, she had published four adult novels; married Francesco Bianco, a dealer in rare books; and given birth to two children, Cecco and Pamela. In the years that followed, the family lived in Paris, then in Italy, and Bianco put her writing aside: "New surroundings, new friends, two small children—all this was far more exciting and interesting than just writing." But when the family returned to London in 1919, and three years later settled for good in America, Bianco was ready to write again and to write something different. She found herself remembering and thinking about treasured family toys—those of her children and those she herself had loved as a child. Out of these memories she wrote *The Velveteen Rabbit* in 1922, based on her own beloved rab-

bit, Fluffy, and her skin horse, Old Dobbin. Her career as a distinguished writer for children was launched. For Bianco, life preceded art. Perhaps this explains why her art, when she did take time away from other interests to create it, ranged so wide and so deep as a representation of human experience.

It is a measure of Bianco's respect for child readers that she produced two allegories among her earliest books for children. *The Apple Tree* (1926) and *The Candlestick* (1929) are Christian allegories that make considerable demands on a child reader's ability to be self-conscious about the act of reading. In *The Apple Tree* a brother and sister watch and wait for the arrival of a personified Easter. Giving up hope of his arrival, they sit down beneath a withered apple tree with a shabbily dressed stranger who has come down the road. The children question the stranger about his life, and his answers provide the informed reader with clues to his identity. But it is not until he shows the children a dead bird, and the brother and sister bring different perspectives to bear on the meaning of its transformation into a dove, that the reader is directly drawn into a debate about whether this man is Easter. Bianco thus leads the reader to reflect on the question of believing in the miracle of Easter. Does the reader side with the sister, a visionary, who concludes, "I think you are Easter," or with the brother, a realist, when he says, "You are a kind man even if you aren't Easter"? Bianco never directly resolves this debate for her readers. However, she does end the narrative with evidence on the sister's side of the argument.

The debate device also appears in *The Candlestick,* where Bianco makes extensive use of personification of commonplace objects to suggest the essence of concepts she wishes to explore. The book is structured around the life of the character David, from childhood to adulthood. Wind debates fire, shells debate kettle, on the various merits of venturing forth into the world versus staying at home. But it is through the candlestick, the object David likes best of all, that Bianco presents the Christian concept of salvation. In her essay "Our Youngest Critics" (1925), Bianco asserts that "children will usually respond immediately to any association of the fantastic with the commonplace." In *The Candlestick,* Bianco depends on this presumed immediacy of response to draw child readers into an exploration of questions about the meaning of life.

In *The Velveteen Rabbit, The Little Wooden Doll* (1925), and *The Skin Horse* (1927), Bianco relies less directly on the Bible as pretext, but rather uses ordinary objects and events, specifically a child's interaction with a toy, in a symbolic way. In each of these books Bianco's child characters remain nameless. The Boy in *The Velveteen Rabbit,* the child in *The Little Wooden Doll,* and both the Boy and the Child in *The Skin Horse* function as Everychild and suggest to the reader that these books are meant to be read for meaning rather than for the action. And in each book, toys—vulnerable as they are to neglect and physical wear and tear—are instruments whereby the theme of the power of love is explored.

Through various structural devices, Bianco focuses and refocuses her readers' attention on ideas of love and rebirth in these narratives. Her first and best-known book for children, *The Velveteen Rabbit,* expounds the shifting meaning of the word "real." "What is REAL?" asks the Rabbit of the Skin Horse. He then proceeds to discover the meaning as he undergoes two transformations. One, the result of being the object of human love and affection, is a reality of an earthly nature. The other, when the discarded stuffed rabbit is transformed into a live one by the nursery magic Fairy, is a reality of a different order. Here Bianco nods in a metaphysical direction. And lest her readers glide over this shift in meaning, she makes the action fade as a verbal exchange between the Rabbit and the Fairy is accentuated: " 'Wasn't I Real be-

fore?' asked the little Rabbit. 'You were Real to the Boy,' the Fairy said, 'because he loved you. Now you shall be Real to every one.' "

In *The Little Wooden Doll* and *The Skin Horse,* Bianco creates enigmatic endings that draw attention to the passage of toy characters from one dimension of being to another. At the outset, *The Little Wooden Doll* makes few interpretive demands on its readers. The story concerns the fate of a little wooden doll, collecting dust in the corner of an attic, who never loses hope of being loved by a child. After her rejection at the hands of two insensitive children, she is restored to her original beauty by her mouse and spider friends and transported by them to the bedside of a little girl who lives in a cottage at the edge of the wood. Bianco interrupts the thread of the action at this point with a conversation between the child and her mother about how the doll came to be there. Since the reader has just read for himself that the mice "set the little doll on a chair by the bedside," this exchange between mother and child does not immediately address a question in the reader's mind. However, near the end of the exchange (and the book) the child asks, "But how is it that her clothes are real?" and the mother answers, "I have always heard that the spiders sew well . . . and when one does a good action, there are those who see to it that it isn't wasted." Unbeknownst to the reader, the doll has apparently undergone a second transformation—her dress of gossamer has been transformed into a dress of real lace. This evidence of a second rebirth, coming as late as it does in the text, is news to the reader and causes him to revise, or at least expand upon, his initial interpretation. How the reader fills in this gap is pivotal in his act of reading and understanding *The Little Wooden Doll.*

Bianco plays with the reader's expectations at the end of *The Skin Horse* as well. The Skin Horse, having outlived his usefulness to the Boy, is given to the Children's Hospital, where he and the Child become best friends. Throughout the year the Child and the Skin Horse share their wishes, yearnings, and dreams. "And then, one day, they came and carried the Child away." In his absence, the Skin Horse gets trodden on by a careless nurse and thrown in the dustbin. A new horse, bought by the repentant nurse, fails to comfort the Child. But on Christmas Eve, the Skin Horse, transformed into a winged Pegasus, comes to the Child in a dream and transports him upward into the sky. The reader, expecting the Child to wake from this wish-fulfillment dream to the hubbub of Christmas morning at the Children's Hospital, is surprised to learn, with a turn of the page, that "the bed in the corner stood empty." Once again, Bianco's reader must fill in the gap and make a choice between natural and supernatural explanations.

Bianco was obviously at home with the intellectuality of these early allegorical works. But she is equally at home in the world of romance and during this same period wrote two superlative tales of adventure, *Poor Cecco* (1925) and *The Adventures of Andy* (1927). In these books children are only mentioned in passing. The reader's attention shifts from concern for the fate of passive toys in human hands to involvement in adventure stories in which toys are the main characters, endowed with active feelings and motivations of their own. Whereas in Bianco's symbolic toy fantasies the reader negotiates the interplay of natural and preternatural worlds, in these tales of adventure the illusion of make-believe is never broken. Here we meet two staunchly independent doll characters—Jensina in *Poor Cecco* and Andromeda in *The Adventures of Andy* —who foreshadow the feminist treatment of female characters in Bianco's later works of realistic fiction. And here also we encounter Bianco as social satirist. Particularly in *The Adventures of Andy,* Bianco satirizes the mass production of toys for children. Through a confrontation between the Fiventens and The Brotherhood of Ancient Toys, Bianco makes a statement about the value of toys that call forth a child's imagination and love.

In *A Street of Little Shops* (1932), *The Hurdy-Gurdy Man* (1933), and *The Good Friends* (1934), Bianco's social criticism takes a comic turn. *A Street of Little Shops* is a masterful collection of stories about "a little street in a little town in the country." Bianco's first-person narrator speaks directly and intimately to the child reader, turning him immediately into confidant and friend. Then the stories unfold. There is the slapstick humor of "Mr. A and Mr. P"; the mockery of pomposity in "The Baker's Daughter"; the ridicule of parsimoniousness in "Mr. Murdle's Large Heart"; the ironic humor of "The Sad Story of Mr. Porium's Family"; the absurdity of exaggerated forgetfulness in "Poor Mr. Fingle"; and finally, the satirization of progress in "The Saddler's Horse" and "Hats for Horses," a theme Bianco explores less effectively in *The House That Grew Smaller* (1931) and *Penny and the White Horse* (1942).

Writing about Walter de la Mare in 1942 ("De la Mare"), Bianco remarked that "more than ever before we have need, today, of the vital quality of imagination and of poetry and of its power to inspire courage and faith, need of 'the music-makers and makers of dreams.' " In *The Hurdy-Gurdy Man,* Bianco caricatures the inhabitants of "a neat and prosperous little town," who, one after the other, rebuff the music-maker, the hurdy-gurdy man. But, as he begins to play his music on the town green, the children hear him and all decorum breaks down. And as the hurdy-gurdy man's monkey makes mincemeat of the town's bylaws atop the village flagstaff, even the most serious-minded townsfolk succumb to the music.

Bianco believed that animism was central to the child's conception of the world. Talking animals, for example, are taken for granted by the human characters (and the reader) in *The Good Friends,* and serve Bianco well as a vehicle for satirizing the limitations of bureaucracy. Bianco characterizes the female protagonist, Mary, as willful, resourceful, and independent—a portrait of females that reverberates throughout Bianco's realistic fiction for children.

In *Winterbound* (1936), Bianco develops the character of Garry, who takes after her absent archaeologist-father. Garry is seen in contrast to her conventionally feminine sister, Kay, in the first chapter: "Nothing could ever spoil Kay's hands, long and sensitive, not like Garry's square blunt fingers that seemed made for doing things and grubbing in the earth." When their mother is called away for the winter, it is sixteen-year-old Garry, younger than Kay by three years, who holds the household together with her enterprising, dependable, and self-reliant ways.

Similarly, *Other People's Houses* (1939) breaks with the tradition of the average success story for girls. The book opens with the protagonist, Dale, in Pennsylvania Station, bidding farewell to her mother and sister. At seventeen, without benefit of college degree or career training, she must take any job she can get in order to earn her living in Manhattan. In the fifth chapter, through Dale's reflections on her mother, Bianco suggests to the reader that this will be a book where both social and literary norms are broken:

"Poor darling, she'd have a thousand fits if she knew what it had led me to," Dale murmured, wondering how it was possible, in this time and age, for anyone to remain so simple and guileless as her mother—just as though she had stepped out of some novel of the eighties, where jobs were referred to as "situations," golden opportunities always opened for the poor but well-bred lady-companion, and everything invariably turned out for the best.

The independent female protagonists that populate Bianco's fictive worlds are, no doubt, reflections of Bianco's own self-image. In the fourth chapter of her autobiographical novel, *Bright Morning* (1942), written for young readers, we get a glimpse of Bianco's view of herself as a young child through the character Chris: "For Chris had never wanted to be the sort of person that heroes died for in battle. If there was to be any battling, or being heroic, she wanted to do it herself."

Bianco's female characters, young and old alike, consistently challenge conventional patterns of female socialization. It might seem surprising, therefore, that in her one and only "book for boys," *Forward, Commandos!* (1944), her male characters engage almost exclusively in the conventionally male activity of war games. Indeed, Bianco makes extensive use of the battle motif in her works, regardless of the sex of her characters. Writing to the editor of the *Horn Book* in 1942, she remarked, "Children are taken up with war and the excitement of it, but it doesn't mean to them what it means to us, unless we make it so." And in this same book, Bianco is among the first writers for children to break with yet another convention through her inclusion of a black character, Banty, as one of the gang—a rare example of interracial friendship in children's fiction of this period.

Bianco had an instinctive grasp of the demands of a young child audience, and in the years immediately before her death in 1944 she directed her fiction toward these young listeners and readers. In her essay "Our Youngest Critics," Bianco wrote of her belief in the young child's love of detail:

Not only is the shape, color, or size of things of such importance to them that they will hold up an exciting narrative in order to have some minor point of this nature determined, definitely and beyond doubt, but they do seem to get a real thrill from facts as facts, apart from any relative value to the story.

In 1941 she put theory into practice with the publication of a little masterpiece, *Franzi and Gizi.* Putting little strain on the listener's ability to follow narrative sequence, Bianco chronicles the activities of a brother and sister from morning to night during a day they spend in the forest. This attempt to develop a form of fiction that would correspond to the young child's conception of the world culminates in the story *Bright Morning,* published in 1942. A catalog of events in the daily lives of two sisters, *Bright Morning* anticipates a reader who will revel in minute detail and immediacy of action.

In addition to these works of fiction, Bianco wrote books about gardening and animals for children. Her skill as a translator made Finnish, Norwegian, French, and African folktales accessible to English-speaking worlds of childhood. Not the least of her contributions to the field of children's literature was her criticism itself. Writing about "The Stories of Hans Andersen" in 1927, she observed that "there has been no writer for children with such amazing range and variety as Andersen. . . . Each [story] is different from the next; each is as spontaneous as though it were the only story he really wanted to write." The same could be said of Margery Williams Bianco's own literature.

Selected Bibliography

WORKS OF MARGERY WILLIAMS BIANCO

The Velveteen Rabbit; or, How Toys Become Real. With illustrations by William Nicholson. London: Heinemann, 1922; New York: George H. Doran, 1922. Modern editions: With illustrations by Michael Green. Philadelphia: Running Press, 1981. With illustrations by Michael Hague. New York: Holt, Rinehart and Winston, 1983. With illustrations by Tien. New York: Simon and Schuster, 1983. With illustrations by Allen Atkinson. New York: Knopf, 1983. With illustrations by Ilse Plume. Boston: Godine, 1983. Also, a videocassette narrated by Meryl Streep. With illustrations by David Jorgensen. New York: Random House, 1984.
The Little Wooden Doll. With illustrations by Pamela Bianco. New York: Macmillan, 1925; New York: Cadmus, 1959.
Poor Cecco. With illustrations by Arthur Rackham. London: Chatto and Windus, 1925; New York: George H. Doran, 1925.
The Apple Tree. With illustrations by Boris Artzybasheff. New York: George H. Doran, 1926.
The Adventures of Andy. With illustrations by Leon Underwood. Garden City, N.Y.: George H. Doran, 1927.
The Skin Horse. With illustrations by Pamela Bianco. New York: George H. Doran, 1927; La Jolla, California: Green Tiger Press, 1982.

The Candlestick. With illustrations by Ludovico Rodo. Garden City, N.Y.: Doubleday, Doran, 1929.

The House That Grew Smaller. With illustrations by Rachel Field. New York: Macmillan, 1931.

A Street of Little Shops. With illustrations by Grace Paull. Garden City, N.Y.: Doubleday, Doran, 1932; Tadworth, England: World's Work, 1958; London: White Lion, 1974; Boston: Gregg Press, 1981.

The Hurdy-Gurdy Man. With illustrations by Robert Lawson. London and New York: Oxford University Press, 1933; Boston: Gregg Press, 1979.

The Good Friends. With illustrations by Grace Paull. New York: Viking Press, 1934; New York: Cadmus, 1940.

Winterbound. With illustrations by Kate Seredy. New York: Viking Press, 1936; New York: Cadmus, 1943–1948.

Other People's Houses. New York: Viking Press, 1939.

Franzi and Gizi. With illustrations by Gisella Loeffler. New York: J. Messner, 1941.

Bright Morning. With illustrations by Margaret Platt. New York: Viking Press, 1942; New York: Collins, 1945.

Penny and the White Horse. With illustrations by Marjory Collison. New York: J. Messner, 1942.

Forward, Commandos! With illustrations by Rafaello Busoni. New York: Viking Press, 1944; New York: Cadmus, 1952.

CRITICAL AND BIOGRAPHICAL STUDIES

Bechtel, Louise Seaman. "A Tribute to Margery Bianco." *The Elementary English Review* (June 1935). Reprinted in *Books in Search of Children,* edited by Louise S. Bechtel. Toronto: Macmillan, 1969. Pp. 67–71.

Commire, Anne. *Something About the Author.* Vol. 15. Detroit: Gale Research, 1979. Pp. 29–35.

Kirkpatrick, D. L., ed. *Twentieth-Century Children's Writers.* New York: St. Martin's Press, 1978. Pp. 121–123. (Includes a complete bibliography of the works of Bianco.)

Kunitz, Stanley J., and Howard Haycraft. *Junior Book of Authors.* 2nd ed. New York: H. W. Wilson, 1951. Pp. 34–36.

Moore, Anne Carroll, and Bertha Mahony Miller, eds. *Writing and Criticism: A Book for Margery Bianco.* Boston: Horn Book, 1951. (Includes "Our Youngest Critics," "The Stories of Hans Andersen," "Hitty, Her First Hundred Years," and "De la Mare.")

—PEGGY WHALEN-LEVITT

WILLIAM BLAKE

1757–1827

WILLIAM BLAKE'S VISION, his grasp of the totality of experience and the states of the soul, his freshness of expression, and his energy of design fascinate both young and not-so-young readers of his work. Blake's evocation of childhood and his understanding of family and individual psychology mark him as one of the first great writers for and about children. But Blake not only wrote children's poetry, he also illustrated his poems; he was perhaps the first true picture-book artist. His influence remains strong in books for children; his vision continues to anticipate our ways of seeing and imagining; and his poems and paintings grow fresher and more mysterious the more we know about them.

Except for three years when he lived in the small Sussex village of Felpham, Blake spent his life in London's "charter'd street[s], near where the charter'd Thames does flow." He was born on 28 November 1757, the third son of James and Catherine Blake; he had five brothers (one died in infancy) and one sister. His father was a hosier situated at 28 Broad Street in the Soho district. Blake's childhood appears to have been free, even Rousseauian. He did not attend school; instead he roamed the green fields that were, in the eighteenth century, within walking distance of Soho, and he learned to read and write at home. As an adult, Blake expressed his opposition to all institutions, as in his poem "The School Boy": "to go to school in a summer morn, / O! it drives all joy away." For Blake, education as practiced in the schools deadens the word and makes the students passive. True understanding could come only through "vision," and vision was open only to the vigorous and active mind. In 1802 Blake remarked in a letter that in childhood he was "famous for" his "Vigor." He also commented often on his visions, the earliest of which may have occurred when he was four. Throughout his life he received visitations from Milton, Ezra, Paracelsus, and many other poets, prophets, and mystics.

Blake's only formal training was in drawing: at ten he was sent to Pars's drawing school in the Strand. From 1772 to 1779 Blake served an apprenticeship with the engraver James Basire. For the rest of his life Blake worked as an engraver, dividing his time between writing, illustrating, and painting his own visionary works and completing the irksome and time-consuming commissions that often plagued him, but that provided for his humble needs. While working for Basire, Blake spent much time in Westminster Abbey and other London churches drawing Gothic monuments, and the style of his own work owes much to the grace and ruggedness of the Gothic world. The clarity of the Gothic line informs all of Blake's graphic work. Also during his years with Basire, Blake wrote poetry. Later, in 1783, four years after Blake left Basire, John Flaxman, a well-known artist and engraver, encouraged Blake to publish his juvenilia; this appeared as *Poetical Sketches*. The poems in this volume are not children's poems, but anticipations of the later *Songs of Innocence and of Experience* (1794) are evident in the "song" that begins "I love the jocund dance" and in the generally playful spirit of "Blind-man's Buff." "How sweet I roam'd from field to field" anticipates several later works, including *For the Sexes: The Gates of Paradise* (c. 1818), an expanded version of the emblem book *For Children: The Gates of Paradise* (1793).

On 18 August 1782 Blake married Catherine Boucher and the two moved to 23 Green Street, just off Leicester Fields. Catherine became a lifelong companion to Blake. He taught her to read and write and to assist in his engraving. Although the couple dearly loved children, they did not have any of their own. In 1784 they moved to 27 Broad Street, where Blake and his partner James Parker set up shop as printsellers. It was probably here that Blake wrote "An Island in the Moon" (1787), a satire he never published. This work is replete with topical references, not least of which are references to children's literature—chapter 9 contains a version of "Frog he would a-wooing go."

Blake was part of the social circle of the Reverend and Mrs. A. S. Mathew, and this circle is probably one source for the characters in "An Island in the Moon." Among the people Blake is likely to have met at the Mathews' house are Anna Laetitia Barbauld, Hannah More, and Thomas Day. In chapter 11 of "An Island," "Mrs. Nannicantipot" (perhaps a portrait of Barbauld) sings a song, later to become the "Nurse's Song" of *Innocence*, reminiscent of Barbauld's second and fifth *Hymns in Prose for Children* (1781). In short, Blake satirizes both educational theories and theorists of his day, as well as other writers for children, like Barbauld and More.

Near the end of the 1780's Blake wrote and illustrated *Tiriel*, which ends with an impassioned criticism of a harsh and repressive educational system. Blake did not engrave this work, but he did engrave *The Book of Thel* (1789). Although this work has never been thought of as written for children, it clearly reflects Blake's interest in those "two contrary states of the human soul," innocence and experience. Northrop Frye calls Thel's world "a world of dissolving and arbitrary fantasy, a looking-glass world of talking flowers," and the hint is important: *The Book of Thel* is Blake's first work appropriate for children.

"Appropriate" is perhaps the most accurate word, since Blake never wrote exclusively for children (even in *For Children: The Gates of Paradise*). He did not produce work for children in the manner of Barbauld, Sarah Trimmer, William Ronksley, or even Isaac Watts, who is Blake's true precursor in poetry for children. But he did envis-

age his audience as including children and he did respect their intellectual (for Blake this means imaginative) capacities. On 23 August 1799 Blake wrote to the Reverend Dr. John Trusler, a patron who niggled at him over the obscurity of his designs:

> But I am happy to find a Great Majority of Fellow Mortals who can Elucidate My Visions & Particularly they have been Elucidated by Children who have taken a greater delight in contemplating my Pictures than I even hoped. Neither Youth nor Childhood is Folly or Incapacity. Some Children are Fools & so are some Old Men.
>
> (*The Complete Poetry and Prose of William Blake*, 1982)

In his annotations to Sir Joshua Reynolds' third *Discourse* (1798), Blake remarks that "Age & Youth are not Classes but Properties of Each Class." In short, Blake felt his work should be accessible to all readers.

Yet Blake's interest in the children's literature of his day is clear. He not only could have met Barbauld and others at the Mathews' house, he also accepted several commissions for children's books. As early as 1780 the publisher Joseph Johnson commissioned Blake to engrave Thomas Stothard's designs for *The Speaker; or, Miscellaneous Pieces Selected from the best English Writers, and disposed under proper heads with a view to facilitate the Improvement of Youth in Reading and Speaking*. Stothard and Blake became friends while Blake was a student at the Royal Academy, and later Stothard illustrated children's books by Day and Barbauld. In 1791 Blake engraved designs for two children's books (the second a translation) by Mary Wollstonecraft, *Original Stories from Real Life* and *Elements of Morality, for the use of children; with an Introductory Address to Parents*.

Since from at least his mid-twenties Blake's interest in education was strong, his interest in art and society fervent, and his knowledge of the moralistic and rationalistic books for children extensive, it is little wonder that he would create a book for and about children that would challenge the conventional children's literature of his day. In 1789 he produced the first half of his great and lastingly influential work for children, *Songs of Innocence*. Blake is responsible for all aspects of the production of this remarkable work: he wrote the text, designed the pages, engraved both text and illustrations on copperplate, printed the plates, and bound and hand-colored them. Twenty-one original copies of *Songs of Innocence* are extant. Blake produced each one by hand, and each time he made the book he tried a new arrangement of the twenty-three poems. A few of the poems—"The School Boy," "The Little Girl Lost," "The Little Girl Found," and "The Voice of the Ancient Bard"—he later placed in his *Songs of Experience* (1794), and this suggests the intimate connection between the two states of innocence and experience. Blake produced the combined *Songs of Innocence and of Experience* in 1794, and subsequently he never printed *Experience* apart from *Innocence*. Twenty-seven copies of the original *Songs of Innocence and of Experience: Shewing the two Contrary States of the Human Soul* still exist.

The introduction to *Songs of Innocence* offers an excellent comment on Blake's concept of poetry and its educational function. Although the poem is well known, it will be useful to have it quoted in full:

> Piping down the valleys wild
> Piping songs of pleasant glee
> On a cloud I saw a child.
> And he laughing said to me.
>
> Pipe a song about a Lamb;
> So I piped with merry chear,
> Piper pipe that song again—
> So I piped, he wept to hear.
>
> Drop thy pipe thy happy pipe
> Sing thy songs of happy chear,
> So I sung the same again
> While he wept with joy to hear
>
> Piper sit thee down and write
> In a book that all may read—
> So he vanish'd from my sight.
> And I pluck'd a hollow reed.
>
> And I made a rural pen,
> And I stain'd the water clear,
> And I wrote my happy songs
> Every child may joy to hear

The force of the last line speaks to all readers for whom the values of spontaneity, liberty, and imagination remain alive. Audible in the poem is the "key of sweet rural joy" (the phrase is Annie E. Moore's), a sound that pervades *Songs of Innocence*. The word "key," like the word "piping" in the poem itself, serves to remind the reader that poetry must be heard. The speaker begins as a piper, then becomes a singer, and is finally a poet (writer), but he writes his "happy songs" so that "Every child may joy to hear." There are music, strong rhythm, and the echoes of nursery rhyme in Blake's *Songs*. (Blake himself set his songs to music and sang them, but unfortunately his musical settings are lost.) Rather than iambic pentameter, the prevailing rhythm in the *Songs* derives from a three- or four-beat, heavily stressed line, often using tumbling trochees and drumming spondees. Energy, not stateliness, is the effect. The world of childhood is a world of joy, of glee, of movement. This accounts for such happy songs of innocence as "Laughing Song," "The Ecchoing Green," and "Spring."

A comforting mutuality is evident in these poems. In "Spring," for example, a series of opposites—sound and silence, day and night, dale and sky, noise and music, human and animal—blend. Lamb and child touch each other tenderly. Here, as in "Laughing Song," anthropomorphism abounds: birds delight, streams run and laugh, and hills respond to human gaiety. In "Laughing Song," "meadows laugh with lively green." Here the synesthetic touch of green laughter and lively color enforces the sense of interconnectedness. The word "ecchoing" in "The Ecchoing Green" reflects this harmonious interplay between the things and beings in nature. These poems celebrate humanity; all the world is a valley of humane and happy life.

But childhood, like adulthood, is not all gaiety. A sense of closure darkens innocence. In "The Ecchoing Green" the children's intense play brings a weariness so deep that they "No more can be merry." Like the day, their "sports have an end." The end stop is firm, firmer than day's end, which is a recurring phenomenon. Even the mutuality of "Spring" hints at the passing of protection into possession; the child's requests, especially in light of Blake's illustration of the poem, which shows the eager desire of the child passing into an enclosed languor, have an understated urgency that suggests a desire turned to self-gratification. The small angel seated on a tendril by the third stanza strengthens this impression.

Innocence, partly because of its intricate connection to experience, has many moods. The child-muse in the introduction responds with laughter, with tears, and with tears of joy to the piper's songs. Those songs, once written as poems, will bring joy to those wise enough to receive them. Blake uses the word "joy" in the way his romantic contemporaries Wordsworth and Coleridge use it: to suggest the state of mind in which the human faculties are integrated and active. Every act, Blake says in his annotations to Lavater's *Aphorisms on Man* (1788), "is Virtue," and in the letter to Trusler quoted earlier, Blake tells his rather dim-witted patron that "that which can be made Explicit to the Idiot is not worth my care. The wisest of the Ancients consider'd what is not too Explicit as the fittest for Instruction, because it rouzes the Faculties to act." Joy results from active faculties. Poetry can only rouse a reader's imagination, his faculties, by allusion, metaphor, image, sound, paradox—the forms of language prior to statement. The reader must have something to figure out. The meaning in a poem such as "Spring" is as much heard and seen as it is passively received. The swift three-beat lines, the liquid *l*, the repetition of "merrily," the sinuous and weaving foliage of the designs, the vision of mother and child, child and lamb, and the inclusion of fairy figures (one plays a flute) all communicate movement, growth, new life, music, and temporality. All of Blake's poems are visionary, expressing themselves to eye and ear simultaneously and presenting a comprehensive view of life.

Seeing comprehensively, Blake is no sentimentalist. Innocence is not all laughter and merriment. It recognizes and sympathizes with grief and care ("On Another's Sorrow"), it is ignorant and gullible, easily manipulated ("The Little Black Boy," "The Chimney Sweeper"), fragile and vulnerable ("The Little Boy Lost"), and easily controlled and oppressed ("The School Boy," "Holy Thursday"). Blake's songs are "happy" because they are prophetic, visions of human possibility that make us "joy to hear" because we can only rejoice to be reminded of the power for change that we have within us. In short, Blake's *Songs of Innocence and of Experience* express human and poetic liberty. They break free of eighteenth-century conventions of children's literature and they speak of the means we have of unbinding ourselves from institutional convention and authority.

For example, a comparison of "The Little Black Boy" with Barbauld's "Hymn VIII" in her *Hymns in Prose for Children* shows how deeply Blake felt and saw the human condition. Barbauld exhorts the "Negro woman, who sittest pining in captivity" to raise her voice to God, for "assuredly He will hear thee." This is, in effect, an encouragement to pas-

sivity, to an acceptance that the black woman's situation is beyond earthly control. There is as much a failure here to understand the social and cultural conditions of captivity as there is a failure to see fairly the black condition in the contemporary nursery rhyme:

> What care I how black I be,
>   Twenty pounds will marry me,
> If twenty won't, why forty shall
> For I am mamma's darling girl.

Blake's poem is remarkable in its difference from this, and in its poignant and incisive comment on the insidious power of cultural conditioning. The second line in which the black boy confesses his outer blackness, but pleads his inner whiteness ("O! my soul is white") powerfully indicates how he has naively and innocently accepted the values of a dominant white society. The poem anticipates with remarkable acuity "The Ballad of Ruby" by May Sarton (from *A Grain of Mustard Seed*, 1971). (Sarton's source is Robert Coles's *Children of Crisis*, 1967.) The innocence of this child moves the reader, who cannot but cherish the little black boy's human warmth and sympathy, expressed in his desire to shade the little English boy from heaven's heat. The mother's innocent desire to protect her child also moves the reader. Even more intense, however, must be the reaction to what happens to innocence. The innocent child and mother accept diminishment without question; they defer their freedom, their participation in community, until after death.

The realization of this double edge to innocence is partly what Blake refers to when the piper in the introduction to *Innocence* speaks of "stain[ing] the waters clear." Poetry educates by staining the reader into clarity. The paradox by its very presence informs the reader of poetry's illuminating function (Blake calls his productions "Illuminated Books"); it speaks not to the reasoning and analytic power of mind, but to the quicksilver imagination, source of what Blake calls "Ideal Beauty," which "in Every Man [is] Born with him." In his annotations to Reynolds, Blake notes that "from my Earliest Childhood" Rafael was never "hidden from Me." He claims that he saw and knew "immediately the difference between Rafael & Rubens." Blake wishes to communicate this way: immediately. To do so, his work must have an impact upon the reader; the reader's imagination must be colored or marked by what he sees and reads. The situation has pedagogic significance, since successful teachers must touch their students with their minds and ideas. Yet the result of this touching is clarity. Young minds are set free, not bonded to another. "Opposition is true friendship," Blake writes in *The Marriage of Heaven and Hell* (begun in 1790, completed in 1793), and this notion of opposition is apparent in the very dialectic of innocence and experience. To stain the waters clear is to set the mind working, seeing freshly, and reevaluating such easily misunderstood concepts as innocence and experience.

Perhaps the ambiguity in Blake's use of the words "innocence" and "experience" is best articulated in "The Lamb" and "The Tyger," two of Blake's most often anthologized poems. As in "Spring," half rhymes convey the childishness of the speaker in "The Lamb." The simple question-and-answer structure dramatizes the "calling," the "voicing" that results in a drawing together. "I" and "you" in the poem become "we," and the safe, protected, comfortable world of innocence sounds clear. Even the teaching situation, which is examined critically in "The School Boy," is without threat and without emphasis on analytic thought in "The Lamb": "Little Lamb I'll tell thee!" The child's telling is both straightforward and allusive; he does not answer his question with a name, but with metaphoric allusion. Both poem and picture are tidy and neatly symmetrical. Each stanza begins and ends with couplets of closely reflective lines. These couplets enclose the stanzas, and this enclosure has its visual counterpart in the thin trees and sinuous vines of the illustration. Lamb and child subtly connect, with a compositional line, to a pair of doves who rest on the roof of a thatched cottage. This is a poem of easy symmetries. Without fear, however, such symmetries become ominous.

In its trochaic tumble, its upbeat line endings, and its mild calling, "The Lamb" conveys its crystalline innocence, but the sense of enclosure the eye perceives contrasts with the easy certainties of the child and his world. Dominating Blake's illustrations are strong horizontal planes that divide and compartmentalize the title, the two stanzas, and the picture of sheep and child at the bottom. The diagonal line connecting lamb, child, and doves counters the strong compartmental vision, but this line remains confined to the lower right-hand section of the plate. Even more interesting is the structure of the poem itself. The two stanzas differ significantly in their line patterns. Stanza one is incremental; its three repetitions of "Gave" move through stages of creation: the giving of life, then of clothing, and finally of speech or "voice." Creation of the lamb calls forth a response, which in its turn calls forth a response from the external world, from "all the vales." This happy creation story is enfolded by the repeated opening and closing lines. The pressure of enclosure intensifies in the second stanza, which has a centering structure. Lines enfold, like the petals of a rose blossom, the central two lines: "He is meek & he is mild, / He became a little child." The symmetry of this stanza is clear and oppressive. The symmetrical pattern of lines reminds us of innocence's vulnerability to control. The reader may see that spontaneity loses ground in the poem, and by implication in the world we know. Child, lamb, and Jesus become sacrificial victims in a world set on the authority of symmetry.

In experience, the world becomes more openly oppressive, but a strong imagination might find solace in the suggestion that the replacing of easy symmetries by fearful ones generates movement and defeats closure. "The Tyger" contrasts with "The Lamb" not only in its aggressive and energetic creation, but also in its potential for autonomy, for liberation. Clearly, the dark forests of fallen desire have replaced the pastoral vales and meads of innocence. The fiery furnace, symbol of both creative heat and destructive tyranny, focuses questions of creation more sharply and more mysteriously than they are focused in "The Lamb." Whereas the speaker of "The Lamb" confidently answers his own questions, the speaker of "The Tyger" has difficulty even completing his questions. The Lamb elicits a protective and encouraging tone in the speaker; the Tyger elicits a frightened and mystified one. The framing stanzas are exact except for the change from "Could" in the last line of the first stanza to "Dare" in the last line of the final stanza. This change slightly shifts the symmetry of opening and closing stanzas, and the word "dare" suggests audacity, defiance, and opposition. The speaker appears to see the Tyger as a threatening predator, as Leviathan, a creature that swallows nature and renders it a nightmarish world of terrifying oppression and aggression. But the Tyger, as symbol of energy and delight, brings a smile to his mysterious creator just as it brings tears to the stars of heaven who have thrown down their spears. This mysterious Tyger might well be wiser than the meek Lamb.

This poem of experience does not simply present a vision of unmitigated gloom. The forests may be dark, but the Tyger burns with gemlike intensity. The ambiguity of the vision is unmistakable when we compare poem and illustration. Blake's illustrated tiger is remarkably unthreatening, even sporting a smile in one copy. What appears to dominate this illustration is the vulnerability of the innocent tiger, hemmed in as he is by spear grass, the text of the poem, and the lugubrious but haunting fairy-tale tree with its bogey face. This poor tiger is assimilated into the tree by the tiger stripes on the base of the tree. The tiger here is as ineffectual as a lamb, and it serves as a contrary to the Tyger in the poem with its liberating potential. However, with little room to soar, a bird, perhaps an eagle, rises from the *T* in the second "Tyger" of the poem's first line to remind us that winged aspiration is still possible. An internal dialectic in both "The Lamb" and "The Tyger" keeps the reader struggling for comprehension, and this struggle, if pursued daringly, must lead to an understanding of innocence and experience and to a transcendence of both.

Experience and innocence are intimately connected and not ends in themselves. Poems from both groups are suitable for children. "The Tyger" has much to appeal to children: strong rhythm, a clear subject, and most important, mystery. The urgent questions of the speaker allow innumerable answers. The response to the Tyger and its creation will be as timid or as daring as the reader is timid or daring. Sadly, the poem appears in most anthologies without Blake's illustration, which, as David Erdman points out, is, like the poem, "one of Blake's contrived enigmas." Surely Blake's intention in contriving his enigmas is to arouse the reader's mental faculties to act. Rather than the passive receptacle of pious lessons the reader of Barbauld's work is expected to be, the reader of Blake's songs is asked to participate in creating meaning.

Here is an example from *Songs of Innocence*:

How sweet is the Shepherds sweet lot,
From the morn to the evening he strays:
He shall follow his sheep all the day
And his tongue shall be filled with praise.

For he hears the lambs innocent call,
And he hears the ewes tender reply,
He is watchful while they are in peace,
For they know when their Shepherd is nigh.

Eighteenth-century pastoral tinged with piety is the convention here. Barbauld's "Hymn III" comes to mind: "Behold the shepherd of the flock, he taketh care for his sheep, he leadeth them among clear brooks, he guideth them to fresh pasture: if the young lambs are weary, he carrieth them in his arms; if they wander, he bringeth them back." Barbauld then asks, "Who is the shepherd's Shepherd?" And she answers: "God is the shepherd's Shepherd." Blake's poem echoes biblical cadences, as does Barbauld's, but the echoes are quieter, less obvious. Also, Blake's "The Shepherd" does not offer a clear moral, only a vision of interplay, lambs and ewes calling and replying, the shepherd nearby to hear his flock and to sing. The attentive reader will stop at the third line of Blake's poem. Shepherds usually lead their sheep (see Barbauld's work, for example); the shepherd in this poem "follows" his sheep. Why? The word "strays" will remind the reader of lost sheep. Does the shepherd act to prevent straying? Why the passive construction in the fourth line? Perhaps even the circular logic of the poem's final two lines has ambiguity of the kind later examined in "The Fly," a poem from *Songs of Experience*. In short, Blake's songs should tease the reader into, and perhaps out of, thought.

Blake's themes in *Songs of Innocence and of Experience* are familiar in children's literature: animals, the seasons, flowers, love, angels, dreams, and, of course, children. Commentators have often remarked on Blake's echoing of nursery rhymes and other earlier children's literature, but it is worth pointing out that the fairy tale also finds a place in Blake's writing. The story (often in ballad form and appearing in chapbooks) known as *The Children in the Wood* or *Babes in the Wood* informs the poems on "lost" children in both *Innocence* and *Experience*. Blake found in *The Children in the Wood* a clear expression of economic ruthlessness and parental jealousy, of nature as fallen space, as the forest of the night. Other fairy tales hinted at in his work are "Rapunzel" and "Sleeping Beauty." The Lyca poems (from *Songs of Experience*) are relevant here, as are poems Blake neither illustrated nor published. He left them in a notebook now known as "The Pickering Manuscript" and housed today in the Pierpont Morgan Library. These works were probably written between 1800 and 1803, and they include "The Mental Traveller," "The Crystal Cabinet," and "Auguries of Innocence." This last work contains lines on cruelty to animals, and others that suggest a connection with the beast fable. In 1793 Blake drew and engraved *For Children: The Gates of Paradise*, a work whose beginning is in the sketchbook once owned by Blake's younger brother Robert. Robert died in 1787; Blake, who was with him when he died, saw Robert's spirit rise through the ceiling "clapping its hands for joy." The little book consists of eighteen plates, with sixteen numbered designs. Each design has a brief legend below. The book was not a success, and Blake put the plates away until 1818, when he revised his book by adding a ten-line prologue, three additional plates of text, and a new title: *For the Sexes: The Gates of Paradise*.

Also about this time, Blake made a small drawing of a title page worded "*For Children/The/Gates/of/HELL*." Blake never completed this work, but the title page reinforces the idea that Blake felt that visions of both heaven and hell, innocence and experience, should be available for children.

In 1790 the Blakes moved from Poland Street, where they had been living since 1787, to Lambeth, number 13 Hercules Buildings. Not far away was the Royal Asylum for Female Orphans, a workhouse and a reminder, if Blake needed one, of society's unkind treatment of charity children (see the two Holy Thursday poems of *Innocence* and *Experience*). In one of his two great epic works, *Milton* (dated 1804, but worked on for several more years), Blake alludes to "Lambeth, ruin'd and given / To the detestable Gods of Priam" and to "the Asylum / Given to Hercules." Despite this, Lambeth was good for Blake, and he stayed there until 1800, when he accepted William Hayley's invitation to live in the coastal town of Felpham and to carry out commissions for Hayley, a minor poet and biographer of William Cowper. Blake went to Felpham with great optimism: "Sussex is certainly a happy place & Felpham in particular is the sweetest spot on Earth," he wrote in May 1801 to his close friend and lifelong patron, Thomas Butts. Almost two years to the day later, in April 1803, Blake speaks of his "three years Slumber on the banks of the Ocean." Only in London, he said, could he "carry on my visionary studies." After settling in Felpham, Blake discovered "on all hands great objections to my doing any thing but the meer drudgery of business" (letter to Butts, 10 January 1803). Hayley could not appreciate Blake's genius, and his idea was to keep Blake busy on works for commission. His intentions were sincere—to assist Blake. The results were unfortunate.

Also unfortunate was the incident in which Blake removed, with physical force, the soldier John Schofield from his garden. Schofield proceeded to accuse Blake of sedition and an unpleasant court case followed.

Blake produced no writing for children after 1800 (one might except *For the Sexes*). Some of his later engraving and watercolor work can, however, be appreciated by children, especially the illustrations to Dante that Blake left unfinished at his death. In the years after 1804 Blake lived frugally and humbly, working with little or no recognition until the 1820's, when a small group of young artists gathered round him at his home in Fountain Court, just off the Strand (Blake lived at 17 South Molton Street from 1803 until 1820). This group included John Linnell, John Varley, and, later, Samuel Palmer and George Richmond. Henry Crabb Robinson also became a supporter, although he gave impetus to the notion of "mad Blake."

Blake died on 12 August 1827. A few months before his death, on 12 April 1827 he wrote to his friend George Cumberland:

I have been very near the Gates of Death and have returned very weak & an Old Man feeble & tottering, but not in Spirit & Life not in The Real Man The Imagination which Liveth for Ever. In that I am stronger & stronger as this Foolish Body decays. . . . God keep me from the Divinity of Yes & No too The Yea Nay Creeping Jesus from supposing Up & Down to be the same Thing as all Experimentalists must suppose

In this fierce belief in the "real man" we have Blake's importance. His idealism was as strong in his old age as it had been in his early manhood. Throughout his life he hated tyranny and falsity, and he remained committed to the belief that "As all men are alike in outward form, So (and with the same infinite variety) all are alike in the Poetic Genius" (*All Religions Are One*, 1788). For him, literature transcends the ideologies of the marketplace and the capitol. For him, the imagination is the creator of reality. And for him, the child is the image of the kingdom of God. Blake and his work are eternally young. Children can have no better introduction to literature than through Blake's *Songs*. They may puzzle over the images, thrill to the music, and even grieve for the lost children of experience. And once they have truly touched Blake's work, they can never forget it.

Selected Bibliography

WORKS OF WILLIAM BLAKE

All Religions Are One. Printed by the author. London, 1788.

The Book of Thel. Printed by the author. London, 1789.

Songs of Innocence. Printed by the author. London, 1789. New York: Dover Publications, 1971. (A facsimile of the copy in the Lessing J. Rosenwald Collection in the Library of Congress.)

The Marriage of Heaven and Hell. Printed by the author. London, 1790–1793.

For Children: The Gates of Paradise. Printed by the author. London, 1793.

Songs of Experience. Printed by the author. London, 1794.

Songs of Innocence and of Experience. Printed by the author. London, 1794. New York: The Orion Press, 1967. Reprinted New York: Oxford University Press, 1977. (A reproduction in the original size of Blake's complete *Songs.*)

Milton. Printed by the author. London, 1804.

For the Sexes: The Gates of Paradise. Printed by the author. London, c. 1818.

The Complete Poetry and Prose of William Blake. Edited by David V. Erdman. Berkeley and Los Angeles: University of California Press, 1965. Rev. ed., 1982.

The Gates of Paradise/For Children/For the Sexes. 3 vols. London: Trianon Press, 1968.

The Illuminated Blake. Annotated by David V. Erdman. London: Oxford University Press, 1975. (Contains all of Blake's illustrated writing.)

CRITICAL AND BIOGRAPHICAL STUDIES

Davis, Michael. *William Blake: A New Kind of Man.* Berkeley: University of California Press, 1977.

Frye, Northrop. *Fearful Symmetry.* Princeton: Princeton University Press, 1947.

Glen, Heather. *Vision and Disenchantment: Blake's "Songs" and Wordsworth's "Lyrical Ballads."* Cambridge: Cambridge University Press, 1983.

Holloway, John. *Blake: The Lyric Poetry.* London: Edward Arnold, 1968.

Leader, Zachary. *Reading Blake's "Songs."* London: Routledge and Kegan Paul, 1981.

Moore, Annie E. *Literature Old and New for Children.* Boston: Houghton Mifflin, 1934.

Pinto, Vivian de Sola. "William Blake, Isaac Watts, and Mrs. Barbauld." In *The Divine Vision*, edited by Vivian de Sola Pinto. London: Gollancz, 1957.

Wilson, Mona. *The Life of William Blake.* London: Nonesuch Press, 1927. Reprinted London: Oxford University Press, 1971.

—RODERICK McGILLIS

ARNA BONTEMPS

1902-1973

IN WRITING FICTION depicting the black experience for young people, Arna Bontemps (pronounced BON-tomp) was a trailblazer. As Arthur P. Davis remarked in *From the Dark Tower,* "Few, if any, books by Negro writers produced expressly for children were in existence in 1932." Bontemps was also a pioneer in writing black history and biography for young people. He led the way in informing not only blacks about themselves but also whites about Afro-Americans. His publications in the middle third of this century formed the necessary foundation for the award-winning black children's authors of the 1970's and beyond. In the words of his own poem, "The Daybreakers," Bontemps was "beating a way for the rising sun."

Any consideration of Arna Bontemps as a writer, specifically a children's writer, must acknowledge his part in creating and being created by the Harlem Renaissance, that great blossoming of black culture in the 1920's. Bontemps's importance as a writer for children is rooted in the underlying concern of this group of black writers and artists using various media to present the black experience to all America. It is just this preoccupation that sets Bontemps apart from other black writers of the period and certainly from other, nonblack children's writers. Bontemps was unique and an innovator.

Bontemps was among the black artists, musicians, and writers who converged upon Harlem in the 1920's, offering their own talents and aspirations, and, through the support of their peers, finding new inspiration. In a real sense, then, they were creating the Renaissance even as they were being brought to life by the movement. As Nathan Huggins wrote in *Harlem Renaissance:*

> . . . to presume to be an actor and creator in the special occurrence of a people's birth (or rebirth) requires a singular self-consciousness. The era produced a phenomenal race consciousness and race assertion, as well as unprecedented numbers of poems, stories, and works of art by black people. Harlem was making it all happen, because black men were coming together there, some intending to build a cultural capital of the black world.
>
> (pp. 3, 83)

For the first time in American history, white intellectuals were "discovering" the Negro; black writers were being regarded seriously by publishers, reviewers, and readers. The publishers Alfred A. Knopf, Boni and Liveright, and Harper and Brothers helped to bring black authors into the public's awareness. In particular, author and critic Carl Van Vechten, in his writing and friendships with black intellectuals, acted as a missionary in focusing attention on their work. And although some have said that the Renaissance flourished largely because of the white intelligentsia's patronage, their hungering for the exotic, and their penchant for the primitive, yet this cultural explosion forced American and world literati to recognize and to appreciate the creative genius of the Afro-American. As Huggins notes:

After a history of struggle, of being an outcast, of being viewed with contempt or pity, the Negro was now courted and cultivated by cultured whites. How grand it was to be valued not for what one might become—the benevolent view of uplift—but for what was thought to be one's essential self, one's Negro-ness.

(p. 118)

The Harlem Renaissance was truly a celebration of blackness.

Otey Scruggs, professor of American history at Syracuse University and specialist in Afro-American history, has suggested that perhaps Bontemps, because he was less flamboyant than some of the Renaissance leaders, has had the greatest staying power and influence. Of course, Bontemps had the advantage of outliving all of the other major figures in the movement, and in later years developed as a highly respected critic and commentator. But it is the thesis of this essay that Bontemps's writing for young people about the black experience provided an excellent medium for carrying out an essential concern of the Harlem Renaissance—the awakening of the American people to a recognition of the Negro and of Negro culture as a dynamic force in American arts and letters.

For children's literature, it is important to note that of all of the writers of the Harlem Renaissance only Bontemps and Langston Hughes produced works for children. Certainly it is Bontemps who deserves continuing credit for having recognized the dearth of young people's materials on black culture and history and for endeavoring throughout his life to fill this gap. As Professor Scruggs notes, his historical and biographical writings for young people and his efforts on behalf of black history have earned him enduring respect among historians and librarians.

Arna Bontemps was a Renaissance man both in the time-honored definition of that term and in the sense of the many-sided nature of black cultural expression in Harlem. A man of many talents, he published in virtually every literary genre. Bontemps was poet, novelist, short-story writer, anthologist, critic, essayist, playwright, historian, folklorist, biographer, and children's author.

Family, geography, education, and tradition all affected Bontemps' formation as a writer. Some of the personal influences important to his development were his father's rejection of things southern and "colored," a stance against which young Bon-

temps felt impelled to rebel; the robust, devil-may-care life-style of his colorful great-uncle Buddy, an anomaly in Bontemps's middle-class-conscious family; his education in Seventh-Day Adventist schools; the fever and fervor of life in Harlem in the 1920's amid other creative young blacks; The Great Depression, which forced Bontemps to leave Harlem for a teaching post in an Adventist school in Alabama; his welcome immersion in the "down home" culture of the rural South; another immersion in a Chicago ghetto where he worked on the WPA Writers' Project; his "oasis" at Fisk University in Nashville, where he settled and which for twenty-two years provided him with the opportunity to become well versed in Negro folklore as he built up the university library's Afro-American collection; his lifelong friendship with Langston Hughes, beginning with their days in Harlem; and his close relationship with his wife and six children.

Arna Bontemps was born in Alexandria, Louisiana, in 1902 and died in Nashville, Tennessee, in 1973. His father, Paul Bontemps, a bricklayer and sometime trombonist, made a good living for his wife, Marie, and their two children. According to family lore, one racial incident too many—the night two white men forced Paul Bontemps off the sidewalk—was the "straw that broke the camel's back," and Paul precipitously moved his family to Los Angeles.

Growing up in Los Angeles young Bontemps became aware of the conflicting strains of "two-ness," first described by noted black social critic, writer, and civil-rights leader W. E. B. Du Bois. The Afro-American, Du Bois had written, is caught in two cultures, and in attempting to become part of the dominant culture he often must deny his African roots. Bontemps's father had been determined to separate himself and his family as far as possible from his unpleasant memories of being regarded as colored and inferior in the South. That meant Bontemps had to play down African-ness, to avoid black speech patterns, to be restrained in order to "fit in." Bontemps mentions that his father's attitude was reflected in his disapproval of Uncle Buddy, Bontemps's great-uncle, a happy-go-lucky character whose relaxed manner and tendency to imbibe definitely ran counter to family values. [But these parental admonitions produced an opposite reaction. Uncle Buddy so impressed young Bontemps as being "real folk"—unpretentious, unthreatened by whites, and refusing to imitate the dominant culture—that he later appears in some of his short stories and as the hero of his first novel, *God Sends Sunday* (1931).]

While growing up in Los Angeles, Bontemps began to sense something missing from the history he learned at school and from the books he devoured in the public library children's room. Were there no Negroes in American history? And why were there no stories about Negro children? These early pressures to suppress one side of his heritage had a lasting effect on Bontemps. Finding and expressing the Negro past were to become his lifelong obsession. His works for young people reveal this deep concern.

Bontemps graduated from Pacific Union College in 1923 and went to work as a mail clerk at the Los Angeles post office. In the summer of 1924 his first poem, "Hope," was published in the NAACP's *Crisis Magazine.* At last he was a published writer, but for bread and butter he accepted a teaching post in the largest Adventist high school, Harlem Academy. And so Arna Bontemps went to Harlem.

It was the best of times and the best of places to be young, gifted, and black. Bontemps found himself in the midst of the whirl of the Renaissance, part of that legendary circle which included, among others, Langston Hughes, Wallace Thurman, Claude McKay, Countee Cullen, Jean Toomer, Charles S. Johnson, Aaron Douglas, Dorothy West, and Zora Neale Hurston. During the next several years Bontemps taught and wrote poetry. But he became dissatisfied with poetry as a medium for expressing the black experience and turned to writing prose fiction. *God Sends Sunday,* the story of a picaresque jockey, was well reviewed, but 1931 was no time for a black writer to earn a living by writing. The Depression had dried up enthusiasm for new writers by shriveling the funds of patrons and stifling publishers' willingness and ability to take risks. The primitive and exotic ways of the Negro seemed no longer to be the stuff needed to sell books. Some called Bontemps's novel the last creative contribution of the Harlem Renaissance.

The Harlem Academy could no longer afford to pay Bontemps, so in 1931 he accepted a post at another church school, Oakwood Junior College in Huntsville, Alabama. This new setting promised new inspiration. Bontemps later wrote rhapsodically about his feelings of being plunged into the black folk culture of the Deep South. Absorbing the verdant, somnolent milieu of rural Alabama; listening to the old folks; and going to the country

churches fed his longing to know and be part of southern Negro life.

It was during his Alabama sojourn that Bontemps first began to write for children. The impetus came from his friend Langston Hughes, who had visited Haiti and asked Bontemps to collaborate with him on a children's book about the island. *Popo and Fifina: Children of Haiti* (1932) was immediately successful. Eight-year-old Popo and his ten-year-old sister, Fifina, are described taking part in the everyday life of a small fishing village: gathering soap-weed, catching crabs, washing dishes at the community fountain, persuading Papa to make a red kite, learning to carve wood at Uncle's cabinetmaking shop. Warm words convey the lushness of this tropical island. Black-and-white illustrations by black artist E. Simms Campbell complete this glimpse into rural life in Haiti. Children's book critic Anne Thaxter Eaton, writing in the *New York Times* in October 1932, stated, "Popo and Fifina prompt us to wish that all our travel books for children might be written by poets." Bontemps, poet, novelist, and short-story writer, was launched as a writer for young people.

Children in his Alabama neighborhood, barefoot and irrepressible, provided him with more story ideas. *You Can't Pet a Possum* (1934) describes Shine Boy's efforts to convince his grandmother to let him keep Butch, a vagrant hound. The story received favorable reviews in the *New York Times* and in the *Saturday Review.* Published after Bontemps had left Alabama but based on the actual escapades of three young farm boy neighbors, *Sad-Faced Boy* (1937) recounts the adventures of Slumber, Rags, and Willie, who run away to get a look at Harlem. Hiding aboard freight trains and hitching a ride in a truck, these three budding street musicians make their way to the many-splendored city, and find a warm welcome from their uncle, a custodian in a high-rent Harlem apartment building. Through their dancing and singing they earn a fair amount of change, but eventually homesickness and the thought of ripe persimmons bring them back to Alabama.

Lonesome Boy, originally written while Bontemps was in Alabama, but published as a children's book in 1955, is a hauntingly mysterious story of a boy struggling to grow up, confronting authority, but unsure of himself. Bubba plays a silver trumpet but ignores his grandfather's warning: "You better mind where you blow that horn, boy!" One night he wanders off to New Orleans and finds lots of jobs playing his horn for fancy parties and riverboat excursions. In a nightmare a faceless chauffeur drives him off to play for a frantic all-night dance, which has been interpreted as a Devil's ball. Bubba wakes up in the morning, apparently realizing that he cannot run from responsibility. The traditional values represented by his grandfather are the essential truths of life, comments Sandra Alexander in her Ph.D. work on Bontemps. Bubba returns home, trumpet now *under* his arm, to find out that his grampa had had the same experience when he was a horn-blowing youngster.

Another story written out of the Alabama experience but not published as a children's book until 1970 was *Mr. Kelso's Lion*. Again the protagonist is a young boy who faces a crisis. Percy goes to Alabama with his grandfather to visit his Aunt Clothilde. It is Percy who must confront the lion in Mr. Kelso's yard. The theme of a child attaining a measure of maturity through coming to terms with obstacles, within or without, real or psychological, occurs in several of Bontemps's works, both fictional and biographical. His belief that young blacks must strive for a sense of self flows through his writings for children and young adults.

The use of dialect in these stories is realistic and tasteful, reflecting southern black speech patterns of the 1930's. The stories are rich in their depiction of important black values such as family closeness, respect for elders and for hard work, rewards for being good, and the conviction that the good old-fashioned virtues of home and family are best. Bontemps's belief in the viability of black culture is revealed in his creative use of black dialect and folklore. He used cadenced, bantering dialogue laced with colloquialisms, folk motifs, and folk speech to create recognizable black characters in his short stories and children's books written out of this southern experience.

Before long Bontemps recognized that Alabama was not the Eden he had first believed. Racial tensions reached a frightening peak during the trial in nearby Scottsboro of nine black youths who had ridden a freight train with two young white women who later accused them of rape. And then the directors of the Adventist school began to question his friendship with black writers, and even wanted him to get rid of the black books in his library. Bontemps decided to leave Alabama. In 1934 he moved with his wife and three children to one room in his father's house in Los Angeles.

There he concentrated on writing for adults. He

wrote what some critics have called his best work. *Black Thunder* (1936), the first black-authored book of historical fiction with a black theme, is the powerful story of the slave Gabriel Prosser, who was the leader of an abortive insurrection in Virginia in 1808. This book was greatly informed by Bontemps's exploration into the Fisk University collection of "slave narratives," stories told by escaped slaves and written down by abolitionists, or stories collected in more recent times from former slaves. This was a rich source of black folklore and history hitherto untapped. Bontemps made extensive use of black folklore motifs in making Gabriel Prosser an archetypal hero. The book was well received. "If one were looking for a sort of prose spiritual on the Negroes themselves, quite aside from the universal dream that they bear in this story, one could not find it more movingly sung," cheered the *New York Times*. Although originally published for the adult market, this work provided young adults with valuable insights into the history of the protest against slavery.

In 1935 Bontemps moved to Chicago as principal of another Adventist school. However, after three years and increasing disinclination to live under the denomination's constraints, he permanently severed his connection with the Adventists. But the Chicago years were productive for his writing and for his future career. With the help of Rosenwald Fund scholarships he was able to obtain a master's degree in library science at the University of Chicago, and was also able to travel to the Caribbean to substantiate his research on another historical novel, *Drums at Dusk* (1939). He published his first anthology of poetry, *Golden Slippers*, in 1941. The book was promoted as the "first collection of Negro poetry suited to young as well as adult readers." Represented in it are such well-known poets as Paul Laurence Dunbar, Langston Hughes, James Weldon Johnson, Claude McKay, Countee Cullen, and Bontemps himself; some lesser known poets; and traditional folk songs and spirituals. This selection provides a valuable introduction to poetry by blacks written before the mid-twentieth century.

Another important outgrowth of his years in Chicago was the development of a mutually fruitful friendship with the white writer Jack Conroy, whom he met while working on the WPA Writers' Project. Together they wrote several books, among them three books for children: *The Fast Sooner Hound* (1942), *Slappy Hooper, the Wonderful Sign*

Painter (1946), and *Sam Patch, the High, Wide and Handsome Jumper* (1951). These three books have the timeless quality of the tall tale. Slappy Hooper's signs were painted so realistically that even the birds were fooled and tried to fly into the painted trees; Sam Patch learned to jump farther and farther until he could beat Hurricane Harry, the Kaskaskia snapping turtle. *Sam Patch* "is all very funny, and ever so well written," wrote L. S. Bechtel in the *New York Times. The Fast Sooner Hound* was the most successful and the most enduring story. An odd-jobs railroad man wagers with his prospective boss that his dog, Sooner, can outrun any train. Sooner even passes up the Wabash Cannon Ball. In reflecting on Bontemps's career as a writer, his collaboration with Conroy undoubtedly enabled him to reach a wider audience of children. Perhaps this was due to Convoy's contacts in the publishing world. Indeed the fact that Convoy was white probably increased the possibility that the books would be noticed by editors.

In 1943 Bontemps left Chicago to become chief librarian at Fisk University in Nashville. He wrote that this was the oasis he had been seeking. The best of all possible worlds for Negroes in the 1940's, the Negro college offered financial security, a congenial community, and professional flexibility to continue his writing while building up the library's collection of works on Negroes. While he tried his hand at playwriting, his primary commitment was to literature for young people, and particularly for adolescents, who he felt had been ignored. Some of his works aimed at this age group are excellent; others suffer from didacticism. But at the time, there was virtually nothing in print on the history and biography of blacks. Bontemps was able to respond to a critical need.

In *Story of the Negro* (1948), which received the Jane Addams Children's Book Award, Bontemps introduces young readers to the drama of black history. The prologue notes the arrival of a Dutch ship at a Virginia port in 1619 with a cargo of twenty black men. Bontemps then provides glimpses of the ancient kingdoms of Africa, including Ethiopia, Timbuctoo, and the Sudanic empires. This book is chiefly about people, black men and women, whose stories, unknown or half forgotten, needed to be told to all young readers. Blacks who played a role in American history are highlighted, as are events from the time of slavery, the slave revolts, the Civil War, the disillusion after Emancipation, the growth of Jim Crow laws, and the con-

tinuing struggle for civil rights. *Story of the Negro* is written anecdotally and is often dramatic and suspenseful—reminiscent of Hendrik Van Loon's *Story of Mankind* (1921). The book was hailed in all of the leading review periodicals. "A primer for white folks, young and old," remarked the *Saturday Review of Literature.*

Shortly thereafter Bontemps published a work of historical fiction for young people about the Jubilee Singers from Fisk University, who for over a hundred years have traveled widely, singing spirituals and raising money for the college. *Chariot in the Sky* (1951) is primarily the story of the beginning of the Fisk Jubilee Singers, and how the original little group of eleven students (several former slaves) introduced to captivated audiences in America and Europe a "new" type of music—the slave song, or spiritual. The Jubilee Singers assured the permanent recognition of the spiritual as basic American folk music. But this is also the story of Caleb, a slave, who is trained to be a tailor, later teaches himself to read, and eventually finds his way to Fisk. Bontemps undoubtedly used some of the materials in the slave narratives to give detail to the story. He incorporated black folklore, excerpts from spirituals, and bits of folk legend, such as the story of the flying Africans. "Freedom is a powerful word, children. Make you fly like a bird sometimes."

During the 1940's blacks believed that World War II would be a turning point, and that the Negro would at last become truly part of American society. Bontemps exemplified this hope in his historical and biographical writing. He published books on George Washington Carver, Frederick Douglass, and Booker T. Washington. He wrote two collective biographies describing living people. *We Have Tomorrow* (1945) introduces to young readers twelve young blacks who had begun to excel in their careers. That they are not all of national significance was Bontemps's point: ordinary people do have a chance. (Among the more well-known blacks in this volume are E. Simms Campbell, cartoonist; Dean Dixon, violinist; Hazel Scott, pianist; and Benjamin Davis, Jr., West Point graduate and later general.) In his note for the eighth printing (1960) Bontemps states: "If deciding on a career and making a start in an unfamiliar field is still hard for some young people today, perhaps the success of these brave ones will still be encouraging." *Famous Negro Athletes* (1964) presents lively sketches of nine towering figures: Joe Louis, Sugar

Ray Robinson, Jackie Robinson, Satchel Paige, Willie Mays, Wilt Chamberlain, James Brown, and Althea Gibson. Another largely biographical work, *100 Years of Negro Freedom* (1961), was written on the eve of the centenary of the Emancipation Proclamation, marking the struggles and achievements of known and lesser-known figures who tried to make real the promise of the proclamation. Frederick Douglass, Booker T. Washington, and W. E. B. Du Bois are treated in detail. Among the many others included are B. P. S. Pinchback, lieutenant governor of Louisiana; Paul Laurence Dunbar, poet; Ralph Bunche, United Nations mediator and Nobel Prize recipient; A. Philip Randolph, head of the Brotherhood of Sleeping Car Porters; and Rosa Parks, heroine of the Montgomery bus boycott. Bontemps is truly perceptive in his short statement on Martin Luther King, Jr., who had just come into the limelight: "His influence is beyond words, deriving from the wisdom of folk who have long recognized the power of the symbol."

What then is the significance of Arna Bontemps for children's literature? The key to his importance lies in his conviction, demonstrated throughout his writing, that black history is important for all young Americans. As Charles Nichols notes in the preface to his compilation of the letters of Bontemps and Langston Hughes: "Perhaps more consistently than many better known black leaders, he [Bontemps] was the 'keeper of the flame.'" Bontemps was a genteel yet adamant crusader, promoting awareness of black history and life for young readers. Early in his career he stated that his own generation was probably beyond saving, but that in young people lay the hope for a better world. Therefore, it was essential to communicate to young people the history and folklore of black America. This conviction was the foundation of his life and his art.

Bontemps's children's books cannot be seen apart from his total literary output. He promoted the cause of black history and culture through his historical novels, his folklore interpretations, his histories and biographies, his anthologies of poetry, and his children's stories. He wanted blacks to know who they were and whence they came in order to better envision where they might go. But Bontemps had more than black readers in mind. Although he believed deeply in the necessity of books on black themes for black readers, he was also committed to bringing about an awareness of the Afro-American to all young readers. As the Harlem Renaissance had aroused interest in the Negro among white literati, so Arna Bontemps saw his children's books, legacy of his experience of the Harlem Renaissance, as reaching white as well as black readers. As the literary parent of such prominent black children's authors as Virginia Hamilton, Mildred Taylor, Walter Dean Myers, Ashley Bryan, and Rosa Guy, Bontemps cleared a path for acceptance of black themes in the wider world of children's literature. Through his more than twenty-five books he "heightened our sense of the range, the peril, the promise of American life in our pluralistic society," declared Charles Nichols. For children's literature on the black experience in the mid- and late twentieth century, Arna Bontemps was truly a trailblazer, "beating a way for the rising sun."

Selected Bibliography

WORKS OF ARNA BONTEMPS

Popo and Fifina, Children of Haiti, with Langston Hughes. With illustrations by E. Simms Campbell. New York: Macmillan, 1932.

You Can't Pet a Possum. With illustrations by Ilse Bischoff. New York: William Morrow, 1934.

Black Thunder. New York: Macmillan, 1936.

Sad-Faced Boy. With illustrations by Virginia Lee Burton. Boston: Houghton Mifflin, 1937.

Golden Slippers. With drawings by Henrietta Bruce Sharon. New York: Harper and Row, 1941.

The Fast Sooner Hound. With illustrations by Virginia Lee Burton. Boston: Houghton Mifflin, 1942.

We Have Tomorrow. With photographs by Marian Palfi. Boston: Houghton Mifflin, 1945.

Slappy Hooper, the Wonderful Sign Painter, with Jack Conroy. With illustrations by Ursula Koering. Boston: Houghton Mifflin, 1946.

Story of the Negro. With illustrations by Raymond Lufkin. New York: Knopf, 1948, 1964.

Chariot in the Sky. With illustrations by Cyrus Leroy Baldridge. Philadelphia: Winston, 1951.

Sam Patch, the High, Wide and Handsome Jumper, with Jack Conroy. With illustrations by Paul Brown. Boston: Houghton Mifflin, 1951.

The Story of George Washington Carver. With illustrations by Harper Johnson. New York: Grosset and Dunlap, 1954.

Lonesome Boy. With illustrations by Feliks Topolski. Boston: Houghton Mifflin, 1955.

Frederick Douglass: Slave, Fighter, Freeman. With illustrations by Harper Johnson. New York: Knopf, 1959.

100 Years of Negro Freedom. New York: Dodd, Mead, 1961.

Famous Negro Athletes. New York: Dodd, Mead, 1964.
Mr. Kelso's Lion. With illustrations by Len Ebert. Philadelphia: Lippincott, 1970.

CRITICAL AND BIOGRAPHICAL STUDIES

Alexander, Sandra C. "The Achievement of Arna Bontemps." Ph.D. dissertation: University of Pittsburgh, 1976.

Bone, Robert. *The Negro Novel in America.* New Haven, Conn.: Yale University Press, 1963.

Bontemps, Arna. "Sad Faced Author." *Horn Book* 15/1: 7–12 (Jan.–Feb. 1939).

Bontemps, Arna. "Why I Returned." *Harper's* 230/1379: 177–182 (April 1965).

Commire, Anne, ed. *Something About the Author.* Detroit: Gale Research: 1971– . (See "Bontemps, Arna," vol. 2, pp. 32–34, and obituary, vol. 24, p. 51.)

Davis, Arthur P. *From the Dark Tower.* Washington, D.C.: Howard University Press, 1974.

Du Bois, W. E. B. *The Souls of Black Folk: Essays and Sketches.* Chicago: A. C. McClurg, 1903.

Huggins, Nathan Irvin. *Harlem Renaissance.* New York: Oxford University Press, 1971.

Lewis, David Levering. *When Harlem Was in Vogue.* New York: Knopf, 1981.

Nichols, Charles H., ed. *Arna Bontemps–Langston Hughes, Letters, 1925–1967.* New York: Dodd, Mead, 1980.

Rider, I. M. "Arna Bontemps." *Horn Book.* 5/1: 13–19 (Jan.–Feb. 1939).

Scruggs, Otey M. "Arna Bontemps: The Harlem Renaissance Remembered." Paper presented at the Syracuse University Afro-American Studies Colloquium (New York), April 1982.

Weil, Dorothy. "Folklore Motifs in *Black Thunder.*" *Southern Folklore Quarterly* 35: 1–14 (March 1971).

—ELIZABETH F. HOWARD

CAROL RYRIE BRINK

1895–1981

IF CAROL RYRIE Brink had never written another book, she would have earned for herself a permanent place in American literary history and in the hearts of young readers with her Newbery Medal–winning novel set in pioneer Wisconsin, *Caddie Woodlawn* (1935). But write other books she did, about thirty altogether, and a host of short stories, articles, plays, and poems, which claimed the attention of critics and the public. About twenty books were intended for a young audience. Like her adult novels, none can boast originality of conception, but all are distinguished by a clear sense of place and of middle-class life and values; a generously detailed, fluid style; and, in particular, a congenial good humor and keen zest for life.

Most of Brink's books had their sources in her own experiences. She was born of pioneer stock on 28 December 1895 in the little town of Moscow, Idaho, when the area still retained much of the wide-open atmosphere and ruggedness characteristic of the Old West. Her father was Alexander Ryrie, a Scotsman who at the age of twenty emigrated to Idaho when it was still a territory. He helped to plan Moscow and became its first mayor. He married the daughter of a pioneer doctor, Henrietta Watkins, whose family, originally from England, followed the young nation's rapidly expanding boundaries westward from New England to Missouri, Wisconsin, and finally Idaho. The West was in Brink's blood. It and small-town life had much to do with establishing her sense of values as well as influencing the subjects and tone of her writings.

By the time she was eight, both of Brink's parents had died. She went to live with her aunt, whose sense of fun Brink fondly recalled, and her grandmother, whose tolerance and philosophical attitude toward life the child early absorbed. Brink remembered that her grandmother, though awkward with the pen, had a natural flair for storytelling and often reminisced about her childhood back in Wisconsin. This maternal grandmother, Caddie Woodhouse, was the source for the character whom two generations of readers have known and loved as Caddie Woodlawn.

A lonely child, Brink early learned to amuse herself by reading, drawing, making up stories, and riding for hours around the Idaho countryside near Moscow. She herself was the prototype of young Chrystal Reese in *Two Are Better Than One* (1968) and *Louly* (1974). She soaked up local atmosphere and recorded details of setting and daily life that were to give to her novels of the West their keen realization of specific place and time.

Brink's interest in writing continued through high school at the Portland Academy in Oregon, where she published some poems, at the University of Idaho, which she attended from 1914 until 1917, and at the University of California at Berkeley, from which she graduated Phi Beta Kappa in 1918. Soon after, she married Raymond Brink, a mathematics instructor she had known for many years, and the couple moved to St. Paul, Minnesota, where they settled and began to raise a son and a daughter. Raymond became a professor of mathematics at the University of Minnesota. His work occasionally took the family to Europe, where they traveled extensively on the Continent and lived for some time in Scotland and France. These years are reflected in such books as *Lad with a Whistle* (1941) and *Family Sabbatical* (1956). As with her books about the West, her ability to observe carefully and to retain and record her impressions with graphic accuracy lends credibility to the stories she wrote based on these experiences.

Brink turned to writing for young people while her own children were still quite young. She wrote first for Sunday school papers, then for national magazines. Longer works for both adults and children followed, stimulated by Brink's research as well as by memories and personal experiences. She continued to write after her husband retired and the couple moved to La Jolla, California. She died in La Jolla on 15 August 1981, leaving behind a large body of variously received writings that show some diversity of technique and subject matter. In addition to the Newbery Medal, she received the Southern California Council of Literature for Children and Young People Award, the Lewis Carroll Shelf Award, and awards for fiction from the National League of American Pen Women.

Critics called Brink's *Anything Can Happen on the River!* (1934) a "first book that shows promise" and felt it boded "well for stories to come." Loosely based on an actual boat trip the Brinks took up the Seine, it describes the lively, post-World War I adventures of orphaned fourteen-year-old Jacques, who, with the help of a burly, good-natured boatman named Lulu; a frail, philosophical traveling puppeteer; and the puppeteer's practical daughter, foils thieves and recovers his own family's lost riverboat. Although the contrived plot relies too much on coincidence, the story's emotional appeal grabs and holds the reader. Its structural and conceptual deficiencies and antiwar didacticism are compensated for by its generous action, intimate views of life on the river, and interesting assortment of carefully individualized, if flat and exaggerated, characters. It foreshadows the wealth of entertainment that would flow from her pen in years to come.

Anything Can Happen on the River! caught but could not retain its reading audience. Not so with *Caddie Woodlawn*, Brink's second published novel. While she was writing the book, Brink corresponded regularly with "Gram" to verify details; the novel was published when the original Caddie was eighty-two. Translated into a dozen languages

and adapted as a play, *Caddie* enjoys the status of a classic today.

A story of pioneer family life and of a girl's growing up, it focuses upon the energetic adventures of eleven-year-old, spunky, redheaded Caddie and her two brothers, the middle children in a large family of settlers in western Wisconsin during the Civil War. Although her wildness offends her Boston-reared mother, Caddie roams the fields, woods, and banks of the Menomonie River with her brothers, one escapade following another. Some activities are humorous, some embarrassing, some mischievous and even dangerous, but all have a peculiar excitement and reflect the inclinations of imaginative and spirited youngsters. Among the many well-drawn episodes, Caddie boldly battles the school bully and generously spends her precious silver dollar on gifts for three motherless, despised, half-breed Indian children. Her most daring exploit involves riding through the night to warn her Indian friends that nervous settlers plan to attack them.

Two interlocking story strands provide unity for the various episodes of the tale. Caddie gradually becomes aware that her hoydenish behavior is considered improper for a well-bred girl, and late in the book she decides to reform after her father has a heart-to-heart talk with her about her actions. Somewhat earlier, when confined to the house after an ice-skating mishap, Caddie investigates the attic and discovers a small pair of scarlet breeches and two little wooden-soled clogs. In response to the children's questions about them, Father tells of his penurious youth as the son of a disinherited English lord. After the death of his own father, he used to dance in the breeches and clogs to support his seamstress mother and himself. Late in the novel, a letter arrives from England informing Father that an inheritance awaits him provided he returns to live in England. Caddie, always a leader, urges Father to keep the family in the United States. To her joy, the family, proud of being Americans, votes unanimously in a democratically conducted election to stay.

Such events as the visit of the circuit rider; the annual passenger-pigeon migration; the speech program on the last day of school; conversations about Lincoln, the war, slavery, and Indians; and details of everyday life provide historical perspective, ground the story firmly in its period, and lift it above the ordinary family adventure story. Incidents that carry the conviction of lived events and the well-rounded character of the heroine have given *Caddie* appeal for readers over a broad age range. *Magical Melons* (1944) offers fourteen more stories about the Woodlawns and their homesteading neighbors. The episodes cover the years from 1863 to 1866 and start when Caddie is ten, one year before the beginning of *Caddie Woodlawn*. The book takes its title from the premier and typical episode in which the children find watermelons hidden in the hayloft out of season, assume they have grown there magically, feast upon them, and then discover to their consternation that the Woodlawns' hired men had put them there as a special family treat. In other episodes of domestic adventure and misadventure, Caddie acquires a pet lamb, Bouncer; the family entertains and helps to provide a home for the area's new young circuit rider, Mr. Ward, and for the shiftless, down-on-their-luck McCantrys; and the children cope with the severe restrictions of straitlaced Cousin Lucy from Boston, who supervises them while the Woodlawn parents travel to St. Louis. Less cohesive than *Caddie*, the book lacks sparkle, seems imitative, and never achieves the popularity of its more spontaneous predecessor.

After *Caddie*, Brink continued the mystery-adventure form begun in *Anything Can Happen on the River!* with *Mademoiselle Misfortune* (1936), also set in France. Its protagonist is winning, like Jacques, but the plot is clumsier and even more melodramatic. Alice Moreau, one of six daughters (their neighbors call them the "six misfortunes") of the former ambassador to Peru, has gained considerable experience in diplomacy from mediating among her siblings. She takes a position as traveling companion with an eccentric American tourist and becomes involved in a conglomeration of unlikely happenings, among them international intrigue over lost Inca treasure. She eventually effects a reconciliation between her father and his estranged son, and restores the family fortunes for good measure. Though Alice's talent at reaching compromises is extended to the point of tedium, she emerges as likable, staunchly independent, and ever resourceful, an older, urban Caddie. She is the strength of the novel, which otherwise exhibits the conventions of the period. The mystery, introduced late in the novel, seems contrived and extraneous, interjected to hold the reader's interest. The chatty style and emphasis on the financial rewards of virtue create an old-fashioned tone.

Brink also early turned her hand to fantasy. The engagingly frivolous *Baby Island* (1937) became immensely popular with young girls and was reprinted over a dozen times. Projecting a strong sense of fun, it relates the adventures of two girls who are shipwrecked while on their way to join their father in Australia. With four babies they have rescued, they are cast up on a desert island; live on shellfish, goat's milk, and roasted bananas; and are eventually rescued when letters they set adrift in cans are discovered. In this whimsical Robinsonnade, Brink intends only to amuse. She parodies the survival-story genre, yet always keeps events logical within the comic framework and retains a gentle humor and richness of small detail.

Tongue-in-cheek style also initiates the comedy in *The Highly Trained Dogs of Professor Petit* (1953), whose adult protagonist is the double of the absent-minded and lovable puppeteer of Brink's first book. Conscientious young Willie finds jobs for the performing dogs of down-on-his-luck Professor Petit in the too-serious little town of Puddling Center, restoring the Professor's fortunes and finding a vocation for himself in the process. Mystery and suspense develop when the Professor's dog Sancho is accused of sheepkilling and the Professor is jailed for the dog's crime. Willie resourcefully uncovers the real culprit, and thus demonstrates that appearances can be deceiving, proves the value of kindness to animals, and shows the people of Puddling Center that performers also contribute valuably to society. He then departs with the exonerated Professor, leaving the town a happier place and the reader with the sense of having completed a thoroughly enjoyable reading experience. The homely philosophy is well masked by the generous action and engaging humor.

An article Brink read about a California boy who built robots led to *Andy Buckram's Tin Men* (1966), her last attempt at fantasy and her only venture into science fiction. Here again Brink's ability to interest her readers comes not from skillful plotting but from her talent in creating interesting, authentic characters and from her felicitously detailed, good-humored style. The robots Andy constructs out of tin cans save his life during a flood. Individualized characters, they grow in interest as the story progresses, becoming more human in nature as they are faced with increasingly difficult challenges, until they become quite the most charming part of the book. When, at story's end, the reader sees them paddling downriver by themselves, striking out bravely on their own, he has no difficulty believing that they can manage their own futures quite well.

Though realistic, *The Pink Motel* (1959) reveals strong fantasy overtones. Brink again plays with the mystery genre in bringing together a thoroughly engaging if unlikely combination of eccentrics in a Florida seaside motel. Lighthearted suspense arises when one of Miss De Gree's valuable poodles disappears and young Kirby gets the opportunity to wear his J. Edgar Hoover Junior G-Man badge and go after the criminals—two bumbling, naive, mock-Al Capone types. Events and characters are overdrawn, but cooperation, resourcefulness, and perseverance save the day and uncover the secret. These are the same solid, traditional values that in varying degrees appear also in Brink's other stories.

After a long hiatus, Brink returned to the family novel in 1952 with *Family Grandstand*, which improvises on the Brinks' own experiences as an academic family living in a university town. Professor Ridgeway teaches history at Midwestern University; his wife writes mysteries; and their three children variously occupy themselves with parties, neighbors, school, and daily problems of a minor nature. The children's activities provide the interest as well as the somewhat tenuous unity of the book. They have two objectives: to help their handyman, a none-too-bright football star, pass chemistry so that he will be eligible to play in a crucial football game, and to earn money to feed their newly acquired dog. Adults are familiar types, but the children come alive: the earnest mediator Susan (an echo of Alice Moreau), conscientious George, and especially little Dumpling, the anxious six-year-old who has a way of coming up with astute, practical solutions to problems and who Susan thinks may be a prodigy. The story suffers from predictability and overextension, but it gives a good description of upper-middle-class life in a university setting during the late 1940's and advocates a sense of community and shared pleasures and the importance of considering the effect of one's actions on others—all supported by Brink's fidelity to the child's point of view and her relaxed style, warm tone, and affection for life. As with most family stories intended for children, the meaning is on the surface, but the total effect makes for pleasing entertainment for late-elementary-school-age readers.

Set one year after the action in *Family Grandstand*, *Family Sabbatical* takes the Ridgeways around

France on Professor Ridgeway's leave from teaching. While Father researches a book on history and Mother writes her novel, the children have various adventures: attending a French school; celebrating holidays; meeting a real princess; and acquiring, growing fond of, and then losing a muddleheaded governess. As they familiarize themselves with local ways and attempt to learn the language, the reader gains a limited but real impression of what it is like to live briefly in a foreign country. Like its predecessor, *Sabbatical* reinforces conventional values of respect, work, concern for others, and doing one's best in whatever situation one finds oneself. Once again the abundance of action, congenial atmosphere, and strong sense of family offset the transparent, hackneyed plotting and incidents and exert the usual comfortable Brink charm.

In addition to the solidly realized *Caddie Woodlawn*, Brink produced several other family period stories and one historical romance, *Lad with a Whistle*. The latter, though consistently interesting, exhibits Brink's usual ineptitude with plot. Resourceful, courageous, orphaned Rob, of Edinburgh, Scotland, ekes out a meager living by playing the fife. Appointed unofficial guardian of the grandchildren of the laird of Kirkness, he unmasks a scheme hatched by the servants to install the housekeeper's smuggler-son as laird. Gothic conventions and melodramatic action abound, but descriptions of the Scottish countryside and Edinburgh and the inclusion of Sir Walter Scott as poet, sheriff, and lawyer help tone down the romanticism and create the semblance of reality.

Three period pieces rose out of Brink's memories of growing up in a small western town: *All over Town* (1939), *Two Are Better Than One*, and *Louly*. The first, for younger readers, describes the fun and excitement that ensue when the two irrepressible sons of Warsaw Junction's new minister involve the tomboy-daughter of the local doctor in their well-intentioned schemes to have fun and help out various townspeople, including their own father. Considerable humor, much of it adult, arises from their efforts to entice local "backsliders" to attend church and thus demonstrate to the church's powers-that-be that the Reverend Dawlish is an effective preacher. The book sports a smashing climax, a fire set at the opera house, followed by a trial in which young Martin's testimony convicts the culprit. The book has plenty of action, humor of situation and character, and even wordplay.

Two Are Better Than One and *Louly* employ less

overt comedy than *All over Town*. They share the same characters and the same small-town setting of Warsaw, Idaho, in 1908. *Two Are Better Than One*, the most complex in structure of Brink's books, presents two interwoven stories within a frame story. Elderly Mrs. Chrystal Banks receives two tiny dolls in the mail for Christmas from a childhood friend, Mrs. Cordelia Crump. This prompts her to recall adventures she and her old friend had had in and around Warsaw when both were thirteen and best friends: selecting frilly hats, dressing up as rag dolls for a masquerade party, attending Sunday school with the Dorcas Club, riding their ponies in the hills, and, especially, composing a book of melodramatic adventures for the dolls. The young, orphaned Chrystal, who lives with her aunt and grandmother, is, of course, Brink herself. But when she and Cordy (the nickname of the young Cordelia Crump) are together, the two girls are almost indistinguishable as characters. The book portrays the era attractively, but the two girls seem quite immature in their attitudes and behavior even by the standards of that more innocent era.

Louly dominates the book of which she is the title character. She runs the family home while her parents visit relatives in Michigan. With the help of Chrys and Cordy, she engineers a camp-out in the backyard, makes up plays to entertain the children, and organizes their entry in the Fourth of July parade. Such activities hold the reader's attention and serve as well to show what life was like for genteel children just after the turn of the century. They also mark the stages of Louly's romance with handsome Eddie Wendell. Though the episodes have a familiar ring, they are spiritedly realized. Louly herself, fun-loving, flirtatious, warm-hearted, yet responsible and ambitious too, is one of the most winning and memorable of Brink's heroines.

Similarly, Minty, the leading character of *Winter Cottage* (1968), carries the book, the barely believable story of a down-on-their-luck Depression family who spend a winter in a northern Wisconsin lake cottage. An organizer like Louly, Minty manages to get her siblings and cloudy-headed father through the winter. Minty would seem entirely too level-headed if it were not for her engagingly romantic fantasies about the cabin owner's daughter, which to the reader's amusement keep her from recognizing the girl when she arrives.

Another strongly drawn, if somewhat less memorable, heroine is Irma of *The Bad Times of Irma Baumlein* (1972), Brink's sole attempt at an amusing psychological problem story. Irma rises above the limitations of plot, too. New in town, shy and lonely, she rashly announces that she has the biggest doll in the world. The rest of the plot centers on her trying to make good her fib, setting in motion a comedy of errors. The style and tone seem typical of children's literature of the 1970's, and Irma's misgivings about what she has done and her ticklish situations relieve the book's didacticism and put the reader firmly on Irma's side.

Brink also edited two anthologies of short stories and wrote two biographies for children: *Narcissa Whitman* (1945), about the wife of Marcus Whitman, pioneer-missionary to the Oregon Territory, and *Lafayette* (1946), about the French soldier-statesman who fought for American independence. Though short picture books, both stories convey much information in a clear and interesting style. The biography of Narcissa Whitman takes her from early youth through schooling, marriage, and work among the Indians of the Northwest to her death in the Indian uprising of 1847. The book about Lafayette has a stronger thematic arrangement, presenting him as a practical idealist and focusing on the activities that opened his eyes to the injustices current in his native France. Both books employ straightforward, concrete language and reveal Brink's respect for the subjects and her audience. Most of Brink's children's books, though they gained enthusiastic followers at publication, have fallen by the wayside. Arch, contrived, dated to late-twentieth-century tastes, they have been supplanted by books more psychologically oriented and dealing with topical social concerns. However, the books more attuned to present-day tastes—*Louly*, *Two Are Better Than One*, *Andy Buckram's Tin Men*, and *Irma Baumlein*—still command an audience. The perennially popular *Caddie* retains its place as a favorite in children's literature, even though it has been castigated for its portrayal of women and Indians.

Brink compensated for her inability to combine episodes into a well-motivated, evenly paced, credibly sustained plot by providing generous detailing of incident and period and writing in a graceful, fluid style. She excelled at creating the Everychild, to whom young readers can relate, and at addressing the secret yearnings of the young for fun and adventure in a world in which good and evil are easily identified and good inevitably wins out. Brink's most substantial writings for the young are her well-researched and clearly envisioned period stories, and it is for the best of these, *Caddie Woodlawn*, that she will be remembered.

Selected Bibliography

WORKS OF CAROL RYRIE BRINK

Anything Can Happen on the River! With illustrations by W. W. Berger. New York: Macmillan, 1934.

Caddie Woodlawn. With illustrations by Kate Seredy. New York: Macmillan, 1935.

Mademoiselle Misfortune. With illustrations by Kate Seredy. New York: Macmillan, 1936.

Baby Island. With illustrations by Helen Sewall. New York: Macmillan, 1937.

All over Town. With illustrations by Dorothy Bayley. New York: Macmillan, 1939.

Lad with a Whistle. With illustrations by Robert Ball. New York: Macmillan, 1941.

Magical Melons. With illustrations by Marguerite Davis. New York: Macmillan, 1944.

Caddie Woodlawn: A Play. New York: Macmillan, 1945.

Narcissa Whitman. With illustrations by Samuel Armstrong. Evanston, Ill.: Row, Peterson, 1945.

Lafayette. With illustrations by Dorothy Bayley Morse. Evanston, Ill.: Row, Peterson, 1946.

Family Grandstand. With illustrations by Jean MacDonald Porter. New York: Viking Press, 1952.

The Highly Trained Dogs of Professor Petit. With illustrations by Robert Henneberger. New York: Macmillan, 1953.

Family Sabbatical. With illustrations by Susan Foster. New York: Viking Press, 1956.

The Pink Motel. With illustrations by Sheila Greenwald. New York: Macmillan, 1959.

Andy Buckram's Tin Men. With illustrations by W. T. Mars. New York: Viking Press, 1966.

Two Are Better Than One. With illustrations by Fermin Rocker. New York: Macmillan, 1968.

Winter Cottage. With illustrations by Fermin Rocker. New York: Macmillan, 1968.

The Bad Times of Irma Baumlein. With illustrations by Trina Schart Hyman. New York: Macmillan, 1972.

Louly. With illustrations by Ingrid Fetz. New York: Macmillan, 1974.

CRITICAL AND BIOGRAPHICAL STUDIES

Hopkins, Lee Bennett. *More Books by More People*. Englewood Cliffs, N.J.: Citation Press, 1974.

Kunitz, Stanley and Howard Haycraft, eds. *Junior Book of Authors*. New York: H. W. Wilson, 1951.

Miller, Bertha Mahony and Elinor Whitney Field, eds. *Newbery Medal Books: 1922–1955*. Boston: Horn Book, 1955.

Rothe, Anna, ed. *Current Biography, 1946*. New York: H. W. Wilson, 1946.

—ALETHEA K. HELBIG

JEAN DE BRUNHOFF

1899–1937

JEAN DE BRUNHOFF was the father of three sons—and an elephant. The Brunhoff *fils*, Laurent, Matthieu, and Thierry, have achieved distinction in their chosen fields of illustration, medicine, and music. But it is Jean's fictional offspring, Babar the elephant, whose name has become an international byword among children and adults since his conception and development in seven picture books written from 1931 to 1937. Unlike other characters in young people's classics—"children" like Alice, Pippi, Wilbur, and Christopher Robin—Babar is a grown-up whom young readers listen to and identify with; they participate in his saga from birth through childhood and youth, to young manhood, marriage, leadership, and eventually, fatherhood. In all this, Babar is a quintessentially French model of inspiring adulthood—authoritative yet loving, principled yet resilient—a perfect Papa and Brunhoff's clear persona.

One of four children, Brunhoff was born in 1899 into the cultivated Parisian home of Maurice de Brunhoff, a publisher of art magazines and cofounder of the French *Vogue*. He graduated from l'École alsacienne in Paris in time to join the French army at the end of World War I; fortunately, he reached the front just as the war ended. To pursue a career in painting, he returned to Paris, where he studied under Othon Friesz, joined and exhibited at the Galerie Champigny, and became established as a painter of portraits and still lifes. In 1924 he married Cécile Sabouraud, a pianist; Laurent was born in 1925, Matthieu in 1926, and Thierry in 1935. The family lived in Paris but spent summers

at Chessy, the house of Cécile's father along the Seine outside Paris. One summer day four-year-old Matthieu was sick, and to comfort him, Mama spun a story about a little elephant. Both boys were charmed by the adventure, told Papa the tale, and begged for illustrations. Brunhoff drew some pictures and expanded the story, soon becoming thoroughly intrigued with the character he named "Babar." At the urging of his brother Michel, an editor at *Le jardin des modes*, he published the illustrated story *Histoire de Babar, le petit éléphant* (*The Story of Babar, the Little Elephant*) in 1931. The book was so immediately popular that Jean produced a second, *Le voyage de Babar* (*The Travels of Babar*), in 1932, a third, *Le roi Babar* (*Babar the King*), in 1933, and a fourth, *ABC de Babar* (*ABC of Babar*), in 1934, all published by Le jardin des modes.

But in the early 1930's Brunhoff learned that he had tuberculosis and was forced to spend periods of convalescence in a Swiss sanitorium, seeing his family only irregularly. As if to fill a mutual void, he continued to produce *Babar* books, publishing *Les vacances de Zéphir* (*Zephir's Holidays*) in 1936, and drafting for serial publication *Babar en famille* (*Babar and His Children*) and *Babar et le Père Noël* (*Babar and Father Christmas*); these three stories were published (the last two posthumously in 1938 and 1941) by Hachette. Brunhoff died on 16 October 1937. His permanent absence from his young family had to be partially filled by the ongoing presence of Babar, the pachydermous picture-book father whom Brunhoff's children also loved.

That Brunhoff lives in his work there is no doubt. The whole ambience of Babar's life-style and home reflects the author's Gallic and personal culture: the centrality of family, order, decorum, and self-control; the importance of music, skiing in the mountains, and good food; and a flair for dressing, playing, and dreaming. Even specific glimpses of the Brunhoffs appear: like Brunhoff himself, the mature Babar is a pipe smoker; Babar wears a cap like Brunhoff's when he skis; Céleste's cloche is just like Cécile's; Babar sits astride a rocking horse like Laurent's; and the character of Babar's faithful dog, Duck, is inspired by the Brunhoffs' family dog. Of course both the Babars and the Brunhoffs have three lively children, a devoted extended family, and a close circle of old friends. All this is not to imply that the books are merely autobiographies. But certainly their emotional proximity to Brunhoff's own environment gives authenticity to the stories' warmth and Brunhoff's power to create an ideal world, at the center of which can only be an ideal family.

The books were translated eventually into fifteen languages, English being one of the first. In America the series was published in the 1930's by Smith and Haas (absorbed by Random House in 1936) and concurrently in England by Methuen; all but *ABC of Babar* were reissued in the U.S. and England in the 1960's. The entire oeuvre has seen new French editions, published by French and European Publications in the 1970's; segments of stories have been excerpted and issued separately as *Le couronnement de Babar* (*Babar's Coronation, 1952*), *L'enfance de Babar* (*Babar's Childhood*, 1951), and *Babar en ballon* (*Babar's Balloon Trip*, 1952). Some, like *Babar aux sports d'hiver* (*Babar at Winter Sports*, 1952), include pictures adapted by Laurent, who revived the series after World War II with *Babar et ce coquin d'Arthur* (*Babar and That Rascal Arthur*, 1946) and perpetuated the Celesteville characters in many volumes that are subtly different from his father's. The *Babar* stories have even been "retold" in *The Babar Story-book*, by Enid Blyton, a curious wartime edition (1942) from Methuen with Brunhoff's pictures "redrawn." Anthologies of Jean's *Babar* saga have appeared in *Trois "Babar" en un* (*Three "Babars" in One*, (1943), *Deux "Babar" en un* (*Two "Babars" in One*, 1945), and *Les aventures de Babar* (*Babar's Adventures, 1959*), a textbook edited by Laurent. Brunhoff's first three stories (though not in facsimile) and three by Laurent appeared in *Babar's Anniversary Album* (1981).

The original books were very large (approximately eleven by fifteen inches); handwritten in round, elephantine, European script; and expensive—high-quality books that children could literally crawl into. Subsequently, the size was reduced to eight by eleven inches, and the typeface was changed to standard fonts; paperback rights further eroded the first volumes' high standards of bookmaking. *Babar's Anniversary Album* is large (9½ by 12½) but sacrifices the aesthetics of script page design, picture reproduction, and even story (it is abridged) to the demands of compendium publishing. Fortunately, the same publisher, Random House, has reissued the original translation of *Histoire de Babar*, *The Story of Babar, the Little Elephant*, in a large facsimile that reproduces the original plates and retains the volume's exceptional artistry.

In spite of their availability and acknowledged excellence, there was little written about the *Babar* books in America, except for reviews, until the 1960's; the most insightful critical attention to Brunhoff's work has appeared since 1975. Most serious readers see a thematic unity to the stories and often focus on their political messages, which do indeed reflect the socialist-idealist milieu of France in the 1930's. Babar's realm is "one of the most successful political ventures of the twentieth century" (Payne), "a benevolent monarchy" (Hurlimann), "an elephant Utopia" (Fisher), "a primer in power politics" (Richardson). Other readers emphasize the books' validity as models of French culture and tradition (Sale); their psychological relevance after fifty years (Sendak); their anthropological affinities (Leach); their philosophical equilibrium (Haskell); or their socio-literary kinship (Hildebrand). All of these themes and more are developed in a manner that is progressive and incremental. Each story introduces, to one degree or another, new facets of Babar's character and new arenas for his personal development. He becomes beneficially civilized as his saga unfolds within an environment that he is instrumental in creating.

Detailed illustrations together with "extreme directness of language" (Hurlimann) make Brunhoff's picture stories seminal models for future picture stories. Early in his career, his brother Michel called Jean a talented colorist, and certainly his extravagant use of color is part of what prompts Maurice Sendak to offer unabashed praise to the body of work that "forever changed the face of the illustrated book." But Sendak also extols Brunhoff's humor, grace, musicality, composition, "sly sense of counterpoint," and unexcelled mastery of scale and double-spread tableaux. The delicacy of Brunhoff's pen in the land of cumbersome animals is exquisite: Babar dances, skis, bikes, and comports himself with attitudinal grace in spite of his bulk. Brunhoff's ingenuity with hats and elephant trunks, his impresario's command of ceremony, and his feel for lyrical movement often force the reader to pause in the narrative and linger over the inexhaustible pictures. But the text soon urges one on, for Brunhoff's sentences are complex enough to be interesting, filled with stimulating cadences of language and vocabulary and a varied, vigorous pace. From endpapers to handlettered text, all reproduced by offset lithography, the books provide a perfect balance of pictures and text.

Of course, translation is always an impediment to experiencing adapted works fully. There is no substitute in any language for the visual-verbal integrity that Brunhoff creates in French. Just the sound of "un beau chapeau melon," "tres heureux," and "la nuit est tombée" is sensually provocative. Concepts like "en famille," "bonheur," and "foyer" are untranslatable, and thus Brunhoff's balanced verbal melodies lose some of their resonance. But given the desirability of an English edition after 50,000 copies had dazzled the French reading public, Merle Haas, the wife of the original publisher, did a good job of capturing the spirit and vivacity of Brunhoff's words. Best of all, she retained the present tense of the French, the spontaneous freshness of "now" in all the books: "In the great forest a little elephant is born. His name is Babar. His mother loves him very much." Laurent achieves the same sense of immediacy in his stories. It is puzzling, then, that the new edition of *Babar's Anniversary Album* uses a banal, flat past tense, with, apparently, the approval of Laurent. The stories lose much of their charm and vigor when the participatory present tense is changed.

Beyond the new editions, adaptations, and translations, Babar lives in various art forms other than print. In 1936 Brunhoff himself decorated, by commission, the children's dining room of the French liner *Normandie*, using large wooden cutouts of the Babar characters. Francis Poulenc celebrated Brunhoff's hero musically in his work for piano and reciter, "Babar the Little Elephant." Originally performed in French in 1945 by Poulenc and Pierre Fresnay, the work has been narrated in English by such notable readers as Noel Coward,

Peter Ustinov, and Werner Klemperer. Equally spirited is the ballet to this music, mounted by the Metropolitan Opera Ballet Company and first performed for American audiences in 1978. Babar was adapted for French television (Tele-Hachette, 1969) and later for American TV, animated movie, and filmstrips; unfortunately, some of these visual attempts seem clumsy compared with Brunhoff's buoyant drawings. Recorded readings of several of the books have been made in English and French by Louis Jourdan, and Paul Bernac's recording of Poulenc's score was recently reissued. Babar-inspired window displays and toy department decorations of Babar dolls, puppets, coloring books, napierie, and clothing have been featured in both American and European department stores. The most recent homage to Babar has been the celebration of his fiftieth birthday with a summer-long exhibition of the Brunhoffs' work at the Centre culturel de Marais in Paris and another exhibition of original Babar watercolors in eight American cities. All in all, the elephant born in 1931 has lived a long, full life and seems in little danger of moving over for another ruler, either from eating a bad mushroom or from neglect.

From the first dazzling page of *The Story of Babar, the Little Elephant*, the reader knows that Babar has an idyllic childhood, complete with love, friends, play, and beauty—and that childhood is abruptly ended when "a wicked hunter . . . [kills] Babar's mother." Babar flees in fright, journeys several days, and comes exhausted to a city where he recovers from his sorrow and desperation as he samples civilization. He meets a new mother figure, the Old Lady (the only major human figure in the series), who "gives Babar whatever he wants," which includes affection, discipline, freedom, and loyalty. As time goes on, Babar absorbs the urban (Paris, surely) culture and becomes well-clothed, educated, and refined. But he often misses his mother and his old home, so much that when his beloved cousins, Céleste and Arthur, appear, he leaves the city and returns to the "great forest" with them— only to find that it has changed. The old king has died, and Babar, innately noble and experienced in the world, is chosen by wrinkled Cornelius and the other elders to become the new ruler. And so, newly affianced to Céleste, he agrees to rule, is married and crowned, and happily looks heavenward in the ultimate gesture of hope and assurance. In this quick-paced chronicle of birth to manhood, the reader meets the series' main characters, sees

Babar becoming a well-bred bourgeois who has set aside despair with optimistic determination, and has the first taste of Brunhoff's spectacular double-spread narratives: Baby Babar witnessing his mother's death, Bon Vivant Babar driving a red roadster, and King Babar dancing at his own coronation.

The end of the first book points smoothly to the second, *The Travels of Babar*, as the two "set out on their honeymoon in a gorgeous yellow balloon" and sail over what must be the Côte d'Azur. But difficulties soon begin: the balloon gets blown off course, and after some strength-and-character-testing adventures, the royal couple is rescued by an ocean liner. Unfortunately, they are mistaken for elephants, for "they have lost their crowns during the storm," and so get sold to a traveling circus where, with great aplomb, they earn their keep by dancing and playing the trumpet. Meanwhile, in the forest lively Arthur has inadvertently started a war with the enemy rhinoceros. Thus, by the time Babar and Céleste escape from the circus, find the Old Lady, and rest from their tribulations by taking a short ski vacation, the Great Forest is in a war-torn shambles: "A few broken trees! . . . There are no more flowers, no more birds." Ever resourceful, Babar sets up a field hospital and a brilliant, memorable strategy to outwit the rhinos. The war ends amid jubilation; all are rewarded (the Old Lady with a "cunning little monkey" later named Zéphir); and the crowned heads settle into their peaceful realm "to try to rule . . . wisely." The adventures of this book show Babar's continuing ability to handle problems, but not his own temper, and establish his need for Céleste's equilibrium and patience. The cast of characters is by now familiar: the Old Lady is reliable, Cornelius worries, and Arthur is mischievous. Skiing seems the ideal way to reinvigorate; and through Babar Brunhoff articulates what between-wars Frenchmen felt—that real war is not a joke.

In *Babar the King* the new kingdom is built with the baggage Babar has collected and is shaped with the ideals he has learned during his honeymoon travels. All the elephants are promised clothes, which give them distinctive identities, and set to work building a city to go with their roles. Céleste-ville emerges as a Utopia of equality, beauty, and utility; it is a city of work—the children go to school and the adults do all the jobs that need doing—and play, from various sports to theater, music, and Great Occasions like promenades and anniversary celebrations. Mischief and a penchant for vanilla

cream are indulged, too, by a firm but kindly Babar. But again, tragedy strikes, in the form of a snake that poisons the Old Lady and a fire that threatens Cornelius. The prospect of losing his sage advisers sends Babar into despair: "What a dreadful day! . . . how worried I am!" But his dreams save him; his friends recover; and in a final tableau, all whom Babar loves—Céleste, Arthur, the Old Lady, Cornelius, and Zéphir—reflect contentedly on the abiding gospel of Babar's kingdom and the philosophical center of Brunhoff's books: "Let's work hard and cheerfully and we'll continue to be happy." In this third book Babar shows an appealing new vulnerability as well as the old recuperative exuberance and a genuine knack for creative kingship. *Babar the King* relies for its richness less on adventurous plot than on carefully conceived setting, and contains Brunhoff's most delightful double spreads. The bulky solemnity of elephants in the park, at the theater, and on parade, and the soaring grace of the elephant-angels of hope show the artist Brunhoff at his polished, witty best.

ABC of Babar does not augment the narrative saga but reinforces delightfully the messages and characters in the previous books. The double-spread pages are gracefully packed with glimpses of the Celesteville folks and activities arranged according to the appropriate letter of the alphabet. There are hints of events current in the real world and in the Brunhoff family and foretastes of scenes and characters that appear in the last three books. The introductory letter from Babar, which urges his "Dear Friends" to discover the words for themselves before consulting the lists at the back, is vintage *père* Brunhoff and gives a warm invitation to this engaging volume.

In *Zéphir's Holidays* the little monkey leaves the ordered world of Célesteville for a free vacation experience. He waves au revoir to Babar, Celeste, the Old Lady, and "his beloved Arthur" and enters another world, Monkeyville, where the houses hang from trees and *he* is the city-bred hero. While out fishing (in a boat sent by Babar), Zéphir catches a little mermaid, Eléonore, who persuades him to throw her back with the promise that when he needs her, she will be there. Upon returning to Monkeyville, he finds that the General's daughter, Isabelle, has been kidnapped, and the soldiers deployed to find her are in disarray. But "Zéphir is the only one who doesn't give up hope," and with the help of Eléonore and the ancient seer Aunt Crustadele, he journeys to the land of the Gogottes (who look rather like Sendak's Wild Things). By dint of art and imagination, Zéphir saves Isabelle just before she turns into stone. The rejoicing is unbounded, and his parents don't even "scold him for having gone off without telling them." Though not using his Babar persona, Brunhoff here says much about the power of art and imagination to solve practical problems. He is suggesting that all is not merely rational, for the regiment fails to find Isabelle in spite of its commonsense approach, while Zéphir and his magical mermaids, his story-telling, dancing, and miming *do* effect a rescue. The setting is not Célesteville's ordinary environment but a more imaginative, even fantastic, one. Brunhoff uses different colors, with oranges replacing reds and further underlining the new locale and the perspective of a holiday from which Zéphir returns with new confidence and power. After all, from every vacation in the entire saga the participants have returned invigorated and energized.

Babar and His Children appeared first in English in black-and-white serial form in the London *Daily Sketch* in 1936; it was published in French in full color in 1938, under the direction of Michel de Brunhoff, who allowed Laurent to finish coloring some of the pictures. In what Hurlimann calls "the most radiant of the Babar books," and certainly Brunhoff's most personal story, Babar becomes the father of not one but three children—and so are introduced Pom, Flora, and Alexander. The babies are eagerly awaited, ceremoniously announced and presented, and lovingly helped through their first years of growing, choking, and falling out of prams by Céleste, Arthur, the Old Lady, Cornelius, and Zéphir, who hold them, play with them, save them from falls and crocodiles, and tuck them warmly into bed. Each child has a distinct personality: "Pom is the greediest . . . and the fattest." To her indulgent parents, "Flora is very good," docile, and a bit of a crybaby; Alexander is the smallest but most adventurous (perhaps the Thierry of the fictional family?). Babar still shows husbandly love and pride, but he reveals a new protective fatherliness that translates into anxiety when his babies are in jeopardy—"Truly it is not easy to bring up a family"—and tender affection—". . . but how nice the babies are. I wouldn't know how to get along without them anymore." The double spreads are not as visually fascinating as in *Babar the King*, but the single page where Babar imagines a baby in the book he is reading, in the letter he is writing, and in the flower he is watering is uniquely memorable. This culminating book makes the reader wonder what can come next. Babar is mature and has every-

thing a person could want, including a complete and complex personality.

And indeed, *Babar and Father Christmas* suffers from a lack of freshness. In Brunhoff's last book, also sterilized and published posthumously with help from Laurent, Babar journeys to the land of Father Christmas so that the children of Célesteville can have the Yule trappings enjoyed elsewhere in the world. Babar leaves his city, endures some minor hardships, and finally falls into Father Christmas' home through a hole in the north snow. After sampling the old man's hospitality, Babar takes him back to Célesteville to rest for the exhausting Christmas preparations; then complete with magic Santa suit, Babar himself delivers gifts in Célesteville while Father Christmas attends to the rest of the world. Somewhat illogically, Father Christmas returns to bring a Christmas tree in a final double spread that shows little of Brunhoff's delicate line, subtle color, and imaginative intricacy. Perhaps because Brunhoff's own beloved governess had died, the Old Lady is missing from this story—and so is the vitality of the other books. The characters are pedestrian and colorless despite their odd names (Lazzari Campeotti, Professor Gillianez); the adventures are tepid; and Babar is static. He seems more like a tourist "doing the sights" than an inspiring adult being creatively influential. His nature is not augmented, either, by this adventure away from home for a less-than-noble reason—bringing commercial Christmas to his Utopian city. Brunhoff's Babar persona seems to have stopped expanding, as if he were running out of creative energy and life. Indeed, a series-like predictability pervades the later books by Laurent, for Babar's character has nowhere to go but on trips, and the stories become ingenious rather than creative. For readers who anticipate each new step in the chronicle of a developing Babar, this story has to be a disappointment.

It is, therefore, the first five narratives that stand as the heart and soul of the *Babar* stories and transmit the statements that are important to Jean de Brunhoff and his readers: the affirmation of family, order, courage, patience, holiday, music, friendship, play, learning, work, goodness, beauty, laughter, imagination; the tolerance of mischief, mistakes, misunderstandings, and hospital stays; and the abhorrence of war, laziness, discouragement, ignorance, despair, cowardice, and anger. That children still respond to Laurent's exotic adventures is due to Jean's inspired creation of character, place, and event in a visual and literary whole that makes his legacy of meaning clear and firm yet not didactic, and filled with beauty, innocence, and humor.

Selected Bibliography

WORKS OF JEAN DE BRUNHOFF IN FRENCH

Histoire de Babar, le petit éléphant. Paris: Éditions du jardin des modes, 1931.
Le voyage de Babar. Paris: Éditions du jardin des modes, 1932.
Le roi Babar. Paris: Éditions du jardin des modes, 1933.
ABC de Babar. Paris: Éditions du jardin des modes, 1934.
Les vacances de Zéphir. Paris: Hachette, 1936.
Babar en famille. Paris: Hachette, 1938.
Babar et le Père Noël. Paris: Hachette, 1941.

ADAPTATIONS IN FRENCH

Trois "Babar" en un. Paris: Hachette, 1943.
Deux "Babar" en un. Paris: Hachette, 1945.
Babar et ce coquin d'Arthur. Paris: Hachette, 1946.
L'enfance de Babar. Paris: Hachette, 1951.
Babar aux sports d'hiver. Paris: Hachette, 1952.
Babar en ballon. Paris: Hachette, 1952.
Le couronnement de Babar. Paris: Hachette, 1952.
Les aventures de Babar. Paris: Hachette, 1959.

TRANSLATIONS AND ADAPTATIONS IN ENGLISH

For a more complete, detailed list of reissues and republications, see Ann Commire's *Something About the Author*, vol. 24, Detroit: Gale Research, 1981. The best American collection of Brunhoff's works and papers resides in the Kerlan Collection at the University of Minnesota. All translations are by Merle S. Haas, unless noted.

The Story of Babar, the Little Elephant. New York: H. Smith and R. Haas, 1933; London: Methuen, 1936. (With an introduction by A. A. Milne.) Reissued in facsimile. New York: Random House, 1984.
The Travels of Babar. New York: H. Smith and R. Haas, 1934. Retitled *Babar's Travels*. London: Methuen, 1935.
Babar the King. New York: H. Smith and R. Haas and Random House, 1935.
ABC of Babar. New York: Random House, 1936. Retitled *Babar's ABC*. London: Methuen, 1937.
Zephir's Holidays. New York: Random House, 1937. Reissued as *Babar and Zephir*. New York: Random House, 1942. Retitled *Babar's Friend, Zephir*. London: Methuen, 1937.
Babar and His Children. New York: Random House, 1938. Retitled *Babar at Home*. London: Methuen, 1938.
Babar and Father Christmas. New York: Random House, 1940.
The Babar Story-book. Retold by Enid Blyton. London: Methuen, 1942.
Babar's Anniversary Album. With an introduction by Maurice Sendak, a picture-essay by Laurent de Brunhoff, and textual changes by Random House editors. New York: Random House, 1981.

CRITICAL AND BIOGRAPHICAL STUDIES

Brunhoff, Laurent de. *Fifty Years of Babar: Watercolors by Jean and Laurent de Brunhoff*. With an introduction by Maurice Sendak. New York: The Arts Publisher and the International Exhibitions Foundation, 1983.
Fisher, Emma. "Laurent de Brunhoff." In *The Pied Pipers*, edited by Justin Wintle and Emma Fisher. New York: Paddington Press, 1974. (An interview.)
Graham, Eleanor. "The Genius of de Brunhoff, the Creator of the *Babar* Books" *Junior Bookshelf* 52: 49–55 (Jan. 1941).
Haskell, Ann S. "Babar at Fifty, Pinocchio at One Hundred" *New York Times Book Review* (Fall 1981).
Hildebrand, Ann M. "Jean de Brunhoff's Advice to Youth: The *Babar* Books as Books of Courtesy." In *Children's Literature*, vol. 11, edited by Compton Rees. New Haven, Conn.: Yale University Press, 1983.
Hurlimann, Bettina. *Three Centuries of Children's Books in Europe*. Cleveland: World Publishing, 1967.
Leach, Edmund. "Babar's Civilization Analyzed" *New Society* (20 Dec. 1962).
Payne, Harry C. "The Reign of King Babar." In *Children's Literature*, vol. 11, edited by Compton Rees. New Haven, Conn.: Yale University Press, 1983.
Richardson, Patrick. "Teach Your Baby to Rule." In *Suitable for Children? Controversies in Children's Literature*, edited by Nicholas Tucker. Berkeley: University of California Press, 1976.
Sale, Roger. *Fairy Tales and After: From Snow White to E. B. White*. Cambridge, Mass.: Harvard University Press, 1978.
Sendak, Maurice. "Homage to Babar on His Fiftieth Birthday." In *Babar's Anniversary Album*. New York: Random House, 1981.

—ANN M. HILDEBRAND

JOHN BUNYAN

1628–1688

FAULTING MUCH OF the children's literature of his day, Samuel Johnson contended that "babies do not want to hear about babies; they like to be told of giants and castles, and of somewhat which can stretch and stimulate their little minds." When Hester Thrale, a friend, reminded Johnson of the many editions and quick sales of juvenile books like *Goody Two-Shoes* (1765), Johnson answered that parents buy such books but children never read them. One of the earliest recorded critical exchanges on children's literature, this conversation highlights the dilemma that children's writers face to this day: Are they writing for a child reader or rather for an adult caretaker who decides what the child will read? A century earlier, the book for children that most decidedly passed the tests of critic, parent, and child had already appeared—John Bunyan's *The Pilgrim's Progress* (1678).

Bunyan's most noted work, *The Pilgrim's Progress* was immediately popular with adults and children. In its first fifteen years of publication, according to Charles Doe, the first editor of Bunyan's works, one hundred thousand copies were sold. Today it has been translated into nearly two hundred languages. In the United States there are dozens of editions currently in print. In England, three centuries after the book first appeared, ten thousand copies are sold annually. Two generations ago one scholar traced more than thirteen hundred editions of Bunyan's narrative, which, although not intended for children, has been widely read by children in England and America since its publication.

Dandling the young daughter of Dr. Thomas Percy on his knee, Samuel Johnson asked her if she had read *The Pilgrim's Progress*. When she confessed she had not, Johnson exclaimed, "*No?* Then I would not give one farthing for you," set her down, and thereafter ignored her.

The historian Macaulay discovered that *The Pilgrim's Progress* delighted peasants in even the wildest parts of Scotland and that in every nursery the story was a greater favorite than *Jack the Giant Killer*. As boys, Benjamin Franklin, Abraham Lincoln, and George Bernard Shaw all read Bunyan. Even fictional children were expected to be familiar with Bunyan. In *Little Women*, by Louisa May Alcott, the March sisters know Bunyan's book intimately, acting out its scenes from cellar to attic even before each one receives her own copy of "that beautiful old story" as a Christmas present. Elsie Dinsmore, Rebecca Rowena Randall, and other model fictional children read *The Pilgrim's Progress*. Even Huckleberry Finn admits, "I read considerable in it now and then. The statements was interesting, but tough."

How was it that an essentially devotional work was as eagerly read by children as were secular tales of giants? First came the approbation of their parents, the gatekeepers of much juvenile literature. Granted that the book was a story, it was, however, an uplifting one studded with biblical allusions. One scholar glossed references to over eight hundred scriptural passages in Bunyan's text—small wonder that it was sanctioned even for the child's (and the family's) Sabbath reading.

But what accounts for the story's enormous appeal to child and adult readers to this day? The first clue to why Bunyan's book would be not only sanctioned by adults but willingly devoured by children is the book's original full title: *The Pilgrim's Progress From This World, to That which is to come: Delivered under the Similitude of a Dream Wherein is Discovered, The manner of his setting out, His Dangerous Journey; And safe Arrival at the Desired Countrey.* The promise of a dangerous journey presages excitement, and an exciting book it is. Once Christian, the main character, leaves the City of Destruction, he confronts an incredible assortment of characters. Of the ninety characters whom Christian meets or hears of, the vast majority are the unsaved, like Mr. Worldly Wiseman, Madam Wanton, my old Lord Lechery, Parson Two-tongues, and Captain Beelzebub. The speech and action of many of these lively characters demonstrate the qualities epitomized in their names.

Action abounds. What child could resist Christian's battle with the foul fiend Apollyon, who is covered with dragon's scales and has the feet of a bear and the mouth of a lion; or Christian's escape from the dungeon in Doubting Castle where he has been imprisoned by Giant Despair? There is nothing recondite in Bunyan's allusions. Preacher that he was, Bunyan used allegory to make the abstract graphic. To bring the action home, however fantastic the struggles and scenes they are staged on familiar English country landscape. For all their allegorical import, the Slough of Despond, the Valley of the Shadow of Death, the Delectable Mountains, and Vanity Fair say as much about Bedfordshire (where Bunyan grew up) as they do about a never-never land.

The language is also rustic. Apollyon urges Christian to "give the slip" to the Lord; a footpath is termed "damned hard." Mr. Heady, a juror in the courtroom of Lord Hategood, finding Faith guilty, labels him "a sorry scrub." And the dialogue is sprinkled with homely proverbs like "a Saint abroad, and a Devil within." Such crudeness and directness sometimes earned Bunyan the scorn of the literati, to whom this Puritan preacher was an unschooled upstart. In his own day Bunyan was called an "illiterate tinker" by Charles II, but to Macaulay and other nineteenth-century critics, *The Pilgrim's Progress,* the product of a natural genius, was the sole English allegory with strong appeal. Bunyan presents allegorized theology, but his point is always within reach, not buried in weighty piles of footnotes. Bunyan delivered on his claim in "The Author's Apology for His Book":

> This book is writ in such a dialect
> As may the minds of listless men affect:
> It seems a novelty, and yet contains
> Nothing but sound and honest gospel strains.

What separates *The Pilgrim's Progress* from other pious works sanctioned for juvenile reading is that however serious the intention, the book reads as adventure story. Many English readers testify that as youths they read *The Pilgrim's Progress* entirely as literal history or simple story, unaware that it was allegory. The book does have most of the qualities associated with medieval romance: action, suspense, violence, lively characters. In "A Few Sighs from Hell; or, The Groans of a Damned Soul" (1658), Bunyan says that he was once heavily absorbed by such romances: "Alas, what is the Scripture, give me a Ballad, a Newsbook, *George* on horseback, or *Bevis of Southampton;* give me some book that teaches curious arts, that tells of old fables; but for the holy Scriptures I cared not."

Bunyan probably read about the medieval heroes Sir Bevis and Saint George in chapbooks. His grandfather was a traveling salesman who sold, among other things, chapbooks. A country boy born in a thatched cottage near Bedford, Bunyan grew up with a passion for sports, games, and fantastic stories before his religious conversion. That rather lengthy process began while Bunyan was at play on the village green. Here he heard the voice of Jesus threaten him with grievous punishment for "ungodly practices." His internal struggle against that conversion is described in *Grace Abounding to the Chief of Sinners* (1666), his spiritual autobiography.

By the time Bunyan was admitted to membership in the Bedford church in 1653 he was already married and a parent, providing for his family as a tinker. Soon after his wife died in 1656, leaving him with four children under the age of nine, he began to preach in public. Before the publication of *The Pilgrim's Progress,* he was just one of dozens of "mechanick preachers," looked down upon by the educated clergy of the Church of England from which they dissented. In 1660, one year after his second marriage, he was put into prison for unauthorized preaching. When Bunyan refused to swear that he would not preach again, he was held in the county jail of Bedford for twelve years. There he wrote and published his spiritual autobiography. A few years after his release, he was jailed again (for six months), during which time he completed *The Pilgrim's Progress.*

Six years later, when *The Pilgrim's Progress, The Second Part* (1684) was published, unauthorized sequels had already appeared and the author was no longer an obscure country preacher. Bunyan's preface warns against such sequels "that counterfeit the Pilgrim and his name [and] Seek by disguise to seem the very same." Taking note of his book's sudden fame in several countries with old and young readers alike, Bunyan promised that this sequel would prove to be "a second store of things as good, as rich, as profitable."

Critics have found Bunyan's "second store" less good and less rich. Part of the problem is that the book covers the same ground Christian already trod, this time with women and children (Christian's wife, Christiana, her companion, Mercy, and Christiana's four sons). The sequel answers the question of what happened to Christian's family whom he left behind to find the Celestial City. (Evidently their fate had troubled readers since the publication of *The Pilgrim's Progress.* Viewing a dramatization of *The Pilgrim's Progress*, one Victorian woman queried, "Are we expected to admire Christian for running away and leaving his family in the City of Destruction?") In the second part, Bunyan presents Christian's wife and family in their travels to the Celestial City. While similar adventures befall them, the pace is more leisurely, and there is considerably less drama. Whereas Christian's struggles take weeks or months at most, the family's narrative covers a lifetime as the sons grow from mere youths stealing apples to married men at book's end. As one critic put it, Christian goes on a pilgrimage, Christiana on a walking tour.

There are monsters and giants enough in the sequel, but they often seem peripheral to the story. The women are left behind while the men go off on a giant hunt. Less dramatic than the original, the sequel reads more like a cautionary fairy tale. Children are shown that taking medicine, although unpleasant, is necessary; they are taught not to steal apples; and they are warned that "nuts spoil tender teeth." Writing a family's narrative for a family audience, Bunyan turns much more didactic. A good example is the House of the Interpreter, where many parables are shown in the form of tableaux. For Christian this was a way station; Christiana's stop is prolonged since, as the Interpreter

tells his female audience: "I chose, my Darlings, to lead you into the Room where such things are, because you are Women and they are easie for you." The action is often extraneous, and the story is interrupted in several places for the children to solve riddles or recite their catechism.

The second part is more cheerful than the first and provides many nice touches. For example, Mr. Great-heart teases the boys who want to lead for jumping to the back of the line when they confront some chained lions. But the didacticism is often heavier than that. For example, when the characters discover that the odious spider is more commendable than human sinners, "this made Mercy blush, and the Boys to cover their Faces. For they all began now to understand the Riddle." What Bunyan calls the "Riddle" is nothing more than the moral—the deceptiveness of appearances. The spider seems loathsome, but man the sinner is the loathsome one. Bunyan takes extra pains to make sure the reader understands such riddles, perhaps as a concession to both his fictive and his target audiences.

However flawed the sequel might be in the eyes of modern critics, *The Pilgrim's Progress* taken as a whole met another test of Dr. Johnson's—the continuing approbation of readers, which he called the certain test of literary merit. Today, centuries after all other Puritan works recommended for children have lost their audience, Bunyan's work endures.

Johnson was right. Babies do not want to hear about babies. Ironically, thanks to Bunyan's childhood reading of adventures and fantasies, which he later forswore, his salvation allegory also stretches and stimulates a child's imagination with adventures involving giants and castles.

So identified is Bunyan solely with *The Pilgrim's Progress* that few besides scholars know of the many other works he penned, such as some deservedly neglected tracts like "A Few Sighs from Hell; or, The Groans of a Damned Soul," "Light for Them That Sit in Darkness" (1675), and "Differences in Judgment about Water-Baptism" (1673).

There is, however, one more work that gains Bunyan the title writer for children. *A Book for Boys and Girls; or, Country Rhimes for Children* (1686), the one work Bunyan intended primarily for young people, is scarcely known today. The book is nonetheless important for several reasons. It is one of the first works in England written specifically for children. Among the first books of juvenile poetry, it influenced Isaac Watts, whose *Divine Songs*

(1715) popularized religious verse for children a generation later.

Bunyan's work is also the first emblem book written for children (an emblem being a description in verse with accompanying morals or mottoes). Since Bunyan's original book was not illustrated, those verse descriptions and the accompanying moral (which Bunyan called the "comparison") had to be quite detailed:

Upon a Horse in the Mill

Horses that work i'th'Mill must hood-wink't be;
For they'l be sick or giddy, if they see.
But keep them blind enough, and they will go
That way which would a seeing Horse undo.

Comparison

Thus 'tis with those that do go *Satan's Round*,
No seeing man can live upon his ground.
Then let us count those unto sin inclin'd,
Either besides their wits, bewitch'd or blind.

(28)

Sometimes Bunyan fused the "comparison" within the verse:

Upon the Boy dull at his Book

Some boys have Wit enough to sport and play,
Who at their Books are Block-heads day by day.
Some men are arch enough at any Vice,
But Dunces in the way to Paradice.

(71)

The rhymes are sometimes forced; the scansion is often as uneven as the choice of subjects. True to the title of the book, there are many verses on natural objects (frogs, cuckoos, swine) and also objects a child would be interested in (tops, hobbyhorses, etc.). Occasionally, Bunyan gets too forced and metaphysical, as in, for example, "Upon the Sight of a Pound of Candles Falling to the Ground." In this poem Bunyan compares the candle that remains upright to Christ, and the candles that are scattered to "The bulk of God's Elect in their lapst State." This is not the easily apprehended allegory we have come to expect from Bunyan. And to modern sensibilities, at least, his subjects are sometimes vulgar (for example, "Upon a Stinking Breath" or "Upon Fly-blows").

Publishers who reprinted Bunyan's verses after his death evidently agreed that some of them were not suitable for or successful with children. In the second edition in 1701, Bunyan's verse for chil-

dren was abridged and retitled *A Book for Boys and Girls; or, Temporal Things Spiritualized.* Of the seventy-four original poems twenty-five were excised, including the two mentioned above. In the third edition (1707) woodcuts were added to the forty-nine remaining poems. Known later in the eighteenth century as *Divine Emblems,* these illustrated editions popularized Bunyan's verse through much of the nineteenth century. Today the book survives only in scholarly reprints. It is ironic that the one work Bunyan wrote for children is today known only to specialist scholars, while *The Pilgrim's Progress,* his narrative for adults, is still read by a young audience.

Some critics question whether *A Book for Boys and Girls* was meant entirely for children, despite Bunyan's clear signal in the title. Of his sixteen prefatory verses only the last two are exclusively directed at child readers. First he addresses "Boys with beards, and Girls that be / Big as old Women, wanting Gravity." But prefaces were seldom written to children before the nineteenth century. Bunyan seems conscious of a dual audience, something true of many children's writers. The publisher John Newbery, for example, in the mid-1700's directed prefaces to parents and governesses and joked about readers six feet high. Children's literature is often, of necessity, a shared literature.

But while keeping an editorial eye on the adult who might buy his verses, Bunyan honed his work for children. Besides the verses centered on everyday objects a child might encounter (lanterns, spectacles, candles, frogs), he included three alphabets, one each in black letter, roman, and italic type; a list of names for boys and girls; Roman and Arabic numerals; rhymed prayers; even a metrical version of the Ten Commandments. Bunyan's verse has been compared unfavorably with that of such seventeenth-century emblem writers as Francis Quarles and George Wither, but they wrote for adults. To compare *A Book for Boys and Girls* with late-seventeenth-century verse versions of Aesop and with Puritan works for children is more just and more revealing. Benjamin Keach's *Instructions for Children* (1664) and Henry Jessey's *A Looking Glass for Children* (1672) came out before Bunyan's book. Keach is best known today for these oft-quoted lines from a poem cautioning a young girl against vanity: "Tis pitty, such a pretty Maid, as I, should go to hell." In Bunyan's poems the child is expected to meditate on death but is never threatened with fire and brimstone. At least as polished as those of his Puritan predecessors, Bunyan's "country rhymes" are considerably less terrifying and much more creative and entertaining.

Spurred perhaps by fellow Puritan versifiers and by the appeal of *The Pilgrim's Progress* to child readers, Bunyan, in *A Book for Boys and Girls,* offered the child a miscellany. The genre of miscellany is what John Newbery secularized and capitalized on in his first publications for children. And at least the trappings of Bunyan's allegory appear in early children's books. In *The Prettiest Book for Children* (1772) the pseudonymous author Don Stephano Bunyano meets a giant named Instruction, governor of the Enchanted Castle. Georgian juvenile books are also replete with allegorical characters like Harry Heedless, Betsy Allgood, Billy Badenough, Dorothy Chatterfast, and Master Anthony Greedyguts.

According to *The Oxford Book of Children's Verse,* Bunyan's poems, along with Watts's songs, mark the beginning of writing for children at their own level. This is no less true of *The Pilgrim's Progress,* written for adults but which children have appropriated. Unlike many other Puritan authors of "improving" literature, Bunyan was able to reach an unsophisticated audience without talking down to them.

And Bunyan did this with literary discards: allegory and emblem. His were the last of the English allegory and emblem books, but they were presented in a new form—the book for children. Just as the medieval romance came to be children's fare, so did allegory and emblem, thanks to the tinker-preacher John Bunyan. In the right hands, the old literary leavings of adults can be transformed into something quite novel and rich in the garden of a child's imagination.

Selected Bibliography

WORKS OF JOHN BUNYAN

Editions of *The Pilgrim's Progress*

The Pilgrim's Progress. London: N. Ponder, 1678.

The Pilgrim's Progress. The Second Part. London: N. Ponder, 1684.

The Pilgrim's Progress. London: Elliot Stock, 1895. (Facsimile of first edition of 1678.)

Pilgrim's Progress by John Bunyan. Retold and Shortened for Modern Readers by Mary Godolphin. With illustrations by Robert Lawson. New York: Frederick A. Stokes, 1939.

The Pilgrim's Progress. Edited by J. B. Wharey and revised by Roger Sharrock. Oxford: Clarendon Press, 1960.

The Annotated Pilgrim's Progress. Edited by Warren W. Wiersbe. Chicago: Moody Press, 1980. (Wiersbe details Bunyan's abundant scriptural references.)

Pilgrim: The Story of The Pilgrim's Progress by John Bunyan. Adapted by Ronald Fuller. With illustrations by Pat Marriott. Owings Mills, Md.: Stemmer House, 1980.

Verse

A Book for Boys and Girls; or, Country Rhimes for Children. London: N. Ponder, 1686.

A Book for Boys and Girls. Edited with an introduction by John Brown. London: Elliot Stock, 1890.

———. Edited with an introduction by E. S. Buchanan. New York: American Tract Society, 1928.

———. Edited with a preface by Barry Adams. New York: Garland, 1978.

———. In *The Miscellaneous Works of John Bunyan, Vol. 6: The Poems,* edited by Graham Midgley. Oxford Text Series. Oxford: Clarendon Press, 1980. (Midgley suggests Bunyan be judged against popular poetic traditions of his day.)

———. In *Masterworks of Children's Literature: 1550-1739,* vol. 1, edited with headnotes by Francelia Butler. New York: Stonehill Publishing and Chelsea House, 1983.

Divine Emblems. Edited with a preface by Alexander Smith. London: Bickers and Son, 1867. (Revision of 1767 edition.)

Other Works

The Miscellaneous Works of John Bunyan. Edited by T. L. Underwood with the assistance of Roger Sharrock. Oxford: Clarendon Press, 1980. (Includes "A Few Sighs from Hell; or, The Groans of a Damned Soul.")

CRITICAL AND BIOGRAPHICAL STUDIES

Brown, John. *John Bunyan (1628–1688): His Life, Times and Work.* 2 vols. London: William Isbister, 1885. Revised by Frank Mott Harrison. London: Hulbert, 1928.

Coats, Robert Hay. "John Bunyan as a Writer for Children." *Westminster Review* 176: 303–307 (Sept. 1911).

Forrest, James F. and Richard Lee Greaves. *John Bunyan: A Reference Guide.* Boston: G. K. Hall, 1982.

Freeman, Rosemary. *English Emblem Books.* New York: Octagon Books, 1966. (Relates *The Pilgrim's Progress* and *A Book for Boys and Girls* to the emblem tradition.)

Furlong, Monica. *Puritan's Progress: A Study of John Bunyan.* London: Hodder and Stoughton, 1975.

Greaves, Richard L. "Bunyan Through the Centuries: Some Reflections." *English Studies* 64: 113–121 (April 1983).

Harrison, Frank Mott. "Editions of *The Pilgrim's Progress* " *The Library* 22: 73–81 (June 1941).

Hill, George B. *Boswell's Life of Johnson.* Oxford: Clarendon Press, 1934.

MacDonald, Ruth K. "The Progress of the Pilgrims in *Little Women.* " In *Proceedings of the Seventh Annual Conference of the Children's Literature Association,* edited by Priscilla A. Ord. Waco, Texas: Baylor University, 1980.

Newey, Vincent. *The Pilgrim's Progress: Critical and Historical Views.* Liverpool: Liverpool University Press, 1980.

Piozzi, Hester Lynch. *Anecdotes of the Late Samuel Johnson LL.D. During the Last Twenty Years of His Life.* Rev. ed., edited by Arthur Sherbo. London: Oxford University Press, 1974.

Sadler, Lynn Veach. *John Bunyan.* Boston: Twayne Publishers, 1979.

Sharrock, Roger. "Bunyan and the English Emblem Writers" *Review of English Studies* 21: 105–116 (April 1945).

———. *John Bunyan.* London: Hutchinson's University Library, 1954. (An authoritative biography by the most notable Bunyan scholar.)

Smith, David E. *John Bunyan in America.* Bloomington: Indiana University Press, 1966. (Invaluable on the reputation and influence of Bunyan in the United States.)

—ROBERT BATOR

FRANCES HODGSON BURNETT

1849–1924

OF THE NUMEROUS children's writers born in the middle of the nineteenth century, very few are still read by children today. Frances Hodgson Burnett is one of that successful few. Her name is often unrecognized by children, but the titles of her books are as familiar as any in children's literature. *Little Lord Fauntleroy* (1886), *The Secret Garden* (1911), and *A Little Princess* (1905) have appeared in numerous editions and also have been seen regularly on movie and television screens.

Frances Hodgson was born in 1849 in Manchester, England, the daughter of a "general furnishing ironmonger" and silversmith who prospered on the trade of the mill owners and new industrialists. Cheetham Hill was a pleasant place to live, but on the death of her father in 1853 the family moved to a poorer and less salubrious area across the river in Salford. They had to struggle to keep up standards and were to know real poverty. The reversal of fortune is a dominant theme of Frances Hodgson Burnett's writing—she never lost her interest in working people, and one aspect of her writing that distinguishes it from that of many of her contemporaries is her genuine belief in the equality of human beings, whatever their external trappings or circumstances. She had a good ear for the different ways that people talk; her interest in dialect (used most effectively by Dickon and Martha in *The Secret Garden*) stems from her early years in Lancashire.

In 1865, just after the Civil War, the family migrated to Tennessee at the rather unwise invitation of an uncle. Frances was fifteen, and it was neces-

sary for her to earn her own living. She tried everything: embroidery, music lessons, poultry keeping. When she decided to try sending a story to a magazine, her letter ended boldly: "My object is remuneration." This was to be her object throughout her long writing career. She was not primarily concerned with self-expression, but she was a born storyteller, and her stories, even when written quickly for compelling financial reasons, nearly always rise above the level of mere potboilers. Her first story appeared in *Godey's Lady's Book* in June 1868. Less than two years later, her mother died, leaving Frances, aged twenty, in charge of her two younger sisters, in an atmosphere of freedom and unconventionality far removed from the life they would have had if they had remained in Manchester. But Knoxville, Tennessee, was not large enough for Frances' ambition. She wanted her "chestnuts off a higher bough" and worked hard to be able to afford to extend her horizons.

In 1872 she returned to England and set the pattern for a transatlantic life and reputation. In all, she crossed the Atlantic thirty-three times. She married her first husband, Swan Burnett, in Tennessee in 1873. A son was born in 1874—the same year that she wrote her first children's story, "Behind the White Brick." In 1875 the family moved to Paris, where Frances supported her husband by writing, while he pursued medical studies. She wrote two stories a month for *Peterson's Magazine* and started her first novel, *That Lass o' Lowries* (1877).

If it had not been for the phenomenal success of

her first full-length children's story, *Little Lord Fauntleroy*, Frances Hodgson Burnett might well have had a secure reputation as a minor Victorian novelist, a follower of Elizabeth Gaskell. Her early adult novels were much praised. Of *That Lass*, the *Boston Transcript* wrote: "We know of no more powerful work from a woman's hand in the English language, not even excepting the best of George Eliot." An article in the July 1883 issue of the *Century* listed Burnett as one of the five novelists in America "who hold the front rank today in general estimation."

At this stage, Burnett had written very little for children—just a few stories in the children's magazine *St. Nicholas*; her success with *Little Lord Fauntleroy* totally changed her career. Though she later wrote some extremely successful adult novels, Burnett was not prepared later in life to work as hard at her craft as she had done in the early years. None of her adult books, not even her most popular one, *The Making of a Marchioness* (1901), has had an influence comparable with her best children's books.

Burnett's life was dramatic and often unhappy. She wrote faster and faster to maintain the way of life to which *Fauntleroy* had introduced her. On the surface she was extremely successful. The young girl who had picked wild grapes on the hillside in Tennessee to pay for the postage on her first stories had gone on to write one of the best-sellers of the century, admired even by Gladstone, the prime minister of England. She became a very rich and famous woman whose opinions on every subject were sought.

But again and again life was a disappointment to her: people did not behave the way she wanted them to. It was only in her books that she could make dreams come true; reality was often harsh. She married twice and yet could write, "I have never had a husband, God knows." Her older son died of tuberculosis at the age of sixteen. Her younger son's life was dogged by his identification with Fauntleroy. As late as 1914, when he met his mother on the quay at New York on her final Atlantic crossing, the newspaper headlines proclaimed "Lord Fauntleroy Greets Mama." A lawsuit toward the end of her life—brought by her nephew's wife for slander—finally shattered Burnett's public image. Of her last novel, *Robin* (1922), the *Times Literary Supplement* wrote: "Lush sentiments flow from her pen with a sweetness that suggests syrup rather than plain ink. This is a pity, because once upon a time Mrs Burnett could write

differently." She could indeed, and her best books survive, not merely as footnotes in the history of children's literature, but as good stories that will always find readers. She died in 1924.

Burnett published more than twenty children's books (some of them collections of short stories), but they are not all worth looking at in detail. *Little Lord Fauntleroy* is almost as important as social history as it is in the history of children's literature. It is impossible to read the book today without preconceived ideas. The word "Fauntleroy" has entered the language, suggesting a mollycoddled namby-pamby, a mother's darling, an overdressed prig, a sissy, a child too good to be true. These associations stem partly from Reginald Birch's illustrations. Fauntleroy's true character is distorted by the trappings of the part—the fancy clothes he wears, and the hair that curls to his shoulders (sweet little girl actresses usually played the role on the stage). Much of the antagonism to Fauntleroy came from men who as boys had been forced to wear Fauntleroy suits—their mothers had hoped that those suits would encourage in them the virtues of Fauntleroy himself.

Cedric Fauntleroy is virtuous, certainly, but not a sissy. He is brave, thoughtful, enterprising, and unaffected. Apart from his inability to spell, he has no apparent faults, which makes it all the more amazing that he comes across as a real boy and in no way simply the embodiment of an ideal. The relationship with his mother, his "Dearest," is overidealized, and the author's comments are often sentimental ("Such a beautiful, innocent little fellow he was too, with his brave, trustful face"). But considering the tone of much writing for children of this period, it is surprising that there is not more of this sort of sentimentalizing. Moreover, Cedric has to be exceptionally charming to make the plot work and to convert his grandfather.

Little Lord Fauntleroy was first published as a book in October 1886, after serialization in *St. Nicholas* magazine. "Mrs. Burnett's juvenile starts with a tremendous rush," her publisher, Charles Scribner, reported. Scribners had to reprint before publication, although the first edition was ten thousand. The reviews were ecstatic, and many of them were far more saccharine than the book itself. In the *Bookbuyer*, Louisa May Alcott commented that she considered writing for children "a peculiarly fitting task for women" and rejoiced to see "our best and brightest consecrating their talents to this useful and beautiful work."

The story of the reformation of an arrogant aristocrat by his democratic young grandson has obviously appeal. All over America, men, women, and children followed Cedric's adventures. One social historian commented, "It does not do to say merely that *Little Lord Fauntleroy* was a great success. It caused a public delirium of joy." Sales soared higher and higher after Burnett's triumphant dramatization of the book in 1888, which was presented throughout Europe, England, and America. *Little Lord Fauntleroy* became one of the biggest sellers of all time, with sales of the English-language editions calculated at well over a million. It was translated into more than a dozen languages. In 1886 it shared the American best-seller list with H. Rider Haggard's *King Solomon's Mines* and Tolstoy's *War and Peace*. Thousands of reluctant small boys were forced into black velvet suits with lace collars.

Burnett had not designed the clothes; children wore them before Fauntleroy. A women's magazine in 1885 (a few months before the story began appearing in *St. Nicholas*) described a style for "a little fellow of seven": a velvet suit with a Vandyke collar; but the suggested color was sapphire blue with a sash of pale pink, which makes Cedric's black and white seem almost austere. But certainly the clothes became identified with the book and the play, and lots of boys hated them all. They preferred to dress like Tom Sawyer or Huckleberry Finn. Girls, however, loved *Fauntleroy*, and so did their parents.

The book's appeal was cleverly double-edged. Readers could enjoy the descriptions of the aristocratic way of life, while sharing Cedric's belief that his friends the grocer and the bootblack were every bit as important as earls. The story's appeal is, of course, the universal one of "rags to riches." The critic Marghanita Laski has described it as "the best version of the Cinderella story in modern idiom that exists." When a rival claimant turns up, Cedric shows that his own character is undeviating and that he will be exactly the same person whether he is an earl or a partner in Hobbs's grocery business. The irony, of course, is that whatever happens he *is* the earl's grandson, for all his splendidly American attitudes. The coincidence of Dick, the bootblack, recognizing the rival claimant's mother as his own sister-in-law is a preposterous one, but by then the reader's belief has been happily suspended. *Little Lord Fauntleroy* is a splendid yarn. The sentimentalizing that readers find nauseating is a minor feature of the book; the story itself is still acceptable to today's taste.

Burnett had started her writing career as a realist.

With *Fauntleroy* she became identified as a romantic. Romanticism was in the ascendant in those years, and she had stepped into line. Andrew Lang, an influential critic, preferred Rider Haggard and Anthony Hope to Thomas Hardy, and Robert Louis Stevenson to Dostoevsky. Thousands of readers on both sides of the Atlantic agreed with him.

In an interview in the February 1886 issue of the *Bookbuyer*, Burnett defined the way she saw the difference between writing for adults and writing for children (although many adult readers made no such distinction and read *Fauntleroy* with relish). She told her interviewer that her early novels had left her "completely exhausted. . . . She had entered into the joys and griefs of the men and women she pictured; she had shared their anxieties, suffered and endured all the trials they had passed through; she was possessed by sensations quite beyond her power to govern." *Fauntleroy*, on the other hand, was easy, "a pleasure to write." It was not surprising that she tried to repeat her success.

Editha's Burglar, which had been written before *Fauntleroy* and had first been published as a story in *St. Nicholas*, appeared both as a play in Boston and in book form in 1888. Editha is as charming as Fauntleroy. When she finds a burglar in the house, she asks him please to burgle as quietly as he can so that he doesn't disturb Mama. Laski considers the burglar's falling in with Editha as not unreasonable. "It was not, after all, as if Mrs. Burnett had made Editha convert the burglar and persuade him to leave his swag behind, a temptation that few Victorian writers could have resisted."

In 1888, *Editha's Burglar* appeared in one volume with another rather short story, *Sara Crewe; or, What Happened at Miss Minchin's*, which had already appeared separately in 1887. To write *Sara Crewe*, Burnett drew on some of her experiences at school in Manchester, but set the scene in London. Sara, a rich, indulged pupil at Miss Minchin's, is reduced to an attic and the life of a small drudge when her father dies, apparently bankrupt. What saves Sara from despair is her imagination. "You can make a story out of anything," as Burnett knew. The moral is the same as that of *Fauntleroy*: true nobility lies not in outward trappings but within oneself.

The transformation of the story into the full-scale novel *A Little Princess* (published in 1905, eighteen years after *Sara Crewe* first appeared in *St. Nicholas*) is an interesting one. In 1902 Burnett turned *Sara Crewe* into a play. It was produced in England under the title *A Little Unfairy Princess* and in New

York as *A Little Princess* and was a great success. E. L. Burlingame, the famous editor at Scribners, then asked the writer to produce a new longer version of the story, incorporating the extra material she had used in the play.

When Burnett was writing the novel, she found that "there were actually pages and pages of things which had happened that had never been put into the play." It is a tribute to the richness of Frances Hodgson Burnett's imagination that the final book is so well balanced; there is no trace of "padding." In the preface she wrote: "I do not know whether many people realise how much more than is ever written there really is in a story. . . . Stories are something like letters. When a letter is written, how often one remembers things omitted and says, 'Ah, why did I not tell that?'" This comparison indicates one of Burnett's strengths. She makes the reader believe that these incidents, however extraordinary, however full of coincidences, really happened. She is recounting, naturally and with consummate skill, what seems like a slice of life. There is always much more behind the story than the mere words on the page; and the child reader, finishing the story, with all the ends perfectly tied up, has the feeling that life itself is richer and more full of possibilities than he had ever imagined.

Laski draws our attention to another virtue of Burnett's best stories. They can be appreciated, at different levels, for a surprising range of years. They can be listened to at about six; they can still be enjoyed by the lone reader at twelve or thirteen, at a time when the child has the ability to realize, for instance, that Sara Crewe's triumph is as much moral as accidental. "Most children's books are simple things, to be fully understood and enjoyed at one stage of development only. *A Little Princess* is something more."

Most of Burnett's stories have an autobiographical interest; but many of them (though the books appear to be for children, with large, clear type and illustrations) are actually stories *about* children rather than *for* children. *The Captain's Youngest*, title story of a collection published in England in 1894, is a particularly vivid example. Its hero is a boy of nine; his adventures in saving his sister from the traditional "fate worse than death" (puzzling to child readers) result in his own death. Deathbed scenes are not uncommon in Victorian children's literature, but the whole feeling of this story is counter to Burnett's usual practice. There are

indeed plenty of offstage deaths of parents (none of the children still have two parents), but she never wrote of the death of a child in her children's books. *In the Closed Room* (1904) is also about children but not for them; of the two children playing at a dolls' tea party in the story, one is a ghost and the other is dead by the end of the book. This was a story written out of anguished memories of her own son's death—a book perhaps for other bereaved parents. Burnett never used the death of a child to move children to tears, the way that, for instance, her friend Kate Douglas Wiggin had done in *The Birds' Christmas Carol* (1887).

Burnett's autobiography, *The One I Knew the Best of All* (1893), was originally intended as a children's book, and superficially it looks like one. She told Burlingame at Scribners that the book had turned out rather differently from the way she had expected: "It is only mature and thinking people who will get the real flavor of the humor and pathos of it. . . . It belongs to the grown-ups—especially those who are interested in children as a sort of psychological study." She subtitled the book *A Memory of the Mind of a Child*. She once defined the aim of her writing: "What we all want is more . . . life, love, hope—and an assurance that they are true. With the best that was in me I have tried to write more happiness into the world." This passage sounds rather anodyne: what makes Burnett a better writer than this extract would suggest is not just her narrative power and her ability to choose the telling detail, but also that special knowledge she always seemed to have of "the mind of a child." In her best books she always makes her characters earn their happy endings.

Reviewing *The Captain's Youngest*, the *Dial*, while conceding that "Mrs. Burnett's graceful style makes everything from her pen agreeable reading," objected to the picture of domestic misery, "which no child should be able to understand; its termination is entirely too tragic." *The Two Little Pilgrims' Progress* (1895), on the other hand, although full of incidental pleasures, can be criticized justly for exactly the opposite reason. The two small pilgrims have things too easy, after the initial rigors of their life with Aunt Matilda. All the hardships are in the compelling beginning—as the children plan, work, and save before running away to the Chicago World's Fair, which they see as the City Beautiful. After that, the lot of the children is too good to be true. The weakest of her full-length children's books, it is a fairy story without real savor. But it is also a celebration of kindness and highlights the fact that everyone—however poor—has something to give to somebody else. It underscores Burnett's belief that human beings can do anything if they try hard enough. Burnett herself called the book a fairy story. "And why not?" she asked. "Fairy stories are happening every day."

All Burnett's stories are fairy tales in a sense. *The Lost Prince* (1915), her last major children's book, is the most romantic of all. A story of Ruritanian politics, it is quite unlike any of Burnett's other books except that once again its basic theme is a reversal of fortune. Its roots lie in the writer's travels in central Europe in the winter of 1913–1914, but also can be traced as far back as 1887, when Burnett came into contact in Florence with young Prince Alexander of Serbia, who was then studying with the same tutors as the Burnett boys. A conversation with her old friend Eleanor Calhoun (an American actress who had become Princess Hreblianovich Lazarowich) about the history of Serbia first gave Burnett the idea for the story. But there was also an interesting seed in an incident in Vienna in October 1913, when a friend bought her a photograph of Van Dyck's portrait of Prince Ruprecht von der Pfaltz of Bavaria, and she saw an uncanny resemblance to her own dead son Lionel: "I found myself looking at my own boy's face in a picture painted three hundred years ago." In a letter the following summer, when she was in the middle of writing *The Lost Prince*, she described it as having in it "the fine, high spirit of a kingly lad —running through centuries like a thread of light and shining over in the Marylebone Road and all sorts of grubby places." The book is much tougher and better than this would suggest. There are some extremely tense and exciting moments in the story, as Marco Loristan, twelve-year-old Samavian exile, travels across Europe with a crippled English boy known as the Rat. Marco has been instructed by his father to alert the Secret Party that the moment has come to reclaim the throne. As the *Oxford Companion to Children's Literature* puts it: "The book contains some of Mrs. Burnett's best character drawing, but the excitement is diminished by her inability to keep from the reader, even in the very first pages, the fact that Marco and his father are themselves the missing royal family." When, on almost the final page, Marco approaches the newly restored monarch, it is not the surprise it should be. But it is a good story all the same, and many children, even in an intensely democratic age, can re-spond to its appeal, for the lost prince and his father are not interested in power or wealth, but in justice, peace, and freedom for everyone.

The Secret Garden is concerned almost entirely with the development and interaction of three children. It has its own dramas and excitements, and the atmosphere of the huge house and garden is romantic and mysterious. As Roger Lancelyn Green put it in his *Tellers of Tales*: "With great skill she has made the story gripping and compelling without her usual melodramatic plot."

It is generally accepted that Burnett's inspiration for *The Secret Garden* came mainly from the rose garden at Maytham Hall in Kent, which she rented for many years. But works of imagination often have many sources, and Philippa Pearce has pointed out convincingly that there are "uncanny resemblances" to the themes and descriptions in her most famous book in a passage in Burnett's autobiography, written eighteen years earlier and referring to a walled garden she had known as a child in Salford:

One or two of the large vacant houses—perhaps all of them—had once had large gardens behind them. Years of neglect and factory chimney smoke had transformed them into cindery deserts, where weeds grew rank in patches where anything could grow at all. . . . Usually the doors of entrance were kept locked, and there was no opportunity of even looking in from the outside. This fact the Small Person had always found enchanting, because it suggested mystery. So long as one could not cross the threshold, one could imagine all sorts of beautifulness hidden by the walls too high to be looked over, the little green door which was never unclosed. It made her wish so that she could get inside. For years she never did so, but at last there came a rumour that the big houses were to be pulled down . . . and then it was whispered about among the Square children that the little green door in the high wall which surrounded the garden behind the big house . . . had been opened and some bold spirit had walked in and even walked out again. And so there arrived an eventful hour when the Small Person herself went in—passed through the enchanted door and stood within the mysterious precincts looking around her. If she had seen it as it really was she would probably have turned and fled. But she did not. . . . She saw a Garden. At least it had been a Garden *once*—and there were the high brick walls around it—and the little door so long unopened, and *once* there had been flowers and trees in it; they had really bloomed and been green and shady there, though it was so long ago. So she wandered about in a dream—"pretending." That changed it all. . . . She bent down and looked the weeds in their faces and touched them tenderly. "Suppose they were roses and pansies and lilies and violets," she said to herself. "How beautiful it would be!"

(*The One I Knew the Best*, chapter 14)

There is nothing sentimental about *The Secret Garden*. It is set far away from Kent in Brontë country—on the Yorkshire moors. Laski has drawn attention to the fact that the beginning of *The Little Princess,* "up to the point where the schoolmistress learns that the father has no money, is the same as that of Charlotte Brontë's unfinished fragment, *Emma.*" The arrival of Mary Lennox at Misselthwaite is strongly reminiscent of Jane Eyre's arrival at Thornfield, and there are other points of resemblance between the two books. Burnett in fact did not know Yorkshire well, and her setting owes more to her reading of the Brontës' books than to real life. She stayed with Lord Crewe at Fryston Hall in 1895, but that is her only recorded visit to the area.

The setting is important, but much more important are the children. The most original thing about the book is that its heroine and one hero are both thoroughly unattractive children. The first sentence makes it compulsive reading: "When Mary Lennox was sent to Misselthwaite Manor to live with her uncle, everybody said she was the most disagreeable-looking child ever seen." Colin is a hysterical hypochondriac, someone who imagines himself into a state of illness. It is the entirely convincing transformation of these two unhappy children that gives the story its tremendous appeal.

Other Victorian writers had made deprived children behave quite inappropriately, but Burnett's instinct has since been confirmed by child psychologists. A child denied love does behave as Mary behaved. But *The Secret Garden* is far more than a parable or demonstration of child behavior. With Burnett the story always came first, and she was far too good a writer to spoil it with propaganda. Only at the beginning of chapter 27 does she lapse, with explicit explanations of her symbolism and a bald definition of what the rest of the book conveys so subtly: "To let a sad thought or a bad one get into your mind is as dangerous as letting a scarlet fever germ get into your body."

It is interesting to see from Burnett's few corrections in the manuscript of the novel (now in the New York Public Library) that several times her alterations are made specifically to achieve a subtler effect. For instance, when Mary asks Dickon whether he thinks Mr. Craven wishes that Colin were dead, Dickon says: "No, but he wishes he'd never been born. Mother, she says that's the worst thing on earth for a child. She says us has all got to be loved an' have fresh air or us can't be healthy." The last sentence was replaced by "Them as is not wanted scarce ever thrives."

The manuscript confirms the sureness of Burnett's touch. Every small change and second thought is an improvement. When Martha first speaks, she originally said: "Mrs. Medlock gave me the place out o' kindness *when mother died.* . . ." It is hard to imagine the book without Mrs. Sowerby. Burnett's handwriting becomes very hurried and careless over Colin and Mary's conversations. As Mary's words tumble over each other, it is clear that Burnett can hardly get them down on paper fast enough. Another interesting change is that when Burnett began writing the manuscript, Dickon was simply Dick—the name of the bootblack in *Fauntleroy*. But the writer eventually decided—after about forty pages—that such an unusual character needed a more unusual name. When Colin first hears it he says, "What a queer name," and it is obviously appropriate that that should be so. But much the most important change was in the title of the book. *The Secret Garden* was first called *Mistress Mary*, surely a title that would have hindered rather than helped. In April 1910, when the story had been taken for serialization by *The American Magazine* ("This is the first instance I have ever known of a child's story being published in an adult's magazine," Burnett wrote), the author was still calling it *Mistress Mary*; there is no record of how it came to have the familiar title.

The Secret Garden has aroused some speculation about its psychological sources. One child psychiatrist (attached to Mount Zion Hospital in San Francisco) made a study of many women's feelings about *The Secret Garden* and identified the silence and secrecy surrounding the garden with the suppression of vaginal awareness—turning Mary's discovery of the keyhole into a masturbatory fantasy. John Rowe Townsend's explanation of the book's power in his *Written for Children* is convincing:

There is something about *The Secret Garden* that has a powerful effect on children's imaginations: something to do with their longing for real, important, adult-level achievement. Self-reliance and cooperation in *making* something are the virtues that Mary and Colin painfully attain.

They heal themselves. It is very much a book of the twentieth century. Far from encouraging the attitudes instilled in Frances Hodgson as a child ("Speak when you're spoken to, come when you're called"), it suggests that children should have faith in themselves, that they should listen not to their elders and betters but to their own hearts and consciences. This is, of course, a suggestion of enormous appeal to children. *The Secret Garden* is undoubtedly Burnett's finest book. Marghanita Laski has called it "the most satisfying children's book I know." Countless people share this view.

Selected Bibliography

WORKS OF FRANCES HODGSON BURNETT

Little Lord Fauntleroy. With illustrations by Reginald Marsh. New York: Charles Scribner's Sons, 1886; London: Warne, 1886.

Sara Crewe; or, What Happened at Miss Minchin's. London: T. Fisher Unwin, 1887; New York: Charles Scribner's Sons, 1888.

Editha's Burglar. Boston: Jordan Marsh, 1888.

Editha's Burglar and Sara Crewe. London: Warne, 1888.

The Two Little Pilgrims' Progress: A Story of the City Beautiful. New York: Charles Scribner's Sons, 1895; London: Warne, 1895.

A Little Princess, Being the Whole Story of Sara Crewe Now Told for the First Time. New York: Charles Scribner's Sons, 1905; London: Warne, 1905.

The Secret Garden. With illustrations by Charles Robinson. New York: Frederick A. Stokes, 1911; London: William Heinemann, 1911.

The Lost Prince. New York: Century, 1915; London: Hodder and Stoughton, 1915.

CRITICAL AND BIOGRAPHICAL STUDIES

Burnett, Vivian. *The Romantick Lady*. New York: Charles Scribner's Sons, 1927.

Carpenter, Humphrey, and Mari Prichard. *Oxford Companion to Children's Literature*. Oxford: Oxford University Press, 1984.

Green, Roger Lancelyn. *Tellers of Tales*. Rev. ed. London: Edmund Ward, 1965.

Kirkpatrick, D. L., ed. *Twentieth-Century Children's Writers*. London: Macmillan, 1978.

Laski, Marghanita. *Mrs. Ewing, Mrs. Molesworth and Mrs. Hodgson Burnett*. London: A Barker, 1950.

Pearce, Philippa. "The Writer's View of Childhood." Lecture to the Library Association, Scarborough, England, 13 September 1960.

Thwaite, Ann. *Waiting for the Party: The Life of Frances Hodgson Burnett*. New York and London: Charles Scribner's Sons, 1974.

Townsend, John Rowe. *Written for Children*. Rev. ed. Philadelphia: J. B. Lippincott, 1979.

—ANN THWAITE

VIRGINIA LEE BURTON

1909–1968

DURING A TWENTY-FIVE-YEAR period from 1937 to 1962, Virginia Lee Burton wrote, designed, and illustrated seven picture books for children and illustrated five books by other authors. Successful stories depend on a strong plot; good character development; and effective setting, style, and theme. The best picture books reflect an integration of text and illustration. Burton incorporated these elements in her work, infusing her plots, characters, and pictures with a zesty and irrepressible humor.

Burton's life sheds light on her development as a writer and offers insight into the subjects and style of her books. Jinnee, as her family and friends called her, lived her first seven years in Newton Center, Massachusetts. Her mother was English, and taught family and friends the folk songs and folk dances of her homeland. She was both poet and musician. Burton's father was the dean of students at the Massachusetts Institute of Technology. When Burton was a teenager, the family moved from the Boston area to California. While a junior in high school, she won a state scholarship to the California School of Arts in San Francisco. She also studied ballet briefly in San Francisco, but gave it up when she returned to Boston with her father in 1928. For the next two years she taught art at Burroughs Newsboys Foundation and at the YMCA and worked as a sketcher for the *Boston Transcript*. At age twenty-one she enrolled in an art course at Boston Museum School and soon married her sculpture teacher, George Demetrios. To-gether they settled in the countryside near Gloucester, some twenty-five miles northeast of Boston, after moving their house away from the noise and traffic of Route 127 to a grassy knoll inland from Folly Cove. This episode provided the inspiration for her award-winning story *The Little House* (1942). (The Cape Ann region of Massachusetts would form the unnamed locale of four of Burton's books.)

Burton not only worked on children's books, but from 1939 to 1941 she also taught a design class in her barn studio. An outgrowth of that class was the incorporation of the Folly Cove Designers. These craftsmen worked individually, but they gathered monthly to critique each other's work and to select designs for block-printing fabrics for dresses and household uses. As a master craftsman and teacher, Burton maintained the high standards in illustrating her books that she espoused in her classes.

Burton approached her books for children with an artist's eye, making the words suit the design of the double-page spread. Her illustrations undulate across the adjoining pages of an open picture book or balance each other visually, working as a duet. The text is integrated with the overall design; lines of type are often arranged symmetrically to form a pleasing visual pattern. "Whenever I can substitute picture for word I do," she once told her editor, Grace A. Hogarth. Burton completed the illustrations for her stories before she wrote the text, since the words proved the more difficult. While this working method allowed her to rework the text to fit the illustrations, it sometimes weakened the story because of incomplete sentence structure and a poor choice of words.

Her first two books, *Choo Choo: Story of a Little Engine Who Ran Away* (1937) and *Mike Mulligan and His Steam Shovel* (1939), were dedicated to her young sons, Aris and Michael. Burton showed the rough dummies of the stories to them prior to sending them to her editor. In *Choo Choo* the unadorned and straightforward plot follows a locomotive engine who is bored by a circumscribed life on designated tracks and so ventures into the unknown.

Choo Choo's prototype was an engine on the Gloucester branch of the Boston and Maine Railroad. By the time coffee-drinking Engineer Jim, Fireman Oley, and Conductor Archibald realize that the young engine is missing, Choo Choo is frolicking far away. Engineer Jim rescues the little engine, which now lacks fuel and is lost among brambles in the darkness. Ultimately, the youngster concludes that running away "isn't much fun" and he reverts to hauling people and freight contentedly. The bold strokes of the black crayon Burton uses to picture the locomotive's antics serve the plot in communicating size and speed. Speed is obvious as the locomotive hilariously causes a pile-up of automobiles and jumps the drawbridge, losing the tender. Pattern as a design element is used effectively in the railroad-track ties. But in this book, as with others, the text is sacrificed to the design. Half sentences (such as "All Shiny and Black") fill the designated length of a line, but communicate poorly. Text arranged as curving railroad tracks on two pages contributes to the design. The initial illustration exuding Choo Choo's pride and purpose contrasts clearly with the closing harsh design of the exhausted adventurer.

Burton's second book, *Mike Mulligan and His Steam Shovel*, continues to number among the most popular children's books written in the twentieth century. In this full-color book, the actions of the incredulous people and the comic situations provide the subjects for Burton's humorous illustrations. The imaginative and action-filled plot concerns a steam shovel that digs the hole for a new town hall. Townspeople of all ages peer into the deep hole, perplexed at how the machine will emerge. A little boy in green overalls points out the absurdity of digging a hole without a plan to get out. It was Burton's neighbor's child, Dickie Birkenbush, who suggested the ingenious twist—the steam shovel converts to a furnace. The relationship of the operator and the personified female steam shovel, Mary Anne, is one of mutual adoration and respect. Burton wanted to teach as well as to entertain. She used her son's toy steam shovel as one model, and also made sketches of real shovels in action to check the accuracy of details in her illustrations. Burton diagrams and reviews Mary Anne's achievements. As with Burton's other machine characters, Mary Anne exhibits very human attributes and a unique personality. Despite lack of dialogue, she communicates with facial expressions, as her machine parts resemble features of the human face, but she remains mute.

Calico the Wonder Horse; or, The Saga of Stewy Stinker (1941), the third Burton book, is a departure from her previous machine-oriented stories. The action is as complex as the title—cowboys chase "the Bad Men," a stagecoach rolls down a narrow mountain road, and cattle stampede, all at a rollicking comic-book pace. *Calico* has the funniest of the Burton texts. A cow pony, Calico, and a cowpuncher, Hank, work together rounding up cattle and ultimately face Stewy Stinker and his four Bad Men. As in every Burton tale, the ending is pleasant. Though the gang cause trouble throughout the story they are ultimately converted to do good deeds. At the conclusion of the story they shake hands with the Cactus County sheriff's posse and promise to behave.

Her purpose in creating *Calico* was purportedly to woo her young sons and their friends away from comic books. Illustrations for the fast action of cowboy Hank and the gang of Bad Men appear horizontally in three or four frames. Reviewers greeted the book as innovative. *The Booklist* reviewer described it as "a western for young readers with a taste for 'the funnies.'" However, the book did not inspire a trend for illustrators; it cost ten times the price and lacked the appeal of the garish comic books.

The two editions of *Calico*, one published in 1941 and the other a decade later, support Burton's contention that she preferred illustrating to writing. While Burton reworked each illustration for the 1951 edition, she left the original text intact. The new line drawings convey even more action, while the text remains the same at the bottom of each frame.

The sixth annual Caldecott Medal went to Burton's fourth book, *The Little House*, in 1943. The book was dedicated to Burton's husband. In a slow-moving, descriptive plot, a little house experiences daily and seasonal cycles. The fifth generation of occupants feel impinged upon by city growth and by urban blight. The great-great-granddaughter of the original owner transports the house from what could be Boston to the countryside, where it remains to enjoy the seasons once again.

Its total design from cover to cover reflects the principles of design important to Burton—color, line, and pattern. Colors are appropriate to the season and mood. While the house remains static, the surrounding countryside changes from winter snow to summer green. While most of the story inspires a bright-yellow sun and a sky-blue background, the brown and black edifices convey the bleakness of city decay. The near-square format widens from nine to eighteen inches when the book opens, and Burton changed the design accordingly. Repeated in the jacket, the front cover introduces the house, set between two apple trees, with twelve daisy-like flowers and a winking sun as part of a circular design. Both title page and dedication page repeat the subject of house and daisies. Similarly, the back cover and jacket repeats a circle, filled with a smiling, satisfied sun. The endpapers have a horizontal pattern, appropriate for the double-page spread, following the historical progression of vehicles from horse-drawn buggy to a truck carrying a horse. Interior illustrations match the text consistently and utilize an appropriate and varying amount of space. In the city scenes, most of the page is illustrated, with the elevated train and tall buildings, similar to Boston, overwhelming the little house. Pattern emerges also in the embellishments to the text, such as robins, fall leaves, and daisies.

Published while the United States was at war with Germany and Japan, this pastoral ending offers hope at a time when peace was threatened. In her Caldecott Medal acceptance speech Burton commented on the importance of illustrations in picture books and school books, rather than on story development. However, the text of *The Little House* was considered strong enough to be printed without the illustrations in at least one anthology of children's literature. Edna Johnson, Evelyn R. Sickels, and Frances Clarke Sayers selected the text of *The Little House* for the third revised edition of their *Anthology of Children's Literature* (Boston: Houghton Mifflin, 1959).

Burton's fifth book, *Katy and the Big Snow* (1943), is about a machine heroine in a snowstorm. Informative and plodding, the plot seems appropri-

ate to a plow moving rather slowly in deep snow. In contrast to the steam shovel in *Mike Mulligan*, the driverless red crawler tractor, Katy, succeeds singlehandedly. The plot is simple, for Katy has little to do until a ten-inch snowstorm with deep drifts challenges her to dig out the town of Geoppolis (modeled on Gloucester). Dialogue is sparse. Katy merely issues the invitation "Follow me" and six times clears the way for city vehicles.

With informative labels and detailed drawings placed on page borders, Burton provides additional information—an explanation of horsepower, a display of tractor accessories, varied tractor maneuvers, an array of department equipment, and several city buildings. The book design is consistent, from the front jacket with its border of telephone poles emerging from a snowdrift and the title page with "K.T." intently plowing to the endpapers showing Katy immersed in snow.

High-minded purpose dominates *Maybelle, the Cable Car* (1952), overwhelming the good features of the book. The dedication of the book to the people of San Francisco and especially to Mrs. Hans Klussman documents the impetus for the book. The cable cars were threatened with extinction, and it was Mrs. Klussman who led the campaign to retain this colorful aspect of San Francisco. On one trip to visit her mother in California, Burton sketched the San Francisco vistas and the cable cars. In the resulting book, the contrived plot pits Maybelle against Big Bill, the bus, who has difficulty in driving down the slippery hill. Details about cable car companies, routes, and mechanical parts and functions are interspersed with panoramic views of the city. There is no character development, but rather character change, with the bully Bill suddenly for no stated reason accepting the cable car. The attempt at suspense in the anticipation of the election results is unsuccessful, and the text, generally adds little to the pictures. To some extent, Burton's illustrations of San Francisco landmarks redeem *Maybelle*. The Golden Gate Bridge, City Hall, and the Ferry Building at the end of Market Street are easily recognizable. Streets such as Sutter, Post, and Geary are in proper parallel order. No longer in print, *Maybelle, the Cable Car* remains a period piece.

In addition to her own seven books as author and artist, Burton illustrated five others. Arna Bontemps was so pleased with the irrepressible humorous illustrations for *Sad Faced Boy* (1937), published the same year as *Choo Choo*, that he asked the Houghton Mifflin editor to commission Burton once again for *Fast Sooner Hound* (1942). She made single drawings, rather than double-page spreads, for Leigh Peck's book *Don Coyote* (1942). In 1949 two more books illustrated by Burton appeared: *The Emperor's New Clothes*, retold by her from Hans Christian Andersen, and *Song of Robin Hood*. The dedication page of the former reveals why she chose it: "With appreciation to my father, who shared his enjoyment of this story with his children." In the story, the crooks' ruse in pretending to weave clothing that could be seen only by those fit to hold high positions is successfully challenged by a little child. Burton's text follows Andersen's, which in turn was based on a Spanish folktale, but much of the subtlety and description intended for adults is absent. She keeps the emperor modest by adding a belt to the otherwise naked body.

Her most ambitious project up to that time was *Song of Robin Hood*, a 128-page book with ballads and verses selected and edited by Anne Malcolmson and then designed and illustrated by Burton. The book, at eleven and one-half inches, is twice as tall as *Mike Mulligan* and *The Little House*, but the illustrations are small, detailed, and decorative. In the preface Burton describes how she designed the volume of five hundred verses. This labor of love necessitated three years of research into English flora and fauna of the Robin Hood era, and meticulous drawings. She even identified the plants and animals drawn for the eighteen ballads, making comparisons between those from England and New England in her notations. Drawing with pen and ink and using scratchboard, she created illustrations that were reproduced in the same minute size. The publication was acclaimed as a Caldecott Honor Book.

Her last book, *Life Story: The Story of Life on Our Earth from Its Beginning Up to Now* (1962), was the most ambitious of her own seven books. She gleaned background information from six years of research in natural history museums and scientific textbooks and then condensed it to a seventy-two-page picture book for children and young adults. Thirty-five full-color illustrations chronicle the earth's evolution. Burton conceived a dramatic presentation for depicting the evolutionary process— she used the device of a stage with a proscenium arch and painted scenes for five acts. Young children lack the ability to conceive of eons of time, but in the gesture of turning the pages they gain a sense of the passage of time, for example how relatively recently prehistoric mankind appeared, presented in Act 4, Scene 1. A narrator describes the occurrences in each scene, but there is no dialogue. Passage of time is conveyed in part by devices such as calendars, clocks, and lengthening shadows. In Act 5 Burton addresses autobiographically the twenty-five years since her family moved their little house to the country. These contemporary scenes bring the child reader from the seeming fantastic to the familiar.

While some passages are poetic, her relentless use of "the" to begin sentences dulls the writing. In this book, too, the lines of type are arranged symmetrically to form a pleasing visual pattern. Like her earlier books, the design encompasses the dust jacket, cover, endpapers, title page, and interior. Even the illustration on the back of the dust jacket is consistent, depicting a smiling sun.

After *Life Story* was completed, Burton continued to work on a book, "Design—and How!" It represented the culmination of twenty-five years of teaching and practicing her principles of design. However, she succumbed to lung cancer at the age of 59 in 1968, and her final book remains unfinished and unpublished.

One or another of Burton's books invariably appears on lists of recommended picture books for the young on school and public library lists. In the mid-1980's, the Children's Literature Association, an organization encouraging the serious study of the subject, selected *The Little House*, in the publication *Touchstones*, as one of their distinguished children's books. Both *The Little House* and *Maybelle* were included in American Institute of Graphic Arts exhibits to recognize excellence in graphic design.

Burton remains a significant author-illustrator of picture books for the young child worldwide, even a half-century after publication. Five of her seven books remain in print today. (The exceptions are *Calico* and *Maybelle*.) British editions were published for *Calico*, *Choo Choo*, *Katy*, *Life Story*, *The Little House*, and *Mike Mulligan*, while the Japanese have published all seven. *The Little House* was published in ten languages between 1944 and 1973: Afrikaans, British, Danish, Dutch, French, German, Japanese, Norwegian, Portuguese, and Spanish. Four Scandinavian editors from Denmark, Finland, Norway, and Sweden also chose *The Little House* and *Mike Mulligan* for an eight-volume co-production for children entitled *Barndomslandet*. The Burton edition of *The Emperor's New Clothes* was published in Zulu and Afrikaans.

Burton's manuscripts and illustrations are distributed among several special collections. Burton presented the *Maybelle* illustrations to the San Francisco Public Library in 1967, the *Katy* originals to the Gloucester Public Library, and the *Song of Robin Hood* ink drawings to the Boston Public Library. Her sons donated *The Little House* originals to the Kerlan Collection at the University of Minnesota and the remaining materials to the University of Oregon.

Burton's greatest contributions to American children's literature are her attention to total book design, to engaging story, and to overt humor. Her roles as designer and mother of two sons assisted her in creating beautiful books within the reach of children's understanding.

Selected Bibliography

WORKS WRITTEN AND ILLUSTRATED BY VIRGINIA LEE BURTON

Choo Choo: Story of a Little Engine Who Ran Away. Boston: Houghton Mifflin, 1937.

Mike Mulligan and His Steam Shovel. Boston: Houghton Mifflin, 1939.

Calico the Wonder Horse; or, The Saga of Stewy Stinker. Boston: Houghton Mifflin, 1941. Rev. ed. Boston: Houghton Mifflin: 1951.

The Little House. Boston: Houghton Mifflin, 1942.

Katy and the Big Snow. Boston: Houghton Mifflin, 1943.

Maybelle, the Cable Car. Boston: Houghton Mifflin, 1952.

Life Story: The Story of Life on Our Earth from Its Beginning Up to Now. Boston: Houghton Mifflin, 1962.

Critical and Biographical Studies

Bader, Barbara. *American Picture Books from Noah's Ark to the Beast Within*. New York: Macmillan, 1976.

Burton, Virginia Lee. "Making Picture Books." In *Caldecott Medal Books 1938–1957*, edited by Bertha Mahoney Miller and Elinor Whitney Field. Boston: Horn Book, 1957.

Burton, Virginia. "Symphony in Comics" *Horn Book* 17: 307–311 (July 1941).

Fisher, Margery. *Who's Who in Children's Books*. New York: Holt, Rinehart and Winston, 1975.

Hogarth, Grace Allen. "Virginia Lee Burton, Creative Artist." In *Caldecott Medal Books 1938–1957*, edited by Bertha Mahoney Miller and Elinor Whitney Field. Boston: Horn Book, 1957.

Kingman, Lee. "Virginia Lee Burton." In *Twentieth Century Children's Writers*, edited by Daniel Kirkpatrick. New York: St. Martin's Press, 1978.

————. "Virginia Lee Burton's Dynamic Sense of Design" *Horn Book* 46: 449–460 (October 1970); 539–602 (December 1970). Reprinted in *Authors and Illustrators of Children's Books*, edited by Miriam Hoffman and Eva Samuels. New York: R. R. Bowker, 1972.

Kunitz, Stanley J., and Howard Haycraft. "Virginia Lee Burton." In *Junior Book of Authors*. New York: H. W. Wilson, 1951.

Ranlett, L. Felix. "Books and Two Small Boys" *Horn Book* 18: 412–416 (November 1942).

—KAREN NELSON HOYLE

LEWIS CARROLL

1832–1898

AS A RESULT of the liberating influences of Felix Summerly's *Home Treasury* series (1844), the Brothers Grimm's *German Popular Stories* (1823), such literary fairy tales as John Ruskin's *The King of the Golden River* (1851), and other similar works, fairy tales and fantasy became accepted in England by the 1860's as the special province of childhood. While didactic stories and moral tales continued as powerful modes in British children's literature, the publication of Lewis Carroll's *Alice's Adventures in Wonderland* (1865) and *Through the Looking-Glass* (1871) set children's literature free from narrowly focused didacticism in unprecedented ways and so exerted a profound and abiding influence upon its subsequent history. Lewis Carroll's *Alice* books occupy a significant place among classics for adults and children and continue to inspire provocative new critical readings.

F. J. Harvey Darton's famous assessment of the *Alice* books has been echoed by dozens of scholars and critics. Darton writes in *Children's Books in England: Five Centuries of Social Life*:

Alice. . . was more than a flare of genius. It was the spiritual volcano of children's books. . . .

It was the coming to the surface, powerfully and permanently, the first unapologetic, undocumented appearance in print, for readers who sorely needed it, of liberty of thought in children's books. . . .

[T]he *Alices* were pure invention . . . [and] led to a prodigious crop of inventions at once; and historically, in the natural course of evolution,

the 'sixties and 'seventies were the due period of ripening.

(pp. 267–269)

The *Alice* books delighted thousands of child and adult readers in the nineteenth century and inspired hosts of children's writers (Edith Nesbit, George Macdonald, and Christina Rossetti, among others); critics have remarked that these two children's fantasies also influenced such twentieth-century writers as T. S. Eliot, Vladimir Nabokov, Franz Kafka, and Samuel Beckett, as well as such children's writers as Maurice Sendak. Moreover, Carroll's books have thoroughly penetrated Western culture. Not only have serious critics given the books extensive attention; filmmakers, television producers, stage directors, advertising directors, and even pornographers turn again and again to Carroll's Alice. After Shakespeare, Carroll is the most often quoted author in English, and in the 1960's and 1970's Alice is said to have inspired rock musicians, some of whom have seen her as an early experimenter in psychedelic experience.

The significance of Carroll's *Alice* books has been analyzed from almost every conceivable perspective. Early reviewers of the works saw them primarily as nonsensical fairy tales and exuberant fun. More recent critics have viewed the books as evidence of Carroll's emotional disturbances, as expressions of his latent religious doubts, as reflections of his views on symbolic logic, as satiric treatments of restrictive Victorian conventions, as treatises on the nature of language, or as Freudian or Jungian parables of growth and child development. All of these sophisticated readings are easily sustained by Carroll's *Alice* books.

For purposes of this discussion it may be instructive to examine the place of these books in the ongoing tension between didactic forces in children's literature on the one hand and defenders of fantasy and imagination on the other. Intensely aware of this controversy and apparently amused by it, Carroll often mocks or parodies moral tales, instructional verse, and school lesson-books in order to reveal fantasy as a mode whereby children may celebrate their own joyously free anarchy. Unlike the heroes and heroines of earlier fairy tales and fantasies in English children's literature, who journey through imaginary worlds to acquire moral virtue or spiritual insight, Carroll's heroine confronts in the fantasy world some of her profoundest wishes and fears, conquers or rejects them, and so grows toward psychological and emotional maturity rather than spiritual wisdom. To some extent Carroll expresses a similar, if darker, vision in his nonsense poem *The Hunting of the Snark* (1876). Thus Carroll realizes an entirely new vision of childhood as a time when children use their imaginations and intelligence not in the service of redeeming themselves as fallen creations but as a way of protecting themselves from stifling adult authority and of acquiring more secure identities for themselves in the face of emotional terrors that threaten to annihilate their sense of self and their initiative.

At the same time that Carroll created his revolutionary image of the child in the *Alice* stories, he also helped to encourage the conventional and idealized Victorian myth of the child in articles, in public addresses, in poems, and in his last fantasies for children, *Sylvie and Bruno* (1889) and *Sylvie and Bruno Concluded* (1893). While Carroll intentionally gave an idealized pastoral vision of childhood and its "golden summer afternoon," his *Alice* fantasies expressed the child's unconscious wishes and fears and thus revealed the minds and imaginations of children more vividly and complexly than any of Carroll's predecessors or contemporaries.

The facts about Charles Lutwidge Dodgson's life are well known, but his life continues to be important in illuminating his works for children. Derek Hudson, Dodgson's most important biographer, stresses the relationship between Carroll's life and his literary work: "The family background explains much in Lewis Carroll's character—his sense of religion and tradition, of loyalty and service; a certain pride in social standing; an innate conservatism that struggled with his own originality of mind."

Dodgson was born in an old parsonage at Daresbury in Cheshire on 27 January 1832, the third child and eldest son of the Reverend Charles Dodgson and Frances Jane Lutwidge. Dodgson appears to have spent a relatively happy childhood in a family of ten children (seven girls and three boys), although he was plagued all of his life with the problem of stammering (except when he was in the company of children).

Dodgson was an avid reader of fairy tales and nonsense rhymes. Hudson stresses that he learned at an early age to entertain children with puzzles, drawings, puppets, plays, and stories. Such inventive play with children (especially with charming little girls) was to remain the central pleasure of Dodgson's emotional life and a vital, moving force in his literary efforts.

As a student, Dodgson proved able and ambitious at Richmond School and at Rugby—both preparatory schools in England. Later Dodgson studied at Oxford, completing his bachelor of arts in 1855 and his master of arts in 1857. He then took deacon's orders in the Anglican church and remained at Christ Church, Oxford, for most of his career, as a lecturer in mathematics and logic. In his rooms at Oxford, Dodgson entertained many child friends. Literally dozens of little girls enjoyed games, picnics, and tea parties with Lewis Carroll, but none of these children proved to be as famous as Alice Pleasance Liddell, daughter of Henry George Liddell, the dean of Christ Church while Dodgson served there.

In July 1862, Dodgson and his friend Robinson Duckworth took Alice and her two sisters, Lorina and Edith, on the now famous boating and picnic expedition to Godstow. During this excursion, Lewis Carroll records in his diaries, he told the children many of the episodes that later appeared in *Alice's Adventures in Wonderland*. Carroll wrote out the stories at the request of Alice and illustrated them himself in an early version entitled *Alice's Adventures Under Ground*. When Dodgson gave a copy to Mrs. George Macdonald to read to her children, her son, Greville, clapped his hands and demanded that sixty thousand copies of it be printed. Carroll apparently initiated publication of the story at Macdonald's insistence. In any event, *Alice's Adventures in Wonderland*, illustrated by Sir John Tenniel and written by "Lewis Carroll," was published in 1865.

It was immediately popular and has remained one of the most influential children's books ever written. Both *Alice* books have been translated into many languages and have been illustrated by dozens of talented artists.

Though the original creative genius manifested in the *Alice* books is beyond question, Carroll's stories do draw upon previously published models to some extent. Strictly speaking both *Alice* books belong to the genre of the dream vision. Donald Rackin explains in his article "Alice's Journey to the End of Night" that virtually all critics agree on this classification and adds that

> if "dream-vision" is understood as serious thinkers (ranging from medieval poets to modern psychologists) have so often understood it, as an avenue to knowledge that is perhaps more meaningful—and frequently more horrifying—than any that the unaided conscious intellect can discover, then it provides an almost perfect description of the very substance of Carroll's masterpiece.

The two *Alice* books bear a strong resemblance, at least structurally, to such medieval dream visions as Chaucer's *The Parlement of Loules*. Yet Carroll humorously turns many conventions associated with the traditional dream vision upside down. In Dante's *Divine Comedy*, the dreamer is conducted to the dream world by a wise and beatific guide; the White Rabbit, Alice's kitty, the Red Queen, and the White Knight of the *Alice* books scarcely qualify as wise spiritual guides. Moreover, the visions of Wonderland and Looking-Glass House are hardly those of a perfectly ordered paradise; rather they are perfectly disordered and chaotic realities that severely challenge Alice's highly conventional modes of making sense. As Nina Demurova writes in her essay "Toward a Definition of *Alice*'s Genre: The Folktale and Fairy-Tale Connections" (in Guiliano's *Lewis Carroll, a Celebration*), the dream vision as Carroll employs it owes more to the English romantic dream vision of the lonely hero's quest, the internalized quest of self-discovery. Yet the tone and the texture of Carroll's fantasies are quite at odds with the "high seriousness" of the romantic quester.

The delightfully bizarre and comic qualities of the *Alice* books are perhaps inspired by more immediate sources in Carroll's life. First, Carroll's particular kind of imagination and his peculiar way of seeing the world were surely encouraged by his father, who also perceived wondrous nonsense and comic possibility in the world around him. When Carroll was eight years old, Hudson writes, he received the following letter from his father:

> . . . I will not forget your commission. As soon as I get to Leeds I shall scream out in the middle of the street, *Ironmongers—Ironmongers*—Six hundred men will rush out of their shops in a moment—fly, fly, in all directions—ring the bells, call the constables—set the town on fire. I *will* have a file & a screwdriver, & a ring, & if they are not brought directly, in forty seconds I will leave nothing but one small cat alive in the whole town of Leeds, and I shall only leave that, because I am afraid I shall not have time to kill it.
>
> (p. 8)

Hudson speculates that this letter was undoubtedly representative of other letters and stories that Carroll heard from his father. The mock violence and comic exaggeration apparent in Mr. Dodgson's letter were also characteristic of the popular writing of the time. As a young man, Carroll contributed humorous verse, prose sketches, and drawings to comic journals. Donald Gray explains in the preface to the Norton Critical Edition of *Alice*:

> From these popular forms of Victorian comic writing Dodgson took over some of their most common practices. The use of parody, for example, and of puns, dialect, and other plays on the sound of words, was frequent in comic journalism and in theatrical burlesque and pantomime. So was the creation of a fanciful grotesquerie—in the cartoons of comic periodicals, for example, and in the plots and staging of burlesque and pantomime—in which ordinary objects and contemporary people and events were jumbled together with talking animals, animated playing cards, and creatures from fairy tale, folklore, and legendary past of a child's history.

In his diaries Carroll mentions attending dozens of pantomimes, featuring "Cinderella," "Puss in Boots," and "Beauty and the Beast," among many other fairy tales. He also mentions a work that may have influenced both him and Charles Kingsley in their depictions of insects and animal characters: William Roscoe's *The Butterfly's Ball and the Grasshopper's Feast* (1807), a long poem describing the humorous revels of sometimes comically arch and imperious butterflies, grasshoppers, trumpeters, and other insects. Roscoe inspired a host of imitators; no doubt these haughtily pretentious animals, insects, and flowers were the source of such *Alice* characters as the elegant Caterpillar, the timorous White Rabbit, the lugubrious Mock Turtle, the Looking-Glass Insects, and the Garden of Live Flowers.

Several comic fairy tales had also been published in the first half of the nineteenth century that probably established a context for the *Alice* books. Catherine Sinclair's interpolated fairy tale in *Holiday House* (1839), "Uncle David's Nonsensical Story About Giants and Fairies," though explicitly didactic, contains many comic and witty conceits. Likewise William Makepeace Thackeray's *The Rose and the Ring* (1855) employs pantomime devices, mock violence, and puns. Both stories were probably well known to Carroll.

Though Carroll had many models for his *Alice* fantasies, he nevertheless celebrated the uninhibited play of the child's intelligence and imagination and sustained a commitment to both the pleasures and terrors of fantasy throughout the *Alice* books. Through parody and burlesque of the didactic tradition and through games, puzzles, and linguistic play Carroll reduces the adult world of authority to an absurdity manageable by children themselves. He does not, as previous British writers of fantasy had, whisk children off to fairyland only to place them under the dominion of powerful authority figures who provide all the answers; solve all the problems; and neutralize the child's spirit, initiative, and curiosity. Rather, Carroll creates for them a fantasy world that renders the arbitrary authority and institutions of adults incoherent and ineffectual and that permits Alice to exercise her own judgments and to make her own decisions.

One of the most prominent features of *Alice's Adventures in Wonderland*, for example, is Carroll's satiric treatment of conventional ways of reading and knowing. He ridicules rote learning, the confining strictures of conventional moral tales, matter-of-fact rational education, and literal-minded conceptions of time and space. The opening paragraph of *Alice's Adventures in Wonderland* reveals Carroll's awareness of children's preferences in literature and their desire to be liberated from didactic children's books, when Alice dislikes her sister's book because "it had no pictures or conversations."

Carroll also alludes directly to the fact-versus-fancy controversy in children's books by emphasizing that Alice is herself the product of an education that crams children's heads with worthless and irrelevant facts. As she falls down the rabbit hole, Alice wonders what latitude or longitude she has reached, though she has no idea what these terms mean. In the Pool of Tears Alice tries to solve the problem of her identity by reference to the multiplication table or geography. When the Mouse tells the "driest" thing he knows in order to dry Alice and the creatures after their immersion in the Pool of Tears, the tale turns out to be a directly quoted passage from the Liddell children's history book. Alice looks for opportunities to show off her knowledge, worries that she will be thought ignorant, and, initially at least, attempts to accommodate herself to the demands of the "adults" in Wonderland. In the scene with the Gryphon and the Mock Turtle, Carroll satirizes school subjects through puns. The Mock Turtle claims that he has studied "Reeling and Writhing, of course, to begin with . . . and then the different branches of Arithmetic—Ambition, Distraction, Uglification, and Derision."

In the same chapter, Alice boasts that she has studied French and music and is indignant when the Mock Turtle asks if she has studied washing. In his extensive punning on school lessons, Carroll subjects both the educational system itself and the child who is its product to playful irony. Alice relies upon facts and the desire to please adults, rather than upon her own good sense and initiative. She is concerned with external appearances and must learn, as the Duchess reminds her, to "take care of the sense and the sounds will take care of themselves." Eventually Alice does take care of the sense by declaring Wonderland and its characters "nonsense." She learns to rely upon her own perceptions of reality and to destroy a dream that is threatening to her sense of self.

Carroll directly parodies the moral tradition in children's literature in many scenes in *Alice's Adventures in Wonderland*. The eighteenth-century children's poet Isaac Watts had written many pious verses for children. Watts's moralistic poem "The Voice of the Sluggard" becomes Carroll's comic "Voice of the Lobster." Alice shows that she has read many cautionary tales for children when she carefully checks a bottle to see whether it is marked "poison."

Carroll also burlesques and mocks the tradition of moral didacticism in the scene in which the Duchess finds a ludicrously inappropriate moral for everything Alice says. By alluding so specifically to the didactic tradition and making fun of it, Carroll emphasizes his awareness that he is writing a book of a very different order and suggests that Alice is in a world where ordinary, mundane rules for children do not prevail. The direct parody of didactic verses and stories and traditional sentimental ones, like Ann Taylor's "Twinkle, Twinkle, Little Star," which becomes "Twinkle, Twinkle, Little Bat," shows that Carroll wishes to make fun of literature that adults think children ought to read rather than books children may wish to read themselves. Carroll invites children to laugh at such forms and to participate in a whole new world of fantasy, one composed of various kinds of play.

But the *Alice* books are more than an adroitly constructed pastiche of parody, burlesque, pantomime, nursery rhymes, and bits of fairy tales that afford children a holiday from the intellectual and moral lessons and demands of the ordinary world. The two books together offer a completed quest in which Alice, if she does not grow to a conventional moral state, confronts and conquers some of her deepest fears, enacts some of her most subversive wishes against the tyranny of adults, and ultimately makes progress in both mental and physical growth.

Alice's Adventures in Wonderland begins as Alice tumbles down the rabbit hole after the elusive White Rabbit. While intentionally pursuing the nervous creature, she clearly does not mean to plunge into a seemingly bottomless black hole. The fantasy begins with that familiar out-of-control sensation of nightmares—the feeling of endlessly falling into darkness. As she falls, Alice consoles herself with language. She wonders about latitude and longitude, assuring herself that "Dinah'll miss me very much to-night, I should think!" Carroll thus shows that language, even the language of nonsense (because Alice does not know the meanings of the words she utters), can help the child conquer uncontrollable fears. Carroll writes in the preface to *Sylvie and Bruno* that the most effective way to deal with "unholy thoughts" is through "useful mental work." In the *Alice* books such mental work also consists of riddles, puzzles, games, and nonsense. Carroll thus creates a new order of fantasy in which the minds and imaginations of children are engaged not only to provide them with amusement but also as a means of standing off their terrors. A telling example of this tendency occurs in the Mouse's "tale," in which the small, helpless creature relates his fears of violent and arbitrary

extinction by reciting a poem whose shape grows ever smaller and trails off almost altogether at the end of the "tail." By imposing his own comic shape and order, that of his tail, upon his worst fears, the Mouse faces up to cunning old Fury, embodies him in a ludicrously humorous form, and through a language puzzle conjures him into nothingness.

After landing from her seemingly endless fall, Alice confronts another nightmare image: a confusing labyrinth of dark passages and locked doors. Carroll thus depicts the child lost in a maze, shut out from the means of finding her way; and he opens the second theme of the quest, Alice's attempt to emerge from confusion and reach a place she selects for herself.

When Alice finally sees a beautiful garden, "she longed to get out of that dark hall, and wander about among those beds of bright flowers and those cool fountains." The garden, the traditional place where children move from innocence to experience, represents a child's vision of adult pleasures and privileges from which he or she is excluded. Her problem, Alice thinks, is to grow enough or to shrink enough to enter the lovely garden. Alice's growth and identity are clearly the major themes of both *Alice* books, and her encounters with the creatures of Wonderland most often show her struggling against adult authority and constraint. She finds herself thrust into the role of mother too soon in the Pool of Tears scene, when the creatures demand that she provide prizes for everyone. She finds herself alternately too small and vulnerable to make progress or too large to fit into the houses of childish adults. She worries about losing her identity altogether in the form of annihilation.

Most of the characters she meets are rude and peremptory. They question her and force her to repeat lessons. She gets useful advice from only two creatures. The Caterpillar tells her that the mushroom will make her grow to the proper size and advises her sagely to keep her temper. The friendly and encouraging Cheshire Cat seems also to side with Alice against the irrational behavior of the other creatures. (Some critics have speculated that the Cheshire Cat is Alice's disembodied intellect, which is elusively and unpredictably out of step with her physical growth.) He encourages Alice to rely upon herself, as she ultimately must do to free herself from the domination of the unreasonably infantile Queen of Hearts: " 'Would you tell me, please, which way I ought to walk from here?' 'That depends a good deal on where you want to get to,' said the Cat." Finally, the Cat helps Alice to outwit the King and Queen of Hearts. His strange habit of disappearing and reappearing, revealing only his head, baffles the Queen's executioners and exposes the fraudulent nature of the Queen's threats to decapitate one and all.

Once in the lovely garden, however, Alice experiences just as much chaos as before. The confused quality of the garden is a telling vision of a child's coming to terms with the fallibility of adults. From the perspective of children, adults, apparently free to do as they please, seem to inhabit an attractively controlled world. Once children reach the garden of adulthood, however, they find it rife with the baffling anxieties, fears, frustrating constrictions, and imperfections that trouble childhood. Carroll thus dissolves the barriers between childhood and adulthood. He reverses adult-child roles, but when Alice finds herself joining the adult game, she is just as muddled as everyone else. In many ways Carroll suggests that we all remain confused children looking for the right rules in an ever-shifting and unmanageable reality.

Like *Alice's Adventures in Wonderland, Through the Looking-Glass* begins with Alice's curiosity, but unlike the confused tumble down the rabbit hole, Alice's entry into the fantasy world of Looking-Glass House seems more controlled and willed. Alice also wishes to escape the restrictions of the ordinary adult world:

> "So I shall be as warm here as I was in the old room," thought Alice: "warmer, in fact, because there'll be no one here to scold me away from the fire. Oh, what fun it'll be, when they see me through the glass in here, and can't get at me!"

Once inside Looking-Glass House, Alice discovers that this fantasy world appears to be governed by much more orderly laws than the chaos that had confused her in Wonderland. But the rules are different from those of the ordinary world. All of reality is inverted. The Red Queen says that the garden is a wilderness compared with the gardens she knows about; she gives Alice a dry biscuit to assuage thirst. And Alice discovers that she must travel backward to get anywhere and that "it takes all the running you can do, to keep in the same place." Despite its inversions, however, the laws governing Looking-Glass House are consistent and orderly. Though short-tempered and peremptory, the Red Queen gives Alice a chance to grow and to win the game (unlike the Queen of Hearts, who

could only utter empty threats and keep the rules of the game a secret in order to preclude anyone else's winning). The Red Queen explains to Alice all of the possible moves in the eight squares and leaves her with some important advice: "Remember who you are!" The Queen thus stresses again that Alice's identity is the central theme of the fantasy.

The nature of identity, reality, and language, and their relationships to each other, receive much attention in *Through the Looking-Glass*. Carroll introduces several possible theories of language in the fantasy. In the Garden of Live Flowers the Daisy suggests that the name of a thing is somehow intrinsically connected with its essence. As she is about to enter this dark wood, Alice worries about her name. When Alice forgets her name in the wood, she and a lovely Fawn (who does not remember who he is either) comfort one another on the way. When the Fawn remembers what he is, he darts away from Alice, realizing that humans and fawns are by their *names* enemies (not by their *natures*, since the fawn and Alice have enjoyed companionship with one another). The poignant scene reveals Carroll's awareness that names and language impart an orderly comfort to our lives but also create painful barriers, isolating us from other beings. Alice looks sadly after the fawn but reassures herself, " 'However, I know my name now . . . that's *some* comfort. Alice—Alice—I won't forget it again.' " The function of language and names raises a difficult question about reality itself. Do we experience reality or merely our artificial linguistic constructs of it? It is a question that Carroll does not answer, but one that continues to trouble Alice throughout the book, and Carroll throughout his life.

Similar questions about identity, reality, and language are raised in the chapters "Tweedledum and Tweedledee" and "Humpty-Dumpty." Tweedledum and Tweedledee, though ill-tempered and irrational, challenge Alice's identity when they tell her that she is only a thing in the Red King's dream and that " 'if that there King was to wake,' added Tweedledum, 'you'd go out—bang!—just like a candle.' " Later in the fantasy Humpty-Dumpty causes Alice to examine the meaning of her name, and he suggests that language itself is only a set of arbitrary signs:

> "When *I* use a word," Humpty-Dumpty said in rather a scornful tone, "it means just what I choose it to mean—neither more nor less."

"The question is," said Alice, "whether you *can* make words mean so many different things."

"The question is," said Humpty-Dumpty, "which is to be master—that's all."

In the context of the fantasy Humpty-Dumpty's last rejoinder is especially significant. The issue is whether Alice will master her fantasy and assert her identity or whether she will allow her fantasy and her uncertainties about her identity to master and perhaps overcome her. One important way that human beings, especially children, make sense of the world, impose meaning on chaotic experience, and finally achieve a sense of personal identity, Carroll suggests, is through language.

One of Lewis Carroll's major achievements in children's literature is his nonsense poetry, most notably the two poems "Jabberwocky" and *The Hunting of the Snark*. Most critics of the nonsense poems contend that they illuminate and extend the major themes and techniques of the *Alice* books. As Edward Guiliano writes in his essay "A Time for Humor: Lewis Carroll, Laughter and Despair, and *The Hunting of the Snark*," the nonsense poems explore "dreams, death, probings into the nature of being, reminders of the inescapability of time, and a quest motif"; he adds of *The Hunting of the Snark* that the "tension between the comic tone and the underlying anxieties is perhaps the poem's most distinguishing and fascinating characteristic." The poems have also been regarded as manifestations of the mind's need to manipulate objects and to create an artificial sense of order in the midst of an unmanageable reality. In her splendid study *The Field of Nonsense*, Elizabeth Sewell argues that the practices and purposes of nonsense are those of a game. The manipulated objects in the game of nonsense, she says, are words, which the mind uses so that "its tendency towards order engages its contrary, the tendency towards disorder, keeping the latter perpetually in play and so in check."

The initial stanza of "Jabberwocky" first appeared in the magazine *Mischmasch* in 1855 as a portion of Carroll's early poem "Stanza of Anglo-Saxon Poetry." In *Through the Looking-Glass* Humpty-Dumpty explains the meanings of some of the words in "Jabberwocky": "'*Brillig*' means four o'clock in the afternoon—the time when you begin *broiling* things for dinner. . . '*slithy*' means 'lithe and slimy.' . . . You see it's like a portmanteau—there are two meanings packed up in one word." Both child and adult readers of "Jabberwocky" understand the poem at one level as "sense" because they have internalized a system of language that tells them which words in a sentence are subjects, verbs, adjectives, etc. The first stanza of "Jabberwocky" clearly establishes setting and mood. The second introduces the comic but terrifying "Jabberwock," with its biting jaws and catching claws. The "beamish boy," the hero of the mock-heroic poem, vanquishes the Jabberwock with his "vorpal sword." According to theories of humor set forth by Freud and Henri Bergson, human beings, especially children, use humorous and wildly exaggerated stories to manage their deepest fears and anxieties; thus in "Jabberwocky" the child reader vanquishes terrors not with a vorpal sword but in naming the terrible foe. In naming the foe a "Jabberwock" or a "Jubjub bird," the child gives form to his or her fears and so masters them, at least temporarily.

A similar but darker vision emerges from *The Hunting of the Snark*, also a mock-heroic poem that features several questers: a Bellman, a Boots, a Barrister, a Banker, a Beaver, and a Butcher, all of whom seek the Snark with ineffectual weapons:

They sought it with thimbles, they sought it with care;
They pursued it with forks and hope;
They threatened its life with a railway-share.
They charmed it with smiles and soap.

Critics of *The Hunting of the Snark* have often seen the Bellman with his bell as the hero of the poem. The Bellman reminds the other comic questers of time. He also identifies and explains the nature of Snarks, which have several "unmistakable marks." According to the Bellman, Snarks taste "meagre and hollow, but crisp"; the Snark frequently gets up so late that it "breakfasts at five-o'clock tea,/ And dines on the following day." Snarks are also fond of bathing machines. Finally, they have ambition. Further, the Bellman notes, there are three categories of Snarks—two harmless and one very dangerous indeed. Common snarks may have "feathers, and bite" or have "whiskers, and scratch." Both types are harmless. But, the captain adds ominously, some Snarks are "Boojums." And "If your Snark be a Boojum! . . . You will softly and suddenly vanish away/And never be met with again." At the end of the quest the poor Beaver does in fact encounter a Snark that is a Boojum:

In the midst of the word he was trying to say,
In the midst of his laughter and glee,
He had softly and suddenly vanished away—
For the Snark *was* a Boojum, you see.

For the Beaver, at least, words cannot finally suffice in the face of terror, extinction, and death.

Lewis Carroll intended *The Hunting of the Snark* to be enjoyed as a hilarious flight of imaginative nonsense. Recent critics and biographers, however, have related the poem to its context in the author's life and have noted the grim implications of the ostensibly comic poem. Carroll recorded in a letter that he conceived the poem as he walked on the Surrey Downs on 18 July 1874:

> I was walking on a hillside, alone, one bright summer day, when suddenly there came into my head one line of verse—one solitary line—"For the Snark *was* a Boojum, you see." I knew not what it meant, then: I know not what it means, now; but I wrote it down: and, some time afterwards, the rest of the stanza occurred to me, that being its last line: and so by degrees, at odd moments during the next year or two, the rest of the poem pieced itself together, that being its last stanza.
>
> (Cohen, p. 234)

The night before this walk, Carroll had been up the entire night nursing a dying cousin, his twenty-two-year-old godson, Charles Wilcox. Thus, Morton Cohen, Martin Gardiner, Edward Guiliano, and other critics of *The Hunting of the Snark* agree that the nonsense of the poem may best be interpreted as Carroll's defense against an all-too-painful reality.

Until recently the two volumes *Sylvie and Bruno* and *Sylvie and Bruno Concluded* have been regarded as inferior in literary quality to Carroll's previously published masterpieces for children. However, the books now have been reprinted in several English editions and also have been translated into several languages. Critics Gilles Deleuzo and Jean Gattégno, moreover, argue that in the *Sylvie and Bruno* books Carroll demonstrates "some entirely new techniques" as he attempts to couple dream and reality. They correctly note that the themes and techniques of these books are radically different from those of the *Alice* books. They are quite wrong, however, in calling such practices in fantasy "entirely new." The *Sylvie and Bruno* books belong to a well-established tradition of nineteenth-century children's fantasy and owe much to such works as George Macdonald's *At the Back of the North Wind* (1871), Mary Louisa Molesworth's *Four Winds Farm* (1887), and Dinah Mulock's *The Little Lame Prince* (1875), in which visions of the fantasy world are closely connected to the conventional morals and values of Victorian society. Hence, as Carroll grew older, he seemingly found it more and more difficult to enter into the consciousness of children and to express their views of adults and their exuberant defiance of adult authority. In *Sylvie and Bruno* and *Sylvie and Bruno Concluded*, Carroll expresses much more conventional ideas about children, fairy tales, and the imagination.

In these books he also attempts to bring the world of dreams and the world of ordinary reality together. In the preface to *Sylvie and Bruno Concluded*, Carroll explains the various psychical states that human beings may experience with varying degrees of consciousness:

(a) the ordinary state, with no consciousness of the Fairies;

(b) the "eerie" state, in which, while conscious of actual surroundings, he is *also* aware of the presence of Fairies;

(c) a form of trance, in which, while unconscious of actual surroundings, and apparently asleep, he (i.e., his immaterial essence) migrates to other scenes, in the actual world, or in Fairyland, and is conscious of the presence of Fairies.

The kindly old gentleman who is the central character in *Sylvie and Bruno* and its sequel is, in the second of these states, in contact with the fairy world and the ordinary world. There are consequently two plots going on concurrently in the stories. The story taking place in the ordinary world is concerned with the old gentleman's friend Arthur Forester, a virtuous young physician, and his love for a morally pure young woman, Lady Muriel, who is engaged to her cousin Eric. Eric senses that Lady Muriel does not truly love him and gallantly releases her from the engagement. Arthur and Lady Muriel declare their love for each other and marry just before the young doctor goes to a plague-stricken fishing village, where he supposedly sacrifices his life ministering to the needs of the sick. The reader is left grieving with Muriel until Eric appears, bringing a very frail and sickly Arthur with him, the news of his death having been a mistake after all. The reader experiences these events through the sympathetic but uninvolved narrator, who is much more intrigued with his imaginary world.

When the old gentleman falls into a dream state,

he enjoys adventures with two lovely fairy children: Sylvie, a beautiful young girl, and her little brother, Bruno. The father of these children has left his post as Emperor of Outlands to become King of Fairyland, putting Sylvie and Bruno in the care of the Lord Chancellor, who promptly declares himself and his wife Emperor and Empress of Outlands and their dull, ill-behaved, and unattractive son, Uggug, the heir to the kingdom. Sylvie and Bruno finally escape from Outlands into an idealized world of nature. In the course of the two volumes these two children often visit the old gentleman narrator and do good deeds for mortals and animals. For example, they cure a cottager of drunkenness and restore domestic tranquillity to his troubled home. They are also responsible for bringing together Arthur and Lady Muriel, but only the Old Gentleman knows of their beneficent deeds or even of their existence, except that upon one or two occasions Sylvie and Bruno pose as ordinary children and take tea at Lady Muriel's home. In *Sylvie and Bruno* and its conclusion Carroll tries to show that the dream world can directly influence the ordinary world for the good. Since neither world is entirely separate from the other, the characters experience no happy release from the cares and restrictions of either world, and Carroll himself exhibits no freedom to deflate pompous adult authority and rules. Trying to write about both worlds at once compels Carroll to remain somewhat solemn about them and restrains his powers of fantastic invention. The reader finds little of the nonsense, jokes, punning, or underlying nightmare that abound in the earlier fantasies. The only hint of Carroll's previous techniques occurs in the comic figure of the mad gardener, who recites nonsense poems whenever he appears.

In the *Sylvie and Bruno* books Carroll continues to be obsessed with dreams and to question concrete reality. He expresses again his apprehension that life is essentially insubstantial and dreamlike. The baffling question of what is dream and what reality in the *Sylvie and Bruno* books, however, is never as troubling and threatening as it is in the *Alice* books, since Carroll depicts both the dream world and the real world as pleasantly ordered spheres where characters worry about conventionally easy moral questions, not complex psychological emotions and fears for which there are no clear-cut solutions. In the *Sylvie and Bruno* books fantasy does not penetrate to the depths of the unconscious but remains serenely on a conventionally conscious surface and so provides beneficent if shallow reassurance to the reader.

In *Sylvie and Bruno* and *Sylvie and Bruno Concluded*, Carroll emphasizes the saintly sweetness of the two children. They are conventionally Victorian in appearance—rosy-cheeked cherubs with masses of curly hair and angelic facial expressions. Bruno speaks an offensively saccharine baby talk, and both children spend most of their time doing good deeds. Infinitely docile, patient, and even-tempered, Sylvie and Bruno pose a pallid contrast to the spirited Alice, who often displays her temper and finally destroys her own dreams when she needs to assert her identity against creatures who threaten and baffle her.

At his best Carroll understood and depicted the child's need to master both internal and external reality through games and fantasy. At his worst he retreats from his own terrors and anxieties, apparently refusing to acknowledge them even in fantasy, and looks to childhood from the perspective of overly sentimental and nostalgic regret. He was responsible at once for liberating the imagination of children, for helping to establish fantasy as a serious literary genre for children's books, for creating a complex and authentic version of the child's consciousness, and for promoting the Victorian cult of the child, a tendency that became pronounced in his work and in comments about it in the last decades of the century.

Selected Bibliography

WORKS OF LEWIS CARROLL

For the most comprehensive account of editions of Carroll's literary works, see *The Lewis Carroll Handbook*, by Sidney Herbert Williams, revised by Roger Lancelyn Green and further revised by Denis Crutch (Folkstone, England: Dawson Press, 1979).

Alice's Adventures in Wonderland. With illustrations by John Tenniel. London: Macmillan, 1865. (First issue recalled because Carroll was not pleased with the printing.) Reprinted London: Macmillan, 1866.
Through the Looking-Glass. With illustrations by John Tenniel. London: Macmillan, 1871.
Alice's Adventures Under Ground. With illustrations by Lewis Carroll. London: Macmillan, 1876. Reprinted in honor of Carroll's centenary. London: Macmillan, 1932. Facsimile edition. Ann Arbor, Mich.: University Microfilms, 1964. Facsimile edition with an introduction by Martin Gardner, additional material

from facsimile edition of 1886, and a history of facsimile editions. New York: McGraw-Hill, 1965.

The Hunting of the Snark: An Agony, in Eight Fits. With illustrations by Henry Holiday. London: Macmillan, 1876. Facsimile edition. New York: Mayflower Books, 1981.

Alice's Adventures in Wonderland and Through the Looking-Glass. With illustrations by John Tenniel. New York and London: Macmillan, 1881. (This edition continues to be reprinted regularly, but see especially the one edited and with an introduction by Roger Lancelyn Green. London: Oxford University Press, 1971.)

Sylvie and Bruno. With illustrations by Harry Furniss. 2 vols. London: Macmillan, 1889–1893. 1-vol. ed., introduced by Edwin J. Kenney, Jr., and part of the series *Classics of Children's Literature 1621–1932*. New York: Garland, 1976. Facsimile edition. New York: Mayflower Books, 1980.

The Nursery "Alice." Twenty colored enlargements from Tenniel's original illustrations, with text adapted to nursery readers by Lewis Carroll. London: Macmillan, 1890. (The 1889 edition was suppressed.) Facsimile of second edition, includes "A Nursery Darling," "Christmas Greetings," and "Cautions to Readers," and is introduced by Martin Gardner. New York: McGraw-Hill, 1966.

The Annotated Alice: Alice's Adventures in Wonderland and Through the Looking-Glass. With illustrations by John Tenniel. Introduced and annotated by Martin Gardner. New York: Clarkson Potter, 1960.

The Annotated Snark: The Full Text of Lewis Carroll's Great Nonsense Epic, The Hunting of the Snark, and the Original Illustrations by Henry Holiday. Introduced and annotated by Martin Gardner. New York: Simon and Schuster, 1962.

Alice in Wonderland: Authoritative Texts of Alice's Adventures in Wonderland, Through the Looking-Glass, [and] The Hunting of the Snark, [with] Backgrounds [and] Essays in Criticism. With illustrations by John Tenniel. Edited and annotated by Donald J. Gray. New York: W. W. Norton, 1971.

COLLECTED WORKS

The Complete Works of Lewis Carroll. Introduction by Alexander Woollcott. With illustrations by John Tenniel. New York: Random House, 1937; London: Nonesuch Press, 1939.

CRITICAL AND BIOGRAPHICAL STUDIES

Ayres, Harry Morgan. *Carroll's "Alice."* New York: Columbia University Press, 1936.

Bowman, Isa. *The Story of Lewis Carroll*. London: J. M. Dent and Sons, 1899. Reprinted as *Lewis Carroll as I Knew Him*. With an introduction by Morton N.

Cohen. New York: Dover, 1972. (Written for young people.)

Burpee, Lawrence J. "Alice Joins the Immortals" *Dalhousie Review* 21/2: 194–204 (1941).

Cohen, Morton N., and Roger Lancelyn Green, eds. *The Letters of Lewis Carroll*. 2 vols. London: Oxford University Press, 1979.

Collingwood, Stuart Dodgson. "Before *Alice*: The Boyhood of Lewis Carroll" *Strand Magazine* 16/96: 616–627 (1898).

———. *The Life and Letters of Lewis Carroll*. London: T. Fisher Unwin, 1898.

Cripps, Elizabeth A. *"Alice* and the Reviewers" *Children's Literature* 11: 32–48 (1983).

Darton, F. J. Harvey. *Children's Books in England: Five Centuries of Social Life*. Rev. ed. by Brian Alderson. Cambridge: Cambridge University Press, 1982.

de la Mare, Walter. *Lewis Carroll*. London: Faber and Faber, 1932. Reprinted New York: Haskell House, 1972.

Dodgson, Charles Lutwidge. *The Diaries of Lewis Carroll*. Edited and supplemented by Roger Lancelyn Green. New York: Oxford University Press, 1954. Reprinted Westport, Conn.: Greenwood Press, 1971.

Empson, William. "Alice in Wonderland." In *Some Versions of Pastoral*. London: Chatto and Windus, 1935.

Greenacre, Phyllis. *Swift and Carroll: A Psychoanalytic Study of Two Lives*. New York: International Universities Press, 1955.

Guiliano, Edward. *Lewis Carroll: An Annotated International Bibliography, 1960–1977*. Charlottesville: University Press of Virginia, 1980. (Printed for the Bibliographical Society of the University of Virginia and the Lewis Carroll Society of North America. Includes editions of Carroll's works as well as articles and books about Carroll.)

———. *Lewis Carroll, a Celebration: Essays on the Occasion of the 150th Anniversary of the Birth of Charles Lutwidge Dodgson*. New York: Clarkson Potter, 1982.

——— and James R. Kincaid, eds. *Soaring with the Dodo: Essays on Lewis Carroll's Life and Art*. Charlottesville: University Press of Virginia, 1982.

Hellems, F. C. R. "Alice and Education" *Atlantic Monthly* 111/2: 256–265 (1913).

Hubbell, George Shelton. "Triple Alice" *Sewanee Review* 48/2: 174–196 (1940).

Hudson, Derek. *Lewis Carroll*. London: Constable, 1954.

"Immortal Alice," written by "a 'Times' Reviewer" *Living Age* 342/4386: 53–57 (1932).

Jabberwocky. (Journal published quarterly by the Lewis Carroll Society of England.)

"Lewis Carroll" *London Times Literary Supplement* 31/1565: 49–50 (1932).

McGillis, Roderick. " 'What *Is* the Fun?' Said Alice"

Children's Literature in Education 17/1: 25–36 (1986).

————. "Tenniel's Turned Rabbit: A Reading of *Alice* with Tenniel's Help" *English Studies in Canada* 3/3: 326–335 (1977).

Moses, Belle. *Lewis Carroll in Wonderland and at Home: The Story of His Life*. New York: Appleton, 1910.

Ovendon, Graham, ed. *The Illustrators of "Alice in Wonderland" and "Through the Looking-Glass."* Introduced by John Davis. London: Academy Editions, 1979; New York: St. Martin's Press, 1979.

Parry, Sir Edward Abbott. "The Early Writings of Lewis Carroll" *Cornhill Magazine* 56/334: 455–468 (1924).

Rackin, Donald. "Alice's Journey to the End of Night" *PMLA* 81: 391–416 (1966). Reprinted in *Aspects of Alice: Lewis Carroll's Dreamchild as Seen Through the Critics' Looking-Glasses 1865–1971*, edited by Robert Phillips and with illustrations by Sir John Tenniel and Lewis Carroll. New York: Random House, 1971.

Reed, Langford. *The Life of Lewis Carroll*. London: Foyle, 1932.

Sewell, Elizabeth. *The Field of Nonsense*. London: Chatto and Windus, 1952.

Skinner, John. "Lewis Carroll's Adventures in Wonderland" *American Imago* 4/4: 3–31 (1947).

Wilson, Edmund. "The Poet-Logician" *New Republic* 71/911: 19–21 (1932).

Woolf, Virginia. "Lewis Carroll." In *The Moment, and Other Essays*. London: Hogarth Press, 1947; New York: Harcourt, Brace, 1948.

—ANITA MOSS

C. COLLODI

1826–1890

INSCRIBED ON A tablet let into the wall at number 2 via Taddea, a moldering stuccoed building in the slums of the ancient San Lorenzo market of Florence, is the meager legend "In this house, in 1826, was born Carlo Lorenzini, called Collodi: father of Pinocchio." This obscure cenotaph was erected in 1940 by a communal deputation *(commissione comunale)* that had been belatedly charged with investigating the history of the author Lorenzini, who was to adopt the pen name C. Collodi at the age of thirty-three.

The *commissione* was able to establish only a scant handful of facts about Collodi's life. These stand in bizarre contrast with the glowing curriculum vitae created over the last ninety-odd years by impressionable Anglo-American scholars, the data for which were most evidently gleaned from the tendentious laudations of reverent Italian biographers who, until rather recently, were rather less than reliable in matters of documentation. The fact remains that C. Collodi was a very ordinary person, in spite of the many wistful claims made posthumously about his life and his career.

Collodi was born on 24 November 1826 to Domenico and Angela Lorenzini, who were employed as servants by the marchese Paolo Garzoni Venturi and later took up actual residence in his household. Although the couple were to spend much of their lives in poverty, they managed to produce nine more children, although of these only two were to survive: Paolo, the industrious son, who went on to eventual prosperity as director of the great Doccia ceramics works at Florence, and

Ippolito, the idler, who, however, was the only one to produce children of his own.

At the age of eleven, Collodi was enrolled at the seminary at Colle Val d'Elsa, where, it was supposed by later scholars, he received the finest of classical educations while studying for the priesthood. However, after only five years of grudging and generally neglected study he quit the seminary, put off probably by monastic restraints imposed upon an adolescent at the wrong time of life. He appears then to have entered another private school, where he spent two years more in a curriculum ponderously entitled *Rettorica e filosofia.* This brings author Collodi to age eighteen with but seven years of the most irregular and indifferent education in the arts and the humanities.

The meagerness of his formal education notwithstanding, Collodi became a reasonably learned man on his own. He managed to develop a keen knowledge and appreciation of literature and at least a practical acquaintance with music and with the theater. It is known, too, that he was something of a linguist, with an understanding of German and with a sufficient fluency in French to enable him to translate eighteenth-century French fairy tales.

Collodi has been depicted as a successful playwright, a first-rate journalist, a distinguished war veteran, and a dedicated civil servant. In fact, he met with little success in any of these ventures. After he left school for good, Collodi evidently worked at the library of the Piatti in Florence until the fateful year 1848, when the Lombardo-Venetian kingdom rose against the stifling rule of

Austria with the help and support of King Carlo Albert of Sardinia. That year Collodi joined the legions of impassioned young Tuscans who went to do intermittent battle on the side of the Sardinian king.

In that same year, between bouts of soldiering Collodi found the time to begin his journalistic career with the establishment of a journal of political satire called *Il lampione* (The Streetlamp). However, within a year the rebellion, King Carlo, and the little propaganda organ were put down by the Austrians and Collodi was reduced to writing on a job basis for other newspapers. When in 1853 he was able to start another less inflammatory journal, *La scaramuccia* (Controversy), it provided such a lean income that he was forced to continue as a hack journalist until 1859, when he joined the forces of the patriot Giuseppe Garibaldi in his campaign against the Austrians.

As he had done in 1848, Collodi once again served only as a part-time soldier with the ragtag citizen army of the Risorgimento until victory in 1861, when Italy was united under the scepter of Vittorio Emanuele II. As a result of this service prideful latter-day Italian scholars have represented Collodi as a wartime hero who was rewarded by appointment to various civil sinecures in which he continued fervently to serve his country, the while continuing to write and to bask in the warmth of his literary successes.

It is a fact that after the resounding success of the Risorgimento, Collodi returned to Florence, where he triumphantly, if only briefly, revived *Il lampione* and took his pen name from the name of a village near Pescia where his mother had been born. He did indeed enter the civil service and at the same time continued to write articles and essays of some political significance, but things were not at all the way popular biographers have put it.

Garibaldi's army, the miserably magnificent *I Mille* (The Thousand), was composed of hot-headed, middle-class idealists and desperate hollow-eyed peasants who were all convinced that revolution and bloodshed offered the only means to deliverance from tyranny and grinding poverty. Their conviction, however, was shattered when it was discovered that victory would bring deliverance and ascendancy not to them, but to an unspeakably arrogant nobility, a corrupt judiciary, and a greedy moneyed elite who were to reap all the benefits for which those patriots had fought.

Collodi, of course, was one of those intellectual idealists who came home from the wars to resume careers in a bright new society. He soon discovered, however, that the new society provided him and his former comrades very little more freedom than they had been permitted by the alien regime they had routed. In the dreary light of this discovery the disillusioned young man seems to have settled for a thoroughly mundane career in the civil service, which allowed some journalistic activity. He was a generally unenthusiastic employee of the state from 1860 until 1881, first in the Commission of Theatrical Censorship, and then in the Prefecture of Florence.

The articles that Collodi wrote during this period were in much the same vein as those of *Il lampione*, petulantly critical of the prevailing social and political conditions. There was little of enduring interest in these articles, although between 1881 and 1892, significantly after the success of *Le avventure di Pinocchio: Storia di un burattino* (*The Adventures of Pinocchio*, 1883), they were collected and published in volumes that were variously entitled *Macchiette* (Caricatures), *Occhi e nasi* (Eyes and Noses), *Storie allegre* (Cheerful Tales), and ponderously, *Divagazione critico-umoristiche*, which translates more comfortably to "Satirical Ramblings."

It was not really until his mature years that Collodi turned to writing for children, and he began modestly, at the age of fifty, by translating eighteenth-century French fairy tales, most notable among which were *Contes de ma Mère l'Oye* (*Mother Goose Tales*), by Charles Perrault. These were published in 1876 under the simple title *I racconti delle fate* (Fairy Tales). In 1877 he wrote and published a story of his own devising, *Giannettino* (Little Johnnie), which was loosely patterned upon the *Giannetto* of the eighteenth-century didactic writer Parravicini. The local success of *Giannettino* thereupon provided impetus to a series of Little Johnnie books, beginning in 1880 with *Il viaggio per l'Italia di Giannettino I* (Little Johnnie's Travels Through [Northern] Italy), and proceeding through such titles as *La grammatica di Giannettino* (Little Johnnie's Grammar, 1882) and *Il viaggio per l'Italia II* (Little Johnnie's Travels Through [Central] Italy, 1885), and *Il viaggio per l'Italia III* (Travels Through [Southern] Italy, 1886). Giannettino was then equipped with *L'abbaco di Giannettino* (Book of Arithmetic, 1885) and *La geografia di Giannettino* (Book of Geography, 1886). As late as 1890, the very year of his death, Collodi produced a final Little Johnnie book, *La lanterna magica di Giannet-*

tino (Little Johnnie's Magic Lantern). It is interesting to note that all of the Little Johnnie books were published as elementary school texts by the Florentine publishing house of Felice Paggi, a pioneer in the large-scale publication of textbooks in Italy. Significantly, it was Paggi who first published *Pinocchio,* and it was Paggi who helped Collodi find his metier in writing books for children.

But there was more to it than that. The Little Johnnie series was written ostensibly for the education of children, to be read by them or to be read to them by literate adults. They seemed also, however, to have served a somewhat sly secondary purpose, one that Collodi more nearly achieved in what was to be his unwitting tour de force, *The Adventures of Pinocchio.* That purpose was to propagate among the largest possible audience his own often extreme ideology beneath the cloak of the entertaining tale.

If Little Johnnie failed to bring fame and riches to his creator, he nevertheless did him a most valuable service. For here and there in the Little Johnnie books were fleeting glimpses of a real growing boy, not the conventional figure of total wickedness or of total virtue, but an urchin whose nature was a balance of puerile meanness and, in the end, deep-seated feelings of compassion and contrition. Whatever Collodi's purpose in choosing a wooden puppet for the hero of his masterwork, the choice was indeed providential, for he was thereby rescued from the inevitable wrath of those Italians whose prideful parental blindness was sure to have prevented their recognizing the potential for wickedness in their own sons. Most appropriately, Pinocchio was born in humble circumstances in July of 1881. Collodi made him the central figure of an unassuming children's story for which he was commissioned by a Roman editorial group that published it in serial form in a weekly gazette for children called *Giornale per i bambini* (The Children's Newspaper). In the beginning the story bore the simple title *Storia di un burattino* (A Tale of a Puppet), and its first installment appeared in the very first issue of the little weekly.

The story begins in the shop of Mastro Cherry, a carpenter who has found a billet of hard pine with which he proposes to make a table leg, but when he sets to work, he is astonished to hear the piece of wood laugh and cry like a child. Mastro Cherry rids himself of the troublesome little log by presenting it to his old friend Mastro Geppetto, who would like to make a wooden puppet that could "dance, fence with a sword, and turn somersaults" on the stage, so he could earn enough money for his "little bit of bread" and his "little glass of wine."

Before Geppetto starts to carve his puppet he has already named it Pinocchio, which literally means "eye of pine" or "pine knot" in Tuscan. Immediately, Pinocchio begins to play cruel pranks on his creator. No sooner has the old man provided Pinocchio with legs and feet than he scampers out the door and down the street with Geppetto limping and bawling after him. The puppet at last is seized by a carabiniere who holds him fast until Geppetto appears to scold him and threaten dire punishment. The assembly of onlookers, however, sides with Pinocchio and persuades the carabiniere to release him and to take, instead, "that mean old Geppetto" off to jail. Here is to be found the first of Collodi's numerous thrusts at the national constabulary and the corrupt judiciary of his time.

Savoring his freedom, Pinocchio returns to Geppetto's house only to confront *Grillo Parlante* (Talking Cricket), a large cricket who lectures him on the evils of childish disobedience. In anger the puppet kills Talking Cricket by bashing him with a mallet, whereupon he ransacks the house for something to assuage his hunger. Finding nothing to eat and being exhausted, he slumps to sleep on a chair with his feet resting on the edge of a smoldering brazier. When Geppetto returns next morning, he finds Pinocchio with his feet burned off.

The old man sets about making new feet for Pinocchio, who now promises to go to school and learn a trade so he can support his "Daddy" in his old age. This proposal, of course, goes counter to Geppetto's original plan to put Pinocchio immediately to work on the stage. But neither Pinocchio nor Geppetto can be blamed for the contradiction; it is the fault of author Collodi, who, in writing a current chapter of his serial, would frequently forget what he had said in previous ones.

Meanwhile, to ready Pinocchio for school, Geppetto fashions clothes and shoes for him from old wallpaper, bread crumbs, and birchbark. Then, as a final unselfish paternal gesture, he sells his only coat to provide Pinocchio with a schoolbook. As the puppet marches confidently off to school, his generally perilous series of adventures begin, while old Geppetto drops from sight, not to be seen again until the penultimate chapter, where he is discovered languishing in the smelly belly of a gigantic shark.

Up to this point, then, it has taken Collodi the space of eight expository chapters—short ones, to be sure—to identify and characterize his puppet protagonist. In those chapters Pinocchio is described as naughty and mischievous. This early characterization has led many critics to represent him, as does the catalogist of the Library of Congress, as "a wooden puppet full of tricks and mischief. . . ." But beyond chapter 4 the puppet cannot be considered mischievous, for "mischief" as committed by a youngster implies only prankishness to one annoying degree and another. And this exactly is his fault up to that time, although his wanton killing of Talking Cricket shows the newly created Pinocchio capable of downright wickedness.

However, from the fourth chapter until the resolution of the last two chapters, while that block-headed puppet-child can be called selfish, ungrateful, irresponsible, disobedient, foolishly gullible, and, at times, untruthful, his nobler thoughts are occupied with the welfare of his old Daddy and how he can please his Fairy benefactress. In spite of his motivation to do the right things, he is too innocent and unschooled in the ways of the world. Thus he can be, and constantly is, lured into the most unpleasant and fearsome situations by conscienceless companions.

Beginning with chapter 9 Pinocchio betrays three of his childish traits—selfishness, ingratitude, and irresponsibility—by selling his schoolbook for the price of admission to a puppet show. The puppets performing on the stage recognize Pinocchio and disrupt the performance to welcome him. For his impudence, the puppetmaster threatens to use Pinocchio's wooden corpus to kindle his kitchen fire, but he is at last mollified by the puppet's flattery and sends him on his way home with a parting gift of five gold pieces!

From this point, Pinocchio's only interest is to get back to Geppetto and support him nobly with his golden treasure. On the way, however, he falls in with the nefarious Fox and Cat, who later disguise themselves and waylay the foolish puppet with the intent to steal his gold. After a frenetic chase into a deep forest, Pinocchio, who has concealed his money in his mouth, is caught by robbers who hang him from the limb of a great oak, planning to return for the gold pieces when he is dead. Collodi and his audience are now arrived at the end of chapter 15, where the author had thought to end his tale. However, the audience set up such a clamor that he was forced to extend the series by another twenty-one installments.

To resuscitate Pinocchio, in chapter 16 Collodi introduces *la bella Bambina dai cappelli turchini* (the beautiful little Girl with the deep blue hair), who rescues the puppet and becomes his "little sister." Later on, when she is grown up, she becomes his *Fata,* or Fairy, who serves then as his "little mother."

Even under the patient care of the Fairy, however, Pinocchio is determined to get back to Geppetto, and in the process he manages to have at least another nineteen hectic chapters of calamitous adventure. Again he is beguiled by the Fox and Cat who finally steal his gold pieces, and when he reports the theft to the authorities, he is thrown into jail for four months for his impertinence. Finally released, Pinocchio has a comically unpleasant experience with a gigantic snake with a smoking tail, and later an angry farmer catches him stealing grapes and punishes him by forcing him to act as a watchdog. When at last he is free, he makes the sad discovery that his Fairy is dead.

As he mourns the death of the Fairy, a huge Pigeon happens by and tells him that old Geppetto is preparing to cross the sea in a small boat to search for his son in the New World. The Pigeon obligingly carries Pinocchio to the seashore, where he dives into the water to try to save his Daddy, but in vain.

After a variety of minor difficulties, the puppet finds his Fairy again, somehow resurrected and grown to "little mother" size. She promises him that if he will be very good and will study hard, he will become a real boy instead of a wooden puppet.

But once again, Pinocchio is led astray by naughty schoolmates and he begins a new series of misadventures. He is persuaded to sneak off to Toyland and enjoys five months of joyous fun, after which he is turned into a donkey and is sold to a circus to be a performer. In his first performance, however, he is lamed by a fall and is sold to a man who wants his skin for a drumhead and throws him into the sea to drown him. Through the magical offices of his Fairy, Pinocchio's donkey skin is stripped off by hungry fishes, but while he is swimming to freedom, he is swallowed by a great Shark.

Not to worry! Pinocchio discovers his Daddy living perilously in the belly of the Shark. From this point on, Pinocchio becomes quite the little man who very rationally takes charge of matters. He rescues the frail old man and nurses him to health, meanwhile performing hard manual labor and weaving baskets to support the two of them. Finally, as a grand reward for his diligence and unselfishness, the Fairy, who is never to be seen again, provides Pinocchio with a house and a large sum of money, and turns him at last into a real boy.

Early in February 1883, the brothers Paggi of Florence, who already had listed in their catalog Collodi's *Racconti delle fate, Occhi e nasi,* and four of the Giannettino books, took over the serialized *Storia di un burattino* and, after minimal editorial adjustment, published it in a single volume with a new title, *Le avventure di Pinocchio: Storia di un burattino.* Collodi, the school dropout, the ineffectual political militant, erstwhile playwright, apathetic civil servant, and penny-a-line journalist, was at last a success—seven years before he died.

In 1892 an astute Englishwoman, Mary Alice Murray, took upon herself the task of translating his masterwork, whereupon it was published in London by the house of Fisher Unwin under the title *The Story of a Puppet; or, the Adventures of Pinocchio.* In the same year, Pinocchio was introduced to American children by Cassell Publishing Company of New York, which served as distributor for Unwin. For what remained of the nineteenth century and for the first third of the twentieth, the story of the marvelous puppet became a favorite not only of children, but of parents required to read it aloud to smaller children who were not yet able to read it for themselves.

Indeed, as thousands of American children and their parents discovered back in the early twenties, *The Adventures of Pinocchio* is not just another condescending collection of fairy stories scribbled out for little kids! It is a *novel,* a novel for children to be sure, but no less a remarkably imaginative and lively apprenticeship novel as thematically developed as, say, the best of the Horatio Alger stories. This is the quaintly heroic tale of the generally intractable, willful, but ultimately golden-hearted wooden puppet, that Pinocchio with whom legions of children of the twenties and thirties grew up.

But not everyone of that period knew the genuine Pinocchio. Scarcely had the first English translation of Collodi's wonderful little work appeared than it was seized by opportunists in the form of well-meaning but often self-righteous pedagogues, who emasculated the story by abridgment and euphemism in their efforts to adapt it more gently to the infant Anglo-American ear and eye. Over the years, then, poor little Pinocchio has been bowdlerized, expurgated, abridged, adapted, dramatized, trivialized, diluted, and generally gutted!

Then there were the pirates, shirtsleeves-printers fancying themselves publishers who churned out scores of inferior versions of the Collodi classic. These rascals not only pirated the adapted editions but often, for the sake of niggardly economy, further truncated and mutilated the adaptations so that what was passed off on an unsuspecting audience as genuine often bore little resemblance to the original beyond the name *Pinocchio* and the fact that the story was concerned with a puppet.

It is sad to think that the father of Pinocchio received relatively little compensation in his native Italy for his labors. It is sadder still to realize that Collodi received absolutely nothing from any other country, including the United States, for his delightful little novel, which, in America at least, has been so prostituted and abused, the while bringing profit to its abusers.

After the tale of the willful marionette was published as a book in 1883, it so caught the fancy of adults who read it to their young that it went through four more editions by 1890, the year in which Collodi died at the age of sixty-four. The shameful fact is that it was not until 1886 that a uniform international copyright system to protect authors from literary theft was provided for by the Berne Convention. Incredibly, however, and to its lasting disgrace, the United States refused to become a party to the convention. It is easy to understand how Collodi's rights to his own work in anything but its Italian form could be blithely and cynically dismissed.

Until 1891 there was no law in the United States that afforded foreign authors protection. Printers and publishers theretofore dealt with such writers by rule of conscience, of which property there seems to have been precious little in the nineteenth century.

For that matter, the Chace Act of 1891 provided a foreign author cold comfort. He could indeed enjoy copyright protection in America if he submitted two copies of his work to the Library of Congress, but only if those copies were printed from type that had been set within the borders of the United States. By the time the Chace Act was passed, Collodi had been dead for a year, and even at that, had he lived, it is unlikely that he could have afforded the expense of having his original work set in type in America on the gamble that it would sell.

But the ultimate destruction of the genuine literary tradition of Pinocchio, not only in America but all over the world, was wrought in 1940 by Walt Disney. In that year, Disney Studios reduced Collodi's *Adventures of Pinocchio* to a mere cartoon absurdity—a fact bitterly resented by every literate adult at the time—by destroying the finely drawn character of the selfish, good-for-nothing knave of a puppet and gratuitously replacing it with that of a preciously cute cartoon creature that came through less as a wooden marionette than as a vaguely naughty-but-nice little boy.

Nor did the cartoonists stop with the destruction of Pinocchio himself. What they did to the subordinate characters! That extraordinary company of human and animal creatures that Collodi had so cannily and skillfully designed to convey to his readers his expression of the social and political evils of his post-revolution Italy simply vanished in Disney's hands and were replaced with the hokey stereotypes so dear to the movie cartoonist. In Disney's asinine version of *Pinocchio,* only eight secondary characters survive, and those not very identifiably: Geppetto, the Fairy, Talking Cricket, the Fox and the Cat, the Pigeon, Lampwick, and the Coachman. These are all that remain of the original delightful cast of nearly fifty characters, which included such marvelous creatures as the puppets, Punchinello and Harlequin; the ferocious puppet-master, Fire Eater; the fierce Green Fisherman; the Snake with the Smoking Tail; the Poodle Coachman; the Gorilla Judge, the Black Rabbit Pallbearers; the Snail Housekeeper; the preachy Firefly; the Owl and Crow consulting physicians; numerous donkeys and a clutch of thieving Polecats. With the very flesh of Collodi's little *romanzo buffo* thus stripped away, Disney's *Pinocchio,* except for its appealing artwork and its charming musical score, is little better than the animated inanity of a Woody Woodpecker cartoon.

Of course, while Disney frequently borrowed themes from folktales and fairy stories—sometimes with considerable success and without causing real damage—it must be noted that *The Adventures of Pinocchio* may not, in any sense, be considered a folktale. The extraordinary concept of a wooden puppet as storybook hero was Collodi's own. Nowhere in the vast folkloric tradition of Italy is there to be found any material that Collodi might have borrowed to flesh out episodes of his novel. Collodi first invented Pinocchio and then invented Pinocchio's world, which he furnished with creatures of his own devising. Just as surely, then, as Mickey Mouse was the brainchild of Walt Disney, Pinocchio was the exclusive product of C. Collodi's genius.

Almost from the time in 1883 when *The Adventures of Pinocchio* was first published in book form,

it has been considered the finest work of its kind in Italian literature. Also, the remarkable tale has become since that time so universally popular that it has been translated into nearly a hundred foreign languages, including Swahili, in which dialect the puppet's name becomes "Pinokyo." But for all its classical status, and its wide appeal, its author cannot, even with the advantage afforded him by the vigorously rich idiom of his native language, be thought of as a great writer, or even as a generally good writer. In the inevitable body of criticism that has developed around Collodi and his masterwork, there has been an abundance of thoughtful, scholarly observation that indicates real appreciation of both strengths and weaknesses in his writing. On the other hand, there are a distressing number of otherwise serious and capable translators and scholars who have been entrapped or misled by Collodi's discrepancies and, out of sheer respect for the man who produced such a classic, have sought determinedly to interpret inconsistency, incongruity, and positively ragged composition as depth of thought and subtlety of expression. They simply refuse to believe that a writer of such stature and reputation could allow careless textual errors to stand when he had every opportunity to discover and correct them before they went into print. The fact is, Collodi was not a writer of stature and reputation. Besides the articles and essays he had published during and after the revolution, he composed, after turning his hand to drama, an uninspired comedy of three acts that seems to have attracted little or no critical notice. His translation of Perrault's "Mother Goose Tales" was, of course, only of local interest, as were his numerous Little Johnnie books. He was, in sum, a part-time journalist of hack grade who seems to have had little urge to correct errors after a piece had been published. Collodi managed to keep his editing to a leisurely minimum, and whatever polish appears upon the rhetoric of *Pinocchio* was undoubtedly imparted by an eloquence bred of his own enthusiasm for his subject.

The pity of the matter is that most Anglo-American critics have never read Collodi's *Pinocchio.* They are ignorant, therefore, of Collodi's actual status as an Italian writer because they have been misled by whole platoons of translators whose own misinterpretations and gratuitous emendations have only aggravated whatever inconsistencies and mistakes of which the author was guilty in the first place.

For example, in the first edition the first sentence of chapter 6 is "Per l'appunto era una nottataccia d'inverno," which translates to "As it happens, it was a nasty winter night." In several subsequent printings, however, *inverno* was changed to *inferno* because someone, presumably a copy editor, found in chapter 7 Pinocchio reporting to Geppetto that he had spent a *nottata d'inferno*—actually a *nasty* night or, at worst, a *devilish* night. Thinking to provide consistency where none was actually required, he went back to the phrase in chapter 6 and changed it to "nottataccia d'inferno" (an awful night in hell). Collodi, of course, failed to notice the change, and the translators who referred to these flawed texts simply compounded the error. Unfortunately, this change lured many a critic to the discovery and interpretation of an imagery of sin and infernal punishment, much as did the author of the pious elaboration of Melville's use, in *Moby-Dick,* of the metaphor "soiled fish of the sea" only later to discover that it should have read correctly "coiled fish of the sea."

Then there is the matter of Collodi's forgetfulness. In chapter 3 he establishes the quaint fact that Geppetto had forgotten to equip his puppet with ears. Toward the end of the story, however, when Pinocchio is being turned into a donkey, he awakens one morning and, in scratching his head, he discovers that "overnight his ears had grown at least five inches longer!" Now the forgetful Collodi finds himself trapped, and must hurriedly and lamely explain that "puppets, from the time they are born, have tiny little ears—in fact, they are so tiny that you can't even see them."

Collodi's memory could even fail him within a single short chapter. In the epigraphic caption of the three-page fifth chapter he refers to Pinocchio's "omelet," but a half-page later the omelet becomes a poached egg. In the very same chapter, he has Pinocchio's nose growing long from the effect of hunger, but a dozen chapters later the growth of the puppet's nose becomes a sign that he is lying.

Among the numerous Collodi inconsistencies, which he seems to have found only too blithesomely easy to ignore, one in particular has reared above all others to confound earnest editors and drive them to wits' end for means to justify it or at least to explain it away. This lapse occurs between the writing of chapter 9 and that of chapter 23. In the earlier chapter, Pinocchio has not yet had a single day of schooling, and being quite unable to read, he must have the sign on the puppet theater read for him. In the latter chapter, the erstwhile illiterate comes upon the grave of the "Girl with the blue hair," his Fairy, and slowly but accurately reads the inscription on the gravestone.

The apparent lacunae in Collodi's memory can be explained, at least in part, by the fact that *Pinocchio* was first a weekly serial. Since he had other matters of livelihood to occupy him as he struggled to get out weekly episodes, he sometimes lost minor threads of his own story, and if ever they were recovered, he seems simply to have neglected to remedy the resulting inconsistencies. To make matters even more difficult for him, the serial tale suffered two long intermissions, the first coming after the publication of the fifteenth chapter, with which Collodi had originally planned to end the story. The second recess occurred after the twenty-ninth chapter, and the final installment did not appear in *Giornale per i bambini* until 25 January, 1883, some 130 weeks after Pinocchio's creation.

It may be wondered why, after nearly a lifetime of expressing political and social dissent, Collodi at last turned to writing stories for children. The fact is that he wrote his *Adventures of Pinocchio* no more especially for children than did Jonathan Swift write his *Gulliver's Travels* for such a select and innocent audience. Instead, he simply reasoned that by publishing chapters of his tale in serial form in a children's weekly paper, he could appeal to the broadest of audiences in that the story would be read not only by literate children, but also by parents who would be required to read it to their pre-school offspring. In this way children could be amused, and adults both entertained and enlightened by Collodi's satire of the injustice imposed upon the weak and the lowly by minions of the new postwar monarchy.

In recent years serious students of Collodi have wondered why it is that since 1892 hardly a year has passed during which some American publisher has not released it in one form or another, yet nobody seems to read it. The truth is, however, that the Murray translation of *Pinocchio* and the Della Chiesà translation of 1925 were widely read and enjoyed by the members of literate families. And the little wooden picaro might well have continued to be a universal hero of childhood had it not been discovered by sundry moral patrolmen of the isolationist 1920's and 1930's that he was an Italian, a pernicious alien whose vicious deportment could somehow infect American youth with the evils that teemed on foreign shores.

The tragic fact of the genuine *Pinocchio* is that it transcended the parochial intellect of the commonplace critic, reviewer, and pedagogue, who, in their misunderstanding of its purpose, its explicitness, and its "barbarism," decided that it was just not suitable fare for American children. What to do, then. with this offensive thing to make it acceptable to everyone excepting, of course, those thinking persons, including children, who would prefer to make such decisions for themselves. The answer was just the fumbling sort that springs most naturally and immediately to the small mind: "Let's level this molehill and rebuild it to suit the demands of propriety."

Thus, *The Adventures of Pinocchio* was rebuilt by revision, adaptation, and general emasculation to the point of utter sterility by the time it fell into Disney hands.

Selected Bibliography

WORKS OF C. COLLODI IN ITALIAN

I racconti delle fate. Florence: Paggi, 1876.

Giannettino. Florence: Paggi. 1877.

Il viaggio per l'Italia di Giannettino I (L'Italia superiore). Florence: Paggi, 1877.

La grammatica di Giannettino, per le scuole elementari. Florence: Paggi, 1882.

Le avventure di Pinocchio: Storia di un burattino. Florence: Paggi, 1883.

Il viaggio per l'Italia di Giannettino II (L'Italia centrale). Florence: Paggi, 1885.

L'abbaco di Giannettino. Florence: Paggi, 1885.

La geografia di Giannettino. Florence: Paggi, 1886.

Il viaggio per l'Italia III (L'Italia meridionale). Florence: Florence: Paggi, 1886.

La lanterna magica di Giannettino. Florence: Paggi, 1890.

EDITIONS OF PINOCCHIO IN ENGLISH TRANSLATION

The following titles have been extracted from a compilation by Richard Wunderlich of significant Pinocchio editions published in the United States.

The Story of a Puppet; or, The Adventures of Pinocchio, translated by M. A. Murray. With illustrations by Enrico Mazzanti. London: T. Fisher Unwin, 1891; New York: Cassell, 1892.

Pinocchio's Adventures in Wonderland, translated by Hezekiah Butterworth. With illustrations. Boston: Jordan, Marsh, 1898.

The Adventures of Pinocchio, translated by Walter S. Cramp. With illustrations by Charles Copeland. Boston: Ginn, 1904. (First American translation.)

Pinocchio: The Tale of a Puppet, translated by M. A. Murray. With illustrations by Charles Folkard. London: J. M. Dent and Sons, 1911; New York: E. P. Dutton, 1911.

Pinocchio: The Story of a Puppet. With illustrations by Maria L. Kirk. Philadelphia and London: J. B. Lippincott, 1920. (The M. A. Murray translation.)

The Adventures of Pinocchio, translated by Carol Della Ciesa. With illustrations by Attilio Mussiano. New York: Macmillan, 1925.

Pinocchio: The Adventures of a Marionette, translated by Walter S. Cramp. With an introduction by Carl Van Doren and illustrations by Richard Floethe. New York: Limited Editions Club, 1937.

Pinocchio: A Story for Children, adapted by Roselle Ross. With illustrations by Henry Muheim. New York: Saalfield, 1939. (First adaption known to embody significant changes in the story.)

Pinocchio. Edited by Watty Piper. With illustrations by Tony Sarg. New York: Platt and Munk, 1940. (An adaptation.)

The Adventures of Pinocchio, translated by M. A. Murray. With illustrations by Fritz Kredel. New York: Grosset and Dunlap, 1946.

Pinocchio, the Adventures of a Little Wooden Boy, translated by Joseph Walker. With illustrations by Richard Floethe. Cleveland and New York: World, 1946.

The Adventures of Pinocchio: Tale of a Puppet, translated by M. L. Rosenthal. With illustrations by Troy Howell. New York: Lothrop, Lee and Shepard Books, 1983.

The Pinocchio of C. Collodi, translated and annotated by James T. Teahan. With illustrations by Alexa Jaffurs. New York: Schocken Books, 1985.

CRITICAL STUDIES OF PINOCCHIO

The following list is based on a compilation made by Thomas J. Morrissey.

Bacon, Martha. "Puppet's Progress." *Atlantic Monthly* 225 (April 1970). Reprinted in *Children's Literature: Views and Reviews,* edited by Virginia Haviland. Glenview, Ill.: Scott, Foresman, 1973.

Budgey, Norman E. Introduction to *The Adventures of Pinocchio,* trans. M.A. Murray. New York: Airmont Books, 1966, pp. 7–11.

Cambon, Glauco. "*Pinocchio* and the Problems of Children's Literature." *Children's Literature* 2: 50–60.

"Carlo Collodi." *Children's Literature Review,* edited by Gerard J. Senick. Detroit: Gale Research, 1983. Vol. 5, pp. 69–87.

Gannon, Susan R. "A Note on Collodi and Lucian." *Children's Literature* 8: 98–102 (1980).

———. "*Pinocchio*: The First Hundred Years." *Children's Literature Association Quarterly* 6: 1ff. (Winter 1981–1982).

Heins, Paul. "A Second Look: *The Adventures of Pinocchio*." *The Horn Book Magazine* 58: 200–205 (April 1982).

Heisig, James W. "Pinocchio: The Archetype of the Motherless Child." *Children's Literature* 3: 23–35 (1974).

Morrissey, Thomas J. "Alive and Well But Not Unscathed: A Response to Susan T. Gannon's '*Pinocchio*: The First Hundred Years.'" *Children's Literature Association Quarterly* 7: 37–39 (Summer 1982).

———, and Wunderlich, Richard. "Death and Rebirth in *Pinocchio*," *Children's Literature* 11: 64–75 (1983).

———. Review of *Pinocchio's Nose*. In *Children's Literature Association Quarterly* 9: 83–84 (Summer 1984).

Van Doren, Carl. Introduction to *The Adventures of Pinocchio*. New York: Limited Editions Club, 1937.

Wunderlich, Richard, and Morrissey, Thomas J. "The Desecration of *Pinocchio* in the United States." *The Horn Book Magazine* 58: 205–212 (April 1982).

———. "*Pinocchio* Before 1920: The Popular and Pedagogical Traditions." *Italian Quarterly* 23: 61–72 (Spring 1982).

—JAMES T. TEAHAN

PADRAIC COLUM

1881-1972

PADRAIC COLUM'S WORDS stir up a strong potion of mists, Irish heroes, bird feathers, and candlelight, all colored by glimpses of his own childhood. His early years remained at the surface of his thoughts, and this is evident even in new printings of his works for both adults and children. To the good fortune of children in Great Britain, Ireland, the United States, the Pacific, and Canada, he wrote prolifically for all ages of readers and lectured extensively throughout his long life.

In reintroducing Colum's *Collected Poems* in 1953, John L. Sweeney said, "It is as an ever new singer in a very old tradition that Padraic Colum will always be remembered." That year Colum received the Gregory Medal awarded him by the Council of the Irish Academy of Letters for very distinguished work. In 1961 he received the Regina Medal, given annually since 1959 by the Catholic Library Association for continued distinguished contributions to children's literature. There were many other awards in the intervening years. Colum, the "ever new singer" in the old tradition of the wandering bard, is remembered in Ireland more for his poetry, but in other countries for his children's books. Because he was gifted in writing in many forms and did so with gusto and good fortune, a simple chronological record of his writing can mislead. He was a consummate circuit rider; new notes and versions of his work are reflections of his "open road."

Colum's writing for children is ripe for republishing for modern generations of readers. The earliest editions of Colum's books are unfailingly the most enjoyable and attractive; libraries remain the best source for these old volumes. Current anthologies include Colum selections. His writing for adults is gaining an appreciative readership as renewed interest in Irish literature grows. The guarantee of a continuing audience for his children's books has something to do with Colum's background and with today's recognition that storytelling is the key to children's literacy and its delight.

In *Padraic Colum: A Biographical-Critical Introduction,* written with Colum's cooperation, Zack Bowen comments: "Just as his subject matter is predominantly Irish, his style can also be generally described as familiar and colloquial. . . . The particular criteria of excellence in evaluating Colum's work are not the normal currency of contemporary literary critics, because few other serious writers attempt what he is doing. . . ." Bowen's term "colloquial" only begins to describe the rhythm and sound of Colum's writing; Padraic Colum also had a strong sense of the visual. In one of his last interviews, he comments: "I have lived in a world of writers, but I have been interested in painting more than in any of the other arts. I would like to know more about music, but, unfortunately I began too late."

Bowen suggests that the study of Colum is a challenge to critics; he wrote concurrently in many genres, for people of all ages, during his long career. With his patience as watcher and listener, his widespread travels, his background as a reader and a linguist, few critics were equal to tracking the length and breadth of his open road.

Sanford Sternlicht in his introduction to *Selected Short Stories of Padraic Colum* (1985) states:

> Storytelling for the young gave Colum the opportunity to relive his own childhood in rural Ireland. Indeed, he began to learn the storyteller's craft as an Irish child sitting by a peat fire and listening to adults spin yarns. However, most of Colum's stories for young people are based on folklore and mythology, not on late-nineteenth-century Irish peasant life. In gifting the young with his storytelling skills Colum chose to serve as a translator of cultural history; Irish, European in general, Ancient Greek, and even Hawaiian.

Colum must never have known a life without impermanence. As a very young boy, he was immersed in a stream of untethered humanity. He said: "I was born in Longford, where my father was Master of the workhouse. He afterwards became Stationmaster at Sandycove, outside Dublin, and I went to the national school at Glasthule. I was the eldest of a family of eight." Consider that the workhouse was meant for impoverished itinerant families. The distinct theme of aloneness in the midst of family upheaval is treated with clarity in Colum's adult novel *The Flying Swans* (1957), in which he recalls his early emotions. He later said: "I never want to live permanently in America or anywhere else, because by nature I am a wanderer. I first went to America in 1914 because I could not earn a living here; I had just married, and there was no living to be had in Dublin." Reminiscences are scattered throughout essays, introductions to anthologies, and his small spiral notebook manuscripts:

> I aged six, and my brother, aged five, are going to school. Before us or alongside of us are a ragged family—father, mother, a boy, and maybe a girl. These have come through the gate of a large-sized building that is our home. That building is the workhouse of the district. My father is master there. That family alongside my brother and me have had a night's shelter there. They are itinerants of some kind, and after doing some jobs on the way—the man may be a tinker or a basketmaker—will spend the night in another workhouse. . . . Never before (and, I may add, never since) did I see a white crow on the shoulder of a boy whose day was to be on the long road that led to towns that were captivating. And here we were, lesson books in hands, going to stand in classes.
>
> (*Something About the Author*, p. 46)

This passage gives an idea of Colum's colloquial style and of what he terms "reverie." Colum the imagemaker is evident also.

Until he was nine, Colum traveled to fairs with Mickey Burns, an uncle who was a buyer of fowl. He was "a man of affairs in the Cavan district . . . [and] a remarkable ballad singer who would regale his young companion with ballads and legends as they strode along the Cavan road." Colum recalled these early years in the introduction to his collection *A Treasury of Irish Folklore* (1954).

Other writers also compiled short biographies of Colum. Cornelia Meigs, in her classic *A Critical History of Children's Literature*, makes several connections clear:

> The Irish Renaissance was a very vital movement in Ireland when Padraic Colum was a young man living in Dublin. Stories and poetry which had been a part of his childhood had given him an early interest in the legends and traditions of Ireland which was stimulated by the Celtic Revival. . . . When he came to America in 1914 he began translating passages from a long Irish folk story . . . to keep from forgetting the language. His translation found its way to the children's page of the New York *Tribune*, where it caught the interest of the Hungarian illustrator Willy Pogány, who suggested that Mr. Colum write a book which he would illustrate. Mr. Colum took his translation, added to it and wove it into the long romantic story full of adventures and enchantment, *The King of Ireland's Son*.
>
> (p. 454)

Colum's years in Dublin were very productive. From his training at the Abbey Theatre, staging and characterization became instinctive writing skills. Besides writing plays (the first was produced in 1903) Colum received a scholarship to read at the National Library of Ireland, courted his future wife, attended Celtic Revival salons, became involved in politics, and wrote his first children's book, *A Boy in Eirinn* (1913), for a series called "The Children of the Nations."

Stephen Brown's critique of the book stated that the author does not "write down" to children. Zack Bowen concedes that "the book does convey the sense of what it is like to be a child" (with some reservations, about its tone of overt patriotism for example). Although it is out of print, *A Boy in Eirinn* deserves mention. Solitary watching echoes here, as in other of Colum's stories; he says, for example, "At night when Finn sat by the fire with the door closed and the candles burning at the window recesses the things of the house became curious." Fireside scenes and candlelight give his cottage interiors a theatrical aspect. In "Art and Infancy" Colum focuses on this aspect of oral story-telling:

> Here sits a child watching a woman knitting. The flame on the hearth rises and sinks down; there are shadows on the walls; the cat drags her kittens about. A man comes in with a load of wood, and a friendly or quarrelsome discussion begins between him and the Knitter. These are types that the child will remember, that he will discover in every literature. As he listens to them he hears about human history and human relationships. Rhymes, fables, lists of straits and capes, conjugations and declensions, become part of what he guesses at. He knows about the world as man first knew about it—as myth.
>
> (*A Half-Day's Ride*, p. 140)

Colum was no less attracted to the myriad distractions of lighting. He explains:

> In every history the children heard or read there was a candle. . . . No explorer or interpreter of the child mind has made enough of the fact that children can be and love to be spectators and audience. . . . I have a notion that what makes children such absorbed spectators and audiences might flourish better by the light of the little candle than under the charming arrangement that holds the electric bulbs in the present-day room.
>
> (ibid., pp. 138–139)

A Boy in Eirinn enabled Colum to document not just rural family life but also the other life, that of the rambles and the open road that took him past castle and round tower ruins and through thickets and hedges full of birds and wildlife. He had watched and listened ever so carefully: "The first birds' nest that Finn was ever shown was upon the old road. It was a robin's, and when he looked in Finn saw a brown, bright-eyed creature that hardly seemed a bird at all. High in the trees there were pigeons and jay-thrushes' nests." Birds were his favorite subjects, but grass, bees, and always "creatures," later used to title a poetry book, found their way into his writing.

This often suited his illustrators, the finest technicians of their day; they approached his writing as worthy of much more than adjunct decoration. Jack B. Yeats, his first illustrator (*A Boy in Eirinn* and *The Big Tree of Bunlahy*, 1933), gives the setting for their collaboration:

> When I search for any artistic influences which may have in some way affected my drawing for children, I remember that I was a child when the books of Randolph Caldecott and Walter Crane were first published; and it would be a shabby-souled child who would not be carried off the ground by *The Three Jovial Huntsmen, John Gilpin, The Hind in the Wood,* and *The Fairy Ship.*
>
> (quoted in Bertha Mahony Miller et al., *Illustrators of Children's Books* [1947], p. 376)

Yeats was not speaking merely of drawings on paper; he intimated that it was important to be "carried off the ground," saying, in effect, that there was a real place for a visual approach to children's books. Where Yeats was writing with pictures, Colum was picturing with writing. It may have been Colum's sense of the theatrical that gave him focus, whether he was describing an interior cottage scene or a walk from one place to another. Very often he would give the details of a scene, letting the meaning fall into place as in a puzzle.

A Boy in Eirinn was more straightforward than some of Colum's other books. The frontispiece was an illustration by Yeats of a moment that did not come often in the lives of many Irish boys. It pictured Finn buying two pieces of gingerbread with an extra penny; Colum did not skip over one of a child's main interests, eating. The fourth chapter, "One of Finn's Days," begins with the fetching of water in a gallon can (from some real distance) for porridge and tea, after which "Finn was given porridge, and when he had taken it he was ready for school and he would start off with two books in his hand and two pieces of bread in his pocket." Formality was not an end sought by either Colum or Yeats: natural landscapes and modest events intrigued them most. Illustrations were titled "When Finn Had a Penny," "Finn and the Gallon Can," "At Night When Finn Sat by the Fire," "St. Bridget's Cross," "It Was As Grand a Fire As Finn Ever Saw," and "Finn's Uncle Bartley."

The poignant comment "Afterwards the house was very lonely . . ." follows the "arrest" episode. The plot is loosely drawn from Colum's own difficult family circumstances (high rents, political jailings, loss of a mother)—worries that children have no control over. Critics felt that this portion of the book weakened its credibility. But the "troubles" of Ireland have not yet been resolved; Colum may have guessed that they would still concern children for a long time.

Colum's first book preceded his move to the United States in 1914. Zack Bowen marks the juncture by saying, "An intimate friend of the giants of modern literature in America and France, as well as in England and Ireland, Colum had a major part in shaping the direction of the Irish theatre and in bringing classical literature to children in comprehensible, appealing form." By 1921 the Colums were established in New York City, a base from which they continued to travel. That year, a second edition of Colum's book *The King of Ireland's Son,* with illustrations by Willy Pogány, heralded a continuing collaboration between the two on mythological tales for some years to come. The magnificent Pogány illustrations were part of the reason that Colum felt it was his finest book for children. Elaborate four-color plates and fine black-and-white full-page chapter title illustrations were interspersed with subchapter beginnings and a title page in Celtic uncials. This edition is extremely rare. By contrast, the third edition, published by Floris Books in 1978, has reduced the book's impact by featuring sketches by G. and W. Knapp aimed at a modern market. In the story "When the King of Cats Came to Visit King Connal's Dominion," Pogány's cat is fierce and ragged, flying over a windswept sea with the bearing of a mystic wildcat. The Knapps' cat has no such enigmatic overtones, thus placing the story in another context.

The *King of Ireland's Son* is constructed as a set of stories within a story, best read in segments by older children. The stories read as a log of the adventures of the son of a heroic family. The book opens:

> Connal was the name of the king who ruled over Ireland at that time. He had three sons, and as the fir trees grow, some crooked and some straight, one of them grew up so wild that in the end the King and the King's Councillor had to let him have his own way in everything. This youth was the King's eldest son and his mother had died before she could be a guide to him.

Many episodes later, in which the King's son repeats the following verse, a resolution of the difficulties comes about:

> His hound at his heel,
> His hawk on his wrist;
> A brave steed to carry him whither his list,
> And the blue sky over him.

As an example of Colum's signature language in folktale, another passage rings out: "[They] took the path that went round the Hill of Horns and at the other side of the hill they found a hut thatched with one great wing of a bird." We find here at least four different frames: the path, the Hill, the other side of the Hill, the hut itself. Alliteration of the repeated "h" and imagery mark Colum's poetic skills.

The traditional writing conventions Colum espoused are summarized in his essay "Story Telling New and Old":

> They have reverie behind them, these stories that have such patterns, such series of happenings, such simplicity of characterization as make it possible to deliver them orally to an unselected audience. This is true of the stories for children that writers such as Hans Andersen and Rudyard Kipling have made up. And the best story-tellers are the men and women who seem to be giving us in stories they are telling fragments of their reverie, this dramatizing of something different from what is in our external consciousness, that makes the story told distinct from the story that is written to be read by the reader.

Colum's "voice" can be found in many works and in his own recorded readings. For a return to readers' theater *A Treasury of Irish Folklore* is the best of anthologies. After publishing this collection Colum expanded on its contents in other works. As he noted in *Irish Folklore,* "The folklore of Ireland—the stories, songs, jests, riddles, usages, charms that make the body of this unwritten literature—is very voluminous."

From 1918 to 1940 Colum produced much of his best writing for children. The security of his affiliation with Macmillan and the encouragement of his editor, Louise Seaman Bechtel, made this period of his life most productive. Bechtel wrote of him:

> For me . . . he epitomized a genius as did not any other living author I knew. His small, erect figure, his noble head with that huge brow, his voice with its pure "Dublin English" accent, were a revelation to one who knew only the "stage Irishman." He

was impractical, forgetful, picturesque, excitable—the traditional poet; but he was also gentle and wise, and had always a commanding dignity.

(*Books in Search of Children*, p. 132)

Colum collected a series of classic tales in 1918 for *The Adventures of Odysseus and the Tale of Troy*, reissued in 1946 under the heading *The Children's Homer*. In 1921 *The Golden Fleece and the Heroes Who Lived Before Achilles* was published. These two titles were published in 1983 as a two-volume paperback set, retaining some of Pogány's illustrations. *The Children of Odin*, also with Pogány illustrations, was published in 1920 and reissued in 1962. Clifton Fadiman included an episode from it in his 1984 anthology, *The World Treasury of Children's Literature*. *The Riverside Anthology of Children's Literature* includes several selections from these books of Colum's. The paperback *Children of Odin* retains some Pogány drawings, but has the flavor of a textbook, as do the other two books in paperback format. Whereas the original editions show extraordinary care in the design detail and serve as "treasured" tales, they have been reduced in character by the changes.

The prose in these books has meaning for children younger than those who now are given Edith Hamilton's *Mythology*, and they expand on the picture book versions of Ingre and Edgar Parin D'Aulaire. Colum's use of reverie sets his versions apart. A comparison of Hamilton's and Colum's tellings of the same stories shows how lyrical the Colum versions are; they are more readable for the young, and more visual. Hamilton describes a passage in the labors of Hercules in this way: "Atlas, who bore the vault of heaven upon his shoulders, was the father of the Hesperides, so Hercules went to him and asked him to get the apples for him." The storytelling style of Colum is direct and familiar, yet lyrical: "Far did Heracles journey; weary he was when he came to where Atlas stood, bearing the sky upon his weary shoulders."

Between 1918 and 1922 Colum produced four children's books with new story-and-picture fusions: *The Boy Who Knew What the Birds Said* (1918), miscellaneous tales; *The Girl Who Sat by the Ashes* (1919), on a Cinderella theme; *The Boy Apprenticed to an Enchanter* (1920), a quest tale involving a search for Merlin; and *The Children Who Followed the Piper* (1922), about three of the children who followed Hermes (a kind of "Pied Piper" figure). Zack Bowen describes these volumes well; they were all illustrated by the American artist Dugald Stewart Walker. A 1968 edition of *The Girl Who Sat by the Ashes* featured illustrations by Imero Gobbato. These were cartoonish in style, not the made-for-the-story romantic drawings and intricately designed captions of the original editions. The originals work better as a fusion of folk drawing with folktale:

Because she used to herd goats in the high places and rocky places, she went by the name of Girl-go-with-the-Goats. But that was not the name that she herself called herself. She called herself Maid-alone.

Her feet were scratched with briars and bruised with stones. She was dressed in rags threaded together. And neither the red of pleasure nor the red of health had ever come into her face.

She lived with her stepmother, Dame Dale, and her two step-sisters, Berry-bright and Buttercup. Now one day as Berry-bright was dizening herself with a necklace of beads and Buttercup was looking at herself in a plate of brass, an old woman came up to the house. Her dress was the queerest that anyone ever saw, a cloak of crow-feathers and nothing else.

"My, my, my," said the old woman as she came into the house. "My, my, my, what became of the big tree that used to grow fornenst your little house?"

(pp. 13–14)

Several generations of child readers have twisted their tongues around words like "fornenst" and "dizening." Like the extra challenge of the words, Walker's pictures require concentration and imagination. Maid-alone and the various types of naming, depending on the eye of the beholder, gave Walker a ticket of freedom in illustrating. The little sketch of the old woman in a dress, which was a cloak of crow's feathers, shows birds in flight as part of the cloak. This is a wonderful image for any illustrator to work with. Was it Colum's? Was it Walker's? Gobbato in his later drawings had fun with it too, but resorted to a pumpkinish and funny view, abandoning the inherently mystic quality of the story line. Walker, knowing of Colum's fascination with birds, pictured all sorts of them—peacocks, geese, swallows, roosters, and more geese.

Two books resulted from a special commission request in Hawaii. They were eventually combined into *Legends of Hawaii* in 1937, still available today.

The conception and execution are unique in publishing. Colum explains in the introduction the extraordinary six months that he spent in entirely new research:

> And now about my own part in the work promoted by the [Hawaiian Legislature's] Commission on Myth and Folk-lore. I went to the Hawaiian Islands in 1923. I learned something of the language; I went through the islands seeking out people who still had the tradition of Hawaiian romance and who could relate it in the traditional way; I placed myself in the hands of the very distinguished group of Polynesian scholars in Honolulu; I made a study of all the material that had been collected.

The initial two books that resulted from the commission, *At the Gateways of the Day* (1924) and *The Bright Islands* (1925), were published by Yale University Press. Although the books did not fully cover Colum's research, he accomplished with them exactly what had been requested—the transformation of existing adult anthropological versions of Hawaiian mythology and native chants, legend, and folklore into stories for Hawaii's children. The Polynesian scholars whom Colum names as his tutors were local citizens, some of them revered Hawaiian teachers with expertise in language, music, dance, storytelling, Hawaiian games, and genealogy. Both Mary and Padraic Colum wrote articles and anecdotes about the period spent in Hawaii, some of which are found in Mary Colum's *Life and the Dream* (1947) and in *A Half-Day's Ride; or, Estates in Corsica* (1932), a book of Padraic's essays.

The subsequent combining of the two books with some changes in text eliminated the illustrations of Juliette May Fraser, Hawaiian painter, muralist, printmaker, and illustrator extraordinaire. Instead, decorations by Don Forrer lend it a textbook quality that puts it in the domain of older students, which was not the commission's original charge. The earlier two titles with Fraser's illustrations were more successful for children and merit rediscovery. Particularly noteworthy is the inside cover mapping for *The Bright Islands,* requested by Colum—he had used the same format in his precursor to *The Children's Homer.*

Changes in Hawaii since the 1930's have been more drastic than most other places in the world. Wars and tourists have uncovered old strengths and new abuses. Arguments are rife as to how to hold on to Hawaiian life and literature, and what should come first and how, and who should be responsible. When Peggy Hickok Hodge wrote her master's thesis, "A Critical Analysis of Padraic Colum's Treatment of Polynesian Legends," she defended the author's work with detailed analysis of source materials and Colum's retellings, along with her own views as to where Colum's previous readings might be responsible for his style elements. To read Hodge's paper is a challenge; it would be simpler to match abbreviated introductory passages with each story.

Years later, in the November 1972 issue of *Honolulu* magazine, Thomas Nickerson wrote a retrospective article on the Colums' stay so many years before—the reception they received from the local viewpoint, some of the objections that surfaced, more on the accolades his work received:

> When Colum died this year, a month past his 90th birthday, the *Honolulu Star-Bulletin* commented, "Many, who knew his work, turned again to his legends . . . and marveled anew at the miracle that brought a poet from so far away to penetrate so deeply into the heart of Hawaii."

Indeed, Colum understood Hawaii much better than Hawaiins knew. His stories need to be read and told away from the hustle and the confusion of conflicting opinions and activities. Even as he retold them, he had to elucidate many names and unfamiliar places; but should not a rescue as important and enigmatic as this, from "The Two Great Brothers," be repeated over and over:

> Kana then went to Kaha-kae-kaea. His brother Ni-he-u was there, wrapped in leaves under the loulu palm. He gave him the Water of Life, and life came back again to Ni-he-u. Afterward Ka-hoa-alii came to where they were. He gave them a canoe made out of white chicken feathers, and in that canoe Kana and Ni-he-u returned to Hawaii. They went to their grandmother's house, and they saw the Sun in the heavens, and the Moon following the Sun, and the Stars with the Moon. And never again were these bright lights taken out of our sky.

During the 1920's and 1930's the Colums wrote, lectured, and entertained continuously. After 1940 they spent fifteen years teaching comparative literature at Columbia University. This post enabled Colum to reach a wide audience on lecture and reading tours. Padraic Colum crossed many cultural barriers for the cause of prose and poetry. His many and various collections of folktales combined excitement and rhythm with a gentle touch seldom achieved by other writers. What Colum wrote about the Irish writer in *A Treasury of Irish Folklore* sings of his own work: "Perhaps we could say that what is startling in Irish wit and humor and exciting in all forms of Irish discourse is the expression of a mind whose spiritual allegiance is to reason and whose linguistic allegiance is to imagination."

Selected Bibliography

WORKS OF PADRAIC COLUM

The first and second titles listed are difficult to find now. Alan Denson's lists in the Spring and Summer 1967 issues of the *Dublin* magazine may help to identify separate editions. The *Longford Leader* issue of 9 October 1981 featured articles on a Colum exhibition at Saint Mel's College, Longford, Ireland, assembled by Marian Keaney, commemorating the centenary of the poet's birth. Other materials may be found in the United States in the Glenn G. Bartle Library of Special Collections, State University of New York at Binghamton.

A Boy in Eirinn. With illustrations by Jack B. Yeats. New York: Dutton, 1913; London: J. M. Dent and Sons, 1915.

The King of Ireland's Son. New York: Macmillan, 1916; London: Harrap, 1920. 2nd ed., with illustrations by Willy Pogány. New York: Macmillan, 1921. 3rd ed., with illustrations by G. and W. Knapp. Edinburgh: Floris Books, 1978.

The Adventures of Odysseus and the Tale of Troy. With illustrations by Willy Pogány. New York: Macmillan, 1918; London: Harrap, 1920. Reissued as *The Children's Homer.* New York: Macmillan, 1946, 1962, 1982.

The Boy Who Knew What the Birds Said. With illustrations by Dugald Stewart Walker. New York: Macmillan, 1918.

The Girl Who Sat by the Ashes. With illustrations by Dugald Stewart Walker. New York: Macmillan, 1919. Reissued, with illustrations by Imero Gobbato. London: Macmillan Collier, 1968.

The Boy Apprenticed to an Enchanter. With illustrations by Dugald Stewart Walker. New York: Macmillan, 1920. (Zack Bowen calls this "one of the best of all Colum's single narrative books for young children.")

The Children of Odin. With illustrations by Willy Pogány. New York: Macmillan, 1920; London: Harrap, 1922. Rev. ed. New York: Macmillan, 1962. (A single selection, "Thor and Loki in the Giant's City," reprinted in *The World Treasury of Children's Literature,* vol. 1, edited by Clifton Fadiman, Boston: Little, Brown, 1984.)

The Golden Fleece and the Heroes Who Lived Before Achilles. With illustrations by Willy Pogány. New York: Macmillan, 1921. Reissued New York: Macmillan, 1957, 1962, 1983.

The Children Who Followed the Piper. With illustrations by Dugald Stewart Walker. New York: Macmillan, 1922.

At the Gateways of the Day. With illustrations by Juliette May Fraser. New Haven, Conn.: Yale University Press, 1924.

The Bright Islands. With illustrations by Juliette May Fraser. New Haven, Conn.: Yale University Press, 1925; London: Oxford University Press, 1925.

A Half-Day's Ride; or, Estates in Corsica. New York: Macmillan, 1932. Reissued Freeport, N.Y.: Books for Libraries Press, 1969. (Contains the essay "Art and Infancy.")

The Big Tree of Bunlahy: Stories of My Own Countryside. With illustrations by Jack B. Yeats. New York: Macmillan, 1933; London: Macmillan, 1934.

Legends of Hawaii. With decorations by Don Forrer and a preface by Padraic Colum. New Haven, Conn.: Yale University Press, 1937.

The Collected Poems of Padraic Colum. Rev. ed., with a preface by John L. Sweeney. Old Greenwich, Conn.: Devin-Adair, 1953.

A Treasury of Irish Folklore. New York: Crown, 1954.

Story Telling New and Old. With decorations by Jay Van Everen. New York: Macmillan, 1968. (This essay first appeared in *The Fountain of Youth,* New York: Macmillan, 1927.)

Selected Short Stories of Padraic Colum. With an introduction by Sanford Sternlicht. Syracuse, N.Y.: Syracuse University Press, 1985.

CRITICAL AND BIOGRAPHICAL STUDIES

Bechtel, Louise Seaman. *Books in Search of Children.* Speeches and essays selected and with an introduction by Virginia Haviland. Toronto: Collier-Macmillan, 1940.

Bowen, Zack. *Padraic Colum: A Biographical-Critical Introduction.* Carbondale: Southern Illinois University Press, 1970; London: Feffer and Simons, 1970.

Brown, Stephen J. *Ireland in Fiction,* vol. 1. Rev. ed. Shannon, Ireland: Irish University Press, 1968.

Colum, Mary. *Life and the Dream.* Garden City, N.Y.: Doubleday, 1947.

Commire, Anne, ed. *Something About the Author.* Detroit: Gale Research, 1980. Vol. 15, pp. 42–51.

Hickey, Des, and Gus Smith. *Flight from the Celtic Twilight.* Indianapolis: Bobbs-Merrill, 1973.

Hodge, Peggy Hickok. "A Critical Analysis of Padraic Colum's Treatment of Polynesian Legends." Unpublished master's thesis, University of Hawaii, 1938.

Hogan, Robert. *The Dictionary of Irish Literature.* Westport, Conn.: Greenwood Press, 1979.

Meigs, Cornelia, ed. *A Critical History of Children's Literature.* New York: Macmillan, 1953.

Nickerson, Thomas. "Man from Donnybrook" *Honolulu* 7/5: 22–32 (Nov. 1972).

Saltman, Judith, ed. *The Riverside Anthology of Children's Literature.* 6th ed. Boston: Houghton Mifflin, 1985. (This book includes seven Colum selections, critical notes quoting Padraic Colum, and a fine chapter on myths, legends, and sacred writings as general background.)

Shulevitz, Uri. *Writing with Pictures: How to Write and Illustrate Children's Books.* New York: Watson-Guptill, 1985.

—DOROTHEA C. WARREN

JAMES FENIMORE COOPER

1789–1851

THE COOPERS WERE English Quakers who came to New Jersey in the late seventeenth century and prospered. William Cooper, James's father, visited upper New York State after the Revolution and with a partner purchased 750,000 acres of prime land near Otsego, where he laid out a town called, naturally, Cooperstown. The twelfth child of thirteen, James, born 15 September 1789, was but fourteen months old when his family moved there in 1790. The elder Cooper, a shrewd businessman, sold off plots from his holdings to eager settlers and soon amassed a considerable fortune. He became a judge, a member of Congress, a powerful force in the New York Federalist party, and the owner of a splendid estate, Otsego Hall.

The part of New York State in which Cooper grew up was no longer frontier. As an early traveler described it, it was "a hilly upland, divided into several ridges separated by deep, broad valleys," centered on Otsego Lake, "a fine sheet of water eight miles long and about one mile broad." Once Iroquois country, it was covered by great forests and fertile farmland, dotted with small lakes, rivers, and creeks. After the opening of the Catskill turnpike in 1802, it became settled into solid town and farmland; Otsego County in Cooper's youth had 22,000 inhabitants.

Young James (he added the middle name Fenimore later, taken from his mother's family) was sent to a private school in Albany and then to Yale College at thirteen, not unusual in those days. Unfortunately for the high-spirited young man, some college pranks that misfired (he took a donkey into

the classroom, among other things) led to his dismissal in his junior year. Judge Cooper, partly as punishment and partly as discipline, sent him to sea as a common sailor; it was planned that he would serve a year or so in a merchantman and then enter the Navy. He did so, was commissioned a midshipman in 1818, and was assigned to a brig on Lake Ontario.

The next year Judge Cooper died, leaving James a $50,000 bequest and a share in a $200,000 legacy. James was, therefore, a rich young man by contemporary standards. He resigned from the Navy and in 1811 married Susan Augusta De Lancey, whom he described in a letter to his father as "a fair damsel of eighteen . . . the daughter of a man of respectable connections and a handsome fortune." The couple built a home in Scarsdale, New York, where the De Lanceys owned land, and James settled down to the life of a gentleman farmer.

Cooper began to write almost by accident. Reading aloud to his wife one evening from a sentimental English novel, he threw it down in irritation, saying, "I could write a better book than that!" When Susan dared him to do so, he started a novel he soon destroyed. But caught up by the challenge, he began another book, modeled on Jane Austen's *Pride and Prejudice* (1813) and *Persuasion* (1818). His wife and friends urged him to publish it, which he did in 1820, calling it *Precaution*. It was published anonymously with a preface suggesting the author was English. The story of parents' attempts to arrange their daughters' marriages, *Precaution* was not a very good novel. It had little action, a great deal of talk, and forgettable characters. Nonetheless, the book did fairly well in the United States and England, and Cooper decided to write another—this one about America. In 1821 he published *The Spy*, the story of Harvey Birch, a double agent who served George Washington and the American cause in the Revolution. *The Spy* had everything the public wanted—adventure, conflict, patriotism, mystery, suspense, and a cast of memorable, well-drawn characters. It not only sold well (8,000 in the first four months) but also was translated eventually into a dozen languages and still remains one of Cooper's most republished novels.

He immediately began another novel, *The Pioneers; or, The Sources of the Susquehanna* (1823), followed by *The Pilot* (1823), based upon the career of John Paul Jones. Thus within three years Cooper introduced three major topics to American fiction—the Revolution, the frontier, and the sea. He wrote, in fact, twenty-eight more novels, experimenting with various themes and styles. *The Pioneers* set the course for *The Leatherstocking Tales* and presented his two most notable and durable characters, the frontiersman and the Indian.

The Leatherstocking Tales, five in all, were written over a twenty-year period (1822–1841) but were not published as a unit in chronological order until 1850–1851, with new prefaces for each and an additional preface for the series. They were written, Cooper explained, in "a very desultory and artificial manner," so that the different books required adjustments to plot and character in order to maintain some consistency. The elements that united them, of course, were Natty Bumppo (under the various names of Hawkeye, Pathfinder, Leatherstocking, and the Trapper) and Chingachgook, the "big Sarpent," his fellow warrior and friend. Cooper knew that in these novels he had touched a theme and characters that lay at the heart of the American experience. His other novels, some of the best writing of his times, faded from view, but the *Tales* endured. They dealt with the westward movement and with the conflict of the two races and two sets of values that marked it—the first thorough, insightful investigation in fiction of this central fact of American history.

The Leatherstocking Tales were written backwards, which lends a certain poignancy to the series for the modern reader who knows how Natty's and Chingachgook's lives end, the one a proud, cantankerous old man, the other a drunken Indian reduced to selling baskets. *The Pioneers; or, The Sources of the Susquehanna*, the first novel, is set at Templeton, New York, in 1793. Its leading citizen, Judge Marmaduke Templeton (who, Cooper maintained, was not modeled on his father), and Natty Bumppo, the old woodsman, clash over Natty's killing of a deer in violation of the game laws.

The plot explores one of the aspects of the westward movement that Cooper observed in the Cooperstown of his youth—that is, the conflict of the individualism of the frontier and the discipline of civilization. Natty "stands in protest," Cooper wrote, "in behalf of simplicity and perfect freedom, against encroaching law and order." But as Judge Templeton tells his daughter, "Society cannot exist without restraints. Those restraints cannot be inflicted without security and respect to the persons of those who administer them." The judge regretfully sentences the old man to the stocks and jail. The "fallen chief," John Mohegan, another of Natty's Indian friends, dies in a fire while Natty, freed from jail, leaves for the unfettered West.

The Last of the Mohicans: A Narrative of 1757 (1826) is a rattling good adventure story—danger, battle, chase, escape, capture, escape—with a love plot and plenty of suspense. The place is the Adirondack foothills, the time the early stages of the French and Indian Wars, when two young women, Clara and Alice Munro, set out to join their father, the British colonel in command of Fort Henry, besieged by the French and Iroquois. Their guides are Hawkeye, already a famed white hunter, and Uncas, his Mohican companion, who has a personal score to settle with Magua, the evil Mingo who tries to betray them all. Uncas, "the last of the Mohicans," dies, but Hawkeye revenges him.

The Prairie: A Tale (1827) was intended to round out the series. The aging Natty, now a trapper, moves across the Mississippi, "driven by the sound of the axe from his beloved forests to seek a refuge" in the denuded plains that stretch to the Rocky Mountains. The rather routine plot is built around the kidnapping of a girl in 1805 and her eventual rescue, but the book is rich in theme and character. Natty is placed against Ishmael Bush and his band of brutal, lawless squatters, who have no law except force and who take "the cream from the face of the earth" by despoiling the land. Hardheart the Pawnee, a heroic Indian, is set against the evil Sioux Mahtoree, as Uncas was against Magua.

Cooper's sales, and his own interest in the characters he had developed in these novels, led him to resume the series with *The Pathfinder; or, The Inland Sea* (1840), which is as much a sea as a forest novel, or, as Cooper called it, "a nautico-lake-savage romance." Natty, now in his mid-thirties, is called simply the Pathfinder. Chingachgook reappears and so does the chase-escape pattern, as Mabel Dunham travels to Fort Oswego to visit her soldier-father. Added are two nautical characters, Charles Cap, a braggart old saltwater sailor, and young Jasper Western, a freshwater sailor on Lake Ontario, the "inland sea" of the subtitle. Arrowhead, a treacherous Iroquois, serves as the red villain, while Mabel so attracts Pathfinder that he offers marriage. But the reader knows that Natty will never leave the forests for a wife and home.

The Deerslayer; or, The First Warpath (1841) completed the *Tales*. The year is 1740, the place Lake Glimmerglass (Otsego), the same country in which Natty was later to be humiliated. A young man of twenty or so, called Deerslayer for his hunting prowess, Natty is traveling in the forest with Hurry Harry March, a powerful, handsome young man who respects nothing but his own strength and prejudices. They find Tom Hutter, an ex-pirate, and his two daughters living in a rude "castle" on the lake, in great danger from a Huron war party. Tom and Harry attack the enemy camp to collect scalps, and in their absence, guarding the girls, Natty kills his first Indian, who, in respect for his warrior skills, before he dies gives him a new name, Hawkeye. Natty then helps his adopted brother, the young Delaware Chingachgook, to rescue his betrothed, the lovely Hist-o-Hist (or Wah-to-Wah, her tribal name) from her Huron captors. Hutter and March are meanwhile captured and released. Natty himself is captured, to be rescued by Chingachgook.

Cooper knew little about Indians firsthand. The few he saw in New York State were disorganized, wandering bands, the last of the "vanishing race." He read industriously in the sources available to him—accounts by such missionaries, travelers, and explorers as Lewis and Clark, Stephen Harriman Long, and Alexander Mackenzie. His most important source was the Reverend John Heckewelder, a Moravian missionary to the Delaware and Mohegan Indians, whose *Accounts of the History, Manners, and Customs of the Indian Nations Who Once Inhabited Pennsylvania and the Neighboring States* (1819) gave

him exactly what he needed. Heckewelder liked the Delawares, with whom he lived. He did not like the Iroquois, or Six Nations, who had conquered and subjugated the Delawares in the seventeenth century.

Heckewelder's distinction between "good" Indians and "bad" Indians provided Cooper with ample material for dramatic conflict and a rationale for his use of the Indian in fiction. The Iroquois became the villainous "Mingoes" of the series, while the Delawares and their allies provided their heroic opposites. He confused their identities a bit. In reality the Mohicans migrated to Wisconsin, where they still are; Uncas was not the last. The Mohegans, a Connecticut tribe, stayed there. Cooper combined them all into Mohicans and Delawares. When Cooper moved Natty westward in *The Prairie*, he simply made the Pawnees the "Delawares of the hills" and the Sioux into western Mingoes, "a treacherous and dangerous race of red devils."

In preparation for the *Leatherstocking* series, Cooper studied Indian customs and beliefs—burial practices, war, the totem system, marriage and family, hunting and woodcraft—and described them fairly and accurately. Those who knew Indian life better than he did, like Governor Lewis Cass of Michigan Territory, had much to say in criticism, for example, that in the world of fiction the representation of the North American Indian has "consistently borne no greater similitude to the red warrior of the woods than it has to a chieftain of Timbuctoo." Cooper, he said, "has dreamed a more consistent dream upon the subject . . . than any other writer of poetry or romance." However, he felt that Cooper relied too heavily on the narrations of Heckewelder "with ardent prejudices in favor of his adopted children; . . . we have seen his wild traditions adopted by the author . . . and made the basis of its [*The Last of the Mohicans*] mythology." Cooper insisted that as a novelist he had the right to draw his characters and plan his plots as he pleased, within reason, "more particularly when the works aspire to the elevation of romance to present the *beau ideal* . . . to the reader." Indians appear as major characters in eleven of Cooper's novels, and whatever his errors of fact or interpretation, his portraits of Indians and Indian life have endured.

When Cooper introduced Natty and Indian John to the public in *The Pioneers*, he extended a long tradition of American writing. The Indian and his culture were objects of fear and fascination to the explorer and settler from their first days of contact. From Captain John Smith's account of his supposed rescue by Pocahontas in 1632, the Indian remained a constant theme in American poetry, fiction, drama, history, and travel literature. Such captivity tales as Mary Rowlandson's *A Narrative of the Captivity and Restauration of Mrs. Mary Rowlandson*, published in 1682 (and others by Jonathan Dickinson and Anna Elizabeth Bleecker), provided popular reading for the next two centuries. Timothy Flint, James Hall, and other western chroniclers also furnished accounts of frontier life that depicted the red man as cruel and unpredictable. The "Indian hater" novel reached its culmination with Robert Montgomery Bird's *Nick of the Woods; or, The Jibbenainosay* (1837), which set the pattern for the lurid dime novels of the latter half of the century. On the other hand, there were such writers as Washington Irving and Maria Child—and later Henry Wadsworth Longfellow—who treated the Indian with respect and compassion. Unlike many of his contemporaries, Cooper recognized the Indian and his culture as different, complex, not easily comprehensible to the non-Indian mind. To Cooper the Indian could be both noble and savage —cruel and demonic in one situation, wise and virtuous in another. His portrait of the Indian determined for a century the way Americans would view Native Americans and their societies.

The people of the early nineteenth century assumed that the Indian was a race doomed to extinction, since he did not possess those qualities— reason and emotional discipline—needed to survive in a biracial society. George Bancroft concluded in his *History of the United States* (1834–1840) that though the Indian was equal to the white man in many ways, he was "inferior in reason and moral qualities." Cooper himself agreed in *Notions of the Americans* (1828) that the red man was bound to disappear before "the superior moral and physical influence of the white."

Natty Bumppo's (and Cooper's) most thoughtful discussion of Indians appears in *The Deerslayer*, as Natty talks with the hunter Harry March. Harry's remarks reflect quite accurately the popular concepts of race of the day. "There's three colors on 'arth," he says, "white, black, and red. White is the highest color, and therefore the best man . . . and red comes last which shows that those that made 'em never expected an Indian to be accounted as more than half human." Young Deerslayer responds, "God made us all white, black, and red, and no doubt has his own wise intentions in coloring us differently. Still, he made us in the main, the same in feelin's. . . . I look upon the red man quite as human as we are ourselves, Harry." Cooper of course faced the same dilemma in his novels as that which faced his times. How could one account for the behavior of "good Indians" who did "bad" things, and vice versa? How did one explain scalping, or torture, or the slaughter of prisoners, for example?

Through Natty, Cooper developed a theory of "gifts" that characterized each race and influenced its behavior and values. Gifts, Deerslayer explains, are the sum of the manners, mores, customs, and traditions—the total cultural environment—in which men and women live. Natty was educated by the Moravian missionaries in his orphaned childhood, and drawing upon this early training, he explains (as Saint Paul did in Romans and Corinthians) that just as each person belongs to a race, so too he or she is a member of the whole body of humanity. "You find different colors on 'arth, as any one may see," he remarks, "but you don't find different natur's. Different gifts, but only one natur'."

When Chingachgook takes a Frenchman's scalp, the act is true to Indian gifts. But Hawkeye will not take a scalp (as Harry March does), for it would violate the white man's inherent code of cultural values. "It is a cruel and inhuman act for a whiteskin," Deerslayer explains, "but 'tis the gift and natur' of an Indian." "I hold," he says, "to a white man's respecting white laws . . . and for a red man to obey his own red-skin usages, under the same privilege." Thus Harry March and Tom Hutter and Ishmael Bush, who should act in accordance with white laws and gifts but instead act by red ones, are more savage than Uncas or Chingachgook. There are, of course, red men who betray their gifts, tribes like the Mingoes who, as Hawkeye says, are "nat'rally perverse and wicked, as there are nations among the whites." Magua, "le Renard Subtil," the villainous Huron of *The Last of the Mohicans*, is an illustration of Indian gifts gone wrong. He is brave, an accomplished orator, a leader among his people. But he is also cruel, treacherous, and completely depraved; his Indian gifts are perverted by his insatiable lust for blood and revenge.

150

If Cooper drew contrasting portraits of Indians to provide some of the character conflicts his plots required, so did he draw Natty Bumppo, the idealized frontiersman, in contrast to the crude and cruel white men who intruded into Natty's forest with ax and gun. From the sad, sympathetic portrait of the old hunter in *The Pioneers* to the young knight of the woods in *The Deerslayer*, Cooper developed the character to represent all that he saw as admirable and American in the westward movement. In *The Pathfinder* Hawkeye is presented to the reader as "a fair example of what a just-minded and pure man might be . . . left to follow the bias of his feelings, amid the solitary grandeur and ennobling influence of a sublime nature." This is the natural man, the "new American" as he might be. Natty was, then, intended to represent the idealized woodsman as he moved westward with the frontier, but he was not to be regarded as a typical historical character. His "moral point of view" (Cooper's phrase) individualized him; he is separated from his fellows by his moral nature. How Natty developed this point of view is explained by his past. He was, after all, educated by the Moravian missionaries and equally influenced by the wilderness in which he grew. His education, he says, "has been altogether in the woods; the only book I read, or care about reading, is the one which God has opened before all creatures. . . . This is the book I read, and I find it full of wisdom and knowledge." This is the Leatherstocking, of course, of the later books of the series, the mythic figure with his famed long rifle, "Killdeer," who set the model for all those frontier heroes who have followed him.

Cooper had a strong visual sense, a recognition of the power of place, or scene, in fiction. As Francis Parkman remarked, scenes from Cooper's novels had "a strange tenacity with which they cling to the memory," and other readers noted that certain images persisted in the mind long after the novel ended. Cooper was thoroughly acquainted with the aesthetics of current landscape painting, particularly with the American Hudson River school, and frequently in his descriptions referred to analogies with specific painters. In chapter 16 of *the Deerslayer*, Natty, from his canoe offshore at night, sees the Indian encampment:

The canoe lay in front of a natural vista, not only through the bushes that lined the shore but of the trees also, that afforded a clear view of the camp.

. . . In consequence of their recent change of ground, the Indians had not yet retired to their huts, but had been delayed by their preparations, which included lodging as well as food. A large fire had been made, as much to answer the purposes of torches, as for the use of their simple cookery, and at this precise moment it was blazing high and bright, having recently received a large supply of dried brush. The effect was to illuminate the arches of the forest, and to render the whole area occupied by the camp as light as if hundreds of tapers were burning. . . .

Deerslayer saw at a glance that many of the warriors were absent. His acquaintance, Rivenoak, however, was present, being seated in the foreground of a picture that Salvator Rosa would have delighted to draw, his swarthy features illuminated as much by pleasure as by the torch-like flame. . . . A boy was looking over his shoulder, in dull curiosity, completing the group. More in the background, eight or ten warriors lay half recumbent on the ground, or sat with their backs inclining against trees, so many types of indolent repose. Their arms were near them, sometimes leaning against the same tree as themselves, or were lying across their bodies, in indolent preparation.

A scene itself could be the inspiration for a chapter or a novel; Cooper's daughter Susan once said that a glimpse of Lake Otsego through the trees was the inception of *The Deerslayer*. He would frame a scene; compose its elements; pose its characters; provide a center for the eye; use color, light, and shadow, all to painterly effect. One may refer to his long description of Glimmerglass in *The Deerslayer*; or to his view of Fort Henry, an island of refuge in the forest-sea of danger; or to Ishmael Bush's sturdy fort on a rock in the boundless, open prairie. In fact, Cooper once planned, but never began, a novel about nature and scenery with no human characters at all.

Cooper's novels, particularly those of the frontier and the sea, were immediately popular at home and abroad. British, French, and German editions appeared as rapidly as American; by the 1850's thirty of his novels had been translated into Italian, Scandinavian, Spanish, and Russian. Thirty-two editions in a variety of other languages appeared over the next century. The *Leatherstocking* series, with their action-filled plots and powerful visual imagery—particularly *The Last of the Mohicans*, *The Pathfinder*, and *The Deerslayer*—naturally appealed most strongly to young readers. British youngsters, like American, played woodsman and Indian, while the French have long known of "Bas-de-cuir" (Leatherstocking) and his battles with "les peaux rouges," as Germans have followed the adventures of Old Shatterhand, a fearless frontiersman resembling Natty. Illustrators for various editions have included such names as F. O. C. Darley, N. C. Wyeth, Reginald Marsh, and John S. Curry.

The dime novels that flooded the popular market after 1860 drew heavily on Cooper's Indians, frontiersmen, and pirates, adapting Natty and his Indian friend, the chase-capture-escape formula, the single-handed duel, the good and bad Indians, the damsel in danger, and the like, and adding violence and villainy to the point of absurdity. A comic book series of the 1940's, *Classics Illustrated*, published seven Cooper novels in abridged form, more than Mark Twain and Herman Melville combined. *The Pioneers*, *The Pathfinder*, *The Deerslayer*, and *The Spy* were all made into movies, while a serial called *Hawkeye, the Last of the Mohicans* ran for thirty-nine episodes at Saturday matinees. At least two television series have been based on the *Leatherstocking* novels, whose plots have been robbed for countless frontier episodes under other names. (Certainly Natty and Chingachgook led to the Lone Ranger and Tonto.) Cooper's novels, or excerpts from them, were required reading in elementary and high schools for many years.

The enduring tradition of the western novel and film also derives directly from Cooper. All the familiar elements are there—Killdeer is the ancestor of the sheriff's six-gun; Natty's faithful companion (red or white) appears in novel after novel; the chase is a standard device as part of the formula of western and adventure tales on film and television; the contrast of nature's Edenic purity with society's fall from grace is part of the western legend; the conflict of the free individual with established order still enchants audiences; the isolated, chivalric hero, dedicated to justice but unable to live within the society he protects, still fascinates the modern reader and viewer.

Cooper began his writing career, under the influence of Jane Austen, as a novelist of social manners. Concerning *The Spy*, he wrote, quoting Henry Fielding, "I am a true historian, a describer of society as it is." As his ideas about fiction developed, however, he moved from social realism toward the kind of novel his era called a "romance." In the contemporary critical sense a romance did not confine itself to the known or probable, but could deal with the possible, using "idealized" and "heroic" (Cooper's words) characters and plots. In a romance, Cooper wrote, the writer is allowed "to take a poetical view of the subject"; he is not a historian, but in a broad sense a poet. A romance need not reflect the actual world, but it must be true to the imagined world the writer creates. The romance is free of what Cooper called that "rigid adherence to truth, an indispensable requisite to history and travel, [which] destroys the charm of fiction." But whatever its relation to reality, fiction in Cooper's view should mean something; it should have some "ultimate moral aim." Sir Walter Scott's works, as much as Cooper admired them, fell short in this respect, for his novels contained "no moral consequences." By this Cooper did not mean an appended, didactic moral, spelled out sermonlike, but rather some concept or principle to be inferred from characters and events.

To the modern reader Cooper's slow-paced narratives and discursive style may seem tedious and outdated. His techniques, drawn from the historical and sentimental traditions of the eighteenth- and early-nineteenth-century novel, unfortunately had fallen into disuse before he completed his work. Twain's essay "Fenimore Cooper's Literary Offenses" catalogued his faults hilariously and not always fairly. It is true that Cooper's plots are loaded with coincidence, melodrama, and complication, but the nineteenth-century reader expected and appreciated such things. The public wanted at least a minor love story, which Cooper inserted, often rather awkwardly, in his already overloaded plots. As Joseph Conrad said of him, "He wrote before the great American language was born and he wrote as well as any novelists of his time." In his time the language of the novel was changing; the American style had not yet developed. Nathaniel Hawthorne and Melville were yet to come, and after them Twain and Walt Whitman and Henry James and William Dean Howells. But within the limits of his fictional techniques and concepts, his stories still generate power. His epic of the wilderness and the people in it, *The Leatherstocking Tales*, remains an important element of the mainstream of American fiction. What appealed to the young reader of Cooper's century—the action-adventure narratives and their vividly conceived characters—still appeals to today's young reader. *The Leatherstocking Tales* have been continuously in print since the first day of their publication. Natty and Chingachgook endure.

Selected Bibliography

INDIVIDUAL WORKS OF JAMES FENIMORE COOPER

Precaution: A Novel. New York: A. T. Goodrich, 1820; New York: AMS Press, 1976.

The Spy: A Tale of the Neutral Ground. New York: Wiley and Halsted, 1821.

The Pioneers; or, The Sources of the Susquehanna. New York: Charles Wiley, 1823. Rev. ed., with illustrations by F. O. C. Darley. New York: W. A. Townsend, 1839. Rev. ed., with historical introduction and explanatory notes by James Franklin Beard. Text established by Lance Schachterle and Kenneth M. Anderson, Jr. Albany: State University of New York Press, 1980.

The Pilot: A Tale of the Sea. New York: C. Wiley, 1823; New York: Heritage Press, 1968.

The Last of the Mohicans: A Narrative of 1757. Philadelphia: H. C. Carey and I. Lea, 1826. Rev. ed., with illustrations by N. C. Wyeth. New York: Charles Scribner's Sons, 1973. Rev. ed., with historical introduction by James Franklin Beard. Text established with explanatory notes by James A. Supperfield and E. N. Feltskog. Albany: State University of New York Press, 1983.

The Prairie: A Tale. Philadelphia: Carey, Lea, and Carey, 1827. Rev. ed., with illustrations by J. S. Curry. Menasha, Wisconsin: Limited Editions Club, 1940.

Notions of the Americans: Picked up by a Travelling Bachelor. Philadelphia: Carey, Lea, and Carey, 1828; New York: Ungar, 1963.

The Pathfinder; or, The Inland Sea. Philadelphia: Lea and Blanchard, 1840. Rev. ed., with illustrations by F. O. C. Darley. New York: W. A. Townsend, 1860. Rev. ed., edited and with a historical introduction by Richard Dilworth Rust. Albany: State University of New York Press, 1981.

The Deerslayer; or, The First Warpath. Philadelphia: Lea and Blanchard, 1841. Rev. ed., with illustrations by N. C. Wyeth. New York: Charles Scribner's Sons, 1925.

COLLECTED WORKS OF JAMES FENIMORE COOPER

The Works of James Fenimore Cooper. 12 vols. New York: G. P. Putnam, 1849–1851. (Cooper's final version.)

Cooper's Novels. 32 vols. With illustrations by F. O. C. Darley. New York: W. A. Townsend, 1859–1861. (The source for most later collected editions.)

James Fenimore Cooper's Works. 32 vols. With an introduction by Susan Fenimore Cooper. Boston: Houghton Mifflin, 1881–1884; New York and Cambridge, Mass.: Houghton Mifflin, 1976.

The Works of James Fenimore Cooper. 33 vols. New York: G. P. Putnam's Sons, 1895–1896.

The Leatherstocking Saga. With illustrations by Reginald Marsh. New York: Avon, 1982.

BIBLIOGRAPHY

Spiller, Robert E., and Philip C. Blackburn. *A Descriptive Bibliography of the Writings of James Fenimore Cooper*. New York: Burt Franklin, 1968.

CRITICAL AND BIOGRAPHICAL STUDIES

Boynton, Henry W. *James Fenimore Cooper*. New York: Century, 1931. (The first complete biography based on the novelist's papers.)

Cass, Lewis. *North American Review* 23: 150–197 (July 1826). (Review of *The Pioneers* and *The Last of the Mohicans*.)

Dekker, George, and John P. McWilliams. *Fenimore Cooper: The Critical Heritage*. London: Routledge and Kegan Paul, 1973. (A selection of reviews and critical essays.)

Grossman, James. *James Fenimore Cooper*. New York: William Sloane Associates, 1949. (A biographical-critical study and an excellent introduction to the man and his work.)

Parkman, Francis. *The Discovery of the Great West*. Boston: Little, Brown, 1869.

Ringe, Donald A. *James Fenimore Cooper*. New York: Twayne Publishers, 1962. (The most useful single volume of criticism.)

Shulenberger, Arvid. *Cooper's Theory of Fiction*. Lawrence: University of Kansas Press, 1957.

Spiller, Robert E. *Fenimore Cooper: Critic of His Times*. New York: Minton-Balch, 1931. (A biography stressing Cooper's role as a social and political critic.)

Twain, Mark. "Fenimore Cooper's Literary Offenses." *North American Review* 161: 1–12 (July 1895).

—RUSSEL B. NYE

JAMES HENRY DAUGHERTY

1887–1974

IN 1975 LYND WARD wrote of James Henry Daugherty:

Using both words and pictures . . . became, for Daugherty, a simple, unified way of working. Had we ever been able to slip inside that head of his and see just how the wheels turned in the process of creation, I suspect we would have found everything so interlocked and so mutually interdependent that it would have been impossible to separate the choice of the right words from the choice of the right visual unit. . . .

This eloquent and resourceful "combined" language, part sound, part image, . . . became both tool and material with which Daugherty achieved something pretty rare in American writing and picture-making—the re-creation of the past in terms that make it pertinent for the present and the future. . . . Daugherty was always . . . the one whose work conveyed the basic quality of the American experience. No one else has rendered [it] with so much gusto and vigor, so much humor, and at the same time concern for the fundamental values.

("A Note on James Daugherty," in
Imprint: Oregon)

Born in Asheville, North Carolina, on 1 June 1887, Daugherty spent his early childhood on farms in Indiana and Ohio, before his father, Charles M. Daugherty, obtained employment with the U.S. Department of Agriculture and moved his family to Washington, D.C. Daugherty's father, a prolific reader, often read aloud to his wife and two sons from the works of Dickens, Thackeray, Chau-

cer, Spenser, and Shakespeare, and especially from *The Library of Poetry and Song*, compiled by William Cullen Bryant in 1870. While his father read, young Jimmie sketched pictures of the characters and events. Daugherty's mother shared Negro spirituals and Uncle Remus stories learned during her Virginia girlhood. Summers were spent in Wilmington, Ohio, with James's mother's family. Here, from his lawyer and farmer grandfather, Daugherty absorbed the folk legends of Daniel Boone and other early frontiersmen. Daugherty's first book, *Their Weight in Wildcats* (1936), was warmly dedicated to his Ohio pioneer grandfather, William B. Telfair.

With such a rich literary life at home, it is not surprising that a one-room school near Lafayette, Indiana, and routine lessons at schools in Ohio and Washington held little appeal. Daugherty's real teacher was his father, who shared his appreciation for the arts not only by reading aloud, but also by regular visits with his son to museums, galleries, and the Library of Congress. He carefully nurtured young Daugherty's budding artistic abilities. After taking free evening art classes at the Corcoran School of Art, Daugherty began study in 1903 under the impressionist Hugh Breckenridge at the Darby Summer School of Painting in Fort Washington, Pennsylvania, followed by a year at the Pennsylvania Academy of Fine Arts.

When father and son were apart, their close relationship was maintained by frequent exchanges of letters. Daugherty's father advised him in a letter of 13 January 1905: ". . . it would be a *most* excellent plan for you to keep up *some* regular course of reading and above all to do some writing . . . unless I am mistaken in you . . . you can do some fine work." This advice may have been prompted by James's lively descriptions in his 7 January 1905 letter to his mother:

> The Academy "fling" is the greatest dance in the world. It is a sort of hop skip and a kick to a fast rollicking tune something like a sailor's horn pipe. The students form like the spokes of a great wheel, holding hands. The music starts and round and round we go faster and faster, shouting and laughing and throwing confetti, until everything is a great whirlpool of dancing legs, laughing faces and brilliant colors. . . .

The reader of Daugherty's books will recognize at once his exuberant prose style, which was not to make its public debut for another quarter of a century.

Early in 1905 Daugherty's father began a two-year assignment in London for the U.S. Department of Agriculture. In June, Daugherty traveled with his friend, sculptor William Hunt Diederich, to London to join his family. During his two years abroad he studied at the London School of Art.

Sometime in 1907

> . . . there appeared at the school a young Californian with a copy of *Leaves of Grass* in his pocket. I had never read a line of it. Was this really my America, this splendor of democracy, this new world of affirmation and fraternity and hope? We read and chanted and roared our favorite passages to our bewildered British comrades.
> *Leaves of Grass* got under my skin and into my bones. For the first time I felt the meaning and power of that majestic word "America," and through Whitman's eyes I dimly glimpsed the grandeur of its possibilities. I must return to my country at once and forever.
>
> ("Introduction" to *Walt Whitman's America*)

In November 1907 he arrived in New York to seek his artistic fulfillment in Walt Whitman's and his own America.

During his first few years in New York, Daugherty shared studios with other struggling young artists and barely subsisted on meager earnings from illustrations for advertising agencies and magazines. In 1913 he was profoundly influenced

by the artistically experimental works exhibited at the Armory Show. He, too, began to explore the possibilities of color and form and to have his work shown. During these financially lean years of artistic discovery Daugherty met Sonia Medvedeva. They were married in 1913; their only child, Charles Michael, was born in November 1914.

In 1918 Daugherty found a new outlet for his talents: wartime camouflaging of naval vessels. During the same period Daugherty's friendship with naval artist Henry Reuterdahl brought him several commissions for naval murals. Both camouflaging and mural-painting required the broad strokes, grand schemes, bold color, and rapid execution that fitted Daugherty's temperament and that characterized his later written and visual creations. After the war he actively sought contracts for advertising art that would use mural techniques.

In 1924 the Daughertys moved to Weston, Connecticut. Daugherty continued to paint, but he found more of his time devoted to magazine and book illustration. In 1925–1926 he did a series of caricatures for the *New Yorker*, signing them "Jimmie the Ink." He illustrated three books in 1925 and another three in 1926, including Stewart Edward White's *Daniel Boone: Wilderness Scout*.

For a friend, critic and librarian Anne Carroll Moore, he illustrated her 1928 edition of Irving's *History of New York*, which gained considerable acclaim. It included "The Artist's Salutation to Father Knickerbocker":

> *We*
> Who step as nimble matadors among Manhattan's plunging traffic—
> *We*
> who mingle in her kaleidoscopic nights—drifting through jewel-bulbed dreams reflected in ever black streets—
> *We*
> of this acid-mouthed, nasal, radio-bawling, jazz-rhythmed, belly-aching decade
> *Open*
> again old Irving's fat volume. . . .

Between 1927 and 1934 the writer Daugherty was still learning the trade as he read and illustrated thirty-one other books, including Carl Sandburg's *Abe Lincoln Grows Up* (1928) and *Early Moon* (1930),

Harriet Beecher Stowe's *Uncle Tom's Cabin* (1852), Stephen Vincent Benét's *John Brown's Body* (1928), and Francis Parkman's *The California and Oregon Trail* (1849). Daugherty's first book as author-illustrator was his picture book *Andy and the Lion* (1938), which achieved immediate success. It was a Caldecott Honor book, and it remains in print to this day.

Daugherty's compilation of frontier tales, *Their Weight in Wildcats*, represents the release of strong emotions stored up from illustrating and researching, retained from all his early childhood reading and his travels, treasured from his romance with American history and folklore. This collection of American yarns received excellent reviews and positive public response. The demand for folktales about American frontier heroes was spreading, and Daugherty's books were just the type to satisfy this new taste.

Daugherty—romantic, folklorist, frontiersman in spirit—made *Daniel Boone* (1939) his tribute to the role of the common people in America's westward expansion. May Massee, Daugherty's editor at Viking Press, wrote in the *Library Journal*, 1 June 1940, about *Daniel Boone*:

> It is a very human story, this story of America, and now that J.D. feels the urge to tell something of what it means to him, he finds that he needs words as well as pictures. The words that come are just as American as the pioneer story; they are a natural combination of Biblical English and the vernacular. The writing ranges from quiet steady narrative, to clipped staccato action, to pure poetry.

Daniel Boone won the John Newbery Medal for 1939.

In 1941 Daugherty created what reviewers called the best picture of Benjamin Franklin for high school readers, *Poor Richard*. They admired, for example, Daugherty's skill in depicting Franklin's mind in this passage:

> There were so many rooms in that luminous mind. Every minute something was going on in each one of them. Nobody knew them all except Ben, but they all had windows and plenty of light and he wanted you to come in and look around. There was no cellar and no attic, no dark unventilated places. All the space was used, in this rooming house under his hat.
>
> (p. 65)

Later in this volume, Daugherty captured the essence of Franklin's *Poor Richard's Almanack* (1732–1757): "Ben's new almanac was a fanciful hodgepodge of gypsy notions, a rag, tag, and bobtail of saws and sayings from Aesop to Rabelais spoken with a Yankee nasal twang. Poor Richard walked into the heart of the American people and stayed there." Daugherty described Franklin's posting to France and his success there with simple familiarity: "With his curious crab-tree walking stick, he was Democracy in person among the powdered wigs and silk coats and gilt swords of the court aristocrats. He had the American flair for dramatic entrance, slyly smiling at himself as he used it." In passages such as these Daugherty drew a quaint and likable portrait of Franklin. He went on to detail the lives of other American historical figures in the same informal style.

Daugherty wrote *Abraham Lincoln* (1943) in the midst of World War II, when America's attention was focused on defeating the enemy. As part of this mobilization there was increased emphasis on pride in the national heritage. In a draft of a letter to Paul McClelland Angle, a Lincoln biographer, Daugherty wrote:

> I understand there is no lack of quantity in the matter of Lincoln biography though one finds considerable variation in quality. In writing for a special group of high school age, I have avoided any psychological rassle dassle or special vocabulary . . . and simply tried to combine good story telling with good history. . . .
>
> [Lincoln's biography] always will be the great American story because it contains all the unsolved mystery of the American destiny, the saga of the average competent democratic person in all his drama, implications, frustrations, grand and individual integrity.

Of Courage Undaunted (1951) took its title from Thomas Jefferson's description of Meriwether Lewis, which Daugherty inserted as an epigraph to his book about the Lewis and Clark expedition. Relying heavily on Lewis and Clark's journals and Jefferson's letters, Daugherty judiciously selected incidents and adeptly sketched character development to convey for the young reader the flavor and excitement of the original documents and the lives of their authors.

In an introductory poem, "The Corps of Discovery," Daugherty pays tribute to the men of the expedition and, by extension, to the American common man of history and his own time:

> Sweating and rank, coarse, muscular, lanky,
>   level-eyed, generous minded, free speaking,
>   slangy—
> you don't have to go far in any city or town to find
>   them;
> no farther than any street corner or factory bench,
>   farmyard, filling station, public high school.
> As Lincoln said, "God must have loved them or he
>   would not have made so many."

He went on to wryly recount the colorful episodes of this dangerous expedition: "The Indians gave the white messengers a feast of stewed dog. The hungry men liked it. It was their first taste of man's best friend." In describing the daily regimen at the journey's beginning, Daugherty noted: "As the men turned out in the gray dawn they sometimes shook a live rattlesnake from a blanket or pillow, where he had crept just to be warm and friendly. That helped to liven one up for the day's work."

Taken as a whole, *Of Courage Undaunted* is one of Daugherty's most powerful and successful works, but it contains elements troubling to the modern student of children's literature.

Among the subjects of interest to today's critic is Daugherty's treatment of the Indian woman Sacajawea. Daugherty remained true to his source materials in noting the poor treatment accorded her, but he also pointed out her courage and importance to the success of the expedition. When the expedition drew to a close, Daugherty summed up her place in it:

> Sacajawea was only a squaw and so received nothing [in recompense]. She said a brief farewell to her captains and stepped out of the story to resume her anonymous place in the life of her tribe. The silent little squaw had patiently toted her baby on her back up rivers and over mountains, guiding and leading, sharing the hunger, cold, and danger without complaint, always to be counted on, asking nothing except to see the great fish and the big salt lake; unrewarded, unforgotten, of courage undaunted.
>
> (p. 154)

Because he was retelling history, not rewriting it, Daugherty did not emphasize the role of women in his biographies of Franklin, Boone, or Lincoln, but he was not unaware of their contributions to

history-making. For Daugherty, Rebecca Boone epitomized the frontier woman, who was expected to leave her home with its meager comforts to set up a new home in the wilderness, and was then left for months and even years to care for her family while her husband pursued adventure and new frontiers.

Daugherty's respect for pioneer women was equally evident in his biography of Dr. Marcus Whitman and his wife, Narcissa, a teacher, missionaries to the Oregon Territory from 1836 to 1847, when they were killed by Indians. Daugherty's major sources for *Marcus and Narcissa Whitman* (1953) were Narcissa Whitman's letters and journals held at the Yale University Library. He was frank in expressing his admiration for Narcissa's personal strength and courage, but he was also keenly aware of the undercurrent of confrontation between the Whitmans and the Indians caused by the threat the missionaries' religious ideals posed to the Indians' culture. Daugherty and the informed reader are never unaware of the impending doom of the mission and missionaries. Only when away from the mission and describing the immigrant train led by Marcus does the tone resume its Daughertyesque cadence. Here he took time out for poetic recognition of the American pioneer woman in his powerfully descriptive "Women of the Wagons":

> Women of the wagons under the faded sunbonnets,
> Forsaking the easier ways, the comforts, the securities,
> For the long trek over the alkali deserts, walking by
>   the ox teams,
> Bending over the campfires, cookstoves, the washtubs.
> Makers of homes in lonely cabins and sod huts,
> Crooning the cradle songs, watchers by bedsides,
>   weepers by graves,
> No whimpering, no whining, when the going was
>   rough,
> Only grateful that the children were safe and the men
>   came through sound and whole.
> Keepers of the faith, the kingdom made without
>   hands,
> Making the wilderness to blossom, making the decent
>   villages,
> The schools, the churches, the democratic community
> With the free ballot, the private individual choice.
> Misshapen hands and bodies worn with hard labor,
> Faces weathered by sun and wind and carved by the
>   years,
> Beautiful beyond the mere flesh, women clothed with
>   the sun,
> Women of the wagons under the faded sunbonnets.

JAMES HENRY DAUGHERTY

In *Trappers and Traders of the Far West* (1952), Daugherty portrayed the heroic fur traders, but he also had an underlying concern for the outcome of their passion "to peel the hides off all the unfortunate fur-bearing animals in North America." The reverse side of the white man's brave pioneering and missionary efforts was the westward expansion of "man the changer, the destroyer, the builder." The trappers traded with the "friendly Walla Wallas, who welcomed the white men and their own extinction with songs and dances and savage hospitality."

For anyone writing about the westward advance of the American frontier perhaps the most difficult subject to treat fairly has been the confrontation of whites and Native Americans over the land. Daugherty did not ignore the issue, but handled it with sensitivity. The rugged pilgrim, explorer, or frontiersman was a recurrent theme in Daugherty's writing on American history, but even as he celebrated in ebullient prose and flowing illustrations the courage and stamina of these men and women in the vanguard of America's westward expansion, Daugherty reminded his reader that this was the settling of untamed but not unclaimed wilderness. The Indian was struggling to preserve his homeland in the face of a ruthless encroachment:

The wise old prophet-chiefs saw their destiny in the sky; they knew their fate was the doom of the buffalo. They saw the last tribes driven like mists down the mountain valleys before the brightness of the pale-faced gods. The axes and arrows of the stone age were useless against the deadly guns and fiery poisons of the white man. Amid their burning villages and the awful butcheries and sickening betrayals of friends and foes, they met the personal tragedy of violent death with a serene indifference.
(*Daniel Boone*, p. 39)

Daugherty's epilogue to *Marcus and Narcissa Whitman* is an eloquent example of his efforts to achieve a balanced interpretation of an aspect of American history which all too many choose to ignore or forget:

Among the some thirty Cayuses who took part in the massacre there were devout Christian Indians, and some had received many kindnesses from the Whitmans. The massacre was not so much an act of personal hatred and vengeance as the last desperate retaliation of a doomed people against their destroyers. For two hundred years the Indians had

been driven relentlessly westward until there was nothing between them and the Pacific Ocean.

The fate of the mission between these ruthless forces was inevitable. The tragedy of the Whitmans was determined from the beginning, by their uncompromising idealism and by the forces of history. At times they were acutely aware that this was so.

The books Daugherty produced in his last years take as their subjects the careers of writers (and in one case a writer-artist, William Blake) he himself had found particularly inspiring. His introductions to these works revealed his personal identification with the minds of his subjects. For example, he wrote of William Blake:

I think that Blake's life and work are important and significant for us today—more so than ever before. It was obviously a battle from first to last, and in the end a great victory for vision and imagination over dullness, doubt, and fear; of individuality and originality over timidity, conformity, and material limitations.

This is why his songs and pictures thrill us today with their mysterious beauty and power, their splendid affirmations, and their wild and vaulting rhythms.

William Blake (1960) was Daugherty's only biography of an artist. *Blake* was a successful venture into a different subject and a different era from those Daugherty had previously treated. His tribute praised Blake's artistic eye, his independence, his vision. For Daugherty, Blake was the poet-artist of integrity and sincerity, with gifts that transcended time, popular trends, and tradition, whether good or bad.

Daugherty's *Walt Whitman's America* (1964), a compilation of both prose and poetry, was warmly reviewed. Daugherty said of Whitman in his introduction:

You will of course choose and reject, agree and disagree with his tumultuous philosophies, but as you read and reread them your thoughts about America will surely expand, for they . . . expand the spirit toward wider horizons along new and unexplored paths; and I think this is good in a world rushing so swiftly toward unlimited possibilities.

Gay Wilson Allen reported in the *New York Times Book Review* in 1964 that Daugherty "illustrates these passages with magnificent drawings which convey the spirit of the poet's themes. These drawings, bold, heroic, and colorful, interpret the poetry and prose better than words."

Daugherty further expanded our democratic vistas with his next book, *Henry David Thoreau, a Man for Our Time* (1967). In his introduction he contemplated Thoreau's diverse background and career:

> Thoreau could always do many things well. He was at different times a carpenter, a gardener, a pencil maker, and a surveyor. He was also a scholar in ancient languages, . . . a poet, a lecturer, a naturalist. . . . Always he kept his daily journal, and this became the treasure house of his thoughts. From these thoughts he took his lectures, essays, and published writings. For Thoreau was above all a writer, a master of words and builder of sentences. And his writings have been read around the world, giving courage and inspiration to men . . . and peoples seeking freedom, independence, and justice.

Daugherty left extensive manuscript drafts of introductions to his works on Whitman, Thoreau, and Emerson that testify to his desire to share their philosophical, literary, and artistic inspiration with a new generation of readers. Self-reliance and freedom of thought were vital concerns to him.

In his last years Daugherty turned to painting once again, and four years passed between *Thoreau* and his anthology of Emerson's writings, *The Sound of Trumpets* (1971). Daugherty's introduction emphasizes the pertinence of Emerson's ideals to current American social problems and their solutions:

> What of his legacy to the 1970s and the years ahead rushing swiftly toward the twenty-first century? Emerson has left us the rich heritage of his wisdom: his faith in the goodness of life and in the reality of the American dream.
>
> Who will say that we shall not use our immense untried spiritual resources to banish war, poverty, ignorance, disease, and to diminish fear and hate with good will, intelligence, and cooperation; to realize humanity's goals of world peace, freedom, justice, and the brotherhood of man in God's image?

Daugherty's collection of some of his own poems, or, as he called them, "Yankee doggerel,"

West of Boston (1956), derived inspiration from the same independent, democratic folk who populate Robert Frost's *North of Boston* (1914). These were not the folk heroes and frontiersmen who appeared in *Their Weight in Wildcats*; they were historical figures who made substantive contributions to the formation and promotion of democratic ideals, along with an occasional renegade or malcontent added for moral contrast. His tribute to Thomas Jefferson is typical:

> His hair was sandy, touched with red;
> It flamed unruly about his head.
> Under the shade of his broad-brimmed hat
> Walked the first American democrat.
>
> He loved the people and children too,
> Virginia's valleys and ridges blue,
> His beautiful home on the little hill,
> And the peaceful village of Charlottesville.
>
> He wrote on parchment with his pen.
> His words still burn in the hearts of men.
> A shining light, a steady flame,
> Burns forever about his name.
>
> ("Independent")

The collection perhaps comes closest to conveying the aspirations that motivated Daugherty in his long career, which ended with his death in Boston on 21 February 1974.

Selected Bibliography

WORKS WRITTEN AND ILLUSTRATED BY JAMES HENRY DAUGHERTY

Their Weight in Wildcats: Tales of the Frontier. Boston: Houghton Mifflin, 1936.
Andy and the Lion. New York: Viking Press, 1938.
Daniel Boone. New York: Viking Press, 1939.
Poor Richard. New York: Viking Press, 1941.
Abraham Lincoln. New York: Viking Press, 1943.
Of Courage Undaunted: Across the Continent with Lewis and Clark. New York: Viking Press, 1951.
Trappers and Traders of the Far West. New York: Random House, 1952.
Marcus and Narcissa Whitman, Pioneers of Oregon. New York: Viking Press, 1953.
West of Boston. New York: Viking Press, 1956.
William Blake. New York: Viking Press, 1960.
Walt Whitman's America. Cleveland: World, 1964.
Henry David Thoreau, a Man for Our Time. New York: Viking Press, 1967.

The Sound of Trumpets: Selections from Ralph Waldo Emerson. New York: Viking Press, 1971.

CRITICAL AND BIOGRAPHICAL STUDIES

Anderson, William Davis, and Patrick J. Groff. *A New Look at Children's Literature*. Belmont, Calif.: Wadsworth, 1972.

Bader, Barbara. *American Picturebooks from Noah's Ark to the Beast Within*. New York: Macmillan, 1976.

Kemp, Edward and Elaine Kemp. "James Henry Daugherty" *Imprint: Oregon* 2: 6–24 (Fall 1975). (Contains a complete bibliography of works written and/or illustrated by Daugherty.)

Kent, Norman. "James Daugherty, Buckskin Illustrator" *American Artist* 9: 16–20 (March 1945).

Lambeck, Frederick. "James Daugherty and His America" *Publishers Weekly* 37: 2135–2136 (1 June 1940).

Levin, Gail. *Synchromism and American Color Abstraction, 1910–1925*. New York: George Braziller, 1978.

Massee, May. "James Daugherty's *Daniel Boone*." *Library Journal* 65/11: 473–474 (1 June 1940).

Titzell, Josiah. "James Daugherty" *Publishers Weekly* 116: 2073–2076 (26 October 1929).

Ward, Lynd. "A Note on James Daugherty" *Horn Book* 16: 239–246 (July–August 1940).

Ward, Lynd. "A Note on James Daugherty" *Imprint: Oregon* 2: 3–5 (Fall 1975).

—EDWARD C. KEMP
AND ELAINE A. KEMP

DANIEL DEFOE
1659?–1731

ROBINSON CRUSOE IS so deeply embedded in our popular literary memory that one need merely say "The Print of a Man's Naked Foot" to evoke the title of the book. After all, as Ian Watt notes in "*Robinson Crusoe* as Myth," "By the end of the nineteenth century, *Crusoe* had appeared in at least seven hundred editions, translations, and imitations, not to mention a popular eighteenth-century pantomime and an opera by Offenbach." The Crusoe myth was further reinforced by "Robinsonnades"—the "wave of German imitations . . . [which] followed in the wake of the novel's publication and continued to 1880" (Stoler).

Another popular identification is most likely that the footprint is that of "my Man Friday," though in fact the print is not Friday's. He doesn't appear until more than three years later than the famous footprint, after Crusoe has been on the island for twenty-two years, living his unthreatened life unaware of cannibals until first seeing them in the eighteenth year. And the third summary-identification of the book is perhaps that "it's about Crusoe's solitary island on which he survives by his mechanical inventiveness."

These three popular notions of the novel probably coalesce into a thumbnail plot summary, thus: A lone white man shipwrecked on an unpopulated island survives through his ingenuity, suffering the pangs of solitude, until another, possibly subservient or primitive, person appears and subsequently becomes Crusoe's devoted servant.

But then come the questions that account for the book's continuing appeal despite shifting emphases that modern readers apply to Defoe's narrative. How did Robinson Crusoe come to be on the island in the first place? What skills, tools, and resources enabled him to survive? How could he endure twenty-four years without talking to another human being and still keep his sanity? Why should his reaction to the footprint be one of terror rather than extreme joy at the prospect of companionship?

Such questions not only inform the plot of the book but also account for its levels of appeal and for Defoe's writing strategies. An actual reading of the book modifies and particularizes the popular "received" notion of *Robinson Crusoe:* A middle-class Puritan young man runs away to sea despite his father's exhortations, is captured and held prisoner by the Moors of Sallee, and eventually escapes— only to be shipwrecked again on an island that is visited, he eventually learns, by cannibals. He builds fortifications, domesticates wild goats, and turns his part of the island into a solitary village. He rescues Friday (Crusoe's name for him, of course), a cannibal in need of Christianizing, from a group of others who intend to have him to dinner, though "not where *he* eats," as Hamlet would say. After further bloody skirmishes against the cannibals in order to rescue some captive Spaniards, Crusoe populates the island with repentant renegades and sails back to England and thence to Lisbon, where he discovers that his investment many years before in the plantations of "the Brazils" has multiplied handsomely and that he's now a reasonably wealthy man. Crusoe rewards those who have looked after his fortune, and—in the fastest settle-up-and-settle-down tradition established by later novelists—he appears to retire gracefully into domestic life. But the end of this history is packed into a few sentences:

> I arriv'd in *England,* the Eleventh of *June,* in the Year 1687 having been thirty and five Years absent. . . .
>
> In the mean time, I in Part settled my self here; for first of all I marry'd, and that not either to my Disadvantage or Dissatisfaction, and had three Children, two Sons and one Daughter: But my Wife was dying, and my Nephew coming Home with good Success from a Voyage to *Spain,* my Inclination to go Abroad, and his Importunity prevailed and engag'd me to go in his Ship, as a private Trader to the *East Indies:* This was in the Year 1694.
>
> In this Voyage I visited my new Collony in the Island, saw my Successors the *Spaniards,* had the whole Story of their Lives, and of the Villains I left there.
>
> (Michael Shinagel, ed., *Robinson Crusoe*, pp. 216, 236)

Despite the assertion of *Crusoe*'s "Editor" that the narrative is "a Just History of Fact; neither is there any Appearance of Fiction in it," one of the critical tempests when the book appeared in 1719 revolved around the question of whether it was a factual travel book, a hoax, pure fiction, or perhaps a direct steal from the then recently published account of Alexander Selkirk's self-imposed exile in the uninhabited Juan Fernández Islands from 1704 to 1709. Selkirk's story was published in 1712 by his rescuer, Captain Woodes Rogers, and by Captain Edward Cooke; and Richard Steele recounted the adventure at some length in his periodical the *Englishman* in December 1713. James Sutherland, in *Daniel Defoe: A Critical Study,* surmises that "Defoe must have known some or all of these accounts," but acknowledges that "it is odd that with his interest in voyages and pirates he made no reference to Selkirk in the *Review* or elsewhere." Sutherland nevertheless maintains that the "traditional view" of Defoe's indebtedness to Selkirk is still unshaken by revisionist critical emphases on mythic or religious interpretations of *Robinson Crusoe.*

Some eighteenth-century critics condemned the book precisely for its "low" qualities: its un-imaginative, prosaic style devoid of allusions except to Bible passages and bereft of any redeeming artistic merits—no "literary" context, no art, no music, no poetry, no wit of the salon. Perhaps all of these lapses are the result of the almost unthinkable situation: man *out* of society. The story "fixes in the mind a lively idea of the horrors of solitude, and, consequently, of the sweets of social life, and of the blessings we derive from conversation, and mutual aid," wrote James Beattie in *Dissertations Moral and Critical.* Small wonder that the literati generally scorned the book, and that literary judgments wandered *ad hominem* away from the persona and toward that partisan pamphleteer hack Daniel Defoe. Literary historians have been able to take some comfort, however, in Alexander Pope's remark that "the first part of Robinson Crusoe is very good.—Defoe wrote a vast many things; and none bad, though none excellent, except this." But then there's enough talk in the novel about "the general Plague of Mankind . . . of not being satisfy'd with the Station wherein God and Nature has plac'd them" to account for the few plaudits from the whatever-is-is-right establishment.

The common readers, however, were another audience. Here at last they discovered a straightforward, enterprising, middle-class hero who talked in a direct, clear (if somewhat conversationally repetitive) manner about combining pragmatic materialism with religious consciousness. In a letter to Walter Wilson (December 1822), Charles Lamb praised *Robinson Crusoe* as "perfect illusion":

> The narrator chains us down to an implicit belief in every thing he says. There is all the minute detail of a log-book in it. Dates are painfully pressed upon the memory. Facts are repeated over and over in varying phrases, till you cannot chuse but believe them. . . . When he has told us a matter of fact, or a motive, in a line or two farther down he repeats it, with his favourite figure of speech, *I say,* so and so, though he had made it abundantly plain before. This is in imitation of the common people's way of speaking . . . and has a wonderful effect upon matter-of-fact readers. Indeed, it is to such principally that he writes. His style is every where beautiful, but plain and homely. *Robinson Crusoe* is delightful to all ranks and classes; but it is easy to see, that it is written in a phraseology peculiarly adapted to the lower conditions of readers. Hence, it is an especial favourite with sea-faring men, poor boys, servant maids, &c. His novels are capital kitchen-reading,

while they are worthy, from their interest, to find a shelf in the libraries of the wealthiest and the most learned.

(ibid. p. 290)

Granting, then, that *Robinson Crusoe* is a planned fiction that has its own internal dynamics and is not simply an ingenious extension of Defoe's own "projecting" personality, it is possible to group its various elements to anticipate several possible levels of reader response. Clearly, some of these elements appeared more pertinent to an eighteenth-century adult reader than they do to a twentieth-century adolescent, whose "island romance" is more likely to be William Golding's *Lord of the Flies.*

On its most theoretical and abstract level, *Robinson Crusoe* can be seen in the context of early-eighteenth-century faith in the natural rationality of human beings if (again, theoretically) they are not corrupted by misleading social and historical institutions. The "Editor" of Crusoe's story assures us that it is aimed as much at "the Diversion, as to the Instruction of the Reader," and Crusoe repeatedly comments on the efficacy of rationality, in one instance supplying a "balance sheet" of credits and debits, fortunes and misfortunes, and concluding—rationally—that "Upon the whole, here was an undoubted Testimony, that there was scarce any Condition in the World so miserable, but there was something *Negative* or something *Positive* to be thankful for in it." Thus "my Reason Began now to Master My Despondency," he records.

Adult readers were made clearly aware, however, that this myth of rationality was to be played off against an older, Puritan skepticism that dwelt on man's fallibility, irrationality, and willfulness. Despite a clear recognition of his society's expectations, "my ill Fate push'd me on," says Crusoe, and

> I was still to be the wilful Agent of all my own Miseries [by] my apparent obstinate adhering to my foolish inclination of wandering abroad and pursuing that Inclination, in contradiction to the clearest Views of doing my self good in a fair and plain pursuit of those Prospects and those measures of Life, which Nature and Providence concurred to present me with, and to make my Duty.
>
> (ibid., p. 32)

If the immediate ideological context for the book was the Age of Reason, its "occasion," as Paul Hunter phrases it in *The Reluctant Pilgrim,* allies it with a Christian, especially Puritan, "guidebook"

tradition of exempla, providences, and allegorical types and antitypes. Hunter writes:

> *Robinson Crusoe* is structured on the basis of a familiar Christian pattern of disobedience-punishment-repentance-deliverance, a pattern set up in the first few pages of the book. Crusoe sees each event of his life in terms of the conflict between man's sinful natural propensity, which leads him into one difficulty after another, and a watchful providence, which ultimately delivers man from himself. Crusoe's continual appraisal of his situation keeps the conflict at the forefront of the action throughout, for his appraisal is not the superficial, unrelated commentary some critics have described, but rather is an integral part of the thematic pattern set up by Crusoe's rebellion and the prophecy of his father that Crusoe "will be the miserablest Wretch that was ever born."
>
> (Hunter, pp. 19–20)

This dimension of *Robinson Crusoe* divides into two subplots: the stages of Crusoe's repentance and his "religious instruction" of Friday, which comes much later in the book.

Perhaps the young Crusoe is not so willful as he describes himself, for when he does "run away" to sea his actual embarking is almost accidental; he notes that he "went casually, and without any Purpose of making an Elopement that time." Whatever his true motives, he's caught in a channel storm that his inexperience leads him to think fatal. "I began now seriously to reflect upon what I had done, and how justly I was overtaken by the Judgment of Heaven for my wicked leaving my Father's House, and abandoning my Duty." He later equates this desertion with "original sin." Now, "I made many Vows and Resolutions, that if it would please God here to spare my Life this one Voyage . . . I would go directly home to my Father, and never set . . . [foot] into a Ship again while I liv'd." He's rebuked as a Jonah by the Captain, and admonished that he "will meet with nothing but disasters and disappointment" for so rejecting his father's good advice.

The account of his later shipwreck in the East Indies is labeled "A Dreadful Deliverance," both words eventually resonating with other, more religious, significance. Here the "dreadful" refers to the physical hardship and mental depression brought about by the immediate event of the wreck; "deliverance" denotes simply Crusoe's physical survival. Although, on the debit side, he

165

notes that "I am singl'd out and separated, as it were, from all the World to be miserable," he reasons that, on the credit side, "I am singl'd out too from all the Ship's Crew to be spar'd from Death."

In a well-known Puritan tradition, he resolves to keep a journal not only of daily events but also, perchance, for recording of divine providences—the first of which is not long in coming. Some stalks of barley spring up, "and I began to suggest, that God had miraculously caus'd this Grain to grow without any Help of Seed sown, and that it was so directed purely for my Sustenance, on that wild miserable Place." But then Crusoe's momentarily touched heart hardens when

> at last it occur'd to my Thoughts, that I had shook a Bag of Chickens Meat [grain] out in that Place, and then the Wonder began to cease; and I must confess, my religious Thankfulness to God's Providence began to abate too upon the Discovering that all this was nothing but what was common.
>
> (Shinagel, p. 63)

"Deliverance" takes on a further meaning in the chapter "Delivered Wonderfully from Sickness," in which Crusoe records his suffering from a violent ague, in the midst of which he has a "terrible vision":

> I saw a Man descend from a great black Cloud, in a bright Flame of Fire. . . . He was all over as bright as a Flame, so that I could but just bear to look towards him; his Countenance was most inexpressibly dreadful, impossible for Words to describe. . . .
>
> . . . he moved forward towards me, with a long Spear or Weapon in his Hand, to kill me; and when he came to a rising Ground, at some Distance, he spoke to me, or I heard a Voice so terrible, that it is impossible to express the Terror of it; all that I can say I understood, was this, *Seeing all these Things have not brought thee to Repentance, now thou shalt die:* At which Words, I thought he lifted up the Spear that was in his Hand, to kill me.
>
> (ibid., p. 70)

Crusoe begins to examine his religious sensibilities, conceding that, until now, he's been going through life with "a certain Stupidity of Soul, without Desire of Good, or Conscience of Evil." "I never had so much as one Thought of it being the Hand of God, or that it was a just Punishment for my Sin." He reproaches himself for his past

"wicked life," but he wonders if his prayer is genuine or "rather the Voice of mere Fright and Distress." Further pondering leads him to reason "that God had appointed all this to befal me"; in despair and anger he cries out, *"Why has God done this to me? What have I done to be thus us'd?"* But, immediately, "My Conscience . . . check'd me in that Enquiry, as if I had blasphem'd." There follows a portentious silence. He is "struck dumb with these Reflections, as one astonish'd, and had not a Word to say, no not to answer to my self, but rose up pensive and sad." Thinking that smoking some tobacco might help his "distemper," Crusoe goes to a chest, "directed by Heaven no doubt; for in this Chest I found a Cure, both for Soul and Body"—the tobacco he was looking for, and a Bible in which he begins to read "casually." Though stumbling on the passage *"Call on me in the Day of Trouble, and I will deliver"* makes "some Impression," his physical deliverance is such an obvious impossibility that Crusoe rather dismisses it, though he kneels down and prays. Later he awakes "exceedingly refresh'd, and my Spirits lively and chearful."

He begins now "seriously to read" in the New Testament, and the terror of his dream-vision is vividly recalled: "the Words, *All these Things have not brought thee to Repentance,* ran seriously in my Thought." What follows is an account of sudden illumination presaging Jonathan Edwards' "divine and supernatural light":

> I was earnestly begging of God to give me Repentance, when it happen'd *providentially* [emphasis added] the very Day that reading the Scripture, I came to these Words, *He is exalted a Prince and a Saviour, to give Repentance, and to give Remission:* I threw down the Book, and with my Heart as well as my Hands lifted up to Heaven, in a Kind of Extasy of Joy, I cry'd out aloud, *Jesus, thou Son of David, Jesus, thou exalted Prince and Saviour, give me Repentance!*
>
> This was the first time that I could say, in the true Sense of the Words, that I pray'd in all my Life; for now I pray'd with a Sense of my Condition . . . and from this Time, I may say, I began to have Hope that God would hear me.
>
> Now I began to construe the Words . . . in a different Sense . . . for then I had no Notion of any thing being call'd Deliverance, but my being deliver'd from the Captivity I was in . . . but now I learn'd to take it in another Sense.
>
> (ibid., p. 77)

Having discovered—and he so admonishes his readers—that "whenever they come to a true Sense of things, they will find Deliverance from Sin a much greater Blessing than Deliverance from Affliction," he recognizes that his physical hardships are "not less miserable," but that his spiritual regeneration now makes it "much easier to my Mind."

Consistent with the tradition of Christian tracts, there are moments of backsliding. But from this time on, Crusoe—in the Puritan phrase, "weaned from this world"—begins to take more delight in it. He embarks on a program of cultivating his kingdom, planting, weaving baskets, and rediscovering the skill of making clay pots.

This suggests yet another way to read *Robinson Crusoe* (and another tension in the web of ideas within the book): as an exemplum of modern— that is, early-eighteenth-century—man's having become economically inept in the new world of specialization. As Sutherland notes:

> When Defoe was writing, the division of labor was already well advanced, and skills which were common even in the Elizabethan age had now become specialized, or had been supplanted by the machine. Even the earliest readers of *Robinson Crusoe,* therefore, were able to find pleasure in Crusoe's primitive carpentry, pottery, bread-making, basket-weaving, etc., with which the growing specialization of industry had begun to make them unfamiliar.
>
> (Sutherland, p. 131)

Forced by the chance of shipwreck to reduce life to its simplest terms of food, clothing, and shelter, Crusoe boasts that

> by stating and squaring every thing by Reason, and by making the most rational Judgment of things, every Man may be in time Master of every mechanick Art. I had never handled a Tool in my Life, and yet in time by Labour, Application, and Contrivance, I found at last that I wanted nothing but I could have made it, especially *if I had had the Tools* [emphasis added].
>
> (Shinagel, p. 55)

One of Defoe's key writing techniques, in fact, develops from this relation to the reader. Crusoe acknowledges that he's puzzled and often frustrated in his attempts to make things; back home

he'd even seen them made, but hadn't paid any attention. How to make a boat? An umbrella that will close? How to fire a clay pot? Weave a basket? Skin a goat? Make butter and cheese? How to know whether wild plants and fruits are safe to eat? Although in some cases he details his process of "reinventing," in others he simply says he managed it— and the reader can play a game of "Now, how would *I* have managed that?" or "I could have shown Crusoe a trick or two!"

This aspect of practical economy has its special appeal. In *"Robinson Crusoe* as Myth," Ian Watt notes that "the dignity of labor is the central creed" of the book, and that Crusoe, "alone on his island, deprived of all assistance from his fellows, and nevertheless able to look after himself, is obviously a figure that will enthral readers of all ages."

One might object, however, that Crusoe *is*— albeit indirectly—assisted by "his fellows," the previous toolmakers. A man out of society, Crusoe is initially dependent on the products of society. Defoe provides his hero with materials from the foundered ship—hatchets, shoes, canvas, guns and gunpowder, and so forth. But Crusoe does not become the inventor of new products, nor does the island supply the necessary raw materials. For example, his gunpowder must be used sparingly; he has neither the chemistry nor an island supply of sulfur and potassium nitrate. He cannot smelt and forge new ironwork; he apparently cannot make paper and ink but must stop his journal when he runs out of both. The situation has implicit in it tragic, ennobling, or simply materialistic and exploitative possibilities.

There is, first, the view that Crusoe's self-interest is hardly "enlightened" and is ultimately isolative and destructive both of his own psyche and of society. His "conversion" experience and his eventual material success do not lead to a more humane, contented, social old age of the sort his father had described. He is a wanderer again. The island solitude has not made him more solicitous of the general welfare but, rather, has turned his thoughts inward, as he describes them in *Serious Reflections During the Life and Surprising Adventures of Robinson Crusoe,* the 1720 essay-sequel to the novel:

> I have frequently look'd back . . . upon the Notions of a long tedious Life of Solitude, which I have represented to the World. . . . Sometimes I have as much wonder'd, why it should be any Grievance or Affliction; seeing upon the whole View of the Stage

of Life which we act upon in this World, it seems to me, that Life in general is, or ought to be, but one universal Act of Solitude. . . . We judge of Prosperity, and of Affliction, Joy and Sorrow, Poverty, Riches, and all the various Scenes of Life: I say we judge of them by our selves. . . .

All Reflection is carry'd Home, and our Dearself is, in one Respect, the End of Living. Hence Man may be properly said to be *alone* in the Midst of the Crowds.

(ibid., p. 263)

Such serious ruminations, and the several implicit or overt theoretical and religious levels of *Robinson Crusoe*, hardly account for its appeal to adolescent readers—though we have noted its "common" style. Leslie Stephen, in "De Foe's Novels," argues that the book "is for boys rather than men" by default; any adult reader would recognize that Crusoe's (or Defoe's) adherence to the notion of rationality destroys the emotive, psychological credibility of the hero, who "takes his imprisonment with preternatural stolidity. His stay on the island produces the same state of mind as might be due to a dull Sunday in Scotland."

Some facts of Selkirk's experience suggest that "he was rapidly becoming a savage," says Stephen; but stolid, unimaginative Robinson Crusoe is incapable of either "enthusiasm" or genuine despair and madness. "He does not accommodate himself to his surroundings; they have got to accommodate themselves to him. . . . Long years of solitude produce no sort of effect upon him morally or mentally." "Everything is capable of a rational explanation, he is sure, if only he had time to attend to it," adds Virginia Woolf in *The Common Reader*. The other side of Defoe's characterization of Crusoe is, however, as both Stephen and Woolf acknowledge, a very high order of verisimilitude—a view proposed by Edgar Allan Poe much earlier. As Woolf points out:

> Thus Defoe, by reiterating that nothing but a plain earthenware pot stands in the foreground, persuades us to see remote islands and the solitudes of the human soul. By believing fixedly in the solidity of the pot and its earthiness, he has subdued every other element to his design.
>
> (Woolf, pp. 74–75)

Which brings us back, in a roundabout way, to that footprint in the sand—so tangibly *there,* but suggesting the absent alien. Although he has longed for companionship, Crusoe's reaction to the sign of an "other" on the island is not one of relief and anticipated reunion but of abject fear, terror "to the last Degree," which "banished all my religious Hope." What we see is the failure of theoretical rationality in the light of actual human behavior. One is reminded of the frenzied philosopher in *Rasselas* (1759), and it may be such moments in *Robinson Crusoe* that prompted Samuel Johnson's praise of the book.

Though his fears persist, Crusoe does not find evidence of cannibals until two years later, when he is "perfectly confounded . . . at seeing the Shore spread with Skulls, Hands, Feet, and other Bones of humane Bodies"; another year goes by before a second sighting; and another fifteen months elapse before Crusoe has a detailed dream-vision of two canoes and eleven savages "with another Savage, who they were going to kill, in Order to eat him." But not until a year and a half later is the dream fulfilled when Crusoe rescues Friday—who "cleverly" beheads one of his captors with Crusoe's sword.

Obviously, from this point on, there is going to be enough action and gore to keep any adolescent reader racing through the novel. It is true that Crusoe has a momentary hesitation about killing more savages. After all, he reasons, their "barbarous Customs were their own Disaster, being in them a Token indeed of God's having left them . . . to such Stupidity, and to such inhumane Courses." (Incidentally, a Puritan reader would no doubt also see in this observation the "antitype" of Crusoe, the "type" of the civilized man.) But such moral niceties disappear when Crusoe discovers that another cannibal expedition to the island is about to execute *white* men, Spanish prisoners! Crusoe, Friday, and one of the released Spaniards kill off at least seventeen of the twenty-one cannibals; and they discover that they have also, to their surprise, rescued Friday's father from the villains. There follow scenes of great solicitude on Friday's part, obviously a contrast to Crusoe's own unfilial behavior years before, although not much is said about this.

Friday, by this time, has been undergoing Crusoe's religious instruction, an interlude that provides both serious and comic debates. Friday reports that there is a God who made all things, and *"all things do say 0 to him."* And there is a place to which all the dead, including the cannibals' victims, will go. But Crusoe finds "it was not so easie to imprint right Notions in his Mind about the Devil," Friday objecting that if God is so powerful, *"Why God no kill the Devil, so make him no more do wicked?"* Crusoe's trying to wriggle out of the question is funny, but of course it's an age-old religious puzzlement. Crusoe admits that he's really a novice, with "more Sincerity than Knowledge" in the debate, and that he's engaged in a process of self-instruction.

The admission is intriguing because it suggests that *Robinson Crusoe* may or should be read not so much for its dealing with the philosophical, religious, and capitalist "issues" we have noted as for the intriguing dynamics of accommodation that occur in the fictional character of the narrator. John Richetti, in *Defoe's Narratives: Situations and Structures,* argues that Defoe's persona creates his own "history" and that paying more attention to this fact helps us find a way through the many partisan critical views that emphasize particular historical ideologies.

The remainder of the novel deals with hair-breadth escapes and comic relief: the adventures of Crusoe and Friday as they cross snow-covered mountains from Spain to France; Friday's treeing a bear—and teasing him for the amusement of Crusoe and the other members of the party; an encounter with wolves; and then, very succinctly, a single sentence that takes the narrator home: "I travell'd from *Toulouse* to *Paris,* and without any considerable Stay, came to *Callais,* and landed safe at *Dover,* the fourteenth of *January.*"

Before concluding—and at the risk of a long digression—it is instructive to contrast *Robinson Crusoe* with the best-known book in the lineage of "Robinsonnades," *The Swiss Family Robinson* (1812–1813). A manuscript novel by Johann David Wyss, a Swiss pastor in Bern, it was edited and completed by his folklorist son, Johann Rudolf Wyss, and translated into English in 1814—perhaps by William Godwin—and published that year by M. J. Godwin under the title *The Family Robinson Crusoe.* As Bettina Hurlimann notes (in *Three Centuries of Children's Books in Europe*) in a wonderful understatement, the book has "a very complicated history." She comments that "Godwin's edition held the field till the late 1840s and from that time on close on three hundred different editions must have been published in England and America. Many of these are based on the famous French edition of the book by the Baroness de Montolieu which expanded certain sec-

tions and provided a more satisfactory ending. Mrs. H. B. Paull . . . was one of the first to use the French version (in Warne's Chandos Classics, 1868)."

But one discovers that an anonymous edition published in 1879 by J. B. Lippincott—and claiming to be a retranslation of Baroness de Montolieu—includes a vast number of episodes not included in "a new and unabridged translation from the original by Mrs. H. B. Paull": Mother and Francis, kidnapped by savages, are rescued by Fritz with the help of a missionary, Mr. Willis; Earnest goes back to Europe to study astronomy with "the celebrated Horner, of Zurich" and returns to the island with his bride, Henrietta Bodmer. They reject the Old World, Mother wondering "what shall we find in Europe to compensate us for what we leave here? —poverty, war, and one of those things which we have here abundantly." They will all live happily ever after in the island paradise that their enlightened industry has subdued. Other anonymous editions add, delete, and completely reword at will. Only the general intentions of the original remain clear.

The title page (reproduced in Hurlimann) of the 1818 two-volume Godwin edition bears the fulsome title: *"The Swiss Family Robinson: or Adventures of a Father and Mother and Four Sons in a Desert Island: being a practical illustration of the first principles of mechanics, natural philosophy, natural history, and all those branches of science which most immediately apply to the business of life."* The two elements that most distinguish *The Swiss Family Robinson* from its predecessor are implicit in this descriptive title: a *community* rather than a solitary individual, and an *educative intention.* Where Crusoe had to invent on the basis of trial and error, and with only vague recollections of having observed crafts in England, this family readily controls its environment—not only making it yield food, shelter, and clothing in abundance, but also providing an aesthetic dimension of daily existence that can only be called high domesticity. If Crusoe is the untutored prisoner of nature, Father in *The Swiss Family Robinson* knows *everything* and is constantly lecturing his boys on applied science. In the Lippincott edition (though not in the "new" Mrs. Paull's), for example, Father explains the principle of a jackscrew, citing Archimedes' lever and concluding that "God, to compensate for the weakness of man, had bestowed on him reason, invention, and skill in workmanship. The result of these had produced a science . . . of *Mechanics.*" Throughout this edition—and sometimes in Mrs. Paull's—Father readily identifies a myriad of plants (and provides taxonomic terms in Latin!), though the ultimate importance of this academic learning is practicality. For example, they discover the *Myrica cerifera*, "from which we shall no doubt be able to make candles" (Paull)—the "candle-berry myrtle, from which a wax is obtained that may be made into candles" (Lippincott).

Interestingly enough, the Lippincott edition adds mini-essays on the nature of fiction, especially applied, of course, to *Robinson Crusoe.* Apparently these are among the "improvements" that this version made to its ostensible source, the edition of Baroness de Montolieu. The most intriguing passage occurs when ten-year-old Jack, worried about "the *anthropophagi,* who eat men like hares or sheep, of whom he had read in some books of travels," is ridiculed by his brother, "who was astonished at his ready belief of travelers' tales, which he asserted were usually false:

> "But Robinson Crusoe would not tell a falsehood," said Jack, indignantly; "and there were cannibals came to his island, and were going to eat Friday, if he had not saved him."
>
> "Oh! Robinson could not tell a falsehood," said Fritz, "because he never existed. The whole history is a romance—is not that the name, father, that is given to works of imagination?"
>
> "It is," said I: "but we must not call Robinson Crusoe a romance; though Robinson himself, and all the circumstances of his history are probably fictitious, the details are all founded on truth—on the adventures and descriptions of voyagers who may be depended on, and the unfortunate individuals who have actually been wrecked on unknown shores. If ever our journal should be printed, many may believe that it is only a romance—a mere work of the imagination."
>
> (Lippincott ed., p. 212)

The contrasts to *Robinson Crusoe* are thus pervasive; one especially notes—since Father is a minister—the absence in *The Swiss Family Robinson* of the religious qualms that inform much of Crusoe's behavior. Yet it might be argued that this difference accounts for the strange power of Defoe's book. If *The Swiss Family Robinson* has retained some status as a children's classic because of the

essentially nonthreatening adventures of its four juvenile heroes, one suspects that its predecessor has remained a classic not simply for its overt adventure but because its fictional strategies shift its meaning out of the book and into the response of any individual reader. The tactic is similar to that found in some modern fiction, such as Jerzy Kosinski's *Steps.* Thus our exasperation with Crusoe's "dullness" and the seeming absence of what we might deem appropriate emotional responses to his danger and solitude derives from reading the book from the perspective of our particular ethical and historical views. If *Robinson Crusoe* may no longer be the "book for boys" it once was (despite its remaining in the public consciousness via numerous edited and illustrated versions for children), its universal human tensions make it an intriguing book for adult reading.

Selected Bibliography

EDITIONS OF ROBINSON CRUSOE

The Life and Strange Surprizing Adventures of Robinson Crusoe. London, 1719.

The Farther Adventures of Robinson Crusoe. London, 1719.

Serious Reflections During the Life and Surprising Adventures of Robinson Crusoe. London, 1720.

Robinson Crusoe. With illustrations by Federico Castellon. New York and London: Macmillan, 1962. (With an afterword on the appeal of the story to children by Clifton Fadiman.)

Robinson Crusoe: An Authoritative Text, Backgrounds and Sources, Criticism. Edited by Michael Shinagel. New York: W. W. Norton, 1975. (With essays and commentary by Ian Watt, James Beattie, and Charles Lamb, among others.)

BIOGRAPHICAL AND CRITICAL STUDIES

Byrd, Max, ed. *Daniel Defoe: A Collection of Critical Essays.* Englewood Cliffs, N.J.: Prentice-Hall, 1976.

De la Mare, Walter, ed. *Desert Islands and Robinson Crusoe.* London: Faber and Faber, 1930; New York: Farrar and Rinehart, 1930.

Ellis, Frank H., ed. *Twentieth-Century Interpretations of "Robinson Crusoe."* Englewood Cliffs, N.J.: Prentice-Hall, 1969.

Hardy, Barbara. "Robinson Crusoe" *Children's Literature in Education* 8/1: 3–11 (1977).

Hoffman, Margit. "Robinsonnades: The A. J. Ahlstrand Collection" *Signal* 17: 61–74 (1975).

Hunter, J. Paul. *The Reluctant Pilgrim: Defoe's Emblematic*

Method and Quest for Form. Baltimore, Md.: Johns Hopkins University Press, 1966.

Hurlimann, Bettina. *Three Centuries of Children's Books in Europe.* Translated by Brian Alderson. Cleveland: World, 1968.

Richetti, John J. "Defoe and the Problem of the Novel." In his *Defoe's Narratives: Situations and Structures.* Oxford: Clarendon Press, 1975. Pp. 1–20.

Stephen, Leslie. "De Foe's Novels." In *Hours in a Library,* vol. 1. London: John Murray, 1917.

Stoler, John A. *Daniel Defoe: An Annotated Bibliography of Modern Criticism, 1900–1980.* New York: Garland, 1984.

Sutherland, James. *Daniel Defoe: A Critical Study.* Cambridge: Harvard University Press, 1971.

Watt, Ian. "*Robinson Crusoe*: Individualism and the Novel" and "*Robinson Crusoe* as Myth." In his *The Rise of the Novel: Studies in Defoe, Richardson, and Fielding.* Berkeley and Los Angeles: University of California Press, 1957.

Woolf, Virginia. *Collected Essays.* 2 vols. New York: Harcourt, Brace, and World, 1967. (Includes *The Common Reader.*)

—J. ROBERT BASHORE, JR.

WALTER DE LA MARE

1873–1956

WALTER JOHN de la Mare was born in the village of Charlton in Kent on 25 April 1873, the sixth child of James Edward de la Mare and Lucy Sophia Browning. The de la Mares were of Huguenot descent. James de la Mare was a civil servant. He was sixty-two when W. J. was born and died four years later, so the young de la Mare was brought up by his mother. Lucy de la Mare was the daughter of a naval surgeon, Dr. Colin Arrot Browning, himself of Scottish descent and distantly related to the poet Robert Browning. After James de la Mare's death the family moved to London. There W. J. became a chorister at St. Paul's Cathedral and received his education at the choir school. While at St. Paul's he founded and edited the *Choristers' Journal*. During the first months of the *Journal*'s existence young de la Mare provided a major portion of its contents and showed promise as a storyteller. Like the Farjeon children's *Weekly* and *Fortnightly*, the *Journal* included stories, competitions, and advertisements. An early issue carried an ad for de la Mare's "marvellously low-priced sheet of rare foreign stamps."

De la Mare left school at Easter 1890, at the age of seventeen, to become a clerk in the city office of the Anglo-American Oil Company. There he stayed for over eighteen years working in the statistics department until in 1908 the government granted him a pension of one hundred pounds a year. During his years as a clerk de la Mare wrote in his spare time and published stories in the *Cornhill, Pall Mall Gazette, Black and White*, and the *Sketch*. The small government pension enabled him to devote himself to writing full-time.

His first published work, a short story called "Kismet," appeared in 1895 in the *Sketch*. All of his early stories were published under the pseudonym "Walter Ramal," Ramal being an anagram of de la Mare. His editor at the *Cornhill* compared his stories to those of Edgar Allan Poe. They give glimpses of the mystery, musical prose, and vivid imagery characteristic of de la Mare's later work. His first book of poems, *Songs of Childhood*, was accepted for publication by Andrew Lang and appeared in 1902. *Henry Brocken*, de la Mare's first novel, followed two years later. In 1910 *The Three Mulla-Mulgars* (later called *The Three Royal Monkeys*) appeared, and in 1913 *Peacock Pie*, a book of rhymes. These last two works established him as a poet/writer of childhood.

De la Mare married Constance Elfrida Ingpen in 1899. They had four children—Dick, Florence, Jenny, and Colin. *The Three Mulla-Mulgars*, considered one of the finest long stories for children ever written, was written for, and read aloud to, the de la Mare children. The book is a quest story that relates the adventures of three royal monkeys, Thumb, Thimble, and Nod, on their perilous journey to the paradisiacal valleys of Tishnar, where they are reunited with their father. Nod, the youngest son, is a nizza-neela, or one who has magic in him. He is keeper of the Wonderstone, which serves as the talisman on their journey. The reader's sympathies go out to little Nod, who, in spite of his magical abilities, shares our human frailties—vanity, impulsiveness, lack of physical strength. But Nod has true courage and before the end of the journey he has triumphed over the flesh-eating Minimuls, the dreadful Immanala, the Meermuts (or phantoms), and the mischievous Water Midden. His friendship with an Oomgar (human), the shipwrecked sailor Andy Battle, is poignant and unforgettable. Elizabeth Nesbitt's evaluation is still wonderfully true:

> *The Three Mulla-Mulgars* seems to me to hold within itself all of Walter de la Mare's great qualities—his power of imagination, his gift of style, his genius for rendering articulate the intangible. But there is in the book a quality still more rare. There is a breadth and depth of compassion for the fears and griefs, the hopes and aspirations of men which gives the book a haunting and elusive significance.
>
> ("The Books of Walter de la Mare," *Horn Book*)

De la Mare was primarily a poet. Influences on his development as a poet were Shakespeare, the works of Christina Rossetti, nursery rhymes, and the Bible. His poems range in subject from animals, nature, and people to fairies and dreamland. They have special appeal for the imaginative child. Leonard Clark called de la Mare "the greatest writer of English lyrical poetry (particularly for children) of the first half of this century" and considered *Peacock Pie* his masterpiece. This collection contains eighty-two poems arranged, in the early editions, under topics: "Up and Down," "Boys and Girls," "Three Queer Tales," "Places and People," "Beasts," "Witches and Fairies," "Earth and Air," and "Songs." A later edition (1961), illustrated by Caldecott Medal recipient Barbara Cooney, has done away with de la Mare's arrangement but includes all of the poems. The poems vary as much in mood as subject, ranging from the nonsense of a fish that talks in "Alas, Alack!" to the dreaminess of "Silver," which in its entirety reads:

> Slowly, silently, now the moon
> Walks the night in her silver shoon;
> This way, and that, she peers, and sees
> Silver fruit upon silver trees;
> One by one the casements catch
> Her beams beneath the silvery thatch;
> Couched in his kennel, like a log,
> With paws of silver sleeps the dog;
> From their shadowy cote the white breasts peep
> Of doves in a silver-feathered sleep;

> A harvest mouse goes scampering by,
> With silver claws, and silver eye;
> And moveless fish in the water gleam,
> By silver reeds in a silver stream.

De la Mare's poems for children reflect the child's playfulness and delight in the sensuous, her pensiveness and wondering. His dream poetry speaks to the child within each of us and the child's wish for oneness with the world.

In an essay entitled "Children and Poetry," the critic of the *Times Literary Supplement* in 1918 wrote:

> Mr de la Mare's verse puts a spell upon them [i.e., children], partly by its music and partly by its rich and quaint fancy. Of these qualities it is probable that the music is the most important. There never was a greater master of delicate and cunning rhythms than Mr de la Mare: and they carry an exquisite vowel melody that haunts the ear of a child who does not even know the meaning of half the words used.
>
> (Clark, p. 29)

De la Mare employed an enormous variety of rhythms and poetic structures. His poems have the effect of a musical composition; the style fits rhythm and theme—he can be forceful and swift or slow and dreamlike. Sound, rhythm, image, and pattern are perfectly matched. De la Mare was a word musician who knew how to use sound to convey an effect; for instance, his use of the letters *b* and *w* to induce sleep in his lullaby "Now Silent Falls" from his only play, *Crossings* (1921):

> Now silent falls the clacking mill;
> Sweet—sweeter smells the briar;
> The dew wells big on bud and twig;
> The glow-worm's wrapt in fire.
>
> Then sing, lully, lullay, with me,
> And softly, lill-lall-lo, love,
> 'Tis high time, and wild time,
> And no time, no, love!

In his analysis of the poem Leonard Clark comments:

> The choice of 'high', 'wild', and 'no' in connection with 'time' is delightful; 'high' time (quite time to go to sleep), 'wild' time (when time finishes as an exact measurement with the coming of dusk and dream) and the sheer inspiration of 'no' time (time

finishes, there is no longer any time, emphasised by the second 'no').

(p. 49)

Bells and Grass (1941) includes selections from two earlier collections, *Songs of Childhood* and *Peacock Pie*, and some new poems. The introduction cites the poet's oft-quoted dictum: "I know well that only the rarest kind of best in anything can be good enough for the young." De la Mare continues:

I *know*, too, that in later life it is just (if only just) possible now and again to recover fleetingly the intense delight, the untellable joy and happiness and fear and grief and pain of our early years, of an all-but-forgotten childhood. I have, in a flash, in a momentary glimpse, seen again a horse, an oak, a daisy just as I saw them in those early years, as if with that heart, with those senses. It was a revelation. But only such poets as William Blake and Vaughan and Traherne have been able to communicate, as if by means of a language within a language, this strange and scarcely earthly rapture, vision, being, grace.

(*Bells and Grass*, pp. 11–12)

Surely de la Mare belongs in this illustrious company.

De la Mare's critical perception is evident in his anthologies, or "interpretations," as they have been called. His introductions and notes about the entries are as treasured as his selections. *Come Hither* (1923) contains 483 poems by some 260 poets and spans six hundred years. De la Mare's notes in the section "About and Round-About" take up almost three hundred pages. The book's subtitle, "A Collection of Rhymes and Poems for the Young of All Ages," indicates that de la Mare had in mind both children and adults.

The poems in *Tom Tiddler's Ground*, on the other hand, were chosen with children in mind. Clark called the collection a miniature *Come Hither* because the idea grew out of that other collection. It was first published in 1931, as three slim books of ninety-six pages each and in a one-volume edition. The following year a new edition appeared with forty woodcuts by Thomas Bewick. " 'Tom Tiddler's Ground,' " we are told in Leonard Clark's foreword to the 1962 edition, "is that no-man's-land where gold and silver can be picked up just for the asking." It is also the name of a very old children's game. Clark commented:

Walter de la Mare would certainly have regarded the world of poetry as the richest kind of Tom Tiddler's Ground because all the treasures of poetry are free and there for the asking. They are compounded, too, of the finest gold and silver, since they are the treasures of man's mind and spirit.

(p. 7)

The collection includes 230 pieces ranging from nursery rhymes and game rhymes of ancient origin to poems by Shakespeare, Blake, Wordsworth, Shelley, Keats, and de la Mare's contemporaries, but none of his own. De la Mare wrote notes for 138 of the poems. The child reader may ignore them, but many children will find them as fascinating as the adult reader finds the notes in *Come Hither*.

In addition to his long story, *The Three Mulla Mulgars*, de la Mare wrote twenty original stories and retold sixty others for children. *Told Again* (1927) is a collection of nineteen tales taken from Aesop, Charles Perrault, the Grimms, and English folklore, all transformed by the poet's imagination. De la Mare kept to the plots, but enlivened the stories with dialogue and description. His versions of "Cinderella and the Glass Slipper" and other favorite fairy tales are probably most enjoyed by children already familiar with the traditional versions. A picture-book edition of the well-loved English folktale *Molly Whuppie*, published separately with full-page color paintings and small silhouettes by the distinguished British illustrator Errol Le Cain, served to call attention to de la Mare's smooth retelling.

De la Mare's *Stories from the Bible* (1929) includes thirty-four narratives taken from the first nine books of the Old Testament and retold in clear prose. In the introduction de la Mare expressed the hope that his book would lead young readers to the original source. There are no finer retellings than his versions of "The Garden of Eden," "The Flood," "Joseph," "Moses," "The Wilderness," "Samson," "Samuel," "Saul," and "David." De la Mare renders immediate what may seem obscure to today's reader. For example, the passage describing the crossing of the Red Sea (Exodus 14: 19–22) in the King James Version reads:

And the angel of God, which went before the camp of Israel, removed and went behind them; and the pillar of the cloud went from before their face, and stood behind them:

And it came between the camp of the Egyptians and the camp of Israel; and it was a cloud and darkness *to them*, but it gave light by night *to these*: so that the one came not near the other all the night.

And Moses stretched out his hand over the sea; and the Lord caused the sea to go *back* by a strong east wind all that night, and made the sea dry *land*, and the waters were divided.

And the children of Israel went into the midst of the sea upon the dry *ground*: and the waters *were* a wall unto them on their right hand, and on their left.

In the hands of the poet this becomes:

The pillar of cloud, that had gone on before the host of Israel, had removed and now stood kindled between the starry skies and the wrath behind them. Between the huge straggling host of the Israelites and the pursuing vanguard of the armies of Pharaoh, there settled a region of dense gloom—illumined, like the smoke of a burning mountain, by the sombre pillar of fire that was the abiding-place of the angel of the Lord. . . .

But with sunset a wind from between east and north had begun to rise, trumpeting mournfully between earth and sky. In the cold of the dark it steadily increased in force and at last grew exceeding strong. It roared under the night, burdened with whispering sand, beneath a sky wildly brilliant with stars, and, in the small hours, lit with the beams of a waning moon.

Sleep came but fitfully to those huddled together about their watch-fires. The women lay in terror of the tumult, clasping their little ones to their breasts, soothing their cries. Yet this was the wind of their great mercy, for in its vehemency it drove back the tumultuous fast-ebbing tide of the sea towards the south-west until its very bed was exposed beneath the stars, and where had been water was now land.

. . . Leading on their timid flocks and their herds and their beasts of burden, they descended the gently sloping sands that had margined the flood-tide the night before, and advanced on to the wind-swept floor of the sea, its salty boulder-strown sands faintly glimmering in the moonlight and the wan of the day.

(*Stories from the Bible* 1961 [1929], pp. 209–211)

Animal Stories (1939) is an anthology of forty-two stories and forty-six rhymes about animals, chosen and in some instances retold by de la Mare. It was de la Mare's intention to show the development of animal stories from Aesop's fables to the works of modern writers. His introduction gives much information about the genre and reveals de la Mare's belief in the kinship of all creatures. The collection comprises such favorites as "The Story of the Three Bears," "Puss in Boots," "Mr. Fox," "The Six Swans," and "Who Kill'd Cock Robin?" It can be seen from these titles that de la Mare interpreted the term "animal" broadly to include birds and fishes. For his own amusement and that of the reader, de la Mare chose Edward Topsell's woodcuts from his *Historie of Foure-footed Beastes* (1658) to illustrate the tales, remarking that "some of them are as pure inventions of his fancy and imagination as are the animals that talk in the tales." De la Mare's retellings are brilliant; for example, "The Hare and the Hedgehog," based on Aesop's fable of the tortoise and the hare. De la Mare's version originally appeared in *Told Again*. He set the tale in an English countryside:

Early one Sunday morning, when the cowslips or paigles were showing their first honey-sweet buds in the meadows and the broom was in bloom, a hedgehog came to his little door to have a look at the weather. He stood with arms a-kimbo, whistling a tune to himself—a tune no better and no worse than the tunes hedgehogs usually whistle to themselves on fine Sunday mornings. And as he whistled, the notion came into his head that, before turning in and while his wife was washing the children, he might take a little walk into the fields and see how the young nettles were getting on. For there was a tasty beetle lived among the nettles; and no nettles—no beetles.

Off he went, following his own little private path into the fields. And as he came stepping along around a bush of blackthorn, its blossoming now over and its leaves showing green, he met a hare. . . .

De la Mare's humorous elaboration has the hedgehog beat the quick-footed but slow-witted hare by positioning his wife (who looks exactly like her husband) at one end of the field while he remains at the other. Every time the hare arrives at either end of the field, he sees the hedgehog, or so he thinks, and hears his mocking "Ahah! So here you are again! At last!"

Between 1925 and 1946 de la Mare's original short stories appeared in several collections: *Broomsticks, and Other Tales* (1925), *The Lord Fish, and Other Tales* (1933), *The Old Lion, and Other Stories* (1942), *The Magic Jacket, and Other Stories* (1943), *The Scarecrow, and Other Stories* (1945), and *The*

Dutch Cheese, and Other Stories (1931). Four of the stories were published as separate books: *Miss Jemima* (1925); *Lucy* (1927); *Old Joe* (1927); and *Mr. Bumps and His Monkey* (1942), also known as "The Old Lion."

Collected Stories for Children, published in 1947, includes seventeen of the original twenty, representing de la Mare's creative work in this genre over a forty-year period. For this book de la Mare received the Library Association's Carnegie Medal (the British equivalent to the American Library Association's Newbery Medal). With the possible exception of "The Scarecrow," which seems a bit cloying, the stories in this collection draw in the reader with their elusive, dreamlike quality. Margery Bianco, in an article in the *Horn Book*, remarked that many of de la Mare's tales have a "queer under-surface quality of reaching out in unsuspected directions." They do not have neat closures. Long after a story has ended it lingers in the mind—the characters are as real as personal acquaintances, the events often puzzling.

The book has a feeling of unity but the stories vary in subject and mood. "Dick and the Beanstalk" is a lively extension of "Jack and the Beanstalk." Dick, a country boy living with his father in the county of Gloucestershire,

> had been sung all the old rhymes and told most of the country tales of those parts by his mother, and by an old woman who came to the farm when there was sewing to be done, sheets to be hemmed, or shirts to be made. . . .
>
> These tales not only stayed in Dick's head, but *lived* there. . . . He not only knew almost by heart what they told, but would please himself by fancying what else had happened to the people in them after the tales were over or before they had begun. . . .
>
> He was what is called a *lively* reader.

(One imagines de la Mare is describing himself as a boy.) Dick happens on an old cottage and nearby "a huge withered tangle of what looked like a coarse kind of withy-wind or creeper. . . [that] went twisting and writhing corkscrew fashion straight up into the air and so out of sight." In a flash he realizes it is Jack's old cottage, and the creeper Jack's famous Beanstalk. So up Dick climbs and whom should he meet at the top but the great-grandson of Jack's Giant and his wife. The Giant decides to go back with Dick to look for the grave

of his great-grandfather and for the harp Jack stole. Dick has no choice in the matter. Once on earth the Giant insists on meeting Dick's father and having "a bite and sup" in Dick's house. The Giant finds the farm to his liking and settles in, causing no end of trouble for Dick and his father. Dick has to be as ingenious as Jack to outwit the Giant and persuade him to go home. Once the Giant is back where he belongs, Dick burns down the Beanstalk, "though he had been wise enough before he had begun gathering together the fuel for his fire to put two or three of the dry bean-seeds into his pocket. Some day he meant to plant them; just to see."

"A Penny a Day" is an enchanting story about good-natured Griselda, who cares for her old grandmother. Things go from bad to worse after Grannie falls ill, and in desperation Griselda makes a bargain with a strange little man. Old Moleskins works for Griselda for "a penny a day," then steals the pennies to test her. Griselda's good nature meets the dwarf's test and he rewards her. He takes her to see the grottoes of the Urchin People under the sea, returns the pennies to her, and gives her some fruit with "a curious magic in it." Griselda finds a sweetheart, Simon, the son of her kind-hearted neighbor, and the farm that once belonged to her great-great-grandfather returns to her through marriage. The story has all the magic of an old fairy tale.

"The Lovely Myfanwy" evokes Shakespeare's *A Midsummer Night's Dream* and *King Lear*. Myfanwy's father is so jealous of any would-be suitor that he keeps his daughter sequestered in his great castle. A juggler (de la Mare liked jugglers and thought they had some unusual power over the things they handled) gains access and gives Myfanwy a colored ball, an English apple, and a silken rope. The apple makes any human who tastes it more himself than ever. Myfanwy's father eats the magic apple and is transmogrified into an ass. Myfanwy's love and a magic carrot restore him to his human form, a much wiser man for the experience and ready to accept the prince, who no longer has to disguise himself as a juggler.

In "Maria-Fly" de la Mare describes with vivid recall the wonder a child feels on seeing for the first time an "ordinary" creature and the inability to communicate that experience to an adult. "Lucy" is the haunting story of Jean Elspeth and her two maiden sisters and the lifelong imaginary playmate Jean created when she was seven years old.

The range of the stories is extraordinary. They

probably appeal as much to adults as to children and are, therefore, "for the young of all ages." They have special appeal for the imaginative child or for the less imaginative child who is fortunate to have an imaginative adult who will read them aloud.

Walter de la Mare died on 22 June 1956. He is buried in St. Paul's Cathedral in London. His biographer and friend, Leonard Clark, wrote that de la Mare "died at the age of eighty-three, a child of mature years." It is said that "writing was his life." Except for one visit to the United States in 1916 he lived in England all of his life, but one might say more truthfully that he lived most intensely in the realm of the imagination. Those who met him recall a person of gentle nobility with eyes that missed nothing. He was a person one did not forget. *Tea with Walter de la Mare*, by Walter Russell Brain, gives impressions of de la Mare as both dreamer and thinker. Brain said his conversations resembled what psychologists call "free association." He had an abiding interest in the interrelationships of brain, mind, and spirit. Near the end of his life he remarked to Brain, "It's the inward life that matters." Occasionally, in his stories, he used words that offend today (e.g., "piccaninnies," "darkey") —he was, after all, a product of the Victorian age—but de la Mare's attitude toward all living creatures, human and animal, was one of respect and sympathy.

Two issues of the *Horn Book* were dedicated to Walter de la Mare. The May–June 1942 issue was published during World War II, when de la Mare was still living. It included pieces by Margery Bianco, Eleanor Farjeon, and Dorothy P. Lathrop. Lathrop recalled the joy of discovering the works of de la Mare when, as a young and inexperienced illustrator, she was invited to make pictures for *The Three Mulla-Mulgars* in 1919. That book became a touchstone for her to compare with other books offered by publishers in the years to come. Miss Lathrop illustrated other works by de la Mare: *Down-Adown-Derry* (1922), *Crossings*, *The Dutch Cheese*, *Bells and Grass*, and *Mr. Bumps and His Monkey*. Jasper, the little monkey in *Mr. Bumps and His Monkey*, is as appealing as Nod, and though the story is shorter and less complex than *The Three Royal Monkeys*, it is written in the same key. To illustrate the story properly, Lathrop decided she needed a living model. Her amusing account of life with a monkey is reminiscent of Robert McCloskey's experience of sharing his apartment with

some young mallards while illustrating *Make Way for Ducklings* (1941). Lathrop's illustrations for de la Mare's works are exquisite—whether full-color paintings or delicate line drawings. There is a touch of mystery in them that is akin to the spirit of the author's work.

A Walter de la Mare issue of the *Horn Book* also appeared in June 1957, a year after the poet's death. In the lead article, "Walter de la Mare," Eleanor Farjeon recounted her first meeting with de la Mare on an autumn afternoon in 1916 and their friendship of forty years. Describing the charm of the houses where de la Mare lived during their forty-year friendship, she wrote: "W. J. could not live anywhere without bewitching the atmosphere and drawing people after him into the magic." The theme that possessed him, according to Farjeon, was "the reality of his dreams compared with the reality of his waking life." Farjeon wrote that children adored his presence among them and enjoyed listening to him reading his poems as he used to do on his visits to schools and libraries.

In this same issue Herbert Read described him as "gentle, sensitive, visionary." Read made a plea for readers not to neglect de la Mare's longer and more difficult poems in which the poet struggled with the meaning of life (for example, "Dreams"), for the more immediate and joyful in appeal that are excessively anthologized.

One of the most interesting articles, "The Books of Walter de la Mare," is written by thirteen editors, authors, storytellers, and librarians who offered tributes to de la Mare in answer to the question: "What is your favorite de la Mare book?" Most refused to limit themselves to one title, naming several. Louise Seaman Bechtel selected *Come Hither* "for the poems chosen, for the marvellous introduction, and for the wide range and brilliance of the rich pages of his notes at the end. It is still the best introduction existing to true poetry in English." David McCord also singled out *Come Hither* and added: "In everything that he did he was a maker of magic." Frances Clarke Sayers picked several, but above all *Early One Morning in the Spring* (1935). This anthology of early memories and writings of various writers (Jane Austin, Henry James, and others) chosen by de la Mare and accompanied by his scholarly notes is a treasure for the adult who has an interest in childhood. Anyone acquainted with the book will share Sayers' enthusiasm. She writes:

It is a handbook on teaching, on childhood, on psychology, with worlds opening up on English literature. I know of no other book which is as strong a restorative as this, when the clamor of theories sounds around the head, or when discouragement sets in and the word seems to be diminishing in power in a push-button world. My copy is interlined and underscored, and yet each time I read it, there is another discovery not yet realized.

This issue also includes a lovely piece by Pamela Bianco, for whom de la Mare wrote verses to go with her drawings of children for *Flora* (1919), and tributes by other luminaries such as Anne Carroll Moore and Bertha Mahony Miller.

Today de la Mare's works are frequently overlooked in favor of more recent authors'. The loss is ours. His fantasies are every bit as good as those by Tolkien, C. S. Lewis, and Lloyd Alexander. His poems and stories are part of the canon of children's literature. It may be that they appeal most to the solitary child, the imaginative child, the future creative adult, but they are very much needed at a time when the visual is stressed and the oral/aural often neglected. The child who has not heard his works read aloud may miss the poet's voice, the beauty of sound and image that was uniquely de la Mare. No one can read de la Mare—or hear his work read aloud—without being enriched in language, imagery, and living.

Selected Bibliography

WORKS OF WALTER DE LA MARE

Verse

Songs of Childhood, under the pseudonym "Walter Ramal." London: Longmans, 1902; New York: Garland, 1976. Rev. ed., published in his own name. London: Longmans, 1916, 1923.

Peacock Pie: A Book of Rhymes. With illustrations by W. Heath Robinson. London: Constable, 1913; New York: Holt, 1925. Rev. ed., with illustrations by Edward Ardizzone. London: Faber and Faber, 1946. Rev. ed., with illustrations by Barbara Cooney. New York: Knopf, 1961.

Flora: A Book of Drawings, by Pamela Bianco with illustrative poems by Walter de la Mare. Philadelphia: Lippincott, 1919.

Down-Adown-Derry: A Book of Fairy Poems. With illustrations by Dorothy P. Lathrop. London: Constable, 1922; New York: Holt, 1922.

Bells and Grass: A Book of Rhymes. With illustrations by F.

Rowland Emett. London: Faber and Faber, 1941. Rev. ed., with illustrations by Dorothy P. Lathrop. New York: Viking Press, 1942.

Fiction

Henry Brocken. London: John Murray, 1904.

The Three Mulla-Mulgars. London: Duckworth, 1910. Rev. ed., with illustrations by Dorothy P. Lathrop. New York: Knopf, 1919. Retitled *The Three Royal Monkees*, with illustrations by Mildred E. Eldridge. New York: Knopf, 1948.

Broomsticks, and Other Tales. With illustrations by Bold. London: Constable, 1925; New York: Knopf, 1925.

Miss Jemima. With illustrations by Alec Buckels. Oxford: Basil Blackwell, 1925; Poughkeepsie, N.Y.: Artists and Writers Guild, 1935.

Lucy. With illustrations by Hilda T. Miller. Oxford: Basil Blackwell, 1927.

Old Joe. With illustrations by C. T. Nightingale. Oxford: Basil Blackwell, 1927.

The Dutch Cheese. With illustrations by Dorothy P. Lathrop. New York: Knopf, 1931. (Includes "The Lovely Myfanwy.")

The Lord Fish, and Other Tales. With illustrations by Rex Whistler. London: Faber and Faber, 1933.

The Old Lion, and Other Stories. With illustrations by Irene Hawkins. London: Faber and Faber, 1942.

Mr. Bumps and His Monkey. With illustrations by Dorothy P. Lathrop. Philadelphia: Winston, 1942.

The Magic Jacket, and Other Stories. With illustrations by Irene Hawkins. London: Faber and Faber, 1943.

The Scarecrow, and Other Stories. With illustrations by Irene Hawkins. London: Faber and Faber, 1945.

The Dutch Cheese, and Other Stories. With illustrations by Irene Hawkins. London: Faber and Faber, 1946.

Collected Stories for Children. With illustrations by Irene Hawkins. London: Faber and Faber, 1947. Rev. ed., with illustrations by Robin Jacques. London: Faber and Faber, 1967.

Play

Crossings: A Fairy Play. With music by C. Armstrong Gibbs and illustrations by Randolph Schwabe. London: Beaumont, 1921. Rev. ed., with illustrations by Dorothy P. Lathrop. New York: Knopf, 1923.

Other Works

Come Hither: A Collection of Rhymes and Poems for the Young of All Ages. Edited by Walter de la Mare. With illustrations by Alec Buckels. London: Constable, 1923; New York: Knopf, 1923. Rev. ed. New York: Knopf, 1928. Rev. ed., with illustrations by Warren Chappell. New York: Knopf, 1957.

Told Again: Traditional Tales. With illustrations by A. H. Watson. Oxford: Basil Blackwell, 1927. Retitled *Told Again: Old Tales Told Again*. New York: Knopf,

1927. Retitled *Tales Told Again*, with illustrations by Alan Howard. London: Faber and Faber, 1959; New York: Knopf, 1959.

Stories from the Bible. With illustrations by Theodore Nadejen. London: Faber and Faber, 1929. Rev. ed., with illustrations by Edward Ardizzone. New York: Knopf, 1961.

Tom Tiddler's Ground: A Book of Poetry. Edited by Walter de la Mare. With illustrations by Thomas Bewick. London: Collins, 1932. Rev. ed., with drawings by Margery Gill. New York: Knopf, 1962.

Early One Morning in the Spring: Chapters on Children and on Childhood as It Is Revealed in Particular in Early Memories and in Early Writings. London: Faber and Faber, 1935; New York: Macmillan, 1935.

Animal Stories: Chosen, Arranged, and in Some Part Rewritten. With woodcuts from Edward Topsell's *Historie of Foure-footed Beastes*. London: Faber and Faber, 1939; New York: Charles Scribner's Sons, 1940.

Molly Whuppie, retold by Walter de la Mare. With illustrations by Errol Le Cain. New York: Farrar, Straus, and Giroux, 1983.

CRITICAL AND BIOGRAPHICAL STUDIES

Bechtel, Louise Seaman, et al. "The Books of Walter de la Mare" *Horn Book* 33/3: 235–241 (June 1957).

Bianco, Margery. "De La Mare" *Horn Book* 18/3: 141–147 (May–June 1942).

Bianco, Pamela. "Walter de la Mare" *Horn Book* 33/3: 242–247 (June 1957).

Brain, Walter Russell. *Tea with Walter de la Mare*. London: Faber and Faber, 1957.

Clark, Leonard. *Walter de la Mare*. London: Bodley Head, 1960; New York: H. Z. Walck, 1961.

Farjeon, Eleanor. "A Pepperpot Question" *Horn Book* 18/3: 149–152 (May–June 1942).

———. "Walter de la Mare" *Horn Book* 33/3: 197–205 (June 1957).

Lathrop, Dorothy P. "Illustrating De La Mare" *Horn Book* 18/3: 188–196 (May–June 1942).

Megroz, R. L. *Walter de la Mare: A Biographical and Critical Study*. London: Hodder and Stoughton, 1924. Reprint Wilmington, Del.: Scholarly Resources, 1972.

National Book League. *Walter de la Mare: A Checklist*. With an introduction by Lord David Cecil and a note on the checklist by Leonard Clark. Cambridge: National Book League at the University Press, 1956.

Read, Herbert. "Walter de la Mare" *Horn Book* 33/3: 209–210 (June 1957).

Reid, Forrest. *Walter de la Mare: A Critical Study*. London: Faber and Faber, 1929; New York: Holt, 1929. Reprint Wilmington, Del.: Scholarly Resources, 1970.

—ELLIN GREENE

CHARLES DICKENS

1812–1870

We are men of secluded habits with something of a cloud upon our early fortunes, whose enthusiasm has not been cooled with age, whose spirit of romance is not yet quenched, who are content to ramble through the world in a pleasant dream, rather than ever waken again to its harsh realities.

(Master Humphrey's Clock,
4 April 1840)

GRAHAM GREENE HAS shrewdly observed that "it is only in childhood that books have any deep influence on our lives." That was certainly true of Charles Dickens. No other literature had a more profound effect on the art of the great novelist than the books he read when a boy. In "A Christmas Tree" (*Household Words*, Christmas Number, 1850), he rapturously recalled all the famous heroes and villains of his little storybooks: Robin Hood, Valentine and Orson, the Yellow Dwarf, Robinson Crusoe, Sandford and Merton. He wrote,

Little Red Riding-Hood comes to me one Christmas Eve to give me information of the cruelty and treachery of that dissembling Wolf who ate her grandmother, without making any impression on his appetite, and then ate her, after making that ferocious joke about his teeth. She was my first love. I felt that if I could have married Little Red Riding-Hood, I should have known perfect bliss.

He always held a sincere affection for

the marvellous bean-stalk up which Jack climbed to the Giant's house! And now, those dreadfully inter-

esting, double-headed giants, with their clubs over their shoulders, begin to stride along the boughs in a perfect throng, dragging knights and ladies home for dinner by the hair of their heads. And Jack— how noble, with his sword of sharpness, and his shoes of swiftness! . . . I debate within myself whether there was more than one Jack (which I am loath to believe possible), or only one genuine original admirable Jack, who achieved all the recorded exploits.

Yet all of these wonders paled for young Dickens when compared to the glories of *The Thousand and One Nights* and "Sir Charles Morell's" *The Tales of the Genii* (actually a series of imitations by the Rev. J. Ridley, said to be "faithfully translated from the Persian Manuscript"). Dickens continued:

Oh, now all common things become uncommon and enchanted to me! All lamps are wonderful; all rings are talismans. Common flower-pots are full of treasure, with a little earth scattered on the top; trees are for Ali Baba to hide in; beefsteaks are to throw down into the Valley of Diamonds, that the precious stones may stick to them, and be carried by the eagles to their nests, whence the traders, with loud cries, will scare them. Tarts are made, according to the recipe of the Vizier's son of Bussorah, who turned pastry-cook after he was set down in his drawers at the gate of Damascus; cobblers are all Mustaphas, and in the habit of sewing up people cut into four pieces, to whom they are taken blindfold.

Yet for Dickens, the marvels he discovered in the romances he read in his childhood were not mere frivolities, were not light diversions without deeper significance. They bore a profound importance in his own life. In a fragment of his uncompleted autobiography, subsequently woven into *David Copperfield* (1850), Dickens confessed to discovering a set of books left by his father in the room that adjoined his own. From here, he recalled, "Roderick Random, Peregrine Pickle, Humphrey Clinker, Tom Jones, the Vicar of Wakefield, Don Quixote, Gil Blas, and Robinson Crusoe, came out, a glorious host, to keep me company. . . . They, and the Arabian Nights, and the Tales of the Genii." Just as they are for his own favorite child, David Copperfield, during David's troubled times with the Murdstones, so they were for Dickens himself in his young years "my only and my constant comfort." He now saw through other eyes. "Every barn in the neighbourhood," David explains, "every stone in the church, and every foot of the churchyard, had some association of its own, in my mind, connected with these books, and stood for some locality made famous in them." These books transformed the everyday world into something wondrous, and thus they consoled him through all the great and small miseries of his own childhood.

Little David Copperfield is well aware that these are clandestine delights. Pious Mr. Murdstone and his hard-hearted sister, had they known of it, would never have approved of the boy's indulging in this frivolous literature. At the time, all these fictions were condemned by the most eminent of contemporary authorities on the education of children. These books were considered sinful, mere trash that corrupted little boys and girls with their absurd notions. Dickens countered these charges. "They kept my fancy alive, and my hope of something beyond that place and time,—they . . . did me no harm; for whatever harm was in some of them was not there for me; *I* knew nothing of it."

What harm they do him, the novel implies, is to turn the boy into a novelist. Once he has begun reading these wild tales of romance, David Copperfield often looks upon the experiences of his own life in terms of characters and incidents from these fictions. When sent away to school, the boy tries to fight back the tears because "neither Roderick Random, nor that Captain in the Royal British Navy, had ever cried, that I could remember, in trying situations"; Mr. Creakle looks upon his pupils at Salem House "like a giant in a story-book surveying his captives"; and when Jack Maldon departs for India David considers him "a modern Sindbad,

and . . . the bosom friend of all the Rajahs in the East, sitting under canopies, smoking curly golden pipes—a mile long, if they could be straightened out." One of the works most frequently referred to throughout Dickens' writings is *The Arabian Nights*. Another is Daniel Defoe's *Robinson Crusoe* (1719), especially in *David Copperfield*: on his arrival by coach in London, with no one to greet him, the boy reflects on how he appears "more solitary than Robinson Crusoe, who had nobody to look at him and see that he was solitary"; when he rents his first apartment in Buckingham Street in the Adelphi, the young man describes how it is "a wonderfully fine thing to have that lofty castle to myself, and to feel, when I shut my outer door, like Robinson Crusoe, when he had got into his fortification, and pulled his ladder up after him"; and when he and Mr. Spenlow hear a case in court, "the evidence was just twice the length of *Robinson Crusoe*, according to a calculation I made." It is not surprising that this romantic young man should color his attractions to women with the same storybook atmosphere. Little Em'ly is "the fairy little woman," and when he first sees his beloved Dora Spenlow, she is to the love-struck David "a Fairy, a Sylph, I don't know what she was—anything that no one ever saw, and everything that everybody ever wanted."

But not all boys are so fortunate as to discover so young such literary treasures as did little David—and Charles. When he goes to Salem House, the only spark of romance in that dreary place is provided by the new pupil, David himself, who offhandedly remarks to J. Steerforth, the head boy, "that something or somebody—I forget what now—was like something or somebody in Peregrine Pickle." Steerforth is unfamiliar with the reference and asks if David has the book with him. Of course he no longer has it or any of the other marvelous books he had found at home in the room adjoining his. But Steerforth must know more and demands that David retell all of these stories to him. "We'll go over 'em one after another," the head boy proposes. "We'll make some regular Arabian Nights of it." For months, David nightly recounts for the other boys all the tales he knows. "Whatever I had within me that was romantic and dreamy, was encouraged by so much story-telling in the dark; and in that respect the pursuit may not have been very profitable to me," he admits. However, in the short run, this special gift redeems David in the eyes of his classmates. In the long run, it serves as his apprenticeship for his future career as a novelist. He can never forget the tales that gave him such comfort as a boy, and he eventually puts them to good use: he learned composition by fitting "my old books to my altered life, and made stories for myself, out of the streets, and out of men and women." By the time he has left school, after completing his studies at the admirable Dr. Strong's, the old feeling for romance has not died within him. For young David, life at this time "was more like a great fairy story, which I was just about to begin to read, than anything else." Sadly, Steerforth, who remains behind at Salem House without the nurturing of David's nightly story-telling, does not turn out well. If David is "the hero of my own life," then Steerforth, his friend and confidant, becomes its villain.

The influences of these romances read in youth can be found everywhere in Dickens' work. *Oliver Twist* (1838), with all of its convenient coincidences and melodrama right out of popular fiction, restores its poor hero like a sexless Tom Jones to his proper place in society. The alliterative name Nicholas Nickleby suggests Peregrine Pickle as well as Roderick Random. Gog and Magog, the giants of Guildhall, are introduced in Dickens' magazine *Master Humphrey's Clock* like modern Scheherazades to relate a new series of tales from the *Arabian Nights*. The confusions induced by Jasper's opium dreams in *The Mystery of Edwin Drood* (1870) also suggest the world of the *Arabian Nights*. Dickens' villains may be found in any storybook: Mr. Squeers is an ogre, with "but one eye, and the popular prejudice runs in favour of two"; Mrs. Pipchin is "this ogress and child-queller"; and Miss Havisham is "the Witch of the place." Mr. Pinch in *Martin Chuzzlewit* (1844) shares David Copperfield's love of the old romances, as we see when he gazes upon a shop

where children's books were sold, and where poor Robinson Crusoe stood alone in his might, with dog and hatchet, goat-skin cap and fowling-pieces. . . . And there too were the Persian tales, with flying chests and students of enchanted books shut up for years in caverns: . . . and there the mighty talisman, the rare Arabian Nights, with Cassim Baba, divided by four, like the ghost of a dreadful sum, hanging up, all gory, in the robbers' cave. Which matchless wonders, coming fast on Mr. Pinch's mind, did so rub up and chafe that wonderful lamp within him . . . and he lived again, with new delight, the happy days before the Pecksniff era.

As John Forster, Dickens' closest friend and biographer, was the first to acknowledge, nowhere in all of the novelist's many works is his love of the books he knew in childhood more evident than in his "Christmas Books." According to Forster, "No one was more intensely fond than Dickens of old nursery tales, and he had a secret delight in feeling that he was here only giving them a higher form." This is certainly obvious from their subtitles: *The Chimes* (1844) is "a goblin story," *The Cricket on the Hearth* (1845) is "a fairy tale of home," and both *A Christmas Carol* (1843) and *The Haunted Man* (1848) are ghost stories. (Today ghost stories are generally considered inappropriate for children, but in Dickens' day these "Winter Stories—Ghost Stories" were recounted around the Christmas fire to every member of the family; his first book, *The Pickwick Papers* [1837], includes a tale within the tale, a Christmas ghost story about the goblins who stole the sexton, which was the model for *A Christmas Carol*.) The first, *A Christmas Carol*, set the tone of all the others in the series. The atmosphere is imbued with an animism one usually finds in storybooks: an ancient church tower strikes the hours "as if its teeth were chattering in its frozen head"; the fire-plug, "being left in solitude, its overflowings sullenly congealed, and turned to misanthropic ice"; the shops have "great, round, pot-bellied baskets of chestnuts, shaped like the waist-coats of jolly old gentlemen, lolling at the doors, and tumbling out into the street in their apoplectic opulence," as well as "ruddy, brown-faced, broad-girthed Spanish onions, shining in the fatness of their growth like Spanish Friars, and winking from their shelves in wanton slyness at the girls as they went by, and glanced demurely at the hung-up mistletoe." Here described is a London where one would not be startled to find the face of an old dead partner in a door knocker. Each of the Christmas books—with the exception of *The Battle of Life* (1846)—is basically the same story, one that might be found in Mother Bunch or Mother Goose: a wretched mortal changes the course of his life through a divine intermediary. It matters little whether it is Marley's Ghost in *A Christmas Carol*, the Goblin of the Bell in *The Chimes*, the Genius of the Hearth and Home in *The Cricket on the Hearth*, or the Phantom in *The Haunted Man*. It might as well be Cinderella's fairy godmother.

Scrooge's sin is that, unlike David Copperfield (or Dickens himself), he let the dreams of his childhood die within him. The first scene with which the

Ghost of Christmas Past confronts the old miser is a view of himself as a boy, alone in the schoolroom reading. Suddenly all the favorite characters of his childhood return in a flood to the aged man. In "a most extraordinary voice between laughing and crying," he shouts:

Why, it's Ali Baba! . . . And Valentine, and his wild brother, Orson! . . . And the Sultan's Groom turned upside-down by the Genii. . . . There's the Parrot! . . . Poor Robin Crusoe, he called him, when he came home again after sailing round the island. . . . There goes Friday, running for his life to the little creek! Halloa! Hoop! Halloo!

And all of this from a man who just hours before had shouted, "Out upon a Merry Christmas!" Clearly it is a buoyant Dickens himself speaking here as much as it is Scrooge.

Scrooge may be redeemed, but not so all of those others in Dickens' fiction who have let the spark of childish merriment go out within them. For these, the flame has been snuffed out early, usually by some zealous schoolteacher. The heartless, humorless instructors of Dickens' world are descendants of Mr. Barlow, the tutor in Thomas Day's popular *The History of Sandford and Merton* (1783–1789), a gentleman Dickens called "childhood's experience of a bore." "What right had he to bore his way into my Arabian Nights?" Dickens demands in *The Uncommercial Traveller* (1861).

He was always hinting doubts of the veracity of Sindbad the Sailor. If he could have got hold of the Wonderful Lamp, I knew he would have trimmed it and lighted it, and delivered a lecture over it on the qualities of sperm oil. . . . I took refuge in the caves of ignorance, wherein I have resided ever since, and which are still my private address.

Sandford and Merton was the prototype for many of the tiresome, didactic children's books that tried to replace the fairy tales and romances popular in Dickens' boyhood. Mrs. Pipchin of *Dombey and Son* (1848) is merely a female Mr. Barlow. Her system of education is "not to encourage a child's mind to develop and expand itself like a young flower, but to open it by force like an oyster." Instead of some delightful children's tales, she teaches with books containing moral lessons "usually of a violent and stunning character: the hero—a naughty boy—seldom, in the mildest catastrophe, being finished off by anything less than a lion, or a bear." Little Paul

Dombey graduates to Doctor Blimber's, an institution that Mrs. Pipchin extols as a place where the students' life is "very strictly conducted, and there is nothing but learning going on from morning to night." Doctor Blimber is just another name for Mr. Barlow. Mercifully Paul Dombey is allowed to die, but others are not so fortunate. Mr. Squeers, proprietor of the notorious Yorkshire school in *Nicholas Nickleby* (1839), brutalizes his charges, in particular the pitiable Smike. Others are social freaks like the Smallweeds of *Bleak House* (1853), "complete little men and women" who "bear a likeness to old monkeys with something depressing on their minds." Their schooling "discarded all amusements, discountenanced all story-books, fairy tales, fictions, and fables, and banished all levities whatsoever." Consequently Judy never hears of Cinderella, and Bart "knows no more of Jack the Giant Killer, or of Sindbad the Sailor, than he knows of the people in the stars."

Dickens' most brutal attack upon this suppression of fancy by contemporary education occurs in *Hard Times* (1854). Here the child is indeed the father of the man. "Now, what I want is Facts," explains Thomas Gradgrind, Sr., the proprietor of a model school of the day.

Teach these boys and girls nothing but Facts. Facts alone are wanted in life. Plant nothing else, and root out everything else. You can only form the minds of reasoning animals upon Facts: nothing else will ever be of any service to them. This is the principle on which I bring up my own children, and this is the principle on which I bring up these children. Stick to Facts, sir!

"The Gradgrind Philosophy" is fully in accord with the designs of that utilitarian age: girl number one and boy number two will become bodies number one and number two of Coketown. Mr. Gradgrind's institution cannot provide even "a little standing-room for Queen Mab's chariot among the Steam Engines." One of Mr. Gradgrind's associates demands,

You must discard the word Fancy altogether. You have nothing to do with it. . . . You don't walk upon flowers in fact; you cannot be allowed to walk upon flowers in carpets. . . . You never meet with quadrupeds going up and down walls; you must not have quadrupeds represented upon walls. You must see, for all these purposes, combinations and modifications (in primary colours) of mathematical figures which are susceptible of proof and demonstration. This is the new discovery. This is fact. This is taste.

Mr. Gradgrind is not amused that a new pupil, Sissy Jupe, is in the habit of reading to her father. "O yes, sir, thousands of times," she confesses. "They were the happiest—oh, of all the happy times we had together, sir!" "And what," he asks, "did you read to your father, Jupe?" "About the Fairies, sir, and the Dwarf, and the Hunchback, and the Genies," she replies, "and about—" "Hush!" he says, "that is enough. Never breathe a word of such destructive nonsense any more." He has instructed his own children well:

No little Gradgrind had ever associated a cow in a field with that famous cow with the crumpled horn who tossed the dog who worried the cat who killed the rat who ate the malt, or with that yet more famous cow who swallowed Tom Thumb: it had never heard of those celebrities, and had only been introduced to a cow as a graminivorous ruminating quadruped with several stomachs.

When asked what a horse is, a student's rote reply is, "Quadruped. Graminivorous. Forty teeth, namely, twenty-four grinders, four eye-teeth, and twelve incisive. Sheds coat in the spring; in marshy countries, sheds hoofs, too. Hoofs hard, but requiring to be shod with iron. Age known by marks in mouth." (The instruction at Dotheboys Hall in *Nicholas Nickleby* is no better. "A horse is a quadruped," lectures the illiterate Mr. Squeers, "and quadruped's Latin for beast, as everybody that's gone through the grammar knows, or else where's the use of having grammars at all? . . . As you're perfect in that, go and look after *my* horse, and rub him down well, or I'll rub you down.")

Still, such instruction proves destructive, leading to bitter resentment. "I wish I could collect all the Facts we hear so much about," says Thomas Gradgrind, Jr., "and all the Figures, and all the people who found them out—and I wish I could put a thousand barrels of gunpowder under them and blow them all up together!" Yes, Tom will have his revenge. And his poor sister, only after hard experience, eventually acknowledges:

If I had been stone blind—if I had groped my way by my sense of touch, and had been free, while I knew the shapes and surfaces of things, to exercise my fancy somewhat, in regard to them—I should have been a million times wiser, happier, more lov-

ing, more contented, more innocent and human in all good respects, than I am with the eyes I have. . . . What I have learned has left me doubting, misbelieving, despising, regretting, what I have not learned.

The moral of the story is that using only facts and no fancy to guide one's life leads only to misery.

Hard Times is certainly the leanest of Dickens' novels, composed with the brevity and clarity of a child's fable. And it is not the subtlest of his fictions, for it is a parable that interplays in an allegorical fashion the fancy of his childhood reading with the harsh economic realities of his day. The names Bounderby, Sleary, Scadgers, and Sparsit suggest the villains of *Pilgrim's Progress*. The monsters Gradgrind and M'Choakumchild, his chief instructor, might have stepped right out of a child's pantomime of "Jack the Giant-Killer." The first impression the five little Gradgrinds have in their own lives is the sight of

a large blackboard with a dry Ogre chalking ghastly white figures on it. Not that they knew, by name or nature, anything about an Ogre. Fact forbid! I only use the word to express a monster in a lecturing castle, with Heaven knows how many heads manipulated into one, taking childhood captive, and dragging it into gloomy statistical dens by the hair.

M'Choakumchild goes after his lessons

not unlike Morgiana in the Forty Thieves: looking into all the vessels ranged before him, one after another, to see what they contained. Say, good M'Choakumchild: When from thy boiling store, thou shalt fill each jar brim full by-and-by, dost thou think that thou wilt always kill outright the robber Fancy lurking within—or sometimes only maim him and distort him!

In *Hard Times* Dickens overplays his irony, sometimes with unctuous sarcasm and at other times with great comic effect, recalling the pages of his favorite storybooks. Particularly clever are his descriptions of the Gradgrinds' scientific studies: "To paraphrase the idle legend of Peter Piper, who had never found his way into their nursery, If the greedy little Gradgrinds grasped at more than this, what was it for good gracious goodness' sake that the greedy little Gradgrinds grasped at?" Why indeed did they grasp at it, for good gracious goodness' sake? Their destiny is Coketown. Yet even this dismal place is painted with Dickens' fancy, albeit with a dash of sarcasm: "The lights in the great factories . . . looked, when they were illuminated, like Fairy Palaces—or the travellers by express-train said so." Mrs. Sparsit deludes herself into thinking she is "the Bank Fairy"; the townspeople see her as "the Bank Dragon." The workers' only refuge (and Mr. Gradgrind's chief torment) is the library in Coketown. No matter how the pedagogue and his many colleagues try to correct the situation, the people still "wondered about human nature, human passions, human hopes and fears, the struggles, triumphs and defeats, the cares and joys and sorrows, the lives and deaths, of common men and women!" And they find all of these human aspirations in the romances in the library. Like David Copperfield and Mr. Pinch and Scrooge and Dickens himself, the workers of Coketown "took Defoe to their bosoms instead of Euclid, and seemed to be on the whole more comforted by Goldsmith than by Cocker."

Dickens thus became the self-appointed defender of the faith of Fancy against the assaults of practicality. He had no patience for any who might, for their own ends, distort the old stories he so loved in his childhood, no matter how well-meaning such people might be. The character of *Hard Times* no doubt evolved in part from the thoughts Dickens expressed in an editorial that appeared in *Household Words* on 1 October 1853. The victim of his attack was his former collaborator, George Cruikshank, who had illustrated *Sketches by Boz* (1836) and *Oliver Twist* years before. Cruikshank was by this time one of England's most popular artists, and he had also become an ardent (and sometimes tiresome) temperance advocate. His teetotalism now colored everything he did: in particular, his recently published *Fairy Library* (1870), comprising the illustrator's retellings of "Cinderella," "Hop-o'-My-Thumb," "Puss-in-Boots," and "Jack and the Beanstalk," was soaked with total-abstinence propaganda. In the Cruikshank version, terrible giants act as they do not because it is their nature but because they drink intoxicating liquors. Dickens, however, termed such changes of the old beloved stories "Frauds on the Fairies."

The novelist "half playfully and half seriously" intended his editorial "to protest most strongly against alteration—for any purpose—of those beautiful little stories which are so tenderly and humanly useful to us in these times when the world

is too much with us, early and late." After all, Dickens pointed out, these simple narratives had had such a profound effect upon him when he was a boy. In their original state, he had discovered an inestimable amount of "gentleness and mercy . . . forbearance, courtesy, consideration for the poor and aged, kind treatment of animals, the love of nature, abhorrence of tyranny and brute force—many such good things have been first nourished in the child's heart by this powerful aid." And their influence persisted in his adult life, helping greatly "to keep us, in some sense, ever young, by preserving through our wordly ways one slender track not overgrown with weeds, where we may walk with children, sharing their delights."

Now more than ever, Dickens argued, these stories needed to remain unaltered to continue "in their usefulness, . . . in their simplicity, and purity, and innocent extravagance, as if they were actual fact." Anyone who even dared to rewrite these tales to suit his own selfish interests, no matter how well-intentioned, was guilty, Dickens believed, "of an act of presumption," and such a person "appropriates to himself what does not belong to him." According to Dickens these hard times, more than any other, needed just such harmless diversion from harsh reality, for "a nation without fancy, without some romance," Dickens warned, "never did, never can, never will, hold a great place under the sun." The world needed any little help it could find, and Dickens' advice to Cruikshank and others was "Leave this precious old escape from it, alone."

Clearly that old romantic Dickens had allowed his sentimentality, his "great tenderness for the fairy literature of our childhood," to distort his memory of that literature. Cruikshank was quick to respond with a mock open letter from Hop-o-My-Thumb to the distinguished novelist, in which the literary midget accuses the literary giant of "suffering that extraordinary seven-league imagination of yours to run away with you into your *own* Fairy Land—thus you have given your *own* colours to that history; and, consequently, a credit and a character which do not belong to them." Cruikshank at least had done *his* homework; unlike Dickens, he had gone back to the old chapbooks to read the authentic tales. And the artist was appalled by what he found: The little hero of "Hop-o'-My-Thumb" was "an *unfeeling*, *artful liar*, and a *thief*"; and "Puss-in-Boots" was "a succession of successful falsehoods—a *clever* lesson in lying!—a system of *imposture*, rewarded by the greatest worldly!—a *use-*

ful lesson, truly, to be impressed upon the minds of children!" How, he asked, could anyone, even Charles Dickens, defend such a tale as "Hop-o'-My-Thumb" in which the Ogre's seven children "bite little children on purpose to suck their blood" and the Ogre himself cuts off the heads of his children one by one? Cruikshank thus felt it necessary not merely to prune but completely to rewrite the old tales, giving some explanation for the few brutalities he still felt compelled to include in the narratives. The artist argued that "if Shakespeare thought proper to alter Italian tales, and even history, to suit *his* purpose, and if Sir Walter Scott used history also in the same way for *his* purpose," then he, Cruikshank, was certainly at liberty to do whatever *he* thought wise in revising nursery tales to make them more palatable for children. However, Dickens was thoroughly justified in objecting to Cruikshank's overt intent, in his *Fairy Library*,

> to inculcate, at *the earliest age*, A Horror of Drunkenness, and a recommendation of Total Abstinence from All Intoxicating Liquors, which, if carried out universally, would not only do away with Drunkenness Entirely, but also with a large amount of Poverty, Misery, Disease, and Dreadful Crimes, also a Detestation of Gambling, and a Love of All That Is Virtuous And Good, and an endeavor to impress on every one the Necessity, Importance, and Justice of Every Child in the land receiving a Useful and Religious Education.

What a burden all of that was for Cinderella and Puss-in-Boots to bear on their frail shoulders! All Cruikshank was really doing was altering the old romances to suit Mrs. Pipchin and her ilk.

In a sense, Dickens never really grew up—or, at least, he never forgot what it was like to be a child. "We have never grown out of the real original roaring giants," he admitted. "We have never grown the thousandth part of an inch out of Robinson Crusoe. He fits us just as well, and in exactly the same way, as when we were only the smallest of the small." And no one else has written better than Dickens on childhood itself.

It is surprising that Dickens did not write more, and better, books for boys and girls. Of course all of his massive novels were devoured in their day as eagerly by children as by their parents, for at that time the great divorce between juvenile and adult literature had not yet been finalized. Yet what Dickens did write specifically for a young audience does not compare favorably with *David Copperfield*, *Oliver Twist*, *Great Expectations* (1862), and all the others. He compromised his vast abilities in speaking down to the little ones. Nevertheless, those writings that can be labeled "children's books" are worthy of some study, if only because they are the work of England's greatest novelist.

A Child's History of England (1852–1854) is an odd effort. Begun in 1843 for his oldest boy, Charles Boz Dickens, it found a wider audience by being serialized in *Household Words* between 1851 and 1853. It was never popular, either as a textbook or even as a mere curiosity; it is largely forgotten today. What Dickens did to British history was no different from what Cruikshank did to fairy tales: he filled it with his own particular and peculiar propaganda. Dickens, for all his romanticism, never dreamed of Camelot. He had no patience with all the medieval humbuggery promoted by Scott and the Pre-Raphaelites. He bore only contempt for "those good old customs of the good old times which made England, even so recently as the reign of the Third King George, in respect of her criminal code and prison regulations, one of the most bloody-minded and barbarous countries on earth." Mindless patriotism was to be found everywhere in tiresome textbooks foisted upon schoolchildren. Dickens was fearful in particular that his own child might "get hold of any conservative or High Church notions." Because "the best way of guarding against any such horrible result, is, I take it, to wring the parrot's neck in his very cradle," Dickens found the time (between installments of *Bleak House*) to produce his revisionist history of England. He desired that his son be "tender-hearted" in his "notions of War and Murder, and may not fix affection on wrong heroes or see the bright side of glory's sword and know nothing of the rusty one."

And what a line of villains has worn the crown of England! Dickens has hardly a good word for any of them: Henry the Eighth, "Bluff King Hal," is no more than "a most intolerable ruffian, a disgrace to human nature, and a blot of blood and grease upon the History of England"; his daughter, "Good Queen Bess," has "a great deal too much of her father in her to please me"; and Dickens neatly sums up the Stuarts as "a public nuisance altogether." (But to his credit, and perhaps to atone for his crude portrayal of Fagin, in speaking of the Jews in this work Dickens "lost no opportunity of setting forth their cruel persecution in old times.'') He even takes the time to describe Joan of Arc, certainly out of place in this history of England, as "a moping, fanciful girl" who, "though she was a very good girl, I dare say . . . was a little vain, and wishful for notoriety." Only Oliver Cromwell stands up somewhat better than do the monarchs of Merry Old England. The sarcasm is so thick at times in Dickens' account that one is almost tempted to defend the atrocities of the aristocracy in order to give some balance to the book. Charles the Second, "with his swarthy ill-looking face and great nose," is depicted as being "surrounded by some of the very worst vagabonds in the kingdom (though they were lords and ladies), drinking, gambling, indulging in vicious conversation, and committing every kind of profligate excess''; for example, his brother James, duke of York, is described as "a gloomy, sullen, bilious sort of man, with a remarkable partiality for the ugliest women in the country." All that Dickens dare say about the current monarch is that Victoria "is very good, and much beloved. . . . God Save the Queen!" But all that one can say on reading such a history is "God Save England!"

Dickens also gave his children *The Life of Our Lord*, written in 1849, but since it was intended solely for his family, it was not published until many years later, in 1934. Like *A Child's History of England*, it is revisionist. Dickens the social reformer is less interested in virgin births and other miracles than in the good works and teachings of Christ. "No one ever lived," he explains, "who was so good, so kind, so gentle, and so sorry for all people who did wrong, or were in any way ill or miserable, as he was." Dickens emphasizes the poverty of Jesus and the fact that he chose his disciples from among the poor. He preaches:

> Heaven was made for them as well as the rich, and . . . God makes no difference between those who wear good clothes and those who go barefoot and in rags. The most miserable, the most ugly, deformed, wretched creatures that live, will be bright Angels in Heaven if they are good here on earth.

The sermon of *The Life of Our Lord* rephrases that of his novels; mercy and kindness are stressed along with the Golden Rule. "Remember!" he tells his children, "It is Christianity TO DO GOOD always —even to those who do evil to us." His retelling of the Christ story is no more than an outline of

good behavior, and could never replace the King James version.

Despite *A Child's History of England* and *The Life of Our Lord*, Dickens' reputation as a children's book author rests primarily on one obscure work, "Holiday Romance" (1868), and even this is known popularly by only a portion of the original. If it is read at all today, it is probably read in the picture book edition of *The Magic Fishbone*, illustrated by F. D. Bedford. Even Dickens' contemporaries recognized this work as a minor effort, for "Holiday Romance" was not published as a separate book until the twentieth century. Its composition was no more than a pleasant diversion from Dickens' responsibilities as editor of *All the Year Round* and from his preparation for the approaching public reading tour of America. In anticipation of his arrival in the United States, "Holiday Romance" was published simultaneously in *All the Year Round* and *Our Young Folks* (January, March, April, May 1868), a children's monthly issued by his Boston publishers. "I hope the Americans see the joke of 'Holiday Romance,' " he alerted its editors.

This work is certainly unlike anything else Dickens ever wrote. Four children on holiday, ages half-past-six to nine, decide to "throw out thoughts into something educational for the grown-up people, hinting to them how things ought to be." They resolve that each must write an original story, each of which must represent a different genre—an adventure yarn, a fairy tale, a pirate story, and a domestic romance. What is so amusing about these four children's stories is that they are supposed to be written in the child's own words. Even Dickens was aware of the risk he was taking in trying something so radically different from anything he or anyone else had done in juvenile literature. He admitted:

> The writing seems to me to be so like children's that dull folks (on *any* side of *any* water) might perhaps rate it accordingly! . . . . It made me laugh to that extent that my people here thought I was out of my wits, until I gave it to them to read, when they did likewise.

Unsure of its reception, Dickens to some extent apologized to his friend Forster for "Holiday Romance," saying, "I hope it is droll, and very child-like; though the joke is a grown-up one."

Not surprisingly, "Holiday Romance" is woven

out of the fragile stuff of Dickens' own childhood imagination. He was particularly proud of the wild adventures he attributed to Captain Boldheart. (He confided to Forster, "You must try to like the pirate story, for I am very fond of it.") Some half-remembered passage in one of the books he discovered when a child, about "Captain Somebody, of the Royal British Navy, in danger of being beset by savages," is transformed into Captain Boldheart and his adventures in foreign lands. "I remember very well when I had a general idea of occupying that place in history at the same age," Dickens wrote a friend. "But I loved more desperately than Boldheart." The sentimental betrothals of his juvenile lovers surely recall his own amorous intentions, before he had reached the age of ten, toward another little girl his own age, Lucy Stoughill. The "dreadful little snapping pug-dog, next door," that torments Princess Alicia and her siblings in "The Magic Fishbone" must be the "puffy pug-dog" owned by the mistress of the school that he and his sister attended when he was six (the woman was later transformed into the frightful Mrs. Pipchin). The adult Dickens gets his revenge upon this hateful cur: the story concludes with the fairy godmother throwing the fish-bone away once it has done its work, whereupon "it instantly flew down the throat of the dreadful little snapping pug-dog, next door, and choked him, and he expired in convulsions."

Many of the other details in "Holiday Romance," if they did not come from direct observation of his own or other children, seem to be Dickens' recollections of what he thought and felt when he himself was a boy. Miss Alice Rainbird, age seven, the supposed author of "The Magic Fishbone," is unschooled in the facts of life: She says that the nineteen children in her story range in age from "seven years to seven months." When trying to describe all of their eyes, she must refer to the standard multiplication table: "their twice seventeen are thirty-four, put down four and carry three, eyes." This pleasant, naive nonsense suggests that of an even more famous Victorian Alice, the heroine of Lewis Carroll's classic tales. (Of course Alice Rainbird is her own heroine, "Princess Alicia," a nice bit of childish arrogance.) The Fairy Grandmarina scolds the King just as Miss Rainbird would like to do (but dare *not* do) to her elders, in the same manner they have treated her: "We hear a great deal too much about this thing disagreeing, and that thing disagreeing. . . . Don't

be greedy. I think you want it all yourself. . . . Don't catch people short, before they have done speaking. Just the way with you grown-up persons. You are always doing it." Part of the delicious humor arises from how seriously the authors take themselves. Dickens' speakers, like all children, yearn to turn the tables, and that is exactly what happens in the romance of Miss Nettie Ashford, age half-past-six, in which boys and girls keep their parents "at school as long as ever they lived, and made them do whatever they were told." All of these four tales are really no more than wish-fulfillments in which the heroes—the authors themselves—triumph over whatever great difficulties they happen to dream up.

"Holiday Romance," written only two years before the author's death, may be seen as a crystallization of his attitudes toward those tales of marvels he had known in his childhood. The young authors of this quartet are as much aware as Dickens himself that romance, if not dead, was surely dying. All the fairies are gone. One of the four children says:

> It must be the grown-up people who have changed all this. . . . We will wait—ever constant and true—till the times have got so changed as that everything helps us out, and nothing makes us ridiculous, and the fairies have come back. We will wait—ever constant and true—till we are eighty, ninety, or one hundred. And then the fairies will send *us* children, and we will help them out, poor pretty little creatures, if they pretend ever so much.

The children's enemies are the Latin-grammar master and Miss Grimmer, proprietress of the private girls' academy. They, like Mr. Gradgrind and Mrs. Pipchin, are the villains, the "wicked fairies" who wish to drive all romance out of childhood. They have forgotten (if they ever knew) what it was like to be a child. Their charges dream of a juvenile utopia "where the children have every thing their own way":

> It is a most delightful country to live in. The grown-up people are obliged to obey the children, and are never allowed to sit up to supper, except on their birthdays. The children order them to make jam and jelly and marmalade, and tarts and pies and puddings, and all manner of pastry. If they say they won't, they are put in the corner till they do. They are sometimes allowed to have some; but when they have some, they generally have powders given them afterwards.

Here, at least, all the little injustices perpetrated against boys and girls may be corrected.

Yet even these romances, the inventions of little children, have been encroached upon by the industrial age. "The Magic Fishbone," which must reflect its young author's world, is very much a Victorian fairy tale. It is a modern "Cinderella" in which destitute Princess Alicia is blessed with a magic talisman by the Good Fairy Grandmarina. Like any heroine in a traditional fairy tale, her fortitude is tested by three opportunities to foolishly waste her one wish. And in the end, she is rewarded for her good judgment with wealth and a prince to marry.

Like the Good Fairy Grandmarina, a Victorian lady of quality "dressed in shot-silk of the richest quality, smelling of dried lavender," all of the traditional fairy-tale elements are clothed in contemporary disguise. The father, King Watkins the First, is petty bourgeois, currently "in his private profession, Under Government," working hard in an office; the Queen is merely "a careful housekeeper" who, like so many of her class at the time, has countless children and is "always having more." Alicia's three temptations to use her magic fishbone are thoroughly mundane: when her mother is ill; when one of her little brothers is bleeding from a cut; and when the baby falls and hurts himself. Even the introduction of the enchanted fishbone is commonplace: on his way to the office the King stops to pick up a pound and a half of salmon at the fishmonger's, the place where he first encounters the Good Fairy Grandmarina.

There are no dragons or giants here. The villain of the piece is poverty. Somehow the family has always been able to get by, usually through the diligence of Princess Alicia. She is forced to use up the one precious wish of the magic fishbone only when there is no other hope. "I am dreadfully poor, my child," her father finally confesses. "I have tried very hard, and I have tried all ways." Now comes the moral of the fable: "When we have done our very, very best, papa, and that is not enough," she acknowledges, "then I think the right time must have come for asking help of others." Herein lies a perfect summary of Dickens' attitude toward social responsibility. No matter how hard life may get at times, one may control almost everything except one's economic circumstances. Even the most virtuous individuals may become victims of poverty. Like Princess Alicia, Dickens himself during his childhood knew firsthand the frustra-

tions of a family in which the father cannot "make a go of it" through his persistent labors. But after one has tried his damnedest and has exhausted all possibilities and yet still has not made a success of it, then, Dickens argued, society must take the responsibility of providing some aid to the needy. Still, all of one's troubles cannot be so easily solved as they are in "The Magic Fishbone"—with a shower of gold coins.

However trivial "Holiday Romance" may seem at first glance, it is still woven out of the fabric of Dickens' greater fictions. It persists with the overriding argument of his writings—that even just a touch of fancy at the right time in one's youth may help one get over the many setbacks, disappointments, and miseries, no matter how great or how small, that one must encounter throughout one's life. "Holiday Romance" may now be largely forgotten, but fortunately, over the years Dickens' works have fallen into the hands of other boys and girls just as those by Defoe, Cervantes, and all the others were discovered by the child Charles Dickens in that little room; and many of these later children, at least through this means, may still wait—ever constant and true—until the times have changed and romance has come back.

Selected Bibliography

WORKS OF CHARLES DICKENS

Sketches by Boz. With illustrations by George Cruikshank. London: John Macrone, 1836.

The Pickwick Papers. With illustrations by R. Seymour and Hablot K. Browne ("Phiz"). London: Chapman and Hall, 1837.

Oliver Twist; or, The Parish Boy's Progress. With illustrations by George Cruikshank. London: Chapman and Hall, 1838.

The Life and Adventures of Nicholas Nickleby. With illustrations by Hablot K. Browne. London: Chapman and Hall, 1839.

A Christmas Carol. With illustrations by John Leech. London: Chapman and Hall, 1843.

The Life and Adventures of Martin Chuzzlewit. With illustrations by Hablot K. Browne. London: Chapman and Hall, 1844.

The Chimes. With illustrations by John Leech, Daniel E. Maclise, Richard Doyle, and Clarkson Stanfield. London: Chapman and Hall, 1844.

The Cricket on the Hearth. With illustrations by Daniel E. Maclise, Richard Doyle, Edwin Landseer, and

Clarkson Stanfield. London: Chapman and Hall, 1845.

The Battle of Life. With illustrations by John Leech, Richard B. Doyle, Clarkson Stanfield, and Daniel E. Maclise. London: Bradbury and Evans, 1846.

The Haunted Man. With illustrations by John Leech, Clarkson Stanfield, Sir John Tenniel, and Frank Stone. London: Bradbury and Evans, 1848.

Dombey and Son. With illustrations by Hablot K. Browne. London: Bradbury and Evans, 1848.

"A Christmas Tree." *Household Words* (21 December 1850).

The Personal History of David Copperfield. With illustrations by Hablot K. Browne. London: Bradbury and Evans, 1850.

A Child's History of England. 3 vols. London: Chapman and Hall, 1852–1854.

Bleak House. With illustrations by Hablot K. Browne. London: Bradbury and Evans; New York: Harper and Brothers, 1853.

Hard Times. London: Bradbury and Evans, 1854.

The Uncommercial Traveller. London: Chapman and Hall, 1861.

Great Expectations. London: Chapman and Hall, 1861.

"Holiday Romance." *All the Year Round* and *Our Young Folks* (January, March, April, May 1868).

The Mystery of Edwin Drood. With illustrations by S. L. Fildes. London: Chapman and Hall, 1870.

The Life of Our Lord. London: Associated Newspapers; New York: Simon and Schuster, 1934.

The Letters of Charles Dickens. 4 vols. London: Oxford University Press, 1965–1977.

CRITICAL AND BIOGRAPHICAL STUDIES

Collins, Philip, ed. *Dickens: The Critical Heritage*. New York: Barnes and Noble, 1971.

Cruikshank, George. *Fairy Library*. London: Bell and Daldy, 1870.

Forster, John. *The Life of Charles Dickens*. London: Chapman and Hall, 1872–1874.

Hearn, Michael Patrick, ed. *The Annotated Christmas Carol*. New York: Clarkson N. Potter, 1976.

Johnson, Edgar. *Charles Dickens: His Tragedy and Triumph*. 2 vols. New York: Simon and Schuster, 1952.

Slater, Michael, ed. *Dickens 1970*. New York: Stein and Day, 1970.

Waugh, Arthur, et al. *The Nonesuch Dickens*. London: Nonesuch Press, 1937.

Wilson, Angus, ed. *The Portable Dickens*. London: Penguin Books, 1983.

———. *The World of Charles Dickens*. New York: Viking Press, 1970.

—MICHAEL PATRICK HEARN

MARY MAPES DODGE

1831–1905

IN LOVE WITH life, joyous, patient, and conscientious, Mary Mapes Dodge exerted an influence on children's literature of the nineteenth century that is beyond question. As editor of *St. Nicholas* magazine, Dodge formed young people's reading tastes for more than thirty years (1873–1905). And her *Hans Brinker,* with over one hundred editions in six different languages, has never been out of print since its publication in 1865. Though less well known, her volumes of poetry also touched young readers and subtly but unmistakably molded their thoughts, as they acknowledged in letters to her.

While most biographers give 1831 as the year of Mary Elizabeth Mapes's birth, research by biographer Catherine Morris Wright suggests that 1830 is a more reliable date. Born to Sophia Furman and James Jay Mapes on 26 January in New York, Mary Elizabeth (known as Lizzie) was educated at home by tutors, governesses, and her father, who instilled in her a love for good literature. Literary people were frequent family guests and encouraged Lizzie's early attempts at writing. At sixteen she gained her first editorial experience on her father's magazine, *The Working Farmer,* begun after the family moved to a farm in New Jersey. In 1851 Lizzie married William Dodge, a moody New York lawyer; they had two sons, James and Harrington. Despondent over financial losses, the death of family friends, and the illness of his son James, William Dodge left the house for a walk late one afternoon in October 1858 and never returned. The circumstances of his disappearance and presumed death

were a secret Dodge revealed to no one. She moved back to a cottage on her parents' farm, determined to support her sons by writing. Following the success of *Irvington Stories* (1864), *Hans Brinker,* and *A Few Friends and How They Amused Themselves* (1869), she became associate editor of *Hearth And Home,* responsible for the juvenile and household departments. Josiah Holland and Roswell Smith, the enterprising new investors in Scribners, noticed her capabilities and invited her to be editor of the children's magazine Scribners planned to start in 1873. Concerned about the status of books and other writings for children, Dodge consented, and with the able assistantship of Frank Stockton and, later, William Fayal Clarke, she created *St. Nicholas,* a magazine that set standards unequaled in the history of children's literature. Yarrow, a cottage at Onteora, New York, in the Catskill Mountains, became Dodge's retreat after family deaths, bouts with serious illness, and years of responsibility depleted her physical stamina. Her urge to write never diminished, however, nor did her delight in receiving guests from literary and publishing circles during her Sunday afternoon "at homes." Children of Onteora picked yarrow blossoms for her funeral service on 23 August 1905—a tribute to a woman who touched the hearts of countless children around the world.

Like so much written for children in the 1800's, the tales in *Irvington Stories* use the motif of a change of heart and its subsequent rewards. Here the stories lack direct sermons; morals are taught "by occasional hints." Lonely and desolate, old Pop, in

"Hermit of the Hills," is reunited with the daughter he once banished for marrying against his wishes. His attitude toward Christmas and children changes when Good Samaritan Elsie treats the wounds he suffered while pursuing troublesome children. Punished for trying to shame his sister out of her babyhood, Tom Laffer in "Cushamee" is tormented by cats, owls, squirrels, and ants in a dream until he learns not to call his sister's innocent sport of playing with dolls "naughty."

Change and reward of a different sort occur in "Captain George, the Drummer Boy, a Story of the Rebellion." George finds the life of a soldier very unlike the glamorous show he expected when he enlisted as a fourteen-year-old in the Regiment of Connecticut Volunteers. But, in spite of torn flags, tired horses, and jaded, weary soldiers, his devotion to country and his deeply felt duty to avenge the death of his father in the Battle of Bull Run take him into battles where he suffers severe leg wounds. His courage and bravery are rewarded with the gift of General Pope's prized sword and scabbard. Dodge's descriptions of the grim horror of battle and of the intense feelings of George and his friend Jessup seem inappropriate for a bedtime story, but they serve well to make the reader believe there has been a change in George from his boyish view of the glamour of war to an adult's realization of both the perils of war and the demands of duty.

Curiously, two of the *Irvington Stories,* reportedly told to her sons at bedtime, have girls as protagonists. In "Learning by Heart" Jenny repeats Bible verses perfectly, but it is Nelly who lives out the meaning of the verses she cannot memorize. In "The Golden Gate" a fearful disease takes the life of both Fleeta and Gretchen. As they approach the gates of Paradise, Fleeta is forced back by an angel, who says that only the truly rich can enter. Gretchen, who has brought no treasures with her but who always shared with the little lame girl who lived downstairs, is allowed to enter. The gate is closed behind her, for Fleeta had never learned to "love one another" and lacks Gretchen's richness of spirit. Nelly and Gretchen fulfill Dodge's belief in the inherent goodness of children and are rewarded accordingly.

"Po-No-Kah" seems at first to reinforce the prevalent nineteenth-century image of murderous redskins who capture and torture children. Three of the Hedden children have gone with Tom Hennessy to explore a stream near their favorite spot in the forest. When they do not return, their parents' turmoil resembles that of the potatoes cooking in their iron pot: ". . . in a high state of commotion, little ones tumbling pell-mell over big ones, big ones rocking mournfully backward and forward in the boiling pot as though they felt sure their end was approaching." Father, neighborly to wounded Po-no-kah "even if he *was* an Indian" seeking provisions and medical help, begins a frantic search for his children. They, in the meantime, have been carried off to be adopted by strange old Ka-te-qua to replace the children she lost. Dodge vividly recounts the torture of Tom and his indoctrination by the Indian tribe: they pierce his nose and ears, paint his body "with every variety of color," hang a cloth about his loins, and finally duck him in the stream to wash out all his white blood. The children live with the Indians long enough "to learn many things . . . they never would have studied in the rough schoolhouse near their pretty home," while the reader wonders what has happened to the heartsick and frenzied parents.

Dodge pauses in the narrative to point out the good side of the Indian character and reminds the reader that "the white man has not always set a good example to his uncivilized brother." Nor are white women's customs of wearing "steel frameworks, made like hen-coops, beneath their skirts," or putting their feet in narrow shoes, or wearing rings in their ears, any less barbarous than the customs of Indian women.

Ka-te-qua dies; spring arrives; winter furs are exchanged for firewater. And while the Indians drink until they can drink no more, Po-no-kah remembers Mr. Hedden's kindness, escapes with the three children, and returns them to their parents, who are "surprised, pleased and grateful."

Dodge shared the popular perception of the Indian, but she also saw beneath the veneer, deep into what makes a person, regardless of skin color or way of living. In a preface to the 1898 revised edition, she wrote: "Po-no-kah shows how certain men . . . have been distinguished by high standards of character even under the most savage conditions"—a statement as true of Tom as it is of Po-no-kah.

"Moral values . . . merge naturally with plot construction and dialogue" in the *Irvington Stories,* according to one of Dodge's biographers, Alice B. Howard, and "the early handling of realism in a day when education insisted on emphasizing moral qualities . . . brought Dodge immediately into the vanguard of the new school of writing." However, when compared with other writers of the time, Dodge appears not to have been the leader acclaimed by Howard. Dodge's stories are not distinctive in style, subject, or tone, and they reflect the same moral values pervading the literature of her contemporaries.

When asked to write a war story with a young soldier as its hero, Dodge refused but offered to write a good story for boys about Holland instead. She had read John Motley's *The Rise of the Dutch Republic* and other treatises on Dutch history, literature, and art, had become acquainted with the Scharff family—immigrants from Holland to Newark, New Jersey—and wanted to write a tale that would give "young readers a just idea of Holland and its resources." The result, reluctantly published by James O'Kane, who thought people would rather read about war than a distant and strange country, was *Hans Brinker; or, The Silver Skates.* On one level biographer Wright describes the book as "a catalogue of Dutch art and architecture, and a guidebook of daily habits and politics" —a trustworthy picture of a country Dodge was not to visit until eight years after her story was written. On another level it is a straightforward, earnest, and simple account of ordinary people, without regard to nationality.

Hans's father, Raff, insensible since a fall from a dike ten years before the story begins, is cared for by Hans, his sister Gretel, and their uncomplaining mother. The skating race, for which Hans and Gretel practice on their wooden skates in hope of winning a prized pair of silver ones, provides the narrative frame for the stop-and-go story. Interspersed between race preparations are long descriptions of Dutch history, of the festival of Saint Nicholas, of the origin of tulips, and of visits to art museums and cathedrals—passages which may have gratified the author somewhat more than her child readers.

In the chapter titled "Glimpses" Dodge uses imagery of sight and vision. To see is to be watchful, especially "on a bright December morning." To have visions is to dream of what might be (as Hans and Gretel do); to perceive is to accept present circumstances (as the mother does). Father Raff's view of his world has been nonexistent since his accident. Mother's perception is limited by her husband's confinement. Hans, able to go on a four-day skating expedition to Haarlem with a group of boys, has unlimited sight. Dodge herself sees from

a distance—even the distance across an ocean to another country. The reader sees near at hand the love, warmth, sense of duty, and pathos of a family in distress.

Gretel's vision of herself and her world is often clouded by tears of discontent. Yet although tears sometimes cloud vision, they can be tears of tenderness and compassion, or scalding tears of recovery rather than of pity. Tearless eyes result from diligence, work, and persistence, and sometimes are produced with the aid of a little "magic" (locating the pot of money).

Ben, linked to the story's outcome and tied "by cousinship to all places and people," is a visitor from England through whom the reader sees the customs and history of Holland. Saint Nicholas sees past deeds of children (including putting snuff on the footstool of the schoolmistress). Injured by overuse, the eyes of the seventeenth-century painter Douw strain to see the broom handle it took him three days to paint. Hans's friend Peter sees, silhouetted against the moonlight through the window of his cold, cheerless room at the Red Lion, the robber who claimed he was only sleepwalking. Hans looks for work. Gretel's friend Hilda peeps, as does Hope, through the window of the Brinker cottage. Dr. Boekman envisions a continuation of his healing powers when he offers Hans an opportunity to study and become a physician. And, as the story ends, Laurens, Dr. Boekman's son, who had fled to England ten years before when he feared he had administered the wrong medicine to his father's dying patient, will move his factory to Amsterdam to make what else but spectacle cases!

To close the eyes is to bring on darkness and memories and still other "glimpses." Raff's accident happened at night, bringing on the gloom of a ten-year illness; at night a robber tried to take money from the boys' skating party; Hans under cover of night sought the doctor to tell him that his lost son had been found; the thousand guilders are dug up at night. It is during a long night that an eight-year-old boy becomes the hero of Haarlem by keeping his finger in the leaky dike (Dodge's story within a story).

Hardly a page is without some reference to the eyes, reducing the imagery to banality and remaining merely a glimpse rather than a deep look through the windows of the soul. Replete with examples of foreshadowing, cliff-hanging suspense, simple characters, accepted moral values, emotions described with control (as dikes control the sea), and a maternal tone, *Hans Brinker* was immediately acclaimed by both readers and critics. It combined the popular Peter Parley travelogue with a domestic tale. Understandably Dodge's writing satisfied readers of the time since she employed conventions and subjects both familiar and accepted. But judged by present-day standards her writing lacks subtlety and originality.

Hans Brinker reportedly had sales of three hundred thousand copies in 1865, with six reviews of the first edition appearing in such magazines as *Harpers* and *Atlantic.* By 1867 it was published in England and was revised for Dutch readers by P. J. Andriessen. Twenty-two separate reviews of the book were published between 1865 and 1881. Today its value seems to be in the scrupulous care given to describing life in a "queer land" rather than in its literary merit.

Games often provided light evening entertainment for both the Mapes and Dodge families and their frequent visitors. As a result, Dodge copyrighted a game called *The Protean Cards; or, Box of Hundred Games* (1879) and wrote a series of stories based on party games for Horace Scudder's *Riverside Magazine* ("Croquet at Midnight," "Bessie's Birthday Party," "Kaleidoscopes and Burglars," and "Holiday Whispers Concerning Games and Toys"). *A Few Friends and How They Amused Themselves* was a compilation of "adult games . . . bringing the reader directly into the parlor." However, children no doubt played many of the games along with the adults.

The quantity of poetry written by Mary Mapes Dodge has been overshadowed by the attention paid to *Hans Brinker* and to her editorship of *St. Nicholas* magazine. The large number of unsigned "filler" rhymes and poems in the magazine suggests the extent of Dodge's poetry writing. The first of her collections specifically for children is titled *Rhymes and Jingles* (1874). The poems, of various lengths and subjects (firecrackers, baby's toes, gardens, a duckling, the frog who wouldn't a-wooing go), were written with an understanding of a child's thoughts and feelings. Her "Snowflakes," at first mistakenly credited to Longfellow, was later set to music and printed in *St. Nicholas.* In it a young girl knows summer has arrived when snowflakes light on her rosy cheeks and melt away. While grandma in "The Minuet" rocks, knits, and thinks about modern hopping, whirling, and bumping, she also recalls when she danced the minuet "long

ago." In "Willy by the Brook" barefooted Willy tells the child reader that he cannot float, fly, or sing like a robin, but he can play his pipe (flute), which helps him "float free on a river of thought." Dodge's editorial notes in *St. Nicholas* reflect her poetic concern for a simple life that leaves time to enjoy the beauty of nature and family relationships. Not all in life is conflict or excitement, she tells children in her poems about flowers, bluebirds, snowflakes, spiders, the seashore, and grandparents.

Edited and partly written by Dodge, *Baby World: Stories, Rhymes, and Pictures for Little Folks* (1884) and *A New Baby World* (1897) invite "babies, large and small, . . . children, one and all," to experience the sights, sounds, puzzles, and people from their "baby world, spick and span," in her book "on the self-same plan." The subject matter ranges from Dobbin the horse and a grandma's nap to a windmill and the punishment given to Leslie for cutting up one of his father's books. Gentleness distinguishes the tone of her writing when Dodge reflects on the happy, playful innocence of childhood, "full of joy / full of merriment, love and light . . . why, we could do nothing but cry all day / If Baby world ever should pass away." Home is recognized as the important center for both emotional security and the everyday events from which life's lessons are learned.

Drawing on the creativity expressed for twenty years on the pages of *St. Nicholas,* Dodge published *When Life is Young: A Collection of Verses for Boys and Girls* (1894). It contains previously unsigned poems, some earlier signed under pen names (Joel Stacy, Nellie Brinckley, Elsie G.) and others signed simply with her initials. A tribute to Hans Christian Andersen (following his death), soap bubbles, Christmas, a Dutch family, and a "pensive cricket" provide subject matter for the poems, which vary greatly in length and style. "The Zealles Xylographer," which she dedicated to the end of the dictionary, shows her playful humor: ". . . in a Xanthic Xebec on the Zuyder Zee . . . in zygomatic pain sang as keen as the zuffolo and blubbered like zeuglodon until xerophthalmia came on." In each volume of collected peoms and stories, at least one piece shows the influence of Dodge's own strict, moralistic upbringing. Here it is found in a poem about Jack and Jill. Mother asks them to fetch water; it is for his defiant "No" that Jack is "rewarded" with his tumble.

Whatever caught Dodge's imagination and fancy

or whatever fit the season of the year was likely to become the subject for a poem, song, or story. Reflecting her own vitality and love of life, she wrote about the wonders of spring, learning to count, serving the worthy poor, waiting for father to come home, the thoughts of grandparents about their grandchildren, and the dangers of swallowing every opinion that was heard. Boys were often characters in her poetry. Style and length were adapted to the space to be filled in *St. Nicholas* (sometimes while the presses waited). Frequent elisions (s'pose, v'lets) created a conversational style and the intimacy with her readers she so desired. Figures of speech, if any, are trite. Most poems have a definite rhyming scheme that to present-day readers seems forced and unnatural. Rhythm, movement, liveliness—yes, but not the precise or vigorous language necessary to make her poems "great." She was, after all, writing for "merryhearted, affectionate, industrious, rosy-cheeked" children who were to be spared the didactic, moralistic fare previously thrust upon them by ministers and mothers who thought it best to teach their children to die bravely rather than to face life confidently. Dodge believed, however, that reading should be for enjoyment and pleasure, not merely instruction and edification.

Expanding and doubling the length of the sketches that first appeared in *St. Nicholas* in *The Land of Pluck: Stories and Sketches for Young Folk* (1894), Dodge described the thrift, patriotism, patience, trust in God, and pluck of the Dutch people who painstakingly wrested their land from the sea. Children read about Holland's windmills, dikes that kept the water level higher than cottage roofs, rigorous laws protecting birds, *iysbrekers* (icebreakers) used to break up canal ice so that barges could move in the winter, looking glasses placed outside houses so that the person inside could see what was going on in the street, and the country's fifteen-year-old leader, Queen Wilhelmina.

With more overt didacticism than is found in many of Dodge's stories and poems, the second part of *The Land of Pluck* contains lessons in love ("The Crow Child," "Wondering Tom"), respect ("Worth Your Weight in Gold"), understanding ("Grandmother"), concern for the poor ("What the Snow Man Did"), thoughtfulness ("Kitty's Canary"), and patience ("A Garret Adventure"). The latter story is unusual in its absence of any severe parental punishment of three boys who tried to make an ice pond in the attic, only to have the water leak through and damage the ceilings of the rooms below. Dodge seems to acknowledge that not all children's actions are misdeeds deserving of punishment; patience solves many troubles.

Called by William Fayal Clarke "the narrative of a boy's chivalrous love for his sister," *Donald and Dorothy* (1883) was said to be one of Dodge's favorite books. It is the story of two children who must find the reason for the visits of the tall, lank Eben Slade to their Uncle George's estate, and solve the mystery of Dorry's identity (is she *Do*rothy *R*eed or her cousin *D*elia *R*obertson?) and her relationship to Donald (are they really twins?). Suspense begins with the title of the first chapter, "In Which None of the Characters Appear," but in which Jack the coachman ("for reasons which you shall know before long") is introduced, along with Nero the dog and a figure who hides in the shrubbery. These characters then retreat into the background while the reader experiences Donald and Dorothy's life with Uncle George—riding horseback, having a house picnic, going by train to New York City, joining the Girls' Botany Club, enjoying a shooting match, and racing boats. For each of these events Dodge interrupts the story's momentum, with only an occasional reference to the mystery yet to be solved. The momentum increases when Slade presents a letter that implies Dorry is his niece, and Donald is pressed into action. Donald receives Uncle George's consent to sail alone to England, leaving Dorothy, wretched and alone, to ponder tearfully, "Who am I?" Feeling "like a Crusader," with Dorothy's happiness as "his Holy-Land," Donald follows a series of clues (a black rag, a sudden glance, a pink ribbon, a key to a necklace) and fortuitous encounters to prove that Dorothy is his sister and they truly are twins and the niece and nephew of George Reed.

The charm pervading this story for nineteenth-century readers was not only its mystery and suspense but also its domestic setting: muffins at an evening meal; games played around the kitchen table; a trunk in the attic holding secrets of Aunt Kate's childhood; Yankee and Doodle, the horses kept in the carriage house. Family members, servants, and friends show concern for each other's welfare. Males are extremely protective of females. Uncle George hides Aunt Kate's diary (which reveals that Aunt Kate was adopted) from Dorothy, who is sent from the house when the men talk about Slade's letter. Donald conceals from Dorothy his anxiety and suspicion about the question of their parentage. His solicitude extends to their former nursemaid Ellen Lee, on whom he must "be judicious not to shower gifts," even after she supplies information confirming his relationship to Dorothy. Carelessly rewarding Ellen Lee might "offend her proud spirit." Yet the girls are not totally passive. Those at the boat race upstage the boys' plans to "accidentally" dump Donald into the lake, and thereby they accomplish their own defiant triumph.

Suspense is alternately quickened and arrested, as the reader is told to wait for further developments, and characters and incidents are dropped into the story. Inconsistent use of a character's name (Dot, Dorry, Dorothy), lack of character development and imagery, and a style of writing that lacks sophistication combine to make *Donald and Dorothy* less successful than *Hans Brinker*. Catherine Morris Wright claims it has "none of the fire and directness, adventure and spirit of *Hans*" and that it may have suffered because of Dodge's "belligerent insistence on a contract clause" with Scribners. She wanted the option of taking her previous manuscripts to another publisher for reissue, a stance that resulted in the book's publication by Roberts Brothers.

An account of Dodge's writing for children must necessarily include her communication with them through the various departments of *St. Nicholas*. "For the Wee Folk," "Jack-in-the-Pulpit," "The Letter Box," "Editorial Notes," and "Books for Boys and Girls" (later called "Books and Music") all came from her pen. Here she could warn readers "not to read any two *new* books in succession" but "to put a good, standard work between them." Here too she voiced no great objection to a reader going to the center of the earth for a *little* while, even though Jules Verne's book had a "great deal of —— stuff" in it. She could also warn Minnie Nichols, who plagiarized another child's story submitted to the magazine, that her fraud was discovered and that she should "never send anything to *St. Nicholas* again." And here she could ask for the wishes, preferences, and needs of the readers for whom the magazine was published.

Since she was possessed with a zest for life and a love of beauty, it is natural that Dodge's ideas came from the real world. Religion, not apparent in her personal life but expected by parents, is neither neglected nor forced upon the child reader. Settings imply a white, middle-class background. Characters are identified at first by their speech (the

newsboy, the Irish maid) and later by their actions. Compared with the dime novels, series books, and adventure, sea, travel, and sensational stories common to the period, Dodge's stories do have simplicity and heartiness, life and joy, and the ever present "hint of morality," but they lack the literary quality that might be expected of someone nurtured on "good" literature. Her vision centered solely on the child, herself a child among children. Dodge's writing skills are far less important to the history of children's literature than her thirty-two years as editor of *St. Nicholas* magazine.

Selected Bibliography

WORKS OF MARY MAPES DODGE

Irvington Stories. With illustrations by F. O. C. Darley. New York: James O'Kane, 1864.

Hans Brinker; or, The Silver Skates: A Story of Life in Holland. With illustrations by F. O. C. Darley and Thomas Nast. New York: James O'Kane, 1865.

A Few Friends and How They Amused Themselves: A Tale in Nine Chapters Containing Descriptions of Twenty Pastimes and Games, and a Fancy-Dress Party. Philadelphia: Lippincott, 1869.

Rhymes and Jingles. New York: Scribner, Armstrong, 1874.

Donald and Dorothy. Boston: Roberts Brothers, 1883.

Baby World: Stories, Rhymes, and Pictures for Little Folks. New York: Century, 1884. (A compilation from *St. Nicholas* edited and partly written by Dodge.)

The Land of Pluck: Stories and Sketches for Young Folk. New York: Century, 1894.

When Life Is Young: A Collection of Verses for Boys and Girls. New York: Century, 1894.

A New Baby World: Stories, Rhymes, and Pictures for Little Folks. New York: Century, 1897. (This edition is three-quarters new material; the rest of the book comprises old favorites and selections from *Baby World*.)

CRITICAL AND BIOGRAPHICAL STUDIES

Blanck, Jacob, ed. *Bibliography of American Literature.* New Haven: Yale University Press, 1957. Vol. 2, pp. 464–473.

Clarke, William Fayal. "In Memory of Mrs. M. M. Dodge" *St. Nicholas* 32: 1059–1071 (October 1905).

Commager, Henry Steele. "Dodge, Mary Elizabeth Mapes." In *Notable American Women 1607–1950: A Biographical Dictionary*, edited by Edward T. James. Cambridge: Harvard University Press, 1971.

Commire, Anne, ed. *Something About the Author*. Detroit: Gale Research, 1980. Vol. 21, pp. 27–30.

Darling, Richard L. *The Rise of Children's Book Reviewing in America, 1865–1881*. New York: R. R. Bowker, 1968. Pp. 228–237.

Doyle, Brian, ed. *The Who's Who of Children's Literature*. New York: Schocken, 1968. Pp. 79–80.

Erisman, Fred. "St. Nicholas." In *Children's Periodicals of the United States*, edited by R. Gordon Kelly. Westport, Conn.: Greenwood Press, 1984.

Griswold, Jerome. *"Hans Brinker*: Sunny World, Angry Waters." In *Children's Literature*. New Haven: Yale University Press, 1984. Vol. 12, pp. 47–60.

Howard, Alice B. *Mary Mapes Dodge of "St. Nicholas."* New York: Julian Messner, 1943.

Johnson, Allen, and Dumas Malone, eds. *Dictionary of American Biography*. New York: Charles Scribner's Sons, 1930. Vol. 5, p. 351.

Kelly, R. Gordon. "Dodge, Mary Mapes." In *Twentieth Century Children's Writers*, edited by D. L. Kirkpatrick. New York: St. Martin's Press, 1978.

Mason, M. E. *Mary Mapes Dodge: Jolly Girl*. Indianapolis, Ind.: Bobbs-Merrill, 1949.

McEnery, Sarah S. "Mary Mapes Dodge: An Intimate Tribute" *The Critic* 290–292, 310–312 (October 1905).

Meigs, Cornelia. *A Critical History of Children's Literature*. Rev. ed. New York: Macmillan, 1969.

Review of *Hans Brinker*. *Atlantic Monthly* 17: 779–780 (June 1866).

Sturges, Florence M. "The St. Nicholas Bequest" *Horn Book* 36: 365–375 (October 1960).

Wright, Catharine Morris. *Lady of the Silver Skates: The Life and Correspondence of Mary Mapes Dodge, 1830–1905*. Jamestown, R.I.: Clingstone Press, 1979.

—HARRIETT CHRISTY

SIR ARTHUR CONAN DOYLE

1859–1930

SIR ARTHUR CONAN Doyle achieved worldwide fame through the creation of his fictional detective, Sherlock Holmes. Doyle's writings, along with the Sidney Paget and Frederick Dorr Steele illustrations for the stories and numerous screen portrayals, have made Holmes's trademarks —the deerstalker cap, magnifying glass, and curved pipe—instantly recognizable to people everywhere.

Doyle's own life was intriguing, and it is clear that many of his own traits are reflected in his fictional creation. He was born in Edinburgh, Scotland, on 22 May 1859, the son of devout Irish Catholics. The Doyle family was talented in the arts: John, Doyle's grandfather, was the well-known political caricaturist "HB"; Doyle's uncle Henry was a talented painter and director of the National Art Gallery of Ireland; his uncle James was a historian and an illustrator; and his uncle Richard created the cover for *Punch* magazine and was a children's book illustrator. Charles Doyle, his father, was the least talented of five brothers and had to struggle to support his seven children, earning extra money by illustrating and painting.

Mary Foley, Doyle's mother, was a descendant of the Percys and Plantagenets, and she taught her son about his knightly ancestors and the historic battles they took part in, instilling in him a sense of honor and chivalry toward women that was later to become part of the character of Sherlock Holmes. Doyle was a robust boy who excelled at sports and enjoyed reading adventure tales by such authors as

Mayne Reid, as well as books of history. He attended Hodder Preparatory School and then Stonyhurst College, both Jesuit institutions.

Although Stonyhurst did not have Christmas vacations, Doyle was given special permission during his last year to go to London to spend the holidays with his uncles. Because of the "pea soup" fog, Doyle's train was involved in two accidents en route. Once he arrived, he visited Madame Tussaud's Wax Museum (especially the famous Chamber of Horrors), the theater, and the Tower of London, among many other sights. London was not a peaceful city at the time; it was filled with violence, murders, burglaries, and lesser horrors, all of which were reported in the newspapers that Doyle read. The city made a vivid impression on him; he later used these impressions and memories to excellent advantage as background for some of the Sherlock Holmes stories.

In 1877 Conan Doyle, as he preferred to be known, entered Edinburgh University to study medicine. There he became student assistant to Dr. Joseph Bell, a surgeon lecturing at the university who possessed keen powers of observation. Dr. Bell's ability to assess a person's occupation from details of his or her dress or mannerisms was later incorporated into the character of Holmes.

During Doyle's medical studies, a classmate offered him his place on board a whaler as medical officer. This experience served as background for "The Adventure of Black Peter," a Sherlock Holmes story with references to whaling and harpooning. His job as medical officer made Doyle financially secure during his last year at the university.

Following his graduation in 1881, Doyle signed on for another few months as ship's doctor on a voyage to Africa. Upon his return he told his family that he could no longer share their Roman Catholic beliefs. During his student days, he had become interested in spiritualism, and his experiences in Africa convinced him that his early religious training was not the answer to all the suffering he had seen. As the years passed, his interest and research led him to become a spiritualist—a believer in the theory that after death one's spirit can communicate with the living through a medium, or third person. Doyle wrote and lectured for the last forty years of his life on this subject, lending his enormous influence to the cause.

In 1881 Doyle entered into a partnership with a Dr. Budd in Plymouth. This association is detailed in Doyle's book *The Stark Munro Letters* (1894). The partnership was unsuccessful, and Doyle then went to Southsea, a suburb of Portsmouth, in 1882. He rented a house at 1 Bush Villas and put up his M.D.'s brass plate, which he used to polish in the middle of the night so that the neighbors wouldn't know he was too poor to have a servant. His practice was slow in developing and his income from it never exceeded three hundred pounds annually.

It was at this point in his life that Doyle began to write in earnest. He sold his first short story in 1879 to *Chambers's Journal*. Between 1879 and 1883 he wrote and sold several short stories, and authored *The Firm of Girdlestone* (1890), which he sent from publisher to publisher in the hope of selling it.

In 1885 Doyle married Louise Hawkins, a member of a patient's family. They had two children, Kingsley and Mary Louise. After Louise's death from tuberculosis in 1906, Doyle married a long-time friend, Jean Leckie, in 1907. They had two sons, Denis and Adrian, and one daughter, who was called Billy.

Doyle decided upon the detective story as a profitable form of writing to help supplement his meager income. In *Memories and Adventures* (1924), he describes how he began formulating the character of Sherlock Holmes:

> Gaboriau had rather attracted me by the neat dovetailing of his plots, and Poe's masterful detective, M. Dupin, had from boyhood been one of my heroes. But could I bring an addition of my own? I thought of my old teacher Joe Bell, of his eagle face, of his curious ways, of his eerie trick of spotting details. If he were a detective he would surely reduce this fascinating but unorganized business to something nearer to an exact science. I would try if I could get this effect. It was surely possible in real life, so why should I not make it plausible in fiction?

Thus was Sherlock Holmes, the world's greatest consulting detective, born. His character was a combination of Joseph Bell, Doyle's much-loved uncle Richard, and the detective characters from Doyle's reading of Edgar Allan Poe, Émile Gaboriau, Wilkie Collins, and Oliver Wendell Holmes.

Like Doyle, Holmes is an avid read of the *Times*. He is physically strong and has athletic ability. He possesses a keen mind with tremendous powers of observation and deduction based on reason. He respects women and treats them with true Victorian courtesy based on romantic ideals of chivalry. Both Doyle and Holmes wrote monographs. Indeed, Doyle's knighthood was a direct result of his pamphlet on the Boer War and his subsequent history of the same subject. (An interesting list of Sherlock Holmes's abilities as observed by Dr. Watson is to be found in the beginning pages of *A Study in Scarlet*, 1888.)

During World War I, Doyle communicated in code with some British prisoners of war in Germany by placing pin pricks under words in books to indicate the message, always beginning with the third chapter of the book. Similar codes are found in Holmes stories; the most intriguing one uses stick figures ("The Adventure of the Dancing Men," from *The Return of Sherlock Holmes*, 1905).

Like Holmes, Doyle enjoyed music, wore smoking jackets, and used a magnifying glass. The daily *Times* served for details of the weather, comings and goings of royalty and high society, theatrical happenings, crimes of note, and other grist for Doyle's mill. If he wrote that Holmes and Watson were going to a concert by Norman-Néurda, there was in fact such a concert.

Doyle's own deductive reasoning is probably best illustrated by the famous case of George Edalji, a man unjustly accused and sentenced to prison, whose exoneration Doyle eventually secured. He was able to do the same many years later for Oscar Slater, who had been sentenced to life imprisonment for murder. Doyle often gave a little advice to police officials, who used him as a consultant unofficially; and he was the deputy lieutenant of Surrey, which automatically involved him in police affairs there. Before police texts were written, the Sherlock Holmes stories were used in training young policemen.

A Study in Scarlet was accepted by Ward, Locke in 1886 and was published in *Beeton's Christmas Annual* at the end of 1887. It came out in book form in 1888. That same year Jack the Ripper, a serial murderer, was abroad in London. Scotland Yard had failed to capture him, and people were fearful. The time was right to create a detective who never failed to solve a crime, particularly when the police could not solve it.

Doyle did more, however, than create a fictional detective; he developed a new idea in writing. In *Memories and Adventures*, Doyle explains how he developed the idea of writing good short stories with the continuity of a central character (rather than a longer story broken up into continuing serial form) to encourage a readership for a magazine and for a character. This had not been done before. Greenhough Smith, the editor of the newly formed *Strand Magazine*, liked Doyle's detective and contracted with him for a series of Sherlock Holmes stories, each story to appear in different issues of the magazine. "A Scandal in Bohemia" appeared in the July 1891 issue and was shortly followed by "A Case of Identity," "The Red-Headed League," "The Boscombe Valley Mystery," "The Five Orange Pips," "The Adventure of the Blue Carbuncle," and "The Adventure of the Copper Beeches." For the first six stories, Doyle was paid about thirty-five pounds each. For subsequent stories he was paid fifty pounds apiece. The first dozen short stories were published collectively as *The Adventures of Sherlock Holmes* in 1892. At the end of 1892 Doyle's second dozen Holmes stories began to appear in the *Strand*; he was paid a thousand pounds for all twelve. This series came out in book form in 1894 as *The Memoirs of Sherlock Holmes*.

Sherlock Holmes brought Doyle fame. With the short story "A Scandal in Bohemia," which had the benefit of a similar sort of scandal in the newspaper headlines of London when it was first published, Conan Doyle became a household word. In this short story, Holmes is asked by a man posing as a member of a European royal family to retrieve an incriminating photograph from the hands of a young woman, Irene Adler. The story shows Holmes in good form, able to solve the problem in a short time using his powers of observation —it takes only a glance for him to recognize that it is the king of Bohemia who is seeking his detective skill in this delicate romantic and political entanglement.

Holmes, disguised as a clergyman, gains entrance into Miss Adler's house by rescuing her from some ruffians (actually his accomplices.) Once there, he fakes a fire alarm, knowing that she will rush to protect her most precious belonging, the picture, and thus reveal its whereabouts. Irene Adler (forever after known as "the woman") outwits Holmes by following him home to 221B Baker Street (as an actress, she too is an expert in disguising herself). In a letter to Holmes and the king, she reveals that she has fled the country with her new husband, keeping the photograph purely for her protection. The king accepts this as an honorable ending, and Holmes sportingly accepts his defeat at the hands of "the woman."

Doyle is a good storyteller, always keeping the reader in suspense. Partly because of his use of real events and actual sites, and his vivid short descriptions that convey the ambience of Victorian England, the backgrounds of the stories are believable. "The Naval Treaty" (from *The Memoirs of Sherlock Holmes*) was based on a newspaper account of a Foreign Office clerk said to have sold secrets to the yellow press. The collection of the Doyle papers contains letters and notes that provide connections between true events and the stories.

In the late 1800's there were few mystery and detective stories. Victorian England was also deeply interested in scientific discovery, and Holmes was a scientific detective. It is not to be wondered at that the Sherlock Holmes stories, with their understandable plots, their excitement, their realistic characters, and, above all, a brilliant consulting detective of the sort people admired, very quickly acquired a readership. From the prince of Wales to the man in the street, people clamored for more short stories about Holmes and Watson. The stories became Doyle's entrée into the political and social world of his time. His writing and lecturing made him rich, and his friends ranged from kings and prime ministers to literary figures and the world's beautiful and famous people. His autobiography includes mention of meetings with Lord Balfour, Theodore Roosevelt, James Barrie, Rudyard Kipling, and George Meredith, among others.

Having read *A Study in Scarlet*, the editor of the American *Lippincott's Magazine* asked Doyle to write a Sherlock Holmes story. The result was *The Sign of the Four*, published in 1890 in both America and England. This was the second long Holmes story as well as the second story about Sherlock Holmes and Dr. Watson. It is a tale of Indian treasure, murder, an unusually terrifying killer, and a thrilling boat chase down the river Thames, with Holmes exhibiting his great detective talents; it is also known for the introduction of Mary Morstan, who becomes the wife of Dr. Watson.

In all Doyle wrote fifty-six short stories (which were later collected into books) about Holmes and Watson, and four longer tales. The books have been translated into over eighty-eight different languages and published in many nations. Of the short stories considered by Sherlockian scholars to be the best, four each are found in the books titled *The Adventures of Sherlock Holmes*, *The Memoirs of Sherlock Holmes*, and *The Return of Sherlock Holmes*. Two others are included in *His Last Bow* (1917). *The Case-Book of Sherlock Holmes*, published in 1927, toward the end of Doyle's life, does not have any of the better Holmes tales. Indeed, it contains eight short stories that are considered the least popular.

This is Doyle's own list of the twelve best Sherlock Holmes short stories: "The Adventure of the Speckled Band" (from *The Adventures of Sherlock Holmes*); "The Red-Headed League" (from *The Adventures of Sherlock Holmes*); "The Adventure of the Dancing Men" (from *The Return of Sherlock Holmes*); "The Final Problem" (from *The Memoirs of Sherlock Holmes*); "A Scandal in Bohemia" (from *The Adventures of Sherlock Holmes*); "The Adventure of the Empty House" (from *The Return of Sherlock Holmes*); "The Five Orange Pips" (from *The Adventures of Sherlock Holmes*); "The Adventure of the Second Stain" (from *The Return of Sherlock Holmes*); "The Adventure of the Devil's Foot" (from *His Last Bow*); "The Adventure of the Priory School" (from *The Return of Sherlock Holmes*); "The Musgrave Ritual" (from *The Memoirs of Sherlock Holmes*); and "The Reigate Squires" (from *The Memoirs of Sherlock Holmes*). In 1944 the Baker Street Irregulars (the oldest American society devoted to the study of Sherlock Holmes) produced their own list of the best stories. This list was identical to Doyle's except for the substitution of "The Adventure of the Bruce-Partington Plans" and "Silver Blaze"—both from *The Case-Book of Sherlock Holmes* —for Doyle's choices of "The Adventure of the Priory School" and "The Reigate Squires" (see the *Baker Street Journal*, vol. 1, no. 4).

It is true that an occasional error exists in the short stories. In "The Man with the Twisted Lip" (*The Adventures of Sherlock Holmes*), for example, Dr. John Watson is referred to as "James" by his wife. There is, in fact, some confusion about whether Dr. Watson had two or three wives.

The Hound of the Baskervilles (1902) is the best-written and best-known Sherlock Holmes story of all the short novels and short stories. It was written after Doyle arranged to have Holmes killed in a struggle with his archenemy, Professor Moriarty, at the Reichenbach Falls ("The Final Problem," *The Memoirs of Sherlock Holmes*). When Holmes was killed, readers of the *Strand* were very upset. Doyle's mother was equally disappointed. In London some people wore mourning bands. Finally Doyle agreed to write another Holmes story, but he made it quite clear that the events of the story took place prior to Holmes's fatal fall at the Reichenbach Falls. Based on a legend Doyle had heard about a Dartmoor family haunted by a dog that had been killed by an evil ancestor of theirs, *The Hound of the Baskervilles* is a wonderful gothic story. Holmes is asked to investigate the death of Sir Charles Baskerville, the attempted murder of the heir, Sir Henry Baskerville, and the old West Country legend concerning a gigantic hellish hound pursing the Baskerville men for several generations. Baskerville Hall is at the edge of the wild, bleak Dartmoor area of England, and Grimpen Mire, a gloomy mist-covered bog that sucks down the unwary man or beast to a terrible death, is close by the Hall. Toward the end of the book, Holmes arranges for Sir Henry to cross the moor at night in the hope of trapping the criminal, but Sir Henry leaves his walk until late and thick white fog begins to cover the moor. Holmes, Watson, and Inspector Lestrade lie in wait. Then Sir Henry bursts through the mists:

> I was at Holmes's elbow, and I glanced for an instant at his face. It was pale and exultant, his eyes shining brightly in the moonlight. But suddenly they started forward in a rigid, fixed stare, and his lips parted in amazement. At the same instant Lestrade gave a yell of terror and threw himself face downward upon the ground. I sprang to my feet, my inert hand grasping my pistol, my mind paralyzed by the dreadful shape which had sprung out upon us from the shadows of fog. A hound it was, an enormous coal-black hound, but not such a hound as mortal eyes have ever seen. Fire burst from its open mouth, its eyes glowed with a smoul-

dering glare, its muzzle and hackles and dewlap were outlined in flickering flame. Never in the delirious dream of a disordered brain could anything more savage, more appalling, more hellish be conceived than that dark form and savage face which broke upon us out of the wall of fog.

This passage is an excellent example of Doyle's style. The alliterative phrase "delirious dream of a disordered brain," for instance, contributes to the mood the author wishes to create, building terror and suspense in the reader. Holmes is exultant, sure that evil is about to be confronted. Yet even the great detective is startled by what he sees. Lestrade, a weak and not very bright investigator, collapses. Dr. Watson springs to his feet at the ready but is frozen for an instant by the awful sight. He remains in character as the sturdy and dependable friend Doyle created, a companion for the indefectible Holmes.

It is impossible to write about Doyle without discussing the unique worldwide literary phenomenon that has grown up around Sherlock Holmes through the years. No other fictional character has become real to so many people around the world, or has been so much written about in detail by others over the last sixty years. In *Sherlock Holmes: The Published Apocrypha*, noted authority Jack Tracy writes:

> It is one measure of Sherlock Holmes's enormous popularity that he is literature's most imitated character. Virtually from the moment of his creation, Sir Arthur Conan Doyle's master detective has been the subject of more satires, parodies, pastiches, and dramatic adaptations than even the most avid "Sherlockian" can count.

Ronald DeWaal has produced two enormous compendiums of the many references to Holmes—whether written or visual, serious studies of the writings or tongue-in-cheek parodies. These number in the thousands.

There are upward of a hundred international societies for devotees of the works about the master detective; many members insist that Dr. Watson wrote the tales and that Doyle was only the literary agent. The most famous of these societies are the Sherlock Holmes Society of London and the Baker Street Irregulars of New York City.

Doyle did not limit his writing to the detective genre. He also wrote adventure stories, historical novels, plays, and science fiction. Most of these other works are no longer popular; they are probably most often read by those who are curious about Doyle's works other than the famous detective tales. They include a series of science fiction stories featuring a hero named Professor Challenger and an exciting adventure novel that is still read by some young people and adults today: *The White Company* (1891). The hero of this historical adventure is Sir Nigel Loring. The story tells of a troop of free bowmen and chivalrous knights fighting in Europe during the fourteenth century. Woven into the background are the ways of life of the nobility, the religious communities, and the common people of that era.

Doyle collaborated in the theater with James Barrie, a good friend, and also wrote a mystery play on his own. In addition, he authored pamphlets and nonfiction books about history and spiritualism. *The Great Boer War* (1900) is one of his best works dealing with an historical subject, in part because Doyle went to South Africa with a hospital unit during this war and witnessed the conflict at first hand.

Doyle was a prolific writer. At his desk, in carriages, on trains, aboard ships, morning, noon, and night, he found time to write. Throughout his adult life, Doyle constantly wrote letters to the *Times* and other leading newspapers in England and elsewhere, and he also produced pamphlets in defense of the government or of causes he felt deeply about that needed public support. By 1890 he was no longer in medical practice, and his writing and, later, lectures were his sole means of support.

It has been noted that children often have taken for their own books written for their elders: *Robinson Crusoe* and *Treasure Island* are two examples. The Sherlock Holmes stories have been similarly enjoyed by children. At late elementary-school age, many children read *The Hound of the Baskervilles*, delighting in the mystery and terror of the hound. Series books are always popular, especially mysteries, so children can continue to enjoy reading about the adventures of Holmes and Watson in the fifty-six short stories. There is also another reason for the popularity of these tales. Sherlock Holmes is a stable figure in an unsettled and often unjust world, as the late Vincent Starrett pointed out in his famous poem about the detective and Dr. Watson, entitled "221B," which appeared in *Profile by Gaslight*: "Here, though the world explode, these two survive, / And it is always eighteen ninety-five."

Writers for children quickly became part of the flood of imitators of Doyle's Sherlock Holmes stories. In 1932, Walter Brooks wrote *Freddy, the Detective*, with Kurt Wiese illustrations that included the symbolic deerstalker cap, magnifying glass, and curved pipe that have come to be associated with Holmes in both the writing and the pictures from the original stories. Other well-known children's authors who have written books featuring detective figures with Holmes-like characteristics include Robert Quackenbush (the Detective Mole and Piet Potter stories), Robert Krauss, Ellen Raskin, Dennis Panek, and Terrance Dicks, to name a few. In the *Basil of Baker Street* series by Eve Titus, the hero, a mouse who lives in the cellar of 221B Baker Street and solves many crimes for the mice of Holmstead, is most likely named for the late Basil Rathbone, who often played Sherlock Holmes in motion pictures. The first really good Sherlock Holmes pastiche for older children, *The Case of the Baker Street Irregular*, was written by Robert Newman and published in 1978. In this full-length book, a boy is brought to London under mysterious circumstances, is rescued by the Baker Street Irregulars, is involved in a subplot concerning a robbery, and finally has his problems solved by the master detective himself.

For forty years, from 1887 to 1927, when the last of the sixty tales, "The Adventure of Shoscombe Old Place," was published, Doyle gave his demanding public a hero who will live as long as people read mysteries. His invention of a central character around whom a series of short individual stories with similar backgrounds are written was a major contribution to literature; few writers can lay claim to have done as much.

For the remainder of his life, Doyle wrote and lectured about spiritualism, although he also maintained his interest in the crimes of the day. In 1924 he created a miniature book for the library of Queen Mary's dollhouse—a short story entitled "How Watson Learned the Trick." The Sherlock Holmes tales were frequently presented in films, beginning in 1903, and Doyle took a keen interest in them. On 7 July 1930, Doyle died at his home in the New Forest area of England, with the family present.

Every year the number of print and nonprint works based on Sherlock Holmes multiplies, while the number of international organizations dedicated to keeping the adventures of the detective and his chronicler alive and well grows along with the number of new readers discovering Doyle's short stories. These new readers will share Watson's excitement, so admirably expressed in "The Adventure of the Abbey Grange" (*The Return of Sherlock Holmes*):

> It was Holmes. The candle in his hand shone upon his eager, stooping face, and told me at a glance that something was amiss.
> "Come, Watson, come!" he cried. "The game is afoot. Not a word! Into your clothes and come!"

Selected Bibliography

WORKS OF SIR ARTHUR CONAN DOYLE

A Study in Scarlet. London and New York: Ward, Locke, 1888.

The Firm of Girdlestone: A Romance of the Unromantic. London: Chatto and Windus, 1890.

The Sign of the Four. London: Spencer Blackett, 1890.

The Adventures of Sherlock Holmes. With illustrations by Sidney Paget. London: George Newnes, 1892.

The Memoirs of Sherlock Holmes. With illustrations by Sidney Paget. London: George Newnes, 1894.

The Stark Munro Letters. London: Longmans, Green, 1894.

The White Company. London: Smith, Elder, 1891.

The Hound of the Baskervilles. With illustrations by Sidney Paget. London: George Newnes, 1902.

The Return of Sherlock Holmes. With illustrations by Sidney Paget. London: George Newnes, 1905.

His Last Bow: Some Reminiscences of Sherlock Holmes. London: John Murray, 1917; New York: George H. Doran, 1917.

Memories and Adventures. Boston: Little, Brown, 1924.

The Case-Book of Sherlock Holmes. London: John Murray, 1927.

The Annotated Sherlock Holmes. 2 vols. Edited and with an introduction by William S. Baring-Gould. With illustrations by Charles Doyle and others. New York: Clarkson Potter, 1967. (Contains the complete stories and four novels.)

CRITICAL AND BIOGRAPHICAL STUDIES

Carr, John Dickson. *The Life of Sir Arthur Conan Doyle*. New York: Harper and Brothers, 1949.

Dakin, E. M. *A Sherlock Holmes Commentary*. New York: Drake, 1972.

DeWaal, Ronald Burt. *The International Sherlock Holmes: A Companion Volume to the World Bibliography of Sher-*

lock Holmes and Dr. Watson. Hamden, Conn.: Archon Books, 1980.

———. *The World Bibliography of Sherlock Holmes and Dr. Watson*. Boston: New York Graphic Society, 1974.

Hall, Trevor H. *Sherlock Holmes and His Creator*. New York: St. Martin's Press, 1977.

Higham, Charles. *The Adventures of Conan Doyle*. New York: W. W. Norton, 1976.

Pearsall, Ronald. *Conan Doyle: A Biographical Solution*. London: Weidenfeld and Nicolson, 1977.

Smith, Edgar W., ed. *Profile by Gaslight: An Irregular Reader About the Private Life of Sherlock Holmes*. New York: Simon and Schuster, 1944.

Starrett, Vincent, ed. *221B: Studies in Sherlock Holmes*. New York: Macmillan, 1940.

Tracy, Jack. *The Encyclopedia Sherlockiana*. New York: Doubleday, 1977.

———. *Sherlock Holmes: The Published Apocrypha*. Boston: Houghton Mifflin, 1980.

—MARY WEICHSEL AKE

ALEXANDRE DUMAS

1802–1870

TWO NOVELS BY Alexandre Dumas have eluded the fate of most works of art, enjoying uninterrupted as well as broad success from the day they were published to the present time. There is every reason to expect their success to endure. *Les trois mousquetaires* (*The Three Musketeers*, 1844), followed swiftly by *Le comte de Monte-Cristo* (*The Count of Monte Cristo*, 1844–1846), first appeared serially in Parisian newspapers. Translated into many languages, the books have been popular on both sides of the Atlantic with people of all ages, education, and social status; even small children parading as Disney Mouscketeers owe Dumas a special debt. There have been many adaptations in various media. In the theater, Eugene O'Neill's father, James, was bound to the role of the count for several decades, and a new stage version attracted critics and public to the Kennedy Center in 1985. There have been at least ten films based on *Musketeers*, several on *Monte Cristo*, as well as adaptations of an excerpt from *Le vicomte de Bragelonne* (*The Viscount of Bragelonne*, 1848–1850), renamed *The Man in the Iron Mask*. Of course, all the stories have made their way to television. Why the immense appeal of these good books that no one would describe as high art? Certainly *Musketeers* appeals to our adolescent dreams of days when knights were bold; for knights one might well read the American idealized cowboy. *Monte Cristo*, one of the great tales of revenge, satisfies the idealist in us, shocked by injustice, willing the triumph of good against seemingly impossible odds.

Dumas's life reads like one of his works of fiction. His father, born in Santo Domingo, was the son of the marquis Antoine-Alexandre Davy de la Pailleterie and his mulatto mistress, Marie-Césette Dumas. A convinced republican, the father abandoned his title, adopted his mother's surname, Dumas, to join the revolutionary army, and became a Napoleonic general at the age of thirty-two. His open dismay when Napoleon became yet another absolute monarch led to his departure in 1801 from the army and his return to his wife and eight-year-old daughter in the small town of Villers-Cotterêts. His son, Alexandre, born a year later, grew up in the kind of heightened times of which great myths are made. As the literature of the period testifies, Dumas's generation was marked indelibly by the era of revolution and by Napoleon, when young men of merit became heroes in the old style and made their fortunes. Their generation had witnessed history, and in Dumas's case the father had helped shape it. How could they not long for glory and excitement in the seemingly dull years of peace that followed? Like Victor Hugo, one of the greatest French poets, Dumas was born in 1802. This was a rich year: Bonaparte had himself elected first consul for life; Madame de Staël's novel *Delphine* appeared and so angered Napoleon that he banished her from Paris; Chateaubriand published *René* (this brief novel was the *Catcher in the Rye* of its day, for it exemplified and marked a generation of young readers).

Dumas left the quiet country town of Villers-

Cotterêts at the age of twenty-one. From then on his life and his literary production proved as outsize as the era into which he was born. He has been named variously "titan" (Maurois), "king of romance" (Hemmings), and "summit of art: you get nothing above Dumas on his own mountain" (George Bernard Shaw). His gigantic *Oeuvres complètes d'Alexandre Dumas* (*Complete Works* in French, beginning in 1851) fill 301 volumes in the standard Calmann-Lévy edition. However, scholars agree that this edition is neither definitive nor complete, and so there is at present no accurate list of Dumas's writings. He is like some latter-day character out of Rabelais with his unbridled imagination; ever-renewed energy and enthusiasm; voracious appetite for food, drink, conversation, work, travel, and women (one wife, innumerable affairs, three illegitimate children). His vigor in all these areas scarcely diminished until his death at the age of sixty-eight.

In 1823, like those heroes of romantic fiction Julien Sorel in Stendhal's *The Red and the Black*, Eugène de Rastignac in Balzac's *Père Goriot*, and his own d'Artagnan, Dumas went to Paris intent on taking it by storm to win wealth, status, and love; he managed it all, though he could not hold on to the money because of his lavish generosity and inept management. He arrived largely uneducated but a new and avid if helter-skelter reader of such works as the Bible and *Arabian Nights*, Goethe's *Sorrows of Young Werther* (the German *René*), the novels of Sir Walter Scott, the poetry of Byron, and the writings of the naturalist Georges-Louis Buffon. He also read chroniclers and memorialists from the medieval Jean Froissart to the duc de Saint-Simon, and his imagination feasted on the French romantic poets. Working as a copyist in the offices of the duke of Orléans (the future King Louis-Philippe), he soon became part of the group of young romantics, settled in with a mistress, (a relationship that resulted in Alexandre Dumas *fils*), and began to write plays and get them performed. In 1829 his career as a writer was launched with the performance of *Henri III et sa cour* (*Henry III and His Court*) at the prestigious Comédie-Française. For the next ten years he produced several plays annually. His success was signaled by his being named Chevalier of the Légion d'Honneur, along with Hugo, in 1837.

His years as a dramatist helped him develop a sense of the dramatic, an ear for dialogue, and the ability to make story and history one. His apprenticeship for the novel came also through travel journalism and from his purportedly nonfiction "historical compilations," starting in 1833 with a book on Gaul and France based on his broad reading of the old chroniclers. His goal was to bring history alive and to use his own reading as a basis for inventing dialogue and delving into character. He made good use of his sense of the public taste, in this case the popularization of historical themes that had led to the vogue of Scott's novels and those of his imitators. Until Dumas, though, the only successful historical novel had been Hugo's *Notre Dame de Paris* (*The Hunchback of Notre Dame*, 1831).

Dumas's public was the growing middle bourgeoisie, literate but not learned, avid for the melodramatic scene and the rousing good story, not keen on ideas or long descriptions à la Scott or Balzac. To reach them, he used the medium that had come into being to meet their needs: the low-priced, mass-audience daily newspaper. In the 1830's, with the increase of literacy in the population, low-priced newspapers sprang up. Rival editors, obliged to maintain and increase circulation, found that they could do so by publishing novels serially. Thus the "feuilleton," or serialized novel, was created. Editors did not encourage Balzac to write for them; he proved too difficult for their readers. They fought to get Dumas and Eugène Sue. These men knew how to get into the action quickly, to end each episode at such a pitch of suspense that readers were compelled to buy the next day's paper to see what happened. Small wonder that Dumas's novels go from one imminent disaster to another until the final triumph.

Inevitably attracted by the broad audience and the rewards open to the writer of feuilletons, Dumas turned his attention to the novel. In 1838, Gérard de Nerval, the great romantic poet, introduced him to August Maquet, lycée teacher of history and would-be writer. In 1842 Dumas's rewriting of a novel by the younger man was published as a feuilleton and set the basis for an extraordinarily successful collaboration. Although Maquet was not Dumas's only collaborator, he was the most important. As the number of his works suggests, Dumas wrote fast, rarely revising, leaving punctuation, accents, and excision of repetitions and obscurities to secretaries. He would talk over the plan of the work with his collaborator, who would then prepare a preliminary draft. This in turn would be entirely rewritten by Dumas, who made the work unquestionably his own through the power of his imagination, his lively dialogue, and his ability to tell a good story.

The Three Musketeers is the first and most important of the d'Artagnan trilogy. The pace never flags in this marvelous adventure story. Despite the rapid succession of exciting incidents, the complexities of situation and plot, the episodic nature of the book, its length (543 pages in the Bantam edition of 1984), even young readers can easily follow it. The fact is that Dumas's narrative strategies carry the reader along. Every incident is dated precisely; place names are given; chapters, generally short, bear titles giving a clue to content. Equally important, for every new situation Dumas provides a brief explanation or a résumé of the background. He also alerts readers to what is going to happen later. Thus what was absolutely necessary in the feuilleton of 1844 is useful for all modern readers. Further, the issues are readily grasped: good (the musketeers and their causes) against evil (their enemies). Character, while never simplistic, is drawn broadly. Dumas does not probe the psyche in depth, but his people act and react plausibly in terms of the world created for them.

The novel starts as it will proceed, with action. In April of 1625 the young hero, d'Artagnan, is on his way from Gascony to Paris to win a place among the King's Musketeers, the handpicked Royal Guard. On the way, he runs afoul of the man with the scar on his face (Rochefort, dreaded agent of Cardinal Richelieu) and catches sight of the woman who will be his nemesis: the woman of unearthly beauty and demonic soul, Milady de Winter. In Paris he quickly proves worthy of friendship with the three musketeers of the title: tragic, noble Athos; Herculean Porthos, who provides comic relief from the tensions of the novel; and Aramis of the religious bent, whose courtliness and courage do not totally conceal a nasty streak.

D'Artagnan will undergo many tests; defend the right causes and defenseless women; conquer evil; and emerge triumphant as a lieutenant in the musketeers, protected by king, queen, *and* cardinal. He will be wiser too, for he will have learned from experience; he will be sadder, because he'll have lost the woman he loves; yet he will be happy in the knowledge that he has triumphantly passed from adolescence into manhood, winning not only the friendship of his peers, but also the respect and admiration of King Louis and Cardinal Richelieu. He will have lived the paradigmatic knight's story

to which the mythical American cowboy also owes so much, as do such modern films as *Romancing the Stone* and *Raiders of the Lost Ark*.

D'Artagnan is completely loyal to his hierarchical superiors. He is faithful to his friends, and they to him. "One for all and all for one!" is their motto, and they stake their lives on it. To act otherwise would be dishonorable, and as that other knight, Shakespeare's Hotspur, said: "Mine honour is my life; both grow in one / Take honour from me and my life is done." The four friends stand together and suffer for each other to defend the queen's honor in the affair of the diamond studs. As a token of love, Anne has given to the duke of Buckingham jewels that had been a gift to her from the king. Richelieu, informed by one of his spies, plots to compromise her. At his request, Milady steals two of the studs from the duke; the cardinal then persuades Louis to insist that his wife wear the complete set at a ball that will shortly take place. Because Anne's lady-in-waiting is Constance Bonacieux, beloved of d'Artagnan, he is enlisted to save her mistress, and his comrades immediately join him. At risk of life and limb, they set off for England at breakneck speed. Three are waylaid by ambushes, but d'Artagnan reaches Buckingham, has the stolen jewels duplicated, and returns to Paris in the nick of time.

Since this is in essence a story of knighthood, and since it is told by a romantic, it is logical that women are portrayed as daughters of Eve (read evil) or of the Virgin Mary: as the cherished inaccessible lady of the heart's desire (Constance) or the spellbinding woman of the body's lust (Milady). There are bad men in the book. Louis XIII is ineffectual in his public and private relationships. Richelieu draws hisses and boos when he secretly plots against Queen Anne and seems to put the lives of d'Artagnan and his friends in jeopardy. Felton is a murderer. But Louis *is* king of France. Richelieu *does* admire and secretly protect the musketeers. Felton—well, what male could have resisted Milady? He is presented as a sternly upright, God-fearing man until, against his will, he succumbs to her enticements and does everything she asks.

That the novel is set in the seventeenth century in a distant land does not usually confuse young readers. It does not matter that many events have a historical basis and that most of the characters have identifiable counterparts in seventeenth-century France, for Dumas makes the past come alive. He achieves this by presenting the past through characters who seem real and by sketching in the background with just enough detail to enlighten nonspecialists without overwhelming them. He does not so much change the known facts as bend them to his purpose. Complex political issues, for example, are reduced to personalities: The handsome duke of Buckingham and the canny Cardinal Richelieu set France and England to war because they are rivals for the love of the French queen, Anne of Austria. Further, history serves as the backdrop against which Dumas's heroes are so magnified as to take the whole stage. The dirt, stench, and disease of semimedieval Paris are totally absent. Despite real place names and people, it is a fairy-tale city. In just such fashion is time suspended and space expanded in tales of knights and cowboys.

Readers of *The Count of Monte Cristo* are also carried off to another world, even though the setting of the novel is Dumas's own nineteenth-century France. *Monte Cristo* stands with the great revenge stories of the ages: Euripedes' *Medea*, Shakespeare's *Hamlet*, Edgar Allan Poe's "Cask of Amontillado." This is not because *Monte Cristo* has equal merit as a work of art or as a probe of the psyche, but because it speaks so powerfully to our need to fantasize impossible victories of the individual against injustice. Is not this the attraction of the American Superman? Because the injustice done the hero, Dantès, is so cruel, the suffering so long, the vengeance so terrible, *Monte Cristo* has a somber texture largely absent from *Musketeers*. This is true in spite of the great adventure tale it is, and of episodes in pure *Arabian Nights* tradition: in the end Dantès sails off into the horizon in the company of a beautiful oriental slave girl who has chosen him over the freedom he has offered her. Therefore the youngest audience for this book should be appreciably older than that for *Musketeers*, which good readers can approach by the sixth grade.

How was the romantic name *Monte Cristo* chosen? The explanation is a romance in itself. In 1842, while Dumas was living in Florence, Jérôme Bonaparte, the emperor's brother, asked him to take his nineteen-year-old son, Prince Louis Napoleon, to visit Elba. A guide pointed out a nearby island, Monte-Cristo, shaped like a sugarloaf, saying that it was excellent for the hunt. According to what Dumas wrote later in his *Causeries* (*Chats*, 1857), he told the prince that in memory of their trip he would one day name a novel *Monte Cristo*.

A major point of departure for the novel was once more the written record, in this case a true story from *Mémoires tirées des archives de la police de Paris* (*Memoirs Drawn from the Archives of the Parisian Police from Louis XIV to the Present*, 1838), by Jacques Peuchet, former keeper of the archives. It is a frightful tale of injustice against a poor shoemaker, Picaud, who spends seven years in prison incommunicado. He inherits a treasure from a fellow prisoner (an Italian) and wreaks bloody vengeance on all those involved in his betrayal.

Using Picaud's story as a basic plot outline, Dumas transformed the victim-turned-brutal-murderer into a man of superior moral, physical, and intellectual qualities. In 1815, on the night of his engagement party, Edmond Dantès, a young sailor soon to be named ship's captain, is carried off to prison in the Château d'If, a real place on an islet off Marseilles. The cause: trumped-up charges of conspiracy with Bonaparte. The perpetrators: jealous friends, as in the Picaud story, and an ambitious young judge. Dantès spends twice as long in prison as Picaud. *His* Italian friend and fellow prisoner is a priest who thoroughly educates him before dying, leaving him a treasure hidden in a grotto of Monte Cristo. Dantès miraculously escapes, able to swim several miles in rolling seas despite fourteen years without any exercise. Now he is not only physically powerful, socially adept, intellectually able, clever, and wise, he is also immensely wealthy. He lavishly rewards faithful friends and neatly arranges revenge. Each enemy is made to become the agent of his own downfall. Dantès, who seems omnipotent, is convinced that he is working out God's own plan, until, at the end, he sees that the price is the suffering of the innocent children of the guilty. As in *The Three Musketeers*, such ambiguity enriches the book and the characterization, reminding us, as do the best knight and cowboy tales, that knights and cowboys are also fallible human beings.

The techniques that work in *Musketeers* function well in *Monte Cristo*: drama, suspense, dialogue, résumés, explanatory chapter titles, allusions to real places and events. But, twice as long and very repetitious, it is usually pruned in translations; pruning can be tricky, however, for readers care about Dantès and want to follow his every gesture, word, and plan.

Dumas has created characters of such appeal that they take on the reality of life. Tourists still visit the Château d'If as if Dantès had lived there. Readers still go on to *Vingt ans après* (*Twenty Years After*, 1845) and to *The Viscount of Bragelonne* out of affection for d'Artagnan.

Surely Dumas the entertainer and his vast production of popular literature need to be explored in terms of what they reveal about the nature and development of the civilization that spawned them. However, it is clear that, born in the age of romanticism, inspired by nostalgia for the heroic days of the French Revolution and of Napoleon, Dumas's novels have an apparently inexhaustible appeal to the romantic in each of us. Certainly their ethic is that of the macho world where men are the "doers" and women—however brave—are the "done unto." This is the world where women are "had" and sex is as much an act of conquest as of love. In any case, the books are a good read, encourage the act of reading, and provoke curiosity about history in a dangerously ahistorical world.

Selected Bibliography

WORKS OF ALEXANDRE DUMAS

The Three Musketeers and *The Count of Monte Cristo* have been translated or adapted into English many times since their publication in Paris. It is a given that some translations are better than others and that abridgments and adaptations mutilate the original. It is also true that a great deal survives in the English renderings of Dumas because of the powerful interest generated by plot, incident, and character.

Editions of *The Three Musketeers*

Les trois mousquetaires. 8 vols. Paris: Baudry, 1844. (Serial publication in *Le siècle*, 1844.)
The Three Musketeers. Translated by Lord Sudley. London: Penguin Classics, 1952.
———. New York: Airmont, 1966. (No translator is listed.)
———. Retold in fifty-two pages by Jane Carruth. With illustrations by John Worsley. London: Award Publications, 1982.
———. Translated by Lowell Bair. New York: Bantam Classics Series, 1984.
———.Adapted for young readers by Vincent Bura-

nelli. With thirteen pages of illustrations by Hieronimus Fromm. Morristown, N.J.: Classics for Kids, 1985.

Other Works

Henri III et sa cour. Paris: Vezard et Cie, 1829.
Le comte de Monte-Cristo. 18 vols. Paris: Pétion, 1845–1846. (Serial publication in *Journal des Débats*, 1844–1846.) Published in English as *The Count of Monte Cristo*. Translated and adapted by Lowell Bair. New York: Bantam, 1981. (While the publisher recommends the book for "grade 6 and up," it is better suited to young people of 14 and older.) Also published with illustrations by Mead Schaeffer. New York: Dodd Mead, 1985. (Reprinted from the 1928 edition. Translator is not listed, but this is a highly abbreviated version with simplified language.)
Vingt ans après. Paris: Baudry, 1845.
Le vicomte de Bragelonne. 26 vols. Paris: Michel Lévy, 1848–1850. An excerpt from part 3 of the D'Artagnan trilogy was published in English as *The Man in the Iron Mask*. New York: Airmont, 1967. (No translator is listed.)
Oeuvres complètes. 301 vols. Paris: Michel Lévy (later Calmann-Lévy), 1851–.
Causeries. Brussels: Hetzel, 1857.

CRITICAL AND BIOGRAPHICAL STUDIES

Hemmings, F. W. J. *Alexandre Dumas: The King of Romance*. New York: Charles Scribner's Sons, 1979.
Maurois, André. *Alexandre Dumas: A Great Life in Brief*. Translated by Jack Palmer White. New York: Alfred A. Knopf, 1966. (Adapted from *The Titans: A Three-Generation Biography of the Dumas*, translated by Gerard Hopkins. New York: Harper and Row, 1957. Excellent as biography and for its style and full bibliography.)
Shaw, George Bernard. *Our Theater in the Nineties*. vol. 3. London: Constable, 1932.
Stowe, Richard S. *Alexandre Dumas père*. Boston: Twayne Publishers, 1976. (A brief, useful survey with an excellent selected and annotated bibliography and a useful chronology.)

—AVRIEL H. GOLDBERGER

ELIZABETH ENRIGHT

1909–1968

THE VERY NAME of Elizabeth Enright triggers a sigh of contented longing, images resonant with happiness, and associations redolent of well-being. She wrote about friendly, comfortable places and imaginative, lively, self-reliant children whose sound, sensible hearts and heads grace them with appreciation and enjoyment of life lived in a beautiful, benign world. It was her hope that childhood might be as secure and satisfying a state as that relished by her characters Garnet Linden, Mab Kendall, the Melendys, and Portia Blake and her cousin Julian Jarmon; this hope tentatively balanced with a conviction that life on a midwestern farm, on Pokenick Island, in the Four-Story Mistake, at Gone-Away Lake must be Reality. Enright is an enchantress, weaving spells with wonderful words. One devoutly wishes her power were as widespread as that of technology, which she described as having teased magic from legend into reality.

Enright, who wrote for children between 1935 and 1965, was well aware that modern science had "wrest[ed] the cloudy symbols [of magic] out of the imagination and convert[ed] them into objects you can buy in a store. Or use in a war." Therefore, she knew it was not possible to promise children security and happiness. In "The Hero's Changing Face" she went on to say:

> But we *can* wish these things for them, and hope them and depict them, so that the child who *enters* a book in a way no adult can finds himself in a world which, though it may contain trial and conflict, also reveals security and reason and humour and a good measure of happiness.

Believing that children's books derive primarily from wish and memory, Enright created par excellence in fiction the "eternal place" she wished for all children.

Security and happiness in Enright's novels are the harmonies effected when children, adults, pets, and physical nature act in concert—reasonably, seriously, yet always with a sense of fun. At the heart of most of her novels is a small community of bright, well-bred children. They are protected by yet act independently of wise adults who respect and like children and are respected and liked by them in return. Though mature, responsible, and frequently elderly, the adults have preserved within themselves the hearts of children. Having lost neither the child's radiant perception of the universe nor her spontaneous alliance with it, they have nevertheless lived long enough to have astonishing tales to tell of what life was like back when. Grown-ups can be counted upon for the right response precisely when it is needed, and thus to hold at bay almost everything that threatens from without. They even counteract childish personal spite, which occasionally ripples the serene flow of Enright's fiction.

The daughter of political cartoonist Walter J. Enright and illustrator Maginel Wright Enright and the niece of Frank Lloyd Wright, Elizabeth unsurprisingly began drawing at an early age, even using her bare knees when she could find nothing else on which to sketch. After her formal training as an artist, she started her career as a magazine and book illustrator. Her own first book, *Kintu: A Congo Adventure* (1935), is the initiation story of a tribal boy she made up to accompany drawings she had made of a witch doctor in a derby, of leopards, and of jungle flora. The story is predictable; the illustrations bold, bright, and flat-textured. Charming but hardly notable, *Kintu* suggests the author's knowledge of children and the acute observation, apt imagery, and humor that characterize her subsequent works. Enright continued to illustrate her own stories through the 1950's, executing characteristic simply lined but detailed drawings having little depth. Sketching few distinguishing features, she nonetheless animates both characters and settings, conveying movement and emotion through posture. When she uses color, she tends toward pure, primary watercolors, selecting shades of similar or contrasting tones to enhance the atmosphere of a scene. Eventually, however, she turned her full attention to writing. Awarded the Newbery Medal in 1939 for *Thimble Summer* (1938), she expressed in her acceptance speech the joy she experienced in writing about children for children. To do so, a writer "naturally goes back to one's childhood to find things. To me the astonishing thing is the way one took life in those years. It was as though a thin, but tough membrane had not yet grown between oneself and the rest of the world."

Enright's major works comprise eight novels and two fairy tales for children. Paradoxically, it is the novels, realized in exquisite circumstantial detail, that idealize childhood. Natural elements like wind, fog, thunderstorms, and drought occasionally ruffle the emotional as well as the physical atmosphere. Foster Blake is almost swallowed by the swamp Gulper, a quicksand bog in *Gone-Away Lake* (1957); Mab Kendall is temporarily lost on the moors in *The Sea Is All Around* (1940); Randy Melendy is very nearly asphyxiated by coal gas in *The Saturdays* (1941). Some few adults are vicious and suspicious of children. In *Spiderweb for Two* (1951) the irascible butcher, Mr. Frederick, is incapable of conceiving that Randy and Oliver, trying to puzzle their way out of the Melendy Maze, are reasonable, honest children. Shiftless, crafty Oren Meeker abuses his nephew, Mark Herron, who is adopted as the fifth Melendy of *Then There Were Five* (1944).

The children themselves are not invariably good-natured. Foster Blake never would have been lost

in the marsh if he had not had to sneak after his sister, Portia, when she refused to take him along. Lonesome when her sister and brothers have gone away to school, Randy Melendy pouts because her father never stays home and doesn't care about his family. "But the thought was so manifestly unjust, so outrageous, in fact, that she felt slightly better for the moment and started to sing as she went upstairs." However, though danger and malevolence threaten children in Enright's novels, evil rarely nicks the microcosms they inhabit; never does it break through. In the fairy tales, on the other hand, Enright incarnates evil in greedy, manipulative giants (*Tatsinda*, 1963), and in careless, insensitive people (*Zeee*, 1965). Though in her novels she could hint that childhood is not an idyll, only in fairy tales could she overtly dramatize evil; only through metaphor did she portray its power. But evil in the fairy tales, because the genre requires it, is always conquered.

The most striking trait of Enright's characters is the robustness of their imaginations. Nourished by story, the characters are never at a loss for something to do; they are empowered to take the stuff of their daily lives—the boring, the perilous, the beautiful—and to transform all of it into amusing games. Casual references to books that are foundations of her children's worlds permeate all the novels. In *Thimble Summer* Garnet Linden and her friend Citronella get locked into the town library one night because, tucked into an obscure window seat, they become so absorbed in their books that they fail to notice the silence and the dusk "sifting into the room." The Melendys celebrate almost any occasion by putting on "shows" that include original fantasies which combine "all the best features of Hans Andersen, Grimm's *Fairy Tales*, *The Arabian Nights*, and Superman." When Mark Herron is adopted by the Melendys, he is "intoxicated" by their books and sits "hour after hour on the floor of the Office, surrounded with crooked columns of books . . . 'This is a good story,' he'd say, lifting his head at last, and looking at the others with eyes still glazed by distance, still focused on the landscape of another world."

Perhaps because she is, atypically for an Enright character, an only child, Mab Kendall is the most endearing example of the child's joy in story. Representative in her intelligence, her independence, her industry, and her indomitability, she plays life as an exciting game. Orphaned at the age of five, Mab has been raised by Aunt Sarah in Golden

Creek, Iowa. At ten she faces transplantation to Aunt Belinda's home on Pokenick Island off the New England coast as an adventure. Mab, whose name is derived from the Welsh word for "youth," is kin to Shakespeare's fairy midwife of dreams of the same name. On the train from Iowa to New Bedford, Mab apologizes for staring at the old lady opposite her. The lady responds, "I like people who look at things wholeheartedly as you do, learning and absorbing them so that their memories are full of accurate impressions." Then she tells Mab stories of her childhood on Pokenick and shares a game that can be played by one alone in a crowd. Mab is a younger version of her traveling companion. Wherever she is, she looks at things wholeheartedly, learning "shape and color by heart, so she [will] never forget it," and on whatever ground her feet are planted, her head inhabits castles in the air. Boarding the ferry from New Bedford, she thinks it is "rather like entering a palace. Mab could imagine page boys running ahead, and scattering rose petals for passengers to step on." After the long journey made "strange and wonderful" by Mab's keen perceptions and Enright's trenchant prose, after a warm welcome from stalwart Aunt Belinda, "stout like a big tree," Mab feels "peaceful and deep and still, as though she had come home from a long perilous journey; like any adventuring voyager from Ulysses to the Jumblies."

Cranky and cramped because she is lonely and bored, one wintry day Mab explores the moors, "a new and spacious place." Pretending that she is the only person left alive after some cosmic cataclysm, she fantasies what she could eat and where she might live. With childlike gravity, she leaves one building standing—the grocery store—and becomes so engrossed in building her snug imaginary house that she loses herself in a forest like that "in a fairy tale [which] seemed to stretch and spread before one's eyes as though it guarded a precious secret." The cause of most of the trials in Mab's world, as in those of Garnet, the Melendys, and the Gone-Aways, is the weather. As January's early dusk falls, apprehension pricks Mab's make-believe: "Overhead and all about her swirled the veils of fog, concealing the road and the village. Behind her lay the woods shadowy and mysterious." Lost, but with the determination and saving humor that had earlier prompted Mab to berate the wind—"Go torment somebody your own size"—she sings loudly to cheer herself up and uses her good sense to break into a beach shack, build a fire,

and find something to eat. Even when her situation is most desperate, the "wide awake corner of her mind said to Mab: this would be a good place to go hunting, there must be hundreds of things to find."

Having secured herself against the storm, Mab tells the room, " 'I don't think I'll ever be scared again. I can take care of myself all right.' Really, she felt very proud and independent." Much later, wakened into a frigid but clear night, Mab can see the lights of the town and starts for home, reminding herself out loud that she is having an adventure —"People don't know enough about the night. They go to bed and sleep through the best part of it, and all the time they're missing things, important things that are happening." Things like the mesmerizing northern lights that "arranged themselves in curious shapes; one minute like a fabric hanging in long folds and then like a huge crown paling and deepening against the stars."

Plucky little Mab, though she isn't "really afraid," skirts the pine forest she'd earlier been lost in, walking "as quietly as possible till she was well beyond" the trees so she won't disturb the "witch that lived in the heart of them, in a hut that stood on chicken feet." Once on the road she pretends she is an escaped prisoner whose head will be chopped off at dawn if she can't get past the cemetery and into town before her pursuers capture her. In so forlorn a place, at so witchy an hour, Mab, as children do, scares herself with her game. When a car comes along, "Her scalp prickle[s], and the fear which had never been very far away [takes] possession of her." The driver of the car, however, is Dr. Norse, out on a night call, who takes Mab home to Aunt Belinda. She, wise woman, wants to hear all about the contrite Mab's adventures.

Near the end of *The Sea Is All Around*, Mab becomes part of a group of amiable, energetic children and collaborates in their make-believe. The camaraderie and practical wit with which the book concludes is as tangible as that which infuses Enright's other novels. It is impossible to resist conjecturing that Mab is Enright's self-portrait of an only child and that the other books derive from her observation of her three sons and their perceptions of the world.

Stories in Enright's novels not only nurture the imagination but also reveal the child in people, regardless of their chronological age; they are the means through which individuals resist conformity to social mores; and they link the present to the past. Storytelling also serves Enright as a major structural device. The plots of most of her novels consist of a loose series of thrilling but not improbable adventures rooted in a particular place, centered in a specific physical and cultural milieu. A favorite technique is the story within a story. Old folks tell stories about past times; young folks listen avidly, and not infrequently they make up yarns for one another. Because Pokenick is an isolated world, it is not surprising that all the adults are exceptional raconteurs, all of whom, like Mab's teacher, narrate events that emphasize "a sense of being at home in the world that most people never have a chance to learn." The Melendy children sit still for little but the fascinating stories told by Father; by Cuffy, their housekeeper and surrogate mother; and by their friends Mrs. Oliphant and Mr. Titus. In *Thimble Summer*, Garnet envies Citronella her great-grandmother: "Grown small with age she [sits], light as a leaf, in a rocking chair," now only sleeping or telling stories of the valley when it was "wild country." "It makes me sleepy to think so far back; more than seventy years ago," she tells the girls. Mr. Pindar Payton and his sister, Minnehaha Payton Cheever, like Gone-Away Lake itself, are remnants of a bygone era, more probable inhabitants of a fairy tale than of a novel. Having fallen upon hard times, they have returned to Lake Tarrigo, where they spent their childhood summers. The Lake now swamp and bog and the mansions slumping in decay, the eccentric pair nonetheless settle in for the rest of their lives, wearing the day-before-yesterday's fashions from abandoned trunks and going forth into and back from the contemporary world by way of Uncle Pin's ancient Machine, "an equipage that looked more like a gigantic insect than a car." The pair know every weed, flower, rock, and bird of Gone-Away and introduce the children to their beauty and usefulness, as well as to the old houses. Aunt Minnehaha, especially, is a never-ending source of stories about the glamour and idiosyncracies of Gone-Away when long ago it was still Tarrigo. Story cements the unique bond between children and old people and roots the present in the past so that both may enrich the future.

Enright obviously makes a game of naming, playing not only on connections between names and classic stories but also on originality, sound, meaning, and gentle irony. One can hear her saying roguishly, and like Portia Blake "rather importantly": " 'I'll have to watch them for awhile until I learn their characters.' . . . She knew she was

supposed to be quite good at naming things." Quite good, and funny too. The names of many of her characters derive from story and history: Mab, Miranda, and Portia; Pindar Payton and Minnehaha Cheever; Daphne Addison and Mr. Titus; Aunt Belinda's cat, Saki, and parrot, Cato; and the Blakes' puppy, Gulliver. Citronella, Garnet's best friend, possesses a euphonious name antithetical to the "fat little girl with red cheeks" who bears it, but her name is as romantic as the stories she loves. The town librarian calls Garnet "Ruby" because "There were so many little girls in Blaiseville with names like jewels that it was very confusing." The name "Citronella" recurs as that of a malodorous mosquito repellent, important in an exciting episode in *Then There Were Five*. Mab Kendall, who wonders about her tutor's curious name, Havana Fish, learns that this daughter of a sea captain, like all her siblings except John, who was born in Elizabeth, is named for the port in which she was born. In *Spiderweb for Two*, many of the rhymed clues to the treasure Randy and Oliver are seeking play on names, most notably one that sends them combing graveyards for a marker bearing the name of a jewel and a bird, Garnet Swan. That names should be unique, fun, and funny is axiomatic for Enright.

Settings in Enright's novels are as vibrant, memorable, and genuine as her characters. All the stories but *The Saturdays* are set in the country, which is Enright's sacred place much as their "Office" is the Melendys', imprinted with individual personalities and interests. In "Realism in Children's Literature" Enright speaks of the importance of detail in fiction. Children, she believed, are insulted by cliché but fascinated by detail in their reading, when it is freshly presented. She emphasizes the writer's responsibility to treat language as children do, that is, "as though it were our own, a perpetually new and valued means of conveying to others our reaction and experience." She acknowledges simile as consonant with the child's mode of perception and as the most effective tool for presenting detail at once fresh and recognizable. Enright's gift for perceiving similarity in disparity and imparting it in the perspicuous image is sure. Many of the images engraved in the reader's mind are mystical moments when characters encounter nature. Mab's new friends take her to their secret "Palace," an ancient stump of a tree cut down years before: "Spreading fungus clung to its sides like terraces and pavilions; the tops of them were hard and rough but underneath they were smooth and pale as cream." The Palace stood in a stagnant pool, "still and strangely rich, the way you might imagine a little pool in the jungles of Ecuador to be." With Candy and Aunt Belinda, Mab awaits the blossoming of Miss Fish's night-blooming cereus: "First one petal, then the next trembled open, like a hand unclosing finger by finger; until at last, frail and exquisite, it bloomed in all its perfection. It's like a promise, or a miracle, Mab thought; it's like the star of Bethlehem." Oliver Melendy, watching for the rare luna moth, "had become moth-sized, too, and felt a thrill of absolute terror when the bat appeared." Never having seen anything so perfect, Oliver is awestricken when the luna appears. Enright's description enraptures the reader too. At the end of the summer, Garnet has an experience that fulfills the promise augured by her discovery of the lovely silver thimble. She comes eye to jewel-eye with a heron, who "stood for a contemplative moment on one foot, still as a bird of carven stone"; for that perfectly still moment the bird becomes Garnet's "companion; a creature who understood and shared her mood of happiness."

Enright's country scenes enable the country-bred reader to see what she has often looked at. The city world of *The Saturdays*, on the other hand, unlocks another magical world for the child who would not otherwise have known the hush of an art gallery, the luxury of tea in an elegant hotel, the excitement of a beauty salon, the scariness of being lost in a huge city at dusk, the compensatory thrill of riding home astride a policeman's horse. Even readers who have never been to a town of more than 25,000 inhabitants experience the headiness of being "all by yourself in a big city for the first time." It is "like the first time you find you can ride a bicycle or do the dog paddle."

Enright is as fascinated by and skilled at rendering houses and rooms as she is the marvels of nature. While the outdoors reveals the handiwork of a beneficent and powerful transcendent force, houses and rooms are symbolic of the interior landscapes of individuals. In two books, *The Four-Story Mistake* (1942) and *Return to Gone-Away* (1961), the family home is a major character as well as the center and source of action in the story. In each book Enright introduces new characters with painstaking descriptions of their abodes. Aunt Minnehaha lives in part of a dilapidated but scrupulously clean old house at Gone-Away; the impression it gives is "one of density. A large herd

of furniture grazed on a red carpet." Then follows an inventory not only of furniture but of wallpaper, pictures, picture frames, plants, vines, covers, and doilies. Like Aunt Minnehaha, who has filed in her orderly mind every fragment of her life, which can be immediately retrieved for a story, the house is crowded with mementos of earlier days. Miss Fish's one room in a boardinghouse is as sparse and virginal as the calm, self-possessed teacher herself. Houses where children live always have inviting attics or top stories burgeoning with boxes, books, toys, trapezes, and pianos, with everything that bespeaks a playland paradise. Even in *Zeee*, the various apartments of the tiny fairy are affectionately described down to the last clamshell bathtub and fishbone footstool.

Zeee and the earlier *Tatsinda*, Enright's two fairy tales, "light, bright, and sparkling," are absorbing tales and pulsate with the same animism as her realistic stories. Yet they are more conventional and didactic, less compelling and memorable than the novels, perhaps because the novels intertwine and cumulatively create a complete world of city, farm, woods, marsh, island, sea, and sky in which live Garnet Linden, Mab Kendall, the Melendys—all the "fairly familiar, possibly dirty, but healthy and reasonable" and, above all, hopeful faces. There they work together toward peace and joy.

Enright concluded in "Realism in Children's Literature" "that there are four things: observation and experience are the blood and bone, while wish and memory are the mind and heart that make book children real." She possessed not only the theory but the art and craft requisite for the creation of real book children, as well as adults, houses, and countryside. If the creation of authentic, consistent new worlds through the imaginative use of simple, concrete language and humor are the hallmarks of literature that becomes classic, then Enright has written children's classics.

Selected Bibliography

WORKS OF ELIZABETH ENRIGHT

Kintu: A Congo Adventure. With illustrations by the author. New York: Farrar and Rinehart, 1935.

Thimble Summer. With illustrations by the author. New York: Farrar and Rinehart, 1938; London: Heinemann, 1939.

The Sea Is All Around. With illustrations by the author.

New York: Farrar and Rinehart, 1940; London: Heinemann, 1959.

The Saturdays. With illustrations by the author. New York: Farrar and Rinehart, 1941; London: Heinemann, 1955.

The Four-Story Mistake. With illustrations by the author. New York: Farrar and Rinehart, 1942; London: Heinemann, 1955.

Then There Were Five. With illustrations by the author. New York: Farrar and Rinehart, 1944; London: Heinemann, 1956.

Spiderweb for Two: A Melendy Maze. With illustrations by the author. New York: Rinehart, 1951; London: Heinemann, 1956.

Gone-Away Lake. With illustrations by Beth and Joe Krush. New York: Harcourt, Brace, and World, 1957; London: Heinemann, 1957.

Return to Gone-Away. With illustrations by Beth and Joe Krush. New York: Harcourt, Brace, and World, 1961; London: Heinemann, 1962.

Tatsinda. With illustrations by Irene Haas. New York: Harcourt, Brace, and World, 1963; London: Heinemann, 1964.

Zeee. With illustrations by Irene Haas. New York: Harcourt, Brace, and World, 1965; London: Heinemann, 1966.

CRITICAL AND BIOGRAPHICAL STUDIES

Cameron, Eleanor. "The Art of Elizabeth Enright" *Horn Book* 45: 641–651 (Dec. 1969); 46: 26–30 (Feb. 1970).

———. "A Second Look: *Gone-Away Lake*" *Horn Book* 60: 622–626 (Sept.–Oct. 1984).

Enright, Elizabeth. "Autobiographical Note" and "Acceptance Paper." In *Newbery Medal Books: 1922–1955*, edited by Bertha E. Miller and Elinor Whitney Field. Boston: Horn Book, 1955. Pp. 168–175.

———. "The Hero's Changing Face." In *The Contents of The Basket*, edited by Frances Lander Spain. New York: New York Public Library, 1960. Pp. 27–34.

———. "Realism in Children's Literature" *Horn Book* 43: 165–170 (April 1967).

—M. SARAH SMEDMAN

JULIANA HORATIA EWING
1841–1885

"I OWE MORE in circuitous ways to that tale than I can tell," Rudyard Kipling wrote in *Something of Myself* (1937) of Juliana Ewing's *Six to Sixteen* (1876). "I knew it, as I know it still, almost by heart. Here was a history of real people and real things." Many writers have testified to the impact Ewing made upon them in childhood, and others have clearly been influenced by her. Edith Nesbit's Bastable stories, though this is rarely acknowledged, clearly stem from "A Great Emergency" (1874), which has the same elements of a child narrator, a child-oriented world where adults are conspicuous by their absence, and the quest for excitement in a life that seems to the characters oppressively secure. The later Victorian and Edwardian stories of family life owe much to those that Ewing had written in the 1870's. Her influence in fact outran her popularity. Her appeal was to the perceptive, not to the masses, and during her lifetime none of her books sold more than a few thousand; today, to most people, she is only a name in reference books. Always a fastidious writer, Ewing is read only by those who are prepared to endure a plot that is often rambling, for the sake of the excellence of the characterization, the beauty of the style, the subtle irony, and the evocation of the English countryside. "These exquisite pieces are too delicately worked for the ordinary style of children of the poor," Charlotte Yonge wrote in 1887 in her pamphlet *What Books to Lend and What to Give*, "though they may be appreciated by those who have time to dream over them, and, as it were, imbibe them."

The second daughter of Margaret Gatty, who was a writer well known in mid-Victorian schoolrooms (her *Parables from Nature* series was a minor classic), Ewing owed much to her mother's loving encouragement. Margaret Scott had married the Reverend Alfred Gatty in 1839. He was then a curate but that same year was offered the parish of Ecclesfield in Yorkshire, a location that all their children were to love with fierce devotion, and which is the background of many of Ewing's books. Margaret Gatty, who if she had had proper opportunities would have been a scientist (she wrote a two-volume work on British seaweeds), turned to writing in a desperate attempt to improve the family finances; Dr. Gatty seems to have had a hazy grasp of finance and lofty notions of how to spend. The education of their four sons, who were variously sent to Eton, Winchester, Marlborough, and Charterhouse, must alone have made substantial inroads into the family income. Every penny that Gatty earned was poured into what her daughter called "the leaky bucket of a large family's expenses." She never enjoyed writing, though she achieved some reputation. In 1866 she took on the editorship of the new children's journal *Aunt Judy's Magazine* (when she was already suffering from the paralysis that was to kill her five years later) with thankfulness that it would bring in a small regular income. Her four daughters undertook the laborious writing and copying the position involved, their mother being unable to use her hands easily. But since Gatty saw her second daughter's career launched from this platform, it made all the drudgery worthwhile.

Juliana Horatia—known to her family as Julie—

was born in 1841. Unlike her mother (who in the family confessions book admitted to wanting to live "somewhere warm, near the sea"), but like all her brothers and sisters, she could think of nowhere she wanted to live other than Ecclesfield. Julie had a busy, happy childhood, though she was delicate and much afflicted with illness. None of the four girls appeared to think there was anything wrong with the fact that most of the family's meager resources were spent on the education and multifarious needs of their brothers, while everyone else went without. The girls muddled along with lessons from their mother or an elder sister, and as soon as they were old enough they acted as unpaid curates to their father or amanuenses to their mother.

> The coming and going of the boys were our chief events. We packed for them when they went away. We wrote long letters to them, and received brief but pithy replies. We spoke on their behalf when they wanted clothes or pocket-money. We knew exactly how to bring the news of good marks in school and increased subscriptions to cricket to bear in effective combination upon the parental mind, and were amply rewarded by half a sheet . . . with brief directions as to the care of garden or collection, and perhaps a rude outline of the head-master's nose.
>
> *(Six to Sixteen)*

Descriptions of the children's activities can be found in many of Ewing's family stories: endless imaginative games, private theatricals, botanical and sketching expeditions in the manner of so many large Victorian families. Each child had his garden. There was also an abundance of dogs, and though the vicarage itself has now been demolished, the graves of the family pets can still be seen against the wall that separates the garden from the churchyard.

> Bury him nobly—next to the donkey;
>   Fetch the old banner, and wave it about:
> Bury him deeply—think of the monkey,
>   Shallow his grave, and the dogs got him out.
>   ("The Burial of the Linnet,"
>   *Verses for Children and Songs for Music*)

Near this place was "Julie's Bower," where on "benches made of narrow boards laid on inverted flower-pots," her sister Horatia in her memoir *Juliana Horatia Ewing and Her Books* (1885) recorded, "we sat and listened to her stories."

Though Gatty in *Aunt Judy's Tales* (1859)—Aunt Judy being the nickname for Julie the storyteller—has the elder sister tell very admonitory tales, Horatia records that they were often fairy tales, inspired by the Grimm brothers, Hans Christian Andersen, and Ludwig Bechstein. (She later wrote many stories based on these models, collected in *Old-fashioned Fairy Tales* in 1882.) Another story, about a deserted windmill on a lonely moor, was the starting point for *Jan of the Windmill* (1876), serialized as *The Miller's Thumb* in *Aunt Judy's Magazine* (1872–1873).

Ewing's first stories were published in the *Monthly Packet*, Charlotte Yonge's journal for young ladies, to which her mother's name gave her an entrée. (This serious, some would say forbidding, periodical devoted itself to the improvement of the upper-middle-class girl.) The first of these stories that is of any distinction is "Melchior's Dream," a powerful parable about family life written in 1861 when she was nineteen, which while owing something to the Sunday tales she read in her youth (like Lucy Lyttleton Cameron's *The Warning Clock*) has an invention and imaginative qualities that are all her own. She was often to return to this theme of the need for love and tolerance and forbearance among brothers and sisters and how difficult it is to achieve (notably in "A Very Ill-tempered Family," 1874–1875). In 1865 she contributed "The Brownies" to Yonge's magazine. This tale of two boys who are persuaded by a wise owl to play the part of house elves, the householder's traditional friend, is perhaps her best-known work today, and from it Baden-Powell took the name that he gave to the junior branch of the Girl Guide movement. Again she takes over the older, didactic tradition in which her mother wrote and turns it into something entirely different, infusing her story with delicate observation of country life and ways. She later wrote other stories about children reformed by fairy methods—"Timothy's Shoes" (1870–1871), "Amelia and the Dwarfs" (1870), and "Snap-Dragons" (1870)—but in all these it is the everyday world and the domestic detail that hold the most interest.

In 1866 *Aunt Judy's Magazine* was founded, and thenceforward she was her mother's principal contributor. Her first offering was the opening episode of *Mrs. Overtheway's Remembrances* (1869), which was serialized from 1866 to 1868. This work, in which an old lady recalls her childhood for the benefit of a lonely small girl, contains some of her finest writing. The story "Mrs. Moss," about the child who longs to meet the great belle of her grandmother's youth (in her ball dress of white brocade embroidered with rosebuds, with a train and bodice of pea-green satin) and who finds a stooping, bearded old woman in dingy brown, conveys with great poignancy a child's sudden bewildered realization that time goes further back than the seeming eternity of seven or eight years. But the style is diffuse and reflective, and it is only the persistent who would be able to read beyond the opening pages.

By the time Julie began *Mrs. Overtheway*, she had met Major Alexander Ewing. Although one might have thought that he had much that would recommend him to the Gattys, his courtship of their second daughter was not at first welcomed. Partly it seems that the parents were genuinely concerned for her health. They may also have been worried about the uncertainty of Major Ewing's future and the fact that they would be losing a valuable pair of hands. All through the summer and autumn of 1866 the arguments went on in the vicarage, but Major Ewing—Rex—persisted, and by November the parents relented; the lovers were allowed to meet again, and their engagement was announced.

Rex and Julie were married on 1 June 1867. They were a well-matched pair, and had many tastes in common—dogs, theatricals, reading and languages, sketching. It is clear, moreover, that married life meant far more freedom to write. As long as Julie stayed at Ecclesfield her life would have been dedicated to her parents.

Rex was in the commissariat department of the army, and their first posting was to Canada, where they lived at Fredericton, New Brunswick, for two years, and where Ewing wrote the last two episodes of *Mrs. Overtheway*, "Reka Dom" (the Russian for River House, about a much-loved childhood home) and "Kerguelen's Land," in which the child Ida's father is miraculously restored to her. She was on the whole very happy in Canada, though acute pangs of homesickness would sometimes sweep over her. It was with much joyful weeping that she returned with Rex to the vicarage in the autumn of 1869 and was given a tremendous welcome by her assembled family and the parish. Stirred by this, she wrote "Christmas Crackers" (1869–1870), a short story in the manner of Andersen, in which a family is gathered around a fire at Christmas, the old dreaming of the past and the young of the future.

The next posting was to Aldershot, England, where they were stationed until 1877. These seven years at an army camp were perhaps the happiest of Ewing's life. She liked the climate and the pine-scented air; she enjoyed theatricals and concerts and regimental balls. But beyond all this she fell in love with the army and its ceremonies, traditions, and ritual. (In those years of peace, when the Napoleonic wars were forgotten and the next European war was many decades away, it must have been easy to overlook the real purpose of soldiers.) These were also her most productive years. She wrote many of the stories that were to appear in *Old-fashioned Fairy Tales*; such fairy stories as "Snap-Dragons," "Amelia and the Dwarfs," "Benjy in Beastland" (1870), and "Timothy's Shoes"; stories of family life like "A Great Emergency" and "A Very Ill-tempered Family"; "Lob Lie-by-the-fire" (1870), which drew upon her interest in the ordinary soldier and barrack-room life; and three full-length books, *A Flat Iron for a Farthing* (1873), *Six to Sixteen*, and *Jan of the Windmill*, as well as much miscellaneous writing, including verse. Nearly all these works made their first appearance in *Aunt Judy's Magazine*.

But *Aunt Judy's* editor was failing. The muscular affliction that had deprived Ewing's mother of the powers of walking and writing had now reached her speech, and though she maintained her indomitable courage and cheerfulness, she could only communicate by using a board on which letters were printed. On 4 October 1873 Margaret Gatty died. Moved by the memory of the generous spirit of her mother and of other women like her whose souls were larger than their purses (she particularly had two aunts in mind), Ewing wrote "Madam Liberality," printed in *Aunt Judy* in December 1873. In her account of a valiant spirit she drew on her memories of the illnesses and disappointments of her own childhood; and thus inadvertently the picture she created seemed, to the family at any rate, to be a self-portrait.

Among the last stories that Ewing wrote from Aldershot was "Our Field" (1876), very short and tailored (as was the frequent practice of the day) to fit some German engravings. She wrote nothing finer than this description of a child's Arcadia—a field that appears to belong to no one, which a family of children (and their dog, of course) take over for their play:

It sloped down hill, and the hedges round it were rather high, with awkward branches of blackthorn sticking out here and there without any leaves, and with the blossom lying white on the black twigs like snow. There were cowslips all over the field, but they were thicker at the lower end, which was damp. The great heat of the day was over. The sun shone still, but it shone low down and made such splendid shadows that we all walked about with grey giants at our feet; and it made the bright green of the grass, and the cowslips down below, and the top of the hedge, and Sandy's hair, and everything in the sun and the mist behind the elder bush which was out of the sun, so yellow—so very yellow—that just for a minute I really believed . . . that everything was turning into gold.

The Aldershot life came to an end early in 1877, and the Ewings moved north to Cheshire, followed the next year by a move to York. Then, in less than six months, news came that Rex had been posted to Malta. The successive moves had taken their toll on Ewing's always fragile health, but with a sister's help she managed to pack up all the furniture and possessions that were to be shipped to Malta. She was to follow when the weather was cooler. It was during this waiting period, the summer of 1879, that news came of the death of the young French Prince Imperial (son of the exiled Napoleon III), killed in a British expedition against the Zulus from which his English companions escaped. All Ewing's emotions about the army and patriotism and the supreme glory of dying to save a friend resurged. The illustrator Randolph Caldecott, whose work she greatly admired, was persuaded to make a drawing around which she would write a story. Caldecott's drawing of a small boy with an aureole of fair hair, riding a red pony and blowing a trumpet that scatters geese and chickens in his path, arrived in August. By 12 September *Jackanapes*, her most famous story, was finished. First published in *Aunt Judy*, it was issued by the Society for Promoting Christian Knowledge (S.P.C.K.) in 1884. With additional Caldecott drawings and after tiresome and worrying financial transactions, "that favourite child of my brain" scored a modest success.

She planned to join Rex in Malta in October, traveling overland by way of Marseilles. But in Paris she became so ill that a sister had to come out to bring her home. She was not only grievously disappointed at not reaching Rex, but also troubled about their finances and about the inconvenience of having had the bulk of her possessions sent on ahead. The doctor she consulted seems to have told her that her illness and back pain were the fancies of a highly strung woman. She hoped that she might be allowed to travel the following year, but

this was forbidden, and when in 1882 Rex was posted to Ceylon, all hope of joining him vanished.

These were not productive years: Ewing was in bad health and in financial difficulties (she said in 1883 that her royalties from ten books came to little over £20), and she was leading a nomadic existence, shuttling between Ecclesfield and various friends and relations. But out of this period came some verses that in addition to those she had written in earlier years were issued separately with illustrations by "André." She also wrote *Daddy Darwin's Dovecot* (1884), perhaps the most polished piece she ever produced.

In the summer and early autumn of 1881 she was staying near her old home and was moved by the beauty of the countryside that she was trying to sketch to attempt to set down some of her feeling for it in a story. A request for a sketch of two gaffers gossiping had gone to Caldecott, and in November 1881 *Aunt Judy* carried the story *Daddy Darwin's Dovecot*. It opens:

> Two gaffers gossiping, seated side by side upon a Yorkshire wall. A wall of sandstone of many colours, glowing redder and yellower as the sun goes down; well-cushioned with moss and lichen, and deep set in rank grass on this side, where the path runs, and in blue hyacinths on that side, where the wood is, and where—on the grey and still naked branches of young oaks—sit divers crows, not less solemn than the gaffers and also gossiping.

It is the story of little Jack March from the workhouse, who yearns to do two things: sing in the church choir and live in Daddy Darwin's Dovecot (a small-holding with a pigeon house). He achieves both and casts behind him the odium of his workhouse origins. As finely and economically wrought as *Jackanapes*, the story is more controlled in emotion and has some memorable vignettes of country life, notably of the parson's daughter, whose duties, anxious thought for the parishioners, and bounty make her a composite portrait of the Gatty daughters.

The Story of a Short Life (1885), included in a S.P.C.K. collected edition with *Jackanapes* and *Daddy Darwin*, was written in 1882, before Ewing finally knew that there was to be no chance of joining her husband. Originally published with the additional title of *Laetus Sorte Mea* ("Happy in my lot"—the motto of the family in the book), it looks back nostalgically to the golden Aldershot days. This explains some of the emotion. The rest presumably stemmed from Ewing's instinct to take refuge from her ill health in dreams about the love and attention (lacking in her case) lavished on the dying Leonard, a beautiful, promising child who falls out of his father's carriage at a military review and is brought to die in the army camp that he so loves. The story's strength is Ewing's sympathy with the ordinary soldier and his life, and in this she foreshadows Kipling, whom she well may have influenced. Its weakness is the otiose deathbed scene. Derived from the deathbed scenes of pious children described by James Janeway in his *Token for Children* (1672) and by his many imitators (the memory of this sort of childhood reading no doubt influenced Dickens when he came to describe the deaths of Paul Dombey in *Dombey and Son* and Little Nell in *The Old Curiosity Shop*, which in their turn were imitated by lesser writers), it lacks all purpose—literary or religious—beyond the wish to draw tears.

The last story of any substance Ewing wrote was "Mary's Meadow" (serialized in *Aunt Judy* between November 1883 and March 1884). Rex had come home; she at last had a home of her own, near Taunton, and the chance to make a garden. "Mary's Meadow" is a fitting finale, for it celebrates two things that Ewing felt deeply—the joy of turning a wilderness into a garden and the joys of family life.

After that she wrote just a few little articles, mostly on the subject of gardens. She also corresponded with Randolph Caldecott (who was dying of heart disease) about illustrations for the S.P.C.K. publications of *Daddy Darwin's Dovecot* and *Lob Lie-by-the-fire* (a collection of several stories). By the beginning of 1885 her health had so deteriorated that there could be no more literary activities. She was in constant pain and an operation was recommended. Ewing died, after a second operation, on 12 May, and was buried with military honors in Trull churchyard near Taunton.

Her literary output was not very large, and she never considered herself a fluent writer. Ewing knew herself to be better at small-scale work; she found it difficult to handle the plot of a longer novel, introducing too many characters and themes. *Six to Sixteen*, which the historian G. M. Young described as one of the best accounts he knew of a Victorian girlhood, took the form of memoirs and was better suited to this discursiveness. Even so, the introduction of the narrator's great-grandparents—exiled French aristocrats (for like many of her class at that time Ewing felt that

there was a mystic virtue attached to high birth)—could only amaze the reader by their total irrelevance to the substance of the story, which takes the narrator from the death of her parents in a cholera epidemic in India, via a deplorable boarding school, to a placidly happy family life in a Yorkshire vicarage that clearly recalls Ewing's own youth.

We and the World (1881), a boy's account of his life, which Ewing began in 1877 and did not finish until 1879, is a less successful attempt at memoirs. The second half of the book describes life at sea, which not surprisingly lacks conviction and fails to hold our attention. But the opening chapters are as entertaining as anything she wrote, with sketches of Yorkshire characters and customs and vignettes of boys determined to be naughty.

The most successful of the three memoir-style novels is *A Flat Iron for a Farthing*, narrated by Reginald Dacre, a motherless only child. His creator does not sentimentalize the situation, and is even prepared to laugh gently at Reginald's occasional affectations of piety and quaint self-absorption, with a detachment she was unable to bring to her account of Leonard in *The Story of a Short Life*. We follow Regie through childhood and schooldays at Eton, to manhood and his marriage to the young woman he had seen as a child buying a toy flat iron. It is a mellow, happy book, in which the author flatters young readers by forbearing to preach on any occasion. She even pokes mild fun at that Victorian sacred cow, Sabbath observance.

Her fourth full-length novel, *Jan of the Windmill*, is more uneven. This story of a foundling brought up by a Wiltshire miller—a child who paints like a genius and who is later united with his true (aristocratic) father through a portrait made by the boy's master—has stagy elements, and the adventures in London show the influence of Dickens' *Oliver Twist*. But the first part, with descriptions of the mill, the Wiltshire downs and vast skies, the tender relationship between Jan the foundling baby and the miller's little son, Jan's first attempts to draw and his growing talent, is memorable.

Part of Ewing's difficulty with the longer books is the serial form in which they were all written. Undeniably Ewing handled the smaller canvas best, as one can see by comparing "A Great Emergency" with, say, *Six to Sixteen*. The action of the first tale takes place over only a few months instead of a decade; the number of characters is reduced to manageable proportions; and the author achieves what she often failed to achieve—a succinct opening. "We were very happy—I, Rupert, Henrietta, and Baby Cecil. The only thing we found fault with in our lives was that there were so few events in them." And a page later Rupert tells the narrator: "You are quite old enough now, Charlie, to learn what to do whatever happens, so every half-holiday, when I'm not playing cricket, I'll teach you presence of mind near the cucumber frame, if you're punctual. I've put up a bench." In search of adventure the narrator runs away on a canal barge with a friend, and comes back to find that in his absence there has been "a great emergency." The house has caught fire, and Rupert and Henrietta between them have rescued their baby brother. (Charlie, Rupert, Henrietta, and Baby Cecil are the precursors of Nesbit's Bastable family.)

Ewing was not a conscious innovator. Nevertheless when one compares her writing with that of her mother (whom in many ways she much resembled), the great differences between the approaches of the two generations toward writing for children is clear. Gatty felt that every occasion must be improved, the moral hammered home. Ewing, who was fundamentally as serious as her mother, and whose religious faith pervaded all that she wrote, did not utter her truths in sermons but rather wove them unobtrusively into the texture of her stories. Born into a generation that was allowed to enjoy childhood, she succeeded perhaps better than any other children's writer in capturing and recording happiness.

Selected Bibliography

WORKS OF JULIANA HORATIA EWING

Nearly all of Ewing's works were first published in magazines, chiefly *Aunt Judy's Magazine*. A full list can be found in *Juliana Horatia Ewing and Her Books*, by Horatia Gatty.

Melchior's Dream and Other Tales. London: Bell and Daldy, 1862.

Mrs. Overtheway's Remembrances. With illustrations by J. A. Pasquier and J. Wolf. London: Bell and Daldy, 1869. (Includes "Mrs. Moss," "Reka Dom," and "Kerguelen's Land.")

The Brownies and Other Tales. With illustrations by George Cruikshank. London: Bell and Daldy, 1870. (Includes "The Brownies," "Christmas Crackers," and "Amelia and the Dwarfs.")

A Flat Iron for a Farthing; or, Some Passages in the Life of an Only Son. With illustrations by Mrs. W. Allingham (H. Paterson). London: Bell and Daldy, 1873. Reprinted London: George Bell and Sons, 1884.

Lob Lie-by-the-fire; or, The Luck of Lingborough and Other Tales. With illustrations by George Cruikshank. London: George Bell and Sons, 1874. Rev. ed., with illustrations by Randolph Caldecott. London: S.P.C.K., 1885. (Includes "Lob Lie-by-the-fire," "Benjy in Beastland," and "Timothy's Shoes.")

Six to Sixteen. A Story for Girls. With illustrations by Mrs. W. Allingham. London: George Bell and Sons, 1876.

Jan of the Windmill: A Story of the Plains. With illustrations by Mrs. W. Allingham. London: George Bell and Sons, 1876.

A Great Emergency and Other Tales. With illustrations by Mrs. W. Allingham. London: George Bell and Sons, 1877. (Includes "A Great Emergency," "A Very Ill-tempered Family," "Madam Liberality," and "Our Field.")

We and the World: A Book for Boys. London: George Bell and Sons, 1881.

Old-fashioned Fairy Tales. London: S.P.C.K., 1882.

Jackanapes. With illustrations by Randolph Caldecott. London: S.P.C.K., 1884.

Daddy Darwin's Dovecot. With illustrations by Randolph Caldecott. London: S.P.C.K., 1884.

The Story of a Short Life. With illustrations by Gordon Browne. London: S.P.C.K., 1885.

Mary's Meadow and Letters from a Little Garden. With illustrations by Gordon Browne. London: S.P.C.K., 1886.

Snap-Dragons and Old Father Christmas. With illustrations by Gordon Browne. London: S.P.C.K., 1888.

Verses for Children and Songs for Music. London: S.P.C.K., 1895. (This book is volume 9 of Ewing's *Works* and includes "The Burial of the Linnet.")

CRITICAL AND BIOGRAPHICAL STUDIES

Avery, Gillian. *Mrs. Ewing*. London: Bodley Head Monograph, 1961.

Gatty, Horatia K. F. *Juliana Horatia and Her Books*. London: S.P.C.K., 1885.

Laski, Marghanita. *Mrs. Ewing, Mrs. Molesworth, and Mrs. Hodgson Burnett*. London: A. Barker, 1950.

Marshall, Emma Martin. "A.L.O.E. (Miss Tucker); Mrs. Ewing." In *Women Novelists of Queen Victoria's Reign*, edited by Mrs. Oliphant et al. London: Hurst and Blackett, 1897.

Maxwell, Christabel. *Mrs. Gatty and Mrs. Ewing*. London: Constable, 1949.

Yonge, Charlotte. *What Books to Lend and What to Give*. London: National Society, 1887.

—GILLIAN AVERY

ELEANOR FARJEON
1881–1965

ELEANOR FARJEON described the milieu in which she and her three brothers grew up as "rich with imaginative suggestion." The Farjeon household was the center of a lively group of writers, musicians, actors, and painters in Victorian London. Eleanor's father, Benjamin Leopold Farjeon, was a popular British novelist. Her mother, Margaret (Maggie), was the lovely, talented daughter of the American actor Joseph Jefferson. Ben and Maggie married in 1877. A year later their first child, Harry, was born in America. The couple then moved to London, where Eleanor (Nellie, Nelly, or Nell) was born on 13 February 1881. Two years later Joseph (Joe) Jefferson was born, and in 1887, with the birth of Herbert (Bertie), the Farjeon nursery was complete. Years later Eleanor relived those magical childhood years in her autobiographical work *A Nursery in the Nineties* (1935).

Farjeon described her father as a "sky-rocket, followed by coloured stars." Benjamin Farjeon was a warmhearted, impulsive (and explosive) man with a playful nature; he knew the pleasure children take in surprises. He bought enticing toys from Cremer's toy shop in Regent Street and amused the Farjeon children and their friends with lantern shows of familiar nursery tales, sometimes deliberately mixing up the slides: "You might see the Big Bad Wolf sitting up in the bed in the Grandmother's nightcap long before he had met Red-Ridinghood in the woods. Then there were screams of laughter."

Farjeon's gentle, fun-loving mother came from a family of actors dating back to the mid-eighteenth century. Maggie entertained her children with bits of Americana and stories of the theater passed down in the Jefferson family, played the piano and the music box for them to dance to, and accompanied herself on the guitar as she sang songs from the American South.

Books, music, and theater were part of the children's everyday world. When Nellie was four, she was taken to see a play, *The Japs*. The leading actor was a friend of the Farjeon family's, and during the performance he came over to the Farjeon box and said, "Hello, Ben." From this experience, Eleanor later wrote, "illusion and reality became indistinguishably mingled forever."

After seeing another play, *The Babes*, Nellie and her older brother, Harry, invented a game they called TAR, after the two main characters in the play, *Tessie* and *Ralph*. This was the beginning of an intense game of make-believe that continued for more than twenty years. In the game of TAR, Nellie and Harry took roles of personages from drama, literature, history, and life. Favorite characters came from *Grimm's Fairy Tales*, Lewis Carroll's *Alice* books, Louisa May Alcott's *Little Women*, *The Three Musketeers*, by Alexandre Dumas, and Shakespeare's *A Midsummer Night's Dream*. Farjeon credited TAR with developing her imagination. It gave her the power "to put in motion, almost at will, given persons within given scenes, and see what came of it."

Equally important for her artistic development was her exposure to books, all sorts of books, including the eight thousand in her father's study and an attic room filled with the overflow. "The Little Bookroom," as the attic room was called, "was yielded up to books as an intended garden is left to its flowers and weeds." Farjeon gave the room's name to the collection of her favorite short stories, her most highly regarded work.

Papa Farjeon read aloud to his children, gave each a new book every Sunday after dinner, and encouraged their literary games. He kept the best of their writings in a book and said he would rather lose a pound note than that book. One of Farjeon's earliest attempts at writing was a collection of stories, "Kitty's Dream," written at the age of six and found among her papers after her death. The title story is about a little girl named Kitty who dreams she is lost in a wood. The use of the dream as a literary device anticipated the author's mature style. In Eleanor Farjeon's stories one finds a curious blend of fantasy and reality. She had the ability to move back and forth between the two smoothly and logically in the telling of a tale.

In the same year that Nellie wrote "Kitty's Dream," she began her first play, *Snow-White*. She finished this play forty years later and included it in *Grannie Gray: Children's Plays and Games* (1939). Farjeon presented the original manuscript to Oxford University Press in 1956 on the occasion of the reprinting of *Grannie Gray*. Her first complete poem was a valentine composed for her sweetheart, Button, written when Nellie was seven. Also when she was seven, her father taught her how to type, correct proofs, and read copy. Benjamin Farjeon held unconventional attitudes toward education. Nellie had no formal schooling; she was educated at home by governesses whom she later characterized in her works of fiction.

In 1891 an essay about her pet sparrow, "Pop," was published in *Little Wideawake: An Illustrated Magazine for Good Children*. Nellie also regularly contributed to her brother Bertie's newspaper, *Farjeon's Fortnightly*, published between the years 1899 and 1901. *Farjeon's Fortnightly* succeeded *Farjeon's Weekly*, which had been published under her brother Harry's editorship from 1897 to 1899. Each issue consisted of eight pages of serials, stories, poems, and literary puzzles. During the years *Farjeon's Weekly* and *Farjeon's Fortnightly* were published, Nellie wrote a fairy tale, "The Cardboard Angel," which was printed in *Hutchinson's* magazine and for which she received three guineas, her first payment for writing.

Harry was then a student at the Royal Academy of Music, and Nellie began writing lyrics for his musical pieces. Together, they wrote an opera, *Floretta* (1897), about a youthful love affair of Henry of Navarre. Though she depreciated this effort—"It was the most artless account of Henry ever written"—the opera was produced and presented at St. George's Hall two years later.

At twenty Eleanor was full of self-reproach at her lack of discipline in writing. Her father's death two years later saved her from remaining a dilettante. The family needed money. Although Ben Farjeon had been a popular and prolific writer, he was never a practical businessman; moreover, he was an impulsive, generous person. On his death the family had to sell household furnishings and most of Ben's library for a fraction of their cost. The situation forced Farjeon to develop her writing skills and make them salable. Success did not come at once. It took thirteen years of personal and professional growth before the critics recognized her work.

Farjeon's development was influenced by her friendship with the English poet Edward Thomas. She was thirty-one when she first met Thomas through her brother Bertie. Their friendship lasted five years, until Edward's premature death in April 1917. The story of their friendship is related in *Edward Thomas: The Last Four Years. Book One of the Memoirs of Eleanor Farjeon* (1958). From Thomas, Farjeon the writer learned to keep her senses fresh and to use words with precision.

The novelist D. H. Lawrence was another early influence. Lawrence, she said, gave her confidence in herself and the power to stand on her own. He stimulated in people a sense of their talents. Lawrence sometimes criticized Farjeon for her facility and sentimentality; however, he admired her best efforts. Critics, too, have remarked on the unevenness of her writing. Her friend and editor Grace Hogarth said that though Farjeon could be an excellent critic of other writers, she could not always judge her own. She hated to discard anything that could possibly turn out in the end to be as good as she wanted it to be. Her weakness may have been rooted in her early lack of discipline or in her profuse nature. Only Bertie was allowed to edit what she wrote. Bertie and Eleanor collaborated on several musical plays, including *The Glass Slipper* (1946). Bertie never tried to curb her enthusiasms but relied on them for impetus; he did the refining.

Another significant person in her life was

George Earle, or "Pod," as he was known to his family and friends. Earle was an English teacher and placed great stress on language: "Words are the flowers of the mind, its fragrance, its pollen." Moreover, Earle deeply admired Eleanor and gave her the intellectual stimulus and emotional devotion she needed for creative work.

Farjeon was never one to analyze the creative act. She mistrusted this approach. She said her imagination was in perpetual flux in which suggestions of all sorts floated like seeds. These seeds developed through an unconscious process described by Farjeon as a state of self-hypnosis: "Under its spell the unpredictable happens, when embryonic thought is transmuted into a miracle of words beyond the most diligent pen-pushing." Part of the creative process was isolating herself. She learned to do this on streetcars, at concerts, and in her cozy cottages. In a broadcast on the BBC in 1961, four years before her death, she remarked that she worked best at night, or behind foggy windows, when she was completely insulated not only from other people, but from awareness of her own identity. She did her most creative writing in what writer Denys Blakelock called "a sort of glorified attic." Her niece Joan, a stage designer, once converted a shed into a writing room, completely redecorated and designed with a whole corner of glass so that Farjeon could sit and look out on an old-fashioned garden. Farjeon was unable to create in this pleasant atmosphere. She preferred a room that was crowded and rather dark, "a glorious jumble of books and papers." To her friend, writer Eileen Colwell, she confided: "When I begin to write, something happens. I am immersed in the world I have created and all my characters are around me." When she wrote *A Nursery in the Nineties*, she said she was not telling a story, or remembering, but was in those days again, reliving them. Perhaps this immediacy is what makes her stories memorable.

Her first book to receive acclaim from the critics was *Martin Pippin in the Apple Orchard* (1921). It was published not as a fairy tale for children but as a fantasy for adults. The seed for this book was sown on a holiday in Brittany, but it did not take root until ten years later. The book consists of six romantic tales framed within the story of Martin Pippin, a wandering minstrel, and his efforts to unite Robin Rue with the lovely Gillian, whose father has locked her in his well house with six young milkmaids. Rebecca West's review in the

New Statesman (3 December 1921) sent the author winging to fame. West wrote:

> The stories themselves, both in their conception and the craft that sets them down on the printed page each as burning bright as a copper beech in noon sunlight, are admirable. They aim at one of the most difficult things in the world, for one would have thought it impossible to write a new fairy story without lapsing either into fatuity or didacticism, and they marvellously succeed. Miss Farjeon has the initial advantage of a richly beautiful style, which loads the pages with colour that is always relevant to form."

Sixteen years after the publication of *Martin Pippin in the Apple Orchard* for an adult audience, Farjeon wrote another set of stories about Martin. *Martin Pippin in the Daisy-Field* (1937), created for a child audience, was written while Farjeon was living in her cottage at Houghton in Sussex. The book is dedicated to "the children of Sussex who skipped in my lane." One of the skippers was Elsie Puttick. Farjeon changed her name to Elsie Piddock and put her in the story "Elsie Piddock Skips in Her Sleep." Farjeon considered this her most perfect story. It is a favorite with storytellers and listeners everywhere. In the tale, Andy Spandy, Skipping-Master for the fairies, teaches seven-year-old Elsie to skip as the fairies skip. At the end of a year she has learned all the fairy skips, and for a prize Andy Spandy gives her a magic skipping rope with one handle made of Sugar Candy and the other of French Almond Rock. Though she sucks them "never so," they never grow less and Elsie sucks sweet all her life. When Elsie grows up and gives up skipping, tales of her marvelous skipping become a legend no one believes except Elsie, who still has the magic skipping rope. At one hundred and nine, she returns to Mount Caburn to save the children's skipping ground, which is threatened by a new squire who wants to build factories there. Elsie ingeniously outwits the squire, and the story ends with her skipping on Caburn still: ". . . if you go to Caburn at the new moon you may catch a glimpse of a tiny bent figure, no bigger than a child, skipping all by itself in its sleep, and hear a gay little voice, like the voice of a dancing yellow leaf, singing: 'Andy Spandy Sugardy Candy French Almond *Rock*! Breadandbutterforyoursupper'sallyourmother's GOT!' " In this story, as in others, Eleanor Farjeon speaks out against greed and materialism.

She shares the child's sense of values and need for justice. Storyteller Eileen Colwell called "Elsie" a brilliantly written story that "links the imaginary world with everyday in a completely satisfying way."

The Little Bookroom (1955) is Farjeon's selection of what she considered her best short stories from her earlier collections, excluding the *Martin Pippin* books. The twenty-seven tales were written over a period of thirty years. The stories are tightly structured and seem chosen as much for their form as their content. In an article solicited by Marcus Crouch on how she came to write these stories, Farjeon gave glimpses into their sources:

> When I was a little girl my favourite treat in Margate was to buy a penny fortune from a gypsy's love-bird like Susan Brown in "The Lovebirds," and when my niece Joan was a still littler girl, demanding stories to be made up on the spur of the moment, "The Lady's Room" became a smash-hit and had to be repeated for a run of quite two years. . . . Curious paragraphs in the corners of newspapers lodged themselves in corners of my mind; the bringing home to England of corn from an Egyptian tomb; the tearful farewell kisses on their fruit-trees of Sicilian peasants fleeting from Etna's stream of lava; the mention of a Russian sentryman who turned out every day to walk so many paces to nowhere and back again, obeying an obsolete order long forgotten; out of these tiny suggestions came "The King and the Corn," "The Girl Who Kissed the Peach-Tree," and "In Those Days."

From these few examples the picture of a fertile imagination emerges.

The British Library Association presented Farjeon with the Carnegie Medal (equivalent to the American Library Association's Newbery Medal) for *The Little Bookroom* in 1955. A year later she received the first international Hans Christian Andersen Medal, presented by the International Board on Books for Young People (IBBY), in cooperation with UNESCO. The citation read in part: "We see in Eleanor Farjeon one of the outstanding children's book writers of our time. *The Little Bookroom* presents a collection of original fairytales—full of beauty and poetry/written in a creative and imaginative language."

Farjeon was very much a theater person; this shows in her stories as well as in her plays. Critics have noted her "instinct for the right word," and her "musicality." Clifton Parker, composer of the music for Farjeon's plays *The Silver Curlew* (1953) and *The Glass Slipper*, remarked: "Eleanor Farjeon had an enormous sense of stagecraft. She knew how to read scripts and about the shaping of a lyric. Her sentences would fall right. She was sophisticated in her sense of lyricism, technically." And Marc Connelly, producer of the New York production of *Two Bouquets* (1936), described her as "an instinctual writer. . . . Each sentence had an architectural structure."

Farjeon possessed a rare understanding of childhood. Selma Lanes, reviewing *Mr. Garden* (1966) in *Book Week*, 7 August 1966, wrote: "As few other authors can, she successfully maintains a dual viewpoint: the sympathies and enthusiasms of childhood combined with the understanding and judgment of a wise and generous grownup." Farjeon's niece Joan described her as "the magic person in my life. Whatever age I was, that was the age she was. She was expansive in every way in a sort of magic way." And Edward Thomas' daughter, Myfanwy, described her as "a person who knew how to reach the heart of a child." Unlike most grown-ups she was comfortable with a child's sense of time. She gives Young Kate, in the story of the same name, time to plant a flower for the Green Woman, to sing a song for the River King, to dance with joy for the Dancing Boy. Her female characters have a sense of self, an independent spirit, a love of freedom. In "The Seventh Princess," the queen ingeniously arranges matters so that her favorite daughter will never bear the burden of queenhood. Human relationships are what counted most for Farjeon in life and in her stories.

The relationship between the very old and the very young, a frequent theme, finds perfect expression in "And I Dance Mine Own Child," the story of ten-year-old Griselda Curfew and her Great-Grandmother Curfew, who is one hundred and ten years old:

> If Griselda's Great-Grandmother had been twice, or thrice, or four times ten years old, there would have been a great deal of difference; for when you are twenty or thirty or forty, you feel very differently from when you were ten. But a hundred is a nice round number, and it brings things home in a circle; so Griselda's ten seemed to touch quite close the ten of Great-Grandmother Curfew, who was a hundred years away, and yet so very near her.

Many of her stories are set within a frame or centered around a character. In *Martin Pippin in the Apple Orchard*, the frame is a singing game, "The Spring-Green Lady." In both Martin Pippin books the stories weave around the minstrel Martin Pippin. *Jim at the Corner* (1934) revolves around the central figure of an old sailor who spins his yarns about life at sea for the little boy Derry. *The Old Nurse's Stocking-Basket* (1931) contains thirteen stories of varying lengths to fit the time it takes the Old Nurse to darn a hole in one of the four children's stockings.

Kaleidoscope (1928), dedicated to "Pod," is a collection of tales based on the stories George Earle told Farjeon of his early life. In her hands these stories became fairy tales. One of them is about a simpleton called Silly Billy. (He and George had been friends.) Billy's one talent is the ability to find mushrooms. One day the boy in the story and his friend, Silly Billy, try to fly a kite without success. At night the boy dreams that the kite is flying and that Silly Billy is flying with it. Along the way Silly Billy plucks mushrooms out of the sky and puts them in his basket. When he gets to heaven, Saint Peter asks him what he has done with his talents. Silly Billy says nothing but shows Saint Peter his basket. The mushrooms have changed to stars. The stories in *Kaleidoscope* are especially childlike. Birthdays "come dressed in gold with their hands full of presents." The child Anthony wonders why people always walk along the road: "Why didn't they sometimes walk up in the air like a bird, or down in the ground like a mole?"

> What is Poetry? Who knows?
> Not a rose, but the scent of the rose;
> Not the sky, but the light in the sky;
> Not the fly, but the gleam of the fly;
> Not the sea, but the sound of the sea;
> Not myself, but what makes me
> See, hear, and feel something that prose
> Cannot: and what it is, who knows?
> ("Poetry")

Farjeon felt that she was most herself in her poetry, and at least one critic agreed, calling her "a poet first and foremost." Her poems vary in subject, mood, meter, and pattern. There is often a touch of mystery or strangeness similar to that found in the poems of her dear friend Walter de la Mare. But there is fun and nonsense, too. Children enjoy her poetry for its rhythmic quality and vivid imagery:

balloons are golden suns and white full moons, meteors slip like skaters on the sky, and:

> The night will never stay,
> The night will still go by,
> Though with a million stars
> You pin it to the sky,
> Though you bind it with the blowing wind
> And buckle it with the moon,
> The night will slip away
> Like a sorrow or a tune.
> ("The Night Will Never Stay")

The Children's Bells (1934), a companion volume in quality to *The Little Bookroom*, consists of over three hundred poems selected from her previous books of prose and poetry for children. It includes the Martin Pippin flower songs, poems from the books about saints, kings, and heroes, and verses to commemorate the passing of the seasons. *The Children's Bells, Silver-sand and Snow* (1951), and *Then There Were Three* (1958) contain the poems Farjeon considered her best. *Then There Were Three* brings together three earlier volumes: *Cherrystones* (1942), *The Mulberry Bush* (1945), and *The Starry Floor* (1949). *Poems for Children*, originally published in 1951 and recently reprinted, includes *Joan's Door* (1926), *Come Christmas* (1927), *Over the Garden Wall* (1933), *Sing for Your Supper* (1938), and an additional twenty poems never before published in an American edition. *Invitation to a Mouse* (1981) is a selection of poems mostly from *Silver-sand and Snow*, chosen by her niece Annabel. The poem heard most often, though perhaps not so often associated with the Farjeon name, is "A Morning Song (For the First Day of Spring)," from *The Children's Bells*, made famous by Cat Stevens' recording.

> Morning has broken
> Like the first morning,
> Blackbird has spoken
> Like the first bird.
> Praise for the singing!
> Praise for the morning!
> Praise for them, springing
> From the first Word.

Farjeon was a prolific writer, and many of her works were reissued, sometimes in slightly altered form. Her range included short stories, novels, verse, musical plays, and history. During her lifetime she published over eighty works. It is not surprising that the results of such prolificacy were uneven in quality. Current assessors of Farjeon's work probably would agree with Naomi Lewis, who wrote in her introduction to *A Book for Eleanor Farjeon* (1966):

> Rereading (for remembered impression is not enough) I, for one, am struck by the inspired craftsmanship of her stories. I would place these above her plays—though she enjoyed writing dialogue, had abundant humour and wit, and understood well the workings of the theatre. I would place them also above her verse for though she wrote many enchanting poems that will always please sensitive children, her facility was not always her friend.

Frances Clarke Sayers, writing about her stories, remarked:

> The miraculous quality is the freshness and originality; the themes, the incidents, the "glad invention" which well up endlessly, tale after tale, story after story, resembling nothing so much as the never-ending variety of melody and theme of Mozart's music. A comfortable practicality, a touch of common earth and ordinary bread and butter give the sanity of salt to her finest fancy. Over and over again the common touch thrusts home the whole airy concept and leaves the reader holding the fantasy so hard by the hand there's no denying the truth of it.

Farjeon was well aware of her limitations. In notes for her last memoir (unpublished), she wrote of her longing to be a poet "first and foremost," adding, "What I did wasn't good enough; presently the effort to write with a genius I didn't possess dwindled into using as well as I could such minor talents as were mine." Minor they may have been, but in her hands they produced miniature gems. "Poetic imagination," "poetry-filled fancy," "a poet's feeling for mood," "sparkling imagery," and similar phrases have been used to describe her work.

The distinguishing mark of Farjeon is *joy*, the child's feeling of exultation for life. Her literary impulse was to waken the reader to a sense of wonder. The underlying theme in her work is "the wise child within." She used the illusions of the theater, its magic and beauty, to illuminate the truth as she knew it. Her gifts were musicality, poetic feeling, and a sense of drama. Farjeon's literary-theatrical-musical childhood milieu directed her talents toward a kind of writing in which fantasy is believable

and reality magical. The rich, imaginative life of TAR developed her gift for characterization and her sense of immediacy. Her childhood imagination informed her creative work as a whole. It influenced her choice of material, the direction of her writing (fantasy), its characteristic form (daydream), and even the conditions necessary for creative effort.

Farjeon always felt that her outside self did not correspond with her inside self. She would never consent to have her photograph taken for publicity purposes because she said that it would spoil the pleasant impression her stories may have made on the reader. To a reporter on the telephone (on the occasion of receiving the Carnegie Medal) Eleanor described herself as "a good-natured and cheerful suet pudding." Yet people coming in contact with her forgot about her weight and plainness and were struck by the luminosity in her face when she entered into conversation. People remarked about her incandescent quality, her versatile mind, her sense of beauty, her gift for friendship, and her freedom from convention. Edward Ardizzone, illustrator of many of her books, thought of her as "a comfortable old nannie" and used her as his model for the Old Nurse in *The Old Nurse's Stocking-Basket*. Ardizzone pictured a younger Nellie in the edition of *The Little Bookroom* that he illustrated.

Farjeon was recipient of the first Regina Medal, presented annually since 1959 by the American Catholic Library Association "to an individual whose lifetime dedication to the highest standards of literature for children had made him an exemplar of the words of Walter de la Mare, 'only the rarest kind of best of anything is good enough for the young.'" The committee chose wisely. Farjeon's stories and poems have secured her a permanent place in the literature of childhood and in the hearts of children everywhere.

Selected Bibliography

WORKS OF ELEANOR FARJEON

Fiction

Martin Pippin in the Apple Orchard. With illustrations by C. E. Brock. London: W. Collins Sons, 1921; New York: Frederick A. Stokes, 1922. Rev. ed., with illustrations by Richard Kennedy. Philadelphia: Lippincott, 1961.

Kaleidoscope. London: W. Collins Sons, 1928; New

York: Frederick A. Stokes, 1929. Rev. ed., with illustrations by Edward Ardizzone. New York: H. Z. Walck, 1963.

The Old Nurse's Stocking-Basket. With illustrations by E. H. Whydale. London: University of London Press, 1931; New York: Frederick A. Stokes, 1931. Rev. ed., with illustrations by Edward Ardizzone. New York: H. Z. Walck, 1965.

Jim at the Corner and Other Stories. With illustrations by Irene Mountfort. Oxford: Basil Blackwell, 1934. Retitled *The Old Sailor's Yarn Box*. New York: Frederick A. Stokes, 1934. Republished as *Jim at the Corner*, with illustrations by Edward Ardizzone. London: Oxford University Press, 1958; New York: H. Z. Walck, 1958.

Martin Pippin in the Daisy Field. With illustrations by Isobel and John Morton-Sale. London: Joseph, 1937; New York: Frederick A. Stokes, 1937; New York: Lippincott, 1963.

The Silver Curlew. With illustrations by Ernest H. Shepard. London: Oxford University Press, 1953; New York: Viking, 1954.

The Little Bookroom. With illustrations by Edward Ardizzone. London: Oxford University Press, 1955; New York: H. Z. Walck, 1956.

The Glass Slipper. With illustrations by Ernest H. Shepard. London: Oxford University Press, 1955; New York: Viking, 1956.

Mr. Garden. With illustrations by Jane Paton. London: Hamish Hamilton, 1966; New York: H. Z. Walck, 1966.

Plays

The Glass Slipper, with Herbert Farjeon. With illustrations by Hugh Stevenson. London: A. Wingate, 1946.

The Silver Curlew: A Fairy Tale. With music by Clifton Parker. London: Samuel French, 1953.

Grannie Gray: Children's Plays and Games with Music and Without. With illustrations by Joan Jefferson Farjeon. London: J. M. Dent and Sons, 1939. Reissued, with illustrations by Peggy Fortnum. London: Oxford University Press, 1956.

Verse

Joan's Door. With illustrations by Will Townsend. London: W. Collins Sons, 1926; New York: Frederick A. Stokes, 1927.

Come Christmas. With illustrations by Molly McArthur. London: W. Collins Sons, 1927. Rev. ed., with illustrations by Rachel Field. New York: Frederick A. Stokes, 1928.

Poems for Children. With illustrations by Lucinda Wakefield. Philadelphia: Lippincott, 1951. Reissued Philadelphia: Lippincott, 1984.

Over the Garden Wall. With illustrations by Gwendolen Raverat. London: Faber and Faber, 1933; New York: Frederick A. Stokes, 1933.

The Children's Bells: A Selection of Poems. With illustrations by Peggy Fortnum. Oxford: Basil Blackwell, 1934. Reissued London: Oxford University Press, 1957; New York: H. Z. Walck, 1960.

Sing for Your Supper. With illustrations by Isobel and John Morton-Sale. London: Joseph, 1938; New York: Frederick A. Stokes, 1938.

Cherrystones. With illustrations by Isobel and John Morton-Sale. London: Joseph, 1942; Philadelphia: Lippincott, 1944.

The Mulberry Bush. With illustrations by Isobel and John Morton-Sale. London: Joseph, 1945.

The Starry Floor. With illustrations by Isobel and John Morton-Sale. London: Joseph, 1949.

Silver-sand and Snow. London: Joseph, 1951.

Then There Were Three: Being Cherrystones, The Mulberry Bush, The Starry Floor. With illustrations by Isobel and John Morton-Sale. London: Joseph, 1958; Philadelphia: Lippincott, 1965.

Invitation to a Mouse, and Other Poems. Chosen by Annabel Farjeon. With illustrations by Antony Maitland. London: Pelham Books, 1981.

Other Works

A Nursery in the Nineties. London: Victor Gollancz, 1935. Retitled *Portrait of a Family*. New York: Frederick A. Stokes, 1936. Reissued London: Oxford University Press, 1960.

Edward Thomas: The Last Four Years. Book One of the Memoirs of Eleanor Farjeon. London: Oxford University Press, 1958.

CRITICAL AND BIOGRAPHICAL STUDIES

Blakelock, Denys. "In Search of Elsie Piddock: An Echo of Eleanor Farjeon." *Horn Book* 44: 17–23 (February 1968).

Colwell, Eileen H. *Eleanor Farjeon*. London: Bodley Head, 1961; New York: H. Z. Walck, 1962.

Crouch, Marcus, and Alec Ellis, eds. *Chosen for Children: An Account of the Books Which Have Been Awarded the Library Association Carnegie Medal, 1936–1975*. 3rd ed. London: The Library Association, 1977. (See section on *The Little Bookroom*.)

Farjeon, Annabel. *Morning Has Broken*. London: Julia MacRae Books, 1986.

Greene, Ellin. *Eleanor Farjeon: The Shaping of a Literary Imagination*. Ann Arbor, Michigan: University Microfilms International, 1980. (Doctoral dissertation.)

Hogarth, Grace. "Remembering Eleanor Farjeon." *Signal* 35: 76–81 (May 1981).

Lewis, Naomi. "Introduction" to *A Book for Eleanor Farjeon: A Tribute to Her Life and Work, 1881–1965*. With illustrations by Edward Ardizzone. New York: H. Z. Walck, 1966.

Sayers, Frances Clarke. "Eleanor Farjeon's 'Room with a View.'" *Horn Book* 32: 335–344 (October 1956).

West, Rebecca. "Notes on Novels." *New Statesman*: 257 (21 December 1921).

—ELLIN GREENE

RACHEL LYMAN FIELD

1894–1942

NEW ENGLAND WAS a prime influence on the writing of Rachel Lyman Field, the first woman to win a Newbery Medal. Though Field spent most of her adult working life in New York City, and California claimed her last years, she was a daughter of New England in spirit, if not in fact, and the villages, islands, and history of the region of her childhood and youth left an indelible mark upon her. Versatile—she was the author of plays, poems, short stories, and novels of history and realism as well as an illustrator—and prolific—she produced over thirty books in less than twenty years—Field drew heavily upon the New England of her heritage for subjects, settings, and themes. The area served as the source of inspiration for the best and most enduring of her work.

Field came from a prominent and well-to-do family, whose contributions to American life and letters must early have inspired her with a sense of her roots, of history, and of the continuity of life, all of which are recurring themes in her work. English settlers on her father's side of the family helped to found Hartford, Connecticut; and her great-grandfather David Dudley Field was an eminent Congregational clergyman and historian of Stockbridge, Massachusetts, among whose sons were Cyrus, an engineer who developed the first Atlantic cable, and Stephen, a Supreme Court justice appointed to the bench by Lincoln.

Field was born in New York City on 19 September 1894, the second surviving daughter of a noted surgeon and medical legal expert, Matthew Dickinson Field, and Lucy Atwater Field, also of respected New England origins. After her father died early in 1895, her mother moved with both daughters to the ancestral home in Stockbridge, a locale that was to provide a rich background for many of Field's stories. She carried away happy memories of life in Stockbridge—details of the broad setting, animals, and people were to flesh out her writing and recur as motifs—but her education in the little village school of two teachers and a dozen pupils presented a continuing trial to the energetic and imaginative child. Although intelligent and quick, with a vivacious personality, she was a poor student. She could not read until she was ten, though she was able to write earlier, perhaps a foreshadowing of her later power over the written word. The stories her mother read to her, acting in school plays, drawing, and memorizing poems fostered a love for theater, art, verse, and story that she never lost.

Concerned about her daughter's lack of academic achievement, Field's mother moved to Springfield, Massachusetts, where she enrolled the child in a larger public school. Always behind in schoolwork there, too—especially in science and mathematics—Field despaired of ever receiving her high-school diploma. Her concern was evidently insufficient to motivate her, an admittedly lazy student, to apply herself to subjects she simply found uninteresting. She developed a love for history, however, and excelled in writing compositions and poems, which occupied her to the exclusion of homework in her other subjects. She delighted in experimenting with forms and techniques, openly imitating English and American writers, and often wrote pieces for her schoolmates, who turned them in as their own. She published in the "League," the young-authors' column of *St. Nicholas*, the leading children's magazine of the time. In her senior year she won $20 in a high-school essay contest, an honor considered of some importance. This demonstrated ability to write won her admission to Radcliffe College, where she spent the World War I years as a special student in English literature and composition. During her last two years at Radcliffe she was a member of Professor George Pierce Baker's famous "English 47" dramatic workshop at Harvard, which produced a number of eminent writers, among them Thomas Wolfe, and where her plays won acclaim upon production and were later published. One of them was *Rise Up, Jennie Smith* (1918), which won the Drama League of America prize for a patriotic play in 1918.

After college she moved to New York City, where she lived for years in an apartment on East Tenth Street, summering four months annually off Maine on Sutton Island in the Cranberry Isles, site of Field family vacations. She later wrote: "I suppose that [small wooded island] more than any one other thing in my life, has helped me with my writing. For it means roots and background to me." In New York, among other editorial positions, she worked five years for Famous Players-Lasky, a leading production company of films for the silent screen. She was responsible for abstracting plots of books and plays, a task, she attested, that sharpened her use of language. In her spare time she wrote poetry, plays, and stories, though without publishing success, until editors, who especially liked the portion about the heroine's childhood in a novel she submitted, suggested she write for children, and thus her career was launched. She went freelance and published her first book of poems, *The Pointed People* (1924), and *Six Plays* (1922), both of which derived from her Radcliffe experience. Following this success, she wrote poems, short stories, plays, and novels steadily and in profusion. Some she illustrated herself; others were decorated by such eminent artists of the period as Elizabeth MacKinstry and Dorothy Lathrop.

Field reached the pinnacle of critical acclaim when she received the Newbery Medal in 1930 for *Hitty: Her First Hundred Years* (1929), the autobiography of a wooden doll. After that she also turned to writing for adults, achieving her greatest financial and popular success with her novels, some of

which were serialized in national magazines and made into movies. In 1935 she married Arthur Pederson, a literary agent, and moved to Beverly Hills, California. The couple adopted a daughter, Hannah, for whom Field wrote the poem *Prayer for a Child* (1944). The poem was published after her death in book form, and its tender, expressive illustrations won the Caldecott Award for Elizabeth Orton Jones. In 1938 Field received honorary Litt. D. degrees from the University of Maine and from Colby College. Field died on 15 March 1942 of pneumonia contracted following cancer surgery, at forty-seven and the height of her career.

Field wrote plays and short stories for children. Her interest in theater resulted in about two dozen one-act plays, some of which she wrote while at Radcliffe. The simple, uncomplicated plots are usually in prose, occasionally in rhyme, and generally involve from four to six actors. She also early aroused the interest of critics for her short stories, which, like her plays, blend fantasy and realism, use stock characters and situations, and exhibit a positive outlook toward a world that offers excitement and plenty of miracles.

Hitty, Her First Hundred Years, the book that is generally conceded to be the apex of Field's contribution to literature for the young, features a protagonist who is prim, proper, and strong-minded in the true Yankee tradition. It also provides Field with a sturdy vehicle for showcasing her love and knowledge of American history. Although *Hitty* was an almost instant hit, the vantage point of more than fifty years raises the suspicion that the novel gained much of its attention because of the romantic aspects of the novel's source, a story often alluded to in published material about Field. The story goes that Field and the artist Dorothy Lathrop discovered the prototype Hitty doll in a New York antique shop. They later found that it was gone from the shop, then bought it when it reappeared, later using it as the focus for the novel. This is the shop in which the Hitty of the novel writes her memoirs.

Hitty herself is a memorable literary figure, but what happens to her is conventional and the figures with whom she associates are mostly stock. The book purports to be the written memoirs of Mehitabel, a six-and-one-half-inch wooden doll jointed at shoulders, hips, and ankles. She was fashioned of mountain ash, a traditional protection against witchcraft and other evils, by an Irish peddler for the daughter of Mr. Preble, a Portland ship's captain in the days of sailing ships and stagecoaches. The wood of which she is made protects Hitty well, carrying her with only minor injuries through a hundred years of perilous adventures on land and sea from her native Maine to the South Seas and India, from New Orleans to Philadelphia to New York, and eventually back again to the very farmhouse where she was made, and then to the antique auction by which she arrives in the New York shop where the author saw the real doll and where Hitty sets down her story in Captain Preble's logbook. Hitty has endured theft, loss, and shipwreck; served as heathen idol and artist's model; been companion to Hindu snake charmer and missionary's daughter; sat for a daguerreotype; attended an Adelina Patti concert; and met John Greenleaf Whittier, who writes a poem for her.

Hitty reports her calamity-filled progress through American history and around the world in animated if excessive detail, never straying from the physical or experiential limitations imposed upon her by her wood-and-peg construction. Though her story is essentially serious and filled with far too many episodes, it moves fast and is lightened by occasional touches of humor arising from Hitty's frequent misunderstandings of what is happening in the human world or from taking people's remarks literally, and also from her own stubborn, self-righteous, judgmental comments about things. That Hitty could recall so much so accurately may give readers pause upon reflection, but while in the book, one responds to the action and the appeal of the dignified, durable doll of independent spirit and forgets about the book's implausible aspects.

Field's next novels, *Calico Bush* (1931) and *Hepatica Hawks* (1932), demonstrate richer characterizations and more cohesive plotting. A historical novel of depth and conviction and without a doubt Field's best fiction for the young, *Calico Bush* drew its inspiration from the sketchily-known life of a Frenchwoman who pioneered on Little Cranberry Island in Maine. Twelve-year-old Marguerite Ledoux, called Maggie, a French indentured servant bound out to English settlers, accompanies them in 1743 to Maine, where they take over the coastal claim they have purchased unseen and which they discover to their dismay lies on ground Indians consider sacred. With the Sargents, Maggie endures a bitter winter, short rations, and the constant threat of Indian attack. Undaunted by their scorn of her language, religion, people, and "Frenchified

airs," she serves them faithfully and well, sensibly making the best of an environment hostile to her both physically and psychically, and winning the affection of the children and the respect of the adults. In an exciting conclusion she resourcefully saves the family from possible massacre, then is offered her freedom and the chance to join the French in Canada. By now, however, she has grown fond of the family who need her and opts to remain with them.

Field dramatizes in vivid and just enough detail the dislike of the settlers for the Indians, the friction between English and French, and the hard lives of the settlers, including such disasters as the death of the Sargent baby from burns and such pleasures as a house-raising and a corn-shelling bee. The character of Aunt Hepsa Jordan stands out, the practical, matriarchal old woman, well "past seventy, but smart's a whip," who lives offshore on Sunday Island. Skilled with herbs, loom, and needle, Aunt Hepsa befriends Maggie, offering advice and consolation; introducing her to the calico bush, the hardy sheep laurel that symbolizes survival; and teaching her to make patchworks, which here clearly represent woman's creative and protective instincts. Field overreaches the demands of realism in affording Maggie opportunities to demonstrate virtue, but the girl's experiences are always possible given the circumstances and are never sensationalized. Although the conclusion is not what readers might wish for Maggie, it accords with Maggie's character and suits the customs of the time.

Hepatica Hawks is a slighter effort than *Calico Bush*; it lacks the rich historical setting, but, on the other hand, adolescents can more readily identify with the protagonist's problems. With honest understanding Field capitalizes on the likenesses that underlie human nature, rather than on the differences that come from outward appearance, in telling the sometimes exciting, always perceptive story of Hepatica Hawks, who at fifteen stands six feet four-and-a-quarter inches tall and is isolated from her peers by her size but is increasingly eager for the companionship of youth her age. She and her father, Hallelujah, the "Human Pike's Peak," are members of Joshua Pollock's World Famous Freaks and Fandangoes, a troupe in which Hepatica is a featured singer and dancer. Conveying some sense of the 1890's and of the itinerant life, Field describes Hepatica's relationships with the group, all adults and the only family the girl has ever known, especially midget Titania Tripp, called T. T., a well-drawn character who mothers her. Moral dilemmas confront Hepatica when irresponsible young Tony Quinn joins them to play banjo and drum, but Hepatica meets each situation with characteristic levelheadedness. Field strays into melodrama at the story's conclusion. Hepatica has been singing for asthmatic T. T. One day she is overheard by a musician who recognizes the possibilities of her true, pleasing tones and secures for her an operatic audition, which, though the girl has had but brief training, she implausibly wins, so that she can now look forward to a career in grand opera.

Even if she had never written fiction for the young, Field would have earned for herself a respected place in children's literature for the poetry she wrote for them, which, in fact, has endured far better than her prose. Her earliest ventures into the genre were both random and thematic collections for the young. *Eliza and the Elves* (1926) comprises eighteen short poems about elves and their doings, intermingled with three short stories. Later Field wrote and illustrated endearing books of stocking-stuffer size for very young children—*An Alphabet for Boys and Girls* (1926) and *A Little Book of Days* (1927), the first with poems for each letter of the alphabet and the second with poems for different holidays. Another, *Christmas Time* (1941), contains a dozen poems for that season. *Susanna B. and William C.* (1934) takes a different tack, containing two rollicking, cautionary nonsense verses that recall Hilaire Belloc's spoofs of didactic writing for children.

Charming and entertaining as these topical collections are, Field's three volumes of assorted poems were, and still are, more highly regarded, and rightly so, for here appears her best work for the young: *The Pointed People*, including poems about elves, among others; *Taxis and Toadstools: Verses and Decorations* (1926), with subjects that range from New York City streets and brownstones to the gardens, forests, and shores of her beloved Maine; and *Branches Green* (1934), which contains many poems about nature. (*Poems*, published posthumously in 1957, contains mostly reissues.)

Field writes directly, unaffectedly for the most part, and affectionately toward audience and subject from her own point of view or from that of an intelligent, observant, sensitive, often wondering child, about mostly familiar things: school, the sea, hills, islands, trees, the circus, dogs, music boxes, clocks, merry-go-rounds, and familiar childhood figures like the ice-cream man. Some poems re-create such activities as gathering cattails or berries or going to the toy shop or to the bank, where

> All that I can ever see
> Even when I stand
> On my toes, and stretch and peer,
> Is a man's plump hand.
> ("At the Bank")

Other poems, like "Summer Afternoon," are conversations:

> "Little Anne! Little Anne!
> Where are you going,
> With your sunbonnet on and your basket new?"
> "Up where the berries hang round and blue,
> That's the place I'm going to!"

But only a few tell stories, among them "The Ballad of Spindle-Wood," "The Gypsies," "Years Ago," and "The Green Fiddler."

Many take place in a fanciful world, but most are realistic. Usually they are reflections or observations in a pensive or whimsical mood about particular situations or objects (although a few are quite humorous) and express the speaker's feelings, often employing wistful questions or pithy statements to conclude the meditation or observation: " 'Still, Pretzel Men can *eat* their rings / And this is not the case with kings'!" ("The Pretzel Man").

Personification appears frequently, as it does in "Where?":

> When winter nights are cold and black,
> And the wind walks by
> Like the battered and wild old tramp he is,
> With a whistle and a sigh—

Sensory imagery abounds, as in "Spring Signs":

> Now is the time that hills put on
> A smoky blue, untinged with green,
> When sorrel-red and cinnamon
> In brief possession hold the scene.

Occasionally there is a startlingly eerie effect: "There are things you almost see / In the woods of evening—" ("Almost").

Her tone is literate, but not literary. Field seldom employs allusion, except to folklore, old tales, or the Bible. Rhythms are regular, three or four beats per line, and rhymes exact, arranged in quatrains

238

and couplets. Her poems are mechanical, and seldom does she vary form and rhythm. "Curly Hair" is typical of the meter and structure she prefers:

> She must have curly thoughts, I know;
> Yet she has never told me so.
> But I can guess because her hair
> Just crinkles crisply everywhere.

Sometimes the poems violate the child's point of view or sound like an adult trying to speak like a child—"By day it's a very good girl am I" ("The Quiet Child")—and a few even insult the child's intelligence, as do "I'd Like to Be a Lighthouse" ("I'd like to be a lighthouse / All scrubbed and painted white") and "Skyscrapers":

> Do Skyscrapers ever grow tired
> Of holding themselves up high? . . .
> Do they ever wish they could lie right down
> And never get up at all?

and "Taking Root":

> If I should sit the summer through
> And never move or stir,
> Could I take root on this pasture slope
> With the bay and juniper?

Field's muse occasionally fails her, or her ear does, and she inverts, leaves out words, or even pads in her attempts to make the verse come out right, "Orchard, meadow and garden through" ("The Catbird"), "For, oh, a parrot's bead-bright eyes / Are keen as wizard's and as wise" ("Parrots"), and "I wouldn't be a private car / In sober black, would you?" ("Taxis").

Field's poems are unabashedly romantic, often sentimental, now and then childish rather than childlike; but the best of them stretch the imagination and invite their audience to see more than meets the eye and hear more than comes immediately to ear. Such poems include "Grandmother's Brook," "General Store," "Old Gardener Time," "The Hills," "For a Dog Chasing Fireflies," "Questions for a Flying Squirrel to Answer," "Marooned," and "Something Told the Wild Geese," probably her best-known poem:

> Something told the wild geese
> It was time to go.
> Though the fields lay golden
> Something whispered,—"Snow."

Such poems fine-tune the senses, touch the heart, and stir the intellect. They are just some of Field's poems that still seem fresh and true today and deserve to be read again and again.

Field's miscellaneous publications for the young range from a book of character sketches entitled *People from Dickens* (1935) through *Ave Maria* (1940), an interpretation of the Schubert music decorated with pictures from Walt Disney's *Fantasia* and featuring new lyrics by Field, to the sentimental *All Through the Night* (1940), a stocking-size retelling of the Christmas story. *The White Cat, and Other Old French Fairy Tales* (1928) contains her adaptations of stories from Madame D'Aulnoy, a rather labored product most remarkable for Elizabeth MacKinstry's quill-pen decorations, which evoke very effectively the stilted elegance of the French court. More notable is *American Folk and Fairy Tales* (1929), a representative collection of authentically American tales: Indian legends, Paul Bunyan and southern mountain stories, and tales from Louisiana, as well as stories derived from Joel Chandler Harris, Nathaniel Hawthorne, Washington Irving, and others, with an introduction by Field attesting to the pleasures these old stories can provide.

Though remembered today mostly for her writing, Field was also an illustrator, pursuing throughout her life the interest in art she displayed in childhood. Through her own work and her support of illustrators, Dorothy Lathrop and Elizabeth MacKinstry in particular, Field helped to promote the use of the reed and quill pen and subtle color techniques reminiscent in their effects of the eminent late-nineteenth-century English illustrators Randolph Caldecott and Walter Crane, which became a fad in her time. But as an artist in her own right, Field never rose above the mediocre. She did the pictures for a dozen books of her own and also illustrated the works of such noted writers of the day as Eleanor Farjeon, Sarah Cone Bryant, and Margery Williams Bianco. Though her color pictures have charm, especially those in her miniature books, her delicate and precise silhouettes are more effective. These cutouts from black paper seem more imaginative, expressive, and technically true than her usual rather stiff line drawings and toneless watercolors. Like her color illustrations, the silhouettes depict chubby-cheeked, round-bodied children dressed in smocks and blousy shirts, full of life and innocence, striking poses or playing happily. But Field has endowed them with more spirit than her watercolors; even her silhouette elves and animals are more alive with energy. The silhouettes also project a timeless quality that the clumsy, peasantish sketches and flat color pictures she used more often do not have.

Field was a leading writer for the young in her time, popular with both critics and audience, to whom her air of romanticism and upper-middle-class respectability appealed. Except for her poetry, however, her work is little read today and is mainly interesting as social or literary history. Her strengths lie in the warmth of her style, her obvious affection for audience and subject, her ability to project an optimistic view of the world, her vigorous diction, her artist's eye for generous and colorful detail, and her fluency. There is, nevertheless, a disturbing unevenness and lack of polish about her writing, perhaps the result of that very ease with words that was part of her charm. Perhaps she simply wrote too much, or perhaps she lacked the necessary vision or the essential know-how of the basics of creative writing, or perhaps she simply did not care enough to give her work the attention that would result in greatness; in any case, much of her work now seems clichéd, dated, and shallow. Such themes as loyalty, neighborliness, respect for the aged and authority, perseverance, and making the best of things are easily grasped; characters lack depth; plotting is slipshod—Field asked little of her readers except that they enjoy her stories. That the best of her children's literature—*Calico Bush*, her three books of assorted poems, and her Newbery-winning book, *Hitty*—are still read today indicates that the enjoyment they offer is not limited to one generation of readers.

Selected Bibliography

WORKS OF RACHEL LYMAN FIELD

Six Plays. New York: Charles Scribner's Sons, 1922.

The Pointed People: Verses and Silhouettes. With illustrations by the author. New Haven, Conn.: Yale University Press, 1924.

An Alphabet for Boys and Girls. With illustrations by the author. Garden City, N.Y.: Doubleday, Page, 1926.

Eliza and the Elves. With illustrations by Elizabeth MacKinstry. New York: Macmillan, 1926.

Taxis and Toadstools: Verses and Decorations. With illustrations by the author. Garden City, N.Y.: Doubleday, Page, 1926.

A Little Book of Days. With illustrations by the author. Garden City, N.Y.: Doubleday, Page, 1927.

The White Cat, and Other Old French Fairy Tales. Selected and arranged by Rachel Lyman Field from Madame la comtesse D'Aulnoy. With illustrations by Elizabeth MacKinstry. New York: Macmillan, 1928.

American Folk and Fairy Tales. Selected by Rachel Lyman Field. With illustrations by Margaret Freeman. New York and London: Charles Scribner's Sons, 1929.

Hitty: Her First Hundred Years. With illustrations by Dorothy Lathrop. New York: Macmillan, 1929.

Calico Bush. With illustrations by Allen Lewis. New York: Macmillan, 1931.

Hepatica Hawks. With illustrations by Allen Lewis. New York: Macmillan, 1932.

Branches Green. With illustrations by Dorothy Lathrop. New York: Macmillan, 1934.

Susanna B. and William C. With illustrations by the author. New York: William Morrow, 1934.

People from Dickens: A Presentation of Leading Characters from the Books of Charles Dickens. Arranged by Rachel Lyman Field. With illustrations by Thomas Fogarty. New York and London: Charles Scribner's Sons, 1935.

All Through the Night. With illustrations by the author. New York: Macmillan, 1940.

Ave Maria: An Interpretation from Walt Disney's "Fantasia." Lyrics by Rachel Lyman Field. New York: Random House, 1940.

Christmas Time: Verses and Illustrations. With illustrations by the author. New York: Macmillan, 1941.

Prayer for a Child. With illustrations by Elizabeth Orton Jones. New York: Macmillan, 1944.

Poems. With illustrations by the author. New York: Macmillan, 1957.

CRITICAL AND BIOGRAPHICAL STUDIES

Horn Book. Rachel Field memorial issue (July–August 1942).

Kunitz, Stanley J., and Howard Haycraft. *Junior Book of Authors*. New York: H. W. Wilson, 1951.

Lane, Margaret. "Rachel Field." In *The Hewing Lectures, 1947–1962*, edited by Siri Andrews. Boston: Horn Book, 1963.

McDowell, Margaret B. "Rachel Field." In *Dictionary of Literary Biography: American Novelists, 1910–1945*, vol. 9, edited by James K. Martine. Detroit: Gale Research, 1981.

Meigs, Cornelia. "Rachel Field." In *Notable American Women, 1607–1950*, edited by Edward T. James. Cambridge: Harvard University Press, 1971.

—ALETHEA K. HELBIG

WANDA GÁG

1893–1946

WANDA GÁG WROTE, or translated, and illustrated ten children's books and an autobiography during a period of eighteen years. She was inspired in part by her father's hope that she become an artist; he had said on his deathbed, "What papa couldn't do, Wanda will have to finish." In the American art world Gág attained only a limited reputation for her prints, including lithographs produced from the 1920's to the 1940's. Karl Kup, curator of the New York Public Library print collection, wrote an article about her in 1947 for *American Artist.* Carl Zigrosser, her agent at the Weyhe Galleries in New York City and later curator of prints at the Philadelphia Museum of Art, included her as one of twenty-four print-makers featured in his book *The Artist in America* (1942). Her prints were purchased by major art museums in America and abroad. Had she painted in oils (she applied for a Guggenheim in 1939 to pursue this medium), she might have achieved greater fame.

However, literary critics gave Gág more attention than did art critics, and creating children's books became Gág's primary livelihood, for two world wars and the Great Depression distracted the public from purchasing fine art. Her writing career was so successful that the prominent children's literature journal the *Horn Book* devoted an entire memorial issue to her in 1947.

Three picture books launched in four years redirected her career. Her first book, *Millions of Cats* (1928), is about a lonely man and wife who want a cat; the second, *The Funny Thing* (1929), is about a cat; the second, *The Funny Thing* (1929), is about an "aminal" who eats good children's dolls; and the third, *Snippy and Snappy* (1931), is about two mice children who explore a home and encounter a mousetrap. A picture-narrative alphabet book (*The ABC Bunny*, 1933) and a folktale (*Gone Is Gone*, 1935) followed. Translations of *Grimm's Fairy Tales* then dominated her attention, although an autobiography based on her early diaries (*Growing Pains*, 1940) and a color picture book about an invisible dog (*Nothing at All*, 1941) were also published in this period. Her last book, *More Tales from Grimm* (1947), appeared posthumously (Gág died in 1946 at the age of fifty-three). In her children's books Gág reiterated principles she adhered to—truthfulness and clarity.

Steeped in the German folktale tradition during her childhood, Gág continued to read folktales as an adult. She later instinctively used a folktale pattern in her own stories. Gág probably never read the Danish folklorist Axel Olrik's "Epische Gesetze der Volksdichtung" (Epic Laws of Folk Narrative), which appeared in *Zeitschrift für deutsches Altertum* in 1909. Although not a traditional folktale, *Millions of Cats* conformed to the thirteen rules espoused by Olrik.

The story progresses from calm to excitement and then recedes, supporting Olrik's "Law of Opening and Closing." The lonely adults talk wistfully about the possibility of having a cat. Tumultuous action follows involving their interactions with the cats. A quiet domestic scene forms the conclusion.

Second, Olrik's "Law of Repetition" is apparent in the repetition of phrases:

Cats here, cats there,
Cats and kittens everywhere,
Hundreds of cats,
Thousands of cats,
Millions and billions and trillions of cats.

In addition, the man repeats the action of selecting cat after cat.

Olrik's laws include narration in a simple, straightforward manner, scenes done in tableau, unity, and finally the featuring of a leading character. According to Olrik, if a story includes a man and woman, the former engages in the formal action, but the latter is more sympathetic. The very old man in *Millions of Cats,* encouraged by the very old woman and their loneliness, sets out in search of a cat. Finding it impossible to select just one, he chooses them all. His wife foresees the dilemma in caring for them, so he then asks which one is the prettiest. Ultimately the cats destroy one another; only the humble, scraggly one survives to bring happiness to the elderly couple. In *Millions of Cats,* Gág's characters and episodes adhere to all Olrik's epic rules, forming a "literary folktale."

Millions of Cats began a reputation for the author-illustrator and initiated the picture-book movement in America. Gág's illustrations reflect the clarity of the text. She used her own cats as models. Other details are equally authentic, even the pictures on the interior walls. She incorporated the text, hand lettered by her brother, Howard, into the illustration layout. Furthermore, she designed as a whole each two facing pages of the opened book, termed a "double-page spread." Future American illustrators of children's books continued this innovation. English-language lists of recommended books for young children usually include *Millions of Cats.* However, while Dutch, Danish, Japanese, and Italian editions exist, the book is not universally translated.

Gág's second picture book, *The Funny Thing,* failed to measure up to the reputation of *Millions of Cats.* Her innate sense of the epic laws of folk narrative is inconsistently applied here. The story begins with too long a description of the "beautiful day in the mountains" and ends abruptly with the comment "So of course he ate no more dolls." The author's voice shifts between narration and interjection ("To come for what do you suppose?" and "We have kind old Bobo to thank for that"). There is no preparation for the ominous "aminal," no further references to Bobo's feeding the animals after the introduction, and nothing to indicate that the doll-eating creature would curl himself around the mountain. Lengthy description, loose organization, and limited dramatic action detract from the book. "Thinking" and "planning" are motifs in Gág's children's books, reflecting her own ideals— in *The Funny Thing* Bobo, the "good little man of the mountains," devises a plan to make the naughty "aminal" forget to eat dolls.

Also completed in 1929, her lithograph *The Stone Crusher* depicts a creature that resembles the "funny thing" somewhat in its dinosaurlike appearance. However, the creature of Gág's book lacks the fearsomeness necessary to motivate Bobo's effort to appease him. The depiction of precise facial expressions and individualized objects inside the mountain where Bobo lives increases the tale's plausibility. Gág draws the exact number of ingredients for jum-jills—seven nut cakes, five seed puddings, two cabbage salads, and fifteen little cheeses.

Although *The Funny Thing* received some short-term adulation, its reputation never matched that of *Millions of Cats.* Artist Lynd Ward commented favorably on the "process of integration" between illustrations and text, summarizing, "No other books have quite that feeling of the artistic whole." Less exuberant, Rachel Field referred to its "grotesque charm" and "conscious and mannered" use of the double-page spread. Faber and Faber, the English company that published *Millions of Cats* within a year of its American edition, delayed publication of the English edition of *The Funny Thing* until 1962. Gág's Guggenheim Foundation fellowship application in 1938–1939 excluded mention of *The Funny Thing.*

Gág's third book, *Snippy and Snappy,* the story of mouse parents who smother their two adventurous children with loving attention, is too saccharine and lacks the integrity and clarity of *Millions of Cats.* While the text and illustrations on the double-page spreads reinforce each other, the text itself is not integrated. Although the loss of the knitting ball distresses Mother Mouse, she inconsistently says to the children, "Never mind if it's lost." Also, the mousetrap is not menacing enough to serve as the pivotal object in the story; indeed, there is not even any reference to a mousetrap in the story until the youngsters encounter it. Clarity is lost because the story is too complicated (with flashbacks, for example) and cluttered with detail. There is an excess of artifacts in the house for the mouse children to mistake—a footstool, a mop, and a lamp are all taken for plants. The refrain "We rolled it up, we rolled it down" is used less effectively than the verse repeated in *Millions of Cats.* Though it could have been effective for repetition, the sentence "There's a snip and a snap and a trip and a trap" appears only once. The book has remained a period piece, for the mice seem too naive and the household artifacts too much a part of the 1930's for a contemporary child reader. Gág's first three picture books were compiled in one volume, as *Wanda Gág's Story Book,* in 1932. The only new illustrations she created were for the cover, endpapers, and title page.

She next wrote *The ABC Bunny,* an alphabet picture story. "It occurred to me one day that it might be fun to do an ABC in rhyme with a continuous idea running through it," Gág reminisced in her autobiography about its genesis. She observed the wild rabbits near her rural home, and she settled on "a bunny for my little hero." The result was more like the nineteenth-century model *A Apple Pie* (1886), by Kate Greenaway, than like C. B. Fall's *ABC Book,* published in 1923. The entries in *The ABC Bunny* follow a sequence of events. Except for the frog's talking to the bunny, it could be classified as nonfiction. The familiar words and clear pictures appeal to the young child. The alphabet story begins rhythmically:

> A for Apple, big and red
> B for Bunny, snug a-bed
> C for Crash! D for Dash!
> E for Elsewhere in a flash.

Gág observed and sketched "greens," quail, and squirrels among the flora and fauna of the New Jersey countryside. Even the dragonfly and ladybug were identifiable as individual insects. "K for Kitten, catnip-crazy / L for Lizard—look how lazy" is typical of her rhyme scheme.

While she illustrated her earlier books with pen and ink, Gág made lithographs for the alphabet book. Drawing on zinc plates with a lithographic crayon was exacting work, for no erasures or changes were possible. Not only did Gág lose a month and a half in repeating the work for the lithographs, but the late June and July heat caused the crayons to melt. Gág's brother and sister assisted in the project: Howard hand lettered the text, while Flavia's musical composition for the endpapers added another dimension.

Contemporary reviews of *The ABC Bunny* were favorable. Alice Dalgliesh, in the *Saturday Review,* characterized it as the "first of all the year," while Bertha Mahony Miller in "Fall Procession of Children's Books," *Scribner's Magazine,* concluded that it belonged to "a small group of the nicest alphabet books." Anne Carroll Moore commented in the *New York Herald Tribune* books section, "No animal has suffered more from commercialized treatment in books and toys than the rabbit, and in restoring him to his place in nature Wanda Gág has made a rich contribution to childhood."

Following four successful picture books, Gág made her first foray into another genre, the folktale, with *Gone Is Gone; or, The Study of a Man Who Wanted to Do Housework* (1935). Her choice of subject matter corresponded with her feminist viewpoint that women's work was equal in importance and difficulty to that of men. It was also consistent with the opinions she expressed in her essay "These Modern Women: A Hotbed of Feminists," published anonymously in 1927 in the *Nation.*

Gone Is Gone was based on a tale told to Gág by her grandmother. As an adult, Gág wrote it down from memory. She assumed that this version of a well-known folk theme was German in origin and perused German folktales unsuccessfully to identify it. The straightforward episodes in the plot and the convincing illustrations of interiors and exteriors contribute to the humor. As the subtitle suggests, a farmer, Fritzl, exchanges daily tasks with his wife, Liesi. While Liesi succeeds out in the field with the scythe, Fritzl fails miserably in caring for their child, milking the cow, and cleaning the house. Gág recalled the peasant immigrants living in "Goosetown," an outlying section of her hometown, New Ulm, Minnesota, as illustration models. The results are gentle and humorous drawings rather than caricatures. The tasks attempted by Fritzl in the story were vividly described in both the text and illustrations, for Gág knew such work intimately. The drawings correspond accurately to the text in every detail, right down to "a sprig of parsley over one ear." As a teenager Gág had assisted her mother in domestic chores and the care of her younger siblings. As an adult she was responsible for her own rural residence: she cared for the house, planted and harvested the garden, and dammed up the brook for a swimming pool—all of which became applicable to the story. The truth and clarity of *Gone Is Gone* appealed both then and now to adults as well as to children.

In 1932 Gág's ink illustration of Hansel and Gretel appeared in the *Children's Book Week* section of the *New York Herald Tribune.* From this impetus, she immersed herself in the translation and illustration of the folktales compiled originally by the Brothers Grimm. She consulted English translations of Grimm by Lucy Crane, Mrs. Edward Verrall Lucas, and Fritz Kredel. Close friends fluent in German also assisted her in translating.

Jacob and Wilhelm Grimm collected and edited two volumes of *Kinder- und Hausmärchen* (1812–1815), or *Household Tales,* first published in Berlin. By the 1930's hundreds of English editions were available. Gág selected sixteen folktales for her *Tales from Grimm* (1936), which she "translated freely," as the title page states. Her feminist convictions emerged in the selection of "Hansel and Gretel," "Clever Else," and "Rapunzel." Her dislike for greedy ambition was evident in "The Fisherman and His Wife." In a letter to a fan Gág stated her aim—"to write readable, live, smooth-flowing prose. . . . Most of the translations seem so stilted and unimaginative to me." Of the seven full-page illustrations in the book, Rapunzel letting down her hair was the only one in color, and it was used for both the jacket and the frontispiece. The ink illustrations were effective in their simplicity. The most perceptive review of this volume appeared in the English journal *Junior Bookshelf,* in which the critic noted that Gág superseded earlier translations by capturing the "spirit of Grimm" and that her illustrations expressed "her own innate appreciation of all folktales."

The fact that *Snow White and the Seven Dwarfs* (1938), "freely translated and illustrated by Wanda Gág," was published hot on the heels of the Walt Disney animated movie version of the tale was no accident. The movie, released over the Christmas holidays in 1937, generated a plethora of books based on the film characters from both the Whitman Company and Walt Disney Enterprises. Anne Carroll Moore was a powerful influence in the children's book world during the 1930's and 1940's, as director of work with children at the New York Public Library, book reviewer for the *New York Herald Tribune,* and contributor to the *Horn Book* magazine. Appalled by the liberties that Disney had taken with the folktale, she suggested that Gág produce a "Snow White" that would be faithful to the Grimms' original.

"Snow White" was not included in her *Tales from Grimm,* published two years earlier. In contrast to the Disney film and other books, she retained the Grimm concept of tidy dwarfs who had no distinct personalities and the use of three disguises by the stepmother and three objects to tempt the girl. Gág's edition reads, "Everything was very small inside, but as neat and charming as could be, and very very clean." The stepmother's three costume disguises hang on pegs in her secret chamber. While the Disney version had only one episode in which the stepmother tempts Snow White to accept a treacherous gift, in Gág's edition, a peddler woman offers bodice laces; an old woman offers a comb; and another old woman offers an apple.

In addition, Gág's version kept the controversial episode of the wicked stepmother's eating what she thought was the heart of Snow White: "She had it cooked and ate it, I am sorry to say, with salt and great relish." Although Gág used the phrase "freely translated" on the title page, her version was a purer rendition of the Brothers Grimm than Disney's version.

Librarians lauded the Gág edition. Moreover, the American Library Association selected the book as one of five runners-up for the Caldecott Medal. Gág, for her part, gave a talk about the importance of fairy tales at the New York Public Library in the fall of 1938, and the following spring it was published as "I Like Fairy Tales" in the *Horn Book.* Yet, ironically, *Snow White* was Disney's first feature-length cartoon, and it has remained one of his most popular cartoon films in the almost fifty years since its release. The Disney books have remained available, while the Gág edition, although still in print, has languished. Following Gág's efforts, Maurice Sendak, Trina Schart Hyman, Nancy Ekholm Burkert, Michael Foreman, and others have illustrated *Snow White,* and their efforts have overshadowed her edition.

Growing Pains, excerpts from the diaries she wrote between ages fifteen and twenty-four, was published when Gág was forty-seven years old. In contrast to her short picture books, her autobiography is very long. The young Gág's perceptions were presented in a clear and integrated manner. Her initial purpose was to write a simple account of daily events, but she could not resist elaborating.

In the very first entry, "Monday, Oct. 12, 1908," the fifteen-year-old began, "I sent one of my pictures to the Journal Junior [a newspaper supplement]." She commented on everyday activities, relationships with friends, and her art accomplishments. Her father had died in May of that year, and though she was still young, she contributed to the family economy as well as to the household tasks. Her brother and four sisters ranged from ages one to thirteen, and her mother, increasingly frail, died in 1917, shortly before Wanda won a scholarship to attend the Art Students' League in New York City.

In the 1930's Gág lent her diaries to adult friends, who concurred with her that they would have an appeal to the reading public. Resisting the temptation to rewrite any passages from an adult perspective, Gág allowed the most scrupulously honest and unsophisticated entries to remain next to the more erudite. The diary is a reliable mirror of these early years, a time when Gág integrated art projects into her everyday household tasks and school work. Observations on life in the German immigrant community of New Ulm are recorded side by side with expressions of her yearnings as a budding artist.

While she chose to publish the diary under her own name, she used pseudonyms to protect acquaintances. "Paula," for example, was her future biographer Alma Scott. Adolph Dehn, a fellow art student who later became famous, gave permission to use his real name. Reviewers of both the first printing and the Minnesota Historical Society reprint of 1984 point out the freshness of the text. Philip Dunaway and Mel Evans selected portions for their *Treasury of the World's Great Diaries* (1957). In 1984, reviewer Phebe Hanson wrote in the journal *Minnesota History,* "It is an endearing and inspirational book, often startlingly contemporary in its insights and outlook."

Gág's fifth and last picture book, *Nothing at All,* focuses on an invisible dog who seeks visibility. In this final fantasy picture book, as in her life, Wanda Gág espoused the work ethic. Like Gág, the dog devises a survival strategy instead of succumbing to tears. The invisible dog works hard to accomplish the task of gaining visibility. Only a few folklore epic laws are used. "I'm busy getting dizzy" occurs twelve times as a magic chant. Didacticism intervenes, evident in passages like "Don't cry, little curly-eared dog. We'll be kind to you. We won't ever hit or kick you, or pick you up by your neck or your tail, or with your legs dangling down." When the two visible dogs leave their houses with the two children, the third dog is left behind. Gág's story continues, "But do you think he sat down and cried? Oh no—he had a plan." The little dog arises at sunrise for nine consecutive mornings and, while whirling and twirling and swirling, chants, "I'm busy . . . getting dizzy." The jackdaw bird taught him the incantation from a book of magic and notes, "You are certainly working hard at your magic task." The dog eventually succeeds in achieving visibility so he can play with the other two dogs and the children.

The seemingly simple plot and pictures make use of white space to describe graphically the invisible dog gaining visibility. Unlike the other Gág books, which were illustrated in black and white, *Nothing at All* has color lithographs. The shape of the book is similar to her first three picture books, and her brother, Howard, hand lettered the text, as he had for the other picture books.

Reviewers heralded the book. Warren Chappell, Anne Carroll Moore in *Commonweal,* Anne Thatcher in *Library Journal,* and others complimented the author-artist. Frances Clarke Sayers, who succeeded Anne Carroll Moore as head of children's work at the New York Public Library, commented in a letter, "There could hardly have been a nicer welcome to New York than *Nothing at All.* As a woman just beginning to realize what I've undertaken to do, I find the incantation of 'I'm busy getting dizzy' a very appropriate accompaniment for these first weeks." *Nothing at All* remained in print into its fourth decade.

Of the four separate editions of stories based on Grimm folktales, *Three Gay Tales from Grimm* (1943) proved the least popular. It contains no readily recognizable folktales, and Gág's illustrations are undistinguished. Gág intended to lighten the burden that Americans carried during World War II by selecting humorous tales. However, the book was doomed from the start. Gág attempted to engage the reader, but she did not succeed, primarily because the reader becomes confused by the number of narrative voices. "Three Feathers" includes reference to *"our* Seppli" and ends, "I don't think so," while "Goose Hans" concludes, "Don't you think so?" While *Three Gay Tales* appeared in an era of increasing feminism, a time when American's women were working on behalf of the war effort, "The Clever Wife" struck a discordant note by featuring a seemingly stupid female character. In addition, the war economy necessitated conservation of natural resources, resulting in small printings, poor paper, and inadequate binding. Therefore the illustrations reproduced in the book lacked the clarity of the original; furthermore, the bindings unhinged. These three folktales might have become part of a larger volume, such as *Tales from Grimm,* but *Three Gay Tales* went out of print.

Four years elapsed between the publication of *Three Gay Tales* and *More Tales from Grimm,* published posthumously. Despite poor health, Gág continued translating and illustrating the Grimm folktales, but she died before completing all of the drawings. The foreword explained that some drawings remained unfinished. The volume, intended as a companion volume to *Tales from Grimm,* published eleven years earlier, contained thirty-two tales. "The Shoemaker and the Elves" and "The Wolf and the Seven Little Kids" were among the more familiar. Since then, artist Margot Tomes has illustrated three of the tales, published individually by the original publishing company, Coward McCann. They are *Wanda Gág's Jorinda and Joringel* (1978), *Wanda Gág's The Sorcerer's Apprentice* (1979), and *Wanda Gág's The Six Swans* (1982).

Though Gág's books received adequate attention from the press, she never won the coveted Newbery Medal, given annually by the American Library Association since 1922 for the most distinguished text; nor did she ever receive the Caldecott Medal, for distinguished illustrations, first given in 1938.

Wanda Gág held to a singular purpose—to create art in a truthful and clear manner. Universal ideals—such as the equality of genders, the wisdom of unsophisticated people, and the importance of planning and perseverance—permeated her work. Her memorable children's picture books, Grimm translations, and autobiography all express the same clear ideals. She applied her high artistic standard to each of the books she wrote, illustrated, and translated. She used some epic laws of folktales instinctively, contributing to the clear narratives in her picture books. Of the ten books intended for children and young adults, all but two, *The Funny Thing* and *Three Gay Tales,* were still in print four decades after their initial publication. *Millions of Cats,* predicted by critics on its publication to become a classic, remains the most popular. It appears consistently on lists of significant picture books for the young and milestones in the history of children's literature.

Selected Bibliography

WORKS WRITTEN AND ILLUSTRATED BY WANDA GÁG

Millions of Cats. New York: Coward McCann, 1928; London: Faber and Faber, 1929.

The Funny Thing. New York: Coward McCann, 1929; London: Faber and Faber, 1962.

Snippy and Snappy. New York: Coward McCann, 1931; London: Faber and Faber, 1932.

Wanda Gág's Story Book. New York: Coward McCann, 1932.

The ABC Bunny. New York: Coward McCann, 1933; London: Faber and Faber, 1962.

Gone Is Gone; or, The Story of a Man Who Wanted to Do Housework. New York: Coward McCann, 1935; London: Faber and Faber, 1936.

Tales from Grimm. New York: Coward McCann, 1936; London: Faber and Faber, 1937.

Snow White and the Seven Dwarfs. New York: Coward McCann, 1938; London: Faber and Faber, 1938.

Growing Pains: Diaries and Drawings for the Years 1908–1917. New York: Coward McCann, 1940; St. Paul: Minnesota Historical Society, 1984.

Nothing at All. New York: Coward McCann, 1941; London: Faber and Faber, 1942.

Three Gay Tales from Grimm. New York: Coward McCann, 1943; London: Heinemann, 1946.

More Tales from Grimm. New York: Coward McCann, 1947; London, Faber and Faber, 1962.

CRITICAL AND BIOGRAPHICAL STUDIES

Bader, Barbara. "Wanda Gág." In *American Picture Books from Noah's Ark to The Beast Within.* New York: Macmillan, 1976. Pp. 32–37.

Cameron, Eleanor. "Wanda Gág: Myself and Many Me's." In *The Green and Burning Tree.* Boston: Little, Brown, 1962. Pp. 295–315.

Cox, Richard W. "Wanda Gág: The Bite of the Picture Book" *Minnesota History* 44: 239–254 (Fall 1975).

Dobbs, Rose, Ernestine Evans, Anne Carroll Moore, Alma Scott, Lynd Ward, and Carl Zigrosser. "Tribute to Wanda Gág" *Horn Book* 23/3: 157–207 (May–June 1947).

Gág, Wanda. "I Like Fairy Tales" *Horn Book* 15/2: 75–80 (March–April 1939).

Klammer, Paul W. *Wanda Gág: An Artist of Distinct Individuality.* New Ulm, Minn.: Brown County Historical Society, 1979.

Scott, Alma. *Wanda Gág: The Story of an Artist.* Minneapolis: University of Minnesota Press, 1949.

Zigrosser, Carl. "Wanda Gág." In *The Artist in America: Twenty-four Close-ups of Contemporary Printmakers.* New York: Knopf, 1942. Pp. 33–44.

—KAREN NELSON HOYLE

KENNETH GRAHAME

1859–1932

ALTHOUGH NOW KNOWN principally for *The Wind in the Willows* (1908), Kenneth Grahame, born in Edinburgh, Scotland, on 28 March 1859, began his writing career with a book of essays for adults, *Pagan Papers* (1893). His subsequent collections of short stories, *The Golden Age* (1895) and *Dream Days* (1898), also for adults, nevertheless had an influence on family novels for children written by others. Two picture books for children, *The Reluctant Dragon* (1983) and *Bertie's Escapade* (1949), illustrated by Ernest H. Shepard, were culled from Grahame's works after his death. Both Shepard and Arthur Rackham were among the many famous artists who tried their hands at illustrating Grahame's complex masterpiece, *The Wind in the Willows*.

Like *Alice's Adventures in Wonderland* (1865), *The Wind in the Willows* is one of those classics of children's fiction written for a specific child—Grahame's son, Alastair. But like many other successful writers for children, Grahame was also profoundly inspired by the "child within": his own conscious and unconscious memory and revitalization of the people, the places, and the feelings of childhood. In Grahame's case, places seem to have loomed large, because people proved distant and difficult after the death of his mother when he was five and his subsequent separation from his grieving father.

Immediately after the combined trauma of the birth of a brother, his mother's death from scarlet fever, and his own bout with the same disease, Grahame, his older sister and brother, and the baby went to live in England with their maternal grandmother, Granny Ingles. They were to visit their father only once after that, in 1866–1867, and then the depressed man disappeared to the Continent. If Grahame's prologue to *The Golden Age* is to be taken autobiographically, the Grahame children, like the orphans in these stories, were treated by their guardians—Granny Ingles and various other relatives—"with kindness enough as to the needs of the flesh, but after that with indifference."

Nevertheless, the Mount, the large house in Cookham Dene on the Thames in which the four children first went to live, along with its Berkshire Downs setting, forms the background for the England Grahame projects in *The Wind in the Willows*, an England of "sunshine, running water, woodlands, dusty roads, winter firesides" (as Grahame wrote to his American editor). To this river landscape and to Ratty in *The Wind in the Willows* Grahame transferred his love of "messing about in boats," first developed on the lochs of Scotland. The two semiautobiographical books that preceded *The Wind in the Willows*—*The Golden Age* and *Dream Days*, both groups of stories for adults about a family of five orphaned siblings—reflect the distress of that period along with its joys.

Grahame himself recognized the truly formative effect of this period and place on his consciousness. As he told Constance Smedley, the European representative of the American magazine *Everybody's*, "The part of my brain I used from four till about seven can never have altered." The year in which *The Wind in the Willows* took shape was the year that Grahame returned with his wife and seven-year-old son to live in Cookham Dene once more.

In spite of the attraction of this place and its

special aura in his memory, Grahame took some forty years to effect this return to Cookham Dene. The absence was not of his own choosing. The Grahame children returned from visiting their father to live in a cottage in Cranbourne, rather than the large house, which had become too expensive to maintain. Shortly thereafter, Grahame and his older brother, Willie, who had until then been tutored only sporadically, were sent off to St. Edward's School in Oxford, where Grahame excelled in both studies and athletics and was allowed to roam throughout the city, exploring not only his old friend, the Thames, but also the walled gardens. The latter atypical taste in a schoolboy is documented by his last essay, published posthumously, "Oxford Through a Boy's Eyes" (*Country Life*, 3 December 1932). Even the death of Willie at sixteen could not cast a pall over Grahame's final prize-winning year at St. Edward's.

The first evidence of Grahame's interest in writing comes from his years at St. Edward's (1868–1876), when he made some anonymous contributions to the school newspaper. Unlike many writers for children, Grahame was not noted for early scribbling or storytelling, but there are tales of his solitary rambles as a child, during which he recited memorized verses to the great outdoors. The predilection for solitude seems to have been a lasting trait. Grahame's definitive biographer to date, Peter Green, who pictures Grahame as a man in conflict between conformity to Victorian mores and rejection of them, uses Grahame's essay "The Fellow That Goes Alone" (a 1913 contribution to his old school magazine) as the key to the solitary aspect of his complex character. Another side, however, enjoyed the kind of conviviality best depicted in Dickens' *Pickwick Papers* (1836–1837)—associated with hearty eating and drinking, in wayside pubs or at picnics, among male comrades and casual friends. That type of conviviality resounds throughout *The Wind in the Willows*.

Perhaps fortunately for the world, since it appears that Grahame might not otherwise have taken to writing fiction, Grahame's family would not allow him to continue his education at Oxford after St. Edward's, but against his wishes insisted that he go to London to take the exam for a gentleman clerkship at the Bank of England. The Grahames' Scots-Calvinist tradition was not in scholarship but in commerce. In his early essays and stories Grahame continued to manifest a bitterness expressed as satire against relatives and their lack of understanding of their young charges, as well as against what Grahame interpreted as their miserliness. This bitterness emerges despite Grahame's avowed dedication to the Stoicism of the Roman philosopher and emperor Marcus Aurelius (A.D. 121–180), from whose *Meditations* he often quotes in these same essays.

Grahame's rebelliousness against the edicts of his relatives was evident only in indirect ways. He did go to London, in 1876; he did become a clerk, in 1879, and eventually, at thirty-nine, one of the youngest secretaries of the Bank of England; he joined the London Scottish regiment, drilling in kilts; and he taught athletics at a workingmen's association—all of which contributed to his young solid-citizen image. But although outwardly he acquiesced, Grahame found an intellectual and social life for himself that at times brought him within the bohemian fringe of his society and gave to his writing for adults a sardonic flavor that remains in the background of *The Wind in the Willows*.

It was his habit, early in his London days, to wander through Soho and to eat in small Italian restaurants there. In one of these restaurants he met the charismatic F. J. Furnivall, renowned literary scholar, holding court for a band of young disciples, which Grahame soon joined. Furnivall not only found in him an eager participant in his enthusiasm for sculling on the river, but also involved Grahame in the New Shakespeare Society and similar literary gatherings, thus continuing an education that the young man felt he had left too soon. To Furnivall, Grahame brought his first efforts, poems and fragments of essays written in a bank ledger in a beautiful clerical hand. For the most part, Grahame thereafter followed Furnivall's advice to stick to prose.

Grahame's first biographer, Patrick Chalmers, had available to him this bank ledger, which has since disappeared. Chalmers' biography, although inaccurate in many respects, is still extremely valuable since it contains some of Grahame's writings for adults that were never published or are otherwise available only in back issues of journals. One of these essays is "By a Northern Furrow" (*St. James Gazette*, 26 December 1888), published anonymously. Grahame was then twenty-nine and had clearly been writing for some time, yet since his St. Edward's days he had apparently never submitted anything for publication.

"By a Northern Furrow" is longer and heavier in tone than his essays gathered later in *Pagan*

Papers, but it is stylistically interesting because it highlights the tendency in Grahame's early writing to spin out in complex sentences a loosely controlled association of eclectic ideas in which literary and artistic allusion is heaped upon allusion. These are all based on a single concrete image: in this case a plowed field on the Berkshire Downs in winter. This tendency sometimes makes his prose seem contrived and precious, but it also gives it a richness and density that, purged of most of its affectation, persists in *The Wind in the Willows*, especially in the descriptions of the river. Those literary allusions that persist there are either buried deep in the complex structure or confined to chapter titles.

The practice of moving out from concrete observed details to many speculative lines of thought, which we find in "By a Northern Furrow" and some of Grahame's later works, seems modeled on the centrifugal structure of works like Sir Thomas Browne's *Urn Burial* (1658). Like Browne (a seventeenth-century physician and metaphysician whom he quotes frequently elsewhere, often without citation), Grahame finds nature evocative and symbolic, although he stops short of any religious mysticism and rejects established churches as enforcers of Victorian morality.

Grahame found a helpful mentor in W. E. Henley (author of the popular poem "Invictus") after he submitted an essay to Henley in the fall of 1890. Henley was then editor of the *Scots Observer* (which became the *National Observer* when Henley brought it to London in the early 1890's). Along with Grahame, Henley was able to attract many of Grahame's distinguished contemporaries to his journal, William Butler Yeats, Joseph Conrad, Stephen Crane, and H. G. Wells among them. Henley published the bulk of Grahame's essays, encouraged him in his move to fiction, and urged him to collect his works in book form. He tried unsuccessfully to persuade Grahame to become a full-time writer.

Although conservative in many ways, Henley was a fierce opponent of organized religion, Victorian prudery, and the destructive role of commerce and industry in modern life. He reinforced these tendencies in Grahame's thinking, encouraging him in his expression of discontent not only with the older generation but also with the modern industrial times and what they had to offer. Unlike Henley, however, who embraced an imperialistic activism close to that of Rudyard Kipling, Grahame expressed his brand of discontent in recurring depictions of pastoral escape. Grahame was, moreover, attracted to the aesthetic writings of John Ruskin, Walter Pater, and William Morris (although he shunned any connection with socialism). For a time he was involved with *The Yellow Book*, a brilliant but short-lived journal (1894–1897), edited by Henry Harland and illustrated by Aubrey Beardsley. Several of Grahame's pieces were published in this journal, known for its "art for art's sake" (rather than for morality's sake) philosophy and considered avant-garde and shocking at the time.

The 1890's was a troubled decade. Neither his visions of escape from modern society nor the antiauthoritarian philosophy of his essays was particularly original to Grahame; they were shared by many of his contemporaries, as was a variety of neopaganism that the title of his first gathering of essays, *Pagan Papers*, reflects. In the late nineteenth century there arose a literary cult of Pan, the pagan god who is conceived as half man, half goat. Pan became a symbol both of the division in man between his intellectual and his sensual self and of the lost connection with the natural, animal world in an industrial society.

In two of the *Pagan Papers* essays, "The Lost Centaur" and "Orion," Grahame expresses the longing for this lost connection in strong terms; in another essay, "The Rural Pan," he presents Pan as a benign, storytelling figure still to be found in the countryside and wayside pubs. The version of Pan that depicts the sensual side of Pan as paternally nurturing rather than sexual is peculiar to Grahame. It finds its fullest expression in the chapter "The Piper at the Gates of Dawn" in *The Wind in the Willows*, in which Pan is depicted as savior of the little otter, Portly. Given Grahame's anticlerical history, to look for Christian allegory, as one does in C. S. Lewis' *The Lion, the Witch and the Wardrobe* (1950) and other Narnia books, would be a mistake. Grahame's life and writings give every evidence that he would prefer to proselytize for a pagan god than for the God of his Scots-Calvinist forebears.

The reviews of *Pagan Papers* were mixed; one reviewer dubbed the pieces "Stevensonettes," comparing them to those of Robert Louis Stevenson in *Virginibus Puerisque* (1876) and elsewhere. This was a facile comparison, based primarily on subject matter, for Grahame and Stevenson took quite different rhetorical stands. For instance, both defend a lack of industriousness; but Stevenson proceeds by earnest argument in his essay "On

Idleness," while Grahame, in "Loafing," wittily and sensuously dramatizes a day in the life of a loafer. Mole's observation in the first chapter of *The Wind in the Willows* that one's leisure is enhanced by watching others work repeats a sentiment from this essay. Taken as a whole, Grahame's essays move toward fiction in their dramatic and evocative qualities.

Grahame does, however, owe an unacknowledged debt to Stevenson's essay "Child's Play," which sparked the notion that, in the minds of children, adults appear as mysterious, alien "Olympians." Grahame enlarges upon this idea in his essay "The Olympians." Five stories and "The Olympians," which later became the prologue to *The Golden Age*, form a group at the end of eighteen essays in the first edition of *Pagan Papers*. They were removed in subsequent editions of *Pagan Papers* and scattered among the other stories in *The Golden Age*, most of which Grahame had also first published piecemeal.

Although almost forgotten now except among critics, for Grahame's contemporaries the stories in *The Golden Age* and those later collected in *Dream Days* were the essence of Grahame's genius. Declared "well-nigh too praiseworthy for praise" by Algernon Charles Swinburne and embraced by Teddy Roosevelt and the German Kaiser Wilhelm (so universal was the appeal to a nostalgia for childhood), *The Golden Age* and *Dream Days* met with immediate success, and Maxfield Parrish's illustrations to later editions added to their popularity. Although both books were written for adults and were told from the point of view of an adult looking back on his childhood, the personalities and antics of Edward, Selina, Harold, Charlotte, and the unnamed narrator as a young boy had an influence on the portrayal of families of children in twentieth-century fiction for children, both realistic and fantastic. Edith Nesbit and C. S. Lewis were highly indebted to these short stories, for instance, for their depictions of imaginative children in large families.

Yet the two volumes hardly constitute novels; they have neither development of character over time nor progressive action; conflicts are resolved within a story or not at all. Some stories have plots, but many are vignettes. It is difficult to determine any ordering principle in the books except that each has a clear ending. The last stories in each volume—"Lusisti Satis" (Enough Play), where Edward goes off to boarding school, and "The Man in the Moon," where the three younger children (the narrator, Harold, and Charlotte) gather around a moonlit funeral pyre on which sacrificial toys are laid—reinforce a pervasive concern with the transitoriness of childhood. As the title *The Golden Age* suggests, adulthood is perceived as a progressive loss of an Arcadian, Edenic world.

Grahame's emphasis differs a great deal from Stevenson's; he harks back to a Wordsworthian romanticism of the sort expressed in "Ode: Intimations of Immortality from Recollections of Early Childhood," where Wordsworth portrays growing up as growing away from the vital sources of the imagination. Phyllis Bixler finds that Grahame, like some of his contemporaries, sentimentalizes this view of childhood. While this may be true for much of the direct commentary in these books, it does not seem to be so for his actual portrayal of children. In "The Olympians" he compares the child to Caliban; indeed his children, boys and girls alike, all partake of the nature of the not-so-noble savage in their self-centered pursuit of their own satisfactions. It is not their innocence but their imaginative fervor that Grahame honors in these stories.

Others, like Roger Lancelyn Green, have suggested that Grahame is original in his realistic and sympathetic portrayal of children as creatures neither excessively good nor excessively bad, capable of both mischief and sensitive suffering. To see Grahame as entirely original, one would have to ignore previous depictions of children in adult literature, like Charlotte Brontë's *Jane Eyre* (1847), George Eliot's *Mill on the Floss* (1860), and Dickens' *Great Expectations* (1861), and in children's literature, like Lewis Carroll's *Alice's Adventures in Wonderland* (1865), Louisa May Alcott's *Little Women* (1868), Richard Jefferies' *Wood Magic* (1881) and *Bevis: The Story of a Boy* (1882), and Mark Twain's *The Adventures of Tom Sawyer* (1876) and *Huckleberry Finn* (1885). The difference in Grahame's work seems to lie rather in the serious attention he gives to rendering the details of both their imaginative play, acted out alone or in groups, and their solitary fantasy lives. While writing as an adult narrator for an adult audience, he maintains an unusual empathy with children that lends a double point of view, delicately balancing the childlike and the adult in most of these stories. This empathy with children seems to be why his children come alive and serve as models for children's writers who came after him, like Nesbit and Lewis.

In spite of the fragmentary glimpses we get of these characters, each of the children emerges as an idiosyncratic personality. Edward, the oldest boy, is an insensitive blusterer, bullying the others into playing his games; Selina, the older girl, is outspoken, maternal toward Harold in particular, and surprisingly passionate about British naval history; the narrator enjoys solitary rambles, is intrigued with ideal rooms and cities, and has a special relationship with Charlotte, his younger sister; Harold, the youngest boy, is an escape artist, howls loudly at will, and invents oddly realistic imaginary situations in which he plays "muffin man" or "club man"; Charlotte always plays Tristram when they dramatize Arthurian tales, is given to verbal faux pas, and delivers odd, conflated versions of well-known tales to her dolls.

The addition of Charlotte to a family that would otherwise resemble quite closely the makeup of Grahame's own is a distancing device that warns us not to draw too close an analogy. Peter Green shows that many of the details of these stories are taken not from Grahame's childhood but from his adult experiences. There are other literary sources that remain to be explored, for the study and criticism of *The Golden Age* and *Dream Days* has been sparse.

From *Dream Days* comes the story within a story of "The Reluctant Dragon," in which a young boy, Saint George, and a literary and sociable dragon put on a fake but artistic battle that fools the villagers into accepting the dragon into their social circle. This story, later published as a separate picture book for children, was a model for a number of revisionist dragon stories (like Nesbit's *The Last Dragon*, 1925). One of the important elements of this tale is the ameliorative ending, in which the boy and Saint George escort the dragon, somewhat the worse for drink, home from the victory banquet. The scene is emblematic of the unity of child and adult in a permissive society that Grahame sees as ideal.

In spite of the adversarial position in which children and adults are shown in "The Olympians," Grahame clearly would have it otherwise. Many of the adults (except for relatives) are shown in a sympathetic light, especially men who are gentlemanly and childlike, courteous and empathetic to children, and willing to join in their imaginative games. One part of Grahame, it seems, could not accept the biblical dictum that men must "put away childish things."

"The Reluctant Dragon" was harbinger of Grahame's move into the animal fable. Grahame, like Richard Jefferies, author of the animal story *Wood Magic* and a number of meditations on nature to which Grahame is indebted, was capable of describing landscapes naturalistically, but depicted animals fantastically in children's stories. Although Grahame persistently denied didacticism or allegory in his animal stories, and in the introduction he wrote to P. J. Billinghurst's *A Hundred Fables of Aesop* (1899) makes fun of the anthropomorphic use of animals, his animal stories can be read at many levels, and his animals are as unnaturalistic as they come. The animal tale, which always lends itself to oblique projections of insights into humanity, allows Grahame to endow animal characters with both adult privileges and childlike personalities. This combination, attractive to Grahame, often makes human beings in real life very unattractive and difficult, but it does so in his stories mainly in the extreme case of Toad, who is both very rich and very infantile.

Grahame's first three books were written during the 1890's, a period that can be described as his own golden age. He was rising rapidly in the bank and leading a social life in London's fashionable literary circles. He traveled extensively on the Continent, especially in Italy, and vacationed in Cornwall on the coast or in the river town of Fowey, where he indulged his boating enthusiasm and from which he drew some river incidents for *The Wind in the Willows*. (The Sea Rat's story also benefited much from these travels.) Yet although he was a handsome and eligible bachelor, many described him as boyish and aloof; his name was attached romantically to no one, and his expressed views of women seemed of the romantic but easily disillusioned variety.

The only one of his works that deals centrally with adult human beings, *The Headswoman*, which appeared as a long story in *The Yellow Book* in 1895 (republished in book form, 1899), is interesting in revealing his views of women. It is the satiric story of beautiful Jeanne, hereditary executioner of an imaginary sixteenth-century French town, who is won away from her profession by the local seigneur, whose head she comes close to chopping off. The satire was generally considered by Grahame's contemporaries to be at the expense of the women's rights movement. On closer examination it seems to be a more general satire on the follies of humanity and its bloodthirstiness. Examined at a still deeper level, *The Headswoman* implies that women are powerful and dangerous enforcers of society's dictates, all the more deadly for their attractiveness.

Grahame's writing clearly exalted the bachelor life and easy camaraderie among men even before his marriage to Elspeth Thompson in 1899, which did nothing to change his mind. It was not a good marriage, although it lasted until the end of Grahame's life in July 1932, despite frequent early separations and the tragic death of their son, Alastair, who was killed by a train (by accident or as a suicide) at the age of twenty.

During the early years of Grahame's marriage he wrote very little; shortly before that he had become secretary to the bank, a job partly public relations, partly liaison between the governor and the board. In 1908 he left the bank on the grounds of ill health, a retirement that may not have been entirely voluntary, for he was seen by some as neglecting his job. Meanwhile, however, he had managed to complete *The Wind in the Willows*. This was at the urging of the avowed feminist Constance Smedley, although the book turned out to be an almost exclusively male tale in which fatherhood, not motherhood, is the nurturing force. It was, of course, inspired by his own young son, but when Grahame proclaimed to his editor that the book was "free of problems, clear of the clash of sex," he was obviously willing it to be different from the life he then was experiencing.

This story of three animal friends, Toad, Mole, and Rat, and their gruff protector, Badger, is given a plot largely by Toad's adventures: running away from his ancestral home in a stolen motor car; being imprisoned and escaping; and having, like Ulysses, to make his hard way back and to purge a home that has been invaded by weasels, stoats, and ferrets from the Wild Wood. Nearly all of Toad's odyssey was first written in letters to Alastair, also known as "Mouse," which were preserved by his governess. (They can be read today in *First Whisper of "The Wind in the Willows,"* 1944.) Toad's boyish enthusiasms and hubris are the main attractions for children in the book. Toad, in his venturesome and somewhat delinquent nature, resembles Bertie the pig, hero of *Bertie's Escapade*, a story Grahame wrote for his son's newspaper about a year before he finished *The Wind in the Willows*.

The mock-epic allusions in *The Wind in the Willows* are clear, but Toad's journey is only one ele- ment of the story. It is enveloped in a larger structure that repeats the theme of finding peace at home, for both Mole and Ratty have their own adventures and temptations, and each makes his separate peace with his home. The prime goal is the acquiring of some "felicitous space" (a term taken from Bachelard) that allows for imaginative growth and development.

Degrees and kinds of security and adventure are examined, contrasted, and tested in the process of this search for felicitous space: the woods are too wild, as Mole learns to his horror; the wide world is full of jails, policemen, and nasty bargewomen, as Toad has reason to discover; the adventurous life of the Sea Rat is not the life of a poetic river Rat; underground homes, while totally safe and sometimes cosy, can be stultifying— Mole's is too small and provincial, Badger's ancient and spacious, but conducive to neither learning nor creativity; anthropomorphic dwellings like Tudor Toad Hall are subject to invasion by the rabble. The island in the midst of the Weir, where Pan abides, is unavailable because it is a place of stasis, heavenly but also deathlike. Only the river, with nourishment for both the body and the imagination of those who live along its banks, is given the seal of approval as completely felicitous space in the book as a whole.

Well into the twentieth century, Tolkien's *The Hobbit* (1937) and A. A. Milne's *Winnie-the-Pooh* series (1926–1928) picked up Grahame's cues and depicted in part or in whole a similar vision of the good life. But even by Grahame's time, the rivers of England were already showing signs of industrial pollution, and the country life, free from urban blight, which had never been as idyllic as he described it except for those who had money, was also becoming a thing of the past. Grahame's book is conservative in a number of ways, and recent readers have questioned both its sexism in largely ignoring females and the elitism in its depiction of the clearly lower-class animals who invade Toad Hall. The character of Badger and the force he is willing to exert upon Toad in order to make him conform imply the price both the individual and society must pay in order to maintain law and order and achieve a serene ending with everyone in his proper place.

The Wind in the Willows is, nevertheless, a "good read" for stylistic and cultural reasons, probably better first read to children than started by children on their own and quickly dropped because it is too difficult. Beyond this there are excellent reasons that the book has gone into over a hundred editions and influenced several generations of writers for children. Not only is it richly written and complexly structured, but the value it places on individual development and growth, its depiction of friendship, and its exaltation of nature are all attractive, and they remain so for both child and adult reader.

Grahame's writing seems to have been the major outlet for the tensions that his life in London aroused in him, but once he had completed *The Wind in the Willows* and moved away from the city, he virtually stopped writing, except for a handful of essays and lectures. He did, however, edit *The Cambridge Book of Poetry for Children*, which first appeared in 1916. Moreover, even in the relatively short time he spent as an author, he produced three books of lasting worth. Two of them, *The Golden Age* and *Dream Days*, influenced the family novel for children (and the latter gave material for a picture book, *The Reluctant Dragon*). One of them, *The Wind in the Willows*, became a children's classic. Grahame's personal problems made his country life quite different from the idyllic one of his last book, yet one likes to think that Grahame, in his retirement from the Wide World, experienced at least some of the joys of rural England he gave so generously to his characters and vicariously to his young readers.

Selected Bibliography

WORKS OF KENNETH GRAHAME

Pagan Papers. London: Elkin Mathews and John Lane, 1893. (Published October 1893 but dated 1894.)

The Golden Age. London: John Lane, 1895; Chicago: Stone and Kimball, 1895. Republished, with illustrations by Maxfield Parrish. London: John Lane, 1900. Republished, with illustrations by Ernest H. Shepard. London: John Lane, 1928.

Dream Days. London: John Lane, Bodley Head, 1898. (Published December 1898 but dated 1899.) Republished, with illustrations by Maxfield Parrish. London: John Lane, 1902. Republished, with illustrations by Ernest H. Shepard. London: John Lane, 1930.

The Headswoman. London: John Lane, Bodley Head, 1898.

"Introduction." In *A Hundred Fables of Aesop*, translated by Sir Robert L'Estrange. With illustrations by P. J. Billinghurst. London: John Lane, 1899.

The Wind in the Willows. New York: Charles Scribner's Sons, 1908. Republished, with illustrations by Ernest H. Shepard. New York: Charles Scribner's Sons, 1933. Republished, with illustrations by Arthur Rackham. New York: Limited Editions Club, 1940. Republished, with illustrations by Michael Hague. New York: Holt, Rinehart and Winston: 1980.

The Cambridge Book of Poetry for Children. Edited by Kenneth Grahame. Cambridge: Cambridge University Press, 1916.

The Reluctant Dragon. With illustrations by Ernest H. Shepard. New York: Holiday House, 1938. Republished, with illustrations by Michael Hague. New York: Holt, Rinehart and Winston, 1983.

First Whisper of "The Wind in the Willows." Edited by Elspeth Grahame. London: Methuen, 1944; Philadelphia: Lippincott, 1945.

Bertie's Escapade. With illustrations by Ernest H. Shepard. Philadelphia: Lippincott, 1949.

CRITICAL AND BIOGRAPHICAL STUDIES

Bachelard, Gaston. *The Poetics of Space*, translated by Maria Jolas. New York: Orion Press, 1964.

Berman, Ruth. "Victorian Dragons: The Reluctant Brood" *Children's Literature in Education* 14: 220–233 (Winter 1984).

Bixler (Koppes), Phyllis. "The Child in Pastoral Myth: A Study in Rousseau and Wordsworth, Children's Literature and Literary Fantasy." Unpublished doctoral dissertation. Lawrence. University of Kansas, 1977.

Buckley, Jerome Hamilton. *William Ernest Henley: A Study in the Counter-Decadence of the 'Nineties*. Princeton: Princeton University Press, 1945.

Chalmers, Patrick Reginald. *Kenneth Grahame: Life, Letters, and Unpublished Work*. London: Methuen, 1933. (Includes "Oxford Through a Boy's Eyes" and "By a Northern Furrow.")

Clausen, Christopher. "Home and Away in Children's Literature" *Children's Literature* 10: 141–151 (1982).

Commire, Anne, ed. "Kenneth Grahame." In *Yesterday's Authors of Books for Children*. Detroit: Gale Research, 1977–.

Cripps, Elizabeth. "Kenneth Grahame: Children's Author?" *Children's Literature in Education* 12: 15–23 (Spring 1981).

Graham, Eleanor. *Kenneth Grahame*. London: Bodley Head, 1963.

Green, Peter. *Kenneth Grahame: A Biography*. London: John Murray, 1959; Cleveland and New York: World Publishing, 1959. (Includes "The Fellow That Goes Alone.")

———. *Beyond the Wild Wood: The World of Kenneth Gra-*

hame, Author of "*The Wind in the Willows*." Exeter: Webb and Bower, 1982.

Green, Roger Lancelyn. *Tellers of Tales*. London: Kaye and Ward, 1969.

Jefferies, Richard. *Wood Magic*. London: Cassell, 1881.

Kuznets, Lois R. *Kenneth Grahame*. Twayne English Authors Series. Boston: G. K. Hall, 1987.

———. "Toad Hall Revisited" *Children's Literature* 7: 115–128 (1978).

Philip, Neil. "Kenneth Grahame's *The Wind in the Willows*: A Companionable Vitality." In *Touchstones:*

Reflections on the Best in Children's Literature. West Lafayette, Ind.: CLA Publications, 1985.

Poss, Geraldine. "An Epic in Arcadia: The Pastoral World of *The Wind in the Willows*" *Children's Literature* 4: 80–90 (1974).

Ray, Laura Krugman. "Kenneth Grahame and the Literature of Childhood" *English Literature in Transition* 20: 3–12 (1977).

—LOIS R. KUZNETS

JACOB AND WILHELM GRIMM

1785–1863 and 1786–1859

IN CHILDREN'S LITERATURE the Brothers Grimm are best remembered today for their *Kinder- und Hausmärchen*, a collection of folktales first published in 1812 and translated under such titles as *German Popular Stories* and *Grimms' Household Tales*. Less well known in English-speaking countries are their *Deutsche Sagen* (*German Legends*, 1816–1818); their essays on fairy lore and children's games; and their studies of medieval literature, comparative mythology, linguistics, law, and romantic theory. Yet all of their diverse scholarly pursuits had a bearing on their folktale collection, particularly on their approaches to fieldwork and on their editing of the tales. A closer investigation of this connection may throw some light on the broader intent behind their efforts, as well as on some of the differences in the temperaments and methodologies of the two brothers, who have almost come to be regarded as identical twins.

Jacob and Wilhelm Grimm were born in Hanau, Germany, in 1785 and 1786. They grew up in Steinau, a small town in which their father had accepted a post as a city clerk. The Grimm family had been associated for several generations with the Protestant clergy and the rising middle class, both of which placed a high value on education. When the father died and left his wife with insufficient means to finance the schooling of the two oldest boys, it was considered self-evident that a well-to-do aunt in Kassel should offer her help. Thus in 1878, when Jacob and Wilhelm were thirteen and twelve years old, both of them moved away from home to Kassel to attend the Lyceum

Fridericianum (later called the Friedrichs-Gymnasium), which would prepare them for their university studies.

They graduated from the gymnasium a year apart from each other, and in that order they also entered the University of Marburg: first Jacob, then Wilhelm. Reunited, they shared the same address, yet maintained their separate interests in law and philology respectively. Among the courses they attended jointly was one in Old Germanic law taught by Friedrich Karl von Savigny, whom they deeply admired. Savigny based his theory of the history of law on some of Johann Gottfried von Herder's concepts pertaining to the language, customs, and folkways of the nation. Through Savigny the brothers received their first inspiration for a close study of folklore and old dialects. They were allowed to browse in Savigny's private library, and discovered there the wondrous world of old chronicles, quaint manuscripts, and German medieval epics. Wilhelm, especially, was so fascinated by these texts that he often copied them purely for the pleasure of reading them again in the privacy of his own study.

When Jacob joined Savigny in 1805 for one year as an assistant in a research project at the University of Paris, it was Wilhelm who urged him to look for and make copies of old manuscripts and medieval poems while there. Jacob himself became fascinated by this topic, and later became involved in independent as well as joint projects with his brother.

Both brothers began to collect oral folklore between 1806 and 1813. During this time, they developed their methods of fieldwork recording and pursued their studies of medieval poetry. While Wilhelm translated Old Danish and Old Scottish ballads and tales, adding his own introductions and commentaries, Jacob published his first essay on *Die Meistersinger von Nürnberg* (*The Master Singers of Nuremberg*, 1811). Together they published *Das Hildebrandslied* (*The Song of Hildebrand*, 1812) and *Das Wessobrunner Gebet* (*The Prayer of Wessobrunn*, 1812), two Old German poems that had received little attention in academic circles. Only then did they bring out *Kinder- und Hausmärchen* (1812–1815)—a work that Wilhelm did not think significant enough to mention in his autobiography. It came into being as a by-product of their other studies, not as a work they considered to be of major importance. Thus their first published works were translations, critical essays, and comparative studies, not folktale collections.

Jacob then joined the diplomatic service and traveled to Paris and Vienna. Wilhelm continued his studies at Marburg, with some interruptions due to frail health. In 1816 they both accepted positions as librarians in Kassel, in the hope that the quiet environment at the Library of King Jérôme would be conducive to a more systematic pursuit of their scholarly work. They were not mistaken. Even though their routine job of cataloguing at times became tedious, it provided them with enough leisure to produce additional volumes and enlarged editions of their folktale collection, to publish the two volumes of the *German Legends*, and to study a number of ancient and modern languages.

Jacob established his academic reputation with the publication of *Deutsche Grammatik* (*German Grammar*, 1819), as well as by his translation in 1824 of a voluminous Serbian grammar. Wilhelm established the framework for a comparative study of folklore by publishing a long essay, "About the Fairies," which he attached to his translation of Thomas Crofton Croker's *Fairy Legends and Traditions of the South of Ireland*. Both appeared in Leipzig in 1826 under the title *Irische Elfenmärchen* and introduced German children to the wondrous world of leprechauns, banshees, phookas, and other creatures of the Irish, Welsh, and Scottish folk traditions. In 1829 Wilhelm published his most scholarly work, *Die deutsche Heldensage* (*German Heroic Legends*), a study of Nordic and Germanic epics and poems that also included a close analysis of fragments and variants related to the *Nibelungenlied*

(*Song of the Nibelungs*). It was on the basis of this last work that he received in 1831 an invitation to lecture on medieval literature at the University of Göttingen, where he became a full professor in 1835.

Jacob had already been called to the University of Göttingen in 1830 as a professor of law and linguistics, mainly on the basis of his work on German grammar and his publication of *Deutsche Rechtsaltertümer* (*German Legal Antiquities*, 1828). Both brothers enjoyed their lectures and their work with students. Jacob published *Deutsche Mythologie* (*Teutonic Mythology*, 1835), and Wilhelm made progress in his comparative literature studies as a by-product of his intensive preparation for his lectures. They might have continued their academic career at Göttingen until their retirement had it not been the irony of fate that these most fulfilling years also became the most upsetting ones of their lives.

During the turmoil of political events, in the course of which Napoleon had overrun Kassel and imposed upon Germany the yoke of French occupation, the Brothers Grimm had done their best to keep alive the spirit of German national self-consciousness. They also contributed actively toward a new constitution that would grant the native population some basic human rights. The study of law under Savigny had convinced the brothers that justice was not a dead paragraph in dusty books but a civil right belonging to all. When the new Hanoverian ruler, Ernst August of Cumberland, on 1 November 1837 imposed his authoritarian will by abolishing overnight all constitutional rights, Jacob and Wilhelm were among the seven dissidents at the University of Göttingen who publicly protested this arbitrary action. In an open address to students and professors, Jacob cited the famous words of Martin Luther: "The freedom of Christian man must give us the courage to resist our ruler, if it turns out that he acts contrary to the spirit of God and if he offends human rights." As a result of their stand on behalf of the principles of democracy, all seven dissidents lost their jobs and were exiled from Göttingen and Hanover.

The period that followed was characterized for Jacob and Wilhelm by financial struggles, but also by the renewed love and support of their friends back in Kassel. A new ray of hope came to them in 1840, when, after three years of unemployment, they received a call from Berlin. The king of Prussia himself, Friedrich Wilhelm IV, in recognition of their scholarly achievements, offered them a generous stipend on the condition that they would spend the bulk of their time compiling a German etymological dictionary, occasionally lecturing at the University of Berlin. They continued their work on this project, almost at the expense of all other interests, past their retirement (1848 for Jacob and 1852 for Wilhelm) and until their deaths. The work was slow and painful; even the patient Jacob at times had visions of getting buried under a "blizzard" of papers swirling around in his study. The first volume was published in 1854 under the title *Deutsches Wörterbuch* (German Dictionary); it covered "A–Biermolke." Wilhelm would have preferred to concentrate instead on medieval literature and folklore studies; only reluctantly and with the encouragement of his brother did he contribute his portion of work to the letter "D," and he died before that volume was completed. Jacob published two more volumes, in 1860 and 1862. He died just after he had finished the entry on the word "fruit," a word that many of his friends came to consider symbolic of his lifelong striving. Jacob knew that he would never finish the dictionary. At the age of seventy-five (three years prior to his death), he wrote to his publisher that an estimated twenty-five thousand more pages in his small handwriting would be needed to do justice to the remaining letters of the alphabet—a task he did not think he was destined to perform. Yet he plodded ahead with undiminished determination, realizing, perhaps, that his spirit would motivate linguists in the decades to come to shoulder the burden that he would leave behind. And so it happened, although it took the best German linguists over a century to complete the sixteen-volume work that the Brothers Grimm had begun.

The *Kinder- und Hausmärchen* had their origins in a collaboration proposed by Clemens Brentano, the brother-in-law of Savigny. Together with L. Achim von Arnim, Brentano had published the first German folk-song collection, *Des Knaben Wunderhorn* (*The Boy's Wonderhorn*, 1805–1808). Impressed by the Grimms' interest in old German manuscripts, he asked them to contribute to his collection of songs and tales, and also to look for folktales among the common people. Both brothers realized that the collection of oral folklore would be of considerable help to their studies of language change and development. Dialects especially, in their retention of archaic expressions, might serve as a living source of comparison with the language

in old manuscripts and medieval poetry. Also, folktales contained clues to myths, customs, traditions, and ancient laws that might be utilized for further studies. Mainly to retrieve such documentary evidence, they recorded the tales in loyalty to the oral tradition. Beyond such professional goals, however, they both realized that the oral language itself, more closely tied to the speech of their forefathers, was more simple and more naive but also more concrete and vivid than modern speech. Like Herder, the Grimms believed that the vernacular language and the dialects came closest to the soul of the nation. Retaining the flavor of this speech was not merely a scholarly or folkloristic endeavor but a patriotic task for both of them. Every turn of speech, every variant of a tale became important, revealing the variations of language and of nature itself. Like nature, the folk language was a God-given organic element, worthy of preservation at a time when modern city life and modern literary taste threatened its survival.

As promised, the Grimms forwarded their collected tales and some tale summaries to Brentano in 1810. Since they feared, however, that Brentano might embellish the tales beyond recognition, they prepared a hasty copy of the collection prior to mailing it to Berlin. As it turned out, Brentano put aside the planned project in favor of his own creative writing—and also lost the Grimms' collection. Yet he not only gave his blessing to the Grimms to proceed with the publication of the folktales on their own terms but also sent them a few unchanged tales that he and his friends had collected. Thus, the extra copy of their manuscript, together with Brentano's own collection and a few tales collected by Arnim and the romantic painter Philip Otto Runge, became the basis for the first volume of the *Kinder- und Hausmärchen*, published in 1812. A second volume with additional tales followed in 1815.

The lost manuscript of the Grimms' first folktale collection was rediscovered in the Oelenberg Monastery in 1927 by Joseph Lefftz. Generally referred to as the *Oelenberg Manuscript*, this document gave scholars an opportunity to prove to what degree and how the Grimms edited the tales before committing them to print. The most obvious change was the translation of the recorded tales from numerous dialects into High German with a colloquial touch. Exceptions were Runge's tales "The Juniper Tree" and "The Fisherman and His Wife," which they retained in the Pomeranian Low German version in which they had received them. In the second edition of 1815 and in later editions, they also included a few tales in the Paderborn dialect, as well as in Austrian and Swiss German. (A selection of these appear in the modern Penguin translation, edited by David Luke, in northeast-Lowland Scots and Dublin Irish.)

A less obvious change had to do with the style of the Grimms' folktale collection in general. Wilhelm, especially, imposed on the tales an oral style, which vastly differed from that of the fashionable literary fairy tales while corresponding closely to the more archaic form of German colloquial speech prevalent in the small towns of Hesse. They proceeded carefully, trying hard not to disturb "nature's work." Besides translating dialects into High German, they also completed or fitted together fragments where they would match "organically" and removed needless repetitions, here and there replacing a drawn-out description with more lively dialogue. Whatever they inserted, however, was not so much their own invention as derived from their close observation of speech patterns among children, simple townsfolk, or older people living in rural areas. Jacob himself contributed a tale to this collection, as did some of his better-educated friends who had preserved their love and memory of the vernacular.

The *Oelenberg Manuscript* contained only about one-third of the tales that appeared in *Kinder- und Hausmärchen* in 1812 and 1815. Of the total of sixty-four tales, Wilhelm had collected fifteen, Jacob twenty-seven, and their friends twelve. Five were based on such literary sources as medieval chapbooks, traditional ballads, and German folk songs. The first volume contained such well-known tales as "The Frog Prince," "Brother and Sister," "Aschenputtel" (the German Cinderella story), "Rumpelstiltskin," and "Snow-White," whereas the second volume related tales like "The Goose Girl," "The Raven," "Jack My Hedgehog," "The Clever Tailor," and "The Old Man in the Forest." Each tale was accompanied by detailed notes, some of which took up more space than the tales themselves. Yet rarely did the Grimms indicate the exact names of the storytellers or the time and circumstances of the recordings. Rather, they would search out variants of the tale known to them from other recordings or readings. Often they would also quote related tale motifs in medieval poetry or similar expressions, rhymes, or sayings found in old German epics or chapbooks. In this connection,

they mentioned the *Edda*, the *Nibelungenlied*, and the works of Hans Sachs, Georg Philipp Harsdörffer, and Jacob Frey, along with many others, some from Italy and France. The variant that they selected, however, in each case was the one that came closest to the current German oral tradition. Although the Grimms had a high regard for the universality of folktale themes, as these became evident from a comparison of German tales with those of other countries and collections, they did not think that in terms of style and conception their collection resembled any other one that they knew. Their collection was unique, they claimed, because it came closest to the unadorned oral tradition. Even though their published tales were not identical to those that they had originally recorded, the Grimms were confident that in both tone and spirit they corresponded to the German folk tradition.

The folktales were rich enough in themselves that they needed no fanciful embellishments, said Wilhelm in his preface to the first edition of *Kinder- und Hausmärchen*. Unlike the folktale collections of Giambattista Basile, Giam Francesco Straparola, and Madame D'Aulnoy, or the fairy tales of Johann K. A. Musäus and Ludwig Tieck, the Grimms' collection preserved a simple and naive style that corresponded to the expression of children. Jacob insisted, in a letter to Sir Walter Scott, that it was a serious mistake to compare their editing to that of Musäus, for example, who had left nothing to the natural poetry of the original tales but had imposed upon them his own philosophy and style. In sharing Herder's belief that the "folk soul" of the nation lay embedded in the native languages and folk traditions, the Brothers Grimm thought that folktales, told in dialectal form and in the vernacular, gave evidence of the nation's roots in the past, thus establishing its identity. In that sense, modern colloquial speech, having preserved some archaic patterns, was also believed to share the virtues of the older Germanic languages, especially in regard to their concrete, vivid, direct, and spontaneous expressions. The vernacular, as the Grimms perceived it, was the language of children and the common folk, but it was also the language of the poet among the people addressing the soul of the nation.

After the first edition of the folktales, Wilhelm became entirely responsible for the revisions of the tales. He brought to this job several unique qualifications. First, he was an intent listener, with a good ear for the sound of native speech. Second, he was a keen observer of children and common folk within their natural environment, and he related to both with ease and kindliness. Third, he had acquired a systematic knowledge of various regional dialects, as well as of Old German, Middle High German, and Gothic. He also knew Old French and Old English well enough to recognize related versions of poems, folk rhymes, and tales. Fourth, his scholarly work with old chronicles, manuscripts, and fragments of medieval poetry had given him the experience of distinguishing between older and more modern versions, between what was genuine and what was added in style and content. Many of his publications were entirely concerned with such matters; they certainly prepared the ground for his selection and editing of oral folklore. Finally, he was a translator with the unique gift of transmitting a work not merely correctly or word by word but by sensing its sound, rhythm, mood, and feeling. Such a talent was needed to translate the folktales from oral into printed language without disturbing their inner core.

Jacob, more scientifically than poetically inclined, tried to restrain his brother from using too much intuition in editing the tales. In that sense, he was more like an archaeologist or a modern folklorist for whom every particle must be recorded and labeled, as it might fill a gap in a larger puzzle. Yet Jacob was not a pedant. He too had a feeling for language and thought that pedantry among scholars and poets introduced a detestable artificiality of style. The Old German language was free of such faults, he argued in one of his speeches, and so were the German tales recited by simple folk and children. In principle, then, he agreed with Wilhelm, who, in the preface to the first edition, said that they had rendered the tales just as they had received them, adding: "It is understood that the expressions and individual details stem from us; but also in this regard we have tried to preserve in the tales the manifold variations of nature."

In translating the *Kinder- und Hausmärchen* for the first time into English in the early 1820's, Edgar Taylor omitted most of the notes. In a later translation, Margaret Hunt supplied them again for the benefit of the English reader, without, however, having digested them properly. Instead of taking account of the sources and variants mentioned, she continued to perpetuate in her preface Edgar Taylor's oversimplified notion that the Grimms had recorded the tales from the oral tradition of the peasant folk, exactly as they had heard them. Mod-

ern translators like Ralph Manheim, Lore Segal, Brian Alderson, or David Luke share a more enlightened view of the Grimms' actual sources, even though they may not agree on every point.

More recently, critics began to realize that some of the Grimms' informants had been small-town residents, and some had even received a higher education. They also noticed that the tales were partly of literary origin; those representing the oral tradition were largely limited to the region of Hesse. Upon further research, they were startled to discover French variants among the folktales and some French Huguenot blood among the informants (namely Old Marie, the housekeeper of the Wild family, and the Hassenpflugs). Some of the severest critics of Jacob and Wilhelm Grimm concluded that the brothers had deceived the public. Their tales neither were printed exactly as they had heard them, nor were they truly peasant and simple folk stories. Also, they were not strictly speaking German tales, for their distribution pattern was limited to one region, and some of the informants might have been raised by nurses who read them the tales of Charles Perrault.

With the exception of the last criticism, all the other points can be answered by referring to the notes that the Brothers Grimm supplied to their first volume, as well as to the extended notes that in 1821 they published in a separate volume (volume 3 of the second edition). They never claimed that they had confined themselves to the peasant population in gathering their tales. They mentioned shepherds, miners, villagers, and some town residents. From their neighbors in Kassel, they obtained tales from the three daughters of the Wild family (one of whom, Dorothea, married Wilhelm in 1825), the Wilds' housekeeper, the Hassenpflug family, Frau Jordis, Minchen Schwertzel, and August von Haxthausen. There were also Colonel Engelhard, Inspector Krause, a soldier, a tailor, and an old woman confined to the local hospital. The Grimms identified these sources with meticulous care, although probably not precisely enough for the modern folklorist, and Wilhelm clearly stated in his preface that most of the tales had been obtained from Hesse. They made no claim for a purely German collection in an ethnic sense, but said that they did hope to retrieve the German elements of their native language. To capture the tales as purely as possible meant to capture the spirit of colloquial speech and the tone of natural storytelling.

The language and age of each folktale were overriding determinants in the selection process. Even in the seventh edition of 1857, in which out of a total of 217 tales they acknowledged that forty-nine were based on literary sources, they emphasized that only tales whose plot, theme, and language pattern proved to be intimately related to the oldest folk traditions were included. In the case of the stories based on literary sources, they had found that they were based on variants still alive in the oral folk tradition. Before they adopted them, however, they carefully removed the overlay of literary adornments and inserted common folk expressions. In this way they supplemented and aligned them with the oral variants, of which sometimes only fragments had remained. In the sixth enlarged edition of 1850, Wilhelm wrote: "I have been constantly trying to integrate into the tales proverbs and quaint expressions of the common people. I always listen for these, ready to record them. Here is an example that may also serve as an explanation. If the farmer wants to express his satisfaction, he says: 'I have to praise this more than the green clover,' and in doing so, he chooses the image of the fresh green field of clover." For this example, too, Wilhelm referred to a medieval literary source, although it is understood that such a colloquial expression was current in his time. Essentially, this work resembled a restoration process, quite different from the literary embellishment of folktales practiced by the Grimms' contemporaries. Tales they considered genuine they tried to return to the oral tradition; others that failed to convince them were kept in their notebooks or desk drawers. Occasionally, a modern folktale editor "rediscovers" such discards in the Grimm archives, not realizing, perhaps, that the Grimms considered them unworthy of printing.

The Brothers Grimm dropped some of Perrault's tales in the second and subsequent editions; from each new edition they omitted some tales. Whenever they were able to establish etymological or mythological evidence of the age of a given tale, they retained it, especially when investigations pointed to an origin in the Germanic North. On this basis, they left intact the tale of "Sleeping Beauty," for example, even though Perrault had published a variant of the tale. In the sleeping princess they recognized the archetype of Brynhild, the sleeping Valkyrie of Norse mythology, whom Odin had punished for her defiance. In the hedge of thorns they saw a reflection of the ring of fire surrounding the mountaintop where she lay under her father's spell, and in the spindle they recognized Odin's "sleep thorn." In their view, such correspondences proved that folktales had descended from older myths.

They were quite aware of the fact that Perrault himself had not always been loyal to the folk tradition. Thus they noted: "It appears as if in some cases Perrault first invented stories before they were disseminated among the people. It is said that [his] 'Tom Thumb' was aimed at becoming an imitation of Homer, for the purpose of making it clear to children what a hard lot Odysseus had with Polyphemos." Nevertheless, they expressed their respect for Perrault in the preface to the 1812 edition of the *Kinder- und Hausmärchen*, while setting his style, with all its limitations, above that of Madame d'Aulnoy. In some cases, as in "Little Red Ridinghood" and "Puss in Boots," where they were unable to trace with certainty some older German or Germanic folk-literature source as proof of an established German oral tradition of a variant, they left open the question of whether the German informants had been directly or indirectly influenced by Perrault, be it in the original or in the German translation. Thus, we read the Grimms' rather frank note on "Little Red Ridinghood" (one of the briefest in the entire first volume): "It may give us something to wonder about that we did not find this folktale anywhere besides in our oral tradition, except in Perrault (chaperon rouge), on which Tieck based his dramatic version." This comment shows two things: first, that the Grimms were looking for literary sources to establish the age of the German oral tradition, and second, that where they were unable to find them, they did not stretch the truth.

The Grimms were not obsessed (as were the Nazis a century later) with proving the Nordic origin of all German folk traditions. Yet their etymological and comparative law and literature studies did supply them with ample evidence of a close cultural interrelationship of such countries of the "Germanic North" as the Netherlands, Germany, Denmark, England, Sweden, Norway, and Iceland. In many folktale variants of these countries, they would often detect the *Edda* or the *Sagas* as the common source. In the tale of "The Golden Goose," for example, they suspected the influence of the Norse myth of Loki clinging desperately to the giant eagle, and in the tale of "The Golden Mountain" they perceived the treasure of the Nibelungs and the motif of Sigurd's magic sword.

Jacob valued the scholarly perspective on folktales and did not think the tales were meant for children. Wilhelm, by contrast, discovered in them the poetic language of the common folk and the naive and natural expression of young children. To this language he responded with the love and perception of a romantic poet. Through his prefaces he expressed his ideas about the folktales' imagery and symbols in very human terms: "Plants and stones talk and know how to express feelings and empathy. The blood itself calls out and speaks, and thus, poetry asserts her laws that later speak in parables." Folktales spoke in a language of contrasts that translated all abstract terms into pictures, which children could clearly understand. The forces of good and evil would take shape and come to life. Warm tears of sympathy would restore the eyesight of a blinded prince, and the loving embrace of an innocent girl would transform the fiercest bear or the ugliest monster. The ethics of folktales were educational in the deepest sense of the word. It was not the clever and calculating fellow who would win out in the end but the one who was pure, unselfish, naive, and loving. There was order after chaos, a sense of justice to set right whatever was wrong. Children needed such a reassurance of universal human values.

That Wilhelm's thoughts were dwelling on children we may also gather from an essay entitled "Children, Their Ways and Customs," which he attached to the second edition of *Kinder- und Hausmärchen*. (Wilhelm himself had four children: Jacob, Hermann, Rudolf, and Auguste. The firstborn, Jacob, named after his brother, died in infancy.) In truly romantic terms, he characterized children as "angelic and unspoiled," imaginative, believing, trusting, and faithful. He especially underscored children's capacity for emotional intensity and their absorption in the present, without overlooking their need for order, discipline, and growth. The lore and language of children reflected their characteristic needs and attitudes, said Wilhelm. In citing diverse medieval poems and epics, he tried to show that children have their own way of looking at and dealing with the world. In the second part of the essay he drew on his own collection of oral lore from playgrounds and sidewalk games, citing counting and nursery rhymes, singing games, customs, and children's celebrations. He also referred to other regions of Germany, which may indicate that he used some references from early returns to Jacob's folklore questionnaire, the *Circular-Brief* (*Round Letter*) of 1815–1816.

What had been drafted as a mere plan by Brentano in a letter to Jacob in 1811 became a reality when Jacob composed and printed the *Round Letter* four years later. His personal notes on a printed copy indicate that he mailed out 365 of these letters to "Friends of German Poetry and History" in various regions in Germany, the Netherlands, Austria, and German-speaking Switzerland. He did not keep a record of the returns, but judging by the increased number of notes appearing in the folktale editions after 1815, and also in the *German Legends*, it is likely that he utilized those that appeared to be reliable and accurate. He asked the recipients of the *Round Letter* to visit museums and archives in their vicinity to record tales and legends that appeared in chronicles, epics, or manuscripts. From the oral folk tradition, to be gathered mostly from women, children, and old and simple folk, they were to record verbatim and "without embellishments or changes" whatever fitted the following categories: folk songs, folk rhymes, jokes, anecdotes, customs, rituals, games, superstitions, proverbs, idiomatic expressions, folktales, variants of folktales, regional legends, and also formulas and stock expressions used in the oral tradition.

The Grimms were probably the first in Europe to employ such a methodology for folklore research; it allowed them to collect and compare variants of folktales and legends on a broad scale. Herder originally had conceived the idea of forming an "Institute of German History and Poetry," but his concept remained a plan, like Brentano's.

The *German Legends* appeared in two volumes in 1816, the first dedicated to folklore with a connection to Germanic and German history. In this volume, Jacob and Wilhelm mainly used literary sources, such as medieval poems, chronicles, manuscripts, and older collections, particularly those of Michael Praetorius, J. R. Wyss, and the theologian Nachtigall, who published under the pseudonym of Otmar. Sometimes they changed the style substantially, if they felt that a printed version had lost its folk character by the addition of too many literary adornments. They arranged these legends in chronological order, in keeping with the historical events to which they were related. Beginning with the Germanic tribes in Roman times, they moved on to relate legends about the Goths, Langobards, and Franks. They omitted the legends of the Nibelungs, since these were well known through the epic. They arranged the regional legends thematically, for such creatures as dwarfs, giants, witches, devils, and monsters were difficult to separate by geographical boundaries. Some regional legends that were a distinct part of the culture of a certain locality, or that were bound up with a definite feature in a peculiar landscape, were grouped together within various subsections of the work. Thus, some of the Swiss legends of freedom fighters, some Thuringian tales involving hunters, and some Harz Mountains tales pertaining to Rübezahl were arranged comprehensively and logically. Some of the better-known legends in these two volumes are those of William Tell, Rübezahl, Saint Genofeva, and Lohengrin. The Grimms were all-encompassing in their attempt to collect traditional local and historical tales related to Germany and German-speaking areas of Europe. Their notes alone make fascinating reading for folklorists, philologists, and interested adults. Yet the episodic character of many of the tales and the sketchy style in which the Grimms recorded them do not make this work easily accessible to children. Perhaps Donald Ward's apt first English translation of the work will stimulate some writers to publish selected legends in children's book versions.

"The legend creates itself in history," Jacob once said. And yet the Brothers Grimm did not believe that history was identical with legends or that legends accurately retold history. What legends did reveal was the spirit of a given time and a given culture. They were less free than folktales and less swift, said Wilhelm: "The folktale flies, yet the legend walks slowly." The plots were episodic, sometimes altogether absent. On the other hand, legends often transmitted a feeling for time and place that was unmatched by any other folklore genre. For that reason, the Grimms hoped their book of legends would bring into focus the splintered and half-forgotten heritage of the German people.

As individuals, Jacob and Wilhelm differed substantially in their attitudes toward folklore, language, and children. In many respects, however, their temperaments and their scholarly approaches complemented each other ideally. As Jacob brought to their work an analytical mind, patience, and a scientific methodology, Wilhelm added to it his feeling for the oral style, his sense of poetry and music, and his love of children. With only a few short interruptions, they lived together under one roof as children, as students, as librarians, as professors, and as researchers, even after Wilhelm got married. As brothers and as scholars, they respected each other in their own unique ways, however, and also kept their own separate offices at home. They were different, but they had more in common. Both were made honorary members of the Philological Society in London in 1846, and to this day in Europe, they are recognized as the founders of German and comparative philology as an academic discipline.

One of their greatest contributions to children's literature was that their publications stimulated other collectors around the world to search out their own native folk heritages. In his preface to the seventh edition of *Kinder- und Hausmärchen* in 1857, Wilhelm pointed with pride to a list of about two hundred folktale collections in many lands that had followed their example. There were flaws in the Grimms' theories and methodologies; their approaches were not always consistent; yet their merit is that they returned to the mainstream of literature what rightfully belonged to children and the common folk.

Selected Bibliography

WORKS OF JACOB AND WILHELM GRIMM

Editions of Kinder- und Hausmärchen

Kinder- und Hausmärchen. Berlin: Reimer, 1812. Subsequent editions were issued as follows: 2nd ed. vol. 1, 1815; vol. 2, 1819; vol. 3, 1821 (consisting of notes). 3rd ed., 1837; 4th ed., 1840; 5th ed., 1843; 6th ed., 1850; 7th ed., 1857. (Twenty-one editions of this work had appeared by 1881. *Kleine Ausgabe*, a short edition inspired by J. Edgar Taylor's English translation and including some illustrations by George Cruikshank, was published in Berlin in 1825 and came out in thirty-six editions before 1887.)

Kinder- und Hausmärchen der Brüder Grimm. Vollständige Ausgabe in der Urfassung. Edited by Friedrich Panzer. Wiesbaden: Emil Vollmer Verlag, 1975. (The text is based on the original edition of the collection and includes some tales in dialect.)

Grimms Kinder- und Hausmärchen. Edited by Heinz Rölleke. 2 vols. Cologne: Diederichs Verlag, 1982; Stuttgart: Reclam, 1984.

Other Works

Anmerkungen zu den Kinder- und Hausmärchen der Brüder Grimm. Edited by Johannes Bolte and Georg Polívka. 5 vols. Leipzig: Diederichs Verlag, 1913–1932. Rev. ed. Munich: Georg Olm, 1963. (A compilation of the Grimms' notes.)

Deutsche Sagen. Edited by Richard Dorson. 2 vols. New

York: Arno Press, 1977. (A reprint of the 1891 edition.)

Translations

The Brothers Grimm: Popular Folktales. Translated and with an introduction by Brian Alderson. With illustrations by Michael Foreman. New York: Doubleday, 1978.

The Complete Grimms' Fairy Tales. Translated by Margaret Hunt. Revised, corrected, and completed by James Stern. With an introduction by Padraic Colum and an essay by Joseph Campbell. With illustrations by Josef Scharl. New York: Pantheon, 1975. (A reissue of the 1944 edition.)

Folktales of Germany. Edited by Kurt Ranke. Translated by Lotte Baumann. With a foreword by Richard Dorson. Chicago: University of Chicago Press, 1966.

The German Legends of the Brothers Grimm. Translated by Donald Ward. 2 vols. Philadelphia: Institute for the Study of Human Issues, 1981.

Grimms' Tales for Young and Old: The Complete Stories. Translated by Ralph Manheim. Garden City, N.Y.: Doubleday, 1977; Doubleday/Anchor, 1983.

Household Stories from the Collection of the Brothers Grimm. Translated by Lucy Crane. With illustrations by Walter Crane. New York: Dover, 1963. (A reissue of the 1886 Macmillan edition.)

Jacob and Wilhelm Grimm: Selected Tales. Translated and with an introduction and notes by David Luke. New York: Penguin, 1983.

The Juniper Tree, and Other Tales from Grimm. Translated by Lore Segal, with four tales translated by Randall Jarrell. Selected by Lore Segal and Maurice Sendak. With illustrations by Maurice Sendak. New York: Farrar, Straus and Giroux, 1973.

The Complete Fairy Tales of the Brothers Grimm. Translated and with an introduction by Jack Zipes. With illustrations by John B. Gruelle. New York: Bantom Books, 1987.

CRITICAL AND BIOGRAPHICAL STUDIES

Bettelheim, Bruno. *The Uses of Enchantment: The Meaning and Importance of Fairy Tales*. New York: Vintage, 1977.

David, A. and M. E. David. "A Literary Approach to the Brothers Grimm" *Journal of the Folklore Institute* 1:5 (1964).

Denecke, Ludwig. *Jakob Grimm und sein Brüder Wilhelm*. Stuttgart: J. B. Metzler, 1971.

Ellis, John M. *One Fairy Story Too Many: The Brothers*

Grimm and Their Tales. Chicago: University of Chicago Press, 1983.

Gerstl, Quirin. *Die Brüder Grimm als Erzieher: Pädagogische Analyse des Märchens*. Munich: Ehrenwirt Verlag, 1964.

Gerstner, Hermann. *Die Brüder Grimm: Biographie mit 48 Bildern*. Gerabronn and Crailsheim: Hohenloher Verlag, 1970.

Gürtler, Hans, and Albert Leitzmann, eds. *Briefe der Brüder Grimm*. Jena: Verlag der Fromannschen Buchhandlung, Walter Biedermann, 1923.

Kamenetsky, Christa. "The Brothers Grimm: Folktale Style and Romantic Theories" *Elementary English* 51:3 (1974).

Lüthi, Max. *Once Upon a Time: On the Nature of Fairy Tales*. Translated by Lee Chadeayne and Paul Gottwald, with additions by the author. Introduction and reference notes by Francis Lee Utley. Bloomington: Indiana University Press, 1976.

————. *Märchen*. Stuttgart: J. B. Metzlersche Verlagsbuchhandlung, 1976.

Leyen, Friedrich von der. *Das deutsche Märchen und die Brüder Grimm*. Düsseldorf: Diederichs Verlag, 1964. (Part of the series *Die Märchen der Weltliteratur*.)

Michaelis-Jena, Ruth. *The Brothers Grimm*. New York: Praeger, 1970; London: Routledge and Kegan Paul, 1970.

Peppard, Murray B. *Paths Through the Forest: A Biography of the Brothers Grimm*. New York: Holt, Rinehart and Winston, 1971.

Pfeiffer, Franz and Karl Bartsch. *Briefwechsel: Mit unveröffentlichten Briefen der Gebrüder Grimm und weiterer Dokumenten zur Wissenschaftsgeschichte des 19. Jahrhunderts*. Edited by Hans-Joachim Koppitz. Cologne: Greven-Verlag, 1969.

Rölleke, Heinz, ed. *Die älteste Märchensammlung der Brüder Grimm*. Cologne: Fondation Martin Bodmer, 1975.

Schoof, Wilhelm. *Zur Entstehungsgeschichte der Grimmschen Märchen*. Hamburg: Hauswedell, 1959.

Steig, Reinhold. *Clemens Brentano und die Brüder Grimm*. Stuttgart: Cotta, 1914.

Thompson, Stith. *The Folktale*. Bloomington: Indiana University Press, 1946; New York: Dryden, 1951.

Zipes, Jack. *The Trials and Tribulations of Little Red Riding Hood*. South Hadley, Mass.: J. F. Bergin, 1983.

Zuckmayer, Carl. *Die Brüder Grimm: Ein deutscher Beitrag zur Humanität*. Frankfurt am Main: Suhrkam, 1948.

—CHRISTA KAMENETSKY

LUCRETIA P. HALE

1820–1900

LUCRETIA PEABODY HALE, chiefly remembered as the author of *The Peterkin Papers* (1880), was born in Boston, Massachusetts, in 1820 and died there in 1900. Her father, Nathan Hale, a nephew of the Revolutionary patriot, was a journalist; he purchased the *Boston Daily Advertiser* and was instrumental in establishing editorial commentaries in newspapers. Along with a sister and two brothers, Lucretia was one of the older Hale children, who called themselves "we four" to distinguish themselves from the younger children, dubbed "the little ones." One of the four older children, Edward Everett Hale, became a Unitarian clergyman and is remembered as the author of *The Man Without a Country.* Journalism, writing, and editing became part of the home activities of the older Hale children, and they produced two family newspapers, the *New England Herald* and the *Public Informer,* the latter published by Lucretia and Edward Everett Hale.

After attending a dame school, Lucretia was taught by Elizabeth Peabody, who held advanced ideas about education, and finally went to George B. Emerson's School for Young Ladies. It was a fashionable school, yet George Emerson believed that girls were as capable of learning as boys, and the graduates of his school were said to have attained the equivalent of a Bachelor of Arts degree. At Miss Peabody's school Lucretia met Margaret Harding, who later became the mother of Eliza Orne White, a writer of stories for children. The two girls played frequently on the Beacon Street Mall of the Boston Common in order to avoid the cows grazing lower down. At Emerson's School for Young Ladies, Lucretia became friendly with Susan Lyman of Northampton, who later married Peter Lesley and went to live in Philadelphia. Lucretia, Margaret, and Susan remained lifelong friends.

Like *Alice in Wonderland, Treasure Island*, and *The Tale of Peter Rabbit*, the Peterkin stories owed their genesis to a particular relationship between author and child. In 1861, while Lucretia was visiting the Lesleys in Princeton, Massachusetts, she entertained young Maggie Lesley, who was ill at the time, with the story of a lady who put salt in her coffee. Meggie's mother was obviously the Lady from Philadelphia, and the Peterkins got their name from the first name of Meggie's father, Peter.

Except for a voyage to Egypt, where her younger brother Charles was American consul general, Hale spent most of her life in Boston and New England, writing for newspapers and magazines, preparing Sunday school and supplementary school textbooks, and editing books of games and needlework. In 1874 she became a member of the School Committee of the City of Boston, on which she served as chairman of the Kindergarten Committee and as a member of the Textbook and Sewing Committee.

Never marrying, Hale remained closely associated with her family for the rest of her life, especially with her brother Edward Everett, and she retained an interest in such educational ventures as vacation schools, kindergartens, cooking schools, and settlement houses. Because of her wit, her contributions to the discussions and conversations of popular study groups and a Sunday-night club were highly prized.

From the time Hale invented her first story to entertain a sick little girl, *The Peterkin Papers* grew by accretion over a number of years. In 1868 "The Lady Who Put Salt in Her Coffee" and five other Peterkin stories were published in *Our Young Folks*; after 1872, when the magazine was sold to Scribners and transformed into *St. Nicholas*, Hale contributed Peterkin narratives sporadically over the following nine years. In 1880 she sent her earlier stories to the James R. Osgood Company for publication as *The Peterkin Papers*, and thus they later became the property of the Houghton Mifflin Company, which succeeded Osgood. In 1883 she completed another collection, *The Last of the Peterkins*, which was published in 1886 by Roberts Brothers. Mr. Niles of that company had originally asked for the first series of Peterkin stories and had been refused, but following her brother's advice Lucretia sent the later collection to Roberts Brothers, which was later absorbed by Little, Brown and Company. As if to accomplish an act of literary integration, in 1960 Houghton Mifflin was able to publish *The Complete Peterkin Papers* with the original illustrations and with an introduction by Nancy Hale, the granddaughter of Edward Everett Hale.

Despite the occasional nature of the production of these stories, seen in the aggregate they are remarkably unified. First, their tone is consistent. For they were tossed off as nonsense stories—to entertain old and young—and they are in fact a series of preposterous episodic adventures. The Peterkins at home and the Peterkins abroad can never cope in a practical or sensible way with the daily mishaps of life. What to do when snowed in, what to do when the dumbwaiter gets stuck, how to cope with moving or with securing enough china for a tea party —these problems are always beyond their power. On this level, the stories capture the Victorian love of nonsense—of reductio ad absurdum—and recall the comparable literary excursions of Edward Lear and Lewis Carroll.

But the stories are also held together by structural unity—one might say by a series of structural unities. Despite the fact that they were produced during different periods of Hale's life, they hang together as the experiences of one family: father, mother, older children, and younger ones, each with his or her own idiosyncrasies. Agamemnon had gone to college at one time and continues throughout his life to rely on such academic paraphernalia as encyclopedias and stray information, while Mrs. Peterkin and Elizabeth Eliza are always indecisive and apprehensive about the least possibility of a domestic mishap. Virtually all we see of the little boys is their ebullient spirit and the fact that they constantly wear rubber boots. The wise Lady from Philadelphia always supplies simple and sane solutions for the agonies of a family that is quietly refined and zany at the same time. She is the *dea ex machina* who untangles the unbelievable snarls, domestic and otherwise, caused by their ineptitude.

Moreover, for each Peterkin volume Lucretia wrote a preface revealing her command of the material that had accrued through the years. In the preface to the first edition she wrote "How the Peterkins Came to Publish Their Adventures," in which the family discusses how to explain to the world what happened to them. At first, "Mrs. Peterkin shrank from this; it would make the whole matter more public than ever." Then the family remembers some of the events that could become subjects for chapters, such as the Fourth of July explosion or the day "when there was no fire, but the engines insisted on coming." In the end they consult the Lady from Philadelphia, who answers, "Yes, of course; publish them."

Similarly, in the preface to *The Last of the Peterkins*, Lucretia effectively disposes of the whole family, very much as Cervantes put an end to the adventures of Don Quixote:

It is feared that Mr. and Mrs. Peterkin lost their lives after leaving Tobolsk, perhaps in some vast conflagration.

Agamemnon and Solomon John were probably sacrificed in some effort to join in or control the disturbances which arose in the distant places where they had established themselves,—Agamemnon in Madagascar, Solomon John in Rustchuk.

The little boys have merged into men in some German university, while Elizabeth Eliza must have been lost in the mazes of the Russian language.

Thus, to the end, Lucretia Hale wrote about the Peterkins tongue in cheek and at the same time retained control of her narrative.

It is interesting to compare her extended narrative control in both sets of Peterkin Papers with the narrative devices in some of her other stories. *The Last of the Peterkins* is accompanied by the subtitle *With Others of Their Kin*, and five unrelated stories and a poem fill out the volume. Consider only three of these narratives. "Lucilla's Diary" is about a wife who keeps a diary while awaiting her husband's return from Texas instead of writing him frequent letters; thus it is only on his return home that he learns that their house has burned down. "Jedidiah's Noah's Ark" tells of a set of toys coming to life, and "Carrie's Three Wishes" is a version of the famous folktale of the old couple who wish—with unfortunate consequences—for a black pudding. The poem—"The First Needle"—explains how a male invention led to female enslavement. Clever, humorous selections suggesting a kind of family kinship with Edward Everett Hale's short story "My Double and How He Undid Me," these narratives demonstrate the kind of anecdotal storytelling material that appealed to Lucretia Hale.

Ultimately, Hale's narrative art was rendered effective by her simple, unassuming, but uncannily witty style. Besides the bizarre adventures and the collection of characters reminiscent of the simpletons and noodleheads of folktales, she could turn out neat, unassuming phrases to convey the absurdly illogical humor engendered by a particular situation. Consider this sample of nonsensical dialogue from "The Peterkins' Journey Again Postponed" (like any other activity the Peterkins undertake, a proposed journey always leads them to further heart-searchings and indecisions):

"Benjamin Franklin came from Philadelphia, or else he went to it," said Agamemnon.

"Oh, yes, I know all about him," said Solomon John; "he made paint-brushes of his cat's tail!"

"Oh, no, that was another Benjamin, I am pretty sure," said Agamemnon.

"I don't know about that," said Solomon John; "but he became a famous artist, and painted the king and queen of England."

"You must have mixed up the Benjamins," said Agamemnon. "I will go and borrow an encyclopedia, and look them out."

"And we will make paint-brushes out of Elizabeth Eliza's cat," exclaimed the little boys; "and we will become famous, and paint the king and queen of England."

"You must not use the whole cat," said Solomon John; "and there is no king of England now."

"And I cannot spare her tail," cried Elizabeth Eliza, starting up in agony for her cat.

"It is only Philadelphia cats that are used for paint-brushes," said Mr. Peterkin.

Except for Mrs. Peterkin, the whole family becomes involved in a farfetched conversation in which the simplicity of the language is used both to hide and to reveal the Peterkins' comical combination of pedantry and naiveté.

Attempts have been made to attribute a serious, albeit satirical, purpose to *The Peterkin Papers*. In her excellent introduction to *The Complete Peterkin Papers*, Nancy Hale says that she detects in them a presentation of the "ludicrous side of Victorian family life," but she admits that "exasperation with the family confines . . . issued forth in a burst of laughter—in the Peterkins." Van Wyck Brooks went further in finding an ideological basis for *The Peterkin Papers*. In *New England Indian Summer, 1865–1915*, he wrote:

> This book was an amicable satire on the well-known culture that was everywhere associated with the name of Boston, and the Peterkins suggested the literary families that also abounded in Boston and its learned suburbs. They might have been drawn from the Alcotts, the Howes, or the Hales.

He further comments that the activities and concepts of the Peterkins "could only have been possible in a world that had known Elizabeth Peabody and the candours of transcendental Concord."

Such commentaries make clear the pragmatic world in which the Peterkins actually lived—a world of horse-drawn vehicles and trips to Boston. At the same time, the telegraph, telephone, locomotive, and fire engine are not ignored, and one is also made conscious of the Centennial celebration in Philadelphia. Interwoven in the stories are strands of such realistic detail, and there are occasional touches of satire as well. For example, "The Educational Breakfast," an alphabetical bill of fare starting with applesauce and ending with zest, touches slyly on the didactic idealism of nineteenth-century New Englanders. The story meanders away from its first theme to recount how Elizabeth Eliza is rendered immobile when the edge of her dress is caught in a locked trunk. By and large, the narratives subsist as extravaganzas intended to elicit laughter.

Selected Bibliography

WORKS OF LUCRETIA P. HALE

The Peterkin Papers. Boston: J. R. Osgood, 1880. Republished with illustrations by Harold Brett. Boston: Houghton Mifflin, 1924.

The Last of the Peterkins: With Others of Their Kin. Boston: Roberts Brothers, 1886; Boston: Little, Brown, 1929.

The Complete Peterkin Papers. With an introduction by Nancy Hale and with the original illustrations. Boston: Houghton Mifflin, 1960.

CRITICAL AND BIOGRAPHICAL STUDIES

Brooks, Van Wyck. *New England Indian Summer, 1865–1915*. New York: Dutton, 1940.

Hale, Edward Everett. *A New England Boyhood*. With a new introduction by Nancy Hale. Boston: Little, Brown, 1964.

Hale, Edward Everett, Jr. *The Life and Letters of Edward Everett Hale*. 2 vols. Boston: Little, Brown, 1917.

Wankmiller, Madelyn Clush. "Lucretia P. Hale and *The Peterkin Papers*" *Horn Book* 34: 95–103, 139–147 (April 1958).

White, Eliza Orne. "Lucretia P. Hale: The Author of *The Peterkin Papers*" *Horn Book* 16: 311–322 (Sept.–Oct. 1940).

—PAUL HEINS

JOEL CHANDLER HARRIS

1848-1908

AN ODD THOUGHT indeed: that white America should become caretaker of the insurrectionist tales of black folk—become their owner and interpreter. And yet we still await the emancipation of the Black Rabbit. Shackled inside an exaggerated slave pidgin and idyllic images of the plantation, he sits hostage in the "big house," kept under guard by Joel Chandler Harris cum "Uncle Remus."

Remus "arrived" with the publication of Harris' first collection of African-American folk materials, *Uncle Remus: His Songs and His Sayings* (1880). A beaming, venerable old darky with "nothing but pleasant memories of the discipline of slavery," Remus came to the rescue of an American imagination stifled with the burden of a national misdeed. For if they would only believe in him, they would have everlasting peace of mind. The cruelties of a slave system—documented and detailed in the published and widely distributed narratives of former captives (who were anything but grateful for the undiciplined thievery of an entire people)—could be forgiven. Remus' white-"toofed" grin was a baptism. America shrugged off its guilt and began to wonder just how horrible a system could be if it produced such lively entertainment. The popular success of *Uncle Remus* was no flash in the pan. Harris had struck a gold mine of psychical need— in the South, where the newly crafted door to self-determination for blacks was being busily unhinged, and in the North, where Jim Crow had migrated aboard the Freedom Train to greet an influx of newly hopeful black folk and oversee de facto segregation and discrimination in the "free states."

What the American journalist Harry Stilwell Edwards foresaw in his gentle plantation tableau (quoted above) was a future in which whites would sort and dispense the remains of the black imagination. Despite the periodic attempts by black artists to reclaim their heritage of resistance, Brer Rabbit and Uncle Remus have remained incompatible yet inseparable companions. *Uncle Remus: His Songs and His Sayings* and the entire Remus saga has become, as much as folklore, a study of the psychological battle of Joel Chandler Harris.

There has been considerable interest in and speculation on the nature and character of both the figure of Remus and his creator; neither is clear-cut or completely attainable. In his essay "Uncle Remus and the Malevolent Rabbit," Bernard Wolfe asserts that the grinning Remus is both servile and sly. At times he is a reflection of the false postures and role-playing commonly employed by the enslaved black, at times a mask behind which Harris works his masquerade.

Born in Putnam County, Eatonton, Georgia, on

9 December 1848, Joel Harris was the illegitimate son of Miss Mary Harris and an Irish day laborer. The father soon deserted them and was never seen again in Putnam County. Joel and his mother survived on her small earnings as a seamstress and the charity of their neighbors, a situation that caused Joel to wonder "which was more respectable— poor folks or niggers." Biographers of Harris attribute his extreme, almost pathological shyness, insecurity, and persistent despondency to these uncomfortable circumstances surrounding his birth and early childhood.

As a boy, Joel camouflaged his public awkwardness by developing a reputation as a mischief-maker whose rough pranks made him the "hellion of the neighborhood." Significantly, the cruel nature of the practical jokes and escapades are suspiciously reminiscent of the havoc and confusion typical of the trickster rabbit. As an adult, too, Harris was never entirely the person he appeared to be. In response to the immediate success of *Uncle Remus,* Harris avoided the public, refused to read his work aloud, and shrugged at fame by consistently disparaging either the work itself (in one letter, he refers to the tales as "the Remus trash") or his own accomplishments as a writer. At the same time, he avidly attempted to manipulate book editors and distributors, urging them to augment their efforts to improve sales. He was shy yet aggressive; confessed terrible loneliness and hopelessness, but always presented a cheerful optimism; professed rather liberal attitudes towards blacks (as compared to others of his era) even while lambasting them between the lines of his fiction. Like Brer Rabbit, Harris was an illusionist; he viewed the world as a pit of antagonists and played them against each other to protect himself. Within the Remus tales, he continues to wreak this same subtle havoc: flattering with the care given to their details, yet betraying their meaning at every turn; drawing Remus with sensitivity in one passage, then minstrelizing him through an exaggerated language or absurd poses in another to remind the reader of his ultimate "inferiority." The works are a misery of contradiction, a masterpiece of deception.

When *Uncle Remus* first appeared, Harris' fictional vision was generally considered to be the most authentic representation of black folk life, as well as an astute study of the psychology of "the negro." This perception of Remus as being realistic, and the folk narratives as being constructed of pure fantasy, provide the basis for the most extreme irony.

Harris was no realist. The author's greater concern is revealed in one of a series of articles written for the *Washington Post* titled "The Negro as the South Sees Him." There he writes:

> It is a common saying in the South that we have very few of the old-time negroes left with us; . . . and we shake our heads sadly and lament the conditions that are so soon to deprive us of one of our most cherished and picturesque relics.
>
> (*Editor and Essayist*, p. 118)

But, optimistic as always, he estimates that there must still be a good number of these "venerable dark[ies] . . . between fifty and seventy years of age, whose tact and conservatism have exerted a tremendous influence on the race." Uncle Remus is not a portrait, as Stella Brewer Brooks has claimed; he is the conjuration of a relic, an incantatory wish-dream calling forth the embodiment of what Zora Neale Hurston labeled the "pet negro" and what Darwin Turner defined as "dutiful genies . . . more faithful than a pet hound."

Rather than a portrait, Remus is a device used to suppress or manipulate truth and substitute the more comfortable image of the passive, simple-natured, nonthreatening negro. The assumption of white superiority upon which the characterization is based is an aspect of the work that is now generally conceded but just as typically dismissed as a minor quirk of "a complicated man full of neurotic conflicts and self-deceiving ways" (Robert Bone). It may be easy for the literary sophisticate to excuse the subtextual racism embedded in the characterization and structure of Harris' story formula, and still savor the rich social commentary available in the folk tales. But Remus is to be found on children's literature bookshelves.

The indisputable indoctrinating function and effect of literature written for children fuels disagreement as to the appropriateness or value of Remus in a juvenile setting. The socializing messages embedded in the story frame are the thinly veiled propagandist doctrines of the post-Reconstruction era. There was never any legitimacy in the absurd celebration of slavery, the lessons in obsequiousness provided by Uncle Remus, or the assumptions of white superiority and privilege. What reason is there to expect that the modern child will be any more immune to these suggestions than the child of one hundred years ago? In a society still dragging its feet towards social and political equity, to preserve Harris' works on the library shelf is an investment in future disharmony. A child might fail to interpret the insurrectionist leanings in the animal tales, but not the unsubtle image of the old "darky." Moreover, the few efforts to "rehabilitate" Remus have merely resulted in presentations such as Walt Disney's "Uncle," who has been "lightened up" and is slightly better dressed.

If *Uncle Remus* serves awkwardly as children's book fare, in fact it is because the creation of the character of Remus was far from child's play. Uncle Remus first appeared not as a storyteller but as a fictional mouthpiece in the pages of the *Atlanta Constitution.* The *Constitution* editors were busily promoting a "New South" philosophy designed to reconcile the estranged North and South on the "issue" of black folk and to, in effect, disfranchise them and establish the narrow margins of their freedom. The *Constitution* regularly disseminated its dogma out of the mouths of fictional negroes; Remus was born out of this tradition. Thus we have Remus holding forth on "Race Improvement":

> You slap de law onter a nigger a time er two, an' larn 'im dat he's got fer to look atter his own ra-shuns an' keep out 'n udder fokes's chick'n-coops, an' sorter coax 'im inter de idee dat he's got ter feed 'is own chilluns, an' I be blessed ef you ain't got 'im on risin' groun'.
>
> (*Uncle Remus*, pp. 235–237)

He has also considered the question of education for negroes:

> W'at a nigger gwinter l'arn outen books? I kin take a bar'l stave an fling mo' sense inter a nigger in one minnit dan all de schoolhouses betwixt dis en de state er Midgigin.... Wid one bar'l stave I kin fa'rly lif' de vail er ignunce.... Put a spellin'-book in a nigger's han's, en right den en dar' you loozes a plow-hand.
>
> (ibid., pp. 259–261)

It is "Remus" who tells us that every negro should "jine de chu'ch" and get religion because " 'lijjun will pay you mo' dan politics" (p. 258). These sketches have been removed from recent revised editions of *Uncle Remus,* but he remains deeply mired in white cultural assumptions, and the problems he presents are not so easily excised.

The dialect sketches were immensely popular, and Harris continued to experiment with his sable spokesperson until he chanced to read an article on negro folklore. Eventually, the "city" Remus became distinct from the "country," tale-spinning

Remus. Harris' first tale, "The Story of Mr. Rabbit and Mr. Fox as Told by Uncle Remus," appeared in July 1879 on the editorial page of the *Atlanta Constitution.* "Brer Rabbit, Brer Fox, and the Tar-Baby" appeared in November of the same year.

Like Harris' creation of the character Uncle Remus, the folk tales of Brer Rabbit were never initially or primarily children's fare, although they were shared with children along with other kinds of tales. These stories from the slaves' African heritage formed an underground communication system; the messages transmitted were sometimes dangerous and therefore required the language of symbols. Surviving within a system that repressed language, discouraged ideas, illegalized education, restricted movement, and even dictated sexual partnerships, the slave—through an act of imagination—violated every restriction that slavery had imposed upon his personal freedom. It was a rebellion against the total control of his mind. Subtle meanings were so well disguised within allegory that some biographers of Harris have speculated that even he, the so-called amanuensis for the black storyteller, was unaware of the intended meanings. This may have been possible at the publication of the first volume of tales, but it is not likely true of his later collections. The classification of the Uncle Remus tales as "humorous" and, later, as literature for children was initially a publisher's decision; Harris himself maintained that "however humorous [the book] may be in effect, its intention is perfectly serious."

Evidently Harris worried a great deal about the "serious" aspects of the tales. He insisted upon the insignificance of his role in the retellings, referring to the stories as "uncooked." He disclaimed the praise of reviewers, saying: "I know it is the matter and not the manner that has attracted public attention." But Harris was wrong in this estimation. Although folklorists and ethnologists were primarily interested in the cultural implications of the tales (and completely uninterested in the literary frame), for others such considerations were minor at best. It seemed that it was very much the "manner" that was endearing to his readers. As Mark Twain wrote in a letter to the author, "The stories are only alligator pears—one eats them merely for the sake of the dressing. 'Uncle Remus' is most deftly drawn and is a loveable creation; he and the little boy and their relations with each other are bright, fine literature ..." (*Life and Letters,* pp. 169–170). In part, the success of *Uncle Remus* was due to Harris' sensitivity to the national mood which, after all, paralleled his own. And it was his talent for rendering convincing details of gesture and the "homely" phrasings and apt metaphors of the untutored that gave the illusion of realism to those who could recognize some of the textures of black life, but not its substance.

It was precisely the observed quality of Harris' details that made his creation so much more believable, and more lasting in its impact, than the black-faced concoctions of other writers of the period. Darwin Turner, in his essay "Daddy Joel Harris and His Old-Time Darkies" (1981), enumerates the distinguishing features of black characters created by Harris as proof that he did "see" the individuality in black people rather than the stock features of Sambo or Aunt Jemina painted by many of his white contemporaries. But it is all an elaborate diversion. For, although Harris remained true, in some degree, to his journalistic instincts—that is, to record what he saw and heard—he lacked a commitment to the substance of the matter. This would have required that he preserve the intent of the original stories—their volatile irreverence, their veiled hatred—as diligently as he reported their plot developments.

But Harris was no realist. And Uncle Remus was no lighthearted frolic; he was a gatekeeper, hired on to keep the blackness of the Rabbit in check, protecting against a threatened foray out of the subtext into the text, out of the subconscious into the conscious minds of both whites and blacks. Harris was writing not to explore his characters (or the minds of his syndicate of black slaves) but to put them to work in the service of his own fictional dream. He was the conjurer of a single image: an ideal paternal estate that he imagined had existed at the Turnwold plantation owned by Joseph Addison Turner, Harris' first tutor, mentor, and father figure.

Harris' four years of apprenticeship as a printer's assistant on Turnwold were pivotal. Later, as he struggled with his own pathology of insecurity, self-consciousness, isolation, and depression, Harris would recall with increasing fondness and longing his brief tenure at the plantation. He used his art to idealize and enshrine a moment of childhood. In "The Oral Tradition," Robert Bone observes that, "whatever the intentions—conscious or unconscious—of Joel Chandler Harris, the Uncle Remus tales confront us with two distinct, and ultimately unreconcilable versions of reality. One is white, the other black. . . . One is nostalgic and sentimental,

the other utterly subversive." But Harris attempts just that, to reconcile the irreconcilable by superimposing his own backward vision onto his black characters.

In recent analyses of these works, the figure of Remus has been increasingly viewed as a key to the psychoanalysis of Harris. Such studies are compelling as they reveal the layers of complexity and contradiction within the so-called simple folk stories collected by a "cornfield journalist." But this type of scholarly study does not alter the stories as they are read by or to children, or as they appear in the images of popular film adaptations. The messages of caste preference insist upon and enforce a clear and negative comparison between the black child listener and the white child. The Uncle Remus tales are often referred to as "universal." The folktales are universal, but the white child at Remus' knee is not. Like Remus, he is particular and static. A relic.

The valuation and classification of children surfaces most clearly when Harris directs the reader to a particular interpretation of the animal fables. In his efforts to conceal the defiance within the tales, Harris inhibits their interpretive depth. Bernard Wolfe views these tactics as Harris' efforts to "exorcise the menace in the Meek." He proposes "Why the Negro Is Black" as an instance of Remus' slipping mask.

In this tale, the little boy asks Remus why his palms are white. The venerable old contented slave responds, "Niggers is niggers now, but de time wuz w'en we 'uz all niggers tergedder. . . . In dem times we uz all black." He then tells the story of a pond that would wash the pigmentation from the skin. The first group of people came out white; the second, "merlatters"; but when the last group arrived, there was only enough water left to "paddle about wid der foots en dabble in it wid der han's." The Remus mischief is revealed in his stress upon the "nigger" origins of all people. The implication is that the differences in people extend no deeper than the skin; therefore, the uneven apportionment of power must be the result of mere luck. This is undoubtedly a commentary on the prevalent fiction, which asserted that the primacy of whites was due to their alleged superior mental and moral capacities. Ironically, Harris was among those whites who clung to this notion. The explanation of the origin of the mulatto "race" is a particularly delicate irony, as Remus thereby neatly sidesteps the bitter issue of institutional rape. Harris is true to the words, but not to their meaning: Remus delivers the story in perfect seriousness of demeanor. It is not the deadpan, mock seriousness he sometimes effects to "put on" the little boy; it is as if Harris would like the reader to believe that the old man takes the tale for factual history. Instead of perceiving the astuteness and sublety of Remus, or piercing his commentary on society, the reader is encouraged to interpret the tale as the quaint simpleminded belief of an ignorant people who simply wish to be made white.

The intelligence within the tales is often no more than a gleaming crack in the Remus facade. For example, the old storyteller can supply a meaningful tale for every occasion of the little boy's misbehavior, suggesting his easy understanding of the potential for truth within the stories. But ask him about Miss Meadows and the Gals, and all he knows is "she was en de tale, honey." Or, when asked the identity of "the man," Remus claims that he is just a man. At these moments, it is difficult to determine who is in control of the deception. Wolfe refers to these "gaps" as indicative that Harris was not so completely taken into the confidence of his informant negroes, and as support of the idea that Harris did not fully comprehend the tale's allegorical significance. The evasiveness is strategic, however. Miss Meadows most certainly represents the violation of racial/sexual taboos, and "the man" quite frankly symbolizes The Man, the white man, the outsider.

But this selective editing on the part of the black informants works both ways. For Harris, it tended to validate his assertion that the tales were harmless pastimes. The gaps suggest that the black storyteller did not, in fact, possess the "key" to his own tales and that he was simply a teller of the tales. Consequently, there could be no malice in them for they were uninterpreted and therefore without significance to their tellers. Of course a storyteller extraordinaire, such as Remus is supposed to be, would have been drummed out of the business had he not known the significance of "Miss Meadows" and "The Man," but this feigned ignorance is reported literally by Harris, who either did not know what was missing or preferred to protect his readers (and himself?) from these particular aspects of the tales. In other matters, Harris is less ginger in his handling.

For example, in *Uncle Remus,* there exists only "Miss Sally's little boy" to receive the tales. But in a later collection, *Uncle Remus and His Friends*

(1892), there is the unusual instance of another child receiving a story from the venerable Uncle. In "Death and the Negro Man" a "Negro boy" is on hand to assist Remus, who is sharpening a dull axe blade. The boy has the job of turning the grindstone. In response to a casual comment by Remus, the boy stereotypically "rolled his eyes and giggled." Remus is so incensed by this behavior that he bears down hard on the axe, so that the grindstone can barely be turned by the little boy. Then he scolds, "Turn it! . . . Turn it! Ef you don't turn it, I'll make you stan' dar plum twel night gwine thoo de motions. I'll make you do like de nigger man done when he got tired er work." Of course the little boy asks for the story, but Remus responds that "tellin' tales is playin' " and refuses to reveal the tale until the boy's task is complete.

Then he tells of an old man who "got so he ain't want ter work. When folks hangs back fum work what dey bin set ter do, hit natchully makes bad matters wuss." The old man of Remus's tale shirks his work and is overheard to say that he hoped " 'Gran'sir Death' " would come and take him off, along with his master and the overseer. As a prank, the master dresses up in a white sheet and "den he cut two-eye-holes in a piller-case" and went to the slave's living quarters. Remus describes the "Affiky nigger" as the Klan-dressed master found him: "wid grease in his mouf en big hunk er ashcake in his han' ." The master bangs on the door proclaiming that he is Gran'sir Death and that he has come for him. The old man is so frightened that he drops his ashcake, rolls his eyes, and "took to de woods." After a week, he returns and becomes the hardest worker on the plantation. Remus claims that "somebody come 'long en try ter buy im, but his marster 'low he won't take lev'm hunder'd dollars for 'im,—cash money, paid down in his han'!"

There is nothing here of the tenderness or genuine concern that Remus displays, even in his rougher moments, with the little white boy. Neither is this tale a veiled allegory; it is blunt and threatening: Negroes who have the temerity to "hang back fum the work what dey bin set ter do" can expect a visit from Gran'sir Death, most likely in the form of a white man dressed in a sheet. It should not be overlooked that Harris has violated a rigid story frame in order to deliver this tale to a "Negro boy." The moral of the tale as told by Remus contradicts the work-saboteur themes so prevalent in the tales of the Rabbit (who never does a lick of work but uses his mind, and his knowledge of the habits and behaviors of others, to shape the world to his liking). Harris becomes a saboteur in his own right, employing the symbols of black people to do the work of the New South propagandist.

In "The Man and His Boots," of the same collection, Harris does not disguise his desire to counteract the subversion in the tales. Remus reports that Miss Sally has expressed disapproval of the tales because they might foster further misbehavior in the little boy. In deference to her controlling influence, Remus delivers a sermonette insisting that people can't do like the animals do because "De creeturs . . . dunno right fum wrong" and "How de name er goodness kin folks go on en steal en tell fibs, like de creeturs done, en not git hurted? Dey des can't do it. Dead dog never dies, en cheatin' never th'ives—not when folks git at it" (*Complete Tales,* pp. 561–562). In this tale, a man tries to use the same trick used by Brer Rabbit in "Mr. Fox Goes A-Hunting, But Mr. Rabbit Bags the Game" (*Uncle Remus*). The trickster man leaves his boot in the road; a second man comes along in a wagon full of valuables. He observes the fine-looking boot but continues on his way, leaving it behind. After all, what can he do with one boot? The trickster runs ahead and places the second boot in the road. This time, the rider leaves his wagon unattended to go back and retrieve the mate. When he returns to find that he has been robbed, he looks at the boots and laughs pretending that he has found ten dollars in each boot. The trickster is foiled when he comes forth and insists that the boots are his and demands their return along with the money. Remus tells the little boy that he doesn't know how long the trickster was imprisoned but " 'fo dey turn him loose dey tuck 'im out en hit 'im thirty nine on de naked hide. . . . Dat what make I say dat folks ain't got no business mockin' de way de creeturs does. Dey er bound ter git cotch up wid" (p. 563).

As an "uncooked" tale, this story was more likely intended to comment on the stupidity that greed engenders. The trickster is foiled not by any weakness in his plan, but by his overreaching nature. Surely the tale was no condemnation of the uses of deception; after all, the tales themselves are a celebration of deception and intrigue.

Harris's moral preachment, delivered through Uncle Remus, reveals his own nagging concern about the "serious" aspects of the tales; that is, the degree to which the violence and subterfuge within the tales might influence or reflect the minds of their black creators—Bernard Wolf's "menace in the Meek."

The published works of Harris are by no means confined to the folklore collections. He was a prolific writer and experimented with the novel and standard short-story form. His other works have not been ignored, but it was Uncle Remus, his companion Rabbit, and the idealization of the utopian plantation myth that etched Harris onto the minds of mainstream America.

As quickly and thoroughly as white America embraced Harris' heavily baggaged versions of the folktales, black Americans seemed to abandon them. They had lost their currency. Modern black writers of adult fiction—for example, Ralph Ellison in *Invisible Man* (1952) or Toni Morrison in *Tar Baby* (1981)—have made excellent use of the complexity of Brer Rabbit; attempts to reinterpret the tales for black children have also been frequent. But the tales have never regained their use or significance within the general black community. Robert Bone contends that black Americans ought to admit the "considerable debt" owed to Harris for the "preservation of their folk heritage." Perhaps. But the "preserving" of the tales seems to have been more a transfer of ownership.

If thanks are in order, so be it. But gratitude cannot stand in the way of efforts to restore lifeblood to the lore and redeem that heritage for the benefit of imaginative freedom. Not much has changed since "way back yander" when the first black man leaped into a pool of water and came out white. If the folk fail to ransom Brother Rabbit—in his substance and import—he may serve to make pickaninnies of us all.

Selected Bibliography

WORKS FOR CHILDREN BY JOEL CHANDLER HARRIS

Uncle Remus: His Songs and His Sayings. With illustrations by F. S. Church and J. H. Moser. New York: D. Appleton, 1880.
Nights with Uncle Remus: Myths and Legends of the Old Plantation. With illustrations by F. S. Church. Boston: James R. Osgood, 1883.
Daddy Jake, the Runaway, and Short Stories Told After Dark. With illustrations by E. W. Kemble. New York: Century, 1889.
Uncle Remus and His Friends: Old Plantation Stories, Songs and Ballads with Sketches of Negro Character. With illustrations by A.B. Frost. Boston and New York: Houghton Mifflin, 1892.
Little Mr. Thimblefinger and His Queer Country: What Children Saw and Heard There. With illustrations by Oli-

ver Herford. Boston and New York: Houghton Mifflin, 1894.

Mr. Rabbit at Home: A Sequel to Little Mr. Thimblefinger and His Queer Country. Boston and New York: Houghton Mifflin, 1895.

Wally Wanderoon and His Story-Telling Machine. With illustrations by Karl Moseley. New York: McClure, Phillips, 1903.

The Tar-Baby and Other Rhymes of Uncle Remus. With illustrations by A. B. Frost and E. W. Kemble. New York: D. Appleton, 1904.

Told by Uncle Remus: New Stories of the Old Plantation. With illustrations by A. B. Frost, J. M. Condé, and Frank Verbeck. New York: McClure, Phillips, 1905.

Uncle Remus and Brer Rabbit. New York: Frederick A. Stokes, 1907.

The Bishop and the Boogerman. With illustrations by Charlotte Harding. New York: Doubleday, Page, 1909.

Uncle Remus and the Little Boy. With illustrations by J. M. Condé. Boston: Small, Maynard, 1910.

Uncle Remus Returns. With illustrations by A. B. Frost and J. M. Condé. Boston and New York: Houghton Mifflin, 1918.

Favorite Uncle Remus. Boston: Houghton Mifflin, 1948.

Seven Tales of Uncle Remus, edited by Thomas H. English. Atlanta: Emory University Press, 1948.

The Complete Tales of Uncle Remus, compiled by Richard Chase. With illustrations by A. B. Frost and others. New York: Houghton Mifflin, 1955.

CRITICAL AND BIOGRAPHICAL STUDIES

Anonymous. "Uncle Remus." In *Critical Essays on Joel Chandler Harris,* edited by R. Bruce Bickley, Jr. Boston: G. K. Hall, 1981.

Abrahams, Roger D. *African Folktales.* New York: Pantheon Books, 1983.

———. *Afro-American Folktales: Stories from Black Traditions in the New World.* New York: Pantheon Books, 1985.

Bacon, A. M. "Work and Methods of the Hampton Folk-Lore Society." *Journal of American Folk-Lore* 11: 17–21 (1898).

Bickley, R. Bruce, Jr. *Joel Chandler Harris: A Reference Guide.* Boston: G. K. Hall, 1978.

———. *Joel Chandler Harris.* Boston: G. K. Hall, 1978.

Bier, Jesse. "Duplicity and Cynicism in Harris's Humor." In *Critical Essays on Joel Chandler Harris,* edited by R. Bruce Bickley, Jr. Boston: G. K. Hall, 1981.

Bone, Robert. "The Oral Tradition." In *Critical Essays on Joel Chandler Harris,* edited by R. Bruce Bickley, Jr. Boston: G. K. Hall, 1981.

Brooks, Stella Brewer. *Joel Chandler Harris—Folklorist.* Athens: University of Georgia Press, 1950.

Brown, Sterling. "Negro Character as Seen by White Authors." *Journal of Negro Education,* 2: 180–197 (April 1934).

Budd, Louis J. "Joel Chandler Harris and the Genteeling of Native American Humor." In *Critical Essays on Joel Chandler Harris,* edited by R. Bruce Bickley, Jr. Boston: G. K. Hall, 1981.

Cousins, Paul M. *Joel Chandler Harris: A Biography.* Baton Rouge: Louisiana State University Press, 1968.

English, Thomas H. "The Other Uncle Remus." *Georgia Review* 21: 210–217 (Summer 1967).

Goldthwaite, John. "The Black Rabbit: Part One." *Signal* 47: 86–111 (May 1985).

Griska, Joseph M., Jr. " 'In Stead of a "Gift of Gab" ': Some New Perspectives on Joel Chandler Harris Biography." In *Critical Essays on Joel Chandler Harris,* edited by R. Bruce Bickley, Jr. Boston: G. K. Hall, 1981.

———. "Selected Letters of Joel Chandler Harris, 1863–1885." Ph.D. dissertation, Texas A & M University, 1976.

Harris, Julia Collier, ed. *Joel Chandler Harris: Editor and Essayist.* Chapel Hill: University of North Carolina Press, 1931.

———. *The Life and Letters of Joel Chandler Harris.* Boston and New York: Houghton Mifflin, 1918.

Hurston, Zora Neale. "The Pet Negro System." In *I Love Myself When I Am Laughing,* edited by Alice Walker. New York: Feminist Press, 1979.

———. *Mules and Men.* Bloomington: Indiana University Press, 1935.

Light, Kathleen. "Uncle Remus and the Folklorists." In *Critical Essays on Joel Chandler Harris,* edited by R. Bruce Bickley, Jr. Boston: G. K. Hall, 1981.

Newell, William Wells. "Editor's Note." *Journal of American Folk-Lore* 11: 291–292 (1898).

Rubin, Louis D., Jr. "Uncle Remus and the Ubiquitous Rabbit." In *William Elliot Shoots a Bear: Essays on the Southern Literary Imagination.* Baton Rouge: Louisiana State University Press, 1975.

Taylor, Ron. "Uncle Remus Lives and Brer Rabbit Survives Thorny Issue." *Atlanta Journal and Constitution* 12-B, 13-B (9 Nov. 1975).

Turner, Darwin T. "Daddy Joel Harris and His Old-Time Darkies." In *Critical Essays on Joel Chandler Harris,* edited by R. Bruce Bickley, Jr. Boston: G. K. Hall, 1981.

Wolfe, Bernard. "Uncle Remus and the Malevolent Rabbit: 'Takes a Limber-Toe Gemmun fer ter Jump Jim Crow.' " In *Critical Essays on Joel Chandler Harris,* edited by R. Bruce Bickley, Jr. Boston: G. K. Hall, 1981.

—OPAL J. MOORE

NATHANIEL HAWTHORNE

1804–1864

THE LITERARY CAREER of the nineteenth-century American novelist Nathaniel Hawthorne reveals a paradox. On the one hand, his lasting reputation rests on several short stories and four novels depicting the evil and guilt of the human heart. In fact, he described his greatest work, *The Scarlet Letter* (1850), as "positively a h-ll-fired story, into which I found it almost impossible to throw any cheering light." On the other hand, he is remembered by historians of children's literature as the first major reteller of the classic Greek legends and myths, works that one contemporary reviewer called "so essentially sunny and happy, that it creates a jubilee in the brain as we read." He also wrote four small books adapting American history for children and contributed short pieces to the children's magazines and annuals of the day. Why should and how could a writer whose adult works reflected the darker side of human experience have undertaken writing projects so apparently contrary to the main bent of his genius? Those questions may be examined by placing Hawthorne's writing for children within the context of his biography and his writing career, by examining in some detail his major children's books, and by considering contemporary and modern critical reactions to these works.

Nathaniel Hawthorne was born in Salem, Massachusetts, on 4 July 1804; among his ancestors was the famous John Hathorne who presided as judge over the notorious Salem witch trials. As a boy, Hawthorne read widely, especially during a two-year period he spent as an invalid. Among his favorite works were Edmund Spenser's sixteenth-century epic *The Faerie Queene*, John Bunyan's seventeenth-century prose narrative *Pilgrim's Progress*, and the plays of Shakespeare. The first two of these are notable for the elements of moral allegory found in them; the characters and incidents were intended to illustrate good and bad behavior and its consequences. Hawthorne was also to write moral allegories. A lifelong reader, he became familiar with the major children's fairy tales popular in the first half of the nineteenth century. He was certainly aware of the great eighteenth- and nineteenth-century novelists and had read widely and deeply in the history and theology of colonial New England.

Not surprisingly, Hawthorne decided while still in his teens to become a writer and in 1828, after his graduation from Bowdoin College in Maine, published his first novel, *Fanshawe*, an unsuccessful imitation of the romances of Sir Walter Scott and of contemporary gothic fiction. Undaunted by the failure of his novel, Hawthorne spent the twelve years after graduation learning his craft. During this period, referred to by biographer Randall Stewart as the "Solitary Years," he wrote and published over fifty stories (mainly on New England history) and sketches (in the manner popular at that time), read voraciously, kept a detailed notebook on his ideas and his observations of scenes and people, and traveled, generally alone, throughout New England.

In 1835 he published his first children's story, "Little Annie's Ramble," a slight sketch of a child's day, and with his sister, Elizabeth, contributed to *Peter Parley's Universal History* (1837), a cut-and-paste history for children. In addition, he jotted in his notebooks such ideas for children's stories as these: "To picture a child's reminiscences at sunset of a long summer's day," and "To describe a boyish combat with snowballs, and the victorious leader to have a statue of snow erected to him."

However, it was not until 1838 that Hawthorne appears to have seriously considered a book-length children's work. He wrote to a college friend, the poet Henry Wadsworth Longfellow, suggesting that the two of them collaborate on a "book of fairy stories." Nothing came of the project. Hawthorne, in the meantime, served as measurer of salt and coal in the Boston Custom House from 1839 to 1841; met his future bride, Sophia Peabody; and in the summer of 1841 lived in the utopian community of Brook Farm. Ideas for children's stories continued to appear in his notebooks: a fairy tale about Echo, a story about wicked gnomes who burrow into people's teeth, and sketches on the life of a city dove and a magic ray of sunshine. His first major children's work was published through the agency of his future sister-in-law, Elizabeth Peabody. Three small books published in 1841, *Grandfather's Chair, Famous Old People*, and *Liberty Tree*, described important events and personages of the Puritan, late colonial, and revolutionary periods. *Biographical Stories for Children* (1842) included stories of such notables as the English writer Samuel Johnson, the Swedish queen Christina, and the revolutionary leader Benjamin Franklin.

Hawthorne married Sophia Peabody in 1842 and moved to Concord, Massachusetts, where he wrote "Rappaccini's Daughter," "The Artist of the Beautiful," and "Egotism; or, The Bosom Serpent." The only children's story to be published during this period was "Little Daffydowndilly," although there are notebook entries for other topics and several descriptions of his own children. From 1846 to 1849 he served as surveyor of the Salem Custom House, a political appointment made in recognition of his loyalty to the Democratic Party. Dismissed from office after a change in political power, he began writing his most famous novel, *The Scarlet Letter*.

With the writing of *The Scarlet Letter*, Hawthorne undoubtedly achieved full control of his creative powers, and certainly acquired great fame. Confidently, he began a four-year period of writing that saw him publish two adult novels (*The House of the Seven Gables*, 1851, and *The Blithedale Romance*, 1852), a collection of short stories (*The Snow Image and Other Twice-Told Tales*, 1851), a collected reprint of his earlier historical books for children (*True Stories from History and Biography*, 1851), a presidential campaign biography for his Bowdoin College friend (*The Life of Franklin Pierce*, 1852), and two retellings for children of classical myths and legends (*A Wonder-Book for Girls and Boys*, 1852, and *Tanglewood Tales for Girls and Boys*, 1853).

As Roy Harvey Pearce, the editor of Hawthorne's children's stories for the scholarly *Centenary Edition of the Works of Nathaniel Hawthorne*, has indicated in the "Historical Introduction" to volume 6, Hawthorne's interest in the Greek myths extended at least back to 1838, when he wrote to Longfellow about a collaborative volume and jotted in his notebook, "Pandora's box for a child's story." Although Hawthorne appears to have maintained interest in the idea during the 1840's, being attracted to the potentially large sales for children's books and the relative ease of writing them, it was not until April 1851, after having completed *The House of the Seven Gables*, that he actually approached the project seriously. His publisher, James T. Fields, had the completed manuscript of *A Wonder-Book* by mid-July, and it was published in November of that year (although it bore an 1852 date). Sales were good: 4,667 in 1851 and 10,349 by 1863 (figures quoted by Pearce). Reviews were favorable, and early in 1853 he wrote *Tanglewood Tales*, which went on to sell 6,930 copies.

These were the last two children's books Hawthorne wrote. In 1853, as a reward for his support of the newly elected president Franklin Pierce, he served four years as American consul in Liverpool, England. The Hawthornes then spent three years in Italy, where he wrote his fourth novel, *The Marble Faun* (1860). The family returned to America in 1860. Four years later, on May 19, 1864, Hawthorne died in his sleep while vacationing in New Hampshire with Franklin Pierce.

In retelling significant historical events for children, Hawthorne conceded that he faced a major challenge. In the preface to *The Whole History of Grandfather's Chair* (the collected version of *Grandfather's Chair, Famous Old People*, and *Liberty Tree*), he writes:

> To make a lively and entertaining narrative for children, with such unmalleable material as is presented

by the sombre, stern, and rigid characteristics of the Puritans and their descendants, is quite as difficult an attempt as to manufacture delicate playthings out of the granite rocks on which New England is founded.

In order to make his history of the colonies up to the time of the Revolution interesting to children, Hawthorne uses three techniques. First, he tells the story through a narrator, an old man speaking to his grandchildren. Such a framework provides a setting similar to that in which his audience would most likely have been used to hearing stories: seated around a revered grandparent. Moreover, the children are characterized as representative types: the older two, Clara and Laurence, are sensitive and thoughtful; Charley is rambunctious and often inattentive; the youngest, Alice, is easily moved emotionally. Second, Hawthorne creates specific incidents, often domestic, to bring his historical personages to life.

Finally, he unifies the story around the old chair in which Grandfather is sitting, connecting the historical elements with "the substantial and homely reality of a fireside chair. It causes us to feel at once that these characters of history had a private and familiar existence, and were not wholly contained within [the] cold array of outward action." The chair, in fact, becomes, during the course of the three sections of *The Whole History*, a symbol of the enduring spirit that led to the creation of the republic. Originally crafted in England, the chair came across the Atlantic with the persecuted Puritans, endured many hardships, underwent several alterations, and was sat in by many of the most famous men of the respective eras discussed, including the father of the new country, George Washington: "He sat down in a large chair, which was the most conspicuous object in the room. The noble figure of Washington would have done honor to a throne. . . . Never before had the lion's head [on Grandfather's chair] . . . looked down upon such a face and form as Washington's." In writing the stories, Hawthorne had two main objectives: to present to children not only the facts of American history but also a basic understanding of the forces that led to the creation of the republic; and to impress upon them important moral lessons.

The topics discussed in *The Whole History of Grandfather's Chair* had also been treated by Hawthorne in many of his short stories: the evil results of witchcraft delusion in "Young Goodman Brown," the terrors of persecution in "The Gentle Boy," and the dangers of mob violence in "My Kinsman, Major Molineux." These and other stories reflected the somber mood so characteristic of the author. Yet in the children's stories this tone is greatly lightened, and many of the more terrifying events of New England history are glossed over or omitted. An example of the difference can be seen by comparing a passage in "Grandfather's Chair" with one in *The Scarlet Letter*. After hearing of the death of Lady Arbella, Clara muses, "How sad is the thought that one of the first things which the settlers had to do, when they came to the new world, was to set apart a burial ground!" In the opening chapter of *The Scarlet Letter* this statement appears: "The founders of a new colony, whatever Utopia of human virtue and happiness they might originally project, have invariably recognized it among their earliest practical necessities to allot a portion of the virgin soil as a cemetery, and another portion as the site of a prison." Significantly, the children's version omits mention of the prison. Such a building, Hawthorne implies in *The Scarlet Letter*, was an inevitable result of the colonists' inability to leave moral evil when they came to the New World. However, discussions of evil do not enter into *The Whole History*.

Grandfather is aware of the innocence of children and does not wish to introduce them before their time to a basic human reality. The old man is reflecting Hawthorne's own view that stories for children, while they should be morally and educationally valuable, should not delve into darker areas that can be understood only by adults. This attitude was, to a great extent, to pervade his major achievement in children's writing, the retellings of the Greek legends and myths.

In *Biographical Stories for Children*, Hawthorne introduced young readers to great people by telling them about childhood incidents that presaged greatness. Its purpose was also avowedly moral, as Hawthorne says in the preface: "This small volume, and others of a similar character, . . . have not been composed without a deep sense of responsibility. The author regards children as sacred, and would not, for the world, cast anything in the fountain of a young heart."

A Wonder-Book contains retellings of six classical legends: Perseus' slaying of the Gorgon Medusa; Midas' acquisition of the golden touch; Pandora's liberation of trouble from a mysterious box; Hercules' quest for the golden apples; Baucis and Philemon's kindly treatment of disguised gods; and Bellerophon's taming of the winged steed Pegasus and the subsequent slaying of the Chimaera. The collection is set within a framework: Eustace Bright, a student at Williams College, tells the stories to a group of young children. *Tanglewood Tales* includes six more Greek legends, but the framework of storyteller and audience is dropped. The stories are about Theseus' slaying of the Minotaur; Hercules' encounter with the pygmies, Cadmus' search for his sister and founding of a city; Ulysses' rescue of his men from the enchantments of Circe; Pluto's abduction of Proserpina; and Jason's quest for the Golden Fleece. Hawthorne's source for these stories was *A Classical Dictionary*, published in 1842 by Charles Anthon, a professor at Columbia University.

In his use of this source, Hawthorne adapted freely, omitting some incidents, bowdlerizing others, and changing the tone. For example, he focuses much of the story of Midas on the foolish king's love of his little daughter, Marygold; the story of Perseus omits references to his divine parentage; Pandora is transformed into a somewhat pettish little girl; and Pluto abducts Proserpina because he wants a child to cheer up his gloomy kingdom. The reasons for these somewhat drastic changes are to be found in Hawthorne's view of the quality of the Greek myths and his attitudes about what constituted acceptable reading for children.

Long before he wrote the tales, Hawthorne had faced what he considered two of the basic difficulties in adapting the Greek myths. First, the classics had a "cold moonshine" or "classic coldness, which is as repellent as the touch of marble." Moreover, they were foreign to the knowledge of contemporary children; they needed to be "modernized." A third major difficulty was expressed in the preface to *Tanglewood Tales*:

> These old legends, so brimming over with every thing that is most abhorrent to our Christianized moral sense—some of them so hideous, others so melancholy and miserable, amid which the Greek Tragedians sought their themes, and moulded them into the sternest forms of grief that ever the world saw; was such material the stuff that children's play things should be made of! How were they to be purified? How was the blessed sunshine to be thrown into them?

In order to overcome these difficulties, Hawthorne gothicized (as he termed it), modernized, and severely edited his material. Modern critics are not certain exactly what Hawthorne meant by gothicizing. Certainly, as Nina Baym has written in *The Shape of Hawthorne's Career*,

> the myths add a note of the supernatural and fantastic, imparting a slight shiver, a hint of moonlight, a touch of magic to the sunny round of homely pleasures. All this is achieved without a trace of the macabre and terrifying, which are hallmarks of the true gothic. Indeed, the myths are gothicized but also tamed.

Thus while the human characters generally act like real people, the events have an aura of mysterious wonder about them. Eustace Bright explains to his youthful auditors that "in the old, old times, a great many things came to pass, which we should consider wonderful, if they were to happen in our own day and country." In addition, the stories make a great deal of the emotions experienced by the characters, a quality also found in gothic fiction.

Modernization of the stories first involved providing a framework in which a contemporary storyteller narrated to children who are not unlike typical mid-nineteenth-century readers. In addition, events and characters were modernized. As critics have often noted, King Midas, the day he has acquired his golden touch, sits down to a hearty New England breakfast: "hot cakes, some nice little brook-trout, roasted potatoes, fresh boiled eggs, and coffee." The children in "The Paradise of Children" play games like those of Hawthorne's readers. Perhaps more important, the characters reflect values appropriate to children of the time. Perseus, Belleraphon, and Theseus display an admirable manliness as they prepare to set out for their adventures in the wide world. It is strongly implied that Proserpina's troubles resulted from not being close to her mother, and the other girls experience difficulties when they do not display appropriate feminine behavior.

Avoiding the grim tone Hawthorne found characteristic of the Greeks usually involved removing undesirable elements and modifying others. It is interesting to note that whereas the Greek myths often contained such intense emotions as jealousy, lust, and revenge, Hawthorne never allows these to appear. Indeed, he often trivializes the negative drives of characters by referring to them as "naughty." The adult passions are also removed by making many of the characters much younger than they were in the Greek originals: they are children, maidens, or youths. In this way Hawthorne was able to avoid discussing the sexual themes often found in the originals.

An examination of how Hawthorne retells the story of Perseus in "The Gorgon's Head" shows more clearly how he handled his material. "The Gorgon's Head" begins simply:

> Perseus was the son of Danae, who was the daughter of a king, and when Perseus was a very little boy some wicked people put his mother and himself into a chest and set them afloat upon the sea. The wind blew freshly and drove the chest away from the shore, and the uneasy billows tossed it up and down, while Danae clasped her child closely to her bosom, and dreaded that some big wave would dash its foamy crest over them both.

Readers familiar with classical mythology will immediately recognize two major omissions. Perseus was in fact the son of Zeus, who had descended upon Danae as a golden shower of rain; and Danae had been imprisoned by her father and later abandoned at sea because the oracle had foretold that her father would be killed by his grandson. Obviously, Hawthorne has removed the sexual elements from the story. He has also omitted the tyrannical grandfather as a character too violent for his audience. But most important, he has made no reference to the gods, effectively removing the story entirely from the realm of mythology. One final point may be made about Hawthorne's opening. The terrors of the ocean voyage are muted; the wind only blows "freshly" and the waves are "uneasy" and have "foamy" crests. In discussing Perseus' quest, Hawthorne deletes sexual references and transforms Perseus into a youthful hero such as one might find in any number of boys' adventure stories of the time.

The tale that Hawthorne creates is perfectly suited for the intended audience: it does not confront the problems of adult evil and sexuality, its monsters are grotesque but not terribly frightening, there is no discussion of the Greek gods, and Perseus is a model hero. In addition, the tale fits mid-nineteenth-century adult notions of what literature should be for children: entertaining, but also morally edifying.

Hawthorne's stories for children were relatively successful financially. Indeed, making money seems to have been one of his motivations for writing them. Although the historical stories exist now only in a scholarly edition, the retellings of the Greek myths and legends frequently have been reprinted in the twentieth century.

Hawthorne himself was extremely pleased with *A Wonder-Book* and *Tanglewood Tales,* telling his friend Richard Henry Stoddard, "I never did anything else so well as these old baby stories." Contemporary reviewers were also enthusiastic. One wrote, "The book will become the children's classic, and, to our taste, is fairly the best of its kind in English literature." A reviewer of *Tanglewood Tales* approved of the stories' moral tone: "It seems to us that if widely read they should exert an admirable influence, not only on the forming morals but the forming taste of children, refining character as well as conveying lessons." Those modern critics who have examined the retellings of myth consider these two volumes to be significant works. In them, Nina Baym notes, Hawthorne "was able to transcend his own temperamental affinity for the dark side of experience and enter into the simple and sunny world view he desired to represent." Hugo McPherson sees the myths as central in Hawthorne's vision, as "serious formulations of Hawthorne's understanding of the self."

While the historical stories are now generally forgotten and the modern age has retold the mythical tales in its own "garniture of manners and sentiment," Hawthorne's place in the history of American children's literature is secure. At a time when the province of writing for children was generally in the possession of inferior talents who almost invariably produced heavy-handed moral tales, Hawthorne was the first major American author to approach the genre seriously. Paperback editions of *A Wonder-Book* and *Tanglewood Tales* are still in print, and modern adapters have often used Hawthorne's versions of Greek myths as the basis for their retellings. As his contemporary reviewers noted, he used the sunnier aspects of his talents to produce, in *A Wonder-Book* and *Tanglewood Tales,* two books that were not only the first of their kind for children but also well-crafted, entertaining stories that, well over a century after their initial publication, maintain their vitality and interest.

Selected Bibliography

WORKS OF NATHANIEL HAWTHORNE

Famous Old People. Boston: E. P. Peabody, 1841.
Grandfather's Chair. Boston: E. P. Peabody, 1841; New York: Wiley and Putnam, 1841.
Liberty Tree. Boston: E. P. Peabody, 1841.

Biographical Stories for Children. Boston: Tappan and Dennet, 1842.

True Stories from History and Biography. Boston: Ticknor, Reed, and Fields, 1851. (A combined volume of the above four titles.) Republished in a scholarly edition with Hawthorne's preface, *The Centenary Edition of the Works of Nathaniel Hawthorne*, vol. 6, edited by Roy Harvey Pearce et al. Columbus: Ohio State University Press, 1972.

A Wonder-Book for Girls and Boys. Boston: Ticknor, Reed, and Fields, 1852.

Tanglewood Tales for Girls and Boys. Boston: Ticknor, Reed, and Fields, 1853. Republished in a scholarly edition, *The Centenary Edition of the Works of Nathaniel Hawthorne*, vol. 7, edited by Roy Harvey Pearce et al. Columbus: Ohio State University Press, 1972. (Combined text of *A Wonder-Book* and *Tanglewood Tales*.)

CRITICAL AND BIOGRAPHICAL STUDIES

Baym, Nina. *The Shape of Hawthorne's Career*. Ithaca, N.Y.: Cornell University Press, 1976.

Crowley, J. Donald. *Hawthorne: The Critical Heritage*. London: Routledge and Kegan Paul, 1970.

McPherson, Hugo. *Hawthorne as Myth-Maker: A Study in Imagination*. Toronto: University of Toronto Press, 1969.

Pearce, Roy Harvey. "Historical Introduction." In *The Centenary Edition of the Works of Nathaniel Hawthorne*, vol. 7: *True Stories from History and Biography*. Columbus: Ohio State University Press, 1972.

Stewart, Randall. *Nathaniel Hawthorne: A Biography*. New Haven, Conn.: Yale University Press, 1948.

—JON C. STOTT

E. T. A. HOFFMANN

1776–1822

> Leave to us Germans all the horrors of delirium, of feverish dreams, and the world of ghosts. Germany is a country more suited for old witches, dead bears' skins, golems of each sex and especially field marshals such as little Cornelius Nepos. Such spectres can only flourish on the other side of the Rhine; France will never be a country for them.
>
> (*Die romantische Schule*, in *Sämtliche Schriften*, p. 465)

EINRICH HEINE WAS thinking primarily of Ernst Theodor Amadeus Hoffmann when he wrote the above words, attempting to introduce German literature and culture to his host country, France. Yet despite the efforts of Heine and others, the reception of Hoffmann might be called a case history of cross-cultural misunderstanding; how one perceives him has depended very much on the place where he has been read. That reception might best be characterized as foreign amusement versus native terror. Anglo-American response to this quintessentially romantic artist has hardly differed, with only random glimpses of Grand Guignol and the grotesque that his German readers see. Encountering the name of Hoffmann in a collection devoted to writers for children, even today German readers might wonder if this is not just one more example of a Hoffmann misunderstood.

To call Hoffmann a children's writer, though not altogether wrong, makes as much sense as calling Picasso a children's painter. The texts clearly designed for a young audience make up a very small part of Hoffmann's total work, and the forms in which they are most likely to be known are adaptations, derivations, trivializations—in short, the amusements of such mediators as Alexandre Dumas *père*, Jacques Offenbach, Tchaikovsky, and Léo Delibes. Yet if one attends to the unmediated Hoffmann, one can find even in the most complex literary fairy tales, with their intricate and involved personal and psychological symbolism, not only a storehouse of children's issues as seen and reworked by Hoffmann the adult attempting to understand the fears and anxieties of his past, but also a set of narratives that has fascinated many generations of children worldwide.

Like his father before him, Hoffmann undertook the study of law, matriculating at the University of Königsberg in 1792. Although Kant was lecturing there at the time, there is no indication that Hoffmann had any interest in Kantian philosophy. If there was any philosophical influence in Hoffmann's life, it was that of Friedrich Schelling's nature philosophy, mediated largely through the writings of Novalis. His major interest during his student days was his music. Then, as well as later, Hoffmann's artistic interests, painting, wide reading (Shakespeare, Laurence Sterne, Tobias Smollett, Rousseau, Jean Paul, Novalis), but especially his music, both composition and performance, would be his defenses against personal loneliness and the banality (and often the mediocrity) of his environment.

Much of Hoffmann's trouble later in life was to stem from his hatred of stupidity and corruption, his refusal to be intimidated or bought out, and the use of his own satiric and artistic talents as a way of venting his anger at authority. The punitive responses of the Prussian bureaucracy paradoxically may have forced him into becoming the artist he was to be by leaving him, after his various transfers or dismissals, with no alternative but his art. His satirical streak, along with his alcoholism and his penchant for affairs with married women, would condemn him in the already precarious conditions of the Napoleonic age to a life of quick exits, exile, wandering, and penury. The pattern, which E. F. Bleiler has defined as "hard work, achievement, trouble, exile or flight, and a new start," began while Hoffmann was still a law student and would end only with his untimely death in 1822. After being tossed about the eastern fringes of the Prussian empire, not always as a result of his own doings, Hoffmann died at the relatively young age of forty-six, in the midst of one more scandal caused by his satirical pen. This time his barbs were aimed at a conservative political opponent who was pushing the investigation of "Father" Friedrich Ludwig Jahn, the fanatical founder of the Turnverein movement, a typical nineteenth-century mixture of jingoism and gymnastics. Because of his massive debts, his long-suffering wife of twenty years, Michaelina Rorer-Trzcínska (Mischa), was forced to relinquish her rights to his literary estate, which Hoffmann had willed to her three months before his death. He died on 25 June 1822 and was buried in Berlin at the cemetery of the Jerusalem Church near the Hallesches Tor.

Almost from the moment of birth the author of "Nussknacker and Mäusekönig" ("Nutcracker and Mouse King," 1816) was to find himself in a threatening and hostile environment, elements of which are reflected in his later work. He was born as Ernst Theodor Wilhelm Hoffmann on 24 January 1776. In honor of Mozart he later exchanged the third given name for "Amadeus." He was the youngest of three children in a family of mixed Polish and German ancestry; only he and his older brother survived childhood. His father, Christoph Ludwig Hoffmann, a lawyer, was also a notorious drinker and a talented but moody man. His mother, Louise Albertine, was a hysterical woman given to violent fits of weeping and depression. The parents were divorced when Ernst was four, and as a result he was separated not only from his father but also from his older brother, Karl, whose custody was given to the father. Louise took Ernst and soon moved to the home of Ernst's maternal grandmother, where he grew up in the company of women: his mother, a slave to bourgeois order; his grandmother; and, later, an insane female roomer, whose mad cries he often heard (she was the mother of Zacharias Werner, the fanatically Christian dramatist and friend of Hoffmann). These surroundings may well account for some of the misogyny in Hoffmann's writings.

Three particularly happy facets of Hoffmann's early years were his musical instruction, his art instruction, and a lasting friendship with Theodor Gottlieb von Hippel. He would later call upon all three to help him in times of need: on music and painting as sources of income when he had been dismissed from one of his posts, either because of a change of governments or because of his incautious and satirical pen; and on Hippel's wealth and influence when all else failed.

In many ways Hoffmann never outgrew his childhood and carried many of his dreams, the reveries as well as the nightmares, with him for the rest of his life, drawing upon them for his adult creations as though he were exorcising the demons of his youth. A study of his childhood not only is enlightening for an understanding of major portions of his own work, but may also grant insight into the inner life of the child, at least of a gifted child in the late eighteenth century. Even a partial inventory of his favorite figures and themes seems to open up onto a child's world. He populates his stories with grown-ups who never seem to have grown up completely, who attract children and confound the adult world with antireason, unpredictability, and playfulness. The theme of the double is reminiscent both of the child's invisible friend, the bad boy or girl who is to blame when things go wrong, and of the child's tendency to split the parent into the kind and loving one and the menacing, vengeful fiend. There are not only many fairy-tale motifs, miraculous transformations, and, sometimes, entry into magic lands, as in "Der goldne Topf" ("The Golden Flower Pot," 1814) and "Prinzessin Brambilla" ("Princess Brambilla," 1820); there are also fears of mutilation, as in "Der Sandmann" ("The Sand-Man," 1815) and of transformation into something less than human, as in "The Golden Flower Pot," "Die Königsbraut" ("The King's Betrothed," 1819), and "Klein Zaches" ("Little Zaches," 1819). Finally, Hoffmann's own life, his attitude toward authority, and his multimedia wizardry—his ability to perform so competently in so many endeavors (law, music, theater direction, painting, and drawing, as well as writing)—is like the acting-out of a child's fantasy life, in which he knows no bounds and does not worry about acquiring skills but simply flouts all boundaries and dares to venture.

Hoffmann's first successful work, *Ritter Gluck* (*Ritter Gluck*, 1809), already included many of the motifs that were to occur in his later works: the detailed and realistic narrative style deployed to describe the fantastic—in this case, the inexplicable reappearance of the composer Christoph Willibald von Gluck twenty-five years after his death; the use of music, not only described in loving detail, but used in gripping and eerie ways to set the scene; and the lack of any explanation for what has clearly been a walk into the "twilight zone": there is simply the mysterious guest's revelation in the last line of the story, "I am Sir Gluck" ("Ich bin der Ritter Gluck").

"The Golden Flower Pot," often considered Hoffmann's best story, is a marvelous narrative about the life of the artist. It combines almost every aspect of German romanticism with the creation within the context of the fairy tale of a typology of bourgeois behavior; a psychology of the artist; orientalism; and an intriguing inversion of the Creation myth, with the snake, Serpentina, representing what is truly divine, poesy. Reversing the biblical narrative, Hoffmann shows the emerging artist, Anselmus, already expelled from paradise, trapped in static and sterile bourgeois society. The narrative goal becomes finding a way back in, a way that is discovered in the seductiveness of art (Serpentina). Hoffmann is at his playful best in this magnificent tale, with its extensive incorporation of what was then contemporary science. Typical is his ability to weave romantic speculative biology, botany, and evolutionary theory, as well as aspects of romantic physics and psychology (electricity, crystallography, animal magnetism), into a highly symbolic narrative in which the real and the fantastic, science and nature, merge. The duel of sorcerer and sorceress at the end of the tale mythicizes the battle between the sexes in ways that may remind modern readers of the duel between Merlin and Mad Madam Mim in *The Sword in the Stone*, the Hollywood version of T. H. White's *The Once and Future King*.

"The Sand-Man," despite its title suggesting the relatively harmless bedtime bugaboo familiar to modern children both German and American, is a frightening tale dealing with narcissism, the psychopathology of art, repressed infantile fear of the father, aggression, and suicide. Sigmund Freud devoted a major portion of an interpretive essay to it in his study "Das Unheimliche ("The Uncanny") and used it as literary evidence for his theory of the castration complex. Insofar as any part of the tale can be considered a children's story, it reflects, especially in the actual fairy tale of the Sand-Man that the old nursery maid tells to the children, the pedagogical tendency to use terror as a deterrent in the moral education of German children in the nineteenth century—a tendency that culminates in the figures of Heinrich Hoffmann's Struwwelpeter and the various creations of Wilhelm Busch, originator of Max and Moritz, the models for the later cartoon characters the Katzenjammer Kids. E. T. A. Hoffmann also created in "The Sand-Man" the figure of Olympia, the "living doll," probably better known to popular audiences through the mediation of Offenbach's *Les contes d'Hoffmann* (*The Tales of Hoffmann*, 1881) and Delibes's ballet *Coppélia* (1870).

"Little Zaches," probably one of the literary models for Günter Grass's little Oskar Matzerath in *Die Blechtrommel* (*The Tin Drum*, 1959), though also not truly a children's story, is nonetheless a tale with pedagogical insight. Ultimately an allegory about good and bad artists (and critics) and an attack on the Enlightenment, it also seems to bring a number of parental attitudes under fire. For example, children may very well turn out to be ugly if one believes they are, but the obverse does not necessarily apply—one cannot necessarily make them beautiful and graceful by saying so. The titular antihero, Little Zaches, a victim of undeserved praise, is misled into believing that his grotesqueries are elegant achievements. His fairy godmother is moved by good intentions, but chooses the wrong message (or raw material). A pessimistic reading of this tale, and none other seems possible, would seem to accord with the moral ascribed to "The Golden Flower Pot" by those who also read that tale pessimistically: the special posture, the frame of mind that makes reality—the washday-workaday world—at all bearable is the power of make-believe; that is the psychological significance of the fairy tale. But ultimately reality always intrudes.

Perhaps the strangest of all of Hoffmann's tales is "The King's Betrothed," the text to which Heine alludes in the opening passage of this article and the basis, in part, for Offenbach's light opera *Le roi carotte* (*The Carrot King*, 1872), the story of a vain young girl who becomes engaged to a carrot and who only barely escapes being pulled down into the carrot king's underground realm, which here, as elsewhere in Hoffmann, represents sterile, unaspiring, vegetative philistinism. The use of ondines, salamanders, kobolds, nymphs, sylphs, and other elemental spirits desiring union with humans, usually in order to acquire a soul, is found throughout German romanticism, in Ludwig Tieck, Joseph von Eichendorff, Adelbert von Chamisso, and Friedrich Fouqué, but nowhere does it reach such heights—or depths—of the ridiculous and absurd as in Hoffmann's tale of the vegetable invasion. While "The King's Betrothed" has in its use of contemporary science, folktale motifs, and mythic material some things in common with Hoffmann's best tales, such as "The Golden Flower Pot," it probably also reflects Hoffmann's deteriorating psychological condition and growing bitterness toward the end of his life. The strong phallicism of the tale suggests once again Hoffmann's affinity with, if not influence on, Günter Grass, in this case in *Der Butt* (*The Flounder*, 1977). Even for Hoffmann, who could be incredibly misogynistic, the treatment of womankind is unusually cruel and demeaning, and parenthood is portrayed as a life-sapping burden.

Fortunately, such a vicious anti–fairy tale was to be balanced out by the much longer and far more artistically successful "Princess Brambilla," a kind of rags-to-riches story and one of Heine's favorites, filled with fantastic figures taken from the Italian commedia dell'arte and inspired by the art of Jacques Callot. The plot is perhaps the romantic and economic narrative that Hoffmann wished for himself, projected into the land of his dreams, Italy. It is one of Hoffmann's happiest creations.

The story for which Hoffmann is best known, at least as a writer for children, is "Nutcracker and Mouse King," but even it is a frightening and at times disturbing tale. The history of its translation and transmission illustrates how Hoffmann's tales have been eviscerated and sugarcoated. The Nutcracker in the German original is awesome, the Mouse King is a truly fiendish and menacing figure, and the battle that takes place between them in the middle of the night is absolutely terrifying. The tale is filled with all sorts of childish fears—things that go bump in the night, horrible transformations of infants into unsightly creatures, limbs that are un-

screwed and pulled out of the body, and a monstrous seven-headed mouse creeping about. The suggestiveness of the relation between Marie and the Nutcracker, with its mixture of mothering and latent eroticism, is obvious and typical of little girls with little doll men, but on another level, remembering that the Nutcracker is the transformation of Drosselmeier's nephew and bears an uncanny resemblance to Drosselmeier himself, there is the further disturbing suggestion, borne out by several passages in the text, that even the relation between little Marie and Godfather Drosselmeier is fraught with vicarious sexual overtones. Though "Nutcracker" definitely was written as a children's tale, a gift for the children of his friends Julius Eduard and Eugenie Itzig (Hitzig), Hoffmann seemed to have an instinctive awareness that even children like to have their flesh creep, that one way of learning to conquer terror is to confront it head on, that children are both violent like Fritz and seductive creatures like Marie-Clara, and that the inner life of a child is filled with something other than dreams of sugar-plum fairies. Finally, Hoffmann may also have meant to write on two levels, as Shakespeare does in *Twelfth Night*.

The "Nutcracker" that most people know is, of course, the adaptation of Hoffmann's tale by Alexandre Dumas *père*, *Histoire d'un casse noisette*, published first in Paris in 1844 in *Le nouveau magasin des enfants* in forty parts, then in book form, by the publisher Hetzel, in 1845. The dust jacket on one of the better-known English translations, by Douglas Munro, characterizes the story this way: "Here is the enchanting world of a late eighteenth-century nursery in Nuremberg and, beyond it, the stranger one of the Land of Toys with its river of essence of roses and its sparkling palaces."

The Dumas version considerably softens the original, although certain macabre aspects are kept and, as a result, stand out by their strangeness. Thus the frightening features of Drosselmeier are conspicuous, and conspicuously unexplained, in the opening of the tale. The sexual overtones are also preserved, such as the symbolic erection at the end of chapter 2 of the Dumas version (chapter 3 of the original).

The animation of the inanimate remains, however, and is stressed, quite appropriately, even before the beginning of the "fantasy" sequence (night in the nursery), affirming the perception so prevalent throughout Hoffmann that there really is no boundary between the "real" world and the "fantasy" world. Thus the brave little Nutcracker turns pale after brother Fritz brutally tests his limits, breaks his jaw, and knocks out three of his teeth; he looks cross and can express pain.

The Dumas retelling still has in common with the original the preindustrial view of war as a romantic spectator sport. Furthermore and understandably, the strong traditional gender roles remain. But in the Dumas version Drosselmeier does not unscrew, that is, dismember, the child in the Princess Pirlipat story, but instead "with a wonderful dexterity he first of all examined the princess's head, and then all her limbs and joints and muscles."

It is the Dumas version on which Tchaikovsky's ballet was largely based. As Maurice Sendak argues in his introduction to the version illustrated by him and newly translated by Ralph Manheim, Tchaikovsky himself seemed to be disappointed with the scenario that had been concocted in 1891 by Ivan Alexandrovich Vsevoloisky, director of the St. Petersburg Imperial Theater, and the choreographer Marius Petipa, which removed the story even further from Hoffmann, but he was able to close the gap a bit by composing "a score that in overtone and erotic suggestion is happily closer to Hoffmann than Dumas." Yet even the ballet omits entirely the fairy tale of the hard nut.

In all fairness, it should be pointed out that the transmission of a truly authentic Hoffmann was probably not possible until well into the twentieth century, that is, not until some rather sweeping changes had been made in societal attitudes about the nature of the psychic life of children, which would lead to more liberal ideas about what is appropriate and inappropriate in the literature we give to or share with them. Also, there has never been a binding obligation of philological fidelity on the part of authors and editors of children's books, and in the case of the transmitted author, especially across several cultures, there is always the possibility of more than one focus of interest. In the case of the Munro edition cited earlier, the translator is interested more in Dumas than in Hoffmann, while the illustrator, Phillida Gili, is expressly interested in the history of toys. The noted children's illustrator Lisbeth Zwerger, who has also provided a version of *Nutcracker and Mouse King*, clearly designates her bibliophile edition of Hoffmann's *Das fremde Kind* (The Strange Child, 1817) "a picture book for grown-ups," and justifies her greatly abridged edition as a pedagogic strategy, offering pictures and enough of the text to which they belong as a way of allowing those who already know Hoffmann to recall a favorite story, while enticing those unfamiliar with Hoffmann to read him in his entirety.

Perhaps the most successful and authentic English version of a Hoffmann text for children is the *Nutcracker* of Sendak-Manheim, a team of one of the most famous children's illustrator-writers with one of the foremost English translators of this century. It is probably not surprising that the artist who was one of the first to depict, visually and psychologically, children as we have finally come to know them in our post-Freudian age, real enfants terribles (*Where the Wild Things Are*, 1963) complete with inner turmoil and even genitals (*In the Night Kitchen*, 1970), would be the one to unveil the "other" Hoffmann and the erotic subtext of *Nutcracker*. A reader interested in finding something of the real Hoffmann lurking behind what Maurice Sendak calls the "confectionary goings-on of this . . . most bland and banal of ballet productions" could do far worse than to read the account of the thinking and discovery that went, first, into his set design for the 1981 Pacific Northwest Ballet *Nutcracker*, and then into the illustrations for the Manheim translation. As Michael Steinberg said in his review for the *New York Times* (11 November 1984), not only have Manheim-Sendak gotten rid of Dumas finally, "to give us, undiluted, the enormously more interesting, complex, even rather sinister Hoffmann," but also, "If mice bother you, don't leaf through this by yourself."

Selected Bibliography

WORKS OF E. T. A. HOFFMANN IN ENGLISH TRANSLATION

The Best Tales of Hoffmann. Translated by Alexander Ewing, J. T. Bealby, et al. Edited and with an introduction by E. F. Bleiler. New York: Dover, 1967. (This is generally recognized as the most useful and felicitous of editions available to the modern reader. E. F. Bleiler's commentary on Hoffmann's life, on the individual works, and on earlier translations is valuable for its succinctness, accuracy, and wealth of information.)

Tales of Hoffmann. Selected and translated with an introduction by R. J. Hollingdale, with the assistance of

Stella and Vernon Humphries and Sally Hayward. London: Penguin Books, 1982. (The chief virtue of this collection is its inclusion of "Mademoiselle de Scudéry" ["Das Fräulein von Scudéry," 1818], one of the most famous of German detective stories, written some twenty years before Edgar Allan Poe [who was influenced by Hoffmann] "invented" the genre. The translator freely admits that he has "editorialize[d]" where he felt that "some speeding up and tightening up was . . . called for.")

The Nutcracker. Translated by Douglas Munro from the French of Alexandre Dumas *père*. With illustrations by Phillida Gili. London: Oxford University Press, 1976.

The Nutcracker. Adapted by Warren Chappell from Alexandre Dumas *père*'s version. With illustrations by Warren Chappell. New York: Schocken Books, 1980. (A children's picture-book version, first published in 1958.)

Nutcracker. Translated by Ralph Manheim. With illustrations by Maurice Sendak. New York: Crown, 1984.

CRITICAL AND BIOGRAPHICAL STUDIES

Daemmrich, Horst S. *The Shattered Self: Hoffmann's Tragic Vision*. Detroit: Wayne State University Press, 1973.

Freud, Sigmund. "The Uncanny." In *Collected Papers*, vol. 4. London: Hogarth Press, 1956.

Heine, Heinrich. *Die romantische Schule*. In *Sämtliche Schriften*, vol. 5, edited by Klaus Briegleb. Munich: Hanser Verlag, 1976.

Hewett-Thayer, Harvey. *Hoffmann: Author of the Tales*. Princeton: Princeton University Press, 1948.

Negus, Kenneth. *E. T. A. Hoffmann's Other World: The Romantic Author and His "New Mythology."* Philadelphia: University of Pennsylvania Press, 1965.

Safranski, Rüdiger. *E. T. A. Hoffmann: Das Leben eines skeptischen Phantasten*. Munich: Hanser Verlag, 1984.

—LEONARD L. DUROCHE

HEINRICH HOFFMANN
1809–1894

PERHAPS NO CHILDREN'S picture book has had a more extravagant history than *Struwwelpeter* (*Slovenly Peter*, 1845), by Heinrich Hoffmann, medical doctor of Frankfurt am Main. Since its first publication in the author's native city, *Slovenly Peter*, the best known of all children's cautionary tales, has appeared in more than six hundred German-language editions as well as in French, Italian, English (several versions), Swedish, Arabic, Esperanto, and Latin translations, among many others. From the time of Sigmund Freud, who wrote inconclusively about its meaning, psychologists and educators have vehemently debated the book's possible effect on children, with some critics condemning it as a sadistic, authoritarian work and others praising it as a tongue-in-cheek entertainment plainly not to be taken at its word. Marxist and other historians have focused on the widely read book as an expression of mid-nineteenth-century Biedermeier values, and of bourgeois culture generally. Slovenly Peter himself has meanwhile assumed the independent life of a cultural icon almost rivaling Lewis Carroll's Alice in the variety of associations that satirists and others have attached to him—in prints, illustrations, toys, advertisements, and book-length homages and parodies.

As an educated man of his time, Hoffmann was not unusual in dabbling in literature. Throughout his adult life he produced occasional poems, aphorisms, and political and social satires, as well as professional papers and the children's books that unexpectedly brought him fame.

As a medical student in Heidelberg from 1829 until 1833, he joined a fraternity with liberal (but at the same time fiercely anti-Catholic and anti-French) views, and became known as the group's poet. As a young man he also met the composer Felix Mendelssohn, who was his contemporary in age and with whom he walked in the forests, which to the German Romantics potently represented transcendent spiritual values. Hoffmann's first published work, *Gedichte* (Poems, 1841), included verses recalling his student days and romantic lyrics in praise of the forest.

After a year of study in Paris Hoffmann returned to his native Frankfurt, where he spent the rest of his long and prosperous life. His first medical assignment was to the city morgue, a circumstance that he was quick to lampoon in a verse about a young doctor so confident of his art that he thinks himself capable of curing even the dead. The peculiar power of this macabre little satire is its cathartic effect: the absurd exaggeration releases the mind from the graphic reminder of mortality. The pictures and verses of *Slovenly Peter* follow a similar pattern.

The young doctor married Therese Donner in 1840, adopting the double-headed surname Hoffmann-Donner (though he signed virtually all of his published works as Heinrich Hoffmann). Their first son was born the following year. At Christmastime of 1844 Hoffmann attempted to purchase a suitable picture book—the boy was then three—and finding nothing that he approved of in the Frankfurt shops, he returned home with a blank book instead and set about making the drawings and verses that were to become *Slovenly Peter*.

Among the books that Hoffmann had had to choose from were, as he recalled years later in an introduction to the fortieth English edition:

> Long tales, stupid collections of pictures, moralizing stories, beginning and ending with admonitions like: "the good child must be truthful," or: "children must keep clean," etc. But I lost all patience when I found a folio volume, where a bench, a chair, a jug, and many other things were drawn, and under each picture neatly written: "half, a third, or a tenth of the natural size." A child, for whose amusement you are painting a bench, will think that a real bench; it has not and need not have an idea of the full size of a real bench. The child does not reason abstractedly [*sic*].

The cautionary tales to which Hoffmann referred were remorselessly humorless in tone, their authors relying on fear or on pious law-giving as instruments for shaping young readers' attitudes and behavior. By considering children's amusement both as a worthwhile end in itself and as the most effective means of offering the young their moral instruction, Hoffmann, though he scarcely meant to do so, helped to redirect children's literature along lines still widely regarded as psychologically valid.

He decided to publish his handmade gift book only after various adult relatives pressed him to do so; he sold the work outright for a modest sum to two friends, Rütten and Löning, who were just then starting out as Frankfurt publishers. To his delight, the first printing of fifteen hundred volumes—the preparation of which Hoffmann had carefully overseen—sold briskly, disappearing from the shops, as he said, "like a drop of water on a hot stove."

The first edition did not bear his name. He had chosen instead to be known by the droll pseudonym Reimerich Kinderlieb, or "Merry Rhymerick, children's friend." With the second printing he edged cautiously away from complete anonymity with the name Heinrich Kinderlieb; only with the fifth printing did he fully acknowledge his authorship. By then Hoffmann had also added four new vignettes to the little book—those concerning Little Pauline (or Harriet in many later editions), Fidgety Philip, Augustus, and Flying Robert. Also starting with the fifth printing, Peter, who originally occupied the last pages, was moved by popular demand of German child readers to the front

and cover. The fifth edition was, moreover, the first to be called *Struwwelpeter*, the book having begun its life with the bland title *Lustige Geschichten und drollige Bilder—für Kinder von 3–6 Jahren* (Pleasant Stories and Funny Pictures—for 3-to-6-Year-Olds) —its subtitle thereafter.

It was most unusual in Hoffmann's time to specify the age level for a children's book. That the author of *Slovenly Peter* thought to do so strongly suggests his awareness of the experimental work of the contemporary German educator Frederich Froebel, founder of the "kindergarten system," as well as perhaps of the writings of Johann Heinrich Pestalozzi, Froebel's mentor and a pioneer of developmental learning theory. Both educators emphasized younger children's sensory awareness as the key to their ability to learn, and thus they stressed the value of brightly colored pictures in books addressed to them, as well as the fruitlessness of instructing by means of logical exposition. Hoffmann evidently helped to popularize these ideas, for his own book gave rise to a new German expression for the ages three to six—the "Struwwelpeter years."

Hoffmann made his pictures first, then invented verses to accompany them. He had had no special training in art, but he clearly was not afraid of embarrassing himself in his own son's eyes by the crudeness of his drawings. Nineteenth- and turn-of-the-century children's classics—*Alice's Adventures in Wonderland*, *The Tale of Peter Rabbit*, and "A Visit to St. Nicholas," among others—were often the work of gifted amateurs, produced for a particular child without prior thought of publication. *Slovenly Peter* belongs to what one suspects was a widespread (although it remains largely unexplored) tradition of homemade books for the young.

We know that Hoffmann had some interest in art, since he modeled Peter directly on the popular lithograph *Les enfants terribles* (1842) by the French satirical illustrator Paul Gavarni, an inspiration for the sake of which he was apparently willing to override his extreme Francophobia. He also must have been acquainted with contemporary German prints; some of his own verses were issued as illustrated broadsides. Günter Böhmer has observed that the prevailing spirit of German popular graphics during the years preceding the revolution of 1848 was one of nonconformity, with the satiric deflation of the social order as one of its chief goals. Though Hoffmann did not support the revolution, his *Slovenly Peter* illustrations nonetheless reflect the irreverent, freewheeling spirit of the art of the time.

Hoffmann plucked the name Slovenly Peter nearly whole from contemporary Frankfurt dialect, which reserved the pejorative *Struwwelkup*, or "Sloppy-head," for a person of Peter's unkempt looks and demeanor. Once, to catch the attention of an anxious child patient who would not be calmed, the canny doctor had made an amusing sketch of such a sloppy-headed boy. The drawing had had the desired mesmerizing effect, so when Hoffmann sat down to make his son's book, he naturally thought to include Peter:

> Just look at him! there he stands,
> With his nasty hair and hands.
> See! his nails are never cut;
> They are grimed as black as soot;
> And the sloven, I declare,
> Never once has combed his hair;
> Anything to me is sweeter
> Than to see Shock-headed Peter.

Such a boy as this, of course, had no hope of receiving Christmas presents—his own copy, let us say, of *Slovenly Peter*—from Saint Nicholas, who rewarded virtuous children but punished the wicked. As if to drive the message home, Hoffmann, in another of the book's verses, called "The Story of the Inky Boys," conjured up the bearded, red-robed saint himself. Saint Nick dips three naughty German children, Ludwig, William, and Kaspar, in an outsize inkpot as fitting punishment for having harrassed a black man. (In later editions not supervised by Hoffmann, the name of Saint Nicholas was changed to that of Cornelius Agrippa, a sixteenth-century German mystic-heretic. The generations after Hoffmann's, it seems, have been less inclined to recall the punitive side of the traditional Saint Nicholas' role; better to attribute, tongue-in-cheek, such disagreeable behavior to one whose character was already under suspicion.)

Hoffmann's young readers, on the other hand, had more than likely received their copies of *Slovenly Peter* for Christmas—a sign from above that they belonged among the worthy. Thus assured of their fundamental goodness—and hence the book's immediate and sensational popularity—readers might feel at liberty to explore, in a more openly playful way than the children's literature of the time generally encouraged, such unruly qualities within themselves as Peter and his fellow mis-

creants illustrated in absurdly exaggerated form. In the character of Peter, Hoffmann created a convincing symbol of the wild, anarchic, unsocialized, or antisocial element of human nature. From this standpoint, *Slovenly Peter* is among the foundation works of a progressive children's literature tradition of which Maurice Sendak's *Where the Wild Things Are* (1963) is a more recent notable example. The nearly simultaneous appearance in Britain of Edward Lear's *A Book of Nonsense* (1846) and, a generation later, of Lewis Carroll's *Alice's Adventures in Wonderland* (1865), both of which also deal memorable blows to the sanctimoniousness of humorless moralizing, further suggests the spirit in which the young of Hoffmann's time were likely to have received his book.

An especially common type of Biedermeier (and Victorian) cautionary tale concerns the disobedient child who plays with matches and thereby burns him- or herself to death. In the context of such didactic lesson-mongering, one can easily recognize Hoffmann's "The Dread Story of Pauline and the Matches" in *Slovenly Peter* for the comic relief it was largely intended to provide.

By far the greatest critical uproar over *Slovenly Peter* has, however, centered on "The Story of Little Suck-a-Thumb," in which a boy named Kaspar (or Conrad in many later editions) refuses to abandon the young child's thumb-sucking habit and suffers the gruesome fate of having both his thumbs cut off by the tailor. As disturbing as the episode is when taken literally, Freud and others have seen in it a still more terrifying parable in which thumb-sucking is to be read as a euphemism for masturbation, for which castration is the indicated punishment. Citing only the verses about Kaspar, historian Peter Gay characterizes the whole of *Slovenly Peter* as a typical expression of male sexual anxiety in a "bourgeois century" marked by rising individual and class expectations. Such a reading of the Kaspar episode may well be justified. The tailor, fairy-tale style, is presented as a sort of magical helper of Kaspar's mother, who has warned her son against thumb-sucking and has predicted the dire consequences of disobedience. It is really she who has laid down the law. Hoffmann (who as a writer was, however, notoriously inconsistent in most matters of politics and ideology) contributed to the anti-feminist literature of his day with a satire, published in 1853, in which married life is compared to a "state of war."

But *Slovenly Peter* as a whole eludes this and other

reductive interpretations. Or rather, Hoffmann's enigmatic achievement was to have furnished grounds enough for both amusement *and* fright to allow either aspect to be emphasized by readers of different temperaments, maturity levels, and, in the case of adults reading aloud to children, motives.

A general practitioner in his first professional years, Hoffmann later specialized in work with the mentally ill. In retirement, as a man in his eighties, he considered his chief accomplishments to have been those concerned with improving the treatment of the insane; in an autobiography of more than two hundred pages, he devoted only ten or so to his books for children. This book was published posthumously, in 1926; its title, *Struwwelpeter-Hoffmann*, was chosen not by the author himself but by his grandson Eduard Hessenberg.

The immense popularity of *Slovenly Peter* has largely obscured the fact that Hoffmann wrote a small handful of other children's books as well. In these later efforts, however, the moralizing impulse that he so deftly subverted in *Slovenly Peter* generally got the upper hand, with unfavorable results. *König Nussknacker und der arme Reinhold* (King Nutcracker and Poor Reinhold, 1851) enjoyed fairly considerable popularity in Hoffmann's lifetime. It is a sentimental work in which nursery toys are brought to life in order to give a poor, sickly boy a joyful Christmas holiday.

In *Bastian der Faulpelz* (Bastian the Lazybones, 1854), the author recounts the sorry fate of a schoolboy who has failed to learn his ABC's. After Bastian meets his early death, the letters of his own name—represented in Hoffmann's haunting if also festive illustrations by a procession of severe-looking elders marching in lockstep—bear his coffin to a grave that, the author adds for good measure, lies beside Slovenly Peter's. This is the first news of Peter's death, for in the earlier book Slovenly Peter is left to slobber for all time in his rough ways. As a boy, Hoffmann had himself been left back in school and had suffered terribly from the disgrace he had thus brought upon his name. *Bastian* is his memory book of the experience, the lesson of which was apparently too emotionally charged for him to recast in a lighthearted vein.

Again, in the satirical *Im Himmel und auf der Erde* (In Heaven and On Earth, 1857), Hoffmann sides in the end with a plodding and pious morality. In heaven, readers learn, there is always work to be done, and woe to the lazy angels who shirk their responsibilities. Their place on high is not secure; let that be a lesson.

Neither *Bastian* nor *Im Himmel* was commercially successful in Hoffmann's time, undoubtedly for the same reasons that they hold little appeal for readers today. Hoffmann thereafter put aside his juvenile writing for twenty years, returning to it only after he became a grandparent.

Prinz Grünewald und Perlenfein mit ihrem lieben Eselein (*Prince Greenwood and Pearl-of-Price, with Their Good Donkey, Kind and Wise*, 1871) may, as the late Swiss critic and editor Bettina Hürlimann said, be Hoffmann's "loveliest" children's book, though if it is, its loveliness is more a matter of its parts than of the work as a whole. An extended verse narrative, *Prince Greenwood* relates the chaotic though at times very amusing story of a callous young prince who is punished for his disdain for the poor by being whisked away (by a magically endowed court donkey) to the depths of the forest, where he is transformed into a beggarly old man, thus to learn lessons in humility and charity. The prince's good sister eventually saves him, though not before the beasts of the forest arrive bearing musical instruments that they play to salute her virtue. The royal children's parents are meanwhile gored to death (by bloodthirsty *Sans-Culottes*—Hoffmann arbitrarily shifts out of fairy tale timelessness for the sake of striking a patriotic blow against the French). Miraculously, at the end of the story, the king and queen are somehow revived. Amid all these complications, concern for the poor is completely forgotten, though the prince, restored to his youth, fortune, and family, lives happily ever after.

Hoffmann left behind many unedited pages of children's verses with illustrations he had roughly sketched in the margins. Two of his grandchildren sorted through these papers, and in 1924 a new Hoffmann picture book was posthumously published, *Besuch bei Frau Sonne* (A Visit to Madam Sun). The verses of *Frau Sonne* lack the psychological edge of *Slovenly Peter*. They are inventive, charming, and for the most part unmenacing trifles:

> Walter in a snow-bound pass
> Found a mammoth stuck in ice.
> Many and many a thousand year
> The creature had been frozen there,
> And now, aroused so suddenly,
> He opens up his eyes and he
> (Despite his age) cries out, "Halloo!
> Now, then, Walter, how d'y'do!"
>
> (Hürlimann, p. 60)

Thus perhaps the aging doctor imagined a grand-child's view of Heinrich Hoffmann, a living dinosaur that moved only with difficulty but, for all that, seemed full of bonhomie and benevolent good cheer for an adventurous, spirited little visitor.

What, though, had become of Hoffmann's once hair-raising wit? It had, for the most part, evidently turned tamer. One example, however, of the earlier, sharper manner is also to be found in *Frau Sonne*. "Rudolph the Runner" is the story of a boy who, refusing to heed his parents' warning not to overexert himself at running, comes apart at the waist and literally runs on ahead of himself.

Rudolph's transgression is not simple disobedience of his elders, but hubris; the boy, we are told, set out to outrun—to "flabbergast"—the Western Wind, i.e., nature itself. The lesson implicit for readers is concerned not only with conformity to the bourgeois preference for restrained and moderate personal behavior (though this message is also plainly indicated) but also with a more general awareness of human limitations within the natural order. Hoffmann, no less than Mark Twain—who translated *Slovenly Peter* into English in the fall of 1891—always wrote most memorably about rule-breakers and mischief-makers, about children, that is, who like Huck Finn were "born to trouble."

Selected Bibliography

WORKS OF HEINRICH HOFFMANN IN GERMAN

Lustige Geschichten und drollige Bilder—für Kinder von 3–6 Jahren. With illustrations by the author. Frankfurt: Litterarische Anstalt (J. Rütten), 1845. (First edition of *Struwwelpeter*.) Later published as *Struwwelpeter: Zur hundertsten Auflage*. With illustrations by the author. Frankfurt: Rütten and Löning, 1876. (100th edition.)

König Nussknacker und der arme Reinhold. With illustrations by the author. Frankfurt: Rütten and Löning, 1851.

Bastian der Faulpelz. With illustrations by the author. Frankfurt: Rütten and Löning, 1854.

Im Himmel und auf der Erde. With illustrations by the author. Frankfurt: Rütten and Löning, 1857.

Prinz Grünewald und Perlenfein mit ihrem lieben Eselein. With illustrations by the author. Frankfurt: Rütten and Löning, 1871.

Besuch bei Frau Sonne. With illustrations based on those of the author. Frankfurt: Rütten and Löning, 1924.

TRANSLATIONS

The English Struwwelpeter; or, Pretty Stories and Funny Pictures. Translator unknown. With illustrations by the author. Leipzig: F. Volckmar, 1848. (First English translation.)

Slovenly Peter; or, Pleasant Stories and Funny Pictures. Translated by Charles T. Brooks. With illustrations by the author. Philadelphia: Willis P. Hazard, 1851. (Earliest American edition listed in the Library of Congress catalog.)

Pierre l'ébouriffé: Joyeuses histoires et images drolatiques pour les enfants de 3 à 6 ans. Translated by Trim. With illustrations by the author. Paris: Librairie Fischbacher, 1860.

Prince Greenwood and Pearl-of-Price, with Their Good Donkey, Kind and Wise. Translated by M. Despard. With illustrations by Eleanor Greatorex. Washington, D.C.: N. Peters, 1874.

Struwwel Peter: A Picture Book for Boys and Girls. Translator unknown. With illustrations by the author. New York: McLoughlin Brothers, 1904.

Slovenly Peter: The Pictures and Verses as Remembered by the Children of Ralph Waldo Emerson. Translated by Annis Lee Furness. With illustrations by Edward Waldo Emerson. Boston and New York: Houghton Mifflin, 1917.

La Struvelpetro: Beletaj rakontoj kaj komikaj bildoj de Dr. Heinrich Hoffmann. Translated into Esperanto by J. D. Applebaum. With illustrations by the author. Frankfurt: Rütten and Löning, 1921.

The Latin Struwwelpeter. Translated by W. H. D. Rouse. With illustrations by the author. London: Blackie and Son, 1934.

Slovenly Peter; or, Happy Tales and Funny Pictures. Freely translated by Mark Twain. With illustrations by Fritz Kredel based on those by the author. New York and London: Harper and Brothers, 1935.

The Mountain Bounder: Rollicking Rhymes and Pictures by Heinrich Hoffmann. Translated from *Besuch bei Frau Sonne* by Jack Prelutsky. With illustrations based on drawings by the author. New York: Macmillan, 1967.

Slovenly Peter; or, Pretty Stories and Funny Pictures for Little Children. Translator unknown. With illustrations by the author. Rutland, Vt.: C. E. Tuttle, 1969.

Struwwelpeter: Merry Stories and Funny Pictures. Translator unknown. With illustrations by the author. London: Pan Books, 1972.

BIOGRAPHICAL AND CRITICAL STUDIES

Böhmer, Günter. *Deutscher Humor im Spiegel der Populärgraphik*. Paris: Centre Cultural Allemand, 1974.

Freud, Sigmund. "Introductory Lectures on Psychoanalysis, Part 3." In *The Standard Edition of the Complete Works of Sigmund Freud*, vol. 16. London: Hogarth Press, 1963.

————. "Three Essays on the Theory of Sexuality." In *The Standard Edition of the Complete Works of Sigmund Freud*, vol. 7. London: Hogarth Press, 1953.

Gay, Peter. *Education of the Senses: The Bourgeois Experience, Victoria to Freud*. New York: Oxford University Press, 1984.

"Herr Hoffmann ist zu gar nichts nütz. . . ." Frankfurt: Heinrich-Hoffmann-Museum, 1984.

Hoffmann, Heinrich. *Struwwelpeter-Hoffmann*. Frankfurt: Englert und Schlosser, 1926.

Hürlimann, Bettina. *Three Centuries of Children's Books in Europe*. Translated and edited by Brian W. Alderson. Cleveland and New York: World Publishing, 1968.

Die Kinder des Struwwelpeter. Frankfurt: Heinrich-Hoffmann-Museum, 1984.

Der Struwwelpeter. Stuttgart: Stuttgarter Kunstkabinett, 1954.

—LEONARD S. MARCUS

LANGSTON HUGHES

1902–1967

LANGSTON HUGHES IS one of the best-known literary exponents of the Harlem Renaissance of the 1920's, and his influence is still evident in the works of contemporary authors and playwrights. Hughes was born in Joplin, Missouri, in 1902. He grew up in Lawrence, Kansas, Lincoln, Illinois, and Cleveland, Ohio, and first came to New York City in 1921 to attend Columbia University for one year. His travels to Africa and Europe after leaving Columbia probably provided the material and helped to shape the insights that were to make his writings so distinctive. Upon his return to the United States, Hughes reentered college; in 1929 he graduated from Lincoln University in Pennsylvania. The young Hughes had a restless, troubled, but eventful youth. By the time he had finished his formal education, he had achieved recognition for his poetry and had been awarded prizes for his writing. Hughes was extremely versatile and prolific, writing poetry, newspaper columns, novels, short stories, plays, a musical, lyrics for popular operas, and both fiction and nonfiction for children. He was, however, primarily a poet, and one of his books of poetry, *The Dream Keeper and Other Poems* (1932) and one of his last, posthumously published works, *Black Misery* (1969), were compiled specifically for children.

The Harlem (or "Negro") Renaissance of the 1920's brought to the forefront of American consciousness an outpouring of literary expression on black themes by young black writers. By combining the popular dialect forms of Paul Laurence Dunbar, the poetic rhythms of Vachel Lindsay, and the free verse forms of Walt Whitman and Carl Sandburg, Hughes shaped his own unique style. The subjects of his poems were frequently based on observations of his family and neighbors as they struggled for survival in a hostile environment.

Hughes was deeply committed to recording the history and preserving the artistic heritage of his people. His nonfiction books for children presented historical information about the origins of Afro-American people and provided informal explanations of their arts and of jazz, as a musical form. He also wrote or colloborated on biographies of blacks whose accomplishments were exemplary, or whose lives could serve as sources of motivation for the young. Most of these books share the concision and cadences of his poetry.

In *The First Book of Negroes* (1952), illustrated by Ursula Koering, the written text is brief. Nevertheless, Hughes manages to weave together past and contemporary history in order to elucidate the topics he chose for discussion. In this short work intended for readers in the third to fifth grades, he describes not only the culture of the Africans, but also the migration of "Negroes" to North and South America and the Caribbean islands. He mentions the ancient kingdoms in Africa, including Ghana, Songhay, and Mandingo. He focuses on notable blacks from these areas, discussing their contributions to history, government, athletics, and the arts. Among those featured are Dunbar, Frederick Douglass, Ralph Bunche, Thurgood Marshall, W. C. Handy, Althea Gibson, Marian Anderson, and Harriet Tubman. It is difficult to separate Hughes's personal view of the social forces that influenced the lives of Afro-Americans, such as the slave trade, the abolitionist movement, or the civil rights legislation of the 1950's, from his presentation of historical facts, which is intensely personal; through the eyes of a child he traces the history and culture of his people from their origins in Africa to their presence on the American continent.

The First Books series was written to meet the publisher's guidelines, which required a fixed length and a manageable vocabulary for young readers. *The First Book of the West Indies* (1956), Hughes's fourth book in the series, contains general information on the geographical characteristics of the different islands and the nature of their populations and customs. In spite of the restrictions imposed by the series format, Hughes includes enough interesting and substantive information, including lists of native plants and of famous men who were born in the islands, to make the book a useful resource for school children. At the same time, Hughes infuses his books in this series with optimistic messages.

He reveals, however, a more stark perspective on the black experience in America in *A Pictorial History of the Negro in America* (1956), written with Milton Meltzer. The photographs, cartoons, and prints that complement the clear, easy-reading textbook are shockingly realistic. The history extends from the arrival of the first shipload of African slaves in Virginia in 1619 to the *Brown* v. *Board of Education of Topeka, Kansas,* Supreme Court decision in 1954, and the book was so popular that it was revised several times before Hughes's death in 1967.

A Pictorial History of the Negro in America is one of two books for children whose authorship Hughes shared. *Popo and Fifina: Children of Haiti* (1932) was the result of a pleasant collaboration with his fellow poet Arna Bontemps. This simple story for young children is set in Haiti; few other authors of children's books at the time attempted to portray the lifestyle of poor blacks in the Caribbean. In *Popo and Fifina,* two children and their parents move from a farm to a small village; Papa Jean earns his living as a fisherman. Through the story of this family, readers are afforded a glimpse of the hardships of life on the island:

Popo and Fifina were walking barefooted behind two long-eared burros down the highroad to the little seacoast town of Cape Haiti. . . . There were by now, too, many people passing along the streets with bundles on their heads. . . . The little house to which Popo and Fifina had come with their parents was just a one-roomed shack with a tin roof. It had no windows, and only one door that was as rough and awkward as the door of a woodshed.

Except for passages in which Hughes compares the life of this family to that of an American family or makes a broad generalization—"All Haitian youngsters learn to carry burdens on their heads" —there is little didacticism in his story. Hughes had spent only a brief time in Haiti, in April 1931, and his impressions of island affairs certainly did not create memories of an idyllic paradise. Yet, although *Popo and Fifina* reveals the poverty of some of the island families, it portrays a warm, loving, hard-working people who still have avenues of hope. His outrage at the disrepair of the historical monuments—themselves symbols of Haitian freedom—at Cap-Haïtien, at the evidence of a corrupting class system, prejudice, and poverty, and at the presence of the American military impelled him to write an article called "People Without Shoes" (October 1931) for the *New Masses,* and further articles in *The Crisis.*

Among the various genres of literary works Hughes produced, his historical books for children are remarkable for their clarity of style and the amount and quality of information they provide. His books about jazz, a music he loved, and his selections of poetry for children are equally informative and sensitive. Unlike his adult works, his writings for the young contain very little social and political protest. *The First Book of Rhythms* (1954) was written to introduce children and young people to a creative way of viewing their world. Hughes discusses the various rhythms of sculpture, painting, the seasons, dancing, poetry, and athletics. In a few words he explains syncopated time, an important and complex component of jazz music. The book was based upon a talk he often gave to groups of children of various ages at schools and other locations.

The First Book of Jazz (1955) is another simple, informative introduction to jazz. Hughes discusses the evolution of jazz from Negro work songs through the jubilees and ragtime to swing and bebop. He explains the emergence of rhythm and blues, "cool" jazz, and "hot" jazz, and relates each development to its particular era. Interspersed with the definitions of musical terms are the music and lyrics for some blues and jazz songs. Hughes also includes some interesting comments about people and places in jazz history; he records that, before Louis Armstrong was twelve, he started to play on a ukulele fashioned from a cigar box, and recalls "Stale Bread," the blind newsboy who conducted a street corner band, and Congo Square, the place where African slaves gathered on Sundays to dance the bamboula. He also describes the themes found in the blues; the songs express sadness and loneliness, but underlying all is the sense of laughter evident in the lyrics:

> I'm going down to the railroad
> And lay my head on the track,
> . . . .
>
> But if I see the train a-coming,
> I'm gonna jerk it back.

Children are introduced to Stephen Foster, one of the great white minstrel writers, who originally called his songs "Ethiopian," and to James Bland, a minstrel man who toured Europe and America and who composed "Carry Me Back to Old Virginny." Hughes lists famous jazz musicians of the past and present, and, of particular interest, one hundred of his own favorite folk, jazz, and blues records—recordings that perfectly illustrate the various stages in the historical evolution of these forms of music.

In *Famous Negro Music Makers* (1955) Hughes presents children with short biographical sketches of people not found in other books. He writes about, among others, the Fisk Jubilee Singers; James Bland; the folk singer Leadbelly; William Grant Still, a composer of symphonic music; the jazz trumpeter Louis Armstrong; the gospel singer Mahalia Jackson; and the opera singer Marian Anderson. Each personality mentioned represents a different form of music. Hughes explores the difficulties these performing artists had, and have, in breaking down the barriers of racial prejudice in the United States.

It was as a poet, however, that Hughes was best known. The editors of *The Brownies' Book,* a children's magazine sponsored by the National Association for the Advancement of Colored People (NAACP) and published monthly between January 1920 and December 1921, gave Hughes his first opportunity to be publish his poems in 1921. These early, unsophisticated works included two poems,

"Winter Sweetness" and "Fairies," and an essay about Mexican games. There were more poems, a one-act play, and a few stories in subsequent issues of *The Brownies' Book,* Hughe's first major poem, "The Negro Speaks of Rivers," appeared in January 1921 in *The Crisis,* the official journal of the NAACP, under the editorial guidance of Jessie Fauset, who was then the literary editor for both magazines. Hughes was to become a true advocate of social causes, and he admired the social realism of Vachel Lindsay's works, including "The Congo," "John Brown," and "Simon Legree." In 1925, when Hughes was working as a busboy in a Washington, D.C., hotel, he recognized Lindsay, who was attending a recital there, and shyly slipped some of his poems to the older poet. Lindsay read the poems at the recital, and this incident marked the beginning of recognition for Hughes's talent.

The music critic Carl Van Vechten dubbed Hughes "The Negro Poet Laureate." The poet William Rose Benét wrote, in a critical review of *The Dream Keeper and Other Poems,* that although the book would not place Hughes among the major poets, at least it displayed his talent as "a melodist." *The Dream Keeper* primarily consists of poems selected expressly for children from *The Weary Blues* (1926) and *Fine Clothes to the Jew* (1927), and includes several additional poems. Most of the poems possess a lyric quality and a simplicity that appeal to young readers and that make them good for reading aloud and memorizing.

The posthumously published *Don't You Turn Back* (1969) contains poems selected by the poet-anthologist Lee Bennett Hopkins, because they were the favorites of children. The title is taken from Hughes's "Mother to Son," in which a black mother urges her son to persevere in spite of hardships:

> So, boy, don't you turn back.
> Don't you set down on the steps
> 'Cause you finds it kinder hard.

Hughes uses the idiom of black speech to deliver a personal message of encouragement to his young readers, for whom, as the mother in the poem points out, generations have endured a life that "ain't been no crystal stair." The poem is graphic, concise, touching, and hopeful. Hopkins divided Hughes's poems into four categories. "My People" includes poems expressive of ethnic or racial feelings. "Prayers and Dreams" is a mixture of lyric verses and poems such as "Prayer Meeting," which first appeared in *The Crisis* in August 1923, and "Feet o' Jesus," which first appeared on the cover of *Opportunity* in October 1926, that stem from his interest in gospel and church music. The last two sections are "Out to Sea" and "I Am a Negro."

Most of Hughes's critics would agree that his poetry is distinctive for its folk quality. He was fascinated by the language of the people of Harlem, whom he described as "not very different from others except in language," adding, "I love the color of their language." His poems reflect the Harlem he found in the 1920's, with its jazz clubs and cabarets. Hughes's use of words itself is often based on jazz, with its improvisational tempos, as in "Negro Dancers," first published in *The Crisis* in March 1925:

> Me an' ma baby's
> Got two mo' ways,
> Two mo' ways to do de Charleston!

These experiments in language forms and rhythms make Hughes's poetry, in the words of one critic, more resonant.

Much of Dunbar's fame was based on his dialect poetry, and Hughes, at the age of fourteen, already reflected the influence of the older poet in an early poem, "Reasons Why" (1932):

> Just because I loves you—
> That's de reason why
> Ma soul is full of color
> Like de wings of a butterfly.

Hughes's interest in the free-verse forms of Sandburg and Whitman marks some of his early poems:

> The mills
> that grind and grind,
> That grind out steel
> And grind away the lives of men
> ("The Mills," in *The Big Sea*)

However, Hughes's use of the rhythms of jazz and Harlem speech patterns soon set his writing style apart from those of his role models.

Another marked characteristic of Hughes's poetry is what might be called its "Negritude"—a concept formulated by Léopold Senghor, Aimé Césaire, and other French-speaking Caribbean and African poets, consisting of a deliberate celebration of black consciousness, black history, and black pride. Senghor, when asked to list American writers whose works exhibited this quality of "Negritude," named Langston Hughes as one. Negritude is akin to the concept popular in the 1970's under the rubric of "soul," which referred to a particular expression of pride in one's identity and an uninhibited freedom to convey innermost feelings. As Senghor observed, the "songs of Langston Hughes are pure, spontaneous, and simple."

Hughes learned early that the writer's best subjects were often those nearest to him. At fourteen, he watched "the brown girls from the South, prancing up and down Central Avenue," and so he wrote about them. He wrote about love, about the mills where his stepfather worked, about the place where he lived at the time, and about Sandburg, one of his early inspirations:

> I know a lover of life sings . . .
> When Carl Sandburg sings.
> I know a lover of all the living
> sings then.
> *(The Big Sea)*

Hughes was a folk poet, interpreting the language and rhythms of the people he observed around him, recording their beliefs, hopes, and fears. In "Baby" (1927), he writes:

> Albert!
> Hey, Albert!
> Don't you play in dat road.

And in "Judgment Day" (1927):

> An' now I'm settin' clean an' bright
> In de sweet o' ma Lord's sight.

Even in poems for children he explored controversial subjects, as in "The Negro," published first in *The Crisis* in January 1922:

> I've been a victim:
> The Belgians cut off my hands in the Congo.
> They lynch me now in Texas.

He personalized daily frustrations and discussed race relations, utilizing his unique ability to bring complex and insightful observations to an imaginative and vivid climax, as in "Good Morning" (1951):

I've seen them come dark
Wondering . . .
The gates open—
but there're bars at each gate.
What happens
to a dream deferred?
Daddy, aint you heard?

And "Merry-Go-Round," which appeared in *Common Ground* in the spring of 1942:

Where is the Jim Crow section
On this merry-go-round,

Where's the horse
For a kid that's black?

Both Bontemps and Countee Cullen were contemporaries of Hughes. With him they were among the greats of the Harlem Renaissance. A comparison of the three poets would readily reveal that Hughes departed from the more standard and structured style of writing of his two contemporaries, even though all three addressed the black experience in their poetry. The difference is already apparent in the early poem "The Negro Speaks of Rivers," in which Hughes writes:

I've known rivers:
. . . .
I bathed in the Euphrates when dawns were young
. . . .
I've known rivers:
Ancient, dusky rivers.

Of the three, Hughes is the most experimental, employing free verse, syncopated rhyme, and rhythms derived from jazz or the music of revivalist church gatherings; he also appears to be most intense in presenting the tensions caused by racial problems, yet the most objective in his perspective. It is possible that, because Hughes had traveled so extensively in his youth, he was better able to record with authenticity and sensitivity a view of the total black culture to which he belonged.

Hughes's literary output has left a permanent imprint on American literature. His gift was to celebrate the values of social and human justice, with originality, clarity, laughter, and deep social awareness. He used his art to describe an America that was little known or understood by a majority of Americans. His methods for bringing about awareness in readers were innovative and effective, even though he principally wrote poetry—a form that some perceive as better suited for idealistic thought and philosophical abstractions than for realistic portrayals and concrete observations. He dared to depart stylistically from the essay form commonly used to express serious concerns, as in "Suicide's Note," which first appeared in *Vanity Fair* in September 1925:

The calm,
Cool face of the river
Asked me for a kiss.

To the purist, the true enigma in his poetry was its combination of simplicity in form and complexity of subject. His imaginative explorations were rooted in reality.

Before his death in 1967 Hughes wrote one other book for the young, *Black Misery,* which was published posthumously in 1969. This book is classed with his poetry, although it is essentially a compilation of one-liners about the "miseries" experienced by children: "Misery is when the kid next door has a party and invites all the neighborhood but you." Some of the situations described in *Black Misery* are unique to black children: "Misery is when you first realize so many things bad have black in them, like black cats, black arts, blackball." Humor tempers some of the bitterness of the insights in this work—insights that definitely present a particular view of childhood: "Misery is when your white teacher tells the class that all Negroes can sing and you can't even carry a tune." *Black Misery* is probably the most satirical work Hughes wrote for and about children. Although not a major work, it is certainly significant because it is among his last and represents his lifetime concern about being young and black in America; in it he articulates what many children feel but are unable to express.

Despite his occasional bitterness, Hughes strongly affirmed the important part humor plays in his writings and in the folk culture of black Americans. Although he abhorred the social inequities he observed, he maintained his optimism and sensitivity about common human frailties. This is particularly evident in his poetry for young people. Hughes defined humor as "laughing at what you haven't got when you ought to have it," continuing, "Humor is our unconscious therapy." José Antonio Fernández de Castro recognized the spontaneity and personal quality of Hughes's poetry—a poetry "filled with laughter, color, sound and splendor—the qualities of the black soul." Hughes himself likened humor to a summer rain in its capacity to "suddenly cleanse and cool the earth, the air and you." For over four decades, Hughes retained a freshness in his poetry:

> To fling my arms wide
> In the face of the sun,
> Dance! whirl! whirl! . . .
> ("Dream Variation")

and he pointed out the wonders of everyday life in each era in which he lived. We define "era" as Donald Dickinson does in his *A Bio-bibliography of Langston Hughes* (1967), which he divides into "1902–1925—Early Years, 1926–1930—The Harlem Renaissance, 1931–1946—Prose and Poetry of Protest, and 1941–1965—Mature Years."

Hughes recorded the pain and poignancy of life for the black population:

> Because my mouth
> Is wide with laughter . . .
> You do not think I suffer after
> I have held my pain
>
> So long?
>
> ("Minstrel Man")

In *The Big Sea* (1940), his first semiautobiographical work, which is more accessible to young adults than to children, Hughes describes his youth and his decision to become a writer when he realized he not only could understand the French of Maupassant but could actually sense the beauty of the falling snow the author was describing. Although Hughes is principally known for writing about the black experience, he has also written a few lyric poems describing some passing scene or some phenomenon in nature: These works include "Winter Moon," which appeared in *The Crisis* in August 1923, and "Long Trip" (1926). Hughes was essentially, however, a "people-watcher," a constant observer of the human scene, recording a mother's love, the exuberance of youth, the pain of violence, or the humiliation of poverty. Hughes also took pleasure in the effects he could achieve with words. He was like a musical arranger producing a particular tonal quality. His poetry closely involves the reader as he or she listens and sounds out the words, trying to capture the poet's rhythm. The oral character of Hughes's poetry gives it an ele-

ment of liveliness that many of his contemporaries, who used more standard and familiar forms and styles, lacked. His subtleties were hidden in the tempo and apparent lightness of the verses—which, in fact, led some critics to see them as trivial.

Many of Hughes's nonfiction books for children are now out of print. *The First Book of Jazz*, however, was revised in 1982. His volumes of poetry are not readily available, but his poems may be found in most outstanding anthologies of American poetry. Describing the culture, experiences, and psychology of black Americans in their various "Harlems," Hughes demonstrated unparalleled pathos, beauty, and understanding in his poetry.

Selected Bibliography

WORKS OF LANGSTON HUGHES

The Dream Keeper and Other Poems. With illustrations by Helen Sewell. New York: Knopf, 1932.

Popo and Fifina: Children of Haiti. With illustrations by E. Simms Campbell. With Arna Bontemps. New York: Macmillan, 1932.

The Big Sea, an Autobiography. New York: Knopf, 1940.

Montage of a Dream Deferred. New York: Henry Holt, 1951.

The First Book of Negroes. New York: Franklin Watts, 1952. With illustrations by Ursula Koering.

Famous American Negroes. New York: Dodd, Mead, 1954.

The First Book of Rhythms. With illustrations by Robin King. New York: Franklin Watts, 1954.

The First Book of Jazz. With illustrations by Cliff Roberts. New York: Franklin Watts, 1955.

Famous Negro Music Makers. With photographs. New York: Dodd, Mead, 1955.

A Pictorial History of the Negro in America. With Milton Meltzer. New York: Crown, 1956; rev. 1963, 1968. Reissued as *A Pictorial History of Black Americans.* With C. Eric Lincoln. With illustrations by E. McKnight Kauffer. New York: Crown, 1973; rev. ed., 1983.

The First Book of the West Indies. With illustrations by Robert Bruce. New York: Franklin Watts, 1956.

Famous Negro Heroes of America. With illustrations by Gerald McCann. New York: Dodd, Mead, 1958.

The First Book of Africa. With photographs. New York: Franklin Watts, 1960.

Black Misery. With illustrations by Arouni. New York: P. S. Eriksson, 1969.

Don't You Turn Back: Poems by Langston Hughes, selected by Lee Bennett Hopkins. With illustrations by Ann Girfalconi. New York: Knopf, 1969.

CRITICAL AND BIOGRAPHICAL STUDIES

Barksdale, Richard. *Langston Hughes.* Chicago: American Library Association, 1977.

Berry, Faith. *Langston Hughes: Before and Beyond Harlem.* Westport, Conn.: Lawrence Hill, 1983.

Dickinson, Donald C. *A Bio-bibliography of Langston Hughes, 1902–1967.* Rev. ed. Hamden, Conn.: Archon Books, 1972.

Jemie, Onwuchekwa. *Langston Hughes: An Introduction to the Poetry.* New York: Columbia University Press, 1976.

Emanuel, James A. *Langston Hughes.* Boston: Twayne, 1967.

Meltzer, Milton. *Langston Hughes: A Biography.* New York: Thomas Y. Crowell, 1968.

Nichols, Charles H., ed. *Arna Bontemps–Langston Hughes Letters, 1925–1967.* New York: Dodd, Mead, 1980.

O'Daniel, Therman B., ed. *Langston Hughes, Black Genius: A Critical Evaluation.* New York: William Morrow, 1971.

—BARBARA T. ROLLOCK

WASHINGTON IRVING

1783–1859

WASHINGTON IRVING HAS become a puzzlement—even an embarrassment—to modern anthologists, and the difficulty is compounded when one searches for works that still appeal to young readers. Abandoning "Rip Van Winkle" and "The Legend of Sleepy Hollow" to junior-high readers, high-school texts include some of Knickerbocker's *History of New York* (1809) and "The Devil and Tom Walker." College anthologies repeat, almost dutifully, "Rip Van Winkle" and "The Legend of Sleepy Hollow," augmented by a page or two of Knickerbocker, "The Adventure of the German Student," and excerpts from "The Author's Account of Himself," which forms the introduction to *The Sketch Book* (1819–1820).

The justification for reading Irving is often essentially his historical interest. He was the first American writer to gain a considerable reputation in England, the British reviewers being delighted to discover "a *mind* working in America . . . on materials . . . of a very singular and romantic kind." Moreover, there was the "remarkable" fact of his "great purity and beauty of diction, on the model of the most elegant and polished of our native writers"; he was seen as an American Addison or Goldsmith. (And, indeed, at one time Irving's work was a model of composition, a handbook of style.)

The praise was a mixed blessing; others complained that Irving was un-American in his imitativeness. Unwittingly contributing to the charge, which has persisted even into twentieth-century criticism, Irving conceded in "English Writers on America" that "we are a young people, necessarily an imitative one, and must take our examples and models . . . from . . . Europe." Thus, so the argument goes, Irving deserted the American concerns of his time, retreating into a sentimental, nostalgic, romantic Anglophilism. Irving's often-quoted contrast between America and Europe seems to support the accusation. "Never need an American look beyond his own country for the sublime and beautiful of natural scenery," he wrote in "The Author's Account of Himself." "But Europe held forth the charms of storied and poetical association. . . . My native country was full of youthful promise; Europe was rich in the accumulated treasures of age. . . . I longed . . . to escape . . . the commonplace realities of the present, and lose myself among the shadowy grandeurs of the past."

The received view of Irving became so consolidated that other, more "American" qualities have been quite obscured. The handbooks stress Irving's "amiable," "gentlemanly" qualities, which precluded his forging a literature of interior conflicts. Much of this is true enough. More damaging is the sweeping assertion by James Hart in *The Oxford Companion to American Literature* that because Irving "saw the European past in an aura of romance . . . [he] consistently avoided coming to grips with modern democratic life." Even those critics who acknowledge that Irving was caught between the old and the new, England and America, classic and romantic, object that these polarities did not produce in his work the kinds of psychic tensions and "tragic vision" that became the mark of later American romantics such as Nathaniel Hawthorne and Herman Melville.

However, a different reading of Irving's American dilemma may account for the persistent appeal of certain sketches—most of which deal with American scenes and characters. Authorially, Irving can be seen as an American "adolescent" whose quest to establish an American "self" took two contradictory directions: one historical and connective, the other essentially psychological and disjunctive. The ambivalence manifested itself in an attempt to attach writing to a "parent" country in order to establish a continuity with the past and, at the same time, to assert its independence from those constraints.

With only a few exceptions, the sketches generated by the first impulse have little appeal for a modern reader. "Westminster Abbey" no doubt could charm the American visitor to that shrine, who finds things tidied up since Irving's time: Elizabeth's scepter and Henry V's head are now both in place. The essay about mutability may speak to a young reader, but most of the other pieces in *The Sketch Book* obviously cater to stock responses and a now-defunct sentimentalism: "The Wife," "The Broken Heart," and "The Widow and Her Son"; the "tourist" sketches—"The Boar's Head Tavern" and "Stratford-on-Avon"; and the Dickensian "Christmas" series. In contrast, the tales that spring from the psychological impulse are still alive— "Rip Van Winkle," "The Legend of Sleepy Hollow," and, later, in *Bracebridge Hall* (1822), "Dolph Heyliger."

What may appear as ambivalence may simply be the expression of Irving's conservative detachment from a peculiarly American nineteenth-century tradition of skepticism about absolute answers, a skepticism we associate with Hawthorne, Melville, and even such nominal optimists as Emerson and Thoreau. The secret is to avoid the acceptance of easy answers, the blandishments of either the mob or the aristocracy, and both the romantic past of England and the romantic material progress of America.

That Irving does not carry skepticism so far as to develop "outcasts of the universe" (Hawthorne), "isolatoes" (Melville), or madmen may be due both to his temperament and to his faith in a genial rationality, which took the form of an insistence that only those characters who control their actions are successful. Interestingly enough, it is in the best-known story, "Rip Van Winkle," that Irving

comes closest to dramatizing the terror of lost identity. Asked who he is, the bewildered old Rip exclaims, "God knows I'm not myself.—I'm somebody else—. . . I was myself last night; but I fell asleep on the mountain—and they've changed my gun—and every thing's changed—and I'm changed—and I can't tell what's my name, or who I am!"

Rip is a special case. Generally, characters who are victimized by their own gullibility are treated comically; those out of their cultural environment are sometimes tragically cut down. Contrast, for example, "The Poor-Devil Author" in *Tales of a Traveller* (1824) and the young Bostonian on the frontier in *The Adventures of Captain Bonneville* (1837). In the first instance, the author, who is working up an epic poem about Jack Straw, one of his "ruffian heroes," meets a man whose "hooked nose," "romantic eye," and "poetical style of head" cause the narrator to "set him down at once for either a poet or a philosopher." The new friends rhapsodize in a pub about "the good old times" of Robin Hood, the author lamenting that "there's no such thing as a dashing, gentleman-like robbery committed nowadays on the King's highway." He expands on the theme, obviously the victim of all the romantic stereotypes: "What a pretty poetical incident . . . for a family-carriage . . . to be attacked . . . by a politely-spoken highwayman . . . who afterwards leaped the hedge and galloped across the country, to the admiration of . . . the daughter." His companion agrees that, yes, Jack Straw and Dick Turpin "are the kind of men for poetry," but that times have sadly changed because of "this cursed system of banking" that has practically eliminated the necessity for travelers to carry their bags of gold with them. Arm in arm, the two leave the pub, the author remarking that anyone would be a fool to resist a holdup to save his purse. He is, of course, struck dumb when his erstwhile friend turns on him, demanding, "Say you so? why, then, . . . disburse! empty! unsack!" Much sobered, the author tells us that he is quite "cured of my poetical enthusiasm for rebels, robbers, and highwaymen."

What a contrast between this sadly comic resolution and the fate of the young Bostonian who, having "seen enough of mountain life and savage warfare, and . . . eager to return to the abodes of civilization," is ambushed by Indians. His horse "wheeled round with affright, and threw his unskilful rider. The young man, . . . unaccustomed to such wild scenes, lost his presence of mind, and stood, as if paralyzed . . . until the Blackfeet came up, and slew him on the spot."

In neither of these sketches is Irving the foolish sentimentalist of the handbooks. A close reading reveals the same fundamental common sense in other sketches that, on the surface, celebrate old times, old books, old customs, and old buildings. "May-Day," as reported in *Bracebridge Hall,* is now "but a faint shadow of the once gay and fanciful rites," and the narrator doubts "whether these rural customs of the good old times were always so very loving and innocent as we are apt to fancy them; and whether the peasantry in those times were really so Arcadian as they have been fondly represented." In "Popular Superstitions" the pseudonymous narrator, "Geoffrey Crayon," admits to having been "so transported by the pleasure of these recollections [of childhood belief in fairy tales], as almost to wish that I had been born in the days when the fictions of poetry were believed." He has a "lurking regret that they have all passed away." Even "English Country Gentlemen," firsthand experience reveals, are not the ideal sort Crayon had imagined. "I have been both surprised and disappointed," he admits, at discovering that he "was often indulging in an Utopian dream, rather than a well-founded opinion."

What we begin to appreciate in this different emphasis is that Irving quickly developed strategies that "distance" the narrator from his story in ways that avoid the usually comic trap into which the listener or reader is led. One such tactic is defensive: the narrative personae of Jonathan Oldstyle, Diedrich Knickerbocker, Geoffrey Crayon, and the Nervous Gentleman intervene between the author and the story so that Irving avoids committing himself. Another tactic is a tradition of storytelling that finds its later examplar in Mark Twain: The focus becomes less the story itself than the way of telling it—the oral tradition, heightening suspense, of a "forgetful" digressive narrator who is often telling a story he's heard from someone else; the false starts; the dialects; the rhythms; and the inconclusive conclusions that leave the baited listener hanging.

Anne Carroll Moore may have been trying to catch this oral quality in *The Bold Dragoon and Other Ghostly Tales by Washington Irving* when she explained that the intention of her editing was "preparing a story to be read aloud by freeing it from sentences and paragraphs which impede its progress as a story." Telling the story—the plot line—and storytelling are not, however, the same. The "impedances" are part of the oral quality and the fun of the hearing. Indeed, much of Irving reads very well aloud. But Moore doesn't emphasize this, and she gives no hint that the last line of "Dolph Heyliger"—that he was a "drawer of the long-bow"—is anything but an additional bit of interesting information. To be such a "drawer" is also, however, to be a straight-faced teller of tall tales, thus raising the question of whether Dolph's ghostly adventure has been simply a joke at the gullible listener's expense.

The pattern is frequently repeated, with teasing delays before we get to the trap, the unexpected suggestion that the whole story may have been a hoax. The teller of "The Adventure of My Uncle" gets momentarily lost and then says, "But all this has nothing to do with my story." The narrator of "The Bold Dragoon" admits that his digression has been "nothing to the purport of my story. I only tell it to show you that my grandfather was a man not easily to be humbugged."

The reader is, of course, the one who's "humbugged." Engrossed in the story, like the listeners within it, he is equally nonplussed by the noncommittal narrator: "And is that all?" asks the "inquisitive gentleman" at the end of "The Adventure of My Uncle." "There was a murmur round the table, half of merriment, half of disappointment," and the Nervous Gentleman himself remarks that "there was an odd expression about [the storyteller's] dilapidated countenance which left me in doubt whether he were in drollery or earnest." "The Bold Dragoon" has a similar ploy. When the narrator concludes that the "whole revel was at an end," the inquisitive gentleman surmises that it must have been a dream, only to be vigorously contradicted: " 'The divil a bit of a dream!' replied the Irishman. 'There never was a truer fact in this world.' " He also admits, though, that his grandfather "was but indifferently acquainted with geography, and apt to make blunders in his travels about inns at night"—especially after such drinking as we've seen at the beginning of the story. At the end of "The Legend of Sleepy Hollow," a "cautious old gentleman" who has heard the story says he's still in doubt about a couple of "points," and is told by the narrator, "Faith, sir, . . . I don't believe one half of it myself." The narrator of "Rip Van Winkle" appends a testimonial by Diedrich Knickerbocker, who assures us that he's "heard many stranger stories than this, in the villages along the Hudson; all of which were too well authenticated to admit of a doubt. I have even talked with Rip Van Winkle myself. . . . The story therefore is beyond the possibility of doubt."

All of these "distancing" storytelling techniques come together in Irving's most inclusive presentation of his ideal middle-class hero, Dolph Heyliger. Despite two rather intrusive interludes, the story is a model of the elements of structure and character that recur in the better-known stories. It is the picaresque adventure of Huck Finn becoming Burgermeister Sawyer.

The hero starts out as a mischievous rogue who is "continually getting into scrapes," an orphaned outsider who is taken advantage of by the "civilized" older folks—including a scolding Frau Ilsé, housekeeper for the eccentric Dr. Knipperhausen. Though Dolph meets ghosts and has a series of bigger-than-life adventures, he keeps a cool head and adapts to whatever necessity arises. A good-natured, realistic opportunist in the face of romantic superstition, Dolph establishes a self-identity, reestablishes his role in society, and is the man in control—even of his own story, since, the narrator assures us, he heard it "at second hand" from Dolph himself, "the ablest drawer of the long-bow in the whole province."

The twists and turns in Dolph's progress are foretold in a dream he has after seeing a ghost at Dr. Knipperhausen's country mansion. Before his adventure is over, Dolph has been swept overboard in a storm on the Hudson, almost fallen into a nest of adders, been shot at, and heard the legend of "The Storm-Ship"—"the ghost-ship," some maintain, of "Hendrick Hudson and his crew of the Half-Moon"—and, along with the reader, vents a good-humored exasperation at being taken the long way around to an anticipated denouement: "Why the plague could not the old goblin have told me about the well at once, without sending me all the way to Albany, to hear a story that was to send me all the way back again?"

Dolph, of course, finds the gold at the bottom of the well, marries Marie, continues to adventure with his father-in-law, and becomes a caring, dutiful son. "Thus did Dolph Heyliger go on, cheerily and prosperously, growing merrier as he grew older and wiser. . . . A great promoter of . . . beef-steak societies and catch-clubs."

We recognize, especially, the characteristic affinities of Dolph to Rip and to Brom Bones of Sleepy Hollow. Rip, despite his domestic laziness, was "a

foremost man at all country frolicks." Brom Van Brunt, too, "was always ready for either a fight or a frolick; but had more mischief than ill will in his composition." "Rip Van Winkle" and "The Legend of Sleepy Hollow" also employ storytelling digressions, the latter somewhat more prominently. Some of these take the form of musing, impressionist color sketches; others are lingering descriptions of tables of cakes and pies. And although the narrator claims he doesn't have "breath and time to discuss this banquet as it deserves," he has effectually delayed the story.

Three other "frontier" works warrant special attention as having probable appeal for adolescent readers. *A Tour on the Prairies* (1835) is not, as sometimes claimed, merely a stereotyped response to the West by an Easterner, although it has its share of the sentimental and picturesque. There are fine descriptions of costume, characters, and scenery. And Irving the realist reports that "the Indian of poetical fiction is like the Shepherd of pastoral romance, a mere personification of imaginary attributes." Unlike Cooper's Indians, who are characterized by Mark Twain as "literary offenses" because they are so stupid and unreal, Irving's are "gossips" and "great mimics and buffoons"; out of the view of white men, they "give full scope to criticism, satire, mimicry, and mirth." *Astoria* (1836), Irving's commissioned recounting of John Jacob Astor's venture into the fur trade beyond the Rockies, is wordy but also has some keenly drawn vignettes of Hawaii, Fort Mackinaw, and frontier St. Louis—and a number of exciting wilderness adventures. One would think that a compilation of these would be well received by young readers. *The Adventures of Captain Bonneville* includes, scattered among its many pages, striking portraits of French and American trappers, sympathetic treatment of several Indian tribes, and probably the fullest demonstration of the author's belief in the importance of training for adaptation to new environments and cultural contexts; consider his observation that "with all their national aptitude at expedient and resource, Wyeth and his men felt themselves completely at a loss when they reached the frontier, and found that the wilderness required experience and habitudes, of which they were totally deficient."

In addition to the sketches discussed here, the following—insofar as they evince the techniques we have briefly explored—are likely to appeal to young readers: from "The Money-Diggers" section of *Tales of a Traveller*, "The Devil and Tom Walker," "Wolfert Webber," and perhaps "Kidd the Pirate"; from *The Alhambra* (1832), the legends of "The Arabian Astrologer," "The Moor's Legacy," and "The Three Beautiful Princesses"; and some parts of Knickerbocker's *History of New York.* The allusive satire of the earlier *Salmagundi* (1807–1808) is probably lost on most readers today, young or old. The histories, which at one time were rather widely read—especially the *Life and Voyages of Columbus* (1828)—have been similarly lost to us. Still, there remains enough good material to explain why Irving has endured despite shifting tastes on the part of critics; he deserves another hearing.

Selected Bibliography

WORKS OF WASHINGTON IRVING

The Works of Washington Irving. 15 vols. Author's rev. ed. New York: G. P. Putnam, 1848–1850. Author's uniform rev. ed. New York: G. P. Putnam's Sons, 1860–1861. (The basis for many subsequent editions.)

The Bold Dragoon and Other Ghostly Tales by Washington Irving. Edited and with an introduction by Anne Carroll Moore. With illustrations by James Daugherty. New York: Knopf, 1930. (Contains "The Bold Dragoon," "The Devil and Tom Walker," "Wolfert Webber," and "Dolph Heyliger.")

Washington Irving: Representative Selections. Edited and with an introduction by Henry A. Pochmann. American Writers Series. New York: American Book Company, 1934. (Contains an annotated bibliography.)

The Complete Works of Washington Irving. Edited by Henry A. Pochmann, Herbert L. Kleinfield, et al. New York: Twayne Publishers, 1978– . (A projected compilation of 28 vols., this scholarly edition will serve on completion as the definitive text.)

Washington Irving's Tales of the Supernatural. Edited and with an introduction by Edward Wagenknecht. With illustrations by R. W. Alley. Owings Mills, Md.: Stemmer House, 1982. (Contains "Rip Van Winkle," "The Legend of Sleepy Hollow," "The Adventure of My Uncle," "The Bold Dragoon," "The Adventure of the German Student," "The Devil and Tom Walker," "The Legend of the Arabian Astrologer," and "The Legend of the Moor's Legacy.")

Washington Irving: Hearthside Tales. Edited and with an introduction by Patrick F. Allen. Schenectady, N.Y.: Union College Press, 1983. (Contains "The Mutability of Literature," "Rip Van Winkle," "The Legend of Sleepy Hollow," "Dolph Heyliger," "The Adventure of the German Student," "Kidd the Pirate," "The Devil and Tom Walker," and "Wolfert Webber.")

CRITICAL AND BIOGRAPHICAL STUDIES

Cairns, William B. *British Criticisms of American Writings, 1815–1833: A Contribution to the Study of Anglo-American Literary Relationships.* University of Wisconsin Studies in Language and Literature, no. 14. Madison: University of Wisconsin Press, 1922.

Hedges, William L. *Washington Irving: An American Study, 1802–1832.* Baltimore, Md.: Johns Hopkins University Press, 1965.

Langfield, William and Philip C. Blackburn. *Washington Irving: A Bibliography* and *A Census of Washington Irving Manuscripts*, edited by H. L. Kleinfield. Port Washington, N.Y.: Kennikat Press, 1968. (A composite volume of two works previously published by the New York Public Library. Particularly useful for citation of illustrated editions of Irving's works.)

Leary, Lewis. "Washington Irving." University of Minnesota Pamphlets on American Writers, no. 25. Minneapolis: University of Minnesota Press, 1963.

Myers, Andrew B., ed. *A Century of Commentary on the Works of Washington Irving* [1860–1964]. Tarrytown, N.Y.: Sleepy Hollow Restorations, 1966.

Pochmann, Henry A. "Washington Irving." In *Fifteen American Authors Before 1900*, edited by Robert A. Rees and Earl N. Harbert. Madison: University of Wisconsin Press, 1971.

Springer, Haskell. *Washington Irving: A Reference Guide.* Boston: G. K. Hall, 1976. (A source book of scholarship, criticism, and reviews published between 1807 and 1974.)

Wagenknecht, Edward. *Washington Irving: Moderation Displayed.* New York: Oxford University Press, 1962.

Williams, Stanley T. *The Life of Washington Irving.* 2 vols. New York: Oxford University Press, 1935.

Williams, Stanley T., and Mary Ellen Edge. *A Bibliography of the Writings of Washington Irving: A Check List.* Folcroft, Pa.: Folcroft Press, 1936.

—J. ROBERT BASHORE, JR.

JOSEPH JACOBS
1854–1916

WRITING IN HER journal on 1 December 1876, about public response to her novel *Daniel Deronda,* George Eliot said:

> I have been made aware of much repugnance, or else indifference, towards the Jewish part of "Deronda," and of some hostile as well as adverse reviewing. . . . Words of gratitude have come from Jews and Jewesses, and these are certain signs that I may have contributed my mite to a good result.
> (quoted by Mayer Sulzberger)

Eliot was not at this time aware of the existence of the young Australian Jew Joseph Jacobs, who was fresh out of Cambridge, in love with literature, and made painfully aware of anti-Semitic feeling in Britain by precisely the adverse criticism of *Daniel Deronda* of which Eliot speaks. Out of this awareness he wrote his own critical essay on *Deronda*, "Mordecai" (*Macmillan's Magazine*, June 1877), which, although Eliot told him she never read criticism of her own works, was probably responsible for his invitation to one of the Sunday-afternoon receptions at the home of Eliot and her companion, George Henry Lewes. Through Eliot, Jacobs met many of the leading writers and artists of the day, especially the Pre-Raphaelites William Morris, Edward Burne-Jones, and Dante Gabriel Rossetti. Through his own warm nature and humor, he became good friends with many of them.

His critical powers, as shown in his volume *Essays and Reviews* (1891), were considerable, and the entry into the literary world opened by Eliot and her acquaintances might have led to true distinction for Jacobs in the field of literary criticism. But so versatile were his talents and so widespread his interests that literary criticism became, like many another field, just one more string to his bow. In none of the many fields that attracted him was his work slipshod or shallow; indeed, he was eminent in at least three of them: Judaic history, folklore, and children's literature. Diversity of interests marked his career from the beginning.

Little is known of his early life in Australia. Born in Sydney to John and Sarah Jacobs, he attended Sydney grammar school before going to England in 1872. According to his daughter, May Bradshaw Hays, he had intended to study law and return to Australia to practice. But at Cambridge he became interested in literature and anthropology (to say nothing of history, mathematics, and philosophy), and upon receiving his B.A. in 1876 he went to London to become a writer. But the *Daniel Deronda* controversy aroused a desire for a deeper knowledge of his own people and culture. In 1877 he went to Berlin to study Jewish literature, bibliography, philosophy, and ethnology at the University of Berlin under such notable Jewish scholars of that time as Moritz Steinschneider and Moritz Lazarus.

Upon his return to England, he again took up anthropology, with Sir Francis Galton as his mentor. The anthropological folklorists had organized the Folk-Lore Society in London in 1878. Through the society, Jacobs met and became friends with Alfred Nutt, who was to publish not only some of

Jacobs' scholarly editions but also his collections of fairy tales (except the last one, *Europa's Fairy Tales*, which was published by G. P. Putnam's Sons in 1916). In the Folk-Lore Society he also met Andrew Lang, with whom he became friendly although they often disagreed, in particular about how folktales had spread throughout the world. Jacobs was a strong and enthusiastic proponent of the "diffusionist" theory; Lang was a cautious but vocal proponent of the theory that held that instead of diffusing outward from a central place of origin, many folktales, however similar to other tales throughout the world, might have arisen independently at different times in different cultures.

Throughout the 1880's and 1890's Jacobs was deeply involved in the study of folklore and in the activities of the Folk-Lore Society. From 1889 to 1900 he edited *Folk-Lore*; this marked a period of outstanding quality for that journal. In 1888 he edited *The Earliest English Version of the Fables of Bidpai; or, The Morall Philosophie of Doni*, volume 3 in Nutt's Bibliothèque de Carabas series. He was later to use this background in his *Indian Fairy Tales* (1892). He edited, also for Nutt, *The Fables of Aesop as First Printed by William Caxton in 1484 with Those of Avian, Alfonso, and Poggio* (1893) in two volumes; volume 1 contained a history of the Aesopic fable. Again, in 1894 he produced *The Fables of Aesop* for children, with no scholarly apparatus but with "A Short History of the Aesopic Fable" appended. He also made a scholarly edition of *The Most Delectable History of Reynard the Fox* (1895). For volume 10 of Nutt's Bibliothèque de Carabas, Jacobs edited *Barlaam and Josaphat* and *English Lives of Buddha* (1896). His output was amazing, for he was, during these same years, also active in various folklorists' controversies, as well as writing articles, reviews, lectures, literary studies, prefaces, and his fine versions of fairy tales and folktales for children.

At the same time, his interest in Jewish history never waned, and he was also active in the Anglo-Jewish community. In 1888 the *Bibliotheca Anglo-Judaica: A Bibliographical Guide to Anglo-Jewish History*, compiled by Jacobs and Lucien Wolf, was published. In 1896 Jacobs conceived *The Jewish Year Book*, which he edited until he left England in 1900. In the 1880's and early 1890's he wrote about Russian persecution of the Jews and was the person perhaps most responsible for drawing the attention of the British public to these atrocities. His many articles on the history of English Jews, his excellent book *The Jews of Angevin England* (1893),

and his researches into the history of Jews in Spain made him the logical candidate for the office of revising editor of *The Jewish Encyclopedia*, the brainchild of Isidore Singer. For this work he moved to New York in 1900. From 1900 to 1916, the year of his death, he lived in New York; he worked on *The Jewish Encyclopedia* and until 1913 was Registrar and Professor of English at the Jewish Theological Seminary.

In his personal life Jacobs apparently enjoyed a happy marriage with his wife, Georgina Horne, and was a devoted father to his three children, May, Sydney, and Philip. Indeed, May describes his nightly homecoming as a child's delight—surprises in his pockets, stories on his tongue. The children were his test cases; on them he tried out the tales he would publish in his fairy tale collections. According to his daughter, he trusted their responses almost absolutely. If they were restless during a story, that story was thrown out. The centrality of these children to the shaping of the fairy tale volumes is reflected in the dedications of three of those works—*English Fairy Tales* (1890): "To my dear little May"; *Indian Fairy Tales* (1892): "To my dear little Phil"; and *More English Fairy Tales* (1894): "To my son Sydney, Ætat. XIII." This deep affection for and compatibility with children extended to the next generation as well: his last fairy tale collection, *Europa's Fairy Tales*, is dedicated to his granddaughter, Margaret, in all her diminutives: "To Peggy, and Madge, and Pearl, and Maggie, and Marguerite, and Peggotty, and Meg, and Marjory, and Daisy, and Pegg, and MARGARET HAYS (How many granddaughters does that make?)."

His cheerfulness, wit, and lively intellect won him many friends in many countries. Foremost among these were Lucien Wolf, who had collaborated with him on the *Bibliotheca Anglo-Judaica* and whose memorial address upon Jacobs' death conveys a sense of deep personal bereavement, and John D. Batten, the illustrator, with whom Jacobs had the most cordial of relationships and with whom he was planning to do yet another fairy tale book when he died. Indications of Jacobs' personal character can easily be inferred from the fact that these men, who had worked with him closely on various projects and had known him almost thirty years, were so devoted to him at the time of his death. Like any scholar who has theories, he was involved in controversies—with Lang, with G. K. Chesterton, and with Israel Zangwill—but they seem not to have led to lasting bitterness. He had a gift for friendship.

Jacobs once joked of himself, deprecatingly, that he was one of the greatest "contributors" to the British Museum Catalogue. Still, although he was honored and respected in every field of his endeavor, he nonetheless evidently never attained the kind of financial security a man of his talents and achievements might have aspired to. He was never poor, but apparently did need the extra income available from translations and reviews.

In the spring of 1914 he journeyed to Nauheim in Germany, seeking treatment for the "heart-weakness" with which his late years had been troubled. The doctors there gave an optimistic prognosis, and he had started to Naples to sail back to America when the mobilization of the German army caused him to be stranded without transport just short of the Italian border. He somehow made his way north to England, where the Battens cared for their sick and exhausted friend until he was well enough to return to America. He lived about a year and a half longer, but friends and family felt that this ordeal might have shortened his life. He died in Yonkers, New York, on 30 January 1916, at the age of 61.

The children's books of Joseph Jacobs are classics of children's literature. Today, more than seventy years after his death, most of the fairy tale books are still in print, and his version of *The Fables of Aesop* is virtually the standard children's text of these pithy tales. Furthermore, many individual tales from his books have been issued separately over the years, often with excellent illustrations; certain of his tales frequently have been anthologized. The continuing popularity of Jacobs' works, over a period during which so many fairy tale collections have come and gone, suggests that these stories have special qualities giving them lasting appeal to generations of children. Yet the actual plots and characters of these tales are much the same, regardless of who retells them; obviously the attractions of the tales are to some extent inherent in themselves. Jacobs did not consider himself the author of these stories. He said he had "collected" or "compiled" them. How could the printed text issued by one "compiler" be significantly better than that of another? How can creativity enter into the retelling of stories already infinitely retold?

In the first place, every compiler of folktales has some license in the area of selection. Some folktales are better than others, at least as tales. Therefore, the success of a collection of folktales or fairy tales depends in large part upon whether the collector has chosen good tales. Second, the tales are incremental and often have, over centuries, both acquired and lost incidents and motifs, some of which are of more value than others. The collector may choose to transmit the story exactly as it was told (as a folklorist would for purposes of scholarly study) or may choose to modify it. Any modifications would require at least the exercise of judgment and taste. Third, these stories were in their earliest originals transmitted orally. Again, the collector must make choices concerning the language in which to publish the story: Should the printed tale reflect the oral tale exactly? Be obviously literary in language and tone? Or be something between the two? In this third area, especially, the collector and editor of fairy tales has the opportunity to display real literary and creative talent.

The first of Jacobs' fairy tale books, *English Fairy Tales*, is one of the best of its kind, and perfectly illustrates the choices Jacobs made in the areas mentioned above. It was harshly criticized in its own time by folklorists, because Jacobs sometimes used "literary" sources, cut or expanded incidents, turned ballads into prose, or otherwise altered the original folklore materials; by literary critics, because in some tales he used dialectal language considered "vulgar," and (scandalous!) he included Scottish tales in an English collection; and by parents, who feared the corruption of their children's language by assimilation of the dialects used in the tales. But the critics were wrong; Jacobs answered them in detail in the revised preface to the third edition of *English Fairy Tales*. Essentially, he averred that he was doing nothing the Grimms hadn't done.

The selections in *English Fairy Tales* make it one of the richest and most varied single volumes in English folk literature. They include legends, beast tales, cumulative stories, nonsense stories, and "drolls." There are few fairies in the entire collection. But there is magic in many of these tales, often of a terrible sort, and there are dragons, imps, brownies, and giants. Jacobs used the term *fairy tale* loosely, as did the Brothers Grimm, to include folktales about the strange, the wonderful, or the absurd. Many of the tales in *English Fairy Tales* are what might be considered old standards of the genre: "Jack and the Beanstalk," "Jack the Giant-Killer," "Henny-Penny," "The History of Tom

Thumb," and so forth. But others are uncommon and had rarely been published before Jacobs produced his very readable versions of them. "The Laidly Worm of Spindleston Heugh," for instance, is a prose version of a ballad that had been made into prose once before, by Alfred Fryer in 1884. But it is Jacobs' version that appears in collections subsequent to *English Fairy Tales*. Similarly, "Earl Mar's Daughter," "Binnorie," and "The Red Ettin" are excellent but rarely anthologized tales.

Some of Jacobs' stories are perhaps uncomfortably bloody or threatening for modern taste. In "The Golden Arm," for instance, the ghost of a dead woman returns to reclaim the golden arm cut away from her corpse by her husband. The last line —"THOU HAST IT!"—is meant to be shouted with stunning force, to startle the tensely listening child. Jacobs, in his notes, justifies the inclusion of the story on the grounds that it is emotionally cathartic and that children know it is just make-believe. Still, it may not be the best of stories for a sensitive child's entertainment. "Mr. Fox" is open to all the criticisms Bluebeard variants invite. "Mr. Miacca" is an "awful warning" story in which a bad little boy, twice captured by Mr. Miacca, who eats bad boys, escapes each time by the use of his wits. This is, of course, very like many of the "Jack tales," and Jacobs has actually made it more comic than threatening. Nevertheless, *English Fairy Tales*, like the Grimms' fairy tales, is vulnerable to the charge that some of the materials are too horrific for the very young.

On the other hand, these selections are unusual in their time for the inclusion of some strong female characters. Cap o' Rushes, Mollie Whuppie, and Kate Crackernuts are all far from passive. They shape their own fates, use their own wits, and need no prince to rescue them (in fact, Kate Crackernuts saves her prince). Stories with strong, independent heroines have always been available to the collector, but many of the Victorian editors either revised them with an eye to appropriate feminine behavior, or simply passed over them. Jacob is clearly not troubled by the so-called vulgar or he would not have told "Tom Tit Tot." Therefore, he revised these stories only for clarity and literary quality, as he did habitually. To what extent his choice of them was influenced by a desire to provide positive images of women, we have no way of knowing.

Jacobs' selections in this volume constitute a varied, balanced whole. The legendary materials of high romance such as "Childe Rowland" are side by side with homely beast fables such as "The Magpie's Nest." Pure absurdity, like "Mr. Vinegar," who lived with his spouse in a vinegar bottle, borders pure magic, like "Nix Nought Nothing." It is perhaps the least predictable gathering of fairy tales ever made.

Jacobs, to the horror of his fellow folklorists, did exercise the reteller's prerogative of altering his sources. In the notes appended to the volume, he always informs the reader of such changes. Some of them are clearly dictated by a Victorian sense of propriety, like his euphemizing of the profession of the midwife in "Fairy Ointment": "Dame Goody was a nurse that looked after sick people, and minded babies." Others are genuine artistic improvements, such as the elimination of too-repetitive incidents in "Childe Rowland," the expansion of what had been a curt and confused travel sequence in "Nix Nought Nothing," and the deletion of an unnecessary moralizing fairy from the chapbook-derived "Jack and the Beanstalk." Jacobs also corrects for verisimilitude: in the oral original of "Mr. Miacca," bad boy Tommy Grimes was a handy carver who carried a carved wooden leg around with him. Jacobs alters this, much for the better, in a way that reveals his own sense of fun: Tommy does not go about always carrying a large wooden leg, but rather has the ingenuity, when Mr. Miacca demands that he thrust out a leg from beneath the sofa where he is trapped, to stick out a sofa leg. This is a far more likely resolution than Tommy's happening to have a wooden leg handy.

The most common alterations Jacobs makes in his sources are in the language. Time and again he notes that he has reduced the dialect of the original. Reduced, but not eliminated: in the preface to *English Fairy Tales* Jacobs strongly emphasizes his intention that the stories be read aloud. He wanted, he says, "to write as a good old nurse will speak when she tells Fairy Tales." Therefore he has eliminated unintelligible dialect phrases, but retained enough dialect to provide a strong oral flavor, a humorous inelegance, and memorable phrasing with the rhythms of real speech. In "Tom Tit Tot," a British folk version of the continental "Rumpelstiltskin," the miller's golden-haired daughter becomes "a gatless girl" whom her mother calls "Darter" and who eats five pies at once. She is expected to spin five skeins of flax a day, not flax into gold; the king whom she weds speaks only a shade less colloquially than his subjects: "Look you here, I want a wife, and I'll marry your daughter." Instead of the dwarf Rumpelstiltskin, the villain is a "little black thing with a long tail" that wants not a baby but the girl herself, and is genuinely menacing: " 'Noo, t'ain't,' that says, and that come further into the room." Even the narrative voice is dialectal, and the repeated "that," referring to the black thing and emphasizing its inhuman aspect, becomes increasingly sinister. Jacobs has softened dialect in "Tom Tit Tot," as in other stories. What would a purely dialectal tale read like? Jacobs never gives us one, but his great contemporary Andrew Lang has one in *The Blue Fairy Book* in which the dialect has been little altered, if at all. A sample from Lang's "The Black Bull of Norroway" will serve to illustrate the difference:

> Lang she sat, and aye she grat, till she wearied. At last she rase and gaed awa', she kendna whaur till. On she wandered till she came to a great hill o' glass, that she tried a' she could to climb, but wasna able. Round the bottom o' the hill she gaed, sabbing and seeking a passage owre, till at last she came to a smith's house; and the smith promised, if she wad serve him seven years, he wad make her iron shoon, wherewi' she could climb owre the glassy hill. . . . There she was telled of a gallant young knight that had given in some bluidy sarks to wash, and whaever washed thae sarks was to be his wife.

Scots dialect is not difficult; the meaning of most of the unfamiliar words in the passage quoted is easily inferred from context. Still, a child might be put off this excellent story by the apparent difficulty of the language. And Jacobs, when he was writing for children, rarely failed to consider his audience.

For legends and saga materials, Jacobs had another style, more elegant but not florid. A comparison of his prose with that of his contemporaries is illuminating. Alfred Fryer had turned the ballad "The Laidly Worm of Spindleston Heugh" (or "Kempe Owein") into prose in *The Book of English Fairy Tales from the North-Country*. Genre transformation can be demanding; if the result is less good than the original one might do best not to meddle. Consider Fryer's account of the transformation of the princess-dragon:

> But soon after her strange disappearance a rumour began to spread through the country that a terrible dragon had taken up its abode in a cave at the foot of a cliff in a dell of the forest called the Spindleston Heugh. For seven leagues in every direction the green grass and the golden corn were withered and blighted by its fiery breath. Awful tales were related of its gigantic size, its fearful aspect, and the wide-

spread devastations it committed. Its scaly hide, covered as if with plates of mail, offered an impenetrable resistance to every weapon; and all efforts to ensnare or destroy it utterly failed. . . . The very name of the monster carried terror with it.

This is literate, grammatical prose, but it is also overwritten and clichéd. Furthermore, Fryer has forgotten that the "monster" is also the heroine. The actual transformation of the princess takes place "offstage" in Fryer, distancing the reader from the event. On the other hand, in *English Fairy Tales* Jacobs shows the transformation more directly:

> So Lady Margaret went to bed a beauteous maiden, and rose up a laidly worm. And when her maidens came in to dress her in the morning they found coiled up on the bed a dreadful dragon, which uncoiled itself and came towards them. But they ran away shrieking, and the Laidly Worm crawled and crept, and crept and crawled till it reached the Heugh or rock of the Spindlestone, round which it coiled itself, and lay there basking with its terrible snout in the air.

This brief passage is not absolutely cliché-free ("beauteous maiden," "dreadful dragon"), but the pictures it conveys are not clichés. That crawling dragon, which eight hours before was a girl—does it come toward the women for help or to devour them? That pathetic progress to the Spindlestone—does it recall a smaller, lighter body? Fear and pity ring in that last sentence, but they are evoked, not described.

In the areas in which a fairy tale collector might demonstrate creativity and originality, Jacobs generally did so to good effect. In the fairy tale books that succeeded *English Fairy Tales*, Jacobs followed essentially the same principles of selection and adaptation. Each has its special qualities, but all are reflective of Jacobs' breadth of knowledge of folk materials and of his highly developed storytelling abilities.

More English Fairy Tales continues *English Fairy Tales* (quite literally; the numbering of the tales picks up at forty-four, where *English Fairy Tales* left off). The two volumes together constitute a treasury of British folklore; they also represent much of the best editing and adapting for children that is available.

Interestingly, *More English Fairy Tales* has distinctive elements. It contains more chapbook material than its predecessor, including the totally unaltered ballad "The Children in the Wood" and the classic "Tom Hickathrift," abridged by Alfred Nutt. For nonsense, "Stupid's Cries," "The Wise Men of Gotham," "The Stars in the Sky," and the ridiculous "Sir Gammer Vans" are but a few of the representatives of the genre. For high romance, the volume has Jacobs' much-anglicized version of "The Black Bull of Norroway," "Tattercoats," and the ballad of "Tamlane" turned into fine prose. There are tales of the strange and supernatural: "The Hedley Kow," "Yallery Brown," and, chillingly, "The Hobyahs." In this volume is published for the first time "Scrapefoot," which may be much closer to the primal story of "The Three Bears" than Robert Southey's version. Here, a nosy fox prowls the bears' castle, breaks furniture, drinks up the milk, is found in the softest bed at last, and is thrown out the window.

Celtic Fairy Tales (1892) is notable for a broad representation of Celtic folk materials, including Irish, Scottish, Welsh, and even one Cornish tale. The heroic and the humorous are cheek by jowl, ranging from the tragic legend "The Story of Deirdre" to the comic cumulative tale "Munachar and Manachar."

Jacobs' most significant artistic achievement in these tales is stylistic. He manages to give the language of the characters regional flavor without slipping into parody or stereotype, even in the comic tales. Again, he uses dialect judiciously, even occasionally retaining an original Gaelic term where the meaning is familiar or easily inferred:

> Well, my dear, it was a beautiful sight to see the king standing with his mouth open, looking at his poor old goose flying as light as a lark, and better than ever she was: and when she lit at his feet, patted her on the head, and "*Ma vourneen*," says he, "but you are the *darlint* o' the world."
>
> ("King O'Toole and His Goose")

More Celtic Fairy Tales (1894) continues this tradition of tasteful style and varied content. Especially striking is Jacobs' abridgement of "The Fate of the Children of Lir," one of the "three sorrowful tales" of Ireland. The interspersed verse of this narrative was naturally attractive to Jacobs, who always believed that most European ballads and folktales had originally been *cantes-fables,* stories constructed of prose intermixed with poetry.

In both of the Celtic collections Jacobs made selective alterations in his sources. These were some-

times motivated by taste, as when he cut an incident from "The Tale of Ivan" (*Celtic Fairy Tales*) because it was "not suited *virginibus puerisque.*" It is curious that he modified the conclusion of "The Ridere of Riddles" (*More Celtic Fairy Tales*) to get rid of the "polygamous complexion," and did not alter "Gold-Tree and Silver-Tree" (*Celtic Fairy Tales*), which contains bigamy. Many of the alterations in these collections were for brevity's sake, since the originals, like "Beth Gellert" (*Celtic Fairy Tales*), are often very long. An interesting example of Jacobs' emending for style is discussed by him in the note to "The Battle of the Birds" (*Celtic Fairy Tales*):

> I have found some difficulty in dealing with Campbell's [Jacobs' source] excessive use of the second person singular, "If thou thouest him some two or three times, 'tis well," but beyond that it is wearisome. Practically, I have reserved *thou* for the speech of giants, who may be supposed to be somewhat old-fashioned.

Indian Fairy Tales is a collection to which Jacobs was able to bring the scholarship that had gone into his 1888 edition of the *The Fables of Bidpai*. In his extensive introduction to the "Notes and References," he wrote that he believed that "30 to 50 per cent" of the "common stock" of European folklore had originated in India and been dispersed to Europe at about the time of the Crusades, chiefly by oral transmission. This volume illustrates Jacobs' eye and ear for a good story, for the selections are very fine and are his usual admixture of comic and serious. But he has altered few of his sources, so that most of the works in this collection are not in Jacobs' own language and do not have his distinctive style. Two exceptions are "The Lion and the Crane," which Jacobs rewrote almost entirely, and "The Soothsayer's Son," which he "considerably condensed and modified."

The last of Jacobs' fairy tale collections, *Europa's Fairy Tales*, is a collection of "common Folk-Tales of Europe," stories that occur, with variations, in many European cultures. Jacobs has attempted here to get back to the common original form of each tale. Therefore, this volume contains many classic fairy tales, even though one may recognize only a few of them by the titles: "Snow White" is here "Snowwhite," "Cinderella" is called "Cinder-Maid," "Puss-in-Boots" is "The Earl of Cattenborough," and "Hansel and Gretel" is "Johnnie and Grizzle." The titles of such materials are infinitely variable, of course, but certain of the titles have become traditional, and alterations in them can jar. The humorous stories in *Europa's Fairy Tales* are excellent: Jacobs' hand had not lost its cunning. "The Master Thief," "Reynard and Bruin," "Day-Dreaming," and "A Visitor from Paradise" all live up to the high standard of comedy in the earlier collections. "Scissors," a tale in which an exasperated husband throws his contentious wife into the river and she drowns, is funny, but perpetuates the stereotype of women as argumentative and unreasonable.

On the other hand, the more familiar fairy tales in the collection seem to have suffered from Jacobs' editing. This volume was meant for Jacobs' grandchild; perhaps he was overprotective of her sensibilities. In the preface he frankly admits to the "Bowdlerization" of some of the tales. Certainly in "Johnnie and Grizzle" he has softened the picture of both parents. In "Beauty and the Beast" no infidelity or forgetfulness on Beauty's part causes the Beast's apparent death. Beauty doesn't have to pay a visit home because her father comes to visit her, and feels better about things because she is so happy! One day, for reasons unknown, the Beast apparently dies. Beauty, grieving, cries that she loved him:

> No sooner had she said this than the hide of the Beast split in two and out came the most handsome young prince who told her that he had been enchanted by a magician and that he could not recover his natural form unless a maiden should, of her own accord, declare that she loved him.

This breathless summary is not at all in Jacobs' usual style. The original tale by Mme. Le Prince de Beaumont is one of the most beautiful, if late, fairy tales of Europe. Jacobs, usually so detailed in his notes, does not really explain his treatment of this story at all. It is a great pity, but his last fairy book does not match the best of the earlier books.

In addition to the fairy tales, Jacobs wrote or edited for children *The Fables of Aesop*, the short, pointed format of which perfectly suited his sense of irony and talent for verbal humor. In 1896 he also produced *The Book of Wonder Voyages*, which contains four mythic journey sagas. "The Argonauts" is Charles Kingsley's version of that tale, reproduced exactly and with reverence. "The Voyage of Maelduin" is adapted and annotated by Al-

fred Nutt. Only in "Hasan of Bassorah" and part of "The Journeyings of Thorkill and of Eric the Far-Traveled" did Jacobs demonstrate his skills. *Wonder Voyages*, by definition, lacks the variety of content that typifies the fairy books, and it has no room for the wit and wordplay that Jacobs enjoyed so much and did best. Jacobs wrote one informational book for children, *The Story of Geographical Discovery: How the World Became Known* (1899). It is readable and informative, but has been out of print for years.

The illustrations of John D. Batten in all six of the fairy books and the *Wonder Voyages* deserve at least a note. They are in the romantic, neomedieval style of the Pre-Raphaelites, with some heroic, neoclassic elements as well (the nude male wrestlers illustrating "The Ridere of Riddles" in *More Celtic Fairy Tales*, for instance). His heroes and heroines have straight noses, delicate lips, graceful bodies; the hair of heroines is usually long and wavy, escaping fillets and rippling in lines that echo the trailing draperies of the costumes. Some of Batten's best illustrations are comic: the dancing silhouettes of "Pride Goeth Before a Fall" and the cavorting lamb of "The Lambikin" in *Indian Fairy Tales*, or his visualization of "The Hobyahs," who look like fat commas with arms and legs and big eyes, in *More English Fairy Tales*. Obviously, he and Jacobs collaborated closely on all of the volumes; Batten is often mentioned in the notes as having been the source of a variant, or having made suggestions about the origins or development of a motif. Jacobs sometimes comments on the illustrations, directing the attention of the reader to some especially interesting detail.

Joseph Jacobs' fairy tale books are in many respects models of how the traditional folktale anthology for children should be made. They are learned volumes, but not pedantic. Jacobs' constant awareness of his audience of children saved him from the excessive reverence for sources that sometimes flawed the artistry of even so great a collector as Andrew Lang. His respect for children prevented condescension; therefore, he provided notes and references to every volume, which are as full of good things and as witty as some of the tales annotated. Although Batten provided clever endpieces warning children away from the notes, these bans probably have as much effect as "Keep off the Grass" signs, and no child will ever be the worse for reading every word of the notes. The prefaces, the tales and illustrations, and the notes and references all combine to make an integrated whole. This unity is the result of Jacobs' singleness of purpose: to give to children the best of folklore as he knew it.

Selected Bibliography

WORKS OF JOSEPH JACOBS

English Fairy Tales. With illustrations by John D. Batten. London: D. Nutt, 1890. 3rd ed., with a revised preface. London and New York: G. P. Putnam's Sons, 1898; New York: Dover, 1967.

Indian Fairy Tales. With illustrations by John D. Batten. London: D. Nutt, 1892; New York: Dover, 1969.

Celtic Fairy Tales. With illustrations by John D. Batten. London: D. Nutt, 1892; New York: Dover, 1968.

More English Fairy Tales. With illustrations by John D. Batten. London: D. Nutt, 1894; New York: Dover, 1967.

More Celtic Fairy Tales. With illustrations by John D. Batten. London: D. Nutt, 1894; New York: Dover, 1968.

The Fables of Aesop. With illustrations by Richard Heighway. London and New York: Macmillan, 1894; New York: Schocken Books, 1966.

The Book of Wonder Voyages. With illustrations by John D. Batten. London and New York: D. Nutt, 1896; New York: G. P. Putnam's Sons, 1967.

The Story of Geographical Discovery: How the World Became Known. London: E. Newnes, 1899; New York: D. Appleton, 1899.

Europa's Fairy Tales. With illustrations by John D. Batten. New York and London: G. P. Putnam's Sons, 1916. Reissued as *European Folk and Fairy Tales*. New York: G. P. Putnam's Sons, 1967.

BIBLIOGRAPHY

Abrahams, I. "Bibliography of Dr. Joseph Jacobs's Contributions to Anglo-Jewish History, Literature, and Statistics" *Transactions of the Jewish Historical Society in England* 8: 150–152 (1915–1917).

BIOGRAPHICAL STUDIES

Dorson, Richard M. *British Folklorists*. Chicago: University of Chicago Press, 1968; London: Routledge and Kegan Paul, 1968.

Hays, May Bradshaw. "Memories of My Father, Joseph Jacobs" *Horn Book* 28: 385–392 (1952).

Kunitz, Stanley, ed. *British Authors of the Nineteenth Century*. New York: H. W. Wilson, 1936.

Sulzberger, Mayer. "Joseph Jacobs" *Publications of the American Jewish Historical Society* 25: 156–173 (1916).

Wolf, Lucien. "Memorial Address" *Transactions of the Jewish Historical Society in England* 8: 147–149 (1915–1917).

Zangwill, Israel. "Memorial Address" *Transactions of the Jewish Historical Society in England* 8: 131–146 (1915–1917).

—MARY E. SHANER

ERICH KÄSTNER

1899–1974

ERICH KÄSTNER IS one of those rare writers who have made their mark as authors of significant books for children as well as for adults. While Kästner's poems and novels for grown-ups reflect the topsy-turvy milieu of the Weimar Republic (the period between 1918 and 1933) and present a biting, satirical view of a world that had lost its meaning, his books for children portray a wholesome environment. Though his stories are not sweet and unproblematic, they still offer hope. Through honesty, courage, trust, decency, and hard work the children manage to restore order, sometimes even in spite of the adults. The difference between the thrust of Kästner's stories for adults and those for young people is best demonstrated by the heroes of his two best-known novels: the adult novel *Fabian: Die Geschichte eines Moralisten* (*Fabian: The Story of a Moralist*, 1931) and the novel for children *Emil und die Detektive* (*Emil and the Detectives*, 1928). The young, intellectual Fabian remains a passive spectator of the corruptions and injustices of this world. At the one moment when he attempts to act by jumping into the river to save a boy from drowning, he himself perishes because he cannot swim. The child is more resilient and safely paddles ashore. In *Emil* the hero has faith in the ultimate good and justice of this world, and in his own ability to right a wrong, because in the end justice must prevail. With the help of the children of Berlin, he eventually catches the thief who had robbed him of his mother's hard-earned money. Virtue is triumphant, and not only is his property restored,

but he also receives a handsome official reward with which he buys his mother a hair dryer for her beauty shop and a much-needed winter coat. This is typical of Kästner's children's stories. They express a basic optimism and belief in the perfectibility of the world. His works for grown-ups, on the other hand, express malaise, ennui, and deep pessimism.

Kästner's career as a writer was a checkered one. He rose to fame quickly in the late 1920's. Because of his commitment to the liberal ideals of the Weimar Republic and his opposition to militarism and fascism, he was enjoined from publishing in Germany during much of the twelve years of Hitler's regime. After 1945 he was esteemed and honored for his integrity during the Nazi period, but during the turbulent 1960's his star began to fade. He was considered too bourgeois and no longer seemed relevant; his works for adults, with the exception of *Fabian* and some of his satirical poems, are now largely ignored. The writer who was once a legend is now only history.

Kästner belongs to that generation of Germans who came of age during World War I; experienced the trauma of the collapsing empire in 1918; and witnessed Germany's struggle with democracy during the 1920's, the oppression of the Hitler regime during the 1930's, the horrors of World War II, and the gradual recovery after 1945. He was a participant in much of modern Germany's history —at times active (during the Weimar Republic), at times passive (during the Third Reich).

Kästner was born in Dresden on 23 February

1899 to parents of modest means. While he and his father (actually his stepfather) always remained somewhat aloof from each other, he had an intense admiration and love for his mother, whom he idealized in many of his works. The bond between the two lasted a lifetime and is reflected in his almost embarrassingly affectionate letters, which were published after his death in the anthology *Mein liebes, gutes Muttchen, Du!* (My Dear, Sweet Mommy, You, 1981), and in his autobiography for young people, *Als ich ein kleiner Junge war* (*When I Was a Little Boy*, 1957).

Kästner grew up in a close-knit family, with many uncles, aunts, and cousins, who also served as models for many of the characters in his books. Money was scarce, and his mother had to work as a hairdresser to pay for Kästner's education. Kästner himself was a model student; however, as he hastened to add, he was never a teacher's pet. Young Kästner was very much like the boy Emil in his first novel for children. After brief military service at the end of the war, Kästner enrolled in a teachers' college. While he never became a classroom teacher, he always remained committed to the concept of nonauthoritarian, humanistic education. He was convinced that "children can only be properly brought up if teachers are properly trained" (*Pinguin*, June 1946). The caring, humane Dr. Bökh, portrayed in *Das fliegende Klassenzimmer* (*The Flying Classroom*, 1933), represents his ideal of the good teacher.

Kästner earned his Ph.D. in German literature in 1925 and went on to become a theater critic and free-lance journalist. His articles and poems were published by some of the leading liberal and left-wing newspapers of Germany. Young Kästner's style in no way suggested a future writer of children's books. It was more fitting for the popular cabaret of the twenties: abrasive, witty, full of sarcasm, with a bitter undertone. He loved to provoke and shock his audience.

Kästner came to the writing of children's books more or less by accident. Edith Jacobsohn, the owner of Williams & Co., one of Berlin's leading publishing houses for youth literature (which had introduced the Dr. Dolittle stories and *Winnie-the-Pooh* to a German audience), asked her friend Kästner if he might not want to write a book for children. His answer was the novel *Emil and the Detectives*, which became an instant success. Not only was the book a best-seller, but a stage and film version were equally well received.

Emil was the beginning of a very productive period of writing, during which Kästner published new stories for young people almost annually, each different from the other, but all reflecting the inimitable style of its author. In 1931 the two novels *Pünktchen und Anton* (*Annaluise and Anton*) and *Der 35. Mai* (*The 35th of May*) appeared, as well as the children's book in verse *Arthur mit dem langen Arm* (Arthur with the Long Arm). In 1932 he added another book in verse, *Das verhexte Telefon* (The Bewitched Telephone), and rewrote *Annaluise and Anton* for the stage, where it enjoyed a successful run. This highly creative period came to a sudden end in 1933, shortly after the publication of *The Flying Classroom*.

The censorship of the Nazis began to weigh heavily on Kästner, whose books had been burned in the infamous auto-da-fé of May 1933. From then on some of his works could only be published abroad. A few "harmless" ones did appear in Germany during those brief periods when he received limited permission to publish in his own country. These were relatively dull stories, themes and variations of familiar tunes, but almost totally devoid of any real "message." Among them is *Emil und die drei Zwillinge* (*Emil and the Three Twins*, 1934), a pathetically poor rehash of the original Emil story. In 1938 he prepared a children's edition of the classic rogue's tale *Till Eulenspiegel* (*Till Eulenspiegel, the Clown*). In 1942 he was asked to write the script for the movie *Münchhausen*. He had to do this under an assumed name because he had been officially blacklisted as politically unreliable by the Nazi authorities. The film became a major motion-picture success and was still shown long after the war.

The retelling of old stories for children became a matter of considerable fascination for Kästner. In 1950 he published an edition of *Der gestiefelte Kater* (*Puss in Boots*), in which he retold the fairy tale on the basis of the original version by Charles Perrault; in 1951 a book version of *Münchhausen* appeared; in 1954 he presented the venerable Schildbürger tales (*The Simpletons*), a collection of folktales originally published in 1598; in 1956 he published a youth edition of *Don Quixote* (*Leben und Taten des scharfsinnigen Ritters Don Quichotte*), followed by *Gulliver's Travels* (*Gullivers Reisen*) in 1961. He even prepared a stage version of J. M. Barrie's *Peter Pan* (1952), which, however, turned out to be a failure.

In 1945, immediately after the war, Kästner

founded and edited the youth magazine *Pinguin*, which was published until 1949. This excellent journal gave voice to Kästner's democratic and humanistic ideas. He also continued to write full-length novels and stories for children, among them *Das doppelte Lottchen* (*Lottie and Lisa*, 1949), *Die Konferenz der Tiere* (*The Animals' Conference: A Story for Children and Other Understanding People*, 1949), *When I Was a Little Boy, Der kleine Mann* (*The Little Man*, 1963), and *Der kleine Mann und die kleine Miss* (*The Little Man and the Little Miss*, 1967). None of these, however, comes close to the novelty and brilliance of the works written between 1928 and 1933. Kästner had grown tired. He was honored for his accomplishments of the past rather than for his current works. He died on 29 July 1974.

Kästner writes for children without any condescension. He speaks to them in a light and chatty tone, as equals. He believes that children have the same rights as adults, and he takes their world seriously. He understands a child's perspective and admonishes his readers never to forget their own childhood. Indeed, he considers the ability to recollect one's own childhood the most important prerequisite for the writing of a good children's book. Only those who have retained a harmonious relationship to their own youth can understand and speak to young people.

Kästner is neither cute nor simplistic. He knows that life, even for young people, is not easy. He is aware of how unhappy children can be and understands that a child's unhappiness is just as real as that of an adult. In the preface to *The Flying Classroom* he writes:

> It never matters in life what makes you sad, but rather how sad you are. Good Lord, children's tears are no smaller and certainly often weigh heavier than the tears of grown-ups. Don't get me wrong, folks! We don't want to be unduly soft. I only think that one must be honest, even if it hurts. Honest to the core!

There are lessons to be learned in Kästner's stories; however, there is little preaching. Usually he relegates his message to the preface, a particular gem in many of his books. Here he directly speaks to his audience, addressing them as his confidants. He combines the absurd with the serious, talking about his travels to the Alps in midsummer, where he went so that the snow on the mountains might get him in the mood to write a Christmas story, and about the fact that life wears mighty big boxing gloves with which it pummels us about. In *The Flying Classroom* he expounds on wisdom and courage, both of which are needed if the world is to progress:

> Courage without wisdom is nonsense; and wisdom without courage is bunk! The history of the world knows many periods when stupid people were courageous, or wise people were cowards. . . . Only when the courageous have become wise, and the wise have become courageous, will we be able to experience . . . human progress.

Kästner's stories reflect the best of the humanistic ideals of the Weimar Republic, but they do not gloss over the injustices and problems that existed. The social environment that he describes is dominated by middle-class values, with a firm belief in the integrity of the family.

In *Emil and the Detectives*, Emil's mother is a widow who (like Kästner's mother) works hard as a hairdresser to support herself and her son. Emil in turn shows his appreciation by being a model student in order to please her. However, he is in no way a sissy. He can be full of mischief, painting a mustache on the monument of a local prince, and he is capable of acting to resolve a crisis. He travels alone to Berlin to visit his grandmother and relatives but is robbed on the train by an unscrupulous man. His anger over the theft is all the greater because he feels himself betrayed and because he knows how hard his mother had worked to scrape together the money. There is an interesting passage about the relativity of money—how much constitutes a lot and to whom. In it Kästner tries to make children aware that to some people even a modest sum may seem like a fortune. In the end the thief is caught with the help of a gang of wholesome kids, who join together to put right what an adult had done wrong. Emil, receiving a reward for having caught a criminal, uses the money to buy his mother a warm coat and an electric hairdryer.

While the plot may be a bit flimsy, the execution of it is not. Kästner successfully combines fantasy and realism. He portrays the big city; loneliness and comradeship; courage, trust, and basic human decency. His heroes are ordinary boys with a deep sense of justice and fairness. There is no violence, and in the end even the police, dreaded initially as authority figures, turn out to be "your friend[s] and helper[s]."

In *Annaluise and Anton*, Kästner juxtaposes a rich family and a poor family. Anton is very much like Emil. He works hard to help his ailing, widowed mother. But Annaluise, the rich girl, seldom sees her parents, who are too busy socializing. They leave her in the hands of a corrupt governess. The two children overcome their social and economic differences through friendship and understanding. They even teach the adults a lesson, which Kästner formulates as follows: "Life is serious and hard. And if people who are well off do not voluntarily help others who are poor, things will one day come to a bad end." Annaluise's parents learn their lesson, offering Anton's family employment and a home. The two families live together in mutual respect—the children have restored a paradise. Kästner concludes by saying: "Earth, so they say, once was a paradise. Everything is possible. Earth could again become a paradise. Nothing is impossible!"

In *The 35th of May*, the author embarks on a fantasy story in which a roller-skating horse takes an uncle and his nephew on a journey to the South Seas. On their way they pass the "Castle of the Glorious Past," in which arrogant old kings and generals fight long-forgotten wars (Caesar and Napoleon argue over strategy, and Hannibal engages Wallenstein in a battle with tin soldiers). It is a chapter that brings home the total absurdity and stupidity of warfare. Horse and riders skate on to the "Topsy-Turvy World," to which one can be admitted only if accompanied by a child. Here we find a correctional institution for difficult parents. Here, too, those who have mistreated their children must endure the same punishments. Kästner draws attention to the battered child—to the boy who is locked out without supper because his math is poor, the girl who is forced to lie to cover up her mother's gambling debts, the children who are beaten and neglected. The parents are dressed in ridiculous children's clothes and act like children in school. In this world the child is the authority figure and must be treated as such. Yet in many ways the children are kinder and fairer than their parents.

From the "Topsy-Turvy World," the travelers reach Elektropolis, the modern, totally mechanized city with moving sidewalks and remote-controlled automobiles. People work only for the fun of it; after all, nature and machines produce in abundance what society needs. Uncle and nephew must admit with shame that "back home" most people still suffer from material want.

The Flying Classroom, perhaps Kästner's best children's story, is set in a boarding school for boys just before Christmas, as the youngsters rehearse a play one of them has written for the school assembly at the end of the term. The play serves only as a connecting link. We are again exposed to the joys and sorrows of young people and to the basic decency that governs their lives. The characters in the story include a boy who has been deserted by his parents, another whose parents are too poor to send him the fare to come home for Christmas, a little fellow who wants to overcome his inborn timidity, and the wonderful teacher Dr. Bökh—affectionately called "Justus" (the Just)—in whom the children can trust and who has never forgotten his own days as a student in the same school. There is bitterness over the injustice of poverty, but love and kindness overcome this injustice. A "hermit," who lives in an old railroad car marked "Non-Smoking," and whom the students affectionately call the "Non-Smoker," turns out to be a long-lost friend of the teacher. He actually is a medical doctor who had withdrawn from society after his wife and child had died—and who now, in an operatic grand finale, is not only reunited with his friend, but is also appointed school physician. There are mean kids who break their word of honor, but they are quickly put in their place. In the end, virtue and decency prevail. The school is a family, and the family remains intact.

Kästner's concern for the family finds its strongest expression in the postwar novel *Lottie and Lisa*, the story of identical twins who bring their divorced parents together again. They do this by means of a deliberate and well-thought-out plan with which the two girls overcome all kinds of obstacles (such as other suitors). What the grown-ups were unable to achieve because of pride, selfishness, and the inability to communicate, the children accomplish through love, trust, devotion, and a firm belief in the inherent goodness of everyone. In addition one needs quite a bit of wit and scheming to achieve one's goals, but the twins are up to all requirements. As is typical of Kästner's books for children, the idealism of young people who have faith in the perfectibility of the world overcomes the pessimism and skepticism of the adults.

Kästner's books for children have a magic all their own. They are attractive volumes, beautifully illustrated. Many show the cartoonist's skills of the whimsical artist Walter Trier, who with just a few lines brings out the characteristic features of Kästner's heroes and of the situations they confront. His portrayals of Emil and his gang of boys, of the thief with the "stiff hat," of Annaluise and Anton with their dog Piefke, are veritable gems of book illustration. Text and illustrations fuse into one harmonious whole. One cannot think of one without the other.

Kästner's stories are heartwarming and sentimental, and they make the reader laugh and cry. But they are never sappy. His books have the admirable flavor of honesty. Kästner is a writer who loves to spin a yarn, but who also likes to develop a character. The child is a human being, not an underdeveloped adult. In his stories he tries to confront children with the problems of real life, so that they may learn judgment and self-reliance. He wants them to be prepared for life and to become responsible citizens in a world that will be better than the one currently occupied by their parents. Emil, Anton, the schoolboys, the identical twins, and all the other heroes are examples. In *Annaluise and Anton*, Kästner tells his readers:

> Perhaps, if you have come to like them [Emil and Anton], you will become like these models: as industrious, as decent, as courageous, as honest. That would be the most wonderful reward for me. Because this Emil, this Anton, and all those like them, will one day become very capable men. Such men are badly needed!

Kästner's readers were often offended by the critical and pessimistic tone of his writings for adults. In one of his best-known poems, he took issue with those who asked, "But where is your positive answer, Mr. Kästner?" ("Und wo bleibt das Positive, Herr Kästner?"). What he tells them is that the world is dark, and therefore the poet cannot paint it bright. Actually, if his readers had been more attentive to Kästner's entire work, they would indeed have found his positive answer: it is manifest in the world of the children, the world of the future generation, which is less corrupt than the present one, the world portrayed in Erich Kästner's books for young people.

Selected Bibliography

WORKS OF ERICH KÄSTNER IN GERMAN

Listed below, besides the collected works of Kästner, are only those works not available in English translation.

Gesammelte Schriften. 7 vols. Zurich: Atrium Verlag, 1959; Cologne: Kiepenheuer und Witsch, 1959. (Vols. 6 and 7 contain Kästner's major works for children, with reproductions of the original illustra-

tions. Includes *Arthur mit dem langen Arm* and *Das verhexte Telefon*.)

Münchhausen, ein Drehbuch. Frankfurt am Main: S. Fischer Verlag, 1960. (The film script.)

Gullivers Reisen. Vienna and Heidelberg: Carl Ueberreuter Verlag, 1961. (A retelling of *Gulliver's Travels*.)

Gesammelte Schriften für Erwachsene. Munich: Droemer Knaur, 1969. (Includes *Peter Pan*.)

Mein liebes, gutes Muttchen, Du!, Dein oller Junge. Hamburg: Knaus, 1981.

WORKS IN ENGLISH TRANSLATION

Emil and the Detectives: A Story for Children, translated by Eric Sutton. With illustrations by Walter Trier. New York: Dodd, Mead, 1930.

Annaluise and Anton: A Story for Children, translated by Eric Sutton. With illustrations by Walter Trier. New York: Dodd, Mead, 1933.

The 35th of May; or, Conrad's Ride to the South Seas, translated by Cyrus Brooks. With Illustrations by Walter Trier. London: Jonathan Cape, 1933; New York: Franklin Watts, 1961.

The Flying Classroom: A Novel for Children, translated by Cyrus Brooks. With illustrations by Walter Trier. London: Jonathan Cape, 1934. Rev. ed. London: Jonathan Cape, 1967.

Emil and the Three Twins, translated by Cyrus Brooks. London: Jonathan Cape, 1935; New York: Franklin Watts, 1961.

Till Eulenspiegel, the Clown, retold by Erich Kästner; translated by Richard and Clara Winston. With illustrations by Walter Trier. New York: Julian Messner, 1957.

The Animals' Conference: A Story for Children and Other Understanding People, translated by Zita de Schauensee. With illustrations by Walter Trier. New York: David McKay, 1949.

Puss in Boots, retold by Erich Kästner; translated by Richard and Clara Winston. With illustrations by Walter Trier. New York: Julian Messner, 1957.

Lottie and Lisa: A Novel for Children, translated by Cyrus Brooks. With illustrations by Walter Trier. London: Jonathan Cape, 1950. Rev. ed. London: Jonathan Cape, 1973.

The Simpletons, retold by Erich Kästner; Translated by Richard and Clara Winston. New York: Julian Messner, 1957.

Don Quixote, retold by Erich Kästner; Translated by Isabel and Florence McHugh. With illustrations by Horst Lemke. London: Jonathan Cape, 1959.

When I Was a Little Boy, translated by Isabel and Florence McHugh. With illustrations by Horst Lemke. London: Jonathan Cape, 1959.

The Little Man, translated by James Kirkup. With illustrations by Horst Lemke. London: Jonathan Cape, 1966.

The Little Man and the Little Miss, translated by James Kirkup. With illustrations by Horst Lemke. London: Jonathan Cape, 1969.

CRITICAL AND BIOGRAPHICAL STUDIES

Benson, Renate. *Erich Kästner: Studien zu seinem Werk*. Bonn: Bouvier, 1973.

Beutler, Kurt. *Erich Kästner: Eine literaturpädagogische Untersuchung*. Weinheim and Berlin: Verlag Julius Beltz, 1967.

Enderle, L. *Erich Kästner in Selbstzeugnissen und Bilddokumenten*. Hamburg: Rowohlt, 1966.

Kiesel, Helmuth. *Erich Kästner*. Munich: C. H. Beck, 1981.

Last, R. W. *Erich Kästner*. Modern German Authors. New Series. Vol. 3. London: Oswald Wolff, 1974.

Mank, Dieter. *Erich Kästner im nationalsozialistischen Deutschland: 1933–1945. Zeit ohne Werk?* Bern: Lang, 1981.

Schneyder, Werner. *Erich Kästner*. Munich: Kindler Verlag, 1982.

Schwarz, Egon. "Erich Kästner: Fabians Schneckengang im Kreise." In *Zeitkritische Romane des 20. Jahrhunderts*, edited by Hans Wagener. Stuttgart: Reclam, 1975, 124–145.

Wagener, Hans. *Erich Kästner*. Berlin: Colloquium Verlag, 1973.

Wiley, R. A. "The Role of the Mother in Five Pre-War Editions of Erich Kästner's Works." *German Quarterly* 28: 22–33 (1955).

Winkelmann, John. *Social Criticism in the Early Works of Erich Kästner*. Columbia: Curators of the University of Missouri, 1953.

—GERHARD H. WEISS

CHARLES KINGSLEY

1819–1875

CHARLES KINGSLEY'S REPUTATION as a children's writer rests entirely upon *The Water-Babies* (1863), which not many children can ever have read to the end. Since it is one of the few Victorian children's books that can be said to be as well known today as it was in its own time, it says much for the potency of the opening of *The Water-Babies* that the book is included with such classics as *Alice's Adventures in Wonderland* (1865), *Treasure Island* (1883), and Edward Lear's *Nonsense* books.

The Water-Babies is an intensely personal book. There is much of Kingsley's own boyhood in it as well as his adult quirks and prejudices, and to understand it one has to know something about the man. He was born on 12 June 1819, the child of a Hampshire squire who had entered the church unenthusiastically when he found that he had no money to live on. When Kingsley was born his father was a curate at Holne on the edge of Dartmoor, and so greatly did his mother love the Devon countryside that she walked about it constantly while she was pregnant, hoping to communicate her feeling for it to her unborn child.

Although Kingsley spent only the first six weeks of his life at Holne, and eight later years of his childhood in Devon, he always thought of himself as a West Country man. After some wanderings the Kingsley family settled at Barnack in Lincolnshire in 1824. Large tracts of the fen country around them were still undrained, and Kingsley felt closest to his father—a remote figure for whom he had little affinity and who repelled any demonstrations of affection—when he was out wildfowling with

him in the marshy wastes. The former squire was a keen sportsman, as his son later was, but the distance between them was great, and Kingsley's lifelong speech impediment seems to have been much aggravated by his terror at having to repeat lessons to his father. (He made a savage attack on the educational practices of his day in *The Water-Babies*, in which the wretched Tomtoddies, crammed with learning by their parents and harassed by the Examiner-of-all-Examiners, turn into turnips and die.) The family left Barnack in 1830, but he remembered the fens with deep affection and made them the scene of *Hereward the Wake* (1866).

The next move was back to Devon, to the fishing village of Clovelly. Kingsley loved the Devon country as passionately as his mother could have wished. He rode with his brothers over the moors that were to play such an important part in *Westward Ho!* (1855), and he discovered among the family's books Richard Hakluyt's accounts of the great Elizabethan navigators and explorers, some of whom, like Drake and Sir Richard Grenville, were West Country men. Kingsley was sent to the grammar school at Helston in Cornwall, a small school whose teachers made allowances for the idiosyncrasies of their pupils and let them wander off on country expeditions. Kingsley wrote home ecstatically about the botanical specimens he had found. He spent two happy years there. But then when he was fifteen his brother died at school, and the following year he was taken from Helston because the family was moving to London, where

Charles Kingsley senior had accepted the living of St. Luke's, Chelsea. Neither the father nor the son enjoyed life there. Unlike the younger Kingsley's contemporary Charlotte Yonge, to whom parish functions were the height of all possible happiness, both male Kingsleys detested them (indeed their strong feelings on the point brought an unusual degree of rapport). "We have nothing but clergymen," wrote Charles junior, "... talking of nothing but parochial schools, and duties, and vestries, and curates, &., &., &. . . . . I begin to hate these dapper young-ladies-preachers like the devil. . . . As you may suppose, this hatred is πατρόθεν [hereditary]." He liked churchy conversation no better when he himself was a clergyman.

Kingsley was sent to King's College, London, and settled down to work (at Greek, Latin, and mathematics) in a way he never had at Helston with its distractions. In 1838 he entered Magdalene College, Cambridge, where for two years he idled, pulling himself together only in his third year. By that time he had rediscovered Christianity (having been latterly repelled both by his father's tepid Low Church practices and by what he regarded as the trite platitudes of the Chelsea "young-ladies-preachers"). In gratitude for his conversion he vowed to take holy orders. He had also fallen in love with Fanny Grenfell, whom he had met when the Kingsley family spent an extended holiday in Oxfordshire. The wooing of Fanny was difficult, as her sisters were possessive and disapproved of the nervous, restless, stammering young man. But his ardor, and hers, eventually won the day, and they were married in 1844.

Very soon afterward Kingsley was presented to the living of Eversley in Hampshire, a parish where he had once been curate and where he stayed for the rest of his life. At the time, Fanny liked the rectory (a large, rambling seventeenth-century house), although she later found drawbacks that gave her husband no little trouble and financial worries to set right. It was a small parish, with only 750 souls in it, and as the previous rector had been lamentably negligent there was much work to be done to woo parishioners back to the church. Kingsley was always at ease with workingmen. Dressed as a sportsman rather than as a clergyman, he strode round the parish (which then included tracts of wild moorland) visiting his flock in their own homes. He organized schooling for them (he found that not one of the villagers could read) and confirmation classes and savings clubs to tide them over in lean times. It was perhaps the happiest period of his life. He enjoyed the activity, and he and Fanny were ecstatically happy in their marriage. They had four children—Rose, born in 1845, Maurice in 1847, Mary in 1852, and Grenville in 1858.

In those early Eversley years Kingsley also met Frederick Denison Maurice (after whom he named his first son), and became deeply committed to Christian Socialism. With Maurice and others he began the periodical *Politics for the People*, which ran to seventeen issues before expiring. Kingsley's articles were signed "Parson Lot"; his views were radical and included the suggestion that cathedrals should be converted to winter gardens for workers. His first novel, *Yeast* (1851), serialized in *Fraser's Magazine* in 1848, arose out of these activities. The plot is minimal; there is much discussion of the degradation of the agricultural laborer, the need for clean water and drains, and the iniquities of the game laws (which, for instance, made it a criminal offense for a cottager to kill the hare that fed off his vegetables). Religious issues of the day were also aired—Kingsley was a violent opponent of Rome and of the Tractarian movement in the Church of England. His second novel, *Alton Locke* (1850), also criticized the living conditions of the poor; it was sparked off by a visit to Jacob's Island, an infamous locality near the London docks, and by the appalling conditions in London tailors' sweatshops. The views he expressed here and from the pulpit brought him much notoriety, as did his novel *Hypatia* (perhaps the best of his fiction, serialized in *Fraser's Magazine* in 1852, and published as a book in 1853), though for very different reasons: this story of fifth-century Alexandria contains scenes of orgy and violence.

By the time he wrote *Hypatia* his involvement with Christian Socialism was beginning to slacken. His money worries were also abating a little, and at last he was able to keep a horse again and to hunt, for he had all the upper-class tastes for blood sports, particularly hunting and fishing, and was suspicious of those who did not share them. A holiday in Devon, where he scrambled over the rocks with Rose and Maurice, produced *Glaucus; or, The Wonders of the Shore* (1855). He believed passionately that a knowledge of and reverence for nature could bring men to God, and his exposition of nature's wonders is interrupted by lengthy sermonizing. (*Madam How and Lady Why*, which he wrote to introduce children to geology in 1869, is an extension of this theme.)

Out of the same holiday in Devon came the far more famous *Westward Ho!*, in which he drew on his love of the Devon landscape and Devon men and those early memories of reading Hakluyt's *Voiages* (1589) when he was a boy in Clovelly. This tale of Elizabethan adventure and discovery, the Spanish wars, and the desperate doings of Jesuits was not written for children but was long regarded as a children's book and had a place in the libraries of boys' schools. Perhaps the child who was skilled at skipping irrelevancies could enjoy the scenes of slaughter and bloodshed and such episodes as the battle with the Spanish treasure fleet, the wanderings in South America, and the rout of the Armada (which Kingsley described in one of the closing chapters as "the battle of Michael and his angels against Satan and his friends," with the English shouts of victory the "prophetic birth-paean of North America"). The book was well received: England was then embroiled with Russia in the Crimean War, so that jingoistic sentiments did not come amiss, although there were some who expressed their distaste. George Eliot, reviewing it for the *Westminster Review*, remarked: "Kingsley sees, feels, and paints vividly, but he theorises illogically and moralises absurdly."

The Heroes (1856), Kingsley's best children's book, was written in the autumn of 1855 and dedicated to Rose, Maurice, and Mary. He undertook this retelling of Greek legends in a fit of irritation with Hawthorne's *Tanglewood Tales* (1853), which he found "distressingly vulgar" and which, though pretty in themselves, undeniably falsify the originals and turn myth into cozy domestic stories, often with a contemporary American setting. As the title suggests, and as best suited his nature, Kingsley chose heroes—Perseus, the Argonauts, Theseus. He did not, like Hawthorne, turn them into children. In this book alone he forbore to lecture and moralize and contented himself with telling a story in a spare dramatic style no doubt intended to suggest Homer. Take the slaying of Medusa, for instance:

> For Medusa's wings and talons rattled as she sank dead upon the rocks; and her two foul sisters woke, and saw her lying dead.
>
> Into the air they sprang yelling, and looked for him who had done the deed. Thrice they swung round and round, like hawks who beat for a partridge; and thrice they snuffed round and round, like hounds who draw upon a deer. At last they

struck upon the scent of the blood, and they checked for a moment to make sure; and then on they rushed with a fearful howl, while the wind rattled hoarse in their wings.

"No one," wrote Roger Lancelyn Green in *Tellers of Tales* (1946), "has caught the magic and the music and the wonder of the old Greek legends as Kingsley did. . . . [He] caught a very echo out of the ancient world [and] gave their first real glimpse of the true Greece to numberless children."

The Heroes was followed in 1857 by a third novel, about contemporary life, *Two Years Ago*, in which Kingsley rode many hobby horses, including sanitary reform, and fired off some broadsides at poets, intellectuals, and Nonconformists. In this book he quotes "Be good, sweet maid, and let who will be clever" from the lines he had written for one of his wife's nieces the year before. Significantly these are put into the mouth of a naturalist; Kingsley is back with his favorite theme—redemption through nature.

In 1858 the Kingsleys' last child was born—Grenville, the much-loved and indulged son to whom *The Water-Babies* is dedicated. Rose, Maurice, Mary, and Grenville had a far happier relationship with their parents than their father with his, and they looked back on their childhood as filled with "perpetual laughter." Charles Kingsley had never outgrown boyishness, and loved romping and practical jokes; he was always accessible to the children. When in 1862 Fanny reminded him that he had promised that the baby should have his book (the other three having *The Heroes*), he strode off to his study and according to Fanny came back in half an hour with the opening chapter:

> Once upon a time there was a little chimney-sweep, and his name was Tom. That is a short name, and you have heard it before, so you will not have much trouble in remembering it. He lived in a great town in the North country, where there were plenty of chimneys to sweep, and plenty of money for Tom to earn and his master to spend. He could not read nor write, and did not care to do either; and he never washed himself, for there was no water up the court where he lived. . . . He cried half his time, and laughed the other half.

Kingsley was never a man to conceal his feelings, and in *The Water-Babies* more of his enthusiasms, his fads, and his often violent prejudices well to the surface than in any other book. There is his insistence on washing and cleanliness; his interest in sanitation and his concern for exploited children; his passion for natural history; his theories on education; his resentment about his own upbringing; and his views on medicine, the stupidity of academics and intellectuals, the iniquitous cheap sweets and children's books of his day—all set down haphazard with gusty vehemence. He gets off squibs at the expense of the Darwin and Huxley school, and he tells his readers what he thinks of the Irish and the Americans, about "frowzy monks" and the absurd new fashion of dining at eight, and that they must see to their horses' comfort before their own after a day's hunting. Only the opening pages are free from digression and have held the imagination of generations of children, primarily for Kingsley's account of the fine June morning when the little chimney sweep sets out with his cruel master to Harthover Place, loses his way in the maze of chimneys, comes down in a little girl's bedroom, is amazed by its cleanness and affrighted by his own reflection, and then is pursued panic-stricken over the moors in the shimmering heat by the owner and his servants until he scrambles down a cliff face to the valley bottom.

But as soon as Tom submerges himself in the stream and becomes a water baby the pace of the narrative slackens, often ceasing altogether, and the lecturing begins, bespattered with allusions to long-forgotten religious and political controversies and topics that few children even at the time could possibly have understood. "Some people think there are no fairies. Cousin Cramchild tells little folks so in his Conversations. Well, perhaps there are none—in Boston, U.S., where he was raised. There are only a clumsy lot of spirits there, who can't make people hear without thumping on the table." Kingsley wanted to have it both ways: he thought that right-minded children should have a sense of wonder and believe in fairies, and he also wanted them to appreciate the marvels of nature. He presented both as universal truths, overlooking the fact that readers might treat his account of the hatching of dragonflies in the same spirit as his account of water babies.

Tom's adventures as a water baby, which occupy by far the greater part of the book, are a form of purification to fit him to be united with Ellie, the little girl whose bedroom he had inadvertently entered in his earth life as a chimney sweep. He meets first the fairy Mrs. Bedonebyasyoudid, who might be said to represent law (Kingsley gleefully sets her to punish the people who had tormented his own childhood—the schoolmasters, the foolish mothers who squeeze their children into uncomfortable clothes, the careless nursemaids, and the doctors, whom she doses with purges and emetics "and no basins"), and then her sister Mrs. Doasyouwouldbedoneby, who conveys her lessons by love. Finally he sets off to the Other-end-of-nowhere, proves himself, and achieves his Ellie and, it is implied, salvation.

In all this Kingsley may well have been drawing unconsciously on his own feelings of sexual guilt and the sense of being unworthy of Fanny that he had expressed to her before he was married and to which he would allude in his attacks of depression. Indeed, *The Water-Babies* does present a tempting field to the amateur psychologist, from the opening motif of Tom descending Ellie's chimney to the obsession with water and cleanliness. Maureen Duffy in *The Erotic World of Faery* (1972) has identified Tom's stealing of sweets from Mrs. Doasyouwouldbedoneby and the prickles that growhim in consequence as masturbation and its punishment.

Kingsley was never an organized writer, but this is the most chaotic and self-indulgent of all his books. Its lasting popularity is puzzling, but can be due only to the originality of the story and the superb narration in the first forty pages. The book also contains three of Kingsley's best-known poems (for all his sometimes voiced scorn of poets, he loved writing verse): the river's song "Clear and cool, clear and cool," the ballad-style "When all the world is young, lad," and Mrs. Doasyouwouldbedoneby's song "I once had a sweet little doll, dears."

By the time *The Water-Babies* was written, Kingsley was an establishment figure, a chaplain to the queen, history tutor to the Prince of Wales and much in favor at court, and Regius Professor of Modern History at Cambridge (a post for which he was intellectually singularly ill-fitted). In 1864 he was rash enough to make offensive references to John Henry Newman in a review and was hopelessly worsted in the exchanges that followed. He was not in good health, and his last novel, *Hereward the Wake*, published in 1866, was written with great effort and only because he needed the money. This story of England at the time of the Norman Conquest and the resistance of its hero, Hereward (called the "Wake" because he was not known to sleep), to the French invaders was long regarded as a children's book; indeed most of the twentieth-century English editions are for schools. Its wordiness must have cast a pall over many a classroom. Less passionate than *Westward Ho!*, it still contains a great deal of bloodshed (and not a few amorous passages as well, for Hereward leaves Torfrida, the wife he had once loved so well, for a new young enchantress). To the adult reader, Hereward is a convincing hero, far more so than Charlotte Yonge's chivalrous lilies; Kingsley shows him first as a reckless young rough, the despair of his mother and the terror of the fens, then (subdued and civilized by his love for Torfrida) the hero of the stand against the French, and finally toppled and ensnared by the wiles of William of Normandy and Alftruda, the woman William offers him.

In 1873 Kingsley became a canon of Westminster, a position that he thankfully supposed would obviate the necessity ever to write again. But Fanny's never-ceasing demands for money sent him on a lecture tour of America the next year. He returned unwell and, finding Fanny ill, nursed her devotedly. He died on 23 January 1875 thinking that she had died before him; in fact she lived until 1892 and wrote a biography of her husband.

At the time of Kingsley's death he was regarded as one of the greatest national figures of his day; now, although Victorian specialists may read *Yeast* and *Alton Locke*, he is remembered chiefly for *The Water-Babies*. Despite its many flaws it is an attractive book, as warmhearted and affectionate as the man who wrote it—and also as muddled.

Selected Bibliography

WORKS OF CHARLES KINGSLEY

Westward Ho! or, The Voyages and Adventures of Sir Amyas Leigh, Knight, of Burrough in the County of Devon, in the Reign of Her Most Glorious Majesty Queen Elizabeth. Cambridge, England: Macmillan, 1855; Boston: Ticknor and Fields, 1855.

The Heroes. With illustrations by the author. Cambridge, England: Macmillan, 1856; Boston: Ticknor and Fields, 1856.

The Water-Babies: A Fairy-Tale for a Land-Baby. With illustrations by J. Noel Paton. London and Cambridge, England: Macmillan, 1863.

Hereward the Wake, the "Last of the English." London and Cambridge, England: Macmillan, 1866.

Madam How and Lady Why. London: Bell and Daldy, 1870.

CRITICAL AND BIOGRAPHICAL STUDIES

Baldwin, Stanley E. *Charles Kingsley.* Ithaca, N.Y.: Cornell University Press, 1934; London: Oxford University Press, 1934.

Chitty, Susan. *The Beast and the Monk: A Life of Charles Kingsley.* London: Hodder and Stoughton, 1974.

Colloms, Brenda. *Charles Kingsley: The Lion of Eversley.* London: Constable, 1975; New York: Barnes and Noble, 1975.

Duffy, Maureen. *The Erotic World of Faery.* London: Hodder and Stoughton, 1972.

Green, Roger Lancelyn. *Tellers of Tales.* Leicester, England: E. Ward, 1946.

Kendall, Guy. *Charles Kingsley and His Ideas.* London and New York: Hutchinson, 1947.

Kingsley, Frances E., ed. *Charles Kingsley: His Letters and Memories of His Life.* London: Henry S. King, 1877.

Martin, Robert Bernard. *The Dust of Combat: A Life of Charles Kingsley.* London: Faber and Faber, 1959.

Pope-Hennessey, Una. *Canon Charles Kingsley: A Biography.* London: Chatto and Windus, 1948.

Thorp, Margaret Farraud. *Charles Kingsley, 1819–1875.* Princeton, N.J.: Princeton University Press, 1937; London: Oxford University Press, 1937. Reprinted New York: Octagon Books, 1969.

—GILLIAN AVERY

RUDYARD KIPLING

1865–1936

JOSEPH RUDYARD KIPLING, who once described England as "the most marvellous of all foreign countries that I have ever been in," was born in Bombay on 30 December 1865. His father, John Lockwood Kipling, was an artist and designer and the principal of the new Jeejeebyhoy School of Art in Bombay; his mother was Alice Macdonald, sister of Lady Burne-Jones. Rudyard, equally comfortable with English and Hindustani, secure in the warm and loving circle of family and friends, spent the first six years of his life in Bombay—a period he always afterward recalled as a personal Golden Age.

In 1871 the Kiplings decided to send Rudyard and his sister, Alice, born in 1868 and nicknamed "Trix," to England—a practice common among British families wishing to protect their children from the many hazards of life in India. Although such children were often lodged with relatives, Rudyard and Trix were taken in as paying boarders by the Holloways of Lorne Lodge, Southsea, whose newspaper advertisement the Kiplings had seen. Trix was usually indulged by this family, but the strong-willed Rudyard, whose miseries were compounded by failing eyesight, was apparently persecuted with all of the zeal and fervor that Mrs. Holloway's brand of evangelical Christianity could inspire. If Bombay had been heaven, Southsea was decidedly not. "I had never heard of Hell, so I was introduced to it in all its terrors," said Kipling over sixty years later, and he recalled those terrors with savage precision in the story "Baa Baa Black Sheep" and in his posthumously published autobi-ography, *Something of Myself for My Friends Known and Unknown* (1937). He spent more than five years in the Holloways' "House of Desolation," from which he was finally delivered in 1877, when he was sent to the United Services College in Devon—a school that he subsequently celebrated in *Stalky and Co.* (1899) and whose headmaster encouraged his literary ambitions.

In 1882 Kipling returned to India, where he went to work for the Lahore *Civil and Military Gazette*. During his "seven years' hard" as a journalist, Kipling accumulated material for his early collections of verse and prose. The gentle satire of *Departmental Ditties and Other Verses* (1886) and the realism of *Plain Tales from the Hills* (1888) and the stories printed for the Indian Railway Library, some of which were later collected in *Wee Willie Winkie and Other Child Stories* (1888) and *Soldiers Three* (1888), made Kipling known outside India and attracted the favorable attention of Andrew Lang, Rider Haggard, and other literati.

He returned to England in 1889 and published his first novel, *The Light That Failed*, in the following year. There he met the American author and publisher Wolcott Balestier, collaborated with him on *The Naulakha: A Story of East and West* (1892), and married his sister, Caroline. A proposed trip to Samoa to visit Robert Louis Stevenson had to be cut short due to the failure of Kipling's bankers. He and his wife settled in Carrie's hometown of Brattleboro, Vermont, where their first child, Josephine, was born in 1894, and where Kipling, seriously turning his attention to literature for children, produced *The Jungle Book* (1894), *The Second Jungle Book* (1895), and *"Captains Courageous": A Story of the Grand Banks* (1897).

The Kiplings went back to England in 1896. When they and their three children returned to America for a visit in 1899, Josephine died of pneumonia in New York, a loss that cut Kipling deeply. In 1901 Kipling published *Kim,* a novel he had begun as early as 1892 and which many consider to be his finest work. The whimsical *Just So Stories for Little Children* followed in 1902, the same year in which Kipling bought "Bateman's," his home in Sussex. Bateman's inspired two collections of short stories based on English history: *Puck of Pook's Hill* (1906) and *Rewards and Fairies* (1910).

Kipling did no more serious writing for children after 1910, and his popularity with many adult readers had begun to decline well before he was awarded the Nobel Prize for literature in 1907. The reasons for this decline had more to do with Kipling's politics than with his literary abilities. *Stalky and Co.,* a collection of irreverent stories celebrating life at a school preparing boys for army careers, and Kipling's scathing criticism of British ineptitude in the Boer War caused some misguided critics to denounce him as a "jingo imperialist." (These critics can hardly have read "Recessional," a poem he wrote for Queen Victoria's Diamond Jubilee in 1897, which is as devastating an exposé of the vanity of power as anything he wrote.) Kipling lost his enthusiasm for politics after the Liberals won the general election of 1906. He lost his only son, eighteen-year-old John, in the Battle of Loos in 1915, and wrote the two-volume book *The Irish Guards in the Great War* (1923) as a memorial, as well as doing work for the Imperial War Graves Commission. Although plagued by chronic ulcers, he wrote some of his most powerful short stories after World War I. His production for children, however, was limited to assembling some of his uncollected stories in *Land and Sea Tales for Scouts and Guides* (1923). Kipling died in 1936. An unfinished autobiography, *Something of Myself,* appeared posthumously in 1937.

Kipling's critical reputation has been slow to recover from the nadir it reached in the 1920's and 1930's. But his unrelenting craftsmanship, his determination to be "master of the bricks and mortar of his trade," compels respect, and his genius as a storyteller, and especially as a teller of stories for children, will surely prove stronger than the murky and sordid vicissitudes of politics. The older generation may know Kipling as a courier of memorable phrases—the most recent edition of the *Oxford Dictionary of Quotations* (1979) lists over three hundred citations of his work—or prize him as the poet who extols the virtues of work, duty, and discipline—qualities most famously praised in "If," in *Rewards and Fairies.* A surer indication of Kipling's enduring popularity is the fact that his stories about Mowgli attained the status of folklore soon after their publication, as Edith Nesbit's mention of them in her books *The Story of the Treasure Seekers* (1899) and *The Would-be-goods* (1901) makes plain. Although Kipling's overall career still awaits judicious critical re-evaluation, the general public—and especially the young public—has long since rendered its own verdict. His status as a writer for children is rightfully secure, and none of his major works has yet gone out of print.

Throughout his career Kipling remained sternly reticent about his private life and detested biography, which he frequently described as "Higher Cannibalism." No doubt he would have approved heartily of the current rejection of the notion that biography is a passe-partout. (In the title of his autobiography, "something" is the operative word.) Still, it is difficult to dismiss the suspicion that so successful a children's writer as Kipling must have remained in creative touch with his own childhood. Even modern psychology confirms what the romantic has always known—that the child is indeed father to the man. In the epigraph to the first chapter of his autobiography Kipling himself concedes: "Give me the first six years of a child's life and you can have the rest." With all due respect for the mysterious evolution of artistic creativity, we can still posit a pattern in Kipling's early life that was to dominate his most significant fiction. All of us mythicize our childhoods; perhaps only for the most creative of us does such mythmaking evolve from neurosis into art.

The most important experience in young Kipling's life was the abrupt rupture of his idyllic existence in Bombay and—his parents seem not to have explained fully the reason for the separation—his inexplicable transportation to the "prison-house" of Lorne Lodge. Sixty years after the event, he recalled in *Something of Myself* the contrast between life in Bombay—"my first impression is of daybreak, light and colour and golden and purple fruits . . . the memory of early morning walks to the Bombay fruit market with my *ayab*"—and the incomprehensible evangelical "Hell" of the Holloways' House of Desolation. His misery is pathetically revealed in the description of his welcome to his mother upon her unexpected return from India: "When she first came up to my room to kiss me good-night, I flung up an arm to guard off the cuff that I had been trained to expect." Bad as they were, however, Kipling's years at Lorne Lodge were not unrelentingly grim. He wrote of his annual stay at the house of his uncle, Sir Edward Burne-Jones: "For a month each year I possessed a paradise which I verily believe saved me." But this "paradise" is significantly absent from his fictional accounts of his own childhood, and the pattern of bliss followed by exile is central to Kipling's fiction. C. S. Lewis observes that what Kipling "loves better than anything in the world is the intimacy within a closed circle," and Angus Wilson gives due attention to "the agonizing sense of personal isolation" that characterizes Kipling's work. The quest for atonement and affiliation, for an end to exile and alienation, is a recurrent theme in Kipling's work throughout his career. Although the imagery in which this quest is presented is seldom religious, the quest itself is religious in its nature and intensity, and the price demanded for an end to alienation is usually death, either literal or metaphoric. Even in his fiction for children this quest is a persistent element, and self-sacrifice, however palliated for the younger reader, is presented as the customary gateway to redemption.

Quest, self-sacrifice, a frontier experience that entails the violation of old boundaries and a journey into the unfamiliar, disease, and death itself are significant features of the first book to draw attention to Kipling as a writer for children, *Wee Willie Winkie*. The hero of the title story, "Wee Willie Winkie," is the six-year-old son of the colonel of the regiment; he confronts a gang of Afghan bandits to rescue the fiancée of one of his father's officers. In "His Majesty the King" an unloved child's theft of a diamond brooch saves his parents' failing marriage. A number of critics deplore the conventionality of some of the tales in this collection, and there is justice to Charles Carrington's dismissal of them as "studio-pieces, not much unlike Mrs. Burnett's *Little Lord Fauntleroy* (1886), the masterpiece among sentimental juveniles." What such critics fail to remark, however, is Kipling's intuitive understanding of the child as outlaw. Though his child protagonists are ultimately reintegrated into society, they, like Jim Hawkins in Robert Louis Stevenson's *Treasure Island* (1883), succeed *because*

they defy discipline and social custom. Although Willie has lived under military discipline all his life, he breaks it to go "beyond the river, which was the end of all the Earth" to rescue Major Allardyce's daughter, and is rewarded by being called by his true name—a symbolic recognition of his manhood. In "His Majesty the King" the boy's fear that his crime is a "black sin" leads to fever, delirium, and, finally, confession, but "his reward was Love, and the right to play in the waste-paper basket under the table 'for always.'"

A similar moral complexity informs "The Drums of the Fore and Aft," the tale of "a brace of the most finished little fiends that ever banged drum or tootled fife in the Band of a British Regiment," who "ended their sinful career by open and flagrant mutiny and were shot for it." Their "mutiny" takes place when their regiment breaks and runs from an Afghan charge, and the two guttersnipes, emboldened by rum from a fallen soldier's canteen, rally their comrades by marching forward playing "The British Grenadiers." Their drunken heroics save the day, win undeserved glory for their brigadier, and secure at last an uncontested place in the regiment for "Jakin and Lew, whose little bodies were borne up just in time to fit two gaps at the head of the big ditch-grave for the dead under the heights of Jagai." Paradoxically, order is maintained only by virtue of the boys' crime, and the law is upheld at the price of their lives.

None of these three tales is simply a story for children, but young Kipling is here feeling his way toward children's literature, finding in stories about children subject matter worthy of serious adult attention. (He made a comparable discovery of the enlisted man as a protagonist in the stories collected in *Soldiers Three*.) Despite occasional lapses into sentimentality or cynicism, these tales explore alienation, violence, sacrifice, and redemption— constant elements in Kipling's work throughout his career. These elements are especially prominent in the best story in *Wee Willie Winkie,* "Baa Baa Black Sheep"—the story, thinly disguised as fiction, of Kipling's years in the House of Desolation with the Holloways in Southsea. Although Kipling is meticulous about exonerating the protagonist's parents, who eventually rescue him as Kipling was himself rescued, the story does not emphasize deliverance and redemption but the price of the experience, the emotional scars that even time will never heal. In this story, the most intimate of all his works of fiction, Kipling broadens his concept of children's literature at the story's close to embrace the Rousseauistic notion of childhood as a lost paradise. The story's protagonist asserts that "it's all different now, and we are just as much Mother's as if she had never gone," but the narrator's concluding comment makes an assertion of a far different sort: "When young lips have drunk deep of the bitter waters of Hate, Suspicion, and Despair, all the Love in the world will not wholly take away that knowledge; though it may turn darkened eyes for a while to the light, and teach Faith where no Faith was."

The essential features of Kipling's mythology of childhood reveal themselves as early as *Wee Willie Winkie.* The crucial experience of childhood is the loss of bliss, followed by a period of exile or outlawry, and leading to a quest for affiliation, for a sense of belonging to a group united by devotion to an ideal. This affiliation compensates the child for the original loss and provides at least some security in the welter of human existence. Although Kipling's success in embodying this myth naturally varied throughout his career—his relish for the discipline by which the outlaw is redeemed has offended many readers—the elements of loss, exile, quest, and redemption, however variously defined, remain central to his conception of children and children's literature.

Nor are these elements restricted to his works of children's literature. They are prominent in Kipling's first novel. *The Light That Failed,* which tells the story of Dick Helgar, an artist disappointed in love and undermined by commercial success as a war artist. Helgar slowly goes blind, abandons women and commercialism, and redeems himself by finding his way to the Sudan to expire cleanly in a friend's arms in battle. Helgar's childhood is a reprise of the House of Desolation episode, but, in this case, neurosis is not elevated into art. *The Light That Failed* is a novel of fearsome misogyny, larded with pretentious pronouncements on art, and fully deserves its customary neglect by the critics. Even its first chapter is far inferior to "Baa Baa Black Sheep" and has little to offer those interested in Kipling as a writer about or for children.

Such is not the case with *The Jungle Book* and *The Second Jungle Book,* the cornerstones of Kipling's reputation as a children's writer and still among the most popular of all his works. The tales of Mowgli, a boy who was lost and raised by a pack of wolves in India's Seeonee Hills, are too well known to require summary. His struggle with the tiger,

Shere Khan, his encounter with greed and human violence when he discovers a forgotten treasure in a long-abandoned city, and his leadership of the wolves in a great battle with a pack of invading wild dogs are among the best of Kipling's adventure stories. Much of the success of these stories is due to the author's wonderful realization of Mowgli's world. Speaking of children's play in *Something of Myself,* Kipling comments on their fondness for imaginary worlds and astutely notes that "the magic . . . lies in the ring or fence that you take refuge in." But it is not only Kipling's success in world-making that compels our attention in these tales. Kipling's scattered references to "the Law of the Jungle" typify his lifelong concern with discipline, and it is worth noting that of all the jungle creatures only the monkeys—who bear an unmistakable resemblance to the British public as Kipling conceived it—scorn "the Law." Nor is Mowgli the only one of Kipling's heroes to enjoy a green world, only to discover eventually that the law of his own nature, which is also the law of his own kind, drives him from it. Even though "it is hard to cast the skin," Mowgli must leave his beloved jungle in order to be reborn as a member of the human community. His ultimate fate, revealed in "In the Rukh," which in fact was written prior to *The Jungle Books* and which is included in *Many Inventions* (1893), is also significant; Mowgli enters the forestry service, where he uses his uncanny skills for the good of all—the sort of fate Kipling preferred for his child heroes until his growing distaste for imperial politics caused him to seek other arenas of fulfillment for them.

Throughout *The Jungle Books,* however, the emphasis is on the social utility of individual courage and enterprise; not only in the Mowgli stories, but also in "The White Seal," "Rikki-Tikki-Tavi," "Toomai of the Elephants," and "Quiquern." Most notable of these stories is "The Miracle of Purun Bhagat," the tale of an Indian statesman who resigns his career to live as a hermit in the Himalayas. Warned of an impending landslide by the animals he has befriended, Purun Bhagat ignores his own safety to carry the word to a nearby village. Once again the hero's life is the price demanded for the common good. The story is remarkable evidence of Kipling's growing disdain for worldly success and power. It is also a more than adequate rebuttal of the complaints one still hears about Kipling's alleged contempt for the peoples of India. Here, as he so often does, Kipling transcends race and culture in the interest of common values and writes sympathetically of a man who, like Kipling himself, had spent a lifetime trying to bridge the gap between East and West.

Kipling's zeal for discipline and work finds less agreeable expression in his next work for children, *"Captains Courageous."* This is the story of Harvey Cheyne, the spoiled and coddled only child of an American millionaire, who is washed overboard while en route to Europe with his overprotective mother. Rescued by a Gloucester fishing boat, Harvey is obliged to spend the season working aboard a ship before he is restored to his grieving parents. This experience matures him both physically and mentally—echoing Thomas Day's three-volume *The History of Sanford and Merton* (1783, 1786, 1789)—and upon his return Harvey is given real work helping to manage his father's sailing ships. Harvey's symbolic death and resurrection conform to one of Kipling's favorite plot scenarios, and his admirable description of life in the Massachusetts fishing fleet reflects his lifelong determination to be the poet of work. But the novel is marred for many readers by its cruel humor (at least in part a reflection of Kipling's ambivalence toward America) and its approval of violence as a pedagogic device. "Dad learned *me* with a rope's end," explains the son of the fishing boat's captain, and that instrument similarly plays a minor, but significant, role in Harvey's education. Harvey's father approves wholeheartedly, but not every reader will agree that all the problems of youth can be solved by hard work and the judicious application of a rope's end; some may well argue that Kipling's studied and doctrinaire unsentimentality is (here as elsewhere) no obvious improvement on the romanticism he deplored.

Criticism of the violence in Kipling's work for children reached a crescendo after the publication of *Stalky and Co.*, a collection of stories describing the adventures of three boys at a fictional school modeled on the United Services College. Rejecting the rigid morality of such previous writers on school life as Frederick William Farrar (whose *Eric; or, Little by Little: A Tale of Roslyn School* [1858] and *St. Winifred's; or, The World of School* [1862] are spoken of with undisguised contempt by Stalky and his comrades), Kipling gleefully explores the natural state of enmity that exists between boys and masters. With cunning and guile and complete disregard for convention, the boys pit their wits against their elders and usually emerge triumphant,

only their headmaster managing to prevail against them. The volume's last story depicts Stalky as a young officer serving on the northwest frontier, using the wiles he learned in his schoolboy campaigns against his masters to good advantage against enemy troops. This story and one other, "The Moral Reformers," in which the school chaplain discreetly encourages the boys to take violent action to "dissuade" a school bully—not the collection's scorn for propriety—brought down a storm of Liberal vituperation. One reviewer denounced the book as a glorification of "boy life in a military nursery"; another denounced its author as a "little rump-fed lord" in whose work "the flag of a Hooligan Imperialism is raised." Once again, however, a close reading of Kipling's work underscores the myopia of his critics, revealing that their criticism is based on sociopolitical rather than literary considerations. It is no exaggeration to claim that the Boer War (1899–1902)—in which the entire British Empire risked the fortunes of war against a hundred thousand Boers—polarized British opinion in much the same way that the opéra bouffe in Vietnam polarized America's.

In his defense, Kipling might have adduced his collection's resemblance to Thomas Hughes's *Tom Brown's Schooldays* (1857); both works show how naturally boyish rebellion may be turned into social usefulness under the tutelage of a semidivine headmaster. Kipling's model was Cormell Price, who was head during Kipling's years at school and to whom *Stalky and Co.* is dedicated. More peevishly he might have argued that it is not the business of military prep schools to produce either chartered accountants or political activists. He might also have politely drawn his critics' attention to "The Flag of Their Country," a story in which the school's students, led by Stalky, desert a "volunteer" drill corps after an address given by a member of Parliament, in which that "Jelly-bellied Flag-flapper" confidently appeals to their undoubted chauvinism. Finally Kipling partisans may note that *Stalky and Co.*, like *Tom Brown's Schooldays*, insists on accepting boys as they really are, not as their doting grandparents (and Talbot Baines Reed, who brought the school story to a perfection of unreality) would wish them to be. In this book Kipling does children's literature a signal service by eschewing his contemporaries' sentimental and distorted images of children and children's lives.

Kipling's best rebuttal of his Liberal critics came in his next work for children, a work that is also the single best thing he ever wrote, the novel *Kim*. It is the story of Kimball O'Hara, an orphan growing up "native" in the streets of Lahore. He befriends Teshoo Lama, an aged priest from Tibet, who is searching for a river whose waters can wash away all sin. In the course of their marvelously described travels and adventures, Kim finds his father's regiment, is persuaded to attend school, is recruited for the "Great Game" of the Secret Service, and is set to spy on some Russian agents. Confronted by these agents, Kim saves the old priest's life and then collapses from cumulative strain and exhaustion. He awakens to learn that the lama has found his river, and that he himself has completed the task assigned him by the Secret Service.

Kipling's own description of the novel as "nakedly picaresque and plotless" is not to be taken any more seriously than is his reference to *Stalky and Co.* as a "truly valuable collection of tracts" on education. The novel is in fact very tightly structured on all levels, and it is through the double quest of the lama and the boy that Kipling's ideal of empire is discerned. The old man, a second father to the orphaned Kim, has much to teach the boy. When they meet, Kim, who does "nothing with an immense success," is a gloriously natural boy, a sort of Stalky in pajamas. From the lama Kim learns to value education, commitment, and self-discipline, all necessary to him in his work for the Secret Service. (All Kim's mentors teach him the value of discipline, and a shared belief in its importance is one of the great bridges joining East and West in the novel.) Furthermore, the lama's quest enables Kipling to set up a series of elaborate parallels in the novel, all of which point to the possibility of a secular career for Kim like the lama's, a career that combines his spirituality with a life of duty and action in this world. Kipling emphasizes the fact that the loving old man recognizes only merit, not color; the lama tells Kim that "to those who follow the Way there is neither black nor white," and matters of caste and creed and color are "nothing." The clear implication is that Kim, after his collapse and symbolic rebirth at the novel's close, will find the same sort of balance in his career of imperial service. All this hardly sounds like the ravings of a jingoistic imperialist, and a century that has found Kurtz's mad order in *The Heart of Darkness* (1899) to "exterminate all the brutes" far more importunate than the lama's vision of a world in which "there is neither black nor white" can ill afford to sneer at Kipling's views in this novel.

Kipling's next work for children, *Just So Stories for Little Children,* has nothing to do with the burdens of empire, but it is a splendid illustration of the superfluity of critical commentary. Like many other such works of children's literature, it is the product of an author writing for the children he knew and loved. In this case Kipling wrote the stories for his own children, embellishing them with wonderful pen-and-ink drawings. As the title suggests, most of the stories explain origins (how the Elephant got his nose, etc.). They reflect the influence of Joel Chandler Harris' *Uncle Remus: His Songs and His Sayings* (1880). The gentle humor of Kipling's stories makes them especially suitable for young children. Much of Kipling's pleasure in writing these stories must have derived from parodying the language of *The Thousand and One Nights* and the *jataka* tales of India. Kipling loved language (and children) too much to fall into the vulgar error that the resilience and beauty of the English language must be beaten into something dull and uniform to be appropriate for young readers. The full magnificence of these stories reveals itself only when they are read aloud; Kipling himself is said to have narrated them superbly. Their language throughout is a tour de force, ranging from the brilliantly nonsensical to the simply unforgettable ("the great grey-green, greasy Limpopo river"). These stories credit children with a sensitivity and responsiveness that many modern authors would do well to contemplate.

The related stories collected in *Puck of Pook's Hill* and *Rewards and Fairies* are Kipling's last significant works for children. (With the exception of "The Son of His Father," those assembled in *Land and Sea Tales for Scouts and Guides* are of little importance.) In these two volumes Kipling expands his grasp of children's literature to include historical material, and he brings to that material the same industry, seriousness, and sense of art he brought to his work for adults. G. M. Trevelyan rightfully praises Kipling's "marvellous historical sense." Kipling himself said that these stories were intended to be read by children "before people realized that they were meant for grown-ups." His statement is particularly true of *Rewards and Fairies;* many of these grim stories are especially poignant simply *because* they are beyond the comprehension of his child-protagonists, Dan and Una.

The adventures begin when Dan and Una enact bits of *A Midsummer Night's Dream* in a fairy ring near their Sussex home, thus summoning up Puck, who becomes their guide to the historical riches of the farm on which they live. Puck first shows them Weland, once worshiped with human sacrifice, but reduced by the time of the Norman Conquest to scratching out a furtive living as a common blacksmith. Weland makes a magic sword, which is carried into battle at Hastings, and later proves crucial in the winning of a great treasure. "The Treasure and the Law," the last of the interwoven stories in *Puck of Pook's Hill,* tells how Kadmiel, who is despised as a Jew and a usurer, sacrifices the treasure to compel King John to sign the Magna Charta. Kipling's account of how "the Sword gave the Treasure, and the Treasure gave the Law" has obvious implications for imperial politics, just as a Norman knight's vision in an earlier story of a day when "there will be neither Saxon nor Norman in England" recalls the pronouncement of the lama in *Kim.* Other stories in this volume deal with Parnesius and Pertinax, two young officers on the Great Wall, who renounce personal ambitions and make common cause with their Pictish enemies against the Viking invaders. Throughout these stories, as in *Kim,* we find the conception of duty and service transcending both self-interest and the claims of individual societies, cultures, and races. In this conception, and in his insistence that the sword should serve the law, not the other way around, Kipling gives us his final opinion of what the British Empire might be—or might have been. Despairing —and with good cause—of contemporary politics, Kipling turned from contemporary to historical settings to embody his vision, a vision that, in many respects, remains richly worthy both of him and his many loving readers.

It is not then too much to claim that Kipling is one of the most influential creators of modern literature for children. Unlike many of his models and contemporaries, he brought a true seriousness to the production of children's literature, a seriousness reflected in his painstaking research and craftsmanship, in the richness and sophistication of his language, and, most remarkably, in the seriousness of his subject matter itself. By his example, he discouraged the earlier authorial condescension to the young reader.

Kipling also found in children's literature a vehicle for some of his highest concerns. Beginning with *Wee Willie Winkie* the themes of courage, loss, and sacrifice are prominent in his writing for and about children. He paid his young audience the great compliment of believing that these matters were not beyond their ken; even the Mowgli stories are both marvelous adventure stories and deft accounts of the loss of innocence—as any comparison with the pallidly imitative *Tarzan of the Apes* (1914) and its sequels, by Edgar Rice Burroughs, will show. His later writings continue to explore various characters' painful alienation and quests for affiliation through work and politics, transcending contemporary struggles to trace this theme throughout British history. Their constant burden is the necessity of the child "working for something beyond and outside and apart from his own self." His gospel of discipline and sacrifice may offend some readers today—"If," for all its merits, is one of the most perfect moral bludgeons ever to have been put into the hands of parents—just as his political opinions offended many readers in his own day. Still, despite the vicissitudes of politics and history, Kipling broadened our perception of the child both as subject and as audience, and his vision remains worthy of both our attention and our respect. For all his limitations he was a gifted and courageous and honest man. We need not accept his beliefs on that account, but we may, at the very least, say of him what one of his characters says of Kim's beloved lama, that perhaps "his gods are not the gods, but his feet are on the Way."

Selected Bibliography

WORKS OF RUDYARD KIPLING

Whatever delights he offers his readers, Kipling is a bibliographer's nightmare. He was a prolific writer—the Sussex edition of his works, whose preparation he oversaw late in life, runs to thirty-five volumes, and his books were widely reprinted (often without his permission). The list below gives only the first publication in book form of those children's works discussed in the text. Serious students will wish to consult James McGregor Stewart's *Rudyard Kipling: A Bibliographical Catalogue,* edited by A. W. Yeats, Toronto: University of Toronto Press, 1960.

Wee Willie Winkie and Other Child Stories. Allahabad: Wheeler, 1888.
Many Inventions. London and New York: Macmillan, 1893; New York: D. Appleton, 1893.
The Jungle Book. With illustrations by J. L. Kipling, W. H. Drake, and P. Frenzeny. London and New York: Macmillan, 1894; New York: Century, 1894.
The Second Jungle Book. London and New York: Macmillan, 1895; New York: Century, 1895.
"Captains Courageous": A Story of the Grand Banks. With

illustrations by I. W. Taber. London and New York: Macmillan, 1897; New York: Century, 1897.

Stalky and Co. London: Macmillan, 1899; New York: Doubleday and McClure, 1899.

Kim. With illustrations by J. L. Kipling. New York: Doubleday, Page, 1901; London: Macmillan, 1901.

Just So Stories for Little Children. With illustrations by the author. London: Macmillan, 1902; New York: Doubleday, Page, 1902.

Puck of Pook's Hill. With illustrations by Arthur Rackham. London: Macmillan, 1906; New York: Doubleday, Page, 1906.

Rewards and Fairies. London: Macmillan, 1910; Garden City, N.Y.: Doubleday, Page, 1910.

Land and Sea Tales for Scouts and Guides. London: Macmillan, 1923. Also published as *Land and Sea Tales for Boys and Girls.* Garden City, N.Y.: Doubleday, Page, 1923.

Something of Myself for My Friends Known and Unknown. London: Macmillan, 1937; Garden City, N.J.: Doubleday, Doran, 1937.

CRITICAL AND BIOGRAPHICAL STUDIES

Birkenhead, Frederick. *Rudyard Kipling.* London: Weidenfeld and Nicolson, 1978. New York: Random House, 1978.

Carrington, Charles E. *Rudyard Kipling: His Life and Work.* London: Macmillan, 1955; Garden City, N.Y.: Doubleday, 1955.

Gilbert, Elliot L., ed. *Kipling and the Critics.* London: P. Owen, 1965; New York: New York University Press, 1965.

Green, Roger Lancelyn. *Kipling and the Children.* London: Elek, 1965.

————, ed. *Kipling: The Critical Heritage.* London: Routledge and Kegan Paul, 1971.

Lewis, C. S. "Kipling's World." In *They Asked for a Paper.* London: Geoffrey Bles, 1962.

Moss, Robert F. *Rudyard Kipling and the Fiction of Adolescence.* New York: St. Martin's Press, 1982.

Rutherford, Andrew, ed. *Kipling's Mind and Art.* Stanford, Calif.: Stanford University Press, 1964.

Wilson, Angus. *The Strange Ride of Rudyard Kipling: His Life and Works.* London: Secker and Warburg, 1977.

Young, W. A., and J. H. McGivering. *A Kipling Dictionary.* Rev. ed. London: Macmillan, 1967; New York: St. Martin's Press, 1967.

—WILLIAM BLACKBURN

ANDREW LANG

1844–1912

IN HIS ONLY autobiographical essay, Andrew Lang, the man who edited a classic collection of fairy tales for children and who created two masterfully whimsical fairy chronicles, wrote modestly of himself that "nothing but a love of books was the gift given to me by the fairies" (*Adventures Among Books,* 1905). If, in fact, it was a modest gift compared with the heroic qualities of the fictive adventurers to whom he was attracted, Andrew Lang made much of the gift he was given. For forty years between 1872, when his first volume of poetry appeared, and 1912, the year of his death, Lang was a dominant figure in the literary and intellectual life of Britain. In all he was the author of 120 books, including translations, poetry, fiction, history, folklore, and essays on many subjects; the editor of or contributor to 150 more books, for which he often supplied analytical introductions; and the writer of thousands of periodical articles.

It was not simply the prodigious output of his long career, however, but the penchant of his genius in discourse and imagination to rise to advocacy that likewise brought Lang so much attention in his day. Among his contemporaries, too, many praised the light touch of his expansive learning and always abundant wit. Richard Le Gallienne wrote respectfully of Lang that "no other such combination of poet, scholar, and journalist has been known in Fleet Street." He esteemed Lang for "wearing his panoply of learning as though it were a garment of iridescent gossamer, turning the dryest subject to favor and to prettiness, particularly the prettiness of an elfish, incalculable wit. . . . His 'leaders' in the *Daily News* read like fairy tales written by an erudite Puck."

Although he was a power with whom to reckon during a time when his opinions were constantly before the public in every literary journal of his day, after his death in 1912 Lang slid rapidly to relative obscurity. This would seem in part a fate of his own choosing, for in order to discourage biographers, Lang requested that his wife destroy his private papers, which she did. Moreover, in all his output Lang wrote no single great book upon which the stature he enjoyed in life could be sustained. It is perhaps posterity's misfortune that writing came so easily to Lang that even in the space of half an hour he could dash off a flawless review while carrying on a conversation at the same time. Had he labored longer at the craft, he might well have produced the monument his genius deserved to leave behind. As the record stands, it remains still for an age free of the battles that heated his own to perform the difficult task of reevaluating Andrew Lang's very real importance to the dynamic history of ideas in which he was so energetic a participant. It is to his credit, at least, that in the scholarly controversies to which he gave himself, which included issues in folklore, Homeric studies, and history, he often made a determinative contribution. His greatest triumph was in the field of folklore, the field in which he would have chosen to make an abiding contribution. Early in his career Lang successfully challenged the then current philological theory of myth propounded by Friedrich Max Müller. In place of Müller's rhapsodic reduction of myth to "the disease of language," Lang formulated for folklore an approach that continues to be fundamental to the comparative method in that field. In Homeric studies, Lang shook the critical orthodoxy that ascribed the Homeric epics to processes of redaction over four centuries and redeemed the single Homer for his day. In history, he promoted the rehabilitation of Joan of Arc and pursued a revisionist history of Scotland.

Andrew Lang was born on 31 March 1844 at Selkirk, in the border country of Scotland, the eldest of eight children in a middle-class family whose comfort was assured by the ignominy of participation in the Highland Clearances only a generation before and whose respectability was established by the academic acclaim of Andrew's uncle, William Young Sellar, whose example Andrew was to follow. His childhood was filled with exploits amid the hills and burns of the border country, where he also imbibed a goodly dose of the folktales and history of the country north of the Tweed. There, too, Lang seems first to have established a habit of indulging his rapacious appetite for reading, for he tells that a nursery legend had it that he "was wont to arrange six open books on six chairs, and go from one to the others, perusing them by turns."

Although he recalls in his autobiographical essay that his reading drifted far afield of school requirements, Lang seems to have managed his academic experience successfully, for in 1861 he matriculated at the University of St. Andrews with what today would be called advanced standing in Latin, Greek, mathematics, logic, and metaphysics; in 1864 he won the prestigious Snell exhibition, which provided him with a scholarship to Oxford; and in 1868 he was elected to the Open Fellowship at Merton College, Oxford, which he kept for seven years. When he left Oxford for a career in literary journalism in London, Lang was uniquely qualified to extol the pleasures of reading and fight the skirmishes of scholarship of his day.

In 1875, after overcoming a threat of consumption in the South of France, where he had befriended Robert Louis Stevenson, Lang moved from Oxford to London and settled with his new wife, Leonora Blanche Alleyne, at 1 Marloes Road, Kensington, where they remained. There he consolidated his love of books and depth of scholarship by means of a remarkable fluency in wrting to support a career as a prominent man of letters. He became an almost immediate success in London as

a journalist, writing for almost every periodical of distinction in England and the United States and offering to the reading public several books on different topics each year until his death.

To assay Lang's contribution to the field of children's literature, one must begin with consideration of his editorship of the Fairy Books. For whatever else can be said about them, like the determinative contributions Lang made to other fields, these books inspired Victorian England to recognize the importance of fairy tales in the reading experience of children. As Roger Lancelyn Green, Lang's biographer, writes, "It would probably be no exaggeration to say that Lang was entirely responsible for this change in the public taste."

That Green could attribute so important a place in literary history to Andrew Lang ought not, however, obscure the fact that in the actual production of the Fairy Books Lang was only a distant supernumerary. Mrs. Lang and a few others (primarily women) were left to do the work of retelling tales and adjusting texts to the anticipated level of their readers. In the preface to the last book in the series, *The Lilac Fairy Book* (1910), Lang wrote of his work on the texts:

> My part has been that of Adam, according to Mark Twain, in the Garden of Eden. Eve worked, Adam superintended. I also superintend. I find out where the stories are, and advise, and in short, superintend. *I do not write the stories out of my own head.* The reputation of having written all the fairy books (an European reputation in nurseries and the United States of America) is "the burden of an honour unto which I was not born."

And yet the power of the Fairy Books to influence public taste owes much to the learned authority of their editor, whose name alone appearing beneath the title would have commended them at the time to adult readers who as parents or guardians would have been expected to purchase the books for their children or charges. Lang's formidable learning is certainly in evidence in the Fairy Books. But he applies his scholarship lightly to the selection of the tales and does not encumber the texts with argument or scholarly apparatus. So scrupulous was Lang to conceal the burden of scholarly considerations from his common readers that, in fact, although he wrote analytical introductions for both *The Blue Fairy Book* (1889) and *The Red Fairy Book* (1890), he allowed them to be published only in limited large paper editions. The prefaces to the popular issues were for the most part simply invitations to readers, with an occasional offhand speculation on the moral truth of the tales or on the puzzle of their origin to whet the appetite for reflection of an inquisitive child or adult shopping for a contribution to the nursery library.

It was, however, as a scholar of folklore that Lang ferreted out the tales in sources from all quarters of the world, such as Perrault, Madame d'Aulnoy, the *Cabinet des fées,* the Brothers Grimm, Asbjørnsen and Moe, *The Book of the Thousand and One Nights,* the U.S. Bureau of American Ethnology's annual reports, and many other collections of *Märchen.* The twelve volumes included an average of thirty-seven stories each. The first books in the collection, of course, contained the best-known and most popular European *Märchen* from the Grimms, Perrault, and Asbjørnsen and Moe, such as the tales of Sleeping Beauty, Rumpelstiltskin, Hansel and Gretel, Puss in Boots, East of the Sun and West of the Moon, Rapunzel, and Snow White; and the best-loved literary tales of D'Aulnoy and Andersen, such as "Beauty and the Beast," "Thumbelina," "The Nightingale," and "The Steadfast Tin Soldier." For the sheer density of popular stories represented in it, the first volume of the collection, *The Blue Fairy Book,* has often been considered as a classic text in its own right. Later books in the collection reach beyond the European repertoire of favorites to include less familiar tales from American Indian tribes, Iceland, Africa, China, Japan, Australia, and India, as well as less familiar tales from countries near at hand, such as France, Ireland, and Wales.

In selection of the tales Lang was guided in part by his folklore scholarship. As a rationale for selection of at least some of the tales, he used the procedures he himself helped devise to compare cultural forms. Clearly he selected some of the stories to demonstrate thematic comparisons. In the analytical introduction to *The Blue Fairy Book,* for instance, Lang pointed out that comparisons can be drawn between the Scottish "Black Bull of Norroway," the Norse tale "East of the Sun and West of the Moon," and "Beauty and the Beast," which first appeared in the *Cabinet des fées.* The publication of the Fairy Books for children was not, however, without criticism among Lang's contemporaries in the field of folklore who would have wished for greater cultural integrity in the collections. In his presidential address to the Folk-Lore Society,

G. Laurence Gomme took both Lang and Joseph Jacobs to task for publishing illustrated editions of folklore for children that promulgated an European ethnocentrism.

The editor, however, placed his responsibility to his audience and for the appeal and accessibility of the tales to English-speaking children above any responsibility to the cultural sources of the tales. In fact, the tales were published without headnotes or footnotes to identify in any way but name the sources from which they were drawn. No attempt was made to present the stories in cultural contexts. Where recurring themes are heard in text after text they, therefore, do not promote cultural comparisons. Rather do they reinforce the thematic material for the sake of the authority and validity of the themes in their own right as elements of good stories worth retelling. Beyond that reinforcement, by their cumulative force, they convey a sense of psychological truth in their descriptions of courage, kindness, and fear, and a sense of spiritual value in their formulations of miraculous acts. For all the eminence of their editor's folklore scholarship, the Fairy Books do not comprise for children an anthropological resource.

It is easy to see in leafing through any of the Fairy Books that Lang admitted stories other than either the authentic cultural transmissions or even the literary revisions of cultural transmissions. Several tales included in the texts are the works of single authors such as Madame d'Aulnoy, Hans Christian Andersen, and Z. Topelius. In these as in the true folktales, however, as Lang rightly discerned, one can yet feel the movement of the same narrative force that spins out a simple tale in which the touch of the miraculous gives transport to a place unknown and a time out of time, where most often courage and cleverness are rewarded and kindness is repaid.

During the years when the Fairy Books were being published, other books edited by Lang were also published for the Christmas trade. Lang himself also wrote a highly praised book entitled *Tales of Troy and Greece* that retold for children the stories of Ulysses, Meleager, Theseus, Perseus, and Jason. The popularity of the Fairy Books, however, far exceeded all of these.

Now that the immediacy of their impact is long past, the Fairy Books still stand as a classic collection, an enduring *Cabinet des fées* for children. The contemporary effort of Brian Alderson, begun in 1975, to reedit the Fairy Books casts a revealing light on the qualities that have helped them to endure. The breadth and richness of the whole is not lost in the new editions, for the overall impact is carried by the sheer idea of the collection. But Alderson's texts attempt to edit out flaws in the originals. Selections critics have generally deemed inappropriate to the books, such as the adventures of Gulliver in Lilliput, are left out. Some texts have been replaced by other versions of the same tales, overlooked by Lang though available in his day, that would be judged by scholars to be more complete or more authentic versions. The contents of the whole have been reordered here and there in accordance with what the new editor considers to be a more forceful structure. Endnotes have been added to justify the changes. And each book has been newly illustrated by a different contemporary illustrator. But this reconstition does not establish the status of the collection with any greater authority than the original texts to which Lang ministered with less weighty research and the light touch of his critical hand. What is most important for a work judged to be a children's classic, the sense of the series' intended audience of children begins to recede with the appearance in these new editions of the scholarly apparatus and new prefaces, though brief, that address themselves to the task of re-editing and not to the task of teasing the reader's curiosity.

Moreover, there are subtle factors that make the originals the yet more satisfying texts and cast upon them the ephemeral halo of a classic work. More than other forms of literature, it would seem that whether or not a collection of folk or fairy tales becomes a classic owes much to the textual form of the book itself, for the tales captured in it represent arrested forms current in ever-changing oral versions and not fixed writings whose words are primary. Just as in a session of storytelling the storyteller must endeavor to set an appropriate atmosphere for the telling, so must a collection of tales put together in a book engender an atmosphere receptive to the miracles and messages they convey. Lang, who was a great collector of books, graced his collection of tales with a bibliophile's sensitivity. The heft of the original books seems just right for their audience of eight-to-eleven-year-olds. The number of stories in each book is sufficiently enticing without becoming overwhelming. Moreover, Lang was fortunate enough to have had the same illustrator for all the books in the collection. (G. P. Jacomb Hood and Lancelot Speed con-

tributed illustrations only to the first and second books, respectively.) The sumptuous abundance of fluid line and imaginative detail in the pre-Raphaelite drawings of H. J. Ford help to create just the right atmosphere to reinforce the incantatory words "Once upon a time. . . ." Despite the fact that Lang as a writer of serious works on many subjects seems at times to have regarded the acclaim of the Fairy Books as his nemesis, they are not an inconsiderable accomplishment for his elfish spirit to have left behind.

Compared with the number of Color Fairy Books that appeared over his name, Lang's own authorship of books for children was far less substantial. Lang's original works for children are also fairy books in the sense that fairies play a part and the fantastic is given full sway. Of these five titles, however, only three merit serious critical mention. The first of his own fairy stories, *The Princess Nobody: A Tale of Fairyland* (1884), was a rather labored attempt to match a text to Richard Doyle's pictures, published originally in 1870, with poems by William Allingham under the title *In Fairyland: Pictures from the Elf World.* The last of Lang's original books of fairy stories, *Tales of a Fairy Court,* was altogether too haphazard an attempt to recover the realm so much more coherently rendered in *The Chronicles of Pantouflia,* written over ten years before.

Lang's first truly successful fairy story for children drew its inspiration from the authentic folk ballads, beliefs, and superstitions of his native countryside along the Scottish border. The literary antecedents of *The Gold of Fairnilee* (1888) are first the old ballads "Tam Lin" and "Thomas Rhymer" and Walter Scott's *Minstrelsy of the Scottish Border* (1802–1803), and after those the stories and narrative poems of James Hogg. The story tells of young Randal Ker, who vanishes at a wishing well one Midsummer's Eve and lives with the fairies underground seven long years. He is won back from the fairy queen in the seventh year of his captivity by his childhood companion, Jean, who plucks the magic roses at the well to summon him back. Randal returns from fairyland with a vial of magic water that enables him to discover the legendary gold of Fairnilee, buried during the Roman occupation. With the gold he rescues his people from famine.

In this little story, Lang assimilated many of the elements and themes of the ballad tradition that was his heritage from childhood. Although the story is in prose, its style is strongly reminiscent of ballad poetry. As in the ballads, the movement of the story proceeds by "leaping and lingering," passing from one scene to another without filling in gaps in time or positing psychological motivation. It is also written impersonally, like ballad poetry, without comment or expressed emotion by the author. Themes in the story, too, are drawn from ballad folklore, as for instance the passage to fairyland, the plucking of flowers to summon an enchanted companion, and the appearance of a revenant, a ghost returning from the dead.

The strength of Lang's tale most certainly derives from the ease with which it assimilates the ballad tradition. That strength, however, produces its own weakness, for so successful is the assimilation that the tale itself seems almost to become absorbed by that tradition.

By contrast, no such absorption lessens the accomplishment of *The Chronicles of Pantouflia,* where Lang draws upon the tradition of the literary fairy tale. The two books that make up the *Chronicles* distinguish themselves in a way that *The Gold of Fairnilee* does not. (Not surprisingly, *The Chronicles* were reprinted in 1981 with excellent new illustrations by Jeanne Titherington that capture the tenor of the text perfectly.)

The Chronicles of Pantouflia, published together first in 1895 with *The Gold of Fairnilee* in *My Own Fairy Book,* appeared originally as two separate volumes, *Prince Prigio* (1889) and *Prince Ricardo of Pantouflia* (1893). Although there are a great many literary references throughout the *Chronicles,* Lang clearly followed the example set by William Makepeace Thackery in *The Rose and the Ring* (1855) in writing these two literary fairy tales. Lang did, however, create a fictive world very much his own.

The two books make a complementary pair. In the first, Prince Prigio is given at birth an unfortunate fairy gift that makes him "too clever." For his presumption he becomes disliked by all until his excessive cleverness is tempered by the accident of falling in love and the discovery of magic behind all his knowledge. Prigio's behavior turns away from the pattern that made his name so apt. He is reformed. With a newfound capacity to believe in things that cannot be explained, Prince Prigio seeks the aid of fairy treasures such as the Cap of Darkness, the Sword of Sharpness, seven-league boots, and a magic carpet to save the land and the people of Pantouflia from a punishing drought brought on by the presence of a firedrake near the kingdom.

For this service, and especially for his newfound wisdom that surpasses cleverness, Prince Prigio (after a happy wedding) becomes a well-loved monarch, as clever as always but appearing not to be.

The second book purports to tell of Prigio's son Ricardo, who is not clever at all. He whiles away his youth rescuing maidens, with the aid of the inherited fairy treasures, from peril of every sort. But his father, now King Prigio, finds too much arrogance in the son's matter-of-fact recourse to the fairy powers and decides to teach him a lesson by replacing the fairy gifts with impotent imitations. Not knowing what has come to pass by his father's will, Ricardo himself is only saved from defeat a number of times by the devotion of one of the princesses he has rescued earlier. With access to magical powers of her own, Jaqueline (an otherwise distant thematic echo of Jean of Fairnilee) conspires to protect her knight against danger. She even submits to personal peril to save his life and so forces upon Ricardo a new nobility. In the end, it is she, her cleverness, courage, and devotion, that are vindicated when all again ends well with a happy marriage and enduring peace.

In the way of burlesque, both tales play freely with a host of elements from fairy tales. This is a high-spirited play in which miracles follow upon the heels of miracles, all reaching toward the delightfully ridiculous. Instead of depicting the rightness of things as in a true fairy tale, these two stories convey a sense of the abiding humor of things. In one sense they might even be read together as an antic coda to the Fairy Books in which for a moment the profound vision embodied in the fairy tales goes out of focus and is turned to jest. But the jest is light, and after the laughter, the stronger vision of the *Märchen* is redeemed in Prince Prigio's reformation and Princess Jaqueline's vindication.

In his work for children, Lang withdrew from advocacy. He edited and wrote for an audience with a "fresh appetite for marvels," who possessed an "unblunted edge of belief," as he stated in his introduction to the large-format paperbound edition of *The Blue Fairy Book.* If his concept of childhood seems too romantic in a harsher age when children are compelled at least to appear more savvy, yet the contribution of his work still seems to support the virtues of imagination and belief, to which it was intended to appeal.

Selected Bibliography

WORKS OF ANDREW LANG

The Princess Nobody: A Tale of Fairyland. With illustrations by Richard Doyle. London: Longmans, Green, 1884.

The Gold of Fairnilee. With illustrations by T. Scott and E. A. Lemann. Bistol, England: J. W. Arrowsmith, 1888.

Prince Prigio. With illustrations by Gordon F. Browne. Bristol, England: J. W. Arrowsmith, 1889.

Prince Ricardo of Pantouflia. With illustrations by Gordon F. Browne. Bristol, England: J. W. Arrowsmith, 1893.

My Own Fairy Book. With illustrations by Gordon F. Browne, T. Scott, and E. A. Lemann. Bristol, England: J. W. Arrowsmith, 1895.

Adventures Among Books. London: Longmans, Green, 1905.

Tales of a Fairy Court. With illustrations by Arthur A. Dixon. London: Collins, 1906.

Tales of Troy and Greece. With illustrations by H. J. Ford. London: Longmans, Green, 1907.

Chronicles of Pantouflia. Bristol, England: J. W. Arrowsmith, 1932. New ed., with illustrations by Jeanne Titherington. Boston: D. R. Godine, 1981.

WORKS EDITED BY LANG

The Blue Fairy Book. With illustrations by H. J. Ford and G. P. Jacomb Hood. London: Longmans, Green, 1889. Reprinted New York: Dover, 1965. With illustrations by Ben Kutcher. London: Longmans, Green, 1948; New York: David McKay, 1948. With illustrations by John Lawrence. Rev. ed. Edited by Brian Alderson. Harmondsworth, England: Kestrel Books, 1975.

The Red Fairy Book. With illustrations by H. J. Ford and Lancelot Speed. London: Longmans, Green, 1890. Reprinted New York: Dover, 1966. With illustrations by Marc Simont. London: Longmans, Green, 1948; New York: David McKay, 1948. Rev. ed. Edited by Brian Alderson. With illustrations by Faith Jaques. Harmondsworth, England: Kestrel Books, 1976.

The Blue Poetry Book. With illustrations by H. J. Ford and Lancelot Speed. London: Longmans, Green, 1891.

The Green Fairy Book. With illustrations by H. J. Ford. London: Longmans, Green, 1892. Reprinted New York: Dover, 1965. With illustrations by Dorothy Lake Gregory. London: Longmans, Green, 1948; New York: David McKay, 1948. Rev. ed. Edited by Brian Alderson. With illustrations by Antony Maitland. London: Kestrel Books, 1978; New York: Viking Press, 1978.

The True Story Book. With illustrations by L. Bogle et al. London: Longmans, Green, 1893.

The Yellow Fairy Book. With illustrations by H. J. Ford. London: Longmans, Green, 1894. Reprinted New York: Dover, 1966. With illustrations by Janice Holland. London and New York: Longmans, Green, 1948. Rev. ed. Edited by Brian Alderson. With illustrations by Erik Blegvard. London: Kestrel Books, 1980; New York: Viking Press, 1980.

The Red True Story Book. With illustrations by H. J. Ford. London: Longmans, Green, 1895.

The Animal Story Book. With illustrations by H. J. Ford. London: Longmans, Green, 1896.

The Pink Fairy Book. With illustrations by H. J. Ford. London: Longmans, Green, 1897. Reprinted New York: Dover, 1967. Rev. ed. Edited by Brian Alderson. With illustrations by Colin McNaughton. London: Kestrel Books, 1982; New York: Viking Press, 1982.

The Nursery Rhyme Book. With illustrations by L. Leslie Brooke. London: Fredrick Warne, 1897.

Arabian Nights' Entertainments. With illustrations by H. J. Ford. London: Longmans, Green, 1898. New York: Schocken Books, 1967.

The Red Book of Animal Stories. With illustrations by H. J. Ford. London: Longmans, Green, 1899.

The Grey Fairy Book. With illustrations by H. J. Ford. London: Longmans, Green, 1900. Reprinted New York: Dover, 1967.

The Violet Fairy Book. With illustrations by H. J. Ford. London: Longmans, Green, 1901. Reprinted New York: Dover, 1967. With illustrations by Dorothy Lake Gregory. London and New York: Longmans, Green, 1947.

The Book of Romance. With illustrations by H. J. Ford. London: Longmans, Green, 1902.

The Crimson Fairy Book. With illustrations by H. J. Ford. London: Longmans, Green, 1903. Reprinted New York: Dover, 1967. With illustrations by Ben Kutcher. London and New York: Longmans, Green, 1947.

The Brown Fairy Book. With illustrations by H. J. Ford. London: Longmans, Green, 1904. Reprinted New York: Dover, 1965.

The Red Romance Book. With illustrations by H. J. Ford. London: Longmans, Green, 1905.

The Orange Fairy Book. With illustrations by H. J. Ford. London: Longmans, Green, 1906. Reprinted New York: Dover, 1968. With illustrations by Christine Price. London: Longmans, Green, 1949; New York: David McKay, 1949.

The Olive Fairy Book. With illustrations by H. J. Ford. London: Longmans, Green, 1907. Reprinted New York: Dover, 1968. With illustrations by Anne Vaughan. London: Longmans, Green, 1948; New York: David McKay, 1948.

The Lilac Fairy Book. With illustrations by H. J. Ford. London: Longmans, Green, 1910. Reprinted New

York: Dover, 1968. With illustrations by Dorothy Lake Gregory. New York: David McKay, 1947.

CRITICAL AND BIOGRAPHICAL STUDIES

Green, Roger Lancelyn. *Andrew Lang: A Critical Biography.* Leicester, England: Edmund Ward, 1946.

Langstaff, Eleanor DeSelms. *Andrew Lang.* Boston: Twayne, 1978.

Tolkien, J. R. R. *Tree and Leaf.* London: George Allen and Unwin, 1964; Boston: Houghton Mifflin, 1965.

—ANDREW LEVITT

ROBERT LAWSON

1892–1957

AS RECIPIENT OF the Caldecott Medal for *They Were Strong and Good* (1940), as illustrator of Elizabeth Janet Gray's Newbery Medal–winning novel about a minstrel boy in medieval times, *Adam of the Road* (1942), as winner of the Newbery Medal for his own *Rabbit Hill* (1944), and as runner-up for that same award for his last book, *The Great Wheel* (1957), Robert Lawson holds a unique place in the history of modern American children's literature. From the 1930's to the 1950's Lawson wrote and/or illustrated more than fifty books for young people, many of which were considered major contributions to the literature. It is the rare American children's book collection that does not have a number of his books on its shelves. Most of them remain in print, and their titles continue to be found on lists of recommended works for children.

Born in New York City on 4 October 1892, Lawson was raised in suburban New Jersey. In his memoir of his childhood, *At That Time* (1947), he recalls a happy youth, surrounded by wealth and servants. His father played the dominating role in the family's life, but it was his mother who had day-to-day influence. These parents and their contrasting personalities had a major impact on Lawson's work.

His mother, so Lawson tells us in the memoir and in his picture-book family history, *They Were Strong and Good,* was raised in a Midwest convent. A mild, gentle woman of great sensitivity, she was a great lover of art and animals. These animals, so Lawson relates (even bees), returned her affection. Standing in sharp contrast was his father. The son of a

fundamentalist preacher who actively fought the power of evil in the rural pre–Civil War South, he owned his own slave (when he was a boy) and fought with the Confederate army. Thus it is hardly a coincidence that in almost all of Lawson's work one finds themes of mild, giving, gentle creatures at odds with contentious, grasping, rebellious spirits.

It was Lawson's mother who urged him to go to art school, and when he graduated from the New York School of Fine and Applied Arts in 1914, he was determined to become an illustrator. For the next three years he worked in the commercial art field as illustrator, stage designer, painter, and even architect. During World War I he served in France, where the military used his skills in camouflage work. In 1922 he married an artist, Marie Abrams. After moving to Connecticut, the two of them paid off their mortgage with a huge production of greeting cards. This was the major source of Lawson's income until 1930, the year that he illustrated his first children's book, Arthur Mason's *The Wee Men of Ballywooden* (1930).

Lawson's development and stature as a commercial artist grew apace. The Society of American Etchers awarded him a prestigious prize in 1931, and he was recognized elsewhere as a special talent in the world of advertising art. In 1935 he developed a new tempera technique, combining Wolf carbon pencil (brushed or rubbed) on smooth Whatman drawing board, a method he used for many of his illustrated books.

Lawson illustrated *The Wee Men of Ballywooden*

with black pen-and-ink drawings. The style, very much influenced by Arthur Rackham, fit the Irish fairy tale and was well received. From then on, an increasing number of book illustrations in a distinct black-and-white style flowed from his pen. Only with *Rabbit Hill,* in 1944, did he switch to gravure reproductions of drawings. But it was in 1937 that Lawson became famous, when he created the black-and-white illustrations for his friend Munro Leaf's text *The Story of Ferdinand* (1936).

Two years later Lawson established himself as a writer with the publication of *Ben and Me* (1939), the first of a number of books that presented the lives of great historical figures "as told by" their pets, such as Benjamin Franklin's cat, Paul Revere's horse, and Christopher Columbus' parrot. By the time of Lawson's death in 1957, he had written and/or illustrated a veritable library of books and had become not just a major contributor but also a much-loved figure in the world of American children's literature. Remembrances, critical commentary, and reviews all note and celebrate the idea that Robert Lawson was a major humorist in the American tradition. The tall tale, the exaggeration of character and event, a prickly, common-man perception of the world, a dry, saucy view of humankind, a love of animals—all were to be found in his works, either in the written word or in his illustrations.

The Story of Ferdinand presents the tale of a pacifist bull, but a pacifist of great strength and passion. The illustrations combine wonderful simplicity, even airiness, with a delightful attention to detail. Everywhere the black line is bold and distinct, by turns realistic, whimsical, frenetic. Lawson was never afraid of strong, direct design, single images on bright white pages. Yet for other books and events, such as the wild battle scene in *Ben and Me,* his life of Franklin, he extended his written words with a riotous carnival of humorous detail and sweeping action.

There is, in the best of Lawson's illustrations, a controlled energy, an awareness of the dramatic quality of black ink on the white page. His male characters stride, their elbows and knees hard at work. His women characters (those he liked) are demure, sweet, pretty. His animals are true to life, but alive to the joke of being the perceptive species. A pert, eager innocence characterizes his children.

His pictures are complex, but at their best they are carefully designed so as instantly to establish the dramatic essence of the moment. Yet they also have the capacity for renewed discovery of detail, the true mark of pictorial works that will engage the young for reading after reading. This style of illustration, upon which Lawson established his own strong, artistic signature, was an extension of a distinguished historical line of American illustrations, exemplified by such artists as Howard Pyle and Henry Pitz of the celebrated Brandywine School of Design. Other books, such as *Rabbit Hill,* contain a much softer line, achieved through pencil in gravure reproduction, very much in keeping with the spirit of generosity evident in the book itself, which depicts the struggle of a community of animals to survive in a shrinking world dominated by people.

Lawson's style of writing was deceptively simple, although he insisted that he never wrote down to children. Often he seemed to speak rather than to write, and his transitions from the real to the unreal are unusually skillful. For example, in *The Fabulous Flight* (1949) the existence of a tiny boy is quickly established with a matter-of-fact directness. Even though it is the important (and fantastic) hinge for the adventure that follows, it is to Lawson's credit that he establishes the crucial point with an absolute minimum of words or rhetorical fuss.

Generally, Lawson was not a subtle writer. His jokes are broad, and his characters are set forth almost crudely. Thus his description of King Ferdinand of Spain from *I Discover Columbus* (1941): "He looked mean. Mean and coarse, and a little stupid. A man of action, perhaps, but very uncouth." Yet, though subtlety was never Lawson's strong point, his most exciting chapter is one that appears in *Rabbit Hill,* when Little Georgie's "Spring Song" is picked up by the entire community until one by one, beast and man, all are singing the song. For Lawson, this is a unique stretch of poetic prose.

On the whole, Lawson's plots develop with a minimum of descriptive prose, dialogue being the great mover. There is no building toward a crescendo of action. Even his adventure tales, like *The Fabulous Flight,* simmer down to a walking conclusion. And, it must be said, that walk sometimes becomes a limp. In *Mr. Twigg's Mistake* (1947), for example, Lawson could not find a solution to the problem of the ever-growing mole. The mole just goes "up and up and over and over, until at last he melted into the low scudding dark clouds." Even in the context of a fantastic tale, such an ending is incomplete.

Lawson normally began with a big, simple idea, an idea that often seems visual in conception. Indeed, Lawson claimed that it was by looking at a picture of Franklin's fur cap and wondering what was in it that he had the notion that Amos ("a mouse") was stationed there. However, Lawson often found it difficult to hold to his original idea. Frequently he became sidetracked. In *Smeller Martin* (1950), the tale of a boy who has the extraordinary ability to distinguish the faintest of smells, Lawson moves away from this core idea so that Smeller and his skills become unnecessary to the unfolding plot. Lawson's lack of focus weakens the book. Similarly, in *Mr. Wilmer* (1945) the central notion of a mild man who discovers he can talk to animals becomes incidental to the resolution of the story. Lawson's visual perception of plot often is not matched by his writer's skills.

While it is true that Lawson was very much a teller of tall tales in the American folk tradition, he was perhaps even more a moralist. But he was a moralist in conflict with his feelings. This applies not just to the tales he wrote but also to the ones he illustrated; such conflict appears to have attracted him. For example, Leaf's book *The Story of Simpson and Sampson* (1941), which Lawson illustrated, is a picture-book tale of twin knights, one perfectly good, one perfectly bad—literally black and white. *Simpson and Sampson* nevertheless concludes with a satisfying mix of good *and* bad.

When Lawson wrote his own texts, this mix of good and bad does not often appear. Rather, he sets forth contrasting lessons. Be trusting and good; things will come; there is enough for all—thus speaks *Rabbit Hill.* In other books, such as *Mr. Revere and I* (1953), *Ben and Me,* and *Captain Kidd's Cat* (1956), one finds a different warning: *don't trust people;* beware, in particular, of people who are making demands or who are not content with their lot. This disparity might be easy to understand as the complacent outlook of a man raised in wealth and comfort, and indeed, we find such self-congratulation in books like *The Great Wheel,* Lawson's story about the invention of the Ferris wheel. It also appears in *The Fabulous Flight.* But Lawson's conservatism turns sharp, even acrimonious, in such works as *Mr. Revere and I,* in which Sam Adams is presented as an unpleasant, self-serving, hypocritical radical. Similarly distasteful characters are the

selfish caretakers in *The Tough Winter* (1954), and in *Smeller Martin* the Lieutenant's vision of life puts the idea baldly: "There's a bad egg in almost every setting, and a vicious pup in every so many litters." And Captain Kidd's downfall was caused, or so Lawson has it, by the fact that "he trusted too many too far."

There is a tendency to group Lawson's books into a variety of types: "true" histories, animal tales, adventure yarns, patriotic works, and picture books. Place the works, however, in chronological order, and one observes a constant swing between Lawson's moral polarities. Thus the utopianism of giving and sharing that appears in *Rabbit Hill* was followed by the naiveté of *Mr. Wilmer,* issued the next year. Then came a transitional work, his autobiography, *At That Time.* Lawson next published the quirky tall tale *McWhinney's Jaunt* (1947), about the eccentric inventor Professor A. A. McWhinney. What followed was the nastiness of *Mr. Twigg's Mistake,* the tale of a gigantic mole, General De Gaulle, and the havoc he brings to the neighborhood.

This shift from light to dark moods may be noted elsewhere. There is increasing nastiness in *Ben and Me,* followed by *They Were Strong and Good,* culminating in the crude *I Discover Columbus.* However, Lawson then wrote *Rabbit Hill,* with all its optimism and sweetness. Lawson certainly had mixed emotions. The darker side of his nature seems to win, but then the bright side rises up again, only to have the struggle begin anew.

In *Smeller Martin,* Lawson was clearly trying to write a book that stressed his positive values. In it he characterizes a potential lynch mob as racist and mindless in its attack upon a gentle black man. But his depiction of both poor blacks and poor whites is at best patronizing. McKinley, the black gardener, is portrayed as a childlike man, and his wife is vague about the number of children they have. McKinley's loyalty goes primarily to the kindly well-off whites who tip him a dollar from time to time. The final story is a bad botch of Lawson's good intent.

But Lawson's stereotyped characters, in both text and illustration, were legion, crude, and, within the context of his stories, unnecessary. For example, in *They Were Strong and Good,* he introduces his father: "When my father was very young he had two dogs and a colored boy." To Lawson ethnic jokes are good jokes. It is disheartening to find in his memoir, *At That Time,* that he and his friends taunted the Chinese and Italians of his town. Lawson speaks of it as harmless, youthful foolishness, but the adult Lawson kept putting the same kind of thing in his books. His slurs spread over a large range of groups: Italians, blacks, Chinese, Jews, Scots. Even the foreign mice in *Ben and Me* are categorized: the Swedish mice are fine; the Russian mice are uncouth; and the Italian and Spanish mice have erratic temperaments. And Gus, the Baltimore seagull who is the real star of *The Fabulous Flight,* views the world like a bigot with wings.

For Lawson women are a fairly useless lot. His female "types" are bland, and when one does have character, as does Captain Kidd's wife, she is in word and image a nag, a shrew, one whose chief desire in life is finding the right size rug. Mr. McWhinney's wife is an imbecile; Paul Revere's mother is a dope; Mother, of *Rabbit Hill,* is a constant worrywart and fussbudget. Best off is Miss Sweeney of *Mr. Wilmer.* Her chief virtue, aside from her good looks, is that she is the perfect secretary, and hence the perfect wife.

All of this combines to create a nasty streak in Lawson's work. Some of it is satirical in intent, but when we consider his work as a body of literature, we must often call Lawson's sense of humor into question. For example, in *I Discover Columbus,* with the exception of the young lovers, the characters are virtually all unpleasant; in fact, the entire story, one of greed, is treated as a joke. The money for Columbus' voyage is raised by theft and fraud by the story's narrator, the parrot, and by Don Issachar, a Jewish pawnbroker whose characterization is nothing less than a classic anti-Semitic portrayal, in act and image. Even in the fanciful *Robbut: A Tale of Tails* (1948), there is a questionable bit of cruelty when one of the tails is chopped off with a shovel. *Captain Kidd's Cat* is a catalog of destructive personalities, liars, and cheats. Uncle Anadias of *Rabbit Hill,* while viewed more kindly by Lawson than most creatures who complain about their lot, causes some uncomfortable moments, particularly in *The Tough Winter,* in which he also appears. Out of sheer meanness, he objects to the other animals joining in for the meager fare of Christmas dinner. Lawson's cast of characters may be unsavory, but it is his persistent portrayal of people who are not satisfied with their condition as being generally bad, even false, people that must be faulted.

Lawson's best book, and the one that will endure, is *Rabbit Hill.* Rich in character, it is a story about established animals who live on the Hill and the way that they deal with the new people who settle the land—how they slowly replace their understandable fears with cooperation and sharing. It is a warm book.

But in Lawson's Newbery acceptance speech for *Rabbit Hill,* one grasps the essence of his contradictions. One of the best characters in the book is Blind Mole, who uses his friend Willie as a seeing-eye mouse. This is a fine, sensitive portrait, fully in keeping with the book's spirit. In his acceptance speech, however, Lawson told his audience that the best way to kill moles is to flip them out of the ground and squash them with a shovel, even as he told his listeners that he himself always let them go. Furthermore, as Lawson was writing *Rabbit Hill,* which may be thought of as a rural idyll, he was penning *Country Colic* (1944), his adult book that recounts, albeit satirically, the miseries of country living. It is as if those different parental elements, his mother's and father's contrasting personalities, were constantly at war within him.

In *The Great Wheel,* Lawson's last book, published after his death, one senses some balance between these contending spirits. Here his ethnic depictions go beyond mere stereotypes and jokes; thus, the "dusky assistants" of *The Fabulous Flight* become "Negroes." Interestingly, the novel centers on a moral choice in which the young Irish hero rejects the money of the urban, industrial age—which is nonetheless described in heroic terms—for a return to rural life and romantic love in Wisconsin, which, perhaps not incidentally, is near Lawson's mother's home, Minnesota. In his last work, Lawson spoke with a gentler voice.

In his Newbery speech, Lawson suggested that he wrote *Rabbit Hill* differently than he wrote his other books. With typical self-deprecating humor, he said he wrote it without careful thought; it grew out of his *feelings.* It is, indeed, in that vein that he was most effective. His illustrations for *The Story of Ferdinand* and his text for *Rabbit Hill* bespeak his capacity for gentleness.

The books of Robert Lawson must be considered central to an understanding of American children's literature of the mid-twentieth century. He was recognized as a major contributor, and both his strengths and faults as a writer may be seen as representative of the period.

Selected Bibliography

WORKS WRITTEN AND ILLUSTRATED BY ROBERT LAWSON

Ben and Me. New York: Little, Brown, 1939.
They Were Strong and Good. New York: Viking Press, 1940.
I Discover Columbus. New York: Little, Brown, 1941.
Rabbit Hill. New York: Viking Press, 1944.
Country Colic. New York: Little, Brown, 1944.
Mr. Wilmer. New York: Little, Brown, 1945.
McWhinney's Jaunt. New York: Little, Brown, 1947.
At That Time. New York: Viking Press, 1947.
Robbut: A Tale of Tails. New York: Viking Press, 1948.
The Fabulous Flight. New York: Little, Brown, 1949.
Smeller Martin. New York: Viking Press, 1950.
Mr. Revere and I. New York: Little, Brown, 1953.
Mr. Twigg's Mistake. New York: Little, Brown, 1953.
The Tough Winter. New York: Viking Press, 1954.
Captain Kidd's Cat. New York: Little, Brown, 1956.

WORKS ILLUSTRATED BY LAWSON

The Wee Men of Ballywooden. Text by Arthur Mason. Garden City, N.Y.: Doubleday, Doran, 1930.
The Story of Ferdinand. Text by Munro Leaf. New York: Viking Press, 1936.
The Story of Simpson and Sampson. Text by Munro Leaf. New York: Viking Press, 1941.
Adam of the Road. Text by Elizabeth Janet Gray. New York: Viking Press, 1942.

CRITICAL AND BIOGRAPHICAL STUDIES

Anonymous. "Robert Lawson." *Art Instructor* 15–21 (November 1938).
Burns, Mary Mehlman. "There Is Enough for All: Robert Lawson's America." *Horn Book* 48: 24–32, 120–128, 295–305 (1972).
Jones, Helene L. *Robert Lawson: Illustrator.* Boston: Little, Brown, 1972.
Lawson, Robert. "The Newbery Medal Acceptance Speech." *Horn Book* 21: 233–238 (July–August 1945).
Madsen, Valden. "Classic Americana: Themes and Values in the Tales of Robert Lawson." *The Lion and the Unicorn* 3: 89–106 (Spring 1979).
Massee, May. "Robert Lawson, 1940 Caldecott Winner." *Library Journal* 66: 591–592 (July 1941).

—AVI

EDWARD LEAR

1812–1888

THE SEARCH FOR symbolic meaning in the work of Edward Lear, the Victorian painter and nonsense writer, often seems as amusing and bewildering as the sea voyage of the Jumblies. Supported by psychoanalytical, philosophical, and sociological findings, twentieth-century scholars incline toward theories that occasionally seem to refer more to the critics' own inventions than to Lear's limericks and story poems. Thomas Byrom, in *Nonsense and Wonder: The Poems and Cartoons of Edward Lear* (1977), views "The Owl and the Pussy Cat" (1870) as "alienation" in a "queer and dislocated landscape." To John Lehmann, author of *Edward Lear and His World* (1977), "The Dong with a Luminous Nose" (1877) is a "macabre Romantic fantasia" with a chorus that emphasizes "the Dong's desolation and sense of abandonment." What these and other treatises regrettably lack, for the most part, is an inquiry into the more crucial exploration of the reasons as to why children—who know nothing of symbolism—respond with *laughter* to the Owl and the Dong; why, indeed, Lear's limericks, alphabets, story poems, and drawings afford joy, rather than pain, to the young.

It is true that the circumstances of Edward Lear's life shaped both his drawing and writing; the background is fascinating, the inquiries fruitful. It is essential that the researcher recognize that Lear's love for birds stemmed from his early work as an ornithological draftsman; that suffering from bouts of epilepsy, asthma, and rheumatism, he left the "smoky-dark Londonlife" to begin his incessant travels; that he detested physical violence, torpidity

and all persons who embodied these traits. But the children who first listened to his "nonsenses," before he was twenty-five years old, and those whom he later met and for whom he drew and wrote his alphabets and story poems had no need to know about Lear's life to respond to the Old Man with a Beard or a

> Pidy,
> Widy,
> Tidy,
> Pidy,
> Nice insidy,
> Apple-pie!

The levels on which literature is read—for Lear has survived while other nonsense versifiers have perished—determine, without doubt, the extent to which readers may return countless times and read anew. Lear is as fresh today as a century ago, and new insights into his melancholy and depressions, his ambivalence towards the "great folk" who supported him physically but stifled him emotionally, are always revealing. If the Owl was able to take along "plenty of money," the researcher recognizes this as a fantasy of the man who was constantly setting up "eggzibissions" of his drawings and paintings to support himself and finance yet another of his journeys. In 1861, writing from St. Leonard's-on-Sea, Lear describes how he spent his days and evenings "prowling in the dark along the melancholy sea." Lear's acute sensitivity about his unattractive nose and poor eyesight, coupled with his fruitless hope to marry, is echoed in "The Dong with a Luminous Nose":

> And now each night, and all night long,
> Over those plains still roams the Dong;
> . . . .
> While ever he seeks, but seeks in vain,
> To meet with his Jumbly Girl again;
> Lonely and wild, all night he goes,—
> The Dong with a luminous Nose!

But what do children find when they hear about the Dong? What they see in the sketch Lear drew for his story poem is a strange figure with an elongated body, buttons about his trousers, playing a "plaintive pipe." On his face is

> a wondrous Nose,
> . . . .
> Of vast proportions and painted red,
> And tied with cords to the back of his head.
> In a hollow rounded space it ended
> With a luminous lamp within suspended,
> All fenced about
> With a bandage stout
> To prevent the wind from blowing it out;
> And with holes all round to send the light
> In gleaming rays on the dismal night.

Certainly this Dong is akin to the spacemen of Halloween, the battery-illuminated whirligigs worn by children going out to trick-or-treat, shedding light on the "Bong-tree" which grows in their own neighborhoods. What the Dong may mean to them is probably

> A lonely spark with silvery rays
> Piercing the coal-black night,—
> A Meteor strange and bright;

and if it "wanders, pauses, creeps,—/Anon it sparkles, flashes, and leaps"; the vividness of the late-night vision can be as compelling as Martian men flashed on the television screen. Surely the invented place names, the humor of the Gromboolian Plain and the Hills of the Cranky Bore, the Jumblies landing "near the Zemmery Fidd/Where the Oblong Oysters grow," and the anapestic rhythms override the use of the letter *o*, whose mournful sounds fascinate as Lear speaks of the "long, long clouds" and the "cruel shore." This is the stuff of poetic craftsmanship, the accompaniment to Lear's narrative. Children, as Paul Hazard

observed, take what is needed. They have not the heart or time to read into the "Dong," or indeed any of the story poems, the suffering of the lonely bachelor wandering along a plain or a rocky shore; the melancholy Lear calling, as in "Calico Pie (1871)," to little birds or mice or fish who "never came back"; the Pobble, in "*The Pobble Who Has No Toes*" (1877), who through ridiculous advice loses his toes.

How is it possible that children laugh at a succession of story poems and limericks wrested from the frustrations and problems that beset Lear? How can the brooding lines, the falling rhythms, fail to work their troubling spell on children? The obvious answer is, of course, that because children have a "universal" and "consistent aversion" to "carefully established reality," as Kornei Chukovsky in *From Two to Five* (1963) has noted, they will gladly subscribe to anything which overturns or attacks reason. Nonsense, in whatever form, drawing or words, is the escape hatch from the trials of life; it is lawless, it is innocent, and, at its very best, it is made by a rational, logical mind that knows the parameters of its power. It is essential, for example, that the Dong be a *dong* and not a man, for both adult and child would weep for a human who loses his Jumbly Girl. At the moment in which the reader cares what happens, in which empathy or sympathy are aroused, nonsense vanishes. And although the Dong and Uncle Arly totter dangerously on the brink of reality, Lear, always in control, has orchestrated with the greatest care. The Dong wears a ridiculous contrivance on his nose; Uncle Arly, although he dies in the end, has a pea-green cricket that settles on *his* nose. Both noses, as it happens deeply meaningful to the scholar, are the stuff which children merely find ridiculous. They do not think of Lear's sensitivity about his ugly, shapeless nose. And so, for over a century, they have laughed!

The genius of the nonsense writer, and Lear in particular, is that he can attack reason through a variety of forms and narratives and drawings, each in tension and balance with each other. Lear recognized that there were many "sagacious persons" who objected to the "perversion of young folks' perceptions of spelling and correct grammar" in his work. He writes of Madame de Bunsen's contention that "she would never allow her grandchildren to look at my books, inasmuch as their distorted figures would injure the children's sense of the beautiful." In the 1960's many parents likewise frowned on Maurice Sendak's "wild things" as much too frightening for young children.

Lear's limericks run the gamut from mere silliness—the old man who made tea in his hat, the old person who rode on the back of a bear, the old lady who taught little ducklings to dance—to depictions of actions that, in the real world, could only be construed as violence:

> There was an Old Man with a gong,
> Who bumped at it all the day long;
> But they called out, "Oh law! you're a horrid old bore!"
> So they smashed that Old Man with a gong.

Several limerick characters die from gluttony, are drowned and meet other dire ends. If scholars read into these deaths the happenings in Lear's life, or trace the changes in his attitudes from his earliest limericks to the last, the findings may be of interest. It is evident, however, that children do not comprehend, nor do they even apprehend, that the "they" of the limericks represent reason, convention, mediocrity and Mrs. Grundy. Nor are they probably aware of Lear's dislike of noise, nor the details of the drawing in which the Old Man's feet and legs are suspended a good twelve inches from the ground whereas the feet of the "they" (the solid citizenry) are planted on terra firma. All that the children find is the comeuppance, the knowledge that *anything is possible* in the nonsense world and it need not be of the highest moral order. Mischief, the antidote to convention and logic, also smashes the "great folk" and the "big folk" who are always sure of their responsibilities and their values. "You are so solid and distinct in going on constantly in doing what is right," Lear wrote to a friend, "I am so fluffy and hazy, and never know what is right and what isn't."

Here is the child speaking, the child in Lear, the child caught in a web of do's and don't's whose escape valve is the world of nonsense. Do children recognize that Lear's understanding was based on his feelings about himself? At the age of seventy-one he wrote in his diary, "Life today is happier than this child deserves." Oftentimes he spoke of himself as a child. He loved children and wished to "make little folks merry." If his own youth had been blighted, he was determined to offer joy to others, to lead them to escape from pain. While Lewis Carroll directly parodied Dr. Isaac Watts's "Against Idleness and Mischief" (1715), in "How

doth the little crocodile," Lear chose another way, for he intensely disliked idleness in both his personal and writing life, but enjoyed mischief and made it incessantly, both with word distortion and drawing pen and in his writing.

Upsetting the rational, reasonable order of the world and its humdrum patterns is consistent in the limericks, the story poems, and the drawings. The world of reality is off limits. Each limerick character, each animal and bird makes an escape in some fashion, sailing off to sea in odd contrivances, hopping the world three times round, accomplishing the impossible in any number of imaginative ways. The people of his drawings seldom touch earth; they fly, they sit in trees, they lie on tables, they dress in odd headgear, they eat inedibles, they effect ridiculous cures. Their bodies are, as Madame de Bunsen observed, distorted. Susan Hyman, author of *Edward Lear's Birds* (1980), notes that "abnormalities of appearance are usually avian in character: frock coats stand out stiffly like tails, arms are flung back like vestigial wings, noses resemble beaks." For just as Lear invested his ornithological drawings with "a measure of his own whimsy and intelligence, his energetic curiosity, his self-conscious clumsiness and his unselfish charm," so did he give to his people characteristics of both bird and beast. It is not necessary that children know about Lear's work at London's Zoological Gardens or the menagerie at Knowsley. They have only to look at the drawings sketched for them to recognize that Lear has played broadly with the characteristics of both species, mixing up arms and wings, noses and beaks!

In a like manner he plays with words, inventing a Bong-tree, a Scroobious Pip, a "slobaciously" shining moon, toadstools that are "oribicular, cubicular and squanbigular," and the marvelous choruses sung by "Mr. and Mrs. Spikky Sparrow" (1871):

> Witchy witchy witchy wee,
> Twikky mikky bikky bee,
> Zikky sikky tee!

Many nonsense writers, of course, invent neologisms, employ alliteration, trade on anthropomorphism, and invest the inanimate with life. Many use anapestic, free-wheeling rhythms and amusing sound patterns. But what others do not have is Lear's unique gift, and that gift is more than imagination, more than mischief and lawlessness, more than a blow to reason, order, and moral consequence. It is the gift that says: Not only is *anything* possible, but there is *hope*. What happens in Lear's work is unique, for there is not a single limerick, story poem, or alphabet that doesn't offer this hope; an ape can tie up his toes in "four beautiful bows"; the old man will keep ringing until someone answers the bell. Hope reaches its quintessence and is stated more directly in the story poems. An Owl and a Pussy Cat, normal enemies in the real world, can sail away with plenty of food and money and music, buy a ring, marry and dance by the light of the moon. That Lear thought of himself as an impecunious owl, that he could never summon the courage to propose to Augusta ("Gussie") Bethell is not important to the young. But that there is hope of escape and happiness is!

In "The Duck and the Kangaroo" (1871), the Duck recognizes that in order to leave his "boring life" in a "nasty pond," to entice the Kangaroo to the world beyond, he must be prepared for the objection that his feet are "unpleasantly wet and cold." He has already "bought four pairs of worsted socks" so both may travel in comfort as they go to "the Dee, and the Jelly Bo Lee" and hop "the whole world three times round." The Daddy Long-Legs and the Fly similarly flee from a world where the length of their legs is not acceptable. "The Nutcracker and the Sugar-Tongs" (1871), aware of their "stupid existence," gallop off with the sole observation that they "will never go back any more!" All have found ways to fulfill their desire for a better life.

There are others who go in search of adventure and return home content that their whims have been satisfied, that an outing has given some new perspective. "The Broom, the Shovel, the Poker and the Tongs" (1871) find that a drive in the park helps to alleviate the gloom of the dark and softens their anger toward each other. Mr. and Mrs. Spikky Sparrow discover that a flight into town to buy "a satin sash of Cloxam blue," slippers, a new gown and a bonnet will make them look and feel quite "galloobious and genteel" and protect them forever from "cold and pain." The Jumblies sail off in a sieve and return from their voyage in twenty years with everything from "a pound of rice" and a "lovely Monkey with lollipop paws" to "forty bottles of Ring-Bo-Ree," and such tales of wonder that those who welcome them back vow to go off and see the sights for themselves. And despite the Chair's complaint to the Table in "The Table and

the Chair" (1871) that "we *cannot* walk," the Table is confident that "It can do no harm to try."

> So they both went slowly down,
> And walked about the town
> With a cheerful bumpy sound
> As they toddled round and round.
> And everybody cried,
> As they hastened to their side,
> "See! the Table and the Chair
> Have come out to take the air!"

The outing is made and they both return, in spite of a small misadventure, to dine and dance upon their heads and toddle off to bed.

Hope is present even in the saddest of Lear's story poems. The Pelicans may never see their Daughter Dell again, but they still chorus:

> Ploffskin, Pluffskin, Pelican jee!
> We think no Birds so happy as we!
> Plumpskin, Ploshkin, Pelican jill!
> We think so then, and we thought so still!

In "The Courtship of the Yonghy-Bonghy-Bò" (1877), the Yonghy-Bonghy-Bò and Lady Jingly Jones, though parted, may mourn for each other. The Pobble who has no toes still returns with his nose intact, and the Dong hopes to "meet with his Jumbly Girl again." The researcher may read into "Mr. and Mrs. Discobbolos" with its catastrophic ending an echo of William Blake's *Songs of Innocence* (1798) and *Songs of Experience* (1794). Lear holds up the other side of the mirror; the world is filled with the discontented and fraught with accident and peril. *Anything* is possible! Those who cannot escape or do not wish to wander, like the Quangle Wangle, can attract others—who come to him—if there is hope and imagination. The old man in the New Vestments learns a lesson about unconventional behavior. The greed or carelessness of limerick characters may result in their demise. But those who make the most of their long noses, those who are curious and even eccentric, are a microcosm of the world as it is. Uncle Arly must die but not before he has enjoyed the benefits of his Railway-Ticket, visited the "Tiniskoop-hills afar," enjoyed the company of his Cricket "Clinging as a constant treasure,—/Chirping with a cheerious measure," and gazed on "golden sunsets blazing."

Lear excels in nonsense because the balance between word and picture continually offers children the apprehension that while anything can happen—

the Discobbolos' tragedy, the "theys" and the drownings—there is comeuppance for the disagreeable and hope for change. His childlike optimism, in spite of his own sad childhood, prevailed. Those who followed him, who understand nonsense and are clever in word invention, alliteration, rhythmical patterns and ludicrous situations, have never equaled Lear because they have neglected to note this unique aspect of Lear's genius. In imitation of Lear, Laura Richards' "The Owl, the Eel and the Warming-pan" (1902) go out together to call on the soap-fat man, find him absent, and turn "the meeting-house upside down." "The Hornet and the Bee" (1902; note the similarity between Lear's "Said the Chair unto the Table" and "Said the bee unto the hornet") is a piracy of "The Courtship of the Yonghy-Bonghy-Bò." The hornet proposes to the bee, but is refused in favor of a Cockychafer who marries the bee and eats her up. Shel Silverstein's "The Toad and the Kangaroo" (1981) involves a contentious discussion between two creatures who argue about names for their future children—Toadaroo or Kangeroad. Disagreeing, they part. Silverstein ends with

> What a loss—what a shame
> Just 'cause they couldn't agree on a name.

Lear, more wisely, never moralizes. William Jay Smith's "The Floor and the Ceiling" (1955) separate in a rage when the Ceiling flies out the door, leaving the house in ruins and the Floor alone. "The Antimacassar and the Ottoman" (1968) express a desire to leave a room they abhor with its ugly objets d'art but fail because they believe they can neither fly nor unpin themselves. Here there is no hope, no belief that the impossible can happen, no will to make a change, and perhaps, more poignantly, no remembrance that real friendship once experienced will sustain those who are left alone in their inevitable moments of sadness.

Children need not know of the great importance Lear placed upon his own friends, but they can certainly apprehend that even Uncle Arly had his Cricket:

> Never—never more,—no! never,
> Did that Cricket leave him ever,—
> Dawn or evening, day or night;—

Even the Yonghy-Bonghy-Bò and Lady Jingly Jones once knew happiness together; even the Dong harbors hope that he will find his Jumbly Girl and relive the joyous moments. Even Mr. and Mrs. Discobbolos once had a secure and happy home, and contentment. But those who have never known the pleasure of friendship have little. Friends who must part or leave each other in anger without sustaining memories are blighted forever.

Will lesser nonsense charm the children of a century from now? This is but a researcher's idle speculation. What is perceived is that the work of Lear has survived not only because it attacks reason but also because it portrays, both graphically and through musical language, the timeless dream of children to make great escapes, to enlist their imaginations in believing that in spite of elongated noses or foreshortened legs, ridiculous behavior or disastrous circumstances, action of some sort is preferable to apathy and idleness. There is a world beyond, Lear seems to tell the children, where I will take you, where anything and everything is possible. I have given you and drawn for you a Bong-tree, an owl who plays upon a guitar, a Duck with worsted socks, the Jumblies and their sea-faring sieve. And you laugh, and through that laughter grow and recognize that the nonsenses abiding in the real world can be overcome by your belief in yourself and your imagination. And the children listen.

Selected Bibliography

WORKS BY EDWARD LEAR

A Book of Nonsense. London: Thomas McLean, 1846. Enlarged ed. London: Routledge, Warne and Routledge, 1861.

Nonsense Songs, Stories, Botany, and Alphabets. London: Robert John Bush, 1871.

More Nonsense, Pictures, Rhymes, Botany, etc. London: Robert John Bush, 1872.

Laughable Lyrics: A Fourth Book of Nonsense Poems, Songs, Botany, Music, etc. London: Robert John Bush, 1877.

Letters of Edward Lear, Author of "The Book of Nonsense," to Chichester Fortescue (Lord Carlingford) and Frances Countess Waldegrave. Edited by Lady Constance Strachey. London: T. Fisher Unwin, 1907.

Later Letters of Edward Lear, Author of "The Book of Nonsense," to Chichester Fortescue (Lord Carlingford), Frances Countess Waldegrave, and Others. Edited by Lady Constance Strachey. London: T. Fisher Unwin, 1911.

Queery Leary Nonsense. Edited by Lady Constance Strachey. London: Mills and Boon, 1911.

Edward Lear's Journals: A Selection. Edited by Herbert van Thal. New York: Coward McCann, 1952.

Teapots and Quails. Edited by Angus Davidson and Philip Hofer. Cambridge: Harvard University Press, 1954.

The Complete Nonsense Book. Edited by Lady Constance Strachey. New York: Dodd, Mead, 1958.

A Book of Bosh: Lyrics and Prose of Edward Lear. Selected by Brian Alderson. Harmondsworth, England: Puffin Books, 1975.

Edward Lear's Birds. Edited by Susan Hyman. New York: William Morrow, 1980.

How Pleasant to Know Mr. Lear! Edward Lear's Selected Works. Edited by Myra Cohn Livingston. New York: Holiday House, 1982.

CRITICAL AND BIOGRAPHICAL STUDIES

Byrom, Thomas. *Nonsense and Wonder: The Poems and Cartoons of Edward Lear.* New York: E. P. Dutton, 1977.

Cammaerts, Emile. *The Poetry of Nonsense.* New York: E. P. Dutton, 1926.

Chesterton, G. K. "Edward Lear." In *A Handful of Authors,* edited by Dorothy Collins. Mission, Kans.: Sheed and Ward, 1953.

Davidson, Angus. *Edward Lear: Landscape Painter and Nonsense Poet.* London: John Murray, 1938.

Lehmann, John. *Edward Lear and His World.* New York: Charles Scribner's Sons, 1977.

Livingston, Myra Cohn. "Nonsense Verse: The Complete Escape." In *Celebrating Children's Books,* edited by Betsy Hearne and Marilyn Kaye. New York: Lohrop, Lee and Shepard Books, 1981.

Noakes, Vivien. *Edward Lear: The Life of a Wanderer.* London: Collins, 1968; Boston: Houghton Mifflin, 1969.

Sewell, Elizabeth. *The Field of Nonsense.* London: Chatto and Windus, 1952.

Smith, William Jay. " 'So They Smashed That Old Man . . .': A Note on Edward Lear." *Horn Book* 35: 323–326 (August 1959).

—MYRA COHN LIVINGSTON

C. S. LEWIS

1898-1963

FEW MODERN AUTHORS of children's books have received the continual praise that has been given to C. S. Lewis. Since the appearance of *The Chronicles of Narnia* in the 1950's he has become—claims Naomi Lewis—"perhaps the best-liked post-war 'quality' writer for children in Britain." In America his reputation is even more solidly established. For many of his enthusiastic readers he is the founder of an ongoing school of fantasy writers originally known as the "Inklings" or the "Oxford Christians"—a literary circle that included Lewis' friends J. R. R. Tolkien and Charles Williams. His impact on the use of allegory and the "philosophical fairy tale" in fantasy fiction for children is rivaled only by that of George MacDonald, Edith Nesbit, and Kenneth Grahame, writers whom Lewis greatly admired and imitated.

For all of this, C. S. Lewis did not consider himself to be a children's writer; he wrote the *Narnia* tales simply "because they were the sort of books he 'would have liked to [have] read when [he] was a child." Lewis says that he "fell in love with the Form [of the fairy tale] itself: its brevity, its severe restraints on description, its flexible traditionalism, its inflexible hostility to all analysis, digression, reflections and 'gas.' " It is the noticeable didacticism, the apparent correspondence in his fairy tales between the content of fairy lore and Christian doctrines, that has been the major point of critical discussion of Lewis as a children's writer. Adult readers (children seem to be less concerned over the "message" in the stories) and critics either are fond of such writing or strongly dislike it.

Most critical evaluations of Lewis have focused on him as a religious writer and on how his teachings are presented imaginatively in his fiction. (Paul F. Ford's *Companion to Narnia* is the best recent study of Lewis' Christian allegory in his fairy tales.) It is interesting, however, that for many readers, especially children who know nothing about Christian doctrines, the *Narnia* tales are enjoyable strictly as fanciful stories. Stories, Lewis believed, should not be dependent on a moral. Thus he writes: "I don't like stories to have a moral: certainly not because I think children dislike a moral. Rather because I feel sure that the question: 'What do modern children need?' will not lead you to a good moral." And he concludes, "The only moral that is of any value is that which arises inevitably from the whole cast of the author's mind."

It can be argued that Lewis' *Narnia* books perhaps have been studied too closely for the allegorical elements in them and not appreciated enough as fairy tales. Both children and adults are often impressed with the imaginative richness of the tales. A striking feature of the *Narnia* stories is Lewis' extensive exploration of the traditional good/evil dualism of the fairy tale. Characteristic of *The Chronicles of Narnia,* and of Lewis' other fiction, is his diverse borrowing from classical sources. Especially in his children's stories he drew heavily from his reading of such writers as Plato, Homer, Dante, and Edmund Spenser, as well as of northern myths. Indeed, Lewis' inexhaustible knowledge of classical, medieval, and Renaissance literature contributed significantly to his creation of the *Narnia* cycle. His anachronistic use in the *Narnia* tales of mythical beings and places greatly disturbed his friend Tolkien, who disliked Lewis' mistreatment (he felt) of the "subcreation process" in his *Chronicles of Narnia*.

Lewis wrote on several occasions about how he came to create the *Narnia* chronicles. They all "began with seeing pictures in my head," says Lewis:

> At first they were not a story, just pictures. *The Lion, the Witch and the Wardrobe* all began with a picture of a Faun carrying an umbrella and parcels in a snowy woods. The picture had been in my mind since I was about sixteen. Then one day when I was about forty, I said to myself: "Let's try to make a story about it." At first I had very little idea how the story would go.
>
> (*Of Other Worlds*, p. 42)

The biographical beginnings of Narnia originated in Lewis' boyhood and youth. Born on 20 November 1898, in the countryside near Belfast, Northern Ireland, Clive Staples Lewis had, for the first few years, an average childhood. When he was nine years old, however, his mother died, an event that no doubt provoked some of what Lewis called his "nightmarish dreams"—such dream images as those in the scene in *The Magician's Nephew* (1955) when Digory gives his dying mother the life-giving apple from Narnia.

Confined to the attic with his brother during long rainy days, Lewis constructed for his own amusement a make-believe "Animal-Land," consisting of anthropomorphic beasts and "knights in armour" as its chief inhabitants. And later, when he was twelve, he built, in childlike imitation of the adult world around him, his fantasy land of Boxon, combined with his brother's India.

Lewis claimed that Boxon had nothing to do with Narnia. Boxoniana animals were little more than "dressed animals" without the true characteristics of different animals. "Animal-Land had nothing whatever," says Lewis, "in common with Narnia except the anthropomorphic beasts. Animal-Land, by its whole quality, excluded the least hint of wonder." The recent publication of Lewis' boyhood world of Boxon reveals his early attempt to combine the beast-fable and the fairy tale. The chief difference between Boxon and Narnia is, as Walter Hooper points out, that Boxon "was created by a boy who wanted to 'grow up,'" but the "Narnia

tales were created by one liberated from this desire." There is a sense in which all the *Narnia* tales are escape adventures from the regimented life of childhood. Independently and together the children—Peter, Susan, Lucy, and Edmund—struggle like Lewis Carroll's Alice to avoid the process of growing up. Narnia is for most adult readers the dream world of forgotten childhood fantasies. It is the element of escape in the stories that is shared most by children and adults alike.

In current critical discussions of children's books that have a wide appeal for both children and adults, it is becoming increasingly relevant to consider such books from both the adult's and the child's point of view. Critics are concerned with the "child's voice" as it is expressed throughout the story. What, for instance, is the relationship between child and adult voices in the *Alice* books? It is interesting that children often understood the hidden meaning in the *Narnia* books better, claimed Lewis, than did adults. Thus he wrote to one young reader: "I'm so thankful that you realized the 'hidden story' in the Narnian books. It is odd, children nearly *always* do, grown-ups hardly ever."

Throughout a recently published collection of Lewis' correspondence with children, there are frequent examples of his intense understanding of a child's mind and evidence that children understood clearly the hidden meaning in the stories. Regarding the point of his stories, Lewis wrote another child inquirer:

> I'm not quite sure what you meant about "silly adventure stories without any point." If they *are* silly, then having a point won't save them. But if they are good in themselves, and if by a "point" you mean some truth about the real world [which] one can take *out of* the story, I'm not sure that I agree. At least, I think that *looking for* a "point" in that sense may prevent one sometimes from getting the real effect of the story in itself—like listening too hard for the words in singing which isn't meant to be listened to that way (like an anthem in a chorus).
>
> (*C. S. Lewis: Letters to Children*, pp. 35–36)

A reader coming to the *Narnia* books for the first time may wonder which story to read first. According to Lewis, one should read the stories in the following order: *The Magician's Nephew*, *The Lion, the Witch and the Wardrobe* (1950), *The Horse and His Boy* (1954), *Prince Caspian* (1951), *The Voyage* of the "Dawn Treader" (1952), *The Silver Chair* (1953), and *The Last Battle* (1956). *The Lion, the Witch and the Wardrobe* is, however, the nuclear story for the remaining six, and most readers prefer to read it first.

Taken as a whole, the seven *Narnia* stories are only loosely related. A summary of the plot of the *Chronicles* reveals their episodic nature (they can be read in any order as long as *The Last Battle* is read last). Also, it is apparent that the myth of Narnia itself was not Lewis' primary motive for writing the stories. He realized, in fact, that the Narnia myth was incomplete and suggested to one child reader who wrote him about securing a map to Narnia: "Why not write stories for yourself to fill up the gaps in Narnian history?" Indeed, there are gaps in the Narnia myth. To simply tell a good story was Lewis' major concern.

In *The Magician's Nephew* the beginnings of Narnia are sketched, and Aslan's singing of Narnia into being is described. We meet Digory Kirke and Polly Plummer, two children who have a series of adventures after they are sent by a scheming old magician into the Woods between the Worlds. The children continue to step from one world to another until they meet the witch Jadis, who has made herself queen of Narnia. The witch and the children return to England, where some comical adventures take place. At the end Jadis confronts Aslan, who restores order and appoints a new king and queen of Narnia.

First-time readers of the seven *Narnia* stories will be impressed with Lewis' creation of mythical beings—the diverse array of ghoulish evil creatures in Jadis' court; the one-footed Dufflepuds in *The Voyage of the "Dawn Treader"*; and the "frog-like creature" Puddleglum, a Marshwiggle, one of Lewis' most original creatures, in *The Silver Chair*. On repeated reading of the stories, however, Lewis' clever ransacking of the traditional myth pot for the content of his stories becomes more annoying and distracts the reader from the development of the plot. The appearances of Father Christmas in *The Lion, the Witch and the Wardrobe* and of the Giant Time in *The Last Battle* seem to break the magic of the stories for the moment. Lewis' nonsensitivity to the distinguishing characteristics of mythical beings (for example his treatment of the dwarfs in *The Last Battle*) suggests that he could not overcome the temptation to alter the nature of mythical beings as he pleased.

Clearly, *The Lion, the Witch and the Wardrobe* is the classic book of the *Narnia* chronicles. The lively pace of the story turns on the child's natural response to ordinary things: " 'What's that noise?' said Lucy suddenly. It was a far larger house than she had ever been in before and the thought of all those long passages and rows of doors leading into empty rooms was beginning to make her feel a little creepy."

In *The Lion, the Witch and the Wardrobe* Lewis introduces the Pevensie children—Peter, Edmund, Susan, and Lucy—who have left London because of air raids during the war and have gone to stay with old Professor Kirke in his country mansion. Lucy is the first to discover the door into Narnia, which actually lies at the back of the wardrobe upstairs. Once in Narnia, she meets Mr. Tumnus, the Faun, and they form an immediate friendship. Jadis, the witch, is in control of Narnia and has caused a perpetual winter to fall on it. The Pevensie children are swept up into the good and evil struggle in Narnia, and through the laws of Deep Magic, known only by Aslan, the land of Narnia and its inhabitants are saved and the children are crowned the country's new rulers.

The unity of the story and its moral—how to learn true courage—is such that neither is sacrificed for the other. The dominance of Aslan (Turkish for "lion") throughout *The Lion, the Witch and the Wardrobe* gives the story a central power and focus that is sometimes lacking in the other stories (for example in *The Silver Chair* and *The Horse and His Boy*).

The next book (in Lewis' preferred order), *The Horse and His Boy*, is less about Narnia and reads more like a conventional fairy tale in the tradition of the *Arabian Nights* saga. It takes place a few years after Peter, Edmund, Lucy, and Susan have become kings and queens of Narnia. The story is mainly about two children, Shasta, the son of a poor fisherman from Calormen (a southern region that is hostile to Narnia), and Aravis, a Tarkheena from the Arabian-like city of Tashbaan, where the god Tash is worshiped. Shasta and Aravis are given the challenge of rescuing Queen Susan, who must marry Prince Rabadash, whom she detests. The children are aided in their mission by the talking horse (Pegasus) named Bree, who turns out to be an animal from Narnia. A battle ensues and Shasta exchanges place with King Lune's son, Corin of Archenland. The Narnians and Rabadash's men clash and Rabadash's forces are defeated. Aravis and Shasta are finally married and, after the death of King Lune, become king and queen of Archenland. Bree and his cohort Hwin, who is also a talking horse, return to Narnia.

In *Prince Caspian* and *The Voyage of the "Dawn Treader,"* Lewis picks up again the history of the Narnia myth. When he wrote *The Lion, the Witch and the Wardrobe* Lewis had no idea how the other stories were to follow. With "some difficulty," claims Walter Hooper, Lewis began to shape the Narnia myth and made several attempts to continue the Narnian adventures. One such attempt, referred to by Hooper as the "Lefay fragment," contains the ingredients of *Prince Caspian* and *The Magician's Nephew.* A reading of this manuscript fragment would suggest that Lewis found it difficult to give the necessary background of the Narnia myth and still maintain the simple structure of the fairy tale, which he wanted to retain. Thus he decided to write a "Return to Narnia" in *Prince Caspian* and follow it with background material on origins in *The Magician's Nephew.* As examples of smoothly integrated myth and fairy tale, the three books—*The Lion, the Witch and the Wardrobe, The Magician's Nephew,* and *Prince Caspian*—are most convincing.

The children return to Narnia in *Prince Caspian,* this time by means of magic at a railway station while they are waiting to return to boarding school. They are whisked off to a ruined castle that turns out to be Cair Paravel, where they had been crowned. From a dwarf they learn what has taken place in their absence. Prince Caspian's uncle, King Miraz, and Queen Prunaprismia have usurped Caspian's throne. The children are given the task of going on a quest to Aslan's How. They must take a path through treacherous mountains. During a night adventure Lucy catches a glimpse of Aslan and encourages the others to search for him. By daybreak the children arrive at the How.

There they find the dwarf Nikabrik arguing with King Caspian and insisting that they summon the white witch for help to save them from Miraz's army. A wild battle occurs and Nikabrik and his cohorts are killed. Peter then sends a challenge to Miraz to meet him in single combat, and there is a long and difficult battle. Finally Peter kills Miraz, and suddenly, when things look desperate for Caspian's forces, the walking trees take over and all the enemies are taken prisoner. The children are returned by the power of Aslan to the railway station.

The next adventure, *The Voyage of the "Dawn Treader,"* takes place one earth year (three Narnian years) later. Edmund and Lucy are visiting their cousin Eustace Clarence Scrubb, a snobbish boy whose parents made him read economics instead of fairy tales. The story begins when the waves from a framed picture of a ship come crashing in, and the children are taken off again to Narnia. Once on the ship, they learn that it belongs to King Caspian, who is looking for the missing lords sent away by King Miraz. Lewis introduces one of his most captivating creatures, the knight-errant mouse Reepicheep, who joins the company for his own reasons.

The Homeric voyage takes the group to places such as Deathwater Island, where they discover a lake that turns everything into gold. At the bottom of the lake they find one of the seven lost lords turned to solid gold. Next, they go to the land of the Dufflepuds, another of Lewis' Homeric hybrid creatures. Arriving at the Island of Darkness, they are given a sumptuous dinner prepared for them by Aslan. They are now among the seven lost lords. After an enchanting voyage through a silvery sea of white lilies, the *Dawn Treader* returns safely to Narnia, and with the kiss of Aslan upon them the children are returned to Cambridge and the picture above their bed.

Like *The Horse and His Boy, The Silver Chair* is a separate adventure; it involves two cousins of the Pevensies, Eustace Scrubb and Jill Pole. Strictly as a fairy tale, *The Silver Chair* is the most rewarding of all the *Narnia* books. In plot and theme it reminds one of George MacDonald's *The Princess and the Goblin* (1872). Eustace and Jill escape from the dreadful Experimental School (Lewis' own recollection of the boyhood school he attended) and find themselves at the castle of Cair Paravel. From the owl Glimfeather they learn how a large green snake killed the queen and how Prince Rilian was persuaded to stay with a beautiful woman with a green dress. All attempts to convince the prince to leave her failed. Again, Aslan, the supreme ruler, sends for Eustace and Jill and requests that they find the prince.

The children are given specific instructions to follow. They are taken by Glimfeather and another owl to Puddleglum, a Marshwiggle, who joins them on their mission. There follows an exciting adventure through a castle inhabited by giants, who plan on having the children for dinner, and at last Prince Rilian is discovered. Unable to recall his past, he is in the power of the wicked witch, who has tied him to a silver chair. In the name of Aslan, the children cut him loose, and the spell over the prince is broken. After freeing the witch's underworld captives, the children discover an opening that leads them to the heart of Narnia and to Cair Paravel. Aslan blows them back to a high cliff and to their school, after allowing them to see King Caspian's new life.

The underlying theme in the seven *Narnia* stories is the idea that myth and fact are uniquely related and that "what is myth in one world may be fact in some other." As Professor Kirke points out to the children in *The Lion, the Witch and the Wardrobe:* "If things are real, they're there all the time." For the child reader it is the recurring conflict between truth and falsity, real and make-believe, reality and appearances, that makes the *Narnia* stories so continually appealing.

The *Narnia* books are Lewis' fictive indictment against the adult refusal to accept the probabilities of Faerie: " 'But do you really mean, Sir,' said Peter, 'that there could be other worlds—all over the place, just round the corner—like that?' 'Nothing is more probable,' said the Professor."

In the *Chronicles of Narnia* Lewis explores the childhood activity of creating, maintaining, and ultimately destroying secondary worlds of fantasy. However, because of his careless use of classical myth, he found it difficult to show the relationship of Narnia to the primary world. His distinction between talking and nontalking animals, for instance, becomes increasingly more muddled, and at the end of *The Last Battle* it nearly breaks down altogether. Repeatedly Lewis wrote to his enthusiastic child readers that Narnia was not to be understood as being the real world. Thus he postulated: "Suppose there were a world like Narnia and it needed rescuing and the Son of God (or the 'Great Emperor oversea') went to redeem *it,* as He came to redeem ours, what might it, in that world, all have been like?"

The relationship between Narnia and the real world becomes notably complicated when one attempts a plot summary of the last *Narnia* book, *The Last Battle.* Lewis tried ambitiously to turn the fairytale structure into a sort of furturistic myth (like the book of Revelation), and in so doing he overloads the basic plot of the story with too much religious and philosophical symbolism (something he also did in the last volume of his space trilogy, *That Hideous Strength*).

Lewis tries in *The Last Battle* to create a counterfeit myth to the story of Aslan. Shift, an ape living in the west of Narnia, convinces an ignorant donkey named Puzzle to wear a lion skin. The ape makes all the talking animals believe that Puzzle is in fact Aslan. Meanwhile, the evil forces have begun to form. King Tirian, last of the Narnia rulers, hears rumors that the talking trees are being cut for the Calormenes, and he and Jewel, the unicorn, kill two Calormenes, for which they are sorry. Because the Pevensies are too old to return to Narnia, only Eustace and Jill are allowed to go. They arrive in Narnia, rescue King Tirian and Jewel, and discover the ape's evil plot, thereby enabling them finally to get possession of Puzzle.

While all of this is happening, Cair Paravel is being overrun by Calormenes. Tirian and the children must stand alone against them. They return to Shift's stronghold, a small stable on a hill where he has kept the donkey and where he displays the donkey in disguise. All who wish are invited to enter the stable and see Aslan face to face. Ginger, a cat and comrade of Shift, enters the stable first but exits terrified. Unexpectantly he comes face to face with Tash and not with Aslan. King Tirian and his friends battle against Shift—each trying to force the other through the stable door. Tirian forces Rishda Tarkaan through the door, and he is confronted by the terrible god Tash. Terrified, Rishda is carried away. Through the tumult is heard the voice of Aslan: "Begone, Monster, and take your lawful prey to your own place."

Tash vanishes and in his place Tirian sees the seven kings and queens before him, with crowns on their heads and dressed in glittering gowns. They turn out to be Peter, Edmund, Lucy, Digory, Polly, Eustace, and Jill. Through the open stable door the children gaze as they see the end of Narnia. Aslan calls the children to go with him "further up and further in": they have not left Narnia after all. They remember that they were in a train wreck back in England and realize that they are alive again after death. And Aslan explains: "The dream is ended: this is the morning."

Much has been written about the role of Aslan in Lewis' *Narnia* books. Without question, his creation of this divine-human superbeast, who is equally the king of beasts and at the same time the stern and loving Lion of Judah, is one of his most moving fictional achievements. Aslan is—in addition to being a symbol of Christ—the model single parent. Through the god–father character of Aslan, Lewis projects his concept of the ideal child–parent relationship, for which as a child he himself had longed:

> "Aslan! Dear Aslan!" said Lucy, "what is wrong? Can't you tell us?"
>
> "Are you ill, dear Aslan?" asked Susan.
>
> "No," said Aslan. "I am sad and lonely. Lay your hands on my mane so that I can feel you are there and let us walk like that."

Aslan's farewell to Edmund and Lucy at the end of *The Voyage of the "Dawn Treader"* is one of the most tender parental scenes in the *Narnia* books. It is, observes Roger Lancelyn Green, "the whole theme and inspiration of Narnia": the child's loving acceptance of divine and human authority as part of growing up. The *Narnia* stories have yet to be fully appreciated for the insights they offer on principles of parent–child psychology. Lewis' understanding of adolescence, for example, is convincingly seen in his treatment of Susan. As the noted Lewis scholar Clyde Kilby pointed out, her failure to get into the new Narnia (*The Last Battle*) is "perhaps the most realistic touch in all the stories." Drawing on George MacDonald's theory of childlikeness as reflective of the human–divine relationship, Lewis creates in Aslan his own version of MacDonald's benevolent Mistress North Wind.

Although Lewis' *Chronicles of Narnia* are still popular and are among the most frequently read fantasies by children and adults today, repeated readings of them reveal certain limitations to a modern reader. In the stories that follow *The Lion, the Witch and the Wardrobe*, action is frequently replaced by chatty dialogue between the children, conversations containing expressions that some modern American children may find strange (for example, the tiresome discussion between Jill and Eustace at the beginning of *The Silver Chair* and the dull opening chapters of *Prince Caspian*). One finds such tedious passages as the children's debate over the meaning of "The Ancient Treasure House":

> "Now," said Peter in a quite different voice, "it's about time we four started using our brains."
>
> "What about?" asked Edmund.
>
> "Have none of you guessed where we are?" said Peter.

> "Go on, go on," said Lucy. "I've felt for hours that there was some wonderful mystery hanging over this place."
>
> "Fire ahead, Peter," said Edmund. "We're listening."
>
> "We are in the ruins of Cair Paravel itself," said Peter.
>
> (*Prince Caspian*, p. 15)

Lewis' labored attempt to bring all the children into the picture only impedes the action of the stories and is painfully reminiscent of E. Nesbit's Bastable children and their stagy discoveries. As adventure stories filled with suspense, the *Narnia* books are hardly equal to the fiction of Robert Louis Stevenson or even some of H. Rider Haggard's stories, which Lewis read and enjoyed.

There is also the question of the myth of Narnia itself. As captivating as parts of the myth may be, taken in its entirety it seems to lack a real beginning, middle, and end. It unfolds in the same episodic way as does Kenneth Grahame's *The Wind in the Willows* (whose treatment of talking animals is far superior). The Narnia myth flows without purpose; it is like the land of Oz, simply an escape world where anything can happen, where one does not have to be concerned about the consequences of growing older.

Of all the themes in the *Chronicles of Narnia* that Lewis touches on, his treatment of death and the implications of immortality is the most notable. Like George MacDonald and his fairy-tale city of Gwyntystorm in *The Princess and Curdie* (1883), Lewis was faced with the ultimate destruction of Narnia. By the time he finished *The Last Battle*, Lewis knew that he had come to the end of the *Narnia* tales; there were no more "pictures." To children who wrote him about more *Narnia* stories he often replied: "I'm afraid the Narnian series has come to an end, and am sorry to tell you that you can expect no more."

It can be argued that *The Last Battle* actually is not a children's book at all. The basic fable plot is overcomplicated by the cataclysmic destruction and re-creation of Narnia. Lewis' parody of the evolutionary claims of modern science, and his attempt to show how pagan myth and Christianity are related (" 'It seems, then,' said Tirian, smiling himself, 'that the Stable seen from within and the Stable seen from without are two different places' "), are more than the fairy-tale structure of the story can tolerate. And yet it is remarkable that Lewis was able to bring about a semblance of unity between myth and fable in the story.

Above all else, Lewis believed that "good Death" was a reality. Thus he approached the Shadowlands described at the end of *The Last Battle* with expectant resolution and confidence. By the time he completed the *Narnia* books in 1956, Lewis was fifty-eight. He was at the height of his literary success as professor of medieval and Renaissance English at Cambridge University and a Fellow of Magdalen College, Oxford. On 23 April 1956 he he married Joy Davidman Gresham and became stepfather to her two sons. Four days later, in reply to a child reader who was concerned if the children in *The Last Battle* actually knew the ending of the Apostles' Creed, "I believe in . . . the resurrection of the body, and the life everlasting," Lewis wrote: "As to whether they knew their Creed, I suppose Professor Kirke and the Lady Polly and the Pevensies did, but probably Eustace and Pole, who had been brought up at that rotten school, did *not.*"

On 22 November 1963, Lewis died at his home at the Kilns, Headington Quarry, Oxford, where he had written so many letters to children who wrote to him about his *Narnia* books. The *Chronicles of Narnia* continue to be Lewis' great literary tribute to the enduring power of a child's mind.

Selected Bibliography

WORKS OF C. S. LEWIS

The Chronicles of Narnia

The Lion, the Witch and the Wardrobe. With illustrations by Pauline Baynes. London: Geoffrey Bles, 1950; New York: Macmillan, 1950. New deluxe ed. with illustrations by Michael Hague. New York: Macmillan, 1983.

Prince Caspian. With illustrations by Pauline Baynes. London: Geoffrey Bles, 1951, New York: Macmillan, 1951.

The Voyage of the "Dawn Treader." With illustrations by Pauline Baynes. London: Geoffrey Bles, 1952; New York: Macmillan, 1952.

The Silver Chair. With illustrations by Pauline Baynes. London: Geoffrey Bles, 1953; New York: Macmillan, 1953.

The Horse and His Boy. With illustrations by Pauline Baynes. London: Geoffrey Bles, 1954; New York: Macmillan, 1954.

The Magician's Nephew. With illustrations by Pauline Baynes. London: Bodley Head, 1955; New York: Macmillan, 1955.

The Last Battle. With illustrations by Pauline Baynes. London: Bodley Head, 1956; New York: Macmillan, 1956.

Other Works

Surprised by Joy: The Shape of My Early Life. New York: Harcourt, Brace and World, 1956.

Letters, edited, with a memoir, by W. H. Lewis. New York: Harcourt, Brace and World, 1966; London: Geoffrey Bles, 1966.

Of Other Worlds: Essays and Stories, edited by Walter Hooper. London: Geoffrey Bles, 1966; New York: Macmillan, 1967.

Boxon: The Imaginary World of the Young C. S. Lewis, edited by Walter Hooper. London: Collins, 1985.

Letters to Children, edited by Lyle W. Dorsett and Marjorie Lamp Mead. New York: Macmillan, 1985.

CRITICAL AND BIOGRAPHICAL STUDIES

Arnott, Anne. *The Secret Country of C. S. Lewis.* Grand Rapids, Mich.: Eerdmans, 1975.

Carpenter, Humphrey. *The Inklings: C. S. Lewis, J. R. R. Tolkien, Charles Williams, and Their Friends.* Boston: Houghton Mifflin, 1979.

Christopher, Joe R., and Joan K. Ostling, eds. *C. S. Lewis: An Annotated Checklist of Writings About Him and His Works.* Kent, Ohio: Kent State University Press, 1974.

Ford, Paul F. *Companion to Narnia.* New York: Harper and Row, 1980.

Green, Roger Lancelyn. *C. S. Lewis.* London: Bodley Head, 1963.

———, and Walter Hooper. *C. S. Lewis: A Biography.* New York and London: Harcourt Brace Jovanovich, 1974.

Hooper, Walter. "Narnia: The Author, the Critics, and the Tale" *Children's Literature* 3: 12-22 (1974).

———. *Past Watchful Dragons: The Narnian Chronicles of C. S. Lewis.* New York: Collier/Macmillan, 1979.

———, ed. *They Stand Together: The Letters of C. S. Lewis to Arthur Greeves (1914–1963).* New York: Macmillan, 1979.

Kilby, Clyde S. *The Christian World of C. S. Lewis.* Grand Rapids, Mich.: Eerdmans, 1964.

———, and Douglas Gilbert. *C.S. Lewis: Images of His World.* Grand Rapids, Mich.: Eerdmans, 1973.

Lewis, Naomi. "C. S. Lewis." In *Twentieth-Century Children's Writers,* edited by D. L. Kirkpatrick. London: St. James, 1978; New York: St. Martin's Press, 1978.

Lindskoog, Kathryn. *The Lion of Judah in Never-Never Land.* Grand Rapids, Mich.: Eerdmans, 1973.

Lochhead, Marion. "Narnia." In *The Renaissance of Wonder in Children's Literature.* Edinburgh: Highgate, 1977; New York: Harper and Row, 1977.

Quinn, Dennis B. "The Narnia Books of C. S. Lewis: Fantastic or Wonderful?" *Children's Literature* 12: 105–121 (1984).

Sammons, Martha C. *A Guide Through Narnia.* Wheaton, Ill.: Harold Shaw, 1979.

Swinfen, Ann. *In Defense of Fantasy: A Study of the Genre in English and American Literature Since 1945.* London: Routledge and Kegan Paul, 1984.

Walker, Jeanne Murray. *"The Lion, the Witch and the Wardrobe* as Rite of Passage" *Children's Literature in Education* 16, no. 3: 177–188 (1985).

—GLENN EDWARD SADLER

HUGH LOFTING

1886–1947

I T IS DIFFICULT to think of an author who provides a purer example of cultural contradictions
than Hugh Lofting. As the creator of the dedicated
naturalist Doctor Dolittle, he could easily be hailed
as a hero among environmentalists. His works demonstrate that he was what Dolittle's wise old parrot,
Polynesia, called a "good noticer"—an indispensable trait in a conservationist. And Lofting's alter
ego, the intrepid Doctor, was both courageous and
ingenious in opposing such outrages in the animal
world as fox hunts, bullfights, and badly managed
pet shops. But at the same time, Lofting was apparently an unwitting originator of regressive, racially
biased children's books.

His extreme blindness to the humanity of African and Native American peoples puts him at the
center of Euro-American ethnocentrism as manifested in children's literature of the 1920's through the
1940's. In a majority of his works, Lofting mocks
the identity of people of color and promotes the
myth of white superiority. From this untenable cultural perspective, he was not able to fulfill the goal
he set for himself: to bring entertainment and life-
enhancing experiences to children. There was little
recognition in the 1920's and 1930's that children,
as a distinct class of readers, included nonwhite
children, and Lofting's personal experience seems
to have been devoid of encounters that would enable him to reject this widespread ethnocentric position.

In a family of six children, Hugh Lofting was the
one with "a strange affinity for animals," as his own
younger son later reported. He was born in 1886

in Maidenhead, England, to an Irish father and an
English mother, and was sent away at the age of
eight to a Jesuit boarding school. He remained in
this relatively secluded environment for ten years,
and although he was of slight build, he developed
an interest in mountain-climbing as well as in
fishing and world travel. In 1904 he was allowed to
indulge his wanderlust by taking up studies in civil
engineering at the Massachusetts Institute of Technology in Boston. He completed his degree at London Polytechnic and began work as a surveyor and
prospector in Canada, then as a railway engineer in
West Africa and in Cuba. He married Flora Small
in New York in 1912, and after service in the Irish
Guards in World War I he returned to New York
with his wife and two children and was granted
American citizenship. Flora Lofting died in 1927;
in 1928 Lofting married Katherine Harrower-Pe-
ters, who died in 1929. In 1935 Lofting married Josephine Fricker; they moved to California,
where their son Christopher was born.

In the monograph "Hugh Lofting," Edward
Blishen speculates that Lofting was headed for a
career as a humorous journalist until he was interrupted by the onset of the war. He had given up
engineering at the time of his marriage and was
trying to succeed as a writer of articles and bur-
lesque-filled short stories. He was, therefore, a
somewhat experienced storyteller by the time he
began shaping the characterization of John Dolittle
from the trenches of France.

Lofting was seriously wounded and as a result
was discharged from the service in 1917. By this

time a sizable collection of illustrated letters from Lofting to his children, Elizabeth and Colin, had accumulated. They centered around a snub-nosed character named Doctor Dolittle, and in a thematic sense, they were inspired by the sufferings of horses observed by Lofting on the battlefield. Lofting had already decided to follow his wife's prompting and turn the Dolittle adventures into a book, but the Atlantic crossing in 1919 speeded up the process. He had a shipmate, novelist Cecil Roberts, who was impressed by the manuscript and recommended Lofting to his own publisher, Frederick A. Stokes. When *The Story of Doctor Dolittle* was published the next year, it was received in professional children's literature circles as a new classic, and Lofting's career as a writer for children was under way.

The paradox of humanitarian and antihumanitarian impulses in much of Lofting's work needs to be studied as both a social and an artistic problem. The social dimension—the characterizations of Third World peoples from a white-supremacist viewpoint—has no redeeming features, as is clear from a study of his works. But the defense of his books typically has rested on artistic grounds, and an analysis of this defense may be useful at the outset. To put the case succinctly, the formalistic "art" argument is weak, primarily because Lofting was not fulfilling even his own stated goals. He was an ardent internationalist, and he opposed racism in the editorial writings he addressed to his peers. If integrity in art depends upon whether or not a work is true to its purpose, then artistic justification for many of Lofting's characterizations is difficult to sustain. His fiction was at odds with his internationalism, unless of course the latter is seen as compatible with the concept of colonialism. This is the crux of the problem when an evaluation of Lofting's art is divorced from a broader context. In the pre–World War II era, such an ironic accommodation between imperialism and concepts of justice was not uncommon in Western thought. And for those working with children, this irony could be maintained so long as it was presumed that child audiences would be generally segregated along racial lines—an assumption that was legally overturned in the 1950's. Historically, a segregated child audience has meant the elevation of one group at the expense of another, an outcome that Lofting probably would have opposed if he had been able to conceive of the possibility of equality and integration of white and nonwhite groups in the first place.

These underlying contradictions in imperialist thought were given concrete shape in *The Story of Doctor Dolittle*. And the problem is seen in literary method as well as in substance. For example, stylistic features of the book emphasize childlike innocence and good faith, whereas the plot is expressive of an arrogant belief in racial and cultural hierarchies. This dichotomy is not based solely upon Lofting's use of the demeaning terms "nigger," "darkie," and "coon"; one seldom finds such epithets isolated from a thoroughly developed set of racial caricatures. In *The Story of Doctor Dolittle* these pejorative labels are connected to a scenario that treats Africans as marginal—as so irrelevant as to have a subhuman status.

After making a few jibes about the snobbery of the English in the first three chapters, Lofting moves Dolittle and his animal entourage to Africa, which has a large and admirable animal population. The immediate focus of dramatic tension is the need to cure a community of ailing monkeys, and this plot line is developed in ways that underscore the marginality of the Africans. The monkeys are cured when animals serve as nurses and "work like niggers." Dolittle is captured by the African king of Jolliginki, and he gains his release only after the Doctor's parrot discovers the king's son pining over Sleeping Beauty. This inspires the plan to turn Prince Bumpo ("this coon") white so he can win Beauty's affection. In the chapter entitled "Medicine and Magic," Doctor Dolittle is doubtful about his ability to change the color of a person's skin, but he remarks, "I suppose it *might* be possible," and the story goes on to report that "he mixed a lot of medicines in the basin and told Bumpo to dip his face in it." Then "a strong smell filled the prison, like the smell of brown paper burning," and the prince's face emerged as "white as snow, and his eyes, which had been mud-colored, were a manly gray!"

It is not surprising that this narrow racial ideal—white skin and gray eyes—was presented to a British and American reading public in the 1920's by a British-American author. But the hazardous experiments in this scene are an unusual twist of plot in any era. They are not like the playful, supernatural happenings typically devised by fictional magicians. In their tenuousness, they are difficult to relate to any context or literary convention. Doctor Dolittle muses: "He *might* stay white—I had never used that mixture before. To tell the truth, I was surprised, myself, that it worked so well." Granted, when the animals argue over whether Bumpo is better-looking now than before this operation, Dolittle lectures them: " 'Handsome is as handsome does.' " But despite the aphorism, the Doctor has a humane dimension here only if one first views Africans as so far outside the realm of humanity that their physical safety can be toyed with in a grossly nonchalant manner.

A review of "anti-Negro" thought during the 1920's throws some light on Lofting's particular blend of dehumanized portraiture and expressions of human sympathy. In *Jim Crow's Defense: Anti-Negro Thought in America, 1900–1930* (1965), I. A. Newby describes three groups that embraced the white-supremacy myth. At one end of the spectrum were people who were vocally hostile to those with an African heritage, and at the other end were "reformers" who felt that environment should be considered alongside heredity in explaining alleged racial inferiority. In the middle was a group whose attitudes are not dissimilar to attitudes found in many British and American children's books of the period. Newby writes that the so-called moderates were no less convinced of a condition of innate inferiority than the hostile extremists, "yet their approach to race problems was fundamentally sympathetic. . . . They were unimpressed by extremists who 'proved' repeatedly that the Negro was inferior, for they assumed his inferiority was self-evident." It is the presentation of racial inferiority as "self-evident" in Lofting's African and Native American realms that makes his mockery so insidious.

Turning to examples of multicultural content in the sequels to *The Story of Doctor Dolittle*, we see a variation in the presentation of Bumpo's character and the introduction of an indigenous Latin American population. In *The Voyages of Doctor Dolittle* (1922), a Native American community on Spidermonkey Island is incredibly dependent on the Doctor as a problem solver. Lofting uses fewer burlesque conventions in depicting this group, but the assumption of childishness and cultural inadequacy is unmistakable.

The African prince is depicted in this sequel as intellectually deficient, a mental infant who employs the malapropisms and grammatical misconstructions that were familiar to audiences of blackface minstrel skits. The prince has been sent to Oxford, but turns up in a "Sambo" costume (frock coat, red cravat, straw hat, green umbrella, and bare feet) and offers to be cook and shipmate on the Doctor's upcoming voyage. He says he doesn't want to neglect his "edification," yet needs an "absconsion" (vacation); he describes a clever action as "stratagenious," and when he is sad, he weeps "from sediment." He is always dangerous as well as ridiculous because his preferred solution to a dispute is to knock opponents over the head, drop them overboard, or salt and eat them.

In *Doctor Dolittle's Zoo* (1925) Bumpo plays a minor role, but the Doctor is still being forced to exclaim, "Oh, Bumpo! Stop, stop, for heaven's sake! . . . You're not in Africa, now, Bumpo. Put him down and let us be going" when the prince is on the point of knocking the villain's "brains out on his own doorstep."

In *Doctor Dolittle's Garden* (1927), Bumpo is again the Dolittle household's chief "bouncer." The narrator explains his particular usefulness in this role: "To be grabbed unexpectedly from under a hedge by a negro of Bumpo's size and appearance was enough to upset any one."

Fantippo is the setting for a second group of Africans—a people delineated as fools rather than bumbling brutes. In *Doctor Dolittle's Post Office* (1923) this group is so fond of sweets they lick the licorice-flavored backing from postage stamps. The king keeps a lollipop on a string around his neck for easy access and for use as a quizzing glass. As he peers through his green "sucker," he considers himself the very image of a fashionable foreign aristocrat.

In the last novel that Lofting completed before his death, *Doctor Dolittle and the Secret Lake* (1948), the king of Fantippo and one of his officials make a brief appearance. Gluttony and ostentation are again highlighted in the portrayal of this mythical —and yet precisely African—people.

"The Green Breasted Martins," a short story published posthumously in the anthology *Doctor Dolittle's Puddleby Adventures* (1952), gave Lofting an opportunity to concoct a third African civilization: the Gambia Goo-Goos. In this story, the author lets his opposition to feminism converge with his racial bias. The extinction of the green-breasted martins appears to be imminent because a "New Woman" has landed in the country of the Goo-Goos—an English citizen with short hair, collar and tie, and a knack for writing books: "As soon as she set foot in Goo-Goo Land she had started bossing the Chief around, telling him how to run his country, how to bring up his children and a whole lot of other things which she thought he ought to know." The Goo-Goo wives consider this boldness to be evidence of magic, and set about killing the green-breasted martins so as to make themselves hats that will match the Englishwoman's magical hat (felt, with a feather ornament). Dolittle promptly saves the martins and the patriarchal social order—and in the process he risks the lives of the entire Gambian community.

The African connection, then, is a prominent feature in *The Story of Doctor Dolittle*, *Doctor Dolittle's Post Office*, and "The Green Breasted Martins." It is less important to the overall narrative in *The Voyages of Doctor Dolittle*, *Doctor Dolittle's Zoo*, *Doctor Dolittle's Garden*, and *Doctor Dolittle and the Secret Lake*. In *The Voyages of Doctor Dolittle* a Native American community shares the brunt of Lofting's demeaning portraiture with Prince Bumpo. The abusive caricatures in his illustrations reinforce the impression that Lofting had an exclusively white readership in mind.

The *Dolittle* books are better read as a set; it is difficult to split them apart. If readers confine themselves to the narratives that exclude references to Jolliginki, Spidermonkey Island, Fantippo, and Goo-Goo Land, they will find certain characterizations thinner than Lofting expected his audience to find them. As in most fiction cycles, character delineation is not repeated in book after book; readers are expected to recall some of the scenes in which major figures expressed their unique personalities. For example, when the dog Jip is using his nose to locate the Doctor's temporary hideout in *Doctor Dolittle's Circus* (1924), the reader needs to know the full range of Jip's powers, which is revealed in the first novel in a marvelously extravagant fantasy about Jip's capacity to follow a scent. The *Circus* scene loses much of its imaginative impact unless the reader can make that association.

The publisher of Lofting's works appeared to be acknowledging this dilemma in 1967 when the company issued excerpts from the *Dolittle* series in *Doctor Dolittle: A Treasury*. On the one hand, the foreword by the publisher claims a sacrosanct status for the entire series: "No quantitative or qualitative measurement can be applied to any body of creative work which has peopled the imaginations and enriched the lives of generations as have the Doctor Dolittle stories." On the other hand, the excerpts in the anthology are expurgated so that all references to Africans (except for one sketch on the title page) are excised. What remains in the *Treasury* are samples of Lofting's imaginative gifts, espe-

cially evident in the pushmi-pullyu episodes, and the juxtaposition of his two styles of writing.

The innovative style of the first novel was not repeated in subsequent volumes, a fact that suggests it may have been heavily dependent upon the circumstances surrounding Dolittle's emergence. With respect to both rhetorical method and subject matter, the conditions of wartime seem to have deeply influenced Lofting. In response to his feelings about wounded, unattended animals, he needed to create an effective fictional advocate for the animal kingdom. He needed someone who could communicate in animal language, and someone not deceived by or enamored of the ways of the world. Warmth, simplicity, and the wit of understatement were natural components of a style that could delineate such a character. At the same time, the letters that were the novel's nucleus may have been instrumental to the work's succinct descriptions and swift narrative pace.

Above all, young children have the pleasure of hearing just a hint of their own language pattern in *The Story of Doctor Dolittle*. Lofting did not resort to the "baby talk" tactic of some nineteenth-century authors in order to produce this effect. He had other kinds of grammatical oddities that gave the third-person narrator a guileless, unschooled dimension. Lines of narration sound as if they might have come from a child's composition exercise, as in "and the money he had saved up grew littler and littler" or "they carried all their luggage down to the seashore and got on to the boat." The Doctor similarly suggests child speech when he asks a youngster in search of his uncle, "Now what was your uncle like to look at?"

Dialogue spoken by the animals blends a more sophisticated tone with a stream of childlike arguments and questions. When the lost child is describing his uncle's ship, the animal chorus is also heard:

"What's 'cutterigsloop'?" whispered Gub-Gub, turning to Jip.

"Sh!—That's the kind of a ship the man had," said Jip. "Keep still, can't you?"

"Oh," said the pig, "is that all? I thought it was something to drink."

(p. 145)

The economy of Lofting's style in the first novel serves him well when he suddenly offers a comically incongruous image. Sparseness makes the humor unusually straight-faced, as when the Queen

Lioness, with a sick cub on her hands, comes "running out to meet [her husband] with her hair untidy," or when the doctor is reminded that he spent his last twopence to buy a rattle "for that badger's baby when he was teething."

In the second novel, *The Voyages of Doctor Dolittle*, economy of expression is replaced by Lofting's more descriptive style, as the elderly Tommy Stubbins, who was once a child assistant to the Doctor, assumes the role of narrator. But even when Lofting backtracks chronologically and uses a time frame in *Doctor Dolittle's Post Office* and *Doctor Dolittle's Circus* that predates the arrival of Stubbins, the special stylistic features of the first book are not recovered. There is an archaic overexplicitness in some passages that creates an aura of condescension, although Lofting insisted that he avoided "talking down" at all costs.

In a formalistic sense, Lofting was at his best when he could combine his innovative style and his fanciful conceptions, as in the beginning of the series. But his inventiveness in using animal lore and imagery was quite consistent. Sometimes the creatures in the Dolittle menagerie were an occasion for wry social comment. For example, in the chapter of *The Voyages* entitled "The Judge's Dog," Dolittle requests that a defendant's dog be permitted to testify in court, and the judge demands proof of the Doctor's power to converse with the beast. He asks the Doctor to inquire of his dog what the judge had for dinner, but the dog goes on to tell of the judge's late-night card parties and carousing. It is clear that the "Not Guilty" verdict results from the judge's desire to muffle the loquacious hound.

In *Doctor Dolittle's Circus*, effective slapstick is drawn from a simple animal image: a seal tossed about like an old sack. It is both credible and absurd when a coastguardsman watches the Doctor throw the seal (disguised now as a lame woman) into the Bristol Channel to return to her family, and then arrests Dolittle for being a Bluebeard and disposing of his wife. If the author had not been a "good noticer," the seal-sack possibilities would have remained unexploited. And if the author had not respected the child's comprehension of simple satire, he would not have made fun of coastguardsmen, judges, or arrogant professionals. In the *Circus*, Lofting makes this quip: "But the leader of the bloodhounds, like many highly trained specialists, was (in everything outside his own profession) very obstinate and a bit stupid."

A look at one of Lofting's most pallid works

points up his difficulty in altering the magical Doctor-animal formula. A novel that is not part of the *Dolittle* series, *The Twilight of Magic* (1930) is a trite, cliché-ridden fantasy set in the Middle Ages. Lofting's procrastination in writing it lends support to the hypothesis that he found it easier to stick to scenarios that enabled him to express his adult interests; he was apparently quite serious when he once remarked that the phrase "juvenile literature" was as unreasonable as the phrase "senile literature."

When Lofting retains the Dolittle character but downplays the animals, his muse still lets him down. For example, in *Doctor Dolittle in the Moon* (1928) he tries to create humor with a variety of "talking" floral species. Some of the plants wave their branches and send out perfumed scents to simulate a kind of Morse code. The result is a vapid fantasy realm that lacks both the tension of querulous nonconformists and the intriguing speculations typical of science fiction.

In *The Story of Mrs. Tubbs* (1923) and *Tommy, Tilly and Mrs. Tubbs* (1936), Lofting keeps an animal cast but contrives for his creatures to assist a woman who exceeds one hundred years of age. Mrs. Tubbs's pets marshall the forces of rats, swallows, and wasps to chase off the man who has evicted their aged friend. And in the sequel they enlist mice to help prepare a basement dwelling place after a storm. Both stories are predictable, banal, and mercifully short.

Lofting tried out additional genres with more success in *Noisy Nora: An Almost True Story* (1929, a picture book), *Gub-Gub's Book: An Encyclopedia of Food* (1932, a set of tales ostensibly by Dolittle's pig), and *Porridge Poetry: Cooked, Ornamented, and Served* (1924, a collection of nonsense verses). All these works include some examples of effective satire, playful spoofing, or ingenious wordplay. In *Porridge*, for example, we meet these eccentrics:

> Betwixt and Between were two betwins,
> Their father's name was Twoddle.
> They've been alike as a pair of pins
> Since they could scarcely toddle.

Only the racism of "Scallywag and Gollywog" and the strained verbal gymnastics on one or two pages mar the poems.

Whenever Lofting introduced multicultural material, he could not harmonize his cultural ideals with his artistic practice. He stated his "one world"

369

principles in an article entitled "Children and Internationalism," in *The Nation* (13 February 1924). In this article, he said that the "race-hatred trafficker [would] finally be swept by the flood of enlightened evolution into the limbo of anachronism" and noted that "all races, given equal physical and mental chances for development, have about the same batting averages." He also said that "it is very wrong to misrepresent things to children"; if they are given the chance to get away from "bigoted misrepresentation . . . , then the children themselves will bring about some form of a rational internationalism."

"Bigoted misrepresentation" was on people's minds to a considerable extent in the 1960's, and one might then expect the creators of the 1967 movie musical *Doctor Dolittle* to have downplayed Lofting's cultural prejudices. However, this motion-picture pastiche of incidents from several *Dolittle* novels adds a number of sexist images as it retains Lofting's white supremacist assumptions. In its own formulaic way, a musical needs a love story as a device to accommodate a series of melodious love songs. But the screenwriter-composer-lyricist, Leslie Bricusse, makes Dolittle's potential lover, Emma Fairfax, a stereotypic shrew in the first half of the film, and in the second half she is alternately a drudge, a dutiful helpmate, a weakling who cringes at the sound of thunder, and a lovesick bawler who almost sinks the fantastic Great Glass Sea-Snail "vessel" in a flood of tears. To some degree, Emma has replaced Prince Bumpo, but there is still a group of African fools and primitives. "William Shakespeare the Ninth," the leader, and the others live on a floating island that rams any ship that crosses its path. The Africans are said to have a rich culture, having looted the doomed ships of their books and artworks. But on the other hand, they are without the intelligence to devise less than barbaric laws. At one moment they are producing *Hamlet*; at another they are following superstitious "signs" and preparing the good Doctor for execution. The film includes songs that would cheer the heart of any devout conservationist (e.g., "Talk to the Animals," which won an Academy Award), but this is not enough to redeem the socially negative content.

Given Lofting's ambivalence about race, it is surprising that today the myth of white supremacy in his works remains largely unchallenged by obdurate Dolittle fans.

If his statements about "one world" had any meaning, they pointed in the direction of defeating complacency about racial myths. And yet when he was completing *Doctor Dolittle and the Secret Lake*, the last book to be published without the help of family collaborators, Lofting was still blending racist derision with condescending goodwill. He shows us the Fantippan king and his admiral through Stubbins' eyes:

> Koko had a nice merry face; and despite some rather childish habits (like his everlasting lollipop and his always wearing his crown, even in a canoe) there *was* something kingly and commanding about his great enormous figure.
>   All [the "Admiral"] wore in the way of a uniform was a rag around his middle and a yachting-cap several sizes too small for him.

In a minor way, Lofting could apparently envision "something kingly" in one of his African characters, but this culturally pluralistic concession is undercut by images frozen within the tradition of the stereotypic black clown. This ambivalence is the paradox of Lofting's era, as well as of his individual career.

Selected Bibliography

WORKS OF HUGH LOFTING

The Story of Doctor Dolittle. With illustrations by the author. New York: Frederick A. Stokes, 1920; London: Jonathan Cape, 1922. Reissued New York: Lippincott, 1967.

The Voyages of Doctor Dolittle. With illustrations by the author. New York: Frederick A. Stokes, 1922; London: Jonathan Cape, 1923. Reissued New York: Lippincott, 1967.

Doctor Dolittle's Post Office. With illustrations by the author. New York: Frederick A. Stokes, 1923; London: Jonathan Cape, 1924. Reissued New York: Lippincott, 1967.

The Story of Mrs. Tubbs. With illustrations by the author. New York: Frederick A. Stokes, 1923; London: Jonathan Cape, 1924. Reissued New York: Lippincott, 1968.

Doctor Dolittle's Circus. With illustrations by the author. New York: Frederick A. Stokes, 1924; London: Jonathan Cape, 1925.

Porridge Poetry: Cooked, Ornamented, and Served. With illustrations by the author. New York: Frederick A. Stokes, 1924; London: Jonathan Cape, 1925.

Doctor Dolittle's Zoo. With illustrations by the author. New York: Frederick A. Stokes, 1925; London: Jonathan Cape, 1926. Reissued New York: Lippincott, 1967.

Doctor Dolittle's Garden. With illustrations by the author. New York: Frederick A. Stokes, 1927; London: Jonathan Cape, 1928.

Doctor Dolittle in the Moon. With illustrations by the author. New York: Frederick A. Stokes, 1928; London: Jonathan Cape, 1929.

Noisy Nora: An Almost True Story. With illustrations by the author. New York: Frederick A. Stokes, 1929; London: Jonathan Cape, 1929.

The Twilight of Magic. With illustrations by Lois Lenski. New York: Frederick A. Stokes, 1930; London: Jonathan Cape, 1931. Reissued New York: Lippincott, 1967.

Gub-Gub's Book: An Encyclopedia of Food. With illustrations by the author. New York: Frederick A. Stokes, 1932; London: Jonathan Cape, 1932.

Tommy, Tilly and Mrs. Tubbs. With illustrations by the author. New York: Frederick A. Stokes, 1936; London: Jonathan Cape, 1937.

Doctor Dolittle and the Secret Lake. With illustrations by the author. New York and Philadelphia: Lippincott, 1948; London: Jonathan Cape, 1953.

Doctor Dolittle's Puddleby Adventures. With illustrations by the author. New York and Philadelphia: Lippincott, 1952; London: Jonathan Cape, 1953, 1966.

Doctor Dolittle: A Treasury. Compiled by Olga Fricker. With illustrations by the author. Philadelphia: Lippincott, 1967; London: Jonathan Cape, 1968.

TRANSLATIONS AND ADAPTATIONS

Berends, Polly Berrien. *Doctor Dolittle and His Friends*. Adapted from the screenplay by Leslie Bricusse. With photographs from the motion picture and illustrations by Leon Jason. New York: Random House, 1967.

Perkins, Al. *Hugh Lofting's Travels of Doctor Dolittle*. With illustrations by Philip Wende. New York: Beginner Books, 1967.

———. *Meet Doctor Dolittle*. With illustrations by Leon Jason. New York: Random House, 1967.

———. *Hugh Lofting's Doctor Dolittle and the Pirates*. With illustrations by Philip Wende. New York: Beginner Books, 1968.

———. *Hugh Lofting's Travels of Doctor Dolittle in English and French*. Translated into French by Jean Vallier. With illustrations by Philip Wende. New York: Beginner Books, 1968.

———. *Hugh Lofting's Travels of Doctor Dolittle in English and Spanish*. Translated into Spanish by Carlos Rivera. With illustrations by Philip Wende. New York: Beginner Books, 1968.

CRITICAL AND BIOGRAPHICAL STUDIES

Blishen, Edward. "Hugh Lofting." In *Three Bodley Head Monographs*. London: Bodley Head, 1968.

Certain, C. C. "Dr. Dolittle, the Children, and the Droll 'Huge' Lofting" *Elementary English* 5: 90–92 (1924).

Chambers, Dewey W. "How Now, Dr. Dolittle?" *Elementary English* 4: 437–439, 445 (1968).

Fish, Helen Dean. "Doctor Dolittle: His Life and Work" *Horn Book* 5: 339–346 (1948).

———. "Dr. Dolittle's Creator" *Saturday Review of Literature* 28–29 (10 January 1948).

———. "Hugh Lofting, 1886–1947." In *Newbery Medal Books: 1922–1955*, edited by Bertha Mahoney Miller and Elinor Whitney Field. Boston: Horn Book, 1955.

Fisher, Margery. "Doctor Dolittle." In *Who's Who in Children's Books: A Treasury of the Familiar Characters of Childhood*. New York: Holt, Rinehart and Winston, 1975.

Lofting, Chris. "Memories of 'Dr. Dolittle' Creator" *Los Angeles Times* (19 November 1967).

Lofting, Colin. "Mortifying Visit from a Dude Dad" *Life* 14: 128–129 (30 September 1966).

Lofting, Hugh. "Children and Internationalism" *The Nation* 3058: 172–173 (13 February 1924).

Moorehead, Caroline. "Hugh (John) Lofting." In *Twentieth-Century Children's Writers*, edited by Daniel Kirkpatrick. New York: St. Martin's Press, 1978. 2nd ed. New York: St. Martin's Press, 1983; London: Macmillan, 1983.

Schlegelmilch, Wolfgang. "From Fairy Tale to Children's Novel: In Honour of Doctor Dolittle's Fiftieth Birthday" *Bookbird* 4: 14–21 (1970).

Shenk, Dorothy C. "Hugh Lofting, Creator of Dr. Dolittle" *Elementary English* 4: 201–208 (1955).

Suhl, Isabelle. "The 'Real' Doctor Dolittle" *Interracial Books for Children Bulletin* 2/1, 2 (1969).

—DONNARAE MacCANN

GEORGE MacDONALD
1824–1905

GEORGE MACDONALD, ONE of the most highly regarded children's writers of the nineteenth century, was born on 10 December 1824 in the farming country of Aberdeenshire, Scotland, in the glens of Strathbogie, Huntly. He incorporated his lifelong fondness for his birthplace into his writings, especially those for children. From reminiscences of his childhood he developed his own definition of "childlikeness." MacDonald's trademark as a children's writer was his ability to link the worlds of the natural and the supernatural—a process that he insisted happened easiest and best in the mind of a child or "childlike" reader. MacDonald's in-depth exploration of child psychology is one of his major contributions as a writer of fairy tale–parables, a hybrid literary form he worked to develop and which later influenced such other writers of fantasy fiction for children as C. S. Lewis, J. R. R. Tolkien, and Maurice Sendak.

MacDonald's strong moral sensitivity, his background in Scottish Calvinism, and his boyhood interest in chemistry and medicine helped to shape his early dual fascination with the metaphysical and visible worlds. At the age of thirteen he became a member of the Huntly Juvenile Temperance Society. In his boyhood letters to his father, for whom he had a deep affection, he expressed both his religious uncertainties and his desire to take to the sea. MacDonald's mother died when he was eight years old, a loss that some critics feel had a lasting effect on him. Although he called upon his early and painful experience with death in his boyhood poetry and in his second novel, *Adela Cathcart* (1864),

actually a collection of fairy tales, parables, and poems, he readily transferred his affections to his stepmother, Margaret McColl, and later to his wife and children.

MacDonald, the second of six sons (two of whom died early), inherited his unusual talent for telling make-believe stories from his father, a master of the kind of spontaneous storytelling one finds in the collection of tales in *Adela Cathcart*. Two of the stories in the novel, "Birth, Dreaming, and Death" and "The Castle: A Parable," illustrate MacDonald's early exploration of metaphysical subjects and experimentation with the philosophical fairy tale, a genre he adapted from his reading of the German romantic writers Novalis (the pseudonym of Friedrich von Hardenberg), Goethe, August Wilhelm von Schlegel, and Ludwig Tieck. Most of all he admired and imitated E. T. A. Hoffmann, the author of *Der goldene Topf* (1814), and Baron de La Motte-Fouqué, whose tale *Undine* (1811) he considered to be "the most beautiful fairy tale." Throughout his long literary career, MacDonald continued to tailor his use of the parable form, writing a kind of crossover story between fairy tale and parable that he called a "double story." Lewis, a great admirer of MacDonald's works, suggests that MacDonald excelled in the "mythopoeic art." And Louis MacNeice claims that "in the realm of parable writing no one went further than MacDonald in the whole of the nineteenth century."

Many of MacDonald's early poems, otherwise not necessarily notable, are parables in verse, based on his boyhood experiences. The world Mac-

Donald knew as a young boy in Huntly, before he left at the age of sixteen to be a student in Aberdeen, had a profound impression on him. The daily struggle of the rural life that he experienced at Upper Pirriesmill, Bleachfield Cottage, later renamed the Farm (called Howglen in *Alec Forbes of Howglen,* 1865), where young George went to live when he was two years old, stimulated his poetic, visionary sense. He had around him all the external makings of a fairy tale—the striking contrast between the reality of menial chores during the day and at night the fantasy world he constructed in his garret bedroom, with its impressive skylight, in which he slept and dreamed (like his child-hero Ranald in *Ranald Bannerman's Boyhood,* 1871) of the sun, moon, and stars dancing together as a celestial family. Across the River Deveron stood the fortresslike ruins of Huntly's Norman castle, and to the north of it, approached "by a great avenue," there was "the large eighteenth century house of stone, Huntly Lodge," described at the beginning of *The Princess and the Goblin* (1871) as "a large house, half castle, half farm-house." Yearly, hundreds of Huntly children would form a procession to the Lodge, which "was built from the stones of the castle in 1757 . . . on a site of what was presumed to be a farm." "Accompanied by a band of music," the children "received a cake, and an orange each from her Grace" (the dowager of Alexander, fourth duke of Gordon), whose funeral MacDonald vividly recalled seeing when he was two-and-a-half years old. Also in *The Princess and the Goblin* MacDonald recalls the thread-spinning factory, where his grandfather Charles Edward had been apprenticed before he became a clerk in one of the largest bleach fields in the Strathbogie area.

MacDonald fictionalized many of the people and events as well as the places of his life in his early semiautobiographical novels: *Alec Forbes of Howglen, Robert Falconer* (1868), and *Gutta Percha Willie: The Working Genius* (1873). His dearly loved paternal grandmother, Isabella Robertson, is the model for Mrs. Falconer in *Robert Falconer.* The daughter of a linen weaver, she lived next door in a stone house that MacDonald's father had built and in which MacDonald had been born. Noted for her religious zeal and her business sense, MacDonald's grandmother seems to have had an intense love for children; at the Farm she was respectfully known as "the real mistress" and is MacDonald's model for other "wise women," grandmother figures who appear throughout his tales. Like Diamond's inquir-

ing conversations with Mistress North Wind in *At the Back of the North Wind* (1871), MacDonald's own talks with his grandmother were filled with admonishment and instruction. Next to his father, she had the most formidable influence on him.

MacDonald never totally forgot those early years in Huntly. Even at the age of fifty-nine, in writing his later Scottish novel, *Donal Grant* (1883), he still nostalgically recalled the world that, as a young boy, he saw and described in his poetry and fiction:

> The wind gave life to everything. It rippled the stream and fluttered the long webs stretched bleaching in the sun: they rose and fell like white waves on the bright green lake of the grass, and women, homely Nereids of the little sea, were besprinkling them with spray. Then there were dull wooden sounds of machinery near, no discord with the sweetness of the hour, speaking only of activity, not labor. These bleaching meadows went a long way by the river-side, and from them seemed to rise the wooded base of the castle.

From these scenes of his boyhood—the bleaching fields around the Farm, the ruined castle nearby, the curious perpetual motion of the thread-spinning factory, and, most important, the transporting power of the wind—MacDonald constructed the symbolic landscapes for his fairy tales. His classic fairy tales for children—the *Princess* books and *At the Back of the North Wind*—have their origins in MacDonald's boyhood in Huntly.

MacDonald's career as a children's writer began informally during his days in Aberdeen. He recounts this period of his life in his less-known children's story *Sir Gibbie* (1879). One of his best attempts at fictionalizing his childhood experiences, it is the story of a mute street urchin who runs through Old Aberdeen, loyally attending to his kind but drunken father, once a man of wealth but now a poor cobbler. After his father's death he flees to the countryside, where he is taken in by cotter Janet and her husband, who become foster parents to him. Eventually he recovers his lost fortune, marries, and lives happily ever after. In *Sir Gibbie* MacDonald's use of a symbolic Christ-child figure as his protagonist at times strains the story's credibility; nevertheless, MacDonald frequently repeated this favorite theme, with variations, in his other stories for children.

According to MacDonald's son Greville a curious event took place during the writer's student days at Aberdeen: in 1842 he skipped a session at King's College and during the summer months went to catalog the collection of a library in "a certain castle or mansion in the far North," the identity of which has never been established. (Most likely it was Sinclair Castle at Thurso, owned then by Sir George Sinclair, who had visited in Germany and owned a library full of volumes of German poetry.) There, according to his son's report, Mac-Donald enthusiastically read the German and English romantic poets—a group that critics, starting with Lewis, have insisted greatly influenced Mac-Donald's writing. Although MacDonald did have a lifelong fondness for mansions, castles, and libraries—a fondness evidenced by his impressive descriptions of these places in *The Portent* (1864), in *Wilfrid Cumbermede: An Autobiographical Story* (1872), and in his "fairie romances" written for adults, *Phantastes: A Faerie Romance for Men and Women* (1858) and *Lilith: A Romance* (1895)—there is no evidence to support any claims that he had an unrequited romance at Thurso, as Robert Lee Wolff has suggested, or even that he ever went to such a place. If he did, his brief time at Thurso did not have the lasting effect on him that his castle-building days at Huntly had, when he learned the art of fantasizing life into fiction.

In 1851 MacDonald, at the age of twenty-seven, married Louisa Powell of Upper Clapton, London. She was the sister of Alexander Powell, the husband of MacDonald's beautiful cousin Helen MacKay, with whom he nearly had a romantic relationship. His marriage launched his literary career, when he published a poem, "Love Me, Beloved," written to his wife as a wedding gift, in *Within and Without: A Dramatic Poem* (1855). Having published an inconsequential volume of *Poems* in 1857, he produced his first major work a year later, titled *Phantastes*. Highly praised by most critics, *Phantastes* marks the beginning of MacDonald's experimentation with the literary parable. In writing this work MacDonald drew upon his reading of romantic poetry—especially Novalis' *Heinrich von Ofterdingen* (1802) and the works of Schiller, Shelley, and Wordsworth—and tried to imitate Edmund Spenser's *The Faerie Queen* (1590) and Hoffmann's *Volksmärchen*. At times he tried in *Phantastes* to combine poetic symbolism and fairy-tale characters in an awkward effort to create a literary myth: a "Vision of Dame Kind," as W. H. Auden has defined it. Auden argues that in this work MacDonald convincingly expresses "an over-whelming conviction that the objects confronting him have a numinous significance and importance, that the existence of everything he is aware of is holy." In a similar estimate of the power of *Phantastes,* Lewis referred to his initial reading of the text as "a baptism of holiness"—a reading experience few modern critics of the romance seem to share.

It is, nevertheless, this numinous sense of a divine influence at work in all living things that Mac-Donald tried to convey in his fairy tales. He intentionally avoided traditional symbolic patterns, choosing rather to devise parables that reflect his own intense belief in the child's ability to overcome evil. With this purpose, he published his first collection of stories for children, *Dealings with the Fairies* (1867). In each of the tales in this volume: "The Light Princess," "The Giant's Heart," "The Shadows," "Cross Purposes," and "The Golden Key," he tried to define the concept of "childlikeness" as a spiritual process of birth, maturation, and future state—the lifelong activity of becoming a child.

Of all MacDonald's shorter fairy tales for children, "The Light Princess" is the best known and most representative. The tale has inspired copious critical interpretations, which often focus on its sexual meaning. John Ruskin, for one, feared that the tale's obvious erotic imagery might have a harmful influence on children. And yet MacDonald's primary concern is not with the princess's sexual drives but with her inability to maintain a proper balance between physical passions and moral imperatives. The story is basically about a little girl who must learn self-sacrifice in order to regain her physical gravity. Through her sacramental act of jumping into the lake—a symbolic baptism—to save the life of the prince, she is spiritually reborn after she has administered last rites to him. Having given freely of herself, she is rewarded by the prince's revival. The princess must then learn the tedious chore of walking, symbolizing the slow process of spiritual growth after the experience of rebirth.

MacDonald wrote "The Giant's Heart," one of his least successful tales, to illustrate his belief in spiritual conversion. The only way to appreciate this tale, as a child or as an adult, is to visualize the comic situation—the scene, for example, of the giant on his knees, "blubbering, and crying, and begging for his heart" from the children Buffy and Tricksey—something that could never happen in fairyland, where giants are not readily converted;

only in MacDonald's tale is a giant made to repent. It is possible that MacDonald had subversive religious intentions, as evidenced by his parody of the confessional sinner's bench. In any case, despite its religious message, the tale is one of MacDonald's few comical ones and is, for all its banality, at times genuinely amusing.

The remaining tales, "The Shadows," "Cross Purposes," and "The Golden Key," are stories an adult will find more interesting than a child reader. In these works MacDonald attempts again to construct fairy tale–parables, which read like preliminary sketches for his longer children's classics. Drawing heavily on the imaginary content of fairy-tale mythology—shadow-spirits, ghosts, goblins, fairies, and various other denizens of Nature—MacDonald tries to create parallel worlds based on such pairs of corresponding opposites as light and darkness, land and water, dreams and reality, and mortal and immortal, and to compose metaphysical parables that illustrate the intermingling of the seen and unseen.

In "The Shadows" old Ralph Rinkelmann becomes King Ralph of Fairyland after he is abducted by the shadow-fairies and taken off to their northern Iceland palace. In "Cross Purposes" the Queen of Fairyland desires "a mortal or two at her Court" because her own subjects are "far too well-behaved," and so she gives orders to Prime Minister Peaseblossom to capture two children, one rich and one poor. The two children, Alice and Richard, are rewarded for "their courage" by being allowed "to visit Fairyland as often as they pleased." Finally, in "The Golden Key," which has justly been labeled a "miniature classic," two children, Mossy and Tangle, experience a Dantean quest, like the title characters of *The Princess and Curdie* (1883), through a network of primal desires and elements of Nature, time, and space.

MacDonald's reputation as a children's writer rests almost solely on his three longer stories for children, *At the Back of the North Wind, The Princess and the Goblin,* and *The Princess and Curdie,* which, according to Naomi Lewis, have "an unquestioned place . . . among the great English children's books which generations of children read again and again" (introduction to the Penguin edition of *The Princess and the Goblin*). The fanciful escapism drawn by MacDonald and his graphic depiction of the workings of the goblin underworld make these stories continually appealing. These three children's classics were all written during what was

undoubtedly the happiest period of MacDonald's life. In the autumn of 1867 the MacDonalds moved to the Retreat, Upper Mall, Hammersmith, London—the house later owned and renamed Kelmscott House by William Morris. There he found adequate space for his large family. Surrounded by eleven children of his own and two adopted children—all of whom provided him with both the inspiration and the subject matter for his writing—he was productive and successful. He wrote his first children's classic, *At the Back of the North Wind,* at the Retreat, where "from his study window looking over the Thames" he could see "a magnolia tree shedding its petals on his front patch of garden."

In 1869 MacDonald had the good fortune of being asked to take over the editorship of the children's magazine *Good Words for the Young,* published by his friend Alexander Strahan. His new position provided him with a ready publishing outlet. In 1868, as a contributor to the magazine, he had already serialized the first half of *At the Back of the North Wind.* As editor, he now went on to serialize the second half. During 1869 and 1870 he also serialized his semiautobiographical childhood romance novel *Ranald Bannerman's Boyhood,* his interpretive commentary on *At the Back of the North Wind.*

Little is actually known about the manner in which MacDonald wrote *At the Back of the North Wind* except that, since the work was published serially, he was constantly under the pressure of meeting publication deadlines and always had to be aware of the impact that each section of the story would have on his readers. For a child, the story is admittedly too long and, at times, overly complicated. MacDonald simply could not resist the temptation to insert smaller fairy tales within the larger framework of his story, including his Sleeping Beauty tale "Little Daylight"—possibly a first draft of his last and most didactic shorter fairy tale–parable, "The History of Photogen and Nycertis: A Day and Night Märchen"—and the less-successful dream-parable "Nanny's Dream." It would have been better for the action of *At the Back of the North Wind* if MacDonald had excluded these minor tales from the story or published them separately, as he did "Little Daylight" and "The History of Photogen and Nycertis." Similarly, the inclusion of his long nursery rhyme "Little Boy Blue" and his most famous children's poem, "Baby" ("Where did you come from, baby dear?"), add little to the story. As examples of light children's verse in the Blakeian tradition, however, they are not all that bad.

Critics of *At the Back of the North Wind* have been interested, for the most part, in MacDonald's treatment of death and in his ability to depict both the ordinary life of Diamond, the child-hero, and his dreamworld encounters with North Wind, "inventing a place with which to contrast the everyday world." Often overlooked by critics, however, the most captivating aspect of the story for a child is Diamond's intimate relationship with North Wind herself, who is his mentor and friend and with whom he forms a sort of Madonna-and-child bond.

As a dream romance, *At the Back of the North Wind* belongs to the long tradition of "secret friend" literature for children, which includes Robert Louis Stevenson's *A Child's Garden of Verses* (1885) and Frances Hodgson Burnett's *The Secret Garden* (1911). One of the most interesting features of MacDonald's classic is his treatment of time from a child's point of view. As Diamond takes his night flights with Mistress North Wind, the barriers of time no longer seem to exist. He is caught up in a fantasy world of endless moral decisions. Diamond's adventures with Mistress North Wind are meaningful to him not only because she takes him to far-off places, a common device in Victorian children's fiction, but also because he forms a deep attachment to her, as MacDonald did to his own grandmother. Tenderly Diamond explains: "It's not for the dream itself—I mean, it's not for the pleasure of it, for I have that, whether it be a dream or not; it's for you, North Wind: I can't bear to find it a dream, because then I should lose you." As Lucy hates to leave her beloved Aslan, at the end of Lewis' *The Voyage of the "Dawn Treader"* (" 'It isn't Narnia, you know,' sobbed Lucy. 'It's *you*. We shan't meet *you* there. And how can we live, never meeting you?' "), Diamond cannot bear to lose his newfound friend.

The critical discussion of MacDonald's major children's books, especially of his *Princess* books, has mainly centered on their psychological, and more recently, their social, implications. MacDonald seems to have been particularly and remarkably aware of the degree to which his characters represent various levels of the subconscious and conscious minds. For example, the goblin figure, who lives in the underworld, symbolizes the degenerate self, and the wise grandmother figure, who resides in her hidden room in the turret, symbolizes the superego. Although both the

Princess books are traditional fairy tales in their explicit polarization of good and evil elements, they read more like metaphysical parables than common fairy tales. The most difficult theological doctrines regarding the origin of evil, the question of predestination, and the nature of free choice are skillfully woven into the tales. These same doctrinal interests were more overtly dealt with in *At the Back of the North Wind*.

As a writer of parables, MacDonald is at his best in the *Princess* books and in *The Wise Woman: A Parable* (1875), a story that is frequently neglected as a transitional fairy tale between the *Princess* books. In tightness of structure and consistency of theme, *The Wise Woman* (later published under other titles) is at times superior to either of the *Princess* books. There is hardly a passage in all of MacDonald's stories for children to equal the entrance of the wise woman, at the end of the novel:

> "Stop!" said a voice of command from somewhere in the hall, and, king and queen, as they were, they stopped at once half way, then drew themselves up, stared, and began to grow angry again, but durst not go farther.
>
> The wise woman was coming slowly up through the crowd that filled the hall. Every one made way for her. She came straight on until she stood in front of the king and queen.
>
> "Miserable man and woman!" she said, in words they alone could hear, "I took your daughter away when she was worthy of such parents; I bring her back, and they are unworthy of her. That you did not know her when she came to you is a small wonder, for you have been blind in soul all your lives: now be blind in body until your better eyes are unsealed."
>
> She threw her cloak open. It fell to the ground, and the radiance that flashed from her robe of snowy whiteness, from her face of awful beauty, and from her eyes that shone like pools of sunlight, smote them blind.

Rosamond, kneeling at the feet of the wise woman, begs her:

> "Oh, my lovely wise woman! do let them see. Do open their eyes, dear, good, wise woman."
>
> The wise woman bent down to her, and said, so that none else could hear, "I will one day. Meanwhile you must be their servant, as I have been yours. Bring them to me, and I will make them welcome."
>
> (*A Double Story*, 1876, pp. 233–235)

In *The Princess and the Goblin* MacDonald treats the same moral issue of conversion. Princess Irene and Curdie, the miner's son, must trust the Wise Woman of their own free will before she can help them conquer the evil goblins and save the kingdom. The story is, like so many of MacDonald's stories, full of the conflicting feelings and desires that arise when children must accept or reject the adult world. Following his account of conversion in *The Princess and the Goblin,* MacDonald continues in *The Wise Woman* to delineate the difficult process of sanctification, or purgation, which the children, Rosamond and Agnes, must undergo as they go through the many rooms in the Wise Woman's house.

Finally, in his parable of city reform, *The Princess and Curdie,* MacDonald attempts to convert the whole kingdom of Gwyntystorm. But like Lewis' Narnia in *The Last Battle* (1956), MacDonald's fictional fairy-tale city is doomed to destruction because human nature, MacDonald believed, is at best corruptible:

> Irene and Curdie were married. The old king died, and they were king and queen. As long as they lived Gwyntystorm was a better city, and good people grew in it. But they had no children, and when they died the people chose a king. And the new king went mining and mining in the rock under the city, and grew more and more eager after the gold, and paid less and less heed to his people.

There were no substitutes, MacDonald believed, for individual free choice and childlike belief. In one of the most convincing passages in the *Princess* books, in *The Princess and the Goblin,* Curdie struggles—as MacDonald felt the child's mind often does—with the tension between belief and disbelief. On the verge of tears, Princess Irene asks Curdie pleadingly, "But don't you hear my grandmother talking to me?" Curdie replies:

> "No. I hear the cooing of a lot of pigeons. If you won't come down, I will go without you. I think that will be better anyhow, for I'm sure nobody who met us would believe a word we said to them. They would think we made it all up. I don't expect anybody but my own father and mother to believe me. They *know* I wouldn't tell a story."
>
> "And yet *you* won't believe *me,* Curdie?" expostulated the princess, now fairly crying with vexation, and sorrow at the gulf between her and Curdie.

> "No. I *can't,* and I can't help it," said Curdie, turning to leave the room.
>
> "What *shall* I do, grandmother?" sobbed the princess, turning her face round upon the lady's bosom, and shaking with suppressed sobs.
>
> "You must give him time," said her grandmother; "and you must be content not to be believed for a while. It is very hard to bear; but I have had to bear it, and shall have to bear it many a time yet. I will take care of what Curdie thinks of you in the end. You must let him go now."

There is not a writer of children's books who could match George MacDonald's ability to explain the experience of being believed or doubted in language that a child could understand. Progressively as the relationship between Princess Irene and Curdie becomes more intimate, one notes MacDonald's special gift for depicting childhood romance. He is "one of the very few children's authors," observes Humphrey Carpenter, "who make a success of portraying romantic feelings between a boy and a girl." He also could depict symbolically the process of the child's self-education so that it was convincing to the child and adult reader alike. Throughout his life he drew on the lessons he had learned as a child and which, as an old man, he still could not forget.

Much has been written of MacDonald's so-called disillusioned old age; indeed it became increasingly difficult for him to maintain his childlike idealism. He had to endure the death of two of his children, and his own health deteriorated. Mary Josephine, his second daughter, died a struggling death from tuberculosis at the age of twenty-four, on 27 April 1878, and his favorite daughter, Lilia Scott, died in his arms at thirty-nine of the same disease, on 22 November 1891. And yet MacDonald still found strength to console his wife and bereaved friends. A year after Mary's death he wrote in an unpublished letter to his dear friend Lord Mount-Temple (9 April 1879):

> How real death makes things look! And how we learn to cleave to the one shining fact in the midst of the darkness of this world's trouble, that Jesus *did* rise radiant! I too have noble brothers to find where the light has hidden them, besides my faithful children, girl and boy. . . . He alone who invented the nursery and its bonds, can perfect what he began there. I, for my part, cry more for a perfecting of my loves than perhaps for anything else. That does make him a real God to us when we feel

that he is the root of all our loving, and recognize him as best of all, causing, purifying, perfecting all the rest. Our perfect God!

Eight years after the death of Lilia Scott, Mac-Donald wrote to Lady Mount-Temple (20 March 1899), after the death of her husband:

I have to be simply the child that tries to be good, and keeps close by his father. One day the door will open and we shall find ourselves at least started for home and the finding of our own. Meantime I must try to be better for the love of my children whom I cannot see, and that will bring me nearer to them. . . . Some day God will, I trust, reveal himself some as he has never done yet, and I shall be as sure as St. Paul. I must try not to stand in the way of his redeeming will with me—for he is doing his best for me as for us all.

Shortly after writing this letter, MacDonald had a stroke that partially paralyzed him, and thus he was forced into silence. For the last five years of his life he waited, like his child-hero Diamond, to be taken to Mistress North Wind's blue ice-cave.

On 18 September 1905 George MacDonald died at Ashtead, Surrey; he was buried beside his wife in Bordighera, Italy. His contribution to the golden age of children's literature was his greatest achievement. In his greatest books—*Phantastes, Lilith,* his masterpiece *At the Back of the North Wind,* and the *Princess* books—he gave to adults and children alike a new dimension to the world of faerie, one that his imitators would find it difficult to equal.

Selected Bibliography

WORKS OF GEORGE MACDONALD

Poems. London: Longman, Brown, Green, Longman, and Roberts, 1857.

Phantastes: A Faerie Romance for Men and Women. London: Smith, Elder, 1858.

David Elginbrod. 3 vols. London: Hurst and Blackett, 1863.

Adela Cathcart. 3 vols. London: Hurst and Blackett, 1864.

The Portent: A Story of the Inner Vision of the Highlanders, Commonly Called the Second Sight. London: Smith, Elder, 1864.

Alec Forbes of Howglen. 3 vols. London: Hurst and Blackett, 1865.

Dealings with the Fairies. With illustrations by Arthur Hughes. London: Strahan, 1867.

Robert Falconer. 3 vols. London: Hurst and Blackett, 1868.

At the Back of the North Wind. With illustrations by Arthur Hughes. London: Strahan, 1871. New ed., with illustrations by Arthur Hughes. London: Blackie and Son, 1886. With illustrations by Maria L. Kirk. Philadelphia: Lippincott, 1909. (This edition was reissued in 1914 as *Stories for Little Folks: At the Back of the Wind,* simplified by Elizabeth Lewis.) With illustrations by Jessie Wilcox Smith. Philadelphia: David McKay, 1919. With illustrations by D. Bedford. New York: Macmillan, 1924. With illustrations by Ernest H. Shepard. London: J. M. Dent and Sons, 1956; New York: Dutton, 1956. With illustrations by the original artists. New York: Franklin Watts, 1960. With illustrations by Charles Mozley. New York: Franklin Watts, 1963. With illustrations by Harvey Dinnerstein and an afterword by Clifton Fadiman. New York: Macmillan, 1964. Edited by Glenn Edward Sadler and with illustrations by Arthur Hughes. New York: Garland, 1976.

The Princess and the Goblin. With illustrations by Arthur Hughes. New York: Routledge, 1871; London: Strahan, 1872; London: Blackie and Son, 1911. With illustrations by Maria L. Kirk, together with the original wood engravings after Arthur Hughes. Philadelphia: Lippincott, 1907. With illustrations by Jessie Wilcox Smith. Philadelphia: David McKay, 1920. With illustrations by Charles Folkard. London: J. M. Dent and Sons, 1949; New York: Dutton, 1949. With illustrations by Nora S. Unwin. New York: Macmillan, 1951. With illustrations by Arthur Hughes. New York: Looking Glass Library, Random House, 1959.

Ranald Bannerman's Boyhood. London: Strahan, 1871. With illustrations by Arthur Hughes. London: Blackie and Sons, 1886.

Wilfred Cumbermede: An Autobiographical Story. 3 vols. London: Hurst and Blackett, 1872.

Gutta Percha Willie: The Working Genius. London: King, 1873. With illustrations by Arthur Hughes. London: Blackie and Son, 1901.

The Wise Woman: A Parable. London: Strahan, 1875. With illustrations by D. Watkins-Pitchford. London: J. M. Dent and Sons, 1965, New York: Dutton, 1965. Reissued as *A Double Story.* New York: Dodd, Mead, 1876. Reissued as *The Lost Princess.* London: Wells, Gardner, Darton, 1895.

Sir Gibbie. 3 vols. Edited by Greville MacDonald. London: Hurst and Blackett, 1879. Edited by Elizabeth Yates. New York: Dutton, 1914. Rev. ed., New York: Dutton, 1963.

Donal Grant. 3 vols. London: Kegan Paul, Trench, 1883.

The Princess and Curdie. With illustrations by James Allen. London: Chatto and Windus, 1883. With illustrations by Maria L. Kirk. Philadelphia: Lippincott,

1908. With illustrations by Frances Brundage. New York: Saalfield Publishing, 1927. With illustrations by Dorothy P. Lathrop. New York: Macmillan, 1943. Rev. ed. London: J. M. Dent and Sons, 1949. With illustrations by Charles Folkard. New York: Dutton, 1951. With illustrations by Nora S. Unwin. New York: Macmillan, 1954. With illustrations by Helen Stratton, New York: Looking Glass Library, Random House, 1960.

A Rough Shaking: A Tale. With illustrations by W. Parkinson. New York: Routledge, 1890.

Lilith: A Romance. London: Chatto and Windus, 1895.

The Fairy Tales of George MacDonald. 5 vols. Edited by Greville MacDonald. London: Fifield, 1904; London: Allen and Unwin, 1920.

The Light Princess. With illustrations by Dorothy P. Lathrop. New York: Macmillan, 1926, 1952. With illustrations by William Pené du Bois. New York: Thomas Y. Crowell, 1962. With illustrations by Maurice Sendak. New York: Farrar, Straus, Giroux, 1969.

George MacDonald: An Anthology. Edited by C. S. Lewis. London: Geoffrey Bles, 1946.

The Complete Fairy Stories of George MacDonald. Edited by Roger Lancelyn Green. With illustrations by Arthur Hughes. London: Gollancz, 1961; New York: Franklin Watts, 1961. (Formerly titled *The Light Princess and Other Tales.*)

The Golden Key. With an afterword by W. H. Auden and illustrations by Maurice Sendak. New York: Farrar, Straus, Giroux, 1967.

The Gifts of the Child Christ: Fairy Tales and Stories for the Childlike. 2 vols. Edited by Glenn Edward Sadler. Grand Rapids, Mich.: Eerdmans, 1973, 1980.

CRITICAL AND BIOGRAPHICAL STUDIES

Auden, W. H. "Introduction" to *The Visionary Novels of George MacDonald*, edited by Anne Fremantle. New York: Noonday Press, 1954.

Bulloch, John Malcolm. "A Bibliography of George MacDonald." *Aberdeen University Library Bulletin* 5: 679–747 (February 1925).

Carpenter, Humphrey. "George MacDonald and the Tender Grandmother." In *Secret Gardens: The Golden Age of Children's Literature.* Boston: Houghton Mifflin, 1985.

Chambers, Diana. "The Fairytales of George MacDonald." Unpublished master's thesis: Columbia University, 1951.

Hein, Rolland. *The Harmony Within: The Spiritual Vision of George MacDonald.* Grand Rapids, Mich.: Eerdmans, 1982.

Hutton, Muriel. "Sour Grapeshot: Fault-finding in 'A Centennial Bibliography of George MacDonald.'" *Aberdeen University Review* 41: 85–88 (Autumn 1965).

Lewis, Naomi. "Introduction" to *The Princess and the Goblin* (Harmondsworth, England: Penguin Books, 1964).

Lochead, Marion. *The Renaissance of Wonder in Children's Literature.* Edinburgh: Canongate, 1977.

MacDonald, Greville. *George MacDonald and His Wife.* London: Allen and Unwin, 1924.

MacDonald, Ronald. *From a Northern Window.* London: James Nisbet, 1911.

MacNeice, Louis. *Varieties of Parable.* London: Cambridge University Press, 1965.

Manlove, Colin N. "George MacDonald's Early Scottish Novels." In *Nineteenth-Century Scottish Fiction*, edited by Ian Campbell. New York: Harper, 1979.

————. *Modern Fantasy: Five Studies.* Cambridge, England: Cambridge University Press, 1975.

Sadler, Glenn Edward. "The Cosmic Vision: A Study of the Poetry of George MacDonald." Unpublished Ph.D. diss.: University of Aberdeen, Scotland, 1966.

————. "George MacDonald." In *Twentieth-Century Children's Writers*, edited by D. L. Kirkpatrick. London: St. James, 1978; New York: St. Martin's Press, 1978.

————, ed. " 'The Little Girl That Had No Tongue': An Unpublished Short Story by George MacDonald" *Children's Literature* 2: 18–34 (1973).

Simpson, Alan. "The Fairytales of George MacDonald." Unpublished B.Litt. thesis: Oxford University, 1954.

Wolff, Robert Lee. *The Golden Key: A Study of the Fiction of George MacDonald.* New Haven, Conn.: Yale University Press, 1961.

—GLENN EDWARD SADLER

FREDERICK MARRYAT

1792-1848

LIVING AT A time when England was gaining dominance as a military and economic power, Captain Frederick Marryat was, in his life, in his character, and in his novels, the embodiment of England's self-image. His own life, up to the time he decided on a second career as a writer, had been one long story of adventure, military achievement, and personal glory. He could in all sincerity present to young readers models of the esteemed English virtues—steadfastness and "backbone," which, combined with practical knowledge, ensured survival in alien environments throughout the world; zest for putting one's abilities—and one's life—on the line in combat with hostile nature or savage peoples; and confidence that an Englishman, by virtue of his innate superiority and certainty that God was on his side, was equal to any challenge.

Life was for the most part very good to Marryat. He was born at Westminster on 10 July 1792 into an accomplished and well-to-do family. He was sent to the best schools, but being a high-spirited boy, he spent more time on pranks and other minor rebellions than on his studies. He ran away to sea several times, only to be captured and returned to academic confinement. His father finally relented in 1806, when the boy was fourteen, and purchased him a commission as naval midshipman. Young Marryat's good fortune continued when his father, a man with connections, obtained for him a highly desirable berth on a famous frigate, the *Impérieuse*, commanded by Lord Cochrane, one of England's most brilliant and admired naval captains during England's successful wars against Napole-

onic France. Under this model officer and in company with an engaging set of shipmates, Marryat experienced over fifty exciting naval adventures. The *Impérieuse* was one of the most active of British fighting ships, and Marryat spent the last ten years of the Napoleonic Wars in patrolling, raiding, capturing enemy ships, storming seaside forts, chasing privateers, as well as surviving storms at sea and near shipwrecks. Marryat rose rapidly through the ranks, became a captain of his own ship, and earned many commendations for his achievements and courageous actions, including leaping into the sea on several occasions to rescue shipmates. He also was wounded once in the leg—not seriously, but enough to give him an honorable scar. In all, it was a dashing and glorious period for Marryat. He had, according to one observer, "prepared himself to write sea stories by making his life a sea story." When he decided to retire from active duty in 1830 at age thirty-eight, he had already published his first adult novel and was ready to begin his second career.

Marryat married in 1819 and would in time have a large family—at least nine children (some biographers say eleven)—and he was continually in need of money. On returning to life on land, he launched himself as a man of letters, working from 1830 to 1848 at miscellaneous journalism (editing the *Metropolitan Magazine* from 1832 until 1835, where some of his stories of sea and land first appeared); writing unsuccessful plays; and producing diaries of his trips through the Continent and North America, along with twenty-four novels. He developed a taste for high society and high living; became estranged from his wife during his later years; made bad investments while living beyond his means; and finally retired to his country home at Langham, where he died on 9 August 1848, leaving his last book unfinished.

Regarding the twenty-four works Marryat published, there is little agreement about which are children's books. Some early critics, taking a dim view of stories of adventure and derring-do, claimed that *all* of them were suitable only for childish minds, whereas many fellow writers, like Charles Dickens, William Makepeace Thackeray, Charles Kingsley, and later Joseph Conrad, looked on his writings with favor. Marryat himself designated several—his last works—as intended for "juveniles": *Masterman Ready* (1841–1843), *The Settlers in Canada* (1844), *The Mission; or, Scenes in Africa* (1845), *The Children of the New Forest* (1847), and *The Little Savage* (1848–1849). To these must be added one more, which, while not written expressly for children, became deservedly popular among young readers—*Mr. Midshipman Easy*. Though published in 1836, it has never been out of print.

Marryat had published over a dozen novels intended for adult readers before he decided in 1840 to write "juveniles," giving as his reason his growing interest in such literature and his need to increase his income. But in deciding to write expressly for children, he had to make some changes in his usual style and subject matter. His first adult writings had been semiautobiographical, and in drawing on his own experiences he included many scenes of extreme savagery rendered in realistic detail, as was appropriate to his times and military adventures. This caused some critics to describe his first novels as "disagreeable" stories featuring unsavory heroes. Indeed, one aspect of the early protagonists had to be changed if they were to meet Marryat's conception of heroes for children. Writing, as he was, in the picaresque tradition of Alain Lesage's *Gil Blas* (1715–1735) and Tobias Smollett's novels, the protagonists were also "picaresque"—a rogue's gallery of opportunistic young rascals, likable enough, but essentially lowlifers, obviously lacking in the moral values he wanted to inculcate in his young readers. Similarly, he had shown less talent for depicting genteel young ladies than the women of the docks and the rough-edged "bumboat women" (who sold items from small boats to the crews of ships at anchor).

When Marryat came to write children's books in later years, he had mellowed considerably, had become serene and philosophical, and filled his books with a high-minded morality and charity not typical of his own early life. As one rather sour critic put it, when Marryat moved from hedonism to didacticism, the world lost a "genial rake" and gained a "pietistic bore." There are, to be sure, many long didactic passages in the children's books that critics, if not children, have found boring. But this cannot be said of *Mr. Midshipman Easy*. Marryat had for some time deplored the inaccuracies and ignorance displayed by previous writers dealing with the sea. He thought himself to be, probably with justification, the first realistic "naval novelist," and his prose style is appropriate to his subject: simple and concise, vividly detailed and well salted with nautical terminology, unflinching in its depiction of *facts*, however unpleasant—all served up with relish and enthusiasm.

Mr. Midshipman Easy is a fast-paced tale of a young fellow who, after getting into many humorous scrapes at home, finally pressures his father into buying him a commission as midshipman (as in Marryat's own life). Jack Easy's mother is a vacuous woman who sits dreamily in corners "waiting for the millennium." The father is obsessed with studying the bumps on people's heads and philosophizing about the rights and equality of man—while his own estate is being exploited by the servants. Jack has many edifying experiences at sea, where he finds that the "equality of man" does not apply to a ship's society—or to any other for that matter. He fights the ship's bully, finds a true friend, engages in love affairs with young women in exotic ports of call, fights rather absurd duels and defeats mutineers, survives storms and bloody battles at sea—all described with cheerful zest. He ultimately returns to put his father's estate in order, having learned that the true mission of man is to find his place in the hierarchical social structure and to do his duty in that calling. It also is apparent (as in all Marryat's books) that money and social influence are crucial in getting on in the world—Jack's life is made easy by the availability of pounds sterling.

There are several elements in this story that reappear in his later works for juveniles. Written in the Robinsonnade tradition (the numerous stories inspired by *Robinson Crusoe*), his novels reflect the conviction that life's essential facts and values are to be discovered in a more or less insular situation: during an extended voyage at sea, on a desert island, or in a cottage hidden in a wild forest, for example. Though the young heroes always come from a good family, their parents are invariably dead, missing, or simply ineffective. This accounts for the traditional father figure—the Wise Old Man—who in Marryat's stories assumes the parental role and takes charge. This figure—"the perfect tutor"—had already been introduced to the reading audience in Jean-Jacques Rousseau's "educational novel," *Émile* (1762), and Thomas Day's popular *History of Sandford and Merton* (1783–1789). He appears in *Mr. Midshipman Easy* as Mesty (short for Mephistopheles), a black African with filed teeth who was a chief in his own land but now is pressed into service for the British. Mesty is a combination of the Wise Old Man, who becomes Jack Easy's able tutor in seamanship and survival at sea, and another popular conception of the time, the Noble Savage, who displays virtues far above those of many of the ship's white crew. Marryat portrays Mesty as an exceedingly competent man, and he shows the same regard for Juno, the black servant who cares for the shipwrecked children in *Masterman Ready*. Juno and Mesty are the subjects of a number of passages affirming the innate good qualities of the dark races and of their ability, sooner or later, to raise their national cultures to the level of the Europeans (though, for the time being, they should "know their place" on the social scale, as should all persons, black or white). The Wise Old Man plays the title role in *Masterman Ready*, and he appears as Jacob Armitage in *Children of the New Forest*, Malachi Bone in *The Settlers in Canada*, and, in a rather bizarre and original form, as the malevolent Jackson in the *The Little Savage*.

The plot in Marryat's stories is essentially the same: the children (and sometimes their families) are displaced from their rightful position in society, which includes inherited wealth and land; they are obliged to live in a primitive fashion for an extended period; and then they regain their social positions and inheritances, and make satisfactory marriages—with everyone the better for the learning experience in contact with bare nature.

Masterman Ready was written at the suggestion of Marryat's children, who had so enjoyed his reading to them of Johann Wyss's *The Swiss Family Robinson* (1813) that they begged him to take up the story where Wyss left off. He tried, but as he says in his preface to *Masterman Ready* (reprinted in the Everyman edition), "I found difficulties which were to me insurmountable, and which decided me not to continue that work, but to write another in the same style." The difficulties included Marryat's indignation at Wyss's lack of verisimilitude (which obviously had not bothered his children): the lack of nautical and geographical accuracy and the incorrectness of much of the fauna and flora found on Wyss's island. So Marryat wrote a more "realistic" book but, in the eyes of some critics, a much duller one, making the "mistake of putting didactic ideal above straight-forward story-telling" (Darton).

In *Masterman Ready* the castaways consist of the parents (the Seagraves) and their four children: William, about ten, Tommy, age six, a girl, Caroline, seven, and a baby boy, Albert, along with the trusty old sailor Ready. Their ship had been abandoned by its mutinous crew, who took the ailing and unconscious captain with them; it was driven on the rocks of a remote island that, fortunately, is a veritable Eden in its plenteous natural resources. The story then tells in meticulous detail how the family, in good Crusoe fashion and under the guidance of the knowledgeable Ready, combines the materials salvaged from the wrecked ship with the island's supply of food sources, and converts the place into a comfortable and relatively secure abode—that is, until they are attacked by hostile natives from a neighboring island and saved in the nick of time by the arrival of the now recovered captain in his new ship.

All of the characters are typical of Marryat: the mother is ineffectual and spends most of her time suffering; the father's knowledge of the world is largely theoretical, and he is soon replaced by the practical Ready; similarly the black servant Juno takes over the mother's role. Ready, in his sixties, is the model old sailor, full of knowledge of nature and of the world in general, but modest, religiously devout, self-sacrificing, kindly, and a born teacher. The bulk of the story describes Ready planning, building, improvising, and lecturing, endlessly lecturing, to the children. The eldest child, William, is a receptive student, the model son, who begs Ready for information and expresses his gratitude when he receives it. Tommy, however, is the opposite—a born troublemaker impervious to instruction. Here Marryat is following, and contributing to, the stereotypical Good Boy/Bad Boy pattern, sometimes referred to as the "Saintly Child," who listens, learns, obeys, and generally incorporates the desired virtues, and the "Depraved Child," who embodies all the faults: he is restless, mischievous, greedy (especially regarding food), and in Tommy's case, he torments small animals. Tommy's punishments arise directly from his crimes: for being greedy he is temporarily deprived of food, and for firing the forbidden gun (almost shooting his sister) he suffers for days from the impact of the gun's recoil.

It is inevitable that Ready and Tommy should clash—they are born antagonists—and it is their conflicts that provide much of the interest in the story. Everyone is extremely pious and well mannered, and Tommy, being hopelessly bad, is resistant to his elders' relentless teachings. At times one cannot avoid sympathizing with him, as when "Sunday was devoted to the usual religious exercises. Tommy stole away out of the tent, while Mr. Seagrave was reading a sermon, to have a peep at the turtle soup, which was boiling on the fire." He is, of course, to be deprived of his share of the soup. Only for his last and most serious offense does Tommy escape punishment. When the family is besieged by the hostile natives, Tommy is responsible for a water shortage and Ready is mortally wounded in the attempt to get water. It is interesting that Marryat allows the boy to remain ignorant (at the kindly Ready's own dying request) of his responsibility for the old sailor's death.

Though it has its interesting aspects and was popular in its day, *Masterman Ready* has not worn well. It is not in the same class with Marryat's best children's books; the later ones are less self-consciously moral and didactic.

The Settlers in Canada appeared in 1844, while Marryat's impressions of his visit to that country were comparatively fresh. (He had visited North America in 1838.) In this story an English family, the Campbells, find that they are not the rightful heirs to their land, and so they decide to emigrate to Canada. In addition to the parents, there are four boys: Henry, who attends Oxford; Alfred, a young naval officer on temporary leave of absence; Percival, a twelve-year-old schoolboy, quiet and studious; and John, ten, who provides most of the interest in the story.

The first part of the story deals with the family's ocean crossing and their settling on the northern shores of Lake Ontario. The rest of the book describes their years in the wilderness and provides the vivid details that are Marryat's forte: descriptions of the glories of the Canadian wilds and of the daily lives of the settlers—the clearing of timber, hunting in the snow, fishing in local streams, the long months of winter, a forest fire, problems with bears, and other adventures.

On the whole, things go well until the family returns to England and to their rightful place as country gentry on their own land. The experiences in the wilderness are edifying for all, but especially for young John. A taciturn and independent young fellow, he is a born woodsman and thrives in the forest. He insists at the outset on having his own rifle and fishing pole, and before the end of the first winter he saves his two girl cousins from a hungry wolf that attacks them after having killed Sancho, the faithful old dog that tried to protect them. One of the girls faints while John dispatches the wolf very coolly, but the boy disdains to make much of the incident when his family praises him. And when saved from the swift torrent of a river, where he is fishing in a small boat, he laughs and insists that his swimming ability would have been equal to the dangers. In his rapid learning of the ways of the wilderness, John has the "perfect tutor" in colorful old Malachi Bone, a seasoned veteran who once served as guide to General Wolfe in the Battle of Quebec. And as is customary in Marryat's novels, the entire family profits from wealthy and influential friends, in this case the governor of Quebec and the soldiers from a nearby fort. *The Settlers in Canada* is a lively, well-written story; the narrative moves rapidly, with vivid local color and exciting episodes that hold a young reader's interest.

The only children's book by Marryat that generally has been looked upon as a failure is *The Mission; or, Scenes in Africa*. Marryat had made brief visits to the west coast of Africa, but most of the book was drawn from secondary sources, including the accounts of travelers and explorers, naturalists, and missionaries. The work has little fictional coherence; in fact it is not so much a story as a series of loosely connected incidents centering around a young protagonist who sets out to discover the fate of a lost female relative. The woman had been shipwrecked on the African coast years before, and it is not known if she is living or dead, or if she became a prisoner or worse—the wife of an African native. The young man ultimately finds a white woman living with the Africans, but not the woman he seeks. The story includes some interesting background descriptions—hunting adventures, Zulu warriors, Dutch Boers, and Hottentot children; however, since it is not drawn from Marryat's own experiences, it lacks the solidity and freshness of detail that characterize his other work, and the narrative rambles rather aimlessly. In the opinion of one modern scholar (Warner), "It would be kindest to draw a veil over *The Mission; or, Scenes in Africa*. It is Marryat's one fiasco in the field of juvenile writing."

The last work published during Marryat's lifetime was *The Children of the New Forest*, which is set in the seventeenth century during Cromwell's civil war. In this story Cromwell's men had killed the parents of an aristocratic country family, the Beverleys, and had burned the ancestral home to the ground. The four children, who were thought to have died in the fire, are hidden and raised in a humble cottage buried deep in the New Forest. Their benefactor is the faithful old forester Jacob Armitage, who raises the Beverleys as his own grandchildren and passes on to them his extensive knowledge of the forest. The two boys, Edward and Humphrey (aged thirteen and twelve at the beginning), become experts at capturing small game in traps, wild cows in pits, and ponies in snowdrifts. They also become accomplished stalkers of deer and practiced marksmen. Meanwhile, the girls (Alice, eleven, and Edith, eight) learn their assigned duties, managing the humble household and cooking up venison stews.

A few years later, after numerous adventures in the forest, the story takes a new turn when the older boy, Edward, leaves the cottage in the care of Humphrey (old Armitage having died) and goes to work for a wealthy landowner, Mr. Heatherstone, a halfhearted supporter of Cromwell and a man of much influence. Suspecting that young Armitage is really a Beverley (aristocratic blood will eventually show) and desiring to help him, Heatherstone takes on Edward as his private secretary, one of whose duties is to travel widely delivering messages. This position enables Edward first to fall in love with Heatherstone's beautiful daughter, Patience, and next to fulfill his aim to fight against the Cromwellian murderers of his father. After a quarrel with the benevolent Mr. Heatherstone, Edward leaves abruptly and travels to the Continent and to other parts of England to assist the deposed king. In this Edward shows two traits that biographers have seen in Marryat himself: a shortness of temper and lack of gratitude toward benefactors, along with great courage and fighting ability. Edward ultimately returns to claim the hand of the forgiving (and well-named) Patience, and to preside over the happy marriages of his younger brother and sisters. All then assume their rightful places in local soci-

ety. This story, like *The Settlers in Canada*, is full of specific, practical information to nourish youthful appetites; it offers interesting characterizations of both adults and children (especially Armitage); and it is relatively free of excessive didacticism. The religious teaching in this story, as in all of Marryat's books for children, takes the form of an unquestioning fatalism. The children are counseled by all their mentors to place their faith in God and accept without complaint whatever destinies He, in His infinite wisdom, decrees.

In *The Little Savage* (published posthumously), Marryat returns to the castaway plot. This work, however, is a far cry from *Masterman Ready*. It has been accurately described as a "more vividly imagined tale" than *Ready* and is "the most sincerely emotional of all the Robinsonnades" (Darton). It also offers an interesting and original variation on the castaway pattern in that the relationship between a young boy and his older mentor is one of hostility and brutality. As the story opens, we find five-year-old Frank Henniker living with a sixty-year-old seaman, Edward Jackson, on a guano island off the coast of Peru. They are the two survivors of a shipwreck that occurred several years earlier, and we learn that Jackson had murdered Frank's father, had treated his mother so brutally that she soon died, and had allowed the ship's captain to fall to his death from a cliff when he could have saved him. The boy, who was born on the island, is growing up wild, ignorant, and undisciplined, with a man who bullies him—presenting an imaginative picture of a childhood where the usual (in Marryat's stories) benevolent influence of nature is overshadowed by the presence of an evil adult. In the boy the savagery of the human animal grows unchecked. One day Jackson is blinded by lightning, putting him at the boy's mercy. There are some strong descriptions of Frank's new sense of power, his "cool ferocity," and of the brutality with which he, in turn, treats his former master. But Frank uses his advantage shrewdly: in exchange for food and water, Jackson must teach the boy "everything," beginning with reading and writing. Frank makes rapid progress, until one day Jackson falls over a cliff and dies, in a retributive manner. With the evil adult out of the way, Frank enjoys a relatively pleasant life amid the flowers and wildlife, making pets of seabirds and a seal who later is killed saving him from sharks.

Frank's lonely idyll is interrupted by the arrival of new castaways: a group of roughneck sailors along with a woman, the widow of a missionary. She immediately begins to mother Frank, and when the two are abandoned by the men, they get along quite well while awaiting rescue and return to England. It is made clear that Frank, in later years, will look back on his sojourn on the island as the happiest period in his life.

Marryat died before finishing this book, which was completed (from chapter 3 of the second volume) by his son Frank S. Marryat, who succeeded in duplicating very closely his father's style. However, the latter part of the story is repetitive and less interesting, since the new author reverts to his father's *Masterman Ready* manner. The story becomes didactic, pietistic, and rather tiresome. It is unfortunate that Marryat did not live to complete the work himself. It contains some of his most original writing, and in the realistic depiction of an isolated human being's gradual transformation from a state of savagery to that of relative civilization, he explores a topic of abiding interest—both in Marryat's time and in our own.

Marryat has been credited with being one of the first to write "true literature" for children. Moreover, his stories have one characteristic that should endear them to all young readers: the child protagonists not only are the recipients of lavish attention and tutoring from their wise mentors, but they also enjoy the adults' respect and confidence. They learn rapidly and early are given responsibilities well beyond what a young person might ordinarily expect. They become accomplished and independent, and function creditably (with the exception of Tommy in *Ready*) in the adult world. They even, at times, assume the parental role—a most satisfying experience that appears frequently in subsequent literature for children.

Selected Bibliography

INDIVIDUAL WORKS OF FREDERICK MARRYAT

Several of these editions contain noteworthy introductions and prefaces: W. L. Courtney (*The Little Savage*, 1898), David Hannay (*Masterman Ready*, 1908), Tony Harrison (*The Mission*, 1970), John Seelye (*Masterman Ready*, 1976), and Oliver Warner (*Mr. Midshipman Easy*, 1954).

Mr. Midshipman Easy. London: J. M. Dent and Sons, 1836. Reprinted in Everyman's Library edition. New York: E. P. Dutton, 1906, 1954. Reprinted in paperback. New York: Penguin, 1983.

Masterman Ready; or, The Wreck of the Pacific. With a preface by the author. 3 vols. London: Longman, Orme, 1841–1843. Reprinted in Everyman's Library edition, 1 vol. London: J. M. Dent and Sons, 1907, 1948. Reprinted, with illustrations by Fred Pegram. London: Macmillan, 1908. Reprinted, with illustrations by John Rae. New York and London: Harper and Brothers, 1928. Reprint of original edition, 3 vols. New York: Garland, 1976.

The Settlers in Canada. 2 vols. London: Longman, Brown, 1844. Reprinted in 1 vol. New York: D. Appleton, 1868.

The Mission; or, Scenes in Africa. 2 vols. London: Longman, Brown, 1845. Reprinted New York: African, 1970.

The Children of the New Forest. With illustrations by Frank Marryat. 2 vols. London: H. Hurst, 1847. Reprinted New York: Penguin, 1984.

The Little Savage. 2 vols. London: H. Hurst, 1848–1849. Reprinted in 1 vol. Boston: Dana Estes, 1898.

COLLECTED WORKS OF FREDERICK MARRYAT

The Novels of Captain Marryat. Edited by R. Brimsley Johnson. 24 vols. London: J. M. Dent and Sons, 1895–1896. Reprinted in 22 vols. London: J. M. Dent and Sons, 1896. Reprinted in 24 vols. Darby, Pa.: Arden Library, 1978.

CRITICAL AND BIOGRAPHICAL STUDIES

Biron, H. C. "Captain Marryat" *National Review* 68: 392–401 (1916).

Conrad, Joseph. "Tales of the Sea." In *Notes on Life and Letters.* London: J. M. Dent and Sons, 1949.

Darton, F. J. Harvey. *Children's Books in England: Five Centuries of Social Life.* London: Cambridge University Press, 1932.

Gautier, Maurice-Paul. *Captain Frederick Marryat: L'Homme et l'oeuvre.* Paris: Didier, 1973.

Hannay, David. *Life of Frederick Marryat.* London: Walter Scott, 1889.

Hannay, J. "Sea Novels: Captain Marryat" *Cornhill Magazine* 27: 170–190 (1873).

Iddesleigh, Sir S. H. "Captain Marryat as a Novelist" *Monthly Review* 16: 123–134 (1904). Also in *Living Age* 243/3146: 212–220 (1904).

Lloyd, Christopher. *Captain Marryat and the Old Navy.* New York: Longmans, 1939.

McGrath, Maurice. "A Century of Marryat" *Nineteenth Century* 106/632: 545–555 (1929).

Marryat, Florence. *Life and Letters of Captain Marryat*. 2 vols. London: Richard Bentley and Son, 1872.

Philip, M. "Cultural Myth in Victorian Boys' Books by Marryat, Hughes, Stevenson, and Kipling." Ph.D. dissertation. Bloomington: Indiana University, 1975.

Sadleir, Michael. "Captain Marryat: A Portrait" *London Mercury* 10/59: 495–510 (1924). An abridged version appears in *Yale Review* 32 (or new series 13)/4: 774–789 (1924).

Warner, Oliver. *Captain Marryat: A Rediscovery*. New York: Macmillan, 1953.

———. "Marryat" *Junior Bookshelf* 17/3: 91–94 (July 1953).

Woolf, Virginia. "The Captain's Death Bed." In *The Captain's Death Bed and Other Essays*. London: Hogarth Press, 1950.

—GLENN S. BURNE

CORNELIA MEIGS

1884-1913

NOT ONLY WAS Cornelia Lynde Meigs a prolific writer, but during her long career she was also enormously popular and highly respected. Besides her six books for adults, she wrote for children thirty-eight books and numerous short stories, many of which were republished in children's schoolbooks. Several of her children's books were republished in second editions, and most had numerous printings—some more than twenty. She received the Drama League Prize for her play, *The Steadfast Princess* (1916), the Beacon Hill Bookshelf Prize from Little, Brown for *The Trade Wind* (1927), an honorary doctorate of humane letters from the University of Plano in Texas, and most important, the prestigious Newbery Medal in 1934 for her biography of Louisa May Alcott, *Invincible Louisa* (1933).

Yet now, not much more than a decade after her death, only *Invincible Louisa* and *A Critical History of Children's Literature* (1953), which she edited and to which she contributed, are still in print, and only a very few of her other books can be found on the shelves of even the largest libraries in the country. Nor has she received critical attention. The book reviews, the newspaper articles, and the informal "appreciations" that were all numerous during her lifetime have stopped and have not been followed by articles of more lasting critical value. Biographical information can be found in such expected places as *The Junior Book of Authors* and *Something About the Author*, but little else has been written about her. Meigs seems a remarkably forgotten author.

This general indifference to her work imparts to the usual questions posed by the literary critic a sense of unusual significance. What was Meigs's contribution to children's literature? What is the nature, what is at the heart, of the worlds her books create? Did her writing or her vision have limitations that in part explain why her books have to a great extent dropped out of sight?

Meigs was born on 6 December 1884 in Rock Island, Illinois, the fifth of six daughters born to Grace Lynde and Montgomery Meigs. Her father was a civil engineer in charge of navigation improvements for a section of the Mississippi River. One of her grandfathers was General Montgomery C. Meigs, quartermaster general of the Union Army in the Civil War, friend of Lincoln, and son-in-law of Commodore John Rodgers, who fought in the War of 1812. Meigs grew up in Keokuk, Iowa. Her mother died when she was seven, so her father was the principal figure in her upbringing. He was a gifted storyteller, and as a child Meigs heard many stories about the War of 1812, the exploration and settling of the Midwest, and the Civil War. Her favorites were tales of naval adventure. These adventure stories, however, were not the only ones important to her childhood; with their father assisting as stage designer and audience, she and her sisters staged plays of the lesser-known works of Alcott. Both sides of her family originated in New England, and many summers and some winters were spent in Vermont and Marblehead, Massachusetts. She followed two sisters to Bryn Mawr College, where she was discouraged from majoring in her first choice, English, and settled on a joint major in history and politics/economics, graduating in 1908.

"It was tolerably plain," as she put it, that she would teach; it was less clear that she would write. After two years as principal of a private school in Keokuk, Iowa, she began teaching English at St. Katharine's School in Davenport, Iowa. In a 1968 interview for the *Rutland Daily Herald*, she explained that it was there, trying out stories on the children, that she "drifted into writing." Her first book, a collection of stories, *The Kingdom of the Winding Road*, was published in 1915. From then on she published one or two works almost every year for the next twenty-five years. Many of those books were written for her nieces and nephews, to whom she was very close. Only in the 1940's did the rate of publication slow down.

From 1932 until 1950, except for a leave of absence during World War II to work as an assistant research analyst for the war department signal corps, she taught at Bryn Mawr College. She is credited for introducing American literature into the undergraduate and graduate curricula, but her major work was as a teacher of writing. She became a full professor of English composition in 1947. On her retirement in 1950 she became college historian and professor emeritus of English composition. The following year, she taught writing at the New School for Social Research in New York City. During the last decades of her life she lived in Havre de Grace, Maryland, and spent summers on her farm in Brandon, Vermont. She died at age eighty-eight in 1973.

The Kingdom of the Winding Road and *The Steadfast Princess*, written at the beginning of Meigs's career, are fantasies; several other books have contemporary settings. But the vast majority—including all her best books—take place in the early seventeenth through mid-nineteenth centuries in New England, the mid-Atlantic states, and the Midwest, and on the seas. Without question she helped define the genre of historical fiction for both young readers (ages eight to twelve) and adolescents. Even her books about modern boys and girls often include stories of the historical past. The three boys who solve the mystery in *At the Sign of the Two Heroes* (1920) are inspired by the memory of Ethan Allen and the days of the Green Mountain boys. In *Rain on the Roof* (1925) the stories the old historian and model shipbuilder, John Selwyn, tells his young friends comprise over a third of the book. In responding to a questionnaire sent to her by Bryn Mawr College in 1970, Meigs described herself as a 'writer of historical fiction for young people" and then, almost as an afterthought, added "and some other," lumping together everything else she wrote in a phrase so offhand that it is ungrammatical.

Her historical studies for adults fit in that "some other" category. She was a careful and serious researcher, but even her adult books are for the general public rather than for the scholarly community. Her interest in history was to popularize it; she was less concerned with refining the picture of the past than she was with making the past live for those of the present. "History is only the past looked at as though it were the present," she stated in a short piece for the Junior Literary Guild's publication *Young Wings*. Meigs's books for children feature many great Americans: George Washington, William Penn, Benjamin Franklin, John Adams, the financier Stephen Girard, the inventor Thomas Davenport, the explorer Zebulon Pike, and the botanist John Bartram, to name just a few. But even in those stories that are clearly period pieces—books like *The Willow Whistle* (1931), *Swift Riverss* (1932), *Wind in the Chimney* (1934), and *Vanished Island* (1941), which do not present a great leader or a turning point in American history—there is still a sense of challenge and excitement about whatever era is being portrayed. "To the people who live in any given period," she stated in her *Young Wings* essay, "their times were as crowded, as bewildering, and wonderful as our time is today." That quality of the wonderful, of the significant masked by the everyday, is a key to the tone of Meigs's historical fiction.

It is also consistent with her interest not simply in the past but specifically in the past from the perspective of young people. The child or adolescent, who is rarely an actor in the great historical events, who is even less likely than the adult to understand the full implications of what is happening, and who is more inclined than the adult to wonder, is someone with whom Meigs identified. "It has seemed to me," wrote Meigs for *Young Wings*, "that history, as seen through the eyes of the young people who lived with it, is the most interesting of all to attempt to call back from the past."

Family loyalty is highly valued in her books, but as we would expect from her taste for excitement, Meigs rarely wrote family stories, though there are exceptions, such as *Wild Geese Flying* (1957). She was more interested in adventure than in family interaction, and adventure is most possible when a child is on his or her own. In some of her stories for younger children, there is one parent, usually a mother, who is part of the story. Even in those stories, however, the major events almost invariably take place when the mother is offstage. Moreover, in many books for younger children and in almost all books for older children, parents are absent or, more commonly, dead.

The worlds of her heroes and heroines are dangerous ones. There are political perils: in *The Two Arrows* (1949) Jan and Ronald are unfairly accused of speaking against King George II, are imprisoned, and are sent as bondservants to the New World. There are economic risks: in *Clearing Weather* (1928) the failure of the shipbuilding business that sustains the port town of Branscomb seems inevitable given the depression and economic disorder of the Colonies following the Revolutionary War. There are dangers from Indians: in numerous stories—*The Willow Whistle, The New Moon* (1924), *Railroad West* (1937), *As the Crow Flies* (1927), *Swift Rivers*, and *Clearing Weather*— murderous Indians threaten the survival of the protagonists. There are hazards from the natural world: nature can be disastrously harsh, with its wild animals, its grand but untamed forests, rivers, and mountains, and its fierce storms. (Almost every protagonist fights through at least one snowstorm.) And, finally, in every story there are threats from characters who are at best selfish and weak and at worst downright evil.

In the face of danger and the emotional and physical hardship that accompanies it, fortitude and courage are critical. If they don't begin by being courageous, all of Meigs's protagonists become so in the unfolding of the story. But fully as important as courage is a lack of pettiness, a generosity of spirit. Meigs's good characters are unfailingly generous to their enemies. "Sam Breen is a neighbor and he needs help," says Sarah in *The Covered Bridge* (1936), explaining why she did not prevent her grandson from running off to help the unpleasant, stingy Mr. Breen save his sheep from the swollen, raging stream that has destroyed his shed. She exhibits this generosity despite the fact that Breen has previously gone out of his way to encourage the failure of Sarah's farm. David, in *The Trade Wind*, comes upon the young Englishman with whom he earlier had exchanged blows while defending the rights of Americans. The Englishman is in command of the battleship *Pegasus*, now a sinking hulk, destroyed by the sea battle that has just ended. Far from gloating over the bad luck of a man who previously treated him ill, David exclaims to him, "They say you were in command during the end of the fight. . . . If you could know how I envy you that hour! Ever since I first saw the *Pegasus*, I have dreamed of standing . . . on her quarterdeck, and taking her into action." In *The Willow Whistle* Eric refrains from any response when the imperious Arickaree boy is thrown by his horse, and the narrator tells us, "There was dumb gratitude" in the Arickaree's eyes "when he saw the white boy take it without a smile, when he understood that Eric would not jeer at his fallen state." The heroes in both *Call of the Mountain* (1940) and *Swift Rivers* rescue their enemies from sure death.

In fact, at times the turning points or happy resolutions of Meigs's plots partly stem from or depend upon an incident of unselfish generosity. In *Clearing Weather* the men on the American ship dress the wounds of a man they assume to be one of the pirates who attacked them and whom they have captured, only to find out that he is the great Manchu gentleman and merchant Leung Tsi-pun, with whom they are seeking to trade. Debby in *Wind in the Chimney* has been helping her mother make a Wheel of Fortune quilt in the hope that, given as a gift, the quilt will persuade Mrs. Bowley to let the Moreland family keep the house that means so much to them. When she is told that the matter is settled and the family must leave, she decides to finish the quilt anyway. To finish it in time, alone —her mother is off nursing the ill child of a woman who has been good to them—is an endurance test. But finish it she does, and when she gives the quilt simply as a gift, not as something that will get her what she wants, it does in fact do just that: "Nothing has ever happened to me that has meant more than this," responds Mrs. Bowley. "Oh, God forgive me, for being a selfish, thoughtless woman." In *The Trade Wind* the Americans aboard a schooner give their cargo—lumber, iron, sailcloth —to a British vessel disabled by a fight with the Spanish, even though the British have no means to pay them. As a gesture of appreciation, the British tell the Americans that they may have whatever cargo (unknown to the British) is on the schooner *Pegasus*, the battleship that so unexpectedly came to their defense against the Spanish. The Americans find, however, that the *Pegasus* is filled with the very guns and ammunition they had failed to pick up in England—guns that they thus succeed in bringing back to America to help in the fight for freedom. In *The New Moon* Dick saves the village of his two Sac-and-Fox Indian friends from their enemies the Sioux and carefully keeps his deed a secret from them. But they find out about it and repay him with enormous rewards: not only do the Indians, unknown to the whites, watch over the whites' sheep and kill the nightly marauding wolves, but the Sac-and-Fox chief also pledges that "he and every chief after him" will ensure that David and his friend Thomas Garrity abide in peace.

In one way Meigs's historical fictions are like the fairy tales she wrote at the beginning of her career. Fortitude and generosity win out, and in the end fate is kind to the good. "Your unchanging ideas of honest dealing will get you nowhere" is the parting remark of the mercenary and manipulative trader Gil Surette to Thomas Garrity in *The New Moon*. But Surette is soon murdered by the Indians he has swindled, and Garrity's honesty bears the fruit of security and peace. Meigs's formula implies a profound optimism about both fate and humankind: in the great scheme of things, good outweighs evil. After narrowly escaping being kidnapped to work as a cabin boy, Hugh in *The Dutch Colt* (1952) is told by his friend Timothy, "There are some very evil men along the docks. . . . I should have warned you, but there's usually a friendly soul at hand to give help if you are in any danger."

As in fairy tales, not only is fate kind to the good but also the protagonists do not go through their trials totally alone. Parents are rarely the source of the hero's or heroine's success, but, unlike fairy tales, in Meigs's stories there are frequently parental figures who either pave the way to success or function in a deus ex machina fashion. In *The New Moon* the orphan Dick finds a friend and mentor in the gruff but kindly Thomas Garrity. In *The Two Arrows* the mysterious Adam Farr, former duke of Kinsdale, who years ago escaped to Maryland as an indentured servant, emerges from the deep forest again and again to give advice or to rescue travelers. In *Master Simon's Garden* (1916) the guiding power of Master Simon, a figure of tolerance in the harshly intolerant world of Puritan New England, exerts influence long after his death. Frequently historical figures act in that role—Ethan Allen in *The Covered Bridge*, Thomas Jefferson in *Fair Wind to Virginia* (1955), Stephen Girard in *The Scarlet Oak*

(1938). It is a common pattern in the stories that make up the collection *Young Americans* (1936). In one of these stories, for example, the heroine Sally goes to William Penn for help:

> The moment she caught sight of his broad forehead and kind dark eyes, she knew that this was not merely a heavy, square-shouldered gentleman doing public business at a tall desk, but a very great man who had all the time in the world to give to her troubles.
>
> ("Dixon's Mill")

The conflation of a fairy-tale formula and history inevitably results in a romanticization of American history, an idealization of its leaders. "Is everyone in Washington as kind as this?" asks Hal in *Fair Wind to Virginia* when he realizes how kind George Wythe and Thomas Jefferson have been toward him. "In a free new country men can afford to be kind," replies his friend. Even General Custer, in *Railroad West*, becomes a gallant figure, not "greedy for glory" but "greedy for danger." The narrator ends *Mounted Messenger* (1943) with an elegy that ties the past to the present:

> And that small plan of bringing the colonies together . . . was to become an idea of union—an idea of men's working and living together for the good of all—that was to reach far beyond the bounds of those thirteen colonies. Those three men [Franklin, Adams, Washington] did not live to see it go farther than their own new, brave country. They would have thought us fortunate, we who may live to see it cover all the kingdoms of the earth.
>
> ("Tidings from the West")

Such unbounded optimism, such uncritical assumptions about the American dream sound naive today. It is a naiveté that overlooks the harsher realities and complexities of this country's history, that depends on a rather extraordinary degree of ethnocentricity. Meigs reveals an affinity with the English; in her books set around the time of the Revolutionary War, the blind British king and his self-serving advisers are always at fault, and the other Englishmen are simply misled. In *Master Simon's Garden* the young British soldier Gerald Redpath explains his feelings about the Americans:

> Many such as I came up from the counties far from London, heard that beyond the seas was a company

of ungrateful rebels who wished to make over our Parliament's laws to suit themselves, and so threw ourselves headlong into our country's service. We were amazed, later, to find that we were facing a spirited people who fought for a splendid cause, one that they, and even we ourselves in the end, knew was a just one.

("Quaker Ladies")

Though tolerance is a theme throughout her works, her respect for many European nationalities is not as invariable as it is for the English. In *The Hill of Adventure* (1922) the Scandinavian immigrants settling in the Midwest are regarded with great suspicion. The wise John Herrick feels that they should be welcome, but his condescension is as clear as the others' suspiciousness. " 'We need them,' he insisted. 'We have to help them and teach them; and their children will be good Americans. There are a few like Thorvik who will cause trouble to the end of the chapter, but we can make something of the rest of them.' "

Meigs's sympathy for Native Americans shows itself in the numerous positive Native American characters in her books; in many of the books the theme of tolerance is realized in friendships between white men and Indians. Nonetheless, her image of the American Indian is obviously racist. For Meigs Indians are crafty children, innocent savages; any book that includes Indians gives evidence of this perspective. Chris and Stuart in *Swift Rivers* discover two Indians who are supposed to be on guard but instead are immersed in a game. We are told:

No white man would spend a long night over such a pastime, growing more and more interested and excited with every turn. Indians are like children in their enjoyment of simple pleasures; they are like the wisest of old men in the wit and craft which they can bring to the pursuit of them.

("Lone Tree Crossing")

Dick, we read in *The New Moon*, sees that the Indians

were close akin to these wild birds passing overhead. Life was sweet to them; it was also uncertain. It was made up entirely of a battle to keep alive, an endless struggle against varied enemies, with the result that anything strange to them must seem hostile and dangerous. Since they held their own lives cheap, they so considered the lives of others.

("Katequa")

Dick's two Indian friends are fascinated by the Bible. "We must go very carefully," Thomas Garrity tells Dick. "Do not confuse them by telling them of things that they cannot yet understand." And the book ends with a final "hymn" to the Indians:

But some day, in just that silent fashion, they would journey away to the westward and never return. And it seemed as though they were to carry away with them into oblivion all that was black and sinister in their way of living, and would leave behind them only their brave tradition of simple courage, of steadfast hearts and love for a wild, free life, a tradition that would touch the valley with magic and romance for all time.

("The Bloom of the Year")

Blacks appear in Meigs's books much less frequently, but here, too, she is clearly racist. One of her few black characters is the deckhand Blackbird in *Vanished Island*. "I likes best of everything," he states near the end of the book, "just to shovel coal and to tote bar'ls ashore, one after the other, just so long's nobody don't ask me to count 'em." Even in *Invincible Louisa* Meigs reveals both racial stereotyping and a sense of white superiority when she describes the blacks Alcott sees in Washington. Women with their toddlers hanging at their skirts and their "unending clatter of cheerful talk"; children running errands, stealing anything, but "always cheerily obliging and goodnatured"—all, adults as well as children, are referred to as "lighthearted children of bondage." Alcott "was not shocked by any of them," Meigs writes, "and grew to feel that, novel as they were to her, she understood them."

Sex stereotyping is also very much part of Meigs's world view. The girls in her books tend to love baking or sewing and weaving. They are gifted nurses. They are *always* a few years younger than the boys. They do good things, but things of a different sort than do boys. In a moment when she intensely misses her brother, Prudence in *Mounted Messenger* is comforted by Mr. Franklin: " 'You must muster all your courage, my dear,' he told her. 'It is his part to go adventuring, and yours to wait bravely until he comes home again.' " In *The*

Dutch Colt both Hugh and Gertrude decide to do something to help Mr. Penn. Gertrude sells the doll bed she loves so much, whereas Hugh sets off to find the colt stolen from Penn's barn, tracks it down in the midst of a snowstorm, steals it back, discovers a young girl being mistreated by her aunt and uncle, and helps in her rescue. In *Railroad West* Anne emerges as a girl with integrity, sensitivity, and courage—making her a good match for the hero, Phil. Part of her value, however, lies in her family connections: she is the younger sister of Phil's gifted, dedicated boss. She proves her mettle, moreover, in a particularly female way, by caring for her brother's children under difficult circumstances, and, after nursing one child who is ill with tuberculosis, by falling ill herself and almost dying. The most valued deeds performed by girls are acts of self-sacrifice. Meigs's early play, *The Steadfast Princess*, presents the prototype of this feminine sacrifice. The climax of the plot occurs when Ursala determines to give herself up in place of the prince in order to make peace between the two hostile countries. She is saved by the prince himself, who claims her as his bride.

Meigs's heroines occasionally may be rebellious, but they are never rebels, and with few exceptions they do not seek adventure. Given this image of girls and Meigs's delight in excitement and challenge, it is understandable that there are relatively few heroines at all in her books. Her stories for adolescents typically feature a boy as the central character, and most of these books don't even include a girl in a secondary position. In her stories for younger readers girls are more often present, but even here there are some books without girls, whereas there is none without a boy.

It was not in writing historical fiction but in writing biography that Meigs revealed her interest in the female experience. She wrote two biographies for young people, *Invincible Louisa* and *Jane Addams* (1970). Both Alcott and Addams were strong, independent, successful women, and Meigs clearly underscores these qualities in her biographies. Alcott herself was an extremely influential figure in Meigs's life; it was Alcott's books and journals, she stated in the *Rutland Daily Herald* interview, that inspired her to write. Like Alcott, Meigs grew up in a family of girls, never married, cared for her father until his death, and was devoted to her sisters' children. When she received the Newbery Medal for *Invincible Louisa*,

she accepted it for both Alcott and herself. Alcott was not a conventional woman of her period, and Meigs was obviously drawn to that fact. But in her biography it is striking how much Meigs eschews or tones down the emotional conflicts in Alcott's life—among others, her combative, yet loving, attitude toward her father, her ambiguous relationship with Ladislas Wisniewski (the model for Laurie in *Little Women*), and her complex feelings about her success. For example, at the end of *Invincible Louisa* Alcott is pictured as having achieved not only success but also a rare kind of peace. Meigs ignores, except for occasional oblique references, the bitterness and resentment that characterized Alcott in her last years. *Invincible Louisa* is a fluid, evocative book, but even here there is evidence of Meigs's tendency to avoid or deny unresolved tensions and injustices.

It is as much a mistake self-righteously to condemn the racial and sexual stereotyping in Meigs's work as it is to condone or overlook it. A previous era's blindness is embarrassingly evident to the next generation, though its own blindness is not. The racist and sexist passages cited above do not do justice to the power of many of Meigs's stories. The limitations of her vision at times make her books disturbing and clearly have been instrumental in the decline of her popularity, but she is nonetheless a gifted storyteller, committed to communicating her idealism and her belief in the American experiment. Many of her books—certainly among them *The New Moon*, *The Two Arrows*, and *Invincible Louisa*—continue to be engrossing and moving to modern readers. Those books and more generally her scholarship and her respect and love for both literature and children—shown so visibly in her section of *A Critical History of Children's Literature*—make her stand out as a significant figure in the field of children's literature. She affirmed the importance of developing imaginations capable of identifying with people of the past as well as of the present, and she helped legitimize children's books as literature.

Selected Bibliography

WORKS OF CORNELIA MEIGS

The Kingdom of the Winding Road. With illustrations by Frances White. New York: Macmillan, 1915. (Short stories.)

Master Simon's Garden. With illustrations by John Rae. New York: Macmillan, 1916.

The Steadfast Princess. New York: Macmillan, 1916. (A play.)

At the Sign of the Two Heroes. Written under the pseudonym Adair Aldon. With illustrations by S. Gordan Smyth. New York: Century, 1920.

The Hill of Adventure. Written under the pseudonym Adair Aldon. With illustrations by J. Clinton Shepherd. New York: Century, 1922.

The New Moon: The Story of Dick Martin's Courage, His Silver Sixpence and His Friends in the New World. With illustrations by Marguerite de Angeli. New York: Macmillan, 1924.

Rain on the Roof. With illustrations by Edith Ballinger Price. New York: Macmillan, 1925.

As the Crow Flies. With illustrations by Lester H. Greenwood. New York: Macmillan, 1927.

The Trade Wind. With illustrations by Henry Pitz. Boston: Little, Brown, 1927.

Clearing Weather. With illustrations by Frank Dobias. Boston: Little, Brown, 1928.

The Willow Whistle. With illustrations by E. Boyd Smith. New York: Macmillan, 1931.

Swift Rivers. With illustrations by Forrest W. Orr. Boston: Little, Brown, 1932. (Junior Literary Guild selection.)

The Story of the Author of "Little Women": Invincible Louisa. Boston: Little, Brown, 1933. Published concurrently as *Invincible Louisa: The Story of the Author of "Little Women."* Boston: Little, Brown, 1933. Published in England as *The Story of Louisa Alcott*. London: Harrup, 1935.

Wind in the Chimney. With illustrations by Louise Mansfield. New York: Macmillan, 1934.

The Covered Bridge. With illustrations by Marguerite de Angeli. New York: Macmillan, 1936.

Young Americans: How History Looked to Them While It Was in the Making. With illustrations by Kurt Wiese. Boston: Ginn, 1936. (Junior Literary Guild selection. Short stories previously published in *St. Nicholas*, the *Portal*, the *Target*, and the *American Girl*.)

Railroad West. With illustrations by Helen Hunt Bencker. Boston: Little, Brown, 1937.

The Scarlet Oak. With illustrations by Elizabeth Orton Jones. New York: Macmillan, 1938.

Call of the Mountain. With illustrations by James Daugherty. Boston: Little, Brown, 1940.

Vanished Island. With illustrations by Dorothy Bayley. New York: Macmillan, 1941.

Mounted Messenger. With illustrations by John C. Wonsetler. New York: Macmillan, 1943.

The Two Arrows. New York: Macmillan, 1949.

The Dutch Colt. With illustrations by George and Doris Hauman. New York: Macmillan, 1952.

A Critical History of Children's Literature: A Survey of Children's Books in English from Earliest Times to the Present. Edited and coauthored by Cornelia Lynde Meigs. With essays by Anne Thaxter Eaton, Elizabeth Nesbitt, and Ruth Hill Viguers. New York: Macmillan, 1953. Rev. ed., published as *A Critical History of Children's Literature: A Survey of Children's Books in English*. New York: Macmillan, 1969. (For adults.)

Fair Wind to Virginia. With illustrations by John C. Wonsetler. New York: Macmillan, 1955.

Wild Geese Flying. With illustrations by Charles Geer. New York: Macmillan, 1957. (A shorter version appeared earlier in *Jack and Jill*.)

Jane Addams: Pioneer for Social Justice. Boston: Little, Brown, 1970. (Junior Literary Guild selection.)

CRITICAL AND BIOGRAPHICAL STUDIES

Arbuthnot, May Hill. *Children and Books*. 3rd ed. Glenview, Ill.: Scott, Foresman, 1964. (Later editions contain less material on Meigs.)

Commire, Anne, ed. "Meigs, Cornelia Lynde, 1884–1973." In *Something About the Author: Facts and Pictures About Contemporary Authors and Illustrators of Books for Young People*, vol. 4. Detroit: Gale Research, 1974.

Hier, Joyce. "Miss Cornelia Meigs, 84, Who 'Drifted Into Writing' in 1912, Is Still with It at Her Brandon Farmhouse" *Rutland Daily Herald* (23 August 1968).

Kunitz, Stanley J., and Howard Haycraft, eds. "Cornelia Meigs." In *Junior Book of Authors*. 2nd ed. New York: H. W. Wilson, 1951.

Meigs, Cornelia. "Treasure Hunt" *Young Wings: The Magazine of the Boys' and Girls' Own Book Club*, Junior Literary Guild (November 1936). Later anthologized as "My Treasure Hunt in History." In *Writing Books for Boys and Girls: A Young Wings Anthology*, edited by Helen Ferris. New York: Doubleday, 1952.

Miller, Bertha Mahony. "Cornelia Meigs: America Speaking." In *Newbery Medal Books: 1922–1955*, edited by Bertha Mahony Miller and Elinor Whitney Field. Boston: Horn Book, 1955.

Viguers, Ruth Hill. "Golden Years and Time of Tumult, 1920–1967." In *A Critical History of Children's Literature*, edited by Cornelia Lynde Meigs et al. New York: Macmillan, 1969.

—SUSAN T. VIGUERS

A. A. MILNE

1882-1956

DOROTHY PARKER DID not like A. A. Milne. Reviewing the New York production of his play *Give Me Yesterday* (1924; published as *Success* in Britain, 1923) in 1931, she wrote:

In a shifting, sliding world, it is something to know that Mr. A. A. ("Whimsy-the-Pooh") Milne stands steady. He may, tease that he is, delude us into thinking for a while that he has changed; that we are all grown up now, and so he may be delicately bitter and even a little pleasurably weary, in front of us; and then, suddenly as the roguish sun darting from the cloud . . . he is our own Christopher Robin again, and everything is hippity-hoppity as of old.
(*The Penguin Dorothy Parker*, p. 437)

In many ways this sums up Milne's situation. Although for two decades he was a great success as an essayist, a light versifier, a novelist, and a playwright, his four major books for children (published between 1924 and 1928) have become classics, transcending the core of whimsy that debilitated much of his writing (and that Dorothy Parker found so risible) and casting a shadow over the rest of his career.

He was, however, a match for Parker, for whatever his faults as a writer, Milne could be an excellent critic. When she arrived at page 5 of *The House at Pooh Corner* (1928) Parker—as Milne put it in his autobiography, *It's Too Late Now* (1939)—"delights the sophisticated by announcing . . . 'Tonstant Weader Fwowed Up' (*sic* if I may)." Milne went on very characteristically:

It is inevitable that a book which has had very large sales should become an object of derision to critics and columnists. . . . No writer of children's books says gaily to his publisher, "Don't bother about the children, Mrs Parker will love it." As an artist one might genuinely prefer that one's novel should be praised by a single critic, whose opinion one valued, rather than be bought by "the mob"; but there is no artistic reward for a book written for children other than the knowledge that they enjoy it. For once, and how one hates to think it, *vox populi, vox Dei.*
(*It's Too Late Now*, p. 238)

Here is Milne in a nutshell: slightly disingenuous, somewhat defensively ironic, but always stylistically adept. As a professional writer, he took professional pride in his work, but all accounts, including his own, suggest that he resented the success of the "juveniles": "No artist but hates to be pinned in a groove like a dead and labeled butterfly. . . ." But as his son, Christopher, pointed out, his public deserted him in the late 1930's because "fluency and grace were not enough." However, it may have been that these books were his best work, and it is only very recently that the critical climate has been one to acknowledge that writings for children can stand alongside any other type of writing in terms of status.

The four "classics" (Milne did write a few unsuccessful pieces for children)—*When We Were Very Young* (1924), *Winnie-the-Pooh* (1926), *Now We Are Six* (1927), and *The House at Pooh Corner*—were immediate best-sellers; the first sold five hundred thousand copies in its first ten years. Together the four books have been reprinted approximately three hundred times in Britain alone, and currently they are available (in whole or in part) in thirty-eight British editions. There is also a *Pooh Cook Book;* a translation into Latin, *Winnie ille Pu;* a philosophical treatise, *The Tao of Pooh,* by Benjamin Hoff; and perhaps the most famous of literary-critical satires, Frederick C. Crews's *The Pooh Perplex.* Rather more important, the books have become part of the currency of a culture, classic in the sense that they have provided a common self-image of childhood for several generations; they are part of family culture, passed on as part of ordinary life. This is particularly true of the verses, for to mutter "What *is* the matter with Mary Jane?" or "I do like a little bit of butter to my bread!" (however curious this may be to an outsider) is to identify an "in" joke—to proffer passwords for admission to a cultural secret society.

This is all the more surprising because, of the small handful of undisputed British classics for children (very few can be added to the Alice books, Beatrix Potter's books, *Treasure Island, The Wind in the Willows,* and possibly *Swallows and Amazons*), Milne's are the most obviously period- and class-bound, the most clearly echoic of a world of nannies and nurseries and the middle-class standards of the 1920's, which one might not expect to be popular in these more democratic days. However, to some extent Pooh Bear escapes this periodization. He is, as Margaret Blount has noted, "the first famous fictional bear. . . . All others owe him something." He stands above his origins and surroundings, as critic Marcus Crouch explains: "In his creation of Pooh [Milne] proved himself one of the supreme myth-makers, for Pooh has proved to be one of those rare characters who develop an existence apart from the books in which they are born."

Rather than being a barrier, the datedness of the language (and of the costumes in the illustrations) seems to have added to the books' appeal. As well as remaining consistently popular with children, they have also enjoyed a series of vogues with adults as Milne's brand of sentimentality and wit has moved in and out of fashion. But they have been sustained by Milne's initial approach. Although taking on what he admitted to be the difficult task of restricting his vocabulary, he did not write down to children. Equally, he had a surprisingly unsentimental view of childhood that, ironically enough, has made his work for children more palatable in the long run than the soft centers of his plays and novels.

Of his thirty-four plays, only four remain in print in Britain (and three of these are usually classified as works for children); of his six novels, only *The Red House Mystery* (1922) survives; and of the three volumes of verse, three volumes of short stories, and approximately nineteen volumes of essays and miscellaneous writing, only *If I May,* from 1920, is still available. But the four Christopher Robin/Pooh books, together with the "adopted" children's book *Once on a Time* (1917) and the adaptation *Toad of Toad Hall* (1929), are perennial successes and sustain Milne's reputation, even if it is not the one he might have wanted.

"It was Milne's misfortune, as a writer if not as a man, to lead a singularly uneventful life." Thus wrote the critic Thomas Burnett Swann, but such a judgment seems to be based on too literal a reading of Milne's misleadingly low-key autobiography. A man who was assistant editor of *Punch* at twenty-four, who saw action as a signaling officer in France in World War I, who was sent home with trench fever, who became an intelligence officer, who after the war became a successful playwright and novelist, and who then went on to make a worldwide reputation as a children's writer can scarcely be said to have had an uneventful time.

Milne's explanation of what might be taken as a rather depressing title for his autobiography is typically clear-sighted: "It means that heredity and environment make the child, and the child makes the man, and the man makes the writer; so that it is too late now—it was probably too late forty years ago—for me to be a different writer."

But that was written in 1938–1939, when he could also say, "It has been my good fortune as a writer that what I have wanted to write has for the most part proved to be saleable"—a situation that did not continue. *It's Too Late Now* is engaging and amiable (except for some rather jaundiced remarks on the fame brought by Pooh and on trends in modern writing); it is also subtly evasive about his personal relationships, especially with his son.

Alan Alexander Milne was born in London and attended a private school run by his father (a self-made man whom he greatly admired); in his autobiography Milne re-creates the school vividly, complete with its science master, who was for a time H. G. Wells. He records his love for his elder brother, Ken, with whom he played and walked and cycled and who later collaborated with him on (unpublished) verses. (Ken died in 1929—a fact not recorded in the autobiography.) Both boys went on to Westminster School, and from there

Ken became (unhappily) a soliciter, and Alan entered Trinity College, Cambridge, to read mathematics. There he edited the *Granta* (his work on this magazine brought him to the attention of the editors of *Punch*) and disappointed his father by taking only a third class honors degree.

He moved to London and became a free-lance writer, selling his first piece, a parody of Sherlock Holmes, to *Vanity Fair.* Just as his money was running out, he began to establish himself as a writer of light verse and articles, and in 1906 he was appointed assistant editor of *Punch;* in 1910 he was invited to join the famous *Punch* table. His own description of himself at this time gives some indication of the kinds of things he was writing:

> [My] levity was no mask put on for the occasion. The world was not then the damnable world which it is today; it was a world in which imaginative youth could be happy without feeling ashamed of its happiness. I was very young, very lighthearted, confident of myself, confident of the future. I loved my work; I loved not working; I loved the long weekends with the delightful people of other people's delightful houses. I loved being in love, and being out of love and free again to fall in love.
>
> (*It's Too Late Now*, p. 197)

Milne's account of the war is as brief as he could make it, reminiscent in tone of that of Ian Hay in *The First Hundred Thousand.* "It makes me almost physically sick," he wrote, "to think of that nightmare of mental and moral degradation"—and this feeling, which led him to write pacifist pamphlets before World War II, led him to minimize his involvement. Rather, he writes about his first "novel," *Once on a Time,* and the first of his plays, *Wurzel-Flummery* (1921).

Of his plays (with one exception), little need be said here. There is no doubt that Milne was a careful theatrical craftsman, but after the early promise of *Mr. Pim Passes By* (1921), which was a great success in 1920, his invention seems to have failed him. As early as 1923, George Jean Nathan could class him as a "lesser British playwright" and say of Milne's plays that "the net impression . . . is a sense of having been present at a dinner party whereat all the exceptionally dull guests have endeavored to be assiduously amusing."

After 1920 only *The Truth About Blaydes* (1921) is worthy of note, apart from two plays removed into the realm of fantasy—*Portrait of a Gentleman in Slippers* (1926) and *The Ivory Door* (1929)—and, of course, his adaptation of Kenneth Grahame's *The Wind in the Willows, Toad of Toad Hall.* The first two are set in the idealized medieval/Arthurian fairytale world of *Once on a Time,* which also occasionally appears in *When We Were Very Young* and *Now We Are Six; Toad of Toad Hall* is an excellent example of his stagecraft.

As is usual when he is playing critic, Milne's introduction to this play is well thought out and sensible. As John Rowe Townsend notes, the play "is excellent Milne but doubtful Grahame, though Grahame seems to have approved of it," and in his introduction Milne dramatized the book from the point of view of a great enthusiast: "I have, I hope, made some sort of entertainment, with enough of Kenneth Grahame in it to appease his many admirers and enough of me in it to justify my name upon the title page."

The problem is, of course, that *The Wind in the Willows* is a very complex book, a mixture of idyll and mysticism, low and high comedy, nostalgia and adventure, and the "animals" change their size and characteristics to suit the moment. Milne appreciated this:

> Of course I have left out all the best parts of the book; and for that, if he has any knowledge of the theatre, Mr Grahame will thank me. . . . There are both beauty and comedy in the book, but the beauty must be left to blossom there, for I, anyhow, shall not attempt to transplant it.
>
> (*Toad of Toad Hall*, pp. v–vi)

With considerable skill, he telescopes Toad's adventures into three acts, either using Grahame's dialogue or neatly echoing its tone. He even manages to include a miniature of the "Dulce Domum" episode, Mole's nostalgic return to Mole End, which would be far too static and reflective to be staged. Despite the fact that Grahame's biographer Peter Greene disapproved of the play, it distills Grahame's comedy and adds a good deal of wit. Marcus Crouch suggests that "to some extent he did injury to the original book by the mere fact of his success, but however far from the spirit of *The Wind in the Willows, Toad of Toad Hall* was, and remained, one of the few really satisfactory plays for children." Unlike Milne's later attempt to adapt *Pride and Prejudice* for the stage, as *Miss Elizabeth Bennet* (1936), *Toad of Toad Hall* stands as a success on its own terms.

But Milne was a literary polymath, and we should not overlook his contribution to the genre of the mystery novel, *The Red House Mystery.* "I wondered," he wrote, "if I could write a detective story about real people in real English," and the result was an amiable work somewhat in the manner of E. C. Bentley's classic *Trent's Last Case.* It makes Milne's best use of the conventional country-house setting, the manly "adventurer," Anthony Gillingham, and his Watson, the not un-Pooh-like Bill Beverly; and its sustained ingenuity has given it a lasting place in the history of that genre.

The relationship between real life and books is at best a tenuous one, and Christopher Milne, with unique authority, points out in his autobiography, *The Enchanted Places,* where his father made direct use of experience in the four children's books. He was the real Christopher Robin, and he suffered a good deal from his fame and from the recordings he made of some of the verses when he was seven. The songs taken from *When We Were Very Young,* perhaps especially "Buckingham Palace," have had lasting significance to generations of children; to Christopher Robin, they were not so entertaining. A. A. Milne claimed that "the publicity which came to be attached to 'Christopher Robin' never seemed to affect us personally," but Christopher Milne explains that what could be kept outside the nursery door could not be kept at bay when he went away to school:

> I vividly recall how intensely painful it was to me to sit in my study at Stowe while my neighbours played the famous—and now cursed—gramophone record remorselessly over and over again. Eventually, the joke, if not the record, worn out, they handed it to me, and I took it and broke it into a hundred fragments and scattered them over a distant field.
>
> (*The Enchanted Places*, p. 164)

Christopher's relationship with his father seems to have been a good one despite the distance imposed by nursery and nanny (as a small child Christopher had only "occasional encounters" with his parents each day). Milne himself wrote, "I am not inordinately fond of or interested in children. . . . I have never felt in the least sentimental about them," but while this may say something about why his children's books have succeeded, it should not be taken as a comment on the real relationship between father and son. (It must be said, however, that apart from an enviable fluidity and elegance of style, both Milnes share a considerable reticence about their feelings.)

The House at Pooh Corner marked, as Christopher Milne puts it, his father's meridian, and his later short stories, novels, and plays were not successes. He may, as Swann says, have been "a happy man but a misplaced writer," or it may have been, as his contemporary Frank Swinnerton wrote of the plays, that "at times his invention is meagre; it is always hampered by a lack of boldness." Certainly the rather scathing conservative comments on the modern world at the end of *It's Too Late Now* suggest a man becoming increasingly uneasy with his world.

In the introduction to *Books for Children,* produced by the National Book League in 1948, Milne warns us, as Elaine Moss points out, "against believing that a book is a *children's* classic if in reality our own pleasure in it has grown through rereadings as we mature." Perhaps we should bear this in mind when approaching Milne's own "classic" works.

We may begin with a book "adopted" by children—or at least appearing on the children's lists—the book Milne dictated to his wife, Daphne, in 1916–1917: *Once on a Time.*

"There are," Milne wrote in *It's Too Late Now,* "I think, some good things in it, but few people have read it, and nobody knows whether it is meant for children or for grown-ups. I don't know myself. But it was the greatest fun to do." In the introduction to the original edition, he was more definite: "This is not a children's book. I do not mean by that . . . 'Not for children' . . . nor do I mean that children will be unable to appreciate it. . . . But what I do mean is that I wrote it for grown-ups. More particularly for . . . my wife and myself."

Set in a fairy-tale land reminiscent of William Makepeace Thackeray's "pantomime" *The Rose and the Ring* (indeed, both books begin with breakfast scenes), a land that combines a modicum of magic and a measure of mild satire, Milne tried to do for the fairy story what he later did for the detective story—to introduce character. Despite the generic characteristics, and whatever the marketing strategy (it was reissued by the New York Graphic Society in 1962, and by Puffin Books in Britain in 1968—two publishers with very different audiences in mind), the audience addressed is clearly adult. The villainous Lady Belvane, for example, reminds the narrator of someone he met "at a country house in Shropshire last summer," and her diary may well reflect a more adult than childlike wit: *"Monday, June first. . . . Became bad. . . . Tuesday,*

June second. . . . Realized in the privacy of my heart that I was destined to rule the country. . . . *Wednesday, June third.* Decided to oust the Princess. *Thursday, June fourth.* Began ousting."

The narrator constantly criticizes his main "historical" source, the history of Euralia by Roger Scurvilegs, and he is ironic at the expense of the inadequate Prince Udo and gently romantic over the hero, Coronel. Despite these obviously adult-oriented elements, it seems that this moderately whimsical (if occasionally inventively weak) tale will no longer be read by an adult audience. It is not simply that adults will now be out of sympathy with whimsy. Rather the label "fairy tale," as Tolkien put it, "banishes it to the nursery." Unfortunately, any child sophisticated enough to understand it would probably be ready for less esoteric introductions to the adult world—and thus its readership will always be restricted.

When We Were Very Young began life with the poem "Vespers," which was first published in *Vanity Fair* and which now resides in the Queen's Dolls' House Library. (Milne gave the rights to his wife—"the most expensive present I had ever given her.") He was then asked by Rose Fyleman to contribute some verses to her new magazine, *The Merry-Go-Round,* an offshoot of Basil Blackwell's pioneering annual *Joy Street.* His first effort was "The Dormouse and the Doctor": "There once was a Dormouse who lived in a bed/ Of delphiniums (blue) and geraniums (red). . . ."

The book that grew from these beginnings is a remarkable mixture, ranging from very limited period pieces to pastorals, comedies, and celebrations of childhood. The wide range of sophisticated verse forms reflects Milne's strongly held view that light verse was a *craft* (hence his dislike of "modern" experimental "free" verse):

> Whatever else they lack, the verses are technically good. The practice of no form of writing demands such a height of technical perfection as the writing of light verse. . . . *When We Were Very Young* is not the work of a poet becoming playful, nor of a lover of children expressing his love, nor of a prose-writer knocking together a few jingles for the little ones; it is the work of a light-verse writer taking his job seriously even though he is taking it into the nursery.
>
> (*It's Too Late Now*, p. 239)

The influences upon Milne have been variously suggested as Mother Goose, Hilaire Belloc, Christina Rossetti, and Robert Louis Stevenson. Certainly Milne shares some of their characteristics, but perhaps a more apt comparison might be with Walter de la Mare, whose slightly off-key tone of mystery is found in *When We Were Very Young* in pieces like "The Wrong House," "Before Tea," and the odd, if deservedly famous, "Disobedience." In this last, James James Morrison Morrison Weatherby George Dupree's mother puts on her golden gown and goes to the end of the town without him—and she "hasn't been heard of since." There is a leap from naturalism to a fairy-tale world in which King John and the court put up a notice, and James James offers what Milne himself pointed out was an egocentric observation: he "told his / Other relations / Not to go blaming *him.*" The adult reader, at least, is left with a disconcerting number of unanswered questions.

But generally, as Sheila Egoff observes, "Milne's own individual talent . . . lies in a keen-edged, comic delight in excessive word play and witty rhyme and an adroit skill with metric patterns." In fact, any enthusiast might be tempted to fill the remaining pages of this article with quotations—again, tokens of admission to a secret society. There are such classic comedies as "The King's Breakfast" or "Bad Sir Brian Botany" (a positively revolutionary tale in which the villagers get their revenge: "Sir Brian had a battleaxe with great big knobs on / He went among the villagers and blipped them on the head . . .") or "Rice Pudding":

> *What* is the matter with Mary Jane?
> She's perfectly well and she hasn't a pain,
> *And it's lovely rice pudding for dinner again!!*
> What *is* the matter with Mary Jane?
>
> (p. 51)

Others have an even more exclusively middle-class air about them: "Buckingham Palace," "Hoppity," and those based on observed childhood, such as "Lines and Squares." Oddly, those that try to express freedom and energy, like "Spring Morning" and "Puppy and I," seem more labored, while "Nursery Chairs" is reminiscent of the worst of Robert Louis Stevenson's *A Child's Garden of Verses* in its archness and artificiality. But if Milne's use of secondhand materials (such as nursery rhymes) is distinctly uneasy, he can produce striking moments of his own, even if they are not of the kind one might ordinarily associate with verse for the very young—for example, from "The Invaders": "Between their shadows and the sun,/ The cows come slowly, one by one. . . ."

For the uninitiated, "Vespers" probably crystallizes the whole problem of Milne. Widely berated for sentimentality, it has frequently been parodied, perhaps most unkindly by the British humorist J. B. Morton ("Beachcomber"). Morton campaigned against what he called "Woogie-Poogie-Boo" books (inventing titles like *When We Were Very Silly*); perhaps the best example of his parody is this verse:

> NOW WE ARE SICK.
> Hush, Hush,
> Nobody cares!
> Christopher Robin
> Has
> Fallen
> Down-
> Stairs.
> (*The Best of Beachcomber*, p. 74)

The real text of "Vespers" begins (perhaps with rather too many "littles"):

> *Little boy kneels at the foot of the bed,*
> *Droops on the little hands little gold head,*
> *Hush! Hush! Whisper who dares!*
> *Christopher Robin is saying his prayers.*
> (p. 99)

Milne defended this and other poems as being "sentimentalized over" by others. "I am glad," he explained, "for the spectacle in real life of a child of three at its prayers is . . . calculated to bring a lump to the throat. But, even so, one must tell the truth about the matter." The truth is that prayers really mean nothing to the child, and he is expressing duty and the "superegotism" of total security rather than love. This is not a personal poem despite the use of the name Christopher Robin; it is a general and somewhat cynical statement about childhood. All this may seem disingenuous to us at this distance, but fashions in sentiment change. Perhaps the problem is, as with Pooh, that we have here an observer as well as an observed: the child's voice or thoughts may be true or blameless enough; it is the adult who is suspect.

Shrewd as are Milne's prefaces to his plays and to other people's books, the introductions to his four children's books are uniformly poor; the very personal introduction to *When We Were Very Young* presents us with a serpentine and mystifying tale of

Christopher Robin and a swan called Pooh. Fortunately, the introduction for *Now We Are Six* is slightly better, and this second collection of verse is also better in general; it includes a similar mixture of styles, but there are fewer failures. Again there are the extended comedies—"King John was not a good man / He had his little ways" or "The Knight Whose Armour Didn't Squeak"; a rather higher proportion of childhood-observed verses like "Busy," "Sneezles," and "The Good Little Girl" ("Have you been a *good* girl, Jane?"); and some small gems like "Buttercup Days":

> Where is Anne?
> Close to her man.
> Brown head, gold head,
> In and out the buttercups.
> (p. 29)

Or "A Thought":

> If I were John and John were Me,
> Then he'd be six and I'd be three.
> If John were me and I were John,
> I shouldn't have these trousers on.
> (p. 69)

Again, there are echoes of de la Mare ("The Little Black Hen" recalls "Off the Ground") and Stevenson ("Swing Song" recalls "The Swing"), but *Now We Are Six* can stand on its own as less dated, more thoughtful, and just as varied and ingenious as its predecessor.

Which brings us to *Winnie-the-Pooh.* Although, like many childhood classics, it has to be approached through a thicket of pleasant associations, the first thing that strikes the adult, soberly rereading it, is how initially inaccessible the stories are. They are buffered by a particularly cumbersome "frame" that, one suspects, is ignored by most readers. As Crouch rather charitably puts it, "The stories began, rather uncertainly, as a kind of private family joke, but Pooh, like all really original characters, took charge and lifted the writing onto a different plane."

Winnie-the-Pooh begins with another "private" introduction in which the toy animals address the author. This immediately undermines the delicate relationships among author, readers, and characters, and it is followed by an opening chapter scarcely distinguishable from the worst of modern computer-printed gift books, in which a specific child's name is inserted on request. (Christopher Robin—a "real" person—is dragged artificially into the fantasy world. When Pooh, in the first story, thinks of Christopher Robin, the real Christopher Robin is allowed to interject, rather embarrassingly: " 'Was that me?' said Christopher Robin in an awed voice, hardly daring to believe it.") Fortunately, apart from occasional short intrusions, this device disappears. Similarly, in the sequel, *The House at Pooh Corner,* apart from an equally inept introduction (which announces somewhat prematurely, in the third line, that the characters are now going to say goodbye), the characters are left in peace.

Christopher Robin becomes absorbed into simple stories of toy animals playing in an idyllic forest, and he generally acts as an omnipotent *deus ex machina*—which may account in some small measure for the popularity of the books. The characters grew out of the real Christopher Robin's real toys (which now reside in Dutton's offices in New York). Milne describes their origins very succinctly in a famous passage:

> My collaborator [as he called his wife] had already given them individual voices, their owner by constant affection had given them the twist in their features which denoted character, and [Ernest] Shepard drew them, as one might say, from the living model. . . . Only Rabbit and Owl were my own unaided work.
>
> (*It's Too Late Now*, p. 241)

Despite his assertion in the introduction to *Once on a Time* that in children's books "if character is to be drawn, it must be done broadly, in tar or whitewash," the characters in the Pooh books are remarkably subtle, given the few words that Milne has available to him, and are shown best in interaction rather than action. To say that Pooh is "a Bear of Very Little Brain," that Piglet is timid, Rabbit bossy, Eeyore gloomy, Tigger bouncy, and Kanga motherly, is to underestimate them. Pooh, who first appeared as the Teddy Bear in *When We Were Very Young* ("He gets what exercise he can / By falling off the ottoman"), has a more complex character than might be supposed. He is not generally very bright—although he has flashes of inspiration—and while he is uniformly amiable, he is also egocentric and greedy. Piglet, who finds it hard to be brave, being such a small animal, acts as his foil in some of the best comic moments:

> "Look, Pooh!" said Piglet suddenly. "There's something in one of the Pine Trees."
>
> "So there is!" said Pooh, looking up wonderingly. "There's an Animal."
>
> Piglet took Pooh's arm, in case Pooh was frightened.
>
> "Is it One of the Fiercer Animals?" he said, looking the other way.
>
> Pooh nodded.
>
> "It's a Jagular," he said.
>
> At this point the Jagular, which is really Tigger and Roo, treebound, calls to them.
>
> "Help! Help!" it called.
>
> "That's what Jagulars always do," said Pooh, much interested. "They call 'Help! Help!' and when you look up, they drop on you."
>
> "I'm looking *down,*" cried Piglet loudly. . . ."
>
> (*The House at Pooh Corner*, pp. 63–64)

Similarly, Rabbit, who has ideas behind which lurks a certain malice (like getting rid of Kanga and Tigger), is best viewed in contrast to Owl, who, in a small splash of literary irony, is hard put to live up to the traditional image of his race. When Rabbit takes Christopher Robin's famous notice "GON OUT / BACKSON / BISY / BACKSON" to Owl for interpretation, we can appreciate the predicament of many a child, slightly outgunned:

> Owl took Christopher Robin's notice from Rabbit and looked at it nervously. He could spell his own name, WOL, and he could spell Tuesday so that you knew it wasn't Wednesday, and he could read quite comfortably when you weren't looking over his shoulder and saying "Well?" all the time and he could—
>
> "Well?" said Rabbit. . . .
>
> Owl looked at him, and wondered whether to push him off the tree; but, feeling that he could always do it afterwards, he tried once more to find out what they were talking about.
>
> (*The House at Pooh Corner*, p. 77)

This is sophisticated writing, the pace, the timing, and the narrative stance all contributing to the comic effect. The subtlety of Milne's control is shown with Eeyore, the dispirited donkey whose gloom is so blatantly egocentric that it very rarely invokes much sympathy. It is interesting to note how closely the authorial voice monitors and tags the dialogue by inserting, in Eeyore's case, more "speech attributions" than are necessary, thus emphasizing the egocentricity. Take the occasion of Eeyore's birthday:

"Good morning, Pooh Bear," said Eeyore gloomily. "If it *is* a good morning," he said. "Which I doubt," said he.

"Why, what's the matter?"

"Nothing, Pooh Bear, nothing. We can't all, and some of us don't. That's all there is to it."

"Can't all *what?*" said Pooh, rubbing his nose. . . .

"Bon-hommy," went on Eeyore gloomily. "French word meaning bonhommy," he explained. "I'm not complaining, but There It Is."

Pooh's response to all this, as those commentators who see him as a mystic bear have been delighted to point out, is to hum a small piece of nonsense (and one which has passed into British folklore):

"Cottleston, Cottleston, Cottleston Pie.
A fly can't bird, but a bird can fly.
Ask me a riddle and I reply:
Cottleston, Cottleston, Cottleston Pie."

"That's right," said Eeyore. "Sing. Umty-tiddly, umpty-too. Here we go gathering Nuts and May. Enjoy yourself."

"I am," said Pooh.

(*Winnie-the-Pooh*, pp. 65–68)

Within the society of the animals there is a hierarchy, with Tigger and Roo taking the parts of the smaller children. Milne, with his sharp eye for childhood, thus allows the child reader to feel superior and to sympathize. Roo, for example, asks his mother if he may go out the next day:

"We'll see," said Kanga, and Roo, who knew what *that* meant, went into a corner and practised jumping out at himself, partly because he wanted to practise this, and partly because he didn't want Christopher Robin and Tigger to think that he minded when they went off without him.

(*The House at Pooh Corner*, pp. 119–120)

The implied reader can thus be an adult or a child, and it is not simply that Milne is able to address two levels of readers; rather, the accuracy of the characterization makes the toys approachable from a variety of readers' levels. This may in turn, as Margery Fisher points out, be a function of the characters' origins:

[Pooh has a] bumbling, loving personality which owed as much to the child's imagination as to the father's invention. Of all the characters . . . Pooh

shows this dual origin most plainly. Piglet's diffidence, his tremulous courage, suggest a mainly adult personalization, and certainly Eeyore's alarmingly gloomy nature, bitterly self-deprecating comments and the embarrassingly incoherent orations he occasionally delivers are not characteristics that a child would claim for a toy, without some prompting.

(*Who's Who in Children's Books*, p. 380)

As with the verses, many of the episodes have passed into the national argot: the heffalump, playing Poohsticks, or the "expotition" to the North Pole. The forest in which the animals play, based in the immediate surroundings of the Milnes' country home, Cotchford Farm in Sussex (which can be seen in Shepard's illustration for "Buttercup Days"), is the equivalent of the nursery and its London surroundings: it has the same underlying security, the same air of eternal innocence, and the same disregard for the niceties of probability. It is, in its way, another forest of Arden.

The House at Pooh Corner, in which we learn what Christopher Robin does in the mornings and in which he and Pooh come to that enchanted place between play and reality, is only partially successful in introducing the problem of growing up. Christopher Robin, "Still with his eyes on the world . . . put out a hand and felt for Pooh's paw." He then fumbles for words to explain, touchingly enough, why it is that he has to go away, and to leave his toys —in effect to take the life that he gives them away from them. But the reader may well be left with only the fumbling. Once again Milne, by trying to direct his fantasy, comes close to fracturing what is, after all, quite a delicate illusion.

In these books Milne was fortunate in his illustrator, Shepard, whose work he is said to have disliked at first. Just as Shepard's drawings for *The Wind in the Willows* have not been seriously challenged by the plethora of recent new editions, so his drawings for the Milne books seem unlikely to be displaced, as Disney's curiously characterless efforts have shown.

Serious if not solemn criticism of Milne tends to labor under the shadow of *The Pooh Perplex*. Crews's satire may warn us away from too much speculation about the origins of Eeyore's character (was he based on the *Punch* editor Owen Seaman or on Milne himself, with his predilection for gloomy workrooms?) or about whether the name of the most nervous beetle, Alexander, is entirely

404

accidental. But it should not take us to the extreme of Townsend, who observes: "The Pooh stories are as totally without hidden significance as anything ever written." They are still the complex work of a complex man, and they include a fascinating series of subtexts that can tell us a lot about the relationships of child, adult, story, and book. Crews uses his insights for humor, but it would be doing Milne an injustice if we did not at least consider recuperating some of those insights in order to sharpen our reading. It may sound pompous to say so, but a genuine critical examination of the books is long overdue.

Milne has been described as a "lightweight of true quality" and as having "perfect vision out of a small window"; in his four children's books his skill and vision were well matched. In *It's Too Late Now* he remarked that "childhood is not the happiest time of one's life, but only to a child is pure happiness possible." Milne has secured his place in literature by contributing to such happiness.

But perhaps Pooh should have the last word— and a word that, like the best children's literature, is profound in its simplicity. At the end of *Winnie-the-Pooh,* Pooh and Piglet are left alone in the golden evening:

"When you wake up in the morning, Pooh," said Piglet at last, "what's the first thing you say to yourself?"

"What's for breakfast?" said Pooh. "What do *you* say, Piglet?"

"I say, I wonder what's going to happen exciting *to-day?*" said Piglet.

Pooh nodded thoughtfully,

"It's the same thing," he said.

(pp. 144–145)

Selected Bibliography

WORKS OF A. A. MILNE

A full bibliography of the works of A. A. Milne can be found in *Twentieth-Century Children's Writers,* edited by D. L. Kirkpatrick. London: St. James, 1978; New York: St. Martin's Press, 1978.

Works for Children

Once on a Time. London: Hodder and Stoughton, 1917; Harmondsworth, England: Penguin Books, 1968. (Though this book was not written for children, it has been "adopted" by them. Pages cited in text are from the Penguin edition, now out of print.)

When We Were Very Young. London: Methuen, 1924; New York: Dutton, 1924.

Winnie-the-Pooh. London: Methuen, 1926; New York: Dutton, 1926. Published in Latin as *Winnie ille Pu.* Translated by Alexander Lenard. New York: Dutton, 1984.

Now We Are Six. London: Methuen, 1927; New York: Dutton, 1927.

The House at Pooh Corner. London: Methuen, 1928; New York: Dutton, 1928.

Toad of Toad Hall. London: Methuen, 1929; New York: Charles Scribner's Sons, 1929. (A play. Pages cited in the text are from the third Methuen edition, 1931.)

Other Works

By Way of Introduction. London: Methuen, 1929; New York: Dutton, 1929. (Essays.)

It's Too Late Now. London: Methuen, 1939. Also published as *Autobiography.* New York: Dutton, 1939.

CRITICAL AND BIOGRAPHICAL STUDIES

Blount, Margaret. *Animal Land.* London: Hutchinson, 1974.

Crews, Frederick C. *The Pooh Perplex.* Milton Keynes, England: Robin Clark, 1979.

Crouch, Marcus. *Treasure Seekers and Borrowers.* London: Library Association, 1962.

Egoff, Sheila, ed. *Thursday's Child: Trends and Patterns in Contemporary Children's Literature.* Chicago: American Library Association, 1981.

Fisher, Margery. *Who's Who in Children's Books.* London and New York: Weidenfeld and Nicolson, 1975.

Hoff, Benjamin. *The Tao of Pooh.* London: Methuen, 1982.

Milne, Christopher. *The Enchanted Places.* London: Eyre Methuen, 1974.

Morton, J. B. *The Best of Beachcomber.* Harmondsworth, England: Penguin Books, 1966.

Moss, Elaine. "A. A. Milne on Books for Children" *Signal* 44: 89–92 (May 1984).

Parker, Dorothy. *The Penguin Dorothy Parker.* New York: Viking Press, 1973.

Stewart, Katie. *The Pooh Cook Book.* London: Methuen, 1971.

Swann, Thomas Burnett. *A. A. Milne.* New York: Twayne Publishers, 1971.

Swinnerton, Frank. *The Georgian Literary Scene.* London: J. M. Dent and Sons, 1938.

Townsend, John Rowe. *Written for Children.* Harmondsworth, England: Penguin Books, 1976.

—PETER HUNT

M. L. S. MOLESWORTH

1839–1921

A PROLIFIC AND professional writer of children's books during the late-nineteenth-century golden age of children's literature, M. L. S. Molesworth provides a transition from earlier moral tales and presages the fashion of domestic fantasies in the twentieth century. Although reticent about her own life, Molesworth profusely detailed the lives of her child characters in approximately eighty-six books of children's fiction. Much to the chagrin of her own children, she often used them as models for her characters. Most of her critics consider her to be an autobiographical writer, yet few facts of her life are known. Some critics, like Roger Lancelyn Green, have blurred the distinction between her life and her works by quoting passages from her books as if they were autobiographical.

Mary Louisa Stewart Molesworth was born in Rotterdam, Holland, on 29 May 1839. But her family soon moved to Manchester, England. She was the second child and eldest daughter of Charles Augustus and Agnes Janet Wilson Stewart, who married around 1835. Of her siblings—John Wilson, Charles, Agnes, William, and Caroline Marion—only Charles had any children, Morier and Noel; Molesworth's second children's book, *"Carrots": Just a Little Boy*, is dedicated to them. Contrary to the speculations of some critics, there is no evidence that she had a lonely childhood. But certainly the central character in her fiction is often a lonely or single young girl who is estranged from family and seeks friends through escape into fantasy.

Taught mostly at home by her well-educated mother, Molesworth may have been a day pupil briefly at a school in Manchester. At age fourteen she went to a boarding school in Lausanne, Switzerland, but soon returned home. In Manchester she took classes from the Reverend William Gaskell, the husband of Elizabeth Gaskell, author of *Cranford* (1853). In a rare bit of autobiography she recalls that she knew French well, Latin less so, and that she found arithmetic very interesting but she did not do well in the subject.

Her father was a self-made man who rejected his family's tradition of pursuing a socially accepted military career. Stewart gave up his commission and went into business as a merchant shipper. Later he became a senior partner in the Manchester firm of Robert Barbour Brothers, merchants and shippers. After settling in Manchester in 1841, his financial condition steadily improved, and he was able to move his family to larger quarters and more prestigious addresses.

Until she was twenty-two Molesworth lived with her family, mainly in the center of Manchester, a leading Victorian industrial city. Her books often contrast life in the city with that in the country, which she experienced during her annual visits to the home of her Scottish maternal grandmother, Mary Black Wilson, between 1841 and 1848. Molesworth fondly remembered the Scottish landscape around Dunfermline and the storytelling skill of her grandmother. The grandmother appears as the white-haired storyteller in *The Tapestry Room* (1879) who tells the traditional story of "The

Brown Bull of Norrowa" that Mary Wilson had told the young Molesworth.

On occasion the Stewart family rented a cottage near the sea at Fleetwood on the Lancashire coast. Although the location was not particularly fashionable, these trips were delightful to the children. Similar locales appear in Molesworth's children's books. All in all, she seems to have had a comfortable and normal upper-middle-class childhood. Perhaps that is why fantasy plays such an important role in the lives of her child characters, who are caught in comfortable but dull routines of daily living. They always seem to be on the lookout for a fairy or some other curious character.

Molesworth read the popular children's literature of her day, but always in her own way. For example, she read Mary Martha Sherwood's *Fairchild Family* (1818) for its adventures, after having skipped the prayers and hymns at the end of each chapter. She disliked the moral sensibility of Maria Edgeworth's stories and John Aikin and Anna Laetitia Barbauld's *Evenings at Home* (1792–1796). But her own fiction is also very moral and maternal in its attitude toward both children and adults. She had rejected Calvinism, the religion she was instructed in during her childhood, and she vowed not to frighten children with religion in her books. She found fairy stories very congenial, especially those of the Grimms, Hans Christian Andersen, and Nathaniel Hawthorne, and was positively influenced by Charlotte Yonge's fiction and by Susan Warner's *Wide, Wide World* (1850). She also liked the portrayal of adventure in Sir Walter Scott's Waverly novels.

Molesworth began as a storyteller to her brothers and sisters, repeating those tales that her grandmother had told, and later drew on other stories that she had read or invented on her own. As a teenager, she published first a translation and then other works for no pay. In her essay "On the Art of Writing Fiction for Children" (1893), she advises writers that translating is the best way to acquire an appropriate style for this kind of writing. She also recommends that the writer follow her example in reading manuscripts first to children.

Before embarking on a career as a serious writer, Mary Louisa Stewart entered into a traditional upper-middle-class marriage to Richard Molesworth. She was engaged to him in 1858, but her parents, especially her mother, did not approve of the match. Richard's prospects, however, were quite good. He was the eldest son of Captain Oliver Molesworth, the third brother of the seventh viscount Molesworth and baron Phillipstown of Phillipstown, Ireland. Since the viscount had no male heirs at the time, it seemed likely that Richard would inherit the titles and estates. He also prospered in his military career. After distinguished service in the Crimea, he was promoted to captain in 1861, and transferred to the Royal Dragoons.

On 24 July 1861 Mary Louisa Stewart married Captain Richard Molesworth at Grosvenor Square Church, Manchester. But the marriage proved far from idyllic. The couple moved with the regiment to Dublin until September 1861, stayed in Birmingham until May 1863, and then went to Aldershot. Molesworth never referred to army life in her work.

During this period two of the Molesworths' seven children were born, Agnes Violet Grace in 1862 and Mary Cicely Caroline in 1863. Then Richard gave up his career, retiring from the army in 1864 with the rank of major and taking eighteen hundred pounds in lieu of commission. Molesworth's father aided the couple financially. They took a house, Tabley Grange, six miles away from her father's West Hall and remained there for five years. In January 1865 Richard was appointed adjutant of the Sixth Royal Lancashire Regiment of Militia. Two more children were born, Juliet in 1865 and Olive in 1867.

Then the family suffered a series of reversals. Samuel Molesworth, the current seventh viscount, fathered a male child in 1868, thereby preventing Richard's inheritance. The Molesworths' daughter Violet died of scarlet fever on 6 April 1869. Her death is fictionalized in the story "Good-Night, Winny," which was included in Molesworth's first book for children, *Tell Me a Story* (1875). Thereafter in her children's books scarlet fever is the disease most frequently mentioned as a threat or the cause of death to small children. A second blow to family happiness in 1869 was the death of a baby son, Richard Walter Stewart, on 20 November at the age of three months.

Evidently the marriage was not going well. In 1870 Molesworth published *Lover and Husband,* the first of her four three-volume adult novels in which the husband and wife are attractive but incompatible. She used the pseudonym Ennis Graham, the name of a friend who had died in Central Africa. The Molesworths next moved to Westfield, a house that Molesworth's father had built for them just a few hundred yards from West Hall. There two more children were born, Richard Bevil in 1870 and Lionel Charles in 1873. But these comfortable domestic arrangements were upset when Charles Stewart died in 1873 and his eldest son soon after in 1874. Molesworth was forced to move with her widowed mother and her family to Edinburgh due to problems of inheritance. Major Molesworth retired permanently in 1874. During this period of financial and emotional stress, Molesworth began her career as a children's writer. *Tell Me a Story* appeared in 1875, *"Carrots"* in 1876, *The Cuckoo Clock* in 1877; these are among her better-known books. *"Carrots"* established her reputation as a children's author. *The Cuckoo Clock* confirmed it.

Molesworth then published another three-volume novel for adults, *Hathercourt Rectory* (1878), and two children's books, *Grandmother Dear: A Book for Boys and Girls* (1878), about her mother, and her most famous children's book, *The Tapestry Room*, set in Normandy, where the family was then living. By 1879 the Molesworths had moved to Caen, France, where their marriage was ended by a legal separation. Richard returned to England, living for a number of years in Brighton. He was made a military "Knight of Windsor" in 1886 and died in 1900.

Molesworth continued to live on the Continent with her mother and children, first in Caen, then in Paris, then in Coburg, Germany, and later in Thüringen, Germany, the setting of several of her children's stories. In Germany she briefly called herself Mrs. von Molesworth. By 1883, the year in which her mother died, she had published eight more books (*Miss Bouverie* [1880] for adults and seven children's books). She returned to London in the autumn of 1885 and lived at 85 Lexham Gardens. She wrote many essays, stories, and children's books, some children's poetry, and an adult novel, leaving the domestic details of the house to Olive, the spinster daughter with whom she lived. In 1890 she moved to 155 Sloane Street, where she settled for the remaining twenty-two years of her life.

In London she became part of the literary establishment and counted Walter Pater, Edwin Arnold, Aubrey de Vere, Rudyard Kipling, Algernon Charles Swinburne, and Theodore Watts-Dunton among her friends. Swinburne compared her favorably to George Eliot in an essay on Charles Reade published in the *Nineteenth Century* in October 1884. Her subsequently published books usually quoted part of his flattering paragraph in the advertising pages on the back. Swinburne wrote, "Any chapter of *The Cuckoo Clock* or the enchanting *Adventures of Herr Baby* [1881] is worth a shoal of the very best novels dealing with the characters and fortunes of mere adults." In 1893 Macmillan published a ten-volume set of nineteen of her most successful books for children. Most reviewers unfailingly praised her insight into the nature of small children, their sorrow and joy over small matters, and her skill in blending the real with the romantic or fantastic.

As Molesworth had first read her stories to her own children in manuscripts concealed in large printed books, so she continued first to read them to her grandchildren. She had considerable financial success; some books went through numerous editions. Except for those titles with the Macmillan imprint, many of her stories appeared as six-part serials in magazines before being gathered into books. The Macmillan titles initially appeared at Christmas each year, eighteen of them with illustrations by Walter Crane, one of the most distinguished nineteenth-century illustrators of children's books. Her last book was *Fairies Afield* (1911).

During her extensive writing career Molesworth published nine novels for adults, a few poems for children, numerous essays on writing and writers like Andersen and Juliana Horatia Ewing, several collections of ghost stories and short stories, and approximately eighty-six books for children. Many of the latter were novels of over two hundred pages each. Of her thirty-three books for Macmillan, which were written at the rate of almost one each year between 1875 and 1911 and which are considered her better books, six were most popular and influential: *Tell Me a Story, "Carrots," The Cuckoo Clock, The Tapestry Room, Christmas-Tree Land* (1884), and *The Carved Lions* (1895).

The plots are typical of Molesworth: while learning to speak correctly, a small child also learns about the real world; a lonely older child takes therapeutic trips to a fantasy world and returns adjusted; and a child copes on his own with troubles in the real world.

Tell Me a Story contains six short stories and an introduction. Several of the book's features are characteristic of much of her children's fiction: her method of introducing a story or stories, her personal approach to readers, and her types of stories. In the introduction the children beg their aunt for a story—the collection is the result. Time and again in her other works, collections of interpolated stories or whole books are the answers to such requests. And the narrator often addresses the child reader or hearer directly, as in "Mary Ann Jolly":

"Am I getting beyond you, children dear? Am I using words and thinking thoughts you can scarcely follow? Well, I won't forget again. I will tell you my simple story in simple words."

In both "The Reel Fairies" and "Con and the Little People," a lonely child finds out by a trip to fairyland that the fairy world is not enough, that despite its enchantment and strangeness, he wants to return to his parents and home. Again and again Molesworth tells us the tale of a child who is good except for one fault. In "Too Bad" Miss Judy's fault is her constant grumbling. Otherwise she is kind-hearted, gentle-mannered, pretty, healthy, and clever. But when, in her fantasy, she changes places with the cottager girl Betsy, whose rural life she envied, she finds out how difficult that life actually is and stops grumbling. As the narrator remarks, " 'And oh, my dears, *real* washing is very different from the dolls' laundressing.' "

In her second book the problem of four-year-old Fabian, nicknamed "Carrots," is his innocence of the world. *"Carrots"* briefly describes the boy's first six years and then concentrates on his and the other children's excitement about the imminent visit of their aunt and her little girl. As in most of Molesworth's books about very young children, she focuses on the small problems typical of their age. Carrots' lisping is amusing to the family, but when he fails to understand that "sovereign" refers to a gold coin and not to face cards, he finds himself accused of stealing by an older brother. Carrots believed the coin he found to be a fairy yellow sixpence. He is cleared when his mother sorts out the linguistic confusion. But the boy is changed; he realizes that "it is possible for our very nearest and dearest to mistake and misunderstand us."

Stories told by the nurse and the other children fill out *"Carrots."* The nurse's story about some children who shaved the family dog while the family was at church exemplifies their thoughtlessness. In contrast, another story, about the lady of the house, who used to wash the best china herself, encourages the children to take proper care of things. Miss Cecil reads an example of an early cautionary story from *Faults Corrected*: "The Bewitched Tongue; or, Think Before You Speak. A Fairy Tale." Its failure to impress the children adds force to Molesworth's argument that such fiction is outdated.

Later Carrots and his sister, Floss, are sent alone by train to stay with an aunt and her young daughter Sybil because their mother has gone abroad for her health. By accident, no one is there to meet the children at Whitefriars, their destination. But they are resourceful. They ask directions and walk several miles to the country house, while imagining themselves to be the children in the chapbook ballad "Babes in the Wood." Unlike those children, however, they arrive safely.

At the end of the book, everyone is happy. The mother does not die as Sybil's retelling of Andersen's story "The Shadow" suggests; instead she is restored like the twin in the aunt's story of "The Two Funny Little Trots." This use of familiar stories of children's literature characterizes Molesworth's fiction. She often suggests that life is quite unlike the familiar tales. Instead its problems can be solved by children with luck and imagination.

In *The Cuckoo Clock* Molesworth employs fantasy to show how young Griselda learns patience. Sent by her widowed father to live with her elderly great-aunts in their old house, Griselda does not feel that she fits in. She resists them and her daily lessons with a tutor, finally throwing a book at the cuckoo in the clock. But the bird appears to her late at night and acts as her guide on a series of imaginative trips that indirectly instruct her in the virtues of punctuality, faithful discharge of duty, and obedience. Griselda wants a playmate, so the bird bandies words with her and takes her to fantastic places inside the clock, which are reminiscent of the scenes on the Chinese cabinet in the grand saloon, like the Land of Nodding Mandarins. Another night his dream pictures of Griselda's own family history draw her closer to the great-aunts. On a third occasion he takes her to Butterfly Land, where the butterflies are busy at work each day painting the flowers of earth, but she rejects their style of life as too laborious.

Finally the cuckoo introduces Griselda to a longed-for real friend and playmate, five-year-old Master Phil. Griselda becomes his teacher, and her need for the cuckoo disappears. The cuckoo says good-bye to her in a dream, for now she has friends to help her "both to work and to play. Better friends than the mandarins, or the butterflies, or even than your faithful old cuckoo." This book is the most successful presentation of Molesworth's belief that a balance of work and play are important to every child. The details of the fantasy worlds are vivid and inventive, yet keyed to objects in the real world.

A similar situation is repeated in a more artificial and fanciful fashion in *The Tapestry Room*. Here the child's guide to the fantasy world is Dudu, an old crow. Jeanne, a seven-year-old girl, feels lonely even though she has pet chickens, a tortoise, a nurse named Marcelline, and devoted parents. She fears that Dudu is a fairy who will harm her, an attitude that exposes her distrust of the imagination. Yet she is discontented and wishes that her parents would turn into playmates her age and that Dudu would lead the way into the castle pictured in the tapestry, even though he may be "a sort of ogre fairy" because he is black and solemn.

When her eight-year-old cousin, Hugh, comes to stay with them, the tapestry room becomes his bedroom. Because Hugh is trusting, Dudu takes him on the first fantastic journey through the tapestry into a corridor of light and beyond to a forest of colored trees. Hugh's coach is pulled by his pet guinea pig and Jeanne's tortoise and is accompanied by Jeanne's pet chickens, which have been transformed into elegant footmen. Jeanne's rooster, Houpet, is the coachman. At this point, Jeanne jumps out of the carriage to join Hugh. The chickens show them a staircase in a hole in the ground, and they climb down expecting a treasure as in the story of Ali Baba in *A Thousand and One Nights.* Instead they find a river and a boat and they row downstream until their boat is caught in the narrows. Talking frogs rescue them with towlines; upon reaching the lake, they are invited by the frogs to hear the swan's song and their croaking accompaniment. Later the frogs offer them "flag-flour cakes" and other delicacies, not worms and such. Awakening, Hugh remembers all their adventures, but Jeanne has only a partial memory of Frog-land. But the nurse, Marcelline, seems to know all. She tells them that people have two selves and that the children's other selves went on the journey.

In the second dream Jeanne is more active. Dressed as a fairy with wings, she appears in the tapestry room, wearing Dudu as her fantastic headdress. She gives a pair of wings to Hugh, and this time they fly together to the castle. There they find a completely white world. Inside the castle is a white-haired old woman at a spinning wheel spinning all the stories of the world. As an example of her craft, she tells them "The Brown Bull of Norrowa," a lengthy version of the "Beauty and the Beast" fable. At the story's conclusion, the old woman suddenly is replaced by Marcelline.

In the third journey Dudu invites the children through a secret passage behind the tapestry and

up to the roof to hear a story about Jeanne and Hugh's great-grandmother and their great-great-aunt. Then Dudu disappears from the house, and the magic is over. But the children have been strengthened in their relationship to each other, to the family, and to the life of the imagination.

Although the theme and incidents are similar to those in *The Cuckoo Clock,* the plot is less natural. For instance, *The Tapestry Room* begins with the thoughts of the crow before he speaks to Jeanne. The lamplit rainbow-colored forest in the Land of the Nodding Mandarins of the first book suggests too closely the Forest of the Rainbow in the second. What enlivens the books are the small details about the domestic pets and the games of the children, as when Jeanne pretends to be a fairy and turns Hugh into a guinea pig or when they disguise themselves as peasants to fool their parents.

Christmas-Tree Land repeats the patterns and themes of both *The Cuckoo Clock* and *The Tapestry Room.* But it is much more abstract, obviously Platonic in its philosophy, and mythic in the manner of George MacDonald. Here too children are separated from their parents and sent to live with an elderly relative who is strict. Rollo and Maia are sent by their widowed father to live with their elderly cousin, Lady Venelda, in her white castle in the German mountains. The opening line reads, "It was not their home." This is the problem they must resolve. But through their application to the lessons organized by Lady Venelda and their fantasy excursions in the forest, the children strike a healthful balance between work and play and make a home for themselves.

What makes the book unusual is the obvious doubling of characters and the relation between the fantasy world and the real world. Before arriving at the castle the children fantasize about how nice it would be to live as a peasant brother and sister in the cottage where they can see smoke come out of the chimney. On their first ramble they find the cottage empty, although there are places set for three people as in the story of the three bears. The second visit brings them face to face with Waldo and Silvia, slightly older doubles of themselves. The adult who lives in the cottage turns out to be a fairy godmother in crimson dress and green cloak, who tells them the lengthy "Story of a King's Daughter," a variant of "Beauty and the Beast." She is an obvious double, or contrast, to the white-robed, logical Lady Venelda. Another time Lady Venelda's physician, who has the confidence of the children's father and acts as his double, shows them the way to the cottage from a secret staircase in the castle. The fairy godmother takes them riding in a diminutive coach to meet Waldo and Silvia. All four enjoy playing with the squirrel family in the treetops, but when Rollo and Maia also learn what hard physical labor Waldo and Silvia have to do, their school lessons seem easy by comparison.

Two final fantastic journeys complete the book. One is the visit of the children to an eagle's aerie for a vegetarian feast. The second occurs on Christmas Eve, when the children follow a robin in the snow after climbing down from a castle window. They find themselves dressed in white cloaks and equipped with wings so that they can fly to a tree. They hear carols and meet Waldo and Silvia. Then their eyes are really opened, and they see a variety of Christmas trees loaded with presents in the valley below. Each tree belongs to a family on earth, as this is Santa Claus's garden. Under their tree they see Papa. Next morning they wake to find Papa has arrived. Lady Venelda compliments their behavior and studiousness. Because their imaginative journeys have supplemented the lessons of the school day, they have made themselves at home in her world. At the same time, they anticipate returning to their real home with their father.

The Carved Lions plays on the same theme of children taken from parents and placed in a cold, unfeeling environment. But Molesworth provides an answer to the problem through realistic, not fantastic, means. There is only one fantastic element: Geraldine's dream of the carved lions talking. Nine-year-old Geraldine, who has been tutored by her mother at home, is to be sent with her brother to a boarding school for two years while her parents are in South America, where her father is to work in a bank. Her eleven-year-old brother, Haddon, nicknamed "Haddie," has been going to day school, so he adjusts easily. The family lives in Great Mexington, a smoky industrial city like Molesworth's hometown of Manchester. They are genteel but poor. The father has made some bad investments and so must now work for a living. They can afford only two servants.

As in earlier books, it is the small things that please both children, such as going with mother to Mr. Cranston's furniture shop with the carved wooden lions on either side of the entry or buying cakes for tea at the confectioner's shop run by a Quaker lady. Geraldine is excited at the idea of going to school at Miss Ledbury's and having lots of friends. But it turns out to be a grim establish-

ment where the girls have to march to class, the governesses censor the girls' letters to their parents, many of the pupils are nouveau riche, and some of the teachers are rather ignorant or critical. Geraldine becomes withdrawn, silent, and dull. She makes only one true friend, the Cranstons' granddaughter, pretty, younger Myra Roby, and has only one sympathetic teacher, Miss Fenimore. Neither returns after Easter.

At this point, Geraldine, who has read *The Wide, Wide World,* by Susan Warner, identifies with its orphan heroine, Ellen, and her trials. She overreacts, runs away in search of Lady Selwood, her mother's rich godmother, and takes refuge in the entryway of Cranston's shop. There she has a dream that the lions carry her and her brother to their parents. Instead she awakens in the Cranstons' bedroom, ill with a bad fever. Miss Fenimore has become the governess to their granddaughter Myra. Geraldine recovers and arrangements are made by her parents for Miss Fenimore to tutor both children. Geraldine reflects that she could have avoided some of her troubles by going to Miss Ledbury, who was old but wished to be fair. She also determines to examine closely any school to which she might send her own children.

The story turns out happily, becoming a domestic romance. The parents are gone three years, not two. But Geraldine goes to live with Myra's parents and shares vacation time at the Cranstons'. Miss Fenimore continues as their governess until the parents return, and then marries. Myra joins Geraldine's prosperous family in London. Haddon and Myra marry. And the narrator reveals that she has written this story for their grandchildren.

As is obvious from the summaries of these six books, the complications and resolutions of plots are highly formulaic in Molesworth's books. Many of her stories extol good sense, include fantastic elements, and end happily. But her emphasis on the interior lives of her characters rather than on exterior details results in types more often than individuals. As Gillian Avery writes, she "is the initiator of the 'nursery world' story books." And she was best known for the title nursery-characters of such books as *"Carrots," Herr Baby, Jasper* (1906), *Hoodie* (1882), and *Mary* (1893). But the fashion for the lisping, prattling four-year-old waned in the early twentieth century. Stories of older mischief-makers caught adult interest. For younger children, animal stories like those of Beatrix Potter and A. A. Milne proved more lasting because they were not dependent on the reader's familiarity with the upper-middle-class English family life-style that began to vanish at the time of World War I. In addition, the domestic feminine realism set forth by Molesworth could not compete with the exotic masculine adventures written by Robert Louis Stevenson, Arthur Conan Doyle, and Rudyard Kipling. Nor could her fairy tales stand up to Andrew Lang's various fairy-tale collections.

But her books did provide models for Edith Nesbit in creating her series of *Bastable* books, various fantastic adventures, and quirky fairy emissaries like the Psammead and the Phoenix. Molesworth's influence can also be seen in Mary Norton's *Borrowers* books. But, more important, she established a pattern for children's books that authors still find viable: the therapeutic journey of children into a fantastic world and their return to the real world stronger and more able to face its problems. This is the pattern, for instance, of P. L. Travers' *Mary Poppins* books, Phillipa Pearce's *Tom's Midnight Garden* (1958), and Nancy Bond's *A String in the Harp* (1976).

The Cuckoo Clock is still in print. And in recent years, *The Tapestry Room, Four Winds Farm* (1887), and *The Children of the Castle* (1890) have joined it in reprints for scholars. *My New Home* (1894), her psychological study of a teenager's development of conscience and maturity, was reprinted in England in 1968. In *A Peculiar Gift,* Lance Salway and other critics acknowledge Molesworth as a critic of nineteenth-century children's literature. Perhaps Molesworth is less well known now than other nineteenth-century children's writers because, as Roger Lancelyn Green writes, "she may be said to have attempted less and achieved that slightly lower aim far more perfectly and completely."

Selected Bibliography

WORKS OF M. L. S. MOLESWORTH

Tell Me a Story, written under the pseudonym Ennis Graham. With illustrations by Walter Crane. London: Macmillan, 1875.
"Carrots": Just a Little Boy. With illustrations by Walter Crane. London: Macmillan, 1876.
The Cuckoo Clock. With illustrations by Walter Crane. London: Macmillan, 1877; New York: M. M. Caldwell, 1877.
Grandmother Dear: A Book for Boys and Girls. With illustrations by Walter Crane. London: Macmillan, 1878.

The Tapestry Room. With illustrations by Walter Crane. London: Macmillan, 1879; New York: Burt, 1879.
The Adventures of Herr Baby. With illustrations by Walter Crane. London: Macmillan, 1881.
Hoodie. With illustrations by Mary Ellen Edwards. London: Routledge and Kegan Paul, 1882.
Christmas-Tree Land. With illustrations by Walter Crane. London: Macmillan, 1884.
The Children of the Castle. With illustrations by Walter Crane. London: Macmillan, 1890.
Mary: A Nursery Story for Very Little Children. With illustrations by L. Leslie Brooke. London: Macmillan, 1893.
The Carved Lions. With illustrations by L. Leslie Brooke. London: Macmillan, 1895.
Jasper: A Story for Children. With illustrations by Gertrude Demain Hammond. London: Macmillan, 1906.
Fairies Afield. With illustrations by Gertrude Demain Hammond. London: Macmillan, 1911.

CRITICAL AND BIOGRAPHICAL STUDIES

Avery, Gillian. *Nineteenth-Century Children.* London: Hodder and Stoughton, 1965. (See chapter 9, "The Nursery World: Mrs. Molesworth.")
Benét, Laura. *Famous Storytellers for Young People.* New York: Dodd, Mead, 1968.
Bull, Angela. "Preface" to *The Cuckoo Clock and The Tapestry Room.* New York: Garland, 1976.
Green, Roger Lancelyn. *Mrs. Molesworth.* London: H. Z. Walck, 1964. (The most trustworthy source about her biography and writing career.)
————. "Preface" to *Four Winds Farm and The Children of the Castle.* New York: Garland, 1977.
————. *Tellers of Tales.* Rev. ed. New York: Franklin Watts, 1965.
Laski, Marghanita. *Mrs. Ewing, Mrs. Molesworth, and Mrs. Hodgson Burnett.* London: A. Barker, 1950. (Provides an interesting comparison but is inaccurate in some details about Molesworth.)
Rosenthal, Lynne M. "Writing Her Own Story: The Integration of the Self in the Fourth Dimension of Mrs. Molesworth's *The Cuckoo Clock" Children's Literature Association Quarterly* 10: 187–192 (Winter 1986).
Salway, Lance, ed. *A Peculiar Gift: Nineteenth-Century Writings on Books for Children.* London: Kestral Books, 1976. (Contains some of Molesworth's essays on writing and children's writers, including "On the Art of Writing Fiction for Children." Also has criticism of her work by contemporaries.)

—HUGH T. KEENAN

L. M. MONTGOMERY

1874-1942

BRITISH AND AMERICAN children have no shortage of literary heroes: King Arthur and Robin Hood, Paul Bunyan and John Henry, the Bastables and the Borrowers, Encyclopedia Brown and Ramona Quimby. Their names are easily remembered, their characters and appearances quickly recognized, and their adventures always enjoyed. In Canada there are few literary heroes for children; in fact, most Canadian children turn to English and American books to find memorable characters. There is one major exception: a skinny, freckle-faced, redheaded orphan girl possessing a strong temper, a sparkling imagination, and a loving heart. She is Anne Shirley, the title character of *Anne of Green Gables*, a book first published in 1908 and still widely read not only by Canadian children but also by children around the world. She was the creation of Lucy Maud Montgomery, a native of Prince Edward Island.

Born on 30 November 1874 in the tiny village of Clifton, Montgomery lived all but four of her first thirty-six years in the rural countryside of the north shore of Prince Edward Island. Both her mother's and father's families had long been influential in the public affairs of the island, and from many of her older relatives she heard the legends and historical events of Canada's smallest province.

Outwardly her young life was relatively uneventful. When Maud (she detested the name Lucy) was two, her mother died of tuberculosis; six years later, her father moved to Prince Albert, Saskatchewan, where he remarried and lived for the rest of his life. The young girl was raised by her grandparents except for a period of sixteen months in 1890–1891, when she lived with her father and stepmother and their children on the Canadian prairies. She attended Prince of Wales College in Charlottetown, Prince Edward Island, during the winter of 1893–1894, where she received a teaching certificate.

Inwardly Montgomery led an intense emotional and imaginative life. Living with older relatives after the death of her mother and the departure of her father, she often felt lonely. She later wrote, "I was shut out from all social life, even such as this small country settlement could offer," and remarked that life with her grandparents was often restrictive. During her stay in Prince Albert she did not get along with her stepmother, often felt overwhelmed by the household duties she performed, and was homesick for Prince Edward Island. About her relationships with adults she was to comment, "I do not think that the majority of grownups have any real conception of the tortures sensitive children suffer over any marked difference between themselves and the other denizens of their small world."

However lonely she became, Montgomery gloried in the scenery of Prince Edward Island: "Life never held for me a dull moment. I had, in my vivid imagination, a passport to the geography of Fairyland." Like Anne Shirley, the heroine of her first novel, she enjoyed responding imaginatively to the beautiful countryside. "Amid all the commonplaces of life," she was to recount, "I was very near to a kingdom of ideal beauty."

Montgomery also read widely, and by the time she entered school was a very competent writer. She remembered having devoured such books as Sir Walter Scott's *Rob Roy*, Charles Dickens' *Pickwick Papers*, and John Bunyan's *Pilgrim's Progress* as well as such favorite nineteenth-century poets as Alfred, Lord Tennyson, John Greenleaf Whittier, Henry Wadsworth Longfellow, and Lord Byron. From an early age she wanted to be a writer: "I cannot remember when I was not writing, or when I did not mean to be an author. To write has always been my central purpose toward which every effort and hope and ambition of my life has grouped itself." At age nine she showed her father a blank-verse poem she had composed and was upset when he told her it was very blank indeed. While she was in Prince Albert, "On Cape LeForce," her poetic account of a Prince Edward Island legend, appeared in the Charlottetown *Daily Patriot*. By the time she had returned to the Island, several of her other short pieces had been published.

Between 1894 and 1911 Montgomery taught school, studied English literature at Dalhousie University in Halifax, worked as a reporter for the *Halifax Daily Echo*, cared for her aged grandmother, and took an active part in church affairs. In a busy and demanding life she steadfastly continued with her literary career. When she was teaching, she would arise at six o'clock, dress, and, tucking her feet beneath her to keep them warm in the unheated room, work at her writing. In 1895 she received her first payment for one of her pieces: five dollars for "Our Charivari," published in *Golden Days*, a Philadelphia magazine. She reported in 1901 that she was making an adequate income from her writing, and in 1904 that she had earned nearly six hundred dollars from the sale of poems and stories.

In 1904, reading over her notebooks, she noticed this jotting: "Elderly couple apply to orphan asylum for a boy. By mistake a girl is sent them." From this forgotten entry, writing in the evenings between April 1904 and October 1905, she created *Anne of Green Gables*. Receiving four rejection slips, she put the manuscript in an old hatbox. When she discovered it again two years later, she considered condensing it into a short story, so that she could get "thirty five dollars for her [Anne] at least." Instead, she revised it and submitted it to the Boston firm of L. C. Page. On 8 April 1907, she received a letter of acceptance, and on 20 June 1908, the date of the publication of *Anne of Green Gables*, she wrote in her journal:

> Today has been, as Anne herself would say, "an epoch in my life." My book came today, "Spleet-new" from the publishers. I candidly confess that it was to me a proud and wonderful and thrilling moment. There, in my hand, lay material realization of all the dreams and hopes and ambitions of my whole conscious existence—my first book. Not a great book, but mine, mine, mine, something which I had created.
>
> (*The Alpine Path*, p. 77)

The book was an immediate success. Within a year Montgomery had received a royalty check for $1,730; the book had received over sixty reviews, nearly all of them favorable; and the publishers had requested a sequel.

As was to be the case throughout her writing career, Montgomery reluctantly approached the writing of a sequel, *Anne of Avonlea* (1909), the story of her heroine's first teaching job. To a friend she wrote: "I had to write it too hurriedly, and the freshness of the idea was gone. It didn't grow as the first book did. I simply built it." Two more books appeared before her marriage in 1911 and her subsequent move to Ontario: *Kilmeny of the Orchard* (1910) and *The Story Girl* (1911). The latter was the author's personal favorite. In it a young woman, Sara Stanley, tells a number of stories, many based on family and local legends Montgomery herself had heard.

Montgomery met her future husband, Ewan Macdonald, when he was the pastor of the Cavendish Presbyterian Church on the north shore of Prince Edward Island. As she was later to tell friends, she had been in love before, with a local farmer who was her social and intellectual inferior; and she had been engaged to a second cousin whom, though he was a social equal, she did not love. Macdonald and she had been engaged since 1906. However, because her sense of duty dictated that she care for her aging grandmother, she did not marry him until 5 July 1911, four months after her grandmother's death. After a honeymoon in England and Scotland, the couple settled in Leaskdale, a small community fifty miles from Toronto, where Macdonald's parish was located. They lived there until 1926, when they moved to Norval, which was closer to Toronto.

After the move to Leaskdale, Montgomery

began the busy life of raising a family, performing the duties of a minister's wife, and writing. In 1912 her first son, Chester Cameron, was born; in 1913 Hugh Alexander was stillborn; in 1915 she had a third son, Ewan Stewart. Over the years, she frequently traveled to literary gatherings in Canada and the United States to read from and to discuss her books. As often as possible she returned to Prince Edward Island, feeling a sense of spiritual restoration after her visits.

The first two volumes to be published after her marriage, *Chronicles of Avonlea* (1912) and *The Golden Road* (1913), are collections of short stories. There followed three more books about Anne: *Anne of the Island* (1915), a description of the heroine's college years; *Anne's House of Dreams* (1917), concerning her life as a young wife; and *Rainbow Valley* (1919), stories about her young children. *Further Chronicles of Avonlea* (1920) was another short-story collection, while *Rilla of Ingleside* (1921) focused on Anne's youngest daughter. Later books about Anne were *Anne of Windy Poplars* (1936), about Anne's life as a school principal, and *Anne of Ingleside* (1939), recalling her life as a young mother.

In 1923 Montgomery published the first of three novels about a new heroine, Emily Byrd Starr. *Emily of New Moon* (1923), *Emily Climbs* (1925), and *Emily's Quest* (1927) are the most autobiographical of the author's books. Orphaned as a young girl, Emily wants desperately to become a writer, but along the way she must face responsibilities and decisions that help her to grow up. Montgomery's two other female heroines are Pat Gardiner (*Pat of Silver Bush*, 1933, and *Mistress Pat*, 1936) and Jane Stuart (*Jane of Lantern Hill*, 1937). During her life Montgomery also published a book of poetry, *The Watchman and Other Poems* (1916), a response to World War I, and two adult novels, *The Blue Castle* (1926) and *A Tangled Web* (1931). *The Road to Yesterday*, which appeared in 1974, is an anthology of short stories, several of which deal with Anne, who as an adult recalls incidents from her childhood.

Although Montgomery was wealthy and famous and apparently contented in her role as mother, minister's wife, and author, the continuing demands for Anne stories weighed heavily on her, and she considered herself a prisoner of her most famous creation. In 1919, after the publication of *Rilla of Ingleside*, she complained: "I have gone completely 'stale' on Anne and must get a new

heroine. Six books are enough to write about any girl." It was with relief that she turned to the Emily series, although nearly sixteen years later public demand forced her to return to her first heroine.

During the 1920's, Montgomery was also involved in a series of costly lawsuits against her Boston publisher, L. C. Page. When she had first signed a contract with them for *Anne of Green Gables*, she agreed to send them "all my books on the same lines for a period of five years." In 1912 they had returned several stories to her, but kept copies that they published without her authorization in 1920. She finally won her suit, but the court proceedings dragged on for nine years, causing her considerable emotional strain and great bitterness.

Although members of her husband's parish remembered her as cheerful and considerate, Montgomery does not appear to have enjoyed the life of a minister's wife. In letters to a Scottish friend, she spoke of disliking the casual mixers and socials that she frequently had to attend. Moreover, in her own reading and thinking, she was far more liberal than was acceptable for a clergyman's wife; but although she discussed her views in personal correspondence, she maintained a completely orthodox persona at home and in the parish.

Finally, she and her husband may not have been ideally suited to each other. In *The Wheel of Things*, her biographer Mollie Gillen writes:

> Perhaps, she should never have married a minister. There was more than a grain of seriousness in her rueful comment to MacMillan [a longtime pen pal] that 'Those whom the gods wish to destroy they make minister's wives!' Certainly she should never have married Ewan Macdonald, whose intense and tragic personal problem—a belief that he was predestined to hell—made itself apparent only slowly to Maud in his increasingly distressing melancholia.
>
> (p. 117)

Although during the last decade of her life the public successes continued—in 1935, for example, she was made a member of the Order of the British Empire—her private life was increasingly gloomy. Her husband's illnesses, the failure of her first son's marriage, a nervous breakdown of her own, and the worsening world situation depressed her greatly. The letters to her friends written during her last two years were increasingly despondent. In November 1941 she wrote: "My husband is very miserable. I have tried to keep the secret of his melancholic attacks for twenty years . . . but the burden broke me at last, as well as other things. And now the war. I do not think I will ever be well again." The woman who had, in over twenty volumes, celebrated the joyousness of childhood and the glorious landscape of Prince Edward Island was to die five months later, on 24 April 1942, in Toronto. A few days later she was buried in Cavendish Cemetery, not far from her birthplace on Prince Edward Island.

The opening sentence of *Anne of Green Gables*, Montgomery's first, best, and most famous novel, provides a metaphor not only for the life of Anne, her redheaded heroine, but also for the lives of her other heroines:

> Mrs. Rachel Lynde lived just where Avonlea main road dipped down into a little hollow, fringed with alders and ladies' eardrops and traversed by a brook that had its source way back in the woods of the old Cuthbert place; it was reputed to be an intricate, headlong brook in its earlier course through those woods, with dark secrets of pool and cascade; but by the time it reached Lynde's Hollow it was a quiet, well-conducted little stream, for not even a brook could run past Mrs. Rachel Lynde's door without due regard for decency and decorum. . . .

At the conclusion of the novel another appropriate metaphor appears. Speaking to Marilla of her plans to become a teacher, Anne remarks:

> When I left Queen's my future seemed to stretch out before me like a straight road. I thought I could see along it for many a milestone. Now there is a bend in it. I don't know what lies beyond the bend, but I'm going to believe that the best does. It has a fascination of its own, that bend, Marilla. I wonder how the road beyond it goes . . . ?

The stream is like the heroines themselves, at first different from others, independent, often impulsive, then gradually maturing, coming to accept and adapt to social roles imposed upon them. The road is made up of the events in their lives. Each road has a common destination: adult fulfillment and marriage. Yet the exact nature of that fulfillment and the incidents that lead to it are generally unknown until they occur.

For Anne Shirley, a Nova Scotia orphan with a lively imagination, a generous heart, an impulsive temperament, and not a little insecurity, the end of the road finds her an established member of her Prince Edward Island community, the wife of Gilbert Blythe, and the mother of a large and generally happy family. But until her marriage at the beginning of the fourth book of the series, *Anne's House of Dreams*, she must undergo several apparent setbacks and must learn to understand herself and her community. The steps in her development make up the first three books and give them both their liveliness and their tensions. Marriage achieved, Anne continues to have adventures and misadventures, but as Montgomery herself acknowledged, these later books lack the spontaneity and vitality of the earlier ones. It is as if, having allowed her heroine to reach her goals, Montgomery discovered there were few major bends in the road, few major discoveries to be made—in short, little of the stuff of which good stories are made.

At the beginning of *Anne of Green Gables*, when the shy Matthew Cuthbert travels to the railroad station to collect the orphan boy whom he and his sister requested, he meets Anne Shirley, whose compulsive talking reveals both her fears of rejection and her strong powers of imagination. Wishing she had a more romantic name, giving new names to the glorious landscape she finds around her, Anne begins to work her way into the heart of the retiring bachelor. However, the process of her socialization is a long and at times difficult one. Marilla, the rigid spinster, is shocked when she discovers that Anne does not know her prayers, but decides to help the girl, who gratefully exclaims, "It's a million times nicer to be Anne of Green Gables than Anne of nowhere in particular."

Her movement toward her goal involves making friends with, as she calls them, "kindred spirits," having disagreements with both adults and children, and getting into many difficulties because of her imaginative nature and impulsiveness. Her troubles arise because, as she tells her best friend, Diana Barry, "there's such a lot of different Annes in me. I sometimes think that is why I'm such a troublesome person. If I was just the one Anne it would be ever so much more comfortable, but then it wouldn't be half so interesting." Her pride leads her to confront Mrs. Rachel Lynde, whom she believes has insulted her, and to break her slate over Gilbert Blythe's head when he teases her because of her red hair. Overimaginative, she frightens herself in the Haunted Wood and is nearly drowned when she pretends to be a lovelorn maiden and floats down the stream in a leaky boat. After inviting Diana to tea, she inadvertently gets her drunk on Marilla's cordial; trying to escape being red-headed, she mistakenly dyes her hair green; and hoping to impress her friends, she breaks an ankle falling from a roof. Yet she good-naturedly views these events as learning experiences and tells Matthew, "Ever since I came to Green Gables, I've been making mistakes, and each mistake has cured me of some great shortcoming." Overstatement though this may be, Anne has changed, as Marilla and Matthew notice.

Anne's life is by no means one of continual blunders; she is good, honest, loyal, and responsible. Although Diana's mother has angrily refused to allow the two girls to see each other, Anne holds no grudges and heroically saves one of the Barry children from a near-fatal attack of croup. Her most responsible act takes place after Matthew has died and Marilla considers selling Green Gables. Anne unhesitatingly gives up the college scholarship she has won and takes a teaching job so that Marilla can keep her home. Anne Shirley the lonely orphan has found her place; she has become Anne of Green Gables.

While noting the generosity of Anne's decision, many readers of *Anne of Green Gables* have felt that the author, by making the heroine grow to responsible young adulthood, was compromising, giving in to accepted attitudes toward fiction for girls. Montgomery, it has been argued, has ended the novel the way she "ought" to, and in the process has "killed" the almost visionary child of the first two-thirds of the book. Certainly the Anne who decides to stay near home at the end of *Anne of Green Gables* and who begins a teaching career in the next book of the series, *Anne of Avonlea*, is far less interesting than the redheaded waif who not only found a home for herself but also profoundly altered for the better the lives of the old, almost reclusive brother and sister who took her in.

By looking at only two of the five sequels, we can see the diminishing power of the novels, a lessening which is best seen in the portrait of Anne. *Anne of Avonlea* begins in late August, as Anne, now seventeen years old, ponders her future as a teacher. She possesses, we are told, "certain rose-tinted ideals of what a teacher might accomplish if she only went the right way about it." Even before

the school term begins, however, Anne's ideas on how to do good sometimes fail the test of reality: for example, with the best of intentions she mistakenly sells her neighbor's cow.

During the year she has to break her vow not to use corporal punishment—strapping recalcitrant Anthony Pye makes a much better student of him. She also befriends Paul Irving, a poetic child who is also an ideal student, and later helps reunite his widowed father with a long-ago sweetheart, Miss Lavender Lewis. Anne is still prone to mishaps: she falls through a shed roof in embarrassing circumstances and greets a famous novelist not knowing that her own nose is scarlet because of a freckle potion she used. Gone, however, is the spontaneous, ingenuous Anne of the first novel. Her adventures seem contrived, her altruism almost too good to be true. Near the end of the novel she is finally given her chance to go to college, and the author remarks: "She had come at last . . . suddenly and unexpectedly . . . to the bend in the road; and college *was* around it . . . but Anne realized as well that when she rounded that curve she must leave many sweet things behind."

Anne's House of Dreams begins with the long-awaited and inevitable marriage between Anne and Gilbert Blythe. The two adjectives "long-awaited" and "inevitable" in themselves indicate the artificiality of the two preceding books, *Anne of Avonlea* and *Anne of the Island*. Events often seem to have been contrived to create conflicts, to prolong the time before the great event. Now married, Anne and Gilbert move to a new home, the house of dreams of the title, where Gilbert has established a medical practice and where Anne has plenty of time to cultivate "kindred spirits." These include Miss Cornelia Bryant, a confirmed man-hater who ends up marrying, and Captain Jim, a lighthouse keeper who has written a book of local legends. The neighbor who most fascinates Anne is Leslie Moore, a beautiful young woman married to a man who has been an imbecile since he was beaten up on a Caribbean island. After a miraculous operation that restores his faculties, he proves to be not the husband, who died of yellow fever, but a long-lost cousin who looks very much like him. This discovery paves the way for Leslie to marry author Owen Ford. (Ford has helped Captain Jim publish his book, which becomes the publishing sensation of the season.) Along the way Anne loses her firstborn, a girl, but she later gives birth to a son, and at the conclusion of the novel she and Gilbert buy and move to a larger house. From this brief summary one can see that Montgomery is more interested in plot manipulations than in further development of Anne's character. Later books about Anne Shirley-Blythe add little that is new to the heroine's portrait.

Emily Byrd Starr, Montgomery's second-best-known heroine, is in many ways like Anne: early orphaned, she leaves her own home, but with her inner pride and determination she achieves fulfillment. At the end of the third and final book of the series, *Emily's Quest*, she marries, after many misunderstandings, the man for whom, it had become apparent in the first book, she was destined. However, Emily is more like her creator than was Anne: she is a writer, struggling to achieve success in spite of the lack of encouragement from her guardians and the fact that she is not only a Canadian writer but a woman as well. Reading the trilogy in the light of Montgomery's autobiographical *The Alpine Path* and later works about her life, one sees exact parallels between the lives of Emily and Montgomery. Indeed, many of the incidents incorporated into Emily's story are taken directly from the author's autobiographical statements. Although Emily's character lacks the ingenuous spontaneity of Anne's, Emily's life as a young woman who grapples with social and family pressures and the demands of various inappropriate suitors is far more interesting.

Early in *Emily of New Moon* the young girl who has experienced "flashes," Wordsworthian visions of higher realities, is sent to live with her maiden aunts, Laura and Elizabeth, at New Moon. Here she is acutely conscious that her adult relatives, with the exception of Uncle Jimmy, consider caring for her a duty. Unhappy at school, she makes friends with Ilse Burnley, daughter of a widowed, bitter, atheist doctor; Teddy, an artistic boy living with his overprotective and jealous widowed mother; and Perry, a hired boy from the wrong side of the tracks.

In the third novel, *Emily's Quest*, Teddy and Emily marry each other, as do Ilse and Perry; and by means of mysterious psychic powers, Emily rescues a boy lost in an abandoned house and stops Teddy from embarking on an ocean liner that is later wrecked. But most important, she perseveres in nurturing her writing talent and becomes a successful author. Encouraged by her uncle and a local teacher, she writes about her own countryside and its people, refusing to move to New York with its greater literary opportunities. She also breaks an engagement with Dean Priest, a much older man who appears to have psychologically manipulated her during much of her life. After marrying Teddy, she moves to a cottage she had as a child, named the Disappointed House. Wisely, Montgomery closed her chronicles of Emily at this point, not creating, as she had done for Anne, tedious, artificial sequels dealing with married life.

Pat Gardiner, heroine of *Pat of Silver Bush* and *Mistress Pat*, hates change and early in the first novel announces, "I don't want to love anyone or anything but my own family and Silver Bush." However, during the course of the two books, she encounters many changes—births, deaths, marriages, and, finally and most devastatingly, the destruction by fire of her beloved home. At the end of *Mistress Pat* she prepares to marry her friend Hilary (Jingles) Gordon, a talented architect, and to move to Vancouver, on Canada's west coast. She states, "I've learned to accept change even though I can never help dreading it." The story outlines are familiar: a special child grows; interacts with her peers; marries a childhood friend after several complications of plot; makes friends with older people; and, at the end, moves from the home she was so attached to. However, approaching the books about Pat after reading the stories of Anne and Emily, the reader is aware that the formula dominates; the liveliness and the sharp perception of character are absent.

Jane Stuart, heroine of *Jane of Lantern Hill* and Montgomery's last major fictional character, is in many ways like Anne Shirley, for she discovers happiness only when she comes to Prince Edward Island. Residing in Toronto with a tyrannical grandmother and a socialite mother, she likes helping others. As she says when she meets Jody, a Toronto neighbor who is soon to become her best friend, " 'Can I help you?' . . . Though Jane herself had no inkling of it, those words were the keynote of her character." When she arrives in Prince Edward Island to spend a summer with her father, she discovers how much she loves the area around Lantern Hill where she and her father set up housekeeping. By the end of the novel she has brought about a reunion of her parents. She has reached her goal—living with her family in a place where she feels she belongs.

Although we have focused on the lives and character development of the Montgomery heroines, it should be noted that their lives do not take place in a vacuum. The girls have young friends who are very important to them: Anne's friend is Diana Barry; Emily has Ilse Burnley; for Pat, there are her sisters; and for Jane, Jody. More important in the life of each of the girls except Jane is the male companion she finally marries. Although the marriages do not take place until after many misunderstandings and near-marriages to unsuitable people, the important point is that each spouse is the right one for the heroine. Gilbert Blythe is a doctor, Teddy Kent an artist, and Hilary Gordon an architect—and they are all intelligent, talented, and, ultimately, totally loving and devoted. In several of the books there are a number of unmarried or unhappily married adults whose lives contrast with those of the happily married heroines: Marilla had long ago rejected Gilbert Blythe's father; Teddy Kent's mother mistakenly believes that her husband died hating her; and Leslie Moore is married to a man who is suffering from brain damage.

The heroines are also surrounded by older people who influence them and whose lives are in turn influenced. Not long after Anne's arrival at Green Gables, Marilla notes, "I can't imagine the place without her." Aunt Josephine, Diana's sometimes grumpy aunt, Mr. James Harrison, the feisty neighbor, and Captain Jim, the lighthouse keeper, are just three of the "kindred spirits" Anne meets. Emily Byrd Starr, during her many years at New Moon, gradually wins the heart of reserved Aunt Elizabeth. Pat can always rely on the advice and love of Judy, the Gardiners' Irish maid.

As important as the people surrounding the heroines is the Prince Edward Island landscape itself. Montgomery, living in Ontario, always felt that her visits to her Island home rejuvenated her, and the houses and landscapes of the various books have a great effect on the fictional characters. This is most evident in *Anne of Green Gables*, in which the insecure orphan immediately responds to the landscape, reacting imaginatively to the areas Matthew drives through on the way home from the railroad station, giving each place they pass through a name that for her captures its essence. Emily discovers how important New Moon is to her, and Pat gives names to the fields and groves surrounding Silver Bush. Leaving the dreary and misnamed Gay Street in Toronto, Jane finds new vitality at Lantern Hill. Growth to maturity means accepting the fact that they must leave places very special to them. After their marriages Anne, Emily, and Pat must move to new homes.

Although L. M. Montgomery wrote many books and created several heroines, it is for one character, Anne Shirley, and one book, *Anne of Green Gables*, that she is principally remembered. While the novels that followed are not without their merits, none of them equals her first in freshness or vitality. Characters and actions become predictable; it is as if the author has established a formula and has merely changed details. The reader who goes through several of the volumes in a short time period becomes confused. Which kindred spirit belongs in which book, which old and grumpy person has mellowed through contact with which heroine, in which book did the central figure drift temporarily away from her intended spouse and for what reason?

However, *Anne of Green Gables* is undeniably a Canadian classic and a classic of international children's literature, and it has been recognized as such from the year of its publication. Mark Twain referred to Anne as "the dearest, and most loveable child in fiction since the immortal Alice." The book has always sold well; has been popular in many countries; has been successfully adapted for stage, screen, and television; and has served as the basis of a musical performed each summer in Charlottetown, Prince Edward Island.

What are the reasons for the popularity of *Anne of Green Gables*? Most important is the character of Anne herself. Like Lewis Carroll's Alice, she is fresh and original; she does not fit the conventional mold of the girl heroine of late-nineteenth-century fiction. Second, she is surrounded by a cast of memorable characters, particularly the adults: gossiping Rachel Lynde, rigid but loving Marilla, tender Matthew, and feisty Aunt Josephine. Third, she is placed in a setting that comes to life because the author has wisely allowed the reader to see it through the wondering eyes of her young heroine. Finally, she has taken these elements and unobtrusively shaped them into a classic fairy tale: the story of the lonely, unwanted orphan who finds happiness and security. This is a plot to which children have responded for generations. In the hands of Montgomery, the pattern was given a specific locale, a fully developed heroine, and emotional intensity. Children and adults everywhere responded immediately to Montgomery's creative handling of the pattern and continue to do so today.

Selected Bibliography

WORKS OF L. M. MONTGOMERY

Anne of Green Gables. With illustrations by M. A. and W. A. J. Claus. Boston: L. C. Page, 1908.

Anne of Avonlea. With illustrations by George Gibbs. Boston: L. C. Page, 1909.

Kilmeny of the Orchard. With illustrations by George Gibbs. Boston: L. C. Page, 1910.

The Story Girl. With illustrations by George Gibbs. Boston: L. C. Page, 1911.

Chronicles of Avonlea. With illustrations by George Gibbs. Boston: L. C. Page, 1912.

The Golden Road. With illustrations by George Gibbs. Boston: L. C. Page, 1913.

Anne of the Island. With illustrations by H. Weston Taylor. Boston: L. C. Page, 1915.

The Watchman and Other Poems. Toronto: McClelland and Stewart, 1916.

Anne's House of Dreams. With frontispiece by M. L. Kirk. New York: Frederick A. Stokes. 1917.

Rainbow Valley. With frontispiece by M. L. Kirk. New York: Frederick A. Stokes, 1919.

Further Chronicles of Avonlea. With illustrations by John Goss. Boston: L. C. Page, 1920.

Rilla of Ingleside. Frontispiece by M. L. Kirk. New York: Frederick A. Stokes. 1921.

Emily of New Moon. With frontispiece by M. L. Kirk. New York: Frederick A. Stokes, 1923.

Emily Climbs. With frontispiece by M. L. Kirk. New York: Frederick A. Stokes, 1925.

Emily's Quest. New York: Frederick A. Stokes, 1927.

Pat of Silver Bush. With frontispiece by Edna Cooke Shoemaker. New York: Frederick A. Stokes, 1933.

Mistress Pat. With frontispiece by Marie Lawson. New York: Frederick A. Stokes, 1936.

Anne of Windy Poplars. With frontispiece by Louise Costello. New York: Frederick A. Stokes, 1936. (Published in England as *Anne of Windy Willows*.)

Jane of Lantern Hill. New York: Frederick A. Stokes, 1937.

Anne of Ingleside. With frontispiece by Charles V. John. New York: Frederick A. Stokes, 1939.

The Road to Yesterday. Toronto: McGraw-Hill Ryerson, 1974.

The Alpine Path: The Story of My Career. Don Mills, Ontario: Fitzhenry and Whiteside, 1974. (Originally published in 1917 in the Toronto magazine *Everywoman's World*.)

CRITICAL AND BIOGRAPHICAL STUDIES

Bolger, Francis. *The Years Before Anne*. Prince Edward Island: Prince Edward Island Heritage Foundation, 1975.

Gillen, Mollie. *The Wheel of Things: A Biography of L. M. Montgomery*. Don Mills, Ontario: Fitzhenry and Whiteside, 1975; London: Harrap, 1976.

Rubio, Mary, and Elizabeth Waterston, eds. *The Selected Journals of L. M. Montgomery*. Vol. 1, *1889–1910*. Toronto: Oxford University Press, 1985.

Sorfleet, John Robert, ed. *L.M. Montgomery: An Assessment*. Guelph, Ontario: Children's Press, 1976.

—JON C. STOTT

E. NESBIT

1858-1924

VICTORIAN LITERARY FAIRY tales tend to have a conservative moral and political bias. Under their charm and invention is usually an improving lesson: adults know best; good, obedient, patient, and self-effacing little boys and girls are rewarded by the fairies, and naughty, assertive ones are punished. In the most widely read British authors of the period—Frances Browne, Dinah Craik, Juliana Ewing, M. L. S. Molesworth, and even the greatest of them all, George MacDonald—the usual tone is that of a kind lady or gentleman delivering a delightfully disguised sermon.

In the final years of Victoria's reign, however, a writer appeared who was to challenge this pattern so energetically and with such success that it makes sense now to speak of juvenile literature as before and after E. Nesbit. Though there are foreshadowings of her characteristic manner in Charles Dickens' *Holiday Romance* (1868) and Kenneth Grahame's *The Golden Age* (1895), Nesbit was the first to write at length for children as intellectual equals and in their own language. Her books were also innovative in other ways: they presented a modern view of childhood; they took place in contemporary England and recommended socialist solutions to its problems; and they used magic both as a comic device and as a serious metaphor for the power of the imagination.

The woman who overturned so many conventions of children's literature was herself a very un-

conventional member of the Victorian upper middle class, into which she was born in 1858. Edith Nesbit was the youngest daughter of John Collis Nesbit, the head of a London agricultural college, who died in 1862, when she was three. After his death, his wife first tried to keep the college going and then spent the next six years traveling from one European city to another in search of inexpensive lodgings and a healthier climate for her invalid daughter, Mary. As a child, Edith was a rebellious, hot-tempered tomboy, and no doubt a trial to her gentle widowed mother. She hated most of the schools she was sent to in England and on the Continent, and declared later that she had "never been able to love a doll." Her passions were reading, riding, swimming, and playing pirates with her older brothers during holidays. She began to compose poems and stories in early childhood, and already at twelve dreamed of becoming a writer; her verses were first published in newspapers when she was only fifteen.

In 1880, at twenty-one, Edith Nesbit married a handsome young businessman named Hubert Bland; she was seven months pregnant at the time. Shortly after the wedding, disaster struck: Bland became seriously ill with smallpox, and his partner disappeared with all the capital of the firm. Somehow Edith had to support herself, her new baby, and her convalescent husband. She did it by painting greeting cards; giving recitations; and turning out a flood of ephemeral verses, stories, essays, and novels. After he had recovered, Hubert Bland also took up the pen, eventually becoming a well-known political journalist; yet throughout their

Some of the observations in this essay were also made by Michael Patrick Hearn in an unpublished essay presented at the December 1977 Modern Language Association conference.

marriage Edith, and not her husband, remained the economic mainstay of their large family.

The work Nesbit produced between the ages of twenty and forty gives almost no sign of what was to come; it is conventional and often, to the modern taste, sentimental. Then suddenly, in 1898, the "Bastable" stories began to appear in the *Pall Mall* magazine; they were published as a book, *The Story of the Treasure Seekers,* the following year. The lively, comic adventures of six modern London children who try to restore the family fortunes were instantly popular and soon became famous. Two equally successful sequels followed: *The Wouldbegoods* (1901) and *The New Treasure Seekers* (1904). What seems to have released Nesbit's genius was the decision to tell her story through the persona of Oswald Bastable, a child much after her own pattern: bold, quick-tempered, egotistic, and literary.

The success of *The Treasure Seekers* made it possible for the Blands to leave London and move to Weld Hall in Kent, a large, beautiful eighteenth-century brick house, which was to be Nesbit's home until almost the end of her life; it became the Moat House of the later Bastable stories. Over the next ten years she produced the books for which she is known today, books full of wit, energy, and invention, far superior to anything she had written before. Nesbit herself, however, seems to have been unaware of her own achievement. She never spoke of her best work as different from the rest, and she continued to turn out pedestrian stories and verses. To the end of her life she regretted that she could not afford to devote herself to what she mistakenly believed to be her real talent, serious poetry.

Throughout their life together the Blands kept open house for their many friends, including famous painters, writers, and politicians, as well as poor relations, abandoned and illegitimate children, and penniless would-be authors, artists, and cranks. H. G. Wells described Weld Hall as "a place to which one rushed down from town at the week-end to snatch one's bed before anyone else got it." Though most of their guests did not know this, the Blands' marriage as well as their house was what today would be called "open," especially at the husband's end. Hubert Bland was constantly unfaithful; his wife, though hurt by his love affairs, usually ended by taking a sympathetic interest in the women involved. She also passed off two of his illegitimate children as her own and raised them along with her three.

As time went on Nesbit also now and then formed romantic attachments—although most of them probably never went beyond enthusiastic friendship. Even in late middle age she was the sort of woman men fall in love with: tall, good-looking, impulsive, charming, and completely unpredictable. Part of her charm was that in some sense she had never quite grown up. As her biographer Doris Langley Moore reports, she "had all the caprices, the little petulances, the sulks, the jealousies, the intolerance, the selfishnesses of a child; and with them went a child's freshness of vision, hunger for adventure, remorse for unkindness, quick sensibility, and reckless generosity." Nesbit's children remembered her as a delightful playmate but a less than perfect mother. Her quick temper and sudden whims made their life interesting but insecure, and her unconventional costume and manner sometimes caused them embarrassment. Her appearance was untidy and strikingly bohemian: she wore loose, trailing, "aesthetic" dress (and sometimes, for bicycling, pantaloons); her arms were loaded with silver bangles; and her abundant dark hair was bobbed. And, in an era when only "fast women" smoked, she was never without tobacco and cigarette papers—a defiance of convention that may have been responsible for her recurrent bronchial troubles and eventually for her death.

Both the Blands were socialists, founders and lifelong members of the Fabian Society. At one time or another Nesbit supported most of the radical causes of her day—and many of its radical fads, including dress reform, psychic research, and the claim that Francis Bacon had written the plays of Shakespeare.

In 1914 Hubert Bland died, and the next few years were a low point in his wife's career. She was frequently ill and unable to work, and many of her friends and relatives were away in the war. Sales of her books fell off, and she had to take in boarders to keep Weld Hall going. In 1917, however, she remarried; her new husband was an old friend, Thomas Tucker, a retired marine engineer who also had been recently widowed. Though she wrote comparatively little, her last years with him were very happy.

Nesbit, it seems, remained emotionally about twelve years old all her life. Perhaps this is why she found it so easy to speak as one intelligent child to another, in a tone now so common in juvenile fiction that it is hard to realize how radical and even shocking it would have seemed at the time. In the late nineteenth century most writing for children was formal, leisurely, and gently didactic. Many writers still used the sort of artificial literary diction that Oswald makes fun of on the first page of *The Story of the Treasure Seekers:*

> I have read books myself, and I know how beastly it is when a story begins, " 'Alas!' said Hildegarde with a deep sigh, 'we must look our last on this ancestral home' "—and then some one else says something—and you don't know for pages and pages where the home is, or who Hildegarde is or anything about it. Our ancestral home is in the Lewisham Road. It is semi-detached. . . .

Nesbit's tone is direct, humorous, and fast-moving, and her children are modern and believable. They are not types imagined by an adult, but individuals coolly observed by their peers, each with his or her faults and virtues and passions. Though she tries to be fair and give everyone an equal chance at adventures, Nesbit clearly prefers boys and girls of her own sort: bold, quick-tempered, egotistic, and literary, like Oswald Bastable. In all her stories the sort of serious, diffident, well-behaved children who would have been the heroes and heroines of a typical Victorian fairy tale are portrayed as timid and dull—though a few of them can, with proper encouragement from their peers, improve, as the "white mouse" Denny does in *The Wouldbegoods.*

The Treasure Seekers and its sequels are firmly rooted in the contemporary world. The Bastable children need to restore the family fortunes because their father's business partner has taken advantage of his illness to abscond to Spain with all the capital of the firm, just as Hubert Bland's partner once did. The children's attempts to earn money by selling patent medicine, starting a newspaper, rescuing an old gentleman from danger (their own pet dog), or finding and marrying a princess tend to produce comic disaster. The story, however, in the tradition of juvenile fiction, ends happily. In the two sequels the Bastables' intended good deeds have a similar effect. By proper Victorian standards they behave badly—often disobeying their elders, digging up gardens, trespassing, and playing practical jokes—but though they are sometimes scolded and punished, they are always forgiven.

The Treasure Seekers was followed by two volumes of humorous fairy tales, *The Book of Dragons* (1900) and *Nine Unlikely Tales* (1901). They differ from most earlier literary fairy stories in that though they may contain magicians and dragons

and kings and queens, they clearly take place in the present. The language in which they are told is also contemporary. Discarding the romantic diction of the traditional literary fairy story and its conventional epithets, the golden hair and milk-white steeds, Nesbit uses Edwardian slang and draws her comparisons from the Edwardian child's world of experience. The dragon in "Uncle James" has "wings like old purple umbrellas that have been very much rained on," and the court officials wear "gold coronets with velvet sticking up out of the middle like the cream in the very expensive jam tarts." And when there is a magical transformation, it often produces very modern results. In "The Cockatoucan" (*Nine Unlikely Tales*) the unpleasant nursemaid Pridmore becomes an Automatic Nagging Machine like the candy dispensers in London railway stations, "greedy, grasping things which take your pennies and give you next to nothing in chocolate and change." What comes out of her are little rolls of paper with remarks on them like "Don't be tiresome."

Though she does not use a first-person child narrator, Nesbit's tone in these literary fairy stories is much like that of Oswald Bastable—contemporary, informal, direct; even today her wholehearted espousal of the child's point of view is striking. In "The Cockatoucan," for instance, she explains why Matilda doesn't want to visit her Great-aunt Willoughby:

> She would be asked about her lessons, and how many marks she had, and whether she had been a good girl. I can't think why grown-up people don't see how impertinent these questions are. Suppose you were to answer, "I'm top of my class, Auntie, thank you, and I'm very good. And now let's have a little talk about you. Aunt, dear, how much money have you got, and have you been scolding the servants again, or have you tried to be good and patient as a properly brought up aunt should be, eh, dear?"

Nesbit's next important book, *Five Children and It* (1902), combines the magical invention of her short tales with the realism and social comedy of the "Bastable" stories, creating a new and influential model for juvenile fantasy. The typical Victorian fairy tale, though it may begin in the real world, soon moves into some timeless Wonderland or country at the back of the North Wind. One of Nesbit's most brilliant moves was to reverse the process, and bring magic into modern London. In this she may have been following the lead of a contemporary writer of adult fantasy, F. Anstey, whose *Brass Bottle* (1900) had brought a genie into the life of an ordinary, contemporary young man. But whatever her sources, Nesbit was the first to imagine for a child audience what would be the actual consequences of magic happenings in the modern world: for example, the delivery by magic carpet of a hundred and ninety-nine Persian cats to the basement dining room of a house in Camden Town, or the transformation of one's brother into a ten-foot boy giant.

Nesbit's other original invention in *The Five Children and It* was the replacement of the traditional good fairy who grants wishes by an ill-tempered, monkeylike creature called the Psammead, who has extendable eyes like a snail's and a horror of water. Other authors of fantasy, of course—notably Lewis Carroll—had already invented strange ill-tempered creatures, but Nesbit was the first to invest such a figure with magical powers and make it central to an otherwise realistic narrative.

The Five Children and It is not only an amusing adventure story but also a tale of the vanity of human—or at least juvenile—wishes. The children in the book want to be "as beautiful as the day"; they ask for a sand pit full of gold sovereigns, giant size and strength, and instant adulthood. Each wish leads them into an appropriate comic disaster. When they become beautiful, for instance, their baby brother does not recognize them and bursts into howls of distrust, and they begin to quarrel among themselves—a not unusual result of such transformations in real life. When the spells end at sunset, the children are always greatly relieved. The reader, of course, has the pleasure of living out these granted wishes in imagination, plus the assurance that his or her unattainable desires are not so desirable after all.

The Phoenix and the Carpet (1904) continues the adventures of the five children, maintaining the comedy and imaginative invention of the original. It introduces another magical creature, the Phoenix, who is better looking and better tempered than the Psammead, but rather vain and self-centered. The central magic device is a secondhand flying carpet that takes the children to France, India, and the South Seas, with humorous consequences.

In the last volume of the series, *The Story of the Amulet* (1906), the Psammead is rediscovered in, and rescued from, a London pet shop. With its help the five children travel in time rather than space, visiting ancient Britain, Egypt, Babylon, and the lost island of Atlantis. *The Story of the Amulet* is unique among Nesbit's books in that it was carefully researched, and each chapter checked by an expert—Dr. Wallis (later Sir Ernest) Budge, the keeper of Egyptian and Assyrian antiquities at the British Museum. In the opinion of many critics, it is Nesbit's best work. It is also the one in which her political beliefs are most evident.

As a Fabian socialist, Nesbit was greatly concerned about the living conditions of the urban poor. One of her recurrent themes is the aesthetic unpleasantness and threat to health of modern cities in general and especially of London, which she called that "hateful, dark, ugly place." Many of us are now so accustomed to the nostalgic, prettified BBC version of Edwardian London that we have forgotten, if we ever knew, that in the early years of this century much of the city was filthy and many of its inhabitants sick or starving, its streets fouled with horse manure and urine, its river polluted, and its air often unfit to breathe. (The pea-soup fogs that lend mystery and charm to the adventures of Sherlock Holmes were in fact a damp, poisonous smog.) In *The Story of the Amulet,* a rash wish brings the Queen of Babylon, whom the children have met in the past, to London. It appalls her:

"But how badly you keep your slaves. How wretched and poor and neglected they seem," she said, as the cab rattled along the Mile End Road.

"They aren't slaves; they're working-people," said Jane.

"Of course they're working. That's what slaves are. Don't you tell me. Do you suppose I don't know a slave's face when I see it? Why don't their masters see that they're better fed and better clothed? . . . You'll have a revolt of your slaves if you're not careful," said the Queen.

"Oh, no," said Cyril; "you see they have votes—that makes them safe not to revolt. It makes all the difference. Father told me so."

"What is this vote?" asked the Queen. "Is it a charm? What do they do with it?"

"I don't know," said the harassed Cyril; "it's just a vote, that's all! They don't do anything particular with it."

"I see," said the Queen; "a sort of plaything."

Later in the same book the Amulet takes the children into a future in which England has become a Fabian Utopia, a city of parks and flowers, with clean air and an unpolluted Thames. People live in beautiful, uncluttered houses and wear loose woolly clothes of the sort favored by William Morris and by the Aesthetic Movement. There are no idle rich: everyone works, and no one goes hungry; the schools are progressive and coeducational; and both men and women care for babies.

With *The Railway Children* (1906) Nesbit returned to the realistic story, producing a work that in some ways anticipates the juvenile "problem novels" of today. The families in all of Nesbit's books tend to be in difficulties, just as the Blands so often were. Sometimes one of the parents is dead; but even if both survive, the father is out of the country, or ill, or has lost his job. The mother too may be ill (in *Five of Us—and Madeline* [1925] she has had a nervous breakdown), or she may be away caring for a sick relative. Often, as a result of these domestic disruptions, Nesbit's children have to leave their family home with the remaining parent, or go and stay with unsympathetic strangers in bleak, unattractive lodgings. Even when the family is intact, they are usually in cramped economic circumstances. The situation is most depressing when they live in town, for, as Nesbit remarks in *Five Children and It,* "London is like a prison for children, especially if their relatives are not rich."

In *The Railway Children* the protagonists not only have fallen upon hard times but also are in serious trouble: their father is in prison. It turns out that he has been mistakenly accused, but the resulting social shame and isolation of the family is real, and the children's efforts to adjust to their changed circumstances and even enjoy themselves are both ingenious and courageous. The tale is unique among Nesbit's family stories in that it is dominated by one child, Roberta, who is almost—but not quite—too good, brave, and kind to be true. *The Railway Children* has proved to be one of the most enduringly popular of Nesbit's books; it has been made into a television play and, more recently, a successful feature film.

In 1907 Nesbit published what may be, next to *The Story of the Amulet,* her most interesting and sophisticated fantasy, *The Enchanted Castle.* Here magic is not so much an imaginative projection of possibilities and the source of amusing adventures as an intensified image of reality. For example, it makes literal the perception that many adults have no idea of what is going on with the children who are living with them, and possibly don't even care. One of the children in the story, Mabel, finds a ring that makes her invisible, but it is soon clear that she was already more or less invisible to the aunt with whom she lives. Mabel's aunt feels not the slightest anxiety about her niece's disappearance, and readily swallows a made-up story about her having been adopted by a lady in a motor car. The other children are shocked by this insouciance, but Mabel explains that her aunt's mind is clogged with sentimental fantasy: "She's not mad, only she's always reading novelettes."

In the most striking episode of *The Enchanted Castle,* Nesbit's Fabian convictions, her comic sense, and her use of magic as a metaphor work together. Mabel and the other children decide to put on a play, and because there are only three grown-ups to watch it, they construct an audience out of old clothes, pillows, umbrellas, brooms, and hockey sticks, with painted paper faces. A magic ring brings these ungainly creatures to life, and they are transformed into awful caricatures of different types of contemporary adults. Eventually, most of the "Ugly-Wuglies" (as Gerald calls them) are disenchanted and become piles of old clothes again, but one remains alive. He is the sort of elderly gentleman "who travels first class and smokes expensive cigars," and Jimmy, the most materialistic of the children, is rather impressed by him: " 'He's got a motor-car,' Jimmy went on, . . . 'and a garden with a tennis-court, and a lake, and a carriage and pair. . . . He's frightfully rich, . . . He's simply rolling in money. . . . I wish *I* was rich.' " Since Jimmy has the magic ring, his wish is instantly granted.

> By quick but perfectly plain-to-be-seen degrees Jimmy became rich. . . . The whole thing was over in a few seconds. Yet in those few seconds they saw him grow to a youth, a young man, a middle-aged man; and then, with a sort of shivering shock, unspeakably horrible and definite, he seemed to settle down into an elderly gentleman, handsomely but rather dowdily dressed, who was looking down at them through spectacles and asking them the nearest way to the railway-station. . . .
>
> "Oh, Jimmy, *don't!*" cried Mabel, desperately.
>
> Gerald said: "This is perfectly beastly," and Kathleen broke into wild weeping.
>
> (*The Enchanted Castle*, pp. 185–186)

In his new persona Jimmy no longer knows the other children and is very unpleasant to them. But he turns out to be well acquainted with the elderly Ugly-Wugly, and they travel up to London together, followed by Jimmy's desperate brother, Gerald. There it appears that both Jimmy and the Ugly-Wugly have offices in the City complete with "a tangle of clerks and mahogany desks." An office boy tells Gerald that in spite of their apparent friendship, the two stockbrokers " 'is all for cutting each other's throats—oh, only in the way of business—been at it for years.' " The whole episode plunges Gerald into a kind of existential crisis:

[He] wildly wondered what magic and how much had been needed to give history and a past to these two things of yesterday, the rich Jimmy and the Ugly-Wugly. If he could get them away, would all memory of them fade—in this boy's mind, for instance; in the minds of all the people who did business with them in the City? Would the mahogany-and-clerk-furnished offices fade away? Were the clerks real? Was the mahogany? Was he himself real?

(ibid., p. 195–196)

Since Gerald is a character in a book, the answer to this last question is no. He is literally no more real than the elderly Ugly-Wugly—he too is a creature composed playfully out of odds and ends and brought to life by a kind of instant magic. But however unreal Gerald may be, Nesbit seems to be suggesting that there is something even more unreal about the average successful businessman. In spite of the pomp and circumstance of his exterior life, the City man is essentially, as Gerald puts it, "only just old clothes and nothing inside." He is an empty assemblage of expensive tailoring—or a greedy little boy who has grown up too fast.

The House of Arden (1908) and *Harding's Luck* (1909), though imperfect, are among Nesbit's most interesting and innovative works. The two stories, in both of which contemporary children travel back into the past, are interlocking rather than consecutive. In the first, Edred and Elfrida, searching for a lost family treasure, take over the bodies and lives of two children who were their ancestors; in *Harding's Luck* Dick does the same. This device is now so common in juvenile fantasy as to have become almost a cliché, but to Nesbit's readers it must have seemed new and exciting.

Another original feature of these two stories is the widening of Nesbit's social range. Before *The Enchanted Castle* all her central characters had been middle-class. Working-class children had been portrayed as aggressive and rude—like the threatening ragamuffins of *The Phoenix and the Carpet*—or else as ignorant and pathetic. The upper class often fared no better. Most of Nesbit's fairy-tale kings and queens were comic bunglers, and her court officials tended to be two-faced frauds with an up-to-date command of smarmy rhetoric. The real-life princess whom Noel had discovered in *The Treasure Seekers* turned out to be a dull, overdressed little girl who was afraid to play in the park.

The children in *The House of Arden,* however, are aristocrats—Edred is the future Lord Arden. He is unusual among Nesbit's heroes in that at the start of the story he is extremely disagreeable: cowardly, mean, and rather stupid. Victorian juvenile literature, of course, is full of children whose characters need improvement; Edred is notable mainly in that it isn't suggested that he should learn to obey and respect his elders. Also, his reformation is not achieved with the help of surrogate parent figures, but through experience and the example of his peers. (Nesbit here anticipates by three years one of the central themes of Frances Hodgson Burnett's masterpiece, *The Secret Garden*.)

Dickie Harding, the crippled hero of *Harding's Luck,* is also a new sort of character. He is almost uneducated and comes from the worst slums of South London, yet he is the most wholly admirable of all Nesbit's child heroes. Dickie not only is intelligent, imaginative, and courageous, but also is capable of self-sacrifice. In his past life he is not a poor, lame orphan, but privileged, healthy, and much loved. Yet he chooses to return to modern times for the sake of Beale, a tramp and part-time thief, and the only person who has ever been kind to him.

After *Harding's Luck* Nesbit's books are less impressive as a whole, but all of them contain good moments, and they continue to exhibit her remarkable sense of how children think, speak, and feel. *The Magic City* (1910), though perhaps the thinnest of her later works, is interesting because it reflects Nesbit's hobby of building miniature towns out of blocks, boxes, china, and all sorts of household bric-a-brac. (She was so successful at this pastime that one of her towns was exhibited to the public.)

The Wonderful Garden (1911) describes the adventures of three children who discover what they believe to be enchanted seeds and a portrait that comes to life. It is married by a condescending attitude toward her characters rare in Nesbit: she lets the reader know that there is no magic, only kindly adults who are indulging the children's fantasies and practicing a theatrical deception on them. In *Wet Magic* (1913) the magic is real, but though the book begins well, with the rescue of a mermaid from a seaside sideshow, Nesbit's imagination flags later on, and here too the end is spoiled for many readers by the casting of a spell that causes the children to forget all their adventures.

Several of the short tales in Nesbit's later collections, *The Magic World* (1912) and *Five of Us—and Madeline*, live up to her earlier standard. They also contain some of the most direct expression of her social views—radical in her own day, but today part of the democratic creed. One striking feature of Nesbit's tales is their implicit feminism. In deference to her husband's views, she never openly supported female suffrage, but her books are full of girls who, though they weep more easily, are as brave and independent-minded and adventurous as their brothers. And the heroines of her short fairy tales seldom sit around waiting to be rescued. In "The Last of the Dragons," for instance *(Five of Us —and Madeline)* the Princess remarks: "Father, darling, couldn't we tie up one of the silly little princes for the dragon to look at—and then *I* could go and kill the dragon . . . ? I fence much better than any of the princes we know." In this story Nesbit also strikes a blow for what is now called male liberation: the princess falls in love with "a pale prince with large eyes and a head full of mathematics and philosophy" who has completely neglected his fencing lessons.

Nesbit's Fabian socialism is also evident in these late stories. "The Mixed Mine" (*The Magic World*), for example, reverses the standard Victorian plot in which a poor child is befriended and reformed by a more privileged one. Here it is the shabby Gustus who shows Edward how to get the best out of a magic telescope that enlarges whatever you look at with it; and it is Gustus who jollies Edward out of his fear of the consequences, remarking finally that his friend is "more like a man and less like a snivelling white rabbit now than what you was when I met you." The implicit Fabian moral seems to be that intelligent artisans can show a scientifically illiterate and scientifically nervous middle class how to use the new technology and increase resources for the good of the whole society. (At the end of the story Gustus and Edward share a treasure and an Oxford education, and plan to start a school for slum children.)

Modern and innovative as Nesbit's books were for her time, in a way they look back to the oldest type of juvenile literature, the traditional folktale. They recall the simplicity and directness of diction, and the physical humor, of the folktale rather than the poetic language, intellectual wit, and didactic intention of the typical Victorian fairy tale.

In Nesbit's stories, as in the traditional tale, magic often seems to be a metaphor for imagination. In the folktale, imagination can turn a cottage into a castle or transform an ugly girl into a beautiful one with a kiss. In the same way it is imagination, disguised as magic, that gives Nesbit's characters (and by extension her readers) the power to journey through space and time: to view India or the South Seas, to visit Shakespeare's London, ancient Egypt, or a future Utopia. Nesbit seems aware of this metaphor in at least some of her tales. "The Book of Beasts" (*The Book of Dragons*), for instance, can be read as a fable about the power of imaginative art. The magic volume of its title contains colored pictures of exotic creatures that become real when the volume is left open. The little boy who finds it releases first a butterfly, then a bird of paradise, and finally a dragon that threatens to destroy his country. If any book is vivid enough, this story says, what is in it will become real to us and invade our world for good or evil.

True imaginative power is strong enough to transform the most prosaic contemporary scene. In the folktale, straw becomes gold, and a pumpkin is changed into a coach. Nesbit's magic is as much at home in a basement in Camden Town as on a South Sea island, and like that of the folktale, it is seldom merely romantic. Though it grants the desires of her characters, it may also expose these desires as comically misconceived.

Socially, too, Nesbit's stories have affinities with folklore. Her adventurous little girls and athletic princesses recall the many traditional tales in which the heroines have wit, courage, and strength. And there is also a parallel with her political stance. The classic folktales first recorded by scholars in the nineteenth century tend to observe the world from a working-class perspective—not unnaturally, since most of them were collected from uneducated farmers, servants, and artisans. The heroes and heroines of these tales are usually the children of poor people. When they go out into the world to seek their fortunes they confront supernatural representatives of the upper class: rich, ugly giants and magicians and ogres. Many of the traditional tales, like Nesbit's, make fun of establishment figures. And as has often been pointed out, the good kings and queens of the folktale seem from internal evidence to be merely well-to-do farmers. (Literary retellings of these stories, however, from Charles

Perrault to the present, usually give their royalty a convincingly aristocratic setting.)

There is no way of knowing whether Nesbit went back to these traditional folktale models consciously, or whether it was her own instinctive attitude to the world that made her break so conclusively with the past. Whatever the explanation, she was riding the wave of the future. And today, when most of her contemporaries are gathering dust on the shelves of secondhand bookshops, her stories are still read and loved by children, and echoed by adult authors. Almost every writer of children's fantasy in this century is—directly or indirectly—indebted to her.

Selected Bibliography

WORKS OF E. NESBIT

Though Nesbit published nearly a hundred books and pamphlets, plus many uncollected verses, essays, and tales, she is remembered today mostly for seventeen books for children, written between 1898 and 1913, many of which are still in print both in England and in America.

The Story of the Treasure Seekers. With illustrations by Gordon Browne and Lewis Baumer. London: T. Fisher Unwin, 1899.

The Book of Dragons. With illustrations by H. R. Millar. London: Harper and Brothers, 1900.

Nine Unlikely Tales. With illustrations by Claude Shepperson, H. R. Miller, et al., and with a frontispiece by A. L. Bowley. London: T. Fisher Unwin, 1901.

The Wouldbegoods. With illustrations by Arthur H. Buckland and John Hassell. London: T. Fisher Unwin, 1901.

Five Children and It. With illustrations by H. R. Millar. London: T. Fisher Unwin, 1902.

The New Treasure Seekers. With illustrations by Gordon Browne and Lewis Baumer. London: T. Fisher Unwin, 1904.

The Phoenix and the Carpet. With illustrations by H. R. Millar. London: George Newnes, 1904.

Oswald Bastable and Others. With illustrations by C. E. Brock and H. R. Millar. London: Wells, Gardner, Darton, 1905.

The Story of the Amulet. With illustrations by H. R. Millar. London: T. Fisher Unwin, 1906.

The Railway Children. With illustrations by C. E. Brock. London: Wells, Gardner, Darton, 1906.

The Enchanted Castle. With illustrations by H. R. Millar. London: T. Fisher Unwin, 1907.

The House of Arden. With illustrations by H. R. Millar. London: T. Fisher Unwin, 1908.

Harding's Luck. With illustrations by H. R. Millar. London: T. Fisher Unwin, 1909.

The Magic City. With illustrations by H. R. Millar. London: Macmillan, 1910.

The Wonderful Garden; or, The Three C's. With illustrations by H. R. Millar. London: Macmillan, 1911.

The Magic World. With illustrations by H. R. Millar and Spencer Pryse. London: Macmillan, 1912.

Wet Magic. With illustrations by H. R. Millar. London: R. Werner Laurie, 1913.

Five of Us—and Madeline. Edited by Mrs. Clifford Sharp. With illustrations by Nora S. Unwin. London: T. Fisher Unwin, 1925.

CRITICAL AND BIOGRAPHICAL STUDIES

Bell, Anthea. *E. Nesbit.* London: Bodley Head, 1960.

Moore, Doris Langley. *E. Nesbit: A Biography.* Rev. ed. New York: Chilton Books, 1966. (An excellent full-length biography and study of Nesbit's work.)

Streatfield, Noel. *Magic and the Magician: E. Nesbit and Her Children's Books.* London: Ernest Benn, 1958. (For child readers.)

—ALISON LURIE

CHARLES PERRAULT
1628–1703

THE SITUATION OF Charles Perrault is unique in literary history. His fairy tales are undoubtedly among the most popular works in the world: millions of people know, or think they know, the stories of Cinderella, Little Red Riding Hood, and Sleeping Beauty, yet few have ever heard the name Charles Perrault. Furthermore, there has been considerable debate over whether Perrault did indeed write the tales or whether they were in fact written by one of his sons. The best evidence indicates that while his *Histoires, ou contes du temps passès, avec des moralitéz* (*Histories or Tales of Past Times, with Morals*, 1697) were published under the name of his son, Pierre d'Armancour, the stories were the work of Perrault in probable collaboration with the talented teenage boy, with whom he had a close relationship. The tales were published near the end of a long career during which Perrault had devoted his talents to works of a quite different nature, little suspecting that these slight tales would have a universal and permanent impact. They seemed, at the time, merely his contribution to a literary form that was a fad of the times.

Charles Perrault, a lifelong Parisian, was born on 12 January 1628. He was educated by his father and also attended the Collège de Beauvoir. He was not an outstanding student, but he was spirited and independent-minded; he argued with his professors and soon dropped out to conduct his own education. This he did with a friend in the Jardin de Luxembourg, reading widely for a few years in any way he saw fit. He began his literary career by engaging in two of the fashionable pursuits of the day—writing parodies of the Latin classics and becoming involved in current literary debates, such as the Quarrel of the Ancients and the Moderns, in which he argued for the superiority of the Moderns. In 1651 he took a law degree at Orléans and was admitted to the bar. Soon wearying of legal practice, he returned to reading and writing; became interested in architecture; held for ten years a government position as superintendant of the royal buildings; and, as a sort of minister of cultural affairs in general, became a regular member of the court of Louis XIV, where he enjoyed considerable favor.

Perrault married late in life, at age forty-four, the beautiful nineteen-year-old Marie Guichon. It was an apparently happy union that produced three sons and, some historians believe, a daughter. When Perrault was fifty his wife died. He was devastated by her death but took over the job of raising and educating his children—which was probably a crucial influence on his composing the fairy tales, since he maintained that such literature was an effective means of instilling values.

When Perrault began writing his tales in the 1690's, the fairy tale was already much in vogue, especially at the court of Louis XIV. The seventeenth century in France was known as the Age of Reason, yet there was wide interest in literature of an allegorical, mythological, and symbolic nature, and during the last two decades of the century it was a popular practice in court circles to tell fairy tales. So the fairy tale was very much in the air

431

when Perrault began publishing his work, but literary history accords him the major credit for recasting the oral tales in a polished literary form.

In 1691 Perrault published the first of his tales, "La marquise de Salusses, ou la patience de Griselidis" ("The Marquise of Salussa; or, The Patience of Griselda"). This story, written in verse form, was not really a fairy tale—in fact, many of his tales, and those of subsequent authors, in no way involve fairies. The events of such stories are, however, highly unusual, sometimes miraculous, and, in the case of Griselidis (the Patient Griselda), incredible. This piece was followed by two other traditional stories, also in verse form, "Peau d'ane" ("Donkey-Skin") in 1692, and "Les souhaits ridicules" ("The Ridiculous Wishes") in 1693. The three were reprinted in 1695 under the title *Contes de ma mère l'oye* (Tales of Mother Goose). Perrault did not invent "Mother Goose"—the term was already in general use to designate oral fairy tales. (The phrase "contes de ma mère l'oye" was also printed on the frontespiece of the *Histoires*, with the result that the latter work came to be known by both titles.)

In 1697 the work appeared that was to earn Perrault immediate and lasting fame as "the father of the literary fairy tale." The tales in *Histoires, ou contes du temps passés, avec des moralitéz*, which were written in prose, appeared under the name of Perrault's son, possibly because Perrault, an established writer of "serious" literature, hesitated to have the fairy tales published under his own name. He anticipated the scorn he would receive from some quarters, as he in fact did from the eminent critic Nicolas Boileau, who scolded him "for having written meaningless and childish stories, unworthy of the attention of a serious writer." Perrault's biographers believe that when Perrault died in 1703 he was probably unaware that he had written an immortal classic. Boileau notwithstanding, the fame of Perrault's tales spread rapidly and far, inspiring a host of admirers and imitators during the eighteenth and nineteenth centuries, along with numerous translations, adaptations, and, inevitably, corruptions. The characters, plots, and phrasings originated by Perrault ("What big teeth you have, grandmother!" and turning into a pumpkin if one doesn't leave a party before a certain hour) have become absorbed into the mainstream of Western culture.

Translations into numerous languages began early in the eighteenth century, the first English version being that of Robert Samber in 1729. His was a relatively faithful "literary" translation that introduced not only Perrault to the English-reading world but also the personage of Mother Goose. Samber's English edition reproduced the frontespiece of the first French edition of 1697. It depicted a peasant woman spinning and entertaining a group of enthralled children sitting by the fireplace. On the wall is a placard that reads "Mother Goose's Tales."

In writing his fairy tales Perrault drew upon the oral tradition and also upon certain writers of the Italian Renaissance whose works, in turn, drew upon Eastern folklore and such tales as the ninth-century Persian *Book of Sindibad*, Gianfrancesco Straparola's *Piacevoli notti* (1550–1553), and Giambattista Basile's *Pentamerone* (1634–1636). From these works and others, Perrault found and used not the exact stories so much as motifs, the basic configurations of plot, character, and theme. He made many changes and additions (which will be noted below) and altered the thematic emphasis to present his own moral implications. Above all, he cleaned up his sources. Many earlier folktales were extremely bawdy, and Perrault considered them unfit in their original condition for his intended audiences of children and members of the courtly salon. In his preface to the *Contes de ma mère l'oye*, Perrault explains the value of his fables: he points out the worthiness of the "morals" found in them, and while acknowledging his debt to his literary forebears who had treated the same motifs, he stresses that his versions were concerned with *bonnes moeurs*, which the earlier writers had neglected. Regarding the influence of fairy tales on children, he states flatly that his stories depict vice punished and virtue rewarded, and that children tend to emulate those characters who are good and therefore successful in life and to dislike and to reject those who are bad and therefore failures. He also admits to presenting his tales in as attractive a form and style as possible to make them enjoyable, but without violating his main self-imposed law: never write anything that would wound modesty or offend decency and decorum. Thus his themes are edifying and his style graceful, urbane, and witty. He reflects the "neoclassical" taste in literary expression: an economical language, carefully chosen to suggest meaning with a minimum of words; a statement of facts; a few descriptive details; and an absence of explanation or analysis. Except for the brief "morals" at the ends of most of his tales, their

CHARLES PERRAULT

meanings, precisely because of their brevity and lack of explanatory details, lie largely in the minds of their audience. Perrault's morals tend to be rather obvious, often reductive and satirical; and they rarely touch the full implications and resonances of the stories. There is one aspect of Perrault's style, however, that generally comes through in the better translations: his ironic tone, his gently suggested mockery of some of the characters and their actions, and of the fairy-tale conventions themselves. And while he may have eliminated the gross and the bawdy, Perrault substituted a sly eroticism implicit both in the situations and in the author's choice of words. His double entendres have been called the author's winking at the adult reader over the heads of his juvenile audience.

The *Histoires, ou contes du temps passés, avec des moralitéz* of 1697 included these eight titles: "La belle au bois dormant" ("The Sleeping Beauty in the Woods"), "Le petit chaperon rouge" ("Little Red Riding Hood"), "La barbe-bleue" ("Bluebeard"), "Le maître chat, ou le chat botté" ("Puss in Boots"), "Les fées" ("The Fairy"), "Cendrillon, ou la petite pantoufle de verre" ("Cinderella"), "Riquet à la houppe" ("Rickey with the Tuft"), and "Le petit poucet" ("Little Poucet" or "Little Thumb").

The first of the stories, "Sleeping Beauty," is a true fairy tale, featuring several fairies and magic spells. In some of the earlier versions using the central motif—a princess doomed to sleep for a hundred years until awakened by a prince—the conduct of the young man is scarcely praiseworthy. He rapes the sleeping girl and leaves her to find, when she finally awakens, that she has borne one or two children. Perrault's prince is more gentlemanly: he braves the briars and thickets that surround Beauty's castle and has relations with her only after she is awake and responsive to his marriage proposal. Perrault then adds a second part to the story, which some critics have found to be extraneous. It depicts the Prince's mother (who comes from child-eating ogre stock) becoming jealous of her son's new wife and children, trying to have them served up in a hash, and being outwitted by a kindhearted cook who substitutes meat from the barnyard. The evil mother, who is eventually destroyed, was often portrayed in earlier versions as the Prince's first wife, which gave a realistic motive for the older woman's savage actions.

Perrault's main contribution to the tale, in addition to providing decorous behavior on the part of the Prince, is the style. Instead of the early folkloristic narration, one finds an irony that is directed at the lovers themselves and at the fairy-tale conventions. When the Good Fairy modifies Beauty's fate (changing death to the long sleep), she also puts to sleep the entire household (except the girl's parents): "All this was done in a moment; the Fairies are not long in doing their business." When the young Prince is confronted by the castle's encircling brambles, "he did not cease from continuing his way: a young and amorous Prince is always valiant." When the entire household is awakened from their long sleep: "As all of them were not in love, they were ready to die of hunger," and the young couple on their first night together "slept very little; the Princess had no occasion." Perrault also makes much of the out-of-date style of clothing necessarily worn by the Princess, "dressed like my great-grandmother." Tellers of fairy tales are not usually so concerned with the passage of real time; the tone and manner of "Sleeping Beauty" are, however, typical of many of his subsequent tales.

"Little Red Riding Hood," one of Perrault's briefest and best-known tales, seems to have come straight from oral tradition—there is no known literary version before Perrault's. The story has since appeared in hundreds of different forms and has attracted a wide spectrum of critical interpretation. The motif of an innocent young girl meeting with and being devoured by a wolf has been seen mythically as the Dawn being consumed by Night; psychologically as a puberty/menstruation rite (the color of the riding hood) or as a seduction story (the girl's willingness to disrobe, jump into bed, and be "devoured"); as a warning against innocence, naiveté, and the thoughtless pursuit of pleasure (Red Riding Hood is unusually beautiful, but receives no guiding instructions from her doting mother and spends much time gathering nuts and flowers and running after butterflies—calling into question her character); as a reflection of contemporary fear of real wolves as well as legendary werewolves (more recently, wolves as Jungian anima figures); and as a cautionary reminder, as suggested by Perrault's moral, that girls should beware of strangers, especially the obliging and gentle, for they are the most dangerous, against whom innocence and virtue have no defenses.

Critics and subsequent writers have found fault with the gratuitous devouring of the grandmother and the brutal abruptness with which Riding Hood meets her fate. Subsequent versions of the tale have differed greatly in showing whether Red Riding Hood deserved to be devoured, whether she should escape or be saved (how or by whom), and whether the wolf should be punished for his evil actions. Some early versions had Riding Hood outwit the wolf and escape safely home, whereas in other, later ones she and her grandmother were exhumed from the wolf's stomach, none the worse for the experience. But the one aspect of Perrault's story that should be beyond negative criticism is his deft handling of the celebrated dialogue between Riding Hood and the wolf, with its ritualistic repetitions leading up to disaster. Repetitious enumerations of parts of the anatomy—arms, legs, ears, eyes, teeth—had appeared in earlier legends and fairy tales, but Perrault's incantatory technique in this tale seems to have been his own invention. It is that dialogue which has provided much of the charm of the tale, and its refrain—"What big teeth you have, grandma!"—has of course become common currency in our culture.

Many scholars believe that "Bluebeard" may be an original invention of Perrault's—with, however, two motifs drawn from popular tradition: the forbidden chamber and the magical key with the indelible spot of blood. These motifs appear in *The Arabian Nights* and *The Pentamerone*, but there is much evidence that the character of Bluebeard was drawn from any one of a number of real-life husbands of monstrous reputation. In Perrault's story Bluebeard gives his new young wife a key to a forbidden chamber, and then leaves the house, thus providing her with an opportunity to succumb to her curiosity. He returns unexpectedly and notes the blood on the key—undeniable evidence that she had discovered the corpses of his former wives. She is spared joining the other murdered wives by the timely arrival of her brothers, who kill Bluebeard.

The reason for the attractive young woman agreeing to marry a man of such repellent aspect, whose previous wives have mysteriously disappeared, is made clear enough: he wins her over by his dazzling wealth and elegant country estates. She decides his beard is not so blue after all. But his motive for murdering his wives is less clear. It has been suggested that "Bluebeard" is a story of "sexual transgression"—that the reader is to understand that during the husband's absence the young wife (and presumably her predecessors) is unfaithful to him. The bloody key and the secret chamber are here seen, in Freudian terms, as distinctly sexual

—an interpretation that has no concrete basis in the story itself but that might be inferred from the many other accounts (*The Arabian Nights*, Greek myth, and the Bible) of women's inability to resist temptation. The fatal effect of this female weakness is an old theme; and while Perrault's version does not insist on the sexual interpretation, it does suggest that the young wife deserves some kind of punishment for her disobedience. On the other hand, Bluebeard has no apparent reason for subjecting his wife to such a tantalizing temptation, and he certainly is not justified in exacting such an extreme penalty. As Perrault says in his moral, modern husbands are more gentle and, even when jealous, do not demand the impossible.

"Cinderella" is probably the world's best-known fairy story—around seven hundred versions have been collected. As was his custom, Perrault made some significant changes in and additions to early versions. For the "helpful animal" who originally came to Cinderella's assistance (usually a bird or some other creature that is understood to be the reincarnation of the dead mother), Perrault substituted the fairy godmother, thus dividing a living mother image into two aspects, the evil and the good (which, according to psychological views, enables the child reader to respond comfortably to the amiable side of the mother while disliking the "evil" side). Perrault also added the magical creation of the carriage, and its horses and footmen, out of the pumpkin and various local rodents. He also devised the enchanted midnight curfew and the all-important glass slipper. Critics argue over the relevance of the fine clothes and elegant carriage, one interesting theory being that of the scooped-out pumpkin/carriage as a womb image, from which Cinderella emerges reborn and, in an important way, reeducated (see Barchilon). A less Freudian view sees the clothes, carriage, and fancy-dress ball at a royal court as part of the realistic detail Perrault lavished on his story, reflecting accurately the aristocratic world and interests of his audience at Louis XIV's Versailles.

The meaning of the midnight deadline has also been variously interpreted, and can be seen as one of those conditions often traditionally imposed on anyone receiving special supernatural assistance. There has also been argument about whether Perrault mistook the word *vair* (fur) for *verre* (glass) in creating his slipper, but it seems apparent that a *glass* slipper was necessary to the story: magic, of course, since it was unbreakable; rigid and unyielding, as it would fit only the precisely appropriate foot, with any misfitting being readily apparent. Freudian critics have, inevitably, made much of the feet and slippers as symbols of genitalia, and of Cinderella's customary unsightly clothes as emblematic of aspects of female biology that the male must learn to accept (see Bettelheim). Whatever the psychological significance, one thing is common to most versions of the story: Cinderella never reveals her identity while she is in her beautiful, enchanted condition, no matter how enamored of her the princely suitors seem to be. They must see her and accept her in her normal humble state. She never reveals her identity until she is so accepted, as if she knows she will never escape her lowly servitude unless she is loved while still in her rags. This is reminiscent of the donkey-skin story, and looks forward in some ways to the later "Beauty and the Beast" of Madame Le Prince de Beaumont (with the roles of course being reversed). One might add that Perrault weakens his version by having one of the Prince's attendants, and not the young Prince himself, discover Cinderella's identity while she is still in her humble clothing.

"Rickey with the Tuft" is another tale with a motif similar to that of "Beauty and the Beast." Perrault's tale was written many years earlier, however, and his special recasting of an ancient theme has no known precedent. Instead of a literal Beast, Perrault depicts an exceptionally ugly man with a brilliant mind. He falls in love with a beautiful but stupid woman. Returning his love, the woman sees only his superiority of mind and character, just as he, because of his passion, sees her as possessing surpassing intelligence. Thus the transforming power of love: the ugly and repugnant become the beautiful and desirable; and Perrault's moral is familiar: beauty, whether of body or mind, lies largely in the eye of the beholder.

"The Fairy" is another tale with a very explicit moral, one that happens to be extremely popular: that goodness and kindness will be recognized and richly rewarded and that evil and selfishness will be punished—which everyone would like to believe. Known to English-language readers as "The Fairy" or "Diamonds and Toads," this tale concerns a kindly but overworked girl who, because of her generosity in giving a drink of water to a poor old woman (a fairy in disguise) is rewarded by having every word that emerges from her mouth accompanied by a flower or a jewel. Her selfish sister attempts to repeat the miracle but cannot refrain

from being hateful to the strange woman. She finds that her words are then accompanied by a spewing forth of snakes and toads. The good daughter is driven out of the house by the angry mother but is not lonely for long. A prince finds her, falls in love with her, and proposes marriage—but only (as Perrault makes clear) after he has calculated that her oral production of jewels would amply compensate for her lack of dowry. The selfish, unproductive sister is later driven out of the house, too, and dies miserably.

"Puss in Boots" and "Little Thumb"(or "Little Poucet") should be considered together. Both Little Poucet and the wily Puss have good reasons for their unscrupulous actions, and the implications of the two stories are similar: that even if you are small and relatively weak, you can succeed in life—if, that is, you are willing to be deceitful and ruthless.

In "Puss in Boots" the reader is introduced to a popular figure in folklore—the helpful animal—who in this instance is combined with another folklore favorite—the trickster. This cat, in the process of gaining riches and power for his destitute master, resorts to a series of con-man operations designed to pass his master off as the wealthy, landowning "Marquis de Carabas." By presenting gifts to the local king, the gullible father of a beautiful daughter, Puss wins his favor; by tricks and by terrorizing some peasants, Puss obtains elegant clothing for his master and the "ownership" of large tracts of productive land; by duping a stupid ogre into giving up both his life and his castle, Puss installs his master in luxury—all of which gains the hand of the beautiful princess. Puss then retires to a life of ease.

Tales like this, depicting adversity and ultimate success, sometimes involve moral choices, sometimes not. There are no moral decisions in "Puss in Boots," no choices between right and wrong—only resourcefulness and cunning. But it can be said on behalf of Puss that his efforts were in a good cause and, as is sometimes the case in trickster operations, the victims, who are often vain, stupid, and greedy, invite exploitation.

The last story in Perrault's *Histoires*, "Little Thumb," is sometimes confused with an English story about another diminutive hero, *The History of Tom Thumbe*, by Richard Johnson (1621). There is a similar motif, but differences in plot and events. Perrault used a number of familiar folklore motifs: the poverty-stricken parents who must abandon their children in a forest; the young hero's leaving

435

a trail, first of pebbles and then of breadcrumbs (unfortunately eaten by birds), to show the way back from dangerous territory; his tricking an ogre into slaughtering his own seven daughters instead of Little Poucet and his brothers; Poucet eventually acquiring wealth and restoring his family to a comfortable life. In Perrault's version Little Poucet, when born, was the size of his father's thumb, but he seems to assume normal if still small size during the story. He manages to wear boots designed for a giant ogre, but, being magic, the boots readily adapt themselves to him. The basis of Poucet's success, other than using his small size to eavesdrop from under adults' chairs, is his willingness to have the ogre's little girls murdered in his place, his successful theft of the ogre's boots, and his extorting from the ogre's wife, already grieving over her murdered daughters, a large amount of gold and silver—which would prevent her husband's death at the hands of "bandits."

In a long closing paragraph Perrault sketches some other of Poucet's reputed deeds, saying that they were accounts of "a great many authors" who did not agree that Poucet took the ogre's money. All agree that Poucet used his magic boots in other ways than to extort gold and silver from the ogre's wife. Perrault grants them their views and points out in his moral that it is often the despised and scorned child who brings good fortune to the entire family; that even if one is very small, sharp wits and courage can win the day where mere brawn will fail. In the first English translation of this tale (Samber, 1729) the hero is called "Little Poucet." By the sixth edition (1764) the name had been changed to "Little Thumb." The name "Hop o' my Thumb" seems to have appeared during the nineteenth century.

During the last hundred years these tales have been subjected to serious critical study from nearly every conceivable point of view. In 1888 Andrew Lang published an edition of Perrault with notes from a folkloric/anthropological viewpoint. Since that time Freudian critics have stressed the sexual content and the importance of such tales in the child's maturing and coping with life's problems. Other critics have discovered mythological patterns, while Jungians have found archetypes and have stressed the role of fairy tales in the "individuation" process. Historical scholars have resisted these "modern" interpretations in favor of seeing Perrault's tales as efforts to indoctrinate the young with the values of French bourgeois-aristo-cratic culture of the late seventeenth century. These stories have also been viewed in their central role in the development of literature for children, of an evolving awareness of the child's nature and needs. It should be pointed out, however, that many of the psychological studies that include Perrault's stories do not consider them as autonomous works of literature; they treat fairy tales in general and are concerned with basic patterns and recurrent motifs. Fairy tales provide "evidence" in the development of critical theories and do not always deal with Perrault's tales specifically as works of art possessing the author's special point of view, language, and tone. Those critics that do study individual stories often choose those works that support a thesis, as with Perrault's presumed hostility toward, or fear of, women; his condescension toward children; his bourgeois-materialist values, to name a few. These elements do exist in the tales, but there is also contradictory evidence—inconsistencies in the author's implied attitudes. It seems that critics have taken the tales far more seriously than Perrault did and are often not as responsive to his humor, his amiable mockery and gentle satirical tone—directed at most all of the characters, situations, and fairy-tale conventions—as he probably hoped his mature audience would be. The importance of his style, his tone in judging the tales, is implied in the foreword to his first published tale of Griselda, addressed to "A Mademoiselle . . . ," in which Perrault observes that he does not expect that Griselda's behavior will be imitated, but that while patience is not necessarily a virtue to be found among Parisian ladies, they have succeeded over the years in instilling it in their husbands.

Selected Bibliography

WORKS OF CHARLES PERRAULT

For a listing of various French and English editions since 1785, including facsimile reprints of the original 1696 and 1697 editions, see Elva S. Smith, *The History of Children's Literature: A Syllabus with Selected Bibliographies*. Revised and enlarged by Margaret Hodges and Susan Steinfirst. Chicago: American Library Association, 1980.

Editions

Contes de fées, with Madame d'Aulnoy and Madame Le Prince de Beaumont. With illustrations by Bertall, Beaucé, et al. Paris: Librairie Garnier Frères, 1856.

Perrault's Popular Tales. Edited by Andrew Lang. London: Oxford University Press, 1888. Reprinted New York: Arno Press, 1977. (Tales in French, with Lang's biographical and critical commentaries in English.)

Perrault: Contes en vers et en prose. Geneva: Skira, 1944.

Translations

Of the numerous translations of Perrault's tales, several are to be especially recommended: those by Richard Howard, Marianne Moore, A. E. Johnson, Geoffrey Brereton, Anne Carter, and Robert Samber (whose 1729 version is the choice in the Opies' *Classic Fairy Tales*). Extracts in this text are from Samber.

Perrault's Complete Fairy Tales. Translated by A. E. Johnson et al. With illustrations by W. Heath Robinson. New York: Dodd Mead, 1961.

The Classic Fairy Tales. Edited by Iona and Peter Opie. With illustrations by Joseph Highmore, Rex Whistler, et al. London: Oxford University Press, 1974.

CRITICAL AND BIOGRAPHICAL STUDIES

Barchilon, Jacques. *Le conte merveilleux français de 1690 à 1790*. Paris: Champion, 1975.

————, and Peter Flinder. *Charles Perrault*. Boston: Twayne Publishers, 1981.

Bettelheim, Bruno. *The Uses of Enchantment: The Meaning and Importance of Fairy Tales*. New York: Knopf, 1976.

Butor, Michel. "On Fairy Tales." In *European Literary Theory and Practice*, edited by Vernon W. Gras. New York: Dell, 1973.

Darton, F. J. Harvey. *Children's Books in England*. Cambridge: Cambridge University Press, 1932, 1958.

Duffy, Maureen. *The Erotic World of Faery*. London: Hodder and Stoughton, 1972.

Heisig, James W. "Bruno Bettelheim and the Fairy Tales" *Children's Literature* 6: 93–114 (1977).

Lüthi, Max. *Once upon a Time: On the Nature of Fairy Tales*. Translated by Lee Chadeayne and Paul Gottwald. New York: Unger, 1970; Bloomington: Indiana University Press, 1976.

Moustakis, Christine, et al. "Fairy Tales: Their Staying Power" *Children's Literature Association Quarterly* 7/2: 2–36 (Summer 1982).

Soriano, Marc. *Les contes de Perrault: Culture savante et traditions populaires*. Paris: Gallimard, 1968.

Taylor, Una Ashworth. "Fairy Tales as Literature (Part 1)" *Signal* 21: 123–138 (Sept. 1976).

Zipes, Jack. *Breaking the Magic Spell: Radical Theories of Folk and Fairy Tales*. Austin: University of Texas Press, 1979.

————. *Fairy Tales and the Art of Subversion: The Classical Genre of Children and the Process of Civilization*. New York: Wildman Press, 1983.

————. *The Trials and Tribulations of Little Red Riding Hood*. South Hadley, Mass.: Bergin and Harvey Publishers, 1983.

—GLENN S. BURNE

BEATRIX POTTER
1866–1943

BEATRIX POTTER SPENT most of her girlhood and young womanhood in her third-floor room in her parents' comfortable Kensington home. Although this seclusion prolonged her adolescence and delayed her declaration of independence from parental restrictions, the time and space allowed her to develop the patience, discipline, and powers of observation that inform both her literary and her artistic styles. At the age of nearly thirty-five she was finally able to break through her parents' protectiveness and began to write and illustrate the exquisitely proportioned nursery classics for which she is famous, completing twenty-one of them between 1900 and 1910. Though she continued to publish these works for most of the rest of her life, she never duplicated the intensity of her early period, during which she wrote and illustrated two books a year. After her marriage to William Heelis in 1913, she wrote and illustrated little, usually culling forgotten projects from her files to satisfy her publishers' requests for more books. Yet in spite of the quantity of work produced in her earlier creative period, the quality of it was not compromised, and it continues to this day to appeal to young audiences. Many of her characters—Peter Rabbit, Mrs. Tiggy-Winkle, Jemima Puddle-Duck, Mr. Tod, Squirrel Nutkin, Tabitha Twitchett, and Hunca Munca, to name a few—have become well-established characters in the English-speaking cultures, in which a good number of her works endure as classics of the nursery.

Helen Beatrix Potter was born on 28 July 1866, the first child of Helen and Rupert Potter. Even as a young child, she spent her time in isolation. Her parents were well-to-do and had extensive connections with famous artists of their time. They were personally acquainted with John Everett Millais and James McNeill Whistler, and Mr. Potter was a talented amateur photographer. Given these contacts, it is not surprising that the daughter became interested in drawing at an early age. She did have some children's books available to her, including the nursery rhymes illustrated by Randolph Caldecott, which later influenced both her writing and her illustrations. Her only constant companions were various animals, starting with a mouse who lived in the nursery wall, but who allowed himself to be tamed. Her relationships with the mouse and with her other pets influenced her artwork, teaching her the necessity for patience and providing the opportunity for the close observation of animal features and habits. Her early seclusion afforded her the time to focus intensely on her art and writing and allowed her to observe the details and minutiae that would make her work so consistent, exquisitely small, and highly valued. Though she did have one younger brother, who was a close companion, when he was old enough to be sent away to boarding school, the older sister was once again left to her own devices in the nursery. The Potter parents remained unworried that such extensive isolation would somehow damage their now adolescent daughter.

Her only sources of diversion were excursions to the Kensington Gardens and to the newly built Victoria and Albert Museum (known then as the

South Kensington Museum) near her home in Kensington. During the outings to the gardens Potter found carefully sculptured natural landscapes, which she used as the backgrounds for her animal studies. In the museum she saw models of animals' skeletons, which allowed her to study animal bone structures closely and thus to draw animals even more accurately.

Although the trips to the museum and the garden were important, the greatest influence on her creative life, as well as on her later personal life, was the family summer vacation. The Potters regularly took prolonged summer holidays either in Scotland or in the Lake District of northern England. During those four months young Beatrix was free to roam the open countryside and, without interruption, to observe and sketch the natural world around her. Given that these holidays were the happiest times of her childhood, it is not surprising that Potter decided later in life to live in the country and to become a farmer and a livestock breeder. It is also not surprising that, though she was city-bred, Potter's best books take place in the country and celebrate the simple pleasures of country living. Both she and the pets she brought back from the country to the Potters' London home felt stifled in the third-floor nursery. During the winter, although she could not literally escape from her confinement, she could roam through the fictional landscapes in her imagination. Through her books she attained the freedom that she cherished and that was otherwise unavailable to her.

Potter thought back to her animals and animal stories when she first had contact with children. Her last governess (companion is perhaps a more appropriate title) was Annie Carter, a young woman only two years older than the nineteen-year-old Potter. When Carter left the Potter home to become Mrs. Moore, the two young women continued what had grown into a friendship. In 1893, when Annie Moore's first child, Noël, became ill with scarlet fever, Potter clearly could not visit the child, so she decided to write him a letter. The letter contained the story of Peter Rabbit in shortened form. The Moore children enjoyed the tale so much that they requested that Potter continue to send them picture-story letters. There is no way of telling how many of these stories Potter wrote because the children either lost them or read them until they fell apart. But scholars are sure that Potter began at least four of the books in the Peter Rabbit series in letters to the young Moores: *The*

Tale of Peter Rabbit (1901), *The Tale of Squirrel Nutkin* (1903), *Tale of Benjamin Bunny* (1904), and *The Tale of Mr. Jeremy Fisher* (1906). Although Noël was only five years old at the time he received the Peter Rabbit letter, he kept it and continued to enjoy it. In 1900, when Potter asked him to lend it to her if he still had it, he was able to comply with her request.

In her twenties Potter had been encouraged by an uncle who was also interested in botany to pursue more actively her scientific interest in fungi—in cataloging their varieties and discovering new species of them, in painting them in scientifically correct detail, and in studying their reproductive systems. In spite of her obvious talent, no one took seriously the work of an untrained artist—a woman, no less—and an uneducated scientist. As well as her drawings of fungi, she had done designs for greeting cards for the firm of Hildesheimer and Faulkner. But Potter's creative involvement in this work was minimal, as the work was done to order; because it did not reflect her talent for drawing animals, she found the task unsatisfying. Then, Canon Rawnsley, a friend of the family, suggested that she publish a small book for children, one that might be popular as a gift book. She recalled the letter to Noël Moore that she had written seven years before and thought she might try converting it into a story. At first publishers showed no interest in her book, and she decided to publish it herself, using her combined earnings from her greeting cards and from a small gift from her father. The first printing of 250 copies sold out to her friends and family and encouraged her to order a second printing of 200 copies. With this edition she reapplied to the one publisher, Frederick Warne, who had earlier shown polite interest, however slight. In its new form the book was good enough for Warne to offer her a contract, with the proviso that the text be more carefully polished and edited and the number of pictures reduced from forty-one to thirty-two, all of them colored. Potter willingly complied with these conditions, although she admitted her doubts that the colors rabbit brown and lettuce green would be interesting enough. The private editions featured black-and-white pictures only, and the addition of color was the publisher's apt suggestion to an unsure first-time author-illustrator. The final result was the nursery classic *The Tale of Peter Rabbit*, in almost exactly the same form in which we know it today.

The narrative incorporates three basically appealing elements. First, Potter has used the archetypal "adventure followed by return home" formula of the boys' adventure book. This formula provides not only the adventure and high-spiritedness for the main character, but also the safe shelter at the end, which is so reassuring to children and adults. Second, she has written a story like the story of David and Goliath, in which the small, quick, and sympathetic hero outwits and defeats the larger, stronger, and malign enemy. Third, Peter is appealing because of his typically human rebellious impulse; he decides to go into Mr. McGregor's garden for no other reason than that his mother has forbidden it, fully aware that he may meet the same fate as his father, who was made into a pie. Most readers would recognize and empathize with his sheer obstinancy in the face of a strict maternal injunction; they might even envy him for proceeding as boldly as he does.

The language, too, has much to do with the book's perennial appeal. Potter's publishers originally had difficulty with what they saw as her overly ornate and complicated diction. But Potter never talked down to her readers, even though she knew that most of them would be children and, therefore, have limited vocabularies. Potter was more concerned with accurate and stirring narration than she was worried about confronting children with unfamiliar vocabulary; if the cadence and diction of such a phrase as "the sparrow implored Peter to exert himself" seemed appropriate, it stood. Potter did not underestimate her young readers' ability to use the pictures and surrounding text to figure out the meanings of words they did not know. As a child she had herself spent many quiet hours trying to deduce what adults were saying from whatever clues she could find in the conversations they conducted around her. She remembered these experiences and probably based her accurate judgment of the child reader's abilities on them.

Potter's illustration is as noteworthy as her language. The soft browns, variegated greens, and understated blues and reds of her watercolors may pale beside the more vivid hues of modern children's books, but her pictures always complement the text rather than compete with it. In fact, they tell the story by themselves, which is especially important for the young child who is not yet able to read the words. They help to clarify the meaning of the occasionally difficult word, to identify the contexts, and to establish the tempo of the story. Most of all, they are lovely. With great precision Potter captures the rabbit's-eye view of the garden in a variety of lifelike colors. She manages to adapt the rabbit's form to express human emotions, capturing the essence of both animal and human life in her animal figures. Finally, the pictures are plentiful and placed opposite the text that they depict. Potter drew and revised extensively in order to get every detail exactly right. She exhibits a remarkable control of watercolor, a very difficult medium to modulate. Her skill is all the more impressive when one realizes that she worked on a very small scale; the pictures in the books are only slight reductions of the originals.

Although *The Tale of Peter Rabbit* is written for young children who are not yet able or are just learning to read, Potter also experimented with books for even younger ones. In *The Story of Miss Moppet* (1906) and *The Story of a Fierce Bad Rabbit* (1906), she forgoes any complicated plot and makes full use of the very young child's willingness to point at and name simple objects. Potter also continued to experiment with more elaborate story lines. Her second book, *The Tailor of Gloucester*, of which she first privately printed five hundred copies in 1902, and which she then edited to the more exacting tastes of her publisher, is a more complicated story about several mice and their interactions with humans and cats. *The Tailor of Gloucester* is a period piece, set in Regency England, with both mice and humans wearing the early-nineteenth-century clothes Potter drew from the clothing collection in the Victoria and Albert Museum. Like *The Tale of Peter Rabbit*, its appeal lies in the marvelous minuteness of its details, in the exactness with which Potter depicts every stitch of an elaborately embroidered Regency waistcoat or a lady mouse's costume, complete with ruffled hat and plume, dainty slippers, and a gown with a wide skirt and puffed sleeves. The story's intrigue centers on the mice's cooperation with the humans who need their help and their success in thwarting the members of their own animal kingdom, especially the cat who threatens them. Its longer text and more complicated action, which involve two separate plots, made Potter think that the book was appropriate for an older audience, but the tale has a timeless quality that makes it just as suitable for the audience of *The Tale of Peter Rabbit*.

Potter's stories about mice continued to be among her best, perhaps because she was fascinated by mice, which live side by side with humans and yet, organized in their own social units, only rarely meet with their neighbors. The idea of this parallel society, which both menaces and helps humans, dominates her best book about mice, *The Tale of Two Bad Mice* (1904). These mice invade and ravage a dollhouse, but then make restitution by coming every morning to do the dolls' housecleaning. The story pokes fun at the sterile, orderly lives of the dolls, who live in a gorgeous but nonfunctional house; they are contrasted with the lithe, active mice, who put the booty they have stolen from the dollhouse to strictly functional uses. For example, dolls do not reproduce, so they have little use for the cradle in their home; the mice put it to much more appropriate and charming use for their tiny progeny.

Much of the pleasure the book provides comes from the mouse's-eye view of the house and the exquisite detail about the life-styles of the mice and the dolls. The fantastic conceit that dollhouses are so neat because mice come to clean them every day adds a charming sense of mystery to the lives of the mice. *The Tale of Two Bad Mice* was Potter's fourth book, and, in the opinion of some critics, far outshines her third book, *The Tale of Squirrel Nutkin*, which is somewhat overladen with nursery rhymes and lacks the colorful detail of the story that followed it.

Although Potter was pleased to get away from the Peter Rabbit books, having tired of that particular animal, her public still appreciated Peter and his siblings above all her other animal characters, and she returned to the rabbits to continue the story of the Peter Rabbit family. *The Tale of Benjamin Bunny* describes the adventures of Peter and his cousin Benjamin when they return to Mr. McGregor's garden to retrieve Peter's clothes. Although Benjamin proceeds boldly, Peter's earlier experiences have scared him, and Peter follows Benjamin's leads timidly and rather unwillingly. They get into trouble and are rescued by Benjamin's father, who soundly whips them and sends them home, where Mrs. Rabbit forgives and welcomes them. The story complements Potter's first book, completing the story, using Peter as a foil for Benjamin, and concluding on the same comforting note. The pictures portray the same rabbit antics and the same details of English gardens that made the earlier book such a popular and critical success.

From the sales of these early books Potter had accumulated enough money to invest in a small farm in Near Sawrey; she had also developed a close relationship with her editor, Norman Warne,

and the two had made plans to marry. His untimely death from leukemia in August 1905, at about the same time as the purchase of the farm, left her saddened, but with a new and welcomed distraction, the farm and its house. Now without Norman Warne's special guidance, but equipped with the lessons of his previous tutelage, she cut herself loose from the editorial apron strings. For the rest of her active creative life, she concentrated on life at the farm, in the farmhouse, and in the village. Her stories became progressively more complicated and more daring as her confidence in her abilities grew.

The Pie and the Patty-Pan (1905), the first of the books based on her life at the farm, is more notable for its pictures of the house than for its story; the loving detail with which Potter portrays her new home, its furnishings, and its flower gardens makes these illustrations some of her most remarkable, colorful, and beautifully composed pictures. The book is the first of a trilogy of cat stories. Cats as rat catchers are an important part of farm life, and Potter was particularly intrigued with those she found already living at her farm. Her tales of the kittens' adventures follow much the same course of events as *The Tale of Peter Rabbit*. The title character in *The Tale of Tom Kitten* (1907), for instance, is unconcerned about his clothing and is reprimanded by his mother. Tom is also the central character in *The Roly-Poly Pudding* (1908; later renamed *The Tale of Samuel Whiskers*), in which he is used as the stuffing for a pudding made by the omnipresent rats of the farmhouse. The rats' dominance of life at the farm is clearly demonstrated as they capture and frighten a kitten and easily steal the other ingredients for the pudding as well as a rolling pin from the kitchen. The plot of *The Pie and the Patty-Pan* is one of Potter's sparsest, but by the time she wrote *The Roly-Poly Pudding* her plot construction and characterization—particularly her portrayal of the obnoxious, but still charming, rats—were far more skillful and subtle.

The characters of Mrs. Tiggy-Winkle, the hedgehog turned country laundress, Jeremy Fisher, the frog turned country gentleman and fisherman, and Mrs. Tittlemouse, the country mouse turned homeowner, are all carefully and aptly chosen for the curious similarities between their animal bodies and the bodies of the human types they are meant to mimic. In each character, the animal likeness is peculiarly able to body forth the foibles of human nature while remaining most clearly animal. Mrs.

Tiggy-Winkle is particularly well chosen; her wrinkled hands and bright eyes characterize both a hedgehog and a sprightly country laundress. The efforts of the title characters in both *The Tale of Mrs. Tiggy-Winkle* (1905) and *The Tale of Mrs. Tittlemouse* (1910) replicate Potter's own exertions to clean and order her country house and to maintain that order against the invasions of dirt, insects, and rodents. In *The Tale of Mr. Jeremy Fisher*, Potter gently pokes fun at the preoccupation with fishing that dominated the lives of the local vacationing gentlemen; even though they pursued their hobby with a vengeance and told preposterous stories about their expeditions, their efforts never yielded them results worthy of the dinner table. Telling the stories of these three wild animals, Potter found much to praise about country life and the coziness of country homes. The pictures, notable for their accurate representation of animals as well as of the details of country homes, clearly reflect her contentedness with the quality of her new life and home.

Potter moved beyond the gates of the farm to describe the village and its inhabitants in *Ginger and Pickles* (1909), named for the general store in her village of animal characters. Ginger and Pickles are the proprietors of the store, a cat and a dog whose business practices of extending unlimited credit and of consuming their own stock without paying for it soon force them to close their doors. In this story Potter experiments with extending the ending beyond the climax of the story. Whereas *The Tale of Peter Rabbit* ends with Peter's return home and a brief description of the rabbits' supper, the ending of *Ginger and Pickles* goes on for twenty pages beyond the climax to explain not only the later careers of Ginger and Pickles but also the ways in which the villagers deal with the closing of the only general store, their sole source of mercantile products. The story is noteworthy for Potter's study of individual villagers and their gossipy, parochial views of life, and for her amassing of characters from earlier books, including Mrs. Tiggy-Winkle, Peter, and Jeremy Fisher, to fill out the population of her animal village.

During this period Potter returned again, at the request of her readers, to her rabbit stories, this time setting a story in Wales, in the garden of her uncle, whom she had visited in 1908 on a summer holiday. *The Tale of the Flopsy Bunnies* (1909) reveals the adult lives of Peter and Benjamin. Peter continues to be careful and industrious, and Benja-

min to be bold and thoughtless, in spite of his new responsibilities as husband and father. Potter is remarkably consistent in her re-creation of the small rabbits as adults. The story again features Mr. McGregor as the rabbits' adversary. The garden, however, is lush with flowers, not the vegetables of the earlier *Peter Rabbit* books, and the illustrations show Potter's increased ability to draw a rich profusion of flora without losing her focus on the animals.

Her last book about the rabbit characters was *The Tale of Mr. Tod* (1912); in it Mr. Tod, a fox, and Tommy Brock, a badger, threaten the young family of Benjamin Bunny. Fortunately, cousin Peter Rabbit's levelheaded thinking saves the day and the little bunnies. But the bones and other grisly remains of the fox's and badger's earlier victims are clearly presented in the drawings of the predators' lairs, and their intent to eat the baby bunnies becomes clear when they imprison their captives in the oven. In this book, among her last, Potter offers a happy ending, but one modified by her frank admission that neither badger nor fox has been permanently vanquished, and that the enmity between predator and prey will continue to be an unpleasant fact of life.

Potter turned to her farm animals to find the central characters for *The Tale of Jemima Puddle-Duck* (1908) and *The Tale of Pigling Bland* (1913). In *The Roly-Poly Pudding* she had started to investigate an unhappy fact of farm life: that some animals die. Although in that story Tom Kitten is rescued before coming to a dire end, both Pigling Bland and Jemima Puddle-Duck are far more seriously threatened, Jemima by the fox disguised as a gentleman with sandy-colored whiskers and Pigling Bland by various butchers, grocers, and thieves. Potter became more willing to investigate the more unpleasant episodes of animal life on the farm and in the wild as her career continued. Although her stories still end happily, Potter's unflinching gaze, taking in both the benign and malign aspects of life, led to these longer, more complicated stories, which endure because of her honesty in dealing with the whole range of animal and human experiences.

In *The Tale of Pigling Bland* the reader finds a foreshadowing of Potter's retirement from active publishing life. The tale is a love story about two pigs, one a pink male like those Potter raised as livestock on her farm, the other a black female like the one she purchased to be a pet. The two pigs wish to live quiet country lives raising potatoes, but their ambition and security are threatened by the thief who steals them both and intends to send them to market. Overcoming a series of obstacles, they escape together and make it to the county line, where they decide to go and live "over the hills and far away." The story was published in the same month that Potter married a country lawyer, William Heelis, whom she had met in the course of doing business at her farm. Potter, who now insisted on being called "Mrs. Heelis," denied the parallel between Pigling Bland's fate and her own. But the similarity between her art and life is hard to ignore, and the escape from the market to a happy married life for both character and author signaled Potter's farewell to her career as a writer and illustrator of children's books and as her parents' dominated daughter.

After her marriage the only book for which she prepared a set of new illustrations and wrote a new story was *The Tale of Johnny Town-Mouse* (1918). Aesop's fable about the town mouse and the country mouse particularly appealed to Potter because her own life spanned both country and city life, so she used his tale as a basis for her own. Potter deliberately slants the story by giving city life, here portrayed as life in Hawkshead, a town near her farm but hardly a large city, very few virtues when compared with the charms of country life. The final choice of home made by Timmy Willie, the country mouse, mirrors Potter's own; again she wished to show her readers the many pleasures she had found in simple, salubrious country living.

The other books of her later period are all taken from the files of half-finished projects she had put aside during her more active publishing period. In the two nursery-rhyme books *Appley Dapply's Nursery Rhymes* (1917) and *Cecily Parsley's Nursery Rhymes* (1922), she reintroduces many of the characters of earlier books as actors in nursery rhymes. All of these verses were written before Norman Warne persuaded Potter to rely on her own powers of invention and composition and to stop mimicking folk rhymes and the verses of Caldecott, Kate Greenaway, and Walter Crane. Derivative as they may be, Potter's rhymes are still charming, and the pictures, coming from her earlier period, are some of her best. *The Tale of Little Pig Robinson* (1930), however, is the least satisfactory of these later books, being an uncomfortable combination of realism, in the mode of *The Tale of Pigling Bland*, and fantasy, in the mode of Edward Lear's "The Owl and the Pussycat" (1871). The story lacks Potter's earlier rigorous editing and meanders verbosely, ending in a fantasy escape that is uncharacteristic.

In all, Potter published twenty-three works in the Peter Rabbit book series. Most of them are designed for very young readers, but some are longer and more involved, such as *The Tale of Mr. Tod* and *The Tale of Pigling Bland*, both of which have fewer pictures and more text. She continued publishing long after her interest waned, partly to sustain her life on the farm and partly to allow her to expand her landholdings. Exchanging her fame as author and illustrator for what she had earlier called "woman's crowning joy," she turned to marriage with her country-lawyer husband with a newly found physical energy. She became an accomplished farmer in her fifties; in her sixties, she became a champion breeder of Herdwick sheep, a hardy variety that could survive the brutal winters of the hills of the Lake District. During this period she also became an active member of the National Trust, seeking both funds and properties that could be preserved for later generations. Although her literary works are part of her legacy, one cannot underestimate the influence she has had on the landscape of England in her tireless efforts to preserve the environment and the way of life she loved. At her death in 1943 she willed all her property to the National Trust, including the house she had made familiar to her readers through her books.

Potter's rural isolation after her marriage led many of her admirers to assume that the author was dead. But when a letter arrived from the United States inquiring about Potter's books and her process of writing and illustrating them, Potter perceived that this admirer was no ordinary reader, but someone who approached children's literature with the seriousness that Potter felt her work deserved. Her correspondence with Bertha Mahony of Boston was continued through further letter-writing and resulted in an increased appreciation of Potter's work in America. In fact, Potter had realized earlier that the American public was a lucrative market, to which she had tried to appeal with *The Tale of Timmy Tiptoes* (1911), the story of an American squirrel. However, because the subject was not as familiar to her as native British squirrels, the drawings are much less accomplished, and neither the drawings nor the descriptions of the characters have the liveliness of her earlier creations.

But Potter did not forget her American fans. When she found that her special project, the National Trust's preservation of open space in the Lake District, needed money to buy more farms, Potter wrote to Mahony, then the editor of the *Horn Book* magazine, sending her a set of sketches drawn after the original Peter Rabbit pictures, which were to be sold for the benefit of this purchase. Potter continued her correspondence with Mahony. As a result, she resumed writing and sketching in order to produce some works to be published exclusively in the United States. *The Fairy Caravan* (1929) was admittedly not Potter's best work. Because she felt it was less satisfactory, less compact, and less true to the animals' natures than her earlier successful works, she permitted the book to be published only by David McKay in Philadelphia, an area where, perhaps, more discriminating eyes would not see it. She also provided sketches, rather than drawings, for the book, and she may have thought that their unfinished quality would not have satisfied a public used to her more polished art. Potter's energy for revising had also waned, and the book rambles on, describing the country highlands with none of the direction or pithy commentary evident in her earlier books. She later published a second book exclusively with McKay; this was *Sister Anne* (1932), a retelling of the Bluebeard story, yet a lame, lifeless version of the original, with none of Potter's own pictures to redeem it.

Following the publication of *The Fairy Caravan*, the publishing house of Frederick Warne, long the supporter and sole producer of Potter's books, insisted that they, too, share in the rare privilege of a new book from their most requested author. *The Tale of Little Pig Robinson* was therefore published simultaneously in Philadelphia and London, and its author's reputation, rather than its literary value, sustained its sales on both sides of the Atlantic. Bertha Mahony also requested a book for the *Horn Book*. Potter responded with *Wag-by-Wall* (1944), a short fairy tale about the highlands where she lived.

Potter's legacy to children's literature is a collection of small books very meticulously written and illustrated, carefully designed in layout and size especially for children. Her books were rapidly adopted as classics, perhaps because there was nothing quite so good at the time, but even today few works rival the excellence of her illustration and writing. She set a high standard for later writers and artists. She deserves to take her place among the major creators of children's books.

Selected Bibliography

WORKS OF BEATRIX POTTER

The Tale of Peter Rabbit. With illustrations by the author. London: privately printed, 1901. Rev. ed. London: Warne, 1902.

The Tailor of Gloucester. With illustrations by the author. London: privately printed, 1902. Rev. ed. London: Warne, 1903.

The Tale of Squirrel Nutkin. With illustrations by the author. London and New York: Warne, 1903.

The Tale of Benjamin Bunny. With illustrations by the author. London and New York: Warne, 1904.

The Tale of Two Bad Mice. With illustrations by the author. London and New York: Warne, 1904.

The Pie and the Patty-Pan. With illustrations by the author. London and New York: Warne, 1905.

The Tale of Mrs. Tiggy-Winkle. With illustrations by the author. London and New York: Warne, 1905.

The Story of a Fierce Bad Rabbit. With illustrations by the author. London and New York: Warne, 1906.

The Story of Miss Moppet. With illustrations by the author. London and New York: Warne, 1906.

The Tale of Mr. Jeremy Fisher. With illustrations by the author. London and New York: Warne, 1906.

The Tale of Tom Kitten. With illustrations by the author. London and New York: Warne, 1907.

The Roly-Poly Pudding. With illustrations by the author. London and New York: Warne, 1908.

The Tale of Jemima Puddle-Duck. With illustrations by the author. London and New York: Warne, 1908.

Ginger and Pickles. With illustrations by the author. London and New York: Warne, 1909.

The Tale of the Flopsy Bunnies. With illustrations by the author. London and New York: Warne, 1909.

The Tale of Mrs. Tittlemouse. With illustrations by the author. London and New York: Warne, 1910.

The Tale of Timmy Tiptoes. With illustrations by the author. London and New York: Warne, 1911.

The Tale of Mr. Tod. With illustrations by the author. London and New York: Warne, 1912.

The Tale of Pigling Bland. With illustrations by the author. London and New York: Warne, 1913.

Appley Dapply's Nursery Rhymes. With illustrations by the author. London and New York: Warne, 1917.

The Tale of Johnny Town-Mouse. With illustrations by the author. London and New York: Warne, 1918.

Cecily Parsley's Nursery Rhymes. With illustrations by the author. London and New York: Warne, 1922.

The Fairy Caravan. With illustrations by the author. London: privately printed, 1929. 2nd ed. Philadelphia: David McKay, 1929.

The Tale of Little Pig Robinson. With illustrations by the author. Philadelphia: David McKay, 1930; London: Warne, 1930.

Sister Anne. With illustrations by Katharine Sturges. Philadelphia: David McKay, 1932.

Wag-by-Wall. With illustrations by the author. Boston: Horn Book, 1944.

CRITICAL AND BIOGRAPHICAL STUDIES

Crouch, Marcus. *Beatrix Potter: A Walck Monograph*. London: Bodley Head, 1960.

Emerson, Ann, ed. *The History of the "Tale of Peter Rabbit."* London and New York: Warne, 1976.

Godden, Rumer. "An Imaginary Correspondence" *Horn Book* 39: 369–375 (1963).

———. "Beatrix Potter" *Horn Book* 42: 390–400 (August 1966).

Greene, Grahame. "Beatrix Potter." In *Collected Essays*. New York: Viking Press, 1969.

Hearn, Michael Patrick. "A Second Look: Peter Rabbit Redux" *Horn Book* 53: 563–566 (1977).

Lane, Margaret. *The Magic Years of Beatrix Potter*. London and New York: Warne, 1978.

———. *The Tale of Beatrix Potter: A Biography*. London and New York: Warne, 1946.

Linder, Leslie. *A History of the Writings of Beatrix Potter*. London and New York: Warne, 1971.

———, ed. *Beatrix Potter, 1866–1943: Centenary Catalogue*. London: Warne, 1966.

MacDonald, Ruth K. *Beatrix Potter*. Twayne English Authors Series, no. 411. Boston: Twayne Publishers, 1986.

Morse, Jane Crowell, ed. *Beatrix Potter's Americans: Selected Letters*. Boston: Horn Book, 1982.

Potter, Beatrix. *The Art of Beatrix Potter: With an Appreciation by Anne Carroll Moore and Notes to Each Section by Enid and Leslie Linder*. Rev. ed. London and New York: Warne, 1972.

———. *The Journal of Beatrix Potter, 1881–1897*. Transcribed by Leslie Linder. London and New York: Warne, 1966.

———. "Roots of the Peter Rabbit Tales" *Horn Book* 5: 69–72 (1929).

Quinby, Jane, ed. *Beatrix Potter: A Bibliographical Check List*. New York: no publisher, 1954.

Sale, Roger. "Beatrix Potter." In *Fairy Tales and After: From Snow White to E. B. White*. Cambridge, Mass.: Harvard University Press, 1978.

—RUTH K. MacDONALD

HOWARD PYLE

1853–1911

HOWARD PYLE WAS born in Wilmington, Delaware, in 1853. His parents, Margaret Churchman Painter and William Pyle, were both Quakers, but they discovered the mystic religion of Swedenborgianism just prior to the Civil War and left the Quaker church. His parents' religious beliefs were practical, and they were good parents. Pyle was encouraged to pursue the great classics, was taught folklore and mythology by his mother, and grew up believing that man should deal fairly with his fellow man. Years later, he would recall how his mother read to him as he sat in front of the fireplace, and how she encouraged his early artistic endeavors. Always surrounded by good literature with the best illustrations, Pyle grew up considering a book's entire format. He later confessed, "In confidence, I still like the pictures in books better than wall pictures."

As a youngster Pyle attended private schools. He was a strong, healthy child who enjoyed roaming about Wilmington on his own. Always an artist at heart, he drew pictures in the margins of his texts and notebooks. Because the family did not have enough money to send Pyle to Europe, then considered the standard training ground for an art student, he broke with the tradition of his day and ultimately created an art training that was uniquely American. As Robert Lawson once commented: "Had Howard Pyle, young, modest, not at all sure of himself, been thrown into this stultifying atmosphere where everything American was considered gauche and crude, there is no knowing what would have happened to the tender bud of his genius."

Genial and industrious, Pyle finished his art training in Philadelphia and moved on to New York, where he began selling pictures to magazine publishers. In 1876 an illustration of his first appeared in *Scribner's Magazine,* and his career as a professional artist began.

Throughout his life Howard Pyle worked vigorously. He produced over thirty-three hundred illustrations and published almost two hundred pieces of writing. Furthermore, he thoroughly researched his subjects before illustrating or writing about them. He taught art to young students at Drexel Institute, Philadelphia, from 1894, gave summer classes at Chadds Ford, and set up and single-handedly ran a private art school at Wilmington. Within thirty years he had trained such illustrators as N. C. Wyeth, Frank Schoonover, and Jessie Willcox Smith. Pyle's students admired his talents both as teacher and as artist. After Pyle's death, Schoonover reminisced about a time filled with hunting, races, bicycle rides and country walks, and pictured Pyle as a romantic who played at Robin Hood in his leisure hours.

Early in his professional career, Pyle returned to the childhood stories his mother had shared with him and began to remold them for American children. In addition, he began to design a unique format for his books. At that time American-made books were weak imitations of European ones; the artwork was largely stilted and stiff. Pyle used models in first sketching sessions, concentrating upon the composition of his scenes. His illustrations, unlike earlier ones by British artists, were full of action and drama. He peopled his scenes with romantic images of his heroes and heroines.

At the same time, Pyle began to rewrite old folktales and to create his own tales, using remnants of the stories he had heard as a child. Although he realized that some critics did not consider folktales acceptable material for children, he was not bothered by this. He wanted to rewrite and illustrate the old stories in a new way so that they would not be completely lost.

One body of literature that interested Pyle was the story, found in early English ballads, of the hero Robin Hood. In 1876 he wrote to his mother, "Children are apt to know of Robin Hood without any clear ideas upon his particular adventures." As a boy Pyle had heard Joseph Ritson's 1795 version of the ballad. It remained with him to his adulthood. His rereading of Ritson as an adult gave him the inspiration for his *Merry Adventures of Robin Hood,* published by Scribners in 1883. In it Pyle systematically developed a very real setting and conjured up a mystical woods. As he wrote in his preface:

> Here you will find a hundred dull, sober, jogging places, all tricked out with flowers and what not, till no one would know them in their fanciful dress . . . wherein no chill mists press upon our spirits, and no rain falls but what rolls off our backs . . . where flowers bloom forever and birds are always singing . . . and ale and beer and wine (such as muddle no wits) flow like water in a brook.

In this passage Pyle shows his woods as a ritualistic place that glorifies the pastoral life. It will have perfect weather, and it will resound with feasting. By the end of the first half of *The Merry Adventures of Robin Hood* Pyle has established his forest. It is this part that children most remember. They have a keen sense of the forest's setting, and they are aware of the typical episodes within the forest: the encounter on the log with Little John; the battles and initiations of the newly discovered recruits; the wooing of Friar Tuck by Robin.

Pyle's Robin Hood is a strong male leader. He does not bother with women (though he promises not to harm them), and he is not subject to anyone else's dictates (though he does claim loyalty to the king). Yet his role as leader does not evolve from his ability to win fights. Indeed, prior to Robin's adventures on his visit to London he is involved in four battles, and he loses each one. What makes him a leader is his "good sweet nature" and his

ability to create a world so serene that neither the weather nor the men under his rule break into storm. All the fighting takes place outside of Robin's realm.

Pyle describes Robin's fights as "merry" adventures or "lusty" encounters. He begins by describing the weather and the greenwood forest, the birds singing in the trees, the peacefulness of Robin and his men in their glen. He allows Robin to venture out on his own, while always reminding the reader that Robin is carrying his trusty horn just in case he can't handle his problems alone. Each time Robin sees an opponent, he challenges him to hand-to-hand combat—not a very wise decision, since he has never yet won—and a fight ensues. Pyle tells the reader each time that Robin has fought well, and then he has Robin use his horn to call reinforcements. Once saved, he commends his opponent, identifies himself, and invites his adversary to join his forces. Only Little John demands that Robin further prove himself in a shooting match; all the others ask for instant acceptance into the clan. Then the merry men return to the glen and feast in celebration. The outlaws' routine is adventurous, but predictable and episodic.

Besides using a consistent plot pattern, Pyle ritualistically repeats certain words to establish the romantic setting as both real and symbolic. In the scenes depicting Robin's cudgel battles, for example, Pyle uses the words "lusty," "tough," and "stout" to describe all the opponents except Robin's cousin, Will Scarlet. In his first three defeats, Robin and his men are described as full of mirth and laughter. Furthermore, those who rob in Sherwood Forest do so in a ritualistic fashion. They entertain only those wealthy enough to have a number of riches to forfeit, and they always follow feasting with business matters. They never blindfold those they rob, yet their glen cannot be found by men of law. Only the truly baptized members of Robin's band can wander freely about the woods and return home again.

Pyle's Robin Hood is the shepherd of his flock, the savior of the innocent who welcomes newcomers to his pastoral scene. His male clan is the ideal of comradeship, of youthful high-spiritedness, of deception, and of verbal and physical daring. Robin Hood and his men live in harmony with nature, forced to seek adventures away from their glen only when boredom strikes. If threatened by the forces of civilization, they retreat into the forest. They are symbols of pastoral freedom and fair play.

The second part of the story deals with Robin's fate outside his glen and is less ritualistic and less romantic. While in London, Robin is almost captured and killed through trickery by King Harry. Robin becomes a hunted man, and is portrayed as a pawn of the queen. When he returns to his glen, he is visited by King Richard, who tells him:

> "Thy danger is past, for hereby I give thee and all thy band free pardon. But, in sooth, I cannot let you roam the forest as ye have done in the past; therefore I will take thee at thy word, when thou didst say thou wouldst give thy service to me and thou shalt go back to London with me."

The tragic end of Robin Hood is placed in the book's epilogue, which explains that Robin's death was caused by his cousin, the prioress of the nunnery of Kirkless. Yet although Robin's death is solemnly portrayed, it is neither melodramatic nor morbid. The reader is reminded that Robin was forgiving and compassionate toward others, and that he died a mortal hero.

Besides the old English hero of ballads, Pyle was interested in oral folktales, which he wanted to recast into modern stories for American children. In his earliest attempts the sources of his adaptations are apparent. For instance, his story "The Skillful Huntsman" is a variation of the European folktale "Clever Gretchen." Pyle's version has more conversation, but the basic plot remains the same. The biggest change is that the story is longer and more casual in tone. Pyle called this rewriting a "shaping" process, and he told his mother, "I shall make note of a great many [tales in Thorp's *Northern Mythology*], hoping that some of the dry grains may fall on ground rich enough to produce a full-grown fairytale or two."

Pyle's first short stories were published in the popular children's periodicals *Harper's Young People* and *St. Nicholas* magazine beginning in 1883, and they were an immediate success. He also published the illustrations that he later used in somewhat altered form in the two collections of his tales *Pepper and Salt; or, Seasoning for Young Folk* (1885) and *The Wonder Clock* (1888). Altogether, these two volumes contain thirty-two stories. Before book publication Pyle greatly revised the stories as well; it is clear that though the plots and characters are the same, he was experimenting with his literary style and developing his storytelling techniques.

The stories in *Pepper and Salt* contain descriptive detail that children find fascinating. Although Pyle did not create his own romantic heroes and heroines, he describes these borrowed characters and their actions vividly. In "Claus and His Wonderful Staff," for instance, he writes:

> Hans and Claus were born brothers. Hans was the elder and Claus was the younger; Hans was the richer and Claus was the poorer—that is the way that the world goes sometimes.
> Everything was easy for Hans at home; he drank much beer, and had sausages and white bread three times a day; but Claus worked and worked, and no luck came of it—that, also, is the way that the world goes sometimes.

Pyle's style is very traditional; his stories read aloud well because of his direct narration. The actions of his main characters are either romantically explained or humorously described. Pyle's prose is so detailed that it needs little visual interpretation. There was no need for him to illustrate many of his scenes because he etched them out in his vigorous storytelling. For example:

> Yes; there they were—little men, little women, little children, and little babies, as thick in the tulip bed as folks at a wedding. The little men sat smoking their pipes and talking together; the little women sat nursing their babies, singing to them or rocking them to sleep in cradles of tulip flowers; the little children played at hide-and-seek among the flower-stalks.

Pepper and Salt contains only eight tales; each is well developed, and the stories combine to complement each other. This collection is Pyle's most finished book in terms of format design. In addition to the tales, Pyle inserted one-page poems surrounded by humorous drawings. They were used to break up the stories and were effective in helping the book maintain a mood of another time, another country.

Immediately after *Pepper and Salt* was published, Pyle began running a second series of short fantasies in *Harper's Young People*. These twenty-six stories were published in *The Wonder Clock*. By this time Pyle's style had evolved into a more sophisticated narrative form. Although each of these tales contains folktale elements, they have remained interesting because they do not depend so much on the traditional folktale formula. Pyle himself considered these his best fairy tales. They lack much of the earthy humor found in *Pepper and Salt,* yet they are entertaining. Many of the stories have intricate plots that abound with activity. Instead of using the traditional three adventures of Western folktales, Pyle's *Wonder Clock* stories are divided into four episodes. Perhaps this division is an allusion to the four quarters within each hour. Also, the heroes in *The Wonder Clock* are not so clever as those in *Pepper and Salt.* They depend upon the advice of others or upon luck. Thus, Peterkin in "Peterkin and the Little Grey Hare" is successful because he does as the hare suggests, and Bearskin, in the story of the same name, is able to marry the princess because he has been saved from his early fate of death and raised by a she-bear. Much more detail is given concerning the plot, but few scenes are as vividly described as they are in *Pepper and Salt.* Stylistically these stories are less robust, less original, and less fun to read aloud. Many of the tales end with moralistic asides to the audience. For instance, in "The Swan Maiden" Pyle concludes:

> After that the prince and the Swan Maiden were married, and a grand wedding they had of it, with music of fiddles and kettle-drums, and plenty to eat and to drink. I, too, was there; but all of the good red wine ran down over my tucker, so that not a drop of it passed my lips, and I had to come away empty. And that is all.

Even the illustrations are heavier in tone and less inviting than those in *Pepper and Salt.* The entire look of the book is more distinctly old-fashioned, and the text is closer in form to the lengthier oral romances.

Some of the tales in *The Wonder Clock* are animal tales. They read much like the early English animal tales found in Joseph Jacobs' collections, and they suggest that the book might be meant for a very young audience. On the whole, however, the tone and length of these tales are more suitable for older children.

In this collection of stories the reader feels that the tale is being told to him. Asides addressed to the listener are quickly delivered throughout and beg for oral interpretation. Thus, in "King Stork" Pyle introduces the main plot, saying:

> The princess of that town was as clever as she was pretty; that was saying a great deal, for she was the handsomest in the whole world. ("Phew! but that is a fine lass for sure and certain," said the drummer.) So it was proclaimed that any lad who could answer a question the princess would ask, and would ask a question the princess could not answer, and would catch the bird that she would be want-ing, should have her for his wife and half of the kingdom to boot. ("Hi! but here is luck for a clever lad," says the drummer.) But whoever should fail in any one of the three tasks should have his head chopped off as sure as he lived. ("Ho! but she is a wicked one for all that," says the drummer.)

A final fairy-tale collection, *Twilight Land,* was published in 1894, but it had neither the early literary verve found in *Pepper and Salt* nor the well-reasoned plot style of *The Wonder Clock.* Instead it contained tales of variable quality whose length far outweighed their interest. In no time these tales became antiquated remnants of a literary fairy-tale imagination run dry. Today *Twilight Land* is out of print.

By the time Pyle had finished the second of his fairy-tale books he had already set his sights on another challenge. He had changed his research interests from the folktale to the stories of King Arthur that he had heard as a youth. By now his personal library included books of illustrations depicting medieval times. He now changed his writing style and his art to reflect another era, another mood.

At the end of 1888 his first chivalric adventure novel, *Otto of the Silver Hand,* was published. This straightforward tale contains a somber picture of German castle life. Set during the twelfth century, *Otto of the Silver Hand* is not based on romantic visions of chivalry. The book has remained in print and is still a noteworthy account of times long past.

Pyle's realistic tale is told in a third-person narrative style. As a story of the darker side of the Middle Ages, *Otto of the Silver Hand* contains chilling scenes of powerful men who govern harshly and are led to acts of greed, violence, and vengeance. The lust for life and spirit of fair play that dominated Robin Hood's adventures have been replaced with the harsh realities of the evils of chivalry. In his foreword, Pyle wrote: "Poor little Otto's life was a stony and a thorny pathway, and it is well for all of us nowadays that we walk it in fancy and not in truth."

Otto is a young boy throughout most of the story. His destiny is controlled by ruthless men who will stop at nothing to gain power over an enemy. Otto's one period of peace comes when he is sent to a monastery. There the gentle life and protective love he experiences nurture his soul. In the end Otto loses his hand and his father to his father's enemy. Pyle writes:

He pressed Otto close to his breast in one last embrace. "My child," he murmured, "try not to hate thy father when thou thinkest of him hereafter, even though he be hard and bloody as thou knowest."

But with his suffering and weakness, little Otto knew nothing of what was passing; it was only as in a faint flickering dream that he lived in what was done around him.

Still, this is not a totally dismal book even though it ends on such a sad note. In the end, Otto marries the daughter of his father's hated rival, rebuilds his father's castle, and carves a new motto over the great gate: A Silver Hand Is Better Than an Iron Hand. Thus, Pyle depicts the end of medieval ignorance through the marriage of two young people who grew up in, but refused to accept, the barbaric society of ruthless killings, and who embraced the wise, peaceful teachings of the monks.

Although Pyle's theme and plot are noteworthy, it is his powerful descriptions and the stark German setting that help create an exceptional book. Pyle begins his drama by saying, "Up from the gray rocks, rising sheer and bald and bare, stood the walls and towers of Castle Drachenhausen." He later describes the scene of the morning meal shared by the baron and baroness, Otto's parents, and tells his reader, "Outside, the rain beat upon the roof or ran trickling from the eaves, and every now and then a chill draught of wind would breathe through the open windows of the great black dining-hall and set the fire roaring." Throughout the story the reader senses the coldness of castle life and the vulgarity of the court. In this book the language is straightforward; Pyle does not attempt to reconstruct a dialect of the Middle Ages, nor does he write with a contemporary American voice. The book can easily be read and understood by today's nine-year-olds.

In 1892 Pyle published a second medieval story. *Men of Iron* is set in England in the year 1400. The father of the hero, Myles, has been involved in a secret plot to take King Henry IV's life and has fled to exile. Meanwhile his son prepares to become a knight. The story is not faithful to historical information concerning the training of a young squire, however. The scenes are not carefully depicted; instead the plot moves quickly along until Myles is able to clear his father's name and marry a young woman from an aristocratic family. Although the characters are more three-dimensional than the ones in *Otto of the Silver Hand*, they are not sympathetic figures. Myles is constantly fighting with his superiors and is intent upon proving that he need not take orders from the older squires. The book reads more like an account of school hazing than one of castle life. Furthermore, Pyle's characters affect a stilted and cumbersome speech pattern that is difficult to read. The book's story has had less success with modern readers, but the skeleton plot was used as the basis for the film *The Black Shield of Falworth* (1954), a swashbuckling story that concentrated upon action rather than characterization.

Howard Pyle's next book, *The Garden Behind the Moon* (1895), is a mystical fantasy based upon his religious beliefs. It was written in response to his son Seller's death, and contains much that is not easily understood by the young reader. Yet, although it is out of print today, it is one of Pyle's finest story creations.

The story can be read at two levels. It is first and foremost an adventure story for youngsters, with a traditional quest plot. David, the young hero, travels to the Garden Behind the Moon and rescues the princess within the garden from death. He returns to earth, waits patiently to be discovered, and in the end marries the princess. The story contains many folkloric elements: the hero is poor but honest; the princess is incapable of saving herself; the boy is guided by several "wise people" in his journey; and the hero must defeat a giant and rescue a treasure in order to win the hand of the princess. Pyle was writing more than a simple adventure story, however, since his hero must travel past death and return to the world of the living with the princess if he is to save her. And David must literally walk through his mentor, the Moon Angel, and travel alone in order to bring back happiness to the world. When writing to Scribner's in 1894 about the manuscript, Pyle said:

> I send it with a curious feeling of reluctance for, in correcting and re-reading it, I have grown very fond of it.
>
> It may be that it will not have the value in your eyes that I hope but, nevertheless, it embodies some of my ripest thought.

The book is laden with Swedenborgian theology, and the tale is a true allegory. As in his other works, Pyle has carefully etched out the characters and their actions in a matter-of-fact way; this time, however, the tale takes place in a magical, imaginary world. David first enters the world of the moon after walking the moon path. Pyle writes:

> Click-clack! What was that? Suddenly a half-door opened and there stood a little old man, as gray as the evening, with long white hair and queer clothes, and a face covered all over with cobwebs of silver wrinkles. It was the Man-in-the-moon, and he was smoking a long pipe of tobacco.
>
> "How do you do, David?" said he. "Will you come in?"
>
> "Why, yes," said David, "I would like to."
>
> "That is good," said the Man-in-the-moon, and he opened the other half of the door. "Now! Give me your hand."
>
> The Man-in-the-moon reached down to David, and David reached up top the Man-in-the-moon. "Now, then!—A long step," said the Man-in-the-moon—and there was David in the doorway of the moon-house.

At the end, Pyle symbolically shows the reader that in real heaven (by Swedenborgian terms) man and woman become one. He stresses this when he ends his story with the opening of the Know-All Book, which contains only the words "When we grow up we shall be married; when we are married we shall grow up; when we are married there shall be joy; hence there shall be joy when we are married."

This story was a departure for Pyle. Although it contains elements of folkloric patterns and religious beliefs, it is Pyle's own story of death and rebirth, of faithfulness and understanding.

The first of Pyle's King Arthur series, *The Story of King Arthur and His Knights,* was published by Scribners in 1903. Pyle devoted his literary efforts to the series until the last book, *The Story of the Grail and the Passing of Arthur,* was published in 1910. In it he wrote his own epitaph, saying:

> Yea; for seven years have I been engaged in writing these books . . . and this book is the last. . . . And I thank God that he hath permitted me to finish this work, for . . . when a man taketh seven years of his life . . . , he knoweth not whether he shall live to complete that which he hath begun.
>
> But so I have completed it, and for that I thank God who permitted me to complete it. Amen.

Although the prose in the Arthurian books is more stilted and less interesting than the straightforward prose found in *Otto of the Silver Hand,* the lyrical retelling of *The Merry Adventures of Robin Hood,* or the simple narrative style of the fairy-tale collections, it is masterful in its blending of French, British, and Celtic legend. The symbolism found in the earier adult renditions is here, as are most of the hero adventures. The conflict between Guinevere, Arthur, and Launcelot is not ignored. However, Pyle refuses to address the possibility of a courtly romantic intrigue between Launcelot and Guinevere. Instead, he writes in the second book, *The Story of the Champions of the Round Table* (1905):

> Now I am aware that there have been many scandalous things said concerning that [Launcelot and Guinevere's] friendship, but I do not choose to believe any such evil sayings. For there are always those who love to think and say evil things of others. Yet though it is not to be denied that Sir Launcelot never had for his lady any other dame than the Lady Guinevere, still no one hath ever said with truth that she regarded Sir Launcelot otherwise than as her very dear friend. . . . I choose to believe good of such noble souls as they, and not evil of them.
>
> (pp. 23–24)

Pyle had hoped to show what "was noble and grand" about chivalry, but at times he found the whole legend bloody and deceitful. The Quaker in him caused Pyle to deliver sermons throughout. In the first book, for instance, he writes at the end of Part 2:

> . . . may God give unto you in your life, that you may have His truth to aid you, like a shining sword, for to overcome your enemies; and may He give you Faith. . . . For with Truth and Faith girded upon you, you shall be as well able to fight all your battles as did that noble hero of old, whom men called King Arthur.
>
> (*Story of King Arthur*, p. 76)

And because Pyle found the male/female controversies within the legends difficult to deal with, he rewrote several until the sexual symbolism completely changed. For instance, in *The Story of King Arthur and His Knights* Pyle skips the fact that Uther Pendragon married Igraine *after* he had slept with her, and that King Arthur is a bastard. He does not explain that Morgana le Fay is Arthur's half-sister, but only says, "Morgana le Fay was a famous sorceress."

452

In spite of these changes, Pyle re-created a British adult hero legend that American children love to read. The characters in the story are all carefully drawn from legend, and the story is presented in a logical chronological sequence. Arthur is clearly the leader, Launcelot the love-driven knight errant, Guinevere the plotting, manipulative female, and Galahad the saintly hero needed to complete the story's Christian cycle. In reference to Galahad's acceptance into the Round Table, Arthur says, "Lo! this youth is he for whom we have been waiting all this time. For so the miracle of the Round Table is fulfilled. . . . For, wit ye, that this is he who shall indeed achieve the Holy Grail."

Galahad is the purest of knights, and his story is suggestive of Christ's trials and triumphs over the worldly evils he encounters. When Galahad sees the Grail making its way to heaven he cries out, "There is nothing remaining for me to live for. So let me depart in peace." Together Galahad and the Grail travel to heaven. Pyle tells his reader that "this was the crowning glory of the reign of King Arthur," and concludes his story with the death of Arthur and of the courtly world.

The final drama in the cycle concerns Launcelot's fall from the court and his battles with the most gentle of knights, Sir Gawaine. In the end, however, Pyle chooses to lay the blame of the court's fall upon Guinevere and Mordred. In his version, Mordred is not Arthur's bastard son with Morgana, but is only his nephew. Thus, Pyle chooses to ignore the incestuous and pagan roots of the story and instead to create a legend in tune with the French and Christian versions.

The legends of Avalon and of the world of spirits who could travel with mortals had strong appeal to Pyle, however. And so he allows Morgana le Fay to take Arthur's body to Avalon, and he concludes:

> And many people declare that they have beheld that land, but always from a distance. . . . But always when they see it it is to behold high towers and glittering pinnacles reaching into the sky; and it is to behold the embowerment of trees, both of forest trees and of shade trees; and it is to behold hill and vale of that mysterious country more beautiful than are the trees and vales of the dark and gloomy earth.

Pyle does not favor Launcelot or Guinevere with such a stately kingdom; he buries both in the Christian fashion. Thus, their story ends with the completion of the cycle, while Arthur's journey to a mysterious land continues his legacy.

When Pyle wrote the concluding episode of King Arthur in *The Story of the Grail and the Passing of King Arthur,* he probably felt at a loss. He had devoted a good share of his last years to working on the medieval sources and legends of the Arthurian myth. Now he would have to find another project. At this point in his career he turned away from children's literature and began to contemplate being a mural painter. He was anxious to travel to Europe, something he had never done. While traveling overseas, he was stricken with a severe attack of renal colic. Although he had times of full activity while in Italy, he never completely recovered. In November 1911 he died in Florence, Italy; he was only fifty-eight years old.

Critics have concluded that Pyle was more than an artist, that his retellings of British legend are exemplary. The Children's Literature Association's canon committee chose both *The Merry Adventures of Robin Hood* and *The Story of King Arthur and His Knights* for their list of important books in the field. Pyle's work is continually cited in standard children's literature textbooks, and his books continue to be found in public libraries.

Howard Pyle's unique contribution to children's literature would not have been possible if he had been only an illustrator. Through his writings he put together noteworthy books containing legendary tales for the young. His own work and his encouragement to American illustrators and writers of children's literature brought him international fame. This legacy lives on today.

Selected Bibliography

WORKS WRITTEN AND ILLUSTRATED BY HOWARD PYLE

The Merry Adventures of Robin Hood of Great Renown in Nottinghamshire. New York: Charles Scribner's Sons, 1883; London: Sampson Law, 1883.

Pepper and Salt; or, Seasoning for Young Folk. New York: Harper and Brothers, 1885.

The Wonder Clock; or, Four and Twenty Marvellous Tales, Being One for Each Hour of the Day. New York: Harper, 1888; London: Osgood, 1888.

Otto of the Silver Hand. New York: Scribner, 1888; London: Sampson Low, 1888.

Men of Iron. New York: Harper and Brothers, 1892; London: Osgood, 1892.

Twilight Land. New York: Harper and Brothers; London: Osgood, 1894.

The Garden Behind the Moon: A Real Story of the Moon Angel. New York: Charles Scribner's Sons, 1895; London: Lawrence Bullen, 1895.

The Story of King Arthur and His Knights. New York: Charles Scribner's Sons, 1903; London: Newnes, 1903.

The Story of the Champions of the Round Table. New York: Charles Scribner's Sons, 1905; London: Chapman and Hall, 1905.

The Story of the Grail and the Passing of King Arthur. New York: Charles Scribner's Sons, 1910; London: Bickers, 1910.

CRITICAL AND BIOGRAPHICAL STUDIES

Abbott, Charles D. *Howard Pyle: A Chronicle.* New York and London: Harper and Brothers, 1923.

Brokaw, Howard Pyle. *The Howard Pyle Studio: A History.* Written for the studio's centennial. Wilmington, Del.: The Group, 1983.

Brown, Ann Barton. *Howard Pyle, a Teacher: The Formal Years, 1894–1905.* Chadds Ford, Pa.: Brandywine River Museum, 1980.

Delaware Art Museum. *Howard Pyle: Diversity in Depth.* Wilmington, Del.: The Wilmington Society of Fine Arts, 1973. (Exhibition catalog.)

Elzea, Rowland. *Howard Pyle.* Toronto: Peacock Press, 1975.

Hilton, Marilyn. "Shining Knight of the Golden Age" *Ontario Library Review* 48 (May 1964).

Kingman, Lee, ed. *The Illustrator's Notebook.* Boston: Horn Book, 1978.

Kunitz, Stanley J., and Howard Haycraft, eds. *American Authors, 1600–1900.* New York: H. W. Wilson, 1938.

Maxim, David. "Medieval Children's Books of Howard Pyle" *California Librarian* (April–July, 1971).

May, Jill P., ed. "Howard Pyle Commemorative Issue." *Children's Literature Association Quarterly* 8: 9–34 (1984).

Michigan State Library. *Biographical Sketches of American Artists.* Lansing, Mich.: State Library, 1912.

Morse, Willard Samuel, and Gertrude Brinklé. *Howard Pyle: A Record of His Illustrations and Writings.* Wilmington, Del.: The Wilmington Society of Fine Arts, 1921.

Nesbitt, Elizabeth. *Howard Pyle.* New York: H. Z. Walck, 1966.

Oakley, Thornton. "Howard Pyle" *Horn Book* 7/2: 91–97 (1931).

Pitz, Henry C. "The Art of Illustration" *Horn Book* 38/5: 454–457 (Oct. 1962).

———. *Howard Pyle: Writer, Illustrator, Founder of the Brandywine School.* New York: Bramhall House, 1975.

Thwaite, Mary F. *From Primer to Pleasure in Reading: An Introduction to the History of Children's Books in England from the Invention of Printing to 1914.* Boston: Horn Book, 1972.

Ward, Lynd. "The Book Artist: Yesterday and Tomorrow" *Horn Book.* 20/3: 231–242 (May 1944).

Weitenkampf, Frank. *The Illustrated Book.* Cambridge, Mass: Harvard University Press, 1938.

White, Gleeson. "Children's Books and Their Illustrators" *International Studio* (New York) 4 (1897).

—JILL P. MAY

ARTHUR RANSOME

1884–1967

MANY WRITERS USE their fiction as a vehicle to test untried experiences in their own lives. With Arthur Ransome it was the opposite: his tumultuous, haphazard life often overwhelmed him, and in his children's books he turned to more straightforward, controlled adventures as a solace.

The self-sufficient and buoyant kind of childhood depicted in Ransome's "Swallows and Amazons" series was both a reflection of and a contrast to his own. Born in 1884 in Leeds, England, where his father taught history at Yorkshire College, Arthur was the eldest of four children. In his boyhood he experienced a deep-seated insecurity and a passion for the English Lake District. These themes colored his future life. His insecurity was mostly due to his father, who showered constant disapproval upon his young son. Arthur's anxiety also stemmed from his extreme shortsightedness, which was not discovered for years.

On the positive side, young Arthur's life was filled with reading. After tackling *Robinson Crusoe*, by Daniel Defoe, at age four, he devoured Rudyard Kipling, Robert Louis Stevenson, Hans Christian Andersen, the Brothers Grimm, Andrew Lang, Lewis Carroll, Juliana Ewing, Charles Kingsley, Charlotte Yonge, and Robert Ballantyne. Later he gave his own child characters an acquaintance with many of these authors. One of the most influential books of his childhood was *Thorstein of the Mere*, by W. G. Collingwood, a Viking saga set around Peel Island in the Lake District, which later became the pivotal place in Ransome's own novels.

An even greater pleasure than reading were the holidays the Ransomes took on Coniston Water. This lake became a sacred place to Ransome, and it is here that the serene parts of his childhood were experienced. As he later stated in the introduction to his books: "We adored the place. Coming to it we used to run down to the lake, dip our hands in and wish, as if we had just seen the new moon. Going away from it we were half drowned in tears." Ransome spent as much of his life as he could visiting and living in the Lake District.

From the ages of eighteen to twenty-four, Arthur lived a self-consciously exultant life as a bohemian in London, working for a publisher and churning out mediocre books to earn money. At this time he formed a most significant friendship, with W. G. Collingwood, painter, former secretary to John Ruskin—and author of Ransome's favorite childhood book, among others. Collingwood's children were Arthur's age and became his second family. He spent all his holidays at their home on Coniston Water, sailing with the son, Robin, in his boat, the *Swallow*, and falling in love with one of the daughters (his suit was later rejected). Much later the children of another Collingwood daughter became the models for the characters in *Swallows and Amazons* (1930).

Ransome's life took a wrong turn in 1909 when he entered into a disastrous marriage. He and his unstable wife, Ivy Walker, had a stormy and uncertain relationship. The birth of a daughter, Tabitha, kept Arthur living with Ivy for four years. After he left, he gradually became estranged from his daughter as well as his wife. He escaped from the marriage in 1913 by going to Russia to learn the language in order to translate Russian fairy tales. Trapped in the country by the revolution, and unable to fight because of poor health, he stayed for most of the next six years as a correspondent for the London *Daily News*. His adventures there, chronicled in detail in Hugh Brogan's biography, were the strangest part of his life. Ransome's eyewitness accounts of the revolution were insightful and accurate. He was acquainted with Lenin (with whom he played chess) and Trotsky and was caught up with the romanticism of the Bolsheviks, although he remained somewhat of a political innocent. Eventually Arthur fell in love with Trotsky's secretary, Evgenia Shelepin. The two escaped dramatically in 1919 and spent the next five years in Estonia until his first wife agreed to a divorce.

In Estonia Ransome had become the Russian correspondent for the *Manchester Guardian*, and upon his return to England he continued as a successful journalist for that paper. Assignments in China, Egypt, and the Sudan, and the writing of books on sailing, fishing, criticism, and politics, kept him from his true vocation of being a novelist. But finally in 1929, at the age of forty-five, he refused the offer of literary editorship of the *Guardian* and left journalism to begin his first children's book, *Swallows and Amazons*.

From 1930 to 1947 twelve children's books by Ransome were published by Jonathan Cape. They slowly became immensely popular. Ransome received honorary degrees and a C.B.E., and the novels were translated into twelve languages. Despite this success, and his generally happy second marriage, the rest of his life contained disappointments. He and Evgenia were curiously restless, moving back and forth between the Lakes, Norfolk, and Suffolk. Arthur's health continued to be poor; plagued by stomach ailments, he was comforted by his abiding enjoyment of sailing and fishing. His wife often criticized his books blindly, baffling and hurting him, and he was never able to break new ground in his writing after the *Swallows and Amazons* series. He died in 1967 at the end of an ill and increasingly cantankerous old age.

Arthur Ransome's dogged perseverance and boyish enthusiasms enabled him to surmount many of the difficulties of his complicated life. In several ways he was a simple man, recognizing in his child friends his spiritual equals. His greatest pleasures were outdoor ones, and it is in his children's books that the happier parts of his life are revealed.

Even if Ransome had never embarked upon his series of realistic novels, he would still have won a place in children's literature for *Old Peter's Russian Tales* (1916). The retellings of the tales he collected combine traditional folktale motifs with uniquely Russian elements: firebirds; czars; samovars; long winters; and the folk figures of Baba Yaga, Vasilissa, and Prince Ivan. The stories are framed by the everyday life of Old Peter and his grandchildren, a device that keeps the tales fresh and child-oriented. They vary in mood between wit and melancholy, and their language is faultless, making the collection both readable and tellable. A second book of Russian stories, *The War of the Birds and the Beasts*, was published for the first time in 1984 to celebrate the author's centenary. The tales, a selection from many unpublished ones found in his archives, are less innocent than those in the first book. Many are sad, violent, or passionate, and the absence of a framing device makes them more suitable for an older audience.

The main body of Ransome's work falls naturally into three groups: eight novels, which are mostly set in the Lake District and carry the same set of main characters over about four years; two "fantasies," *Peter Duck* (1932) and *Missee Lee* (1941); and two books set in the Norfolk Broads, *Coot Club* (1934) and *The Big Six* (1940).

The first book of the principal sequence, *Swallows and Amazons*, introduces the central family of the series: John, Susan, Titty, and Roger Walker. They are staying with their mother at the Lakes and obtain permission to sail their borrowed boat, the *Swallow*, to Wild Cat Island and camp there alone for the rest of the summer. There they encounter two tomboyish girls, Nancy and Peggy Blackett, whose boat, the *Amazon*, flourishes a skull-and-crossbones flag. The "Swallows" and the "Amazons" fight an organized war for the island. The two groups become united, however, against the Blacketts' Uncle Jim ("Captain Flint"), who accuses John of tampering with his houseboat.

There has been much speculation about whether the four Walkers were modeled on real children. Hugh Brogan's biography and Christina Hardyment's sleuthing reveal how much they were based on the Altounyans, the five children of Dora Collingwood. Taqui, Susie, Titty (her real name was Mavis, but she was nicknamed after the folktale "Titty Mouse and Tatty Mouse"), Roger, and Brigit spent most of the year in Aleppo, but often came to England for holidays with their Collingwood grandparents, and were also close to the Ransomes. "Uncle Arthur" owned one of the boats they used, named the *Swallow* after the one that once belonged to their Uncle Robin. Touched by the Altounyans' birthday present to him of a pair of Turkish slippers, Ransome decided to write a book about the children to remind them of the Lakes when they were back in Syria. In a childhood memoir, *In Aleppo Once* (1969), Taqui describes their wonder at receiving *Swallows and Amazons* and realizing it was about them. It was dedicated "to the six, for whom it was written in exchange for a pair of slippers." In old age, however, Ransome suppressed this dedication and claimed in his *Autobiography* (1976) that the characters were entirely imaginary. He seems to have thought that the Altounyans would cash in on their connection with the stories, a belief that was all the more unfair because of their discomfort with being identified with the characters. Ransome's fictional creations had become so real to him that any suggestion that they stemmed from actual children made him jealously protective.

Although it is now obvious that the Walkers began as models of real children, like all literary characters they assumed a life of their own and are probably a mixture of the Altounyans, the young Collingwoods, and Arthur and his siblings as children. Stalwart and ethical John, practical Susan, imaginative Titty (upon whom the author centers almost all the emotion in the series), and clownish Roger—each is so consistently presented that their predictability becomes an assuring presence.

The other two main characters in *Swallows and Amazons*, Nancy and Peggy, are equally strong creations. Ransome first conceived them when he glimpsed two girls in red caps playing by the side of Coniston Water. Nancy's real name in the story is Ruth, but she calls herself Nancy because she is an Amazon pirate and pirates are "ruthless." She is just as able a sailor as John, and her colorful language and inventive, wild nature are an invitation to adventure to the milder Walkers. Chattering, prosaic Peggy is completely reliant upon her daunting older sister. She, Susan, and Roger serve as foils to the stronger personalities of John, Titty, and Nancy, who are the head, heart, and hands of the series.

Swallows and Amazons is a leisurely book. The first seven chapters describe settling in on the island and are filled with Ransome's characteristic details of sailing and camping. The conflicts between the

Swallows and the Amazons and with Captain Flint, however, keep the story moving. Titty captures the *Amazon*, and Captain Flint makes peace with John. The last episode, however, where Titty and Roger discover the trunk that local ruffians have stolen from Captain Flint's houseboat, seems one excitement too many, as if the author did not want his story to end.

A major feature of the early books is that these children are not just enjoying sailing and camping, they are playing games while they do so. Thus, at the beginning of *Swallows and Amazons*, the Walkers make up ship's papers, where John becomes the Captain, Susan the Mate, Titty the Able Seaman, and Roger the Ship's Boy. These roles remain consistent throughout the series; characters reply, "Aye, aye, sir," so often that the reader forgets it *is* a game. Nancy and Peggy are also a Captain and a Mate, as well as being pirates.

In the second book, *Swallowdale* (1931), the sailors become grounded. The *Swallow* is "shipwrecked" and the *Amazon* off limits because of the visit of Nancy and Peggy's great-aunt, who restricts them to a tame life of best frocks and "no piracy except just now and then between meals." The Swallows decide to be explorers instead, camping out in a valley they name Swallowdale, with the Amazons visiting when they can escape.

Swallowdale is the longest book of the series and has the least plot. Sometimes it becomes ponderous, but its length gives Ransome an opportunity to dwell on his beloved countryside. By the end of the novel the Lake District landscape has so saturated the story that the area deserves the epithet "Ransome Country" that has sometimes been applied to it.

In *Swallowdale*, also, the characters of the Walkers become fully rounded, especially that of Titty. Her fantasy life is expanded; she now has an imaginary friend, "Peter Duck," an old sailor she and the others made up for a story they composed during the previous winter. Titty's imagination becomes too much for her when she tries some magic. She creates a candle-grease statue of the great-aunt, intending to melt the wax just enough to make the real aunt uncomfortable enough to leave. When Titty accidentally drops the image into the fire she believes she has killed her. It takes much reassurance by Susan to convince her she hasn't.

The 1930's proprieties forced upon Nancy and Peggy point out the need the children feel to separate themselves, almost as a tribe, from the adults, or "natives," as they call them. Great-aunt Maria is the worst kind of native; their mothers are the best kind but are still firmly on the other side. In this book, however, the one adult in the series who is allowed to enter fully into their activities, Captain Flint, begins to do so. His reassuring background presence, as when he helps to repair the *Swallow*, extends the children's freedom. Captain Flint's writing, sailing, and traveling career are obviously modeled after Ransome himself; it is as if the author were physically present in the stories.

Winter Holiday (1933) and *Pigeon Post* (1936) are examples of Ransome at his best. The children's growing competence with their environment enables the author to give them more challenges, and the addition of two new characters completes the group, resulting in a greater diversification of roles and a larger pool of resources upon which to draw for the adventures.

Winter Holiday takes place the winter after the events in *Swallowdale* and is based on Ransome's experiences at boarding school in Windermere during the "Great Frost" of 1895, when the whole lake froze solid. The Swallows and Amazons make friends with Dick and Dorothea Callum, who are also spending their holiday on the lake, a holiday that is extended when Nancy contracts mumps and the others are kept away from school in quarantine. As the lake gradually freezes, they plan an expedition to the "North Pole." It is the newcomers, Dick and Dorothea, who prove themselves by sailing to the Pole in their ice sledge through a blizzard.

Unlike the other children, Dick and Dorothea are not accustomed to the country; they are timid and awkward, but eager to learn. Scientific, bespectacled Dick becomes a vehicle for Ransome's delight in technical details, through his complete absorption in whatever passion he has at the moment. His older sister, Dorothea, is the opposite: a budding young novelist, she invests each situation with romance. The humor of the characters' desperate attempts to create excitement in a restricted winter environment, the suspense of the race to the Pole, and the beauty of a transformed landscape combine to make *Winter Holiday* a deeply satisfying story.

Pigeon Post deserved the Carnegie Medal (the first ever awarded) it won in 1937. It is the most typical of Ransome's books: set in the summer in the Lakes, with the full cast of characters participating in an exciting adventure, a search for gold. A scene of solitary courage, when frightened Titty

decides to use her newly discovered talent for water divining so that the others can camp in the dry fells, is remarkable for its combination of restraint and emotion.

We Didn't Mean to Go to Sea (1937) differs from the previous books in that it is not set in the Lakes and is a more dramatic adventure. Here no games overlay the activities because the experience itself—the Walkers forced in a fog to sail a large boat across the North Sea to Holland—is exciting enough.

The story is John's and Susan's, and they each pass its trials. John, after steering the small ship through a storm, deserves his father's praise, "You'll be a seaman yet, my son." Susan fights her terrible seasickness and her agony over breaking their promise not to go outside the harbor, and becomes "once more the mate, with a job to do."

Many critics consider this to be Ransome's finest novel. It is certainly the most accessible to modern children, with its carefully paced suspense and mixture of real danger and such domestic details as the rescuing of a kitten. The adventure is realistic in every detail; before beginning to write it Ransome tried the journey in his boat the *Nancy Blackett*.

The novel that immediately follows, *Secret Water* (1939), is very much a book of transition, with new characters introduced and familiar ones growing up. Although it contains much humor and drama, it is not up to Ransome's best work. There are too many echoes of *Swallows and Amazons*. As the Amazons did in the first book, a group of strangers, the Eels, leave their emblem in the camp and start a conflict. The adventure is too adult-oriented to be exciting. The Walkers, later joined by the Blacketts, are set down alone on the coast of Suffolk, with a blank chart to be filled in. Fulfilling their father's, not their own, goal of charting the land makes the atmosphere tame and artificial. The new characters introduced—Daisy, Dum, Dee, and Don, known as the "Eels"—are too one-dimensional to be interesting. The addition of Bridget, the youngest Walker, adds much humor, but having someone that young along to look after slows up the action considerably.

Nancy is in conflict with the Walkers because she wants to have a war with the Eels instead of charting and surveying. Here the aging of Ransome's characters is apparent: John and Susan, matured by their experience in *We Didn't Mean to Go to Sea*, seem too old for games; Nancy is confused and rebellious; and Titty shows new leadership abilities when trapped by the tide with Roger and Bridget.

Ransome shifts emphasis from the Walkers to the Blacketts and Callums, and also back to the Lakes, in *The Picts and the Martyrs* (1943). The story takes place the summer after the adventures in *Secret Water*. Nancy and Peggy are left alone with the cook when their mother is sent away to convalesce after an illness. Great-aunt Maria arrives unexpectedly to take care of them, and the visiting Dick and Dorothea are forced to hide out in the woods. It is in this book that Nancy also matures, persuading the others that "there's lots and lots to do without adventures." She does her best to please her aunt so that her mother will not be blamed for leaving them on their own. So well does she succeed that the great-aunt praises her in a letter. In the end Nancy realizes that she shares her formidable relative's stubbornness and self-possession.

The last book, *Great Northern?* (1947), takes place in a new setting, this time the Scottish Hebrides. Captain Flint and all of the children except Bridget are on a cruise, when they become involved in stopping an egg collector from finding the nest of a pair of great northern divers. Ransome treats this adventure as the most important they have had. Titty reflects on its seriousness as she and Dick frantically search for the stolen eggs: "This was a matter of life and death. Quick! Oh, quick! Life and death!" Dick and Titty find the eggs and return them to the nest. The series ends in a life-affirming moment as, blinking back tears, the two of them watch the birds come back.

The eight books in the first group can be easily viewed as one long story. Then the maturing of the characters is apparent, and along with this a movement from imaginative games to reality; the books become more and more realistic as they spread geographically from the small island all the way to Scotland.

The imaginative element of the series is the greatest difference between Ransome and his many imitators. There are two types of games: private ones, such as Titty pretending to be a cormorant, and communal ones, such as the most basic game of being sailors. The communal games are intrinsically connected to the action and form the theme of each of the earlier books. They are what the children call their "real" life: "What are you?" Nancy asks Dorothea. "In real life, I mean. We're sailors and explorers."

The games help the characters grow up because in them the children mirror adult roles. It is significant that after the sailor hierarchy is set up in the first book Ransome never again refers to his characters as "the children." Thus, in *We Didn't Mean to Go to Sea*, one reason the Walkers survive is that the younger ones are used to obeying their Captain and Mate, much more than they would likely obey an older brother and sister. And in *Pigeon Post* Titty recalls all her past and present roles to give her courage to pick up the hazel stick that she knows will work for her as a dowsing rod: "She, an able-seaman, an explorer, a mining prospector."

Once even Nancy, in *The Picts and the Martyrs*, has grown beyond games, Ransome seems momentarily unwilling to let his characters grow up. In a puzzling turnabout Nancy declares: "And now at last we're free to start stirring things up. We'll hoist the skull and cross-bones again the moment we've had our grub." Newly mature, teenage Nancy is not likely to do this. It is as if there are two endings to the sequence: one, in *The Picts and the Martyrs*, where the characters endlessly create adventure with "five more weeks of the holidays still to go"; and the other, in *Great Northern?*, where there are no more games and where reality itself is an adventure.

An intriguing aspect of the children's imaginations occurs in the second group of books, *Peter Duck* and *Missee Lee*. These novels have been called "realistic fantasy"; they are supposed to be stories the children have made up about themselves. Both concern Captain Flint, the Walkers, and the Blacketts on their ship the *Wild Cat*. In *Peter Duck* they race to the Caribbean to beat a crew of pirates to a treasure, and in *Missee Lee* they are captured by a female Chinese pirate. *Peter Duck* contains some of the most impressive sailing passages in the series, and Missee Lee is a memorable heroine. But Ransome has already created such convincing characters, it is jarring to lift them to another plane of reality. The reader becomes bewildered: *Are* these adventures supposed to have really happened? Read separately from the others, the two novels succeed as *Treasure Island*–like improbable adventures; indeed, *Peter Duck* was the first of Ransome's books to become popular. Viewed in relation to the other books, however, they do not succeed as either reality or fantasy. The books are interesting failures and proof of how well the others work. Ransome's characters do not need to voyage to a desert island or to a distant land, for they have discovered how to create excitement in their own environment.

The last of the three groups of books, *Coot Club* and *The Big Six*, are dominated by their Norfolk

Broads setting. Except for Dick and Dorothea, the characters are new: Tom Dudgeon, the doctor's son; Port and Starboard (twin girls), his neighbors; and Joe, Bill, and Pete, young sons of boatbuilders. In the first book they help Tom escape from the wrath of the "Hullabaloos," noisy barge people who are disturbing coots' nests. The second is a first-rate mystery, as the "Big Six"—Dick, Dorothea, Tom, Joe, Bill, and Pete—try to discover who is casting boats adrift.

The two books are permeated with meticulous details of sailing and birds. They do not contain much game playing, other than that of being detectives, but are gentler stories that effectively evoke an area of England different from the Lakes.

Arthur Ransome's books have long been labeled "holiday adventures" and praised for being the first novels to depict children coping without their parents in an outdoor setting. The books' enormous popularity continued right up to the 1960's. Children all over the world addressed letters to their favorite characters in envelopes decorated with skulls and crossbones or labeled "Pirate Post." Two adolescents at boarding school, Katherine Hull and Pamela Whitlock, were so influenced by the novels that they sent Ransome one of their own. *The Far-Distant Oxus* (1937) had similar games and adventures set in Devon, and Ransome went to great efforts to get it published.

The main reason the books were so popular was no doubt the freedom and competence the author gave his characters. In *Swallows and Amazons*, the telegram from their father that first grants the Walkers this freedom—"BETTER DROWNED THAN DUFFERS IF NOT DUFFERS WONT DROWN"—exemplifies the rare respect that adults have toward children in Ransome's world. The children won't drown because they are too competent to be duffers; Nancy and Peggy, brought up on the shores of the lake, are just as adept. With practical Susan to remind them of bedtimes, and adults close at hand to turn up with porridge after a storm, the freedom is extended by being rooted in security.

Another appeal is the intense reality of the children's activities. The many technical details are a hallmark of the series; what is astonishing is how unobtrusively Ransome integrates them into the narrative. By the end of the series the reader has painlessly absorbed information about sailing in all types of boats, camping, cooking, fishing, swimming, tracking, fell climbing, birds, knots, astronomy, signaling, water divining, surveying, mapping, fingerprinting, photography, eels, netting, and even Latin.

The landscape is also accurately described, although the author played his own games with it, letting his characters rename the area, and combining Peel Island, on Coniston Water, with Blakeholm, on Windermere, to create Wild Cat Island. Generations of readers, armed with the endpaper maps, have visited the Lakes to discover the real places. Ransome's economical prose manages to capture details of landscape with scarcely any description. His illustrations—flat perspectives of horizontal bodies of water broken by perpendicular masts of boats and rounded hills—evoke the area perfectly. He excused the nonprofessionalism of his illustrations by stating that they were done by Nancy, but the amateur quality of his drawings is appropriate to their simplicity.

The books' decline in popularity must be due in part to their daunting length. The author's straightforward prose and suspenseful plots still carry most of the stories forward, however, despite their bulk. Ransome has sometimes been criticized for depicting children who are too competent and well-behaved to be true. This has never seemed to bother his readers and may even add to the books' appeal. The characters *are* ideal, because they are so civilized. Their resourcefulness, good humor, and self-reliance are shown so convincingly that these qualities become possibilities. Ransome depicts children in the way they would like to think of themselves if given the same freedom.

Selected Bibliography

WORKS OF ARTHUR RANSOME

Russian Folktales

Old Peter's Russian Tales. With illustrations by Dmitri Mitrokhin. London: T.C. and E.C. Jack, 1916; New York: Frederick A. Stokes, 1917. Paperback ed., with illustrations by Faith Jaques. Harmondsworth, England: Penguin Books, 1974. Republished Salem, N.H.: Merrimack, 1984.

The Fool of the World and the Flying Ship. With illustrations by Uri Shulevitz. New York: Farrar, Straus, Giroux, 1968. (A story from *Old Peter's Russian Tales.*)

The War of the Birds and the Beasts. With illustrations by Faith Jaques. London: Jonathan Cape, 1984.

Swallows and Amazons Series

Swallows and Amazons. London: Jonathan Cape, 1930. Rev. ed., with illustrations by Clifford Webb and maps by Stephen Spurrier. London: Jonathan Cape, 1931. Rev. ed., with illustrations by Helene Carter. Philadelphia: Lippincott, 1931. Rev. ed., with illustrations by the author. London: Jonathan Cape, 1938. Reprinted (paperback edition) Harmondsworth, England: Penguin Books, 1962; Salem, N.H.: Merrimack, 1981.

Swallowdale. With illustrations by Clifford Webb. London: Jonathan Cape, 1931. Rev. ed., with illustrations by Helene Carter. Philadelphia: Lippincott, 1932. Rev. ed., with illustrations by the author. London: Jonathan Cape, 1938. Reprinted (paperback edition) Harmondsworth, England: Penguin Books, 1968; Salem, N.H.: Merrimack, 1980.

Peter Duck. With illustrations by the author. London: Jonathan Cape, 1932. Rev. ed., with additional illustrations by Helene Carter. Philadelphia: Lippincott, 1933. Reprinted, with illustrations by the author. Harmondsworth, England: Penguin Books, 1968; Salem, N.H.: Merrimack, 1980.

Winter Holiday. With illustrations by the author. London: Jonathan Cape, 1933. Rev. ed., with additional illustrations by Helene Carter. Philadelphia: Lippincott, 1934. Reprinted, with illustrations by the author. Harmondsworth, England: Penguin Books, 1968; Salem, N.H.: Merrimack, 1980.

Coot Club. With illustrations by the author. London: Jonathan Cape, 1934. Rev. ed., with additional illustrations by Helene Carter. Philadelphia: Lippincott, 1935. Reprinted, with illustrations by the author. Harmondsworth, England: Penguin Books, 1969; Salem, N.H.: Merrimack, 1980.

Pigeon Post. With illustrations by the author. London: Jonathan Cape, 1936. Rev. ed., with illustrations by Mary E. Shepard. Philadelphia: Lippincott, 1937. Reprinted, with illustrations by the author. Harmondsworth, England: Penguin Books, 1969; Salem, N.H.: Merrimack, 1980.

We Didn't Mean to Go to Sea. With illustrations by the author. London: Jonathan Cape, 1937; New York: Macmillan, 1938. Reprinted (paperback edition) Harmondsworth, England: Penguin Books, 1969. Rev. ed., with an introduction by Beryl B. Beatley. Boston: Gregg Press, 1981. Rev. ed. Salem, N.H.: Merrimack, 1983.

Secret Water. With illustrations by the author. London: Jonathan Cape, 1939; New York: Macmillan, 1940. Reprinted (paperback edition) Harmondsworth, England: Penguin Books, 1969; Salem, N.H.: Merrimack, 1980.

The Big Six. With illustrations by the author. London: Jonathan Cape, 1940; New York: Macmillan, 1941. Reprinted (paperback edition) Harmondsworth, England: Penguin Books, 1970; Salem, N.H.: Merrimack, 1980.

Missee Lee. With illustrations by the author. London: Jonathan Cape, 1941; New York: Macmillan, 1942. Reprinted (paperback edition) Harmondsworth, England: Penguin Books, 1971; Salem, N.H.: Merrimack, 1980.

The Picts and the Martyrs; or, Not Welcome at All. With illustrations by the author. London: Jonathan Cape, 1943; New York: Macmillan, 1943. Reprinted (paperback edition) Harmondsworth, England: Penguin Books, 1971; Salem, N.H.: Merrimack, 1980.

Great Northern? With illustrations by the author. London: Jonathan Cape, 1947; New York: Macmillan, 1948. Reprinted (paperback edition) Harmondsworth, England: Penguin Books, 1971; Salem, N.H.: Merrimack, 1980.

Swallows and Amazons Forever! With illustrations by the author. Harmondsworth, England: Penguin Books, 1983. (A paperback abridgment of *Coot Club* and *The Big Six,* by Neil Philip.)

CRITICAL AND BIOGRAPHICAL STUDIES

Avery, Gillian. *Childhood's Pattern: A Study of the Heroes and Heroines of Children's Fiction, 1770–1950.* London: Hodder and Stoughton, 1975.

Bodger, Joan. *How the Heather Looks: A Joyous Journey to the British Sources of Children's Books.* New York: Viking Press, 1965.

Brogan, Hugh. *The Life of Arthur Ransome.* London: Jonathan Cape, 1984.

Hardyment, Christina. *Arthur Ransome and Captain Flint's Trunk.* London: Jonathan Cape, 1984.

Hunt, Peter. "Ransome Revisited: A Structural and Developmental Approach" *Children's Literature in Education* 12/1:24–33 (1981).

Ransome, Arthur. *The Autobiography of Arthur Ransome,* edited by Rupert Hart-Davis. London: Jonathan Cape, 1976.

Senick, Gerard T. "Arthur Ransome." In *Children's Literature Review,* vol. 8. Detroit: Gale Research, 1985.

Shelley, Hugh. *Arthur Ransome.* London: Bodley Head, 1960; New York: H. Z. Walck, 1964.

—KIT PEARSON

MARJORIE KINNAN RAWLINGS

1896-1953

IN THE NEARLY fifty years since Marjorie Kinnan Rawlings' novel *The Yearling* (1938) was published, it has joined the distinguished ranks of *Robinson Crusoe* (1719), *Two Years Before the Mast* (1840), and *The Last of the Mohicans* (1826)—all books not originally intended for children that nevertheless have become classic "boys' books." During her lifetime, Rawlings published nothing intended for children. *The Secret River* (1955), a picture book, was published posthumously, but it is a slight story of a child who saves her father and her forest community from "hard times" by catching a large number of catfish in a river that she can never find afterward. It is written in a very simple style with the somewhat condescending tone typical of many books of the mid twentieth century intended for young children, and is more notable for its illustrations by Leonard Weisgard than for its fanciful text. *The Yearling*, however, has retained a faithful audience of young, and older, readers not only because of its touching story of a lonely boy and his pet deer but also because of its strong characterization of the independent Florida "Crackers" and its vivid evocation of the wild beauty of the Florida scrub country.

Rawlings was not a native of the northern Florida country she loved and made famous. She was born in Washington, D.C., on 8 August 1896. In 1914 she moved to Madison, Wisconsin, with her recently widowed mother and her brother, so that she could enter the University of Wisconsin. In college Rawlings was an excellent and prominent student. She was chosen for Mortar Board, a

women's honor society, and for Phi Beta Kappa; she was an active member of Red Domino, the campus dramatic group, writing and acting in a number of productions. After her graduation in 1918, she worked as a publicist for the Young Women's Christian Association at the national headquarters in New York City. In 1919 she married her college friend Charles A. Rawlings, a writer and boating enthusiast. For the next nine years she did advertising and newspaper writing, most notably a syndicated poetry column called "Songs of the Housewife," and struggled to preserve a marriage that was evidently never happy and was becoming increasingly difficult.

Hoping that a change of scene would give their relationship a new start, in 1928 Rawlings and her husband moved to a seventy-two-acre orange grove at Cross Creek, Florida, land purchased with a small sum of money she had inherited. At first, two of her husband's brothers were also involved in running the orange grove, but they soon departed, and Charles Rawlings, always more interested in boats and maritime pursuits, moved to the coast. The Rawlingses were divorced in 1933, and Marjorie Rawlings continued to manage the citrus grove by herself. Although she was married again in 1941 to Norton Sanford Baskin, a hotel owner in St. Augustine, and changed her main residence to the east coast of Florida, she continued to own her home at Cross Creek and frequently returned there for the solitude and inspiration she needed to write. She died of a cerebral hemorrhage on 14 December 1953 in St. Augustine and was buried in Island

Grove, Florida. Her modest home at Cross Creek has become a state museum that is open to the public.

Beginning in her college days, Rawlings wrote and attempted to publish fiction. It was not until she moved to Florida that any of her work was purchased; her first success was "Cracker Chidlings: Real Tales from the Florida Interior," a series of sketches based on her observations of her Florida neighbors and acquaintances, which ran in *Scribner's Magazine* in February of 1931. The term "Cracker," as Rawlings uses it, refers without derogatory connotations to the country people of northern Florida. Her association with the magazine and with the press was of paramount importance to the rest of her writing career. Her work came to the attention of Scribners' editor Maxwell Perkins, who began working with her as he worked with such famous authors as Ernest Hemingway, Thomas Wolfe, and F. Scott Fitzgerald, and who became her friend and mentor for the rest of his life. In 1931 she placed second in the Scribner Prize Contest with "Jacob's Ladder," a long story, or novella, which was published in the April issue of *Scribner's Magazine*, included in her 1940 story collection *When the Whippoorwill—*, and republished as a separate volume in 1950 by the University of Miami Press. She continued to write and sell short stories, and in 1933 Scribners published her first novel, *South Moon Under*. *Golden Apples*, her second novel, was published by Scribners in 1935.

These early writings foreshadow *The Yearling* in setting and in type of character, but they fall short in total conception, in development of characterization, and in style. "Cracker Chidlings" is a series of brief pieces about Florida people and places, and as such presages her most successful books, but it reflects the point of view of an outsider who finds the locals quaint and amusing. "Jacob's Ladder" has a more sympathetic tone. It describes the wanderings of a young woman and her man from one disaster to another. They survive without a home, frequently even without food or shelter, through the birth and death of their baby, until the young woman takes the situation into her own hands. She insists that they return to the cabin that is rightfully hers and confront her brutal father.

By the time of the writing of *South Moon Under* Rawlings's almost condescending attitude had changed to one of understanding and admiration for the enduring spirit and simple life of the Florida natives. This novel, her most successful except for *The Yearling*, tells the story of three generations of

a family of bootleggers who live and work in the cypress swamps along the Ocklawaha River. The Lantrys and the Jacklins, who regard the making of moonshine not as a criminal activity but as a way of life, are more fully drawn than Florrie and Mart of "Jacob's Ladder." But all these characters exhibit the stoic acceptance of hardship and the appreciation of the unusual beauty of their wild and forbidding environment that Rawlings develops further in the characters of *The Yearling*.

In *Golden Apples* Rawlings attempted a more ambitious plot, but even she admitted in a letter to Perkins that the novel is "interesting trash instead of literature." Her main character is a young English remittance man, Richard Tordell, who is exiled to the Florida scrub land that was abandoned years ago by a relative. Although he despairs at first and hates the area, he gradually becomes more interested and ambitious. The foil for Tordell is a local orphan, Luke Brinley, who, with his sister, has taken up squatter's rights in the decaying house on the land. Brinley stays to become servant to the new owner, and his sister becomes Tordell's mistress and, eventually, shunned wife. Rawlings made a trip to England in 1933 to collect background material for her protagonist and interviewed the survivors of a colony of Englishmen who had owned orange groves in northern Florida before the "Big Freeze" of 1885. But despite her considerable efforts, her main character never comes to life. The chief interest in the novel centers on Luke, a sensitive but stoic survivor who recalls Lantry Jacklin in *South Moon Under* and, in some ways, foreshadows both Jody and Penny Baxter in *The Yearling*.

The substitution of journalistic research for the imaginative creation of character may be one of the defects that doomed Rawlings' last and most ambitious novel, *The Sojourner* (1953), which is set in upstate New York. The novel was not completed until fifteen years after the publication of *The Yearling*; during this time she had become quite wealthy and famous and had published a collection of short stories, *When the Whippoorwill—*, and two semiautobiographical books, *Cross Creek* (1942) and *Cross Creek Cookery* (1942), all three successful with both critics and the public. *The Sojourner* is a long novel, covering the life span of Ase Linden, whom Rawlings patterned after her own maternal grandfather Traphagen. She used information collected from boxes of her grandfather's letters and ledgers, and, as a consequence, Ase never emerges as a vivid character from the wealth of facts about farming and family life gleaned from this material. Moreover, it is a doctrinaire book, a sort of allegory, with Ase cast as Everyman, as the ideal husbandman in tune with the soil and with nature. As with all allegories, the characters are more types than individuals. Her biographer Gordon E. Bigelow says in *Frontier Eden: The Literary Career of Marjorie Kinnan Rawlings*: "The book represents a noble attempt to write the great American novel, but it must be counted more a failure than a success."

Rawlings's present reputation rests almost entirely on the merits of those of her stories, novels, and nonfiction pieces that are set in northern Florida, and her name is included in lists of important writers of children's literature solely on account of *The Yearling*. Ironically, she insisted that the book was not for a young audience. Perkins had suggested in 1933, after the publication of *South Moon Under*, that she write a story in the pattern of *The Adventures of Huckleberry Finn*, and she tried to do so for some time without success. "Do you realize how calmly you sat up there in your office and announced that you were expecting a boy's *classic* of me?" she wrote accusingly in a letter to him. Toward the end of 1935 she mentioned the idea in another letter: "At present, I don't have the enthusiasm. . . . My material seems very thin." By January of 1936, however, she had changed her mind: "The feeling for the boy's book, the particular thing I want to say, came to me. It will not be a story for boys, though some of them might enjoy it. It will be a story *about* a boy—a brief and tragic idyll of boyhood." She proposed a length of about fifty thousand words. The story grew in the next year, and in November she wrote Perkins again, insisting that it was not a book for children:

> What I am concerned about is that the forthcoming book should not be labeled a "juvenile," because I think it will only incidentally be a book *for* boys. I hope there will be nostalgic implications for mature people for we never *feel* more sensitively than in extreme youth, and the color and drama of the scrub can be well conveyed through the eyes and mind of a boy. . . . But it is important that no announcement ever be made, anywhere, that the book is a "juvenile."

Despite its publication and success as an adult novel —it received general critical acclaim, was a bestseller, was awarded the Pulitzer Prize in 1939, and was made into a motion picture in 1946—*The Year-* *ling* now often appears on children's lists in libraries and publishers' catalogs and is probably read much more by young people than by adults. Its basic plot has strong appeal. Jody is a lonely eleven-year-old boy, the only child of small, wiry Penny Baxter and his mountainous wife, Ora, to survive infancy. When Jody acquires Flag, a fawn, the pet satisfies a need for affection that grim Ma Baxter has never fulfilled. For a year the two are constant companions on the isolated scrub farm, surrounded by miles of forest, but when, as a yearling, Flag destroys the crops on which the family's precarious living depends, he must be shot. Though Jody runs away in despair, he returns to face the hard responsibilities of his life. He is now mature enough to begin taking over from his aging and ailing father. As with any tale of a beloved pet, the story could have been written as a tearjerker. Rawlings resisted the temptation admirably. The novel does have strong feeling, but with the possible exception of the final sentence—"Somewhere beyond the sinkhole, past the magnolia, under the live oaks, a boy and a yearling ran side by side, and were gone forever"—there is no sentimentality.

In the development of this simple plot alone *The Yearling* might well have a place in children's literature. Essentially an initiation story, the novel culminates in a conflict that has been foreshadowed in a number of other encounters Jody has with death and with the threat of death. Early in the book he and Penny hunt Old Slewfoot, the giant bear that has killed their brood sow. In the fearful battle with the bear, old Julia, the hound, is badly mauled and brought near death. Later in the book a terrible flood kills most of the wildlife, and the disease that follows destroys more. Penny is bitten by a rattlesnake and nearly dies. Fodder-wing, the youngest of the Forresters, who, although they live four miles away, are the Baxters' nearest neighbors, does die, and Jody sits with his body through the night and attends the simple funeral. These episodes not only prepare the way for Flag's inevitable death, but also make Jody's ultimate acceptance of hardship and responsibility more credible by showing his gradual development from a fun-loving child who runs off from hoeing the corn to make a flutter-mill in the stream to a youth who accepts the necessity of sacrificing his pet.

The real strength of the book, however, lies not in the plot but in the characterization and in the evocation of the setting. Jody himself is an endearing boy, wide-eyed with wonder at the beauties and mysteries of nature, delighted with his fawn, puzzled by the apparent contradictions and arbitrary events of life, and stoic in the hardships that the family must endure. Ma Baxter is a believable character and even wins the reader's grudging respect as, in her own humorless way, she copes with her hard life. Minor characters are also convincingly and interestingly portrayed, particularly the boisterous, hard-drinking Forresters and feminine, flirtatious Grandma Hutto, who serves as foil for Ma. But it is Penny Baxter whose character is most highly developed and essential to the novel. Despite his small stature, Penny has the strength of personality to make a living in the arid region, to defend Jody's interests against Ma's insistence on duty, and to earn the respect of his neighbors. At the same time, he is sensitive to the beauty of the scrub and feels a kinship with the animals who live there. Even the Forresters defer to him in matters of hunting and listen breathlessly to his stories. For Jody he is mentor and role model, not only in his approach to practical matters but also in his philosophical attitude toward life. In one of his final speeches in the book, after Jody has returned nearly starving, Penny sums up his philosophy of life:

> "Ever' man wants life to be a fine thing, and a easy. 'Tis fine, boy, powerful fine, but 'tain't easy. Life knocks a man down and he gits up and it knocks him down again. I've been uneasy all my life.
> . . . I wanted to spare you, long as I could. I wanted you to frolic with your yearlin'. I knowed the lonesomeness he eased for you. But ever' man's lonesome. What's he to do then? What's he to do when he gits knocked down? Why, take it for his share and go on."

Set in the decade after the Civil War, *The Yearling* gives a memorable picture of the time and of the frontier life in the wild scrub country. The novel is full of vivid scenes. There are two bear hunts, both described with an intensity that evokes the sounds and the smells of the woods, the feel of swamp water in the shoes, and the characters' terror at the sheer power of Old Slewfoot. There are scenes of pure beauty, like the one in which Penny and Jody witness the dance of the whooping cranes:

> The dancers raised their wings and lifted their feet, first one and then the other. They sunk their heads deep in their snowy breasts, lifted them and sunk them again. They moved soundlessly, part awkwardness, part grace. The dance was solemn. Wings fluttered, rising and falling like out-stretched arms.

The outer circle shuffled around and around. The group in the center attained a slow frenzy.
> . . . The birds were reflected in the clear marsh water. Sixteen white shadows reflected the motions. The evening breeze moved across the saw-grass. It bowed and fluttered. The water rippled. The setting sun lay rosy on the white bodies. Magic birds were dancing in a mystic marsh.

One unforgettable scene takes place at the home of the Forresters, where Jody is spending the night with Fodder-wing. The household is roused by a "varmint hunt" in the middle of the night. The six big, black-bearded, older Forrester sons, stark naked, drink moonshine and make music with their fiddles, mouth organs, and drums, thunderous and out of tune, while their wizened parents placidly ignore the commotion and Jody and Fodder-wing crouch on the floor watching.

An equally memorable, though quieter, scene occurs when Jody wakes after falling asleep by the stream:

> When he awakened, he thought he was in a place other than the branch bed. He was in another world, so that for an instant he thought he might still be dreaming. The sun was gone, and all the light and shadow. There were no black boles of live oaks, no glossy green of magnolia leaves, no pattern of gold lace where the sun had sifted through the branches of the wild cherry. The world was all a gentle gray, and he lay in a mist as fine as spray from a waterfall. The mist tickled his skin. It was scarcely wet. It was at once warm and cool. He rolled over on his back and it was as though he looked up into the soft gray breast of a mourning dove.

An important element that contributes to the realism of the setting is Rawlings' remarkably convincing handling of the Cracker dialect. On their way to the Forresters', Penny cautions Jody, "Now don't you torment Fodder-wing," whose wits are "addled," and explains, "He's the second settin' and he ain't to blame for hatchin' out peculiar." Grandma Hutto, who has no love for Ma Baxter, tells Jody, "Your father married a woman all Hell couldn't amuse." Jody's appetite is also the subject of numerous exchanges. "The time it takened me," Ma complains, "to make that pone—and you destroyin' it before I git my breath—" Another time Penny remarks, "Where you put it all, I cain't see. But I'm proud I got it to give to you. There was times when I were a boy, they was sich a passel of us, my own belly lay mighty flat." The rhythms and phraseology of the dialogue are essential parts of the characterization, well suited to the period and shifting subtly from one individual to another. Through the characters' own words, as well as through her descriptions, Rawlings expresses the hardships and the beauty of life in the northern Florida scrub country.

Marjorie Kinnan Rawlings' legacy to children's literature essentially consists of just one book, *The Yearling*, but it is a book that even after fifty years still lives through its strong characters, its telling metaphor, and its vivid scenes.

Selected Bibliography

WORKS OF MARJORIE KINNAN RAWLINGS

"Cracker Chidlings: Real Tales from the Florida Interior." *Scribner's Magazine* 89: 127–134 (February 1931).

"Jacob's Ladder." *Scribner's Magazine* 89: 351–366, 446–464 (April 1931). Published separately Miami, Fla.: University of Miami Press, 1950.

South Moon Under. New York: Charles Scribner's Sons, 1933.

Golden Apples. New York: Charles Scribner's Sons, 1935.

The Yearling. With decorations by Edward Shenton. New York: Charles Scribner's Sons, 1938.

When the Whippoorwill—. New York: Charles Scribner's Sons, 1940.

Cross Creek. New York: Charles Scribner's Sons, 1942.

Cross Creek Cookery. New York: Charles Scribner's Sons, 1942.

The Sojourner. New York: Charles Scribner's Sons, 1953.

The Secret River. With illustrations by Leonard Weisgard. New York: Charles Scribner's Sons, 1955.

The Marjorie Kinnan Rawlings Reader. Edited by Julia Scribner Bingham. New York: Charles Scribner's Sons, 1956.

CRITICAL AND BIOGRAPHICAL STUDIES

Bellman, Samuel I. *Marjorie Kinnan Rawlings*. New York: Twayne Publishers, 1974.

———. "Marjorie Kinnan Rawlings: A Solitary Sojourner in the Florida Backwoods." *Kansas Quarterly* 2: 78–87 (Spring 1970).

———. "Writing Literature for Young People: Marjorie Kinnan Rawlings' 'Secret River' of the Imagination." *Costerus: Essays in English and American Language and Literature* 9: 19–27 (1973).

Bigelow, Gordon E. *Frontier Eden: The Literary Career of Marjorie Kinnan Rawlings*. Gainesville: University of Florida Press, 1966.

———. "Marjorie Kinnan Rawlings' Wilderness." *Sewanee Review* 73: 299–310 (Spring 1965).

——— and Laura V. Monti. *Selected Letters of Marjorie Kinnan Rawlings*. Gainesville: University of Florida Press, 1983.

Evans, Harry. "Marjorie Kinnan Rawlings." *Family Circle* (7 May 1943, 14 May 1943).

Pope, Vernon. "Marjorie Rawlings Hunts for Her Supper." *Saturday Evening Post* 215: 26–27, 58–59 (30 January 1943).

—AGNES REGAN PERKINS

LAURA E. RICHARDS

1850–1943

B Y THE MIDDLE of the last century, an American ideal of child nurture had coalesced. The model childhood of late Victorian America began with two intelligent, devoted parents in whom rationality and emotional warmth existed side by side in judicious proportions; it included brothers and sisters, for sociability and to forestall selfishness; and it was set in a home with space and scope for active play and expanding imaginations.

Family life in such a home was child centered but not child dominated, recommended child nurture called for both affection and discipline. Unlike the nanny-reared offspring of Britain's Victorian upper middle class, American children of the ideal would see a good deal of their parents, who always took time for family life, even as they met their responsibilities to their jobs and to society. Children would grow up surrounded by noble ideals and models of excellence, knowing that father was a pillar of the community, learning from mother the joys of music, art, and literature.

Given the realities of nineteenth-century house keeping, a model household had to be reasonably affluent, with servants enough to free both parents and children from consuming drudgery. Yet the children would surely learn that happiness did not depend upon riches; family affection, love of nature and art, and a developed sense of duty to others were the ingredients of true contentment. Born to a happiness so constituted, children would perpetuate it, carrying the blessings of a well-ordered childhood into their adult lives and to the next generation.

If such a childhood was not the lot of every American child, neither was it wholly a pipe dream. Laura E. Richards enjoyed an upbringing very like the ideal, and her long, productive life as a woman and as a writer bore its imprimatur to the end. She was born Laura Elizabeth Howe in Boston, on 27 February 1850, fourth child (of six) and third daughter of her remarkable parents. Her father, Samuel Gridley Howe, was director of the Perkins Institution and Massachusetts School for the Blind, "practical founder," his daughter wrote, of the institute, and the first teacher to find a way through the terrible isolation surrounding a blind deaf-mute. Laura was named for Laura Bridgman, the young woman her father "brought into communication with her fellow beings" in spite of her triple handicap.

Her mother, Julia Ward Howe, is today remembered primarily as the author of the "Battle Hymn of the Republic," which does scant justice to a woman of broad interests, numerous talents, and many accomplishments. Mrs. Howe was a published poet and essayist and a lifelong student of philosophy and literature. She knew well a half dozen languages, both classical and modern. In her later years she was active in a variety of public causes, including women's suffrage and the peace movement. She lived to be over ninety—as did her daughter—and, like her daughter, was thoroughly engaged in life and service to her fellow human beings to the end.

The household presided over by this interesting pair was described by Richards in two autobiographical works. *When I Was Your Age* (1894) was written for children in her best lighthearted, affectionate manner. "There were five of us," she begins (one child had died very young) and goes on to sketch the separate personalities and the common activities of a lively group of children, especially the games, stories, and plays they made up for themselves. She gives in its entirety her sister Julia's *The Offers*, a play consisting of a series of admirably terse dialogues between a most taciturn maiden and her several suitors. It is characteristic of Richards' sense of humor that she includes this hilarious childish effort; it is characteristic of the family that the manuscript was preserved. Doubtless to the joy of her child readers, Richards also recounted some of the creative mischief of the ménage—Flossy and Julia drinking train oil under the impression it was syrup; Laura falling into the sugar barrel; six-year-old Harry upending four-year-old Laura into the horse trough for no more sinister reason than a healthy curiosity about the results. (She withheld mention of Harry dropping wet sponges from the top of the stairwell onto the heads of visitors until she wrote for adults, who were presumably past corruption by such an example.)

But the book is as much a loving portrait of the parents as of the children. They adored their father, who was never "out of patience" with his offspring. "He loved to play and romp with us," and for all his high works and demanding duties, "no finger-ache of our father's smallest child ever escaped his loving care, no childish thought or wish ever failed to win his sympathy." Writing of their mother, Richards paid tribute to her intellectual achievements while acknowledging that, during these years, "Our mother's genius . . . was tied to our little string, and we never doubted (alas!) our perfect right to pull her down to earth whenever a matter of importance—such as a doll's funeral or a sick kitten—was at hand."

Stepping Westward (1931) is a fuller autobiography, written for adults, again in an easy, anecdotal style. In this book Richards rounds out the description of her early years—there is a whole chapter on what she read while growing up, and another on the pictures that filled the walls of her family home —but the basic story is the same. It is an account of a childhood that matched the ideal at nearly every point, a family life full of affection, tolerance, and joy and lived in a home in which noble ideals and intellectual effort were as familiar as food and drink. Richards' tribute here to her parents is en-

hanced, if anything, by detail; her love and respect for them both as parents and as people is unwavering; her appreciation of a childhood "cradled . . . in poetry, romance and philanthropy" runs throughout the book.

In 1867 Laura's acquaintance with the world was vastly expanded when she, her sister Julia, and her mother accompanied Dr. Howe on an extensive trip through Europe to Crete, where Dr. Howe oversaw the distribution of supplies to a people engaged in a terrible war for independence. In 1869 she became engaged to Henry Richards, a young architect whose family she had known since childhood. They were married two years later and went to live in the "Old Part" of Green Peace, her childhood home in the south of Boston, while her parents continued to live in the "New Part."

The next four years saw the birth of three of her seven children and the beginning of her long career as a published writer. The first writing was of verses:

> I had always rhymed easily; now, with the coming of the babies, and the consequent weeks and months of quiet, came a prodigious welling up of rhymes. . . . I wrote, and sang, and wrote, and could not stop. The first baby was plump and placid, with a broad, smooth back which made an excellent writing desk. She lay on her front, across my lap; I wrote on her back, the writing pad quite as steady as the writing of jingles required.
>
> (*Stepping Westward*, p. 156)

Many verses produced in this manner were published in the newly established *St. Nicholas* magazine, with John Ames Mitchell as illustrator. They included some of the best-loved of her humorous rhymes, "Little John Bottlejohn," "The Shark," and "The Queen of the Orkney Islands," all republished later in *Tirra Lirra* (1932).

In 1876 a depression in the architectural business, together with a request for her husband to take over the family paper mill, precipitated a decision by the Richards to leave Boston and take up residence in Gardiner, Maine. In the summer of that year they moved to the town that was to be their home for the rest of their lives. The yellow house overlooking the Kennebec River in which they settled their growing family soon became a center for literary and civic activity in the region.

Richards' life was always busy and full. After the move to Maine, four more children were born:

Julia Ward in 1878, Maud in 1881 (died 1882), John in 1884, and Laura Elizabeth in 1886. In addition, and true to her heritage, Richards became an active contributor to her new community, lending support and often leadership to many public causes and civic projects.

Through it all she wrote and wrote. At first it was mostly the verses that came so easily to her and for which there was a ready market in children's magazines; but soon she began to publish prose stories as well. Her first published book, *Five Mice in a Mouse-trap* (1880), is a collection of anecdotes about five children, told by "the Man in the Moon." The narrative consists of mildly whimsical observations of the doings of charming children; the tone is conventionally parental and Victorian. *Sketches and Scraps*, illustrated by her husband and published in 1881, has greater claim to originality, as the first book of nonsense ever written by an American and published in the United States. In 1885 Richards edited and "mostly wrote" *Four Feet, Two Feet, and No Feet* (published 1886), "a venture into the realm of natural history, where I did not really belong," she remarked in *Stepping Westward*. That same year saw the publication of the first of the "Toto" stories (*The Joyous Story of Toto*), "two merry little tales" she wrote as an antidote to her grief over the death of her infant daughter Maud; the second, *Toto's Merry Winter*, appeared in 1887.

In 1889 Richards' novel *Queen Hildegarde* launched her as an author of girls' stories. She wrote many more over the next forty-five years; indeed, in her own lifetime her literary reputation rested primarily on these books. Though she never entirely stopped writing verse, Richards' shift to prose was major. In this she was apparently strongly influenced by the advice of the well-known Maine author Sarah Orne Jewett, who suggested that she should choose between verse and prose and that her strongest talents were for prose. As it happens, posterity has reversed the judgment. The verse has had a long and lively existence in compilations and anthologies, while the prose has quietly disappeared into the obscurity of historical collections.

Queen Hildegarde is typical in most ways of all of Richards' girls' stories, and a good example of the qualities that have dated them so conclusively. The story line is slight: Hildegarde is the daughter of affluent, amiable parents, who, as the story opens, are discussing their pending trip to California and whether or not Hildegarde will go with them. At fifteen Hildegarde is beautiful, all too popular with her rather frivolous friends, and slightly discontented. Mother decides, and Father concurs, that Hildegarde is in need of some moral adjustment, best accomplished by sending her to spend the summer with her mother's old nurse and her farmer husband. Hildegarde is shocked by this decision, but acquiesces. She does not fight it, since her mother's rule, "gentle though it was, was not of the flabby, nor yet of the elastic sort." Like Richards', Hildegarde's first lessons had been "truthfulness and obedience"; so she goes, a little sulkily, to the farm to be rescued from the pernicious influence of "fashion."

The farm is, of course, the quintessence of ideal country simplicity, but Hildegarde finds her hosts entirely too bucolic for her city tastes. She decides, the first evening, on a demeanor of icy distance, which she intends to last the summer. It doesn't last the night. From the window of her room Hildegarde hears the good-hearted Hartleys discussing her mother's concern for her character. Much ashamed, she apologizes the very next morning, asking the Hartleys' help to make her more like her mother.

For the rest of the novel Hildegarde behaves like what she is, that is, Richards' ideal of young womanhood. There is more than a faint flavor of class consciousness in the ideal: Hildegarde has "delicate, high-bred" features, perfect manners, and a keen sense of responsibility toward those less fortunate than herself. She meets and promptly undertakes to teach and improve an ambitious but underprivileged local lad. When she discovers that he has a crippled sister, she befriends her, too, and by summer's end has arranged for an operation for the girl and higher education for the boy. In between, after a villain steals the Hartleys' mortgage money, Hildegarde finds a long-lost treasure that saves the day.

In short, *Queen Hildegarde* is sentimental, as are all Richards' girls' novels. *Three Margarets* (1897) and its sequels are somewhat more believably plotted, but the atmosphere of privilege is much the same, as it also is in the *Honor Bright* (1920) and *The Merryweathers* (1904) series. In all of these books Richards' impulse to teach marks her characterizations both of the model girls who are the protagonists of the stories and of the model mothers (or aunts) who, though not central to the action of the plot, are very much at the center of their families' lives. These idealized women rule gently but firmly, often giving voice to Richards' philosophy of life and child nurture. So Aunt Faith in *Three Margarets* suggests how Margaret may help to improve her two cousins: "Neither of these children is to be led by precept, I think," but an example of Margaret's own ways, "the ways of pleasantness and peace," will, she believes, reform them in time. As for the Cuban-bred girl's rudeness to servants, Aunt Faith points out that "she was brought up without learning any respect for the dignity of labour," thus signaling her own attitude toward labor as well as underscoring the importance of wise adult tutoring in a child's life.

All of these novels offer a model of family life that plainly had its counterpart in Richards' own life, both as a child and as a mother. The same values appear again and again: responsibility, self-control, pleasant manners, and a tolerant concern for others are basic to good character; music, poetry, and intelligent reading are basic to a good life. Richards often specified the reading she thought essential: Shakespeare, the Bible, Sir Walter Scott, "the great ballads, the Norse sagas, the *Iliad* and the *Odyssey*, the *Lays of Ancient Rome*"—all literature, of course, that she knew as a child.

However popular they were in their own time, the girls' stories are museum pieces today. Though the writing is competent, the way of life attractive, and the values admirable, there is an opaque quality to the novels. They seem to take place in a never-never land from which the ordinary human experiences of strife, disappointment, failure, and frustration are barred. Where the human frailties of Louisa May Alcott's March girls reach across the years to capture readers even now, Richards' adolescents seem impregnably gilded with both virtue and privilege; their assured good fortune smothers the empathy of a modern reader. They are beyond belief—and thus beyond interest.

Also girls' stories, but in a slightly different category, are several novels set in Maine in which the idealized girls are of humbler origins than are the genteel, affluent Hildegardes and Margarets. *Melody* (1893) and *Marie* (1894) are two brief novels whose heroines represent a type evidently dear to Richards' heart. They are both unsophisticated, intensely musical, innocent, romantic figures, whose role in the lives of others is akin to saintly. In fact, Melody, a blind girl with an exquisite voice, functions as a female Christ figure in her Maine village, comforting the dying, giving hope and joy to the

living, reforming the villain of the story with a single eloquent speech. Marie opens the worlds of art and nature to a husband imprisoned by his overly rigid religious beliefs.

Richards herself referred to *Melody* as "wildly sentimental"—if anything, an understatement; she may not have seen that her most famous book was no less so. *Captain January* (1890), twice made into successful film drama (1924 and 1936), is the story of a child rescued from shipwreck and raised by an old sea captain-turned-lighthouse-keeper. Star Bright, as the Captain names her, is another of Richards' highly romanticized children:

> a little girl about ten . . . with a face of almost startling beauty. Her hair floated like a cloud of pale gold about her shoulders: her eyes were blue . . . violet. Wonderful eyes, shaded by long, curved lashes of deepest black, which fell on the soft, rose-and-ivory tinted cheeks.

Though not the saint that Melody was, Star is an object of awe and adoration for the simple folk who live around her Maine island; the class difference between Star and everyone else is always clear.

In the plot Star is recognized—most improbably—by her dead mother's sister, who immediately makes plans to adopt her, that she may live with "her own people" and be properly educated. Mournfully, for he adores the child, Captain January agrees, telling Star that she is of "gentlefolk" and should have "gentle raisin'." However, in a melodramatic scene Star adamantly refuses to leave her island home or be parted from the old man she loves. "You may kill me," she says, "and take my body away, if you like. I will not go while I am alive." Everyone gives up in the face of such resolution; the aunt departs, and life returns to its quiet, idyllic round. The book ends, however, as Captain January dies, having arranged that Star will now leave the island to live with her relatives and receive the education suitable to her birth.

Nearly forty years after the publication of *Captain January*, Richards wrote a sequel called *Star Bright* (1927). Unhappily, all the faults and none of the strengths of the first book are in *Star Bright*. In this second book Star is in her teens and living with her relatives. Whimsical as a child, she is now fey to an alarming degree, bursting into Shakespearean quotes whenever agitated—which is often. She wants to return to her island, and, of course, that is what happens. Deliverance takes the form of Bob Peet, once a notably monosyllabic fisherman's son, but now rehabilitated by education and success as a ship's captain into a suitable candidate for marriage with Star.

A romantic novel about children depends for its success upon the lovableness of its main character—consider *Little Lord Fauntleroy*, *Anne of Green Gables*, or *Rebecca of Sunnybrook Farm*. *Captain January* was neither as successful nor as enduring as these, but it was helped by the characterization of the Captain and by the theme of the love between an old man and a child. In *Star Bright*, Richards insists that Star is still adorable, but it is an unworkable proposition. By Richards' own standards Star is no longer a child, and the carry-over of her self-absorbed, impetuous ways only makes her seem selfish and occasionally a little nuts. It is clear that she belongs to the "child woman" ideal; it is less clear why that ideal should have appealed to Laura Richards.

Sentimental as all the Maine tales are, a redeeming feature is the occasional touch of local color, which Richards could render expertly. Whenever a character tells a story, whether funny or exciting or reminiscent, the romantic fog clears, and the prose is brought abruptly to life by the colorful speech and genuinely individual point of view. Captain January's account of the shipwreck that brought him his adored Star Bright is the best and liveliest writing in the book. It may have been these passages that moved Sarah Orne Jewett, an accomplished local colorist herself, to encourage Richards' prose efforts.

Finally, Richards wrote several biographies of famous women cast in the semifictional form popular in the early twentieth century. Like the girls' novels, these were successful at the time, but are now entirely out of style. The author's voice is intrusive, with direct addresses to the reader ("think of it children!") calling attention to the remarkable or the outrageous, and her point of view is historically naive. In *Florence Nightingale* (1909), for example, she suggests that the world's evils are swiftly cured once people are informed of them. When the "people of England" learned of the hospital conditions in the Crimea, Richards writes, "a great cry of anger and sorrow . . . went up from the whole country." The real difficulties of creating a coherent hospital system out of bureaucratic and medical chaos are minimized and, therefore, so is the force of character and the political acumen it took to do it. It is unlikely that anyone other than an occasional historian of children's literature will read these biographies again.

But the verse survives. Richards was, as she said herself, a born rhymer, with a sure sense of rhythm and beat. She came by it naturally enough; here is Julia Ward Howe's versified memoir of the trip to Crete:

"Who were the people you saw, Mrs. Howe,
When you went where the Cretans were making a
    row?"
Kalopothakis, Diomondakis
Nikolaides, P'raskevaides,
Anagnostopoulos, Paparipopoulos,
These were the people that met Mrs. Howe,
When she went where the Cretans were making a
row.

(quoted in *Stepping Westward*, p. 89)

Richards shared her mother's taste for multisyllabic names strange to American ears:

A Mesopotamian Mameluke
    Was pricking it over the plain;
He met a Wallachian Hospodar,
    Riding about in the rain.
(originally published in
St. Nicholas magazine and
reprinted in *Tirra Lirra*)

And her meters were strong and sure, though not particularly inventive. She was fond of ballad forms, limericks, and tetrameters, all of which she handled with aplomb; she liked nonsense words and used them often, no doubt inspired by Lewis Carroll and Edward Lear. She in turn may have influenced Ogden Nash: it would be hard to guess which of them had written "An elderly lady named Mackintosh, / She went out to ride in a hackintosh." (It was Richards.) But her meter and rhyme are just very good, not superlative. She hadn't the delicate ear of A. A. Milne at his best; she certainly wasn't as subtly witty and endlessly complex as Carroll. What she was, was good-humored, mildly irreverent, and funny in a way most children enjoy, as much now as then.

The verses have what the prose lacks: the imprint of Richards' lively sense of humor. When she spoke to children through verse, Richards seemed to feel a kinship with her audience, and she left aside, for the most part, the sentimentality and the mild moral earnestness that has blighted her prose for a later age. (There are a few exceptions; she wrote some sentimental verses, but these are rarely included in today's collections.) She could draw upon a fund of genuinely childlike silliness with a poem like the famous "Eletelephony" (first published in *Child Life* and later reprinted in *Tirra Lirra*):

> Once there was an elephant,
> Who tried to use the telephant—
> No! No! I mean an elephone
> Who tried to use the telephone—

Or as in "After a Visit to the Natural History Museum" (first published in *The Piccolo* in 1906 and later reprinted in *Tirra Lirra*), which commemorates a visit to the natural history museum, with introductions to the Ptoodlecumtumpsydyl and the Ichthyosnortoryx.

More surprising, she could assume a child's moral stance, as she did in many poems that dispensed justice swiftly and remorselessly, with a casual violence one scarcely expects of the author of *Captain January*. The four squaws in "An Indian Ballad" who would have done in the beautiful Michiky Moo meet the very ends they had planned for her:

> Away went the braves, without question or pause,
> And they soon put an end to the guilty squaws.
> They pleasantly smiled when the deed was done,
> Saying, "Ping-ko-chanky! oh! isn't it fun!"
>
> (*Tirra Lirra*)

And when the seven little tigers who meant to eat the Aged Cook ("The Seven Little Tigers and the Aged Cook") instead dine on one of their own number (neatly dispatched by the cook), no one finds fault with this merciless but just conclusion. As for Ponsonby Perks, who fought with the Turks, "He killed over forty / Highminded and haughty, / And cut off their heads with smiles and smirks"— all without further comment from Richards ("Nonsense Verses," 2).

Richards' offhand chauvinism toward other peoples and places, while it was entirely characteristic of her time, offends many present-day readers. Yet some other qualities in her poetry still please. There is a broad streak of cheerful irreverence running through Richards' rhymes, an engaging sentiment that might successfully have leavened her

prose. Victorian solemnity is at a minimum in "Jumbo Jee," a poem that tells of three kings celebrating their accomplishment—building a tower to a monstrous height—with ginger wine:

> They drank to the health of Jumbo Tower
> Until they really could drink no more;
> And then they sank in a blissful swoon,
> And flung their crowns at the rising moon.
>
> ("Nonsense Verses," 2)

And no sentimentality mars the brief but interesting tale of Winifred White ("Nonsense Verses," 4):

> Winifred White,
> She married a fright,
> She called him her darling, her duck, and delight;
> The back of his head
> Was so lovely, she said,
> It dazzled her soul and enraptured her sight.

The professions are not sacrosanct. Speculating on "The Baby's Future" in *In My Nursery* (1890), Richards is hard on lawyers and flippant about doctors, who

> will dose you with rhubarb, and calomel too,
> With draughts that are black and with pills that are blue;
> And the chances will be, when he's finished with you,
> You'll be worse off then when he began.

Writing verse, Laura Richards drew on the liveliest legacy of her happy childhood; romance and philosophy gave way to high spirits and humor. Her nonsense rhymes, many of which are still on library shelves in the collection *Tirra Lirra*, have a perennial appeal for the young and have kept alive the name and the spirit of a happy woman.

Selected Bibliography

WORKS OF LAURA E. RICHARDS

Fiction

Five Mice in a Mouse-Trap. By the Man in the Moon. Done in the Vernacular, from the Lunacular. With illustrations by Kate Greenaway et al. Boston: Dana Estes, 1880.

The Joyous Story of Toto. With illustrations by E. H. Garrett. Boston: Roberts Brothers, 1885.

Toto's Merry Winter. Boston: Roberts Brothers, 1887.

Queen Hildegarde: A Story for Girls. Boston: Dana Estes, 1889.

Captain January. Boston: Estes and Lauriat, 1890. Reprinted, with illustrations by Frank T. Merrill. Boston: Estes and Lauriat, 1893. Rev. ed., with stills from the Shirley Temple film. New York: Random House, 1959.

Melody: The Story of a Child. Boston: Estes and Lauriat, 1893.

Marie. Boston: Estes and Lauriat, 1894.

Three Margarets. With illustrations by Ethelred B. Barry. Boston: Estes and Lauriat, 1897.

The Merryweathers. With illustrations by Julia Ward Richards. Boston: Dana Estes, 1904.

Honor Bright: A Story for Girls. With illustrations by Frank T. Merrill. Boston: L. C. Page, 1920.

Star Bright: A Sequel to "Captain January." With illustrations by Frank T. Merrill. Boston: L. C. Page, 1927.

Verse

Sketches and Scraps. With illustrations by Henry Richards. Boston: Dana Estes, 1881. Reprinted Ann Arbor, Mich.: University Microfilms, 1967.

In My Nursery. Boston: Roberts Brothers, 1890.

The Piccolo. Boston: Dana Estes, 1906.

Tirra Lirra: Rhymes Old and New. With illustrations by Marguerite Davis and foreword by May Lamberton Becker. Boston: Little, Brown, 1932. Rev. ed., with foreword by May Hill Arbuthnot. Boston: Little, Brown, 1955.

Nonfiction

Four Feet, Two Feet, and No Feet; or, Furry and Feathery Pets, and How They Live. Edited by Laura E. Richards. Boston: Estes and Lauriat, 1886.

Florence Nightingale, Angel of the Crimea: A Story for Young People. New York: Appleton, 1909. Revised and edited by Rowena Keith Keyes. New York: Appleton, 1931.

Autobiographical Works

When I Was Your Age. Boston: Estes and Lauriat, 1894.

Stepping Westward. New York: Appleton, 1931.

CRITICAL AND BIOGRAPHICAL STUDIES

Eaton, Anne T. "Laura E. Richards" *Horn Book* 17/4: 247–255 (1941).

MacLeod, Anne Scott. "Laura (Elizabeth) Richards." In *Twentieth-Century Children's Writers*, edited by D. L. Kirkpatrick. 2d ed. New York: St. Martin's Press, 1983.

Richards, Laura E., ed. *Laura Richards and Gardiner*. Gardiner, Me.: Gannett Publishing, 1940. (Collected papers.)

Viguers, Ruth H. "Laura E. Richards: Joyous Companion." In *The Hewins Lectures: 1947–62*, edited by Siri Andrews. Boston: Horn Book, 1963.

—ANNE SCOTT MACLEOD

ELIZABETH MADOX ROBERTS

1881-1941

THE FACT THAT Elizabeth Madox Roberts' *Under the Tree* (1922) was permitted to go out of print for a number of years and has never been available in paperback says much about the present-day lack of interest in substantive poetry for children, in poetry that goes beyond trendy subjects, usually humorous and set in clever rhythm and rhyme. For years selections from *Under the Tree* were included in virtually all major textbooks and anthologies used in children's literature courses, and the collection was recommended on their reading lists. The most popular poems were widely anthologized in children's poetry collections. Today the book is omitted from all but a few textbooks, and if any of Roberts' poems appear in contemporary anthologies, the entries are usually the short and easily understood "Firefly" and "The People."

When *Under the Tree* was published, it met with considerable critical acclaim. Louis Untermeyer, for one, said, "Few American lyricists have made so successful a debut." In 1956 Harry M. Campbell and Ruel E. Foster, in their book-length analysis of Roberts' work, stated that the "poems are little flowers that flare up in our imaginations and then glow for a long time in our memories. We will not forget them." Even as late as 1983 David McCord called *Under the Tree* "undiminished" and declared that Roberts "is the only poet . . . writing in the English language . . . who possessed and consistently used the undisguised, uninterrupted voice of childhood, . . . not only the vocabulary but the attitude and voice inflection of a small girl lost in wonder."

That "lost in wonder" element (which Glenway Westcott called the "plain wonderland of a more normal and realistic Alice") is surely the central reason that *Under the Tree* will endure despite the vagaries of fashion. Roberts' ability to grasp the child's vision, along with her high degree of craftsmanship, was what Robert Morss Lovett must have seen in her first poems when he encouraged her to come to the University of Chicago in 1917 at age thirty-six. His trust was well placed. By 1921 she had graduated with a bachelor of philosophy degree in English with honors, and by 1922 she had published *Under the Tree*, a collection of fifty-two poems, for which she won the Fiske Poetry Prize.

Elizabeth Madox Roberts was born on 30 October 1881 in Perryville, Kentucky, into a family who traced their origins on both sides to pioneers who had migrated over Boone's Trace to the Kentucky wilderness. Although both parents had been schoolteachers, by 1884 the family had moved to Springfield (population twelve hundred), where her father opened a grocery store and worked as a civil engineer. Springfield was deep in the heart of rolling farmland, where once a month farmers came to town to shop, exchange news, and trade horses or mules.

The second of eight children, Elizabeth early on relieved the drudgery of the family's household chores by creating a fantasy family. She and her brothers and sisters played at being the rich Wilsons, a family who had everything the Robertses lacked, never having to touch "dishwater and strong soap." The Wilsons provided the children, as well as their parents, with much delight. (It must be a Wilson who reappears as "The Richest Woman in the World" in *Under the Tree*.) But even at this age Elizabeth's imagination and sensitivity turned toward real people. She never forgot, for example, an old black carpenter, "Uncle Wilse," who had "been a king in Africa" and "slowly and with labor and pain" built his house, his mansion. When he died the structure was not finished, but he had painted it red and the roof was on. Even then she knew that she was only "a little girl trying to climb out of my sordid world by the way of high towers [like] Uncle Wilse with his mansion. . . . He was a better builder than I."

Sensitivity to the joys and sorrows of those close to her, coupled with a keen memory, constitute the core of Roberts' understanding of the hard yet full world of her childhood. This sensitivity, along with a fascination for the thrill of the *story* (in the form of myths her father remembered from *Bulfinch's Mythology* and his retelling of his adventures in the Civil War), laid early foundations for her appreciation of language and literature. Her maternal grandmother's accounts of their ancestors' struggles at Harrod's Fort and the Wilderness Trace further enriched the child's mind and heart. Although she did not read much as a child because her father's books had been lost in a fire, she said later that she grew up on "phantom books" in the voices of her father and grandmother, voices she ultimately made her own.

She wrote her first story at age eight, her first poem at eleven. In spite of receiving scant encouragement, when she saw a picture of Elizabeth Barrett Browning with the word "poet" under it in a *McGuffey Reader*, she said, "That's what I am, a poet."

Although her early memories were filled with unending toil, there were pleasant times too, when the family went on all-day trips through the countryside to see a new bridge or trestle that her father had built, or when she played in the graveyard high above the town and looked down on their house (as the child does in "On the Hill" in *Under the Tree*), or when she observed the nightly rite of her father milking the cow and filling her mug with the foaming milk (as the father does in "Milking Time"). But there were dark memories too, of lynch mobs and "night riders." Elizabeth never forgot the terrible juxtaposition of good and evil, light and dark that she knew in her formative years. It was the rich vein, the deep source from which she mined her powerful, poetic novels.

Springfield had no public schools, so she attended Professor Grant's Academy, where the more well-off children laughed at her ragtag clothes, but where she first displayed her intellectual prowess. In 1897 she was sent to Covington to complete high school. Although she lived with an aunt, she was intensely homesick for the Pigeon River country, so she returned, as she would throughout her life, as soon as she could.

Although she entered the University of Kentucky in 1900, she soon withdrew, probably because of illness and lack of money. For the next several years she longed to learn more about literature and art and to know people who valued these things as she did. Nonetheless, during this period, while she was teaching school privately and in nearby villages, she steeped herself in the language, lore, and people that she would use in her later work.

From 1910 through 1916 she made periodic trips to Colorado to stay with relatives. During one of these visits she wrote seven poems to accompany a series of wildflower photographs by Kenneth Hartley. The resulting book, *In the Great Steep's Garden*, was published privately in 1915. In 1912, while visiting her sister and brother at the University of Kentucky, she showed her poetry to Professor James T. Cotten, who was a friend of Professor Lovett's at the University of Chicago. With Lovett's encouragement, she enrolled at Chicago in 1917 and quickly became known as a writer of consequence.

This period marked her transition from a would-be poet to a nationally published poet, most notably in *Poetry*, the most prestigious poetry magazine in the country. Among her Chicago friends was Westcott, who called her a "young Southern woman, alone absolutely original, . . . untouched by but kindly toward our half-grown baseness." Her circle of literary friends included Janet Lewis, Monroe Wheeler, Yvor Winters, Vincent Sheean, and Sterling North, all of whom were drawn together by their common interest in literature and art. Although Elizabeth remained essentially a private person, she at last had the stimulation and support of the kind of people she had been seeking.

At the urging of these friends, she began to share her children's poems with them. Some of the poems had been written during summers in Springfield, others in Lovett's English courses. A year after she graduated from the university, the poems collected in *Under the Tree* were published by B. W. Huebsch. This slim volume of outwardly matter-of-fact poems, which Untermeyer said had "unusual delicacy . . . with the light of early wonder shining behind them," launched her professional writing career.

By the fall of 1922 she was back in Springfield at work on her first and greatest novel, *The Time of Man*. Already plagued with bouts of serious illness that continued for the rest of her life, Roberts worked diligently at the novel, always taking time to walk the country roads; to note the changes in nature as well as in the houses, barns, and people; and to listen to the speech, often poetic, of those around her. In 1926 the Viking Press published *The Time of Man*, which won her great acclaim. Sherwood Anderson said, "A wonderful performance. I am humble before it." A critical and financial success, the book was featured as the October selection of the Book-of-the-Month Club and was later received enthusiastically in England. German, Swedish, Spanish, Danish, and Norwegian editions followed, as did a Modern Library edition.

Roberts turned to writing with all of her energy. As early as 1923 she had been working on her second novel, *My Heart and My Flesh*, while still working on the first. In 1927 the second book was published, and five others followed: *Jingling in the Wind* (1928), *The Great Meadow* (1930), *A Buried Treasure* (1931), *He Sent Forth a Raven* (1935), and *Black Is My True Love's Hair* (1938). She also published two books of short stories, *The Haunted Mirror* (1932) and *Not by Strange Gods* (1941), as well as three books of poems, *In the Great Steep's Garden*, *Under the Tree*, and *Song in the Meadow* (1940). In addition to receiving the Fiske Prize in 1922, Roberts also won the John Reed Memorial Prize in 1928, the O. Henry Memorial Award in 1932, and the Poetry Society of South Carolina's 1931 award.

Throughout her writing career, Roberts' work was gravely hampered by periods of debilitating illness, diagnosed by at least one specialist as Hodgkin's disease. By 1937 she was spending winters in Florida trying to regain her strength, but returning to Kentucky whenever she could.

Although the popularity of her novels had begun to decline by the mid-1930's, she was still an important figure in American literature when death came in Orlando, Florida, on 13 March 1941. Willard Thorp labeled her one of the three best regional novelists—the other two being Sarah Orne Jewett and Willa Cather—that America had produced. Frederick P. W. McDowell said, "She probed more deeply into the psychic realms than any Southern novelist before the generation of Thomas Wolfe,

William Faulkner, Katherine Anne Porter, Eudora Welty, and Caroline Gordon." *Time*'s obituary called her "one of America's most distinguished women writers." According to Earl H. Rovit, Roberts' work was always "musical patterning," and her "view of words was that of a poet." He pointed out that "metaphor was pervasive" in all of her work, but the realities of life were never lost on her. Whether she was writing a novel or a poem, Roberts never lost sight of her Kentucky roots, those realities in which she as an artist tried for, in her own words, "great precision, . . . the point where poetry touches life," and life is transcended.

During her lifetime it was her novels that brought the highest praise, but if McCord is correct, her book of poems for children, *Under the Tree*, is her "one undoubted masterpiece." Not all critics agree with McCord. Carpenter and Prichard in *The Oxford Companion to Children's Literature* suggest that the book is overrated. They say that its "language is simple almost to the point of banality." Campbell and Foster counter this accusation by saying that the language is simple, to be sure, but its clarity and directness give it a "physical exactness, the exact look and 'feel' of an object or scene"; it is this simplicity that guards these poems from "sentimentality, coyness, and posturing." They point out that Roberts never allows "adult condescension" to interfere with the control of the poems, which are tight, traditional quatrains in iambic tetrameter in either *abab* or *abcb* rhyme schemes.

Not all critics agree on Roberts' ability to universalize. McDowell, who praises her novels for this attribute, says that only four of the poems in *Under the Tree* ("August Night," "Cold Fear," "In the Night," and "The Dark") universalize the child's experience in the way that Walter de la Mare's poems "convey truth about life in general." But Campbell and Foster refute this assessment by comparing Roberts' "pristine world" to the "innocence of Blake's world, . . . a child's world which . . . is a man's world too. As the little girl probes her village world, she is man probing the pitiless universe." They say that in the child's being "poignantly aware of the grand mysteries of the universe," she recreates the archetypal experience for us all.

Most critics agree that Roberts' attention to minutiae accurately reflects the way a child sees the world. McDowell believes that her observations are so true to the child's perceptions that she "assimilated [these perceptions] without discord or hint of patronizing"; in doing so she captures the child's "concentrated and unconventional reactions to the world." He calls *Under the Tree* the poet's "first clear impression," in which she took the small incidents of childhood and made them glow, making the "very dust of the ground . . . other-wordly," luminous.

In "Autumn Fields" the child sees a tramp "with sticktights on his clothes." In "The Worm" she sees a worm that "puckered in a little wad . . . and went back home inside the clod." In "Mr. Wells" she first smells the camphor balls on Mr. Wells's clothes, and then she sees him, who "wears his whiskers in a bunch." In "Miss Kate-Marie" she watches the Sunday-school teacher's tongue "always wriggling out and in." In "The Butterbean Tent" she observes that "a cricket-like thing that could hop went by" and hears that "hidden away there were flocks and flocks / Of bugs that could go like little clocks."

But what she observes almost always impinges on larger, more intuitive feelings. When Father (in "Father's Story") sings or tells the children the story of the Trojan War, "I push my finger into his skin, / To make little dents in his big rough face." When the child goes to church (in "The Pulpit") she hears Dr. Brown preaching and making "the shivery bells begin to ring," but she thinks about those who live in the "little pulpit house." Do they have a cat? Say their prayers? She asks "what their little dreams are like / And what they wonder all about." It is typical of Roberts' child that as she listens to Father's stories, she also explores his face. As she hears the preacher's voice, she constructs a "pulpit house" and questions whether its inhabitants have pets, say prayers, dream dreams, wonder. While rooted in immediacy, Roberts' child almost always stands on the brink of an intuitive experience that goes beyond the "real." This juxtaposition of the ordinary with things of the spirit, "this seizing of experience," as McDowell says, "is often translated into fantasy when imagination becomes impatient with facts and invests them with a significance of its own devising."

Similarly, in *Under the Tree* it is often a larger vision that grows out of the "very dust," the minute detail, the small experience that provides the child of the poems with a philosophical stance. In "The Worm" a child says, "I wonder if / He knows that he's a worm." In "Autumn Fields" the child sits by the tramp "to see the things that he had seen," to smell the "shocks and clods / And the land where

he had been." In "The Hens" the child observes a hen say her "little asking words." But when the hen pushes her head into her wing, "nothing answered anything." In "August Night" the child, lying in the grass, sees the stars that were "beyond the tree, beyond the air / And more and more were always there." The stars become like dust to her, a dust so infinite that it makes her cry because she cannot know them all.

In "Christmas Morning" the transcendence is complete. The child imagines that the Nativity is happening in their own barn, where she goes to see and to touch the Christ child. In the near perfect closing words, "poetry touches life" indeed:

> While Mary put the blanket back
> The gentle talk would soon begin.
> And when I'd tiptoe softly out
> I'd meet the wise men going in.

In some of Robert Louis Stevenson's poems for children, he moves the reader from the here to the far away (most notably in "Boats Sail on the Rivers"). In "On the Hill" Roberts uses a similar device but brings the experience back to the child's inner being. The children in the poem are picking strawberries on the hill above the town. When the child looks down, she surveys the fields, road, courthouse, bridge, and blacksmith shop, until finally she sees the church steeple and then their own house.

> I saw it under the poplar tree,
> And I bent my head and tried to see
> Our house when the rain is over it,
> And how it looks when the lamps are lit.
> I saw the swing from up on the hill,
> The ropes were hanging very still.
> And over and over I tried to see
> Some of us walking under the tree . . .
> And how it looks when I am there.

Under the Tree is how it looked when Roberts was there, how it looked and smelled and sounded and felt to be a sensitive child "lost in wonder" in a Kentucky town near the turn of the century. *Under the Tree* is also a book of rare substance and beauty that comes as close to the heart of the universal child, the child of no time, of no place, as any book in American literature.

Emily Dickinson's world, as described by Carl Van Doren, was one "in which all thoughts are alive. Everything is achingly alive." Rovit says that Roberts most closely resembles Dickinson: "Like Emily Dickinson, Miss Roberts' universe is a soul-centered universe, all the components of which make sense . . . when they are organized into a pattern by the creatively perceiving spirit."

In *Under the Tree* the components of a child's universe are revealed and organized by Roberts' perceiving spirit. That *Under the Tree*, her only book for children, her "one undoubted master-piece," should have ever gone out of print and never appeared in soft cover, while dozens of lesser works continue to dominate best-seller lists, speaks volumes about the precarious state of worthwhile poetry for today's children. It is not *Under the Trees* that is lacking.

Selected Bibliography

EDITIONS OF ELIZABETH MADOX ROBERTS' POEMS FOR CHILDREN

Under the Tree. New York: Huebsch, 1922. Enlarged edition, with illustrations by F. D. Bedford. New York: Viking Press, 1930. (This edition contains seven new poems: "The Twins," "The Richest Woman in the World," "Uncle Mells and the Witches' Tree," "The Dark," "Number Song," "Cold Fear," "Firefly Song.") Enlarged edition, with illustrations by F. D. Bedford and an afterword by William H. Slavick. Lexington: University Press of Kentucky, 1985. (Reprinted from the Viking edition.)

CRITICAL AND BIOGRAPHICAL STUDIES

Campbell, Harry M., and Ruel E. Foster. *Elizabeth Madox Roberts: American Novelist*. Norman: University of Oklahoma Press, 1956.

McDowell, Frederick P. W. *Elizabeth Madox Roberts*. New York: Twayne Publishers, 1963.

McCord, David. "Elizabeth Madox Roberts.' In *Twentieth-Century Children's Writers*, edited by Daniel Kirkpatrick. 2nd ed. New York: St. Martin's Press, 1983; London: Macmillan, 1983.

Rovit, Earl H. *Herald to Chaos: The Novels of Elizabeth Madox Roberts*. Lexington: University of Kentucky Press, 1960.

Thorp, Willard. *American Writing in the Twentieth Century*. Cambridge, Mass.: Harvard University Press, 1960.

Westcott, Glenway. *Elizabeth Madox Roberts: A Personal Note*. New York: Viking Press, 1930.

—GRAYCE SCHOLT

CHRISTINA ROSSETTI

1830–1894

CHRISTINA ROSSETTI, BORN 5 December 1830, was the quiet, somewhat reclusive daughter of Gabriele Rossetti, an Italian political exile and man of letters living in London. Her two brothers were William Michael, a civil servant, member of the Pre-Raphaelite Brotherhood, and editor of many literary works including those of his famous brother and sister, and the Pre-Raphaelite painter and poet Dante Gabriel. Her sister was Maria Francesca, who joined the Anglican sisterhood of All Saints in 1873. Nature and art, along with a deep spiritual commitment, are the most pervasive influences on Rossetti's work. And although she had no children of her own—she never married despite two proposals (one by the painter James Collinson and the other by the scholar and linguist Charles Bagot Cayley)—she did write several important books for children. By writing for children, Rossetti and many of her female contemporaries not only could participate in a didactic tradition that presented authors as educators, but also could find a means of liberating themselves from the conventional attitudes toward women and of expressing their own desires.

Rossetti's work for children clearly illustrates the tension between duty and desire. As early as 1850 she wrote a story for girls titled *Maude: Prose and Verse* (the book was not published until 1897, three years after her death), whose heroine struggles with "a divided heart and a reproachful conscience." Maude feels a deep ennui that derives from the pull between unworldly spirituality and playfulness and desire. Despite its topical interest, *Maude* is not a successful work; Rossetti's most im-

portant works for children are "Goblin Market" (1862), *Sing-Song: A Nursery Rhyme Book* (1872), and *Speaking Likenesses* (1874).

Although she had been writing verse for many years and even had a small volume, *Verses,* published by her maternal grandfather, Gaetano Polidori, in 1847, Rossetti did not publish her first important volume of poetry, *Goblin Market, and Other Poems,* until 1862, after considerable encouragement from her brother Dante Gabriel. The title poem of this volume is perhaps Rossetti's best-known work, and it has achieved a strong reputation as a poem for children. Georgina Battiscombe refers to it as "a fairy tale with overtones." With a technical brilliance that gives the poem a sprightly and haunting quality, Rossetti tells the story of two sisters living an isolated and pastoral existence. The poem begins with a long cry from the goblin men exhorting anyone within hearing to buy their fruits. The two sisters, Lizzie and Laura, hear the goblins, warily huddle together, and attempt neither to look at the goblins nor to listen to their cry. Laura, however, cannot resist temptation. She seeks out the goblins and buys their fruit with a "golden curl" from her head. Having tasted the goblin fruit, Laura finds that she cannot rest and that she cannot satisfy her craving for more of it. She begins to neglect her duties and to pine away until she is "knocking at Death's door." Lizzie now decides she must act to save her sister, and proceeds to put herself in the goblins' way. When she offers to pay them for the fruit with a coin, the goblins become agitated and accuse her of being "uncivil." They aggressively force their fruits against Lizzie's mouth until the juices run down her chin and neck. She successfully resists their advances and the goblins disappear. Lizzie hurries home, where she embraces Laura and the two sisters kiss. Lizzie's sacrificial act saves her sister and the poem ends with a vision of the two sisters years later, married and with children of their own.

The poem is ostensibly a fairy tale about fall and recovery, a tale such as the Grimms' "Faithful John," in which acts of love, loyalty, and self-sacrifice result in the defeat of evil and the restoration of order and family. Readers may accept the story as an allegory in which false desire—the fleshly, earthly, selfish desire of the goblins—is overcome by true desire—the spiritual and selfless desire of Lizzie to save her sister. Christian overtones sound through the poem. From this perspective the poem fits into the didactic tradition of children's literature that began with such writers as Anna Laetitia Barbauld, Sarah Trimmer, and Catherine Sinclair. Works for children in this tradition leave no doubt as to the lesson young readers are supposed to learn. "Goblin Market" appears to allow the reader to rest comfortably with the lesson that "there is no friend like a sister." This concluding moral statement, however, is too slight, too narrow for the richness of language and incident that has gone before—not unlike the conclusion of Coleridge's "The Rime of the Ancient Mariner" (1798), in which the moral sentiment of "He prayeth best, who loveth best / All things both great and small" strikes us as inadequate to explain the macabre supernatural incidents that constitute the poem's action.

Jonathan Cott points out that Victorian children's books "almost always had a moral or religious basis, but it was often just this conflict between morality and invention (or morality and eroticism in Christina Rossetti's *Goblin Market*) that created some of this era's greatest works." He refers to "Goblin Market" as "probably the most extreme and most beautifully elaborated example of repressed eroticism in children's literature." That the poem is erotic has been clear to readers at least since 1893, when Laurence Housman illustrated it with delicate, sinuous, and sensual designs. Rossetti herself must have been aware of the sexual implications of such passages as the one in which the goblins glide "like fishes" up to Lizzie and

> Hugged her and kissed her,
> Squeezed and caressed her:
> Stretched up their dishes,

> Panniers, and plates:
> "Look at our apples
> Russet and dun,
> Bob at our cherries,
> Bite at our peaches,
> Citrons and dates,
> Grapes for the asking,
> Pears red with basking
> Out in the sun,
> Plums on their twigs;
> Pluck them and suck them,
> Pomegranates, figs."

If "Goblin Market" were only an expression of repressed eroticism, it probably would have little interest for children; just as the moral statement reduces the poem, so too does a reading that takes the sexual theme either literally or biographically. Jeannie Watson is one commentator to argue that the didacticism of "Goblin Market" is undercut by what she refers to as "the goblin fruit of a fairy tale." Fairy tales often subvert their own moral tags, and more often than not they use sex. For example, in the well-known story "The Frog Prince," the frog's desire to sleep with the princess is also a desire to gain power over her, and the princess becomes an object of desire that binds. True desire unbinds and liberates the loved one instead of diminishing him or her; the princess is right to reject obedience to father, frog, and patriarchy. In "Goblin Market" the leering goblins desire to control both Laura and Lizzie. Their design is to suck life and vitality from the sisters as they pretend to offer plump ripe fruits. This fruit is forbidden in the sense that to eat it is to lose any sense of independence or selfhood. Its attraction is the attraction of nonbeing, an end to the quest for self-definition. But the cessation of such a quest or the adoption of a received identity cannot satisfy anyone for long. Sex as it is portrayed in "Goblin Market" is a metaphor for diminishment. In the poem a child's fear of the rigidity and stultifying effect of gender roles receives haunting expression. Laura's willingness to pay the goblin's price is a betrayal of her female identity; she gives the goblins what they desire and loses her voice and will. In short, she is diminished as an individual.

The demands of patriarchy are surely in Rossetti's mind in "Goblin Market." The traditional fairy tales upon which she draws—especially those of the Brothers Grimm—show an acute interest in female identity. In many of the tales (see, for example, "The Rabbit's Bride," "Fred and Kate," or "The Robber Bridegroom"), male attitudes and male tyranny push females to the edge of hysteria. "Goblin Market" shows what happens when the female succumbs to the male and his conception of the world as a marketplace. When Laura arrives home after tasting the goblin fruit, Lizzie reminds her of the fate of a girl named Jeanie, who met the goblins in the moonlight and ate their fruits and wore their flowers, then pined away and died. Her grave lies barren. Laura too becomes barren after eating the goblin fruit; she loses her voice. In a male world the female cannot speak, cannot assert her independence. Lizzie, perhaps Laura's other self, restores her sister's voice, and Laura becomes a storyteller with children of her own. That Laura and Lizzie are married at the poem's end is in keeping with the biblical overtones of the poem. We might recall "Snow White" or "The Sleeping Beauty," where marriage signals a renewal of the kingdom, a transformation of the land. Rossetti, as so often in her poetry, renders an otherworldly vision tangible.

But such complexity does not necessarily make a children's poem. What makes "Goblin Market" a poem for children is its sense of fun, its play with language. The opening lines set the tone:

> Morning and evening
> Maids heard the goblins cry:
> "Come buy our orchard fruits,
> Come buy, come buy:
> Apples and quinces,
> Lemons and oranges,
> Plump unpecked cherries,
> Melons and raspberries,
> Bloom-down-cheeked peaches,
> Swart-headed mulberries,
> Wild free-born cranberries,
> Crab-apples, dewberries,
> Pine-apples, blackberries,
> Apricots, strawberries;—
> All ripe together
> In summer weather."

The catalog continues for fifteen more lines. The whole passage establishes the tone of wonder and the sense of fecundity familiar in works for children. It conveys the sense of the world's richness, the wonder of nature's bounty. Children find comfort in the repetitive act of collecting, and the catalogs of things often found in children's books convey a sense of stability. To collect is to put a stay to confusion. Rossetti's poem, however, is more complex than many children's works, and the reassurance of the catalog is ironic. The goblins'

catalog of fruits seems to reassure the reader by drawing together fairy-tale and commercial discourses. Yet these discourses are opposites, just as morning and evening are opposites. The goblins try to disguise their intent, but their language gives them away.

The passage appears to flow smoothly, but the shifts from two- to three- to four-beat lines bring momentary hesitation. Instead of freeing, the goblins' words fix, enclose, suspend, and exhaust their listeners. The long twenty-nine-line bark of the goblins begins and ends with the exhortation to "come buy." In all there are only six different rhymes in this passage, and the rhyme on "buy" ("cry," "fly," "by," "try," and "eye") sounds at the beginning, middle, and end of the passage, effectively enclosing and fixing it. The most often repeated rhyme, on "berries," clogs the lines. "Cooing all together," the goblins sound "kind and full of loves," but their cloying sweetness is deceiving. Tucked into the middle of this list of fruits is the familiar *carpe diem* warning: "Morns that pass by, / Fair eves that fly." Here is the nub of the goblins' argument: Come buy before it is too late. But their offer of fruits from apples to citrons mutes this hint of change and decay. Nursery rhyme and fairy tale unlock the word hoard and play with language; the goblins' list purports to do the same, while in truth it is merely a huckster's cry. The catalog fills the mind with the fullness of nature, yet it can, like innocence, deceive. The language the goblins sell betrays the sense of community that fairy tales and nursery rhymes promote. Laura restores this at the end when she gathers the little ones about her and bids them "cling together." The final words of the poem, Laura's words, speak of sisterhood, of the importance of friendship and community. The poem shows, through its similes, its repetitions, its verbal echoes, that sisterhood is as much figurative as actual.

The lists of exotic and familiar fruits show Rossetti's delight in nature as well as in words. Rossetti also has a fondness for animals. Her goblins are men, but they also have a variety of animal-like attributes. One has a cat's face, another a tail. One crawls like a snail, another walks like a rat, and yet another is furry like a wombat. They bark, mew, and hiss. Their animal qualities suggest their earthly and predatory natures. They assimilate their victims into the order of nature, whereas Lizzie, by her act of self-sacrifice, humanizes the natural order and demonstrates higher values than aggression, power, and greed. The natural world the goblins inhabit is that of fairy tale or that in which William Blake's tiger roams. Nature, for Rossetti, can only please when it schools us in a respect for the divine.

There are no wombats or animal-like goblins or other threatening creatures in Rossetti's second volume for children, her collection of original nursery rhymes, *Sing-Song: A Nursery Rhyme Book.* The book appeared during a period of extreme discomfort in Rossetti's life, a time when she suffered from various illnesses, including neuralgia and Graves' disease, whose symptoms included vomiting, swelling throat, and fainting fits. This makes all the more remarkable, as Annie E. Moore says, the "fresh air of English meadows and the serene security of home" that pervade the untitled poems in the book. Moore notes that *Sing-Song* contains no weird creatures, but that "cows and lambkins and sitting hens; birds and flowers, wind and sun; cherries, pancakes, and bread and milk; play-time, work time and tender care at bedtime" are the subjects of the book. Other interests also predominate: a desire for stasis, an awareness of class divisions, an acceptance of suffering, an exploration of fantasy, and an understanding of pastoral. The natural world Rossetti depicts in *Sing-Song,* like that of Blake in *Songs of Innocence* (1789), is innocent and fragile:

> Growing in the vale
> By the uplands hilly,
> Growing straight and frail,
> Lady Daffadowndilly.
>
> In a golden crown,
> And a scant green gown
> While the spring blows chilly,
> Lady Daffadown,
> Sweet Daffadowndilly.

Several poems describe the seasons, dubbing spring and summer the times of desire: "If only we could stop the moon / And June!" The end of summer brings longing for its return:

> Fly away, fly away over the sea,
> Sun-loving swallow, for summer is done;
> Come again, come again, come back to me,
> Bringing the summer and bringing the sun.

Longing and desire are most evident in verses about mothers. The second poem in *Sing-Song,* "Love me,—I love you," expresses the mother's

desire for affection as much as it expresses her affection for her baby. The fourth poem in *Sing-Song* deals with a baby's death, but the focus of the poem is the mother's desire for security:

> Our little baby fell asleep,
> And may not wake again
> For days and days, and weeks and weeks;
> But then he'll wake again,
> And come with his own pretty look,
> And kiss Mamma again.

The tenderness of a mother's love moves the reader in a poem like "Your brother has a falcon," and the ambivalent feelings of a mother who finds her child both a "trouble and treasure" fade under deep love in "Crying, my little one, footsore and weary?" Rossetti does not shy away from such hard themes as poverty, grief, wandering, and woe.

On the whole, such subjects receive imaginative treatment in *Sing-Song.* Some poems, however, continue the didactic tradition. Practical and moral lessons permeate the book. There are lessons in addition ("1 and 1 are 2—"), clock and calendar time ("How many seconds in a minute?"), the use of money ("What will you give me for my pound?"), the seasons ("January cold desolate"), and colors ("What is pink? a rose is pink"). Some poems decry cruelty to animals in the tradition of Sarah Trimmer: "Hurt no living thing," "If the sun could tell us half." "Seldom 'can't'" instructs a child against disobedience and negative thinking. Work, charity, and selfishness are the subjects of "I planted a hand":

> I planted a hand
> And there came up a palm,
> I planted a heart
> And there came up balm.
>
> Then I planted a wish,
> But there sprang a thorn,
> While heaven frowned with thunder
> And earth sighed forlorn.

This poem also shows Rossetti's interest in the interplay between symbolic and literal meanings. Here the hand and heart are abstractions, metonymic expressions for work and charity, but they produce something concrete: trees. The palm and the balm are not only abstract expressions of peace and healing, they are also trees. Rossetti manages the conceit of planting admirably.

486

Her interest in language also manifests itself in an acute awareness of the child's verbal world. Some rhymes overtly encourage the young reader to play with words:

> A city plum is not a plum;
> A dumb-bell is no bell, though dumb;
> A statesman's rat is not a rat;
> A sailor's cat is not a cat;
> A soldier's frog is not a frog;
> A captain's log is not a log.

The words are not so much referential as they are metaphoric. One purpose of this poem is to educate the reader in poetic discourse. Another means of accomplishing the same end is to place in the foreground the devices of sound, repetition, and meter. Meaning results from the reader engaging the poem as discourse, as a form of communication that differs from statement. Poems communicate through their formal patterns and their sounds perhaps more than through their semantic content, and the reader must interpret these formal elements. This is particularly true of poetry for young children, which emphasizes rhyme and which often uses nonsense words. Any interpretation we might produce from our reading of Rossetti's poems derives from formal elements. Take, for example, this poem:

> "Kookoorookoo! kookoorookoo!"
> Crows the cock before the morn;
> "Kikirikee! kikirikee!"
> Roses in the east are born.
>
> "Kookoorookoo! kookoorookoo!"
> Early birds begin their singing;
> "Kikirikee! kikirikee!"
> The day, the day, the day is springing.

More obviously than other poems in the book, this poem derives from such traditional nursery rhymes as "Cock-a-Doodle-Doo! / My Dame Has Lost Her Shoe," "Titty Cum Tawtay," and "Bow, Wow, Wow." The voice that speaks the poem produces two sound words that are similar, yet oppose each other. The consonants are the same, but the vowel sounds differ. The last line with its three repetitions of "day" reinforces a sense of sprightliness, as do the alliteration and assonance in the second and fourth lines. The energetic bounce of the poem's rhythm not only suggests the liveliness of the new morn, but also connotes springtime and the pasto-

ral freshness so pervasive in *Sing-Song.* Although there is no mention of God or the Christian stories in *Sing-Song,* an aura of spirituality is apparent in the poem. We begin to suspect a spiritual meaning in the line "Roses in the east are born," especially when we consider that roses and other flowers figure in at least fifteen poems in the volume. The poem, then, is a celebration of birth, a new morning, spiritual vitality, and natural harmony. The "kookoorookoo" and "kikirikee" are not exclusively the voices of specific birds, and the speaker of the poem is not a specific individual. This is, like all nursery rhymes, a collective song, but here it is a collective hymn of praise to a world that reflects the divine.

One of the best-known poems in *Sing-Song* suggests the presence of the divine. "Who has seen the wind?" gives simple yet intense expression to the numinous:

> Who has seen the wind?
> Neither I nor you:
> But when the leaves hang trembling
> The wind is passing thro'.
>
> Who has seen the wind?
> Neither you nor I:
> But when the trees bow down their heads
> The wind is passing by.

The addition of syllables in the third and fourth lines of the first stanza accurately suggests the passing wind, and the half stress on "hang" effectively modulates the breeze. The third line of the second stanza has four stresses to convey the strength of the wind that bends the branches; reverence infuses the line. Rossetti describes the wind as *inspiritus,* the breath of the divine, using the image both to emphasize the pastoral harmony of her world and to show the darker side of pastoral innocence. "O wind, where have you been?" and "O wind, why do you never rest?" depict both sweetness and restlessness. The images of the wind and sea combine to evoke death in "The wind has such a rainy sound."

Despite the themes of death and parting that appear throughout *Sing-Song,* the dominant mood is joyous:

> "Goodbye in fear, goodbye in sorrow,
> Goodbye, and all in vain,
> Never to meet again, my dear—"
> "Never to part again."

"Goodbye to-day, goodbye to-morrow,
Goodbye till earth shall wane,
Never to meet again, my dear—"
"Never to part again."

Two voices speak. One voice, that which speaks the first three lines of each quatrain, is melancholy. The second voice, however, transforms the first speaker's message to one of cheer. Like the child in Wordsworth's "We Are Seven" (1798), the second speaker does not accept discontinuity. By using verbal repetition and interlocking rhymes, Rossetti focuses on the form of the poem, drawing the two quatrains together. Battiscombe's assertion that for Rossetti "death is the bringer of joy" is pertinent to *Sing-Song.* Here she presents death as a positive aspect of life. In part, she accomplishes this by identifying death as a natural aspect in a larger pattern. A child may die, but in this the child is like a rose: "I have but one rose in the world, / And my one rose stands a-drooping." Ships may go down, but so do apples in the orchard tumble from their tree. A baby dies, and its father and mother sigh; flowers also "bloom to die," accepting the way of things, for "If all were sun and never rain, / There'd be no rainbow still." Finally, death is but a sleeping: "Our little baby fell asleep, / And may not wake again / For days and days, and weeks and weeks." But the poem assures us that he will "wake again." Death sends a child's soul "home to Paradise" and leaves his "body waiting here."

Just as Rossetti delights in wordplay, in the intricacies of form and allusion, and in the openness of meaning, her notion of death is equally at variance with discontinuity and finality. *Sing-Song* contains several poems that compare sleep with death and that offer hope for angelic care after death. The book's final poem may be read as a summary of this theme:

Lie a-bed,
Sleepy head,
Shut up eyes, bo-peep;
Till daybreak
Never wake:—
Baby, sleep.

Death, like sleep, is a comforting time of preparation and waiting for a grand new morning. In "Lie a-bed," the masculine rhymes and strong, end-stopped third and last lines signal finality, closure,

death. But the two halves of the little poem are hooked together with the rhyme of "bo-peep" and "sleep." "Bo-peep" reminds us we are in the world of nursery rhyme where rhyme is strongly musical; the words have a non-referential significance and power. If we should catch a somber note here, if we should allow our minds to play on the meaning of "wake" and consider its two senses of emerging from sleep and watching over the body of a dead person, then we might also consider the wake of the poem, the track it leaves behind, the residue in the mind. We might hear that coupling of "peep" and "sleep," a sound connection that suggests a seeing in sleep. During sleep, we catch glimpses of the greater reality to come; we peep into our future. During our nightly dreams, we peep into our unconscious. Coming at the end of a book so concerned with the possibility of death, this little lullaby allows us a peep into the mystery of sleep both in its nightly and in its deathlike aspects. This baby will not sleep the sleep of death, but may or may not sleep until the next morning or the final morning. The sense of closure in all lullabies is premature, since there is always more to come, more to sing.

Even in Rossetti's didactic poems we can discern the play with closure and its opposite. The poem explaining time begins with the smallest unit of clock time: "How many seconds in a minute? / Sixty, and no more in it." The sense of closure is bluntly conveyed by the phrase "and no more in it." Time circumscribes experience; we have twenty-four hours in a day "for work and play," and "the almanack makes clear" there are twelve months in a year. Yet time cannot circumscribe experience; the poem's final couplet reads, "How many ages in time? / No one knows the rhyme." The two words "time" and "rhyme" are united and remind us that neither completes anything. Rhyme is part of a poem's time, its musical beat, but it also has nothing to do with measurable clock or seasonal time. Rhyme is as timeless as language and sound. Time, on the other hand, is rhymeless in the sense that it cannot be packaged in couplets since "no one knows the rhyme"; paradoxically, "time" and "rhyme" perform the coupling the poem says is impossible.

In *Sing-Song,* as in "Goblin Market," Rossetti is less concerned with allegory or didacticism than she is with intensity of form and language. She chooses her forms, whether fairy tale or nursery rhyme, carefully. These forms feature play, repetition, song, and language.

Rossetti's last book for children, *Speaking Likenesses,* which the *Times Literary Supplement* called "a peculiarly revolting book," does much the same. It contains three unconnected stories told to a group of children by an officious aunt. The first story, by far the longest, tells of eight-year-old Flora's birthday party. After much bickering among the children present there, Flora goes off by herself and falls asleep to dream of another birthday party that is a grotesque extension of the first. The dream, of course, makes Flora a better child. The second story recounts little Edith's attempt to boil a kettle, and the third is a Christmas tale about Maggie's trip to the country to return some presents left behind at her grandmother's shop by a well-to-do country doctor. Her journey is dangerous; she must learn to avoid temptation and to see through false appearances. The first story is the most fully developed. Rossetti's interest in all these stories is in challenging conventions, but her methods are still playful. The narrator, for example, is a source of fun, and we should be careful not to assume that the aunt speaks for Rossetti. True, the narrator's tone is didactic, but the children who form her audience manage to undercut her intentions.

Clara, Jane, Laura, Ella, and Maude continually interrupt their aunt's storytelling. They comment on the oddness of a name, they ask for clarification, or they point out improbable assertions. The cumulative effect is to emphasize the separation between the irritable, presumptuous, and matter-of-fact aunt and the curious children who remain receptive to fancy and wonder. For example, when the narrator describes the sunny afternoon of Flora's birthday in the first of the book's three stories, she remarks that "bell flowers rang without clappers." Before she can complete her sentence, Maude interrupts to ask whether bell flowers can ring without clappers. The narrator shrugs the question off with the reply: "Well, not exactly, Maude: but you're coming to much more wonderful matters!" In other words, "Don't ask difficult questions, and attend to the rest of my story."

Yet there is a strangeness in the narrator's attitude to storytelling; she urges her listeners to occupy themselves with sewing, painting, or darning while they listen. When Jane and Laura become engrossed in the fantastic room with animated furniture described in the first story, the narrator admonishes them not to "*quite* forget the pocket-handkerchiefs you sat down to hem." Sitting down to hear a story is apparently too idle an occupation for this aunt. Many writers for children in the nineteenth century distrust fantasy, and here Rossetti pokes fun at the aunt's similar attitude. When Jane asks whether the furniture that arranges itself flat against the walls also flattens itself across the door, her aunt answers briskly: "Why, yes, I suppose it may have done so, Jane. . . . At any rate, as this is all make-believe, I say No. Attention!" At one point in the third story, the narrator interrupts herself to ask the children if they know what would happen to the story's heroine if she were to sleep out in the cold winter weather, thus raising the subject of death.

This is the last interruption that occurs. The book ends without a return to its narrative frame. Each of the first two stories ends abruptly, followed, apparently a day later, by a conversation between the children and their aunt concerning the next story. Are we to assume at the end of the third story that there is no next day? The disjunction between the opening, in which the narrator tells the "dear little girls" to gather around her, and the end, when Maggie and her granny go quietly to bed, is clear. The book begins with a call to story and it ends within the world of story. What matters is story, not the narrator's lessons on acoustics or her warning that one should never put an empty kettle on a fire. The children's interruptions show their interest and engagement in the stories; they ask for details when their aunt appears insufficiently clear. Along with Laura they ask, "And please, Aunt, be wonderful."

Just as the narrative frame draws attention to the act of storytelling, the stories themselves draw attention to form, to the play of allusion, to the interruptions of linear narrative. In the second story Edith and the kettle are "spending one warm afternoon together in a wood" that has, "by some freak," one vine that grows among the beech trees and silver birches and that dangles "bunches of pale purple grapes among its leaves and twisted tendrils." Just where the vine grows, a party is to take place, and Edith decides to take the kettle there and light the fire to boil it. First, however, she eyes the grapes and longs to grasp a cluster. Then she turns her attention to the fire, but fails to start it with her six matches. Various animals attempt to help her and also fail. Just before the enterprise ends with the arrival of Nurse, a fox bustles up, brushes the dust from Edith's frock, attempts vainly to reach the grapes and then trots away, muttering, "They must be sour." The allusion is clearly to Aesop's fable. Were we to look for a moral in this story of Edith and the kettle, this famous fable provides one: Some people blame circumstances when they fail through their own incapacity and some people take disappointment with indifference. Edith sits down to cry. Yet to point out such a moral contrast is to ignore the more obvious nonsense. The fox trots in and out of the scene. What he signals is "fable." The fable's first function is fun, and as several versions of Aesop indicate (most notably the 1692 translation by Roger l'Estrange), the moral explanation is simply unsatisfactory, or even inapplicable. What matters in Rossetti's story is the frog who could not boil the kettle, the toad whose father lived in a stone, and the other animals who help so ineffectually.

Rossetti inverts the Aesop fable. The fox is unconcerned about not reaching the grapes; Edith is in despair. This does not suggest a more acute moral in the Rossetti story but rather a play with the form of fable. The whole story is free association, made up as the aunt speaks; she states at the beginning that she does not know the story of the frog who couldn't boil the kettle, but that she will try to tell it anyway. In short, there is a nod in the direction of Lewis Carroll in *Speaking Likenesses.* Rossetti wrote to her publisher, Alexander Macmillan, that *Speaking Likenesses* was "merely a Christmas trifle, would-be in the *Alice* style." Most readers have found the book a pale shade of *Alice,* yet it does have certain similarities: a dreamlike atmosphere, fantastic creatures and talking animals, animated objects, the uncovering of desire, and the nakedness of fear. The first story in *Speaking Likenesses,* about Flora's birthday party, provides the clearest example.

The quaint children in Flora's dream—the boys Hooks, Angles, and Quills, and the girls Sticky, Slime, and Queen—play two games: "Hunt the Pincushion" and "Self-Help." The nightmarish quality some readers perceive in Carroll's *Alice's Adventures in Wonderland* (1865) is evident here in the two games, which express sexual violence and a disturbing disrespect for humanity. The first game treats human beings as objects, things without feeling or dignity; it reverses the fairy-tale convention of imagining inanimate objects as animate. This misimagining is central to Rossetti's point. In Carroll's first *Alice* book, inanimate objects such as mallets and balls become hedgehogs and flamingos.

The Queen of Hearts presides over a lively game in which there are no rules and no ill consequences. "Hunt the Pincushion," however, reverses this. The hunt is no longer an innocent search for an object; it is a bloody sport. Rossetti clarifies the sexual implications of the game and draws attention to its nastier aspects. In the description of both games, Rossetti puts forth a feminist critique of the customs of her culture. The players of "Hunt the Pincushion" select "the smallest and weakest player (if possible let her be fat: a hump is best of all)," and they "chase her round and round the room." The pincushion is female. In "Self-Help" the "boys were players, the girls were played." Rossetti also satirizes the whole notion of self-help, made popular by Samuel Smiles's *Self-Help, with Illustrations of Character and Conduct* (1859). The unpleasant implication for females in Smiles's assertion that the "energy of will may be defined to be the very central power of character in a man" is uncovered in Rossetti's imaginary game. In Flora's dream self-help becomes a situation in which the man helps himself at the expense of the woman.

Most readers of *Speaking Likenesses* will be brought up short by the descriptions of these games. Rossetti's satire and innuendo halt the reader, or ought to. Rossetti indicates her intent by having the narrator interrupt the narrative to say: "Don't look shocked, dear Ella, at my choice of words." What these shocking words are we can only suppose, since the description of "Self-Help" that immediately precedes this interruption is harmless enough. Certainly the description of "Hunt the Pincushion" contains shocking words:

> Quills with every quill erect tilted against her, and needed not a pin: but Angles whose corners almost cut her, Hooks who caught and slit her frock, Slime who slid against and passed her, Sticky who rubbed off on her neck and plump bare arms, the scowling Queen, and the whole laughing scolding pushing troop, all wielded longest sharpest pins, and all by turns overtook her.

The passage that follows, in which the narrator reflects on the effect of the game upon the "stickers," combines colloquial expressions ("cutting corners") with tautologies ("pricking quills," "catching hooks"), and alliteration ("particular personal pangs"). The narrator directs our attention to vocabulary and to stylistic effects, and in doing this she impedes narrative. This combination of interest in form and language, cultural critique, and sexual politics makes *Speaking Likenesses* appear dated and difficult. It is understandably neglected; it demands more from its reader than the general run of children's books. Yet, like "Goblin Market" and *Sing-Song*, it is difficult only for the reader who expects simple narrative or clear didacticism. All three works do appear conventionally didactic and traditionally narrative in impulse, yet they are also disturbing and confusing. What appears straightforward is, upon reflection, askew. The reader confronts nursery rhyme and fairy tale in a new guise, one that consciously plays with traditional form and themes.

Selected Bibliography

WORKS OF CHRISTINA ROSSETTI

Goblin Market, and Other Poems. With illustrations by D. G. Rossetti. London and Cambridge, England: Macmillan, 1862. Reissued with illustrations by Laurence Housman. London: Macmillan, 1893.

Sing-Song: A Nursery Rhyme Book. With illustrations by Arthur Hughes. London: G. Routledge and Sons, 1872; Boston: Roberts Brothers, 1872.

Speaking Likenesses. With illustrations by Arthur Hughes. London: Macmillan, 1874.

Maude: Prose and Verse by Christina Rossetti, 1850. Chicago: Herbert S. Stone, 1897.

CRITICAL AND BIOGRAPHICAL STUDIES

Battiscombe, Georgina. *Christina Rossetti: A Divided Life*. London: Constable, 1981.

Cott, Jonathan, ed. *Beyond the Looking Glass: Extraordinary Works of Fairy Tale and Fantasy*. With an introduction by Jonathan Cott and a special introductory essay by Leslie Fiedler. New York: Stonehill, 1973.

Moore, Annie E. *Literature Old and New for Children*. Cambridge, Mass.: Houghton Mifflin, 1934.

Watson, Jeannie. " 'Men Sell Not Such in Any Town': Christina Rossetti's Goblin Fruit of Fairy Tale" *Children's Literature* 12: 61–77 (1984).

—RODERICK McGILLIS

JOHN RUSKIN

1819–1900

JOHN RUSKIN, KNOWN after 1843 as the author of *Modern Painters,* is probably the most famous art critic of Victorian England. Because he came to believe that the art of a society reflects its moral qualities as well as its aesthetic sensibilities, he developed into a severe critic of the industrialized society of nineteenth-century England. His contributions to children's literature do not usually receive extensive consideration in summaries of his life's work, but they are of real interest both because of his own writing for children and because of his influence on the achievements of others in this field.

Ruskin began life with the advantages of wealth. His father, a wine merchant, gave his son an education, travels in Europe, and financial support for his career. Disadvantages of his birth and family were a possibly hereditary mental instability and a rigidly disciplined upbringing that allowed little close association with other children. By his teens, the precocious child was already devoting his talents to writing. About 1836 he tried to impress a girl near his own age, Adèle Domecq, daughter of a French partner in his father's business, by composing poems and a tragic prose tale, *Leoni,* all very full of current clichés. Adèle, much more sophisticated, was merely amused by the absurdities.

The embarrassment from this experience turned Ruskin away from romantic fiction, but five years later circumstances encouraged him to write a work really intended for a child. In 1841 a distant relative, Euphemia ("Effie") Gray, visited the Ruskins. An attractive girl of thirteen, she was capable of sharing some of John's interests. At this date Romantic revival of the Middle Ages, represented by works like Scott's *Ivanhoe,* was still strong. In particular, in 1823 the German folktales of Jacob and Wilhelm Grimm had been translated by Edgar Taylor into English with great success. Both John and Effie liked them. She challenged him to write a story in the manner of the Brothers Grimm for her amusement. By his own statement written more than forty years later, he was also influenced by the early works of Dickens, and by the love of Alpine scenery developed during family travels. The result was *The King of the Golden River: A Tale of Stiria,* completed rapidly in 1841.

To place this tale chronologically in Ruskin's career, it was not actually published until December 1850, with only minor changes from the original manuscript. Effie married Ruskin in 1848 and shared an unhappy marriage that was annulled in 1854, but seems to have had no influence on the work after 1841. It is not even clear what she thought of it. The tale was very popular, thanks in part to the illustrations by Richard Doyle of *Punch.*

In *The King of the Golden River* the Alpine setting in Ruskin's Styria is really an Alpine province of Austria; the story mentions mountains and a glacier, and the river of the title springs in a beautiful cataract from near the summit of a mountain. But the elements that make this work what Victorians called a fairy tale are the supernatural elements—not necessarily fairies—for which the German stories furnish examples in both characters and plot.

To begin with time and place, the date of the

story is only "once upon a time," a vaguely medieval past. The location in Styria is really as unidentifiable as a kingdom in any folktale; no town or mountain is specifically named. The Golden River cannot be identified with any real river. The hero's home, the Treasure Valley, is only a mountain valley kept fertile by rains—it cannot be pinpointed on a map. The religion is Roman Catholic, as would be true for medieval Austria, but it is not stressed except to provide the "holy water" important for the plot.

The treatment of characterization is typical of folktales. The Treasure Valley is owned by three brothers (a number often significant in such tales). The two eldest, Schwartz and Hans, are brutal, hardhearted, avaricious. Gluck, only twelve years old, is unselfish and generous, qualities that in folktales often characterize the youngest son, who usually becomes the hero. All three brothers always act in accordance with the original conception of their characters; they do not develop.

The story's action begins with the appearance of the supernatural. On a stormy day, Gluck is hospitable to a small elderly gentleman of comical appearance, but the elder brothers try to force the stranger out of doors. Supernatural beings can be dangerous, however; the comical visitor is Southwest Wind, Esq., who promptly ruins the Treasure Valley and turns it into a desert by withholding the rains. The brothers are driven to become goldsmiths in an unnamed town.

The elder brothers have learned nothing. They compel Gluck to melt down his cherished golden mug, made in the likeness of a bewhiskered face. The melting frees another supernatural being, a dwarf who announces that he is the King of the Golden River. In gratitude for being freed from enchantment, the King tells Gluck that if anyone climbs to the source of the Golden River and casts therein three drops of holy water, for him only the river shall turn to gold. But such quests may have deadly perils: anyone attempting the quest has only one chance, and if he casts unholy water into the source, he shall become a black stone. Naturally, first Hans and then Schwartz go on the quest and fail before young Gluck can try.

The quest requires the seeker to overcome physical obstacles and pass crucial tests of character. In a difficult crossing of a glacier, each brother loses all his supply of water except a flask of the required holy water. Each brother then suffers intense thirst that tempts him to drink from his flask. Three times each brother sees a small dog or a human being begging for water. Each elder brother callously keeps the water for himself; each elder brother casts his "holy water" into the source, and is transformed into a black stone.

But Gluck's sheer goodness meets all tests, even to pouring his last drops of holy water down the throat of a dying dog. The dog is only a disguise adopted by the King of the River. Resuming his real shape, he assures Gluck of his favor. The latter timidly asks why his brothers were transformed into stones in spite of casting holy water into the river. The King expounds Ruskin's moral: "Water which has been refused to the cry of the weary and dying is unholy, though it had been blessed by every saint in heaven; and the water which is found in the vessel of mercy is holy, though it had been defiled with corpses." The King gives Gluck three drops of pure water to cast into the river, which works underground to a new cataract falling into the Treasure Valley to restore fertility to its soil and make Gluck as prosperous as he is good.

Ruskin's debt to Dickens in this tale is hard to detect. It may be seen in the theme of a likable young hero in difficult circumstances, or it may have inspired the vein of humor, such as the touch of caricature in the description of Southwest Wind, Esq., with his conical hat.

One point has aroused some curiosity among students of Ruskin. Why are there no feminine characters in a tale written to amuse a thirteen-year-old girl? In many tales from Grimm, the hero or heroine is rewarded with a happy marriage, sometimes even with a royal spouse. Effie might have had a princess to identify with, but nothing is said of Gluck's ever marrying. He is evidently an orphan, but no Dickensian pathos for the loss of his mother is part of his troubles. Scholars interested in Ruskin's personality are apt to connect the lack of women in this fairy tale with his embarrassment by Adèle Domecq, but such arguments are speculative. It should be said that readers, especially very young ones, may not expect a love story. The plot is complete in itself: a likable youngster mistreated by obnoxious brothers ultimately wins a happiness he has deserved, a theme that has pleased both young and old readers of many folktales, whether or not a spouse or a mother shares the happiness.

One merit of *The King of the Golden River*, as of other works by Ruskin, owes nothing to folktale: his skill with words. In this story his style can be colloquial in some conversations, but at climaxes it can appeal to both sight and hearing by means comparable to the word-painting found in elevated passages of *Modern Painters.* One brief example will have to do: as Schwartz nears the source of the Golden River, he mocks the likeness of his brother Hans, crying for water. "And the bank of black cloud rose to the zenith, and out of it came bursts of spiry lightning, and waves of darkness seemed to heave and float between their flashes over the whole heavens." Under this sky Schwartz presses on to his doom. But beautiful flowers and a sunny sky match the goodness of Gluck's deeds. In his later years, Ruskin is considered to have made less use of deliberately poetic passages, but he never completely lost his gift of eloquence until his mind failed in old age.

Ruskin wrote only this one fairy tale. In his discussion of this work in *Praeterita,* he wrote that *The King of the Golden River* had been rightly pleasing to nice children and good for them, but, he surprisingly added, "it is totally valueless for all that." In 1868, eighteen years after the publication of his *King of the Golden River,* he wrote "Fairy Stories," an introduction to a new edition of Edgar Taylor's *German Popular Stories,* in which he criticizes some unnamed contemporaries for warping genuine original folktales to make some moral point. Insistence on too explicit a moral, Ruskin maintains, may harm a child's imagination and falsify its understanding of good and evil.

This introduction to Taylor's edition of the Brothers Grimm is proof that although Ruskin gave up writing fairy tales after *The King of the Golden River,* he did not lose interest in books for youthful audiences, either his own writings or works of his contemporaries. His *Ethics of the Dust* (1866) is in a fringe area of children's literature— semi-fictional dialogues based on Ruskin's experiences teaching at a progressive girls' school at Winnington Hall in the Lake District. Ruskin's introduction acknowledges that the characters and speeches are rarely literal reports, but he is himself "The Old Lecturer" and Van Akin Burd's *The Winnington Letters* identifies the originals of some of the girls, aged nine to twenty. The work theoretically introduces the pupils to the scientific study of crystals; actually it covers a wide range of literature and mythology with some moral implications. Ruskin tried to make learning pleasant by putting some humor and individual characterization into this semi-dramatic form, but not always successfully. Although the subtitle, "Ten Lectures to Little Housewives," may to feminists seem patronizing, Ruskin was nevertheless part of the movement to expand the range and depth of education for women. *Ethics of the Dust* was not a success in 1866, but after 1883 it became relatively popular and continued to be reprinted into the twentieth century.

During the last decade of Ruskin's active career, before repeated attacks of insanity finally in 1889 ended his ability to work, his importance for children's literature is hard to evaluate because the available evidence is often incomplete or ambiguous. His interest in works for children, including the art that illustrated such works, very probably increased as part of the interest in education already evident in *Ethics of the Dust* and other publications like *Sesame and Lilies* (1865). His comments, both public and private, may well have had influence to be recognized in the history of children's literature. In particular, Kate Greenaway, whose drawings of children have their admirers today, became Ruskin's close friend, even his disciple. In addition, their relationship led to a lecture, "Fairy Land: Mrs. Allingham and Kate Greenaway," delivered by Ruskin as part of a series called *The Art of England,* presented at Oxford in 1883, in which discussion of Greenaway's art led to some general consideration of what works intended for children ought to be.

One serious difficulty in evaluating Ruskin's influence on Miss Greenaway's art and therefore on her many followers is that her charming children with their quaint and decorous costumes were already enjoying tremendous popularity by 1878. Ruskin's first letter to her was written early in 1880. It is therefore impossible that his praise of her art created her vogue or that his criticism of it affected much of her best-known work. It is true that a close friendship grew up between them, and that he mixed warm praise of her work with many suggestions for improvement. He found her children charming, but more decorative than true to life. To the end of their correspondence he constantly urged her to portray anatomical details more accurately and to show children as they really were. He also maintained that her drawings from nature should be more realistic. Some of her later work, such as her illustrations for Robert Browning's *Pied Piper of Hamelin* in 1888, may show an effect of Ruskin's suggestions, but other late illustrations look much like her earlier ones. Which did her followers copy?

The lecture at Oxford already mentioned was a direct address to a public audience, but again its significance for Greenaway's reputation and for children's literature in general is uncertain. Students checking twentieth-century appraisals of Ruskin's works will find that the 1883–1884 lectures draw comparatively little space or praise. Some scholars even suggest that the eulogies of Greenaway and other artists show that Ruskin had lost some of his critical powers. However, the printed lectures sold well enough to indicate that some readers were seriously interested. A main part of the content, in addition to praise of Greenaway, is Ruskin's insistence that it is vital to give children the very best training possible in intellect, aesthetic sensitivity, and moral character. The freedom of the creative imagination is invaluable in a child's development. Children should have the chance to know the beauty of the unspoiled earth. Supplying children with the best possible books was part of Ruskin's battle against the defects he found in an industrialized society.

In summary, it cannot be claimed that John Ruskin's contribution to children's literature is the most important achievement of his career, but it is noteworthy. *The King of the Golden River* still gives pleasure to readers. Ruskin's very real love of children finds expression in his insistence that educators, writers, and artists should all give their best to any works intended for children. He has a respectable place in the history of children's literature.

Selected Bibliography

WORKS OF JOHN RUSKIN

Editions of *The King of the Golden River*

The King of the Golden River; or, The Black Brothers: A Legend of Stiria. With illustrations by Richard Doyle. London: Smith, Elder, 1851. With illustrations by Maria L. Kirk. Philadelphia: J. B. Lippincott, 1921. With illustrations by Arthur Rackham. London: G. Harrap, 1932; Philadelphia: J. B. Lippincott, 1932. With illustrations by Fritz Kredel. Cleveland and New York: World, 1946.

Collected Works

The Works of John Ruskin. Edited by E. T. Cook and A. D. O. Wedderburn. 39 vols. London: George Allen, 1902–1912. (The definitive edition; includes publishing histories.) Vol. 1, pp. 238–304. *Leoni: A Legend of Italy.* Vol. 1, pp. 305–354. *The King of the Golden River; or, The Black Brothers: A Legend of Stiria.* Vol. 18, pp. 189–368. *The Ethics of the Dust: Ten Lectures to Little Housewives on the Elements of Crystallisation.* Vol. 19, pp. 231–239. "Fairy Stories": A Preface to "German Popular Stories" (1868). Vol. 25, pp. 303–304. *Praeterita,* vol. 2, chap. 4, sec. 34. Vol. 33, pp. 327–349. *The Art of England.* Lecture 4, "Fairy Land: Mrs. Allingham and Kate Greenaway." Vol. 37. *The Letters of John Ruskin,* vol. 2, 1870–1889. (Includes numerous letters to Kate Greenaway from 1880 to 1889.)

BIOGRAPHICAL AND CRITICAL STUDIES

Burd, Van Akin, ed. *The Winnington Letters: John Ruskin's Correspondence with Margaret Alexis Bell and the Children at Winnington Hall.* Cambridge, Mass.: Harvard University Press, 1969.

Hearn, Michael Patrick. "Mr. Ruskin and Miss Greenway [*sic*]." *Reflections on Literature for Children,* edited by Francelia Butler and Richard Rotert. Library Professional Publications / 18: 181–189 (1984).

Rahn, Suzanne. "The Sources of Ruskin's *Golden River.*" *Victorian Newsletter,* no. 68: 1–9 (Fall 1985).

—LOWELL P. LELAND

FELIX SALTEN

1869-1945

SIEGMUND SALZMANN, THE son of Philipp and Marie (Singer) Salzmann, was born 6 September 1869 in Budapest, Hungary. His parents moved with their small son to Vienna soon afterward, and the young Salzmann grew up in the stimulating cultural environment that also nurtured Sigmund Freud, Arthur Schnitzler, Hugo von Hofmannsthal, and Arnold Schoenberg. Salzmann's parents were not wealthy, and the youngster was largely self-taught. The family was of Jewish origin; when Salzmann began writing he adopted the name Felix Salten as a token of his assimilation into German culture. He joined the circle of intellectuals known as *Jung Wien* (Young Vienna) and was particularly close to Schnitzler and Hofmannsthal, as their correspondence shows. In 1902 Salten married Ottilie Metzl, an actress.

Before World War I he published numerous short novels, essays, and plays and was a regular theater critic and contributor to the *feuilleton* sections of several Viennese newspapers, the *Wiener Allgemeine Zeitung, Die Zeit,* and the *Neue Freie Presse.* In 1906 he served as an editor for the *Morgenpost* in Berlin. Most of his fiction described and commented upon the bourgeois and aristocratic society found in the closing years of the Central European monarchies; these works range from *Wiener Adel* (Viennese Aristocracy, 1905) to *Der Schrei der Liebe* (The Cry of Love, 1928), a collection of short novels, including *Die Kleine Veronika* ("Little Veronica"), an erotic story of a teenage girl from the country. Some of his most notable cultural and critical essays were collected and published in 1921

as *Schauen und Spielen: Studien zur Kritik des modern Theaters* (Shows and Plays: Studies in the Criticism of the Modern Theater); they deal with such luminaries as Gerhard Hauptmann, Frank Wedekind, Richard Wagner, Henrik Ibsen, Oscar Wilde, George Bernard Shaw, and Leo Tolstoy. A six-volume set of Salten's collected works appeared between 1928 and 1932 in Vienna, but none of these was translated into English, and they are rarely read today.

Unlike his compatriot Theodor Herzl, Salten did not become a Zionist. Assimilation within the context of German-Jewish culture remained his ideal. A *New York Times* correspondent wrote in 1929 that Salten was "as truly typical a Viennese as anyone who came into the world within sight of the shadow of the spire of St. Stephen's Cathedral [a Viennese landmark]." Nevertheless, some of his writings during the 1920's did exhibit Jewish interests, including the biblical novel *Simson* (*Samson and Delilah,* 1928) and a group of travel essays concerning Palestine entitled *Neue Menschen auf alter Erde* (New Men in an Ancient Land, 1925).

Salten's lasting literary fame came with his animal stories, the most successful of which was *Bambi: Eine Lebensgeschichte aus dem Walde (Bambi: A Life in the Woods),* published in German in 1923 and translated into English by Whittaker Chambers in 1928. *Bambi* was first published as an adult novel, and early American reviewers treated it as such. John R. Chamberlain titled his *New York Times* review of the book "Poetry and Philosophy in a Tale of Forest Life," and in it said, "He has given us the life story of a forest deer, and Felix Salten's comprehension of the entire universe as well. Here is a rationale of life." William Rose Benét said in his review for the *Saturday Review of Literature,* "The description of the hunt transmits its cataclysmic murderousness, from the point of view of the wild animals, most strikingly. This portion of the tale is, indeed, a triumph." The review in London's *Spectator* was even more explicit. It commented, "This is not a book for children alone. . . . Indeed, it may be too heartbreaking for the majority of children."

As a German author, Salten was writing about the forest he was familiar with, not the forest of America. His story is harsh, but the hunters in general are not the villains in it. When Salten typically speaks of "He," he is describing the poacher rather than the forester who hunts during hunting season and otherwise cares for the forest and its inhabitants. Thus he is suggesting that those who break the law and who shoot the "king's deer" are criminals who cause the animals to face constant fear, never to rest easy. However, even the forester is viewed apprehensively by most of the animals. They chide Gobo for his trust in man. When describing his experiences at the home of the forester, Gobo says, "You all think He's wicked. But He isn't wicked. If He loves anybody or if anybody serves Him, He's good to him. Wonderfully good! Nobody in the world can be as kind as He can."

Salten's description of the authorized hunt is somber. At that time Bambi loses his mother, sees Gobo fall with weakness and fright, and watches several others, including Friend Hare, die. Salten writes: "Then Friend Hare and two of his cousins rushed past them across the clearing. Bing! Ping! Bang! roared the thunder. Bambi saw how Friend Hare struck an elder in the middle of his flight and lay with his white belly turned upward. He quivered a little and then was still. Bambi stood petrified." Later, when Bambi meets Friend Hare's wife, she is gasping for breath.

> "Can you help me a little?" she said. Bambi looked at her and shuddered. Her hind leg dangled lifelessly in the snow, dyeing it red and melting it with warm, oozing blood. "Can you help me a little?" she repeated. She spoke as if she were well and whole, almost as if she were happy. "I don't know what can have happened to me," she went on. "There's really no sense to it, but I just can't seem to walk. . . ."

> In the middle of her words she rolled over on her side and died.

This authorized hunt goes on for eleven pages. In the end, the hunter and his killings vanish, and the hunt is never explained. Brutal as the authorized hunt is, it somehow seems fairer, because it is quick and final, than the constant threat of the poacher, who enters the woods quietly, without warning, or with some cunning device that adds to his guile. His threat is a psychological as well as physical one because he preys upon the very instincts of the wild animals. For example, when mating season comes and Bambi hears what he believes is Faline's call, the old stag takes him to the place where the call originates. Bambi sees the poacher calling softly in Faline's voice. Salten says that Bambi was "so terrified that he began to understand only by degrees that it was He who was imitating Faline's voice." Once he understands, "Cold terror shot through Bambi's body." Later, when Bambi finds Faline, he begs her not to call him again and concludes, "I can't resist your voice."

The deer continually talk of Him, of His "third arm," and of His meanness. There is no off season for the animals; the poacher takes no vacation from hunting. And he comes alone to the forest, much like a guerrilla soldier who fights and withdraws. This kind of hunter does not let the deer learn the rules of the hunt; he does not observe the conventions of disciplined war. In the end, Bambi stands with the old stag over a dead poacher and learns that the poacher is not a god. Bambi says, "There is Another who is over us all, over us and over Him." In the strictest sense the other one is God, but in another sense Salten could have been referring to the forester and to the organized laws within the hunting code.

The theme of the hunt, which so dominates the story, is not an element that would appeal to children. Rather, it is Salten's adroit use of human personalities to characterize the animals that gives a childlike charm to the story. The forest banter begins on the first page, when the magpie sees Bambi and chatters:

> "How amazing to think that he should be able to get right up and walk! How interesting! I've never seen the like of it before in all my born days. Of course, I'm still young, only a year out of the nest, you might say. But I think it's wonderful. A child

like that, hardly a minute in this world, and beginning to walk already! I call that remarkable. Really, I find that everything you deer do is remarkable. Can he run, too?"

Later Bambi sees his father for the first time and asks his mother:

"Will my father speak to me?"

"Of course he will," his mother promised. "When you're grown up he'll speak to you, and you'll have to stay with him sometimes."

Bambi walked silently beside his mother, his whole mind filled with his father's appearance. "How handsome he is!" he thought over and over again. "How handsome he is!"

Throughout the book these basic emotional responses to others and to the shared situations cause the reader to believe in the forest scene that is created. Yet the animals are definitely fantasy creatures, for their reactions to situations are altogether human. Their constant philosophical discussions in the evening hours remind the adult reader that Salten's own discussions with his compatriots in *Jung Wien* were probably philosophically based. For example, when the adult deer discuss Him they search for logical explanations concerning His behavior and for a real understanding of what the "third arm" really is. At other times the conversations resemble those Salten might have heard when he was growing up in the Jewish community. After the hare first meets Bambi and talks to his mother about the "young prince," Bambi's mother says of him, "He is so suave and prudent. He doesn't have an easy time of it in this world." Later, when the mothers show off their young offspring and Bambi's Aunt Ena calls Bambi a "lovely child," his mother replies, "O well, we have to be content."

It is this feeling of community, along with the vivid descriptions of nature and the passing of seasons, that would appeal to the young reader. Yet Margaret Blount, in her discussion of the book as children's literature, observes that "the story is accurate besides being sad and beautiful" but goes on to say, "The dialogue gives it an inner unreality." To the child this is an animal story that contains real personalities. It is no more unreal than Kenneth Grahame's *The Wind in the Willows* or E. B. White's *Charlotte's Web*.

What separates *Bambi* from these two animal sto-

ries is that it contains adult interpretations of the hunt and the hunter. Indeed, it is too somber in detail to have been written intentionally for children. What keeps the book alive in the hearts of children is Salten's positive presentation of his two heroes, Bambi and Faline. Bambi is the shy, cautious deer who grows up to understand the forest because he has known the forest's despair and the deer's longing to understand the rules of the hunt. Bambi's choice of Faline as his mate is predestined, since she is the only young roe deer that the reader gets to know. She is more venturesome than Bambi when they are young, but by the end of the book she has grown to trust Bambi, and she is more subdued in her behavior. And, while the story is laden with killings and maimings, it ends happily, with Bambi discovering his own two offspring. Bambi has become the old stag by the end, and he asks his children, "Can't you stay by yourself?" just as the old stag had once asked him. The story has come full circle with this new generation. The child reader is aware that new generations of deer will come to the forest and face the same trials that Bambi faced. Because Bambi has survived, children assume that the new deer will also.

In 1937, the Walt Disney production crew for the animated film version of *Bambi* began their story conferences. The movie was not released until 1942, three years after Salten's sequel, *Bambis Kinder: Eine Familie im Walde* (*Bambi's Children: The Story of a Forest Family*, 1940), was published in America. In 1938 the Nazis had taken over Austria and Felix Salten had fled. Already all of his works had been banned in Germany. *Bambis Kinder* was published in Zurich during 1940. The sequel presents a more carefully defined picture of the two types of hunters. Here Salten carefully defines the forester as the protector of the forest and thus, inadvertently, the savior of the animals. Bambi's family is constantly saved from domesticated animals and from poachers by the hunter. However, Salten makes it perfectly clear that the forester would love to hunt Bambi. When he sees Bambi in the forest hill during the winter, for instance, Salten writes that the hunter says, "Glory be! What an animal! I hope I see him later on when he has his points." Man remains an outsider in the forest, an intruder who sometimes helps but who can never be completely trusted.

This book also contains an official hunt, but this time the game warden is heard telling the hunters,

"Remember, gentlemen, you're using shot. No large game. And leave the owls alone." This time, however, the hunt lasts only five pages, and Bambi and his family are absent from the violent scene. When they return home, Faline asks, "Why must this happen, Bambi? Why must we always undergo this terror?" Bambi is unable to answer her. The story shows both the human and the animal points of view, but in the end the reader sympathizes with the animals.

The story itself has less appeal than *Bambi;* in the sequel the setting is less realistic and the storytelling is more affected. The deer are pictured as having a family structure that is loyal and that binds them together: Bambi constantly comes to the aid of his family and saves them from destruction. His cousins face death and react with the human emotions of rage and jealousy. Thus, when Rolla accidentally brings an enemy into Faline's hiding place, she is chastised. The scene could be an allegorical portrayal of the realistic drama faced by members of fleeing Jewish families during Salten's time.

> "You have sacrificed my son," she cried in her bitterness.
> "I didn't know!" wailed Rolla.
> "You didn't know!" Faline's eyes flashed. "The first law of motherhood is to protect the young. You are a murderess as surely as if you killed yourself."
> "Mother!" protested Gurri.
> "Be quiet, child!" snapped Faline. "Let this creature realize the extent of her crime. Every time she looks at Boso let her remember the price we paid."

All of the animals engage in conversations that are totally inappropriate for them, and the deer fluctuate between being representatives of a humanized animal colony and the idealized noble beasts who are never killers but are always the prey of others. At times the story's impact is lost in absurd conversations. For instance, when the animals first learn about the dog who has turned wild, the conversation turns to matters outside the animal world. The deer admit that they have never heard of the nth power, and the screech-owl explains, "It's a great pity that you never studied algebra. It would have been very simple to describe the wolf as a fox to the nth power."

Perhaps Salten realized that his largest American audience was made up of children. In any event, this story is less harsh, more moralistic, and less realistic than the first story. It ends in much the same way, this time with Bambi returning to take the children and teach them the lore of the forest. The book's ending is less positive than the conclusion of *Bambi,* for Faline is left behind by her family. Yet she is aware that the children will return to visit. To the finches she says, "They go, and the better they are, the more we miss them. But they must go. That is the fate of all parents." In the final scene, Bambi returns to Faline: "She saw a well-beloved shadow move with usual silence just where the tree trunks stood in mist. With light and quickened step she went toward it." In *Bambi's Children* the family circle remains unbroken. The separations that come are natural ones. Man, the hunter, has not brought death to Bambi, his mate, or their children. The story's ending is pleasing to the child reader, but it is too idyllic for the mature audience.

In 1948 the Disney book *Walt Disney's Bambi* was published, and in America Bambi's story became less the vision created by Felix Salten and more the interpretation created by the Disney staff. Disney did not list Salten as a consultant for the film or as a story adapter. It is possible that he consulted Salten while the author visited America for a brief time during the late 1930's, but if so, Salten's advice was not acknowledged by the company. Several changes were made in the story through the Disney process. The family connections are stressed much less; Friend Hare is exchanged for a more joyful, lovable hare and is renamed "Thumper"; new creatures such as Flower, the skunk, abound; and new man-made events, including a forest fire, have been introduced. Still, the story's original portrayal of the life struggle is there. And in Disney's version Bambi's story ends with the birth of the fawns, much as it did in the original. Although the concept of the poacher has been ignored, the hunter is very real. Once again, man is not depicted as the friend of the forest folk.

In 1939, when Robert de Graff launched the first mass-market paperback line in the United States, Pocket Books, he released *Bambi*. Salten's tale continues to be in print in English, French, and German editions.

That same year Salten returned to Europe and settled in the Swiss-German city of Zurich. He continued to write animal stories during the war years. On 8 October 1945, Salten died in Zurich after a long illness. At one time several of his animal tales were in print in America, but they have now been largely forgotten. Only *Bambi* has remained alive to children, because in it Salten created a compelling animal survival story with sympathetic characters. At the same time, the book has remained important to adult critics because of the moral implications it contains.

Selected Bibliography

WORKS OF FELIX SALTEN IN GERMAN

Bambi: Eine Lebensgeschichte aus dem Walde. Berlin: Ullstein, 1923; P. Zsolnay, 1926.

Fünfzehn Hasen: Schicksale im Wald und Feld. Berlin: P. Zsolnay, 1929.

Florian, das Pferd des Kaisers. Berlin: P. Zsolnay, 1933.

Die Jugend des Eichörnchens Perri. With illustrations by Ludwig Heinrich Jungnickel. Berlin: P. Zsolnay, 1938.

Bambis Kinder: Eine Familie im Walde. Zurich: A. Müller, 1940.

Renni der Retter: Das Leben eines Kriegshundes. Zurich: A. Müller, 1941.

ENGLISH TRANSLATIONS

Bambi: A Life in the Woods, translated by Whittaker Chambers. With an introduction by John Galsworthy and illustrations by Kurt Wiese. New York: Simon and Schuster, 1928; London: Jonathan Cape, 1928. New ed., with illustrations by Barbara Cooney. New York: Simon and Schuster, 1970.

Fifteen Rabbits, translated by Whittaker Chambers. With illustrations by John Freas. New York: Simon and Schuster, 1930. Reissued New York: Delacorte, 1976.

Florian, the Emperor's Stallion, translated by Erich Posselt and Michel Kraike. Indianapolis and New York: Bobbs-Merrill, 1934.

Perri: The Youth of a Squirrel, translated by Barrows Mussey. With illustrations by Ludwig Heinrich Jungnickel. Indianapolis and New York: Bobbs-Merrill, 1938.

Bambi's Children: The Story of a Forest Family, translated by Barthold Fles. Edited by R. Sugden Tilley. With illustrations by Erna Pinner. Indianapolis and New York: Bobbs-Merrill, 1939.

Renni the Rescuer; A Dog of the Battlefield, translated by Kenneth C. Kaufman. With illustrations by Diana Thorne. Indianapolis and New York: Bobbs-Merrill, 1940.

Walt Disney's Bambi. Retold by Idella Purnell. Boston: Heath, 1944.

Walt Disney's Bambi, adapted by Bob Grant from the Disney motion picture. New York: Simon and Schuster, 1948.

BIOGRAPHICAL AND CRITICAL STUDIES

Blount, Margaret. *Animal Land: The Creatures of Children's Fiction.* New York: William Morrow, 1975.

"Felix Salten." In *International Dictionary of Central European Emigrés 1933–1945.* Munich: K. G. Saur, 1983.

"Felix Salten." In *Something About the Author,* edited by Ann Commire. Detroit: Gale Research, 1971. Vol. 25, pp. 207–211.

"Felix Salten." In *Twentieth-Century Authors,* edited by Stanley Kunitz and Howard Haycraft. New York: H. W. Wilson Company, 1942.

—JILL P. MAY AND GORDON R. MORK

CARL SANDBURG
1878–1967

EVER SINCE CARL Sandburg first burst upon the literary scene with nine poems in the March 1914 issue of *Poetry: A Magazine of Verse*, critics have disagreed about his work. For example, although his poem "Chicago" shocked the traditionalists, it delighted the avant-garde of the day, who were trying to break away from conventional patterns and subjects. In time he became a public personality upon whom honors were heaped, but for all his life his work was controversial. This varied critical response has been true of his books for children as well as of his works for adults. The one thing all critics seem to agree upon is that his writing is peculiarly American and could not have been done by anyone less conscious of his country.

Of the eleven books by Sandburg published for children, only the three *Rootabaga* books—*Rootabaga Stories* (1922), *Rootabaga Pigeons* (1923), and *Potato Face* (1930)—are collections originally written specifically for young people. *Abe Lincoln Grows Up* (1928) and *Prairie-Town Boy* (1955) are taken from books written for adults; *Early Moon* (1930) and *Wind Song* (1960) are collections of poems, most of which were first published elsewhere, although some were composed for children. *Rootabaga Country* (1929) and *The Sandburg Treasury* (1970) are combinations of earlier books. *The Wedding Procession of the Rag Doll and the Broom Handle and Who Was in It* (1967) is a picture book made from one of the *Rootabaga* stories, and *Rainbows Are Made* (1982) is a selection by Lee Bennett Hopkins of seventy Sandburg poems, mostly from books originally published for adults, and organized into six sections, each introduced by one of the "Tentative Definitions of Poetry" from the thirty-eight that precede *Good Morning, America* (1928). *The American Songbag* (1927) and *The New American Songbag* (1950) are collections of folk songs published for adults, often used with children but never reprinted in special editions for them.

In *Always the Young Strangers* (1953), which came out on Sandburg's seventy-fifth birthday, he tells the story of his humble beginnings and his first twenty years. *Prairie-Town Boy*, published two years later and much shorter (and in many ways more readable), is not just a reduction of this long autobiography, but a rearrangement and a reordering of much of the material, with many of the stories about people from the area dropped and paragraphs from later chapters pulled into a more clearly chronological order. The result is a book that still gives a picture of the town on the plains of Illinois and the way of life in the late nineteenth century, but is more clearly focused on young Sandburg.

Sandburg was born on 6 January 1878 of Swedish immigrant parents in Galesburg, Illinois, the second child of seven and the oldest son. His father worked most of his life for fourteen cents an hour in the shops of the "Q," the Chicago, Burlington, and Quincy Railroad. An honest and undemonstrative man, he was kindly but never understood his son; never was able to pronounce the name "Charlie," which young Carl Sandburg adopted at six; never approved his son's passion for reading; and never agreed with his desire to write, asking disapprovingly, "Sholly, is there any money in this poetry business?" *Prairie-Town Boy* omits the most poignant episode concerning Sandburg's father: the story of the "sleeping mortgage" that came to light on a house he had bought in good faith. He had to pay it off with interest—an incident that changed him and made him suspicious that the American Dream was not for the foreign born. The children's book does describe the death of two younger brothers from diphtheria and Carl's closeness to his mother, his older sister, Mary, and his brother Mart. Two younger sisters are scarcely mentioned in either book. *Prairie-Town Boy* gives a good sense of Sandburg's hunger for learning; he had to stop school at eighth grade and pick up secondhand what he could from Mary's high-school textbooks. The book shows his restlessness, as he drifted from one job to another, went hoboing as far west as Colorado, and later joined the army during the Spanish-American War, which took him on a miserable long march in the Puerto Rican jungles where he fought mud, mosquitoes, and lice, but no enemy. The book ends with his return and his matriculation at Lombard College in Galesburg, where as a veteran he was offered a year's free tuition.

Prairie-Town Boy is not an exciting book, but it is simple and honest. Sandburg's biographer Richard Crowder calls the first autobiographical work, *Always the Young Strangers,* "unquestionably the best book" of the prose works; he points out that its effect comes from an unsentimental reporting of facts. Both books give a memorable picture of a small Midwestern American town in the last two decades of the nineteenth century, a picture drawn without sentimentality but with warmth and nostalgic humor and none of the satire of Sinclair Lewis and some other chroniclers of the Midwest.

Sandburg left Lombard College without graduating, but the experience was important in his life. There, with the encouragement of his favorite professor, Philip Green Wright, he started to put his thoughts on paper, and his first works were published at Wright's Asgard Press. In the next twelve years he worked as a reporter and a columnist on a variety of newspapers in Chicago, as a district organizer for the Social-Democratic party in Wisconsin, and as private secretary to the mayor of Milwaukee. He also met and married Lillian "Paula" Steichen, and their first two daughters, Margaret and Janet, were born.

With the publication of his first poems in *Poetry*

and, two years later, his first volume of poetry, *Chicago Poems* (1916), Sandburg became widely known in the literary world. He continued, however, to work on newspapers in Chicago until 1932 and to supplement his income with lectures and performances, always feeling a pressing need because another child, Helga, was born in 1920, Margaret had developed an epileptic condition, and Janet suffered debilitating headaches as the result of an accident. These problems made him feel responsible for supporting his two elder daughters for life, and poetry, as his father had suspected, did not pay well. In 1932 he moved to Harbert, Michigan, devoting all his time to writing and lecturing. In 1945 the family moved to Flat Rock, North Carolina, where Sandburg died in 1967. Throughout his long life he continued to write and to give public performances, winning many honors, including Pulitzer Prizes in both history and poetry. Nevertheless, the decade from 1922 to 1932 was in many ways the most fruitful. During this period, besides producing several volumes of poems, he wrote most of his most memorable children's books: all the *Rootabaga* books, *Abe Lincoln Grows Up, The American Songbag,* and *Early Moon.* Only *Prairie-Town Boy* and *Wind Song* were published later in his life.

Among the wider reading public, Sandburg's massive life of Lincoln is his best-known work. Strangely enough, he started this as a children's book. In a letter to his friend and biographer Harry Golden, he traces the evolution of the idea:

> While I was writing the *Rootabaga Stories* for children I got to thinking about the many biographies I had read in grade school. It came over me that there was not in the school libraries nor in the public libraries a book about Abraham Lincoln. . . . As I sat up to my typewriter I had in mind the young people who had listened to me in the *Rootabaga Stories* and I kept them somewhat in mind in the early chapters of the finished book, *Abraham Lincoln: The Prairie Years.*

Although he warned his publisher that "it might run a little longer" than the four hundred manuscript pages first discussed, he did not at first envision the long and detailed study of Lincoln's early years that was eventually published, much less the final six-volume biography that covers all of Lincoln's life.

The children's biography was not entirely forgotten: the first twenty-seven chapters of *Abraham Lincoln: The Prairie Years* (1926) were reduced to twenty-six and published in 1928 as *Abe Lincoln Grows Up.* The changes from the adult version are not great. Chapter 16 in *The Prairie Years,* about the illegitimate birth of Lincoln's mother, Nancy Hanks, and her cousin, Dennis Hanks, is omitted entirely. Most of the other omissions are of minor material that editors must have considered to be improper for children, including a description of frontier church services and hysterically religious women from chapter 1; several sentences about the trial of Lucy Hanks, Lincoln's grandmother, for "immoral tendencies" from chapter 2; several pages about hijinks indulged in by young Abe from chapter 15; the story of Mike Fink's threatening to shoot or burn his wife for making eyes at men on other boats from chapter 21; and a few phrases and one long paragraph in which rape is mentioned from chapter 22. For the most part, however, Sandburg's picture of the boy Lincoln is the same for children as it is for adults.

Perhaps this picture is more true to Sandburg's boyhood than to Lincoln's. In his own autobiography he is continually recalling his wonder and puzzlement over the meaning of words. In *Abe Lincoln Grows Up* he portrays Lincoln as having the same curiosity:

> Words like "independent" bothered the boy. He was hungry to understand the meanings of words. He would ask what "independent" meant and when he was told the meaning he lay awake nights thinking about the meaning of the meaning of "independent." Other words bothered him, such as "predestination." He asked the meaning of that and lay awake hours at night thinking about the meaning of the meaning.

In *Prairie-Town Boy* he tells of how he learned to recognize his first printed words from the Swedish-language Bible:

> Mary and I heard father read a chapter by the light of a small kerosene lamp. Several times that week I went to where the Book lay on the top of a bureau, and I opened it and turned the pages. I asked my mother to point out certain words I remembered.

He pictures young Abe in much the same way:

> How many times he had gone to the family Bible, opened the big front cover, and peeped in at the page which tells what the book is! . . . And then pages and pages filled with words spelled out like the words in the spelling-book he had in school. So many words: heavy words—mysterious words!

Some critics have found the Lincoln biography overly fictionalized and romantic. It is true that Sandburg occasionally lapses into rhapsodic paragraphs, like the last in chapter 14:

> In the short and simple annals of the poor, it seems there are people who breathe with the earth and take into their lungs and blood some of the hard and dark strength of its mystery. During six and seven months each year in the twelve fiercest formative years of his life, Abraham Lincoln had the pads of his foot-soles bare against clay of the earth. It may be the earth told him in her own tough gypsy slang one or two knacks of living worth keeping. To be organic with running wildfire and quiet rain, both of the same moment, is to be the carrier of wave-lines the earth gives up only on hard usage.

Most of the book, however, is factual and full of specific detail. No conversations, he says, have been quoted that he did not hear from or read about in reliable sources. Much of the information comes from public records, from firsthand view of the country described, and from the memories of men and women who had known Lincoln personally. If occasionally it sounds semiautobiographical, it may be that he and Lincoln had much in common. Among the many biographies of Lincoln now available to young people, Sandburg's still ranks with the best, not only for its portrait of a great man in his formative years but also for the sense it gives of America at the time, of the way the pioneers in the Midwest lived, talked, suffered, and played.

In 1927 Sandburg published another peculiarly American book, *The American Songbag.* Although not primarily for children, this collection of folk songs is often used as a source book for young people's study of both music and ballad. The original impetus for the compilation came in the period when Sandburg was bumming his way around the country, riding the rails and sleeping in hobo jungles. He had played the guitar from the time he was a young man, and he picked up lyrics and tunes wherever he went, later incorporating them into his lecture programs. Interest in the American folk song had already been awakened by John Lomax and other field collectors, but Sandburg's collection supplemented their work and reached a wider audience. Frequently those who attended his programs contributed other songs and readers sent songs from their own localities and occupations. In 1950 a revision, with many additions, was published as *The New American Songbag.*

From the first Sandburg's own poems have aroused great admiration and great scorn, but none of his critics has denied that they are distinctively American and that many of them are strongly reflective of his Midwestern background. The two collections for children he assembled, *Early Moon* and *Wind Song,* contain poems that are generally shorter than the average in his adult books, but that otherwise exhibit both the strengths and weaknesses of his poetry as a whole.

Although he claimed not to have any connection with the Imagists, many of the poems in these two books are clearly imagistic, with what Crowder calls their "emphasis on single-minded clarity" showing "no effort to comment," in the pattern adopted from Oriental verse by many poets of the period. Typical are his much-anthologized "Fog" and "Lost" and the less often reprinted "Nocturn Cabbage," "Goldwing Moth," and "Splinter":

> The voice of the last cricket
> across the first frost
> is one kind of good-by.
> It is so thin a splinter of singing.

As Mark Van Doren, one of Sandburg's most perceptive critics, points out, Sandburg "feels free only when he thinks he has escaped from form. He seems to have known nothing about the freedom that flows from mastery of form." Although some of his early verses, before *Chicago Poems,* are in regular meter and rhyme, he typically rejected metrical form. All the poems in *Early Moon* and *Wind Song* are in free verse. Van Doren observes that the rhythm is the rhythm of prose, but "the rhythm was there, and in a sufficient number of cases it was so distinctly and powerfully there that we never hesitated to call him a poet."

Sometimes the prose rhythm is effective and sometimes it is not. Among the poems most often anthologized for children are some that can only be described as prosy and unmusical, most notably "Arithmetic," "Little Girl, Be Careful What You Say," "Boxes and Bags," "Paper I," and "Paper II." When the prose rhythm works, however, it can be powerful, as in "Buffalo Dusk":

> The buffaloes are gone.
> And those who saw the buffaloes are gone.
> Those who saw the buffaloes by thousands
>   and how they pawed the prairie sod
>   into dust with their hoofs, their
>   great heads down pawing on in a great
>   pageant of dusk,
> Those who saw the buffaloes are gone.
> And the buffaloes are gone.

(Early Moon)

Frequently, as in "Buffalo Dusk," the rhythm works by repetition in a circular pattern. "Milk-White Moon, Put the Cows to Sleep" starts by repeating the title and ends, a dozen lines later, "Put the cows to sleep, milk-white moon. / Put the cows to sleep." Similarly, in "Evening Waterfall," which describes a waterfall of warblers' songs in the dusk, the opening lines are repeated at the end: "What was the name you called me?— / And why did you go so soon?"

Sandburg admired Walt Whitman and often seems to be striving for a Whitmanesque effect, as in "Ripe Corn," "Hits and Runs," and the longer poem "Lines Written for Gene Kelly to Dance To." This last also illustrates his inclination for picking subjects that were not formerly considered appropriate for poems, like "New Farm Tractor," which starts: "Snub nose, the guts of twenty mules are in your cylinders and transmission."

Somewhat more jarring is his propensity for slang, a habit that annoyed even Amy Lowell, whose enthusiasm for Sandburg's work during his early period was influential in getting him accepted in the literary world. Nothing dates faster than slang, and when it is out of date it seems embarrassingly self-conscious. Take, for instance, "Phizzog," which starts: "This face you got, / This here phizzog you carry around, / You never picked it out for yourself, at all, at all—did you?"

In the years since their first publication, the poems from both *Early Moon* and *Wind Song* have consistently appeared in anthologies for children, as have selections from *Abe Lincoln Grows Up.* This is not true of the *Rootabaga* tales. Such widely used collections as Johnson, Sickels, and Sayers' *Anthology of Children's Literature* did not include a selection until the fourth edition in 1970; the *Arbuthnot Anthology* in its several editions had no example, although its successor, *The Scott, Foresman Anthology of Children's Literature,* published in 1984, contains "How They Bring Back the Village of Cream Puffs

When the Wind Blows It Away." It is hard to tell whether this reflects a renewal of interest in the stories or just the personal taste of the compilers. Like most of Sandburg's other writing, the *Rootabaga* tales have always had strongly partisan supporters and detractors.

Even when the first volume, *Rootabaga Stories,* was published in 1922, it received widely varying evaluations. A writer in the *Literary Review* called it "a most delightful book," and one in the *New York Tribune* said: "It is like no other book. It is nonsensical and wise; it is laughing and serious; it is crude and polished; it has the windiness of the prairies and the stillness of blue mist and mountains. It makes America thrilling." The critic in the *Survey* was equally enthusiastic, saying that the stories are shaped by "shrewd humor and real thought" and adding that "the poet gave them . . . the quality of folk-fables, of folk-ballads, a quality that is at the same time irrepressibly, reprehensibly American."

At the same time, other periodicals panned the book. The reviewer in the *Nation* asked indignantly, "What shall the intelligent child make of this?" and sourly commented, "Perhaps this is funny: 'The zizzy is a bug. He runs zigzag on zigzag legs, eats zigzag with zigzag teeth, and spits zigzag with a zigzag tongue.' " The reviewer in the *Dial* said flatly, "They do not come off," and, after a highly negative description, decided that the stories "turn out, when all is over, not to mean a great deal." The same sharp divergence of opinion also greeted *Rootabaga Pigeons,* published the following year, and *Potato Face,* a smaller collection published in 1930.

Of major modern critics of children's literature, only John Rowe Townsend devotes more than a passing mention to the stories, and even he treats the stories as if they were all of a kind, without noticing, or at least without explaining, that they vary greatly both in quality and kind. Some are what later became known as "shaggy dog" stories, tales with no point or discernible meaning. Some follow folktale patterns; others have a strong, almost fablelike theme; some are thoughtful, others silly; some are slangy and haphazard, others poetic.

All the *Rootabaga* tales share an essentially oral character. Originally, they *were* oral, stories told by Sandburg to his three daughters. He described their genesis to Harry Golden: "The children asked questions, and I answered them." Another friend, May Massee, then editor for the American

Library Association Booklist, however, was helping get the tales into readable shape, and saw beyond this apparent ease of composition: "Carl has never worked so hard on anything; he's been doing them for several years but has only just got them to the point where he's willing to let go." By 1921 he was incorporating three or four into the recitals and lectures that he frequently gave to supplement his salary. Many of them are structured as stories within stories, stories told by the Potato Face Blind Man or occasionally by other characters. Sometimes they are even presented as stories within stories within stories, that is, as stories that a character tells which another character has told to him. These frames add to the oral quality, as do the frequent repetitions, the zany names—Gimme the Ax, the Village of Cream Puffs, Dippy the Wisp, Slip Me Liz, Bozo the Button Buster—and the non sequiturs that create a sense of spontaneity.

Typically, the Potato Face Blind Man, who used to play an accordion on the Main Street corner nearest the post office in the Village of Liver-and-Onions, is approached by one or more girls who ask him questions, and he tells them a story. There is a warm, affectionate tone to most of these encounters, as in "Moonlight, Spiders, Rats and Elephants," from *Potato Face:*

> Three girls came skipping along trying to make foot tracks in the moonlight as if it were snow. And they spoke to the Potato Face Blind Man sitting in front of the post office. They told him about the moonlight and the white wool clouds.
>
> They said, "We are the Balloon sisters. Our father is the balloon man who makes the balloons."
>
> The Potato Face said he had been wondering for a long time who makes the balloons and he was glad to meet the Balloon sisters.

"How Pink Peony Sent Spuds, the Ballplayer, up to Pick Four Moons," from *Rootabaga Pigeons,* ends: "So the Potato Face came to a finish with his story. Blixie Bimber kissed him good night on the nose, saying, 'You loosened up beautiful tonight.' " The names of the girls vary, but the tone is much the same in story after story.

Some of the tales have stronger structures than others. "How Bimbo the Snip's Thumb Stuck to His Nose When the Wind Changed," from *Rootabaga Stories,* is in the traditional cumulative story pattern: Bimbo's father, Bevo the Hike, finding his son in the predicament described in the title, sends for the ward alderman, who sends for the barn boss of the street-cleaning department, who sends for the head vaccinator of the health department, who sends for the big main fixer of the weather bureau, who advises them to hit the thumb six times with the end of a traffic policeman's club. The policeman can't leave his post unless a monkey comes to take his place; the monkey cannot direct traffic without a ladder and a whistle; an old widow directs Bevo to an umbrella handle maker, who will not lend his ladder and whistle unless they can be back in time for a special job that night, and so on.

Several other stories employ the device of a magic token that produces marvellous happenings for whoever owns it. These include "The Story of Blixie Bimber and the Power of the Gold Buckskin Whincher," "The Story of Jason Squiff and Why He Had a Popcorn Hat, Popcorn Mittens, and Popcorn Shoes," and "The Story of Rags Habakuk, the Two Blue Rats, and the Circus Man Who Came with Spot Cash Money," all in *Rootabaga Stories.* Another story that has a recognizable pattern from traditional fantasy literature is "Three Boys with Jugs of Molasses and Secret Ambitions" in *Rootabaga Stories,* a story in which the boys, playing in spilled molasses, become small as potato bugs and have adventures in a miniature land under the potato plants until they are sprayed with Paris green and regain their original size.

A few of the tales have strong themes and, in spite of their nonsense, are didactic in purpose, if not in tone. Both "The Spink Bug and the Hunk" in *Potato Face* and "How Two Sweetheart Dippies Sat in the Moonlight on a Lumberyard Fence and Heard About the Sooners and the Boomers" in *Rootabaga Pigeons* are actually antiwar fables. The spink bug is covered with white splashes and black alphabets, while the hunk is covered with white spots and black numbers, so naturally they hate each other. As they talk over plans for their fight, however, they discover they are more alike than different, so they part, each agreeing to write the other "a letter sometimes in the gloaming when the thoughts come." The sooners and the boomers do have a war, several wars, in fact, the first to decide whether the pigs should be painted pink or green, the next to decide whether the pigs should be painted checks or stripes, and others to decide about such momentous subjects as "whether telegraph pole climbers must eat onions at noon with spoons, or whether dishwashers must keep their

money in pig's ears with padlocks pinched on with pincers." Eventually the sooners and the boomers are all lost or scattered and the pigs are all gone, so the wars end.

The distinguishing quality of the *Rootabaga* tales is their language. Sometimes the fun arises from wordplay, as in "The Huckabuck Family and How They Raised Popcorn in Nebraska and Quit and Came Back," from *Rootabaga Pigeons:*

> The next year came. It was the proudest of all. This was the year Jonas Jonas Huckabuck and his family lived in Elgin, Illinois, and Jonas Jonas was a watchman in a watch factory watching the watches.
>
> "I know where you have been," Mama Mama Huckabuck would say of an evening to Pony Pony Huckabuck. "You have been down to the watch factory watching your father watch the watches."
>
> "Yes," said Pony Pony. "Yes, and this evening when I was watching father watch the watches in the watch factory, I looked over my left shoulder and I saw a policeman with a star and brass buttons, and he was watching me to see if I was watching Father watch the watches in the watch factory."

Some critics have compared the stories to Kipling's *Just So Stories for Little Children* (1902), and there is an occasional resemblance. In the last tale in *Rootabaga Stories,* "How the Animals Lost Their Tails and Got Them Back Traveling from Philadelphia to Medicine Hat," the animals form a committee to deal with their problem:

> So the Committee of Sixty-Six had a meeting and a parleyhoo to decide what steps could be taken by talking to do something. For chairman they picked an old flongboo who was an umpire and used to umpire many mix-ups. . . . He was from Massachusetts, born near Chappaquiddick, this old flongboo, and he lived there in a horse chestnut tree six feet thick halfway between South Hadley and Northampton.

The rhythm is similar to Kipling's in, for example, "How the Rhinoceros Got His Skin" and the purpose, to provide the pleasure of repetitious, sonorous nonsense phrases rolling off the tongue, is similar to that in Kipling's "How the Camel Got His Hump" and "How the Whale Got His Throat." Most of the *Rootabaga* tales, though, seem less carefully planned and more extemporaneously told.

As in his poems, Sandburg sometimes uses contemporary slang in the stories. Gimme the Ax in the first of the *Rootabaga Stories* sells everything he owns for "spot cash money"; Ezekiel the spotted rat in *Potato Face* says, "I seen what I seen, that's what I seen, you big gazook." In "How Hot Balloons and His Pigeon Daughters Crossed Over into the Rootabaga Country," from *Rootabaga Pigeons,* Sandburg revels in slang:

> "I'll say it's a hot job," said the gringo, answering the snoox.
>
> "We'll give this one the merry razoo," said the snoox to the gringo, working overtime and double time.
>
> "Yes, we'll put her to the cleaners and shoot her into high," said the gringo, answering the snoox, working overtime and double time.

Just as often, the stories, despite their nonsense, have a poetic quality, a feeling for the beauty of the prairies and the wide-open spaces of the American Midwest. At the opening of "How Dippy the Wisp and Slip Me Liz Came in the Moonshine Where the Potato Face Blind Man Sat with His Accordion," in *Rootabaga Pigeons,* it has just rained:

> And after the rain, the sky shook loose a moon so a moonshine came with gold on the rainpools.
>
> And a west wind came out of the west sky and shook the moonshine on the tops of the rainpools.
>
> Dippy the Wisp and Slip Me Liz came, two tough pony girls, two limber prairie girls, in the moonshine humming little humpty dumpty songs.

One of the most poetic of the *Rootabaga Stories,* and a favorite of many readers, is the romance of the White Horse Girl, who "rode one horse white as snow, another white as new-washed sheep wool, and another white as . . . a silver ribbon of the new moon," and the Blue Wind Boy, who "liked to walk with his feet in the dirt and the grass listening to the winds." The two lovers set off together "to go where the white horses come from and where the blue winds begin."

Some critics and some children find the *Rootabaga* tales silly and their nonsense tiresome and repetitious. Others delight in their playfulness and consider the books enduring classics. As with virtually all of Sandburg's writing, however, they agree that the stories are undeniably American. The reviewer in the *New York Times* in 1922 said of *Rootabaga Stories:*

> Carl Sandburg . . . has gone to the American prairies, to the Middle West towns and cities, to the great American corn belt, and conceived a series of tales that smack mightily of American soil. Even to the cadences of his prose . . . the reader will find an American spirit. Such tales . . . could have been conceived in no other locale than the United States.

Except for E. B. White's *Charlotte's Web* (1952) and possibly L. Frank Baum's *Oz* books (1900–1919), both quite different sorts of stories, this could have been said of no other American fantasies until very recent times. For that contribution alone, Sandburg must be considered historically important. For his tales, poems, folk songs, biographies, and autobiographies for young people, all American in an essential way, he deserves a prominent place in the history of children's literature.

Selected Bibliography

WORKS OF CARL SANDBURG

Chicago Poems. New York: Holt, 1916.

Rootabaga Stories. With illustrations by Maud and Miska Petersham. New York: Harcourt, Brace, 1922.

Rootabaga Pigeons. With illustrations by Maud and Miska Petersham. New York: Harcourt, Brace, 1923.

Abraham Lincoln: The Prairie Years 2 vols. New York: Harcourt, Brace, 1926.

The American Songbag. New York: Harcourt, Brace, 1927.

Abe Lincoln Grows Up. With illustrations by James Daugherty. New York: Harcourt, Brace, 1928.

Good Morning, America. New York: Harcourt, Brace, 1928.

Rootabaga Country. With illustrations by Peggy Bacon. New York: Harcourt, Brace, 1929.

Early Moon. With illustrations by James Daugherty. New York: Harcourt, Brace, 1930.

Potato Face. New York: Harcourt, Brace, 1930.

The New American Songbag. New York: Broadcast Music, 1950.

Always the Young Strangers. New York: Harcourt, Brace, 1953.

Prairie-Town Boy. New York: Harcourt, Brace, 1955.

Wind Song. New York: With illustrations by William A. Smith. Harcourt, Brace, 1960.

The Wedding Procession of the Rag Doll and the Broom Handle and Who Was in It. With illustrations by Harriet

Pincus. New York: Harcourt, Brace, and World, 1967.

The Sandburg Treasury. With illustrations by Paul Bacon. New York: Harcourt Brace Jovanovich, 1970.

Rainbows Are Made. Edited by Lee Bennett Hopkins. With illustrations by Fritz Eichenberg. New York: Harcourt Brace Jovanovich, 1982.

CRITICAL AND BIOGRAPHICAL STUDIES

Crowder, Richard. *Carl Sandburg.* New York: Twayne, 1964.

Golden, Harry. *Carl Sandburg.* Cleveland and New York: World, 1961.

Sandburg, Helga. *A Great and Glorious Romance: The Story of Carl Sandburg and Lillian Steichen.* New York: Harcourt Brace Jovanovich, 1978.

Townsend, John Rowe. *Written for Children: An Outline of English-Language Children's Literature.* Rev. ed. Philadelphia and New York: Lippincott, 1974.

Van Doren, Mark. *Carl Sandburg, With a Bibliography of Sandburg Materials in the Collections of the Library of Congress.* Washington, D.C.: Library of Congress, 1969.

—AGNES REGAN PERKINS

RUTH SAWYER

1880–1970

RUTH SAWYER CAME by her storytelling talent quite naturally. Her grandmother, the Lucinda Wyman for whom a character in three of Sawyer's autobiographical novels is named, sang ballads to her husband's fifing while she washed the dinner dishes. Sawyer's father often read aloud to his children from the works of Robert Louis Stevenson and Mark Twain, and her mother sang ballads to her and read from the Bible, rejoicing in the sheer wonder of the ancient stories and in the great beauty of their resonant language. The influence of Sawyer's Irish nurse, Johanna, was also powerful. Her accounts of fairies and wee men from her native Donegal awakened in the intelligent and imaginative child the love for traditional tales and the pleasure in storytelling that were to direct her life. The strong Irish flavor of much of Sawyer's work also attests to the strength of Johanna's influence.

Sawyer was the youngest child by several years and the only daughter of the five children of Francis Milton Sawyer, an importer, and Ethelinda Smith Sawyer. Both her parents were of respected New England stock. She was born on 5 August 1880 in Boston, but grew up near Central Park on New York's Upper East Side. The family spent summers in their cottage at Haddock Harbor on the coast of Maine, a place that held great joy for Sawyer and that, like her New York home, frequently served as a setting in her books. Later in her life Sawyer recalled her childhood as a happy time. She often tagged after her older brothers; the very warm, real, and attractive boy protagonists in her books probably derive from her memories of the close

relationships she had with them. From her earliest years family life was important to her.

Her father, who was often abroad on buying trips, died when Sawyer was fourteen. She knew him less well than she did her tiny, fun-loving, outgoing mother, whose influence on her life and work was much stronger. Her mother and her mother's prim and proper relatives provided prototypes for the characters in Sawyer's stories. Since Sawyer's mother often accompanied her father abroad, Johanna, the Irish nurse, assumed a significant position in the child's life. She was to be replicated in Sawyer's stories as a nurse, a housekeeper, or a similar selfless mother figure who nurtures, sustains, and puts others ahead of herself. These are also the qualities that epitomize femininity in Sawyer's original writings.

Sawyer was educated at a private school in New York City and then attended the Garland Kindergarten Training School in Boston for two years. Fired with enthusiasm, she left Boston at age twenty to help organize kindergartens in Cuba for orphans of the Spanish-American War. It was there that her career was launched. The storytelling and story collecting she did in Cuba won her a scholarship to Columbia University, where she studied folklore and storytelling, receiving a B.S. in education from Teachers College in 1904. She began storytelling professionally for the New York Public Lecture Bureau in 1908, telling stories in schools and missions, for the foreign born and for those down on their luck and in trouble. She started the storytelling program in the New York Public Li-

511

brary in 1910. She describes these experiences vividly in her book about storytelling, *The Way of the Storyteller* (1942).

At the same time she began doing features for the *New York Sun*. While on assignment in Ireland in 1905, and again in 1907, she collected Irish tales. She sold her first Irish story to the *Atlantic Monthly* in 1905. Listening to the *seanachies* (traditional Irish tale tellers) in Ireland further attuned her mind, ear, and heart to the flavor and spirit of true traditional storytelling, reinforced her affection for Irish stories, and undoubtedly contributed to the distinctive authenticity of her story collections and her written narrative style.

In 1911 she married Dr. Albert Durand, an ophthalmologist, and went to live in Ithaca, New York. The couple had two children—a son, David, born in 1912, and a daughter, Margaret, born in 1916. Margaret became the wife of Robert McCloskey, the illustrator with whom Sawyer collaborated on her Southern-mountain runaway pancake story, *Journey Cake, Ho!* (1953). The Durand home in Ithaca became a social center for students, where they often also welcomed eminent visitors. Like the Sawyers, the Durands enjoyed doing things as a family; in particular, their summers in Maine and their Christmases were special occasions for celebration, as they also are in Sawyer's books.

Even after she became an established writer, Sawyer continued to lecture on the subject of storytelling and to tell stories for universities, the government, and various other groups and agencies. She made collecting trips to Spain and other parts of Europe and to South America and Mexico. The result of all this activity was a rich outpouring of more than two hundred short stories, articles, tales, poems, and books. The Durands later settled at "Gull Rock" in Hancock, Maine, where Sawyer died on 3 June 1970, leaving behind a rich legacy of written and oral stories that bear eloquent witness to her ability to convey the emotional power of a narrative.

Sawyer's writing career spanned over fifty years, nearly every one of which saw the appearance of a novel, a picture book, a collection of stories, or a record of personal experience. The years before 1936, or the first half of her writing life, were mostly devoted to producing adult works, including a book of stories, a dozen romances and domestic novels, and many magazine articles and short stories. Formulaic success stories, her adult novels

enjoyed only ephemeral popularity. They tell the stories of young women who succeed in careers or overcome adversity through hard work and considerable luck, have a series of love affairs, and eventually settle down to appropriately domestic lives with virtuous young men who have proved themselves worthy of love. Sentimental, episodic, and filled with improbable coincidences and conventional characters, these novels promote old-fashioned virtues and traditional morality for women. Such contemporary reviewers' comments as "delightful," "charming fairy tale," "abundance of sugar," "welcome relief from the sordid," and "moral is rather obtrusive" still aptly describe the immediate impact of Sawyer's adult novels.

Typical is *Leerie* (1920), a hospital story. Like Leerie the lamplighter in Stevenson's poem "The Lamplighter," Sawyer's Sheila O'Leary, a dedicated, spirited young nurse, brings light into the lives of those around her. After energetically coping with several particularly trying cases, she feels a strong call to go to France to help with the war effort. There she amply demonstrates her heroism and skill and then returns to marry her sweetheart, grateful that she has had the chance to give her best to her countrymen. The development of Leerie's romance and the unraveling of the mystery about her expulsion from the hospital give a tenuous unity and some spice to the episodes detailing Leerie's unselfish devotion and inventive service. The message the *Catholic World* reviewer found in the book, that "happiness comes from making others happy," is repeated in Sawyer's other adult novels. Other dominant themes in her adult work include the importance of individual perseverance, the value of home and family, and the evils of accumulating wealth; these themes recur in her juvenile work.

The settings of Sawyer's early adult books foreshadow those she uses in her later juvenile fiction: various university towns, New York City, Boston, Ireland, Maine, Haddock Harbor. *Gallant: The Story of Storm Veblen* (1936) is set at Haddock Harbor and narrates the story of the daughter of Norwegian immigrants who wins a journalism scholarship to go to New York City and eventually marries her crippled childhood sweetheart. Set partially in the same place is *Gladiola Murphy* (1923), which traces the adventures of the daughter of a family of ne'er-do-wells, who runs away to Boston and becomes a lady. The same character appears in

Sawyer's later juvenile works, in *The Year of Jubilo* (1940) and again in *Maggie Rose* (1952), as the title character.

The selfless nurse Nora Kelley, narrator of *Herself, Himself and Myself* (1917), is drawn from Johanna, Sawyer's childhood nurse. Other spinoffs of this character are vigorous Patsy O'Connell, the Irish actress in *Seven Miles to Arden* (1915), an overextended pun on Shakespeare, and indomitable old Bridhe Donnoghue of *The Luck of the Road* (1934), an improvisation on the German folktale "The Bremen Town Musicians." The mingling of pathos and humor, the embedding of extant folk stories into a larger narrative, the strong Irish tone, and the sense of play are still other characteristic features of Sawyer's work that also appear later in her stories for the young.

Sawyer's early works for children have not endured any more successfully than her early works for adults. *This Way to Christmas* (1916), however, along with *Maggie Rose*, enjoys a brief renaissance each year at Christmastime for its colorful evocation of the old-fashioned Yuletide spirit. Broadly autobiographical, the sentimental *This Way to Christmas* tells how young David goes to stay with his former nurse, Johanna, and her husband, Barney, in the New England mountains while his parents are in Europe during the war. Accompanied by an Irish fairy man, he encounters neighbors, among them a German flagman, a black lumber camp cook, and a gypsy trapper, who tell him stories from the folklore of their native regions.

The Tale of the Enchanted Bunnies (1923), another fantasy, describes the good times two little children have when a collection of china bunnies comes alive at the top of the world. The plot wears on as the various characters tell the stories of their lives, with Sawyer clearly straining to produce the kind of amusing, uplifting, wholesome story that readers of her day deemed appropriate for children. Today few people read *A Child's Year-Book* (1917), a dozen short lyrics for young children. The mechanical and uninspired verses are decorated with Sawyer's own cutouts, making it an attractive, if slight and dated, specialty book.

Some of Sawyer's later writing also seems contrived and overly sentimental. Her interest in the British royal house is evident in *Maggie Rose*, where she borrows a princess's name for her sturdy protagonist, and in *A Cottage for Betsy* (1954), where she evidently sympathizes with the newly married Princess Elizabeth's need for a private life free of royal responsibilities. The first story concerns the efforts of the eight-year-old third child of the shiftless Bunker family to have a proper celebration for her birthday on Christmas Eve, one that will not "shame Him." Quite predictably, the child's efforts incite her slovenly parents to clean up their lives. The second story, *A Cottage for Betsy*, is a romantic fairy tale that follows the adventures of a young queen and her loving and sensible consort, Michael, in a kingdom reminiscent of Ireland. With the help of an understanding prime minister, they steal away in disguise to a cottage by the sea. There their friendship with some children brings about a reconciliation between the villagers and an embittered, ostracized former sailor.

Sawyer wrote two novels about boys whose experiences improve their characters. *Old Con and Patrick* (1946) has a strong Irish flavor and is even more sentimental, wholesome, and uplifting than the previous two stories. Ten-year-old Patrick Boyle, paralyzed from polio, feels sorry for himself until with the help of Old Con, his grandfather, and Bill the Birdman, an ornithologist, he learns to use his head and his hands again. He wins a prize for his drawings of wildlife. The plot of *The Little Red Horse* (1950) is awkwardly structured. In this story, five-year-old Michael, reluctantly vacationing with his parents in Florida, is told he may not have the little red toy horse that belongs to Granny, the lady who owns the Island Inn. Michael overcomes his fear of the sea, finds a prize shell, and then, after taking the little red horse, inexplicably gives it to the ocean. Sawyer's characters are often hollow, her incidents contrived, but, as in her adult novels, the storytelling exerts a distinct charm. If Sawyer's muse occasionally failed to inspire her with original ideas, it still endowed her with considerable narrative skill.

Those children's books that arose out of Sawyer's personal experiences at home and abroad have justly enjoyed greater popularity than most of her early work. Her trip to Spain in 1931–1932 inspired *Toño Antonio* (1934), the amusing story of a boy who travels to Málaga with a herd of playful goats after his family has come upon hard times. Based upon a chance meeting with a shepherd boy at a bakery shop, *Toño Antonio* has a valid and compelling motivation, conveys a strong sense of the pre–Civil War Spanish countryside, and captures the indomitability of the Spanish character, features that more than make up for the patness of the book's conclusion.

The Least One (1941), a story about the close relationship between Paco, the son of a Mexican burden-bearer, and his little gray burro, Chiquitico, the youngest and least esteemed of his father's pack animals, grew out of the affection Sawyer developed for the small, spirited boys she met while collecting tales in Mexico. Desolate when his beloved burro disappears, Paco prays to the good San Francisco, patron of animals, and, at the feast of the blessing of the animals, his burro miraculously reappears. One of the most appealing of Sawyer's books, this warm, genuine account of the home life, religious customs, and social attitudes of Mexican peasants is told in a simple, straightforward style that uses the cadences of Mexican speech. *The Least One* was selected by UNESCO for translation into several languages. Like *Toño Antonio*, the story is strengthened by an effective use of setting, a faithful representation of the nature of little boys, and a magnetic language based on vocal rhythms and inflections.

Less successful than these works but still more convincing than her earlier books are *The Enchanted Schoolhouse* (1956) and *The Year of the Christmas Dragon* (1960)——possibly because both stories use folkloric material. In the first, an Irish fairy man accompanies young Brian Boru when he emigrates to Maine and helps the children of Lobster Cove get a new schoolhouse. The second story exhibits a similar joy in story for story's own sake, telling about a little Chinese boy who tames a dragon with rice cakes and then rides him across the Pacific to Mexico. It is an active and amusing tale that also purports to explain why some Mexicans have Asian features and why Chinese paper dragons appear in Latin-American festivals.

Among the most highly acclaimed of Sawyer's writings for the young are the two autobiographical novels *Roller Skates* (1936), for which she won the John Newbery Medal, and its sequel, *The Year of Jubilo*. In *Roller Skates*, Sawyer uses a persona, the free-spirited ten-year-old Lucinda Wyman, to record vividly and sensitively the year she spent with the genteel Misses Peters in the 1890's while her parents were traveling in Europe. Lucinda spends her time on skates, whizzing around New York City and involving herself in the lives of the people she meets, most of whom are drawn from real life.

The large, assorted, and skillfully drawn cast of characters includes Patrick Gilligan, the warm and expansive Irish hansom-cab driver; the Browdowskis, a struggling young couple whose pretty four-year-old daughter, Trinket, dies; Mr. Night Owl, a reporter for the *New York Sun*; domineering, stuffy, and proper Aunt Emily and her meek and prissy daughters; young Tony Coppino, who runs his father's fruit stand and whom Lucinda assists against vandals; and, in particular, perceptive, kind-hearted, diplomatic Uncle Earle, who dubs Lucinda "Snoodie," rescues her from Aunt Emily's improving clutches, and introduces her to Shakespeare. A dynamic and sturdy character, Lucinda learns to reach out to people, gains some control over her restlessness and impulsiveness, and acquires a better self-image.

This very entertaining, occasionally humorous, and sometimes melodramatic novel comes alive with the sights, smells, and sounds of the city and with the vividly drawn, thoroughly engaging heroine. The ethnic characters are presented without condescension or exaggeration; the dialogue rings true; and the episodes, if occasionally too cliché or fortuitous, move rapidly and project a joy of living that builds as the story progresses. Although some adults complained because the book portrays the death of a child and a murder, subjects then deemed unsuitable for a story of family and neighborhood life, both events are tastefully handled and their melodrama, and that of other incidents as well, seems true to the point of view of a somewhat protected, healthily imaginative child of Lucinda's years and social class. Many references to familiar classics and cultural functions add a strong literary flavor and a good historical sense of the period. If dated, the book carries the conviction of actual lived experience, conveyed in just the right words by an accomplished storyteller.

The Year of Jubilo takes Lucinda to Maine, after Mr. Wyman's business fails and he dies. Lucinda, now almost fourteen, her three older brothers, and their mother, whom they affectionately call Grasshopper, move to their cottage at Haddock Harbor on Penobscot Bay. Their main problem is survival, and as they cope with their straitened circumstances, they grow closer as a family, develop new spiritual and economic resources, and have some lively times as well. They come to call this time together their Year of Jubilo, for an old song they often sing together.

The story is told from Lucinda's point of view and shows her slowly, and sometimes painfully, leaving behind her "Wymans' Tag" reputation and gaining acceptance as a person in her own right. She pluckily applies herself to learning to cook, makes friends with the haunting, preternaturally wise young Gladiola Murphy, and gradually, if reluctantly, comes to terms with her superior and bossy older brother. Staunch Maine natives parade through the story and help to ground it in reality. But some episodes are unlikely, and some are excessively sentimental; life never seems quite as hard for the Wymans as it must have been for the Sawyers. *The Year of Jubilo* seems to have been concocted primarily to provide wholesome, uplifting reading for young adolescent girls and to illustrate such virtues as obedience, hard work, self-control, and confidence in the future. Compared with the sprightly *Roller Skates, The Year of Jubilo* lacks conviction, even if it is true to this stage in Lucinda's life.

Daddles: The Story of a Plain Hound-Dog (1964) is also about the Wymans. Published two dozen years after *The Year of Jubilo*, it describes for younger readers two years in the life of eight-year-old Lucinda, called by her nickname Snoodie, and Peterkin, her older brother. While vacationing at Haddock Harbor, they adopt Daddles, a nondescript beagle hound of which they become very fond. The dog joins them in adventures in the countryside, some with neighbors met earlier in *The Year of Jubilo*. This is a pleasant story. Its narrative has a quiet credibility and makes use of some of Sawyer's stock settings, incidents, characters, and themes: the circus; the silent, secluded thinking place in the woods; music and singing among family and close friends; the shiftless local family; and the importance of obedience, responsibility, and family ties.

In addition to her creative writing, Sawyer maintained her interests in storytelling and story collecting. *Picture Tales from Spain* (1936) consists of eleven vivid and humorous traditional stories found on her trip to Spain in 1931–1932. Among them are such Sawyer favorites as "The Frog," "The Terrible Carlanco," "Chick, Chick, Halfachick," "La Hormiguita and Perez the Mouse," and one especially loved, "The Flea," a tale she herself told with such gusto and affection that it has become permanently linked with her name.

Her spirited version of the traditional Southernmountain pancake story, *Journey Cake, Ho!*, illustrated with sly humor by Robert McCloskey, remains dear to the hearts of younger children. Worthy of more attention than it has received is

Dietrich of Berne and the Dwarf King Laurin (1963), a collection of traditional stories she found in the Tyrol, lovingly and knowledgeably assembled from fragmentary sources to present a unified account of stalwart Theodoric the Great, an emperor of Rome in the fifth century.

Sawyer especially enjoyed the Christmas season, and two of her collections of folktales are perennial holiday favorites: *The Long Christmas* (1941) and *Joy to the World* (1966). The first book contains thirteen tales from eight European countries and an equal number of ballads and carols, arranged to parallel the celebration of "long Christmas," which in old England and other parts of Europe lasted from Saint Thomas' Day on 21 December to Candlemas on 2 February. Sawyer's nicely balanced use of flavorful old language and dialect and her careful attention to rhythm and details of plot capture the traditional ethnic setting and hearty festival spirit. Here appear, among others, "Schnitzle, Schnotzle, and Schnootzle" from Austria, "The Crib of Bo' Bossu" from Brittany, and her own Christmas classic, "The Voyage of the Wee Red Cap," a tale she heard from an itinerant tinker at a crossroads in Ireland and included in her novel *This Way to Christmas* as well.

Joy to the World offers six more tales and six carols from several different European countries. The collection provides a rich source for storytelling material. Read aloud, the stories are especially beautiful, for Sawyer was exceptionally skillful at putting down on paper versions of oral stories that are both faithful and usable. *This Is the Christmas: A Serbian Folk Tale* (1945), a single traditional story Sawyer found in her travels, is about a blind gypsy boy who is rewarded for his patience and virtue by a visit from the Christ Child. This tale further illustrates Sawyer's unusual ability to transmit the spirit of folk narrative.

Eleven more traditional stories are included in *The Way of the Storyteller*, which has become a Bible for those who practice that ancient art. Here Sawyer presents her philosophy of storytelling and gives advice about telling tales and putting together a story hour. Also important for understanding Sawyer's work is the lively and graphic *My Spain* (1967), a book of observation and personal experience, in which she describes her year of travel through Spain. The book has appeal for children as well as adults. It not only helps the reader to appreciate her methods of gathering and learning stories but also dramatically demonstrates her ability to catch and hold the reader when she speaks from personal experience. It further reveals why her autobiographical novels have more narrative power than her purely imaginary stories.

In addition to the Newbery Medal, in 1965 Sawyer also received the Laura Ingalls Wilder Award in honor of her many books and her work as a storyteller and the Regina Award from the Catholic Library Association as a "tribute to one who has dedicated a lifetime to children's literature." In May 1965 a special storytelling festival was held in her honor in Provincetown, Massachusetts.

Sawyer's writings are marked by warmth of tone, love of life, and confidence in the innate goodness of people. They exalt the old-fashioned virtues of industry, perseverance, responsibility, and faith in God. Regardless of their genre, her works are characterized by a strong sense of the storytelling situation, a sharp eye for ethnic detail, a keen ear for the cadence of common speech, and a leisurely and loving narrative manner.

In spite of its strong narrative sense, most of her fiction seems quaint by today's standards and has limited interest for contemporary readers. Still, her more pragmatic contributions to oral storytelling and to the literature of the Christmas season keep her name alive. Sawyer's unique ability to invest old narratives and legends with new life made her the acknowledged great lady of American storytelling, and therein lies her chief claim to immortality in the field of children's literature.

Selected Bibliography

WORKS OF RUTH SAWYER

Seven Miles to Arden. New York: Harper and Brothers, 1915.

This Way to Christmas. New York: Harper and Brothers, 1916.

A Child's Year-Book. With illustrations by the author. New York: Harper and Brothers, 1917.

Herself, Himself and Myself. New York: Harper and Brothers, 1917.

Leerie. With illustrations by Clinton Balmer. New York: Harper and Brothers, 1920.

Gladiola Murphy. New York: Harper and Brothers, 1923.

The Tale of the Enchanted Bunnies. With illustrations by the author. New York: Harper and Brothers, 1923.

The Luck of the Road. New York: Appleton-Century, 1934.

Toño Antonio. With illustrations by F. Luis Mora. New York: Viking Press, 1934.

Gallant: The Story of Storm Veblen. New York: Appleton-Century, 1936.

Picture Tales from Spain. With illustrations by Carlos Sanchez. Philadelphia: Lippincott, 1936.

Roller Skates. With illustrations by Valenti Angelo. New York: Viking Press, 1936.

The Year of Jubilo. With illustrations by Edward Shenton. New York: Viking Press, 1940.

The Least One. With illustrations by Leo Politi. New York: Viking Press, 1941.

The Long Christmas. With illustrations by Valenti Angelo. New York: Viking Press, 1941.

The Way of the Storyteller. New York: Viking Press, 1942.

This Is the Christmas: A Serbian Folk Tale. Boston: Horn Book, 1945.

Old Con and Patrick. With illustrations by Catnal O'Toole. New York: Viking Press, 1946.

The Little Red Horse. With illustrations by Jay Hyde Barnum. New York: Viking Press, 1950.

Maggie Rose: Her Birthday Christmas. With illustrations by Maurice Sendak. New York: Harper and Brothers, 1952.

Journey Cake, Ho! With illustrations by Robert McCloskey. New York: Viking Press, 1953.

A Cottage for Betsy. With illustrations by Vera Bock. New York: Harper and Brothers, 1954.

The Enchanted Schoolhouse. With illustrations by Hugh Troy. New York: Viking Press, 1956.

The Year of the Christmas Dragon, With illustrations by Hugh Troy. New York: Viking Press, 1960.

Dietrich of Berne and the Dwarf King Laurin: Hero Tales of the Austrian Tirol. Collected and retold by Ruth Sawyer and Emmy Mollès. With illustrations by Frederick T. Chapman. New York: Viking Press, 1963.

Daddles: The Story of a Plain Hound-Dog. With illustrations by Robert Frankenberg. Boston: Little, Brown, 1964.

Joy to the World: Christmas Legends. With illustrations by Trina Schart Hyman. Boston: Little, Brown, 1966.

My Spain: A Storyteller's Year of Collecting. New York: Viking Press, 1967.

CRITICAL AND BIOGRAPHICAL STUDIES

Haviland, Virginia. *Ruth Sawyer*. New York: H. Z. Walck, 1965.

Kunitz, Stanley J. and Howard Haycraft, eds. "Ruth Sawyer." In *Junior Book of Authors*. Rev. ed. New York: H. W. Wilson, 1951.

McCloskey, Margaret Durand. "Our Fair Lady!" *Horn*

Book 41: 481–486 (October 1965). (The entire issue honors Ruth Sawyer and Laura Ingalls Wilder.)

Overton, Jacqueline. "Roller Skates." In *Newbery Medal Books: 1922–1955, with Their Authors' Acceptance Papers and Related Material Chiefly from the Horn Book Magazine*, vol. 1, edited by Bertha Mahony Miller and Elinor Whitney Field. Boston: Horn Book, 1955. (The volume includes book notes, biographical sketch by Josephine Overton, excerpt, and acceptance paper by Sawyer.)

Robinson, Beryl. "Ruth Sawyer." *Horn Book* 45: 347, 431 (August 1970).

———. "To Ruth Sawyer." *Horn Book* 41: 478–480 (October 1965).

—ALETHEA K. HELBIG

KATE SEREDY

1896–1975

K ATE SEREDY'S NATIVE Hungary set the direction of her life and left an indelible mark upon her career. She traveled to the United States when she was twenty-six and subsequently spent forty years of her working life and published all her writings there; yet both her writing and her illustrations strongly reflect the influence of her birthplace. Her pictorial style of writing; her deeply felt sympathy for the people and creatures of the land and for the earth itself; her affinity for oral stories; her reliance on ethnic material for subjects and settings; her recurring choices of themes, such as the hatred of war and the promotion of traditional values; and the origins of some of her characters—all these elements have their roots in her early years.

Seredy was born on 10 November 1896 in Budapest, the daughter of Louis Peter Seredy, a teacher and storyteller, and Anna Irany Seredy. She recalled that her parents' house was a simple place, though comfortable and beautiful, with good books and artwork lining the walls. It was a home filled with fine music and the lively conversation of her family and their friends. From this intellectually charged atmosphere she gained not only a respect for ideas but also a love of good workmanship and a skillful use of language that were to influence her illustration and writing.

A beloved and devoted educator, Louis Seredy gave endless hours not just to the academic side of his vocation but to its human demands as well. Seredy recalled that the scores of boys her father counseled invariably left his modest study with a new sense of purpose. He helped them recognize their inner resources and encouraged them to make the most of their advantages and talents. His literary derivatives are Márton Nagy, the "Good Master" in the book of the same name (1935); the stalwart Prince Alexander, wise father of the unfortunate Prince Michael in *The Chestry Oak* (1948); and the determined, caring Mr. Smith in *A Brand-New Uncle* (1961).

When Seredy was nine she reluctantly accompanied her father and some of his artist friends on a trip to the Hungarian countryside to study peasant art and customs. She remembered herself as a pale and scrawny, spoiled and willful city child. She refused to drink milk fresh from the cow and insisted on eating sausages, which were not good for her. Although fussed over by a buxom, kindly peasant woman and comforted at night by featherbeds above and beneath, she refused to enjoy the trip. But her memories of the experience—her impressions of the life and atmosphere of the plains, the herdspeople, the animals, and the native folk arts her father's friends admired and pored over—later provided the basic plot, the main characters, and the scenes of country life in *The Good Master*. Seredy later commented that "all I did was put a frame to the picture that many unknown Hungarian peasants painted for me many years ago." *The Singing Tree* (1939), *The Chestry Oak*, and several picture books adorned with Central European motifs also seem to owe their provenance to that childhood experience.

Seredy had already started to draw by the time

she entered grade school. After high school, she attended the Academy of Art in Budapest for six years, receiving a teacher's diploma, and spent her summers studying art in Paris, Rome, and Berlin. Her instructors held her to high standards, insisting especially that she perfect her knowledge of anatomy. The effect of their teaching can be seen in the strong composition that characterizes her best illustrations, in particular the powerful pictures of *The White Stag* (1937).

During World War I Seredy served for two years as a nurse in front-line hospitals, an experience that left her ill in body and spirit and a confirmed pacifist. What she went through during the conflict undoubtedly produced the strong antiwar emphasis and the stress on international understanding and cooperation so evident in her writing.

Seredy visited the United States in 1922, then decided to make her home there. Although she was already a published illustrator in Hungary, she had difficulty in establishing herself in the United States. During her early years in this country she earned a living at factory work and by decorating lampshades, stenciling greeting cards, and painting sheet music covers. She moved on gradually to fashion design and magazine covers, and eventually to primary texts and tradebook illustrations. Willy Pogány, another Hungarian immigrant and a successful illustrator, gave her a boost toward more serious illustrating.

She gradually overcame her language handicap, learning the hard way, by trial and error. An afternoon's conversation with May Massee of Viking Press in the early 1930's, during which Seredy told stories of her Hungarian childhood, so delighted the editor that she suggested that Seredy set her memories down on paper. The result was *The Good Master*, the first book Seredy both wrote and illustrated, and the young immigrant's career as a writer for children was launched. In twelve years Seredy had become so proficient in her adopted tongue that in style, idiom, and structure the book seems to have been written by a native speaker.

Seredy lived for a while in an old house in New Jersey, which provided the inspiration for *Listening* (1936). Then she bought a farm near Montgomery, New York, which afforded firsthand background for her American farm novels. When caring for the old farmhouse and running its one hundred acres proved too demanding, she let the land lie fallow. Twenty years later she moved to the nearby town of Hamilton. After giving up farming, she devoted herself full-time to her work, becoming one of the most prominent writers and illustrators of the mid-twentieth century and reaching the zenith of recognition in 1938 with her Newbery Medal–winning *The White Stag*. She continued to write and illustrate until a few years before her death in 1975.

Seredy's most highly acclaimed works—*The Good Master*, *The Singing Tree*, *The Chestry Oak*, and *The White Stag*—improvise upon her memories of her Hungarian childhood and the stories her father had told her of her country's past. *The Good Master*, still her most popular book, is the episodic, loosely autobiographical account of wild, spoiled, motherless, nine-year-old Cousin Kate of Budapest, who goes to live with her Uncle Márton Nagy (who is known as the Good Master for his wise and understanding ways), his wife, and their son, Jancsi, ten, on their horse and sheep ranch on the Hungarian plains just before World War I. As the year moves from Easter to Christmas, Kate gradually becomes absorbed in the joys and responsibilities of farm life. Under the patient, firm guidance of Uncle Márton, and through her new relationship with sturdy Jancsi and the loyal and capable hands who tend the stock, Kate becomes less cranky and hyperactive and assumes her share of the chores.

The book reaches a mild, overforeshadowed climax near Christmas. Kate's father, Sándor, arrives for a visit, disguised as Mikulás (St. Nicholas), and distributes gifts to the children of the village. He expresses amazement at the positive changes the months have wrought in his daughter and decides to stay permanently as village schoolmaster—reemphasizing the book's major themes: the superiority of life on the land to that in the city and the importance of patience and firmness in rearing children—and the Nagy family is joyfully reunited on the family homestead.

The taming-of-the-shrew plot lacks invention and tension. The story grips initially, with Jancsi's ironic musings about Cousin Kate, presumably delicate from measles. But by the end of chapter 2 Kate's character has already undergone considerable reformation, and thereafter interest centers on the children's adventures about the ranch and countryside, episodes consistently lively but occasionally illogical. For example, Kate appears unfamiliar with the traditional Easter customs but quite capably dances the peasant *csárdás* at the fair. The author's earnest tone suggests a didactic intent—to introduce young readers to life on the plains, to glorify living close to the soil, and to promote traditional prudential values. Uncle Márton is too patient and understanding; the dialogue is often stilted; and the folk stories related by herders and Márton, though they contribute atmosphere and linkage to Hungary's past, seem deliberately interjected, too literary, and poorly meshed with the plot.

The book's staying power arises from its round and winning child characters, its abundant action, gentle humor, and warm tone, and the author's skill at creating the moment. Staunch Jancsi appears as his father's younger counterpart in his well-developed sense of responsibility and love for the soil and animals. He is somewhat naive, a trifle vain, and occasionally chauvinistic toward Kate, but he has a good sense of fun. And although he deliberately keeps Kate in the saddle much too long for her first riding lesson, later he bravely and resourcefully plunges his horse into the river to rescue her when a dangerous current seizes her.

Kate is winsome if overdrawn, her screaming monkey voice and angelic face that heralds trouble too often repeated. But her life-loving, fun-seeking, tomboyish nature and her refusal to conform to her aunt's ideas of femininity make her a consistently interesting heroine. She deliberately splits her skirts to match Jancsi's pantaloons, tricks him into smearing himself with Easter egg dye, and unconventionally requests spurs as her gift from Uncle Márton at the fair. With true grit and undaunted spirit she exposes the fakery of the acts at the fair and keeps her head when kidnapped by thieving gypsies, thus becoming the means by which they are brought to justice.

Not only does *The Good Master* feature likable, fully fleshed-out young protagonists, it also never lacks for adventures, some spiced with humor and all action-filled. Kate runs off with a wagon and four, having boldly dumped overly trusting Jancsi into the dust; Jancsi teaches Kate to ride; they hunt crawfish and unsuspecting Kate gets her fingers pinched; they visit shepherds, horsemen, and a miller; they participate in the Easter festival where the boys sprinkle the girls with water; and in a particularly exciting scene, they avert a horse stampede.

Moreover, the story exhibits Seredy's flair for creating pictures with words. Jancsi and the Good Master ride out of the yard for the annual roundup

... while the morning dew was still sparkling on the grass. ... Narrow paths forked out of the main

road, leading to white cottages nestling under shade trees. From the distance they looked like small white mushrooms under their heavy thatched roofs. ... Soon they could see the river Tisza, like a wide blue ribbon on the green velvet of the fields.

Seredy often uses color words and draws upon nature for imagery.

Equally vivid are action scenes, such as the boldly sketched passage in which arrogant Kate straddles the smoky kitchen beam, "skinny legs dangling, munching one end of a long sausage," while Father (Uncle Márton) gets "red and redder in the face" and Mother is "wringing her hands, trying to calm Father," and all the time Kate continues "screaming like a tin whistle" in an ecstasy of dominance. In this instance, the graphically described scene is echoed in a carefully patterned black-and-white toned illustration that is triangular in shape, with Kate at the apex and Father, Jancsi, and Mother below gazing helplessly up at her—a small masterpiece of mood and situation as well as of design. Throughout the story, vividly portrayed scenes of daily domestic ranch and peasant life and festivals make the family and times seem real and alive, exude affection for life, and alleviate the didacticism.

The more serious *Singing Tree*, sequel to *The Good Master*, takes the Nagys through World War I. At first the conflict means little to the children, something they only hear about in vague conversations between Márton and Sándor about matters that seem irrelevant compared with the more important problems of running the ranch. Seasonal activities proceed much as usual, and the still-spunky Kate even helps to reform proud, spoiled Lily Kormos, daughter of the local judge, in an ironic rerun of her own story. Gradually, however, the war intrudes upon their lives, as herdsmen, villagers, and ranchers are called up for service, including Sándor, soon a prisoner of war in Russia, and then Márton, whose letters suddenly cease without explanation. Jancsi runs the ranch quite capably with the assistance of a manual prepared by his foresighted father, along with the advice of wise old Moses Mandelbaum, the village storekeeper, whose charity to all constitutes an obvious rebuttal to anti-Semitism.

Because he needs workers, Jancsi applies for and receives six Russian prisoners of war, all peasants and workingmen who fit in quite nicely with the family—especially the burly, bearish, light-hearted Grigori, to whom Kate even entrusts her precious chickens. Later the ranch becomes a haven for Jancsi's grandparents, some neighbors, and six German war orphans—an assemblage that pushes hard a thesis of international cooperation and understanding. Coincidence restores Márton: the children encounter him in a military hospital, a victim of amnesia. The continuing problem of survival gives the book more unity than its predecessor. Kate remains a strong personality, and Seredy's picture-making style conveys clear views of ranch and community life. Although the reader never fears that things won't go all right for the Nagys, there is the sense that war is horrible and that it brings much hurt to common people and families.

The Chestry Oak, set during World War II and also in Hungary, continues the antiwar theme introduced in *The Singing Tree*. This stark, message-laden novel follows for four years the varying fortunes of young Prince Michael of Chestry, in a remote valley in Hungary. Before the Nazis commandeer the Chestry Castle as headquarters, Michael has been living happily with his father, Prince Alexander, a character identical to the Good Master, and his loving, devoted Nana. When the Russians bomb the region, the horse (an animal of mythological significance to the Hungarians) that is to carry the boy to safety with the Underground throws him, after which Michael undergoes a series of vicissitudes, finally encountering an American soldier named Brown, who arranges for him to join his family in the United States. The fractious horse also eventually reaches America and serves to substantiate Michael's story of his true identity. Michael, however, feels comfortable with the Browns, a typical American farm family, and elects to remain with them. He plants an acorn from the mighty Chestry oak on the Brown place, symbolizing loyalty to his adopted homeland.

Although the plot relies heavily on coincidence, Seredy's style reveals a rhythm and euphony absent from her earlier writing. The strongest part of the book concerns details of life in the castle and the upbringing of the prince. Michael's Nana, Mari Vitez, the wise and sturdy peasant woman chosen at his birth to be his nurse, stands out among Seredy's characters. She is portrayed with depth and believability as a firm mother figure, devoted to Michael and faithful to the Chestrys. She instills in him ideals of loyalty to country, family, and people and continues to tell him stories of the old days to keep alive traditional values, which his Nazi tutor, who arrives after the German takeover, deliberately works to eradicate. Though slow-moving and contrived, the book suggests currents of human emotion and projects a sense of what war is really like, something *The Singing Tree* fails to achieve.

The White Stag stirringly retells Seredy's father's favorite story, that of the legendary founding of Hungary. It follows a family of heroes over four generations: Old Nimrod, Mighty Hunter before the Lord; his twin sons, Magyar and Hunor; Hunor's son, Bendeguz; and Bendeguz's son, Attila, who in turn lead their people at the command of their god, Hadur, from their ancient homeland in Central Asia steadily westward until they reach their promised land along the Danube. They are guided by visions of a red eagle, a flaming sword, and a magnificent white stag—the symbols of Hadur, conquest, and faith in an ideal.

Seredy herself speaks as storyteller in this spirited re-creation of wars and hardships. The high diction, the biblical intonations, and in particular the vividly drawn scenes heighten the dramatic conflict, the irony, and the deep tragedy of the ancient legend. Concerns weigh heavily on Old Nimrod as the story begins. He "leaned wearily against the stones of the sacrificial altar," with "sadness in his face," since "the altar stones were cold to his touch . . . [and] there was nothing to offer on the altar," for the tribe is near starvation. He prays in sonorous tones: "O Powerful Hadur, have pity on me and my people. . . . I am suffering with shame, for I have nothing to offer Thee." This serious, somber note persists throughout the tale, which moves with epic grandeur and skillful storytelling appeal to both eye and ear. Nimrod's sacrifice of his horse, the terrible gale out of which appear two mighty eagles, the twins' encounter with the Moonmaidens, and the tender romance and dramatically described wedding between Bendeguz and the proud and beautiful captive Alleeta are just a few of the book's powerfully drawn scenes.

Terrible irony ensues when Alleeta dies at Attila's birth and Bendeguz vows to mold his son into a war machine the like of which the world has never known. Under Attila's leadership, the people follow the white stag through the Carpathians and into the homeland Hadur promised them. The story ends with a vivid scene: Attila standing on the highest step of an altar to Hadur, slashing the air with his sword, flames of fire rising behind him "like great flaming wings." He is "King of the Promised Land, Attila the Conqueror." Seredy leaves the story of the violence and bloodshed that follow to the reader of history, concluding her legend on the optimism of a journey of many decades that is finally completed.

By contrast with these strongly conceived books, Seredy's novels with American settings seem contrived, shallow, and dated. The most convincing of the longer ones, with its strong sense of history and closeness to nature, is the earliest, *Listening*, the story of the old Dutch colonial house in the Ramapo Mountains of New Jersey in which Seredy lived for a time. Uncle George, an artist, tells his niece and his twin sons stories about the people who built the house, tracing its history from its Dutch beginnings in 1656 and showing how each generation has added to it. Interspersed among the historical vignettes are domestic activities of an entertaining if inconsequential nature.

The theme of the earth providing salvation and refuge appears also in *The Open Gate* (1943), a detailed story set on a New York farm just before World War II. An overdrawn, enterprising grandmother manipulates her son into buying a farm after he loses his position as an advertising manager in New York City. In *The Good Master* Jancsi can tell from the angelic look on Kate's face that she has skulduggery in mind; in *The Open Gate* Gran assumes a mask of innocent indifference or becomes atypically laconic when she is up to something. Gradually the family settles in and makes a go of things, even becoming involved in the lives of neighbors, among them Mike the Slovak, who relates stories of misfortune in the old country.

Similarly, *A Brand-New Uncle*, in which a near-delinquent boy finds friends and new hope in grandparents who have run away from the demands of their numerous offspring, falls short of its potential, being marred by sentimentality and moralizing. Its characters seem tailor-made to convey the message that love and caring can effect great changes in behavior. Both text and illustrations project a comic tone that trivializes the characters' problems.

Seredy's shorter writings also do not achieve the standard of her early books. A glimpse from a train window of a sad-eyed lad amid tumbledown shacks resulted in *A Tree for Peter* (1941), the sentimental account of how a simple tramp brings joy to a small boy's life and transforms a shantytown by giving the boy a little red shovel and a Christmas tree. In

The Tenement Tree (1959) Tino makes up stories about what he sees in and around the big old tree near his artist Aunt Trina's house. The slim text serves to showcase the finely conceived, realistic pictures of animals that constitute most of the book. The picaresque *Philomena* (1955) harks back to Seredy's European origins in telling of a sturdy Bohemian girl who seeks employment in Prague and ends up finding a long-lost aunt. The book belabors the theme that life in the country is superior to that in the city, Philomena's conversations with her Babushka in heaven may seem condescending to the audience, and the plot moves from one set of coincidences to another.

Seredy published two picture-story books, *Gypsy* (1951) and *Lazy Tinka* (1962). The former is told from the viewpoint of Gypsy, a cat, tracing her life from kittenhood to motherhood. It is most notable for the strongly composed portraits that capture the grace, awkwardness, and attitudes typical of cats. In the second book, slovenly little Tinka predictably learns from association with wild creatures that everyone must make the most of what he or she has been given. The illustrations in this work seem gaudy and slipshod in workmanship.

Although best known for her writing for children and young people, Seredy also won acclaim as an artist for children. She illustrated her own books, almost always in black and white. The drawings for those with American settings tend to be realistic and tinged with the comic, while those with Hungarian backgrounds are more stylized and romantic. Fluid with circles and curves, these reveal a strong sense of design, careful attention to composition, unusual perspectives, and an almost palpable vitality. Seredy drew heavily on Central European ethnic motifs for her decorations for *The Good Master* and *The Singing Tree*, and these, together with the skillfully executed full- and half-page pictures of people and activities, add much to the sense of immediacy, warmth, and authenticity of these books. Seredy's masterpiece of illustration, however, is *The White Stag*, whose magnificent, vigorous, stylized compositions of heroes, horses, and stag perfectly catch the exuberance of a young nation in the making.

Seredy also illustrated books by such notable writers as Carol Ryrie Brink, for whom she did *Caddie Woodlawn* (1935), which won the Newbery Medal. Seredy's pictures catch the energy and spirit of the book's protagonist; most unforgettable is the illustration in which Caddie and the school bully,

Obediah Jones, square off and have it out with flailing fists and flying feet. Seredy also illustrated for other authors prominent in mid-century, including Mabel Leigh Hunt, Blanche Thompson, Margery Williams Bianco, and Eva Roe Gaggin. Seredy's highest recognition as an illustrator of books for others came for her delicately colored, Central European ethnic pictures in Ruth Sawyer's *The Christmas Anna Angel* (1944), which was a runner-up for the Caldecott Medal.

Except for *The White Stag* and *The Chestry Oak*, Seredy's writings make few demands upon the reader, being for the most part lighthearted stories of domestic and community life. In the mode of the 1930's and early 1940's, she tends to belabor her themes. While such values as love of family, respect for authority and the aged, pleasure in hard work, and faith in God and the future reappear throughout her writings, emphasized themes involve confidence in the ultimate goodness of human nature and a deep affection for the soil. The greatest evil is war, and the earth, horses, and trees are symbols of the good life. While characters tend to be types, those in the earlier books are more believable—some are even memorable—and plots, if thin, generally sustain interest. The best of Seredy's writing has rich visual qualities with details drawn from nature and from folk life and art. Seredy herself testified that all her writings started with pictures, and this is probably why their visual quality is so strong.

In addition to receiving the Newbery Medal, *The White Stag* was elected to the Lewis Carroll Shelf. Two books, *The Good Master* and its sequel, *The Singing Tree*, received Newbery honor status. Except for *The Good Master*, however, Seredy's books are seldom read today and are mainly interesting as social and literary history, although *The White Stag* deserves more attention than it has received lately; it is a worthy retelling of a little-known story and the only book of its type to win a Newbery. Nevertheless, Seredy's chief claim to fame as a writer of children's literature rests upon the family novels set in her native Hungary, especially *The Good Master*.

Selected Bibliography

WORKS WRITTEN AND ILLUSTRATED BY KATE SEREDY

The Good Master. New York: Viking Press, 1935; London: Harrap, 1937; New York: Dell, 1963.
Listening. New York: Viking Press, 1936.
The White Stag. New York: Viking Press and Puffin, 1937; London: Harrap, 1938.
The Singing Tree. New York: Viking Press, 1939; London: Harrap, 1940; New York: Dell, 1973.
A Tree for Peter. New York: Viking Press, 1941.
The Open Gate. New York: Viking Press, 1943; London: Harrap, 1947.
The Chestry Oak. New York: Viking Press, 1948. London: Harrap, 1957.
Gypsy. New York: Viking Press, 1951; London: Harrap, 1952.
Philomena. New York: Viking Press, 1955; London: Harrap, 1957.
The Tenement Tree. New York: Viking Press, 1959; London: Harrap, 1960.
A Brand-New Uncle. New York: Viking Press, 1961.
Lazy Tinka. New York: Viking Press, 1962; London: Harrap, 1964.

CRITICAL AND BIOGRAPHICAL STUDIES

Higgins, James E. "Kate Seredy: Storyteller" *Horn Book* 44/2: 162–168 (1968).
Kassen, Aileen M. "Kate Seredy: A Person Worth Knowing" *Elementary English* 45: 303–315 (1968).
Kirkpatrick, D. L., ed. *Twentieth-Century Children's Writers*. 2nd ed. London: Macmillan, 1983.
Kunitz, Stanley J., and Howard Haycraft, eds. *Junior Book of Authors*. New York: H. W. Wilson, 1934, 1951.
Markey, Lois R. "Kate Seredy's World" *Elementary English* 29: 451–457 (1952).
Miller, Bertha E. Mahony, and Elinor Whitney Field, eds. *Newbery Medal Books: 1922–1955*. Boston: Horn Book, 1955.
Seredy, Kate. "The Country of 'The Good Master'" *Elementary English Review* 13: 167–168 (May 1936).

—ALETHEA K. HELBIG

ANNA SEWELL

1820–1878

ANNA SEWELL WROTE only one book, *Black Beauty.* Written during the seven years of her last illness (she died three months after it appeared in 1877), this book is still read by children all over the world who know nothing about its author. It is said to be the sixth best-seller ever written in the English language, and its sale of forty million copies to date equals that of the entire works of Charles Dickens.

The story of Sewell's life is a strange one. In 1820 she was born in Great Yarmouth in Norfolk, England, to a Quaker couple, Isaac and Mary Sewell. Isaac's ancestors had been Quaker shopkeepers in the town since George Fox's times, when the newly-founded Quakers were being persecuted by the authorities. When Anna was a few months old her father opened a small shop in the City of London, but he totally lacked any business ability and soon lost everything. The family had to move to Hackney, an area of London that was virtually a slum. By this time Anna had a younger brother, Philip.

Mary Sewell, Anna's mother, was a woman of character. There was no money for schooling, so she educated the children herself, and the effect of her strict Quaker training on Anna and Philip cannot be too much emphasized. Mary Sewell took literally the Quaker advice "to seek out and alleviate suffering." Furthermore, she was of the era of Shaftsbury and William Wilberforce and had a natural passion for improving the poor, of whom there were plenty in cholera-ridden Shoreditch, just down the road. Anna and Philip, in their turn, were

encouraged to make sacrifices, and once gave up a seaside holiday to raise money for famine relief in Ireland. But it was the suffering of animals that affected Anna most. As a small girl she once said to a man who requested the blackbird he had shot in her garden, "Thee cruel man, thee shan't have it at all."

Horses had been Anna's special passion since the age of two, when she had insisted on being carried daily to feed the horses on the cab rank in Bishops gate. When she was a child she spent holidays at Dudwick Farm in Norwich. Those holidays represented a turning point in Anna's life, for she learned to ride her Uncle Wright's carriage horses and to drive her Aunt Wright's pony. She also painted watercolor landscapes with a passion unusual in a Victorian miss, and she looked forward eagerly to starting school at last when she returned home.

And then the shutter fell on Sewell's life. Running home from school on a rainy day, she fell and irreparably damaged both ankles. She was never to walk easily again. In later life, like many other middle-class Victorian spinsters, she became a prisoner on a couch, guarded by her adoring and powerful mother, her only escape an occasional pilgrimage to a European spa. As she grew older she began to have headaches and to experience difficulty concentrating. No one will ever know if Sewell's lifelong maladies were real or imagined.

Mary Sewell's position was now supreme. Isaac had long since become a mere cipher in his own household. Having failed at all branches of haberdashery, he was now failing as a bank manager, moving from branch to branch at increasing speed. Fortunately, moving all over England suited his wife. Every neighborhood was a new field in which she could seek out poverty and evil. Anna, by this time thirty-eight years old, seemed to find strength to face the challenge of rural misery and opened a Working Man's Evening Institute where she taught three nights a week, in all weathers. On one occasion she amazed her audience by dissecting a bullock's eye.

Sewell drove the family pony chaise to these meetings. Her mother's friend and biographer, Mrs. Boyly, described a ride to the station:

> Anna seemed simply to hold the reins in her hand, trusting to her voice to give all needed directions to her horse. She evidently believed in a horse having a moral nature, if we may judge by her mode of remonstrance. "Now thee shouldn't walk up this hill—don't thee see how it rains?" "Now thee must go a little faster—thee would be sorry for us to be late at the station."

Another passenger praised her ability to detect approaching lameness from the slightest change in the rhythm of hoofbeats.

At this time the indefatigable Mary Sewell began a career as a writer of "Homely and Improving Ballads for the Working Classes." *Our Father's Care,* the story of a homeless London child, sold a million copies. Mary Sewell's transformation into a bestselling author certainly influenced Anna. She read everything her mother wrote and criticized her work with characteristic and indeed somewhat alarming honesty.

When Anna Sewell was fifty, a serious illness confined her not just to a sofa but to bed permanently. By this time the family had moved back to Norfolk, to The White House, just outside Norwich, to be near Sewell's brother Philip and his seven motherless children. Because she could no longer assist her mother in a practical way, Sewell started to turn over the idea of a "little Book" about a horse. The horse was almost certainly based on Philip's fine black carriage horse, Black Bess, but a conversation from her window with a cab driver also had something to do with it. The man told her much that shocked her about the lives of London cab drivers and their horses. Like her mother, Sewell was inspired to write by the desire to help the poor and oppressed.

When she started to compose *Black Beauty* Sewell was too weak to hold a pen. She spent much of the first year of her illness forming scenes in her head and dictating them to her mother, who took them down in pencil on scraps of paper. In later years she could sometimes write unaided. When the book was finished, Mary Sewell sold it outright to her own publisher, Jarrold of Norwich.

Black Beauty entered the world modestly on 24 November 1877, in a cheap edition with one illustration. It was an immediate and tremendous success. Why? To start with, *Black Beauty* is not a book about a horse. It is a book by a horse. The title page of the first edition reads:

> Black Beauty
> His grooms and companions
> The autobiography of a horse
> Translated from the original equine
> By Anna Sewell

Anna Sewell had imaginatively entered the mind of a horse and lived his life from foalhood to old age.

Black Beauty starts his career as the darling of a wealthy and aristocratic family, the Gordons of Birtwick Park. Squire Gordon is the best of all possible squires and John Manly, his coachman, the best of all possible grooms (even if he does quote from the Bible excessively). At four years old Black Beauty is an exceptionally fine-looking gelding with a coat that shines like a rook's wing and a mane as fine as a lady's hair. He has a "sweet good-tempered face" and a "fine intelligent eye," and his character is as perfect as his appearance. Though he is "as fleet as a deer and has a fine spirit, . . . the lightest touch of the rein will guide him." Black Beauty's companions at Birtwick Park are Ginger, the spirited but hot-tempered mare who has never known kindness, and the dappled gray Merrylegs.

For Black Beauty, as for Sewell herself, tragedy comes with a fall. The drunken stableman Reuben Smith, by galloping the horse home at midnight, causes him to injure his knees on a bad road. From this point on, Black Beauty is "blemished" and therefore unfit to stand in a gentleman's stables. Chapter 27 is entitled "Ruined, and Going Downhill"; the fine black horse drops rapidly down the social scale, even working as a job horse in a drive-yourself firm. He reaches rock bottom as a London cab horse and finally collapses pulling a heavy load up Ludgate Hill. But he is rescued and ends his days happily with the three Misses Blomefield on the very boundary of Birtwick Park, dreaming of the old days and his "old friends under the apple trees."

Only Sewell ever imagined what it *feels* like to be a horse, to have a bit in your mouth:

> A great piece of cold hard steel as thick as a man's finger . . . pushed into one's mouth, between one's teeth and over one's tongue, with the ends coming out at the corner of your mouth, and held fast there by straps over your head, under your throat, round your nose, and under your chin; so that no way in the world can you get rid of the nasty hard thing.

Even more immediate was the description of working with the dreadful fixed bearing rein, or checkrein, designed to keep a horse from lowering its head. Indeed, some say Sewell's chief aim in writing the book was the abolition of the bearing rein, used on all the fashionable carriage horses of her time:

> That day we had a steep hill to go up. Then I began to understand what I had heard of. Of course, I wanted to put my head forward and take the carriage up with a will, . . . but no, I had to pull with my head up now. . . . Day by day, hole by hole our bearing-reins were shortened.

Modern children like *Black Beauty* because, unlike the ballads of Mary Sewell, it contains facts rather than sentiment. Flower, the harness expert, wrote of Sewell's book when it appeared, "It is written by a veterinary surgeon, by a coachman, by a groom; there is not a mistake in the whole of it." Even today, a child lucky enough to win a dream pony could equip himself tolerably for the care and management of it with only *Black Beauty* as a guide.

But *Black Beauty* does not succeed merely because it is accurate; it is a book full of drama and even death. Grown men admit to having wept over the chapter entitled "Poor Ginger." Ginger's road to ruin also ends between the shafts of a London cab, and one day Black Beauty finds himself standing next to her in a cab rank:

> "It was Ginger! but how changed! The beautifully arched and glossy neck was now straight, . . . the clean straight legs were swelled; . . . the face, that was once so full of spirit and life, was now full of suffering. . . . A short time after this, a cart with a dead horse in it passed our cab-stand. The head hung out of the cart-tail, the lifeless tongue was slowly dropping with blood. . . . I believe it was Ginger."

But all is not doom and gloom. There are memorable scenes of excitement: the moonlight gallop to fetch the doctor, the tale of the flooded bridge, the fire at the coaching inn. And not all cabmen are cruel. Cheerful Jerry Barker, with little enough for his wife and two children, is the best of masters to his horses and would never underfeed them or make them work on a Sunday.

In the United States the book set a world publishing record. A million copies were circulated within two years of its appearance on 1 April 1890, and the book continued to sell at the rate of a quarter of a million copies a year for twenty years. The man responsible for this massive achievement was George T. Angell, the founder of the Massachusetts Society for the Prevention of Cruelty to Animals. Angell, the son of a Baptist minister of Southbridge, Massachusetts, was a remarkable man. By the time he was forty-five he had made enough money at the bar to retire and devote himself to good works. For years Angell had been anxious to find a book that would do for horses what *Uncle Tom's Cabin* had done for slaves, and when *Black Beauty* was brought to his attention he decided to print an edition of ten thousand copies at once. He then appealed for funds to give away thousands more to "all drivers of horses." He even encouraged the makers of Frank Miller Harness Dressing to bring out fifteen tons of their own version of the book, in which chapter headings were decorated with a row of horses wearing rugs printed with Frank Miller's name. A leading Boston newspaper accused Angell of pirating the book (which indeed he had done), selling it at a quarter of its proper price, and paying nothing to the author. As he reported in his *Autobiographical Sketches and Personal Recollections* (1891), Angell defended himself in a letter to the paper. His main points were as follows:

> . . . The English publisher paid Miss Sewell *just twenty pounds* for the book. By the payment of *twenty pounds* it became his property, *and no one but the English publisher gets a sixpence from the profits.* . . . As there is no American copyright on this book, we must undersell every other publisher. . . . The sending of . . . *"Black Beauty"* into every American home may be . . . an important step in the progress, *not*

only of American, but the world's, humanity and civilization.

In England, meanwhile, deluxe illustrated editions were beginning to appear. The first of these was the 1894 edition, with line and wash illustrations by John Beer; a 1912 edition included color illustrations by Cecil Aldin as well as a biographical introduction. In 1915 Lucy Kemp-Welch produced by far the finest illustrations ever, some in color.

When Jarrold's copyright expired in 1927 almost every famous name in British publishing jumped on *Black Beauty*'s bandwagon, and since then barely a year has passed without a new edition appearing. The only exception was the period of World War II, when even the Everyman edition became unobtainable. To compensate for this dearth, no fewer than three editions appeared in 1947. By 1954 the book was available in thirty-five editions from twenty-five English and American publishers. Today there are few bookstores on either side of the Atlantic that do not offer a choice of paperback editions of *Black Beauty*. Black Beauty is known to French readers as Prince Noir, to Spanish readers as Azabache and to Italians as Re Moro. The famous horse has been the star of at least four films, and he frequently appears on the television screen. His story has also been adapted many times for radio and issued on records and cassettes.

Black Beauty, in effect, started a new category of book, the animal story. There had been animal stories, of course, since Jean de La Fontaine, indeed since Aesop. Sewell would have read Robert Ballantyne's *The Dog Crusoe* and would have known the talking cab horses of George MacDonald's *At the Back of the North Wind.* But these added up to only a handful of books, whereas after *Black Beauty* such books proliferated. Soon Jarrold was offering a long animal list, including *The Uses and Abuses of Domestic Animals* (uniform with *Black Beauty*) along with books about the adventures of a polar bear, a Persian cat, and two dogs. One of the dogs, the Canadian dog in *Beautiful Joe,* has a life that closely resembles that of Black Beauty except that it is led in reverse order: Joe starts his life in the home of a cruel milkman and ends it in the family of a kind minister. In this century, both Beatrix Potter and Kenneth Grahame have owed much to Sewell.

But Sewell was no more concerned with worldly success than was Angell. She was concerned for the better treatment of horses and above all the aboli-

tion of the bearing rein, and in this she virtually succeeded. By the early years of the twentieth century the strength of public feeling against the cruel device was so strong that only undertakers persisted in using it; in 1914 The Royal Society for the Prevention of Cruelty to Animals persuaded even them to abandon it. By then Anna had lain in the little burial ground at Lammas for thirty-five years.

The horses that had pulled her own hearse had not suffered. Bayly, her mother's biographer, was not present on the day of the funeral, but Mrs. Buxton, the wife of the local squire, was. She was standing near the window of the upstairs drawing room at The White House, where the guests were gathering to follow the cortege to Lammas. Mary Sewell, who was beside her, glanced out of the window as the horse-drawn hearse drew up outside. "Oh this will never do!" she exclaimed to herself, and hastened downstairs. Soon a top-hatted figure was seen moving down the train of horses removing the bearing rein of each one in turn.

Selected Bibliography

EDITIONS OF BLACK BEAUTY

Black Beauty. London: Jarrold, 1877. Boston: American Humane Education Society, 1890. With illustrations by John Beer. New York: E. P. Dutton, 1894. With illustrations by Cecil Aldin. London: Jarrold, 1912. With illustrations by Lucy Kemp-Welch. London: J. M. Dent and Sons, 1915. With recollections of Anna Sewell by Margaret Sewell. London: G. G. Harrap, 1935. With illustrations by Fritz Eichenberg. New York: Grosset and Dunlap, 1945. With an introduction by May Lamberton Becker and illustrations by Wesley Dennis. New York: World Publishing, 1946.

CRITICAL AND BIOGRAPHICAL STUDIES

Baker, Margaret Joyce. *Anna Sewell and Black Beauty.* London: George C. Harrap, 1956.

Bayly, Marie. *The Life and Letters of Mrs. Sewell.* London: James Nisbet, 1888.

Chitty, Susan. *The Woman Who Wrote Black Beauty.* London: Hodder and Stoughton, 1971.

Sewell, Joseph S. *A Quaker Memoir.* London: n.p., 1902.

Sewell, Mary. "Reminiscences of Mary Sewell." Unpublished.

—SUSAN CHITTY

JOHANNA SPYRI

1827–1901

TODAY FEW PEOPLE realize that modest, introspective Johanna Spyri, the author of *Heidi,* was a truly talented, prolific writer. As the author of thirty stories for children and young adults, Spyri portrayed the vibrant Swiss countryside and its people in vivid prose. Drawing on her own experiences, Spyri created a lasting contribution to children's literature.

Johanna Spyri was born in the rural village of Hirzel on 12 June 1827. Her father, Dr. Johann Jakob Heusser, for whom she was named, was the local physician. Her mother, Meta Schweizer, developed a fine reputation as a local poet and lyricist. Like her beloved character Heidi, Johanna had gray eyes and brown hair. Her family called her "Hanneli" or "Hanni." The household included her two brothers, Theodor and Christian; her three sisters, Anna, Ega, and Meta; her grandmother; two aunts; and two female cousins. As a child, Johanna was more interested in nature, frolicking out-of-doors, creative drama, storytelling, and music than she was in academics.

Bernhard Spyri, her brother's classmate, often came to visit the family in Hirzel, and in 1852, while she was continuing her education in Zurich, Johanna married him. Spyri was a lawyer and publicist who later became the town clerk of Zurich. The Spyris were friends with the members of a cultural group in Zurich that included the poet Conrad Ferdinand Meyer and the composer Richard Wagner. In 1855 their only child, Bernhard Diethelm Spyri, was born. Young Bernhard developed his musical talent and studied law, but he died of tuberculosis

in 1884. Later that same year Johanna Spyri also mourned the death of her husband.

It was not until 1870 that Johanna Spyri began writing for publication. Her decision to write was directly influenced by two historical events: the establishment of the International Red Cross in Geneva and the Franco-Prussian War. A devout Christian, Spyri wanted to raise funds in order to help the wounded soldiers and war orphans coming into Switzerland. Her lasting motivation to write fictional stories was twofold: to donate all of her royalties to charities and to write about the grave conditions of orphans. In 1871 her first story for adults, *Ein Blatt auf Vronys Grab* (A Leaf on Vrony's Grave), was published anonymously. In 1880 *Heidi's Lehr- und Wanderjahre* (Heidi: Her Years of Wandering and Learning) was published, also anonymously. In 1881 the second Heidi story, *Heidi kann brauchen, was es gelernt hat* (Heidi Makes Use of What She Has Learned), accredited her authorship for the first time. (The two stories are now published as one book.) In 1886 she moved to Zeltweg 9 near Zurich's municipal theater. She became an invalid but continued to write until her death on 7 July 1901. Her last story, *Die Stauffer-Mühle (Jörli; or, The Stauffer Mill),* was published in Berlin during that same year. Spyri preferred to stay out of the limelight, and through the years her personal papers and manuscripts have been lost or destroyed. Therefore, the recollections of her family and close friends provide all that is known about her life.

The Alpine region of Canton Graubunden (the

Grisons) in eastern Switzerland is the setting for *Heidi,* Spyri's most famous work. Heidi, a small, robust orphan, is brought by Aunt Dete to live with her reclusive grandfather in his mountain chalet. Grandfather (called "Alm-uncle" by the villagers) is feared for his antisocial behavior, but Heidi changes him into a tender, caring man. She befriends the goatherd Peter, his mother and grandmother, and an assemblage of goats. Self-centered Aunt Dete reappears and tricks Heidi into leaving her mountain home to go to Frankfurt and become a companion to Klara, the sickly daughter of a wealthy German man. Heidi poignantly touches the lives of several people in Frankfurt: the kindly doctor, Klara's grandmamma, and Herr Sesemann, Klara's father. But homesickness overwhelms her, and she returns to her grandfather and friends on the mountain. Later Klara joins Heidi at the chalet and is restored to good health. The story ends as Heidi and her grandfather deepen the bonds of friendship with their German guests.

The convincing characters and picturesque setting of *Heidi* reflect the experiences of Spyri's own childhood. Like little Heidi, Spyri preferred a simple, quiet life close to nature. The kindly doctor in the story is much like her own father. Klara's grandmamma and Peter's grandmother are storytellers, much as Spyri's own grandmother was. Spyri's insights into Heidi's feelings of homesickness and Heidi's and Peter's poor adjustments to school were also drawn from her own experiences. Spyri chose the area near the city of Maienfeld (in eastern Switzerland) as the setting for the story and named the quaint fictional village Dorfli. It was much like the village of Jenins, which Spyri frequented between 1846 and 1852.

Spyri's unique style of writing brings to life a spiritual theme with basic story elements. Her devout Christian faith strengthened and shaped the spiritual theme in her writing. Examples of beautiful religious verses are featured in each story, evidence that her fine talent as a writer was not limited to prose. The spiritual overtones in her work reflect a universal faith in God that transcends any particular Christian denomination.

Close examination of a variety of her stories reveals how the setting, characters, plot, and conclusion vividly typify Spyri's writing style. At the mere mention of the word "Switzerland," one imagines a breathtaking view of majestic mountains rising above sloping green pastures with grazing cattle and wooden huts, with clear brooks winding through pines to a village below. This was Johanna Spyri's homeland. For readers of the nineteenth and twentieth centuries, Spyri's settings form an image so powerful that one feels directly transported to Switzerland. Drawing from her experiences and travels in the Engadine area of Switzerland, northern Italy, France, and Germany, Spyri uses specific details to depict a place for her audience. For example, in "Am Silser- und am Gardasee" ("The Story of Rico") she describes the Maloja Pass leading from Sils and St. Moritz in the upper Engadine area, where Rico lives. Rico journeys alone to Italy, passing through Lake Como and Lake Garda to Peschiera, a quiet community where most of the story takes place. Rarely does Spyri use a fictional name; each place mentioned in a story is identifiable on a map.

Spyri clearly establishes the cultural and historical dimensions of her setting, describing life in late-nineteenth-century Switzerland. Influenced by the diverse cultures of three bordering countries, she describes the contrasting standards of the social classes without discrediting any of them. Personal prejudices and diverse backgrounds are transformed to camaraderie as Spyri integrates her characters. Rich and poor, handicapped and able-bodied people all appear together. Her characters are placed in a variety of settings: wealthy estates, isolated villages, castles, vineyards, high mountain pastures, and holiday resorts. She realistically and historically portrays the conditions of orphans wandering about Switzerland looking for places to call home, an actual circumstance in Switzerland following the Franco-Prussian War.

Spyri uses colloquial language to familiarize the reader with local culture. In "In sicherer Hut" ("A Mountain Miracle," also titled "Little Miss Grasshopper"), young Seppli longs for a "peitsche" (whip) with a "zwick" (gusset), described in the story as a large goat whip with a yellow tassel. In a few of the stories she refers to local folk songs from various regions. Even the names of her characters identify the area of Switzerland they are from, including the German names Rudi and Kaspar, the French names Ninette and Michel, and the Italian names Peppino and Rico. Frequently, Spyri uses the diminutive form of a child's name, adding the Swiss "li" suffix, as in the names Wiseli, Fränzeli, and Jörli.

Spyri's most commendable skill as a writer is her capacity to create a diversity of believable characters in her narratives. Critics acclaim her talent for developing accurate, vivid personalities. The reader empathizes with the plights of the characters and thus is born a feeling of comradeship. She also stages fictionalized conflicts with such mastery that readers perceive them as real and identify with the characters and their problems.

Wo Gritlis Kinder hingekommen sind and *Gritlis Kinder kommen weiter* (combined in one volume in English as *Gritli's Children: A Story of Switzerland,* 1883–1884) together provide one of the finest examples of Spyri's ability to develop a complex set of characters in a multifaceted plot while keeping the reader's curiosity aroused throughout a story. The story takes place in northern Switzerland and southern Germany along the Rhine River. Several households of children are introduced. The wealthy Mrs. Stanhope, accompanied by her nurse and her fragile daughter, Nora, travel to Buchberg hoping to restore Nora's failing health. In Switzerland Nora is befriended by the four energetic Kellers: Oscar, the leader of a secret club; Fred, a naturalist; Emmi, a creative artist; and Riki, a little tattletale. Nora derives the greatest comfort, however, from her friendship with Elsli, a poor, delicate girl burdened with constant responsibilities for her own four younger siblings. Nora dies peacefully, and out of Elsli's and Mrs. Stanhope's grief comes a new beginning for them. Given her parents' permission, Elsli returns with Mrs. Stanhope to Germany and is followed by her artistic brother, Fani. Both siblings along with the neighboring Keller children remain at Lindenhalde-on-the-Rhine during the summer holiday. Bedlam results as each child becomes unhappily involved with an individual struggle related to the conflicts of the other characters, but bright futures await them all at the end of the story when each conflict is resolved.

Spyri's heroine Heidi has captivated readers with her innocence, compassion, amiability, and honesty, but her lesser-known works also portray believable and similarly candid characters. In "Lauris Krankheit" ("Lauri's Rescue") Spyri introduces the young hero as he is naively misguided into a life of deceit. Lauri flounders throughout most of the story. He is an accomplice in an attempted robbery; during the robbery, Schnufferli, a small dog that Lauri loves, is killed. Lauri, ashamed and grief-stricken, runs away and hides from his family and friends. Finally, he confesses his part in the crime, and is reunited with his family. As he grows up, he becomes a fine example to younger children; his virtuous qualities overshadow his former behavior.

Spyri's family and friends could identify characters and events that directly influenced her writing. Many of her stories portray a grandparent who nurtures and cares for the child and then dies, leaving the child feeling lonely and vulnerable. As a child Spyri was deeply affected by the death of her own grandmother. In *Gritli's Children,* Fred Keller, the young naturalist, is much like Spyri's younger brother, Christian. In "Vom This, der doch etwas wird" ("Tiss: A Little Alpine Waif," also called "Without a Friend"), the kind cheesemaker, Franz Anton, recalls the friendly cowherd named Franz Antoni whom Spyri visited in the mountains as a child. In "Beim Widen-Joseph" ("The Pet Lamb,") Spyri re-creates her own joy at discovering a real, live lamb under the Christmas tree and caring for it during her youth.

Spyri generates empathy between reader and characters as her plot unfolds. Children can identify with the characters because their personal conflicts are universal by nature: they include the problems of finding one's purpose in life and finding a secure environment to grow in, the necessity of feeling loved and needed, and the difficulties of dealing with such sources of unhappiness as homesickness, dishonesty, disloyalty, cowardice, death, and separation. In "Moni der Geissbub" ("Moni, the Goat Boy"), for example, Moni has been framed by Jordie, a dishonest playmate. He debates whether he should reveal that Jordie has found and kept a valuable necklace. Jordie's threat endangers the life of Moni's favorite goat, but Moni finally chooses to disclose the injustice. The necklace is returned to the owner; the goat is not slaughtered; and Moni realizes that his fears of the consequences were greatly exaggerated.

In *Cornelli wird erzogen* (*Cornelli,* 1890) the author displays great empathy for the irrational fears of childhood. Cornelli, a blithe spirit, meets her comeuppance in a prissy, stifling governess who tells her that she will grow horns if she continues to disobey and sulk around the house. Sensitive and shy, Cornelli believes the governess, becomes withdrawn and despondent, and refuses to have the front locks of her hair cut because she fears that her ugly horns will become visible for everyone to see. When Cornelli moves to her friend's home, where she is nurtured and respected, she changes back into a happy, carefree girl.

Although they are not without loss or sadness, all of Spyri's stories conclude happily. The traumatic realities of death or separation are revealed early in the story, and the main character then confronts and overcomes the trauma optimistically. Spyri's use of coincidence combines with suspense and surprise in many stories. In *Jörli; or, The Stauffer Mill* the orphan Jörli must find a new home after his foster grandfather dies. He sets out with his only inheritance, his father's mandolin, and journeys to the home of a miller and his wife. Coincidentally, Jörli displays an innate aptitude for mill work, and it is revealed at the end of the story that the miller and his wife are Jörli's real grandparents—a discovery that is confirmed when they find the name of Jörli's father written on the inside of the mandolin.

Spyri followed the conventions established for late-nineteenth-century writers and at the same time gave expression to her own ideas. She worked within the conventions of the literature of her time by including an invalid and an orphaned character in each story, to show death as a release from earthly misery and to convey a spiritual message. It is important to realize that she began writing at a time when literature was beginning to move away from didacticism and children's writers were beginning to recognize the value of creativity and imagination. Therefore, the originality of her stories bridges two eras of children's literature.

As translations of *Heidi* poured from publishing houses around the world in the 1880's, Spyri's literary prominence grew, and she gained notable status in the first Golden Age of children's literature. Modern critics have compared her works to those of her literary contemporaries. Her development of female characters is compared to Louisa May Alcott's, and her use of the elements of setting and plot have been ranked with Robert Louis Stevenson's historical fiction. Her exploration of the themes of death and spirituality has been seen as similar to Hans Christian Andersen's: both authors see death as a release from the poverty and pain of earthly life and an accession to the hope of a new, peaceful, eternal life.

Nevertheless, the literature of Johanna Spyri has received much critical attention over the years, some of it quite harsh. Several modern critics claim that her work is outdated, too didactic, and too sentimental, or that it does not portray realistically the harsh life of the Swiss peasant characters. These critics attribute the lasting popularity of *Heidi* to the fact that it has appeared on lists of favorite books for such a long time. Still, other critics argue for the value of *Heidi* and its popularity on the basis of the literary merit of Spyri's work. By viewing her writing in a historical context, as children's literature has evolved, one can easily determine and appreciate the valuable literary contribution that Spyri has made to the world.

Selected Bibliography

WORKS OF JOHANNA SPYRI IN ENGLISH TRANSLATION

Editions of Heidi

Heidi. Translated by Louise Brooks. New York: Platt and Peck, 1884.

Heidi: A Story for Children and for Those That Love Children. Translated by Helen B. Dole. Boston: Ginn, 1899.

Heidi. Translated by Elisabeth P. Stork. With illustrations by Maria L. Kirk. Philadelphia and London: Lippincott, 1915.

————. Translated by Philip Schuyler Allen. With illustrations by Maginel Wright Enright. Chicago and New York: Rand McNally, 1921.

————. With illustrations by Jessie Wilcox Smith. Philadelphia: David McKay, 1922. Reissued New York: Charles Scribner's Sons, 1958.

————. With illustrations by Gustaf Tenggren. Boston: Houghton Mifflin, 1923.

————. With illustrations from the motion picture starring Shirley Temple. New York and Akron, Ohio: Saalfield, 1937; New York: Random House, 1959.

————. With illustrations by Troy Howell, New York: Julian Messner Division, Simon and Schuster, 1982.

————. With illustrations by Ruth Sanderson. New York: Knopf, 1984.

Other Works

Red Letter Stories. Translated by Lucy Wheelock. Boston: Lothrop, 1884. (Includes "Lisa's Christmas" and "Basti's Song in Altdorf.")

Rico and Wiseli. Translated by Louise Brooks. Boston: DeWolfe Fiske, 1885. Reissued New York: Thomas Y. Crowell, 1922.

Uncle Titus: A Story for Children and for Those Who Love Children. Translated by Lucy Wheelock. Boston: Lothrop, 1886.

Gritli's Children: A Story for Children and for Those Who Love Children. Translated by Louise Brooks. Boston: Cupples and Hurd, 1887.

Swiss Stories for Children and for Those Who Love Children. Translated by Lucy Wheelock. Boston: Lothrop, 1887. (Includes "Lisa's Christmas," "Rosenresli," "Toni," "Basti's Song in Altdorf," and "In Safe Keeping.")

Dorris and Her Mountain Home. Translated by Mary E. Ireland. Richmond, Va.: Presbyterian Committee of Publication, 1902.

Cornelli. Translated by Elisabeth P. Stork. With illustrations by Maria L. Kirk. Philadelphia and London: Lippincott, 1921.

Mäzli: A Story of the Swiss Valleys. Translated by Elisabeth P. Stork. With illustrations by Maria L. Kirk. Philadelphia and London: Lippincott, 1921.

Moni, the Goat Boy and Other Stories. Translated by Helen B. Dole. With illustrations. New York: Grosset and Dunlap, 1923. (Includes "Moni, the Goat Boy," "Trini, the Little Strawberry Girl," "Tiss, a Little Alpine Waif," "Jo, the Little Machinist," and "What Sami Sings with the Birds.")

Vinzi: A Story of the Swiss Alps. Translated by Elisabeth P. Stork. With illustrations by Maria L. Kirk. Philadelphia and London: Lippincott, 1923.

Dora. Translated by Elisabeth P. Stork. With illustrations by Maria L. Kirk. Philadelphia and London: Lippincott, 1924.

Gritli's Children: A Story of Switzerland. Translated by Elisabeth P. Stork. With illustrations by Maria L. Kirk. Philadelphia and London: Lippincott, 1924.

Veronica. Translated by Louise Brooks. New York: Grosset and Dunlap, 1924.

Arthur and Squirrel. Translated by Helen B. Dole. With illustrations. New York: Thomas Y. Crowell, 1925.

Children of the Alps. Translated by Elisabeth P. Stork. With illustrations by Margaret J. Marshall. Philadelphia: Lippincott, 1925. (Includes "Francesca in Hinterwald," "The Fairy of Intra," and "Gay Little Herbli.")

Eveli: The Little Singer. Translated by Elisabeth P. Stork. With illustrations by Blanche Greer. Philadelphia and London: Lippincott, 1926. (Includes "Eveli, the Little Singer," "Peppino," and "The Stauffer Mill.")

Maxa's Children. Translated by Clement W. Coumbe. New York and Akron, Ohio: Saalfield Publishing, 1926.

Castle Wonderful. Translated by Helen B. Dole. New York: Thomas Y. Crowell, 1928.

Jörli; or, The Stauffer Mill. Translated by Elisabeth P. Stork. Philadelphia and London: Lippincott, 1928.

Children of the Alps. Translated by Helen B. Dole. With illustrations. New York: Grosset and Dunlap, 1929. (Includes "Eveli and Beni," "Lauri's Rescue," and "Jörli's Mandolin.")

In the Swiss Mountains. Translated by Helen B. Dole. With illustrations by Sybil Tawse. New York: Thomas Y. Crowell, 1929. (Includes "Ehel," "The Fairy of Intra," and "Happy Heribli.")

Renz and Margritli. Translated by Helen B. Dole. With illustrations. New York: Thomas Y. Crowell, 1931.

Eric and Sally. Translated by Helen B. Dole. With illustrations by A. A. Dixon. New York: Thomas Y. Crowell, 1932. (Includes "Eric and Sally," "Peppino," and "Pino's Good Fortune.")

The Pet Lamb and Other Swiss Stories. Translated by M. E. Calthrop and E. M. Popper. With illustrations by Michael Ross. London: J. M. Dent and Sons, 1956. (Includes "The Pet Lamb," "Toni the Woodcarver," "Basti and Franzeli," "A Mountain Miracle," "Moni the Goatherd," "Granny's Golden Rule," "Good-for-Nothing Batty-Matt," and "The Bird's Message.")

All Alone in the World: The Story of Rico and Wiseli's Way. Translated by M. E. Calthrop. With illustrations by Michael Ross. London: J. M. Dent and Sons, 1958; New York: Dutton, 1959.

CRITICAL AND BIOGRAPHICAL STUDIES

Anonymous. "Heidi—or the Story of a Juvenile Best Seller" *Publishers Weekly* 318–321 (5 July 1953).

———. "Johanna Spyri Anniversaries 1976–1977–1980." Newsletter, English text. Zurich: Johanna Spyri Foundation (July 1976).

Casper, Franz. "Johanna Spyri, Children's Writer (1827–1901)" *Pro Helvetia* 8: 68.

Dahme, Lena F. *Women in the Life and Art of Conrad Ferdinand Meyer.* New York: Columbia University Press, 1936. Reissued New York: AMS Press, 1966.

Egoff, Sheila, ed. *Thursday's Child: Trends and Patterns in Contemporary Children's Literature.* Chicago: American Library Association, 1981.

Enright, Elizabeth. "At 75, Heidi Still Skips Along." In *Children and Literature (Views and Reviews),* edited by Virginia Haviland. Glenview Ill.: Scott, Foresman, 1973.

Smith, James Steel. *A Critical Approach to Children's Literature.* New York: McGraw-Hill, 1967.

Ulrich, Anna. *Recollections of Johanna Spyri's Childhood,* translated by Helen B. Dole. New York: Thomas Y. Crowell, 1925.

Zipes, Jack. "Down with Heidi, Down with Struwwelpeter, Three Cheers for the Revolution" *Children's Literature,* 5: 162–180 (1976).

—CATHERINE EAYRS

ROBERT LOUIS STEVENSON
1850-1894

THE CHILDHOOD OF Robert Louis Stevenson probably has been more familiar to readers of all ages than that of any other author. Later generations of children have identified themselves with the child in *A Child's Garden of Verses* (1885) —sick in bed, marching his lead soldiers, sailing little ships, planting trees and houses in "the pleasant Land of Counterpane," or, like Louis, watching for Leerie the lamplighter. The Stevensons had "a lamp before the door." In the verses we see the reality of Stevenson's life as a small boy: he plays, often alone, surrounded by the cold and darkness of an Edinburgh winter, except when he joins the adults, his only companions, in the circle of light and warmth around lamp or hearth.

Stevenson was baptized Robert Lewis, after the names of his grandfathers, but his father changed the spelling out of dislike for another man named Lewis. The name was still pronounced Lewis by the family. His mother was Margaret Isabella, daughter of the Reverend Lewis Balfour; his father was Thomas Stevenson, a civil and marine engineer well known for his technical books. Both parents were deeply religious, strictly conventional in their views, and devoted to their frail child. A country girl, Alison Cunningham, joined the household as Louis' nurse before he was two years old; he called her "Cummy," and it was to her that he dedicated *A Child's Garden of Verses.* She was the tireless guardian of the little invalid, whose nights were often made hideous by paroxysms of coughing. It was Cummy who carried him to the window to look out at lights burning in other windows or who read

the Bible and *Pilgrim's Progress* to pass the wakeful hours. But all was not solemn. Cummy told hair-raising tales of the bloody history of Scotland and, when Louis was well, took him shopping for "penny dreadfuls" full of mysterious houses and graveyards. As mental and emotional food for a small boy, all of this sometimes led to childish nightmares; in later life it helped to shape the plots of his novels.

From time to time Louis went to school with other boys; in the summer he spent weeks in the country at Colinton Manse, where there were Balfour cousins and the opportunity to climb trees, play in the hayloft, and make little boats to sail down the river. Louis learned to compete with his cousins after his own fashion and at the age of six won a prize offered by a Balfour uncle for the best history of Moses to be written by one of the children. Except for the terrors of an easily overwrought imagination and the constantly threatening bouts of illness, Louis' childhood was relatively happy.

The doctors could do nothing but treat his symptoms—the cough, fevers, and loss of weight—but somehow, with unceasing care from his father and mother as well as from Cummy, and with frequent visits to resorts in a mild climate, Louis survived into his teenage years. In spite of a nervous, high-strung disposition, he was intensely affectionate and expected the best of his fellow man; his spirit, if not his body, was tough.

At sixteen Louis willingly entered the University of Edinburgh, planning to follow in his father's footsteps as an engineer; at the same time he was trying to learn to write by imitating the style of eminent authors, one after another. Later he defended this practice and considered it no hindrance to originality. For pleasure he read Alexandre Dumas, Captain Marryat, W. H. Kingston, and R. M. Ballantyne, whose stories were set in foreign lands and were popular with all boys. Louis actually met Ballantyne, who had already written *Coral Island* and *The Dog Crusoe.* Thus the theme of islands and castaways ran strongly in Louis' mind from an early date.

Thomas Stevenson was pleased with his son's literary talent, taking it for granted that writing was a gentleman's hobby. He assumed that Louis was seriously preparing for a career like his own. But Louis, old enough and almost well enough to free himself of the bondage of home, was skipping classes at the university and exploring the seamy side of Edinburgh, following a pattern set by many other young men. The difference between him and the others was his sympathy for outcasts wherever he found them—in back streets, saloons, or brothels. He instinctively treated social inferiors with delicacy and generosity.

During holidays Louis' father sent him to inspect the lighthouses and harbors of the Orkneys and Hebrides, but he surveyed them as an artist and writer rather than as a would-be engineer; he was later to describe these wild coasts in his novels of adventure. Gradually Thomas Stevenson realized that his son would never fit his own mold, and in spite of their deep love for each other there were serious disagreements and painful controversies. The pretense of preparing for an engineering career was dropped when a severe illness sent Louis on a six-month sojourn on the Riviera. When he returned, still willing to opt for a "respectable" vocation, he began to study for the bar. By 1875 he had qualified as advocate and enjoyed the meetings of the Speculative Society, known as "the Spec," a prestigious literary and debating club to which he was admitted through family influence.

In the meantime Louis' personal life had entered a new phase. His cousin, the artist Bob Stevenson, who was three years older, bohemian, and wildly exotic in manners and dress, came to Edinburgh from Cambridge and captivated Louis. They became notorious for their outrageous scrapes and bizarre clothing, worn, as Stevenson said, "from a hankering after social experiment and adventure and a dislike of being identified with any special

class or caste." His velveteen jacket and day laborer's knotted scarf and his long hair under a low, broad-brimmed hat became his trademark.

His father gave him a small allowance, and when he could afford it he went off vagabonding with friends, carrying no luggage. In the summer of 1876 he joined Bob Stevenson near Paris at Grèz-sur-Loing in the forest of Fontainebleau, where they met Fanny Van de Grift Osbourne. She was an American woman, the admired center of the artists' colony at Grèz, separated from her ne'er-do-well husband, Sam Osbourne, and living abroad with her two children; another child had recently died. Fanny was eleven years older than Louis, but he had had satisfying friendships with older women before this, and he fell in love with Fanny. She was small, dark-skinned, with exquisite little hands and feet—an exotic flower, "a tiger lily," as he later called her in a love poem. Her American informality and freedom of manner added to her attraction in his eyes. She was to become his mistress, wife, nurse, cook, gardener, factotum, editor, and "violent friend," as he once described her to J. M. Barrie. With Fanny came a ready-made family: a seventeen-year-old daughter, Belle, and Lloyd, the eight-year-old son who soon took Louis for an adored older brother. It was to him that Stevenson would dedicate *Treasure Island* (1883).

When Fanny's husband withdrew financial support, she returned to California with the children to arrange for a divorce. Early in August 1879 she cabled Stevenson, and he left Scotland at once, without telling his parents. There would have been a harrowing scene, and he was determined to go. On 7 August he sailed from Port Clyde, Glasgow, traveling second class but barely separated from the steerage filled with emigrants and their children. In *The Amateur Emigrant* (1895), *Across the Plains* (1892), *The Silverado Squatters* (1883), and essays and letters to friends at home Stevenson recorded the trip and the American year that followed. Throughout there are vignettes of Stevenson with American children, clearly showing his interest, understanding, and affection for them. One cannot adequately judge him as a writer *for* children without taking account of his relationships *with* them. He tells how on board ship he feared for children whose own mothers complacently watched them "climb into the shrouds or on the rails while the ship was swinging through the waves." He also tells how, ill after a terrible day and night in New York, he went with a crowd of emigrants to board a westbound train; while most of the passengers sat up for a day and a night without food, Stevenson made friends with a Dutch widow and her three children, buying fruit and candy for them at Pittsburgh and sleeping on the floor of the train to give them more room. On 30 August, having ridden four trains, he reached San Francisco, literally more dead than alive.

He found Fanny in Monterey, surrounded by or in touch with the group who became Stevenson's adopted family: Nellie, Fanny's younger sister, who was being courted by Adolpho Sanchez, a gentleman bartender; Belle, who had just eloped with a young artist, Joe Strong; and Lloyd. It was to Lloyd that Stevenson gave his greatest affection.

There were delays about the divorce. As Stevenson wrote to a friend, he was "a mere complication of cough and bones," and Fanny questioned whether she should marry him after all. While she made her decision, he went on a camping trip into the hills behind Monterey and lay half-conscious for two nights under a pine tree. A retired sea captain turned goat herd found him and kept him for two weeks in his cabin. Stevenson, recuperating by a miracle, gave reading lessons to the ranch children, two little girls whose mother was away and ill. Even in extremis he could never turn away from a child.

Fanny did decide to push on with the divorce and to marry Stevenson, who now undertook to explain matters to Lloyd. They had enjoyed walks on the beach among the live oaks and pines, so this seemed like the best place for the crucial conversation with the vulnerable boy of eleven. Lloyd later told how they had tramped along side by side for some time before Stevenson found the right words, tactful, sympathetic, but straightforward: "I want to tell you something. You may not like it, but I hope you will. I am going to marry your mother." A few moments later Lloyd simply put his hand into Stevenson's, and they walked on.

In the fall Fanny moved to a house in Oakland where she and Sam had lived. Stevenson spent the winter in a boardinghouse in San Francisco, almost without funds and writing desperately, resolved not to accept money from his parents. He was on a starvation diet, concealing the truth from Fanny and making friends among writers and artists to whom she introduced him. Often he sat in Portsmouth Square, telling stories to children. The youngest child of his landlady, a four-year-old boy named Robbie, was especially attached to him, call-

ing him "de author." In March Robbie nearly died of pneumonia, and Stevenson sat up with him, night after night. Robbie recovered, but Stevenson had overtaxed his limited strength. He was prostrated with a high fever, coughing, and cold sweats. Fanny had him moved to a hotel in Oakland where he suffered the first of the lung hemorrhages that repeatedly brought him to the point of death in the following years. When he could move to Fanny's house, she nursed him devotedly and undoubtedly saved his life. Here children came in to see the author and to play a storytelling game. Lloyd's contributions were always sea adventures; he also had a toy printing press for which Stevenson suggested ideas.

In May 1880 Stevenson and Fanny were married and set off on a strange honeymoon, taking Lloyd, his dog, and the printing press with them. They spent the summer above the Napa valley at an abandoned mine called Silverado on the slope of Mount St. Helena, where they could live free of charge. Fanny found ingenious ways to make an old bunkhouse into comfortable living quarters, and in the high, pure air Stevenson regained a semblance of health. His cure was facilitated by reconciliation with his parents, who had never given up hope that the rift could be healed. Just a year after his departure from Scotland, Stevenson returned there to introduce Fanny and Lloyd to the older Stevensons. Their meeting was such a success that several summers were spent together.

On a rainy day in Braemar, Scotland, in 1881, Stevenson drew a map of a "treasure island" to amuse Lloyd. As he drew, a story "came alive" to him. The family was delighted with the opening chapters, and Lloyd helped to finish the map while Thomas Stevenson contributed the idea of the apple barrel scene, the name *Walrus* for Flint's old ship, and the list of things found by Jim Hawkins and his mother in Billy Bones's sea chest. The British magazine *Young Folks* accepted the story when they had seen the first chapters, paying Stevenson £34 7s.6d., and began serial publication in the issue of 1 October 1881 under the title *The Sea Cook,* by "Captain George North." After this hopeful beginning Stevenson suffered from writer's block, which was not broken until the following winter in Davos, Switzerland, where he had gone with Fanny and Lloyd. Davos was recommended for tubercular patients, but it was depressing, so Stevenson relieved the tedium by finishing *Treasure Island.* Now the writing came easily, "like small talk," as he said in an 1894 essay, "My First Book." In Davos he also wrote some comic verses illustrated by woodcuts and titled *Moral Emblems* (1882), for Lloyd's printing press. Today this edition of *Moral Emblems* is a rarity much prized by collectors of Stevensoniana.

Thomas Stevenson gave Fanny a house on the sunny south coast of England, in Bournemouth; they called it Skerryvore in honor of the elder Stevenson's famous lighthouse off the Hebrides. Here Stevenson's parents and many other visitors came, some of them literary lights like William Ernest Henley and Henry James. John Singer Sargent painted a striking portrait of Stevenson at Bournemouth, in which he is an extravagantly thin figure pacing nervously while Fanny sits in the background, one little bare foot exposed from beneath an Indian sari that almost completely veils her.

The illness and hemorrhaging persisted, and there were winters when Stevenson and Fanny retreated to the warmth and seclusion of Hyères on the French Riviera, but in both Bournemouth and Hyères he was producing books, essays, and poems, some of them intended for young readers. One was a medieval romance, *The Black Arrow* (1888), a novel of the Wars of the Roses that was serialized in *Young Folks* as written by "Captain George North." In Hyères, while he "was sick and lay a-bed" in pain, he drafted most of *A Child's Garden of Verses;* about half of these first appeared as *Penny Whistles.* He finished the collection in Bournemouth and wrote *Kidnapped* (1886) there. Then came *The Strange Case of Dr. Jekyll and Mr. Hyde* (1886), the aftermath of a nightmare at Bournemouth. (Stevenson later wrote about the important role that his dreams played in his life as a writer.) Financial rewards poured in at last. Sales were amazing.

The search for a perfect climate continued. In 1887, after the death of Thomas Stevenson, Louis returned to the United States with Fanny and Lloyd. In New York he found that he was a celebrity. *Dr. Jekyll* was being performed to standing-room-only audiences in Boston and was about to open on Broadway. The sculptor Augustus Saint-Gaudens came to Stevenson's hotel to work on the famous medallions that show the author writing in bed, pen (or cigarette) in hand. The press swarmed in. The strain was too much; the Stevensons decided to try the cure at a new resort for tubercular patients at Saranac Lake in the Adirondacks. There, during the autumn and a sub-zero winter, Stevenson's health did improve. It was in Saranac that Lloyd began to write *The Wrong Box* (1889), which Stevenson as collaborator later finished in Hawaii.

The end of their wanderings was in sight. The American publisher S. S. McClure came to Saranac Lake, offering Stevenson a handsome contract to write some travel letters, perhaps to be followed by an American lecture tour with photographic slides. The Stevenson chartered a yacht, the *Casco,* and set sail from San Francisco for the South Pacific. The final chapter of Stevenson's life was spent surrounded by a large family on Upolu in the Samoan islands. At the foot of wooded Mount Vaea Stevenson built Vailima, a fine house that became a center of hospitality for friends, relatives, and, most of all, Samoans. Stevenson ardently championed the cause of human rights for native chiefs who had been jailed by the Samoan government: he took food and clothing to them in prison, and he sent a doctor. They adored him; he was their counselor, their father, their "Tusitala," the "teller of tales." In that hot, moist island where work was avoided whenever possible, the chiefs worked for a month to cut a road through the jungle to Vailima; they called it the Road of the Loving Heart.

Stevenson continued to write at Vailima, but only one of these works was for young readers—*Catriona* (1893), a sequel to *Kidnapped,* titled *David Balfour* (1893) in the American edition. However, a case could be made for including *Prayers Written at Vailima* (1904) among Stevenson's works written for children. The collection is childlike in tone, suggesting the household where Tusitala gathered his Samoan "children" around him with the rest of his family at the end of the day.

On the evening of 3 December 1894, Stevenson died suddenly of a cerebral hemorrhage. At sunrise the next day, Samoan men began to clear a path to the top of Mount Vaea, and they dug his grave at the summit. Inscribed on his tomb are the words of his "Requiem," begun years earlier on his life-threatening trip "across the plains." In 1914 Fanny too died of a cerebral hemorrhage; her ashes were buried beside him.

When Robert Louis Stevenson used the word "children," he meant little children, and for this audience he wrote only *A Child's Garden of Verses.* Some critics have suggested that even these simple poems are written about children rather than for them, but this judgment ignores the fact that many of the verses are known by heart among English-speaking children almost as soon as they know

Mother Goose. The book opens with the famous dedication to Alison Cunningham and, in poems such as "The Lamplighter," "Winter-time," and "North-west Passage," Stevenson recalls his early childhood in Edinburgh. The summer poems picture bright days in the country at Colinton Manse; "Foreign Lands" (as they are seen from the cherry tree), "The Swing," and "From a Railway Carriage" are among the most familiar of these, the latter two being especially memorable for their properly suggestive rhythms.

In addition to its simple word pictures, *A Child's Garden of Verses* also offers some acute psychological studies in miniature. Stevenson often reveals his penetrating and subtle insight into the mind of the child at play. Several of his essays—"Child's Play," "A Penny Plain and Twopence Coloured," and "The Lantern-Bearers"—demonstrate a keen awareness of the difference between the imagination of the adult and that of the child, who acts out whatever he imagines, and in *A Child's Garden of Verses,* "Pirate Story," "A Good Play," "Marching Song," and "My Bed Is a Boat" are examples of this. Other verses explore the differences in the expectations and obligations that divide the child's world from the adult world. Here Stevenson acknowledged a debt to the Scottish child versifier Marjorie Fleming, who died in 1811 before her ninth birthday. She was known and loved on both sides of the Atlantic for what Mark Twain called her "little perfunctory pieties and shop-made holinesses," mixed in with her "stunning and worldly sincerities." In a letter of 1894 Stevenson wrote to a friend, "Marjorie Fleming I have known, as you surmise, for long. . . . Your note about the resemblance of her verses to mine gave me great joy, though it only proved me a plagiarist." The resemblance lies in such poems as his "Whole Duty of Children," "System," and "Good and Bad Children," which have come in for harsh criticism by some solemn latter-day educators who have questioned their effect on the social consciences of children, as if children were not bright enough to see a joke.

A final group of Stevenson's verses are poems filled with what has often been called a "sense of wonder." In "Travel" the child longs to go "where the golden apples grow;— / Where below another sky / Parrot islands anchored lie." In "The Land of Nod" he goes "All alone beside the streams / And up the mountain-side of dreams." "Escape at Bedtime" takes him out under the night sky, where he

finds the pail by the wall "half full of water and stars." Often Stevenson plays games with a double perspective of adult time and child time, as in the envoi "To My Name-Child." The name-child is "little Louis Sanchez," the son of Fanny's sister Nellie, born years after the older Louis had left Monterey. In the poem the poet foresees that the baby Louis will someday be able to read "this rhyming volume" printed in London while he is "still too young to play." Then time folds in upon itself and Louis *can* read the verses, but the poet tells him to put down his book and go out to play:

> And remember in your playing, as the sea-fog
>   rolls to you,
> Long ere you could read it, how I told you
>   what to do;
> And that while you thought of no one, nearly
>   half the world away
> Some one thought of Louis on the beach of
>   Monterey!

In his *Intimate Portrait of Robert Louis Stevenson,* Lloyd Osbourne recalls how shortly before his death Stevenson predicted that he would be remembered for "no more than a handful of stories for boys." By "boys" he meant those about the age of Lloyd, who was thirteen when Stevenson wrote *Treasure Island.* But old boys as well as young boys read this book when it was published, and the old boys made enthusiastic comments. Andrew Lang compared *Treasure Island* to the *Odyssey* and *Tom Sawyer;* William Gladstone read it through in one night; W. B. Yeats wrote that his grandfather, a great sailor, was reading it on his deathbed.

The quality of *Treasure Island* is, in fact, undisputed. It rests not only on the excitement of the subject—pirates, murder, hidden treasure—but also on dramatic visualization of scenes, the series of "small, bright, restless pictures" with which Stevenson thought a novel should progress. Blind Pew panics on the moonlit road just before the revenuers run him down; the "brown old seaman" with the saber cut across one cheek stares out to sea from a cliff near the Admiral Benbow Inn, his spyglass under his arm and his great cape blowing in the wind; Jim Hawkins aims down with two pistols from the rigging of the *Hispaniola* as the pirate Israel Hands aims his dirk for an upward throw; Long John Silver with his parrot on his shoulder ploughs his way across the island on the final search for the treasure, pressing heavily forward on wooden leg and crutch while Jim, a captive, resists the tug of the rope with which Silver has tethered him.

To populate and enact such vivid scenes as these, Stevenson developed three-dimensional, ambivalent, contradictory human characters. Long John, that smoothly plausible villain, is a masterpiece of characterization. Stevenson admitted to Henley, "He has his moments has Long John. Let the Heathen rage; Long John'll do." Consummate liar, traitor to all but his own schemes, and murderer, Silver still attracts Jim by his native intelligence, his cheerfulness, and the easy kindness he displays when it suits him to be kind. Silver is a bad man not without redeeming traits, just as Doctor Livesey and Squire Trelawney are good men not without faults. Jim, young, guileless, untried by experience, and not without faults himself, learns the fallibility of all men and returns home the wiser. N. C. Wyeth's illustrations for *Treasure Island* surpass all others, as does his work for *Kidnapped, David Balfour,* and *The Black Arrow.*

Kidnapped produced Alan Breck Stewart, a character who is the equal of Long John Silver in human ambiguity. Alan is the political enemy but devoted personal friend of a young Scot, David Balfour. Alan is sturdy and brave as well as quirky and contentious, always spoiling for a fight, a Catholic Highlander true to the lost cause of Bonnie Prince Charlie. David is a Protestant Lowlander, more canny and cautious, who learns from Alan the will to survive through courage, daring, and endurance. Together, as fugitives from the law, they make a "flight through the heather," the wild Scottish moors, like hunted animals, sealing their comradeship forever yet often quarreling. *Kidnapped* is not as tightly plotted as *Treasure Island* and is more difficult for readers of any age because of its generous use of Scottish dialect and because the details of Scottish history are not well enough known, at least among American readers. Yet *Kidnapped* is appealing because of the same qualities that make *Treasure Island* such good reading. As the story opens, David crawls blindly on a stormy night up a dark stairway in the house of his evil old uncle. Suddenly a flash of lightning reveals that he has reached the top step, beyond which the stairway is unfinished; he has come within an inch of pitching down to his death. In another unforgettable scene David and Alan Breck defend themselves in the roundhouse of the brig *Covenant* against a crew of no fewer than fifteen; every thrust and parry of

swordplay is described with zest, every phrase honed to a sharp edge. The effect is a tour de force. "The characters," Stevenson said, "took the bit in their teeth; all at once they became detached from the flat paper, they turned their backs on me bodily; and from that time my task was stenographic—it was they who wrote the remainder of the story." He composed a couplet for a presentation copy of *Kidnapped* to a friend: "Here is the one sound page of all my writing, / The one I'm proud of and that I delight in."

Stevenson meant *Kidnapped* to be part of a longer story, but he did not take the tale up again until he began to write the sequel, *David Balfour,* in Samoa. It first appeared serially in *Atalanta,* a magazine for girls, and was published as a book in 1893 with the title *Catriona* in England and *David Balfour* in America. It is possible to fault this late work for its lack of unity, since its two parts are only loosely connected in plot. Part 1 concerns David's decision to volunteer as a witness on behalf of two Highlanders accused of "the Appin murder," in which King George's "factor," a Campbell, has been shot to death. Both suspects are Stewarts; one is Alan Breck, David's bosom friend from *Kidnapped.* In his attempt to free these men, David risks his own life and becomes disenchanted with the self-serving and politically biased men who administer the law in posts of high responsibility. He risks his life again to help Alan escape to France, where he can take refuge with his Stewart chieftain; here Alan disappears from the story until the very end. Part 2 takes place in Holland, where David has gone to study law at the university in Leyden. Under his protection is the beautiful Catriona, the daughter of James More, a sly and conniving sycophant who is secretly plotting to betray Alan Breck to his enemies. David, deeply in love with Catriona from the opening pages of the book, is scrupulously careful of her innocence and helplessness alone in a foreign land. They pose as brother and sister and behave as such. Catriona tries to remain loyal to her rascally father but finally has to admit his worthlessness. In a climactic scene Alan Breck reappears and fights James More; David and Catriona come between them, and Catriona is wounded by David's sword. James More conveniently dies soon afterward, and David and Catriona return to Scotland to live happily ever after.

Two themes give *David Balfour* what unity it possesses: law as a profession and the romance of David and Catriona. Both suggest connections with

Stevenson's own experience. Stevenson did become an advocate, and Fanny's independence and integrity seem to be reflected in Catriona. "I should have been a man child," she says. "Well I know it is good to sew and spin, and to make samplers, but if you were to do nothing else in the great world, I think you will say yourself it is a driech [dreary] business." David calls Catriona violent in her friendship; Stevenson called Fanny "a violent friend." If the romance between Catriona and David is moving, and it is, it owes much to its real-life model. Catriona is so openhearted and impulsive that long before a word of love is spoken between them, she kisses David's hand as he leaves for Leyden, perhaps never to be seen again. When, after all, he takes her with him to join her father in Holland, she is so brave that she jumps without help from the ship into the boat that waits below, plunging about in a high sea. It is clear that Stevenson was in love with this girl of his imagination for the same reasons that made him love Fanny.

Strange as it may seem today, *The Black Arrow*, a story of the Wars of the Roses, was well received by the young readers who had enjoyed *Treasure Island*. *Young Folks* published *The Black Arrow* as written by "Captain George North," but Stevenson's literary friends advised him to delay book publication for fear that it might damage his reputation as a writer. He had written at such speed that he forgot one character completely and wrote to his editor, "I had, I blush to say it, clean forgot him. Thanks to you, Sir, he shall die the death." Greater difficulties are the complexity of the historical background and of the moral ambiguities, which are here carried to such extremes that the reader hardly knows how to feel toward the characters. For example, the hero, Dick Shelton, switches his allegiance from Lancaster to York only to find that his leader, the duke of Gloucester, is a villain, while the Lancaster leader is admirable. Disguises abound—Joanna Sedley, the heroine, appears as a boy. One theme that makes *The Black Arrow* pertinent in today's world is its recognition of the inherent evil of war and of the indiscriminate horror that war metes out to the innocent victims on both sides of a conflict.

If Stevenson and his stepson Lloyd Osbourne had written a story line for burlesque, *The Wrong Box* might have been the result. They were not writing for a juvenile audience, but young readers who happen to discover this book today find it very funny. It is impossible to describe the plot—there is none. There is only action—kaleidoscopic action—involving a corpse and a cast of characters ranging from eccentrics to madmen, most of whom turn up in disguise. In 1966 Bryan Forbes directed this comic masterpiece with a galaxy of stars, including Ralph Richardson, John Mills, Michael Caine, and Peter Sellers. *The Wrong Box* deserves to be starred on reading lists for teenagers.

The Strange Case of Dr. Jekyll and Mr. Hyde, though not written for young readers, has long been one of their favorites. Stevenson's original idea was "to write about a fellow who was two fellows." The story was meant to be merely a thriller, but Fanny objected that he could not publish such a horror story without giving it a moral. Reluctantly, Stevenson burned the manuscript and rewrote it, at white heat, in three days. *Dr. Jekyll* (Stevenson said that the name should be pronounced with a long *e*) was an instant success. Sales were phenomenal; money poured in. Stevenson said years later that *Dr. Jekyll and Mr. Hyde* was the worst thing he had ever written, but neither the critics nor the public have agreed; for teenagers it has remained as popular as *Dracula* and *Frankenstein*, and "Jekyll and Hyde" has become idiomatic in English for "split personality". The movies, of course, have added to the fame of the book; John Barrymore, Fredric March, and Spencer Tracy have all played the part.

But the lasting significance of *Dr. Jekyll and Mr. Hyde* gives it a quality far above the run-of-the-mill horror story; in this case, Fanny's editorial advice was right. Step by step, the psychological tension mounts as Stevenson tightens the screw. The doctor grows obsessed with his discovery of a mind-changing, body-changing drug; the dosage of the drug that reverses the change has to be increased; the change into Mr. Hyde begins to occur spontaneously, even without the drug; Mr. Hyde sinks deeper and deeper into corruption; too late, he abhors himself but can no longer obtain the drug that will allow him to return to the life of the law-abiding, kindly Dr. Jekyll—there is no way out but suicide.

In his lifetime there was already a Stevenson cult, which included his friends, some (though not all) literary critics, and a wide reading public of both adults and children. Andrew Lang judged Stevenson to be the best historical novelist since Sir Walter Scott and William Makepeace Thackeray. Barrie called the initials R. L. S. "the best loved in recent literature." G. K. Chesterton praised the "economy of detail" and "suppression of irrelevance" that still make his best books readable, even by the young, who like a writer to get on with the story.

Yet Stevenson once wrote to his wife that his fame would not last four years after his death. He would have been surprised to know that in 1950, centenary celebrations of his birth took place all over the English-speaking world, that landmarks connected with his life are carefully preserved from Scotland to Samoa, and that important library and museum collections are devoted to him. The centenary of his "American year," 1979–1980, was widely memorialized in the United States, and in 1980 Edinburgh's Canongate Tolbooth Museum mounted a stunning exhibit marking the return of Scotland's native son with his American wife. The exhibit was titled "A Spirit Intense and Rare." R. L. S. was also a youthful spirit all his days and gave young readers some gifts that seem likely to keep their freshness and vitality in the future. Clifton Fadiman has confidently listed *Treasure Island* among ten books by writers in the English language that will still give pleasure five hundred years hence.

Selected Bibliography

WORKS OF ROBERT LOUIS STEVENSON

Moral Emblems: A Collection of Cuts and Verses. Privately printed. Davos Platz, Switzerland: S. L. Osbourne, 1882; New York: Charles Scribner's Sons, 1897.

The Silverado Squatters: Sketches from a California Mountain. London: Chatto and Windus, 1883.

Treasure Island. London: Cassell, 1883. With illustrations by N. C. Wyeth. New York: Charles Scribner's Sons, 1911. Reprinted New York: Charles Scribner's Sons, 1981.

A Child's Garden of Verses. London: Longmans, Green, 1885; New York: Charles Scribner's Sons, 1885.

Kidnapped. London: Cassell, 1886. With illustrations by N. C. Wyeth. New York: Charles Scribner's Sons, 1913. Reprinted New York: Charles Scribner's Sons, 1982.

The Strange Case of Dr. Jekyll and Mr. Hyde. London: Longmans, Green, 1886.

The Black Arrow: A Tale of the Two Roses. With illustrations by Will Low and Alfred Brenon. London: Cassell, 1888; New York: Charles Scribner's Sons, 1888. With illustrations by N. C. Wyeth. New York: Charles Scribner's Sons, 1916. Reprinted New York: Charles Scribner's Sons, 1987.

The Wrong Box, with Lloyd Osbourne. New York: Longmans, Green, 1889.

Across the Plains, with Other Memories and Essays. London: Chatto and Windus, 1892; New York: Charles Scribner's Sons, 1892.

Catriona: A Sequel to "Kidnapped," Being the Memoirs of the Further Adventures of David Balfour at Home and Abroad. London: Cassell, 1893. Published in the American edition as *David Balfour.* New York: Charles Scribner's Sons, 1893. With illustrations by N. C. Wyeth. New York: Charles Scribner's Sons, 1937.

The Amateur Emigrant. Chicago: Stone and Kimball, 1895.

Prayers Written at Vailima. New York: Charles Scribner's Sons, 1904; London: Chatto and Windus, 1905.

CRITICAL AND BIOGRAPHICAL STUDIES

Aldington, Richard. *Portrait of a Rebel: The Life and Work of Robert Louis Stevenson.* London: Evans, 1957.

Balfour, Graham. *The Life of Robert Louis Stevenson.* 2 vols. London: Methuen, 1901; New York: Charles Scribner's Sons, 1901.

Butts, Dennis. "The Child's Voice" *Junior Bookshelf* 29: 331–337 (December, 1965).

————. *R. L. Stevenson.* New York: H. Z. Walck, 1966. (A Bodley Head monograph.)

Cohen, Morton N. "A Voyage Back to *Treasure Island*" *Junior Bookshelf* 23: 122–129 (March 1959).

Colvin, Sidney, ed. *Letters of Robert Louis Stevenson to His Family and Friends.* 2 vols. New York: Charles Scribner's Sons, 1899.

Daiches, David. *Robert Louis Stevenson and His World.* London: Thames and Hudson, 1973.

Field, Isobel Osbourne Strong. *This Life I've Loved.* London: Joseph, 1937.

Furnas, J. C. *Voyage to Windward: The Life of Robert Louis Stevenson.* New York: William Sloane Associates, 1951.

Gosse, Edmund. "Stevenson's Relations with Children" *Youth's Companion* (13 June 1899).

Hodges, Margaret. "The American Children of Robert Louis Stevenson" *Horn Book* 55/6: 641–647 (Dec. 1979).

Mackay, Margaret. *The Violent Friend: The Story of Mrs. Robert Louis Stevenson.* Garden City, N.Y.: Doubleday, 1968.

Osbourne, Lloyd. *An Intimate Portrait of Robert Louis Stevenson.* New York: Charles Scribner's Sons, 1924.

Shaffer, Ellen. "Robert Louis Stevenson and the Silverado Museum" *Top of the News* 30: 169–175 (January 1974).

Stern, Gladys Bronwyn. *He Wrote "Treasure Island": The Story of Robert Louis Stevenson.* London: Heinemann, 1954.

Stevenson, Robert Louis. "Child's Play" *Cornhill* 38: 352–359 (Sept. 1878).

———. "The Lantern-Bearers" *Scribner's Magazine* 3: 251–256 (February 1886).

———. "My First Book: *Treasure Island.*" In *Writings,* vol. 2. New York: Charles Scribner's Sons, 1894.

———. "A Penny Plain and Twopence Coloured" *Magazine of Art* 7: 227–232 (April 1884).

—MARGARET HODGES

FRANK R. STOCKTON

1834–1902

FRANK R. STOCKTON is one of those unfortunate writers whom many have heard of but few actually have read. If he is known at all, it is through one short story, "The Lady, or the Tiger?" (*Century,* November 1882)—that famous puzzler that has been foisted upon reluctant high-school students ever since it became public domain. Yet in Stockton's own time he was universally acknowledged as one of the country's leading men of letters. In 1899, when the influential journal *Literature* conducted a poll to determine which ten writers should constitute an American Academy, Stockton ranked above Henry James and Bret Harte (only William Dean Howells, John Fiske, Mark Twain, and Thomas Bailey Aldrich were considered his contemporary superiors). Howells himself proclaimed Stockton "an author who has done more than any other (except Mark Twain) to lighten the heart of his generation." Stockton's chief publishers, Charles Scribner's Sons, thought enough of his reputation to issue a special edition of his collected works. He was so popular that soon after his death appeared *The Return of Frank R. Stockton* (1913), a peculiar collection of dull letters and several stories claimed to have been dictated from beyond the grave.

Stockton was best known to his contemporaries as a humorist, but his fairy tales (which he preferred to call "fanciful tales") had their admirers, most notably L. Frank Baum, who wrote *The Wonderful Wizard of Oz* (1900). Stockton's publishers issued an anthology of the best of these children's stories in a sumptuous volume entitled *The Queen's*

Museum and Other Fanciful Tales (1887), illustrated in full color by Frederick Richardson and published as one of Scribners' Illustrated Classics. Their "classic" status, however, has long been in doubt. Stockton was ignored in the first edition of Cornelia Meigs's *Critical History of Children's Literature,* once considered the Bible of the field. Only recently and reluctantly have Stockton's fairy tales been acknowledged by juvenile literature specialists. This revival of interest in his work arose in the 1960's when Maurice Sendak illustrated two of his best stories, "The Griffin and the Minor Canon" (October 1885) and "The Bee-Man of Orn" (November 1883). Unfortunately, these pretty storybooks proved to be two of the least popular of this popular artist's efforts, and few of Stockton's juvenile works are presently in print. He deserves better than that, for he wrote some of the wittiest children's stories in American literature.

Stockton had a largely uneventful life. Even his biographer Martin I. J. Griffin had to admit that his subject had "sometimes an exasperating story, because, like all good men, he had a placid and industrious life." He was born (on 5 April 1834, in Philadelphia). He married (on 30 April 1860, Mary Ann Edwards Tuttle, who later wrote as "Marian Stockton"). He had no children. And he died (on 20 April 1902, while on a visit to Washington D.C.).

He also wrote and wrote and wrote and wrote. His wife once confessed that "his life was, in great part, in his books." He was by nature a storyteller, a fabricator, an inventor. All of his best efforts were romances, pure escapist fiction. He said that he was concerned with only two subjects: "one, the world of fancy invaded by the real; the other, the world we live in as seen through spectacles of more or less fantastical colors." In these concerns lie both his strengths and his severe limitations as an adult author, for while he could tell the most beguiling yarn, Stockton was alarmingly limited in describing the vagaries of human psychology and experience. The quaint particularly appealed to him. He could write effortlessly about fairies, ghosts, pirates, and the rural South, and his handling of such marvelous stuff was peculiarly his own. His work is aligned with other traditions as well: *The Great War Syndicate* (1889), with its prophetic Peace Queller, has affinities to H. G. Wells; and *The Great Stone of Sardis* (1898) recalls Jules Verne in its quest for a great crystal at the center of the earth. But what distinguishes Stockton from other writers is what Howells described as "that quiet confidence that every intelligent person enjoys an absurdity reduced from the most logical argument; and prefers the wildest caper of the fancy performed with a countenance of the gravest sobriety." Typical of Stockton's approach is *The Casting Away of Mrs. Lecks and Mrs. Aleshire* (1886); one of his most popular works for adult readers, it is the story of how two very proper New England ladies adjust to being marooned on a desert island in the South Pacific. It might be easy to conclude that Stockton's dependence upon the odd in his fictions came from his own deformity; from childhood he suffered from a severe limp due to one leg being shorter than the other. But in his whimsical art he never struggled with life as it is. His work is never more than charming and enchanting. And that may be why he is such a superior writer for children.

Even as a boy, Stockton loved to make up stories, and he was not the only one in his family with literary ambitions. His father, concerned with Methodist Church reform, wrote principally on ecclesiastical matters; and an elder sister had some success in placing her sentimental verses in magazines. But Frank's taste in reading was closest to that of his younger brother John, his constant companion in his childhood. They hated to come to the end of a beloved book, so like many other young writers, they composed new conclusions to the stories they were sharing. They continued to write and even submitted their early work to publishers while attending Central High School in Philadelphia. Frank did publish his first story while still a student;

it was awarded a prize by and appeared in the *Boys' and Girls' Journal* of Philadelphia.

On graduation Frank and his brother had to find trades. Frank was apprenticed to learn engraving on wood while John learned the same craft on steel. They continued to write, and with other Central High School graduates they formed their own literary society, exchanging one another's work for criticism. Frank always enjoyed fairy tales best, especially those of Hans Christian Andersen, but he detested the silly winged sprites who swarmed through children's stories and who had nothing better to do than to lecture naughty boys and girls on how to mend their evil ways. He resolved to create his own branch of fairy lore. He wanted

> the fanciful creatures who inhabited the world of fairy-land to act, as far as possible for them to do so, as if they were inhabitants of the real world. I did not dispense with monsters and enchanters, or talking beasts and birds, but I obliged these creatures to infuse into their extraordinary actions a certain leaven of common sense.

He therefore peopled his own experiments in the form with

> little beings of every temper and turn of mind, all suitably dressed in jerkins and breeches, and hats and feathers, and gowns and bodices, but with never a wing-hole in any garment. They were little men and women, more gifted in many ways than we, but on whom we could look with true brotherly and sisterly sympathy.

His fellow members of the literary club were so enthusiastic about his little fairy tales that they urged him to submit them for publication. However, the society soon folded, and Stockton put the stories aside as he pursued his career as a wood engraver.

He did submit and sometimes sell other work, principally humorous sketches, and when his brother became an editor of the *Philadelphia Morning Post* Stockton found a ready market for his early literary work. Surprisingly, while he certainly had some artistic ability himself, Stockton never illustrated any of his own stories. His eyesight was poor, and was no doubt aggravated by the exacting labors of wood engraving, so once he began selling his writing regularly he gave up art for literature. Still struggling as a free-lance writer, he pulled out his old fairy tales and sent them to the recently founded children's monthly the *Riverside Magazine* of Boston. There was no better place than this to launch the career of a new writer for boys and girls, for its editor, Horace E. Scudder, sought only the best for his young readers. His authors included such prominent literary figures as Edward Everett Hale, Sarah Orne Jewett, Helen Hunt Jackson, and Mary Mapes Dodge. He secured pictures from such eminent artists as Winslow Homer, John La Farge, Thomas Nast, and F. O. C. Darley. Scudder also had the good judgment to solicit contributions directly from Andersen himself in Europe, so that several of the Danish poet's fairy tales made their first appearance in print in English in an American children's magazine.

Scudder also published one of Stockton's adolescent fairy tales, "Ting-a-Ling," in the November and December 1867 numbers of the *Riverside*. It is included with some other stories in the first of Stockton's books, a collection of loosely connected short stories for children issued as *Ting-a-Ling* in 1870. These ornate, somewhat self-conscious confections are certainly a youthful effort, but they do contain many of the distinctive characteristics of the author's mature work. Their enchanted atmosphere is an odd borrowing from various literary traditions. While the general setting of *Ting-a-Ling* is decidedly out of the *Arabian Nights,* its diminutive hero is clearly an Elizabethan fay: he cavorts among the flowers with his companions Parsley and Sourgrass, and he pays tribute to his queen, who like Shakespeare's Mab is attended by golden moths and dragonflies. Ting-a-ling's bosom friend, Tur-il-i-ra, however, is a giant right out of the tales of the Brothers Grimm. These airy creatures are menaced by nightmarish beasts and bogies, some of whom apparently are created entirely from Stockton's own imagination. These include the Nimshee, an ocean spirit similar to a banshee, and the prong-horned Yabouks, "those sanguinary monsters which impale their victims on the great horn upon their noses, holding back their heads and opening their mouths to let the blood slowly trickle down their throats."

However derivative these tales may at first appear, they are saved from being mere pastiche by Stockton's marvelous sense of humor. Even here, in these early exercises, his highly refined, understated comedy is evident everywhere in his storytelling. The grisly and alarming beheading of Nerralina is accepted so matter-of-factly by the Prince that one knows immediately that nothing

terrible will result. The now headless girl becomes a "running gag" in the first tale. The fairies finally reattach her head, but not before a mischievous gnome turns it backward; but all is set right in the end, with her first kiss. *That* turns her head around! Stockton also makes the most of the incongruities in size between those two great friends Ting-a-ling the fairy and Tur-il-i-ra the giant; thus, while Ting-a-ling can scarcely finish three grains of rice for dinner, Tur-il-i-ra satisfies his hunger with "a pair of roast oxen, besides a small boiled whale, and a great plate of fricasseed elks. As for vegetables, there were boat-loads of mashed potatoes, and turnips, and beans; and there was a pie which was as big as a small back-yard."

In *Ting-a-Ling,* Stockton does not always seem to be aware of his intended audience. For example, what are children to make of the heartless disposal of Ting-a-ling's little girlfriend Ling-a-ting? One day, when the Princess Aufalia is weeping in her garden, the two fairies amuse themselves by balancing the prettiest tears that they can find; unfortunately, the one that the luckless Ling-a-ting is juggling bursts and drowns her. That is the end of her! Perhaps an adult may smile at this wry conceit, but children are perhaps too literal for this, and certainly the drowning of Ling-a-ting dampens the good humor of the rest of the story. Never strong on plot, the tales here, as everywhere in Stockton's work, tend to go off in every unexpected direction, no doubt confusing some young readers. However, Stockton was such a deft and delightful storyteller that his writing is never dull, so the reader usually remains engaged right up to the unpredictable conclusions. Even with all of its faults, *Ting-a-Ling* was still an auspicious introduction of this distinctive voice to nineteenth-century American letters.

Of course, at this time the sporadic sale of short stories to the periodicals could hardly pay all of Stockton's bills. Setting his career in wood engraving behind him, he went to New York City to become an editor. In 1868 Orange Judd, a publisher of numerous agricultural journals and books, founded a general-interest weekly called *Hearth and Home.* His editors included Harriet Beecher Stowe, author of *Uncle Tom's Cabin* (1852), and Mary Mapes Dodge, who had just come out with *Hans Brinker; or, The Silver Skates* (1865). Dodge, who was responsible for the children's page, needed an assistant, and Stockton got the job. His chief duty was to provide "fillers" on everything from pest control to interior decoration. He also was one of the magazine's major contributors to the boys' and girls' page. Here too his subjects could be dull; he ground out such pieces as "After Turtles' Eggs" (30 October 1869), "The Tale of a Trap" (9 September 1871), and "A Trip to Blodgett's Island" (12 October 1872). Some of these texts were written merely to describe some stock cuts taken from other, usually foreign, publications. Fortunately, Stockton could write on any topic and make it of some immediate interest.

He also used the children's page of *Hearth and Home* for further experimentation with original fairy tales. Pixies and giants are again introduced for the humor of their differences in size. Unfortunately, unlike the best of the *Ting-a-Ling* tales but like so many children's stories of the day, Stockton's little fancies primarily preach good behavior. Consequently, such a tiresome tale as "How Little Misty Came Out All Right" (2 April 1870) is marred by such twee characters as Little Misty, Isty, and Cutely. Others are elaborations of Mother Goose rhymes: "The Fairy and His Bell" (9 July 1870) refers to the famous line "Rings on her fingers and bells on her toes" and "The Naiad and the Dryad" (6 August 1870) is a slight fantasy woven around Little Bo-Peep. Many of these contributions to *Hearth and Home* are no better than parodies of traditional fairy tales, but here and there is a touch of the distinctive Stockton voice. Particularly fine is "The Tender Heart" (18 February 1871), a Valentine's Day tale about a giant's vain love for a girl of normal size. But that was the exception. Many of his contributions to *Hearth and Home* are indistinguishable from the pious drivel served up to boys and girls by the periodicals of the day.

Scribners was impressed by what Dodge was doing with *Hearth and Home* and hired her to found her own children's magazine, *St. Nicholas.* She was given carte blanche by her new employers, and she brought Stockton with her as her editorial assistant. She also stipulated that she be required to come to the office only once a week, and therefore the bulk of the labor of putting out *St. Nicholas* was left to Stockton. Dodge's special skill was in obtaining contributors. Leaving the journal in Stockton's capable hands, she went off on an extended European vacation. In England she contacted such distinguished authors and artists as George MacDonald, Alfred Lord Tennyson, Lewis Carroll, Christina Rossetti, and Kate Greenaway. Back home she secured work from Louisa May Alcott,

Thomas Bailey Aldrich, Henry Wadsworth Longfellow, John Greenleaf Whittier, Kate Douglas Wiggin, and Howard Pyle.

Scribners soon lost interest in *St. Nicholas* and sold it to the Century Company, also in New York. Happily the new owners did not change editors, and *St. Nicholas* soon became the preeminent American children's magazine. Established with the November 1873 issue, it did not have a worthy rival until six years later, when *Harper's Young People* was founded. At first the editors did have difficulty filling its pages with enough suitable material, and much of the copy in the early numbers was the work of Dodge and Stockton themselves, printed under several pseudonyms. Stockton signed this hack work either "Paul Fort" or "John Lewees," from the names of his siblings, Paul, John, and Louise. "Paul Fort" was responsible largely for slight sketches and fiction, "John Lewees" for informational articles. Again, much of this was merely filler written to accompany previously prepared wood engravings cribbed from European books and magazines. As late as 1882, long after Stockton had resigned as one of its editors, work continued to appear under these pseudonyms in *St. Nicholas.* Even as Frank R. Stockton, he published considerable hack work to accompany whatever the editors found in the public domain, and he did this not only for *St. Nicholas;* he also produced for Scribners two children's books, *Roundabout Rambles in Lands of Fact and Fancy* (1872) and *Tales Out of School* (1875), miscellanies of the oddest assortment of subjects derived from all kinds of cuts from the publisher's illustration files. Justifiably forgotten, these eclectic volumes show that Stockton was willing to write on anything that was requested of him.

Stockton appeared to one friend at this time as

> having a sallow skin, dark eyes, straight black hair, a nose a bit awry and a sensitive mouth whose twitchings gave notice of a good story. He was lame . . . but there was always dignity in his limping walk. He laughed much and enjoyably but almost noiselessly at the humor of other persons as well as his own—a real achievement for a humorist.
>
> (introduction to *The Storyteller's Pack*)

With only slight but significant variation did he appear to a fellow editor at the Century Company:

> His features were strong, his eyes dark and unusually large, and his voice was grave, deep in tone,

even musical. His face in repose was sad, and had about it the drawn look of those who know habitual pain, though I am sure that he always spoke of himself as being in the best of health. His laugh, though hearty at times, had the peculiar characteristic of being almost soundless.

(ibid.)

Stockton's was a most wry, understated humor that might reveal itself in the most unexpected ways. He enjoyed naming his chickens after literary friends, including Dodge. Once when she asked him how her namesake was doing, he sighed, "Imagine my surprise when Mary Mapes Dodge turned out to be Thomas Bailey Aldrich!" Another time, on departing the office in haste, Dodge forgot her galoshes. Stockton immediately wrapped them up and sent them on by messenger, enclosing one of the magazine's printed rejection slips, with one sentence underlined: *"Many articles must be returned for reasons which have no connection with their literary worth."*

In 1876 Stockton was forced to resign from *St. Nicholas.* He and Dodge remained on cordial terms, and he continued to contribute to her magazine as late as 1898. The reason for his leaving was that he could not take the strain of his office work. He was suffering from further deterioration of his eyesight, a malady common among wood engravers that often led to total blindness for the "woodpecker." At this point Stockton had to give up all reading and writing.

Of course he still had to earn a living, so he dictated his stories and articles to his wife, and later to a secretary. He also had to rely on others to read to him. He generally devoted two to three hours in the morning to reciting what he had worked out in his head the previous day. "First I lasso an idea," he described his method of composition. "It may be a startling climax—an effect, the causes leading up to which will of themselves develop a narrative." Except for occasionally jotting down notes for a story, he did most of his writing in his head. "I never take the trouble to work out the details," he admitted. "I crowd the interest in characters toward a certain fixed point in the narrative. Occasionally they protest and declare that they would not do what I make them do." He rarely consulted others' books, he explained, "because the ideas evolved are the offspring of another mind. I always feel however new the thought that comes to me may be, that the author I am reading had had it in his mind and rejected it."

While certainly more comfortable with the short story, Stockton did publish several serials on widely varying subjects in *St. Nicholas.* He often traveled for his health, gathering local color along the way for future writing. *What Might Have Been Expected* (serialized from November 1873 to October 1874; published as a book in 1874) is typical of the Reconstruction fiction in children's magazines, a sympathetic but still patronizing picture of the Southern "darky." *A Jolly Fellowship* (serialized from November 1878 to October 1879; published as a book in 1880) is a pleasant boys' shipboard yarn, inspired by the Stocktons' recent voyage to the Bahamas. *Personally Conducted* was a series of travel sketches he published from time to time in *St. Nicholas,* between November 1884 and March 1888 (published by Scribners in 1889). Knowing his love for the swashbucklers of the Spanish Main, Dodge readily accepted Stockton's "Buccaneers of Our Coast" (serialized from November 1897 to July 1898, issued by Macmillan in 1898 as *The Buccaneers and Pirates of Our Coast*). But perhaps Stockton was just too sweet-natured to give a rousing, vivid account of these romantic thieves; his pirate portraits are surprisingly tame and consequently inferior to those Pyle was publishing in the popular magazines at the same time. Stockton also attempted a historical novel for boys and girls, *The Story of Viteau* (serialized from November 1882 to April 1883; published as a book in 1884), set in the age of Louis IX, but he clearly was not really at home in medieval France. It is evident in all of these dated works that at least here Stockton was writing merely to suit the marketplace.

His heart lay elsewhere, and it is in his fanciful tales that one finds the quintessential Stockton as a children's author. But even here he developed slowly. Only after several years of fits and starts in the pages of *St. Nicholas* did Stockton introduce his particular brand of fairy tale with "Sweet Marjoram Day" (later "The Reformed Pirate") in the December 1877 issue. Of course Stockton had already written many other fairy tales for Dodge's magazine, but these earlier ones were composed to fit the pictures and thus constrained the full flowering of Stockton's wild invention. "Sweet Marjoram Day," which depicts the ridiculous consequences of a little girl's determination to visit the tiny cottage of two fairy sisters, marks the beginning of Stockton's classic period. He did not write many fanciful tales. He published only twenty-one in *St. Nicholas* or, sometimes, in *Harper's Young People,* off and on between December 1877 and January 1888. Yet this relatively slim body of work is the most significant contribution to the American fairy-tale genre prior to the publication of *The Wonderful Wizard of Oz* in 1900.

There is nothing self-consciously American about Stockton's stories. Giants, dwarfs, sphinxes, dryads, gnomes, griffins, witches, and magicians wander here and there in his Old World landscape. He does introduce some new types of fairy folk (for example, a "gudra" is a giant dwarf), but there is nothing obviously Yankee from which he wove his enchantments. Stockton did not merely transplant European myths to New England soil as did Nathaniel Hawthorne in *The Wonder Book* (1852) and *Tanglewood Tales* (1853). He did not attempt to introduce indigenous legends as did Washington Irving with "Rip Van Winkle" and "The Legend of Sleepy Hollow" (1820). Edmund Wilson found Stockton's stories

> really admirable, . . . but they have none of the authentic glamour of myths—their success, in fact, depends on the fact that Stockton is not trying, like Hawthorne and Irving, to fit out America with a needed mythology, but merely by writing about the fairies so soberly and dryly as he did about contemporary American life aiming at an effect of irony.

However, it is in his distinctive use of fairy lore that Stockton made his most original contribution to the form.

One cannot expect much from Stockton's plots; he was always weak on form and structure in his short stories. This problem of composition may have been due to his particular method of writing: dictation has its limitations, and seems to have caused his tales to wander much as the mind wanders. Also, he relies too much on the basic plot of the fairy tale—the quest. While a great deal goes on in a Stockton story, not much really happens. He was certainly aware of this limitation. One of his best stories, "Prince Hassak's March" (December 1883), is almost a self-parody of the typical Stockton narrative. Prince Hassak of Itoby decides to visit his uncle, the King of Yan, saying:

> I shall march from my palace to that of my uncle in a straight line. I shall go across the country, and no obstacle shall cause me to deviate from my course. Mountains and hills shall be tunnelled, rivers shall be bridged, houses shall be levelled; a road shall be cut through forests; and, when I have finished my march, the course over which I have passed shall be a mathematically straight line. Thus will I show to the world that, when a prince desires to travel, it is not necessary for him to go out of his way on account of obstacles.

At first his path appears to be another Sherman's March to the Sea or the route of the Transcontinental Railroad, but of course, on only the second day Stockton starts dropping obstacles in the Prince's way, wildly throwing him off his determined course for days. The author even provides a complete and clear map of the Prince's mad march.

Stockton could no more write in a mathematically straight line than Prince Hassak could march in one; he constantly diverts from the path he originally sets out on, and one never knows what will happen next or how on earth the author will resolve all the strands of story he scatters along the way. For example, who could have predicted that Nassime would eventually marry the fairy Lorilla in "The Floating Prince" (December 1880)? Some stories are really two tales in one; for example, "The Bee-Man and His Original Form" (November 1883; later titled "The Bee-Man of Orn") is as much the history of the Languid Youth as that of the Bee-Man himself. Surprises are waiting at every bend in the road. Of course all does ultimately end well in most of his children's stories—these are fairy tales after all. Stockton once observed:

> When people who are really in earnest, especially people in fiction, go forth to find things they want, they generally find them. And if it is highly desirable that these things should be out of the common they are out of the common. A great deal of what happens in real life, and almost everything in literature, depends on this principle.

At least everything in *his* literature depends on it.

There is always a good dose of wry irony underlying Stockton's tales, but with one or two possible exceptions there is no tragedy. "He had not the heart to make his stories end unhappily," his wife once explained. "He knew that there is much of the tragic in human lives, but he chose to ignore it as far as possible, and to walk in the pleasant ways which are numerous in this tangled world." But his otherwise generous spirit did not prevent the author from occasionally inserting barbed observations on human stupidities. He was too much of an artist to ignore them all.

In reading through his fanciful tales for children, one is immediately struck by how free of true villainy they are; there is no sense of menace here. They are also refreshing to read after plowing through the didactic, earnest drivel that filled much of *St. Nicholas* at that time; Stockton's tales are cleansed of the fierce Puritan morality of the run-of-the-mill children's literature of that century. In Stockton's fairyland Good no longer battles toe-to-toe with Evil. His witches, goblins, and monsters are so civilized, so *moderne,* and his giants are always accommodating. When the fairy cries, in "The Poor Count's Christmas" (December 1881), "How glad I am that your grandfather's uncle died!" the giant hastens to correct her: "You shouldn't say that. It isn't proper." The Reformed Pirate of "Sweet Marjoram Day" is likewise a master of politesse, and the robbers in "The Christmas Truants" (*Harper's Young People,* 7 December 1886) eagerly change places with the schoolboys. And in "The Battle of the Third Cousins" (September 1885), the virile warrior is the sworn enemy of his relative until he gets to know and love the twelve-year-old boy. There are no bloodcurdling characters or incidents, no real dangers in Stockton's fairy realm. Even the Gorgoness of "The Philopena" (May 1884) is not the horrid creature of Greek and Roman myth. "My impulses, I know, are good," she sighs, "but my appearance is against me." Stockton's is a Peaceable Kingdom in which every creature appears to be in harmony with everyone else.

Of course there are certain types who occasionally must cause discord among their fellows. Chief among these nuisances are schoolteachers. Stockton clearly shared with many of his young readers their disdain for the classroom. "Happening to pass a house with open windows," Stockton noted in one of his adult works, "I heard the sound of children's voices speaking in unison, and knowing that this must be a school, I looked in, compelled entirely by that curiosity which often urges us to gaze upon human suffering." Not surprisingly, buoyant truants abound in Stockton's children's stories. Prince Terzan, in "The Sisters Three and the Kilmaree" (October 1882), must suffer a long round of ridiculous instruction, being "passed from professor to professor, from teacher to teacher, each one trying to keep him as long as possible, and to teach him as much as he could." And once he has graduated, "the professors wished him to begin all over again"!

In "The Accommodating Circumstance" (*Harper's Young People,* 22 July 1884), the tables are turned: the Baron comes upon a "School for Men" where "the principal thing we try to teach . . . is the proper treatment of boys." One of the young instructors explains that this institution has been "established by boys for the proper instruction and education of men. We have found that there are no human beings who need to be taught so much as men." Beneath such wall mottoes as "The Boy: Know Him, and You Are Educated" and "Respect Your Youngsters," the Baron studies "sixteen rules which proved that boys ought to be consulted in regard to the schools they were sent to, the number of their holidays, the style of their new clothes, and many other things which concerned them more than any one else." One adult who should have been sent to this "School for Men" is the jailer of "Prince Hassak's March," who incarcerates seventeen individuals, most of them boys and girls, for a wide range of crimes: "The first was highway robbery, the next forgery, and after that followed treason, smuggling, barn-burning, bribery, poaching, usury, piracy, witchcraft, assault and battery, using false weights and measures, burglary, counterfeiting, robbing hen-roosts, conspiracy, and poisoning his grandmother by proxy." The Potentate finds these strange offenses for little children. "They often begin that sort of thing very early in life," says the jailer, as if paraphrasing some nineteenth-century pedagogue. "It is best to take them young, my lord. They are very hard to catch when they grow up."

In Stockton's world there are some who are never pleased with the way things are; these busybodies cannot leave well enough alone. The Bee-Man of Orn is contented with his lot in life until a Junior Sorcerer informs him that he has been transformed and must be turned back into his former shape. The poor Bee-Man then suffers many dangers to discover who or what he once was—only to learn that his former shape was that of a baby. He returns to this former state and grows up to be exactly the same man he was at the story's beginning! The Queen of "The Queen's Museum" (September 1884) tries to force her people to admire her collection of buttons and buttonholes, but soon discovers that "we cannot make other people like a thing simply because we like it ourselves." Even the little girls in "Sweet Marjoram Day" and in "The Clocks of Rondaine" (December 1887 to January 1888) are busybodies who cause no end of troubles for others through their odd whims.

The true villain in Stockton's fairyland is Human Folly. The Ninkum (for nincompoop) in "The Castle of Bim" (October 1881) seeks a wonderful place that no one else has ever heard of. Along the way he convinces a citizen of another town to accompany him in his quest. The man tells him:

> In our city, we try to be governed in everything by the ordinary rules of common sense. In this way we get along very comfortably and pleasantly, and everything seems to go well with us. But we are always willing to examine into the merits of things which are new to us, and so I would like to go to this curious castle.

However, after many more miles of travel, the Ninkum is asked whether he really knows the way to the Castle of Bim. "I do not know the exact way," he confesses. "I have thought a great deal on the subject, and I feel sure that there must be such a place, and the way to find it is to go and look for it." Otherwise sensible people are misled by simpletons. In "The Philopena," people trust in the advice of the Absolute Fool because he always sounds so logical and sane at first, but his pronouncements end in disaster. Filamina, in "The Magician's Daughter and the High-Born Boy" (November 1880), is burdened with six foolish requests made by a merchant who wants to recover some lost rubies that he says are as big as cherries, a beautiful damsel who seeks her lost lover, a covetous king who demands the kingdom next to his own, a young man who wants to know how to make gold out of old iron bars and horseshoes, a general who wishes to learn the secret of vanquishing another army, and an old woman who would like to discover a good way to make root beer. In the end good common sense is the only magic that can fulfill their requests. In "The Banished King" (December 1882), the foolish monarch goes out into the world to learn why everything goes wrong in his kingdom; in his absence, everything runs smoothly under his queen's wise rule, for the problem all along was the silly king himself. Clearly Stockton had as little respect for governments as for schools. But there is no real malice in his observations. Stockton merely pokes fun at others, and there is no animosity in his gentle jibes. His fanciful tales can hardly be called satires.

Men have their praiseworthy characteristics as well as their flaws. Stockton frequently considers the quality of generosity, particularly in his holiday stories such as "Shamruch; or, The Christmas Panniers" (*Harper's Young People,* 20 December 1881) and "The Poor Count's Christmas" (December 1881 and January 1882), published at that time of year when his young readers were likely to give as much as they received. Also, for fairy tales, Stockton's stories are remarkably free of any romantic passion. Howells noticed that this writer "is rarely more droll than when he lets his lovers disport themselves as lovers. It sometimes seems as if he looked up his lovers' words in the dictionary." In "The Accommodating Circumstance" the Baron woos Litza completely matter-of-factly: " 'Why, you have given me yourself!' he cried, delighted. 'So it appears,' said Litza. . . . 'And will you marry me?' he cried. 'If you wish it,' said Litza. So that matter was settled." At first glance "The Sisters Three and the Kilmaree" and "The Philopena" seem to be conventional romances, except that Stockton introduces so many twists and turns in trying to get his lovers together that in fact these are parodies of the form. Husbands and wives frequently have no understanding of one another. The Banished King is so out of touch with his queen that he has no idea that she can rule much better than he ever could. "If you have made up your mind," sniffs the Countess in "The Poor Count's Christmas," "I suppose there is no use in my saying anything more about it." "Not the least in the world" is the reply, which silences her.

If there is only one real love story among Stockton's fanciful tales, it must be "Old Pipes and the Dryad" (June 1885), which may also be his only tragedy for children. Although the kiss that the Dryad bestows on the piper makes him grow ten years younger, Old Pipes and the Dryad are not really lovers. Still, there is a strong bond between these two peculiar souls—call it platonic. The Echo-dwarf acts like the villainous Yellow Dwarf in Madame D'Aulnoy's fairy tale, trying to break up the hero and heroine, and he nearly succeeds. It is Nature, however, who parts the two. The Dryad knows that the piper will return in the spring to release her from her wooden prison. "But, to his sorrow and surprise," Stockton concludes, Old Pipes "found the great tree lying upon the ground. A winter storm had blown it down, and it lay with its trunk shattered and split. And what became of the Dryad, no one ever knew." Stockton already had recorded the similarly sad end of another spirit, the Water Sprite of "The Philopena," who pines when taken from her home, the Land of the Lovely Lakes:

> The more she thought about it, the more she grieved; and one morning, unable to bear her sorrow longer, she sprang into the great jet of the fountain. High into the bright air the fountain threw her, scattering her into a thousand drops of glittering water; but not one drop fell back into the basin. The great, warm sun drew them up; and, in a little white cloud, they floated away across the bright blue sky.

That is certainly an odd way to finish an otherwise whimsical tale, but here Stockton returns to the preciosity of his heartless dismissal of Ling-a-ting in *Ting-a-Ling.* It is jarring without being true tragedy, for it is so out of character with the story before it. However, the loss of Old Pipes's Dryad is a poignant conclusion to the tale of that most unlikely couple.

Stockton was capable of some bitterness, too, even in a children's story. His masterpiece is perhaps "The Griffin and the Minor Canon," which is strikingly different from his other fanciful tales due to its cynicism. In what appears as an otherwise delightful fairy story, Stockton touches on some of the ugliest attributes of human nature—ingratitude, selfishness, and cruelty. The only decent person in the whole town is the Minor Canon, "a man of good sense," the Griffin calls him, and *he* is driven from the village. His neighbors' spiritual neglect is indicated early, when the Minor Canon conducts afternoon services with only "three aged women who had formed the week-day congregation." The Griffin learns to feel contempt for these townspeople. He chastises them for treating his friend so shabbily:

> Here was your Minor Canon, who labored day and night for your good, and thought of nothing else but how he might benefit you and make you happy; and as soon as you imagine yourselves threatened with a danger . . . you send him off, caring not whether he returns or perishes, hoping thereby to save yourselves. . . . Go, some of you, to the officers of the church, who so cowardly ran away when I first came here, and tell them never to return to this town under penalty of death. And if, when your Minor Canon comes back to you,

you do not bow yourselves before him, put him in the highest place among you, and serve and honor him all his life, beware of my terrible vengeance! There were only two good things in this town: the Minor Canon and the stone image of myself over your church-door.

It is unusual for Stockton to preach so much in one of his children's stories. His tales are always moral, even if not heavily laden with strict morality, but he preferred that his readers figure out his teachings for themselves. "Some people work out one kind of moral, and others work out another kind," he noted. He did not wish to have to attach some little lesson to the end of each story; that was as tiresome as "being asked to make bread for the man who buys my wheat." Surely much of the subtler observation of human character in his fanciful tales must have been lost on most boys and girls. "Children liked the stories," his wife admitted, "but the deeper meaning underlying them all was beyond the grasp of a child's mind." Perhaps to be sure his moral was not lost, at least in this story, Stockton has his Griffin preach for him this one time.

The author may have been well aware that his work was changing in tone; perhaps he feared he was losing his child audience. Anyway he wrote only three more fanciful tales beyond "The Griffin and the Minor Canon": two minor holiday stories, "The Christmas Before Last" (December 1885) and "The Christmas Truants," and the admirable "The Clocks of Rondaine." Clearly he had other things to write at this time. However, although he abandoned juvenile literature (except for some few unmemorable efforts), he thought enough of these short stories for girls and boys to include them in his collected works. Maybe some modern readers, young or old, will return to this remarkable contribution to American children's literature. After all, as Howells asked, "Where . . . in our literature shall we find such a body of honest humor, with its exaggeration deep in the nature of things, and not in the distortion of the surface?"

Selected Bibliography

WORKS OF FRANK R. STOCKTON

Short stories mentioned in this essay were originally published in *St. Nicholas* unless otherwise indicated. Most of these stories were later published individually or in the collections listed below.

Ting-a-Ling. With illustrations by E. B. Bensell. Boston: Hurd and Houghton, 1870.

Roundabout Rambles in Lands of Fact and Fancy. With illustrations. New York: Scribner, Armstrong, 1872.

What Might Have Been Expected. With illustrations. New York: Dodd, Mead, 1874.

Tales Out of School. With illustrations. New York: Scribner, Armstrong, 1875.

A Jolly Fellowship. With illustrations. New York: Charles Scribner's Sons, 1880.

The Floating Prince and Other Fairy Tales. With illustrations. New York: Charles Scribner's Sons, 1881.

The Story of Viteau. With illustrations by R. B. Birch. New York: Charles Scribner's Sons, 1884.

A Christmas Wreck and Other Stories. New York: Charles Scribner's Sons, 1886.

The Bee-Man of Orn and Other Fanciful Tales. New York: Charles Scribner's Sons, 1887.

The Queen's Museum and Other Fanciful Tales. New York: Charles Scribner's Sons, 1887.

Personally Conducted. With illustrations by Joseph Pennell et al. New York: Charles Scribner's Sons, 1889.

The Clocks of Rondaine and Other Stories. With illustrations by Bashfield, R. B. Birch, et al. New York: Charles Scribner's Sons, 1892.

The Great Stone of Sardis. New York: Harper and Brothers, 1898.

The Buccaneers and Pirates of Our Coast. With illustrations by G. Varian and B. West Clinedinst. New York: Macmillan, 1898.

The Poor Count's Christmas. With illustrations by E. B. Bensell. New York: Frederick A. Stokes, 1927.

The Griffin and the Minor Canon. With illustrations by Maurice Sendak. New York: Holt, Rinehart and Winston, 1963.

The Bee-Man of Orn. With illustrations by Maurice Sendak. New York: Holt, Rinehart and Winston, 1964.

CRITICAL AND BIOGRAPHICAL STUDIES

Bowen, Edwin W. "Frank R. Stockton." *Sewanee Review* (1920).

"Frank R. Stockton." *St. Nicholas* 6: 46–47 (1878).

Griffin, Martin I. J. *Frank R. Stockton: A Critical Biography.* Philadelphia: University of Pennsylvania Press; London: Oxford University Press, 1939.

Howells, William Dean. "Fiction, New and Old." *Atlantic Monthly* 87 (1901).

———. "The Novels and Stories of Frank R. Stockton." *Book Buyer* 20: 19–21 (1900).

———. "Stockton and His Works." *Harper's Weekly* 41: 538 (1897).

———. "Stockton's Stories." *Atlantic Monthly* 59: 130 (1887).

"Introduction" to *The Storyteller's Pack: A Frank R. Stockton Reader.* New York: Charles Scribner's Sons, 1968.

Stockton, Frank R. "How I Served My Apprenticeship As a Man of Letters." *Youth's Companion* 70: 119 (1896).

———. "Looking Back at Boyhood." *Youth's Companion* 65: 213–215 (1892).

Stockton, Marian E. "A Memorial Sketch of Mr. Stockton." In *The Novels and Stories of Frank R. Stockton,* Shenandoah Edition, vol. 23. New York: Charles Scribner's Sons, 1904.

—MICHAEL PATRICK HEARN

JONATHAN SWIFT

1667–1745

CHILDREN'S LITERATURE NOT by intention but by acceptance, *Gulliver's Travels* undeniably appeals to children. That appeal stretches back to 1726, the year Jonathan Swift's satire first appeared as *Travels into Several Remote Nations of the World,* by Lemuel Gulliver. Whether intended for them or not, literature claimed by children (like the medieval *Robin Hood,* the eighteenth-century *Robinson Crusoe,* or the twentieth-century *Watership Down*) becomes theirs by annexation. Once they find what they are looking for, juvenile audiences can easily scamper over such barriers as an author's intention. So it was for *Gulliver's Travels* two and a half centuries ago.

Pretending not to know that Swift was the author of the anonymously published travels, the poet and playwright John Gay wrote to him on 17 November 1726 about their instant popularity with adult and juvenile readers:

> About ten days ago a Book was publish'd here of the Travels of one Gulliver, which hath been the conversation of the whole town ever since: The whole impression sold in a week. . . . From the highest to the lowest it is universally read, from the Cabinet-council to the Nursery.
>
> (*Correspondence,* edited by Harold Williams)

Within a month ten thousand copies were sold. Many editions and abridgments quickly appeared.

The first of the pirated abridgments, which was put out by J. Stone and R. King only one year after the original, does not appear to have been intended exclusively for children, although the printers claimed to have omitted passages "which the Generality of Mankind have thought immodest and indecent." To that end there is some trimming of the text. For example, Gulliver's reference to "the Necessities of Nature" (defecating) is left out of Lilliput. But his urinating on the burning Lilliputian palace is retained, as are many of the book's references to excrement. Finding little censorship, one scholar (Rogers) suspects the reference to "immodest" material was simply a ploy to remind readers of its existence and to entice them to buy the book.

Gulliver's Travels came out a generation before John Newbery and other enterprising publishers in England began to market secular books that children would no longer have to borrow from adults. Besides original storybooks, such as *The History of Little Goody Two-Shoes* (1765), they put out special juvenile editions of books child readers had already borrowed from adults. While featuring more illustrations than their adult counterparts, these children's editions were abridgments. In 1772 Francis Newbery (John Newbery's nephew) advertised *The Adventures of Captain Gulliver,* perhaps the first such abridgment for young readers of Swift's novel. Most early versions for children stress the word "adventures" in their titles rather than "travels," presumably to make the book more attractive to young audiences.

And though profusely illustrated, the juvenile versions were not always accurately or carefully illustrated. For example, in a New England edition the Lilliputian temple looks suspiciously like a Congregational church, presumably because the printer had such a woodcut handy, and the rope dancing at court is pictured with children, not courtiers, playing games. A typical early version for children was *The Adventures of Captain Gulliver in a Voyage to the Islands of Lilliput and Brobdingnag. Abridged from the Works of the Celebrated Dean Swift. Adorned with Cuts*. The book was printed around 1789 in London by Elizabeth Newbery, the widow of John Newbery's nephew Francis. Adorning woodcuts, however crude or inexact, were no small feature in the successful merchandising of books for children in the eighteenth century.

For the adult reader, however, illustrated editions were available as early as 1727. The original text featured four maps, two plans, and a frontispiece. In Swift's day illustrations did not stamp a novel as suspect fare for adults, as the "G" rating of a movie does today. Only a twentieth-century bias automatically stamps an illustrated edition as suitable only for the young.

Yet another way *Gulliver's Travels* reached universal popularity was through the chapbook editions available from the mid-1700's. A typical title was *The Travels and Adventures of Capt. Lemuel Gulliver. Shewing How he was cast upon unknown Land, where the Inhabitants were but six Inches high; the Customs of the Country, Court, King &c. And the Author's Exploits, and surprising Return*. Only twenty-four pages, this undated chapbook (*ca.* 1750) featured on its cover the quintessential illustration of a supine Gulliver surprised and ensnared by the Lilliputians. Because of their extreme brevity, the chapbooks were necessarily savagely truncated, though earthy and sexual references were not always excised, as in many Victorian and contemporary editions for youth.

Whether in the children's editions or the chapbooks, then as now, books 1 and 2 of *Gulliver*, the voyages to Lilliput and Brobdingnag, are the real attraction. The third book, the voyage to Laputa and other lands, is sometimes retained in truncated form for its nonsensical qualities, but book 4, the voyage to the land of the Houyhnhnms, the perennial line of scrimmage for Swiftian scholars, is often dropped altogether (critics see it as Swift's most complex and least fathomable voyage). Whether because editors find the final section of *Gulliver* too pessimistic or too subtle, in juvenile editions children often do not get to read about Gulliver's final voyage.

Such tampering with his text, even for a young audience, would hardly have gained Dean Swift's approbation. When his original publisher toned down his satire for political reasons, Swift complained to his friend Charles Ford in a letter dated 20 November 1733: ". . . the whole Story is taken out of several passages, in order to soften them. Thus the Style is debased, the humor quite lost, and the matter insipid."

Was the "whole story" taken out of juvenile editions of *Gulliver?* Is the humor quite lost? Accustomed as we are today to heavily annotated editions, that is hard to judge. The modern adult reader is constantly barricaded from the text by walls of footnotes. Less reverent, young readers find few (if any) footnotes to distract them in juvenile editions, or they can, without guilt, ignore masses of footnotes in adult editions. The juvenile reader is freer to enjoy Swift's work than the scholar sifting every allusion for a topical reference to Georgian England. While it is useful to know that Flimnap is a caricature of Sir Robert Walpole, first prime minister of England, do child readers have to know about Walpole's career to laugh at Flimnap's antics? Do they need specifics of the Treaty of Utrecht to enjoy Lilliputian naval battles?

While there are thickets of topicality aplenty for scholars to explore, *Gulliver's Travels,* unlike Swift's more sophisticated and erudite "The Battle of the Books" (1704), is a general satire applicable to all mankind, not simply to select eighteenth-century courtiers. F. R. Leavis points out that, with the exception of book 4, an adult's reading of *Gulliver* will not be of a different order from the child's. While the adult might be more aware of the political satire in Lilliput, the politics of the court of Queen Anne and George I are not very well known today. Today's reader, whether child or adult, enjoys Swift in the same way.

Enjoy is a key term. Swift's satire is taken so somberly by some scholars that we forget that our first reading of *Gulliver* (as child or adult) was undoubtedly joyful. George Orwell, for example, received a copy for his eighth birthday and read it with inexhaustible fascination. In "Politics vs. Literature" he explains why children find the book absorbing:

> A child, when it is past the infantile stage but still looking at the world with fresh eyes, is moved by horror almost as often as by wonder—horror of

snot and spittle, of the dogs' excrement on the pavement, the dying toad full of maggots, the sweaty smell of grown-ups, the hideousness of old men, with their bald heads and bulbous noses.

If Orwell is right, children would be better served by adult editions than by children's editions, which have some of the less pleasant details omitted.

In their scrutiny of Swift, today's adult readers often lose sight of what Swift's contemporaries and young readers for over two centuries have experienced—rollicking humor and delightful detail. One of Swift's contemporaries labeled *Gulliver's Travels* a "merry work," a perspective adult readers often lose sight of. Rebutting colleagues who were surprised that he laughed aloud while reading Gulliver's adventures, one critic countered, "What should I have done? Blown my brains out?"

Whether in editions for children or adults, what makes *Gulliver* a merry book, albeit one with a serious intention? Throughout, there is the central conceit of topsy-turviness. In the first book Gulliver towers over minuscule creatures with whom a child, living in a world of veritable giants himself, can empathize. Book 2 turns the twelve-to-one scale upside down. Tall as church steeples, the Brobdingnagians now tower over Gulliver. To Samuel Johnson this switch in perspective was little to get excited about. "When once you have thought of big men and little men, it is very easy to do all the rest." Surprised by this assessment, James Boswell defended Swift, but was unable to budge Johnson from his opinion that *The Tale of a Tub* (1704) was Swift's sole masterpiece. Johnson got taken in by the simplicity of the conceit. Swift makes his satire look deceptively easy. William Hazlitt's answer to Johnson was that it does not matter whether the excellence of *Gulliver* lies in conception or execution, that Swift deserves no pooh-poohing since his toying with scale delights both adult and child.

What in *Gulliver's Travels* delights children? In Lilliput and Brobdingnag, besides the cunning peeps through two ends of a telescope, it is what accompanies that vision—the heaps of carefully worked out details. The Lilliputian chains that confine Gulliver in the temple resemble those worn on ladies' watches. The creatures are so small that Gulliver is able to slip five of the little beasties in his pocket, and their children can play hide and seek in his hair. It takes three hundred of their tailors to make Gulliver a suit, and 120 waiters to serve him a single meal. Twenty-four horses drill in formation on Gulliver's handkerchief.

In Brobdingnag, where, tables turned, Gulliver is now Lilliputian, the giant's handkerchief used to transport him is one foot thick. Such ingeniously calculated specifics fascinate, whether the hogsheads of wine Gulliver downs with one gulp or the twenty or thirty fowl he scoops up with the tip of his knife. In the land of the giants serving dishes are twenty-four feet in diameter, and the smallest cup holds two gallons. And here Gulliver is wedged into a marrowbone by a jealous dwarf and nearly drowns in a creamer. Apparently Swift knew of Tom Thumb, the chapbook hero who experienced similar mishaps, like falling into a pudding.

Throughout the book, such details are piled matter-of-factly with mathematical precision. Gulliver even details the torrents of urine he voids and the number of Lilliputian wheelbarrows required to haul away his excrement. Dr. Johnson, who disliked the book so much that Boswell asked whether he harbored some animosity against Swift, found great merit in the inventory of articles the Lilliputians make of the Man-Mountain's pockets, especially the description of his watch, which, since he consults it so often, they conjecture is his God. Children are no less interested in copious details of everyday objects and happenings, maybe even more so, as George Orwell has observed.

Some of the very details children would be interested in, especially allusions to bodily functions, are removed in typical modern juvenile versions. While their editors claim such abridgment merely cuts down on difficult and abstract passages, one result is the elimination of sexual, gross, or earthy material. Many children's versions eliminate the passage in which Gulliver's excrement is hauled away in wheelbarrows. That passage was also excised in the first adult abridgment of *Gulliver*. Gulliver's memorable voiding of urine on the palace fire is routinely bowdlerized today but was not excised in Georgian children's versions. References to breast-feeding are also cut, as is another reference to Gulliver's discharging "the Necessities of Nature." Swift and his contemporaries were evidently less squeamish. When asked by a publisher what scenes should be illustrated, Swift suggested including the dousing of the palace fire. While this scene was depicted in two adult editions of the late eighteenth and early nineteenth centuries, these illustrations were later suppressed.

In light of today's frankly realistic young-adult novels, which are avidly read by prepubescents, the attempts to purge Swift's situational or linguistic coarseness seem misguided. Certainly there are confusing passages that benefit from retelling or annotation. Thus, adult versions of *Gulliver* often come heavily annotated, but one questions whether whole sections need to be chopped out of what is a 250-page storybook.

Swift's language, even though occasionally vulgar and therefore chastened in contemporary juvenile editions, delights the youngest of readers. The child might miss the parody in the litany of titles of the Emperor of Lilliput, but who among us, child or adult, can miss the fun of "Mully Ully Gue"? Children relish nonsensical Swiftian wordplay like the "Luggnaggians" or the land of "Glubbdubdrib."

That Swift, childless and unmarried, who wrote nothing exclusively for children, continually delights that audience with comic hijinks is but one irony in Swift's life. Born in Ireland of English parents, he looked down upon the land of his birth, regarding his church positions in Ireland as exile in a "land of slaves." Yet it was here he wrote *Gulliver* and became heralded as an Irish patriot for *The Drapier's Letters* (1724), which was instrumental in saving the Irish from a debased coinage. Once a Whig, he became, during the reign of Queen Anne, the literary Tory spokesman. Engaged in intense friendships with several women, he never married. A clergyman who aspired to be a poet and to obtain a bishopric, he became dean of Dublin's Saint Patrick's Cathedral and is best known for his prose masterpieces. He craved literary fame, yet published all his major works anonymously. Swift, according to his many friends, was "formed for mirth and society," but he died alone and aphasic, no longer able to manage himself or his duties. However, he did not die a raving lunatic, as Thackeray and other critics of his work gleefully assumed. And his decline occurred some twenty years after he composed *Gulliver's Travels,* which belies the popular misconception of him as a misanthrope who vented his spleen in book 4 of that work.

No other work of Swift would appeal to children, certainly not the mock-heroic "The Battle of the Books" or the coolly savage "A Modest Proposal" (1729), with its detached persona calmly discussing roasting babies "hot from the knife" (even some college students are not yet ready for that satiric tract). Children would like some parts of *Directions to Servants* (1745), his humorous guide on how to be an incompetent servant.

One of Swift's friends wished him a press run as big as John Bunyan's. Bunyan's *Pilgrim's Progress* (1678), Daniel Defoe's *Robinson Crusoe* (1719), and Swift's *Gulliver's Travels* are the big three of the early classics for children. First appearing during the period of the Restoration and the early eighteenth century, they still enjoy universal popularity.

Defoe's travel book certainly influenced Swift. And just as there were Robinsonnades, there was Gulliveriana, in the new children's books beginning to be marketed in England about the time of Swift's death. In John Newbery's *The Newtonian System of Philosophy* (1761) the Lilliputian Society gathers to hear scientific lectures. And the first periodical for children, *The Lilliputian Magazine,* was put out by Newbery in 1752. One can spot the Swiftian touch in children's books to this day. (Pauline Clarke's *The Return of the Twelve,* Mary Norton's *The Borrowers,* and E. B. White's *Stuart Little* feature Lilliputian characters). In the *Butter Battle Book* (1984), by Dr. Seuss, the Zooks and the Yooks battle over which side of a slice of bread one should butter. This put-down of war by Seuss, a former Swift scholar, recalls Lilliput's Big-Endians and Little-Endians. And "Lilliputian" has become a household word.

Johnson, no fan of the book, admitted that Swift's satire was so new and strange it filled readers with mingled merriment and amazement. "Criticism was for a while lost in wonder," he complained. Today, just the opposite is true. Wonder is often lost in criticism. In 1805 Richard Payne Knight noted what is still true, that children who read *Gulliver* without suspecting that it is satire are "more really entertained and delighted, than any learned or scientific readers, who perceived the intent from the beginning, have ever been." Young readers form an interpretive community capable of putting wonder back into the criticism of *Gulliver's Travels.* Swift would have savored this delicious irony.

Selected Bibliography

EDITIONS OF GULLIVER'S TRAVELS

Gulliver's Travels. Edited by Padraic Colum. With illustrations by Willy Pogany. New York: Macmillan, 1917.

Gulliver's Travels into Several Remote Nations of the World. With illustrations by Arthur Rackham. London: J. M. Dent and Sons, 1919; New York: E. P. Dutton, 1919.

Gulliver's Travels. Edited by May Lamberton Becker. With illustrations by R. M. Powers. Cleveland: World Publishing, 1948. (Typical of the modern expurgated texts for children.)

Gulliver's Travels. With illustrations by David Small. New York: William Morrow, 1953. (Retold and abridged.)

Gulliver's Travels: An Authoritative Text, the Correspondence of Swift, Pope's Verses on Gulliver's Travels and Critical Essays. Edited by Robert A. Greenberg. Rev. ed. New York: Norton, 1970.

Gulliver's Travels: A Casebook. Edited by Richard Gravel. London: Macmillan, 1974.

Gulliver's Travels: A Facsimile Reproduction of a Large-paper Copy of the First Edition, 1726, Containing the Author's Annotations. Edited by Colin McKelvie. Delmar, N.Y.: Scholars' Facsimiles and Reprints, 1976.

The Annotated Gulliver's Travels. Edited by Isaac Asimov. New York: Clarkson Potter, 1980. (Useful for historical illustrations by various illustrators.)

Gulliver's Travels. Adapted for young readers by Vincent Buranelli. With illustrations by Hieronimus Fromm. Morristown, N.J.: Silver Burdett, 1984. (A severe reduction of the voyage to Lilliput.)

CRITICAL AND BIOGRAPHICAL WORKS

Berwick, Donald M. *The Reputation of Jonathan Swift: 1781 1882.* Princeton: Unpublished Ph.D. dissertation, 1937. Reprinted New York: Haskell House, 1965.

Brady, Frank, ed. *Twentieth-Century Interpretations of "Gulliver's Travels": A Collection of Critical Essays.* Englewood Cliffs, N.J.: Prentice-Hall, 1968.

Eddy, William A. *Gulliver's Travels: A Critical Study.* Princeton: Princeton University Press, 1923. (For source study and imitations of *Gulliver's Travels.*)

Ehrenpreis, Irvin. *Swift: The Man, His Works, and the Age.* 3 vols. Cambridge: Harvard University Press, 1962, 1983.

Hunting, Robert. *Jonathan Swift.* New York: Twayne, 1967.

Kosok, Heinz. *Lemuel Gullivers Deutsche Kinder; Weltliteratur als Jugendbuch.* Wuppertal, Germany, 1976. (Available in only a few U.S. libraries, this short

work is a rare, if not the only, study of *Gulliver's Travels* as a work for children.)

Leavis, F. R. "The Irony of Swift." In *Fair Liberty Was All His Cry: A Tercentenary Tribute to Jonathan Swift,* edited by A. Norman Jeffares. New York: St. Martin's Press, 1967.

Lenfest, David S. "A Checklist of Illustrated Editions of *Gulliver's Travels, 1727–1914*" *The Papers of the Bibliographical Society of America* 62: 85–123 (1968).

Lock, F. P. "The Text of *Gulliver's Travels.*" *MLR* 76: 513–533 (1981). (Compares the 1726 first edition with the George Faulkner edition of 1735.)

Orwell, George. "Politics vs. Literature: An Examination of *Gulliver's Travels.*" In *The Orwell Reader.* New York: Harcourt, Brace, 1961.

Pickering, Samuel, Jr. "Gulliver and the Lilliputians" *AB Bookman's Weekly* 73: 175–198 (9 Jan. 1984). (Traces the influence of *Gulliver's Travels* on early children's books.)

Rogeres, Pat. "Classics and Chapbooks." In *Books and Their Readers in Eighteenth-Century England,* edited by Isabel Rivers. New York: St. Martin's Press, 1982.

Traugott, John. "The Yahoo in the Doll's House: *Gulliver's Travels,* the Children's Classic." In *English Satire and the Satiric Tradition,* edited by Claude Rawson. Oxford: Basil Blackwell, 1984. (Excellent on the psychological appeal of Swift's work to a child's fantasies.)

Tuveson, Ernest Lee. *Swift: A Collection of Critical Essays.* Englewood Cliffs, N.J.: Prentice-Hall, 1964.

Voigt, Milton. *Swift and the Twentieth Century.* Detroit: Wayne State University Press, 1964.

Welcher, Jeanne K., and George E. Bush, Jr., eds. "Lilliputiana for Children." In *Gulliveriana.* Delmar, N.Y.: Scholars' Facsimiles and Reprints, 1976. (Vol. 6, book 3, part 5.)

Williams, Harold, ed. *The Correspondence of Jonathan Swift.* 5 vols. Oxford: Clarendon Press, 1963–1965.

Williams, Kathleen. *Swift: The Critical Heritage.* London: Routledge and Kegan Paul, 1970. (Contains reprints of William Hazlitt's *Lectures on the English Poets* [1818] and Richard Payne Knight's *An Analytical Inquiry into the Principles of Taste* [1805]. Very useful on historical reaction to *Gulliver's Travels.*)

—ROBERT BATOR

J. R. R. TOLKIEN

1892–1973

ON 15 OCTOBER 1937, John Ronald Reuel Tolkien wrote to his editor, Stanley Unwin of Allen and Unwin, thanking him for the encouraging words in his last letter about the popularity of *The Hobbit,* which had been published recently. "The reviews," Tolkien added, "in the [London] Times and its Literary Supplement were good—that is (unduly) flattering." Unwin was also already anxious to discuss a possible sequel, and Tolkien responded:

> I cannot think of anything more to say about *hobbits.* . . . I have only too much to say, and much already written, about the world in which the hobbit intruded. . . . But if it is true that *The Hobbit* has come to stay and more will be wanted, I will start the process of thought, and try to get some idea of a theme drawn for treatment in a similar style and for a similar audience. . . . One reader wants fuller details about Gandalf and the Necromancer. But that is too dark . . . though actually the presence (even if only on the borders) of the terrible is, I believe, what *gives* this imagined world its verisimilitude. A safe fairy-land is untrue to all worlds.

Tolkien had originally told the story of the hobbit Bilbo Baggins and his adventures aloud to his children. When he began writing a formal version of *The Hobbit* with a view toward, perhaps, getting it published one day, he approached it in what was for him a typically equivocal fashion. Perhaps some of his roundaboutness was caused by discovering how much more of *The Hobbit* there was than there had

been when he first made up bits of the story to amuse his children. He all but stopped working on it three-quarters or so of the way through, after a highly important scene (the death of the dragon Smaug) but by no means a decisive one. But he did have it typed, even in its unfinished state, and then the pages lay in a drawer while he attended to other, more important things—giving lectures (for he was a professor at Oxford University), marking student papers and exams, and meeting with the Inklings, his beer-and-conversation circle of literary friends. This circle included, among others, C. S. Lewis, who was also the critic responsible for those "unduly flattering" reviews of *The Hobbit,* and Charles Williams, the author of a number of mystical-supernatural novels that few people could make head or tail of when they were first published. The existence of Professor Tolkien's "hobbit tale" was known to a few friends: the Inklings, for example. Lewis borrowed and read it in 1932, and praised it highly (this was twenty years before he would begin his immensely popular Narnia series). Some friend of a friend at last mentioned it to someone who worked at Allen and Unwin, and, intrigued, the someone asked to read it. Perhaps only because the Tolkiens were always short on money—there were four children to support on a don's meager salary—J. R. R. Tolkien finally sat down to write the closing chapters of *The Hobbit.*

But perhaps the major reason he had not done so before was that his heart was not entirely in it. He was fond of his hobbits, who were "just rustic English people, made small in size because it reflects the generally small reach of their imagination—not the small reach of their courage or latent power" —and who, he admitted, were much like himself:

> I am in fact a hobbit in all but size. I like gardens, trees, and unmechanized farmlands; I smoke a pipe, and like good plain food . . . and even dare to wear in these dull days, ornamental waistcoats. I am fond of mushrooms (out of a field); have a very simple sense of humour (which even my appreciative critics find tiresome). . . . I do not travel much.

But his real literary love was his imaginary languages, together with the world and its mythos that had grown up around those languages to give them a home: this was the world "in which the hobbit intruded," but the hobbits themselves were only a side issue.

Many years after he first began the creation of this vast mythology-history, he described his early, youthful concept of what the work was at last to be:

> Do not laugh! . . . once upon a time . . . I had a mind to make a body of more or less connected legend, ranging from the large and cosmogonic to the level of romantic fairy-story . . . which I could dedicate simply: to England; to my country. It should possess the tone and quality that I desired, somewhat cool and clear . . . (the clime and soil of the North West, meaning Britain and the hither parts of Europe; not . . . the Aegean, still less the East), and, while possessing (if I could achieve it) the fair elusive beauty that some call Celtic (though it is rarely found in genuine ancient Celtic things) it should be "high". . . . I would draw some of the great tales in fullness, and leave many only placed in the scheme.

He called his young self "absurd" for such a goal; and yet he worked on his beloved languages, and the legends and lives of the people who spoke them, all his life; and many of his readers would say today that his goal was not absurd at all. Long before *The Lord of the Rings* was thought of, some of these stories had evolved into *The Silmarillion*, although the book by that title was not published till after Tolkien's death.

"Middle-earth is *our* world," he wrote. "I have (of course) placed the action in a purely imaginary (though not wholly impossible) period of antiquity, in which the shape of the continental masses was different." And as he worked he came to feel that he was only recording a story, a history, that existed somewhere: perhaps not in our world as we know it, but somewhere.

> The tales arose in my mind as "given" things, and as they came, separately, so too the links grew. An absorbing, but continually interrupted labour (especially, even apart from the necessities of life, since the mind would wing to the other pole and spread itself on the linguistics): yet always I had the sense of recording what was already "there", somewhere: not of "inventing".

The emphasis here should be on "continually interrupted." Tolkien accepted a teaching post, married, had children; and with all these things came an increasing number of responsibilities and obligations, which left him less and less time for Middle-earth. He also had other creative work that drew him, for he was a scholar in a wide range of areas having to do with languages. "I am a philologist," he wrote, "and all my work is philological." When he was not yet twenty he worked for a while on the *New English Dictionary*, whose editor said of him:

> His work gives evidence of an unusually thorough mastery of Anglo-Saxon and of the facts and principles of the comparative grammar of the Germanic languages. Indeed, I have no hesitation in saying that I have never known a man of his age who was in these respects his equal.

As an undergraduate, Tolkien studied classical languages as well as English literature and linguistics; he later became Professor of Anglo-Saxon at Oxford at an unusually early age. And at Oxford he stayed for the rest of his working life, later being elected Merton Professor of English Language and Literature.

He spent a great deal of his limited free time in scholarly research; he was, furthermore, a perfectionist whose work was always in progress. His essays on Chaucer's "Reeve's Tale" and on *Beowulf* are still studied; and yet the greater part of his original research was never put in final, publishable form. He did fresh new translations of the medieval English poems *Sir Gawain and the Green Knight*, *Pearl*, and *Sir Orfeo*; and yet *Gawain* and *Pearl* were not published till after his death, because he was never nearly enough satisfied with his introductory notes to be willing to turn them over to a publisher. He was not a very organized worker—imaginative and diligent and often charismatic, but not very organized. Christopher Tolkien, his third and youngest son and his literary executor, has his life's work cut out for him by taking on the prodigious task of setting his father's papers in order.

But Tolkien did finish his children's book, *The*

Hobbit, and it was successfully published. And Tolkien did listen to Allen and Unwin's requests for another hobbit book. The letter of 15 October 1937 continues:

> I hope I am not taking myself too seriously. But I must confess that your letter has aroused in me a faint hope. I begin to wonder whether duty and desire may not (perhaps) in future go more closely together. I have spent nearly all the vacation-times of seventeen years examining, and doing things of that sort, driven by immediate financial necessity. . . . Writing stories . . . has been stolen, often guiltily, from time already mortgaged, and has been broken and ineffective. I may perhaps now do what I much desire to do, and not fail of financial duty. Perhaps!

He began, very tentatively, on a story that would have both hobbits and some more of the world of his *Silmarillion* in it. On 4 February 1938, he wrote again to Allen and Unwin: "I enclose a copy of Chapter I 'A Long-Expected Party' of possible sequel to *The Hobbit.*" And on 13 October of the same year he wrote:

> I have worked very hard for a month . . . on a sequel to *The Hobbit.* It has reached Chapter XI (though in rather an illegible state): I am now thoroughly engrossed in it, and have the threads all in hand—and I have to put it completely aside, till I do not know when.

Furthermore, now that he had opened the door to the world of *The Silmarillion,* he found that it poured into his new story:

> When I spoke . . . of this sequel getting "out of hand", I did not mean it to be complimentary to the process. I really meant it was running its course, and forgetting "children", and was becoming more terrifying than the Hobbit. It may prove quite unsuitable. . . . However, you will be the judge of that, I hope, some day! The darkness of the present days has had some effect on it. Though it is not an "allegory".

Months, sometimes years, passed when he did not touch the little heap of manuscript pages that would eventually become *The Lord of the Rings.* In his foreword to *The Fellowship of the Ring* he tells the story of his long labor:

> Those who had asked for more information about hobbits eventually got it, but they had to wait a long time; for the composition of *The Lord of the Rings* went on at intervals during the years 1936 to 1949. . . . The delay was, of course, also increased by the outbreak of war in 1939, by the end of which year the tale had not yet reached the end of Book I. In spite of the darkness of the next five years I found that the story could not now be wholly abandoned, and I plodded on, mostly by night, till I stood by Balin's tomb in Moria. There I halted for a long while. It was almost a year later when I went on and so came to Lothlórien and the Great River late in 1941. In the next year I wrote the first drafts of the matter that now stands as Book III, and the beginnings of Chapters 1 and 3 of Book V; and there as the beacons flared in Anórien and Théoden came to Harrowdale I stopped. Foresight had failed and there was no time for thought.
>
> It was during 1944 that, leaving the loose ends and perplexities of a war which it was my task to conduct, or at least to report, I forced myself to tackle the journey of Frodo to Mordor. These chapters, eventually to become Book IV, were written and sent out as a serial to my son, Christopher, then in South Africa with the RAF. Nonetheless it took another five years before the tale was brought to its present end. . . . Then when the "end" had at last been reached the whole story had to be revised, and indeed largely re-written backwards.

He did indeed recast much of the book and reworked much of what he had already written, both before and after he began *The Lord of the Rings* itself: this was only too typical of his work habits anyway. But one of the most extraordinary bits of this rewriting is a thunderingly complete revision of one chapter of *The Hobbit,* which by this time of course was not only already published but well on its way to becoming a minor classic.

The original version of the chapter "Riddles in the Dark" introduced Gollum as a nasty little creature who lives in the bottom of a mountain inhabited by the goblin Orcs. Gollum will reappear as one of the most fascinating characters in *The Lord of the Rings,* but for now he is only rather slinky and icky, with a hissing way of talking. He challenges Bilbo to a riddle game and promises him a "present" if he should win: the gold ring that is Gollum's most prized possession. This is a little implausible even without any knowledge of the later Gollum in *The Lord of the Rings,* for he is at once a creature not to be trusted, and his begging Bilbo's pardon when he finds the ring missing (because Bilbo had found it earlier and, without thinking, put it in his pocket) sounds very odd. But once Tolkien understood the significance of Bilbo's gold ring in what would be the War of the Ring, this scene no longer worked at all, any more than a historical novel about the exploits of Alexander the Great could include his use of machine guns.

And so by as neat a bit of authorial hocus-pocus as has ever been demonstrated, he rewrote that chapter to suit his new understanding of the Ring, inserted it defiantly into a new edition of *The Hobbit,* and added to the prologue of *The Fellowship of the Ring* a beautiful disclaimer about how this important material change came to be.

But Tolkien did finish *The Lord of the Rings* at last —more or less. On 31 October 1948, he wrote, "I managed to go into 'retreat' in the summer, and am happy to announce that I succeeded at last in bringing 'Lord of the Rings' to a successful conclusion." This turned out to be a trifle premature: Tolkien bogged down in the heavy task of typing the fair copy ("professional typing by the ten-fingered was beyond my means"); and true to form he found some further rewriting he had to do in the process. On 24 February 1950, he wrote again to Allen and Unwin: "For eighteen months now I have been hoping for the day when I could call [*The Lord of the Rings*] finished. But it was not until after Christmas that this goal was reached at last." Still he could not resist declaring, "It is finished, if still partly unrevised." He would say later, "I don't suppose there are many sentences that have not been niggled over."

The claim has been made often enough in the ensuing years that Tolkien's *The Lord of the Rings* began the new popularity of fantasy, or specifically of "high fantasy," that has not even yet reached its peak. The claim has been made so very often that few people pay much attention to it anymore. But it is true. The son of Stanley Unwin, of Allen and Unwin, who had given his eager ten-year-old's approval to *The Hobbit* years before, was a first reader of *The Lord of the Rings.* He called it "a brilliant and gripping story" but: "Quite honestly I don't know who is expected to read it: children will miss something of it, but if grown ups will not feel infra dig to read it many will undoubtedly enjoy themselves."

Allen and Unwin was seriously worried about the book's audience, particularly given its length. Tolkien's trilogy also began the fashion for fantasy trilogies, the irony of this being that Tolkien did not want to see his work split up into separate books at all, and fought the idea as long as he could, until he was made to understand that it would be three volumes or nothing. It was almost nothing even then, for he wanted to demand that *The Silmarillion* be published in tandem with *The Lord of the Rings,* and when Allen and Unwin demurred Tolkien almost went to another publisher. Once things were settled with Allen and Unwin there were further battles about giving the three volumes separate titles, which he also did not want, for unlike many of the later trilogies, *The Lord of the Rings* is one long narrative with no real breaks. He never was happy with the title of the third book, which, he said, gave too much of the plot away.

The Lord of the Rings was not an overnight bestseller. As Allen and Unwin didn't know quite what it was or whom to sell it to, it was hard to know how to advertise it. Furthermore, there were still wartime shortages to contend with, and publishers producing the most mainstream types of fiction were under pressure. But Allen and Unwin took the risk, and *The Fellowship of the Ring* came out in the summer of 1954, with the other two volumes following shortly. Critical reaction was a trifle confused—critics guessed no better than Allen and Unwin what sort of beast they had by the tail—but generally positive: positive enough to bring respectable sales. Six weeks after the appearance of the first thirty-five hundred copies of *Fellowship* a reprint was ordered. Houghton Mifflin, the American publisher of *The Hobbit,* brought *Fellowship* out that fall in the United States, where the critics were even more confused; but W. H. Auden wrote in the *New York Times,* "No fiction I have read in the last five years has given me more joy," and American readers also began to buy copies of this curious new literary phenomenon.

And the rest, as they say, is history.

There is nothing like *The Lord of the Rings.* There are greater mythologies and (perhaps) greater novels, but there is nothing else quite like what Tolkien accomplished in his long, tumultuous history of the War of the Ring. The fact that even now, over thirty years since *The Lord of the Rings* first appeared, almost every new science fiction or fantasy novel over a certain number of pages has nailed to its brow the tribute "comparable to *The Lord of the Rings!*" is the best indication of the greatness and essential, unassailable originality of Tolkien's immense work.

The Lord of the Rings not only caught and claimed the public eye for new works of fantasy, but also brought some of Tolkien's literary neighbors and forebears to a wider audience. There was renewed interest in the latter nineteenth-century and earlier twentieth-century writers of fantasy, including C. S. Lewis' mentor George MacDonald and Lewis' and Tolkien's friend Charles Williams. The success of Tolkien's work with college students and other persons of little discretionary income who liked to read played a significant part in the sudden appearance of paperback editions of Lord Dunsany and William Morris and James Branch Cabell, among others, including a few, like E. R. R. Eddison, who proved unreadable in spite of the enthusiasm for rediscovering old masters. Some of these paperbacks made inexpensive editions available for the first time, and in some cases the books had long been entirely out of print.

This is not to say that, despite the splendor of *The Lord of the Rings* and of what it accomplished, as a novel it is without flaws. My personal dislike for Samwise Gamgee only grows with age and rereading: Sam is a maudlin re-creation of a phony element of a way of life that never existed. He is capable of little but forelock-pulling, bursting into tears, admirable rabbit stews, and a blindness of loyalty and selflessness of devotion that give those old clichés an awful new lease on life. I was appalled to discover that Tolkien claimed to prefer Sam above his other characters; he was also exceedingly fond of that embarrassing creation Tom Bombadil, whose beard is long and whose boots are yellow. Tom capers, refers to himself in the third person, and has a reprehensible habit of breaking into doggerel when he might decently restrain himself to simple prose.

Tolkien's poetry is at its best what T. S. Eliot calls "verse"; but more of it (and not only in Bombadil's mouth) is little more than doggerel, although to many seventh-graders (myself once included) it is better than Keats, and perhaps gives them (as it did me) a better attitude toward trying Keats later in life.

Tolkien was also far from being a great prose stylist. No one who had more thrilling words at his command would let his chief wizard, at a life-or-death cliff-hanger moment beside Balin's tomb in deep Moria, declare stolidly: "What it was I cannot guess, but I have never felt such a challenge. The counter-spell was terrible. It nearly broke me. For an instant the door left my control and began to open!" Any high school student steeped in *Star Wars* and Dungeons and Dragons could do as well. It could be argued that literary "style" was one of the last things on Tolkien's mind and that he tried

very hard to write plainly and to avoid the "forsoothly" style so many second-rate fantasy writers (and high school students steeped in *Star Wars* and D & D) adopt so eagerly. But that does not cover all the ground. Poor Gandalf, who was just quoted being stolid halfway through *The Fellowship of the Ring*, is called on to pontificate at an even more life-or-death cliff-hanger moment in *The Return of the King:*

> Maybe I can [help Faramir], but if I do, then others will die, I fear. Well, I must come, since no other help can reach him. But evil and sorrow will come of this. Even in the heart of our stronghold the Enemy has power to strike us: for his will it is that is at work.

Rubbing it in, Tolkien adds, "Then having made up his mind he acted swiftly." Rule one in any basic creative writing class is not to let your characters hang around chatting in clichés, especially at crucial points; and this has been true since Homer.

Tolkien has another shortcoming in common with other, lesser writers: characters who grow too heroic grow increasingly difficult to deal with. Frodo, as the Ring inevitably burns away the heavier bits of his personality, becomes rather too transparently spiritual, as Tolkien himself recognized: "[Frodo] is not so interesting because he has to be highminded, and has (as it were) a vocation." Strider, when he ceases to be Strider and becomes Aragorn, ceases also to be either human or interesting beyond a certain bleak, unvarying nobility. Gandalf the White is not in all things as satisfactory as Gandalf the Grey was; and characters who first come on stage as heroic or superhuman, like Elrond, never become real or interesting in the first place.

Nor does Tolkien have an easy time with his occasional anxious attempts at humor. There is so little humor in most of *The Lord of the Rings* (except for some more or less successful offhand remarks from various hobbits) that when Aragorn suddenly becomes wry for the space of half a page in "The House of Healing" midway through *The Return of the King,* the poker-faced dignity of the Heir of Elendil almost can't stand it, and the reader feels unsettled for the rest of the chapter. Tolkien was correct, however, when he protested somewhat wistfully—for he was taken up on his humorlessness straightaway—that he felt the *Fellowship* to be lighter and jollier than the rest, as the War of the

Ring progresses to its terrible conclusion. For all the slightly coy busyness of the hobbits ("I am personally immensely amused by hobbits as such, and can contemplate them eating and making their rather fatuous jokes indefinitely; but I find that is not the case with even my most devoted 'fans' ") there is a real, homely, welcoming quality of the Shire and its hobbits and a real, if small and dry, humor about living with or in spite of your neighbors that is enjoyable even when a little overextended. *The Lord of the Rings* might be far more nearly another *Silmarillion* without the hobbits, and that would have been a tragic pity—and then Tolkien might be no better known than, say, William Morris, who wrote beautiful, dignified fairy stories about beautiful, dignified, two-dimensional people.

There are also virtually no women of any species in Tolkien's huge tale: not only are all the Nine Walkers of the Fellowship of the Ring—that great symbolic army of the free peoples of Middle-earth united against Sauron, the Enemy, who had been the Necromancer—male, but even Sam's pack pony is named Bill. And while Galadriel has a few oracular lines, Arwen, who is Aragorn's great love and the motive force (we are told) for many of his most valiant deeds, is not ever enough of a character even to be called cardboard. This is a great waste, for her story—of giving up her Elvish heritage forever to marry the man she loves—could be a great and tragic and beautiful one in hands able or willing to shape it. All we are given is: "None saw her last meeting with Elrond her father, for they went up into the hills and there spoke long together, and bitter was their parting that should endure beyond the ends of the world." This is begging the question with a vengeance. There is Lady Eowyn's brief, glorious moment in battle with the Nazgûl king, which I hope has illuminated many a young reader's dreams as it did mine; but she alone is not enough.

But in the end none of it matters; *The Lord of the Rings* rises above its failures, its blind spots, its ineptnesses, its clichés. As many times as I have read it—times without count—I rarely have concentration to spare for faulting it while I'm in the midst of reading. It's not till I'm done, and coming down a bit from the high it invariably provokes, that it occurs to me that Sam has grown no less insufferably irritating, or that the Orcs, in less polite hands than those of an Oxford don, might have been a good deal nastier than they are; or that how Gandalf finally did get the best of the Balrog is

never satisfactorily explained. If the book had been a magazine serial with fortnightly deadlines, if we did not know that Tolkien wrote *The Lord of the Rings* from front to back and back to front many times, I would suspect that Gandalf's deus ex machina reappearance was an awkward afterthought mugged in when, as in the case of Arthur Conan Doyle and Sherlock Holmes, Tolkien's public protested his killing off one of his best characters. The trusting reader emits the same sort of "Huh? What did I miss?" upon the abrupt reference, most of the way through *The Return of the King,* to Sam's sweetheart Rosie: she surfaces in the story as if Tolkien had suddenly realized that Sam is going to have to live on in the Shire by himself and he'll need something to occupy his time usefully—and a wife sounds like a good idea.

It's much easier to point out the flaws in Tolkien's grand conception than to set down in cold black-and-white why it is, finally, grand; but there are at least three obvious reasons. The simplest one derives from Tolkien's scholarship: the fact that he was able to translate his fascination with the myths and languages of northwestern Europe into utterly convincing place-names and proper names and geographies and cultures for his own private world. The second is a development of one aspect of the first: Tolkien's sense of the specifics of countryside, of the shifting landscapes over which the story plays itself out. The last, and perhaps the most important, is the force of the telling of the tale—the force of Story.

Tolkien had a very strong feeling for the personal importance of the landscape. Much of the Shire is consciously based on the West Midland farmland in which he spent much of his boyhood; and during and after World War II one of the things that appears again and again in his letters is his fear that the last of the old "unmechanized" countryside will disappear. Humphrey Carpenter in his excellent (if frustratingly brief) biography of Tolkien discusses this aspect of Tolkien's mental makeup at some length, for it is a thread running through all of Tolkien's life and work, similar in some ways and occasionally parallel to his devout, lifelong Catholicism. Both his love of the land of England and his love for his God contribute to the resonances of *The Lord of the Rings;* for as the landscape of Middle-earth was real to him, as three-dimensional as his own back garden, so too was the struggle between Good and Evil: not an abstruse argument for philosophers, but a real question fought daily in the hearts and lives of real people.

One of the first charms of *The Fellowship of the Ring* to new readers who have no idea what they may be getting into lies in the descriptions of the Shire: "The flowers glowed red and golden: snapdragons and sunflowers, and nasturtians trailing all over the turf walls." Not just flowers that happen to be red and yellow; specific flowers with specific names. When the hobbits go for walks—and later when they go on their great adventure—the roads they walk on are described as steep or rocky, wet or dry, wide or narrow, clear or confused; and Tolkien gives his readers the points of the compass and the phases of the moon, not obtrusively, but as walkers and adventurers would notice them. (I, who have no sense of direction and am always surprised by the full moon when it appears, was delighted to read in Tolkien's letters, edited again by the admirable Mr. Carpenter, that he had a fair amount of difficulty keeping proper track of such things himself, and got sometimes in tangles.)

One of the final horrors of the story, and ironically the one that perhaps strikes deepest, occurs at the very end of *The Return of the King,* when the little band of hobbits comes home again, whole and (relatively) hale, against all odds—to find that Mordor's minions have been busy even in the Shire. The land has been ruined, and the inhabitants are frightened and cowed; there are smokestacks where there used to be fields, and fences where there had been none. They arrive at Bilbo and Frodo's old home, Bag End:

> "They've cut it down!" cried Sam. "They've cut down the Party Tree!" He pointed to where the tree had stood under which Bilbo had made his Farewell Speech. It was lying lopped and dead in the field. As if this was the last straw Sam burst into tears.

Sam would burst into tears, but no one who has come over nine hundred pages with the hobbits will not be tempted to join him. The reader's mind goes back to the first chapter of *The Lord of the Rings,* "A Long-Expected Party": "There was a specially large pavilion, so big that the tree that grew in the field was right inside it, and stood proudly near one end, at the head of the chief table. Lanterns were hung on all its branches." This is the tree under which Bilbo gives his speech, and from which he disappears out of the Shire, leaving the Ring and,

unknowingly, its heritage, to his nephew Frodo. In chapter 2, "The Shadow of the Past," Gandalf first tells Frodo *of* the Ring that has come to him from Bilbo. Frodo protests:

> "I was not made for perilous quests! I wish I had never seen the Ring! . . . Why was I chosen?"
> . . . "But you have been chosen," said Gandalf.
> . . . "Have you decided what to do?"
> "I should like to save the Shire, if I could," [replied Frodo]. . . . "I feel that as long as the Shire lies behind, safe and comfortable, I shall find wandering more bearable; I shall know that somewhere there is a firm foothold, even if my feet cannot stand there again."

Even in the War of the Ring such things as the fate of an old beloved tree matters, and Tolkien makes the reader see that they matter: and just as *The Lord of the Rings* is about honor and fate, and risking all for a forlorn-hope quest against an Enemy, so too it is about how even if good triumphs something is lost in the process. Even though a magnificent Elvish tree (planted by Sam) grows where the Party Tree once stood, still the Party Tree is gone forever —as much that was wise and beautiful has been lost forever to Middle-earth.

But Tolkien is good not only at evocative descriptions of countryside similar to that dearest to his comfortably middle-class English heart. One of the eeriest scenes in *The Lord of the Rings* occurs before the Gates of Moria, where Gandalf is stymied by the magical doors' instruction to "speak friend and enter" and a piece of the landscape comes to horrible life; and the desolation that Frodo and Sam meet on their grim journey toward Mordor, land of the Enemy, is only too vivid.

> In a chill hour they came to the end of the watercourse. The banks became moss-grown mounds. Over the last shelf of rotting stone the stream gurgled and fell down into a brown bog and was lost. . . . On either side and in front wide fens and mires now lay, stretching away southward and eastward into the dim half-light. . . . Far away, now almost due south, the mountain-walls of Mordor loomed, like a black bar of rugged clouds floating above a dangerous fog-bound sea.

The reader is every bit as bone- and soul-weary as Frodo and Sam by the time they stand on the slopes of Mount Doom in the heart of Mordor for the final confrontation with the Lord of the Rings.

Diana Wynne Jones has written an excellent essay entitled "The Shape of the Narrative in *The Lord of the Rings,*" which is contained in an otherwise indifferent-at-best collection of essays on Tolkien entitled *This Far Land.* I recommend Jones's piece for a better overview of the effect of Tolkien's scholarship on the shape of his narrative than I can provide; but anyone who has read *Beowulf* or *The Ring of the Nibelung* will see a familiar background shimmer in *The Lord of the Rings.* At the same time, many people have read and loved the legends of northern Europe; it is Tolkien's genius that the singular fire of myth burns in his own work —that the liveliness of Story entered what he had made.

The Fellowship of the Ring starts with a party in a small, backwater sort of place called Hobbiton, where a lot of small, backwater sorts of people (or hobbits) are "fond of simple jests at all times, and of six meals a day (when they could get them)." The first whiff of Story is in a bit of Bilbo's verse: "The Road goes ever on and on / Down from the door where it began. / Now far ahead the Road has gone, / And I must follow, if I can. . . ."

The plot develops with speed: Frodo will have accepted his "perilous quest" by the middle of the next chapter, and by the third chapter the dread Black Riders, the Enemy's direst servants, make their first appearance. Except for a few quieter moments, in Rivendell or Lothlórien, for example, where the wisest of the Elves still live, or in Ithilien, Gondor's sad and doomed but still lovely land on the borders of Mordor, there is barely a letup for nine-hundred-odd pages. Even in Rivendell there is Elrond's Council, where the Fellowship of the Ring is chosen and formed; and in Ithilien the Ring is discovered by one who might have the right to take it from Frodo, for his own purposes.

Even when Tolkien's characters are faltering, or indulging in awkward dialogue, the Story flings the reader along, on to the next thing, and the next after that; and you find frequent unexpected tributaries feeding into the river of next-things you're now hurtling down, and eventually you lose the banks on either side and simply cling to your book-raft till it's all over. The point where I lose the literary banks of the story-river is early in the third volume, at the siege of Gondor. Till then I've been paying some, if irregular, attention to the landscape and the sentence structure. But about the time the defenders of the city of Minas Tirith close the Gate, saying, "There is no news of the Rohirrim. . . . Rohan will not come now. . . . The Orcs of the Eye

. . . hold the northward road. The Rohirrim cannot come," I lose my grip and the phone can ring till it falls off my desk or the house burn down around my ears and I won't notice or care. And I even know that the Rohirrim, the Riders of Rohan, are going to show up in the next chapter to succor their old allies. The siege of Gondor and the final assault of Mount Doom together make one of the best sustained exciting bits of any book I've ever read, and between the closing of the Gate of Minas Tirith and Frodo standing composedly at the edge of the Cracks of Doom and saying, "I am glad you are here with me. Here at the end of all things, Sam," I'm sure there are sentences I've still never read for frantic need to get on to the next ones.

There are scenes that stand out from the tumult and shouting: Eowyn facing the Nazgûl captain is the chief of these, but the Riders of Rohan "singing as they slew" is blood-chilling even though they're the good guys and are slaying the Orcs of the Eye, of Mordor; and even though any reader paying any kind of attention knows that Gollum has to turn up one last time to make life more complicated for Frodo and Sam, it's still a shock when it happens. But I admit I've long harbored a grudge that we hear only hastily and secondhand of Aragorn's terrifying victory at the head of the Grey Company of the dishonored Dead.

And if Tolkien has trouble writing convincing descriptions of ordinary folk like Sam and Frodo, or traditional-style (not to say stereotyped) heroes like Aragorn, or traditional (not to say better avoided) mythic creations like Tom Bombadil, he is also capable of inventing other characters of vigorous originality. The Ents doubtless owe something to their author's general sensitivity to natural landscape, and there have been other tree-people from the Greek dryads to the Oakmen of the north of England. But none of these has quite the deep, treeish resonances of Tolkien's Ents, those tree-guardians who in their anger against Saruman, the tree-killer, do what the entire White Council of wizards cannot do. The tale of the ruin of Isengard, unlike the blurry story of Aragorn and the Grey Company of the Dead, is all the more sharply framed for being told by Merry and Pippin after it has occurred, while they are sitting with Aragorn, Gimli, and Legolas among the flotsam and jetsam.

And then there is Gollum. If *The Lord of the Rings* were far less of an achievement than it is, it would be worth reading for Gollum alone: Gollum, that small, wiry, slinking, paddlefooted, luminous-eyed wretch who first appeared in *The Hobbit* as the keeper of the Ring. He is almost a hobbit, very nearly a monster, very nearly a villain and yet almost a hero—he has a creepy charisma uniquely his own, and it is hard to forget him and his weird whispering *my precioussss* even in the many chapters when he does not appear.

He serves also as something of a touchstone for those who come in contact with him. In that fateful second chapter of *Fellowship,* Frodo says of Gollum to Gandalf:

"For now I am really afraid. . . . What a pity that Bilbo did not stab that vile creature, when he had a chance!"

"Pity?" [said Gandalf.] "It was Pity that stayed his hand. Pity, and Mercy: not to strike without need. . . . Be sure that he took so little hurt from the evil, and escaped in the end, because he began his ownership of the Ring so. With Pity."

And, perhaps alone among Tolkien's characters, who do tend to stand for Good or Evil a trifle opaquely, Gollum maintains a precarious balance between goodness and wickedness that remains in doubt till his very last moment, when he confronts Frodo at the Cracks of Doom.

Tolkien did write things other than *The Lord of the Rings. The Hobbit,* its precursor, is the most famous of these. I've never really warmed up to *The Hobbit,* which has a sad habit of falling into archness, although there are some splendid things in it. The landscape already has the ability to snatch you out of your reading-chair, or wherever you happen to be—at poolside, sick in bed, or hanging from a subway strap at rush hour—and thrust you into an alien country; and you get to meet Gandalf for the first time.

Tolkien himself eventually grew embarrassed about the coy tone of some of *The Hobbit,* which, he explained,

was a fragment, torn out of an already existing mythology. In so far as it was dressed up as "for children", in style or manner, I regret it. So do the children. . . .

When I published *The Hobbit* . . . I was still influenced by the convention that "fairy-stories" are naturally directed to children (with or without the silly added waggery 'from seven to seventy'). And I had children of my own. But the desire to address children, as such, had nothing to do with the story. . . . But it had some unfortunate effects on the mode of expression, which . . . I should have corrected.

A light is shed on some of Tolkien's later thinking about *The Hobbit* in one of the pieces in *Unfinished Tales,* which was published not long after *The Silmarillion.* Christopher Tolkien explains in the introductory notes to "The Quest of Erebor" that "there is more than one version" (and no conclusion to any of them) of the scene in which Gandalf tries to explain to Frodo and the other Fellowship hobbits how he came to send Bilbo off with Thorin Oakenshield in the first place—one of the most obvious weaknesses of *The Hobbit,* and one that leaves a gap in the plot large enough to drive a dragon through. Why would a wizard like Gandalf, high in the counsels of the great, send off so foolish a creature, hobbit or otherwise, to help the exiled King Under the Mountain's quest to win back his own? Tolkien's permanent inability to bring any of his work quite up to his grim standard of absolute perfection could be the reason he never settled on any version of this explanation; but in this case I think he did not wrench it into the shape he wished because he couldn't. He had already done one notable bit of revisionist history, for "Riddles in the Dark": there are limits.

The Silmarillion, the first volume of Tolkien's writing to appear after his death, with an introduction by his son Christopher, will appeal most to those who privately prefer the appendixes at the back of *The Return of the King* to the story, and whose favorite bedtime reading is *The Golden Bough.* But it is a fascinating book in its way, if it is not the page-turner that *The Lord of the Rings* is. Tolkien believed that *The Silmarillion* and *The Lord of the Rings* were equally important in his history of Middle-earth, and he probably preferred *The Return of the King*'s appendixes himself. Those who have fallen under the spell of the tale of the Ring should give themselves the opportunity to struggle through at least enough of *The Silmarillion* to find out if they want more.

If they do want more, there are, besides *Unfinished Tales,* four volumes of *The History of Middle-earth.* The first two volumes are *The Book of Lost Tales,* parts 1 and 2—"The Book of Lost Tales" being Tolkien's original name for the epic he planned to write, which became the tale of Middle-earth. Just out as I write this is volume 3, *The Lays of Beleriand;* volume 4, *The Shaping of Middle-earth,* is "in preparation," by the indefatigable Christopher Tolkien.

If restless readers want something that is a little lighter going, there are several overlapping collections of Tolkien's shorter works. *The Tolkien Reader* contains his much-prized essay "On Fairy-Stories." There is so little intelligent writing on fantasy even now (Tolkien's essay was composed in the late 1930s) that "On Fairy-Stories" is perhaps better thought of than it would be if it had more stringent competition; it is nonetheless a thought-provoking piece, if a little rambling where it should be exact and declamatory for the sake of hiding gaps in logic. "On Fairy-Stories" and a short story called "Leaf by Niggle," both contained in *The Tolkien Reader,* have also been published alone together as *Tree and Leaf;* and there is a brief introduction to the pair of them in which Tolkien explains that he sees them *as* a pair: the essay describes what he has called "sub-creation," and the story is an example of the process of composing a leaf to hang on that particular tree. Tolkien wrote in the prologue to *The Fellowship of the Ring:* "I cordially dislike allegory in all its manifestations, and always have done so since I grew old and wary enough to detect its presence. I much prefer history, true or feigned." Of *The Lord of the Rings* I believe him—beyond the fact that particular stories tend to find authors to tell them who are already preoccupied with the significant elements of the particular stories. About "Leaf by Niggle" I cannot say fairly that I believe it is "history, true or feigned," but as a useful anatomical skeleton on which to point out the parts of Story defined by the essay it is interesting.

This is not a complete list of Tolkien's published works, but several others should be mentioned. "Smith of Wooton Major" is a rather somber—some might say flat-footed—old-fashioned fairy tale; "Farmer Giles of Ham" is a funny, satirical story on the nature of heroes and of dragons, and contains one of the most engaging dogs to be found in all literature. *The Adventures of Tom Bombadil and Other Verses from the Red Book* is best enjoyed with the illustrations of Pauline Baynes, so the fretful reader can look at the illustrations. In truth old Tom ("Come derry-dol, merry-dol, my darling") is less fretful-making when he's deliberately set out as poetry. And at least two more of the entertainments he invented for his children have found their way to print, *Mr. Bliss* and *The Father Christmas Papers.*

I cannot judge the strength or accuracy of his scholarly work, although reading his translation of *Pearl* several years after struggling through the grindingly boring translation available to us in a college course on medieval English poetry made the poem suddenly come into the light of my careless modern intellect. I felt belatedly sorry for the professor, who could read it in the original, trying to get through to us. And I have not yet read all of *The Lays of Beleriand* and will be very embarrassed if it makes me eat my words about Tolkien's poetry.

I would like to finish by making some grandiloquent claim for Tolkien's work so breathtaking in its arrogance that any readers reaching the end of this essay who have never read *The Lord of the Rings* will be so morally outraged that they must rush out and find it at once. But it's hard to come up with anything so extravagant that there isn't some truth to it. *The Lord of the Rings did* cause a revolution in both popular fiction and serious literature, and in critical thought about both; it does stand alone on the peak of its particular artistic mountain, although the foothills and lower slopes are lately getting pretty crowded. I know there are people who cannot read *The Lord of the Rings:* the stilted language, the relentless quaintness of the hobbits, the blunt confrontation between Black and White with no patience or subtlety for the presence of shades of gray—I understand the reasons even as I discount them. I know there are people who cannot enter the world of Middle-earth, and I pity them as I pity people who don't like to read at all. *Silmarillion* or no *Silmarillion,* the center of Tolkien's work for the average, unphilological reader is *The Lord of the Rings,* and he should be content for it to be so. *The Lord of the Rings* is one of the finest books—if not the finest book—to put in the hands of any eager, wistful junior high school student who has begun to suspect there's something more to life than Steven Spielberg; and it will lift the heart and touch the soul of anyone of any age who can suspend disbelief long enough to step through Tolkien's enchanted portal and welcome what will be found on the other side.

Selected Bibliography

WORKS OF J. R. R. TOLKIEN

The Hobbit; or, There and Back Again. With illustrations by the author. London: Allen and Unwin, 1937; Boston: Houghton Mifflin, 1938.

"Leaf by Niggle." *Dublin Review* 432: 46–61 (January 1945).

Farmer Giles of Ham. London: Allen and Unwin, 1949; Boston: Houghton Mifflin, 1950.

The Fellowship of the Ring: Being the First Part of The Lord of the Rings. London: Allen and Unwin, 1954; Boston: Houghton Mifflin, 1955.

The Two Towers: Being the Second Part of The Lord of the Rings. London: Allen and Unwin, 1954; Boston: Houghton Mifflin, 1955.

The Return of the King: Being the Third Part of The Lord of the Rings. London: Allen and Unwin, 1955; Boston: Houghton Mifflin, 1955.

The Adventures of Tom Bombadil and Other Verses from The Red Book. With illustrations by Pauline Baynes. London: Allen and Unwin, 1962; Boston: Houghton Mifflin, 1962.

Tree and Leaf. London: Allen and Unwin, 1964; Boston: Houghton Mifflin, 1964.

The Tolkien Reader. Edited by Owen Lock. New York: Ballantine Books, 1966.

Smith of Wootton Major. With illustrations by Pauline Baynes. London: Allen and Unwin, 1967; Boston: Houghton Mifflin, 1967.

The Father Christmas Letters. Edited by Baillie Tolkien. London: Allen and Unwin, 1976; Boston: Houghton Mifflin, 1976.

The Silmarillion. Edited by Christopher Tolkien. London: Allen and Unwin, 1977; Boston: Houghton Mifflin, 1977.

Unfinished Tales. Edited by Christopher Tolkien. London: Allen and Unwin, 1980; Boston: Houghton Mifflin, 1980.

Letters of J. R. R. Tolkien. Edited by Humphrey Carpenter, with the assistance of Christopher Tolkien. London: Allen and Unwin, 1981.

The Monsters and the Critics, and Other Essays. Edited by Christopher Tolkien. London: Allen and Unwin, 1983; Boston: Houghton Mifflin, 1983.

The History of Middle-earth. Edited by Christopher Tolkien. London: Allen and Unwin; Boston: Houghton Mifflin. Vol. 1. *The Book of Lost Tales. Part One.* 1983. Vol. 2. *The Book of Lost Tales. Part Two.* 1984. Vol. 3. *The Lays of Beleriand.* 1985. Vol. 4. *The Shaping of Middle-earth.* 1986.

CRITICAL AND BIOGRAPHICAL STUDIES

Carpenter, Humphrey. *J. R. R. Tolkien: A Biography.* London: Allen and Unwin, 1977; Boston: Houghton Mifflin, 1977.

Giddings, Robert, ed. *J. R. R. Tolkien: This Far Land.* New York: Barnes and Noble, 1984.

Helms, Randel. *Tolkien's World.* Boston: Houghton Mifflin, 1975.

Isaacs, Neil D., and Rose A. Zimbardo, eds. *Tolkien and the Critics: Essays on J. R. R. Tolkien's The Lord of the Rings.* Notre Dame, Ind.: University of Notre Dame Press, 1963.

Kocher, Paul. *Master of Middle-Earth: The Achievement of J. R. R. Tolkien.* Boston: Houghton Mifflin, 1972.

Lobdell, Jared. *England and Always: Essays on The Lord of the Rings.* Grand Rapids, Mich.: William B. Eerdsmans, 1981.

———, ed. *A Tolkien Compass.* LaSalle, Ill.: Open Court, 1975.

Tyler, J. E. A., ed. *Tolkien Companion.* New York: Avon Books, 1977.

—ROBIN McKINLEY

MARK TWAIN

1835–1910

MARK TWAIN MUST be laughing now, to think that he is known today primarily (if not exclusively) as a writer of boys' stories. If there was any branch of American letters that he detested, it was juvenile books. "I have no love for children's literature," he admitted to his brother Orion in 1871. He said that he knew of none that he "thought was worth the ink it was written with, and yet . . . such literature is marvelously popular and worth heaps of money." While preparing *The Adventures of Tom Sawyer* (1876), Twain insisted to William Dean Howells that his new story "is *not* a boy's book at all. It will only be read by adults. It is only written for adults." Howells, however, found the manuscript

> altogether the best boy's story I ever read. . . . But I think you ought to treat it explicitly *as* a boy's story. Grown-ups will enjoy it just as much if you do; and if you should put it forth as a study of boy character from the grown-up point of view, you'd give the wrong key to it.

Twain quickly came around to Howells' opinion of the work, but only reluctantly. "Mrs. Clemens decides with you," he reported back to his friend, "that the book should issue as a book for boys, pure and simple—and so do I. It is surely the correct idea." And Howells proved to be right, for from the start the book has been as popular with adults as with boys and girls. But issuing a book for children is not the same as writing it for them. Twain vacillated over what he thought his story's true audience was. He felt forced to defend himself in the preface, stating, "Although my book is intended mainly for the entertainment of boys and girls, I hope it will not be shunned by men and women on that account, for part of my plan has been to try to pleasantly remind adults of what they once were themselves." But he came to believe that that had been his sole plan all along. In 1902 he jotted in his notebook, "I have never written a book for boys; I write for grown-ups who have *been* boys. If the boys read it and like it, perhaps that is testimony that my boys are real, not artificial. If they are real to the grown-ups, that is proof."

Of course the children's literature from which Twain wished to disassociate his own efforts consisted mainly of the pious Sunday-school tracts that he hated in his own childhood (and which he so brutally burlesqued in his early sketches "The Story of the Good Little Boy" and "The Story of the Bad Little Boy," both written in 1865). These writings argued that the obedient child would always prosper and the vagrant one would surely come to a horrible end. Resistance to such well-meaning polemics was shared by Twain's contemporary Thomas Bailey Aldrich. He tried to correct this misconception of childhood in *The Story of a Bad Boy* (1869). Actually Aldrich's reminiscences concerned "not such a very bad, but a pretty bad boy; and I ought to know, for I am, or rather I was, that boy myself." His purpose was

> partly to distinguish myself from those faultless young gentlemen who generally figure in narratives

of this kind, and partly because I really was *not* a cherub. . . . I didn't want to be an angel and with the angels stand; I didn't think the missionary tracts . . . were half so nice as *Robinson Crusoe;* and I didn't send my little pocket-money to the natives of the Feejee Islands, but spent it royally in peppermint-drops and taffy candy.

Aldrich's now obviously innocent attitude must have appeared heretical in nineteenth-century puritanical America's juvenile literature, but all that Aldrich was attempting in his story was a Yankee equivalent of Thomas Hughes's *Tom Brown's School Days* (1857), the first full-blooded portrait of a schoolboy in British juvenile letters; Aldrich even quoted from the famous novel in chapter 10 of his work. Drawing on his own childhood experiences just as Hughes had done, Aldrich was trying to depict "a real human boy, such as you may meet anywhere in New England, and no more like the impossible boy in a story-book than a sound orange is like one that has been sucked dry." Hughes, however, a prominent Muscular Christian, chronicled his personal spiritual awakening through the fictional Tom Brown. "Why," he confessed in the preface to the sixth edition, "my whole object in writing at all was to get the chance of preaching!" Fortunately Aldrich had never gone through any such religious crisis in his boyhood, so neither does Tom Bailey.

The Story of a Bad Boy was widely popular and inspired a minor American genre, the bad boy's book. Howells found the story "a new thing . . . in American literature, an absolute novelty." Twain, however, was not at first impressed with Aldrich's effort. In 1869, he admitted that "for the life of me I could not admire the volume much." But in 1893, by which time he had become friends with its author, Twain was far more generous toward the book, rapturously writing Aldrich that on rereading it,

> by the time I had finished it . . . worked its spell, and Portsmouth was become the town of my own boyhood—with all which that implies and compels; the bringing back of one's youth, almost the only time in one's life worth living again. . . . I enjoyed it— every line of it; and I wish there had been more.

The Adventures of Tom Sawyer may be seen in part as Twain's initial response to *The Story of a Bad Boy.* The similarity between the names of the two young heroes, Tom Bailey and Tom Sawyer, is not coinci-

dental. Both writers cover much the same ground, describing a boy's early fistfights, first loves, running away from home—the common experiences of nineteenth-century American boyhood.

Like Tom Bailey, Tom Sawyer may be a bad boy, but he is not evil. Of course Twain's hero breaks most of the cardinal rules of the Sunday-school tracts. He steals, he lies, he smokes, he fights, and he plays hooky. In St. Petersburg, Tom Sawyer stands somewhere between the model boy and the juvenile pariah. Willie Mufferson "always brought his mother to church, and was the pride of all the matrons. The boys all hated him, he was so good. And besides, he had been 'thrown up to them' so much." Huckleberry Finn, however, "was cordially hated and dreaded by all the mothers of the town, because he was idle and lawless and vulgar and bad—and because all their children admired him so . . . and wished they dared to be like him." Throughout the story Tom Sawyer is torn between respectable and unrespectable society, but he is mischievous rather than wicked, merely, as his Aunt Polly explains, "full of the Old Scratch."

Just as Aldrich drew on his own childhood back in Portsmouth, New Hampshire, Twain recalled the locale, incidents, and people of his early years in Hannibal, Missouri. Tom Sawyer, of course, is Sam Clemens himself. His mother was the model for Aunt Polly, his brother Henry for Sid Sawyer. Huckleberry Finn was based upon Tom Blankenship, the son of the town drunkard. It was Henry who pointed out to Mrs. Clemens the change in color of the thread in Sam's collar. It was Sam himself who fooled his mother by shouting, "Look behind you!" as he scrambled over the back fence to escape a switching. And it was Sam who fed painkiller to the family cat.

But *Tom Sawyer* is not just a series of reminiscences, as was Aldrich's *Story of a Bad Boy.* It is the *adventures,* not the *life,* of Tom Sawyer. It is Twain's first attempt at a purely fictional work written entirely on his own. As the story grew, Twain relied less and less upon his own experiences. The narrative is episodic and formless. "Since there is no plot to the thing," Twain admitted to Howells, "it is likely to follow its own drift, and so is as likely to drift into manhood as anywhere—I won't interpose." The author obviously was the last one who knew where his story was heading. It developed into no more than a string of what Huck Finn calls "stretchers," with just enough truth in them to make them plausible. *Tom Sawyer* is a series of wish fulfillments, derived from the daydreams of a boy in the American Southwest before the Civil War. Although he hates school, Tom is a voracious reader of popular romances and dime novels. Much of his imaginative life is drawn from such trash. Yet unlike other boys in his time and place, Tom Sawyer lives out these adventures. He does save a damsel in distress. He does find buried treasure. He does become a local hero. Certainly one of the peculiar powers of the narrative and one of the principal reasons for its continued appeal to boys and girls is that none of the wonderful events is so far removed from life that it could not have happened. All things seem possible for Tom Sawyer.

Twain once described the book as "simply a hymn, put into prose form to give it a worldly air." It does contain several of the most memorable scenes of an idyllic boyhood in all American children's literature: the whitewashing of Aunt Polly's fence, the puppy love of Tom and Becky, the camping out on Jackson's Island. While Twain carefully introduces the reader to the secret rituals, superstitions, and language of a child growing up along the banks of the Mississippi in the early nineteenth century, *Tom Sawyer* does not pretend to be a realistic novel. An idealized world is described here. Nowhere is it more evident than in the inflated style of the nostalgic narrator. Typical of Twain's strain to achieve a conventionally artistic tone is the opening of the chapter on Tom's whitewashing of the fence: "The sun rose upon a tranquil world, and beamed down upon the peaceful village like a benediction." Such descriptions throughout the narrative seem artificial, especially when followed by the vivid conversations.

While certainly livelier than that in any previous work of juvenile literature, even the dialogue cannot be judged purely authentic. Once he had decided to tailor his story for the children's book trade, Twain, under Howells' supervision, carefully "tamed the various obscenities" that littered the manuscript. Now there was no place for such an expression as "comb me all to hell." Howells thought that Twain's original description of the dog and the pinch bug in church, in which "the poodle went sailing down the aisle with his tail shut down like a hasp," was "awfully good but a little too dirty." Likewise Howells confessed to being "afraid of the picture incident," where Tom and Becky discover the frontispiece of a nude man in the schoolteacher's anatomy book. Twain obediently toned down the episode, apparently the only

reference in all of his works to any childish sexual curiosity. These boys and girls are true innocents. When Tom tells Huck of his plans for a robber gang, he says that the cavern will be just perfect to hold their "orgies." But when asked what that means, Tom simply confesses, "I dono. But robbers always have orgies, and of course we've got to have them, too." And obviously not even Huck Finn knows what they are. Clearly Twain was compromising his efforts to fit the current conventions of literary decorum. Still, his story retains enough of the flavor of the actual language of the common people in a small Mississippi River town to elevate his book above the dead literature of his day.

On the surface, perhaps, *Tom Sawyer* is indeed an idyllic vision of the author's own boyhood. But Twain was ambivalent about his early years. "As to the past," he wrote bitterly to an old school friend during the year *Tom Sawyer* appeared, "there is but one good thing about it, and that is that it *is* past." To dwell in the memories of one's childhood seemed to Twain to be standing "dead still in the dreaminess, the melancholy, the romance, the heroics, of sweet but sappy sixteen. Man, do you know that this is simply mental and moral masturbation?" Not all of his recollections of Hannibal were pleasant. There is a dark side to its society, which Twain weaves into the fabric of his novel. And it is not just the graverobbing and the killing of Dr. Robinson that indicate there is something terribly wrong with this town.

The children seem largely divorced from adult concerns. When left alone, they function perfectly within a world all of their own creation. *Tom Sawyer* is a subversive and cynical book, perhaps the first in American literature to consider the eternal battle between the generations. In Tom Sawyer's world the constant torments of childhood are those dealt out by adults. Nothing seems to delight a man or woman more than to disrupt a boy's or girl's play with some pointless errand. Twain was, of course, not the first writer to describe the secret life of children, but even in *Tom Brown's School Days* Hughes was careful to assure the young reader that there were always present in the background the benevolent and intelligent principles of Dr. Arnold for the students to fall back on when necessary. There is no one the boys and girls of St. Petersburg can truly admire. Everyone is either a scoundrel or a fool. Aunt Polly believes that "she was endowed with a talent for dark and mysterious diplomacy, and she loved to contemplate her most transparent devices as marvels of low cunning.'' She is always outwitted by the boy. The schoolteacher is a tyrant. Judge Thatcher is a pious old windbag. The local doctor is a graverobber. There is no one in a position of authority who is worthy of a boy's respect. The villagers are moral hypocrites. They express ''a strong desire to tar and feather Injun Joe and ride him on a rail, for body-snatching, but so formidable was his character that nobody could be found who was willing to take the lead in the matter, so it was dropped.'' Once an innocent man is finally cleared of murdering Dr. Robinson, Twain notes sarcastically, ''As usual, the fickle, unreasoning world took Muff Potter to its bosom and fondled him as lavishly as it had abused him before.'' They cannot even administer proper legal justice. When Injun Joe is finally convicted of Dr. Robinson's murder, a petition for his pardon circulates among the townspeople. Twain reports:

> Many tearful and eloquent meetings had been held, and a committee of sappy women been appointed to go in deep mourning and wail around the governor, and implore him to be a merciful ass and trample his duty under foot. Injun Joe was believed to have killed five citizens of the village, but what of that? If he had been Satan himself there would have been plenty of weaklings ready to scribble their names to a pardon petition, and drip a tear on it from their permanently impaired and leaky waterworks.

And these same people had been so eager to tar and feather him not so long ago and just for graverobbing!

The only character with any moral courage is Tom Sawyer. It is he who stands up to Injun Joe. He even proves his inherent nobility by taking the blame for Becky's tearing of the schoolteacher's anatomy book. His heroism is infectious. Even Huckleberry Finn, which ''ain't a name to open many doors,'' as the Welshman states, demonstrates his bravery by saving the Widow Douglas from Injun Joe's wrath. Of course the intentions behind Tom's good deeds are questionable. He is noble in spite of his elders' earnest teachings. Still, as the story progresses, his naturally anarchic spirit is tamed as he is slowly drawn into respectable society, or ''sivilized,'' as Huck Finn would say. But this is always on Tom's terms. Even at the end, when he fantasizes about organizing his own robber band, Tom's full reform is doubtful.

Twain knew when it was time to finish the adventures of Tom Sawyer. He abruptly concluded his book:

> It being strictly a history of a *boy,* it must stop here; the story could not go much further without becoming the history of a *man.* When one writes a novel about grown people, he knows exactly where to stop—that is, with a marriage; but when he writes of juveniles, he must stop where he best can.

Behind this tongue-in-cheek attitude lay a definite literary dilemma for the writer. Twain really was not yet ready to say good-bye to his creation. He thought that ''it might be worthwhile to take up the story of the younger ones again and see what sort of men and women they turned out to be.'' Or maybe ''by and by, I shall take a boy of twelve and run him through life (in the first person) but not Tom Sawyer—he would not be a good character for it.'' All that Twain was certain of was that Tom Sawyer had changed for him through the writing of his book. Twain had to admit to Howells that he felt a ''strong temptation to put Huck's life at the Widow's into detail, instead of generalizing it in a paragraph.'' He therefore began a sequel, ''a kind of companion'' to *Tom Sawyer,* but after completing four hundred pages of manuscript Twain threw ''Huck Finn's Autobiography'' aside in disgust. ''I like it only tolerably well,'' he confessed to Howells, ''and may possibly pigeonhole or burn the manuscript when it is done.'' For the time being, Twain did not finish it, but merely put it aside.

Instead he wrote *The Prince and the Pauper* (1882), Mark Twain's bid for literary respectability. This ''yarn for youth,'' as he called it, is not what one expects from the author of *The Innocents Abroad* (1869), *Roughing It* (1872), and *The Adventures of Tom Sawyer.* On the surface, it is an exciting swashbuckling romance worthy of Alexandre Dumas or Sir Walter Scott, one that Tom Sawyer himself would have enjoyed reading. So uncharacteristic was the new work that Twain at first did not want to issue it under his old pseudonym, ''such grave and stately work being considered by the world above my proper level.'' He need not have worried. *The Prince and the Pauper* was immediately embraced by genteel American society. Unlike his previous comic works, this ''historical tale of three hundred years ago,'' written ''simply for the love of it,'' was not hawked from door to door by an army of aggressive book agents but was published by a reputable Boston house. Even the pictures were different, grave and stately pen-and-ink drawings replacing the often crude, outrageous wood engravings of Mark Twain's subscription books.

Unlike *Tom Sawyer, The Prince and the Pauper* was unquestionably a book *for* boys and girls. The story was affectionately dedicated to "those good-mannered and agreeable children," his daughters, Susy and Clara Clemens. Prominent literary friends urged its author to serialize the new novel in *St. Nicholas,* the most prestigious juvenile magazine of the day. (Twain refused only because he thought publication in a monthly would hurt the sale of the book. Again Howells went over the manuscript to ensure that none of Twain's spontaneous vulgarity would infect this high-minded effort, and when Howells protested that it lowered the "dignity" of the novel, Twain dutifully excised one chapter, "The Whipping Boy's Story," an overwrought sadistic little yarn about some bees and nettles and an enraged bull. (Twain did retain, against Howells' wishes, Tom Canty's response to learning that the funeral of Henry VIII would not take place for some time: "Will he keep?")

"I have wanted papa to write a book that would reveal something of his kind sympathetic nature," Susy Clemens admitted in a portrait of her father written when a little girl, "and *The Prince and the Pauper* partly does it. The book is full of lovely charming ideas, and of the language! It is *perfect.*" And she was not the only one who thought *The Prince and the Pauper* a decided literary advance for Mark Twain. It is a carefully researched historical novel for young people, with a mock-authentic document from the period at the front and scholarly notes at the back. It certainly gives the appearance of accuracy. But the language is *not* perfect. It is what the nineteenth-century public expected Elizabethan parlance to be. Twain employs an artificially archaic style, forced particularly in the dialogue. It is the speech one heard on the nineteenth-century stage. Typical is Prince Edward's evaluation of Henry VIII: "Fathers be alike, mayhap. Mine hath not a doll's temper. He smiteth with a heavy hand, yet spareth me: he spareth me not always with his tongue, though, sooth to say." It is not surprising that the novel was successfully adapted to the American stage within a few years of its publication.

Twain, however, was aware of how the British courtier or commoner had spoken three hundred years before. While researching *The Prince and the Pauper,* he amused himself by writing *1601,* a slight bit of classic American ribaldry, Rabelaisian in its perversity, published privately and anonymously in a few copies for select friends. It describes in Shakespearean prose a discussion among the lords and ladies of the court of Queen Elizabeth I about who among them "did breake wind" before her majesty. But *The Prince and the Pauper* was a book for boys and girls, so its language was cleansed of all blasphemy and obscenity.

At first glance, *The Prince and the Pauper* appears to be just another of the countless Victorian novels about merry old times in Merrie Olde Englande. But Twain had no sympathy for the current Anglophilia among Yankees. This humorist from the Missouri backwoods had no need for the medieval revival. He despised the English monarchy. He had a serious purpose in writing *The Prince and the Pauper,* "to afford a realizing sense of the exceeding severity of the laws of the day by inflicting some of their penalties upon the King himself and allowing him the chance to see the rest of them applied to others." Twain came up with a clever device through which he could expose the ugly underbelly of British society. Always fascinated with doubles, Twain has a pauper exchange clothes and ultimately stations with a prince, the future King Edward VI of England. "It may be history, it may be only legend, a tradition," Twain suggested in the book's preface. "It may have happened, it may not have happened: but it *could* have happened." Of course it could *not* have happened. The tale is derived from popular romance, the conflicts of mistaken identities. Although King Alfred is said to have once disguised himself as a commoner to learn what his people were thinking, there is nothing in British history to suggest that any of the events of Twain's novel ever happened. *The Prince and the Pauper* is purely the American's invention. He chose this particular prince from among all the monarchs of Britain "to account for certain mildnesses which distinguished Edward VI's reign from those that preceded and followed it."

Like most of Twain's novels, *The Prince and the Pauper* has often been misunderstood by its public. Or, at the least, its more serious aspects have been ignored in favor of the wild adventures in Twain's tale. It is remarkable how easily the characters are duped into thinking the pauper is a prince and the prince a pauper. It does not say much for mankind. (Only Tom Canty's mother recognizes her son, but she is quickly rebuked.) The plot reveals Twain's cynicism with regard to human nature; Edward slowly gains in strength of character as he observes the injustices done to his people, and Tom Canty regresses as he is beguiled by the vast power of his new office.

Although he shrouds the events with a veil of gentility, Twain nevertheless serves up some strong stuff for babes. *The Prince and the Pauper* is not a children's book typical of its period. It questions not only British law but also filial piety. Neither prince nor pauper has a father worthy of his respect, and Tom Canty's grandmother is no better than her brutal son. The law, the family, even religion are criticized in Twain's story for boys and girls. There is a disturbing incident with a hermit, one who has cut himself off from all human companionship with nothing but Roman Catholic dogma to occupy his mind; after befriending the fugitive Edward, the old man, mumbling something about being "an archangel—but for [Henry], I should be pope," ties up the boy, intending to slay him. Likewise, the public execution of two heretics is mercilessly described by Twain:

> The women bowed their heads, and covered their faces with their hands; the yellow flames began to climb upward among the snapping and crackling fagots . . . just then two young girls came flying through the great gate, uttering piercing screams, and threw themselves upon the women at the stake. Instantly they were torn away by the officers, and one of them was kept in a tight grip, but the other broke loose, saying she would die with her mother. . . . She was torn away once more. . . . Both the girls screamed continually, and fought for freedom; but suddenly this tumult was drowned under a volley of heart-piercing shrieks of mortal agony.

Such distressing descriptions of atrocities are hardly what one would expect to find in a well-known example of the genteel tradition in American juvenile literature. Yet *The Prince and the Pauper* was universally accepted and recommended to boys and girls for their story hours. Perhaps parents were not fully aware of what their youngsters were actually reading. Perhaps Twain distanced the material from his own day so convincingly that the public considered it no more than a reconstruction of the long-dead past in a faraway country.

But there was no such distance in Twain's next major work of fiction. Having worked intermittently over the last eight years on the manuscript, Twain finally published *Adventures of Huckleberry Finn* in early 1885. This new book, seemingly a companion to *Tom Sawyer,* was also set in the Slave South of thirty or forty years before and was issued during the twentieth anniversary of the end of the American Civil War. In spite of the editing and approval of Howells, Mrs. Clemens, and other discriminating readers, Twain's story is anything but genteel. It is the autobiography of a poor-white-trash boy, told completely in his own idiom. American slavery, only faintly visible in the background of *Tom Sawyer,* is explored in all its ugliness throughout *Huckleberry Finn.* It was Twain's fervent plea for physical and spiritual freedom from what his young hero calls "sivilization." Reviewers found the book offensive, and the Concord Free Public Library made national news when it banned the novel for being "immoral," "coarse," and "the veriest trash." "If Mr. Clemens cannot think of something better to tell our pure-minded lads and lasses," protested Louisa May Alcott, the famous author of *Little Women* (1868), "he had best stop writing for them."

But *was* he writing for lads and lasses? Although it was begun as a sequel to *Tom Sawyer,* during many years of composition *Huckleberry Finn* developed into a work considerably different from its predecessor. *Huckleberry Finn* is a bitter satire of the various social levels in the American South. Twain did not conceal the violence of this society. Family feuds, lynchings, and thirteen corpses pass freely through the adventures of the fourteen-year-old boy and his friend Jim, a fugitive slave. If Twain had intended the book for children, he would probably have submitted excerpts to *St. Nicholas* rather than to its adult counterpart, the *Century.* (The publisher did not help matters by offering the title as "another boy's book" in a package with *Tom Sawyer* and *The Prince and the Pauper.*) For the rest of his life, Twain was harassed by attempts to censor the work. Finally he replied sarcastically:

> I wrote *Tom Sawyer* and *Huck Finn* for adults exclusively, and it always distresses me when I find that boys and girls have been allowed access to them. The mind that becomes soiled in youth can never again be washed clean. I know this by my own experience, and to this day I cherish an unappeasable bitterness against the unfaithful guardians of my youth, who not only permitted but compelled me to read the unexpurgated Bible before I was 15 years old. . . . If there is an unexpurgated Bible in the Children's Department, won't you please

... remove Tom Sawyer and Huck from that questionable company?

The objections to Twain's book continue today, although liberals have replaced conservatives as censors; Twain's attack on American slavery, so bold in its time, is now considered by some educators to be "racist trash." As for the children themselves, most likely they respond to *Huckleberry Finn* just as Huck Finn did to John Bunyan's *Pilgrim's Progress* (1678): "The statements was interesting, but tough."

Twain's next novel, *A Connecticut Yankee in King Arthur's Court* (1889), has suffered much the same fate as *Huckleberry Finn.* Today it is almost universally acknowledged as a children's classic. Evidently those who recommend the book have either not read it or are merely recalling the much sunnier movie adaptations with Will Rogers and Bing Crosby. Its odd current reputation may also be due in part to the general opinion that the legends of the Round Table belong in the nursery. But just as Malory did not write for babes, Twain's powerful satire of the Age of Chivalry is lost on most children. Of course there is indeed much to laugh at in many of the clashes between Hank Morgan, Twain's "champion of hard unsentimental common-sense and reason," and the various proponents of medieval superstition he encounters. Twain, however, felt no need when speaking through his Connecticut Yankee to soften his opinions of man's past stupidities. *A Connecticut Yankee in King Arthur's Court* is something of a cross between *The Prince and the Pauper* and *Huckleberry Finn,* but with an edge. "*Any* kind of royalty, howsoever modified," he concludes, "*any* kind of aristocracy, howsoever pruned, is rightly an insult." The Roman Catholic Church is seen as "that awful power. . . . In two or three little centuries it had converted a nation of men to a nation of worms." And what is a child to think of the disgusting scene at the "Ogre's Castle"? A princess leads Hank Morgan to a pigsty that she says is actually an enchanted castle and throws herself in the mud: "And when I saw her fling herself upon those hogs, with tears of joy running down her cheeks, and strain them to her heart, and kiss them, and caress them, and call them reverently by grand princely names, I was ashamed of her, ashamed of the human race."

Twain was most bitterly cynical in exploring the injustices of British law. On being seized and sold as a slave, the Connecticut Yankee comes upon a scene as horrific as the burning of the heretics in *The Prince and the Pauper.* A young girl of eighteen, with a baby in her arms, is to be hanged for stealing a piece of linen. After the priest's prayer, her executioners have trouble adjusting the noose, for

> she was devouring the baby all the time, wildly kissing it, and snatching it to her face and her breast, and drenching it with tears, and half moaning half shrieking all the while, and the baby crowing, and laughing, and kicking its feet with delight over what it took for romp and play. Even the hangman couldn't stand it, but turned away.

And the children are no better than the adults. While going through the wood, Hank Morgan encounters "a small mob of half-naked boys and girls . . . scared and shrieking. The eldest among them were not more than twelve or fourteen years old. . . . The trouble was quickly revealed: they had hanged a little fellow with a bark rope, and he was kicking and struggling, in the process of choking to death." On cutting the poor boy down, Hank Morgan observes, "It was some more human nature, the admiring little folk imitating their elders; they were playing mob, and had achieved a success which promised to be a good deal more serious than they had bargained for."

Not even Hank Morgan is sinless in Twain's embittered portrait of mankind. The conflict between the Victorian progressive ideas of the Connecticut Yankee and the entrenched feudalism of King Arthur's England leads to Armageddon. Hank Morgan successfully brings electricity to the Dark Ages and with it the horrors of modern warfare. With the help of nineteenth-century technology, in the form of electrified wire fencing and machine guns, the Connecticut Yankee swiftly conquers the knights errant. "Land, what a sight!" reports Hank Morgan.

> We were enclosed in three walls of dead men! . . . I shot the current through all the fences and struck the whole host dead in their tracks! *There* was a groan you could *hear!* It voiced the death-pang of eleven thousand men. . . . The thirteen gatlings began to vomit death into the fated ten thousand. . . . Within ten short minutes after we had opened fire, armed resistance was totally annihilated, the campaign was ended, we fifty-four were masters of England! Twenty-five thousand men lay dead around us.

A shocking vision for a children's book! Chivalry is dead, killed by Yankee military know-how gone mad.

After several halfhearted fits and starts, Twain once again revived Tom Sawyer and Huck Finn in 1893. He had to. Threatened with bankruptcy due to impractical investments, the writer turned to that despised branch of letters, juvenile literature, to help him out of his financial difficulties. He had recently become friends with Mary Mapes Dodge, editor of *St. Nicholas,* and she was eager to have him contribute to her successful magazine. Within two months, he dashed off *Tom Sawyer Abroad,* for which she paid him $5,000 when it appeared in *St. Nicholas* from November 1893 through April 1894. Twain had high hopes for this new children's story. If it proved successful, he was ready to pour out a long line of Tom Sawyer travel books, merely "adding 'Africa,' 'England,' 'Germany,' etc., to the title page of each successive volume in the series." Unfortunately *Tom Sawyer Abroad* is but a pale imitation of the worst portions of *Huckleberry Finn.* As the earlier novel satirizes the absurdities of Dumas's romances in the "evasion" of its final chapters, the new story parodies Jules Verne's *Cinq Semaines en Ballon* (*Five Weeks in a Balloon,* 1863). *Tom Sawyer Abroad* is an impossible adventure tale in which Tom, Huck, and Jim travel to Africa in a hot-air balloon. Still smarting from the criticism of *Huckleberry Finn,* Twain was perfectly willing to tailor the new book to the children's fiction market. Again recounted in the first person by Huck Finn himself, the text went through numerous revisions before appearing in the juvenile monthly. "I have tried to leave all improprieties out," Twain proudly admitted. "If I didn't, Mrs. Dodge can scissor them out." What the editor considered to be proper and improper differed from Twain's opinion. She "scissored out" references to drunkenness, death, and religion, and "nigger" became "darky." But she need not have bothered. *Tom Sawyer Abroad* is an unresolved yarn because even its author lost interest in it by mid-adventure.

If *Tom Sawyer Abroad* is to be remembered at all, it is for the occasional philosophical clashes between Tom and Huck. Again common sense triumphs over romanticism as Huck plays Sancho Panza to Tom's Don Quixote. Huck is baffled when Tom says that he has discovered the exact location of a house described in *The Arabian Nights,* the evidence being a single brick. To test Tom's discovery, Huck puts

another brick considerable like it in its place, but he didn't know the difference. . . . Instink tells him where the exact *place* is for the brick to be in, and so he recognizes it by the place it's in, not by the look of the brick. If it was knowledge, not instink, he would know the brick again by the look of it the next time he seen it—which he didn't. So it shows that for all the brag you hear about knowledge being such a wonderful thing, instink is worth forty of it for real unerringness.

Huck, like Twain himself, does not value knowledge for its own sake but for how it can be used in his own life. Tom asks his friend if he knows what a crusade is. "No," Huck replies,

I don't. And I don't care to, nuther. I've lived till now and done without it, and had my health, too. But as soon as you tell me, I'll know, and that's soon enough. I don't see any use in finding out things and clogging up my head with them when I mayn't ever have any occasion to use 'em.

Because of such philosophical asides in the children's story, Huck's criticism may be applied to *Tom Sawyer Abroad* itself. "I conceive that the right way to write a story for boys," Twain explained while working on the tale, "is to write so that it will not only interest boys but will strongly interest *any man who was a boy.* That immensely *enlarges the audience.*" Of course Twain was just reversing the process he used for *Tom Sawyer,* preparing a book for adults that also appealed to children. Unfortunately *Tom Sawyer Abroad* interests neither.

When reissued in book form in 1896, the slim *Tom Sawyer Abroad* was enlarged by being paired with "Tom Sawyer, Detective," a short story that first appeared in *Harper's Monthly* in August and September 1896. But Twain's undistinguished mystery story, capitalizing not only on the author's best-known characters but also on the current Sherlock Holmes craze, gained nothing by being narrated by Huck Finn. This tale was based upon an actual Swedish case and could have been set anywhere—not just in Missouri. Twain just could not say good-bye to Huck and Tom. They briefly reappeared in drafts of his last major work, a novel he may never have intended to publish. It was to be a summary of his final thoughts on all the inequities of life, the last philosophical grumblings of a bitter old man. It was to be written "without reserves— a book which should take account of no one's feelings, and no one's prejudices, opinions, beliefs, hopes, illusions, delusions . . . without a limitation of any sort." It was a misanthropic exercise, an attempt to define "what I think of Man, and how he is constructed, and what a shabby poor ridiculous thing he is, and how mistaken he is in his estimate of his character and powers and qualities and his place among the animals."

The Mysterious Stranger, as this manuscript was titled when it was posthumously published in 1916, is a literary fraud. It does not properly represent the author's intentions for his uncompleted novel, for it was invented to meet the needs of a specific market. By the time of his death in 1910, Twain was universally considered to be the most popular American writer of boys' books, and his publishers were eager to release a new Christmas book by their famous writer. Therefore Albert Bigelow Paine, Twain's biographer and literary executor, and himself an author of children's books, went through Twain's papers and, extracting one of the drafts, tacked on an ending from another manuscript. It was then issued as a sumptuous children's gift book, with handsome but irrelevant color plates by N. C. Wyeth, who illustrated *Treasure Island* in 1911. Obviously his publishers misread Twain's parable as a fairy tale, but Twain's divine messenger was no fairy godmother. True, the early drafts did introduce Tom Sawyer and Huck Finn to Satan, Jr., but *The Mysterious Stranger* is no more a children's book than is *Huckleberry Finn.* Set in the Middle Ages, in Eseldorf (Assville) in Austria, it returns to themes touched upon but usually tempered in his earlier fiction. It is a dark, disturbing work in which Satan tests and tricks poor mortal boys, confronting them with the futility of their existence. "There is no God," Satan proclaims, "no universe, no human race, no earthly life, no heaven, no hell. It is all a dream—a grotesque and foolish dream. Nothing exists but you. And you are but a *thought*—a vagrant thought, a useless thought, a homeless thought, wandering forlorn among the empty eternities!" The only answer, the only comfort is to welcome death when it comes. *The Mysterious Stranger* is a defeatist tract as pedantic as any of the Sunday-school texts that Twain so hated when he was a boy back in Hannibal. His lifelong argument with the Protestant God forced him to make a complete turnaround from a skeptic to a preacher of a new religion of fatalism.

And still his books, both those written specifically for children and those that were not, are passed on to young readers with complete approval. Perhaps no other American author is so widely misunderstood as Mark Twain. He is still considered the greatest of writers for boys, but this popular picture, promoted and trivialized by stage and screen adaptations of his books, is as thorough a whitewash of Twain's true meaning as the job Tom Sawyer did on Aunt Polly's fence. How many people, child and adult, standing in awe before the actual homes of the fictional characters in Hannibal, Missouri, have grasped the depth and the despair of these novels? Yes, Mark Twain must be laughing now.

Selected Bibliography

WORKS OF MARK TWAIN

The Innocents Abroad. With illustrations by True W. Williams et al. Hartford, Conn.: American Publishing Company, 1869.

Roughing It. With illustrations by True W. Williams et al. Hartford, Conn.: American Publishing Company, 1872.

Mark Twain's Sketches, New and Old. With illustrations by True W. Williams. Hartford, Conn.: American Publishing Company, 1875.

The Adventures of Tom Sawyer. With illustrations by True W. Williams. Hartford, Conn.: American Publishing Co., 1876.

A Tramp Abroad. With illustrations by W. F. Brown, True W. Williams, B. Day, W. W. Denslow, et al. Hartford, Conn.: American Publishing Co., 1880.

1601. West Point, N.Y.: Academie Presse, 1882.

The Prince and the Pauper. With illustrations by Frank T. Merrill. Boston: James R. Osgood, 1882.

Life on the Mississippi. With illustrations by E. H. Garrett, A. B. Shute, et al. Boston: James R. Osgood, 1883.

Adventures of Huckleberry Finn. With illustrations by E. W. Kemble. New York: Charles L. Webster, 1885.

A Connecticut Yankee in King Arthur's Court. With illustrations by Dan Beard. New York: Charles L. Webster, 1889.

Tom Sawyer Abroad. With illustrations by Dan Beard. New York: Charles L. Webster, 1894.

The Tragedy of Pudd'nhead Wilson and the Comedy of Those Two Extraordinary Twins. Hartford, Conn.: American Publishing Co., 1894.

"Tom Sawyer, Detective." With illustrations by A. B. Frost. *Harper's Monthly,* August and September 1896.

Tom Sawyer Abroad; Tom Sawyer, Detective; and Other Stories. With illustrations by Dan Beard and A. B. Frost. New York and London: Harper and Brothers, 1896.

The Mysterious Stranger. Edited by Albert Bigelow Paine.

With illustrations by N. C. Wyeth. New York and London: Harper and Brothers, 1916.

Mark Twain's Letters. Edited by Albert Bigelow Paine. 2 vols. New York and London: Harper and Brothers, 1917.

Mark Twain's Speeches. With an introduction by Albert Bigelow Paine and an appreciation by William Dean Howells. New York and London: Harper and Brothers, 1923.

Mark Twain's Notebook. Edited by Albert Bigelow Paine. New York and London: Harper and Brothers, 1935.

Mark Twain's Letters to Will Bowen. Edited by Theodore Hornberger. Austin: University of Texas Press, 1941.

Life on the Mississippi. With an introduction by Edward Wagenknecht and with suppressed passages edited by Willis Wager. With illustrations by Thomas Hart Benton. New York: Limited Editions, 1944.

The Letters of Mark Twain. Edited by Dixon Wecter. New York and London: Harper and Brothers, 1949.

The Autobiography of Mark Twain. Edited by Charles Neider. New York: Harper and Row, 1959.

Mark Twain–Howells Letters. Edited by Henry Nash Smith, William M. Gibson, and Frederick Anderson. 2 vols. Cambridge, Mass.: Harvard University Press, 1960.

Mark Twain's Letters to His Publishers. Edited by Hamlin Hill. Berkeley and Los Angeles: University of California Press, 1967.

Mark Twain's Hannibal, Huck and Tom. Edited by Walter Blair. Berkeley and Los Angeles: University of California Press, 1969.

The Mysterious Stranger. Edited by William M. Gibson. Berkeley and Los Angeles: University of California Press, 1969.

What Is Man? and Other Philosophical Writings. Edited by Paul Baender. Berkeley and Los Angeles: University of California Press, 1973.

Mark Twain's Notebooks and Journals. Berkeley: University of California Press. Vol. 1. Edited by Frederick Anderson, Michael B. Frank, and Kenneth M. Sanderson. 1975. Vol. 2. Edited by Frederick Anderson, Lin Salamo, and Berend L. Stein. 1975. Vol. 3. Edited by Robert Park Browning, Michael B. Frank, and Lin Salamo. 1979.

Life As I See It. Edited by Charles Neider. New York: Harper and Row, 1977.

Early Tales and Sketches. Vol. 1, *1851–1864.* Edited by Edgar Marquess Branch, Robert H. Hirst, and Harriet Elinor Smith. Berkeley and Los Angeles: University of California Press, 1979.

The Adventures of Tom Sawyer; Tom Sawyer Abroad; Tom Sawyer, Detective. Edited by John C. Gerber, Paul Baender, and Terry Firkins. Berkeley and Los Angeles: University of California Press, 1980.

The Annotated Huckleberry Finn. Edited and annotated by Michael Patrick Hearn. New York: Clarkson Potter, 1981.

CRITICAL AND BIOGRAPHICAL STUDIES

Blair, Walter. *Mark Twain and Huck Finn.* Berkeley: University of California Press, 1960.

Brooks, Van Wyck. *The Ordeal of Mark Twain.* Rev. ed. New York: Dutton, 1933.

DeVoto, Bernard. *Mark Twain at Work.* Cambridge, Mass.: Harvard University Press, 1942.

———. *Mark Twain's America.* Boston: Little, Brown, 1932.

Hinz, Joseph. "Huck and Pluck: 'Bad' Boys in American Fiction" *South Atlantic Quarterly* 53:120–129 (1952).

Howells, William Dean. *My Mark Twain; Reminiscences and Criticisms.* Harper and Brothers, 1910.

Kaplan, Justin. *Mark Twain and His World.* New York: Simon and Schuster, 1974.

———. *Mr. Clemens and Mark Twain.* New York: Simon and Schuster, 1966.

Meltzer, Milton. *Mark Twain Himself: A Pictorial Biography.* New York: Thomas Y. Crowell, 1960.

Paine, Albert Bigelow. *Mark Twain: A Biography.* 2 vols. New York: Harper and Brothers, 1912.

Sanderlin, George. *Mark Twain: As Others Saw Him.* New York: Coward, McCann and Geoghegan, 1978.

Stone, Albert E., Jr. *The Innocent Eye: Childhood in Mark Twain's Imagination.* New Haven, Conn.: Yale University Press, 1961.

Webster, Samuel Charles, ed. *Mark Twain, Business Man.* Boston: Little, Brown, 1946.

Wecter, Dixon. *Sam Clemens of Hannibal.* Boston: Houghton Mifflin, 1952.

—MICHAEL PATRICK HEARN

HENDRIK WILLEM VAN LOON

1882-1944

He was a giant of a man with a mind and a heart to correspond. He abominated dullness and he used his pen and colored inks in free, storytelling drawings to add sparkle to all his texts. His books are not only fascinating to the young—they are a challenge to artists and authors. It is impossible to reckon how much dullness we have been spared because Hendrik Willem van Loon showed how to make books lively. The long shelf beginning with *History with a Match* on to *The Story of Mankind,* the song collections, the biography, history, geography; all were decorated, illustrated, made more truly provocative by his drawings—a great soul; a gifted artist.

(May Massee, in *Illustrators of Children's Books, 1744-1944* [1947])

HENDRIK WILLEM van Loon was born in Rotterdam, Holland, on 14 January 1882, the only son and second child of Hendrik Willem van Loon and Elisabeth Johanna Hanken. From earliest childhood he was captivated by history, geography, ships, technology, drawing, and music. He played the violin well. At the age of ten he decided that he wanted above all else to be "a very famous historian." The family moved to The Hague when he was eight years old; there his education was directed by his uncle, Jan Hanken, a respected member of society, who saw to it that the boy was removed as much as possible from the influence of a paranoid father. Overindulged and protected by his mother, young van Loon was imaginative, self-centered, and inclined to hypochondria—a pawn in the struggle between an antagonistic father and a too-loving mother. He attended several boarding schools, including the famous Noorthey School, where he excelled in Latin and Greek and polished his English. His love of that language was furthered by an intuitive teacher who had him read William Makepeace Thackeray's *Henry Esmond.*

Van Loon was totally unprepared for his mother's death on 3 May 1900. One of her last letters to him showed that she had, too late, realized the effect of her overindulgence on the boy. Gerard van Loon, Hendrik Willem van Loon's son and biographer, records a letter that shows her concern: "O, what a miserable letter I received this morning. Do I have to remind you that you have so much that others don't and you seem to forget how it is with your father and how difficult things are for me. . . . Don't you ever think about anything but yourself?" It was a letter that van Loon kept with him all his life.

Life with his father was intolerable, particularly after his father's second marriage, and on the advice of family and friends young van Loon left Holland for the United States, where he attended a new college—Cornell, in Ithaca, New York. He was accepted as a sophomore in the law school, which at that time was open to undergraduates. The young Dutchman chose law not because he wished to practice but because he felt its breadth of studies would best prepare him for a career in journalism. After one year he left Cornell for Harvard, in spite of the fact that that university did not recognize his academic credits. However, the ultimate realization that he would have to complete four more years of undergraduate work, coupled with the difficulty of meeting living expenses in Cambridge, persuaded van Loon to return to Cornell. He received a B.A. degree from that institution in June 1905.

Through the good offices of a well-known educator and former president of Cornell, Andrew White, van Loon found a job at the New York cable desk of the Associated Press. From there he was sent to Washington for what proved to be a short stay. Russia was making news—the January massacre of workingmen before the Winter Palace in St. Petersburg was followed by a great general strike—and Melville Stone of the Associated Press soon assigned van Loon to St. Petersburg.

Before leaving the country, van Loon married Eliza Bowditch, daughter of a distinguished Boston family, whom he had met a year earlier while traveling from Holland to the United States. The two had been drawn together by a mutual love of music, books, and travel, and a deep-seated grievance against one parent—his against his father, hers against her volatile German mother. Each saw in marriage the answer to a need for escape and security. Van Loon had no easy time winning the Bowditch family's consent to the marriage; fortunately, Dr. Bowditch liked him and overruled the objections of his wife and other members of the family. With high hopes, van Loon and Eliza set off together for St. Petersburg, Warsaw, and Moscow. Their first child, Henry Bowditch van Loon, was born in Warsaw.

As the excitement in Eastern Europe abated, van Loon lost his interest in journalism and thought seriously of teaching. On the advice of friends, he went to the University of Munich, where he received his doctorate in history in 1911 and where his second child, Gerard Willem van Loon, was born. The death in March 1911 of Eliza's father meant that van Loon had lost a wise counselor and an influential supporter in academic circles. Nonetheless, van Loon wished to return to the United States to teach in a university or college. Eliza had no desire to go home; only signs of approaching war made her accept her husband's decision. The couple decided to live in Washington—away from her mother—on their return, and van Loon managed to be appointed Washington correspondent for the *Amsterdam Handelsblad.* He wrote occasional articles and set to work turning his Munich dissertation into his first book, *The Fall of the Dutch Republic* (1913).

Money was not plentiful. When van Loon's prospects were at a low ebb, Houghton Mifflin offered him a contract for the book while rejecting two other manuscripts he had hastily prepared. The book appeared in 1913 and received generally favorable reviews. Only Dutch critics and his friend and mentor, Cornell professor George Burr, took the author to task for some geographic and historical inaccuracies, a characteristic failing that recurred in van Loon's other works. The book, unfortunately, was of too limited an interest to sell.

The ensuing years were difficult. Van Loon had not found regular employment, much less fame, and was forced to dip into Eliza's income to live. He lectured at Cornell, where he was a natural performer, captivating his audience with his charm, wit, and easy, authoritative manner. However, the fees barely covered his expenses. He changed publishers, leaving Houghton Mifflin after the company had accepted his second book, *The Rise of the Dutch Kingdom, 1795–1813* (1915), and went to Doubleday, where neither he nor the book fared well. In the meantime he had received an offer to teach at the University of Wisconsin in Madison. By the time he decided to accept the offer, the position was filled, and he was left with a six-week summer lectureship there on art history. That summer the heir to the Austrian throne was slain and in a matter of weeks war broke out. An outburst of patriotism (and no job) led van Loon to go to Holland, and before the ship had docked he was back with the Associated Press. He filed dispatches, corrected proofs for *The Rise of the Dutch Kingdom,* saw some fighting, and returned to America for the publication of the book in March 1915.

From 1915 to 1918 van Loon lectured, wrote, and finally obtained a lectureship at Cornell, from which he shuttled back and forth to New York and the offices of the *Nation* and the *New Republic.* He also became an American citizen. His *Golden Book of the Dutch Navigators,* his first children's book (though it is not acknowledged as such), was brought out by Century in 1916; his *Short History of Discovery,* first titled *History with a Match, Being an Account of the Earliest Navigators and the Discovery of America,* was published by David McKay in 1917. This was his first book avowedly written for children, with simple, wide-spaced text and each page facing a full-page illustration drawn with a match dipped into colored india inks. Sophisticated and humorous, it did not go unnoticed by the new children's book specialists. Anne Carroll Moore of the New York Public Library admired the book, commenting in her *Roads to Childhood* (1921) that the book "has interested many children as a picture book and is a delight to the grown-up." Despite her acclaim, the book was not a commercial success, partly because publishers of that time did not as a rule devote energy and money to the promotion of children's books.

The poor performance of his students on their examinations forced van Loon to leave Cornell. He went again to Europe, leaving his wife and children behind. When he returned, he found that his marriage had been shattered beyond repair: Eliza had discovered that he had been involved with another woman. Even prior to this she had suffered much, emotionally and financially, for she had been forced to use her own income to provide for the family's needs. Most difficult for her was van Loon himself. He had never outgrown the effect of his mother's spoiling and overprotectiveness; he was self-centered, he always needed to be at center stage, and he was a hypochondriac, subject to acute bouts of recurring deep depression or "melancholia," for which his remedies were either total immersion in a writing project or flight. He needed a mother and a nurse—roles Eliza could not fill, struggling as she was to raise two children.

When he was dangerously near the end of his tether, van Loon was rescued by an enterprising young publisher, Horace Brisbin Liveright, who offered him one hundred dollars as an advance on receiving from him a manuscript for an illustrated history for children, *Ancient Man* (1920), the first of a projected series of short histories, the second of which was to be titled "The Classical World." At this time he met Eliza Helen Criswell, also known as Jimmie, James, or Jim. She filled the roles of listener, nurse, and typist; while van Loon worked at odd jobs to support himself, she typed the manuscript for *Ancient Man.* It was published in 1920, in time for the Christmas market. Liveright promoted it so well, according to Gerard van Loon, that it was selling at the rate of one hundred copies a day. By January 1921 orders for others in the series were coming in. There were other results, too. In March 1921 van Loon was offered a position in Yellow Springs, Ohio, as head of Antioch College's social-science department, at a salary of four thousand dollars a year.

The success of *Ancient Man* and an unexpected surge of American interest in the past—stimulated by the publication in England and the United States of H. G. Wells's popular *Outline of History*—prompted Liveright to tell van Loon not to continue with the series but to produce instead an illustrated history of the world for children, to be titled *The Story of Mankind.* The scheduled publication date was November 1921. Spring and summer were frantic as van Loon, with the help of Jimmie, now his second wife, worked to complete the manuscript. In late August 1921 they moved to Antioch.

Before the publication of *The Story of Mankind,* Liveright astutely sent copies of the book to important critics, many of whom had never before reviewed a book for children. Favorable reactions poured in between December 1921 and January 1922. Anne Carroll Moore, in *The Bookman,* described it as "The most invigorating and, I venture to predict, the most influential children's book for years to come." J. Salwyn (the *Nation*), Austin Hays (the *New York Times*), and Charles A. Beard (the *New Republic*) hailed it. Gerard van Loon quotes the following from a letter sent to his mother by his father:

> I humbly wonder that I ever wrote it for it was a fiendish job, and now that people are saying things about it, I wonder whether it can all be true? . . . I get letters these days from people who are totally unknown to me like Stuart Walker and Wyeth, the illustrator, and Donald Ogden Stewart . . . and two letters from Mencken using large words like "stupendous" and the first edition was half sold out the first week and I really wonder is the thing going to succeed at last? For the little bit of glory that is coming in so unexpectedly has not given me the assurance that it will MEAN anything. People have said nice things about my books before. I never had quite the avalanche of approval but to what will it lead?

It led, in 1922, to van Loon's being awarded the first John Newbery Medal by the Children's Library Association for his "distinguished contribution to American literature for children." The account of the event given in the August 1922 issue of *Library Journal* is a succinct note that at the close of the first session of the Children's Library Association Meeting, Clara W. Hunt of the Brooklyn Public Library and Chairman of the Association presented the medal to Dr. van Loon, who "informally replied in a merry vein." Fame was his at last.

The Story of Mankind is an extraordinary book. Van Loon was a great popularizer, a raconteur with an uncanny ability to sense the kind of details that would appeal to children and adults alike. It was said that his mind was crammed with bits and pieces of information gathered from a wide variety of sources. He had a broad understanding of history and an infectious liking for it. He was able to describe to children and adult lay audiences the great events of the past and the great ideas that had formed the Western world and to connect the rise and fall of nations with economic, social, and political developments. Occasionally his love of story led him to insert fictional incidents into his works. In *The Story of Mankind* there is a chapter entitled "Joshua of Nazareth," which tells of Jesus and the apostle Paul in two letters, the first purportedly from one Æsculapius Cutellus, a Roman physician, to his nephew, a Roman officer serving in Syria, and the second from the nephew to his uncle. Such improvisation makes interesting reading, but it is not history. Interpolations of this nature infuriated Dutch historians, one of whom wrote for the influential *De Gids* a scathing review of the Dutch translation. One of van Loon's great grievances against the Dutch was that they did not value his work; recognition in America did not mean recognition in Holland.

Reviewing a new work, *Van Loon's Geography,* for the *New York Herald-Tribune* in September 1932, Carl Van Doren reflected on the success of *The Story of Mankind:*

> It looked like a book for children and was that too. It was sparkling with pictures . . . pictures that at first appeared scratchy and casual and then were suddenly seen to illuminate the text and to reinforce the meaning of the historian. . . . The American public called for thirty-two printings in five years and after eleven years still goes on reading *The Story of Mankind.* It has been translated into so many languages that only Upton Sinclair can count them. At least outside Russia it has become the chief historical primer of the age.

Van Loon walked away from Antioch College without finishing the term, leaving behind him outraged students who went on strike in protest at his departure; he and Jimmie went to Baltimore on the strength of a letter from H. L. Mencken suggesting that he take a job on the editorial staff of the *Baltimore Sun.*

Meanwhile Liveright had not been idle. He had conceived the idea of having van Loon write a history of the Bible. This van Loon was reluctant to do, but, feeling indebted to Liveright, he overrode his better judgment and wrote *The Story of the Bible,* which appeared in 1923. There was protest, for

many took umbrage at his discussion of evolution and his attitude toward Genesis in *The Story of Mankind.* Reviews were mixed. Unable to accept either miracles or metaphysics, van Loon had omitted, among miraculous events, the crossing of the Red Sea, the Virgin Birth, and the Resurrection, although, strangely enough, he depicted Jesus with a halo. He was able to show enthusiasm for his subject only when he dealt with such historical details as a Babylonian origin for the Ten Commandments or the effect of Christianity on the course of human events. Bertha Mahony, in *Realms of Gold in Children's Books* (1929), described the work as "a free telling of the Bible story, such as might be made by a father well versed in history, but telling the story to his children on a desert island far from the Bible itself and other sources of historical accuracy." Gerard van Loon suggests that the critic who commented that the book offered the shell but not the spirit of the Bible came nearest to pinpointing the cause of its failure.

In any case, however, van Loon's financial affairs were such that he no longer had to teach and no longer had to face semi-isolation in such places as Yellow Springs and Baltimore. He and Jimmie visited Holland; there van Loon took Jimmie to Veere, a village in Zeeland, where they were to buy a house, and where van Loon would later write much of the material for a book for adults, *R. v. R.: The Life and Times of Rembrandt van Rijn* (1930). On their return to the United States, they moved to Westport, Connecticut. At the instigation of Liveright he undertook to write a history of America, and at the same time he vented his spleen against intolerance, in two separate works—*Tolerance* (1925), for adults, and a little satire entitled *The Story of Wilbur the Hat* (1925), for children. *Wilbur* is indeed a slight work. Few critics had much to say about the account of the rise and fall of a pompous hat from Boston. Moore found the pictures delightful and referred to them with affection in her memorial to van Loon in *Horn Book* (May–June 1944): "And there was *The Story of Wilbur the Hat* . . . it contains some of the most arresting of van Loon's drawings. . . . Who can forget the picture of those men on the high ladder putting a piece of music together in the sky?" Mark Van Doren (in the *Nation,* April 1925) and the critic for the *New Republic* (June 1925) thought otherwise, the latter commenting that "it's too bad, on the whole, that Mr. van Loon was not satisfied with the fun and drawing of Wilbur, without insisting on the fun of publishing it."

America was published in 1927 by Boni and Liveright. It is an unconventional, idiosyncratic history, scant on dates and dwelling only on the events, presidents, and people of interest to the author. It ends with the Civil War and van Loon's ruminations over the choices facing American youth in 1927. His biases, such as dislike of the Puritans, are reflected throughout. In her review of the book for the *New York Herald-Tribune,* Rebecca West commented that "it has no heights . . . no moments of inspiration." However, an unidentified reviewer in *Horn Book* (November 1927) called it a book to be read by every American with profit, for no reader will be left "in a passive state of mind." *America* was included in the issue's list of "Twenty-Five Outstanding Books of the Fall and Spring." That there was disagreement among *Horn Book* staff is revealed in the February 1928 issue, for an unsigned critic decried the book for its flippant tone and cynicism. Josephine Adams Rathbone, in her essay "The Story of America: *America* by Hendrik van Loon" (1931), notes that the work is not for small children, who "need heroes, and to deprive them past of romance and glamour, even in the interest of truth, is for them a dubious gain." Rathbone assigns *America* to a new category of historical writing, the "Human Nature School," and calls it "a book to be read by the younger, if not the youngest generation. It is alive, vivid, dramatic. Underneath its occasionally flippant surface there is courage, a feeling for realities, a true sense of values and a candid presentation of opposing opinions that may act as a wholesome corrective for readers of high-school age to the type of history produced to meet the demands of superpatriots."

Next, the prolific van Loon turned his energies to writing for Liveright a book about inventions that he titled "Multiplex Man." His concept was ingenious, for he chose to suggest that the development of technology was a logical extension of "man's powers"—eyes, skin, hands, feet, nose—eyes leading to the invention of the telescope and microscope, skin to the making of clothes, houses, heat, and so forth. The end result, he hoped in the foreword, would indicate

> along which lines we may hope for the ultimate emancipation of mankind from that cruel tyranny which for so many hundreds of thousands of years has turned this earth into a shambles, and which was the direct and inevitable outcome of man's cowardice when face to face with his prejudices and his ignorance.

He was enraged when an editor at Liveright changed the title to *Man the Miracle Maker* (1928), and subjected the book to judicious editing. It must be noted that this careful editing spared van Loon the scathing criticism given the book when the unedited version was published in England and Holland. As for its reception in the United States, the author was disappointed. He had hoped for controversy, but there was none. The *New York Herald-Tribune* found it "a successful combination of information, illustration and sound social philosophizing" and the *New York Times* called it "entertaining"; Van Loon had heard these sentiments before. Only in the intellectual community in Germany was van Loon acclaimed a man ahead of his time in his understanding of technology and its potential dangers.

Also published in 1928 was *The Life and Times of Pieter Stuyvesant,* an adult work that had been rejected by Liveright and was published by Henry Holt and Company. It is a slight, dull work that contributes little new or important information. Its critical reception was poor. Van Loon's lack of interest in the subject was apparent.

Van Loon had prodigious energies and spent them freely. He developed an intimacy with his sons, both of whom stood loyally by him in the midst of his chaotic personal life. He traveled widely, lectured, wrote numerous articles, and, in spite of illness, was able to complete for Liveright his fictionalized adult biography of Rembrandt. Its interest, beyond that of the subject, lies in the amount of autobiographical information that van Loon (consciously or not) reveals in the character of the fictional physician-narrator. As Gerard van Loon has noted, precise information about his father's life is difficult to locate. For reasons best known to himself, van Loon, "who had spent his life distilling the 'why's' of history from the vast accumulation of human data, had preferred for deep-rooted, personal reasons to keep the 'why's' of his own life a secret—even from himself." The biography, massive as it was, received favorable reviews. It achieved its greatest success in Germany, where Mosse, the German publisher, had the wisdom to cut it drastically before publishing it in 1933 as *Der Überwirkliche* (The Superreal). At first incensed, van Loon eventually forgave Mosse the editing, and when he himself revised the book for the Heritage edition, he followed the German version.

Liveright, to whom van Loon owed so much, finally succumbed to alcoholism and a penchant for gambling and womanizing, and was forced to leave the firm. After his departure, van Loon took his *Geography* to Simon and Schuster, who issued it in 1932. Three weeks before its official publication, it became a best-seller, remaining at the top of the national nonfiction best-seller list until well into 1933. A generous compendium of history, geography, economics, and politics, it is written so clearly and entertainingly that Fanny Butcher of the *Chicago Daily Tribune* commented, "The simplest reader can understand it and be thrilled by *Van Loon's Geography* and the sophisticated can, and will find it a book exciting and stimulating for its very great simplicity." The author's note "that we are all of us fellow-passengers on the same planet and the weal and woe of everybody else means the weal and woe of ourselves" captured the imaginations of its readers as successfully as had the optimism of *The Story of Mankind.* By the time the British edition, retitled *The Home of Mankind,* appeared in 1933, 138,000 copies had been sold in the United States and translations into German, Spanish, Hungarian, Italian, Portuguese, and Swedish were in progress. Only the geographers sounded a sour note—maps were too sketchy, mountains were misplaced, and rivers flowed in wrong directions. To these cries of outrage van Loon was indifferent. To him concepts were always more important than data. However, Simon and Schuster felt differently and subsequently no longer accepted Jimmie's reliability in checking details.

During the 1930's and 1940's van Loon busied himself with writing, traveling, and lecturing. He saw early on the danger of Hitler's Germany and spoke out in warning. When Hitler closed down Jewish publishing houses, van Loon refused to have any of his books published in Germany. He became a broadcaster for NBC, leaving that post only after he had thoroughly antagonized American isolationists and supporters of Germany by revealing unpalatable truths about that country. He became lecturer in history for New York radio station WEVD and, in 1933, dean of faculty of its University of the Air. He took part in such popular radio quiz programs as *Information Please,* and played the violin in an orchestra. Sandwiched in between these activities was the writing of *The Arts,* published by Simon and Schuster in 1937. Prior to the book's release, van Loon was made an Officer of the Order of Orange Nassau, an honor rarely awarded by the Dutch to a foreigner, much less an expatriate. Due to the absence of the Dutch ambassador, who had been called back to Holland, the impor-

tant ribbon was placed in his buttonhole by Eleanor Roosevelt.

Van Loon's last important work for adults was his *Lives* (1942). Planning it helped him through the inactivity following a massive heart attack and offered him an outlet for his anguish over the destruction of Rotterdam and Middelburg. It was his literary memorial to Holland and especially to his favorite corner of it, Veere. Both *The Arts* and *Lives* were highly praised. On the morning of his sixtieth birthday, six months after he had been gravely ill, van Loon received a cablegram from London with the news that Queen Wilhelmina had conferred upon him the Order of the Netherlands Lion, the highest honor he could ever have hoped for. He had at last received full recognition from his native land.

Meanwhile van Loon had not completely abandoned writing children's books. In 1933 he produced a gently ironic, delightfully illustrated little book entitled *Re: An Elephant up a Tree,* in which he explained why elephants chose to be elephants. Gerard van Loon suggests that Simon and Schuster only published the book to keep his father happy. *Around the World with the Alphabet* was published in 1935; it is sophisticated and clever, and its pictures, as always in van Loon's works for the young, enhance its appeal. For Dodd, Mead he completed three of a projected series of biographies: *Thomas Jefferson: The Serene Citizen from Monticello* (1943), *The Life and Times of Simon Bolivar* (1943), and *The Adventures and Escapes of Gustavus Vasa,* published posthumously in 1945. The Jefferson and Bolivar biographies were released by Dodd, Mead in 1962 in a single volume entitled *Fighters for Freedom: Jefferson and Bolivar.* He combined his gifts as illustrator with those of Grace Castagnetta, a talented musician, to produce four songbooks: *Christmas Carols* (1937), *Folk Songs of Many Lands* (1938), and *The Songs America Sings* (1939), published by Simon and Schuster; the last, *Christmas Songs,* was brought out in 1942 by the American Artists' Group. These are delightful family books and, though out of print, still have charm for the family of today.

Hendrik Willem van Loon died of heart failure on 11 March 1944. He was sixty-two years old. The New Haven Railroad ran two special cars from New York to Old Greenwich, where the funeral was attended by four hundred notables from the literary and social worlds of the day.

Van Loon was a man of considerable charm; he was capricious, capable of both kindness and cruelty, dificult, passionate, unreliable in his relationships, a showman, and a storyteller. He married three times, divorced his third wife, Frances Ames Goodrich, and returned to Jimmie, his second wife, with whom he spent the rest of his life in a common-law arrangement. His two sons stood by him loyally. Moore's tribute to van Loon in "The Three Owls' Notebook" (*Horn Book,* May–June 1944) shows him at his best: a man whose charm, wit, and showmanship illuminate his best work.

Three of van Loon's books remain in print, including his Newbery Medal winner, *The Story of Mankind.* Revised and updated for a number of editions, the first by his son, Gerard Willem van Loon, the 1984 edition by a team of scholars, with new illustrations by Arthur Simon, the book is still a readable introduction to world history for the young. For adults, his *Arts* and *R. v. R.: The Life and Times of Rembrandt van Rijn* are still available. Advances in scientific knowledge and rapid changes in global politics have rendered his other books out of date. Even the biographies for children are too superficial for youngsters living in the age of television and instant information. Yet his basic message is as crucial today as ever, warning that our planet is fragile, that nature must be respected, and that the machine must be mastered. As Alden Whitman noted in reviewing Gerard Willem van Loon's biography of his father for the *Saturday Review* (May 1972), Van Loon was, indeed, a "Roman candle," dazzling, "filling the skies while he lived."

Selected Bibliography

WORKS WRITTEN AND ILLUSTRATED BY HENDRIK WILLEM VAN LOON

The Golden Book of the Dutch Navigators. New York: Century, 1916.

History with a Match: Being an Account of the Earliest Navigators and the Discovery of America. Philadelphia: David McKay, 1917. Retitled *A Short History of Discovery from the Earliest Times to the Founding of Colonies on the American Continent.* Philadelphia: David McKay, 1918.

Ancient Man: The Beginning of Civilization. New York: Boni and Liveright, 1920.

The Story of Mankind. New York: Boni and Liveright, 1921.

The Story of the Bible. New York: Boni and Liveright, 1923.

The Story of Wilbur the Hat. New York: Boni and Liveright, 1925.

America. New York: Boni and Liveright, 1927. Retitled *The Story of America.* Garden City, N.Y.: Garden City Publishing, 1934.

Man, the Miracle Maker. New York: Horace Liveright, 1928.

Re: An Elephant Up a Tree. New York: Simon and Schuster, 1933.

Van Loon's Geography. New York: Simon and Schuster, 1935.

Around the World with the Alphabet. New York: Simon and Schuster, 1935.

Christmas Carols, with Grace Castagnetta. New York: Simon and Schuster, 1937.

Folk Songs of Many Lands, with Grace Castagnetta. New York: Simon and Schuster, 1938.

The Songs America Sings, with Grace Castagnetta. New York: Simon and Schuster, 1939.

Christmas Songs, with Grace Castagnetta. New York: American Artists' Group, 1942.

Thomas Jefferson: The Serene Citizen from Monticello. New York: Dodd, Mead, 1943.

The Life and Times of Simon Bolivar. New York: Dodd, Mead, 1943.

Adventures and Escapes of Gustavas Vasa. New York: Dodd, Mead, 1945.

Fighters for Freedom: Jefferson and Bolivar. New York: Dodd, Mead, 1962.

CRITICAL AND BIOGRAPHICAL STUDIES

Commire, Anne, ed. *Something About the Author,* vol. 18. Detroit, Mich.: Gale Research, 1980.

Mahony, Bertha E., and Elinor Whitney. *Realms of Gold in Children's Books.* Garden City, N.Y.: Doubleday, Doran, 1929.

Rathbone, Josephine Adams. "The Story of America: *America* by Hendrik van Loon." In *The Three Owls: A Book about Children's Books, Their Authors, Artists and Critics,* edited by Anne Carrol Moore. Vol. 3. New York: Coward-McCann, 1931

Van Loon, Gerard Willem. *The Story of Henrik Willem van Loon.* Philadelphia and New York: J. P. Lippincott, 1972.

Van Loon, Hendrik Willem. *Report to St. Peter.* New York: Simon and Schuster, 1947. (Unfinished autobiography, published posthumously.)

—MARGARET COUGHLAN

JULES VERNE

1828–1905

JULES VERNE, "father of science fiction," ranks as one of the all-time great writers for children. No author has so well prepared young people for life in the space age and for high technology. No writer has so neatly introduced so many children to such adult problems as calculating escape velocity, sailing under the polar ice caps, and saving the whale. Few novelists have made boys and girls so aware that "progress" can be a mixed blessing—that unless we marry science to ethics, humanity is doomed. And since Verne used the adventure story as his medium for painless education in science—even in social science—we must credit him too with introducing millions of children to the joys provided by plot, characterization, setting, theme—in short, to the glories of language.

But that is all just a reminder of what everybody knows. To discuss Verne judiciously, on a professional level, we must add something that not everybody knows: Verne is one of the few children's authors whom children can take with them as they grow up. To explain this accolade, which surprises many readers, we must add two serious qualifications to our discussion of his impact on children.

First, Verne actually wrote very few books exclusively for children. Rather, it was characteristic of his genius that he conceived and rendered novels that simultaneously entertain and edify both children and adults. Many of his stories originally ran serially in such publications as the children's review *Magasin d'education et de récréation* (Magazine of Recreation and Education), the magazine *Musée des familles* (The Family Museum), or the adult periodi-

cals *Le Temps* (The Times) and *Journal des débats* (Journal of Discussions). No matter which, by the time the yarn appeared in book form, it was being discussed by everyone—from schoolboys in Paris and ironmasters in Indret to the scientist Joseph Bertrand and the feminist author George Sand. In Europe today Verne's works appear in both juvenile and adult formats, the difference being discernible mainly in design and illustration. In France, Verne is a perennial subject for critics of all persuasions: structuralist, psychoanalytic, sociological, aesthetic, and theological.

Second, until recently Verne's situation was quite different in the English-speaking world. Early English translations of Verne classics, rushed into print in the late nineteenth century, were crudely inaccurate and incomplete. Crucial theoretical, technical, and political passages were cut. Verne's precise mathematical schemes were hamstrung with errors, his characterization, even his humor, eviscerated. And so, as the level of popular education rose, readers of English, unaware that a cheap trick had been played on them, patronizingly came to regard Verne as fit only for children. Verne's reputation in America bottomed in 1961 when *Galaxy* magazine ridiculed him for, among other things, having Captain Nemo say, in *Vingt Mille Lieues sous les mers* (*Twenty Thousand Leagues Under the Sea*, 1870) that *his* iron is .7 to .8 the density of water. (In the original French, of course, Nemo says 7.8.)

But late in the twentieth century, more responsible American and British critics have turned the

591

tide. Their exposés of "standard" translations have prompted conscientious publishers to commission new English versions. These are rehabilitating Verne's reputation in the English-speaking world. No longer should American whiz kids be able to "discover" that Verne made myriad errors in logic, arithmetic, and terminology. Rather, like those two boys destined to become great space scientists—the German Wernher von Braun (1912–1977) and the Russian Konstantin Tsiolkovsky (1857–1935)—American youngsters can now discover, with each rereading, that Verne deepens as they themselves mature.

Verne's first major work, *Cinq Semaines en ballon (Five Weeks in a Balloon),* published directly in book format in 1863, was an instant best-seller in both the juvenile and adult markets. It provided Verne with a guaranteed income from his writing: publisher Jules Hetzel put him under virtually a lifetime contract at fees just under those Hetzel paid Honoré Balzac and George Sand. The novel's success also provided its author with welcome proof that now he could use its original formula for a series of novels: "Voyages Extraordinary: Worlds Known and Unknown." The formula: involve the hero in that type of scientific problem and in that area of exploration most in the news at the time, and extrapolate from present knowledge in both science and exploration so as to offer predictions of future developments. Thus what is now called "science fiction" was created.

In 1863 the formula pointed to the future of air travel and of Africa. All France was abuzz with the latest project of Felix Tournachon, who in a balloon trip over Paris in 1858 had pioneered aerial photography. Nadar, as he preferred to be called, was then building *The Giant,* a balloon as tall as Notre Dame, with a two-story gondola. Meanwhile, all Europe was awaiting word from the John Speke–James Grant Expedition, then deep in Africa trying to establish the sources of the Nile.

The scientific problem Verne took on was the difficulty of steering balloons over long distances. The usual procedure was to throw sand-ballast overboard to ascend and to release gas from the balloon-bag to descend, until the crew found themselves carried by an air current going their way—a tedious, unreliable, wasteful, haphazard procedure, often ending in total stultification if not disaster.

Verne's hero, Dr. Samuel Ferguson, invents a coil to heat the gas in his balloon *Victoria* so that as the gas expands, the balloon becomes lighter, and he can raise it directly to the height of the prevailing trade wind. To stay at that altitude, he keeps the gas at an even temperature. To descend, he cools it until it condenses and the balloon becomes heavier. In this way Dr. Ferguson, his friend the big-game hunter Dick Kennedy, and his servant Joe pick up the trade wind from the southeast over Zanzibar, fly as planned north-by-northwest over the sources of the Nile and the Congo jungles, and descend in Senegal.

Predictions? Speke returned from Africa to discover that all France already knew that the Nile originates in Ripon Falls: Ferguson had said so! And within a few years overpopulated Europe would be scrambling for land in Africa, just as Ferguson predicts. And Verne even has his balloonists anticipate a dread that would not seize humanity at large for decades to come: "By dint of inventing machinery," Kennedy says, "men will finally be eaten up by it. . . . The end of the world will come when some enormous boiler will explode and blow up the world!" Joe is more specific: "I bet the Yankees will have a hand in that." Ferguson underlines the message: "Yes, they *are* great boiler-makers."

Notice how Verne seduces his audience: He predicts some development they themselves will live to see. Thus he gains their confidence when he extrapolates far into the future.

In their conversations the three characters—such a trio is Verne's typical core group—educate us not only in science but in morality. They explicitly abhor the West's vain worship of gold, and they educate us implicitly by showing the advantage of close friendship. These are two of Verne's most persistent moral themes.

Five Weeks in a Balloon poses one problem that must be put into context for juvenile readers. Verne usually distributes among his characters the full range of sociopolitical views, from the most vulgar and prejudiced to the most advanced and sophisticated. Joe expresses the typical nineteenth-century view of white supremacy over blacks, but Ferguson predicts a great future for African culture, which has been so maligned by Western culture. In *Five Weeks* Verne also begins his lifelong habit of eliciting the reader's interest in the victims of colonialism, here the Senegalese under el-Hadj-Omar.

In his next book, Verne's formula pointed to geology and paleontology. For just as Speke had traced the Nile back to its source, so men like

Charles Lyell, Alfred Wallace, and Charles Darwin were seeking, in rock and fossil, the origin of the earth's formations and of its living forms. Lyell's and Darwin's findings had traumatized the Christian world, provoking bitter debate in print and in lecture halls over the validity of the creation story told in Genesis. Now, Verne must have reasoned, if strata deep beneath the earth's skin contain all the answers, why not send an expedition down *inside* the planet? In his day several thinkers hypothesized that volcanoes were really openings in a vast network of tunnels connecting all the world's volcanoes with each other.

One character in this work, *Voyage au centre de la terre* (*Journey to the Center of the Earth,* 1864), had, clearly, to be a scientist. Who else would update the reader on the age of the earth? But—and here Verne's artistic instincts served him well—suppose the narrator were a teenager? Notice the rich emotional counterpoint: While the scientist leads the party in its probe of Nature, the teenager, in an adolescent identity crisis, probes his own nature. As the expedition seeks the secrets of the evolution of reality organic and inorganic, the narrator seeks the secret of evolution from youth to adulthood.

As Verne worked out the story, Professor Lidenbrock and his nephew Axel find, in an old Icelandic book, instructions for descending into the earth's interior via a volcano in Iceland. The professor urges Axel to go with him. Axel resists until Gräuben, his girlfriend, says that if he goes, he will return a man. So now Verne has added anthropology, with its universal rites of initiation, to geology and paleontology to create a great fugue of natural and social sciences.

At one point in their descent, Axel is separated from Lidenbrock and their phlegmatic guide, Hans. Axel gropes through dark tunnels and finally is on the verge of an emotional breakdown. Verne anticipates psychiatrist R. D. Laing, who believes that a breakdown can be a breakthrough. In a state of raw nerves, Axel rediscovers his instincts, his primal oneness with the earth, and he takes the pulse of Nature. He first follows a stream, then, ear pressed to rock strata, detects faint echoes of Lidenbrock's faraway movements. Thus Axel not only locates his party, he also finds a fuller, more integrated, more mature self. In one of his best lyric passages, Verne reinforces Axel's discovery that Nature and humankind are consubstantial by describing a fjord in terms of human architecture.

Already enthralled by their identification with Axel's quest, juvenile readers thrill to two grandly conceived sequences. The reunited party discovers an underground sea in which dinosaurs are fighting, while on a distant shore the superspelunkers spot sheeplike creatures herded by an anthropoid twice the height of man. This phantasmagoric "outer reality" is balanced by the "inner reality" of Axel's famous dream: "My imagination carried me off through the wondrous hypotheses of paleontology." He drifts through evolution in reverse, "back to the scriptural periods of creation," back to the time when the earth was just a gaseous mass. "My body was volatilized," he says. Verne has added a fourth voice to his fugue of sciences: depth psychology, the study of how "inner" and "outer" lose their meanings as modifiers of "reality."

The entire trip, of course, is typical of Vernean mythic withdrawal from ordinary reality, first a return to the womb of earth for all three men and then a return to the womb of wombs—the beginning—for Axel. Readers agree with Gräuben at the end: Axel is a hero.

Exploring the unconscious is just one of the ways *Journey* anticipates twentieth-century concerns. Fossil evidence of *Gigantopithecus,* a twelve-foot-high anthropoid, has been found in China. And geologist Norbert Casteret, in *Ten Years under the Earth* —his very title pays tribute to Verne—verifies Verne's assumption that underground passages do extend for great distances. Reading *Journey* as a child led Casteret to his calling. How many children today will find themselves in a Verne classic?

Meanwhile, in America, in the just-ended Civil War, eight thousand cannons had fired six million shells. The Union and Confederate armies had suffered one casualty for every three men. Verne wondered how this death technology could be reconverted to peacetime industry, all these destructive powers rechanneled into creative work. The result was *De la Terre à la lune* (*From the Earth to the Moon,* 1865).

The novel opens in the lounge of the Baltimore Gun Club, an association of artillerists, ballistics experts, and war profiteers who can now "muster . . . one arm for every four men, only two legs for every six." They are miserable because the advent of peace has nipped their militarist careers in the bud. But Impey Barbicane, president—one of the few members with all four limbs—proposes that they extend their talents to fire a cannonball at the moon. Step by step they solve all the technical problems involved, including the best place for launching their shell, the velocity it will need to escape gravity, its trajectory, and the length of time it will take to reach its target. Their nine-hundred-foot cannon has been cast—buried upright in the earth itself—when they get a telegram from Ardan (anagram for Nadar), a French daredevil, saying that they should "replace the spherical shell with a cylindro-conical projectile" so that he can "be inside when she leaves." After he arrives in his adopted country—like Lafayette, he is made an honorary citizen—he finds Barbicane involved in a duel. Ardan persuades both duelists that it's less dangerous to join him as passengers on the moon shot. The novel ends with the trio propelled moonward, exact whereabouts unknown.

From the Earth to the Moon is a rare blend of highly mathematical science fiction with social satire, especially on militarists: "They did unto others what they would not have others do unto them." Verne also becomes the first author systematically to apply the science of ballistics to the problem of lifting human beings into outer space. He correctly calculates (with the help of his cousin, a mathematics professor) that "any projectile aimed at the moon with an initial velocity of twelve thousand yards per second will arrive there out of scientific necessity." He hits on what has proved to be a typical flight time for manned spacecraft: ninety-seven hours and twenty minutes. He correctly predicts, for the proper scientific reasons, that America would launch its moon shot from Florida: his launching site is only 137 miles from Cape Kennedy (in today's city of North Port). He anticipates the size and weight of our Apollo capsule. He prophesies the use of rockets as retrojets: a self-fulfilling prophecy, since it inspired early space scientists such as Tsiolkovsky and Hermann Oberth to work on rockets as the main motive power for space.

As a social prophet, Verne divines that it would be the users and makers of weapons—the military-industrial complex—who would launch the space age; that the space effort would provide a ritualization of war, a peacetime spillover for the pent-up energies of the world's military juggernauts. He even calculates the sudden huge economic and demographic growth of Florida that would result.

Children respond warmly to the powerful appeal of two archetypal themes implicit in the plot: preparation for a journey into the unknown and arrival of an "outsider" who sets things straight. Before Ardan's appearance, Gun Clubbers cannot see their project as anything but target practice on a cosmic scale. They are stick figures struggling with narrowly technical questions. Barbicane is a walking timepiece, living proof of the grim efficacy of the work ethic. His sidekick Maston is a chauvinist who won't hear of accomplishments by any nationality but his own. But when Ardan ("ardent") brings flesh and blood into the situation, the project becomes humanistic as well as scientific. Barbicane slows down to enjoy people. Maston becomes a hero-worshiper of a foreigner. Activity once all form and content expands to include style.

The sequel *Autour de la lune* (1870)—literally, "around the moon"—appeared in its first English version together with the first book as *From the Earth to the Moon; and a Trip around It* (1873). But when it is published (and discussed) separately it is usually titled *Around* [or *All around*] *the Moon.* In this second story we learn that the trio has not landed on the moon because their course is altered by a passing asteroid. They simply loop the moon and splash down 250 miles off the coast of California. As Colonel Frank Borman would write to Verne's grandson in 1969, "Our space vehicle [Apollo 8] splashed down in the Pacific a mere two and a half miles from the point mentioned in the novel."

Both the Confederate States and France had by the mid-nineteenth century experimented with submarines. "I hope," George Sand wrote to Verne, that soon "your characters will travel in one of those submersible boats which your imagination and knowledge will make perfect." How well she knew his genius for extrapolating from the known to the still unknown and for ramifying all the implications of an "if." Verne had already amassed the "knowledge." His "imagination," his sensibilities in politics and depth psychology as well as in hydrodynamics, were at their best when, crisscrossing the English channel in his small boat *Le Saint Michel,* he composed *Twenty Thousand Leagues under the Sea.*

Just as he had extended the horizons of the first space effort from the narrowly artillerist to the broadly humanistic, so now Verne expanded the possibilities of the submarine. His *Nautilus* is not simply—like all large submarines today—a sneak-attack vessel. It is also a luxury underwater hotel and research laboratory the likes of which is still not yet, more than a century later, matched in reality.

Verne puts his splendid invention in the hands of a bitter genius, Captain Nemo, generally regarded as one of the great characters in world literature. Scientist, inventor, musician, philosopher, he has forsworn relations with terrestrial institutions and lives only where governments cannot obtrude their tyrannies. Yes, Nemo is an anarchist, equipped even with a black flag that he unfurls when he discovers—and takes possession of—the South Pole. For children, *Twenty Thousand Leagues* may be their first sympathetic glimpse at radical politics as well as at the staggering problems of oceanography.

The story is told by Professor Aronnax, who, as the novel opens, has completed his research in "les mauvaises terres du Nébraska," that is, the Badlands (rendered fatuously in the "standard" translation as "the disagreeable territory of Nebraska"). Aronnax joins the staff of the USS *Lincoln,* a warship ordered to seek and destroy a mysterious whale-like monster that has been sighted by—and has often collided with—ships in all of the Seven Seas. Aronnax and his servant Conseil make friends with Ned Land, aboard as expert harpooner. When the *Lincoln* discovers and attacks the huge "whale," that monster cripples the warship, and the trio, thrown overboard, are picked up by the "monster's" captain, Nemo. He is obliged to keep them with him in order to keep his submarine secrets safe from the powers he hates. This infuriates Ned but compromises Aronnax: he is now the first marine scientist able to study the oceans *in* the ocean.

Thus Verne invents an ideal scenario for the education of his readers. Nemo and Arronax discuss the theories of the American oceanographer Matthew Maury and future possibilities like undersea towns and new foods derived from sea flora. The professor answers Ned's questions about the growth of pearls and Conseil's about the growth of coral. The trio discuss the classifying of sea species, how life springs up on an islet of naked rock, and ecological problems triggered by the extermination of the dugong, manatee, and whale. However, Verne does most of his teaching not by stating but by demonstrating; his characters exit through an air lock to walk the ocean floor, wearing prototype aqualungs; they ride out a hurricane; and they tackle the terrifying problem of thawing the *Nautilus* out of a capsized iceberg. When it finally becomes clear that Nemo is fighting a naval war of vengeance against some nation (the trio can't discover which), Aronnax agrees to Ned's plans for escape.

As with Axel and Barbicane, the careers of these characters impress moral as well as scientific lessons on young minds. Nemo stands for Faustian science, pursued for secret, personal gain, Aronnax for Baconian science, pursued for the world's benefit. Although successful and apparently justified in inflicting massive and ingenious retaliation on his (to us still unidentified) enemy, Nemo nevertheless suffers remorse over his part in the unending violence. Aronnax muddles through a full-blown identity crisis: he retreats like Jonah from world affairs into the whale's belly, switches loyalty from friend Ned to friend's enemy Nemo, learns that friendship is more valuable than scientific knowledge acquired under dubious auspices, and frees himself from attachment to Nemo as a "perfect father" figure. Verne's characterization is revealed through psychological methods far in advance of 1870 or even of much juvenile fiction today, exploring slips of the tongue, dreams, and unconscious allusions.

Nemo provides the mystery again in *L'Île mystérieuse (The Mysterious Island,* 1875). Cyrus Smith, captain of engineers in the Union army, leads a reporter, a sailor, a black servant, and a teenager in their escape by balloon from a Confederate prison. They are carried by a storm all the way to a seemingly uninhabited Pacific isle. Under Smith's leadership, they more than survive—they not only eat well but also manufacture hats, candles, bricks, and pottery, build a residence high up in a cliffside (which they can get to easily on an elevator run by waterpower), stake out a farm, and set up a telegraph system to keep in touch with their farm crew. But they survive some crises only with some mysterious protection: Quinine appears by the bedside of a man sick with fever, and pirates attacking them are blown up or drop dead. Their secret benefactor proves to be Nemo and the island his secret headquarters, which he defends with torpedoes and Verne's anticipation of electric stun guns. Verne's scientific point is nowhere better made: All mysteries have a rational explanation. On his deathbed Nemo explains that he is an Indian prince, hero of the ill-fated Sepoy Revolt, who fled beneath the waves and was hunted by—and sank—British warships.

Children love *The Mysterious Island* as the last in that series that Verne called the "Robinsonades," beginning with Daniel Defoe's *Robinson Crusoe,* renewed with Johann Wyss's *Swiss Family Robinson,* and culminating in the most scientific version, Verne's. The juvenile reader identifies most with Herb Brown, the fifteen-year-old who gets his first lessons in applied math and science from Captain Smith.

While the Nemo novels are justly considered Verne's masterpieces, it was his pleasant entertainment *Le Tour du monde en quatre-vingt jours* (*Around the World in Eighty Days*, 1873) that earned him both world fame and his fortune. The story was serialized in *Le Temps;* summaries were telegraphed everywhere as world news; and after the novel appeared in book format, a stage version, which ran in Paris for fifty years, brought a "rain of gold" into the family coffers.

In this novel, Phileas Fogg bets his London friends that he can circle the globe in eighty days. He survives a rapid series of frustrations and breakneck triumphs as he races from continent to continent by railroad, elephant, canal boat, and steamship, only to arrive back home believing he has lost: he has traveled for eighty-one days. Finally he realizes that by traveling east around the world, he has gained a day. He dashes to his club just in time to collect his wager. He also wins the hand of Aouda, widow of the rajah of Bundelkund. (Between quick looks at his timetable he had saved her from sure death.) The sweet love between the British Fogg and the Indian Aouda is Verne's romantic answer to British prejudice against intermarriage with natives.

The novels I have reviewed here are the Verne books most popular with children. All seven were written for both adult and juvenile audiences. Oddly enough, the only two novels that Verne wrote expressly for children have never really caught on in England or America. *Un Capitaine de quinze ans* (*Dick Sands, the Boy Captain*, 1878), a classic on the Continent, may have failed in the United States because of its unequivocal stand against oppression of blacks. Reissue in a new and complete version might give it a second chance in the improved racial climate in America today. *Deux ans de vacances* (*Two Years Holiday*, 1888), a story about rivalries and politics among schoolboys marooned on a desert island, could never compete today with a far superior treatment of the same subject, William Golding's *Lord of the Flies*, which *Holiday* may have inspired (in his essays Golding reveals an intimate knowledge of Verne).

In any event, the seven novels treated here amply represent the themes and subject matter, the approach and scope of Jules Verne. One question remains. For how long can we expect his popularity as a writer for children to last? Is it doomed to die as more and more of his predictions come true? Will he, like them, become passé?

No. Even if Verne had ventured no predictions at all, he would still be a best-selling author as one of our best teachers of the history of science and of the scientific method. He succeeds in this role because he puts exciting science into an exciting human, social, comic, tragic context. But he did venture predictions, by the thousands. So the more his predictions do come true, the more his books teach the reliability of the scientific method: The stock in trade of science is its ability to predict events, and hence Verne becomes more and more an exemplar of its long-range success. Of course, there still are, as we have indicated with the submarine, scores of Vernean predictions that remain mere unfulfilled ambitions, ambitions for new Tsiolkovskys to live by.

An equally intriguing possibility is that, with the issuance of *complete* modern versions of Verne, novels now relatively unknown in the Anglo-American world, such as *La Maison à vapeur* (*The Steam House*, 1880) and *Robur le conquérant* (*The Clipper of the Clouds*, 1886), may help juvenile readers become more aware of Verne as a social prophet as well as a science prophet. His *Les Naufragés du Jonathan* (*The Survivors of the Jonathan*, posthumous, 1909), for example, explores the psychosocial problems of organizing a new *polis* from scratch. *Les Cinq Cents Millions de la Bégum* (*The Begum's Fortune*, 1878) and *L'Étonnante Aventure de la messian Barsac* (*The Barsac Mission*, posthumous, 1919) actually foresee the permanent (not just 1930's–1940's) danger of alliance between science and the more fascistic elements of international finance. Anglo-American children would then have access to the ultimate Verne, the writer who saw science and politics in one dynamism and could not prophesy about one without the other.

Selected Bibliography

WORKS OF JULES VERNE IN FRENCH

Cinq Semaines en ballon. Paris: Hetzel, 1863. With illustrations by Édouard Riou. Paris: Hetzel, 1867.

Voyage au centre de la terre. Paris: Hetzel, 1864. With illustrations by Édouard Riou. Paris: Hetzel, 1867.

De la Terre à la lune. With illustrations by de Montaut. Paris: Hetzel, 1866.

Autour de la Lune. With illustrations by Émile Bayard and Alphonse de Neuville. Paris: Hetzel, 1870.

Vingt mille lieus sous les mers. With illustrations by Édouard Riou and Alphonse de Neuville. Paris: Hetzel, 1870.

Le Tour du monde en quatre-vingt jours. Paris: Hetzel, 1873. With illustrations by Alphonse de Neuville and L. Benett. Paris: Hetzel, 1874.

L'Île mysterieuse. Paris: Hetzel, 1874–1875. With illustrations by Ferat (1875).

Un Capitaine de quinze ans. With illustrations by Meyer. Paris: Hetzel, 1878.

Les Cinq Cents Millions de la Bégum. Paris: Hetzel, 1878. With illustrations by L. Benett. Paris: Hetzel, 1879.

La Maison à vapeur. With illustrations by L. Benett. Paris: Hetzel, 1880.

Robur le conquerant. With illustrations by L. Benett. Paris: Hetzel, 1886.

Deux ans de vacances. With illustrations by L. Benett. Paris: Hetzel, 1888.

Les Naufragés du Jonathan. With illustrations by George Roux. Paris: Hetzel, 1909. (Published posthumously and hence perhaps written in part by Michel Verne.)

L'Étonnante Aventure de la mission Barsac. With illustrations by George Roux. Paris: Hachette, 1919. (Published posthumously and hence perhaps written in part by Michel Verne.)

WORKS OF JULES VERNE IN ENGLISH TRANSLATION

Early translators of Verne often violated the scientific and political integrity of the originals; unfortunately, many of these mistranslations persist. In the following list, the original "standard" translations are followed by whatever recent reliable versions are at present available.

Five Weeks in a Balloon, translator unknown. London: Chapman and Hale, 1870. (Replete with errors, which were blamed on Verne as early as 1874.)

Journey to the Centre of the Earth, translator unknown. London: Griffith and Farran, 1872. (Contains unacknowledged cuts.) *Journey to the Center of the Earth,* translated by Robert Baldick. London: Penguin Books, 1962. (Recommended.)

From the Earth to the Moon Direct in 97 Hours 20 Minutes; and a Trip around It, translated by Louis Mercier and Eleanor E. King. (Omits almost a quarter of the original.) London: Sampson Low, Marston, 1873.

The Annotated Jules Verne: From the Earth to the Moon, translated and edited by Walter J. Miller. New York: Thomas Y. Crowell, 1978. (Recommended.)

Twenty Thousand Leagues under the Sea, translated by Mercier Lewis. London: Sampson Low, Marston, 1873. (Lewis cut almost a quarter from the original and mistranslated hundreds of figures and phrases.)

Twenty Thousand Leagues under the Sea, translated by Philip Schuyler Allen. With illustrations by Milo Winter. Chicago: Rand McNally, 1922. (A reworking of the Lewis translation and hence incomplete, with passages of exposition recast as dialogue.)

Twenty Thousand Leagues under the Sea, translated by Mendor T. Brunetti. New York: Signet Books, 1969. (Recommended.) *The Annotated Jules Verne: Twenty Thousand Leagues under the Sea,* edited by Walter J. Miller. New York: Thomas Y. Crowell, 1976. (Recommended.)

Around the World in Eighty Days, translated by Mercier Lewis. London: Sampson Low, Marston, 1874. (Lewis' only complete and correct translation.)

The Mysterious Island, translated by W. H. G. Kingston. London: Sampson Low, Marston, 1875. (Kingston imposed his own views on political passages.)

Dick Sands, the Boy Captain, translated by Ellen E. Frewer. London: Sampson Low, Marston, 1879.

The Begum's Fortune, translated by W. H. G. Kingston. London: Sampson Low, Marston, 1880.

The Steam House, translated by A. D. Kingston. London: Sampson Low, Marston, 1881.

The Clipper of the Clouds, translator unknown. London: Sampson Low, Marston, 1887.

Two Years Holiday, translator unknown. London: Sampson Low, Marston, 1889.

The Survivors of the Jonathan, translator unknown. London: Arco, n.d.

The Barsac Mission, translated by I. O. Evans. London: Arco, 1965.

CRITICAL AND BIOGRAPHICAL STUDIES

Allotte de la Fuÿe, Marguerite. *Jules Verne,* translated by Erik de Mauny. London: Staples Press, 1954; New York: Coward-McCann, 1956. (First published in France, 1928; first "family" biography, by Verne's niece by marriage. Highly sentimental treatment that suppresses much important information.)

Asimov, Isaac. "An Introduction to This Edition." In *A Journey to the Centre of the Earth,* translator unknown. New York: Heritage Press, 1966. (Introduction recommended, but not this reprint of the "standard" translation.)

Bleiler, E. F. "Jules Verne." In *Science Fiction Writers,* edited by E. F. Bleiler. New York: Charles Scribner's Sons, 1982.

Born, Franz. *Jules Verne, The Man Who Invented the Future,* translated by J. Biro. Englewood Cliffs, N.J.: Prentice Hall, 1964. (Children's biography, somewhat novelized.)

Casteret, Norbert. *Ten Years Under the Earth.* London: Thames and Hudson, 1938. (Account of work inspired by his childhood reading of *A Journey to the Center of the Earth.*)

Chesneaux, Jean. *The Political and Social Ideas of Jules Verne,* translated by Thomas Wikely. London: Thames and Hudson, 1972.

Clarke, A. C. "Introduction." In *From the Earth to the Moon and Round the Moon,* translator not identified (Mercier and King translation). New York: Dodd, Mead, 1962. (Introduction recommended, but not this reprint of the "standard" translation.)

Costello, Peter. *Jules Verne: Inventor of Science Fiction.* London: Hodder and Stoughton, 1978. (Excellent materials on Verne's sources.)

Jules-Verne, Jean. "Introduction." In *From the Earth to the Moon and Around the Moon,* by Jules Verne, translator not identified (Mercier and King translation). New York: Limited Editions, 1970. (Introduction recommended, but not this reprint of the "standard" translation.)

Jules-Verne, Jean. *Jules Verne,* translated and adapted by Roger Greaves. New York: Taplinger, 1976. (Second "family" biography, by Verne's only surviving grandson; many valuable personal criticisms and memories of Verne.)

Ley, Willy. "Jules Verne: The Man and His Works." In *Dr. Ox's Experiment,* by Jules Verne, translator unknown. New York: Macmillan, 1963.

Miller, Walter James. "Jules Verne in America: A Translator's Preface." In *Twenty Thousand Leagues under the Sea,* by Jules Verne, with an afterword by Damon Knight. New York: Thomas Y. Crowell, 1965. (The first exposé of the "standard" translations.)

Moré, Marcel. *Le très curieux Jules Verne.* Paris: Gallimard, 1960.

———. *Nouvelles explorations de Jules Verne.* Paris: Gallimard, 1963.

Vierne, Simone. *Jules Verne et le Roman initiatique.* Paris: Sirac, 1973. (Study of initiation ritual in Verne's stories, such as *Journey to the Center of the Earth.*)

—WALTER JAMES MILLER

H. G. WELLS
1866-1946

IN THE HISTORY of science fiction H. G. Wells enjoys a prominent place: some commentators praise him as one of the founders of the genre; others hail him as the Shakespeare of modern science fiction. This lofty reputation does not mean that Wells attained prominence in no other area; much of his realistic and comic fiction was, and is, incisive and delightful, and his commentary on sociological and historical topics was eagerly read by countless thousands. Still, what ensures his fame is his science fiction, or, as he called it, scientific romances. Moreover, five of them, *The Time Machine* (1895), *The Island of Doctor Moreau* (1896), *The Invisible Man* (1897), *The War of the Worlds* (1898), and *The First Men in the Moon* (1901), because they are his most imaginative and least ideological novels, have proved attractive to young readers over the years.

Herbert George Wells was born on 21 September 1866 in Bromley, Kent, to Joseph and Sarah Wells. Bertie, as his parents called him, physically resembled his father and shared with him a distinct mental keenness and a taste for free, imaginative reading. His deeply religious, orthodox mother was intensely devoted to her children; although cherishing her devotion, Bertie rejected not only his mother's brand of Christianity but also every other kind. The father, a better cricketer than shopkeeper, saw his hardware business collapse, forcing his wife to reenter service as housekeeper to her former employers at Up Park, Sussex, where she had once worked as a lady's maid. The boy was sent to a local school, where he flourished, but upon the advent of the family's financial difficulties he was apprenticed to a draper. For the next several years Bertie alternated between several apprenticeships, which he keenly disliked, and periods of idleness at Up Park, where he read and absorbed the relatively liberal thinking found upstairs.

In 1883 Wells became an assistant schoolmaster and one year later won a scholarship to the South Kensington Normal School of Science, later named the Imperial College of Science and Technology. For three years he studied science, in particular biology, which he took from Thomas Henry Huxley, the champion of Darwinism, whom Wells always spoke of as the greatest man he ever met. As a student Wells also wrote humorous and satiric essays and occasionally attended socialist gatherings, where he met George Bernard Shaw and others instrumental in founding the Fabian Society. On leaving school without passing his final exams—a deficiency he subsequently remedied by first-class honors in zoology at the University of London—he reentered teaching, to which he returned once again after a period of ill health and convalescence. In October 1891 he married his cousin Isabel Mary Wells, but the marriage failed, which led to his unconventional, if not radical, views on sexual matters. Abandoning his wife in 1894, he eloped with and later married Amy Catherine Robbins, who, despite her husband's infidelities, remained loyal and supportive.

During this period Wells began to write seriously, published a science textbook, and by the mid-1890's was earning enough money from his writing to give up teaching. The 1895 publication of *The Time Machine* brought fame while the subsequent appearance of seven other novels and six collections of short fiction ensured fortune by the first years of the new century. A versatile author, Wells exhibited an extraordinary range of style and topic, turning out scientific romances, realistic and comic novels, and much nonfiction. By World War I, however, Wells had shifted from imaginative fiction to the propagandistic and nonfictional. This shift, it has been charged, signaled his demise as an artist and the ascendancy of the popularizing preacher.

World War I precipitated in Wells a preoccupation with the need for global unification and the belief that humanity had to adapt its political and educational institutions to the major changes occurring in the world or risk extinction. Global institutions, he argued, should be set up to force and oversee disarmament and peace, husband natural resources, and organize transportation networks. Further, history needed to be studied on a global basis. Influential books of this period that disseminated his ideas worldwide were *The Outline of History* (1920), *The Science of Life* (1929–1930), and *The Shape of Things to Come* (1933). A pacifist, he changed his views with the rise of Hitler. Unfortunately, frequent bouts of ill health slowed him down considerably in his last years. On 13 August 1946 he died in London, his reputation as a writer in eclipse and his status as a world-respected commentator suspect. Recently, however, renewed attention has been paid to Wells the artist.

Since its publication *The Time Machine* not only has become Wells's most popular novel but also has been hailed as his best work. That his very first science fiction novel should enjoy widespread popularity as well as critical esteem is no surprise: Wells worked hard at his story, seeing it through seven drafts. It was almost as if he sensed that public acceptance (or rejection) of the novel would be tantamount to approval (or disapproval) of both his decision to become a writer and the viability of science fiction as a literary genre.

The Time Machine is not long, nor is its plot complicated. The time traveler, having invented a machine that allows traveling through time, uses his invention to journey into the future. Arriving in 802701, he finds himself among a graceful, beautiful, and manifestly human people, the Eloi, who he initially decides dwell in a golden age. Further ob-

servation, however, reveals that the golden age is seriously tarnished inasmuch as the Eloi are feckless and unable to control their lives. He is surprised to learn of another people, the Morlocks, ugly, fearsome, subterranean, and, the time traveler discovers to his horror, preying upon the Eloi for their food. A final horror is the realization that both Eloi and Morlock are descendants of the human race and represent the natural culmination of the stratification of society rampant in the late nineteenth century. Barely escaping from the Morlocks, the time traveler hurls himself farther into the future, where he witnesses the final days of earth. Returning to his own time just long enough to record his travels, he disappears, again journeying into time.

The Time Machine is, first of all, an exciting adventure story. Suspenseful scenes when the time traveler escapes from the Morlocks and from the sluglike creature he encounters at the end of the world; the horror experienced at the slowly growing awareness of the truth concerning the Eloi and the Morlocks; and the foreboding description of the imminent end of life on earth are especially effective and readily accessible to virtually all readers. The slight characterization is dramatic and, as in all of Wells's science fiction, tends to the general and abstract without becoming allegorical. With the exception of the encounter with Weena, an Eloi woman he saves from drowning, the first-person narrator's comments are not introspective or personal; instead Wells focuses on the narrator's observations of the strange and unexpected and his attempts to make sense of them.

The appeal of *The Time Machine* stems, too, from Wells's success in utilizing the new genre of science fiction to point out to his contemporaries their misunderstanding and abuse of Darwinism to justify then-current social structures. Inadequately grasping evolution and the natural origin of species, many people confused these theories with meliorism and believed that the changes over time in the status of the white races, which had brought them global power, were the outcome of a successful struggle with the environment and implied the whites' survival as the fittest and best, and, furthermore, that evolution, which had already brought the white races this far, would impel them to even dizzier heights in the future. The Eloi-Morlock relationship is Wells's satiric commentary on this self-flattering misunderstanding of Darwinism. Through the time traveler, readers are to perceive that both Eloi and Morlocks—the former, pitiful, feckless, and undeniably human in appearance; the latter, cannibalistic and ugly because of being forced to live underground—descend from the human race. Also, the relationship between them— slave and master, prey and predator—is a reversal of the social classification enforced during Wells's time. Further, the description of the end of life on earth illustrates convincingly and hauntingly that, according to Darwin, devolution as well as evolution might occur. That is, instead of constant improvement and "good times" for humanity, the future might see regression and a return to "bad times."

Finally, *The Time Machine* is important because in it for the first time science and fiction are blended into a harmonious whole. It is true that previous writers used science as subject matter; for instance, Mary Shelley in *Frankenstein* (1818) investigated the possibility of artificially creating life. But Wells was the first to incorporate science—specifically the inevitability of change, evolution, and the importance of the future, where the predicted and actual results of change might be looked for and evaluated—or its methodology into the very fabric of his narrative. Hence the time traveler's determination to make sense of what he observes by tentatively drawing up an explanation and his willingness to discard it in light of new data and to find a second explanation are instances of the scientific method— creating a hypothesis, testing it against the observed data, and discarding it if found wanting. Moreover, in his description of the imminent end of life on earth, Wells reverses popular understanding of taxonomy and the development of the human species from its origin in the sea; hence it is both shocking and scientific that a sluglike creature is the last being alive.

Whether *The Time Machine* is pessimistic is debatable. What is not debatable is the pessimism of Wells's second scientific romance, *The Island of Doctor Moreau*. Somewhat longer than its predecessor and less tightly written, the novel still fascinates with its story of a medical genius who almost succeeds in surgically altering animals into human beings. Told by Edward Prendick, who is the only human survivor of Moreau's vivisectionist laboratory on a lonely South Pacific island, the story focuses on the doctor's attempt first to complete his experiments in the surgical alteration of animals and then to prevent the collapse of the society he

has set up, a collapse that accelerates as the human-like creatures revert to their animal natures. The novel is clearly shocking and violent, but the violence is not gratuitous; how else are animals to act when they are hurt while being surgically altered to resemble human beings and then revert in anger and vengefulness to their animality? In fact, the violence, regardless of what some adults might prefer to believe or refuse to accept, is an attractive feature to some young readers. Further, the shock and violence of detail and subject matter dramatically underscore the novel's provocative intent, an intent shared with *The Time Machine:* Wells sought to remind readers that Darwinism argues that humanity in its origin is animal and that, regardless of how far the human species may have evolved from that origin, within its basic nature there still remain distinctly animal traits.

Wells himself wryly noted toward the end of his life that to many young people he was just the author of *The Invisible Man.* It is easy to understand this novel's attraction for youth then and now. Both as novel and film, the plot has capitalized on the sensationalism and irony inherent in a story that seeks to gratify a sentiment more than one adolescent has expressed: Oh, if only I had the power to make myself invisible—not the way I feel when I am being ignored by everybody, but really invisible—then I'd be able to make people notice me. This sentiment is pretty much what eventually dominates Griffin, the invisible man. Originally a scientist seeking to learn whether through chemical analysis and synthesis he can achieve invisibility, Griffin is dismayed to learn that being invisible actually means being radically naked and exposed to the push and shove of society. Coming to the quiet village of Iping, Griffin soon upsets its calm with his frantic attempts to remain isolated long enough to learn how to regain visibility and then to seek revenge upon those unwilling to give him what he wants, which is power. Fittingly, in an especially sobering scene at the end he is trampled and crushed to death, ironically only then regaining visibility. Another strength of the novel is its realistic, almost Dickensian scenes of city and village life, which render plausible as well as offset the extraordinary phenomenon of the invisible man. Also striking is Wells's insistence, manifest in much of his writing, that power without moral control is dangerous and irresponsible. Through much of the book,

Griffin has the reader's sympathy, but by the end, because of his cruelty and arrogance, he has forfeited all of it. In his quest for immunity to visible sight, he has surely lost another, perhaps more important kind of sight.

The War of the Worlds may be Wells's most recognized work today because of the famous Orson Welles radio broadcast, which continues to be re-broadcast, and the several film versions of both the novel and the radio broadcast. For the same reasons, the novel paradoxically may go unread inasmuch as many think they already know the story and need not bother taking the time to read it. Yet the novel is quite readable. Set in the quiet suburbs around London at a time when people felt almost smugly satisfied about themselves and the future, the story concerns an invasion of earth by Martians. The invaders immediately reveal both their hostility and technological superiority as they quickly spread through the countryside, overcoming all resistance. Total defeat seems inevitable, when suddenly the Martians die from infection by earth bacteria.

The continuing impact of this novel stems from three sources. First, the description of the Martians and their implacable hostility is striking, regardless of how often Wells's achievement has been imitated. Second, the scenes of violence and destruction in town and country and of the crowds fleeing the invaders—which were nothing but sensational when they first appeared—demonstrate Wells's skill in first imagining and then re-creating what the Western world had not yet experienced. Today, readers are still impressed, recognizing the scenes of warfare and streaming refugees as harbingers of what now actually happens far too often. Finally, the novel is a vivid lesson in what colonization and subjugation mean to those colonized and subjugated by a people convinced of its moral and cultural superiority and indifferent to the freedom and rights of the vanquished.

The last of Wells's scientific romances readily accessible to young readers is *The First Men in the Moon.* The Wells most evident in the novel is the one who subsequently came to be prominently associated in the popular mind with speculation and prediction about the future, new technology, and possible social reorganization. As science fiction, the novel, too, was influential in suggesting that science fiction typically is a predictive fiction rather than a discursive and critical one, a notion many

still entertain to the detriment of science fiction. It is true that in *The First Men in the Moon* Wells is almost uncanny in some of his descriptions, and his gift for imagining what does not yet exist and skill in describing it vividly and plausibly are most evident. For instance, before flight of any kind was practical and the only flights to the moon were fantastic ones, Wells laid out plausibly and convincingly the stages of space flight—lift-off, weightlessness, zero gravity, radio communication, reentry, and splashdown. Even more impressive than descriptions of spacecraft and flight are those of the dawning of day upon the moon and the emergence of life on its surface, which in their detail and lyricism rank as some of the most stimulating, imaginative passages in all science fiction. Also contributing to the novel's success is its characterization: Cavor, the almost comic scientist-inventor, who is left behind on the moon, and Bedford, the writer who comes along partly because he sees in the lunar flight a way to get rich, are vividly drawn. The final strength of the novel is its last section, which purports to be Cavor's message to earth describing the Selenites and their society. This section is best read as Wells's satiric commentary on any society, real or proposed, that overorganizes its citizens, seeking to train and educate them for every possible specialized task. The novel, in short, is both fascinating technological speculation and hardy intellectual fare.

It is not likely that Wells will ever regain the eminence he once enjoyed as a man of letters and as a spokesperson for stimulating and provocative positions on a wide range of topics. But it is likely that, given the current acceptance of science fiction as both art and vehicle for serious investigation of ideas and trends, his reputation as a major science fiction author will remain intact. For as more than one critic has pointed out, it is to Wells's achievement in his scientific romances that one must look for the initial definitive demonstration that science fiction can embody science that stimulates wonder and challenges thought, as well as fiction that entertains. Even further testimony to Wells's achievement in his early science fiction is that these novels, which clearly speak to adult readers, are also readily accessible to young ones without the necessity for extensive commentary or explanation. In a famous debate with Henry James concerning the role of the writer, Wells proudly, if not defiantly, announced that he was not an artist, which he considered to be a kind of dilettante who owes no responsibility except to his or her art—a definition, incidentally, reflecting Wells's youthful disdain for the Pre-Raphaelites —but a journalist, that is, someone who wants to get across his or her ideas to as many readers as possible. Hence, one suspects, Wells would have taken pleasure in learning that eighty years after they were written his early novels are read and enjoyed by both young and old. At the same time, one also suspects, Wells would not have been upset, in spite of his avowed preference for being considered primarily a journalist, to discover that on the basis of his early science fiction he would ultimately be praised as an artist.

Selected Bibliography

WORKS OF H. G. WELLS

Works. 24 vols. London: Essex, 1926–1927.
Seven Science Fiction Novels. New York: Dover, 1950. (Includes the five novels discussed in this essay. These are also usually available in paperback.)
Twenty-eight Science Fiction Stories. New York: Dover, 1952.

CRITICAL AND BIOGRAPHICAL STUDIES

Bergonzi, Bernard. *H. G. Wells: A Collection of Critical Essays*. Englewood Cliffs, N.J.: Prentice-Hall, 1976.
Hammond, J. R. *An H. G. Wells Companion: A Guide to the Novels, Romances and Short Stories*. New York: Barnes and Noble; London: Macmillan, 1979.
Haynes, Roslynn D. *H. G. Wells, Discoverer of the Future: The Influence of Science on His Thought*. New York: New York University Press, 1980; London: Macmillan, 1980.
Hillegas, Mark R. *The Future as Nightmare: H. G. Wells and the Anti-Utopians*. New York: Oxford University Press, 1967.
Mackenzie, Norman and Jeanne. *The Time Traveller: The Life of H. G. Wells*. London: Weidenfeld and Nicolson, 1973.
McConnell, Frank. *The Science Fiction of H. G. Wells*. New York: Oxford University Press, 1981.
Scholes, Robert, and Eric S. Rabkin. *Science Fiction: History, Science, Vision*. New York: Oxford University Press, 1977.
Suvin, Darko, and Robert M. Philmus, eds. *H. G. Wells and Modern Science Fiction*. Lewisburg, Pa.: Bucknell University Press, 1977.

—FRANCIS J. MOLSON

KATE DOUGLAS WIGGIN

1856-1923

K ATE DOUGLAS WIGGIN was born in Philadelphia, Pennsylvania, on 28 September 1856. She grew up in Maine and was educated first at Gorham Female Seminary, then at Morison Academy in Baltimore and Abbot Academy in Andover, Massachusetts. She did not attend college but instead went to Mrs. Severance's Kindergarten Training School in Los Angeles, California. At that time she had to make a career for herself as quickly as possible in order to support her mother, younger sister, and stepbrother.

Wiggin came from a distinguished New England family, particularly on her father's side. Her paternal grandfather, Noah Smith, was a member of the Maine legislature who became Speaker of the House and secretary of state in Maine. After his career in the state legislature, he was the secretary of the United States Senate and then legislative clerk of the Senate. Her father was a lawyer, evidently of some promise, but he died while quite young, leaving a wife with two children. Wiggin's mother remarried a country doctor whose health failed when Kate was a young teenager. The family moved to Santa Barbara, California, in an effort to improve the health of her stepfather, but he died within a year.

Wiggin was brought up in a family of voracious readers. Her mother particularly loved the works of Dickens, and she read them to her family every night. When Wiggin was a child she was the traveling companion of Dickens when he made a journey from Portland, Maine, to Boston. Her other literary influences included the collected works of

Shakespeare (a volume she said she wore out), the fairy tales of Hans Christian Andersen, and the Bible, which she knew virtually by heart.

With the death of her stepfather in Santa Barbara, the family was left destitute, partly because he had made many foolish investments in California real estate. At this period, Wiggin became involved in the Froebelian Kindergarten Movement, and after she graduated from Mrs. Severance's Kindergarten Training School she went to San Francisco to set up free kindergartens. In 1878 she founded, with Felix Adler, the Silver Street Free Kindergarten, the first free kindergarten west of the Rockies. Through her kindergarten work, she was able to pull her family out of debt and to pay off the mortgages on their property.

Wiggin's first two books, *The Story of Patsy: A Reminiscence* (1883) and *The Birds' Christmas Carol* (1887), were written and privately printed to raise money for the Silver Street Kindergarten. Neither of these books had a wide circulation—the press runs were very small—but one day, out of curiosity, Wiggin sent *The Birds' Christmas Carol* to Houghton, Mifflin and Company of Boston. The senior member of the firm, Henry A. Houghton, took the book home and read it to his children. Because of their positive response, he published the book. It became a success and launched Wiggin's career.

In 1881 Wiggin married Samuel Bradley Wiggin, an acquaintance she had met when she lived in Maine. He graduated from Dartmouth and upon completion of his legal training moved to San Francisco to practice law. After they were married he moved his practice to New York City, and Wiggin left San Francisco to set up housekeeping with him. She continued her activities in free kindergartens, both in New York and in San Francisco, though not as extensively as when she was single. Then in 1889 her husband suddenly died.

Through her work raising money for free kindergartens, Wiggin came into contact with many wealthy people. Because of the evangelical nature of the Free Kindergarten Movement, she often traveled around the country and also to Europe. On one of her trips to England, she met on shipboard George Christopher Riggs, a wealthy New York industrialist. He fell in love with her, and they were married in 1895. Wiggin had no children by either marriage. The closest she came to becoming a mother was when, on a speaking engagement in England, a poor woman offered to give her her crippled baby because neither the woman nor her husband wanted it. To Wiggin's later regret, she did not accept the offer, perhaps because of the severe and paralyzing headaches that plagued her all her life.

The combination of literary success (Wiggin was awarded an honorary Doctor of Letters by Bowdoin College in 1904) and a wealthy marriage opened the doors to the best social circles in both America and Europe. Wealthy Americans at that time looked to England as a center of social and literary culture, and Wiggin spent much time living in England, where she had friends among the English aristocracy. She also knew and was influenced by American and English writers who lived in London at the turn of the century, notably Henry James, Mark Twain, William Dean Howells, John Masefield, and Lady Gregory. Needless to say, she was Anglophilic in her tastes and inclinations; she even preferred English food to American.

Wiggin published not only children's books but also books for adults, some of which were fairly successful, such as *The Old Peabody Pew: A Christmas Romance of a Country Church* (1907). She gave public readings in which she often shared the platform with such authors as Rudyard Kipling and Mark Twain. Her nonfiction writings consisted primarily of professional books in the kindergarten field.

Her most important children's writings are *The Birds' Christmas Carol*, *Rebecca of Sunnybrook Farm* (1903), *Mother Carey's Chickens* (1911), and also *The Arabian Nights: Their Best-Known Tales* (1909),

which she edited with her sister, Nora A. Smith, and which was illustrated by Maxfield Parrish.

The Birds' Christmas Carol, Wiggin's first success, is a sentimental story about a child's life and death. It is related to the Puritan tradition of "joyful death" books, associated primarily with James Janeway and later with Cotton Mather, which are case histories of the deaths of sick children made joyful through their Christian faith; at the turn of the century, it was fashionable for children's authors to kill off their child characters at the end of their books.

The Birds' Christmas Carol opens with the mother of the Bird family giving birth on Christmas day to a baby girl. The mother hears Christmas carolers outside her window and decides to name the newborn baby Carol. Carol is a sweet but sick child and is adored by the other local children, primarily the poor neighbors, the Ruggleses. On her tenth birthday (which of course is also Christmas Day), Carol dies after attending a joyful dinner party with all the other children. The book is suffused with transcendental and mystical Christianity, a sensibility Wiggin derived not only from her native New England religious heritage but also from the writings of Ralph Waldo Emerson, whose lectures she attended in her youth.

The birth of the child Carol reflects Wiggin's idea of the glory of motherhood and of large families. Wiggin describes postpartum bliss with these words: "Mrs. Bird lay in her room, weak, but safe and happy, with her sweet girl baby by her side and the heaven of motherhood opening again before her." As is characteristic of children's fiction of the period, the view of women is one-dimensional; they bloom best while they are reproducing.

Wiggin is best remembered for *Rebecca of Sunnybrook Farm*, which was first published in 1903. This book has become so famous that the phrase "Rebecca of Sunnybrook Farm" is often used to denote a type of woman who exudes pastoral innocence and sweetness. This image of Rebecca probably derives more from Shirley Temple's portrayal of her in the movie of the same name than from the character of Rebecca in the novel.

The novel begins with Rebecca at age ten going to live with her two maiden aunts, Miranda and Jane Sawyer, in the town of Riverboro. Rebecca wants to get away from Sunnybrook Farm so she can go into the world and work to pay off the mortgage that her widowed mother has inherited from a romantic but improvident husband, her mother having been left with not only a mortgage but also seven children to support. This part of the book clearly relates to Wiggin's own experience of trying to support a mother and two younger siblings and pay off the family's debts at the age of seventeen.

In her autobiography, *My Garden of Memory* (1923), Wiggin said that she conceived the story of Rebecca in a kind of "waking dream," and she wrote it while recovering from a fever. By 1903 things had worked out well for Wiggin in her kindergarten profession, in her second marriage, and in her writing, so that the novel can be seen as a semiautobiographical affirmation of her own life story.

In the novel, Rebecca desires success so she can remove the burden of the farm from her mother and family. Far from being a lover of nature, Rebecca is overjoyed when at the end of the story Sunnybrook Farm is sold to a railroad and is to be destroyed. The next to last chapter is entitled "Good-by, Sunnybrook"; in it her mother gets a good price for the farm, the burden of country life is removed, and the family goes to live in the aunts' house in Riverboro.

Like many successful women in the inhibited Victorian period, Wiggin clung to the fantasy of herself as an innocent little girl. Similarly, as a character, Rebecca never matures psychologically although she grows from being a girl of ten to a so-called woman of eighteen. She changes outwardly as her spelling and grammar improve and as she becomes tidier in her behavior and more socially conscious and conforming. But she still remains a little girl. Wiggin emphasizes this point in the book, and this is perhaps the message that comes through most clearly: Do not become a mature woman.

Although Rebecca is somewhat of a local phenomenon in intelligence, she succeeds in each of her plans, whether selling soap to help out a poor family or paying off the mortgage on Sunnybrook Farm, through the help of a magical father figure, Adam Ladd. On their first meeting Rebecca wistfully calls him "Mr. Aladdin" because he "miraculously" aids her by buying three hundred cakes of Snow-White and Rose-Red brands of soap. At the end of the story, with Rebecca graduated from school as a young woman of eighteen, Wiggin leads the reader to believe that Adam Ladd and Rebecca

will marry. To Wiggin's credit as a writer, she only cleverly suggests the marriage through the medium of the story of Aladdin and the Princess from *The Arabian Nights*. Adam Ladd has purchased a copy of this book for Rebecca to read, and thumbing through it he reads the account of Aladdin and the Princess. The quotation from *The Arabian Nights* in chapter 30 indicates that Ladd identifies the Princess with Rebecca and Aladdin with himself, an association that Wiggin also wants the reader to make.

It is significant that Adam Ladd's attraction for Rebecca is grounded in her little-girl psychology. At one point in the story Rebecca becomes jealous of him when she sees him escorted by the beautiful and precocious Hulda Meserve, a girl slightly older than Rebecca. Adam Ladd notices Rebecca's jealousy and puts her fears to rest by telling her that she will have nothing to worry about if she will always remain a little girl:

> Adam put a finger under Rebecca's chin and looked into her eyes; eyes as soft, as clear, as unconscious, and child-like as they had been when she was ten. He remembered the other pair of challenging blue ones that had darted coquettish glances through half-dropped lids, shot arrowy beams from under archly lifted browns, and said gravely, "Don't form yourself on her, Rebecca; clover blossoms that grow in the fields beside Sunnybrook must n't be tied in the same bouquet with gaudy sunflowers; they are too sweet and fragrant and wholesome."

Rebecca's model of wholesomeness and virginal childlikeness has become an ideal for generations of adolescent American girls approaching womanhood, and the "little girl" has always been an alluring figure in the imagination of American males. Adam Ladd represents the archetypal paternal lover, from Daddy Long Legs to the contemporary "sugar daddy." Wiggin certainly had her own father-lover-husband and magical protector in George Riggs, her second husband, whom she admired and called "a man's man."

Today, four of Wiggin's books are in print: *Rebecca of Sunnybrook Farm*, *The Birds' Christmas Carol*, *The Village Watch-Tower* (a collection of stories, 1895), and *Pinafore Palace: A Book of Rhymes for the Nursery* (1907). Still excerpted in anthologies is *Mother Carey's Chickens*, a work of fiction that shares with *Rebecca of Sunnybrook Farm* the still current interest in the fragmented family. The book is essentially an encomium to family. It begins with a description of the Careys; perhaps a more idealized or sentimental portrait of a family has never been written. The parents are described as perfect:

> Mrs. Carey did not wear her usual look of sweet serenity, but nothing could wholly mar the gracious dignity of her face and presence. As she came down the stairs with her quick, firm tread, her flock following her, she looked the ideal mother. Her fine height, her splendid carriage, her deep chest, her bright eye and fresh color all bespoke the happy, contented, active woman.

And Captain Carey is seen through the eyes of his children as a

> gay, gallant father, desperately ill and mother nursing him; father, with the kind smile and the jolly little sparkles of fun in his eyes; father, tall and broad-shouldered, splendid as the gods, in full uniform; father, so brave that if a naval battle ever did come his way, he would demolish the foe in an instant; father, with a warm strong hand clasping ours on high days and holidays, taking us on great expeditions where we see life at its best and taste incredible joys.

The crisis alluded to is Captain Carey's illness from typhoid fever. He dies from it, and his death creates a domestic imbalance. But Mother Carey and her four children are filled with enough spirit to triumph over poverty and the absence of a father. As the novel progresses the Careys not only overcome each difficulty that confronts them but are also able to support and reform a spoiled cousin, Julia, who is taken into the family group when she is left destitute.

Despite the book's moral and sentimental idealism, there are flashes of humor and bright characterization, as in this strange description in chapter 5 of the selfish person who is not part of a family: "Miserable, useless, flabby paws, those of the non-joiner; that he feeds and dresses himself with, and then hangs to his selfish sides, or puts behind his beastly back!"

The Arabian Nights, edited by Wiggin and her sister, Nora A. Smith, is also an important book in Wiggin's canon, although it is not as well known as her fiction. It is interesting primarily because it is illustrated by Maxfield Parrish. Although Wiggin

and her sister knew the great translations of *The Arabian Nights* by Sir Richard Burton and John Payne, they chose to butcher their version for the sake of innocence. Wiggin says in the preface that she has followed Andrew Lang, who "says amusingly that he has left out of his special versions 'all the pieces that are suitable only for Arabs and old gentlemen,' and we have done the same." In spite of the bowdlerization of the stories, the Parrish illustrations make the book a classic; his combination of chiaroscuro and bold colors stimulates the imagination and enlarges the text.

Although Wiggin's work is too often sentimental and didactic, she wrote with humor and had a talent for characterization. Her writings have influenced the social attitudes of generations of children and are an interesting reflection of her age.

Selected Bibliography

WORKS OF KATE DOUGLAS WIGGIN

The Story of Patsy: A Reminiscence. San Francisco: C. A. Murdock, 1883; London: Gay and Bird, 1889.

The Birds' Christmas Carol. San Francisco: C. A. Murdock, 1887; London: Gay and Bird, 1891. (Still in print in 1987 with Houghton Mifflin.)

The Village Watch-Tower. Boston: Houghton Mifflin, 1895.

Pinafore Palace: A Book of Rhymes for the Nursery. New York: McClure, 1907.

Rebecca of Sunnybrook Farm. Boston and New York: Houghton Mifflin, 1903; London: Gay and Bird, 1907. (Seven editions were still in print in 1985, including a Houghton Mifflin edition in America and a Black edition in England.)

The Arabian Nights: Their Best-Known Tales, edited with Nora A. Smith. With illustrations by Maxfield Parrish. New York: Charles Scribner's Sons, 1909; London: Laurie, 1909.

Mother Carey's Chickens. Boston: Houghton Mifflin, 1911. Retitled *Mother Carey*. London: Hodder and Stoughton, 1912.

My Garden of Memory: An Autobiography. Boston: Houghton Mifflin, 1923; London: Hodder and Stoughton, 1924.

CRITICAL AND BIOGRAPHICAL STUDIES

Benner, Helen F. *Kate Douglas Wiggin's Country of Childhood*. Orono: University of Maine Press, 1956.

Boutwell, Edna. "Kate Douglas Wiggin: The Lady with the Golden Key." In *The Hewlins Lectures*, edited by Siri Andrews. Boston: Horn Book, 1963.

Brooks, Van Wyck. *New England Indian Summer*. New York: Dutton, 1940.

Butler, Francelia. "Preface" to *Rebecca of Sunnybrook Farm*. London and New York: Garland, 1976. (Facsimile edition.)

Commire, Anne, ed. *Yesterday's Authors of Books for Children*, vol. 1. Detroit: Gale Research, 1977.

Jordan, Elizabeth. *Three Rousing Cheers*. New York: Appleton-Century, 1938.

Moss, Anita. "Kate Douglas Wiggin." In *Dictionary of Literary Biography*, vol. 42. Detroit: Gale Research, 1985.

Smith, Nora A. *Kate Douglas Wiggin as Her Sister Knew Her*. Boston: Houghton Mifflin, 1925; London: Gay and Hancock, 1925.

Wells, Carolyn. *The Rest of My Life*. Philadelphia: Lippincott, 1937.

—FRANCELIA BUTLER

OSCAR WILDE

1854-1900

READERS WHO ASSOCIATE Oscar Wilde's name mainly with flamboyance and degradation are unprepared for Wilde's stories written for children. These unique and beautiful tales dramatize the difficulty of living by Christian ideals.

George Woodcock, in his critical biography *The Paradox of Oscar Wilde* (1949), focuses on the contradictions in Wilde's life. He acknowledges that Wilde was "a strange combination of adolescence and maturity," a man who was emotionally immature, with serious character weaknesses, but at the same time a gifted man who was capable of showing deep wisdom. Wilde's maxim that "one's real life is often the life one does not live" expresses his awareness of his own complexity.

Wilde's public and literary reputation was consciously built on his skill with language. William Butler Yeats, in his *Autobiography* (1916), called Wilde "the greatest talker of his time." Yeats said that before he met Wilde he had never before "heard a man talking with perfect sentences, as if he had written them all overnight with labour and yet all spontaneous." Possessing a natural dramatic flair, Wilde preferred a live audience. When he had to write, usually to earn money, he could produce work rapidly because he had told and retold his stories many times before he prepared them for publication.

He was born in Dublin on 16 October 1854, and was christened Oscar Fingal O'Flahertie Wills Wilde, a name full of stories. "Oscar" was for the son of Ossian, a third-century Irish warrior poet, and for Wilde's godfather, the reigning king of

Sweden, whose successful cataract operation was performed by Wilde's father, a leading ear and eye surgeon (who had also treated Queen Victoria and Napoleon III of France); "Fingal" was the central hero of Ossianic legend; "O'Flahertie" was the famous O'Flahertie of Galway; and "Wills" was a Wilde family name.

His interest in fairy and folk tales came from his intellectual, unconventional parents. His formidable mother, a fervent Irish nationalist who wrote under the pen name Speranza, and his physician father were researchers and authors of books and articles on Irish history, folklore, and legends. Their house was often filled with famous visitors, many of them literary personalities, whose conversation and stories the three Wilde children absorbed. Oscar Wilde's later interest in the poor also stems from these early years, when his mother wrote about starving children in some of her own poems.

Wilde acquired a solid grounding in the classics. At Trinity College, Dublin, he won the Berkeley Gold Medal for Greek. At Oxford University, in addition to winning the Newdigate Prize for English verse, he earned a double first in classics. He read Homer in the original, not as an academic exercise but rather for pleasure. Walter Pater and John Ruskin influenced him in his aesthetic formulations and probably awakened his social conscience. John Cardinal Newman, whom Wilde called "that divine man," attracted him for his distinctive approach to Catholicism. Wilde considered conversion to Catholicism at various times in his

611

life. He was intensely interested in the life of Christ, and at times even identified with him; finally in 1900, on his deathbed, he became a Catholic convert.

Throughout his life, Wilde was principally a storyteller, whether in the form of drama, fiction, poetry, or conversation. When two sons were born, the issue of Wilde's marriage in 1884 to Constance Lloyd, it was natural that they would become his dearest audience. Unlike many Victorian parents, he loved playing with and reading to his children. Indeed he once wrote, "It is the duty of every father to write fairy tales for his children," a practice that he followed with his own children. In the autobiography *Son of Oscar Wilde* (1954) Wilde's son Vyvyan Holland recalls that his father told rather than read many of his own stories to his two young sons, so that he could adapt the stories to fit their understanding.

Fortunately for twentieth-century fathers, the nineteenth century left behind a legacy of literary fairy tales for reading to children, among them nine stories by Wilde, published in two separate volumes. *The Happy Prince and Other Tales* was published in 1888 and included five stories: the title story, "The Nightingale and the Rose," "The Selfish Giant," "The Devoted Friend," and "The Remarkable Rocket." In 1891 he published *A House of Pomegranates,* which brought together "The Young King," "The Birthday of the Infanta," "The Fisherman and His Soul," and "The Star-Child."

The question of Wilde's intended audience for the tales has been an ongoing concern of critics. His son Vyvyan describes the stories in *The Happy Prince* as "really poems in prose more than fairy tales for children" and goes on to say that "the remarkable thing is that they appeal equally to children and adults." He calls *The House of Pomegranates* "a book of short stories—one can hardly call them fairy tales" and agrees with those critics who claim that no child could understand them. Some critics have complained that the stories are too sophisticated for children and too contrived for adults. Responding to the critics of his own day, Oscar Wilde wrote that he addressed himself to "children of all ages, to the unripe and the adult alike" and that the tales were written "for those who have kept the childlike faculties of wonder and joy and who find simplicity in a subtle strangeness." In a letter to a friend he seemed to settle the question of audience when he wrote that the stories were written "not for children, but for childlike people from eighteen to eighty."

Many of Wilde's biographers and critics, unfortunately, have slighted his children's stories, sometimes using them only as evidence to support theses about Wilde's perversions. More perceptive critics, however, have acknowledged that the tales are miniature masterpieces, delicate, imaginative, and sometimes irreverent, their satire distanced by a quasi-biblical tone and a highly ornamental, rhythmic prose.

Critics aside, the continued popularity of the tales attests to their success. They have been immensely popular with generations of children in the United States and in Europe. Russian and German translators and critics have called the tales masterpieces. Individual stories have been issued in a vast number of beautifully illustrated editions and included in hundreds of anthologies. Collections continue to be published, and the stories have been illustrated by many important artists, beginning with Walter Crane, illustrator for the first edition of *The Happy Prince.* The tales have been adapted for recordings, radio, theater, mime, dance, film, and television. "The Happy Prince," for example, has been made into a cartoon, a movie, a play, and an opera in one act for children. "The Birthday of the Infanta" has been performed as a ballet and "The Nightingale and the Rose" as a stage play. "The Selfish Giant" was performed by the Budapest Opera as a ballet in Philadelphia in 1963, and in 1980 an animated film based on the same tale was broadcast on Canadian television.

The stories vary considerably as to reading level and complexity of subject matter. In some collections put together for very young children, Wilde's long descriptive and philosophical passages have been omitted, ostensibly to make the tales more accessible. But this kind of tampering has been severely criticized. As recently as 1985, critic Michael Patrick Hearn complained in the *New York Times Book Review* (11 August) that one new picture-book edition of "The Selfish Giant" was "sponged of Wilde's Christian morality," and another eliminated the Christian ending, which prompted Hearn to ask, "If Wilde's preachings are so offensive, then why reillustrate his stories?"

The stories in *The Happy Prince* are shorter and less complicated than those in *The House of Pomegranates.* In the latter collection, for example, the story entitled "The Fisherman and His Soul" barely qualifies as a children's story except perhaps for mature teenagers. Multi-leveled, with deep psychological overtones, this story—the longest in the collection —tells of a young fisherman who wrestles with problems of Love, Soul, and Heart but resolves none of them. The ending is ambiguous, the style, highly ornate.

An approach that Wilde said he had used in one of his tales could be said to apply to all of them. He said he did not start with ideas and search for a form but began "with a form and strove to make it beautiful enough to have many secrets and many answers." He borrowed elements from classic folk-fairy and saints' tales, such as the protagonists whose struggles usually come in threes (three tasks, three dreams, three visits) and who get help from unexpected sources (the supernatural, animals, plants). He made strange worlds familiar. Flowers, birds, and objects like sundials and Roman candles talk as humans do. Exotic and familiar settings transport readers to barnyards, to seventeenth-century Spanish palaces, to the bottom of the sea, where mermaids dwell.

In all of the tales a strong note of idealism is struck. Suffusing the tales is the spirit of Jesus, symbolizing the highest ideals to which man can aspire. Qualities Wilde associated with Jesus—his tolerance, charity, unselfishness, love—are contrasted with worldly behavior—selfishness, meanness, stupidity, possessiveness, and hypocrisy. Jesus appears in only one of Wilde's tales, "The Selfish Giant," but God's presence is felt in most of the tales. In "The Selfish Giant" Jesus appears in the guise of a small child bearing the prints of two nails on his palms and feet; he comes to lead the Selfish Giant to repentance. In "The Happy Prince," only God expresses approval of the good deeds planned by the Happy Prince's statue and executed by the swallow. In "The Young King," the Bishop refuses to crown the young King who appears at his coronation in goatherd's dress. Only divine intervention reveals to the Bishop the young King's angelic nature and thus saves the King's life. When the glory of God fills the cathedral with "a marvellous and mystical light," the Bishop cries, "A greater than I hath crowned thee."

A striking feature of Wilde's tales is his frequent departure from the classic fairy-tale ending, in which the good nearly always triumph and the wicked perish. More than one critic has been bothered by the conclusions of Wilde's tales. Wilde's stories end happily only when Jesus (or God) intervenes. In the world of men, virtue is usually defeated. The nightingale dies in her sacrificial act of love; the gentle, lovable dwarf, whose only "sin" is ugliness, dies of a broken heart; the Star-Child, who transforms his kingdom by his "love and loving kindness and charity," rules only three years before he dies, and "he who came after him ruled evilly."

Successful survivors are generally uncaring, unfeeling, selfish, and egotistical. "The Birthday of the Infanta" ends when the Infanta is told that the dwarf's heart is broken. In the last lines of the tale, she "frowned, and her dainty rose-leaf lips curled in pretty disdain. 'For the future let those who come to play with me have no hearts,' she cried, and she ran out into the garden." In "The Remarkable Rocket," a witty study of vanity, the self-deceived, self-absorbed Rocket is extinguished with nobody present to see his last "fizz," but he is convinced that he will create "a great sensation"; unaware of his self-deception, he never suffers for his false pride. In "The Devoted Friend," the egotistical, grasping Miller exploits his friendship with Hans; he never does him a good turn but rather makes heavy demands on him in the name of friendship, even brings on his death, and then says without irony about himself, "One always suffers for being generous." In the story that frames "The Devoted Friend," the Water-rat, a close duplicate of the Miller, defines a devoted friend as one who is "devoted to me, of course."

But if those characters who practice Christian ideals are not rewarded by the world, they triumph inwardly; in this way their tales provide the final satisfaction that fairy tales by their very nature require. The young King and the Star-Child, for example, are, by their experiences with poverty and injustice, transformed into caring human beings whose inner beauty shines forth. By contrast, those who triumph by worldly standards are shown up for what they really are: the Rocket is clearly self-deceived, the Miller is egotistical, the Infanta is heartless, and the professor's daughter is mercenary. Those with worldly values win worldly prizes but not the respect of readers.

Wilde wrote that his stories were "an attempt to mirror modern life in a form remote from reality —to deal with modern problems in a mode that is ideal and not imitative." Social issues concerned him, particularly poverty and injustice. In many of his children's stories he contrasts the lives of those who live well with those who are exploited to make the lives of the rich possible. In an essay published in 1890 entitled "The Soul of Man Under Socialism," Wilde calls for a society in which every man can live well enough to develop the "treasury house" of his soul, according to the teachings of Jesus. "The true perfection of a man lies not in what man has, but in what man is," Wilde asserts. A state built on the labor of slaves, he says, is despicable because it prevents segments of the population from living life "intensely, fully, perfectly." The capitalist system, as he saw it, prevents rich and poor alike from heeding Christ's admonition to "Be thyself"—the rich are too busy accumulating and protecting their wealth, and the poor are too tired and too hungry to think about perfecting their souls.

Many of Wilde's tales present dramatically or poetically the points argued in his essay. "The Selfish Giant," for example, contrasts an ill-spent life with one well spent. The Giant represents the wealthy man whose heart is frozen because he focuses his life on the protection of his private property. To keep out the young children who play in his beautiful garden after school is over, the Giant erects a large "Trespassers Will Be Prosecuted" sign. For his selfishness, perpetual winter comes to his garden, driving out the other seasons. However, with the help of the Blessed Child, whom he does not recognize as Christ but whose power he feels, the Giant has a change of heart, and children and the other seasons come into his garden again. He begins to live fully now that he lovingly shares his garden with the children. The Child promises the Giant he will have a garden in Paradise after his death, and death comes to him that afternoon.

But the two tales that most vividly portray the disparity between the suffering poor and the rich are "The Happy Prince" and "The Young King." The Happy Prince during his reign was isolated in his walled palace, unaware of the suffering outside. From his present vantage as a statue in the square, he sees the ugliness, misery, and poverty in the streets and houses. He says, "When I was alive and had a human heart . . . I did not know what tears were for, for I lived in the Palace of Sans Souci, where sorrow is not allowed to enter." Even though his heart is now made of lead, he can weep. He can try to alleviate suffering by the only means he has, that is, by distributing the jewels and gold

leaf that cover him. He comes to realize that without means the poor can only live meanly.

The strongest expression of Wilde's concern over social and economic inequality is offered in the tale "The Young King." In three vivid, terrible dreams the King witnesses in turn the poverty, suffering, and loss of life that have come about in order to make his coronation robe, his scepter, and his crown. In one dream the weaver of his robe tells him:

> In war the strong make slaves of the poor. We must work to live, and they give us such mean wages that we die. We toil for them all day long, and they heap up gold in their coffers, and our children fade away before their time, and the faces of those we love become hard and evil. We tread out the grapes, and another drinks the wine. We sow the corn, and our own board is empty. We have chains, though no eye beholds them; and we are slaves, though men call us free.

So struck is the Young King by what he witnesses that he refuses to be crowned with the official vestments and chooses instead a shepherd's cloak, a rude staff, and a circlet of wild briar, signifying his identification with the poor in his kingdom. Ironically, it is God alone, not the poor or the churchmen, who appreciates his symbolic act.

Although the tales contain a strong indictment of a social system and although they consistently maintain a tone of Christian socialism, they are more than moral medicine. Morals in the tales are not forced upon readers. Part of the story "The Devoted Friend" concerns itself with stories that have morals. The Linnet who tells the story annoys the Water-rat, who says "Pooh" to her story with a moral. The Duck maintains that telling stories with moral endings is "always a very dangerous thing to do." And for the only time in any of his children's stories, Wilde shifts here from the third-person to the first-person narrative form and ends the story with the line "And I quite agree with her."

The tales are masterpieces of storytelling. They successfully arouse sympathy for social inequities, but they do so as art, not polemic. They draw readers in immediately; keep them wanting to know what happens next; with great economy present strong and memorable characters, images, and settings; offer witty dialogue; and use language artfully.

Through personification, for example, Wilde

charms the reader to his side of an argument. In "The Nightingale and the Rose," this brief conversation contrasts the cynic and the romantic:

"He [the Student] is weeping for a red rose," said the Nightingale.

"For a red rose!" they [the natural inhabitants of the garden] cried; "how very ridiculous!" and the little Lizard, who was something of a cynic laughed outright.

But the Nightingale understood the secret of the Student's sorrow, and she sat silent in the oak-tree, and thought about the mystery of Love.

In "The Remarkable Rocket" Wilde provides a brief conversation that humorously captures the limitations of two of its characters. The little Squib brags that, having seen the King's garden, he has really traveled. "Travel improves the mind wonderfully, and does away with all one's prejudices," he says. The Roman Candle answers, "The King's garden is not the world, you foolish squib. The world is an enormous place, and it would take three days to see it thoroughly."

A brief conversation from "The Happy Prince" illustrates Wilde's economic rendition of time, place, and character:

"He [the statue] looks just like an angel," said the Charity Children as they came out of the cathedral in their bright scarlet cloaks, and their clean white pinafores.

"How do you know?" said the Mathematical Master, "you have never seen one."

"Ah! but we have, in our dreams," answered the children; and the Mathematical Master frowned and looked very severe, for he did not approve of children dreaming.

In a revealing tirade by the flowers against the birds and lizards in "The Birthday of the Infanta," Wilde captures the arrogance, smugness, and insularity of a group that thinks of itself as upholding a standard for the world:

"It only shows," they said, "what a vulgarising effect this incessant rushing and flying about has. Well-bred people always stay exactly in the same place, as we do. No one ever saw us hopping up and down the walks, or galloping madly through the grass after dragon-flies. When we do want change of air, we send for the gardener, and he carries us to another bed. This is dignified, and as it should be. But birds and lizards have no sense of repose, and indeed birds have not even a permanent address. They are mere vagrants like the gipsies, and should be treated in exactly the same manner." So they put their noses in the air, and looked very haughty.

Wilde's tales are an antidote for modern children, many of whom are dulled by film and television images that leave little room for the imagination. In Wilde's stories children find drama, vitality, wit, action, good characters and evil characters, sparkling dialogue, and, most especially, compassion for those who, like themselves, are so often oppressed. Children do not know and probably would not care that Oscar Wilde was a poseur, a dandy, a decadent. They appreciate his fresh and original stories. They feel his championing of the best in the human spirit.

Selected Bibliography

WORKS OF OSCAR WILDE

The Happy Prince and Other Tales. With illustrations by Walter Crane and G. P. Jacomb Hood. London: David Nutt, 1888. With illustrations by Charles Robinson. Boulder: Shambhala Publications, 1980.

A House of Pomegranates. London: Osgood, McIlvaine, 1891. Reprinted Portland, Me.: T. B. Mosher, 1906.

Fairy Tales. With illustrations by Charles Mozley. London: Bodley Head, 1960. Retitled *The Complete Fairy Tales of Oscar Wilde.* New York: Franklin Watts, 1960.

The Complete Works of Oscar Wilde. With an introduction by Vyvyan Holland. London: Collins, 1966.

The Fairy Stories of Oscar Wilde. With an introduction by Naomi Lewis and illustrations by Harold Jones. London: Gollancz, 1976; New York: Peter Bedrick Books, 1986.

The Complete Shorter Fiction of Oscar Wilde. Edited by Isobel Murray. Oxford and New York: Oxford University Press, 1979.

The Birthday of the Infanta and Other Stories by Oscar Wilde. With illustrations by Benny Montresor. New York: Atheneum, 1982.

The Young King and Other Fairy Tales. With an introduction by John Updike and illustrations by Sandro Nardini and Enrico Bagnoli. New York: Macmillan, 1982.

CRITICAL AND BIOGRAPHICAL STUDIES

Brasol, Boris. *Oscar Wilde, the Man, the Artist, the Martyr.* New York: Octagon Books, 1975.

Cohen, Philip K. *The Moral Vision of Oscar Wilde.* Rutherford, N.J.: Fairleigh Dickinson University Press, 1978.

Hardwick, Michael. *The Drake Guide to Oscar Wilde.* New York: Drake Publishers, 1973.

Holland, Vyvyan. *Oscar Wilde: A Pictorial Biography.* London: Thames and Hudson, 1960.

————. *Son of Oscar Wilde.* London: R. Hart-Davis, 1954; New York: E. P. Dutton, 1954.

Hyde, H. Montgomery, ed. *The Annotated Oscar Wilde.* London: Orbis Publishing, 1982.

Kronenberger, Louis. *Oscar Wilde.* Boston: Little, Brown, 1976.

Pearson, Hesketh. *The Life of Oscar Wilde.* London and New York: Harper and Brothers, 1946.

Woodcock, George. *The Paradox of Oscar Wilde.* London: Boardman, 1949.

—ANNA Y. BRADLEY

LAURA INGALLS WILDER

1867–1957

NEAR THE END of John Steinbeck's "The Leader of the People," an old wagon boss reminisces about the mythic undertaking that he calls "westering." It was, he says, an expression of the American people's yearning westward, "but it wasn't getting [there] that mattered, it was movement and westering." *Westering* may be Steinbeck's coinage, but one notable expression of its essential quality can be ascribed to Laura Ingalls Wilder. In eight semiautobiographical novels Wilder distills the essence of "westering" and presents a capsule history of one family's response to one of the formative experiences of American life.

Born Laura Elizabeth Ingalls on 7 February 1867 in Pepin County, Wisconsin, Wilder was the second of four daughters of Charles and Caroline Ingalls. She spent the greater part of her youth on the American frontier: the family moved in the early 1870's from Wisconsin to the Indian Territory of southern Kansas (just north of the present Kansas-Oklahoma border, about forty miles from Independence, Kansas), back to Wisconsin, thence to Minnesota, and finally to the Dakota Territory (now South Dakota), where in 1879 they became the first residents of the settlement of De Smet. Her formal education, fragmentary at best, ended in 1882, when she won a teaching certificate and began work in the territorial schools.

Her teaching career came to a close in 1885 when she married Almanzo James Wilder. Although Wilder had been a successful homesteader in the region, he seemed unable to progress as a farmer and family man. The financial difficulties created by a series of bad crops were aggravated by the birth of a daughter in 1886, a stroke suffered by Almanzo following a bout with diphtheria in 1888, the birth and death of a son in 1889, and, just weeks later, a fire that destroyed the Wilder house. The Wilders continued farming in and around De Smet until 1894, when they moved to Mansfield, Missouri, which became their permanent home.

In 1910 Wilder began work with the Missouri Home Development Association, but a developing career as a journalist proved more profitable; she became a columnist (eventually a contributing editor) for the *Missouri Ruralist* and later contributed articles to the *St. Louis Star* and various magazines. She also began work on an autobiography, "Pioneer Girl," which remains unpublished; however, with the editorial assistance of her daughter, Rose Wilder Lane, she later incorporated portions of the manuscript into the first of her "Little House" books, *Little House in the Big Woods* (1932).

The critical and popular success of this volume prompted Wilder to continue the recasting of her childhood memories. Of the seven succeeding volumes published in her lifetime, six deal with the Ingalls family's slow movement westward, following them from Laura's childhood days in Wisconsin to her marriage in Dakota Territory. The exception is *Farmer Boy* (1933), relating episodes from her husband's boyhood in New York State. Two of the books, *On The Banks of Plum Creek* (1937) and *The Long Winter* (1940), were runners-up for the Newbery Medal, and Wilder herself received the first Laura Ingalls Wilder Award, given by the

American Library Association in 1954. She died on 10 February 1957 in Mansfield.

Laura Wilder in many ways resembled the Laura of the "Little House" books. She was in most respects a highly traditional woman of the late nineteenth and early twentieth centuries, accepting her role as wife, mother, and homemaker with ease, just as does the fictional Laura. At the same time, however, the strong-willed independence of the fictional Laura is equally present in Wilder. She clearly was the moving spirit in the Wilder household; Almanzo never fully regained his strength after the stroke he suffered in 1888, and the burden of leading the family often fell squarely upon his wife. Her journalistic work, moreover, broadened her horizons, so that when she came to write the "Little House" books she brought to them not only her memories of frontier existence but a knowledge of the demands and frustrations of life in the depression-era United States. Thus, as she combined past and present, independence and frustration, she made of the "Little House" books a revealing record of the United States in a protracted time of transition.

On the surface, *Little House in the Big Woods* seems little more than an anecdotal, third-person account of a year in the life of a frontier family. As its leisurely story unfolds, the book introduces the Ingalls family—Pa (Charles), Ma (Caroline), Mary, Laura, and Carrie—and follows them through the varied activities of frontier life. Pa spends his days in the woods of Wisconsin hunting meat for the family and his nights maintaining his traps, his rifle, and his farm equipment. Ma works through a regular weekly cycle of chores—mending, washing, cooking, and baking—interrupted periodically by seasonal needs: sugar-making in the spring, cheese-making in the summer, salting meat and preserving vegetables in the autumn. The girls help in ways suited to their ages, and in leisure times amuse themselves with improvised toys and activities. The result is an accretive, deceptively simple portrayal of a year (approximately 1872) in the life of a single, isolated family, concretely depicting the activities necessary to survival on the American frontier.

From that concreteness comes much of the book's importance. Wilder details the day-in, day-out demands made upon the family by the exigencies of frontier life and suggests the personal qualities essential for survival under frontier conditions. Pa and Ma Ingalls are resourceful and re-

silent; recognizing and accepting the commitment that the frontier requires, they achieve a life that is only marginally above the subsistence level, yet demonstrate to their children and to the reader that the human spirit can be enhanced rather than crushed by frontier circumstances. The Ingallses confront the challenges squarely, and through their small victories the reader, like the fictional Laura, learns the importance of conscientiousness, industriousness, and ingenuity—the very qualities that, according to historian Frederick Jackson Turner, the frontier contributes to the American experience.

The other side of that experience, life in a more established context, appears in *Farmer Boy*. Less episodic than *Little House in the Big Woods*, *Farmer Boy* shares the earlier book's affection for the land and its devotion to the inherent values of American life. Its setting is the Wilder farm near Malone, New York; its events extend from approximately late 1866 through 1867; and its focus, like its predecessor's, is upon everyday family life.

The Wilders, however, are more affluent and settled than the Ingallses: Father Wilder is a prosperous landowner whose crops and horses provide a steady income, and Mother Wilder, as efficient a homemaker as Ma Ingalls, is herself a small-scale capitalist, selling surplus butter to a jobber from New York City. A steady stream of peddlers and buyers passes by the farm, bringing news and entertainment as well as goods, and the family itself regularly attends church in Malone, only five miles away, and makes frequent journeys into the town to take part in such community activities as the county fair or a Fourth of July celebration.

The Fourth of July celebration links this book with *Little House in the Big Woods*. Nine-year-old Almanzo gets a lesson in the labor theory of value when his father explains money to him in terms of time, work, and potatoes; the silver coin in his hand translates into hours of effort in the fields. He then comes to see that effort in the context of the nation. The explorers opened the country, his father tells him, and the hunters and trappers made the first settlements, but the farmers settled the land, cleared it, cultivated it, and made it America. The energies of the frontiersman, complemented by the civilizing activities of the farmer, have made a nation of a wilderness. It only remains for Wilder, returning to the chronicles of her family, to illustrate how this process takes place.

Little House on the Prairie (1935) is a story of

movement, personal and national. Set in approximately 1874, it begins in the Wisconsin forests of *Little House in the Big Woods*, where there is discontent in the Ingalls family. Pa, chafing at the influx of settlers, yearns to go West, toward open spaces free from the oppressive crush of a growing population. Ma resists; their home is snug and comfortable. But Pa prevails, and the family moves on to a new home in the Indian Territory—the Osage Diminished Reserve of southern Kansas and northern Oklahoma, near the Missouri border.

Here Pa revels in the rough-and-ready environment, where he is able once again to live the individual, unfettered life that he cherishes. Yet, as Wilder slowly makes clear, that life has undergone some telling changes. The family is no longer totally independent. Pa borrows nails to finish the cabin roof and has to call upon a distant neighbor for help in digging a well. He travels forty miles to town for supplies that they cannot produce: white flour, white sugar, and glass for the windows. And he must yield to the power of the United States government, abstract though it seems; federal troops oust the white settlers from the Indian Territory, and the family is forced to take to the road once more.

In *Little House on the Prairie* Wilder records the changing circumstances of family and nation alike. Whereas Pa and Ma once had only to contend with the forces of nature, now they must confront the concurrent force of the national government; they cling to their individualistic skills but feel the first pressures of involvement in a complex society. That society, moreover, is itself in flux, as John Mason Peck suggests in his *A New Guide for Emigrants to the West* (1836), for the waves of settlement that move westward leave behind irrevocable changes. As yet unaware that they are a part of this process, the Ingallses see only the diminishing of game, the uprooting of the Indian by white settlers, and the sudden manifestation of federal authority. Partly fearful, partly tolerant of the Osage Indians who live throughout the region, and having comparatively little real knowledge of them, the family find themselves even more perplexed by the national government. Having encouraged them to settle the new territory, it now forces them out. They retain their optimism, to be sure, but the reader sees them in an altered light. As they set out to travel still farther westward, they seem less stalwart adventurers than unwitting participants in a national event.

The extent to which circumstances have changed becomes clearer in *On the Banks of Plum Creek*. Set in the period between 1874 and 1875, the book picks up where the preceding one ends, as the Ingallses, evicted from the Indian Territory, find a new homestead in Minnesota. Their intention is to buy some land, build a house, and resume the life that they left behind. That life, however, as each developing episode makes clear, is increasingly a thing of the past. Try though they may to preserve the frontier ways, the family must yield to the forces of change.

Some of the forces are economic. For the first time, Pa cannot afford to build a house from scratch; he must take over the dugout home of the Norwegian immigrant whose farm he buys. The house he finally builds is one of machine-cut lumber (obtained on credit), equipped with bought shingles, prehung windows, and a cast-iron cookstove. Pa himself is no longer the roving frontiersman; he hunts and fishes when he can but turns his principal energies to farming. Significantly, his crops are for investment rather than subsistence; he is, in fact, a capitalist, and when grasshoppers devastate the first year's wheat, he is left unable to pay off his debts.

Other forces are social: for the first time the family encounters a relatively settled population. Laura and Mary are sent to school and find themselves among strangers. They quickly become accepted members of the group but still learn of snobbery and bullying. Yet not all the social encounters are unpleasant: the family attends church for the first time in Laura's experience; Sunday school becomes a part of their life; and the church Christmas party gives them a sense of social cohesiveness that no earlier episode has supplied. Each experience, however, further documents the degree to which civilization is altering frontier life.

On the Banks of Plum Creek, therefore, records the end of one era and the beginning of another. The Ingallses in many respects remain a frontier family: their fortunes depend upon Pa's initiative, and they themselves are sensitive to the subtle presence of land and climate. Yet to a degree neither apparent nor possible in the earlier books, they are becoming a settled, socialized family. They have, by unconscious choice, surrendered their independence for the corresponding benefits of society: education, religion, and social involvement. As they live with the consequences of their choice, they dramatize a critical stage in the westering of the American nation.

619

The next stage of that progress appears in *By the Shores of Silver Lake* (1939). It is 1879, and the Ingalls family's circumstances have deteriorated. A new child—Grace—has arrived; Ma, Mary, and Carrie have survived a bout of scarlet fever, but complications of the illness have blinded Mary; crops have been marginal at best; and the family, deeply in debt, cannot even pay the doctor. A solution appears when Pa wins a job as timekeeper with a railroad crew in western Dakota; though he goes farther West, he goes as a wage earner rather than an independent frontiersman, and the irony is not lost on Wilder.

The changes implicit in Pa's altered status extend throughout the book, which becomes a chronicle of compromises. Pa finds a homestead, but must vie with other settlers to file for it. The family spends an isolated winter in borrowed quarters, living as caretakers in the railroad surveyors' house. In the spring, Ma and the girls, now town dwellers, support the family by running a boardinghouse, accepting the unpleasant realities of humanity in the mass for the sake of the money that they can earn, and Pa himself becomes a small-scale landlord.

The degree to which Wilder intends the story as a record of social and national change is dramatized in a telling episode close to the book's center. Laura, stricken by wanderlust and panicked by time's passing, pleads with her parents to move on. Ma is aghast; Pa is understanding. He tells Laura that he shares her feeling, but reluctantly confesses that he has struck a bargain with Ma. She will accede temporarily to his longings to roam, but once they find and file for a homestead, moving is to stop and the girls are to be educated. Moreover, he continues, since Ma had once been a teacher, she is determined that one of the girls will become one as well. As the eldest, Mary was appointed; now that she is blind, the responsibility devolves onto Laura. In one brief scene Wilder makes her point. Societies, like persons, grow up. They gain in maturity and responsibility, but they lose in other ways —as in the vanishing of game and the sacrificing of freedom. Pa and Ma have made their accommodation to adulthood; now Laura must do the same. They have come West to grow up with the country and must accept the consequences of national as well as human maturation.

The Long Winter subtly shifts the focus of Laura's story, for Almanzo Wilder, who appeared briefly in the preceding book, now emerges as an important character. The Ingallses, meanwhile, alarmed by predictions of a hard winter, move from their claim shanty into town. A succession of blizzards blocks the railroad, isolates the community, and shuts off the supply of food and fuel, and the townspeople come close to starvation, surviving only because Almanzo and a friend make a heroic trip through snow and subzero temperatures to bring back a supply of wheat.

Throughout the narrative Wilder dwells upon the costs of civilization. De Smet is now a town rather than merely a settlement; it boasts a railroad depot, a grocery, a lawyer's office, and a tailor's shop, and its very solidity gives the populace a sense of communal security. Yet when the storms come, the townspeople discover the fragility of their ties to civilization and their inability to withstand the power of nature. In surrendering frontier independence for the conveniences of community, they put themselves at the mercy of external agencies; their wherewithal comes not from their own energies, but from the railroad and its suppliers. Progress does, indeed, have its price.

Reinforcing this theme is a concern for cooperation. No longer are the townspeople discrete entities; instead, they have become an interdependent community. When the merchant who financed Almanzo's trek puts an inflated price on the wheat, the hungry men agree that he is entitled to a profit but point out that his survival as storekeeper is dependent on their goodwill and custom. The townspeople need wheat; the merchant needs customers. Neither can survive without the other, and each must accommodate the other. The problem is settled amicably, but Wilder's point remains vivid: whereas frontier survival required individual skills, survival in a social context depends upon cooperation and combined effort. Just as the innocent freedom of childhood gives way to the obligations of maturity, the simple efforts of the frontier give way to the complexities of national society.

The Long Winter, with its leitmotiv of community interdependence, is followed by *Little Town on the Prairie* (1941), which focuses not upon family life in the big woods or survival on the prairie but upon the burgeoning of De Smet as a town and the increasing socialization of its citizens. Signs of growing community pervade the story. The adjoining areas are organized into a county, and Pa becomes a commissioner. A school board (of which Pa is a member) is created to oversee the children's education. There is even leisure time: parties, rare in frontier days, become commonplace for the young people, and the adults amuse themselves with a succession of "literaries," ranging from a raucous minstrel show to an evening of public recitation where the schoolchildren show off their learning. Little remains of the rampant individualism so visible in the earlier books.

Corresponding changes come to the Ingallses, who embark upon yet another transition. This transition, however, is cultural and emotional rather than geographical, for now the family is settled. Pa has made his peace with civilization, and is content to earn his living as a carpenter. Laura, too, is a wage earner, working as a seamstress to bolster the family's income. Every spare dollar must be saved for tuition, since Mary attends a college for the blind in Iowa; even so, the family enjoys relative affluence. They have occasional small luxuries, and Laura is able at one point to squander twenty-five cents for printed visiting cards.

Their emotional transition is equally profound. Laura, almost fifteen, is close to adulthood. Her teaching career is upon her, thanks to her performance at the school recitation and a nearby community's sudden need for a teacher. Vaguely depressed by the pervasive ugliness of the weather-beaten town, frustrated by her circumstances, and frightened by the prospect of her impending responsibilities, she sees the adult world in a new and unflattering way. Compensating for these disillusionments, however, is her romance with Almanzo. Their paths cross with increasing frequency until Almanzo asks if he may walk her home from a revival meeting. One walk leads to another, Almanzo asks her to go sleigh riding, and one more transition—in Laura's life as much as the family's—commences.

The transition begun in *Little Town on the Prairie* is completed in *These Happy Golden Years* (1943). Its themes continue those of the preceding book—transition, maturation, and the inevitable cost of progress—but they now are couched in individual terms. The story is Laura's, not the town's; the changes are personal, not societal, and are summed up in the departures that open and close the book. In the first, Laura leaves her home to take up schoolteaching, still stunned by her transition from pupil to teacher. In the second, she leaves again, this time for good, as Almanzo's wife. The narrative that connects the two is one of romance and discovery, but most of all it is one of growing up.

Laura's maturation emerges through her work and in her courtship. Teaching forces her to con-

front the responsibilities of adulthood. Unsettled by the unhappy and half-crazed family with whom she boards, frustrated by a rowdy youngster, and desperately homesick, she longs to give up the job and go home. Yet even as she toys with rebellion, she knows she cannot quit. She has agreed to carry out a specific task for specific payment, and her sense of duty carries her through. Just as teaching helps her to an adult's understanding of duty and responsibility, the transition from girl to wife leads her to a comparable understanding of human relations: marriage vows take on a fuller meaning as she and Almanzo debate the word *obey*, and her memories of life with Pa and Ma emerge as a solid foundation for her new life. She is at last an adult, prepared to accept the responsibilities of maturity as readily as the joys.

That Wilder sees Laura's life within a national context is patent. "Going West to grow up with the country" is one of the oldest themes in American literature, and her awareness of it is clear in the careful paralleling of national, local, and individual growth throughout the books. Laura grows from a child in Wisconsin in 1872, four years before the Centennial Exposition, to a wife in De Smet in 1884, barely six years before the Federal Census Bureau proclaimed the frontier closed. She does, indeed, go West to grow up with the country, and her transition from child to adult echoes the nation's transition from an adolescent, rural society to an adult, settled one.

In the years following Wilder's death, three other books appeared under her name, assembled from a travel diary, an unfinished manuscript, and packets of letters. The first, *On the Way Home* (1962), is a journal she kept as she and Almanzo traveled by wagon from De Smet to Mansfield. The second, *The First Four Years* (1971), continuing the story of Almanzo and Laura as a married couple, records several important events, notably the birth of their two children, Almanzo's illness, and the devastating fire; but this book was never completed. The last, *West from Home* (1974), reprints letters giving impressions of San Francisco and the Panama-Pacific International Exposition of 1915. Each adds somewhat to the reader's knowledge of Wilder, but the eight "Little House" books remain her monument.

Of the permanence of the "Little House" books there is little question. Their remaining in print for over forty years is evidence enough of the degree to which Wilder's work has captured the imagination of American readers, while a popular television series, though debasing the books themselves, has familiarized a generation of viewers with at least the names of the principal characters. Behind that popularity, however, are qualities that readers may not consciously recognize, yet which provide a solid foundation for the overt acclaim. Whatever else they accomplish, the "Little House" books work on two levels, operating within the genre of the juvenile domestic novel to present a distinctively mythic vision of the American experience.

In a literary sense, the books continue the tradition of the realistic domestic story established by Louisa May Alcott in the "Plumfield" trilogy. Their homely incidents show appealing characters going about everyday activities and dealing forthrightly with the problems of life. The characters themselves, though essentially good, are nevertheless flawed enough to come alive as rounded human beings: Pa, though he is devoted to his family, chafes at the confinement of domesticity and longs for the open frontier; Ma, for all her gentility, can be sharp-tongued and domineering and holds a deep-seated prejudice against Indians; and Laura knows the secret pleasures of harboring a grudge. But these flaws only accentuate the characters' virtues, so that one comes away from the books with a sense of having accompanied a living family as they triumph over adversity. Artistic in their artlessness, the "Little House" books speak quietly but eloquently for the simple virtues of industry, responsibility, and family cohesiveness.

Yet the importance of the books extends beyond their portrayal of family life, for they also convey a history of the American frontier. Frederick Jackson Turner, speaking in 1893, called the map of the United States a palimpsest from which one might read the history of the generations that had gone before. The "Little House" books give Turner's metaphor life, showing that palimpsest as it is being written, preserving for later generations of readers times, places, and experiences that are long since gone. They evoke once again the nineteenth-century appeal of the call of free land. They dramatize, as the Ingallses grope their way westward, the compelling power of the westering urge. And, above all, they illustrate how independence and custom, nature and civilization commingle to give the American character its distinctive traits. They are, in sum, a contribution to American letters that stands as significantly as history as it does as literature.

Selected Bibliography

WORKS OF LAURA INGALLS WILDER

Dates given are those of first publication; the original eight "Little House" books were reissued by Harper and Row in 1953 in a collected edition with illustrations by Garth Williams.

Little House in the Big Woods. With illustrations by Helen Sewell. New York: Harper and Brothers, 1932.

Farmer Boy. With illustrations by Helen Sewell. New York: Harper and Brothers, 1933.

Little House on the Prairie. With illustrations by Helen Sewell. New York: Harper and Brothers, 1935.

On the Banks of Plum Creek. With illustrations by Helen Sewell and Mildred Boyle. New York: Harper and Brothers, 1937.

By the Shores of Silver Lake. With illustrations by Helen Sewell and Mildred Boyle. New York: Harper and Brothers, 1939.

The Long Winter. With illustrations by Helen Sewell and Mildred Boyle. New York: Harper and Brothers, 1940.

Little Town on the Prairie. With illustrations by Helen Sewell and Mildred Boyle. New York: Harper and Brothers, 1941.

These Happy Golden Years. With illustrations by Helen Sewell and Mildred Boyle. New York: Harper and Brothers, 1943.

On the Way Home: The Diary of a Trip from South Dakota to Mansfield, Missouri, in 1894. Illustrated with photographs from the Wilder family album. New York: Harper and Row, 1962.

The First Four Years. With illustrations by Garth Williams. New York: Harper and Row, 1971.

West from Home: Letters of Laura Ingalls Wilder to Almanzo Wilder, San Francisco, 1915. Edited by Roger Lea MacBride. Illustrated with photographs. New York: Harper and Row, 1974.

CRITICAL AND BIOGRAPHICAL STUDIES

Anderson, William T. " 'It is better farther on' " *American West* 21: 35–42 (1984).

Bosmajian, Hamida. "Vastness and Contraction of Space in *Little House on the Prairie*" *Children's Literature* 11: 49–63 (1983).

Erisman, Fred. "The Regional Vision of Laura Ingalls Wilder." In *Studies in Medieval, Renaissance, American Literature*, edited by Betsy Colquitt. Fort Worth: TCU Press, 1971.

Holtz, William. "Closing the Circle: The American Optimism of Laura Ingalls Wilder" *Great Plains Quarterly* 4: 79–90 (1984).

Jacobs, William Jay. "Frontier Faith Revisited" *Horn Book* 41: 465–473 (1965).

Lee, Anne Thompson. " 'It's better farther on': Laura Ingalls Wilder and the Pioneer Spirit" *Lion and the Unicorn* 3: 74–88 (1979).

Moore, Rosa Ann. "Laura Ingalls Wilder's Orange Notebooks and the Art of the Little House Books" *Children's Literature*, 4: 105–119 (1975).

———. "The Little House Books: Rose-Colored Classics." *Children's Literature* 7: 7–16 (1978).

———. "Laura Ingalls Wilder and Rose Wilder Lane: The Chemistry of Collaboration" *Children's Literature in Education*: 11: 101–109 (1980).

Segal, Elizabeth. "Laura Ingalls Wilder's America: 'An Unflinching Assessment' " *Children's Literature in Education* 8: 63–70 (1977).

Wolf, Virginia. "Plenary Paper: The Magic Circle of Laura Ingalls Wilder" *Children's Literature Association Quarterly* 9: 168–170 (1984–1985).

Zochert, Donald. *Laura: The Life of Laura Ingalls Wilder*. Chicago: Henry Regnery, 1976.

—FRED ERISMAN

CHARLOTTE MARY YONGE

1823–1901

"IN THY LAW is my Delight" appears on the title page of the biography of Charlotte Yonge that Christabel Coleridge wrote two years after Yonge's death, and these words summarize Yonge's credo and permeate all that she wrote. Her readers are always conscious that they are being led in the ways of the law—not only the law of the church but the law of the upper-middle-class society of her day—and sometimes it seems that Yonge equated the one with the other; having absorbed the views of her parents in early childhood, she never allowed herself to reassess those values. "What she was at fifteen, that she was, with modifications, at fifty," Coleridge wrote, adding, "and she lived so much in the life of her family that her history cannot be picked out and separated from theirs." Her outlook was essentially early Victorian, and though her writing career stretched from 1844 to 1901 her attitudes changed little. This for many of her modern admirers is her great charm, together with her very real power of creating characters and evoking a way of life now totally vanished, which even in her own day existed only in a very small section of society—the educated squirearchy with High Church affiliations.

Yonge was born on 11 August 1823. Her father, William Yonge, came of an old Devon family, had served as an army officer in the Peninsular War, and had been present at the battle of Waterloo (a source of great joy to his daughter, who was always to view martial deeds with almost mystic rapture). He had married Fanny Bargus, the daughter of a prosperous clergyman, in 1822, after a courtship of

five years. His mother-in-law, Mrs. Mary Bargus, by then a widow, was reluctant to allow her daughter to marry an army officer, and William's father refused to countenance his son giving up his profession. Matters remained thus at an impasse until Mrs. Bargus bought a small property at Otterbourne, near Winchester, where she proposed that she and the young couple settle. William thereupon resigned his commission to take on the role of landowner—though since the property had very little land attached, he often must have found time heavy on his hands. And there Mrs. Bargus ruled the household until the end of her days.

Yonge's grandmother was a strong-willed old woman who nearly succeeded in preventing the publication of Yonge's first book, *Abbeychurch* (1844), because she felt it was unladylike to earn money from one's own labors. The family deferred to her in all things (her son-in-law even concealed his interest in art lest she condemn it as an extravagant taste), and it is interesting to note that the dutiful acceptance of maternal tyranny and the obligation to sacrifice one's own interests were to play a large part in Charlotte's message to her readers. In the early books it is felt to be such an accepted part of every family's way of life that it does not even need to be discussed, but as the century moved on and young women began to show signs of independent thinking, it was part of her mission to youth to show them that (in Coleridge's words)

the newest *youngest* thing was to do home and family duties more perfectly. What greater happiness can be given to youth? The fact was the keynote of her character, and produced that atmosphere of mingled ardour and submission in which she lived all her life, while all other contemporary and contending inspirations were so entirely outside her ken that she did not so much oppose them as remain in ignorance almost of their existence, and certainly of their force.

(*Charlotte Mary Yonge*, p. 145)

William and Fanny Yonge's only other child, Julian, was not born until six years after Charlotte, so that she was for a time an only child, and her experience of large families derived from visits to Yonge cousins in Devon. The dominant influence in her early life was her father, a grave and serious man with a strong sense of duty. Charlotte said of him that she loved his approval and dreaded his disapproval more than anything else. It was he who, after the first nursery teaching by her mother, gave her her lessons. "He was the most exact of teachers, and required immense attention and accuracy," Charlotte recalled in her autobiography, which is also included in Coleridge's biography. Though she thought of her childhood as a happy one, outsiders viewed it as lonely and repressive, and undoubtedly it contributed to the diffidence and awkwardness that dogged her all her adult life. Her parents had such a horror of encouraging vanity that she grew up wondering if she were not mentally deficient and certain that she was very ugly. Until her father died when she was thirty-one, her status in the household was that of a child, and to the end of her life she saw everything from a child's point of view. In her novels she examines the duty that a child owes its parents, but never what the parents owe their child. They could, she implied, exact anything they willed from their offspring; their wishes were overriding even when they apparently conflicted with religious duties. In *The Castle Builders* (1854), for instance, Frank Willoughby, who has always intended to take holy orders, is told by his father that he has to go into the Guards; he says, "I have told my father that of course he must dispose of me as he likes."

The other formative influence in Charlotte Yonge's life was John Keble, the leader of the Oxford Movement, who, along with Edward Pusey, had stayed within the Church of England when John Newman and many others had converted to Catholicism. In 1836 he came to be vicar of the nearby church of Hursley, in whose parish Otterbourne stood, and stayed there until the end of his life in 1866. William Yonge discussed with him his great schemes to build a new church for Otterbourne (a church for which he was his own architect), and sent the fifteen-year-old Charlotte to him to be prepared for confirmation. In her autobiography she referred to it very soberly as an "especial blessing of my life. . . . It was a great happiness." She was always deeply reserved when it came to discussing her inner feelings, but in fact this was the turning point of her life. Keble's firm direction saw to it that her religious fervor had solid intellectual foundations. She had a strong historical sense, and he instructed her in the faith and the rites of the Church of England by linking them with the doctrines and liturgies of older churches. Like him she was to stay loyal to the Church of England, and her last book had the title *Reasons Why I Am a Catholic and Not a Roman Catholic*. He remained a lifelong friend and adviser to whom she would confide plans for her latest book and ask for criticism, though even he could not, he confessed, stop her from writing far too much. Her father was her other mentor in literary matters, and to a certain extent after he died this role was filled by the Moberlys of Winchester, whom she had known since she was twelve, when Dr. Moberly became headmaster of Winchester College. Their large family was, in her eyes, the ideal one.

Yonge had always told herself stories as a child, inventing families and their histories as she paced round the shrubbery. All that has survived from those early years is *Le château de Melville*, a compilation of little stories written in schoolroom French that she and her mother published privately in 1838 to raise money for the parish school. Her first public appearance in print was with *Abbeychurch*, subtitled *Self-control and Self-conceit*, in which the main dramatic action derives from the uproar that ensues when a group of young people go to a lecture on chivalry at the local Mechanics' Institute, thereby rubbing shoulders not only with vulgar social climbers (Miss Yonge always regarded the parvenu with the greatest abhorrence) but also with people of dangerous radical tendencies. ("It gave me a great moral shock," she said later, "when I first found out that a Radical could be a good person.")

Her second book was *Scenes and Characters* (1847), the first of the long series of family chronicles that was to gain her a devoted following, although the Mohun family have never been as much loved by Yonge cognoscenti as the Mays and Underwoods of later tales. In 1850 came *Henrietta's Wish*, in which a sixteen-year-old girl shoulders a crushing load of responsibility for the disasters that come to her family (in reality brought about by a neurotic mother and an interfering grandmother) after she expresses a wish that her mother move back to the family's former home in Sussex. The same year saw the publication of the first of her tales about village schoolchildren, *Langley School*.

The first of Yonge's books to become a best-seller was *The Heir of Redclyffe* (1853), one of the best-known books of its time. The story tells of the generous and good young Sir Guy Morville, wrongly supposed to be an inveterate gambler (in fact he has paid the debts of a disreputable uncle and given money to found an Anglican sisterhood); he forgives the injury done to him by his accuser, his cousin Philip, and nurses the latter through a fever, but then catches the fever himself and dies. Yonge succeeded in capturing the public's imagination with this novel, which invested sound church principles and moral rectitude with heady romance; and the young women of the day were in raptures over Guy, a young man of such delicacy and virtue that he fears to take a horse with him when he goes up to Oxford lest his groom should be corrupted by the loose morals of a university town. But the book was also read by men of affairs, including bishops and statesmen; Dante Gabriel Rossetti wept over it, and fan letters came from royalty. Overwhelmed by all the acclaim, the author sought out John Keble to get assurance that to enjoy praise was not necessarily vainglorious. She never enjoyed publicity; the repressions of her childhood had handicapped her with paralytic shyness and self-consciousness, an embarrassment to others as well as to herself. Besides, she held that she wrote not for herself but for the honor and glory of the church.

William Yonge died in 1854, and in 1862, a few years after Julian brought his young wife to live at Otterbourne House, Charlotte and her mother moved a few hundred yards up the village street to Elderfield, the house where Yonge remained until the end of her life. Her days were very full. There were her daily church and parish duties, and her duties to her mother. She had taken a Sunday-school class from the age of seven and always maintained a devoted interest in the parish school, where she gave much time to teaching children. (She wrote over thirty lesson books covering a wide range of subjects from the church catechism to natural history, which were intended for parish schoolrooms, private schoolrooms, and teachers.) From 1851 she edited the *Monthly Packet*, a Church of England publication for girls designed to be "a companion in times of recreation, which may help you to perceive how to bring your religious principles to bear upon your daily life." Many of her stories were first published there, among them *The Little Duke* (1854), *The Lances of Lynwood* (1855), *The Daisy Chain* (1856), and *The Trial* (1864). When in 1890 the proprietors of the *Monthly Packet* decided that she should be replaced by a younger editor, she took on the new Mothers' Union publication, *Mothers in Council*. From 1859 to 1874 she acted as "Mother Goose" to a group of ardent young women who called themselves her "goslings" and who, eager for self-improvement, modeled themselves on her heroines and even had their own journal, the *Barnacle*.

She was also writing. The year 1873, for instance, saw the publication of five books: *The Pillars of the House*, one of her best (as well as longest) novels; *Aunt Charlotte's Stories of English History for the Little Ones* (she wrote many such history books, covering a wide sweep of centuries and countries); a two-volume life of John Coleridge Patteson, a missionary bishop of Melanesia (she took a devoted interest in foreign missions and was a great admirer of Bishop Patteson); a melodrama, *Lady Hester*; and a book of eighteenth-century memoirs, which she had edited and translated from the French. She kept up this huge and varied output until the end of the century, writing with great ease and fluency, sometimes working on three books simultaneously, taking up another sheet for the third while she waited for the ink on the first two to dry. She never moved far from Elderfield and only once left England, to stay with a French Huguenot family; she was always deeply reluctant to venture into society she did not know, and was hostile to new experience. "It would be useless to deny that this environment produced limitations when in her turn she became the leader and the oracle," said Christabel Coleridge, one of her "goslings"; Ethel Romanes, another disciple, wrote sadly of her isolation and of the fact that after the death of Keble (the year also that the Moberlys left Winchester) Yonge never met her intellectual equals, let alone superiors. "To be surrounded by a circle of admirers, all decidedly inferior to oneself, is good for no-one." By the time she died, in 1901, though she had her devoted middle-aged following, she had long ago lost touch with youth and found it hard in the family chronicles (where her original characters were now mothers and aunts) to write of the late-Victorian young with sympathy. She was buried at Otterbourne on the thirty-fifth anniversary of the death of John Keble, and her coffin was followed by the schoolchildren she had so often led into church.

Her writing for children falls into two categories, the "drawing-room books" and the stories for cottage homes. She herself had made this distinction in the pamphlet *What Books to Give and What to Lend*, which she wrote in 1887 as a guide for prizegiving and parish libraries. Though by this date the curriculum in parish and national schools was changing, so that working-class children could be assumed to know enough history to be given historical tales, she felt that books about upper-class families could "answer no end, except to depict pleasures [they] can never share, raise hopes it is impossible for [them] to realize," in the words of Barbara Hofland's much earlier children's book *Rich Boys and Poor Boys* (1833). Conversely she held that the upper-class child would not derive any useful lesson from tales of cottage life.

For drawing rooms, therefore, and for such young women as her "goslings," she wrote her stories of family life, which still have their admirers. The best known of these is *The Daisy Chain*, the saga of the May family, whose mother dies in an early chapter in a carriage accident. As with all Charlotte Yonge's novels, the plot is subservient to the characters, though in this particular case she keeps better control over them than in, say, *Magnum Bonum* (1879), where her enthusiasm for inventing cousinhoods and dynasties led her to assemble an enormous cast that became impossible to manipulate.

The Daisy Chain is notable for the attractive figure of Dr. May, impetuous and boyish and sadly perplexed by the difficulties of bringing up his motherless brood; and for Ethel, in some ways a self-portrait. Ethel is a more favorable self-portrait than Yonge allowed in *The Clever Woman of the Family* (1865), where the enthusiastic and awkward Rachel Curtis has to be civilized by friendship with an older woman, an invalid, and *Heartsease* (1854), in which Theodora, who takes herself and the family honor very seriously, is horrified when her brother marries the despised Violet, who is gentle and unassuming—but it is Violet who becomes the dominant power for good in the fam-

ily while Theodora, until she learns humility, alienates them. Ethel May, a gawky fifteen-year-old when *Daisy Chain* opens, is allowed to grow into a very likable young woman—one we know will be a much-valued aunt and sister, though not a mother. One of the first lessons that she learns is to accept a woman's role and to put aside her efforts to keep pace with her brother in learning. As the years move on the church of Cocksmoor is built and dedicated, and the children grow up (most of them satisfactorily, though Harry is given to boisterous behavior that delays his confirmation and Tom, a brilliant scientist, who is the one most alienated from the family spirit, causes anxiety). Margaret, the eldest, injured in the carriage accident that killed her mother, dies after seven years of being an invalid, leaving her engagement ring to be set round the new church's chalice. Richard, the eldest son, becomes the incumbent of the church.

The Trial, *Daisy Chain*'s sequel, might be called a very early example of detective fiction; it was Yonge's only attempt at this genre, and boasted one of her better plots. Leonard Ward, the son of Dr. May's former partner, is unjustly accused of murder, but his death sentence is commuted to penal servitude. The May family is convinced of his innocence, and Tom succeeds in bringing the real murderer to justice. Leonard comes back from prison shattered by the experience—here the author shows startling imaginative insight—and feels so tainted by it that he hesitates to offer himself for work in the mission field.

In *The Pillars of the House* Yonge creates a family that became as beloved as the Mays, although the book is far longer than its predecessors, with an almost overwhelming cast. The Underwood family has been dispossessed of its rightful inheritance, the estate of Vale Leston, through a flaw in a will. The father, an impoverished curate dying of consumption in an industrial town, baptizes his last two children (twins) from his deathbed. ("My full twelve, and one over, and on Twelfth-day.") His wife, bedridden and half-imbecilic from bearing thirteen children in seventeen years, dies three years later. Meanwhile the full responsibility for the family has fallen upon "the pillars of the house": Felix, age sixteen, and Wilmet, one year younger. Felix gives up his idea of taking holy orders and apprentices himself to a printer (this meek acceptance of the stigma of trade seeming to Charlotte Yonge the ultimate in sacrifice), and the strong-minded Wilmet succeeds in managing the household, one of whom, Geraldine, is a cripple with a tubercular ankle joint, and the youngest of whom is mentally handicapped. The author sees them through grinding poverty to their restoration to the Underwood family property. Felix turns into a model squire, devoting himself to the parish church and to good works, but an unavailing attempt to rescue Theodore, the mentally afflicted twin, from a drowning accident brings on an illness from which he dies a year later. The book dwells much on Yonge's favorite theme of sacrifice. There is not only Felix's sacrifice; Geraldine insists on having her foot amputated so that she will be more useful, and Lance the choirboy refuses the chance of a musical career because "you must know that the fever and transport that comes of one kind of music has nothing good in it." But there is also Angela, one of Yonge's most spirited children, who refuses to work a problem from Colenso's *Arithmetic* because she says the author is a heretic (the Church of England had indeed excommunicated Bishop John William Colenso in 1864).

Magnum Bonum has one of Yonge's most attractive families, at least in the earlier pages—the young, widowed Carey Brownlow and her six children, whom she leads on delightful escapades to the scandal of her more staid relations. Yonge may have found Carey Brownlow too scandalous, for she sobers her down with much tribulation and brings her to repentant middle age, by which time the book has become dull and clogged with a preposterous subplot about a missing will as well as far too many characters. The "magnum bonum" of the title is an unlikely medical secret that the dead father has left to be brought to fruition only by a genuinely lofty-souled researcher. It is stolen by the always difficult Janet (here Yonge takes another swipe at girls with intellectual aspirations), who comes to a very bad end in America.

There were other family stories like *Hopes and Fears* (1860), *The Young Step-Mother* (1861), and *The Three Brides* (1876), all suffering from lack of organization but all having their admirers, as did even the late novels like *The Two Sides of the Shield* (1885), *Beechcroft at Rockstone* (1888), and *Modern Broods* (1900), in which Yonge takes up the lives of characters introduced in much earlier books. But these were less and less read by children. Her true children's books are technically much more satisfactory, being shorter and with more manageable numbers of characters. Outstanding is *Countess Kate* (1862), the story of a little girl who becomes a

peeress in her own right, is wrenched away from her adoptive family, and is carried off by aunts she has never seen to be educated for her new station in life. The aunts have no understanding of the needs of children, and Yonge here goes as far as she ever does to admitting that authority can sometimes be wrong. Kate Caergwent is one of her most convincing children, very like the young Charlotte herself in her passionate feelings, her vehemence, and her awkward clumsiness, all of which can be endearing as well as infuriating to adults.

The Stokesley Secret (1861) is equally good; it is an account of a nursery full of boisterous children, each one of whom takes on shape and individuality in a drama about saving pocket money to buy an old woman a pig, a brother who steals the money, another brother who longs for him to be drastically punished, and the final attainment of the pig. There are a few more stories of this sort of simplicity, like *P's and Q's* (1872) and *The Six Cushions* (1867), but these turn on matters of more limited appeal, such as whether a father's permission can be given for attendance at early communion and the difficulties that six girls have, because of their mothers' demands, in finishing the cushions they have undertaken to embroider for their church.

Otherwise, for stories of everyday life that are intended for the younger child, we must turn to those that Yonge wrote for village schools, like *Langley School*, *Leonard the Lion-heart* (1856), *Friarswood Post-Office* (1860), *Cheap Jack* (1881), *Langley Little Ones* (1882), *The Little Rick-burners* (1886), and many others. These are vigorous, concise, and readable; not only do they show her flair for depicting character, they also possess simple and uncluttered plots. And there are absorbing details of Victorian cottage life—remarkable considering that in obedience to the wishes expressed by her parents when she was a child, Yonge never in her life entered a cottage and, because of similar embargoes on talking to the villagers, found it very difficult in later life to communicate with village children unless teaching a class. These books concern a remote world where the squire rules, and his wrath (as in "A Patchwork Fever," in *Langley School*) can make a village tremble, and where there are dauntingly high standards to which the girls especially are expected to conform. The tone became less severe in later books, all of which show her invariably keen insight into childhood's nature.

The historical tales, which were read long after the domestic stories were forgotten by children, were written for both the drawing room and the cottage. There are over thirty of them, and they range from the early Christians to figures in the nineteenth century; there is scarcely a period of European history that Yonge did not cover. All of these works have some merit, for she could communicate her ardent love of history and imbue even distant centuries with life. But though she took great care with background detail, the characters always seem early Victorian. *The Dove in the Eagle's Nest* (1866), for example, set in fifteenth-century Germany, is suffused with Tractarian ideals. Christina, a gentle burgher girl of Ulm (who has watched the Ulm cathedral being built, as Charlotte had watched the building of the Otterbourne church) is carried off to the mountain stronghold of a lawless baron to be a companion to his ailing little daughter. Christina brings gentleness, compassion, and a sense of religion to the savage household. When the daughter dies, Christina marries the son, who disappears soon afterward in one of the habitual skirmishes in nearby disputed territory. She bears twin boys, Friedmund and Eberard, who grow up to resemble Yonge's pattern youths—chivalrous, bookish, and devoted to their mother. "Nurtured in mountain solitude, on romance transmitted through the pure medium of his mother's mind, and his spirit untainted by contact with the world, Friedmund von Adlerstein looked on chivalry with the temper of a Percival or Galahad, and regarded it with a sacred awe." Both boys are wounded, Friedel mortally, while fighting the family's hereditary enemy; yet even in dying, Friedel sings to his much-loved brother to take the latter's mind off the pain of his wounds—a deathbed scene that must have drawn as many tears as Guy Morville's. Christina's husband then returns as it were from the dead, having spent the lost years as a galley slave of the Turks, chained next to a German friar who has brought him to adore the will of God. The book ends with the family embracing the new Lutheran creed.

This type of the idealized warrior, who was to appear so often in the historical tales, was perhaps based on Yonge's feelings about her father, whom she had hero-worshiped. We meet another such character in another very popular novel, *The Lances of Lynwood*, a story of feudal England and the French wars in the reign of Edward III. Here the hero is Sir Eustace Lynwood, who is delicate and bookish in childhood and who grows to be a courageous and ever-chivalrous knight, having steeped himself in youth in the romances of ancient chivalry.

Other historical romances written more for the castle than for the cottage included *The Chaplet of Pearls* (1868), a story of sixteenth-century France at the time of the St. Bartholomew massacres; *The Caged Lion* (1870), a story of James I of Scotland in which Henry V appears in an extremely idealized light; and *Unknown to History* (1882), subtitled *A Story of the Captivity of Mary of Scotland*. All these continued to be reprinted well into this century and were to be found on the shelves of many schools. But the story that persisted the longest was *The Little Duke*. Set in tenth-century Normandy, it is the story of the boyhood of Richard the Fearless, great-grandfather of William the Conqueror. His father is treacherously killed by the Count of Flanders; the child becomes duke of Normandy and learns, even while he stands beside the body of his dead father, that he must lay aside hatred and vengeance and offer love and mercy to his enemies. In later books the weight of antiquarian detail became excessive and daunting; here the author sketches with a very light hand, and many young readers were to remember the opening scene in the smoky hall of Bayeux Castle and the coronation in which the crown has to be held steady on Richard's eight-year-old head.

Yonge had few imitators. Even the band of "goslings," some of whom became professional writers, recognized that she represented an earlier age. She is, however, still read, if not by children then by those with an interest in minor Victorian fiction and in Tractarian ideals.

Selected Bibliography

WORKS OF CHARLOTTE MARY YONGE

Abbeychurch; or, Self-control and Self-conceit. London: James Burns, 1844. Reissued New York: Garland, 1975.

Scenes and Characters; or, Eighteen Months at Beechcroft. With illustrations by W. J. Hennessy. London: Mozley, 1847.

Henrietta's Wish; or, Domineering. London: Masters, 1850.

Langley School. London: Mozley, 1850.

The Heir of Redclyffe. London: J. W. Parker, 1853. Reprinted New York: Garland, 1975.

The Castle Builders; or, The Deferred Confirmation. London: Mozley, 1854. Reprinted New York: Garland, 1975.

Heartsease; or, The Brother's Wife. London: J. W. Parker, 1854.

The Little Duke; or, Richard the Fearless. With illustrations by Jane Blackburn. London: J. W. Parker, 1854.

The Lances of Lynwood. With illustrations by Jane Blackburn. London: J. W. Parker, 1855.

The Daisy Chain; or, Aspirations. New York and London: J. W. Parker, 1856.

Leonard the Lion-heart. London: Mozley, 1856.

Friarswood Post-Office. New York and London: Mozley, 1860.

Hopes and Fears; or, Scenes from the Life of a Spinster. London: J. W. Parker, 1860.

The Stokesley Secret. London: Mozley, 1861.

The Young Step-Mother. London: Longmans, Green, 1861.

Countess Kate. With illustrations by Gwen Raverat. London: Mozley, 1862. Reprinted New York: Random House, 1960.

The Trial: More Links of the Daisy Chain. New York and London: Macmillan, 1864.

The Clever Woman of the Family. New York and London: Macmillan, 1865. Reissued New York: Garland, 1975.

The Dove in the Eagle's Nest. New York and London: Macmillan, 1866.

The Six Cushions. London: Mozley, 1867.

The Chaplet of Pearls; or, The White and Black Ribaumont. New York and London: Macmillan, 1868.

The Caged Lion. New York and London: Macmillan, 1870.

P's and Q's; or, The Question of Putting Upon. London: Macmillan, 1872.

Aunt Charlotte's Stories of English History for the Little Ones. London: Lasley, 1873.

The Pillars of the House; or, Under Wode, Under Rode. London: Macmillan, 1873.

The Three Brides. New York and London: Macmillan, 1876.

Magnum Bonum; or, Mother Carey's Brood. London: Macmillan, 1879. Reissued New York: Garland, 1975.

Cheap Jack. London: W. Smith, 1881.

Langley Little Ones. London: W. Smith, 1882.

Unknown to History: A Story of the Captivity of Mary of Scotland. London: Macmillan, 1882.

The Two Sides of the Shield. New York and London: Macmillan, 1885.

The Little Rick-burners. London: Skeffington, 1886.

Beechcroft at Rockstone. New York and London: Macmillan, 1888.

Modern Broods; or, Developments Unlooked For. New York and London: Macmillan, 1900.

CRITICAL AND BIOGRAPHICAL STUDIES

Avery, Gillian. *Nineteenth-Century Children*. London: Hodder and Stoughton, 1965.

Battiscombe, Georgina. *Charlotte Mary Yonge: The Story of an Uneventful Life*. London: Constable, 1943.

————, and Marghanita Laski, eds. *A Chaplet for Charlotte Yonge*. London: Cresset Press, 1965. (Published for the Charlotte Yonge Society. Contains a complete bibliography, miscellaneous writings of Charlotte Yonge, and genealogical tables of characters in the linked novels.)

Coleridge, Christabel. *Charlotte Mary Yonge: Her Life and Letters*. New York and London: Macmillan, 1903.

Maison, Margaret M. *Search Your Soul, Eustace*. London: Sheed and Ward, 1961.

Mare, Margaret and Alicia C. Percival. *Victorian Bestseller: The World of Charlotte M. Yonge*. London: Harrap, 1947.

Romanes, Ethel. *Charlotte Mary Yonge: An Appreciation*. London: Mowbray, 1908.

Tillotson, Geoffrey, and Kathleen Tillotson. *Mid-Victorian Studies*. London: Athlone Press, 1965.

—GILLIAN AVERY

LIST OF CONTRIBUTORS

LIST OF CONTRIBUTORS

MARY WEICHSEL AKE. Librarian/Media Specialist, Walt Whitman Elementary School, Littleton, Colorado. Author of "The Touchstones in the Classroom," in *Touchstones: Reflections on the Best in Children's Literature.* **Sir Arthur Conan Doyle.**

MARILYN F. APSELOFF. Associate Professor of English, Kent State University. Author of *Virginia Hamilton: Ohio Explorer in the World of Imagination* and numerous articles on fiction, poetry, and various other subjects pertaining to children's literature. **Edward Ardizzone.**

GILLIAN AVERY. Lecturer, Department of External Studies, Oxford University. Author of *Nineteenth Century Children; Childhood's Pattern; Victorian People; Mrs Ewing.* Editor of Gollancz Revivals. Author of children's books. **Juliana Horatia Ewing, Charles Kingsley, Charlotte Mary Yonge.**

AVI. Writer, librarian, lecturer, critic. Author of many works of fiction for young people, including *The Fighting Ground, Bright Shadow, S.O.R. Losers, Man from the Sky.* Winner of the O'Dell Award, Christopher Award, ALA Notables, IRA Children's Choice, MWA Special Awards. **Robert Lawson.**

J. ROBERT BASHORE, JR. Professor Emeritus of English and former director of University Honors Program, Bowling Green State University. **Daniel Defoe, Washington Irving.**

ROBERT BATOR. Professor of English, Olive-Harvey College of the City Colleges of Chicago. Author of *Shared Prose: Process to Product* and, with Mits Yamada, *Blue Pencil* (software). Editor of *Signposts to Criticism of Children's Literature* and *Masterworks of Children's Literature: 1740–1836* (2 volumes). **John Bunyan, Jonathan Swift.**

WILLIAM BLACKBURN. Associate Professor of English, University of Calgary, Alberta. Author of numerous articles on children's literature, Renaissance literature, and Oriental studies. **Rudyard Kipling.**

ANNA Y. BRADLEY. Retired teacher of English at Mott Community College, Flint, Michigan. **Oscar Wilde.**

GLENN S. BURNE. Professor of English, University of North Carolina at Charlotte. Author of *Remy de Gourmont. His Ideas and Influence in England and America, Julian Green,* and *Richard F. Burton.* **Frederick Marryat, Charles Perrault.**

FRANCELIA BUTLER. Professor of English, University of Connecticut. Books include *The Lucky Piece* (novel), *Indira Gandhi, Children's Literature: A Conceptual Approach.* Books edited include *Masterworks of Children's Literature 1550–1736, Sharing Literature with Children.* Editor-in-chief of *Children's Literature* (annual), 1972–date. Co-editor, with Richard Rotert, of *Reflections on Literature for Children* and *Triumphs of the Spirit in Children's Literature* and, with Richard Rotert and Anne Jordan, of *The Wide World All Around.* **Kate Douglas Wiggin.**

SUSAN CHITTY. Author of biographies: *The Woman Who Wrote "Black Beauty"* (Anna Sewell), *The Beast and the Monk* (Charles Kingsley), *Gwen John, Now to My Mother* (Antonia White). Also three novels and numerous articles. Forthcoming biography of Edward Lear. **Anna Sewell.**

HARRIETT CHRISTY. Instructor of Children's and Young Adult Literature, University of Wisconsin–Eau Claire. Author of essays on nineteenth-century children's magazines. **Mary Mapes Dodge.**

MARGARET COUGHLAN. Reference specialist, children's literature, Library of Congress. Publications include *Creating Independence, 1763–1789; Background Reading for Young People; Folklore from Africa to the United States.* Co-author of *Children's Literature: A Guide to Reference Sources, Yankee Doodle's Literary Sampler.* **Hendrik Willem van Loon.**

LEONARD L. DUROCHE. Associate Professor of German and Comparative Literature, University of Minnesota. Author of *Aspects of Criticism* and of articles on spatial perception and existential experience in literature. **E. T. A. Hoffman.**

CATHERINE EAYRS. Elementary instructor, Saint Pius X Grade School, Rochester, Minnesota. **Johanna Spyri.**

FRED ERISMAN. Lorraine Sherley Professor of Literature and Chairman of the English Department, Texas Christian University. Co-editor, with Richard W. Etulain, of *Fifty Western Writers.* Author of *Barnboken I USA* (with Zena Sutherland), *Frederic Remington,* and numerous articles on children's literature, regional literature, detective and suspense fiction, and the Western. **Laura Ingalls Wilder.**

ELLIN GREENE. Freelance library and educational consultant, lecturer, storyteller. Formerly Associate Professor, University of Chicago. Author, with Augusta Baker, of *Storytelling: Art and Technique* and, with George Shannon, of *Storytelling: A Selected Annotated Bibliography.* Author of numerous articles on children's literature in professional journals. **Walter de la Mare, Eleanor Farjeon.**

AVRIEL H. GOLDBERGER. Professor of French and Chair of the French Department, Hofstra University. Translator of Germaine de Staël's *Corinne, or Italy,* with introduction and notes. Author of *Visions of a New Hero,* and papers on André Malraux, translation, and Mme de Maintenon. Director of Hofstra Conferences on Malraux, Stendhal, and nineteenth-century women writers. **Alexandre Dumas.**

ERIK HAUGAARD. Author of *The Little Fishes, The Untold Tale, Leif the Unlucky, The Samurai's Tale,* and other juvenile novels. Translator of *The Complete Fairy Tales and Stories of Hans Christian Andersen.* **Hans Christian Andersen.**

MICHAEL PATRICK HEARN. Author of *The Annotated Wizard of Oz, The Annotated Christmas Carol, W. W. Denslow, The Art of the Broadway Poster,* and *The Annotated Huckleberry Finn.* Editor of the Critical Heritage Edition of *The Wizard of Oz* and *The Andrew Lang Fairy Tale Book.* **L. Frank Baum, Charles Dickens, Frank R. Stockton, Mark Twain.**

ETHEL HEINS. Lecturer, critic, reviewer. Adjunct Professor, Center for the Study of Children's Literature, Simmons College. Former editor, *Horn Book Magazine.* **Ludwig Bemelmans.**

PAUL HEINS. Lecturer and critic, children's literature. Adjunct Professor, Center for the Study of Children's Literature, Simmons College. Editor of *Crosscurrents of Criticism.* Former editor, *Horn Book Magazine.* **Lucretia P. Hale.**

ALETHEA K. HELBIG. Professor of English, Language, and Literature, Eastern Michigan University. Author of numerous articles and of *Nanabozboo, Giver of Life.* Co-author, with Agnes Perkins, of *Dictionary of American Children's Fiction, 1859–1959: Books of Recognized Merit* and *Dictionary of American Children's Fiction, 1960–1984: Recent Books of Recognized Merit.* Co-compiler, with Helen Hill and Agnes Perkins, of *Straight on till Morning: Poems of the Imaginary World* and *Dusk to Dawn: Poems of Night.* **Carol Ryrie Brink, Rachel Lyman Field, Ruth Sawyer, Kate Seredy.**

ANN M. HILDEBRAND. Associate Professor of English, Kent State University. Author of essays and reviews on various topics, primarily in children's literature. **Jean de Brunhoff.**

MARGARET HODGES. Professor Emeritus, School of Library and Information Science, University of Pittsburgh. Author of books for young readers, including *Baldur and the Mistletoe, Fire Bringer, High Riders, Knight Prisoner, Little Humpbacked Horse, Saint George and the Dragon.* Co-editor of *Elva S. Smith's History of Children's Literature,* revised and enlarged edition. **Asbjørnsen and Moe, J. M. Barrie, Robert Louis Stevenson.**

ELIZABETH F. HOWARD. Associate Professor of Library Science, West Virginia University. Author of articles and reviews in various journals and compilations. **Arna Bontemps.**

PETER HUNT. Lecturer in English and Director of Studies, University of Wales, Cardiff. Author of more than forty articles on children's literature and three novels, *The Maps of Time, A Step off the Path,* and *Backtrack.* **A. A. Milne.**

CHRISTA KAMENETSKY. Professor of English, Central Michigan University. Publications include *Children's Literature in Hitler's Germany: The Cultural Policy of National Socialism* and numerous articles in professional journals. **Jacob and Wilhelm Grimm.**

HUGH T. KEENAN. Associate Professor of English, Georgia State University. Author of essays on Old English, Middle English, and children's literature. Editor of *Papers by Medievalists, Typology and Medieval Literature, Narrative Theory and Children's Literature,* and *Joel Chandler Harris: The Writer in His Time and Ours.* **M. L. S. Molesworth.**

EDWARD C. KEMP. Librarian, Professor Emeritus, University of Oregon. Co-author of bio-bibliographical essays on James Henry Daugherty and Berta and Elmer Hader. **James Henry Daugherty.**

ELAINE A. KEMP. Librarian, University of Oregon. Co-author of bio-bibliographical essays on James Henry Daugherty and Berta and Elmer Hader. **James Henry Daugherty.**

LOIS R. KUZNETS. Associate Professor of English, San Diego State University. Author of *Kenneth Grahame* (Twayne English Author Series) and various other articles on and reviews of children's literature in professional journals. **Kenneth Grahame.**

LOWELL P. LELAND. Emeritus Professor of English, Bowling Green State University. **John Ruskin.**

ANDREW LEVITT. Mime, Greensboro, North Carolina. **Andrew Lang.**

MYRA COHN LIVINGSTON. Poet, author, Senior Instructor, University of California Los Angeles Extension. Author of *The Child as Poet: Myth or Reality?*, *Worlds I Know and Other Poems*, *Celebrations*, *How Pleasant to Know Mr. Lear*, *A Learical Lexicon*, and many other books. Compiler of twenty poetry anthologies. Numerous articles and essays in various periodicals. **Edward Lear.**

ALISON LURIE. Professor of English, Cornell University. Author of seven novels, three books for children, and many articles on and reviews of children's literature. Co-editor of *The Garland Library of Children's Classics.* **E. Nesbit.**

DONNARAE MACCANN. Doctoral candidate in American Studies, University of Iowa, and columnist for *Wilson Library Bulletin* and *Children's Literature Association Quarterly.* Co-author of *The Child's First Books* and co-editor of *The Black American in Books for Children* and *Cultural Conformity in Books for Children.* Advisory board member, Council on Interracial Books for Children, and executive board member, Children's Literature Association. **Hugh Lofting.**

RUTH K. MACDONALD. Associate Professor of English, New Mexico State University. Author of *Literature for Children in England and America, 1646–1774, Louisa May Alcott, Beatrix Potter, Dr. Seuss (Theodore Seuss Geisel).* **Louisa May Alcott, Beatrix Potter.**

ANNE SCOTT MACLEOD. Professor of Children's Literature, University of Maryland. Author of *A Moral Tale: Children's Fiction and American Culture, 1820–1860,* and numerous articles on children's literature, especially in relation to culture. **Laura E. Richards.**

LEONARD S. MARCUS. Humanities Faculty, School of Visual Arts, New York. Children's book reviewer for *Parenting.* Book review editor for *The Lion and the Unicorn.* Author of a forthcoming biography of Margaret Wise Brown. Contributor to *New York Times Book Review, Washington Post Book World, Smithsonian, Dictionary of Literary Biography, Small Press, Children's Literature, Art in America.* **Heinrich Hoffmann.**

RODERICK MCGILLIS. Associate Professor of English, University of Calgary, Alberta. Editor of the *Children's Literature Association Quarterly.* Articles on William Wordsworth, George MacDonald, Lewis Carroll, and others. **William Blake, Christina Rossetti.**

JILL P. MAY. Associate Professor of Education, Purdue University. Publications Chair of the Children's Literature Association. Editor of *Children and Their Literature: A Readings Book.* Co-editor of *Festschrift: A Ten Year Retrospective.* Author of numerous articles on children's literature, including several papers on Howard Pyle. **Howard Pyle, Felix Salten.**

ROBIN MCKINLEY. Author of *Beauty, The Door in the Hedge, The Blue Sword, The Hero and the Crown.* Editor of *Imaginary Lands.* Numerous articles and reviews in periodicals. **J. R. R. Tolkien.**

WALTER JAMES MILLER. Poet and Professor of English, New York University. Editor of *The Annotated Jules Verne: Twenty Thousand Leagues Under the Sea* and *The Annotated Jules Verne: From the Earth to the Moon.* **Jules Verne.**

FRANCIS J. MOLSON. Professor of English, Central Michigan University. Author of the chapter on children's and adolescent science fiction in *Anatomy of Wonder* and of various essays and papers on children's literature, in particular science fiction and fantasy. **H. G. Wells.**

GORDON R. MORK. Associate Professor of History, Purdue University. Author of *Modern Western Civilization: A Concise History* and articles dealing with German and Jewish culture. **Felix Salten.**

OPAL J. MOORE. Fiction writer. Instructor, Virginia State University. Author, with Donnarae MacCann, of a series of articles on cultural pluralism in children's literature. **Joel Chandler Haris.**

ANITA MOSS. Associate Professor of English, University of North Carolina at Charlotte. Editor

(U.S. and Canada) of *Children's Literature in Education.* Author of *E. Nesbit* (Twayne English Author Series). Co-editor, with Jon C. Stott, of *The Family of Stories: An Anthology of Children's Literature.* Author of numerous articles and reviews of children's literature. Winner of the Children's Literature Association's award for the best article in children's literature for 1983. **Lewis Carroll.**

RUSSEL B. NYE. Distinguished Professor Emeritus of English, Michigan State University. Author of *George Bancroft: Brahmin Rebel* (Pulitzer Prize) and numerous books on American history and culture, including *The Birth of the New Republic* and (on American popular culture) *The Unembarrassed Muse.* Co-editor of *The Democratic Experience.* **James Fenimore Cooper.**

KIT PEARSON. Writer for children and librarian, Burnaby Public Library, Vancouver, Canada. Occasional critic and teacher of children's literature. Author of *The Daring Game* and *A Handful of Time.* **Arthur Ransome.**

AGNES REGAN PERKINS. Professor of English, Eastern Michigan University. Co-author, with Alethea K. Helbig, of *Dictionary of American Children's Fiction, 1859–1959: Books of Recognized Merit* and *Dictionary of American Children's Fiction, 1960–1984: Recent Books of Recognized Merit.* Co-compiler, with Helen Hill, of *New Coasts and Strange Harbors: Discovering Poems* and, with Hill and Helbig, of *Straight on Till Morning: Poems of the Imaginary World* and *Dusk to Dawn: Poems of Night.* **Marjorie Kinnan Rawlings, Carl Sandburg.**

BARBARA T. ROLLOCK. Formerly Coordinator of Children's Services, the New York Public Library. Editor of *The Black Experience in Children's Books* (bibliography). Author of numerous articles on and reviews of children's books. Alternate delegate to UNICEF representing the International Board on Books for Young People. **Langston Hughes.**

GLENN EDWARD SADLER. Associate Professor of English, Bloomsburg University. Author of numerous articles on George MacDonald and C. S. Lewis. Editor of George MacDonald's *The Gifts of the Child Christ: Fairy Tales and Stories for the Childlike.* **George MacDonald, C. S. Lewis.**

GRAYCE SCHOLT. Instructor of Children's Literature; Language, Literature and Philosophy Division, Charles Stewart Mott Community College. Author of poems and articles in various journals. Co-author, with Jane M. Bingham, of *Fifteen Centuries of Children's Literature: An Annotated Chronology of British and American Works in Historical Context.* **Hilaire Belloc, Elizabeth Madox Roberts.**

MARY E. SHANER. Professor of English, University of Massachusetts. Contributing editor to *The Riverside Chaucer.* Co-editor of *Masterworks of Children's Literature: The Twentieth Century* (vol. 8). Author of various essays and reviews in the fields of medieval studies and children's literature. **Joseph Jacobs.**

M. SARAH SMEDMAN. Associate Professor of English, University of North Carolina at Charlotte. Author of articles, essays, and reviews in various journals, reference works, and critical anthologies. **Elizabeth Enright.**

JON C. STOTT. Professor of English, University of Alberta. Member of founding board and first president, Children's Literature Association. Author of *Children's Literature from A to Z: A Guide for Parents and Teachers* and, with Anita Moss, *The Family of Stories: An Anthology of Children's Literature;* and numerous articles on children's literature. **Nathaniel Hawthorne, L. M. Montgomery.**

JAMES T. TEAHAN. Professor of English Literature and former chairman of Faculty of English Language and Literature, Farah Pahlavi University, Tehran, Iran. Editor of *An Annotated Introduction to English Verse.* Translator and editor of *The Pinocchio of C. Collodi.* **C. Collodi.**

ANN THWAITE. Editorial board, *Cricket,* the magazine for children. Author or editor of thirty children's books and of the biographies *Waiting for the Party: The Life of Frances Hodgson Burnett, Edmund Gosse: A Literary Landscape,* and *A. A. Milne: His Life* (forthcoming). **Frances Hodgson Burnett.**

SUSAN T. VIGUER. Associate Professor of English, Philadelphia Colleges of the Arts. Author of *With Child: One Couple's Journey to Their Adopted Children* and articles on and reviews of English Renaissance drama, aesthetic education, and children's literature. **Cornelia Meigs.**

DOROTHEA C. WARREN. Adjunct Instructor of English, Kent State University. Columnist and reviewer. **Padraic Colum.**

PEGGY WHALEN-LEVITT. Author of *The Critical Theory of Children's Literature: A Conceptual Analysis* (forthcoming) and of various articles on and reviews of children's literature in professional journals. **Margery Bianco Williams.**

GERHARD H. WEISS. Professor of German, University of Minnesota. Co-author of *Begegnung mit Deutschland.* Author of articles on German literature and German culture. Former editor of Minnesota Monographs in the Humanities and of *Die Unterrichtspraxis.* **Erich Kästner.**

INDEX

INDEX

641